AMERICAN GOVERNMENT

Institutions and Policies

SEVENTH EDITION

James Q. Wilson
University of California, Los Angeles

John J. DiIulio, Jr.
Princeton University

HOUGHTON MIFFLIN COMPANY   Boston   New York

Sponsoring Editor: Melissa Mashburn
Editorial Assistant: Vikram Mukhija
Senior Project Editor: Janet Young
Editorial Assistant: Carrie Wagner
Senior Production/Design Coordinator: Carol Merrigan
Manufacturing Coordinator: Florence Cadran
Marketing Manager: Sandra McGuire

Cover design: Judy Arisman, Arisman Design
Photo credits appear on page A83.
Cover photograph: *Lincoln Memorial, Washington, D.C.,* FPG International.

Printed in the U.S.A.

Library of Congress Catalog Card Number: 97-72562

ISBN: 0-395-85763-5

123456789-QH-01 00 99 98 97

For Roberta, Matthew, Rebecca, Annie, and Bob.
And Winston, Clementine, and Sarah.
J.Q.W.

Dedicated to the memory of Aaron H. Crasner.
J.J.D.

James Q. Wilson
is an emeritus professor of management and public policy at the University of California, Los Angeles. From 1961 to 1987, he was a professor of government at Harvard University. Raised in California, he received a B.A. degree from the University of Redlands and a Ph.D. from the University of Chicago. Wilson is the author or coauthor of fourteen books, including *Moral Judgment* (1997), *The Moral Sense* (1993), *Bureaucracy* (1989), *Crime and Human Nature* (1985, with Richard J. Herrnstein), *Thinking about Crime* (1983), and *Political Organizations* (1974).

Wilson has served in a number of advisory posts in the federal government. He was chairman of the White House Task Force on Crime in 1967, chairman of the National Advisory Council on Drug Abuse Prevention in 1972–1973, a member of the Attorney General's Task Force on Violent Crime in 1981, and a member of the President's Foreign Intelligence Advisory Board in 1986–1990.

In 1977 the American Political Science Association conferred on him the Charles E. Merriam Award for advancing the art of government through the application of social science knowledge and in 1990 the James Madison Award for distinguished scholarship. In 1991–1992 he was President of the Association.

He is a Fellow of the American Academy of Arts and Sciences and a member of the American Philosophical Society. When not writing, teaching, or advising, he goes scuba diving. He says that it clears the brain.

John J. DiIulio, Jr.
is a professor of Politics and Public Affairs at Princeton University, teaching in both the Princeton Politics Department and the Woodrow Wilson School of Public and International Affairs. He is also Douglas Dillon Senior Fellow in Public Management at the Brookings Institution, and director of the Partnership for Research on Religion and At-Risk Youth. Raised in Philadelphia, he received a B.A. from the University of Pennsylvania and a Ph.D. from Harvard University. He is the author, coauthor, or editor of nine books, including *Making Health Reform Work* (with Richard P. Nathan); *Improving Government Performance* (with Donald F. Kettl and Gerald J. Garvey); *Deregulating the Public Service; Governing Prisons;* and *Courts, Corrections, and the Constitution.*

DiIulio has served on the National Commission on the State and Local Public Service and advised officials at the National Performance Review, the Office of Management and Budget, the General Accounting Office, the Office of National Drug Control Policy, the U.S. Justice Department, and other federal agencies.

In 1995 the Association of Public Policy Analysis and Management conferred on him the David N. Kershaw Award for outstanding research achievements by a scholar under age 40, and in 1987 he received the American Political Science Association's Leonard D. White Award in public administration. In 1991–1994 he chaired the latter association's standing committee on professional ethics. He spends all his free time with family and old friends from Philadelphia.

Preface

The Seventh Edition of *American Government* has been substantially revised to reflect major changes that have occurred in national politics. The Republicans won control of Congress in 1994 and retained it in 1996, the procedures by which the House of Representatives operates were substantially altered, an important federal program (Aid to Families with Dependent Children) was converted into a block grant to the states, and both a Democratic president and a Republican Congress agreed on a budget plan that (if their predictions turn out to be correct) will produce a balanced budget by the year 2002.

Important as these changes were, the overall tone and thrust of the book required little alteration. The essential processes of American politics remain unchanged, still governed, as always, by the Constitution, slow judicial modifications in its meaning, and popular attitudes toward politics and policies that have not altered much in several decades.

As before, we stress the history of our institutions and comparisons with other democratic nations. In some ways, the rest of the world is becoming a bit more like the United States. More nations are democratic today than ever before, and several of those that have always been that way are creating (as did Canada) new constitutions. Market economics now has a wider appeal in Europe and Latin America than once was the case. The former Soviet Union is struggling to find its democratic sea legs and something resembling an open economy. The global economy has brought every nation closer together and made a quiver in one place resonate loudly in many.

We extensively revised Chapters 11, 17, and 19, the chapters on Congress, welfare policies, and civil rights. In the Seventh Edition we have also added a new feature called "Who Governs? To What Ends?" that examines key legislation and asks who is responsible, focusing on the interplay of policy elites, political institutions, and public opinion. The themes introduced in the Sixth Edition—more attention to critical thinking, an emphasis on the differences between direct and representative democracy, attention to crime and criminal justice, and recognition of the growing importance of immigrants—have proved valuable and are retained in the Seventh.

Many of the unique features in previous editions have been retained here, including two in particular. The boxes headed "Politically Speaking" that give the origin of certain common political terms (such as *litmus test, lame duck, logrolling, boycott,* and *muckraker*) have proved to be useful ways of making unfamiliar words accessible and interesting. Another series of boxes headed "What Would You Do?" presents to the student material very much like presidential decision memorandums (albeit ones for a variety of political actors). Should we send troops? rule a state statute unconstitutional? take money from a political action committee? These boxes can be the basis of classroom debates or term papers.

The lists of "Political Trivia" and "Laws of Politics" remain; students (like the authors of this text) seem to have an unflagging appetite for such minutiae and folk wisdom.

Finally, the Summary, Suggested Readings, and lists of Key Terms at the end of each chapter continue to serve as easy references and help students review for examinations.

Supplements

The outstanding ancillary program that has always supported *American Government* has been improved and enlarged.

For the Instructor: The **Instructor's Guide** revised by MaryAnne Borrelli of Connecticut College helps instructors using the Seventh Edition to plan their course, lectures, and discussion sections. Professor Borrelli has thoroughly integrated the *Instructor's Guide* with the textbook so that instructors will be able to capitalize upon the richness of *American Government*. Elements new to the edition are summarized, and the resources and references sections as well as the Video and Film Guide have been completely updated.

The **Test Item File** revised by J. Edwin Benton of the University of South Florida contains over 4,000 questions. Each chapter has multiple-choice, true/false, and essay questions—averaging 180 items per chapter—designed to aid in your class testing of *American Government,* Seventh Edition. The file is available in print or in electronic form for Windows and for the Macintosh.

The **Transparency Package** contains fifty full-color transparencies from the illustration program of *American Government,* Seventh Edition.

For the Student: The **Student Handbook** has been thoroughly updated by J. Edwin Benton of the University of South Florida to help students using *American Government,* Seventh Edition, master the facts and principles introduced in the text. For each textbook chapter, the handbook includes focus points, a study outline, key terms, notes about possible misconceptions, a data check, examination practice, and special application projects, as well as answers to all chapter exercises (excluding the essay questions). It is ideal for class preparation, reviewing class reading, and especially preparing for examinations.

New! **Guide to the Internet** with an introduction by James Q. Wilson, is a brief, useful guide to surfing and browsing the Internet. It introduces students to using the Internet for political research and lists various web sites along with addresses and descriptions of each site.

New! **Wilson/DiIulio American Government Web Site** <http://www.hmco.com/college> will allow students and instructors access to text-specific materials. The web site includes chapter outlines and summaries, links to web sites mentioned in the text, and other additional resources.

For the Instructor and the Student: *New!* The **Houghton Mifflin American Government Web Site** located at <http://www.hmco.com/college> contains a complete array of resources to accompany our American government titles, including an extensive **Documents Collection** with accompanying discussion questions and web exercises, various instructor's resources, web-based research activities, an annotated collection of links to innovative and useful web sites, and a downloadable, updated version of the award-winning **Crosstabs,** a computerized software program allowing students to cross-tabulate survey data on the 1996 presidential election and the 1994–95 voting records of members of Congress in order to analyze voter attitudes and behavior.

Acknowledgments

A number of scholars reviewed the Sixth Edition and made many useful suggestions for the Seventh. They include Sam Van Leer, Jr., University of California, Berkeley; Walter A. Rosenbaum, University of Florida; Richard Himelfarb, Hofstra University; Eugene R. Goss, Long Beach City College; James Penning, Calvin College; Jack Riley, Coastal Carolina University; Nat Cipollina, City University of New York, Baruch College; and Stephen S. Smith, Winthrop University.

Other scholars read, at the authors' request, particular chapters and made useful suggestions: Aaron Friedberg of Princeton University, Don Kettl of the University of Wisconsin, Tom Mann of the Brookings Institution, and Richard Nathan of the State University of New York at Albany.

We also owe thanks to Meenchshi Bose, Fred Dews, Carey R. Macdonald, Tara Adams Ragone, and Cynthia D. Terrels.

J.Q.W. and J.J.D.

Contents

PART ONE

The American System
1

1 The Study of American Government   3
What Is Political Power?   4
What Is Democracy?   5
Direct Versus Representative Democracy:
    Which Is Best?   7
How Is Power Distributed in a Democracy?   7
Political Change   12
Finding Out Who Governs   15

2 The Constitution   19
The Problem of Liberty   19
The Constitutional Convention   24
The Challenge   29
The Constitution and Democracy   32
The Constitution and Liberty   35
The Motives of the Framers   41
Constitutional Reform—Modern Views   44

3 Federalism   51
Governmental Structure   52
The Founding   56
The Debate on the Meaning of Federalism   59
Federal-State Relations   61
The Slowdown in "Free" Money   68
Federal Aid and Federal Control   69
A Devolution Revolution?   75
Congress and Federalism   80

4 American Political Culture   85
Political Culture   86
Comparing America with Other Nations   90
The Sources of Political Culture   94
Mistrust of Government   99
Political Efficacy   102
Political Tolerance   103

PART TWO

Opinions, Interests, and Organizations
109

5 Public Opinion   111
What Is Public Opinion?   112
The Origins of Political Attitudes   114
Cleavages in Public Opinion   121
Political Ideology   130
Political Elites, Public Opinion, and Public
    Policy   139

6 Political Participation   143
A Closer Look at Nonvoting   143
The Rise of the American Electorate   146
Who Participates in Politics?   152

7 Political Parties   163
Parties—Here and Abroad   163
The Rise and Decline of the Political Party   166
The National Party Structure Today   172
State and Local Parties   178

The Two-Party System   183
Minor Parties   186
Nominating a President   189
Parties Versus Voters   191

8 *Elections and Campaigns*   *195*

Presidential Versus Congressional Campaigns   196
Primary Versus General Campaigns   199
Money   207
What Decides the Election?   215
Election Outcomes   224
The Effects of Elections on Policy   229

9 *Interest Groups*   *235*

Explaining Proliferation   235
The Birth of Interest Groups   236
Kinds of Organizations   239
Interest Groups and Social Movements   244
Funds for Interest Groups   249
The Problem of Bias   250
The Activities of Interest Groups   252
Regulating Interest Groups   262

10 *The Media*   *267*

Journalism in American Political History   269
The Structure of the Media   275
Rules Governing the Media   279
The Effects of the Media on Politics   283
Government and the News   285
Interpreting Political News   287

PART THREE

Institutions of Government   *297*

11 *Congress*   *299*

The Evolution of Congress   302

Who Is in Congress?   307
Getting Elected to Congress   314
The Organization of Congress: Parties and Caucuses   319
The Organization of Congress: Committees   329
The Organization of Congress: Staffs and Specialized Offices   332
How a Bill Becomes Law   334
How Members of Congress Vote   343
Reforming Congress   346
Ethics and Congress   354

12 *The Presidency*   *363*

Presidents and Prime Ministers   363
Divided Government   365
The Evolution of the Presidency   367
The Powers of the President   374
The Office of the President   376
Who Gets Appointed   382
Presidential Character   384
The Power to Persuade   386
The Power to Say No   392
The President's Program   395
Presidential Transition   400
How Powerful Is the President?   405

13 *The Bureaucracy*   *409*

Distinctiveness of the American Bureaucracy   409
The Growth of the Bureaucracy   411
The Federal Bureaucracy Today   414
Congressional Oversight   429
Bureaucratic "Pathologies"   432
Reforming the Bureaucracy   435

14 *The Judiciary*   *439*

The Development of the Federal Courts   441
The Structure of the Federal Courts   447
The Jurisdiction of the Federal Courts   450
Getting to Court   453
The Supreme Court in Action   457

The Power of the Federal Courts   459
Checks on Judicial Power   463

PART FOUR

The Politics of Public Policy
471

15 *The Policy-Making Process*   *473*

Setting the Agenda   474
Making a Decision   477
Majoritarian Politics: Distributed Benefits, Distributed Costs   479
Interest Group Politics: Concentrated Benefits, Concentrated Costs   480
Client Politics: Concentrated Benefits, Distributed Costs   481
Entrepreneurial Politics: Distributed Benefits, Concentrated Costs   482
The Case of Business Regulation   483
Perceptions, Beliefs, Interests, and Values   491

16 *Economic Policy*   *499*

Economic Health   500
Economic Theories and Political Needs   504
The Machinery of Economic Policy Making   507
Spending Money   510
The Budget   511
Levying Taxes   516

17 *Social Welfare*   *523*

Social Welfare in the United States   524
Two Kinds of Welfare Politics   532
Toward a New Welfare Politics   534

18 *Civil Liberties*   *545*

Politics, Culture, and Civil Liberties   546

Interpreting and Applying the First Amendment   550
What Is Speech?   553
Who Is a Person?   556
Church and State   557
Crime and Due Process   562

19 *Civil Rights*   *571*

The Black Predicament   572
The Campaign in the Courts   574
The Campaign in Congress   581
Women and Equal Rights   588
Women and the Economy   592
Affirmative Action   594
Gays and the Supreme Court   599

20 *Foreign Policy*   *603*

Kinds of Foreign Policy   604
The Constitutional and Legal Context   606
The Machinery of Foreign Policy   612
Foreign Policy and Public Opinion   615
Cleavages Among Foreign-Policy Elites   619
The Beginning of a New Era   624

21 *Military Policy*   *631*

The Structure of Defense Decision Making   632
The Defense Budget   636
What Do We Buy for Our Money?   643
Congress Versus the Executive   647

22 *Environmental Policy*   *651*

The American Context   652
Entrepreneurial Politics: Pollution from Factories   653
Majoritarian Politics: Pollution from Automobiles   656
Interest Group Politics: Acid Rain   658
Client Politics: Agricultural Pesticides   661

The Environmental Uncertainties   662
The Results   664

PART FIVE

The Nature of American Democracy
667

23 **Who Governs?**   669

Four Kinds of Politics   670
Competing Theories of Political Power   676

24 **To What Ends?**   683

Competing Interests   684
Restraints on the Growth of Government   684
Consequences of Activist Government   685
The Influence of Structure   687
The Influence of Ideas   688

PART SIX

State and Local Government
693

25 **State and Local Government**   695

State Constitutions and Political Philosophy   696
The Legal Basis of State and Local
    Government   698
The Structure of State Government   703
The Structure of Local Government   713
Politics and Policies   717
Taxes and Tax Revolts   719
State Policies and Federal Politics: The Case of
    Crime Control   720

Appendix

The Declaration of Independence   A1
The Constitution of the United States   A4
The *Federalist* No. 10   A21
The *Federalist* No. 51   A26
Presidents and Congresses, 1789–1997   A30

Glossary   *A33*

References   *A47*

Index   *A61*

Photograph Credits   *A83*

AMERICAN GOVERNMENT

Institutions and Policies

PART ONE

The American System

"In framing a government which is to be administered by men over men, the great difficulty lies in this: You must first enable the government to control the governed; and in the next plave oblige it to control itself."

— FEDERALIST NO. 51

1

The Study of American Government

★ Formal authority

★ Legitimacy of government

★ Forms of democracy

★ Democratic centralism

★ Participatory democracy

★ Representative democracy

★ Majoritarian politics

★ Theories as to who rules

★ Political power

There are two questions about politics: Who governs? To what ends?

We want to know the answer to the first question because we believe that those who rule—their personalities and beliefs, their virtues and vices—will affect what they do to and for us. Many people think they already know the answer to the question, and they are prepared to talk and vote on that basis. That is their right, and the opinions they express may be correct. But they may also be wrong. Indeed, many of these opinions *must* be wrong because they are in conflict. When asked, "Who governs?" some people will say "the unions" and some will say "big business"; others will say "the politicians" or "the people" or "the special interests." Still others will say "Wall Street," "the military," "crackpot liberals," "the media," "the bureaucrats," or "white males." Not all these answers can be correct—at least not all of the time.

The answer to the second question is important because it tells us how government affects our lives. We want to know not only who governs, but what difference it makes who governs. In our day-to-day lives, we may not think government makes much difference at all. In one sense that is right, because our most pressing personal concerns—work, play, love, family, health—are essentially private matters on which government touches but slightly. But in a larger and longer perspective, government makes a substantial difference. Consider: in 1935, 96 percent of all American families paid no federal income tax, and for the 4 percent or so who did pay, the average rate was only about 4 percent of their incomes. Today almost all families pay federal income taxes, and the average rate is 20 percent of their incomes. Through laws that have been enacted since the 1930s, the federal government has taken charge of an enormous amount of the nation's income, with results that are still being debated. Or consider: in 1960, in many parts of the country, blacks could ride only in the backs of buses, had to use washrooms and drinking fountains that were labeled "colored," and could not be served in most public restaurants.

Such restrictions have been almost eliminated, in large part because of decisions by the federal government.

It is important to bear in mind that we wish to answer two different questions, and not two versions of the same question. You cannot always predict what goals government will establish knowing only who governs, nor can you always tell who governs by knowing what activities government undertakes. Most people holding national political office are middle-class, middle-aged, white Protestant males, but we cannot then conclude that the government will only adopt policies that are to the narrow advantage of the middle class, or the middle-aged, or whites, or Protestants, or men. If we thought that, we would be at a loss to explain why the rich are taxed more heavily than the poor, why a War on Poverty was declared, why constitutional amendments giving rights to blacks and women passed Congress by large majorities, or why Catholics and Jews have been appointed to so many important governmental posts.

This book is chiefly devoted to answering the question, Who governs? It is written in the belief that this question cannot be answered without looking at how government makes—or fails to make—decisions about a large variety of concrete issues. Thus, in this book we shall inspect government policies to see what individuals, groups, and institutions seem to exert the greatest power in the continuous struggle to define the purposes of government. We shall see that power and purpose are inextricably intertwined.

What Is Political Power?

By **power** we mean the ability of one person to get another person to act in accordance with the first person's intentions. Sometimes an exercise of power is obvious, as when the president tells the air force that it can or cannot build the B-1 bomber. More often, power is exercised in subtle ways that may not be evident even to the participants, as when the president's economic advisers persuade him to impose or lift wage and price controls. The advisers may not think they are using power—after all, they are the president's subordinates—but if the presi-

dent acts in accord with their intentions as a result of their arguments, they have used power.

Power is found in all human relationships, but we shall be concerned here only with power as it is used to affect who will hold government office and how government will behave. This fails to take into account many important things. If a corporation closes a factory in a small town where it was the major employer, it is using power in ways that affect deeply the lives of people. When a university refuses to admit a student or a medical society refuses to license a would-be physician, it is also using power. But to explain how all these things happen would be tantamount to explaining how society as a whole, and in all its particulars, operates. We limit our view here to government, and chiefly to the American federal government. However, we shall repeatedly pay special attention to how things once thought to be "private" matters become "public"—that is, how they manage to become objects of governmental action. Indeed, one of the most striking transformations of American politics has been the extent to which, in recent decades, almost every aspect of human life has found its way onto the governmental agenda. In the 1950s the federal government would have displayed no interest in a factory closing its doors, a university refusing an applicant, or a profession not accrediting a member. Now government actions can and do affect all these things.

People who exercise political power may or may not have the authority to do so. By **authority** we mean the right to use power. The exercise of rightful power—that is, of authority—is ordinarily easier than the exercise of power that is not supported by any persuasive claim of right. We accept decisions, often without question, if they are made by people who we believe have the right to make them; we may bow to naked power because we cannot resist it, but by our recalcitrance or our resentment we put the users of naked power to greater trouble than the wielders of authority. In this book, we will on occasion speak of "formal authority." By this we mean that the right to exercise power is vested in a governmental office. A president, a senator, and a federal judge have formal authority to take certain actions.

What makes power rightful varies from time to time and from country to country. In the United

Dramatic changes have occurred in what people believe it is legitimate for the government to do. We now submit to searches before boarding an aircraft, unthinkable before hijackings made such government regulations seem necessary.

States we usually say that a person has political authority if his or her right to act in a certain way is conferred by a law or by a state or national constitution. But what makes a law or constitution a source of right? That is the question of **legitimacy**. In the United States the Constitution today is widely, if not unanimously, accepted as a source of legitimate authority, but that was not always the case.

Much of American political history has been a struggle over what constitutes legitimate authority. The Constitutional Convention in 1787 was an effort to see whether a new, more powerful federal government could be made legitimate; the succeeding administrations of George Washington, John Adams, and Thomas Jefferson were in large measure preoccupied with disputes over the kinds of decisions that were legitimate for the federal government to make. The Civil War was a bloody struggle over the legitimacy of the federal union; the New Deal of Franklin Roosevelt was hotly debated by those who disagreed over whether it was legitimate for the federal government to intervene deeply in the economy.

In the United States today no government at any level would be considered legitimate if it were not in some sense democratic. That was not always the prevailing view, however; at one time people disagreed over whether democracy itself was a good idea. In 1787 Alexander Hamilton worried that the new government he helped create might be too democratic, while George Mason, who refused to sign the Constitution, worried that it was not democratic enough. Today virtually everyone believes that "democratic government" is the only proper kind. Most people probably believe that our existing government is democratic; and a few believe that other institutions of public life—schools, universities, corporations, trade unions, churches—should be run on democratic principles if they are to be legitimate. We shall not discuss the question of whether democracy is the best way of governing all institutions. Rather we shall consider the different meanings that have been attached to the word *democratic* and which, if any, best describes the government of the United States.

What Is Democracy?

Democracy is a word used to describe at least three different political systems. In one system the government is said to be democratic if its decisions will

Before Boris Yeltsin came to power in Russia, the old Soviet Union was run on the principle of what the communists called "democratic centralism."

serve the "true interests" of the people, whether or not those people directly affect the making of those decisions. It is by using this definition of democracy that various authoritarian regimes—China, Cuba, and certain European, Asian, and Latin American dictatorships—have been able to claim that they were "democratic." Presidents of the now-defunct Soviet Union, for example, used to claim that they operated on the principle of **democratic centralism,** whereby the true interests of the masses were discovered through discussion within the Communist party and then decisions were made under central leadership to serve those interests. The collapse of the Soviet Union occurred in part because many average Russians doubted that the Communist party knew or would act in support of the people's true interests.

Second, the term *democracy* is used to describe those regimes that come as close as possible to Aristotle's definition—the "rule of the many."[1] A government is democratic if all, or most, of its citizens participate directly in either holding office or making policy. This is often called **direct** or **participatory democracy.** In Aristotle's time—Greece in the fourth century B.C.—such a government was possible. The Greek city-state, or *polis,* was quite small, and within it citizenship was extended to all free adult male property holders. (Slaves, women, minors, and those without property were excluded from participation in government.) In more recent times the New England town meeting approximates the Aristotelian ideal. In such a meeting the adult citizens of a community gather once or twice a year to vote directly on all major issues and expenditures of the town. As towns have become larger and issues more complicated, many town governments have abandoned the pure town meeting in favor of either the representative town meeting (in which a large number of elected representatives, perhaps two or three hundred, meet to vote on town affairs) or representative government (in which a small number of elected city councillors make decisions).

The third definition of democracy is the principle of governance of most nations that are called democratic. It was most concisely stated by the economist Joseph Schumpeter: "The democratic method is that institutional arrangement for arriving at political decisions in which individuals [that is, leaders] acquire the power to decide by means of a competitive struggle for the people's vote."[2] Sometimes this method is called, approvingly, **representative democracy;** at other times it is referred to, disapprovingly, as the elitist theory of democracy. It is justified by one or both of two arguments: First, it is impractical, owing to limits of time, information, energy, interest, and expertise, for the people to decide on public policy, but it is not impractical to expect them to make reasonable choices among competing leadership groups. Second, some people (including, as we shall see in the next chapter, many of the Framers of the Constitution) believe that direct democracy is likely to lead to bad decisions, because people often decide large issues on the basis of fleeting passions and in response to popular demagogues. This fear of direct democracy persists today, as can be seen from the statements of those who do not like what the voters have decided. For example, politicians who favored Proposition 13, the referendum measure that in 1978 sharply cut property taxes in California, spoke approvingly of the "will of the people." Politicians who disliked Proposition 13 spoke disdainfully of "mass hysteria."

Direct Versus Representative Democracy: Which Is Best?

Whenever the word *democracy* is used alone in this book, it will have the meaning Schumpeter gave it. As we shall see in the next chapter, the men who wrote the Constitution did not use the word *democracy* in that document. They wrote instead of a "republican form of government," but by that they meant what we call "representative democracy." Whenever we refer to that form of democracy involving the direct participation of all or most citizens, we shall use the term *direct* or *participatory democracy*.

For representative government to work, there must, of course, be an opportunity for genuine leadership competition. This requires in turn that individuals and parties be able to run for office, that communication (through speeches or the press, and in meetings) be free, and that the voters perceive that a meaningful choice exists. Many questions still remain to be answered. For instance: How many offices should be elective and how many appointive? How many candidates or parties can exist before the choices become hopelessly confused? Where will the money come from to finance electoral campaigns? There is more than one answer to such questions. In some European democracies, for example, very few offices—often just those in the national or local legislature—are elective, and much of the money for campaigning for these offices comes from the government. In the United States many offices—executive and judicial as well as legislative—are elective, and most of the money the candidates use for campaigning comes from industry, labor unions, and private individuals.

Some people have argued that the virtues of direct or participatory democracy can and should be reclaimed even in a modern, complex society. This can be done either by allowing individual neighbor-

In ancient Athens citizens participated directly in politics by meeting in the Agora.

hoods in big cities to govern themselves (community control) or by requiring those affected by some government program to participate in its formulation (citizen participation). In many states a measure of direct democracy exists when voters can decide on referendum issues—that is, policy choices that appear on the ballot. The proponents of direct democracy defend it as the only way to ensure that the "will of the people" prevails.

How Is Power Distributed in a Democracy?

Representative democracy is any system of government in which leaders are authorized to make decisions by winning a competitive struggle for the popular vote. It is obvious then that very different sets of hands can control political power, depending on what kinds of people can become leaders, how the struggle for votes is carried on, how much freedom to act is given to those who win the struggle, and what other sorts of influence (besides the desire for popular approval) affect the leaders' actions.

In some cases the leaders will be so sharply constrained by what most people want that the actions of officeholders will follow the preferences of citizens very closely. We shall call such cases examples of *majoritarian politics*. In this case elected officials are the delegates of the people, acting as the people (or a majority of them) would act were the matter put to a popular vote. The issues handled in a majoritarian fashion can only be those that are sufficiently important to command the attention of most citizens, sufficiently clear to elicit an informed opinion from citizens, and sufficiently feasible to address so that what citizens want done can in fact be done.

Direct or participatory democracy can still be found in the New England town meeting.

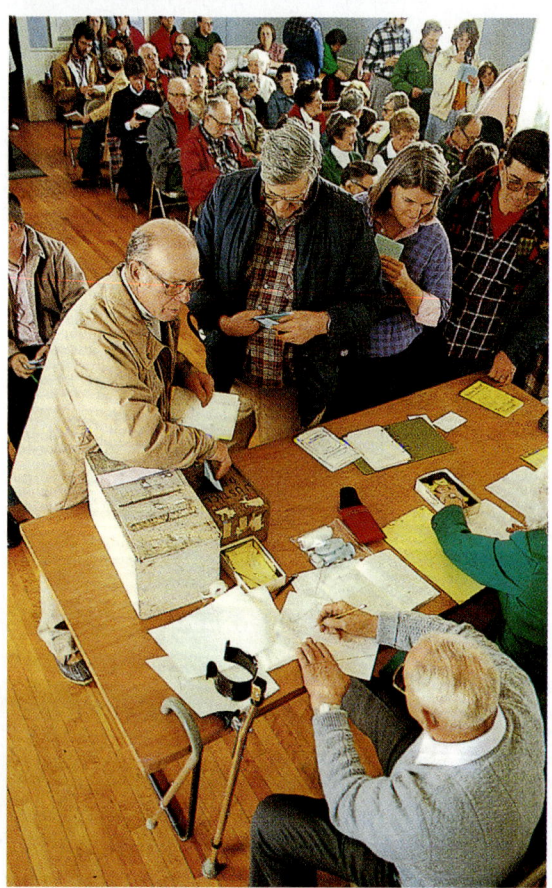

When circumstances do not permit majoritarian decision making, then some group of officials will have to act without knowing (and perhaps without caring) exactly what people want. Indeed, even on issues that do evoke a clear opinion from a majority of citizens, the shaping of the details of a policy will reflect the views of those people who are sufficiently motivated to go to the trouble of becoming active participants in policy-making. These active participants usually will be a small, and probably an unrepresentative, minority. Thus the actual distribution of political power, even in a democracy, will depend importantly on the composition of the political elites who are actually involved in the struggles over policy. By **elite,** we mean an identifiable group of persons who possess a disproportionate share of some valued resource—in this case, political power.

Four Theories of Who Governs

At least four theories purport to describe and explain the actions of political elites. One theory is associated with the writings of Karl Marx. To **Marxists**—or at least to some of them, since not all Marxists agree—government, whatever its outward form, is merely a reflection of underlying economic forces, primarily the pattern of ownership of the means of production. All societies, they claim, are divided into classes on the basis of the relationships of people to the economy-capitalists (the bourgeoisie), workers, farmers, intellectuals. In modern society two major classes contend for power—capitalists and workers. Whichever class dominates the economy also controls the government, which is nothing more than a piece of machinery designed to express and give legal effect to underlying class interests. In the United States the government "is but a committee for managing the common affairs of the whole bourgeoisie."[3] To a traditional Marxist it would be pointless to study the government since, as it is controlled by the dominant social class, it would have no independent power. There are many variations, some quite subtle, on this fundamental argument, and some newer Marxists find it more interesting to study how the government actually operates than did Marx himself, for whom government was a mere "epiphenomenon." But even neo-Marxists believe that the answer to the questions of

Thinking CRITICAL

Do We Want Push-Button Democracy?

The choice between representative and direct democracy is a profound one. Today many Americans are dissatisfied with representative government, which, they argue, acts too slowly, serves only special interests, and is unresponsive to majority opinion. During the 1992 presidential campaign, independent candidate Ross Perot promised to bring televised town hall–style meetings to the nation. Viewers would listen to experts debate an issue and then "vote" via toll-free telephone services capable of processing tens of thousands of calls per minute. Although he came in third in the 1992 election behind Bill Clinton and George Bush, Perot received 19.2 million votes, or 19 percent of all votes cast.

This type of "push-button" democracy is rapidly becoming technologically feasible, but is it desirable? Is government by electronic plebiscite preferable to government by deliberative institutions? Do you believe that most citizens have the time, information, interest, and expertise to make reasonable choices among competing policy positions? Or do you suspect that even highly educated people can be manipulated by demagogic leaders who play on their fears and prejudices?

How you respond to such questions ought not to depend on how you feel about any particular public figure,

whether you like watching television, or how much you enjoy playing with computers. Rather, your answer ought to depend primarily on what you believe about the arguments for and against representative government versus direct democracy. For example, it is true that representative democracy often proceeds slowly and prevents sweeping changes in policy. But it is also true that a government capable of doing great good quickly can also do great harm quickly.

Representative democracy is often plagued by special interests, but it is by no means clear that direct democracy would solve rather than exacerbate this problem. For example, in California in 1990 about $125 million was spent to influence voters on initiatives (laws and amendments proposed by citizens with a required number of signatures on a petition and then decided by popular vote). That is more than was spent in 1990 by all special interests to lobby California legislators on all legislation (over one thousand bills).

Majority opinion figures in the enactment of many government policies, but few Americans would want the protection of their civil rights or civil liberties—the right to a fair trial; the freedoms of speech, press, and religion; or the right to vote itself— to hinge on a majority vote.

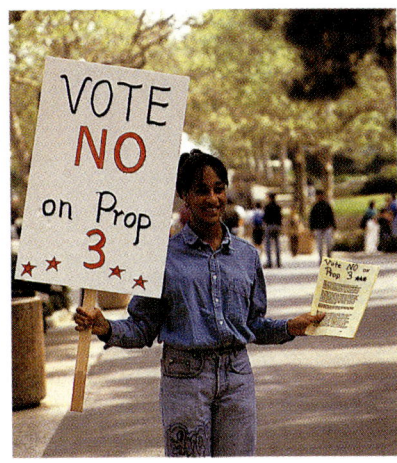

When people vote on referenda, the "special interests" are *us*.

As we will discuss in Chapter 2, the Framers of the United States Constitution believed strongly that government should mediate, not mirror, popular views, and that elected officials should represent, not register, majority sentiments. They favored representative democracy as a way of minimizing the chances that power would be abused either by a tyrannical popular majority or by self-serving office holders.

who really governs, and to what ends, is to be found in the pattern of economic interests, especially those represented by the large corporation.

A second theory, closely related to the first, argues that a nongovernmental elite makes most of the major decisions but that this elite is not com-

posed exclusively, or even primarily, of corporate leaders. C. Wright Mills, an American sociologist, expresses this view in his book *The Power Elite*.[4] To him, the most important policies are set by a loose coalition of three groups—corporate leaders, top military officers, and a handful of key political lead-

Karl Marx (left) (1818–1883), a German philosopher and radical political leader, was the founder of modern socialist thought. A brilliant, complex, and vituperative writer, Marx was best known for his *Communist Manifesto.* His major work was *Das Kapital,* a four-volume analysis of nineteenth-century capitalism.

Max Weber (right) (1864–1920), a German scholar, was a founder of sociology. Trained in law and history, he produced a major analysis of the evolution of modern society, which stressed the role of bureaucracy.

ers. Different people have different versions of the "power elite" theory. Some would add to the triumvirate listed by Mills the leaders of the major communications media; others would add major labor leaders or the heads of various special-interest groups. The essential argument is the same, however: government is dominated by a few top leaders, most of whom are outside the government and enjoy great advantages in wealth, status, or organizational position. They act in concert, and the policies they make serve the interests of the elite. Some people have such leaders in mind when they use the term *the Establishment,* though when that expression was first coined it referred to the influence exercised by Wall Street lawyers who alternated between governmental and private employment.[5]

A third theory directs attention to the appointed officials—the **bureaucrats**—who operate government agencies from day to day. Max Weber, a German historian and sociologist who wrote in the early years of this century, criticized the Marxist position because it assigned exclusive significance to economic power. Weber thought Marx had neglected the dominant social and political fact of modern times—that all institutions, governmental and nongovernmental, have fallen under the control of large bureaucracies whose expertise and specialized competence are essential to the management of contemporary affairs. Capitalists or workers may

come to power, but the government agencies they create will be dominated by those who operate them on a daily basis. This dominance would have advantages, Weber thought, because decisions would be made more rationally; but it would also have disadvantages, because the political power of the bureaucrats would become "overtowering."[6]

A fourth answer has no single intellectual parent but can be described loosely as the **pluralist** view. Political resources, such as money, prestige, expertise, organizational position, and access to the mass media, are so widely scattered in our society and in the hands of such a variety of persons that no single elite has anything like a monopoly on them. Furthermore there are so many governmental institutions in which power may be exercised—city, state, and federal governments and, within these, the offices of mayors, managers, legislators, governors, presidents, judges, bureaucrats—that no single group, even if it had many political resources, could dominate most, or even much, of the political process. Policies are the outcome of a complex pattern of political haggling, innumerable compromises, and shifting alliances.[7] Pluralists do not argue that political resources are distributed equally—that would be tantamount to saying that all decisions are made on a majoritarian basis. They believe that political resources are sufficiently divided among such different kinds of elites (businesspeople, politicians,

What the Majority Wants: Of Government and Baseball

The choice between representative and direct democracy is central to governance. According to public opinion surveys, a majority of Americans would

- sentence all rapists to death

- oppose extending civil rights laws to homosexuals

- not allow anyone accused of a violent crime to get out on bail while awaiting trial

- spend less on foreign aid

- oppose military intervention if Arab forces invaded Israel

- spend more government money on medical care, protecting the environment, big cities, and transportation

- spend either the same amount or less government money on welfare, unemployment insurance, and programs that benefit minority citizens

- oppose the construction of nuclear power plants

- oppose giving financial aid to Russia

- have rejected the Marshall Plan (the financial support America gave to rebuild Europe after World War II)

- favor term limits for members of Congress

- favor amending the Constitution to require a balanced budget

Most Americans are in the majority on some issues but not on others. (Are you in the majority on some, all, or none of the issues listed above?) Thus, for most Americans, simply knowing what the majority wants is not a way to resolve the tension between direct and representative democracy.

As it is in government, so it is in major-league baseball. Most baseball fans like getting a chance to vote on which players merit selection to the All-Star teams. In 1992 at the All-Star break, Edgar Martinez of the Seattle Mariners was hitting .319 (third in the American League), with forty-six runs batted in, and fourteen home runs; he was a standout fielder. Wade Boggs of the New York Yankees was hitting .268 (sixty-fourth in the American League), with just twenty-five runs batted in, and only six home runs; he was having an average year fielding. But Boggs received 1.2 million votes versus Martinez's 500,000. Boggs played third base on the All-Star team; Martinez watched the game on TV. Direct democracy in baseball appeals to the fans, but does it produce the best All-Star teams?

SOURCE: Adapted from Christopher J. Georges, "Perot or Con," *The Washington Monthly* (June 1993): 38–43, and *The Gallup Monthly Poll* (April 1993): 31–34.

union leaders, journalists, bureaucrats, professors, environmentalists, lawyers, and whomever) that all, or almost all, relevant interests have a chance to affect the outcome of decisions. Not only are the elites divided, they are responsive to their followers' interests, and thus they provide representation to almost all citizens affected by a policy.

Contemplating these contending theories may lead some people to the cynical conclusion that, whichever theory is correct, politics is a self-seeking enterprise in which everybody is out for personal gain. Though there is surely plenty of self-interest among political elites (at least as much as there is among college students!), it does not necessarily follow that the resulting policies will be wholly self-serving. For one thing, a policy may be good or bad independently of the motives of the person who decided it, just as a product sold on the market may be useful or useless regardless of the profit-seeking or wage-seeking motives of those who produced it. For another thing, the self-interest of individuals is often an incomplete guide to their actions. People must frequently choose between two courses of action,

neither of which has an obvious "payoff" to them. We caution against the cynical explanation of politics that Americans seem especially prone to adopt. Alexis de Tocqueville, the French author of a perceptive account of American life and politics in the early nineteenth century, noticed this trait among us.

> *Americans . . . are fond of explaining almost all the actions of their lives by the principle of self-interest rightly understood. . . . In this respect I think they frequently fail to do themselves justice; for in the United States as well as elsewhere people are sometimes seen to give way to those disinterested and spontaneous impulses that are natural to man; but the Americans seldom admit that they yield to emotions of this kind; they are more anxious to do honor to their philosophy than to themselves.*[8]

The belief that people will usually act on the basis of their self-interest, narrowly defined, is a theory to be tested, not an assumption to be made. Two examples of how such an assumption can prove misleading will suffice for now. In the 1960s leaders of the AFL-CIO in Washington were among the most influential forces lobbying Congress for the passage of certain civil rights bills. Yet at the time they did this, the leaders did not stand to benefit either personally (they were almost all white) or organizationally (rank-and-file labor union members were not enthusiastic about such measures).[9] Another example: In the late 1970s, many employees of the Civil Aeronautics Board worked hard to have their agency abolished, even though this meant that they would lose their jobs. To understand why they took these positions, it is not enough to know their incomes or their jobs; one must also know something about their attitudes, their allies, and the temper of the times. In short, political preferences cannot invariably be predicted simply by knowing economic or organizational position.

Direct Democracy and the Computerized Presidency

Shortly after being elected to office, President Clinton starred in a television program that was billed as a "nationwide electronic town meeting" on jobs and the economy. The White House communications staff also employed a former disc jockey to develop "BC TV" (Bill Clinton TV), an interactive cable television station that would provide twenty-four-hour coverage of the presidency. Subscribers to major on-line computer services such as CompuServe can now punch in the command "GO WHITEHOUSE" to hook into the "White House forum," send or receive messages and information on dozens of subjects, or gain instant access to presidential speeches and photographs. During the Reagan years (1980–1988), the White House operators received five thousand calls on a busy day. But in the first months of the Clinton presidency, about forty thousand calls a day lit up the White House switchboard.

Political Change

The question of who governs will be answered differently at different times. Circumstances change, as does our knowledge about politics. As we shall see in

Part Three, the presidency and Congress in the second half of the nineteenth century were organized rather differently from how they are today. Throughout this book we shall make frequent reference to the historical evolution of institutions and policies. We shall do this partly because what government does today is powerfully influenced by what it did yesterday, and partly because the evolution of our institutions and policies has not stopped but is continuing. If we get some sense of how the past has shaped the government, we may better understand what we see today and are likely to see tomorrow.

When we view American government from the perspective of the past, we will find it hard to accept as generally true any simple, mechanistic theory of politics. Economic interests, powerful elites, entrenched bureaucrats, and competing pressure groups have all played a part in shaping our policies, but the great shifts in the direction of that policy respond to changing *beliefs* about what government is supposed to do.

In the 1920s it was widely assumed that the federal government would play a small role in our lives. From the 1930s through the 1970s it was generally believed that the federal government would try to solve whatever social or economic problem existed. From 1981 through 1988 the administration of Ronald Reagan sought to reverse that assumption and to cut back on the taxes Washington levied, the money it spent, and the regulations it imposed. It is clear that no simple theory of politics is likely to explain both the growth of federal power after 1932 and the effort to cut back on that power starting in 1981. Every student of politics sooner or later learns that the hardest things to explain are usually the most important ones.

Take the case of foreign affairs. During certain periods in our history we have taken an active interest in the outside world—at the time the nation was founded, when France and England seemed to have it in their power to determine whether or not America would survive as a nation; in the 1840s, when we sought to expand the nation into areas where Mexico and Canada had claims; in the late 1890s, when many leaders believed we had an obligation to acquire an overseas empire in the Caribbean and the Pacific; and in the period from the 1940s to the 1960s, when we

Direct political action can be peaceful or violent, as when abortion-rights advocates march (top) or opponents bomb an abortion clinic (bottom).

CRITICAL Thinking

Raising Taxes

From the birth of the nation to the present, few issues have excited more debate than taxation. The signers of the Declaration of Independence charged the king of Great Britain with "imposing taxes on us without our consent." Today, many Americans would make the same charge against their own elected representatives.

Americans seem especially unhappy with their federal tax burden: 80 percent rate the value they get from taxes paid to Washington as only fair or poor, and nearly three-quarters favor having all citizens vote on all proposals to raise federal taxes. But when asked which federal programs should be cut, solid majorities say no to cuts in Social Security, Medicare, Medicaid, environmental spending, unemployment insurance, student loans, and more.

How different do you suppose the distribution of federal tax burdens and benefits would be if average Americans had to approve or reject all major tax and spending proposals? When it comes to specific proposals for raising (or lowering) federal, state, or local taxes on income, property, sales, or "sins" (for example, taxes on cigarettes and liquor), how might one find out "who governs" and "to what ends"?

For starters, consider the federal income tax. For most of American history, there was no federal income tax. The Sixteenth Amendment to the Constitution, ratified in 1913, authorized Congress "to lay and collect taxes on incomes." As you might guess, not everyone was for it. Over the last eight decades, the federal income tax system has changed repeatedly in response to new economic ideas and competing political pressures. Today the federal government taxes income at five different rates that vary according to citizens' income level and marital status (see table below).

For example, let's say you graduate from college and land a job that pays you a taxable income of $31,000 a year. Under present federal tax laws, if you remained single you would owe Uncle Sam 15 percent on the first $23,350 of your taxable income ($3,502) and 28 percent on the next $7,650 of your taxable income ($2,142), for a total of $5,644. (That's not counting either the $2,371 you will have automatically deducted from your pay-

check for Social Security and Medicare or any of the state and local income, property, or other taxes you would be required to pay.) Should you ever be so prosperous as to make over $256,500 a year, you would pay about forty cents of every extra dollar you earned to the Internal Revenue Service.

The present federal income tax system is "progressive," meaning that rates rise with income. Some argue that the system should be more steeply progressive (it once was); others insist that the top federal tax rate should be lower than 39.6 percent (it once was); and still others favor a "flat tax," under which all citizens would pay at the same rate (such as 20 percent) on all taxable income above a certain minimum.

What do you think? In your view, who should make decisions about taxation, and what would constitute a fair income tax system? Jot down your preliminary answers to the questions posed above, think up and answer related questions of your own, and then return to review and critique what you wrote after you have finished reading this book.

Federal Income Tax Rates

Taxable Income, by Filing Status

Rates	Married filing jointly	Head of household	Single	Married filing separately
15%	0–$39,000	0–$31,250	0–$23,350	0–$19,500
28	$39,000–$94,250	$31,250–$80,750	$23,350–$56,550	$19,500–$47,125
31	$94,250–$143,600	$80,750–$130,800	$56,550–$117,950	$47,125–$71,800
36	$143,600–$256,500	$130,800–$256,500	$117,950–$256,500	$71,800–$128,250
39.6	over $256,500	over $256,500	over $256,500	over $128,250

SOURCES: *The American Enterprise*, March/April 1995, pp. 101, 103; *The Public Perspective*, April/May 1995, p. 5; *The American Enterprise*, July/August 1996, p. 19; *Consumer Reports Books: Guide to Income Tax 1996* (Consumers Union, 1995), p. 35.

openly accepted the role of the world's police officer. At other times America has looked inward, spurning opportunities for expansion and virtually ignoring events that in other periods would have been a cause for war, or at least mobilization.

Deep-seated beliefs, major economic developments, and widely shared (or competing) opinions about what constitutes the dominant political problem of the time shape the nature of day-to-day political conflict. What this means is that, in any broad historical or comparative perspective, politics is not just about "who gets what," though that is part of the story. It is about how people, or elites claiming to speak for people, define the public interest. Lest one think that such definitions are mere window dressing, signifying nothing of importance, bear in mind that on occasion men and women have been prepared to fight and die for one definition or another. Suppose you, the reader, had been alive in 1861. Do you think you would have viewed slavery as a matter of gains and losses, costs and benefits, winners and losers? Some people did. Or do you think you would have been willing to fight to abolish or preserve it? Many others did just that. The differences in these ways of thinking about such an issue are at least as important as how institutions are organized or elections conducted.

Finding Out Who Governs

Ideally political scientists ought to be able to give clear answers, amply supported by evidence, to the questions, How is political power distributed? and To what purposes will it be used under various circumstances? In reality they can (at best) give partial, contingent, and controversial answers. The reason is to be found in the nature of our subject. Unlike economists, who assume that people have more or less stable preferences and can compare ways of satisfying those preferences by looking at the relative prices of various goods and services, political scientists are interested in how preferences are formed, especially for those kinds of services, such as national defense or pollution control, that cannot be evaluated chiefly in terms of monetary costs.

Understanding preferences is vital to understanding power. Who did what in government is not

hard to find out, but who wielded power—that is, who made a difference in the outcome and for what reason—is much harder to discover. *Power* is a word that conjures up images of deals, bribes, power plays, and arm-twisting. In fact most power exists because of shared understanding, common friendships, communal or organizational loyalties, and different degrees of prestige. These are hard to identify and almost impossible to quantify.

Nor can the distribution of political power be inferred simply by knowing what laws are on the books or what administrative actions have been taken. The enactment of a consumer-protection law does not mean that consumers are powerful any more than the absence of such a law means that corporations are powerful. The passage of such a law could reflect an aroused public opinion, the lobbying of a small group claiming to speak for consumers, the ambitions of a senator, or the intrigues of one business firm seeking to gain a competitive advantage over another. A close analysis of what the law entails and how it was passed and administered is necessary before much of anything can be said.

This book will avoid sweeping claims that we have an "imperial" presidency (or an impotent one), an "obstructionist" Congress (or an innovative one), or "captured" regulatory agencies. Such labels do an injustice to the different roles that presidents, members of Congress, and administrators play in different kinds of issues and in different historical periods.

The view taken in this book is that judgments about institutions and interests can be made only after one has seen how they behave on a variety of important issues or potential issues, such as economic policy, the regulation of business, social welfare, civil rights and liberties, and foreign and military affairs. The policies adopted or blocked, the groups heeded or ignored, the values embraced or rejected—these constitute the raw material out of which one can fashion an answer to the central questions we have asked: Who rules? and To what ends?

The way in which our institutions of government handle social welfare, for example, differs from the way other democratic nations handle it, and it differs as well from the way our own institutions once treated it. The description of our institutions in Part Three will therefore include not only an account of how they work today but also a brief historical background on their workings and a comparison with similar institutions in other countries. There is a tendency to assume that how we do things today is the only way they could possibly be done. In fact there are other ways to operate a government based on some measure of popular rule. History, tradition, and belief weigh heavily on all that we do.

In any event the place to begin a search for how power is distributed in national politics and what purposes that power serves is with the founding of the federal government in 1787: the Constitutional Convention and the events leading up to it. Though the decisions of that time were not made by philosophers or professors, the practical men who made them had a philosophic and professorial cast of mind, and thus they left behind a fairly explicit account of what values they sought to protect and what arrangements they thought ought to be made for the allocation of political power.

SUMMARY

There are two major questions about politics: Who governs? To what ends? This book will focus mainly on answering the first.

Four answers have traditionally been given to the question of who governs.

- The *Marxist*—those who control the economic system will control the political one.
- The *elitist*—a few top leaders, not all of them drawn from business, make the key decisions without reference to popular desires.
- The *bureaucratic*—appointed civil servants run things.
- The *pluralist*—competition among affected interests shapes public policy.

To choose among these theories or to devise new ones requires more than describing governmental institutions and processes. In addition one must examine the kinds of issues that do (or do not) get taken up by the political system and how that system resolves them.

The distinction between different types of democracies is important. The Framers of the Constitution intended that America be a representative democracy in which the power to make decisions is determined by means of a free and competitive struggle for the citizens' votes.

KEY TERMS

power *p. 4*

authority *p. 4*

legitimacy *p. 5*

democracy *p. 5*

democratic centralism *p. 6*

direct or participatory democracy *p. 6*

representative democracy *p. 6*

elite *p. 8*

Marxists *p. 8*

bureaucrats *p. 10*

pluralist *p. 10*

SUGGESTED READINGS

Banfield, Edward C. *Political Influence.* New York: Free Press, 1961. A method of analyzing politics—in this case, in the city of Chicago—comparable to the approach adopted in this book.

Crick, Bernard. *The American Science of Politics.* London: Routledge & Kegan Paul, 1959. A critical review of the methods of studying government and politics.

Marx, Karl, and Friedrich Engels. "The Manifesto of the Communist Party." In *The Marx-Engels Reader,* edited by Robert C. Tucker. 2d ed. New York: Norton, 1978, 469–500. The classic statement of the Marxist view of history and politics. Should be read in conjunction with Engels, "Socialism: Utopian and Scientific," in the same collection, 683–717.

Mills, C. Wright. *The Power Elite.* New York: Oxford University Press, 1956. An argument that self-serving elites dominate American politics.

Schumpeter, Joseph A. *Capitalism, Socialism, and Democracy.* 3d ed. New York: Harper, 1950, Chs. 20–23. A lucid statement of the theory of representative democracy and how it differs from participatory democracy.

Truman, David B. *The Government Process.* 2d ed. New York: Knopf, 1971. A pluralist interpretation of American politics.

Weber, Max. *From Max Weber: Essays in Sociology.* Translated and edited by H. H. Gerth and C. Wright Mills. London: Routledge & Kegan Paul, 1948, Ch. 8. A theory of bureaucracy and its power.

2

The Constitution

★ Revolution fought for liberty

★ Colonists' views on government

★ Problems with the Confederation

★ Innovative state constitutions

★ Shays's Rebellion

★ Framing the Constitution

★ *Federalist* papers

★ Checks on popular rule

★ Protecting liberty

★ Need for Bill of Rights

★ Position on slaves and women

★ Motives of the Framers

★ Constitutional reform

The goal of the American Revolution was liberty. It was not the first revolution with that object; it may not have been the last; but it was perhaps the clearest case of a people altering the political order violently, simply in order to protect their liberties. Subsequent revolutions had more complicated, or utterly different, objectives. The French Revolution in 1789 sought not only liberty, but "equality and fraternity." The Russian Revolution (1917) and the Chinese Revolution (culminating in 1949) chiefly sought equality and were little concerned with liberty as we understand it.

The Problem of Liberty

What the American colonists sought to protect when they signed the Declaration of Independence in 1776 were the traditional liberties to which they thought they were entitled as British subjects. These liberties included the right to bring their legal cases before truly independent judges rather than ones subordinate to the king; to be free of the burden of having British troops quartered in their homes; to engage in trade without burdensome restrictions; and, of course, to pay no taxes voted by a British Parliament in which they had no direct representation. During the ten years or more of agitation and argument leading up to the War of Independence, most colonists believed that their liberties could be protected while they remained a part of the British Empire.

Slowly but surely opinion shifted. By the time war broke out in 1775, a large number of colonists (though perhaps not a majority) had reached the conclusion that the colonies would have to become independent of Great Britain if their liberties were to be assured. The colonists had many reasons for regarding independence as the only solution, but one is especially important: they no longer had confidence in the English constitution. This constitution was not a single written document but rather a collection of laws, charters, and traditional understandings that proclaimed the liberties of British subjects. Yet these liberties, in the eyes of the colonists, were regularly

19

Even before the Revolutionary War, many felt that some form of union would be necessary if the rebellious colonies were to survive. In 1774 the *Massachusetts Spy* portrayed the colonies as segments of a snake that must "Join or Die."

violated despite their constitutional protection. Clearly, then, the English constitution was an inadequate check on the abuses of political power. The revolutionary leaders sought an explanation of the insufficiency of the constitution and found it in human nature.

The Colonial Mind

"A lust for domination is more or less natural to all parties," one colonist wrote.[1] Men will seek power, many colonists believed, because they are ambitious, greedy, and easily corrupted. John Adams denounced the "luxury, effeminacy, and venality" of English politics; Patrick Henry spoke scathingly of the "corrupt House of Commons"; and Alexander Hamilton described England as "an old, wrinkled, withered, worn-out hag."[2] This was in part flamboyant rhetoric designed to whip up enthusiasm for the conflict, but it was also deeply revealing of the colonial mind. Their belief that English politicians—and by implication, most politicians—tended to be corrupt was the colonists' explanation of why the English constitution was not an adequate guarantee of the liberty of the citizens. This opinion was to persist and, as we shall see, profoundly affect the way the Americans went about designing their own governments.

The liberties the colonists fought to protect were, they thought, widely understood. They were

based not on the generosity of the king or the language of statutes but on a "higher law" embodying "natural rights" that were ordained by God, discoverable in nature and history, and essential to human progress. These rights, John Dickinson wrote, "are born with us; exist with us; and cannot be taken away from us by any human power."[3] There was general agreement that the essential rights included life, liberty, and property long before Thomas Jefferson wrote them into the Declaration of Independence. (Jefferson changed "property" to "the pursuit of happiness," but almost everybody else went on talking about property.)

This emphasis on property did not mean that the American Revolution was thought up by the rich and wellborn to protect their interests or that there was a struggle between property owners and the propertyless. In late eighteenth-century America most people (except the black slaves) had property of some kind. The overwhelming majority of citizens were self-employed—as farmers or artisans—and rather few people benefited financially by gaining independence from England. Taxes were higher during and after the war than before, trade was disrupted by the conflict, and debts mounted perilously as various expedients were invented to pay for the struggle. There were, of course, war profiteers and those who tried to manipulate the currency to their own advantage, but most Americans at the time of the war saw the con-

WILLIAM WALCUTT, *PULLING DOWN THE STATUE OF GEORGE III AT BOWLING GREEN*, 1857

The American colonists' desire to assert their liberties led in time to a deep hostility to British government, as when these New Yorkers toppled a statue of King George III, melted it down, and used the metal to make bullets.

flict clearly in terms of political rather than economic issues. It was a war of ideology.

Everyone recognizes the glowing language with which Jefferson set out the case for independence in the second paragraph of the Declaration:

> We hold these truths to be self-evident, that all men are created equal, that they are endowed by their Creator with certain unalienable Rights, that among these are Life, Liberty, and the pursuit of Happiness.—That to secure these rights, Governments are instituted among Men, deriving their just powers from the consent of the governed—that whenever any Form of Government becomes destructive of these ends, it is the Right of the People to alter or to abolish it, and to institute new Government, having its foundation on such principles, and organizing its powers in such form, as to them shall seem most likely to effect their Safety and Happiness.

What almost no one recalls, but what are an essential part of the Declaration, are the next twenty-seven paragraphs, in which Jefferson listed, item by item, the specific complaints the colonists had against George III and his ministers. None of these items spoke of social or economic conditions in the colonies; all spoke instead of specific violations of political liberties. The Declaration was in essence a lawyer's brief prefaced by a stirring philosophical claim that the rights being violated were **unalienable**—that is, based on nature and Providence, and not on the whims or preferences of people. Jefferson, in his original draft, added a twenty-eighth complaint—that the king had allowed the slave trade to continue *and* was inciting slaves to revolt against their masters. Congress, faced with so contradictory a charge, decided to include a muted reference to slave insurrections and omit all reference to the slave trade.

The Real Revolution

The Revolution was more than the War of Independence. It began before the war, continued after it, and involved more than driving out the British army by force of arms. The *real* Revolution, as John Adams afterward explained in a letter to a friend, was the "*radical change in the principles, opinions, and sentiments, and affections of the people.*"[4] This radical change had to do with a new vision of what could make political authority legitimate and personal liberties secure. Government by royal pre-

NORTH AMERICA IN 1787

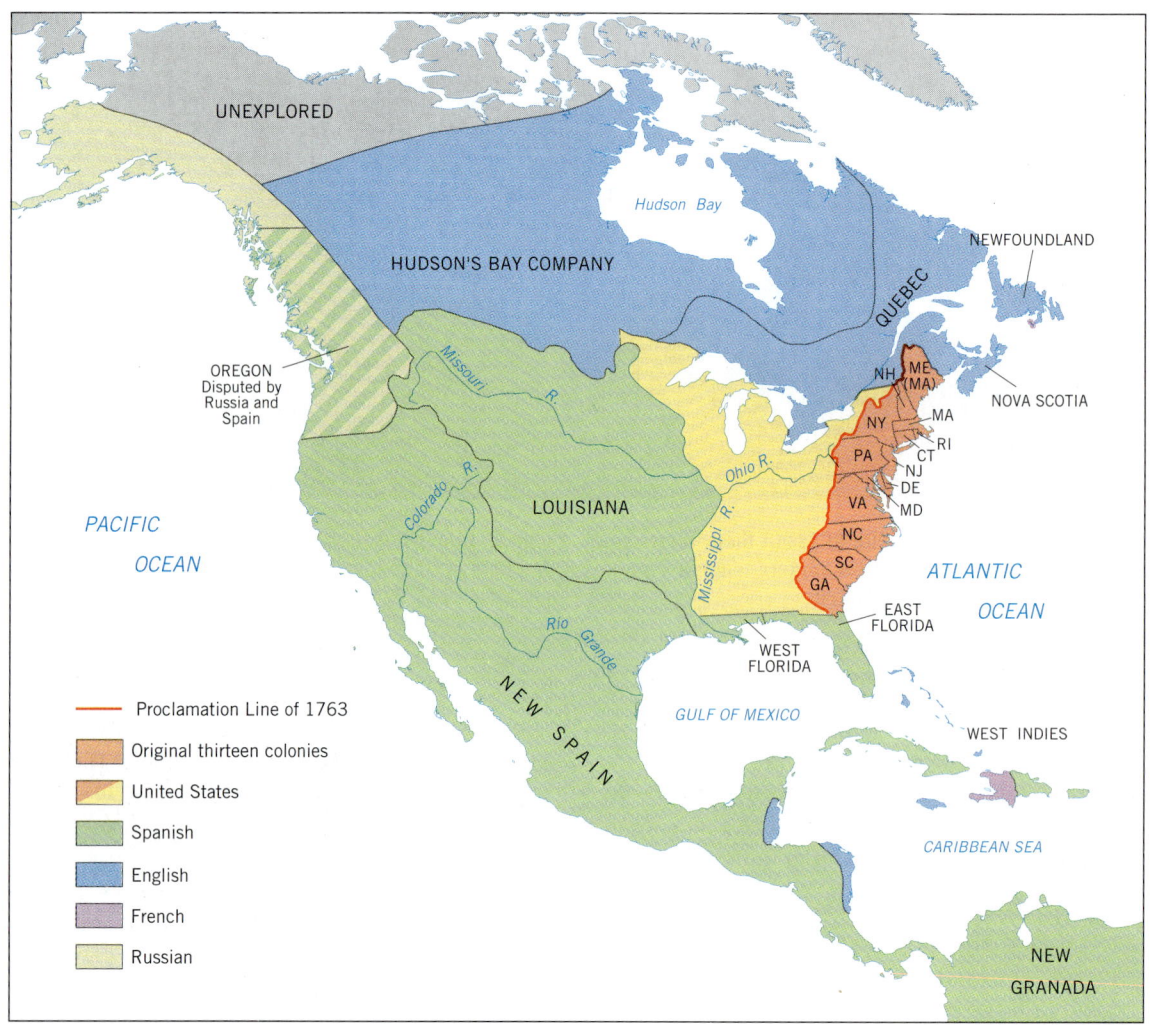

rogative was rejected; instead legitimate government would require the consent of the governed. Political power could not be exercised on the basis of tradition but only as a result of a direct grant of power contained in a written constitution. Human liberty existed before government was organized, and government must respect that liberty. The legislative branch of government, in which the people were directly represented, should be superior to the executive branch.

These were indeed revolutionary ideas. No government at the time had been organized on the basis of these principles. And to the colonists such no-

tions were not empty words but rules to be put into immediate practice. In 1776 eight states adopted written constitutions. Within a few years every former colony had adopted one except Connecticut and Rhode Island, two states that continued to rely on their colonial charters. Most state constitutions had detailed bills of rights defining personal liberties, and most placed the highest political power in the hands of elected representatives.

Written constitutions, representatives, and bills of rights are so familiar to us now that we forget how bold and unprecedented those innovations were in 1776. Indeed, many Americans did not think they would succeed: such arrangements would be either so strong that they would threaten liberty or so weak that they would permit chaos.

The eleven years that elapsed between the Declaration of Independence and the signing of the Constitution in 1787 were years of turmoil, uncertainty, and fear. George Washington had to wage a bitter, protracted war without anything resembling a strong national government to support him. The supply and financing of his army were based on a series of hasty improvisations, most badly administered and few adequately supported by the fiercely independent states. When peace came, many parts of the nation were a shambles. At least a quarter of New York City was in ruins, and many other communities were nearly devastated. Though the British lost the war, they still were powerful on the North American continent, with an army available in Canada (where many Americans loyal to Britain had fled) and a large navy at sea. Spain claimed the Mississippi River Valley and occupied what are now Florida and California. Men who had left their farms to fight came back to discover themselves in debt with no money and heavy taxes. The paper money printed to finance the war was now virtually worthless.

Weaknesses of the Confederation

The thirteen states had formed only a faint semblance of a national government with which to bring order to the nation. The **Articles of Confederation,** which went into effect in 1781, created little more than a "league of friendship" that could not levy taxes or regulate commerce. Each state retained

John Hancock was proud to have signed the Declaration of Independence, but thought so little of the presidency under the Articles of Confederation that he never bothered to accept the job.

The Articles of Confederation had made it plain that the United States was not to have a true national government but was to be governed by a compact among sovereign and independent states.

Independence Hall in Philadelphia, where the Declaration of Independence and the Constitution were signed.

its sovereignty and independence, each state (regardless of size) had one vote in Congress, nine (of thirteen) votes were required to pass any measure, and the delegates who cast these votes were picked and paid for by the state legislatures. Congress did have the power to make peace, and thus it was able to ratify the treaty with England in 1783. It could coin money, but there was precious little to coin; it could appoint the key army officers, but the army was small and dependent for support on independent state militias; it was allowed to run the post office, then, as now, a thankless task that nobody else wanted. John Hancock, who in 1785 was elected to the meaningless office of "president" under the Articles, never showed up to take the job. Several states claimed the unsettled lands in the West, and they occasionally pressed those claims with guns. Pennsylvania and Virginia went to war near

Pittsburgh, and Vermont threatened to become part of Canada. There was no national judicial system to settle these or other claims among the states. To amend the Articles of Confederation, all thirteen states had to agree.

Many of the leaders of the Revolution, such as George Washington and Alexander Hamilton, believed that a stronger national government was essential. They lamented the disruption of commerce and travel caused by the quarrelsome states and deeply feared the possibility of foreign military intervention, with England or France playing one state off against another. A small group of men, conferring at Washington's home at Mount Vernon in 1785, decided to call a meeting to discuss trade regulation. That meeting, held at Annapolis, Maryland, in September 1786, was not well attended (no delegates arrived from New England), and so another meeting, this one in Philadelphia, was called for the following spring—in May 1787—to consider ways of remedying the defects of the Confederation.

The Constitutional Convention

The delegates assembled at Philadelphia for what was advertised (and authorized by Congress) as a meeting to revise the Articles; they adjourned four months later having written a wholly new constitution. When they met, they were keenly aware of the problems of the confederacy but far from agreeing as to what should be done about those problems. The protection of life, liberty, and property was their objective in 1787 as it had been in 1776, but they had no accepted political theory that would tell them what kind of national government, if any, would serve that goal.

The Lessons of Experience

They had read ancient and modern political history, only to learn that nothing seemed to work. James Madison spent a good part of 1786 studying books sent to him by Thomas Jefferson, then in Paris, in hopes of finding some model for a workable American republic. He took careful notes on various confederacies in ancient Greece and on the more modern confederacy of the United Netherlands. He reviewed the history of Switzerland and Poland and the ups and downs of the Roman republic. He concluded that there was no model; as he later put it in one of the *Federalist* papers, history consists only of beacon lights "which give warning of the course to be shunned, without pointing out that which ought to be pursued."[5] The problem seemed to be that confederacies were too weak to govern and tended to collapse from internal dissension, while all stronger forms of government were so powerful as to trample the liberties of the citizens.

State Constitutions   Madison and the others did not need to consult history, or even the defects of the Articles of Confederation, for illustrations of the problem. These could be found in the government of the American states at the time. Pennsylvania and Massachusetts exemplified two aspects of the problem. The Pennsylvania constitution, adopted in 1776, created the most radically democratic of the new state regimes. All power was given to a one-house (unicameral) legislature, the Assembly, the members of which were elected annually for one-year terms. No legislator could serve more than four years. There was no governor or president, only an Executive Council that had few powers. Thomas Paine, whose pamphlets had helped precipitate the break with England, thought the Pennsylvania constitution was the best in America, and in France philosophers hailed it as the very embodiment of the principle of rule by the people. Though popular in France, it was a good deal less popular in Philadelphia. The Assembly disfranchised the Quakers, persecuted conscientious objectors to the war, ignored the requirement of trial by juries, and manipulated the judiciary.[6] To Madison and his friends the Pennsylvania constitution demonstrated how a government, though democratic, could be tyrannical as a result of concentrating all powers into one set of hands.

The Massachusetts constitution, adopted in 1780, was a good deal less democratic. There was a clear separation of powers among the various branches of government, the directly elected governor could veto acts of the legislature, and judges served for life. Both voters and elected officials had to be property owners; the governor, in fact, had to own at least £1,000 worth of property. The principal officeholders had to swear that they were Christians.

The presiding officer at the Constitutional Convention was George Washington (1732–1799). He participated just once in the debates, but the effect of his presence was great. He was a national military hero, and it was generally expected that he would be the nation's first president.

Shays's Rebellion   But if the government of Pennsylvania was thought to be too strong, that of Massachusetts seemed too weak, despite its "conservative" features. In January 1787 a group of ex-Revolutionary War soldiers and officers, plagued by debts and high taxes and fearful of losing their property to creditors and tax collectors, forcibly prevented the courts in western Massachusetts from sitting. This became known as **Shays's Rebellion,** after one of the officers, Daniel Shays. The governor of Massachusetts asked the Continental Congress to send troops to suppress the rebellion, but it could not raise the money or the manpower. Then he turned to his own state militia, but discovered he did not have one. In desperation private funds were collected to hire a volunteer army, which marched on Springfield and, with the firing of a few shots, dispersed the rebels, who fled into neighboring states.

Shays's Rebellion, occurring between the aborted Annapolis and the coming Philadelphia conventions, had a powerful effect on opinion. Delegates who might have been reluctant to attend the Philadelphia meeting, especially those from New England, were galvanized by the fear that state governments were about to collapse from internal dissension. George

Shays's Rebellion in western Massachusetts in 1786–1787 stirred deep fears of anarchy in America. The ruckus was put down by a hastily assembled militia, and the rebels were eventually pardoned.

Commonwealth of Massachusetts,

By BENJAMIN LINCOLN, Esquire,

Commanding General of the Troops now in the Field, by Order of

GOVERNMENT.

Whereas there are some of the Citizens of this Commonwealth, who have acted in Arms as Non-Commissioned Officers and Privates against the Government of this State, who have caused it to be represented, that they would willingly return to their Allegiance and Duty, could they hope for a Pardon.

To all such I declare, That if they will come in, surrender their Arms, and take and subscribe the Oath of Allegiance to this Commonwealth, that they will be recommended to a Pardon.

B. LINCOLN.

Dated at Head-Quarters, Pittsfield, *February* 19, 1787.

Washington wrote a friend despairingly: "For God's sake..., if they [the rebels] have *real* grievances, redress them; if they have not, employ the force of government against them at once."[7] Thomas Jefferson, living in Paris, took a more detached view: "A little rebellion now and then is a good thing," he wrote. "The tree of liberty must be refreshed from time to time with the blood of patriots and tyrants."[8] Though Jefferson's detachment might be explained by the fact that he was in Paris and not in Springfield, there were others, like Governor George Clinton of New York, who shared the view that no strong central government was required. (Whether Clinton would have agreed about the virtues of spilled blood, especially his, is another matter.)

The Framers

The Philadelphia convention attracted fifty-five delegates, only about thirty of whom participated regularly in the proceedings. One state, Rhode Island, refused to send anyone. The convention met during a miserably hot Philadelphia summer, with the delegates pledged to keep their deliberations secret. The talkative and party-loving Benjamin Franklin was often accompanied by other delegates to make sure that neither wine nor his delight in telling stories would lead him to divulge delicate secrets.

Those who attended were for the most part young (Hamilton was thirty; Madison, thirty-six) but experienced. Eight delegates had signed the Declaration of Independence, seven had been governors, thirty-four were lawyers and reasonably well-to-do, a few were wealthy. They were not "intellectuals," but men of practical affairs. Thirty-nine had served in the ineffectual Congress of the Confederation; a third were veterans of the Continental army.

Some names made famous by the Revolution were conspicuously absent. Thomas Jefferson and John Adams were serving as ministers abroad; Samuel Adams was ill; Patrick Henry was chosen to attend but refused, commenting that he "smelled a rat in Philadelphia, tending toward monarchy."

The convention produced not a revision of the Articles of Confederation, as it had been authorized to do, but instead a wholly new written constitution creating a true national government unlike any that had existed before. That document is today the world's oldest written national constitution. Those who wrote it were neither saints nor schemers, and the deliberations were not always lofty or philosophical—much hard bargaining, not a little confusion, and the accidents of personality and time helped shape the final product. The delegates were split on many issues—what powers should be given to a central government, how the states should be represented, what was to be done about slavery, the role of the people—each of which was resolved by a compromise. The speeches of the delegates (known to us from the detailed notes kept by Madison) did not explicitly draw on political philosophy or quote from the writings of philosophers. Everybody present was quite familiar with the traditional arguments and, on the whole, well read in history. But though the leading political philosophers were only rarely mentioned, the debate was profoundly influenced by philosophical beliefs, some formed by the revolutionary experience and others by the eleven-year attempt at self-government.

From the debates leading up to the Revolution, the delegates had drawn a commitment to liberty, which, despite the abuses sometimes committed in its name, they continued to share. Their defense of liberty as a natural right was derived from the writings of the English philosopher John Locke and based on his view that such rights are discoverable by reason. In a "state of nature," Locke argued, all men cherish and seek to protect their life, liberty, and property. But in a state of nature—that is, a society without a government—the strong can use their liberty to deprive the weak of theirs. The in-

Patrick Henry   **James Madison**   **Thomas Jefferson**

Edmund Randolph   **John Locke**   **William Paterson**

The Federalist Papers

In 1787, to help win ratification of the new Constitution in the New York state convention, Alexander Hamilton decided to publish a series of articles defending and explaining the document in the New York City newspapers. He recruited John Jay and James Madison to help him, and the three of them, under the pen name "Publius," wrote eighty-five articles that appeared from late 1787 through 1788. The identity of the authors was kept secret at the time, but we now know that Hamilton wrote fifty-one of them, Madison twenty-six, and Jay five, and Hamilton and Madison jointly authored three. The two most famous articles—Numbers 10 and 51—were by Madison alone (and are reprinted here in the Appendix).

The *Federalist* papers probably played only a small role in securing ratification. Like most legislative battles, this one was not decisively influenced by philosophical writings. But these essays have had a lasting value as an authoritative and profound explanation of the Constitution. Though written for political purposes, the *Federalist* has become the single most important piece of American political philosophy ever produced. Ironically Hamilton and Madison were later to become political enemies; even at the Philadelphia convention they had different views of the kind of government that should be created. But in 1787–1788 they were united in the belief that the new constitution was the best that could have been obtained under the circumstances.

James Madison

John Jay

For the Independent Journal.

The FŒDERALIST. No. X.

To the People of the State of New-York.

AMONG the numerous advantages promised by a well constructed Union, none deserves to be more accurately developed than its tendency to break and control the violence of faction. The friend of popular governments, never finds himself so much alarmed for their character and fate, as when he contemplates their propensity to this dangerous vice. He will not fail therefore to set a due value on any plan which, without violating the principles to which he is attached, provides a proper cure for it. The instability, injustice and confusion introduced into the public councils, have in truth been the mortal diseases under which popular governments have every where perished; as they continue to be the favorite and fruitful topics from which the adversaries to liberty derive their most specious declamations. The valuable improvements made by the American Constitutions on the popular models, both ancient and modern, cannot certainly be too much admired; but it would be an unwarrantable partiality, to contend that they have as effectually obviated the danger on this side as was wished and expected. Complaints are every where heard from our most considerate and virtuous citizens, equally the friends of public and private faith, and of public and personal liberty; that our governments are too unstable; that the public

Alexander Hamilton

stinct for self-preservation leads people to want a government that will prevent this exploitation. But if the government is not itself to deprive its subjects of their liberty, it must be limited. The chief limitation on it, he said, should derive from the fact that it is created, and governs, by the consent of the governed. People will not agree to be ruled by a government that threatens their liberty; therefore the government to which they freely choose to submit themselves will be a limited government designed to protect liberty.

The Pennsylvania experience as well as the history of British government led the Framers to doubt whether popular consent alone would be a sufficient guarantor of liberty. A popular government may prove too weak (as in Massachusetts) to prevent one faction from abusing another, or a popular majority can be tyrannical (as in Pennsylvania). In fact the tyranny of the majority can be an even graver threat than rule by the few. In the former case there may be no defenses for the individual—one lone person cannot count on the succor of public opinion or the possibility of popular revolt.

The problem, then, was a delicate one: how to devise a government strong enough to preserve order but not so strong that it would threaten liberty. The answer, the delegates believed, was not "democracy" as it was then understood. To many conservatives in the late eighteenth century, democracy meant mob rule—it meant, in short, Shays's Rebellion (or if they had been candid about it, the Boston Tea Party). On the other hand, *aristocracy*—the rule of the few—was no solution, since the few were likely to be self-seeking. Madison, writing later in the *Federalist* papers, put the problem this way:

> *If men were angels, no government would be necessary. If angels were to govern men, neither external nor internal controls on government would be necessary. In framing a government which is to be administered by men over men, the great difficulty lies in this: you must first enable the government to control the governed; and in the next place oblige it to control itself.*[9]

Striking this balance could not be done, Madison believed, simply by writing a constitution that set limits on what government could do. The example

of British rule over the colonies proved that laws and customs were inadequate checks on political power. As he expressed it, "A mere demarcation on parchment of the constitutional limits [of government] is not a sufficient guard against those encroachments which lead to a tyrannical concentration of all the powers of government in the same hands."[10]

The Challenge

The resolution of political issues, great and small, often depends crucially on how the central question is phrased. The delegates came to Philadelphia in general agreement that there were defects in the Articles of Confederation that ought to be remedied. Had they, after convening, decided to make their business that of listing these defects and debating alternative remedies for them, the document that emerged would in all likelihood have been very different from what in fact was adopted. But immediately after the convention had organized itself and chosen Washington to be its presiding officer, the Virginia delegation, led by Governor Edmund Randolph but relying heavily on the draftsmanship of James Madison, presented to the convention a comprehensive plan for a wholly new national government. The plan quickly became the major item of business of the meeting; it, and little else, was debated for the next two weeks.

The Virginia Plan

When the convention decided to make the Virginia Plan its agenda, it had fundamentally altered the nature of its task. The business at hand was not to be the Articles and their defects, but rather how one should go about designing a true national government. The Virginia Plan called for a strong national union organized into three governmental branches—the legislative, executive, and judicial. The legislature was to be composed of two houses, the first elected directly by the people and the second chosen by the first house from among the people nominated by state legislatures. The executive was to be chosen by the national legislature, as were members of a national judiciary. The executive and some members of the judiciary

CRITICAL Thinking

How to Read the Federalist *Papers 10 and 51*

James Madison is rightly regarded as the single most important mind behind the Constitution, and his ideas are worth knowing first-hand. The Appendix to this book contains reprints of Madison's *Federalist* papers 10 and 51. After you have finished this chapter, turn to the Appendix and try to read them. On your first reading of the papers you may find Madison's language difficult to understand and his ideas overly complex. The following pointers will help you decipher his meaning.

In *Federalist* No. 10, Madison begins by stating that "a well constructed Union" can "break and control the violence of faction." He goes on to define a "faction" as any group of citizens who attempt to advance their ideas or economic interests at the expense of other citizens, or in ways that conflict with "the permanent and aggregate interests of the community" or "public good." Thus, what Madison terms "factions" are what we today call "special interests."

One way to defeat factions, according to Madison, is to remove whatever causes them to arise in the first place. This can be attempted in two ways. First, government can deprive people of the liberty they need to organize: "Liberty is to faction what air is to fire." But that is surely a cure "worse than the disease." Second, measures can be taken to make all citizens share the same ideas, feelings, and economic interests. However, as Madison

observes, some people are smarter or more hard working than others, and this "diversity in the faculties" of citizens is bound to result in different economic interests as some people acquire more property than others. Consequently, protecting property rights, not equalizing property ownership, "is the first object of government." Even if everyone shared the same basic economic interests they would still find reasons "to vex and oppress each other" rather than cooperate "for their common good." Religious differences, loyalties to different leaders, even "frivolous and fanciful distinctions" (not liking how other people dress or their taste in music) can be fertile soil for factions. In Madison's view people are factious by nature; the "causes of faction" are "sown" into their very being.

Madison thus proposes a second and, he thinks, more practical and desirable way of defeating faction. The way to cure "the mischiefs of faction" is not by removing its causes but by "controlling its effects." Factions will always exist, so the trick is to establish a form of government that is likely to serve the public good through the even-handed "regulation of these various and interfering interests." Wise and public-spirited leaders can "adjust these clashing interests and render them all subservient to the public good," but, he cautions, "Enlightened statesmen will not always be at the helm." (Madison implies that

"enlightened statesmen"—such as himself, Washington, and Jefferson—were at the "helm" of government in 1787.)

Madison's proposed cure for the evils of factions is in fact nothing other than a republican form of government. Use the following questions to guide your own analysis of Madison's ideas. Why does Madison think the problem of a "minority" faction is easy to handle? Conversely, why is he so troubled by the potential of a majority faction? How does he distinguish direct democracy from republican government? What is he getting at when he terms elected representatives "proper guardians of the public weal," and why does he think that "extensive republics" are more likely to produce such representatives than small ones?

When you are finished with *Federalist* No. 10, try your hand at *Federalist* No. 51. You will find that the ideas in the former paper anticipate many of those in the latter. And you will find many points on which you may or may not agree with Madison. For example, do you agree with his assumption that people—even your best friends or college roommates—are factious by nature? Likewise, do you agree with his view that government is "the greatest of all reflections on human nature"?

By attempting to meet the mind of James Madison, you can sharpen your own mind and deepen your understanding of American government.

were to constitute a "council of revision" that could veto acts of the legislature; that veto, in turn, could be overridden by the legislature. There were other interesting details, but the key features of the Virginia Plan were two: (1) a national legislature would have

supreme powers on all matters on which the separate states were not competent to act, as well as the power to veto any and all state laws, and (2) at least one house of the legislature would be elected directly by the people.

The New Jersey Plan

As the debate went on, the representatives of New Jersey and other small states became increasingly worried that the convention was going to write a constitution in which the states would be represented in both houses of Congress on the basis of population. If this happened, the smaller states feared they would always be outvoted by the larger ones, and so, with William Paterson of New Jersey as their spokesman, they introduced a new plan. The New Jersey Plan proposed to amend, not replace, the old Articles of Confederation. It enhanced the power of the national government (though not as much as the Virginia Plan), but it did so in a way that left the states' representation in Congress unchanged from the Articles—each state would have one vote. Thus not only would the interests of the small states be protected, but Congress itself would remain to a substantial degree the creature of state governments.

If the New Jersey resolutions had been presented first and taken up as the major item of business, it is quite possible that they would have become the framework for the document that finally emerged. But they were not. Offered after the convention had been discussing the Virginia Plan for two weeks, the resolutions encountered a reception very different from what they would have received if introduced earlier. The debate had the delegates already thinking in terms of a national government that was more independent of the states, and thus it had accustomed them to proposals that, under other circumstances, might have seemed quite radical. On June 19 the first decisive vote of the convention was taken: seven states preferred the Virginia Plan, three states the New Jersey Plan, and one state was split.

With the tide running in favor of a strong national government, the supporters of the small states had to shift their strategy. They now began to focus their efforts on ensuring that the small states could not be outvoted by the larger ones in Congress. One way was to have the members of the lower house elected by the state legislatures rather than the people, with each state getting the same number of seats rather than seats proportional to its population.

The debate was long and feelings ran high, so much so that Benjamin Franklin, at eighty-one the oldest delegate present, suggested that each day's meeting begin with a prayer. It turned out that the convention could not even agree on this: Hamilton is supposed to have objected that the convention did not need "foreign aid," and others pointed out that the group had no funds with which to hire a minister. And so the argument continued.

The Compromise

Finally a committee was appointed to meet during the Fourth of July holidays to work out a compromise, and the convention adjourned to await its report. Little is known of what went on in that committee's session, though some were later to say that Franklin played a key role in hammering out the plan that finally emerged. That compromise, the most important reached at the convention, and later called the **Great Compromise** (or sometimes the Connecticut Compromise), was submitted to the full convention on July 5 and debated for another week and a half. The debate might have gone on even longer, but suddenly the hot weather moderated, and Monday, July 16, dawned cool and fresh after a month of misery. On that day the plan was adopted: five states were in favor, four opposed, and two not voting.* Thus, by the narrowest of margins, the structure of the national legislature was set, as follows:

- A House of Representatives consisting initially of sixty-five members apportioned among the states roughly on the basis of population and elected by the people

- A Senate consisting of two senators from each state to be chosen by the state legislatures

The Great Compromise reconciled the interests of small and large states by allowing the former to predominate in the Senate and the latter in the House. This reconciliation was necessary to ensure that there would be support for a strong national government from small as well as large states. It represented major concessions on the part of several groups. Madison, for one, was deeply opposed to the idea of having the states equally represented in the

---

* The states in favor were Connecticut, Delaware, Maryland, New Jersey, and North Carolina. Those opposed were Georgia, Pennsylvania, South Carolina, and Virginia. Massachusetts was split down the middle; the New York delegates had left the convention. New Hampshire and Rhode Island were absent.

Senate. He saw in that a way for the states to hamstring the national government and much preferred some measure of proportional representation in both houses. Delegates from other states worried that representation on the basis of population in the House of Representatives would enable the large states to dominate legislative affairs. Although the margin by which the compromise was accepted was razor-thin (five states in favor, four opposed), it held firm. In time most of the delegates from the dissenting states accepted it.

After the Great Compromise many more issues had to be resolved, but by now a spirit of accommodation had developed. When one delegate proposed having the Congress choose the president, another, James Wilson, proposed that he be elected directly by the people. When neither side of that argument prevailed, a committee invented a plan for an "Electoral College" that would choose the president. When some delegates wanted the president chosen for a life term, others proposed a seven-year term, and still others wanted the term limited to three years without eligibility for reelection. The convention settled on a four-year term with no bar to reelection. Some states wanted the Supreme Court picked by the Senate; others wanted it chosen by the president. They finally agreed to let the justices be nominated by the president and then confirmed by the Senate.

Finally, on July 26, the proposals that were already accepted, together with a bundle of unresolved issues, were handed over to a "Committee of Detail" of five delegates. This committee included Madison and Gouverneur Morris, who was to be the chief draftsman of the document that finally emerged. The committee hardly contented itself with mere "details," however. It inserted some new proposals and made changes in old ones, drawing for inspiration on existing state constitutions and the members' beliefs as to what the other delegates might accept. On August 6 the report—the first complete draft of the Constitution—was submitted to the convention. There it was debated, item by item, revised, amended, and finally, on September 17, approved by all twelve states in attendance. (Not all *delegates* approved, however; three, including Edmund Randolph, who first submitted the Virginia Plan, refused to sign.)

The Constitution and Democracy

A debate continues to rage over whether the Constitution created, or was even intended to create, a democratic government. The answer is complex. The Framers did not intend to create a "pure democracy"—one in which the people rule directly. For one thing the size of the country and the distances between settlements would have made that physically impossible. But more important, the Framers worried that a government in which all citizens directly participate, as in the New England town meeting, would be a government excessively subject to temporary popular passions and one in which minority rights would be insecure. They intended instead to create a **republic,** by which they meant a government in which a system of representation operates. In designing that system the Framers chose, not without argument, to have the members of the House of Representatives elected directly by the people. Some delegates did not want to go even that far. Elbridge Gerry of Massachusetts, who refused to sign the Constitution, argued that though "the people do not want [that is, lack] virtue," they are often the "dupes of pretended patriots." Roger Sherman of Connecticut agreed. But George Mason of Virginia and James Wilson of Pennsylvania carried the day when they argued that "no government could long subsist without the confidence of the people," and this required "drawing the most numerous branch of the legislature directly from the people." Popular elections for the House were approved: six states were in favor, two opposed.

But though popular rule was to be one element of the new government, it was not to be the only one. State legislatures, not the people, would choose the senators; electors, not the people directly, would choose the president. As we have seen, without these arrangements, there would have been no Constitution at all, for the small states adamantly opposed any proposal that would have given undue power to the large ones. And direct popular election of the president would clearly have made the populous states the dominant ones. In short the Framers wished to observe the principle of majority rule, but they felt that, on the most important questions, two kinds of majorities were essential—a majority of the voters and a majority of the states.

The power of the Supreme Court to declare an act of Congress unconstitutional—**judicial review**—is also a way of limiting the power of popular majorities. It is not clear whether the Framers intended that there be judicial review, but there is little doubt that in the Framers' minds the fundamental law, the Constitution, had to be safeguarded against popular passions. They made the process for amending the Constitution easier than it had been under the Articles but still relatively difficult.

An amendment can be proposed either by a two-thirds vote of both houses of Congress *or* by a national convention called by Congress at the request of two-thirds of the states.* Once proposed, an amendment must be ratified by three-fourths of the states, either through their legislatures or through special ratifying conventions in each state. Twenty-seven amendments have survived this process, all of them proposed by Congress and all but one (the Twenty-first) ratified by state legislatures rather than state conventions.

In short the answer to the question of whether the Constitution brought into being a democratic government is yes, if by *democracy* one means a system of representative government based on popular consent. The degree of that consent has changed since 1787, and the institutions embodying that consent can take different forms. One form, rejected in 1787, gives all political authority to one set of representatives, directly elected by the people. (That is the case, for example, in most parliamentary regimes, such as Great Britain, and in some city governments in the United States.) The other form of democracy is one in which different sets of officials, chosen directly or indirectly by different groups of people, share political power. (That is the case with the United States and a few other nations where the separation of powers is intended to operate.)

Key Principles

The American version of representative democracy was based on two major principles, the separation of powers and federalism. In America political power was to be shared by three separate branches of government; in parliamentary democracies that power was concentrated in a single, supreme legislature. In America political authority was divided between a national government and several state governments—**federalism**—whereas in most European systems authority was centralized in the national government. Neither of these principles was especially controversial at Philadelphia. The delegates began their work in broad agreement that separated powers and some measure of federalism were necessary, and both the Virginia and New Jersey plans contained a version of each. How much federalism should be written into the Constitution was quite controversial, however.*

Government and Human Nature

The desirability of separating powers and leaving the states equipped with a broad array of rights and responsibilities was not controversial at the Philadelphia convention because the Framers' experiences with British rule and state government under the Articles had shaped their view of human nature.

These experiences had taught most of the Framers that people would seek their own advantage in and out of politics; this pursuit of self-interest, unchecked, would lead some people to exploit others. Human nature was good enough to make it possible to have a decent government that was based on popular consent, but it was not good enough to make it inevitable. One solution to this problem would be to improve human nature. Ancient political philosophers such as Aristotle believed that the

* There have been many attempts to get a new constitutional convention. In the 1960s thirty-three states, one short of the required number, requested a convention to consider the reapportionment of state legislatures. In the 1980s efforts were made to call a convention to consider amendments to ban abortions and to require a balanced federal budget.

* To the delegates a truly "federal" system was one, like the New Jersey Plan, that allowed for very strong states and a weak national government. When the New Jersey Plan lost, the delegates who defeated it began using the word *federal* to describe their plan even though it called for a stronger national government. Thus men who began as "Federalists" at the convention ultimately became known as "Antifederalists" during the struggle over ratification.

Checks and Balances

he Constitution creates a system of *separate* institutions that *share* powers. Because the three branches of government share powers, each can (partially) check the powers of the others. This is the system of **checks and balances.** The major checks possessed by each branch are listed below.

CONGRESS

1. Can check the president in these ways:
   a. By refusing to pass a bill the president wants
   b. By passing a law over the president's veto
   c. By using the impeachment powers to remove the president from office
   d. By refusing to approve a presidential appointment (Senate only)
   e. By refusing to ratify a treaty the president has signed (Senate only)
2. Can check the federal courts in these ways:
   a. By changing the number and jurisdiction of the lower courts
   b. By using the impeachment powers to remove a judge from office
   c. By refusing to approve a person nominated to be a judge (Senate only)

THE PRESIDENT

1. Can check Congress by vetoing a bill it has passed
2. Can check the federal courts by nominating judges

THE COURTS

1. Can check Congress by declaring a law unconstitutional
2. Can check the president by declaring actions by him or his subordinates to be unconstitutional or not authorized by law

In addition to these checks specifically provided for in the Constitution, each branch has informal ways of checking the others. For example, the president can try to withhold information from Congress (on the grounds of "executive privilege"), and Congress can try to get information by mounting an investigation.

The exact meaning of the various checks is explained in Chapter 11 on Congress, Chapter 12 on the presidency, and Chapter 14 on the courts.

first task of any government was to cultivate virtue among the governed.

Many Americans were of the same mind. To them, Americans would first have to become good people before they could have a good government. Samuel Adams, a leader of the Boston Tea Party, said that the new nation must become a "Christian Sparta." Others spoke of the need to cultivate frugality, industry, temperance, and simplicity.

But to James Madison and the other architects of the Constitution, the deliberate cultivation of virtue would require a government too strong and thus too dangerous to liberty, at least at the national level. Self-interest, freely pursued within reasonable limits, was a more practical and durable solution to the problem of government than any effort to improve the virtue of the citizenry. He wanted, he said, to make republican government possible "even in the absence of political virtue."

Madison argued that the very self-interest that leads people toward factionalism and tyranny might, if properly harnessed by appropriate constitutional arrangements, provide a source of unity and a guarantee of liberty. This harnessing was to be accomplished by dividing the offices of the new government among many people and giving to the holder of each office the "necessary means and personal motives to resist encroachments of the others." In this way "ambition must be made to counteract ambition" so that "the private interest of every individual may be a sentinel over the public rights."[11] If men were angels, all this would be unnecessary. But Madison and the other delegates pragmatically insisted on taking human nature pretty much as it was, and therefore they adopted "this policy of supplying, by opposite and rival interests, the defect of better motives."[12] The **separation of powers** (see box) would work, not in spite of the imperfections of human nature, but because of them.

So also with federalism. By dividing power between the states and the national government, one level of government can serve as a check on the other. This should provide a "double security" to the rights of the people: "The different governments will control each other, at the same time that each will be controlled by itself."[13] This was especially likely to happen in America, Madison thought, because it was a large country filled with diverse interests—

rich and poor, Protestant and Catholic, northerner and southerner, farmer and merchant, creditor and debtor. Each of these interests would constitute a **faction** that would seek its own advantage. One faction might come to dominate government, or a part of government, in one place, and a different and rival faction might dominate it in another. The pulling and hauling among these factions would prevent any single government—say, that of New York—from dominating all of government. The division of powers among several governments would give to virtually every faction an opportunity to gain some—but not full—power.

The Constitution and Liberty

A more difficult question is whether the Constitution created a system of government that would respect personal liberties. And that in fact is the question that was debated in the states when the document was presented for ratification. The proponents of the Constitution called themselves the **Federalists** (though they might more accurately have been called "nationalists"). The opponents came to be known as the **Antifederalists** (though they might more accurately have been called "states' righters"). To be put into effect, the Constitution had to be approved at ratifying conventions in at least nine states. This was perhaps the most democratic feature of the Constitution: it had to be accepted, not by the existing Congress (still limping along under the Articles of Confederation), nor by the state legislatures, but by special conventions elected by the people.

Though democratic, the process established by the Framers for ratifying the Constitution was technically illegal. The Articles of Confederation, which still governed, could be amended only with the approval of all thirteen state legislatures. The Framers wanted to bypass these legislatures because they feared that, for reasons of ideology or out of a desire to retain their powers, the legislators would oppose the Constitution. The Framers wanted ratification with less than the consent of all thirteen states because they knew that such unanimity could not be attained. And indeed the conventions in North Carolina and Rhode Island did initially reject the Constitution.

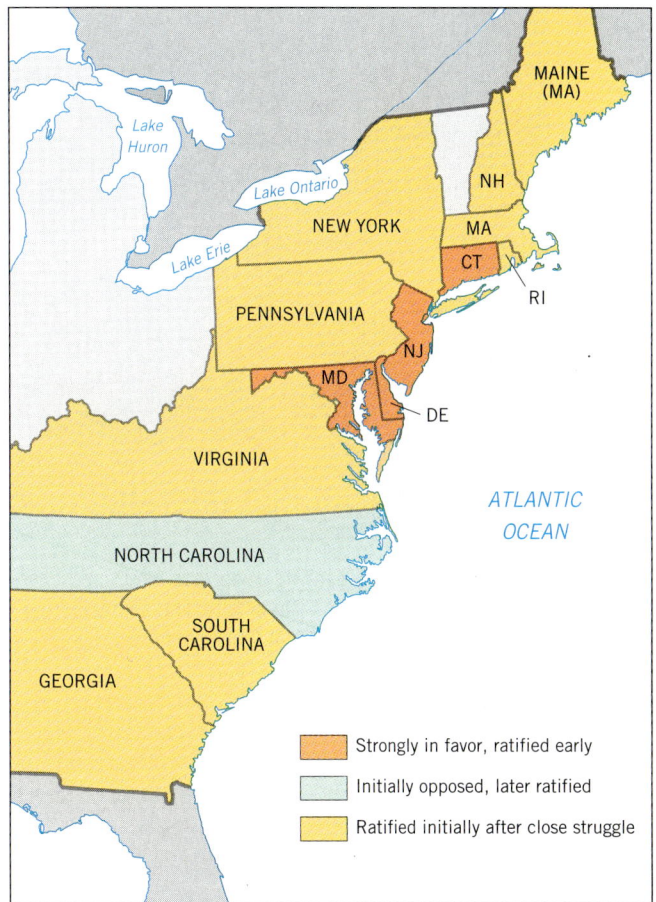

RATIFICATION OF THE FEDERAL CONSTITUTION BY STATE CONVENTIONS, 1787–1790

Strongly in favor, ratified early

Initially opposed, later ratified

Ratified initially after close struggle

The Antifederalist View

The great issue before the state conventions was liberty, not democracy. The opponents of the new Constitution, the Antifederalists, had a variety of objections but were in general united by the belief that liberty could be secure only in a small republic in which the rulers were physically close to—and closely checked by—the ruled. Their central objection was stated by a group of Antifederalists at the ratifying convention in an essay published just after they had lost: "a very extensive territory cannot be governed on the principles of freedom, otherwise than by a confederation of republics."[14]

These dissenters argued that a strong national government would be distant from the people and

By steadily moving westward, Americans both searched for economic opportunity and sought to protect their freedom from government. Here George Caleb Bingham depicts Daniel Boone escorting settlers through the Cumberland Gap.

would use its powers to annihilate or absorb the functions that properly belonged to the states. Congress would tax heavily, the Supreme Court would overrule state courts, and the president would come to head a large standing army. (Since all these things have occurred, we cannot dismiss the Antifederalists as cranky obstructionists who opposed without justification the plans of the Framers.) These critics argued that the nation needed, at best, a loose confederation of states, with most of the powers of government kept firmly in the hands of state legislatures and state courts.

But if a stronger national government was to be created, the Antifederalists argued, it should be hedged about with many more restrictions than those in the constitution then under consideration. They proposed several such limitations, including narrowing the jurisdiction of the Supreme Court, checking the president's power by creating a council that would review his actions, leaving military affairs in the hands of the state militias, increasing the size of the House of Representatives so that it would reflect a greater variety of popular interests, and reducing or eliminating the power of Congress to levy

taxes. And some of them insisted that a *bill of rights* be added to the Constitution.

James Madison gave his answer to these criticisms in *Federalist* papers 10 and 51 (reprinted in the Appendix). It was a bold answer, for it flew squarely in the face of widespread popular sentiment and much philosophical writing. Following the great French political philosopher Montesquieu, many Americans believed that liberty was safe only in small societies governed either by direct democracy or by large legislatures with small districts and frequent turnover among members.

Madison argued quite the opposite—that liberty is safest in *large* (or as he put it, "extended") republics. In a small community, he said, there will be relatively few differences in opinion or interest; people will tend to see the world in much the same way. If anyone dissents or pursues an individual interest, he or she will be confronted by a massive majority and will have few, if any, allies. But in a large republic there will be many opinions and interests; as a result it will be hard for a tyrannical majority to form or organize, and anyone with an unpopular view will find it easier to acquire allies. If Madison's argument seems strange or abstract, ask yourself the following question: If I have an unpopular opinion, an exotic lifestyle, or an unconventional interest, will I find greater security living in a small town or a big city?

By favoring a large republic, Madison was not trying to stifle democracy. Rather he was attempting to show how democratic government really works, and what can make it work better. To rule, different interests must come together and form a **coalition**—that is, an alliance. In *Federalist* No. 51, he was arguing that the coalitions that formed in a large republic would be more moderate than those that formed in a small one because the bigger the republic, the greater the variety of interests, and thus the more a coalition of the majority would have to accommodate a diversity of interests and opinions if it hoped to succeed. He concluded that in a nation the size of the United States, with its enormous variety of interests, "a coalition of a majority of the whole society could seldom take place on any other principles than those of justice and the general good." Whether he was right in that prediction is a matter to which we shall return repeatedly.

The implication of Madison's arguments was daring, for he was suggesting that the national government should be at some distance from the people and insulated from their momentary passions, because the people did not always want to do the right thing. Liberty was threatened as much (or even more) by public passions and popularly based factions as by strong governments. Now the Antifederalists themselves had no very lofty view of human nature, as is evidenced by the deep suspicion with which they viewed "power-seeking" officeholders. What Madison did was take this view to its logical conclusion, arguing that if people could be corrupted by office, they could also be corrupted by factional self-interest. Thus the government had to be designed to prevent both the politicians and the people from using it for ill-considered or unjust purposes.

To argue in 1787 against the virtues of small democracies was like arguing against motherhood, but the argument prevailed, probably because many citizens were convinced that a reasonably strong national government was essential if the nation were to stand united against foreign enemies, facilitate commerce among the states, guard against domestic insurrections, and keep one faction from oppressing another. The political realities of the moment and the recent bitter experiences with the Articles probably counted for more in ratifying the Constitution than did Madison's arguments. His cause was helped by the fact that, for all their legitimate concerns and their uncanny instinct for what the future might bring, the Antifederalists could offer no agreed-upon alternative to the new Constitution. In politics, then as now, you cannot beat something with nothing.

But this does not explain why the Framers failed to add a bill of rights to the Constitution. If they were so preoccupied with liberty, why didn't they take this most obvious step toward protecting liberty, especially since the Antifederalists were demanding it? Some historians have suggested that this omission was evidence that liberty was not as important to the Framers as they claimed. In fact, when one delegate suggested that a bill of rights be drawn up, the state delegations at the convention unanimously voted the idea down. There were several reasons for this.

First, the Constitution, as written, *did* contain a number of specific guarantees of individual liberty, including the right of trial by jury in criminal cases and the privilege of the writ of habeas corpus. The liberties guaranteed in the Constitution (before the Bill of Rights was added) are listed below.

- **Writ of habeas corpus*** may not be suspended (except during invasion or rebellion).

- No **bill of attainder** may be passed by Congress or the states.

- No **ex post facto law** may be passed by Congress or the states.

- Right of trial by jury in criminal cases is guaranteed.

- The citizens of each state are entitled to the privileges and immunities of the citizens of every other state.

- No religious test or qualification for holding federal office is imposed.

- No law impairing the obligation of contracts may be passed by the states.

* For a definition of this and the following terms used in connection with certain rights, see the Glossary.

The Bill of Rights

The First Ten Amendments to the Constitution Grouped by Topic and Purpose

PROTECTIONS AFFORDED CITIZENS TO PARTICIPATE IN THE POLITICAL PROCESS

Amendment 1: Freedom of religion, speech, press, and assembly; the right to petition the government.

PROTECTIONS AGAINST ARBITRARY POLICE AND COURT ACTION

Amendment 4: No unreasonable searches or seizures.

Amendment 5: Grand jury indictment required to prosecute a person for a serious crime.

No "double jeopardy" (being tried twice for the same offense).

Forcing a person to testify against himself or herself prohibited.

No loss of life, liberty, or property without due process.

Amendment 6: Right to speedy, public, impartial trial with defense counsel and right to cross-examine witnesses.

Amendment 7: Jury trials in civil suits where value exceeds $20.

Amendment 8: No excessive bail or fines, no cruel and unusual punishments.

PROTECTIONS OF STATES' RIGHTS AND UNNAMED RIGHTS OF PEOPLE

Amendment 9: Unlisted rights are not necessarily denied.

Amendment 10: Powers not delegated to the United States or denied to states are reserved to the states.

OTHER AMENDMENTS

Amendment 2: Right to bear arms.

Amendment 3: Troops may not be quartered in homes in peacetime.

Second, most states in 1787 had bills of rights. When Elbridge Gerry proposed to the convention that a federal bill of rights be drafted, Roger Sherman rose to observe that it was unnecessary because the state bills of rights were sufficient.[15]

But third, and perhaps most important, the Framers thought they were creating a government with specific, limited powers. It could do, they thought, only what the Constitution gave it the power to do, and nowhere in that document was there permission to infringe on freedom of speech or of the press or to impose cruel and unusual punishments. Some delegates probably feared that if any serious effort were made to list the rights that were guaranteed, later officials might assume that they had the power to do anything not explicitly forbidden.

Need for a Bill of Rights

Whatever their reasons, the Framers made at least a tactical and perhaps a fundamental mistake. It quickly became clear that without at least the promise of a **bill of rights**, the Constitution would not be ratified. Though the small states, pleased by their equal representation in the Senate, quickly ratified (in Delaware, New Jersey, and Georgia, the vote in the conventions was unanimous), the battle in the large states was intense and the outcome uncertain. In Pennsylvania Federalist supporters dragged boycotting Antifederalists to the legislature in order to ensure that a quorum was present so that a convention could be called. There were rumors of other rough tactics.

In Massachusetts the Constitution was approved by a narrow majority, but only after key leaders promised to obtain a bill of rights. In Virginia James Madison fought against the fiery Patrick Henry, whose climactic speech against ratification was dramatically punctuated by a noisy thunderstorm outside. The Federalists won by ten votes. In New York Alexander Hamilton argued the case for six long weeks against the determined opposition of most of the state's key political leaders; he carried the day, but only by three votes, and then only after New York City threatened to secede from the state if it did not ratify. By June 21, 1788, the ninth state—New Hampshire—had ratified and the Constitution was law.

Despite the bitterness of the ratification struggle, the new government that took office in 1789–1790, headed by President Washington, was greeted enthusiastically. By the spring of 1790 all thirteen states had ratified. There remained, however, the task of fulfilling the promise of a bill of rights. To that end James Madison introduced into the first session of the First Congress a set of proposals, many based on the existing Virginia bill of rights. Twelve were approved by Congress; ten of these were ratified by the states and went into effect in 1791. These amendments did not limit the power of state governments over citizens, only the power of the federal government. Later the Fourteenth Amendment, as interpreted by the Supreme Court, extended many of the guarantees of the Bill of Rights to cover state governmental action.

The Constitution and Slavery

Though black slaves amounted to one-third of the population of the five southern states, nowhere in the Constitution can one find the words *slave* or *slavery*. There are three provisions bearing on the matter, all designed to placate the slave-owning states. The apportionment of seats in the House of Representatives was to be made by counting all free persons and three-fifths of all "other persons." This meant giving a few extra seats in the House to those states that had a lot of "other persons"—that is, slaves. Congress was forbidden from prohibiting the "importation" of "persons" (that is, slaves) before the year 1808. And if any "person held to service or labour" (that is, any slave) were to escape from a slave-owning state and get to a free state, that person would not become free but would have to be returned to his or her master.

To some the failure of the Constitution to address the question of slavery was a great betrayal of the promise of the Declaration of Independence that "all men are created equal."[16] For the Constitution to be silent on the subject of slavery, and thereby to allow that odious practice to continue, was to convert, by implication, the wording of the Declaration to "all white men are created equal."

The Constitution was silent on slavery, and so buying and selling black slaves continued for many years.

It is easy to accuse the signers of the Declaration and the Constitution of hypocrisy. They knew of slavery, many of them owned slaves, and yet they were silent. Indeed, British opponents of the independence movement took special delight in taunting the colonists about their complaints of being "enslaved" to the British Empire while ignoring the slavery in their very midst. Increasingly, revolutionary leaders during this period spoke to this issue. Thomas Jefferson had tried to get a clause opposing the slave trade put into the Declaration of Independence. James Otis of Boston had attacked slavery and argued that black as well as white men should be free. As revolutionary fervor mounted, so did northern criticisms of slavery. The Massachusetts legislature and then the Continental Congress voted to end the slave trade; Delaware prohibited the importation of slaves; Pennsylvania voted to tax it out of existence; and Connecticut and Rhode Island decided that all slaves brought into those states would automatically become free.

Slavery continued unabated in the South, defended by some whites because they thought it right, by others because they found it useful. But even in the South there were opponents, though rarely conspicuous ones. George Mason, a large Virginia slaveholder and a delegate to the convention, warned

prophetically that "by an inevitable chain of causes and effects, providence punishes national sins [slavery] by national calamities."[17]

The blunt fact, however, was that any effort to use the Constitution to end slavery would have meant the end of the Constitution. The southern states would never have signed a document that seriously interfered with slavery. Without the southern states there would have been a continuation of the Articles of Confederation, which would have left each state entirely sovereign and thus entirely free of any prospective challenge to slavery.

Thus the Framers compromised with slavery; political scientist Theodore Lowi calls this their Greatest Compromise.[18] Slavery is dealt with in three places in the Constitution, though never by name. In determining the representation each state was to have in the House, "three-fifths of all other persons" (that is, of slaves) are to be added to "the whole number of free persons."[19] The South originally wanted slaves to count fully even though, of course, none would be elected to the House; they settled for counting 60 percent of them. The convention also agreed not to allow the new government by law or even constitutional amendment to prohibit the importation of slaves until the year 1808.[20] The South thus had twenty years in which it could acquire more slaves from abroad; after that, Congress was free (but not required) to end the importation. Finally, the Constitution guaranteed that if a slave were to escape his or her master and flee to a nonslave state, the slave would be returned by that state to "the party to whom . . . service or labour may be due."[21]

The unresolved issue of slavery was to prove the most explosive question of all. Allowing slavery to continue was a fateful decision, one that led to the worst social and political catastrophe in the nation's history—the Civil War. The Framers chose to sidestep the issue in order to create a union that, they hoped, would eventually be strong enough to deal with the problem when it could no longer be postponed. The legacy of that choice continues to this day.

The Motives of the Framers

The Framers were not saints or demigods. They were men with political opinions who also had economic interests and human failings. It would be a mistake to conclude that everything they did in 1787 was motivated by a disinterested commitment to the public good. But it would be an equally great mistake to think that what they did was nothing but an effort to line their pockets by producing a government that would serve their own narrow interests. As in almost all human endeavors, the Framers acted out of a mixture of motives. What is truly astonishing is that economic interests played only a modest role in their deliberations.

Economic Interests at the Convention

Some of the Framers were wealthy; some were not. Some owned slaves; some had none. Some were creditors (having loaned money to the Continental Congress or to private parties); some were deeply in debt. For nearly a century scholars have argued over just how important these personal interests were in shaping the provisions of the Constitution.

In 1913 Charles Beard, a historian, published a book—*An Economic Interpretation of the Constitution*—arguing that the better-off urban and commercial classes, especially those members who held the IOUs issued by the government to pay for the Revolutionary War, favored the new Constitution because they stood to benefit from it.[22] But in the 1950s that view was challenged by historians who, after looking carefully at what the Framers owned or owed, concluded that one could not explain the Constitution exclusively or even largely in terms of the economic interests of those who wrote it.[23] Some of the richest delegates, such as Elbridge Gerry of Massachusetts and George Mason of Virginia, refused to sign the document, while many of its key backers—James Madison and James Wilson, for example—were men of modest means or heavy debts.

In the 1980s a new group of scholars, primarily economists applying more advanced statistical techniques, found evidence that some economic considerations influenced how the Framers voted on some issues during the Philadelphia convention. Interestingly, however, the economic position of the *states*

Elbridge Gerry (left, 1744–1814) was a wealthy Massachusetts merchant and politician who participated in the convention but refused to sign the new constitution.

James Wilson (right, 1742–1798) of Pennsylvania, a brilliant lawyer and terrible businessman, was the principal champion of the popular election of the House. Near the end of his life he was jailed repeatedly for debts incurred as a result of his business speculations.

from which they came had a greater effect on their votes than did their *own* monetary condition.[24]

We have already seen how delegates from small states fought to reduce the power of large states and how those from slaveowning states made certain that the Constitution would contain no provision that would threaten slavery.

But contrary to what Beard asserted, the individual interests of the Framers themselves did not dominate the convention except in a few cases where a constitutional provision would have affected them directly. As you might expect, all slaveowning delegates, even those who did not live in states where slavery was commonplace (and several northern delegates owned slaves), tended to vote for provisions that would have kept the national government's power over slavery as weak as possible. However, the effects of other personal business interests were surprisingly weak. Some delegates owned a lot of public debt that they had purchased for low prices. A strong national government of the sort envisaged by the Constitution was more likely than the weak Continental Congress to pay off this debt at face value, thus making the delegates who owned it much richer. Despite this, the ownership of public debt had no significant effect on how the Framers voted in Philadelphia. For example, five men who among them owned one-third of all the public securities held by all the delegates voted against the Constitution. Nor did the big land speculators vote their interests. Some, such as George Washington and Robert Morris, favored the Constitution, while others, such as George Mason and William Blount, opposed it.[25]

In sum, the Framers tended to represent their states' interests on important matters. Since they were picked by the states to do so, this is exactly what one would expect. If they had not met in secret, perhaps they would have voted even more often as their constituents wanted. But except with respect to slavery, they usually did not vote their own economic interests. They were reasonably but not wholly disinterested delegates who were probably influenced as much by personal beliefs as by economics.

Economic Interests and Ratification

At the popularly elected state ratifying conventions, economic factors played a larger role. Delegates who were merchants, who lived in cities, who owned large amounts of western land, who held government IOUs, and who did not own slaves were more likely to vote to ratify the new Constitution than were delegates who were farmers, who did not own public debt, and who did own slaves.[26] There were plenty of exceptions, however. Small farmers dominated the conventions in some states where the vote to ratify was unanimous.

Though interests made a difference, they were not simply elite interests. In most states the great majority of adult white males could vote for delegates to the ratifying conventions. This means that women and blacks were excluded from the debates, but by the standards of the time—standards that did not change for over a century—the ratification process was remarkably democratic.

The Constitution and Equality

Ideas counted for as much as interests. At stake were two views of the public good. One, espoused by the Federalists, was that a reasonable balance of liberty, order, and progress required a strong national government. The other, defended by the Antifederalists, was that liberty would not be secure in the hands of a powerful, distant government; freedom required decentralization.

Today that debate has a new focus. The defect of the Constitution, to some contemporary critics, is not that the government it created is too strong but that it is too weak. In particular the national government is too weak to resist the pressures of special interests that reflect and perpetuate social inequality.

This criticism reveals how our understanding of the relationship between liberty and equality has changed since the Founding. To Jefferson and Madison citizens naturally differed in their talents and qualities. What had to be guarded against was the use of governmental power to create *un*natural and undesirable inequalities. This might happen, for example, if political power was concentrated in the hands of a few people (who could use that power to give themselves special privileges) or if it was used in ways that allowed some private parties to acquire exclusive charters and monopolies. To prevent the inequality that might result from having too strong a government, its powers must be kept strictly limited.

Today some people think of inequality quite dif-

Were Women Left Out of the Constitution?

In one sense, yes: Women were nowhere mentioned in the Constitution when it was written in 1787. Moreover, Article 1, which set forth the provisions for electing members of the House of Representatives, granted the vote to those people who were allowed to vote for members of the lower house of the legislature in the states in which they resided. In no state at the time could women participate in those elections. In no state could they vote in any elections or hold any offices. Furthermore, wherever the Constitution uses a pronoun, it uses the masculine form—*he* or *him*.

In another sense, no: Wherever the Constitution or the Bill of Rights defines a right that people are to have, it either grants that right to "persons" or "citizens," not to "men," or it makes no mention at all of people or gender. For example:

- "The *citizens* of each State shall be entitled to all privileges and immunities of citizens of the several States." [Art. I, sec. 9]

- "No *person* shall be convicted of treason unless on the testimony of two witnesses to the same overt act, or on confession in open court." [Art. III, sec. 3]

- "No bill of attainder or ex post facto law shall be passed." [Art. I sec. 9]

- "The right of the *people* to be secure in their persons, houses, papers, and effects, against unreasonable searches and seizures, shall not be violated." [Amend. IV]

- "No *person* shall be held to answer for a capital, or otherwise infamous crime, unless on presentment or indictment of a grand jury. . . . nor shall any *person* be subject for the same offense to be twice put in jeopardy of life or limb; . . . nor be deprived of life, liberty, or property, without due process of law." [Amend. V]

- "In all criminal prosecutions the *accused* shall enjoy the right to a speedy and public trial, by an impartial jury." [Amend. VI]

Moreover, when the qualifications for elective office are stated, the word *person*, not *man*, is used.

- "No *person* shall be a Representative who shall not have attained to the age of twenty-five years." [Art. 1, sec. 2]

- "No *person* shall be a Senator who shall not have attained to the age of thirty years." [Art. 1, sec. 3]

- "No *person* except a natural born citizen, . . . shall be eligible to the office of President; neither shall any *person* be eligible to that office who shall not have attained to the age of thirty-five years." [Art. 2, sec. 1]

In places the Constitution and the Bill of Rights used the pronoun *he*, but always in the context of referring back to a *person* or *citizen*. At the time, and until quite recently, the male pronoun was often used in legal documents to refer generically to both men and women.

Thus, though the Constitution did not give women the right to vote until the Nineteenth Amendment was ratified in 1920, it did use language that extended fundamental rights, and access to office, to women and men equally.

Of course what the Constitution permitted did not necessarily occur. State and local laws denied to women rights that in principle they ought to have enjoyed. Except for a brief period in New Jersey, no women voted in statewide elections until, in 1869, they were given the right to cast ballots in territorial elections in Wyoming.

When women were first elected to Congress, there was no need to change the Constitution; nothing in it restricted office-holding to men.

When women were given the right to vote by constitutional amendment, it was not necessary to amend any existing language in the Constitution, because nothing in the Constitution itself denied women the right to vote; the amendment simply added a new right:

- "The right of citizens of the United States to vote shall not be denied or abridged by the United States or any state on account of sex." [Amend. XIX]

SOURCE: Adapted from Robert Goldwin, "Why Blacks, Women and Jews Are Not Mentioned in the Constitution," *Commentary* (May 1987): 28–33.

ferently. To them it is the natural social order—the marketplace and the acquisitive talents of people operating in that marketplace—that leads to undesirable inequalities, especially in economic power. The government should be powerful enough to restrain these natural tendencies and produce, by law, a greater degree of equality than society allows when left alone.

Ways of Amending the Constitution

*U*nder Article V there are two ways to *propose* **amendments** to the Constitution and two ways to *ratify* them.

TO PROPOSE AN AMENDMENT

1. Two-thirds of both houses of Congress vote to propose an amendment, *or*

2. Two-thirds of the state legislatures ask Congress to call a national convention to propose amendments.

TO RATIFY AN AMENDMENT

1. Three-fourths of the state legislatures approve it, *or*

2. Ratifying conventions in three-fourths of the states approve it.

SOME KEY FACTS

• Only the first method of proposing an amendment has been used.

• The second method of ratification has been used only once, to ratify the Twenty-first Amendment (repealing Prohibition).

• Congress may limit the time within which a proposed amendment must be ratified. The usual limitation has been seven years.

• Thousands of proposals have been made, but only thirty-three have obtained the necessary two-thirds vote in Congress.

• Twenty-seven amendments have been ratified.

• The first ten amendments, ratified on December 15, 1791, are known as the Bill of Rights.

To the Framers liberty and (political) equality were not in conflict; to some people today these two principles are deeply in conflict. To the Framers the task was to keep government so limited as to prevent it from creating the worst inequality—political privilege. To some modern observers the task is to make government strong enough to reduce what they believe is the worst inequality—differences in wealth.

Constitutional Reform—Modern Views

Almost from the day it was ratified, the Constitution has been the object of debate over ways in which it might be improved. These debates have rarely involved the average citizen, who tends to revere the document even if he or she cannot recall all its details. Because of this deep and broad popular support, scholars and politicians have been wary of attacking the Constitution or suggesting many wholesale changes. But such attacks have occurred. During the 1980s—the decade in which we celebrated the bicentennial of its adoption—we heard a variety of suggestions for improving the Constitution, ranging from particular amendments to wholesale revisions. In general there are today, as in the eighteenth century, two kinds of critics: those who think the federal government is too weak and those who think it is too strong.

Reducing the Separation of Powers

To the first kind of critic the chief difficulty with the Constitution is the separation of powers. By making every decision the uncertain outcome of the pulling and hauling between the president and Congress, the Constitution precludes the emergence—except perhaps in times of crisis—of the kind of effective national leadership the country needs. In this view our nation today faces a number of challenges that require prompt, decisive, and comprehensive action. Our problem is gridlock. Our position of international leadership, the dangerous and unprecedented proliferation of nuclear weapons among the nations of the globe, and the need to find ways of stimulating economic growth while reducing our deficit and conserving our environment—all these situations require that the president be able to formulate and carry out policies free of some of the pressures and delays from interest groups and members of Congress tied to local interests.

Not only would this increase in presidential authority make for better policies, these critics argue, it would also help the voters hold the president and his party accountable for their actions. As matters now stand, nobody in government can be held responsible for policies: Everybody takes the credit for successes and nobody takes the blame for failures.

The Twenty-seventh Amendment: A Rip Van Winkle Ratification

The Twenty-sixth Amendment to the Constitution gave citizens of the United States who are eighteen years of age or older the right to vote. It cleared Congress on March 23, 1971, and was ratified by the states on June 30, 1971. Since 1971 five other proposed constitutional amendments have come to a vote in one or both chambers of Congress:

- *Equal Rights Amendment* Cleared Congress in 1972; ratification deadline extended by Congress in 1978; deadline expired in 1982 after thirty-five states (of thirty-eight needed) had approved it.

- *Voting representation in Congress for the District of Columbia* Cleared Congress in 1978; ratification deadline expired in 1985 after sixteen states (of thirty-eight needed) had approved it.

- *Prohibition of busing for school desegregation* House rejected in 1979.

- *Balanced Budget Amendment* Passed Senate in 1982, but rejected in House.

- *Denial of a constitutional right to abortion* Senate rejected in 1983.

Most amendments proposed in recent times have been sent to the states with a seven-year deadline for ratification; however there is no constitutional requirement that Congress impose such deadlines. A dozen amendments sent to the states in 1789 had no deadline; ten of them became the Bill of Rights (see box on page 38). The other two were a proposal to change the apportionment of the House and a proposal to keep congressional pay increases from taking effect until after an election has intervened. The former proposal was never ratified. The latter, after a 203-year ratification process, became the Twenty-seventh Amendment in 1992.

The Twenty-seventh Amendment states: "No law varying the compensation for the services of Senators and Representatives, shall take effect, until an election of Representatives shall have intervened." Between 1789 and 1992 forty states (of thirty-eight needed) ratified the amendment. The amendment was certified by the United States Archivist on May 18, 1992, and printed in the *Federal Register* the day after. On May 18, 1992, the Senate passed two resolutions recognizing the amendment by a vote of 99–0. On May 19, 1992, the House passed a resolution recognizing it by a vote of 414–3. And on May 20, 1992, both chambers of Congress passed resolutions endorsing the amendment.

But Congress did not need to pass any resolutions in order to make the amendment official. Because there is no limit on the amount of time it can take to ratify an amendment (unless Congress specifically imposes a deadline), the Twenty-seventh Amendment automatically became law once the requisite thirty-eight states had ratified it. Still, some members of Congress recommended holding hearings on the 203-year-old amendment's constitutionality, but because of the political furor over congressional pay increases, they did not do so. Despite its Rip Van Winkle–like ratification, the Twenty-seventh Amendment is now as much a part of the Constitution as the Bill of Rights.

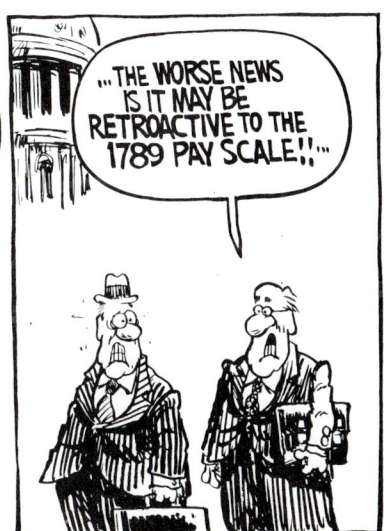

Typically the president, who tends to be the major source of new programs, cannot get his policies adopted by Congress without long delays and much bargaining, the result of which often is some watered-down compromise that neither the president nor Congress really likes but that each must settle for if anything is to be done at all.

Finally, critics of the separation of powers complain that the government agencies responsible for implementing a program are exposed to undue interference from legislators and special interests. In this view the president is supposed to be in charge of the bureaucracy but in fact must share this authority with countless members of Congress and congressional committees.

Not all critics of the separation of powers agree with all these points, nor do they all agree on what should be done about the problems. But they all have in common a fear that the separation of powers makes the president too weak and insufficiently accountable. Their proposals for reducing the separation of powers include the following:

- Allow the president to appoint members of Congress to serve in the cabinet (the Constitution forbids members of Congress from holding any federal appointive office while in Congress).

- Allow the president to dissolve Congress and call for a special election (elections now can be held only on the schedule determined by the calendar).

- Allow Congress to require a president who has lost its confidence to face the country in a special election before his term would normally end.

- Require the presidential and congressional candidates to run as a team in each congressional district; thus a presidential candidate who carries a given district could be sure that the congressional candidate of his party would also win in that district.

- Have the president serve a single six-year term instead of being eligible for up to two four-year terms; this would presumably free the president to lead without having to worry about reelection.

- Lengthen the terms of members of the House of Representatives from two to four years so that the entire House would stand for reelection at the same time as the president.[27]

Some of these proposals are offered by critics out of a desire to make the American system of government work more like the British parliamentary system, in which, as we shall see in Chapters 11 and 12, the prime minister is the undisputed leader of the majority in the British parliament. The parliamentary system is the major alternative in the world today to the American separation-of-powers system.

Both the diagnosis and the remedies proposed by these critics of the separation of powers have been challenged. Many defenders of our present constitutional system believe that nations, such as Great Britain, with a different, more unified political system have done no better than the United States in dealing with the problems of economic growth, national security, and environmental protection. Moreover, they argue, close congressional scrutiny of presidential proposals has improved these policies more often than it has weakened them. Finally, congressional "interference" in the work of government agencies is a good way of ensuring that the average citizen can fight back against the bureaucracy; without that so-called interference, citizens and interest groups might be helpless before big and powerful agencies.

Each of the specific proposals, defenders of the present constitutional system argue, would either make matters worse or have, at best, uncertain effects. Adding a few members of Congress to the president's cabinet would not provide much help in getting his program through Congress; there are 535 senators and representatives, and probably only about half a dozen would be in the cabinet. Giving either the president or Congress power to call a special election in between the regular elections (every two or four years) would cause needless confusion and great expense; the country would live under the threat of being in a perpetual political campaign with even weaker political parties. Linking the fate of the president and congressional candidates, by having them run as a team in each district, would reduce the stabilizing and moderating effect of having them separately elected. A Republican presidential candidate who wins in the new system would have a Republican majority in the House; a Democratic candidate winner would have a Democratic majority. We might as a result expect dramatic changes in policy as the political pendulum swings back and forth. Giving presidents a single six-year term would indeed free them from the need to worry about reelection, but it is precisely that worry that keeps presidents reasonably concerned about what the American people want.

Making the System Less Democratic

The second kind of critic of the Constitution thinks the government does too much, not too little. Though the separation of powers at one time may have slowed the growth of government and moderated the policies it adopted, in the last few decades government has grown helter-skelter. The problem, these critics argue, is not that democracy is a bad idea but that democracy can produce bad, or at least unintended, results if the government caters to the special-interest claims of the citizens rather than to their long-term values.

To see how these unintended results might occur, imagine a situation in which every citizen thinks the government grows too big, taxes too heavily, and spends too much. Each citizen wants the government made smaller by reducing the benefits other people get—but not by reducing the benefits he or she gets. In fact such citizens may even be willing to see their own benefits cut, provided everybody else's are cut as well, and by a like amount.

But the political system attends to individual wants, not general preferences. It gives aid to farmers, contracts to industry, grants to professors, pensions to the elderly, and loans to students. As someone once said, the government is like an adding machine: during elections candidates campaign by promising to do more for whatever group is dissatisfied with what the incumbents are doing for it. As a result most elections bring to office men and women who are committed to doing more for somebody. The grand total of all these additions is more for everybody. Few politicians have an incentive to do less for anybody.

To remedy this state of affairs, these critics suggest various mechanisms, but principally a constitutional amendment that would either set a limit on the amount of money the government could collect in taxes each year or require that each year the government have a balanced budget (that is, not spend more than it takes in in taxes), or both. In some versions of these plans an extraordinary majority (say, 60 percent) of Congress could override these limits, and the limits would not apply in wartime.

The effect of such amendments, the proponents claim, would be to force Congress and the president to look at the big picture—the grand total of what they are spending—rather than just to operate the adding machine by pushing the "add" button over and over again. If they could only spend so much during a given year, they would have to allocate what they spend among all rival claimants. For example, if more money were to be spent on the poor, less could then be spent on the military, or vice versa.

Some critics of an overly powerful federal government think these amendments will not be passed or may prove unworkable; instead they favor enhancing the president's power to block spending by giving him a **line-item veto**. Most state governors can veto a particular part of a bill and approve the rest, using a line-item veto. The theory is that such a veto would better equip the president to stop unwarranted spending without vetoing the other provisions of a bill. In 1996 President Clinton signed the Line Item Veto Act, passed by the 104th Congress. But despite its name, the new law did not give the president full line-item veto power (only a change in the Constitution could confer that power). Instead, the law gave the president authority to selectively eliminate individual items in large appropriations bills, expansions in certain income-transfer programs, and tax breaks (giving the president what budget experts call *enhanced rescission authority*). But it also left Congress free to craft bills in ways that would give the president few opportunities to veto (or *rescind*) favored items. For example, Congress can still force the president to accept or reject an entire appropriations bill simply by tagging on this sentence: "Appropriations provided under this act (or

As governor of New Jersey, Christine Todd Whitman can veto specific items in a spending bill passed by the legislature.

title or section) shall not be subject to the provisions of the Line Item Veto Act." A federal court has declared that this law is unconstitutional. The Supreme Court will act after the line item veto is used.

Finally, some of these critics of a powerful government feel that the real problem arises not from an excess of "adding-machine" democracy but from the growth in the power of the federal courts, as described in Chapter 14. What these critics would like to do is devise a set of laws or constitutional amendments that would narrow the authority of federal courts.

The opponents of these suggestions argue that constitutional amendments to restrict the level of taxes or to require a balanced budget are unworkable, even assuming—which they do not—that a smaller government is desirable. There is no precise, agreed-upon way to measure how much the government spends or to predict in advance how much it will receive in taxes during the year; thus, defining and enforcing a "balanced budget" is no easy matter. Since the government can always borrow money, it might easily evade any spending limits. It has also shown great ingenuity in spending money in ways that never appear as part of the regular budget.

The line-item veto may or may not be a good idea. We will not know until it has been in effect at the federal level for a number of years since the states, where some governors have long had the veto, are quite different from the federal government in power and responsibilities. We might well discover that the president will use it not to spend less but to spend more—by threatening, for example, to veto something of modest cost that Congress wants in order to get Congress to vote for a far more costly item that the president wants.

Finally, proposals to curtail judicial power are thinly veiled attacks, the opponents argue, on the ability of the courts to protect essential citizen rights. If Congress and the people do not like the way the Supreme Court has interpreted the Constitution, they can always amend the Constitution to change a specific ruling; there is no need to adopt some across-the-board limitation on court powers.

Who Is Right?

Some of the arguments of these two sets of critics of the Constitution may strike you as plausible or even

entirely convincing. Whatever you may ultimately decide, decide nothing for now. One cannot make or remake a constitution based entirely on abstract reasoning or unproven factual arguments. Even when the Constitution was first written in 1787, it was not an exercise in abstract philosophy but rather an effort to solve pressing, practical problems in the light of a theory of human nature, the lessons of past experience, and a close consideration of how governments in other countries and at other times had worked.

Just because the Constitution is over two hundred years old does not mean that it is out of date. The crucial questions are these: How well has it worked over the long sweep of American history? How well has it worked compared to the constitutions of other democratic nations?

The only way to answer those questions is to study American government closely—with special attention to its historical evolution and to the practices of other nations. That is what this book is about. Of course, even after close study, people will still disagree about whether our system should be changed. People want different things and evaluate human experience according to different beliefs. But if we first understand how, in fact, the government works and why it has produced the policies it has, we can then argue more intelligently about how best to achieve our wants and give expression to our beliefs.

SUMMARY

The Framers of the Constitution sought to create a government capable of protecting both liberty and order. The solution they chose—one without precedent at that time—was a government that was based on a written constitution that combined the principles of popular consent, the separation of powers, and federalism.

Popular consent was embodied in the procedure for choosing the House of Representatives but limited by the indirect election of senators and the Electoral College system for selecting the president. Political authority was to be shared by three branches of government in a manner deliberately intended to produce conflict among these branches. This conflict, motivated by the self-interest of the people occupying each branch, would, it was hoped, prevent tyranny, even by a popular majority.

Federalism came to mean a system in which both the national and state governments had independent authority. Allocating powers between the two levels of government and devising means to ensure that neither large nor small states would dominate the national government required the most delicate compromises at the Philadelphia convention. The decision to do nothing about slavery was another such compromise.

In the drafting of the Constitution and the struggle over its ratification in the states, the positions people took were chiefly determined not by their economic interests but by a variety of factors. Among these were profound differences of opinion over whether the state governments or the national government would be the best protector of personal liberty.

KEY TERMS

unalienable rights   *p. 21*

Articles of Confederation   *p. 23*

Constitutional Convention   *p. 24*

Shays's Rebellion   *p. 25*

The *Federalist* Papers   *p. 28*

Great Compromise   *p. 31*

republic   *p. 32*

judicial review   *p. 33*

federalism   *p. 33*

separation of powers   *p. 34*

checks and balances   *p. 34*

faction   *p. 35*

Federalists   *p. 35*

Antifederalists   *p. 35*

coalition   *p. 37*

writ of habeas corpus   *p. 37*

bill of attainder   *p. 37*

ex post facto law   *p. 37*

bill of rights   *p. 38*

amendment   *p. 44*

line-item veto   *p. 47*

SUGGESTED READINGS

Bailyn, Bernard. *The Ideological Origins of the American Revolution.* Cambridge, Mass.: Harvard University Press, 1967. A brilliant account of how the American colonists formed and justified the idea of independence.

Becker, Carl L. *The Declaration of Independence.* New York: Vintage, 1942. The classic account of the meaning of the Declaration.

Farrand, Max. *The Framing of the Constitution of the United States.* New Haven, Conn.: Yale University Press, 1913. A good, brief account of the Philadelphia convention, by the editor of Madison's notes on the convention.

Federalist papers. By Alexander Hamilton, James Madison, and John Jay. The definitive edition, edited by Jacob E. Cooke, was published in Middletown, Conn., in 1961, by the Wesleyan University Press.

Goldwin, Robert A., and William A. Schambra, eds. *How Capitalistic Is the Constitution?* Washington, D.C.: American Enterprise Institute, 1982. Essays from different viewpoints discussing the relationship between the Constitution and the economic order.

———. *How Democratic Is the Constitution?* Washington, D.C.: American Enterprise Institute, 1980. Collection of essays offering different interpretations of the political meaning of the Constitution.

McDonald, Forrest. *Novus Ordo Seclorum.* Lawrence: University of Kansas Press, 1985. A careful study of the intellectual origins of the Constitution. The Latin title means "New World Order," which is what the Framers hoped they were creating.

Robinson, Donald L., ed. *Reforming American Government.* Boulder, Colo.: Westview Press, 1985. Collection of essays advocating constitutional reform.

Storing, Herbert J. *What the Anti-Federalists Were For.* Chicago: University of Chicago Press, 1981. Close analysis of the political views of those opposed to the ratification of the Constitution.

Wood, Gordon S. *The Creation of the American Republic.* Chapel Hill, N.C.: University of North Carolina Press, 1969. A detailed study of American political thought before the Philadelphia convention.

———. *The Radicalism of the American Revolution.* New York: Alfred P. Knopf, 1992. Magisterial study of the nature and effects of the American Revolution and the relationship between the socially radical revolution and the Constitution.

3

Federalism

★ Contrast of federal and unitary systems

★ Intent of Founders to disperse power

★ "Necessary and proper" clause

★ *McCulloch* v. *Maryland*

★ Dual federalism

★ National supremacy

★ Politics of federal grants

★ Intergovernmental lobbies

★ Block grants and revenue sharing

★ Federal aid and federal control

★ Mandates and conditions of aid

★ Congress: representatives *to* Washington, not *of* Washington

★ Increased nationalization

Since the adoption of the Constitution in 1787, the single most persistent source of political conflict has been the relations between the national and state governments. The political conflict over slavery, for example, was intensified because some state governments condoned or supported slavery, while others took action to discourage it. The proponents and opponents of slavery were thus given territorial power centers from which to carry on the dispute. Other issues, such as the regulation of business and the provision of social welfare programs, were in large part fought out, for well over a century, in terms of "national interests" versus "states' rights." While other nations, such as Great Britain, were debating the question of whether the national government *ought* to provide old-age pensions or regulate the railroads, the United States debated a different question—whether the national government *had the right* to do these things. Even after these debates had ended—almost invariably with a decision favorable to the national government—the administration and financing of the programs that resulted have usually involved a large role for the states.

Today an effort is under way to scale back the size and activities of the national government and to shift responsibility for a wide range of domestic programs from Washington to the states. In recent years the effort to devolve onto the states the national government's functions in areas such as welfare, health care, and job training has become known as **devolution**. In the 104th Congress (1994–1996), Republican majorities in the House and Senate made proposals, several of them enacted into law, to accelerate the devolution of national power. Many of these proposals involved giving the states **block grants**—money from the national government for programs in certain general areas that the states can use at their discretion within broad guidelines set by Congress.

In 1908 Woodrow Wilson observed that how we structure the relationship between the national government and the states "is the cardinal question of our constitutional system," a question that cannot be

51

Republican candidates for Congress gather to endorse the Contract with America that promised more devolution.

settled by "one generation, because it is a question of growth, and every successive stage of our political and economic development gives it a new aspect, makes it a new question."[1]

As the nation approaches the twenty-first century, is the American political system in the early stages of a "devolution revolution" that will make the states, not the national government, the dominant force in domestic affairs? Do most Americans support devolution? Why do some leaders hope for this historic change as ardently as others oppose it? What, if any, differences are recently enacted devolution reforms likely to make in who governs and to what ends? Before one can begin to address these questions, it is important to master the basic concepts and understand the political history of federalism.

Governmental Structure

Federalism refers to a political system in which there are local (territorial, regional, provincial, state, or municipal) units of government, as well as a national government, that can make final decisions with respect to at least some governmental activities and whose existence is specially protected.[2] Almost every nation in the world has local units of government of some kind, if for no other reason than to decentralize the administrative burdens of governing. But these governments are not federal unless the local units exist independently of the preferences of the national government and can make decisions on at least some matters without regard to those preferences.

The United States, Canada, Australia, India, Germany, and Switzerland are federal systems, as are a few other nations. France, Great Britain, Italy, and Sweden are not: they are **unitary systems,** because such local governments as they possess can be altered or even abolished by the national government and cannot plausibly claim to have final authority over any significant governmental activities.

The special protection that subnational governments enjoy in a federal system derives in part from the constitution of the country but also from the habits, preferences, and dispositions of the citizens and the actual distribution of political power in society. The constitution of the former Soviet Union in theory created a federal system, as claimed by that country's full name—the Union of Soviet Socialist Republics—but for most of their history, none of these "socialist republics" were in the slightest degree independent of the central government. Were the American Constitution the only guarantee of the independence of the American states, they would long since have become mere administrative subunits of the government in Washington. Their independence results in large measure from the commitment of Americans to the idea of local self-government and from the fact that Congress consists of people who are selected by and responsive to local constituencies.

"The basic political fact of federalism," writes David B. Truman, "is that it creates separate, self-sustaining centers of power, prestige, and profit."[3] Political power is locally acquired by people whose careers depend for the most part on satisfying local interests. As a result, though the national government has come to have vast powers, it exercises many of those powers through state governments. What many of us forget when we think about "the government in Washington" is that it spends much of its money and enforces most of its rules not on citizens directly but on other, local units of government. A large part of the welfare system, all of the interstate highway system, virtually every aspect of programs to improve cities, the largest part of the effort to supply jobs to the unemployed, the entire program to clean up our water, and even much of our military manpower (in the form of the National Guard) are enterprises in which the national government does not govern so much as it seeks, by regulation, grant, plan, argument, and cajolery, to get the states to govern in accordance with nationally defined (though often vaguely defined) goals.

In France welfare, highways, education, the police, and the use of land are all matters that are directed nationally. In the United States highways and some welfare programs are largely state functions (though they make use of federal money), while education, policing, and land-use controls are primarily local (city, county, or special-district) functions.

Federalism: Good or Bad?

A measure of the importance of federalism is the controversy that surrounds it. To some, federalism means allowing states to block action, prevent

On the Evolving Meaning of Federalism

*I*t is customary in textbooks to distinguish among three forms of government—the unitary, the federal, and the confederal—and to claim that the United States is an instance of the federal form.

These three terms describe different places in which political sovereignty can be located. **Sovereignty** means supreme or ultimate political authority: a sovereign government is one that is legally and politically independent of any other government. A unitary system is one in which sovereignty is wholly in the hands of the national government, so that the states and localities are dependent on its will. A **confederation** or **confederal system** is one in which the states are sovereign and the national government is allowed to do only that which the states permit. A **federal system** is one in which sovereignty is shared, so that on some matters the national government is supreme and on others the states are supreme.

These definitions, though neat and systematic, do not correspond either to the intentions of the Founders or to the realities of American politics. The Founders at the Philadelphia convention, and later in the *Federalist* papers, did not make precise distinctions among these three kinds of governments. Indeed, there is some evidence that they took *confederal* and *federal* to mean much the same thing. Nor did they establish a government in which there was a clear and systematic division of sovereign authority between the national and state governments. They created something quite new—a government that combined some characteristics of a unitary regime with some of a confederal one.

In this text little is made of the conventional definitions and distinctions. Instead a federal regime is defined in the simplest possible terms—as one in which local units of government have a specially protected existence and can make some final decisions over some governmental activities. Where "sovereignty" is located is a matter that the Founders did not clearly answer, and no one else has been able to answer since.

progress, upset national plans, protect powerful local interests, and cater to the self-interest of hack politicians. Harold Laski, a British observer, described American states as "parasitic and poisonous,"[4] and William H. Riker, an American political

Federalism has permitted experimentation. Women were able to vote in the Wyoming territory in 1888, long before they could do so in most states.

scientist, argued that "the main effect of federalism since the Civil War has been to perpetuate racism."[5] By contrast another political scientist, Daniel J. Elazar, believes that the "virtue of the federal system lies in its ability to develop and maintain mechanisms vital to the perpetuation of the unique combination of governmental strength, political flexibility, and individual liberty, which has been the central concern of American politics."[6]

So diametrically opposed are the Riker and the Elazar views that one wonders whether they are talking about the same subject. They are, of course, but they are stressing different aspects of the same phenomenon. Whenever the opportunity to exercise po-

litical power is widely available (as among the fifty states, three thousand counties, and many thousands of municipalities in the United States), it is obvious that in different places different people will make use of that power for different purposes. There is no question that allowing states and cities to make autonomous, binding political decisions will allow some people in some places to make those decisions in ways that maintain racial segregation, protect vested interests, and facilitate corruption. It is equally true, however, that this arrangement also enables other people in other places to pass laws that attack segregation, regulate harmful economic practices, and purify politics, often long before these ideas gain national support or become national policy.

For example, in a unitary political system, such as that of France, a small but intensely motivated group could not have blocked civil rights legislation for as long as some southern senators blocked it in this country. But by the same token it would have been equally difficult for another small but intensely motivated group to block plans to operate a nuclear power plant in their neighborhood, as citizens have done in this country but not in France. An even more dramatic illustration involved the efforts of citizens in England, France, and the United States to prevent the Concorde supersonic transport from landing at airports near certain populated areas. Such groups had no success in England or France, where the national government alone makes these decisions. But they enjoyed considerable (albeit temporary) success in the United States, where they were able to persuade the New York Port Authority to deny landing rights to the Concorde. British and French officials were incredulous that such matters could be decided by local authorities. (Eventually the courts ruled that these restrictions had to be lifted.)

The existence of independent state and local governments means that different political groups pursuing different political purposes will come to power in different places. (While groups opposed to the Concorde had the most influence in New York, those welcoming it were most influential in Dallas.) The smaller the political unit, the more likely it is to be dominated by a single political faction. James Madison understood this fact perfectly and used it to argue (in *Federalist* No. 10) that it would be in a large (or "extended") republic, such as the United

CRITICAL Thinking

Federalism American-Style: Should Who Gets What Depend on Where?

Ronald A. Harmelin learned about federalism the hard way. On June 27, 1991, the U.S. Supreme Court ruled 5 to 4 that the life-without-parole prison sentence imposed on him by the state of Michigan did not violate the Constitution. In 1978 Michigan adopted a law requiring a mandatory life sentence for persons convicted of possessing more than 650 grams (about one and one-half pounds) of cocaine. Mr. Harmelin had 672.5 grams of cocaine in the trunk of his car when the police stopped him for running a red light. When he was convicted in 1986, Michigan was the only state to impose a mandatory life sentence for the possession of this amount of cocaine. For the same crime under the federal sentencing guidelines he would have received about ten years. In Alabama and some other states he would have received only about five years.

Politics, argued the political scientist Harold Lasswell, is about deciding "who gets what." In a federal system, many decisions about who gets what depend on who lives where. Criminal justice furnishes some of the most dramatic examples: a conviction for first-degree murder in some states means the death penalty, but a conviction for the same crime in other states normally means only ten years (or fewer) behind bars.

Criminal justice is not the only area in which who gets what depends on who lives where. States differ widely in the benefits they pay to persons on public assistance, the degree to which they restrict minors' access to abortion, the extent to which they regulate corporations in the name of environmental protection, the restrictions (if any) they place upon parents wishing to legally educate their children at home (through "home-schooling" ordinances), and much more.

Federalism permits intrastate as well as interstate differences both in where certain laws are applied and in per capita spending on public services. For example, in 1996 Pennsylvania and Tennessee were two of twenty-seven states that permitted citizens who meet certain basic requirements to carry firearms. But while Tennessee's "right-to-carry" permit program applied statewide, Pennsylvania's did not extend to persons in big cities such as Philadelphia.

Likewise, a study by the Congressional Research Service documented big intrastate gaps in public school expenditures. In at least ten states the average annual expenditures per pupil in the ten wealthiest school districts were twice or more the expenditures of the ten poorest school districts. For example, in New York the ten wealthiest school districts spent an annual average of about ten thousand dollars per student while the ten poorest spent barely four thousand dollars per student. Similarly, average annual spending per pupil in Texas ranges from about twenty-seven hundred dollars in some school districts to nearly ten thousand dollars in others.

Much else depends on the state and local government under which you happen to live or under whose jurisdiction you happen to be passing: whether you can legally drive faster than fifty-five miles per hour on designated highways without risking a speeding ticket, whether you can purchase a bottle of beer at a neighborhood restaurant or have to go dry, whether you can get divorced quickly or have to show grounds, and whether your property taxes are light or heavy.

Other countries that have federal systems limit the extent of such differences more than we do in the United States. What criteria should be used in deciding which matters of public law and policy are allowed to vary, and to what degree, among and between states and localities? Who should decide? Congress? Federal and state judges? Governors? State legislatures? City officials? Trying to answer such questions is one way to begin to come to grips with the pros and cons of federalism American-style.

SOURCES: *Governing* (April 1993): 23; Jill Zuckerman, "The Next Education Crisis," *Congressional Quarterly Weekly* (March 27, 1993): 749–754; Linda Greenhouse, "Mandatory Life Term Is Upheld in Drug Cases," *New York Times* (June 28, 1991).

States as a whole, that one would find the greatest opportunity for all relevant interests to be heard. When William Riker condemns federalism, he is thinking of the fact that in some places the ruling factions in cities and states have opposed granting equal rights to blacks. When Daniel Elazar praises federalism, he is recalling that, in other states and cities, the ruling factions have taken the lead (long in advance of the federal government) in developing measures to protect the environment, extend civil rights, and improve social conditions. If you live in California, whether you like federalism depends in part on whether you like the fact that California has, independent of the federal government, cut property taxes, strictly controlled coastal land use, heav-ily regulated electric utilities, and increased (at one time) and decreased (at another time) its welfare rolls.

Increased Political Activity

Federalism has many effects, but its most obvious effect has been to facilitate the mobilization of political activity. Unlike Don Quixote, the average citizen does not tilt at windmills. He or she is more likely to become involved in organized political activity if he or she feels there is a reasonable chance of having a practical effect. The chances of having such an effect are greater where there are many elected officials and independent governmental bodies, each with a relatively small constituency, than where there are few elected officials, most of whom have the nation as a whole for a constituency. In short a federal system, by virtue of the decentralization of authority, lowers the cost of organized political activity; a unitary system, because of the centralization of authority, raises the cost. We may disagree about the purposes of organized political activity, but the fact of widespread organized activity can scarcely be doubted—or if it can be doubted, it is only because you have not yet read Chapters 6 and 9.

It is impossible to say whether the Founders, when they wrote the Constitution, planned to produce such widespread opportunities for political participation. Unfortunately they were not very clear (at least in writing) about how the federal system was supposed to work, and thus most of the interesting questions about the jurisdiction and powers of our national and state governments had to be settled by a century and a half of protracted, often bitter, conflict.

The Founding

The goal of the Founders seems clear: federalism was one device whereby personal liberty was to be protected. (The separation of powers was another.) They feared that placing final political authority in any one set of hands, even in the hands of persons popularly elected, would so concentrate power as to risk tyranny. But they had seen what happened when independent states tried to form a compact, as under the Articles of Confederation; what the states

FIGURE 3.1 Lines of Power in Three Systems of Government

UNITARY SYSTEM

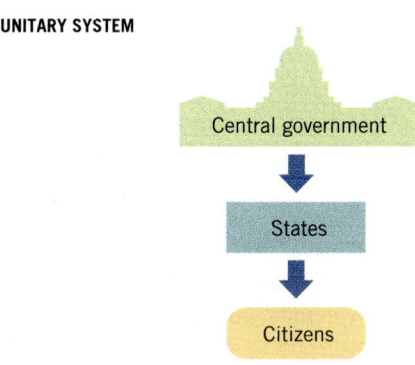

Power centralized.
State or regional governments derive authority from central government.
Examples: United Kingdom, France.

FEDERAL SYSTEM

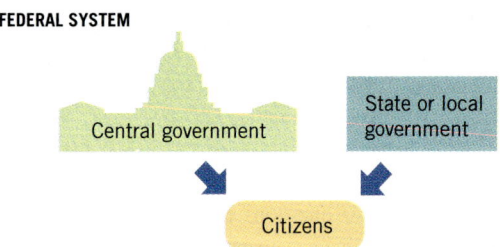

Power divided between central and state or local governments.
Both the government and constituent governments act directly
    upon the citizens.
Both must agree to constitutional change.
Examples: Canada, United States since adoption of Constitution.

**CONFEDERAL SYSTEM
(or CONFEDERATION)**

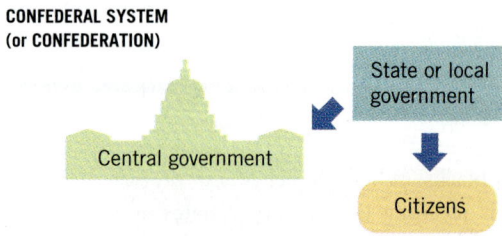

Power held by independent states.
Central government is a creature of the constituent governments.
Example: United States under the Articles of Confederation.

The States and the Constitution

*T*he Framers made some attempt to define the relations between the states and the federal government and how states were to relate to one another. The following points were made in the original Constitution—before the Bill of Rights was added.

RESTRICTIONS ON POWERS OF THE STATES

States may not make treaties with foreign nations, coin money, issue paper currency, grant titles of nobility, pass a bill of attainder or an ex post facto law,* or, without the consent of Congress, levy any taxes on imports or exports, keep troops and ships in time of peace, or enter into an agreement with another state or with a foreign power.
[Art. I, sec. 10]

GUARANTEES BY THE FEDERAL GOVERNMENT TO THE STATES

The national government guarantees to every state a "republican form of government" and protection against foreign invasion and (provided the states request it) protection against domestic insurrection.   [Art. IV, sec. 4]

An existing state will not be broken up into two or more states or merged with all or part of another state without that state's consent.
[Art. IV, sec. 3]

* For definitions of *bill of attainder* and *ex post facto law,* see the Glossary.

Congress may admit new states into the Union.
[Art. IV, sec. 3]

Taxes levied by Congress must be uniform throughout the United States: they may not be levied on some states but not others.
[Art. I, sec. 8]

The Constitution may not be amended to give states unequal representation in the Senate.   [Art. V]

RULES GOVERNING HOW STATES DEAL WITH EACH OTHER

"Full faith and credit" shall be given by each state to the laws, records, and court decisions of other states. (For example, a civil case settled in the courts of one state cannot be retried in the courts of another.)   [Art. IV, sec. 1]

The citizens of each state shall have the "privileges and immunities" of the citizens of every other state. (No one is quite sure what this is supposed to mean.)   [Art. IV, sec. 2]

If a person charged with a crime by one state flees to another, he or she is subjected to extradition—that is, the governor of the state that finds the fugitive is supposed to return the person to the governor of the state that wants him or her.
[Art. IV, sec. 2]

---

put together, they could also take apart. The alliance among the states that existed from 1776 to 1787 was a confederation: that is, a system of government in which the people create state governments, which, in turn, create and operate a national government (see Figure 3.1). Since the national government in a confederation derives its powers from the states, it is dependent on their continued cooperation for its survival. By 1786 that cooperation was barely forthcoming.

A Bold, New Plan

A federation—or a "federal republic," as the Founders called it—derives its powers directly from the people, as do the state governments. As the Founders envisioned it, both levels of government, the national and the state, would have certain powers, but neither would have supreme authority over the other. Madison, writing in *Federalist* No. 46, said that both the state and federal governments "are in fact but different agents and trustees of the people, constituted with different powers." In *Federalist* No. 28 Hamilton explained how he thought the system would work: the people could shift their support between state and federal levels of government as needed to keep the two in balance. "If their rights are invaded by either, they can make use of the other as the instrument of redress."

It was an entirely new plan, for which no historical precedent existed. Nobody came to the Philadelphia convention with a clear idea of what a federal (as opposed to a unitary or a confederal) system would look like, and there was not much discussion at Philadelphia of how the system would work in practice. Few delegates then used the word *federalism* in the sense in which we now employ it (it was originally used as a synonym for *confederation* and only later came to stand for something different).[7] The Constitution does not spell out the powers that the states are to have, and until the Tenth Amendment was added at the insistence of various states, there was not even a clause in it saying (as did the amendment) that "the powers not delegated to the United States by the Constitution, nor prohibited by it to the states, are reserved to the states respectively, or to the people." The Founders assumed from the outset that the federal government would have only those powers given to it by the Constitution; the Tenth Amendment was an afterthought, added to make that assumption explicit and allay fears that something else was intended.[8]

The Tenth Amendment has rarely had much practical significance, however. From time to time the Supreme Court has tried to interpret that amendment as putting certain state activities beyond the reach of the federal government, but invariably the Court has later changed its mind and allowed Washington to regulate such matters as the hours that employees of a city-owned mass-transit system may work. The Court did not find that running such a transportation system was one of the powers "reserved to the states."[9]

Elastic Language

The need to reconcile the competing interests of large and small states and of northern and southern states, especially as they affected the organization of Congress, was sufficiently difficult without trying to spell out exactly what relationship ought to exist between the national and state systems. For example, Congress was given the power to regulate commerce "among the several states." The Philadelphia convention would have gone on for four years rather than four months if the Founders had decided that it was necessary to describe, in clear language, how one was to tell where commerce *among* the states ended and commerce wholly *within* a single state began. The Supreme Court, as we shall see, devoted over a century to that task before giving up.

Though some clauses bearing on federal-state relations were reasonably clear (see the accompanying box), other clauses were quite vague. The Founders knew, correctly, that they could not make an exact and exhaustive list of everything the federal government was empowered to do—circumstances would change, new exigencies would arise. Thus they added the following elastic language to Article I: Congress shall have the power to "make all laws which shall be necessary and proper for carrying into execution the foregoing powers."

The Founders themselves carried away from Philadelphia different views of what federalism meant. One view was championed by Hamilton. Since the people had created the national government, since the laws and treaties made pursuant to the Constitution were "the supreme law of the land" (Article VI), and since the most pressing needs were the development of a national economy and the conduct of foreign affairs, Hamilton thought that the national government was the superior and leading force in political affairs and that its powers ought to be broadly defined and liberally construed.

The other view, championed by Jefferson, was that the federal government, though important, was the product of an agreement among the states; and though "the people" were the ultimate sovereigns, the principal threat to their liberties was likely to come from the national government. (Madison, a strong supporter of national supremacy at the convention, later became a champion of states' rights.) Thus the powers of the federal government should be narrowly construed and strictly limited. As Madison put it in *Federalist* No. 45, in language that probably made Hamilton wince, "The powers delegated by the proposed Constitution to the federal government are few and defined. Those which are to remain in the State governments are numerous and indefinite."

Hamilton argued for national supremacy, Jefferson for states' rights. Though their differences were greater in theory than in practice (as we shall see in Chapter 12, Jefferson while president sometimes acted in a positively Hamiltonian manner), the differing interpretations they offered of the Constitution were to shape political debate in this country until well into the 1960s.

The Debate on the Meaning of Federalism

The Civil War was fought, in part, over the issue of national supremacy versus states' rights, but it settled only one part of that argument—namely, that the national government was supreme, its sovereignty derived directly from the people, and thus the states could not lawfully secede from the Union. Virtually every other aspect of the national-supremacy issue continued to animate political and legal debate for another century.

The Supreme Court Speaks

As arbiter of what the Constitution means, the Supreme Court became the focal point of that debate. In Chapter 14 we shall see in some detail how the Court made its decisions. For now it is enough to know that during the formative years of the new Republic, the Supreme Court was led by a staunch and brilliant advocate of the Hamilton position, Chief Justice John Marshall. In a series of decisions he and the Court powerfully defended the national-supremacy view of the newly formed federal government.

The most important decision was in a case, seemingly trivial in its origins, that arose when James McCulloch, the cashier of the Baltimore branch of the Bank of the United States, which had been created by Congress, refused to pay a tax levied on that bank by the state of Maryland. He was hauled into state court and convicted of failing to pay a tax. In 1819 McCulloch appealed all the way to the Supreme Court in a case known as *McCulloch* v. *Maryland.*

Thomas Jefferson (1743–1826) was not at the Constitutional Convention. His doubts about the new national government led him to oppose the Federalist administration of John Adams and to become an ardent champion of states' rights.

The Court, in a unanimous opinion, answered two questions in ways that expanded the powers of Congress and confirmed the supremacy of the federal government in the exercise of those powers.

The first question was whether Congress had the right to set up a bank, or any other corporation, since such a right is nowhere explicitly mentioned in the Constitution. Marshall said that, though the federal government possessed only those powers enumerated in the Constitution, the "extent"—that is, the meaning—of those powers required interpretation. Though the word *bank* is not in that document, one finds there the power to manage money: to lay and collect taxes, issue a currency, and borrow funds. To carry out these powers Congress may reasonably decide that chartering a national bank is "necessary and proper." Marshall's words were carefully chosen to endow the **"necessary and proper" clause** with the widest possible sweep:

> *Let the end be legitimate, let it be within the scope of the Constitution, and all means which are appropriate, which are plainly adapted to that end, which are not prohibited, but consistent with the letter and spirit of the Constitution, are constitutional.*[10]

The second question was whether a federal bank could lawfully be taxed by a state. To answer it, Marshall went back to first principles. The government of the United States was not established by the states, but by the people, and thus the federal government was supreme in the exercise of those powers conferred upon it. Having already concluded that chartering a bank was within the powers of Congress, Marshall then argued that the only way for such powers to be supreme was for their use to be immune from state challenge and for the products of their use to be protected against state destruction. Since "the power to tax involves the power to destroy," and since the power to destroy a federal agency would confer upon the states using it supremacy over the federal government, the states may not tax any federal instrument. Hence the Maryland law was unconstitutional.

McCulloch won, and so did the federal government. Half a century later, the Court decided that what was sauce for the goose was sauce for the gander. It held that, just as state governments could not tax federal bonds, the federal government could not tax the interest people earn on state and municipal bonds. In 1988 the Supreme Court changed its mind and decided that Congress was now free, if it wished, to tax the interest on such state and local bonds. Municipal bonds, which for nearly a century were a tax-exempt investment protected, so their holders thought, by the Constitution, were now protected only by politics. So far Congress hasn't wanted to tax them.[11]

Nullification

The Supreme Court can decide a case without settling the issue. The struggle over states' rights versus national supremacy continued to rage in Congress, during presidential elections, and ultimately on the battlefield. The issue came to center on the doctrine of **nullification.** When Congress passed laws (in 1798) to punish newspaper editors who published stories critical of the federal government, James Madison and Thomas Jefferson opposed the laws, suggesting (in statements known as the Virginia and Kentucky Resolutions) that the states had the right to "nullify" (that is, declare null and void) a federal law that, in the states' opinion, violated the Constitution. The laws expired before the claim of nullification could be settled in the courts.

Later the doctrine of nullification was revived by John C. Calhoun of South Carolina, first in opposition to a tariff enacted by the federal government

At one time the states could issue their own paper money, such as this New York currency worth 25 cents in 1776. Under the Constitution this power was reserved to Congress.

and later in opposition to federal efforts to restrict slavery. Calhoun argued that if Washington attempted to ban slavery, the states had the right to declare such acts unconstitutional and thus null and void. This time, the issue was settled—by war. The northern victory in the Civil War determined once and for all that the federal union is indissoluble and that states cannot declare acts of Congress unconstitutional, a view later confirmed by the Supreme Court.[12]

Dual Federalism

After the Civil War the debate about the meaning of federalism focused on the interpretation of the commerce clause of the Constitution. Out of this debate there emerged the doctrine of **dual federalism,** which held that though the national government was supreme in its sphere, the states were equally supreme in theirs, and that these two spheres of action should and could be kept separate. Applied to commerce, the concept of dual federalism implied that there was such a thing as *inter*state commerce, which Congress could regulate, and *intra*state commerce, which only the states could regulate, and that the Court could tell which was which.

For a long period the Court tried to decide what was interstate commerce based on the kind of business that was being conducted. Transporting things between states was obviously interstate commerce, and so subject to federal regulation. Thus federal laws affecting the interstate shipment of lottery tickets,[13] prostitutes,[14] liquor,[15] and harmful foods and drugs[16] were upheld. On the other hand, manufacturing,[17] insurance,[18] and farming[19] were in the past considered *intra*state commerce, and so only the state governments were allowed to regulate them.

Such product-based distinctions turned out to be hard to sustain. For example, if you ship a case of whiskey from Kentucky to Kansas, how long is it in interstate commerce (and thus subject to federal law), and when does it enter intrastate commerce and become subject only to state law? For a while the Court's answer was that the whiskey was in interstate commerce so long as it was in its "original package,"[20] but that only precipitated long quarrels as to what was the original package, and how one is to treat things, like gas and grain, that may not be

shipped in packages at all. And how could one distinguish between manufacturing and transportation when one company did both or when a single manufacturing corporation owned factories in different states? And if an insurance company sold policies to customers both inside and outside a given state, were there to be different laws regulating identical policies that happened to be purchased from the same company by persons in different states?

In time the effort to find some clear principles that distinguished interstate from intrastate commerce was pretty much abandoned. Commerce was like a stream flowing through the country, drawing to itself contributions from thousands of scattered enterprises and depositing its products in millions of individual homes. The Court began to permit the federal government to regulate almost anything that affected this stream, so that by the 1940s not only had farming and manufacturing been redefined as part of interstate commerce,[21] but even the janitors and window washers in buildings that housed companies engaged in interstate commerce were now said to be part of that stream.[22]

The current Court interpretation of various laws pertaining to commerce is immensely complex, difficult to summarize, and impossible to explain. (For example, lawyers are said to engage in interstate commerce but professional baseball players are not, so that federal antitrust laws affect the former but not the latter.)[23] It would be only a mild overstatement, however, to say that the doctrine of dual federalism is virtually extinct and that, provided it has a good reason for wanting to do so, Congress can pass a law that will regulate constitutionally almost any kind of economic activity anywhere in the country.

Federal-State Relations

Though constitutionally the federal government may be supreme, politically it must take into account the fact that the laws it passes have to be approved by members of Congress selected from, and responsive to, state and local constituencies. Thus what Washington lawfully may do is not the same thing as what it politically may wish to do. For example, in 1947 the Supreme Court decided that the federal government and not the states had supreme authority over

CRITICAL Thinking

The Tenth Amendment: Sleeping Giant?

The Tenth Amendment to the Constitution reads, "The powers not delegated to the United States by the Constitution, nor prohibited by it to the States, are reserved to the States respectively, or to the people."

In the one hundred years after Chief Justice John Marshall left the Court in 1835, the Tenth Amendment was frequently invoked by proponents of states' rights to limit powers expressly granted to Congress, including the powers to regulate interstate commerce, to enforce the equal-protection clause of the Fourteenth Amendment, and to impose and collect taxes. But after the late 1930s and President Franklin D. Roosevelt's New Deal, the Tenth Amendment was virtually forgotten. In 1993, the U.S. Advisory Commission on Intergovernmental Relations declared that a series of U.S. Supreme Court decisions stretching into the 1980s had "reduced the status of the states to that of 'interest groups' operating and competing in the national political process."

But in the 1992 case *New York* v. *United States*, the Court struck down a federal law that required the states to regulate low-level radioactive waste produced within their borders, holding that the law infringed on state sovereignty: "States are not mere political subdivisions of the United States." Likewise, in the 1995 case *United States* v. *Lopez*, the Court invalidated the 1990 Gun-Free School Zones Act. The Court ruled that making it a federal crime to carry a gun within one thousand feet of a school

could not be justified as a rational extension of congressional authority to regulate interstate economic activity, for the statute "would convert congressional authority under the commerce clause to a general police power of the sort retained by the states." In 1997, the Court refused to allow Congress, in the Brady bill, to require local law enforcement officers to do background checks on people trying to buy guns (*Printz* v. *United States*).

Moreover, in recent years a number of state leaders have asserted Tenth Amendment rights. For example, after the 1994 elections, thirty of the nation's Republican governors met and signed "The Williamsburg Resolve," drafted by Governor George Allen of Virginia: "Here and in other colonial capitals, the nation's founders first debated the idea of independence and the fundamental principles of freedom. . . . Chief among [the checks and balances the founders established] were to be the State governments, whose co-equal role was expressly acknowledged in the Tenth Amendment to the Constitution." And in 1995 Colorado legislators passed this joint resolution: "The state of Colorado hereby claims sovereignty under the Tenth Amendment to the Constitution of the United States over all other powers not otherwise enumerated and granted to the federal government by the United States Constitution, including at least sovereignty over its people and its natural resources."

Clearly, the Tenth Amendment is no longer a political sleeper, but is it a sleep-

ing giant? How, if at all, might renewed interest in its twenty-eight words change the course of federal-state relations? If the doctrine of nullification (states' declaring acts of Congress unconstitutional) is null and void, then what do champions of the Tenth Amendment mean by "state sovereignty" and the states' "co-equal role"? How, if at all, might adherence to the Tenth Amendment narrow the scope of congressional power to regulate interstate commerce and thereby revive the doctrine of dual federalism (the idea that the national government and the states are each supreme in their respective spheres)? Is there any activity you can think of that does not somehow involve "interstate commerce"? Getting dressed in the morning—in a shirt made in China and shipped from outside the state? Buying a watch in one state—containing parts made in another?

Find out whether the Tenth Amendment has been debated by leaders in your home state. What arguments have they made about it, and which points, pro and con, do you find most persuasive?

SOURCES: Edward S. Corwin, *The Constitution and What It Means Today* (Princeton, NJ: Princeton University Press, 1978), p. 443; *Federal Regulation of State and Local Governments* (U.S. Advisory Commission on Intergovernmental Relations, July 1993), p. 7; Linda Greenhouse, "Blowing the Dust Off the Constitution That Was," *New York Times*, May 28, 1995, sec. 4, pp. 1, 6; W. John Moore, "A Landmark Decision? Maybe Not," *National Journal*, May 6, 1995, p. 1131; *The American Enterprise*, March/April 1995, p. 30.

oil beneath the ocean off the nation's coasts.[24] Six years later, after an intense debate, Congress passed and the president signed a law transferring title to these tidelands oil reserves back to the states.

Grants-in-Aid

The best illustration of how political realities modify legal authority can be found in federal **grants-in-aid.** The first of these programs began even before the Constitution was adopted, in the form of land grants made by the national government to the states in order to finance education. (State universities all over the country were built with the proceeds from the sale of these land grants; hence the name *land-grant colleges.*) Land grants were also made to support the building of wagon roads, canals, railroads, and flood-control projects. These measures were hotly debated in Congress (President Madison thought some were unconstitutional), even though the use to which the grants were put was left almost entirely to the states.

Cash grants-in-aid began almost as early. In 1808 Congress gave $200,000 to the states to pay for their militias, with the states in charge of the size, deployment, and command of these troops. However, grant-in-aid programs remained few in number and small in price until the twentieth century, when scores of new ones came into being. In 1915 less than $6 million was spent per year in grants-in-aid; by 1925 over $114 million was spent; by 1937 the figure was nearly $300 million.[25] The greatest growth began in the 1960s: between 1960 and 1966 federal grants to the states doubled; from 1966 to 1970 they doubled again; between 1970 and 1975 they doubled yet again. By 1985 they amounted to over $100 billion a year and were spent through more than four hundred separate programs. The five largest programs accounted for over half the money spent and reflected the new priorities that federal policy had come to serve: housing assistance for low-income families, Medicaid, highway construction, services to the unemployed, and welfare programs for mothers with dependent children and for the disabled.

The grant-in-aid system, once under way, grew rapidly because it helped state and local officials resolve a dilemma. On the one hand they wanted

Some of the nation's greatest universities, such as the University of California at Berkeley, began as land-grant colleges.

access to the superior taxing power of the federal government. On the other hand prevailing constitutional interpretation, at least until the late 1930s, held that the federal government could not spend money for purposes not authorized by the Constitution. The solution was obviously to have federal money put into state hands: Washington would pay the bills, the states would run the programs.

There were four reasons why federal money seemed, to state officials, so attractive. First, the money was there. During most of the nineteenth century and the early decades of the twentieth, the federal government was taking in more money than it was spending. The high-tariff policies of the Republicans produced a large budget surplus; in the 1880s Washington literally had more money than it knew what to do with. Some went to pay off a big part of the national debt, some was given to Civil War veterans as a pension, and some went to the states or was otherwise used for internal improvements.[26]

By the mid-twentieth century, when budget surpluses had pretty much become a thing of the past, a second reason for turning to Washington became evident: the federal income tax. Inaugurated in the 1920s, it proved to be a marvelously flexible tool of public finance, for it automatically brought in more money as economic activity (and thus personal income) grew.

Third, the federal government, unlike the states, managed the currency and thus could print more money whenever it needed it. (Technically it borrowed this money, and of course it paid interest on what it had borrowed, but it was under no obligation to pay it all back, because, as a practical matter, it had borrowed from itself.) The size of the federal public debt stayed more or less constant, or even declined, in the second half of the nineteenth century. By the mid-twentieth century people no longer worried about the national debt so much, or at least they worried about it for reasons other than the fear of being in debt. Thus the federal government came to accept, as a matter of policy, the proposition that when it needed money, it would print it. States could not do this: if they borrowed (and many could not), they had to pay it all back, in full.

These three economic reasons for the attractiveness of federal grants were probably not as important as a fourth reason: politics. Federal money seemed to a state official to be "free" money. If Alabama could get Washington to put up the money for improving navigation on the Tombigbee River, the citizens of the entire nation, not just those of Alabama, would pay for it. Of course, if Alabama gets money for that purpose, every state will want it (and will get it). Even so, it was still an attractive political proposition: the governor of Alabama did not have to propose, collect, or take responsibility for federal taxes. Indeed, the governor could denounce the federal government for being profligate in its use of the people's money. Meanwhile he would cut the ribbon opening the new dam on the Tombigbee.

That every state had an incentive to ask for federal money to pay for local programs meant, of course, that it would be very difficult for one state to get money for a given program without every state's getting it. The senator from Alabama who votes for the project to improve navigation on the Tombigbee will have to vote in favor of projects improving navigation on every other river in the country if the senator expects his or her Senate colleagues to sup-

port such a request. Federalism as practiced in the United States means that when Washington wants to send money to one state or congressional district, it must send money to many states and districts.

In 1966, for example, President Lyndon Johnson proposed a "Model Cities" plan, under which federal funds would be spent on experimental programs in a small number of large cities that had especially acute problems. When the bill went to Congress, it quickly became clear that no such plan could be passed unless the number of cities to benefit was increased. Senator Edmund Muskie of Maine, whose support was crucial, would not vote for a bill that did not make Augusta, Bangor, and Portland eligible for aid originally intended to help New York, Chicago, and Philadelphia.[27]

FIGURE 3.2 The Changing Purposes of Federal Grants to State and Local Governments

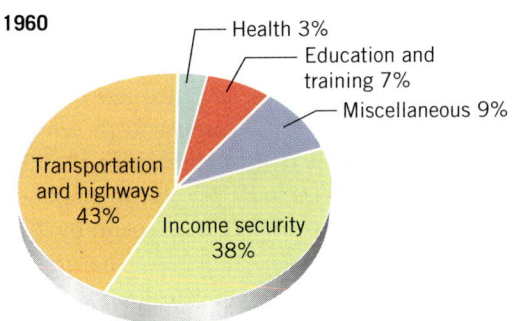

1960

- Health 3%
- Education and training 7%
- Miscellaneous 9%
- Transportation and highways 43%
- Income security 38%

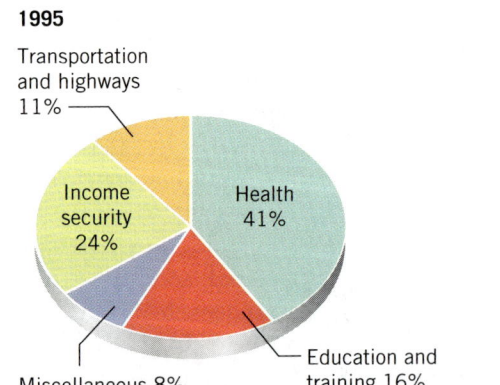

1995

- Transportation and highways 11%
- Income security 24%
- Health 41%
- Miscellaneous 8%
- Education and training 16%

SOURCE: *Budget of the U.S. Government, Fiscal Year 1996*, Table 12.3.

Meeting National Needs

Until the 1960s most federal grants-in-aid were conceived by or in cooperation with the states and were designed to serve essentially state purposes. Large blocs of voters and a variety of organized interests would press for grants to help farmers, build highways, or support vocational education. During the 1960s, however, an important change occurred: the federal government began devising grant programs based less on what states were demanding and more on what federal officials perceived to be important *national* needs (see Figure 3.2). Federal officials, not state and local ones, were the principal proponents of grant programs to aid the urban poor, combat crime, reduce pollution, and deal with drug abuse. Some of these programs even attempted to bypass the states, providing money directly to cities or even to local citizen groups. These were worrisome developments for governors, who were accustomed to being the conduit for money on its way from Washington to local communities.

TABLE 3.1 Federal Aid to State and Local Governments, 1955–1995

| Year | Total Federal Aid (in billions)[a] | Federal Aid as a Percentage of | |
		Federal Outlays	State and Local Outlays
1955	$15.1	4.7%	10.1%
1960	29.1	7.6	14.7
1965	41.8	9.2	15.3
1970	73.6	12.3	19.2
1975	105.4	15.0	23.0
1980	127.6	15.5	26.3
1985	113.0	11.2	21.0
1990	119.7	10.8	20.0
1995	175.3 (est.)	15.3 (est.)	NA

[a] In constant 1987 dollars.

SOURCE: Total aid figures, percentages of federal outlays, and 1995 estimates from *Budget of the U.S. Government, Fiscal Year 1993*, Table 12.1, part 5, 164–165. Percentages of state and local outlays 1955–1985 from *Budget of the U.S. Government, Fiscal Year 1991*, Table 12.1, A-321. Percentage of state and local outlays in 1990 from *Budget of the U.S. Government, Fiscal Year 1994*, 79.

FIGURE 3.3 Federal Aid to State and Local Governments, 1980–1994

Total federal aid to state and local governments, in billions of constant 1987 dollars, and the aid as a percentage of total federal spending, for each fiscal year.

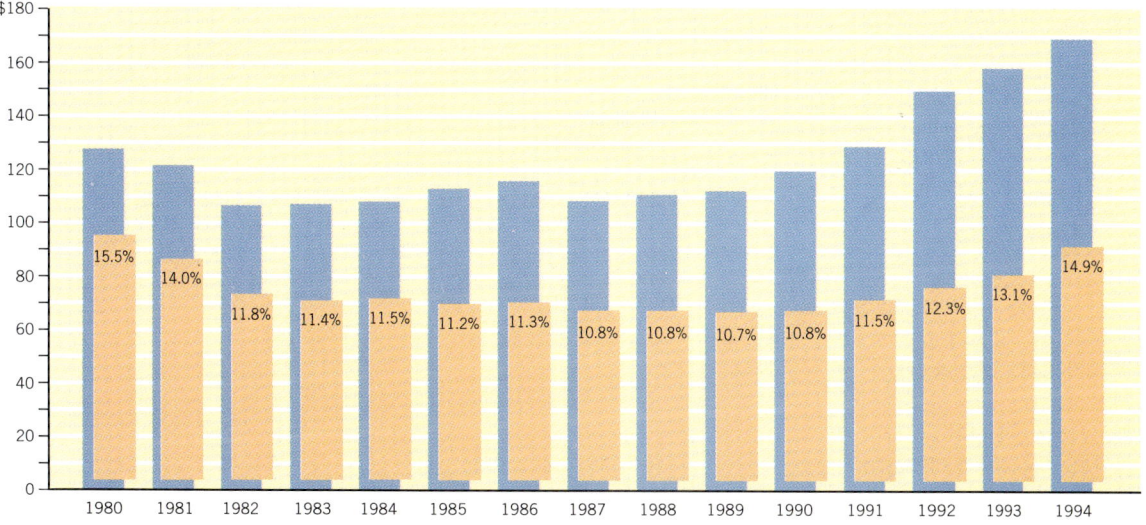

NOTE: Data for 1992, 1993, and 1994 are estimated.

SOURCE: *Budget of the U.S. Government, Fiscal Year 1991 Supplement*, Table 12.1, 164–165.

The rise in federal activism in setting goals and the efforts, on occasion, to bypass state officials occurred at a time when the total amount of federal aid to states and localities had become so vast that many jurisdictions were completely dependent on it for the support of vital services. Whereas federal aid amounted to less than 2 percent of state and local spending in 1927, by 1970 it amounted to 19 percent and by 1980 to 26 percent (see Table 3.1 and Figure 3.3, page 65). Some older, larger cities had become what one writer called "federal-aid junkies," so dependent were they on these grants. In 1978 in Detroit 77 percent of the revenue the city raised came from Washington.[28]

The Intergovernmental Lobby

State and local officials, both elected and appointed, began to form an important new lobby—the "intergovernmental lobby," made up of mayors, governors, superintendents of schools, state directors of public health, county highway commissioners, local police chiefs, and others who had come to count on federal funds.[29] The five largest of these lobbies employed, in 1990, over four hundred people and spent about $45 million (see Table 3.2), nearly half of which came from the federal government. Even this has proved insufficient. After all, national organiza- tions of governors or mayors can press for more fed- eral money but not for increased funding for any particular state or city. Thus over thirty-one individ- ual states, more than two dozen counties, and over one hundred cities have opened their own offices in Washington. Some are small, some share staff with other communities, but a few are quite large. Texas alone employs two dozen people in Washington to look after its interests.

The purpose of this intergovernmental lobby was the same as that of any private lobby—to obtain more federal money with fewer strings attached. For a while the cities and states did in fact get more money, but by 1980 federal grants had stopped growing.

Categorical Grants versus Revenue Sharing

The effort to loosen the strings took the form of shifting, as much as possible, the federal aid from **categorical grants** to block grants or to **revenue sharing.** A categorical grant is one for a specific pur- pose defined by federal law: to build an airport or a college dormitory, for example, or to make welfare payments to low-income mothers. Such grants usu- ally require that the state or locality put up money to "match" some part of the federal grant, though

TABLE 3.2   State and Local Governments Lobby in Washington

Organization	Number of Employees 1990	Approximate Budget 1990	Percentage of Budget from Federal Governments 1980	1990
National Governors' Association (55 state and territorial governors)	100	$10 million	42%	33%
National Conference of State Legislatures (50 state legislatures)	140	$10 million	36	15
National League of Cities (14,700 cities)	65	$8 million	43	2
U.S. Conference of Mayors (1,000 large cities)	50	$7 million	60	35
National Association of Counties (2,000 counties)	70	$10 million	30	9

SOURCE: Compiled by Xandra Kayden.

Federal aid now supports almost every local government program, including school lunches.

the amount of matching funds can be quite small. (In the federal highway program Washington pays about 90 percent of the construction costs and the states only about 10 percent.) Governors and mayors complained about these categorical grants because their purposes were often so narrow that it was impossible for a state to adapt federal grants to local needs. A mayor seeking federal money to build parks might have discovered that the city could get money only if it launched an urban renewal program that entailed bulldozing several blocks of housing or small businesses.

One response to this problem was to consolidate several categorical or project grant programs into a single block grant devoted to some general purpose and with fewer restrictions on its use. Block grants (sometimes called "special revenue sharing" or "broad-based aid") began in the mid-1960s, when such a grant was created in the health field. Though many block grants were proposed between 1966 and 1980, only five were enacted. Of the three largest, one consolidated various categorical grant programs aimed at cities (Community Development Block Grants); another created a program to aid local law enforcement (Law Enforcement Assistance Act); and a third authorized new kinds of locally managed programs for the unemployed (CETA, or the

Comprehensive Employment and Training Act). In 1981 President Reagan persuaded Congress to raise the number of block grants to nine. In 1987 block grants accounted for about 12 percent of all federal aid programs.

Revenue sharing (sometimes called *general revenue sharing,* or GRS) was even more permissive. Adopted in 1972 with the passage of the State and Local Fiscal Assistance Act, GRS provided for the distribution of about $6 billion a year in federal funds to the states and localities, with no requirement as to matching funds and freedom to spend the money on almost any governmental purpose. Distribution of the money was determined by a statistical formula that took into account population, local tax effort, and the wealth of the state in a way intended to send more money to poorer, heavily taxed states and less to richer, lightly taxed ones. In 1986 the program was ended after having distributed about $85 billion over a fourteen-year period.

In theory block grants and revenue sharing were supposed to give the states and cities considerable freedom in deciding how to spend the money while helping to relieve their tax burdens. To some extent they did. However, neither the goal of "no strings" nor the one of fiscal relief was really attained. First, the amount of money available from block grants and revenue sharing did not grow as fast as the states had hoped nor as quickly as did the money available through categorical grants. Second, the federal government steadily increased the number of strings attached to the spending of this supposedly "unrestricted" money. Thus, between 1993 and 1995 the number of federal grants to state and local governments increased from 599 to 633. The entire growth was in categorical grants (from 578 to 618); no new block grants were established. In 1995 as in 1975, roughly 85 to 90 percent of total federal grant dollars were in categorical programs.

The Slowdown in "Free" Money

Block grants grew more slowly than categorical grants because of the different kinds of political coalitions supporting each. Congress and the federal bureaucracy liked categorical grants for the same reason the states disliked them—the specificity of these programs enhanced federal control over how the money was to be used. Federal officials, joined by liberal interest groups and organized labor, tended to distrust state governments. Whenever Congress wanted to address some national problem, its natural inclination was to create a categorical grant program so that it, and not the states, would decide how the money would be spent.

Moreover, even though governors and mayors like block grants and revenue sharing, these programs cover such a broad range of activities that no single interest group has a vital stake in pressing for their enlargement. Revenue sharing, for example, provided a little money to many city agencies but rarely provided all or even most of the money for any single agency. Thus no single agency acted as if the expansion of revenue sharing were a life-and-death matter. Categorical grants, on the other hand, are often a matter of life and death for many agencies—state departments of welfare, of highways, and of health, for example, are utterly dependent on federal aid. Accordingly the administrators in charge of these programs will press strenuously for their expansion. Moreover, categorical programs are supervised by special committees of Congress, and as we shall see in Chapter 11, many of these committees have an interest in seeing their programs grow.

As a result of the political differences between categorical grants and block grants or revenue sharing, the amount spent on the former tends to increase faster than the amount spent on the latter. Between 1975 and 1978 the amount spent on revenue sharing increased by 11 percent, but that spent on categorical grants increased by 56 percent.[30] One observer explained: "You dilute the constituency when you make aid more general. Say you had a program to control a disease. You'd get everyone in the country interested in that disease to focus on that one subject, and a congressman to become the champion of it. . . . There just is not that much sympathy to increase revenue sharing."[31] So little support did general revenue sharing have that, in their debate over the 1986 budget, almost the only thing Democrats and Republicans could agree on was abolishing revenue sharing, which they did.

Not only did general revenue sharing lack a constituency, but it was a wasteful way of trying to help poor communities. The waste resulted from the fact that *every* community—some thirty-nine thousand in all—got revenue-sharing money whether it was rich or poor. Paw Paw, West Virginia, a town devastated by a loss of jobs, received only $11,874 from revenue sharing, but that amounted to more than one-third of all the tax money it collected, and was enough to pay the salary of its lone police officer. Beverly Hills, California, a city so affluent and exclusive that, as the joke goes, the police department has an unlisted phone number, also got revenue-sharing money.

Rivalry Among the States

The more important that federal money becomes to the states, the more likely they are to compete among themselves for the largest share of it. For a century or better, the growth of the United States—in population, business, and income—was concentrated in the industrial Northeast. In recent decades, however, that growth—at least in population and employment, if not in income—has shifted to the South, Southwest, and Far West. This change has precipitated an intense debate over whether the federal government, by the way it distributes its funds and awards its contracts, is unfairly helping some regions and states at the expense of others. Journalists and politicians have dubbed the struggle as one be-tween "Snowbelt" (or "Frostbelt") and "Sunbelt" states.

Whether in fact there is anything worth arguing about is far from clear: the federal government has had great difficulty in figuring out where it ulti-mately spends what funds for what purposes. For example, a $1 billion defense contract may go to a company with headquarters in California, but much of the money may actually be spent in Connecticut or New York, as the prime contractor in California buys from subcontractors in the other states. It is even less clear whether federal funds actually affect the growth rate of the regions. The uncertainty about the facts has not prevented a debate about the issue, however. That debate focuses on the formulas written into federal laws by which block grants are allocated. These formulas take into account such factors as a county's or city's population, personal income in the area, and housing quality. A slight change in a formula can shift millions of dollars in grants in ways that favor either the older, declining cities of the Northeast or the newer, still-growing cities of the Southwest.

With the advent of grants based on distribu-tional formulas (as opposed to grants for a particu-lar project), the results of the census, taken every ten years, assume monumental importance. A city or state shown to be losing population may, as a result, forfeit millions of dollars in federal aid. There are over one hundred programs (out of some five hun-dred federal grant programs in all) that distribute money on the basis of population. When the direc-tor of the census in 1960 announced figures showing that many big cities had lost population, he was gen-erally ignored. When he made the same announce-ment in 1980, after the explosion in federal grants, he was roundly denounced by the mayors of those cities.

Senators and representatives now have access to computers that can tell them instantly the effect on their states and districts of even minor changes in a formula by which federal aid is distributed. These formulas rely on objective measures, but the exact measure is selected with an eye to its political conse-quences. There is nothing wrong with this in princi-ple, since any political system must provide some benefits for everybody if it is to stay together. Given

the competition among states in a federal system, however, the struggle over allocation formulas be-comes especially acute. The results are sometimes plausible, as when Congress decides to distribute money intended to help disadvantaged local school systems in large part on the basis of the proportion of poor children in each school district. But some-times the results are a bit strange, as when the for-mula by which federal aid for mass transit is determined gives New York, a city utterly dependent on mass transit, a federal subsidy of two cents per transit passenger but gives Grand Rapids, a city that relies chiefly on the automobile, a subsidy of forty-five cents per passenger.[32]

Federal Aid and Federal Control

So important has federal aid become for state and local governments that mayors and governors, along with others, began to fear that Washington was well on its way to controlling other levels of government. "He who pays the piper calls the tune," they mut-tered. In this view the constitutional protection of state government to be found in the Tenth Amend-ment was in jeopardy as a result of the strings being attached to the grants-in-aid on which the states were increasingly dependent.

Block grants and revenue sharing were efforts to reverse this trend by allowing the states and locali-ties freedom (considerable in the case of block grants; almost unlimited in the case of revenue shar-ing) to spend money as they wished. But as we have seen, these new devices did not in fact reverse the trend. Until 1978 block grants and revenue sharing increased until they amounted to 27 percent of all federal grants to states and localities but then began to decline, so that by 1986 they accounted for only 18 percent of such aid. Categorical grants—those with strings attached—continued to grow even faster.

There are two kinds of federal controls on state governmental activities. The traditional control tells the state government what it must do if it wants to get some grant money. These strings are often called **conditions of aid.** The newer form of control tells the state government what it must do, period. These rules are called **mandates.** Sometimes the mandates

TABLE 3.3	Major Mandate Enactments Regulating State and Local Governments, 1982–1991
1982	Surface Transportation Assistance Act Voting Rights Act Amendments
1983	Social Security Amendments
1984	Child Abuse Amendments Hazardous and Solid Waste Amendments Highway Safety Amendments Voting Accessibility for the Elderly and Handicapped Act
1985	Consolidated Omnibus Budget Reconciliation Act
1986	Age Discrimination in Employment Act Amendments Asbestos Hazard Emergency Response Act Commercial Motor Vehicle Safety Act Education of the Handicapped Act Amendments Emergency Planning and Community Right-to-Know Act Handicapped Children's Protection Act Safe Drinking Water Act Amendments
1987	Civil Rights Restoration Act Water Quality Act
1988	Drug-Free Workplace Act Fair Housing Act Amendments Lead Contamination Control Act Ocean Dumping Ban Act
1990	Americans with Disabilities Act Cash Management Improvement Act Clean Air Act Amendments Education of the Handicapped Act Amendments Older Workers Benefit Protection Act
1991	Social Security Fiscal Budget Reconciliation Act

SOURCE: Adapted from Timothy J. Conlan and David R. Beam, "Federal Mandates: The Record of Reform and Future Prospects," *Intergovernmental Perspective* (Fall 1992): 8.

must be observed only if the state takes any federal grants, but sometimes the mandates have nothing to do with federal aid—they apply to all state governments whether or not they accept grants.

Mandates

Most mandates concern civil rights and environmental protection. States may not discriminate in the operation of their programs, no matter who pays for them. Initially the antidiscrimination rules applied chiefly to distinctions based on race, sex, age, and ethnicity, but of late they have been broadened to include physical and mental disabilities as well. Various pollution-control laws require the states to comply with federal standards for clean air,

pure drinking water, and sewage treatment.[33]

Stated in general terms, these mandates seem reasonable enough. It is hard to imagine anyone arguing that state governments should be free to discriminate against people because of their race or national origin. In practice, however, some mandates create administrative and financial problems, especially when the mandates are written in vague language, thereby giving federal administrative agencies the power to decide for themselves what state and local governments are supposed to do.

In 1980 there were thirty-six mandates affecting state and local governments, twenty-two of them enacted in the 1970s. Both the Reagan administration and the Bush administration opposed the growth of mandates. Nevertheless, between 1981 and 1986 some 140 regulations, representing nearly six thousand new requirements on state and local government, were added to eighteen existing mandates. And between 1982 and 1991 Congress passed twenty-seven additional mandates (see Table 3.3).

All mandates are not created equal. Some mandates take the form of regulatory statutes and amendments that expand on previous legislation; the 1982 Voting Rights Act Amendment was based on federal civil rights laws dating back to the 1960s. Other mandates represent new areas of federal involvement. For example, the 1986 Handicapped Children's Protection Act introduced federal regulations intended to improve the life prospects of disabled youngsters. Some mandates are easy to understand, simple to administer, and relatively inexpensive; for example, the 1988 Ocean Dumping Ban Act, which prohibits any additional dumping of municipal sewage sludge in ocean waters. However, many mandates are hard to interpret, difficult to administer, and have high or uncertain costs. The 1990 Americans with Disabilities Act (ADA), which required businesses and state and local governments to provide the disabled with equal access to services, employment, buildings, and transportation systems, was one of twenty mandates signed into law by President Bush in 1990. Unfortunately the ADA was enacted with no clear-cut definition of "equal access," no unambiguous blueprint of how it was to be administered, and no reliable estimates of how much it would cost to implement.

Republican leaders in the 104th Congress promised to roll back mandates. They took special aim at requirements from Washington that dictate actions by state and local governments without providing the money to carry them out. For example, in 1993 the U.S. Conference of Mayors claimed that it cost 314 cities $6.5 billion to comply with just ten federal laws that contained such "unfunded mandates."[34] In 1995 Congress passed and President Clinton signed a law that directed the Congressional Budget Office to identify any bill, amendment, or conference report that would impose a new mandate of more than $50 million on state and local governments. But the law neither repealed existing unfunded mandates nor prohibited new ones, and it exempted all anti-discrimination legislation.

Mandates are not the only way in which the federal government imposes costs on state and local governments. According to a 1994 study by the U.S. Advisory Commission on Intergovernmental Relations, certain federal tax and regulatory policies make it difficult or expensive for state and local governments to raise revenues, borrow funds, or privatize public functions. Other federal laws expose state and local governments to financial liability, and numerous federal court decisions and administrative regulations require state and local governments to do or not do various things, either by statute or through an implied constitutional obligation.[35]

It is clear that the federal courts have helped fuel the growth of mandates. As interpreted in this century by the United States Supreme Court, the Tenth Amendment provides state and local officials no protection against the march of mandates. Indeed, many of the more controversial mandates result not from congressional action but from court decisions. For example, many state prison systems have been, at one time or another, under the control of federal judges who required major changes in prison construction and management in order to meet standards the judges derived from their reading of the Constitution.

School-desegregation plans are of course the best-known example of federal mandates. Those involving busing—an unpopular policy—have typically been the result of court orders rather than of federal law or regulation.

Judges—usually, but not always, in federal courts—have ordered Massachusetts to change the way it hires fire fighters, required Philadelphia to institute new procedures to handle complaints of police brutality, and altered the location in which Chicago was planning to build housing projects. Note that in most of these cases nobody in Washington was placing a mandate on a local government; rather a local citizen was using the federal courts to change a local practice.

The Supreme Court has made it much easier of late for citizens to control the behavior of local officials. A federal law, passed in the 1870s to protect newly freed slaves, makes it possible for a citizen to sue any state or local official who deprives that citizen of any "rights, privileges, or immunities secured by the Constitution and laws" of the United States.[36] In 1980 the Court decided that this law permitted a citizen to sue a local official if the official deprived the citizen of *anything* to which the citizen was entitled under federal law (and not just those federal laws protecting civil rights).[37] For example, a citizen can now use the federal courts to obtain from a state welfare office a payment to which he or she may be entitled under federal law. No one yet knows how this development will affect the way local government operates.

Conditions of Aid

By far the most important federal restrictions on state action are the conditions attached to the grants the states receive. In theory accepting these conditions is voluntary—if you don't want the strings, don't take the money. But when the typical state depends for a quarter or more of its budget on federal grants, many of which it has received for years and on which many of its citizens depend for their livelihoods, it is not clear exactly how "voluntary" such acceptance is. During the 1960s some strings were added, the most important of which had to do with civil rights. But beginning in the 1970s the number of conditions proliferated. One study of federal grant programs in five large states found that between 1951 and 1978 over a thousand conditions had been added to these programs; nearly 90 percent had been added after 1971.[38]

With more federal aid has come more federal control. City transportation systems getting federal money must be accessible to disabled persons.

Some conditions are specific to particular programs. For example, if a state does not establish a highway-beautification program, it will lose 10 percent of its federal highway aid money.[39] Others are general, covering most or all grants. For instance, if a state builds something with federal money, it must first conduct an environmental-impact study, it must pay construction workers the "prevailing wage" in the area, it often must provide an opportunity for citizen participation in some aspects of the design or location of the project, and it must ensure that the contractors who build the project have nondiscriminatory hiring policies.

The states and the federal government, not surprisingly, disagree about the costs and benefits of such rules. Members of Congress and federal officials feel they have an obligation to develop uniform national policies with respect to important matters and to prevent states and cities from misspending federal tax dollars. State officials, on the other hand, feel these national rules fail to take into account diverse local conditions, require the states to do things that the states must then pay for, and create serious inefficiencies.

The dispute over the best way to make city transit facilities accessible to disabled persons illustrates the difficulty of reconciling national objectives and a decentralized system of government. In 1973 Congress passed the Rehabilitation Act, which forbids discrimination against disabled people in any program receiving federal aid. Since there was virtually no discussion of this provision as the bill moved through Congress, no one was quite certain what it would mean when applied to a city transit system receiving federal money. Narrowly read, the law might mean only that the city could not refuse to hire an otherwise qualified disabled person to work in the transit system. Broadly read, it might mean that the buses and subway cars in the city had to be made physically accessible to disabled persons.

Under pressure from organizations representing the disabled, various federal agencies decided that the law should be given the broader interpretation. Accordingly they issued regulations requiring that city transit systems receiving federal aid equip their buses and subway cars with devices to lift wheelchairs on board.

Disabled people were pleased with these rules, believing that the benefits to them were well worth the cost. State and local officials took a different view. The then mayor of New York City, Edward Koch, argued that rebuilding existing buses and subways and buying new ones would make each trip by a wheelchair user cost thirty-eight dollars. It would be cheaper, he said, for the city to give free taxicab rides to every disabled person, but the federal regulations would not permit that. Billions would be spent by cities for a program to benefit 2 percent of the transit users, deserving though they may be.[40]

(In 1981 the Reagan administration relaxed the requirement that buses be able to lift wheelchairs aboard.)

What local officials discovered, in short, was that "free" federal money was not quite free after all. In the 1960s federal aid seemed to be entirely beneficial; what mayor or governor would not want such money? But just as local officials found it attractive to do things that another level of government then paid for, in time federal officials learned the same thing. Passing laws to meet the concerns of national constituencies—leaving the cities and states to pay the bills and manage the problems—began to seem attractive to Congress.

One's perspective depends on what office one holds, as is revealed by this statement of Mayor Koch, who once had been a congressman from New York:

> *As a member of Congress I voted for many of the laws imposing grant conditions, and did so with every confidence that we were enacting sensible permanent solutions to critical problems. It took a plunge into the mayor's job to drive home how misguided my congressional outlook had been. The bills I voted for came to the floor in a form that compelled approval. After all, who can vote against clean air and water or better access and education for the handicapped? But as I look back it is hard to believe I could have been taken in by the simplicity of what the Congress was doing and by the flimsy empirical support . . . offered to persuade the members that the proposed solution would work throughout the country.*[41]

As is evident from the mayor's remarks, the tensions in the federal system do not arise from one level of government or another being callous or incompetent, but from the kinds of political demands with which each must cope. Because of these competing demands, federal and local officials find themselves in a bargaining situation in which each side is trying to get some benefit (solving a problem, satisfying a pressure group) while passing on to the other side most of the costs (taxes, administrative problems).

The bargains struck in this process used to favor the local officials, because members of Congress

Federal Mandates: Golf Courses and Alarm Boxes

During the debate on the Americans with Disabilities Act (ADA), no one mentioned golf courses. Nevertheless, the ADA has changed the way that public golf courses are administered. There is an Association of Disabled American Golfers and a National Blind Golfers Association. The March 1993 issue of *Golf Course News* offered the following guidelines to public golf course operators, who must comply with the ADA:

- Reserve one or two handicapped parking spaces near the bag drop rather than next to the clubhouse.

- Cut out spots on raised curbs so carts can pass through.

- Build ramps to tees where possible.

- Provide a spot for disabled golfers to get in and out of the bunker.

- Keep bunker grades no more than one foot of elevation for every five feet of length.

- Install a Telecommunication Device for the Deaf (TDD) in the reservation office so the hearing impaired can make tee-time reservations by phone.

Likewise, no one mentioned alarm boxes during the debate over the ADA. But in 1996 Federal District Court Judge Robert W. Sweet ordered the New York City Fire Department to halt its plan to replace the city's 16,300 antiquated alarm boxes with public telephones wired to an emergency system. Judge Sweet ruled that because deaf and hearing-impaired people may be unable to use the phones to call for help, the plan violated the ADA's guarantee of "equal access to public services." Rather than appeal his ruling, New York Mayor Rudolph W. Giuliani directed city officials to meet with Judge Sweet and try to persuade him that the new phone system was usable by the deaf, who could tap a special fire alarm code over the system.

SOURCES: Joanne Desky, "Park Facilities Meet ADA Challenges: Even Public Golf Course Managers Must Comply," *PA Times*, 16, no. 5 (May 1, 1993): 1, 16; Don Vannatta, Jr., "U.S. Judge Says Removing Alarm Boxes Discriminates Against the Deaf," *New York Times*, February 14, 1996, p. B3.

were essentially servants of local interests: they were elected by local political parties, they were part of local political organizations, and they supported local autonomy. Beginning in the 1960s, however, changes in American politics that will be described

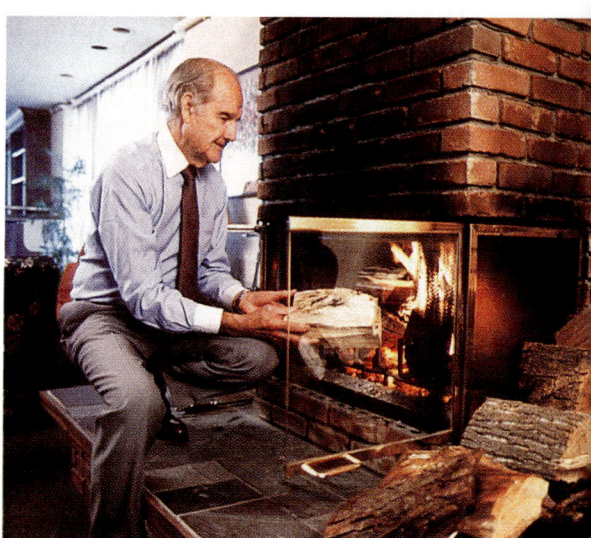

When George McGovern was a senator (left), he voted for many federal regulations that he later found burdensome when he became an innkeeper in Connecticut (right).

in later chapters—especially the weakening of political parties, the growth of public-interest lobbies in Washington, and the increased activism of the courts—shifted the orientation of many in Congress toward favoring Washington's needs over local needs.

Various presidents have tried to reverse this trend, but with little success. President Nixon proclaimed the "new federalism" and helped create revenue sharing and block grants, but as we shall see, federal mandates and conditions of aid grew rather than declined during his administration.

In 1981 President Reagan asked Congress to consolidate eighty-three categorical grants into six large block grants, none of which would seriously restrict how the states could spend the money. Congress went along in name only—it consolidated fifty-seven programs into nine small block grants, each of which had many restrictions attached. The debate over this plan showed that what is at stake is not simply differing views on how best to "streamline" or make "more efficient" the way in which federal money supports local programs, but rather competing philosophies of governance.

The Reagan administration believed that giving money without strings to the states was good because state governments are generally more conservative than the federal government. The reasons are that state governments must have balanced budgets (and thus cannot spend on social programs by running up deficits) and that liberal interest groups are less influential at the state level than at the national level. The critics of the Reagan view distrusted state governments for the very reason he admired them—they are less responsive to liberal causes. And members of Congress, whether they are liberal or conservative, are exposed to the demands of state officials who wish to have particular federal programs that benefit them protected by "categorization."

In general, the states did not respond to Reagan-era block grants and budget cuts simply by slashing programs. A state-by-state study led by Richard P. Nathan found that "state and local government responses to the 1981 federal aid cuts—through replacement funding, through a wide variety of financial coping and delaying measures, and through administrative reforms"— actually produced "higher service levels than otherwise would have been the case."[41] Likewise, another study concluded that, on balance, the Reagan block grants had promoted greater state flexibility in program design, reduced administrative costs, and necessitated little reduction in services despite the fact that states had to operate with about 13 percent fewer federal dollars.[42]

Thus, it appears that in the 1980s cutbacks in the amount of federal money, coupled with changes in state governments, led many states to experiment with new ways of delivering services. In the 1990s, the states once again became "laboratories," trying out new ideas in areas such as welfare, child care, education, and many more.

A Devolution Revolution?

The Reagan administration never attempted the sort of sweeping efforts to devolve federal power to the states that defined much of the legislative activity of the 104th Congress. The politics of federalism is a pendulum that over the last half century has swung between giving the states a lot of leeway and giving them very little. The Reagan administration gently nudged the pendulum in the direction of greater state autonomy. But the leaders of the first Republican-dominated House in forty years pushed for devolution with all their might.

Block Grants for Entitlements

Consider what happened with block grants. Basically, there are three types of block grants: *operational grants,* for such purposes as running state child care programs; *capital grants,* for such purposes as building local wastewater treatment plants; and *entitlement grants,* for transferring income to families and individuals. Since 1966 a total of twenty-three block grants had been enacted, and fifteen were still in place when the new Congress came to power. But all of these block grants, including all nine of the Reagan-era block grants, were for operating and capital purposes; none were for major entitlement programs. Thus, in 1995, of the $38.4 billion in federal block grant money, 29 percent was for operating programs, 67 percent was for capital programs, and only 4 percent was for entitlement programs. Block grant programs represented about 15 percent of the $238.5 billion in federal grants to states, localities, and nonprofit organizations.

The federal government's two biggest grant-in-aid programs—Aid to Families with Dependent Children (AFDC), often referred to simply as "welfare", which provides cash assistance to the poor, and Medicaid, which finances the majority of medical

The Complex Web of Federal, State, and Local Agencies

The Case of Oakland, California Not only does federalism lead to variation in public policy, it also increases the difficulty of managing complex programs. To get an aircraft hangar and a ship terminal built in a way that would help reduce minority unemployment in Oakland, California, the following groups and agencies had to cooperate.

Federal
- Economic Development Administration (EDA), U.S. Department of Commerce
- Seattle Regional Office of the EDA
- Oakland Office of the EDA
- U.S. General Accounting Office
- U.S. Department of Health, Education and Welfare
- U.S. Department of Labor
- U.S. Navy

Local
- Mayor of Oakland
- Oakland City Council
- Port of Oakland

Private
- World Airways Company
- Oakland business leaders
- Oakland black leaders
- Conservation and environmental groups in Oakland

There were at least seventy important decisions to which some or all of these groups had to agree. After four years, the terminal was only partially built, the plans for the hangar were not yet complete, and only a small number of jobs for minorities had been created. As this case suggests, in America's federal system it is rarely possible to get independent organizations to agree by "issuing orders," least of all when they belong to legally distinct levels of government.

SOURCE: Jeffrey L. Pressman and Aaron B. Wildavsky, *Implementation* (Berkeley, University of California Press, 1973), 95–96, 102–107.

Critical Thinking

Devolving Welfare

On August 22, 1996, President Clinton signed the Personal Responsibility and Work Opportunity Reconciliation Act. The bill converts Aid to Families with Dependent Children (AFDC) into a block grant program, cuts federal spending on many types of antipoverty programs, ends the post-1935 federal guarantee of cash assistance for poor children, and gives states virtually unlimited authority to run their own welfare programs. Among the major provisions of the bill are the following:

- The head of every family on welfare must work, either at a regular job or in community service, within two years or lose benefits. States that fail to put at least half of adult welfare recipients to work within two years are subject to some loss of federal funds.

- Lifetime welfare benefits are limited to five years or fewer, at the discretion of the states, which can make hardship exemptions available for up to 20 percent of families on welfare.

- States can provide payments to unmarried mothers under age eighteen only if they stay in school and live with an adult. States that reduce their rates of out-of-wedlock births among welfare mothers receive bonus payments.

- Future legal immigrants are ineligible for most welfare benefits during their first five years in America.

- Food stamps are limited for adults not raising children.

- Federal spending on welfare is cut by about $55 billion over six years.

In thinking critically about welfare and other complex and controversial political issues, it is always a good idea to examine the fine print of new laws, especially ones that hinge on complicated but consequential arrangements between Washington and the states. Did the historic welfare reform act of 1996 actually "end welfare as we know it"?

Not exactly. On the day the bill was signed, some forty-three states, representing 95 percent of all welfare recipients, had already been granted federal waivers to run experimental welfare programs. Under the new law, states with waivers were allowed to operate their welfare programs regardless of whether they complied with the new federal requirements. For example, the new law required that between 1997 and 2002 a state's "work participation rate" among adult welfare recipients must reach at least 50 percent. It specified that after 1999 a welfare recipient must work at least thirty hours a week for a state to count him or her as working. But the law also specified that states operating under waivers need not meet this requirement for a period of from five to eleven years.

Still, the debate over the new law was intense. People disagreed strongly on devolving welfare. Some argued that devolving welfare would trigger a race to the bottom in which many states, either immediately or during the next eco-

and long-term care services for low-income and disabled adults and children—were not created as block grant programs. Together, AFDC and Medicaid accounted for half of all federal grant-in-aid spending. Both AFDC and Medicaid were operated as entitlement programs. Each state was entitled to federal dollars for AFDC and Medicaid based on the amount of money it paid to poor families and individuals. In turn, each state determined the level and range of benefits eligible individuals received, within a framework defined by federal laws and regulations.

The Reagan administration once considered making AFDC a block grant program in exchange for centralizing Medicaid, but this "swap and turn back plan" was never even introduced in Congress. In contrast, Republicans in the 104th Congress made a flurry of proposals for making *both* AFDC and Medicaid into block grant programs, as well as federal job training, vocational education, employment, child care, foster care, school nutrition, and food programs. All told, these proposals, had they been enacted, would have increased federal block grants to about $183 billion and catapulted the amount of block grant funds in income-transfer programs from only 4 percent to nearly 79 percent.

In the end, the devolution revolutionaries of the

nomic recession, would slash benefits and services for the poor and push millions of women and children into poverty. Others argued that devolving welfare would free the states to streamline welfare bureaucracies, push millions of able-bodied adults into economic self-sufficiency, and help cure any number of social problems, from family disintegration to teenage pregnancy, that were ostensibly fueled by the existing welfare system.

But how devolved was welfare before 1996, and how much did state welfare benefits and programs vary before the new law was passed? The best one-word answer is "lots." For example, in 1995 the maximum monthly AFDC and food stamp benefit for a family of three ranged from $1,223 in Alaska to $424 in Mississippi. In ten states the benefit was $800 or above, while in thirteen states it was $600 or below. Expenditures for low-income housing and medical coverage also varied greatly, as did the quality and range of state and local welfare-related social services (child care, remedial education, job training).

In fact, "who gets what" on welfare in this country has long depended largely on "who lives where." But should it? Should it be possible under federal law for poor U.S. citizens living in one state to receive much in the way of public cash assistance and services while equally poor U.S. citizens in another state receive less?

Any judgment about devolving welfare, like any judgment about the worth of federalism itself, is fundamentally about important competing values. And very few of us have consistent values. If we favor equal treatment of individuals by government, we will prefer uniform national policies instead of diverse state ones. But if we also favor personal liberty and local diversity, we also will support devolution and be suspicious of Washington.

As you think about devolving welfare, and as you wrestle with other key issues of federalism and public policy, consult the Constitution. You will discover that the Founders did not produce a document that drew clear lines between national and state responsibilities. They left them vague and subject to political determination. Over two hundred years of political history have not clarified them very much or made it possible to devise some "rational" scheme for deciding which government will do what.

If you doubt it, just ask President Clinton. He came to office in 1992 armed with a detailed blueprint for sorting out Washington's proper role. The blueprint listed criminal justice as an area in which "no federal role is justified" and welfare as one in which "federal action is strongly justified." By 1996, however, the president had approved major expansions in the federal role in crime control and signed into law the further devolution of welfare.

104th Congress did not succeed in turning Medicaid into a block grant program. But, as the "Devolving Welfare" feature above explains, they did succeed with AFDC and a number of related programs. And they did put the devolution of Medicaid and other important federal programs squarely on the national political agenda, possibly to stay.

What's Driving Devolution?

The drive for devolution has complex roots, but three reasons stand out: the beliefs of devolution's proponents, the realities of deficit politics, and the views of most citizens. According to R. Kent Weaver, the House Republicans who spearheaded the devolution effort harbored a "deep-seated ideological mistrust of the federal government reinforced by the belief that governments closer to the people were more responsive to popular sentiment, and more likely to constrain the growth of programs that were wasteful and redistributive."[43] At the same time, by 1994 many governors of both parties were convinced that the time had come to let state capitals take the lead in figuring out how best to address social problems and administer public health and welfare programs.

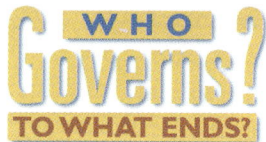

Medicaid versus AFDC

Medicaid is the eight-hundred-pound gorilla of federal-state relations. For example, in 1995 the federal contribution to Medicaid totaled $89 billion—roughly 40 percent of all federal grants to state and local governments and more than six times as much as the federal government spent on Aid to Families with Dependent Children (AFDC). At the state level, Medicaid expenditures rose from about 11 percent of all state spending in 1988 to 20 percent in 1994. Indeed, by 1996 about half of every new dollar of state revenue was being spent on Medicaid. Many leading health policy experts agreed that Washington—in particular, the Health Care Finance Administration (HCFA), the federal agency that oversees and regulates state health care programs—was largely to blame for Medicaid's spiraling costs and administrative inefficiencies. In the 1990s, HCFA granted many states waivers to experiment with new approaches to Medicaid. In 1994, Florida's assistant secretary for Medicaid, Gary Clarke, summarized the case for devolving Medicaid:

> The federal rules on Medicaid are 694 pages long. The federal/state Medicaid manual encompasses six large texts. One chapter alone has been revised twelve times [in the last five months]. For every problem, [the federal] government thinks there ought to be a new statute or regulation.

Thus, the case for devolving Medicaid would appear to be at least as compelling as the case for devolving AFDC. Yet the devolution of Medicaid in the 104th Congress ended with waivers, while the devolution of AFDC ended the program and replaced it with a big new welfare block grant (see "Devolving Welfare" on pages 76–77). Why?

One answer is that who governs and to what ends often depends on whose ox is being gored—or whose program is being cut and redesigned.

Take AFDC. In 1992 President Clinton campaigned successfully on a pledge to "end welfare as we know it." In 1994 Republicans won control of Congress after pledging in their "Contract with America" to "discourage illegitimacy and teen pregnancy" by denying increased aid to mothers who have more children while on welfare, denying benefits to mothers under eighteen altogether, requiring welfare recipients to find work within two years, and cutting welfare spending overall. In abolishing AFDC, both the Democratic president and the Republican Congress were responding to polls showing that upwards of 65 percent of Americans supported reducing welfare payments and shifting responsibility for welfare programs to the states.

Moreover, as suggested by the accompanying table, the general public had come to perceive welfare as a perverse, Washington-run system of government hand-outs that had created a permanent and undeserving underclass. Various congressional defenders of AFDC attempted to rebut this perception. For example, they stressed that the program provided cash assistance to 4.2 million single mothers and 9.4 million children, and that most adults who received AFDC for five years or more were poor minority women who did not have a high school education.

Despite its much bigger budgetary drain and much tighter bureaucratic stranglehold on the states, Medicaid was not substantially cut *or* devolved. A key reason is that Medicaid recipients include not just the poor but also the middle-class and elderly Americans who rely on the program for long-term nursing home care. A 1996 study commissioned by the American Association of Retired Persons (AARP), one of the most power-

But deficit politics also played a role. Congressional Republicans sought not only to fund entitlement programs with block grants instead of categorical grants but also to make major cuts in entitlement spending. For example, one of their bills would have reduced Medicaid spending by $163 billion and various welfare entitlements by $175 billion over seven years. In the words of Richard P. Nathan, there is probably no way any big "federal deficit-reduction targets can be met without striking a deal whereby governors get more power in exchange for going along with growth caps on grants-in-aid.

ful lobbying organizations in the country, made clear that "Medicaid performs a substantial safety net function for the middle class as well as for the poor." As we will see in Chapter 6, middle-class and older Americans vote and otherwise participate in political activities more than poor and younger Americans.

Thus during the 1994 congressional elections Medicaid, unlike AFDC, figured only tangentially in the Republicans' "Contract with America." Once in power, Republicans gradually backed off any all-encompassing plans for cutting Medicaid. As R. Kent observed, they feared alienating middle-class voters and appearing "callous in meeting the needs of clientele for whom the public shows substantial sympathy," namely, elderly but not affluent people in nursing homes.

Find out more about Medicaid and AFDC. How, if at all, have the programs overlapped? (Hint: In 1994 about $17 billion in federal dollars and another $13 billion in state spending went to AFDC recipients on Medicaid.) Do you know anyone who has received benefits from either or both programs? How big is the nation's elderly (over age 65) population, and is it growing? Which agencies administer health and other programs for the elderly in your home state? If you represented your district in the House and were running for re-election, how likely do you think you would be to vote "yes" on far-reaching proposals to reduce Medicaid benefits while giving the states autonomy over the program? Why? Finally, how might who governs on Medicaid, and to what ends, change over the next decade or so?

SOURCES: Gary Clarke, as quoted in National Commission on State and Local Public Service, *Frustrated Federalism: Rx for State and Local Health Reform* (Albany, NY: Rockefeller Institute of Government, 1993), p. 27; Joshua M. Weiner et al., *Spending Down on Medicaid* (Washington, D.C.: American Association of Retired Persons, June 1996); R. Kent Weaver, "Deficits and Devolution in the 104th Congress," unpublished draft, Brookings Institution, April 1996, pp. 17, 25, 29.

Percentage saying item is a "very serious" problem	*Blacks*	*Whites*
People abuse the system by staying on too long and not trying hard enough to get off.	72%	72%
Welfare is passed on from generation to generation, creating a permanent underclass.	62	68
The system gives people benefits without requiring them to do work in return.	60	66
People cheat and commit fraud to get welfare benefits.	69	62
Welfare encourages teenagers to have kids out of wedlock.	59	61
The system costs taxpayers too much.	55	59
The system does not give people the skills and help they need to get off welfare.	66	53
The system gives out benefits too easily, without making sure applicants deserve them.	50	51

SOURCE: Chart adapted from *The Values We Live By: What Americans Want From Welfare Reform* (New York, NY: Public Agenda Foundation, 1996), p. 40. Reprinted with permission.

Once you put a growth cap on these programs, you have to give the states added flexibility to meet them. Whether you call this a block grant or not does not matter. The result is programs that look and function like block grants."[44]

As Figure 3.4 (page 81) suggests, most Americans favor devolution, at least in principle. But it remains unclear how deep public sentiment in favor of devolution runs when "shifting responsibility to the states" also means cutting specific program benefits. For example, when asked in 1995 which federal programs "should be cut back in order to reduce the fed-

The federal government helps shape the character of cities by giving money to build parts of the federal highway system.

eral budget deficit," most Americans opposed cuts in Medicaid (73 percent), environmental spending (67 percent), unemployment insurance (64 percent), and many other programs. The one main exception was AFDC (only 35 percent opposed cutting it).[45]

Congress and Federalism

It is not yet clear whether the devolution movement will gain momentum, stall, or be reversed. But whatever the movement's fate, the United States will not become a wholly centralized nation. There remains more political and policy diversity in America than one is likely to find in any other large industrialized nation. The reason is not only that state and local governments have retained certain constitutional protections but also that members of Congress continue to think of themselves as the representatives of localities *to* Washington and not as the representatives *of* Washington to the localities. As we shall see in Chapter 11, American politics, even at the national level, remains local in its orientation.

But if this is true, why do these same members of Congress pass laws that create so many problems for, and stimulate so many complaints from, mayors and governors? One reason is that members of Congress represent different constituencies from the same localities. For example, one member of Congress from Los Angeles may think of the city as a collection of businesspeople, homeowners, and taxpayers, while another may think of it as a group of blacks, Hispanics, and nature lovers. If Washington wants to simply send money to Los Angeles, these two representatives could be expected to vote together. But if Washington wants to impose mandates or restrictions on the city, they might very well vote on opposite sides, each voting as his or her constituents would most likely prefer.

Another reason is that the organizations that once linked members of Congress to local groups have eroded. As we shall see in Chapter 7, the political parties, which once allowed many localities to speak with a single voice in Washington, have decayed to the point where most members of Congress now operate as free agents, judging local needs and national moods independently. In the 1960s these needs and moods seemed to require creating new grant programs; in the 1970s they seemed to require voting for new mandates; in the 1980s they seemed to require letting the cities and states alone to experiment with new ways of meeting their needs.

There are exceptions. In some states the parties continue to be strong, to dominate decision making in the state legislatures, and to significantly affect the way their congressional delegation behaves. Democratic members of Congress from Chicago, for example, typically have a common background in party politics and share at least some allegiance to important party leaders.

But these exceptions are becoming fewer and fewer. As a result, when somebody tries to speak "for" a city or state in Washington, that person has

FIGURE 3.4   Devolution in the Polls: The States Over Washington

QUESTION

*Which do you favor — concentration of power in
the federal government or in the state government?*

QUESTION

*Would you still favor shifting responsibility for
programs from the federal government to state
governments if it meant your state taxes would
increase to offset a decrease in your federal taxes?*

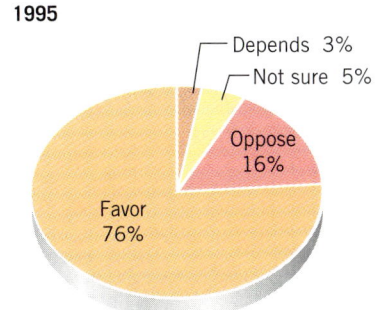

QUESTION

*What if some of the tax dollars that go to the federal government now went to your state government instead?
Generally speaking, do you think that would result in better government services, or in worse government
services, or wouldn't it have much impact on the quality of government services?*

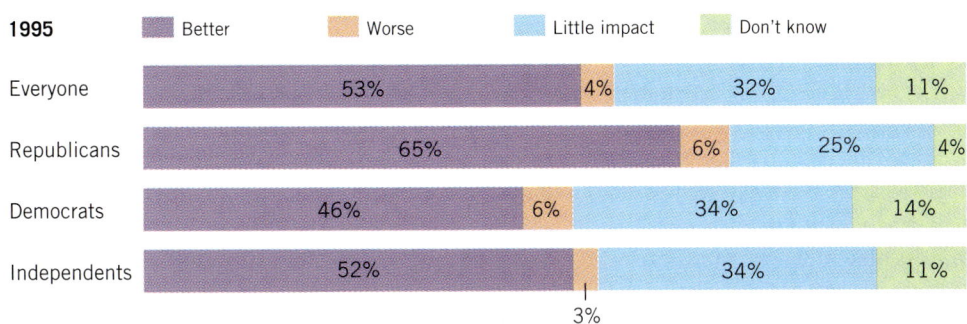

* Asked of those who favored giving states more responsibility (75%). Survey by the Hart and Teeter research Companies for the Council for Excellence
in Government, March 16–18, 1995.

SOURCE: Polling results on devolution as compiled by Richard P. Nathan, Director, Rockefeller Institute at SUNY-Albany, with the assistance of the
Roper Center for Public Opinion Research at the University of Connecticut. Data for bottom graph: Survey by the *Los Angeles Times,* January 19–22,
1995, as published in *The Public Perspective* (Storrs, CT: The Roper Center for Public Opinion Research, University of CT), April/May 1995, p. 28. © The
Public Perspective. Reprinted by permission.

little claim to any real authority. The mayor of
Philadelphia may favor one program, the governor
of Pennsylvania may favor another, and individual
local and state officials—school superintendents, the
insurance commissioner, public-health administrators—may favor still others. In bidding for federal
aid, those parts of the state or city that are best organized often do the best, and increasingly the best-
organized groups are not the political parties but
rather specialized occupational groups such as doctors or schoolteachers. If one is to ask, therefore,
why a member of Congress does not listen to his or
her state anymore, the answer is, "What do you
mean by *the state*? Which official, which occupational group, which party leader speaks for the
state?"

FIGURE 3.5 From Which Level of Government Do You
Feel You Get the Most for Your Money?

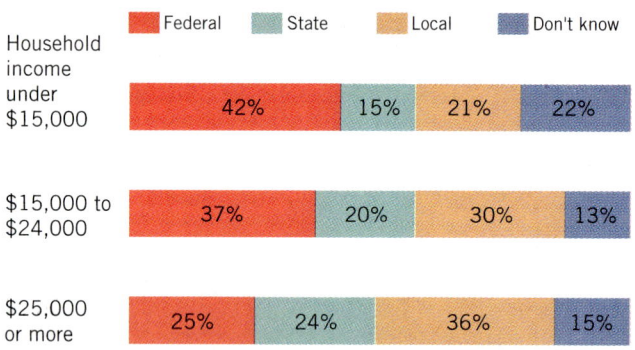

Household
income
under
$15,000 — Federal 42% / State 15% / Local 21% / Don't know 22%

$15,000 to
$24,000 — Federal 37% / State 20% / Local 30% / Don't know 13%

$25,000
or more — Federal 25% / State 24% / Local 36% / Don't know 15%

SOURCE: Advisory Commission on Intergovernmental Relations (1982): *Changing Public Attitudes on Governments and Taxes,* as cited in David C. Nice, *Federalism: The Politics of Intergovernmental Relations* (New York: St. Martin's Press, 1987), p. 210.

Finally, Americans differ in the extent to which we like federal as opposed to local decisions. As Figure 3.5 shows, when people are asked which level of government gives them the most for their money, relatively poor citizens are likely to mention the federal government first, whereas relatively well-to-do citizens are more likely to mention local government. If we added to income other measures of social diversity—race, religion, and region—we would probably see even sharper differences of opinion about which level of government works best. It is this social diversity, and the fact that it is represented not only by state and local leaders but also by members of Congress as well, that keeps federalism alive and makes it so important. Americans simply do not agree on enough things, or even on which level of government ought to decide on those things, to make possible a unitary system.

SUMMARY

States participate actively both in determining national policy and in administering national programs. Moreover, they reserve to themselves or the localities within them important powers over public services, such as schooling and law enforcement, and important public decisions, such as land-use control, that in unitary systems are dominated by the national government.

How one evaluates federalism depends in large part on the value one attaches to the competing criteria of equality and participation. Federalism means that citizens living in different parts of the country will be treated differently, not only in spending programs, such as welfare, but in legal systems that assign in different places different penalties to similar offenses or that differentially enforce civil rights laws. But federalism also means that there are more opportunities for participation in making decisions: in influencing what is taught in the schools and in deciding where highways and government projects are to be built. Indeed, differences in public policy—that is, unequal treatment—are in large part the result of participation in decision making. It is difficult, perhaps impossible, to have more of one of these values without having less of the other.

From the 1930s to the present, American politics and public policy became decidedly more nationalized, with the federal government, and especially the federal courts, imposing increasingly uniform standards on the states in the form of both mandates and conditions of aid. Efforts begun in the 1960s and 1970s to reverse this trend by shifting to revenue sharing and block grants have been only partially successful. In the mid-1990s, a political movement to devolve power from Washington to the states gained momentum. But whether this devolution revolution will effect large and lasting changes in federal-state relations remains to be seen.

KEY TERMS

devolution   *p. 51*

block grants   *p. 51*

federalism   *p. 52*

unitary systems   *p. 52*

sovereignty   *p. 53*

confederation or confederal system   *p. 53*

federal system   *p. 53*

"necessary-and-proper" clause   *p. 60*

nullification   *p. 60*

dual federalism   *p. 61*

grants-in-aid   *p. 63*

categorical grants   *p. 66*

revenue sharing   *p. 66*

conditions of aid   *p. 69*

mandates   *p. 69*

SUGGESTED READINGS

Beer, Samuel H. *To Make a Nation: The Rediscovery of American Federalism.* Cambridge, Mass.: Harvard University Press, 1993. The definitive study of the philosophical bases of American federalism.

Diamond, Martin. "The Federalist's View of Federalism." In *Essays in Federalism,* edited by George C. S. Benson. Claremont, Calif.: Institute for Studies in Federalism of Claremont Men's College, 1961, 21–64. A profound analysis of what the Founders meant by federalism.

Elazar, Daniel J. *American Federalism: A View from the States.* 2d ed. New York: Crowell, 1972. A sympathetic analysis of historical development and present nature of American federalism.

Grodzins, Morton. *The American System.* Chicago: Rand McNally, 1966. Argues that American federalism has always involved extensive sharing of functions between national and state governments.

Melnick, R. Shep. *Between the Lines: Interpreting Welfare Rights.* Washington, D.C.: Brookings Institution, 1994. An examination of how trends in statutory interpretation have affected broader policy developments, including the expansion of the agenda of national government, the persistence of divided government, and the resurgence and decentralization of Congress.

Peterson, Paul E., Barry G. Rabe, and Kenneth K. Wong. *When Federalism Works.* Washington, D.C.: Brookings Institution, 1986. A careful analysis of how various federal grant-in-aid programs actually work.

Pressman, Jeffrey L., and Aaron B. Wildavsky. *Implementation.* Berkeley: University of California Press, 1973. An excellent case study of how federalism affected the implementation of a single economic development project in Oakland, California.

Riker, William H. *Federalism: Origin, Operation, Significance.* Boston: Little, Brown, 1964. An explanation and critical analysis of federalism here and abroad.

Wright, Deil S. *Understanding Intergovernmental Relations.* 2d ed. Monterey, Calif.: Brooks/Cole, 1982. Useful survey of how state and local officials try to influence federal policies.

4

American Political Culture

★ Tocqueville's observations

★ Culture and the political system

★ Americanism

★ Culture and the economic system

★ Sources of political culture

★ Legitimization of an opposition party

★ Influence of religious heritage

★ The culture war

★ Trust in government

★ Increase in cynicism

★ Political efficacy

★ Support for civil liberties

I f the Republic, created in 1787, had depended for its survival entirely on the constitutional machinery designed by the Founders, it probably would not have endured. That machinery has been copied by many other nations, notably those of Latin America, but in virtually no other country have such devices as federalism, an elected president, a bicameral legislature, and the separation of powers produced a political system capable of both effective government and the protection of liberty. In many nations (such as Argentina, Brazil, and the Philippines) that adopted the American model, there have been, at best, brief periods of democratic rule interrupted by military takeovers, the rise to power of demagogues, or the spread of wholesale corruption. The Constitution of the United States, like an old wine, has rarely survived an ocean crossing.

Alexis de Tocqueville, the perceptive French observer of American politics, noticed this as early as the 1830s. One reason a democratic republic took root in the United States but not in other countries that copied its constitution was that this country offered more abundant and fertile soil in which the roots could grow.[1] The vast territory of the United States created innumerable opportunities for people to acquire land and make a living. No feudal aristocracy monopolized the land, the government imposed only minimal taxes, and few legal restraints existed. As one place after another filled up, people kept pushing west to find new opportunities. A nation of small, independent farmers, unlike the traditional European one of landless peasants and indentured servants, could make democracy work.

But other nations that were similarly favored did not achieve the same result. As Tocqueville noted, much of South America contains fertile lands and rich resources, but democracy has not flourished there.[2] Had he returned to the United States fifty years later, when the frontier was no longer expanding and Americans were crowding into big cities, he would have found that democratic government was still more or less intact.

The Constitution and the physical advantages of the land cannot by themselves explain the persist-

Alexis de Tocqueville (1805–1859) was a young French aristocrat who came to the United States to study the American prison system. He wrote the brilliant *Democracy in America* (2 vols., 1835–1840), a profound analysis of our political culture.

ence of the nation's democratic institutions. In addition we must consider the customs of the people—what Tocqueville called their "moral and intellectual characteristics"[3] and what modern social scientists call our political culture.

Political Culture

If you travel abroad, you will quickly become aware that other people often behave differently from Americans. Spaniards may eat dinner at 10:00 P.M., whereas Americans eat at 6:00 or 7:00 P.M. Italians may close their shops for three hours in the middle of the day, while American shops are open continuously from 9:00 to 5:00. The Germans address people more formally than Americans, using last names

when we would use first names. Japanese business executives attach a lot of importance to working together as a group, while their American counterparts often are more individualistic. In these and countless other ways, we can observe cultural differences among people.

Such differences are not limited to eating, shopkeeping, or manners. They include differences in political culture as well. A **political culture** is a distinctive and patterned way of thinking about how political and economic life ought to be carried out (see the accompanying box). Beliefs about economic life are part of the political culture because politics affects economics.

Americans do not judge their political and economic systems in the same way. As we shall see, this difference makes them somewhat unique, for in many other nations people apply the same standards to both systems. For example, Americans think it very important that everybody should be equal politically, but they do not think it important that everybody should be equal economically. By contrast people in some other nations believe that the principle of equality should be applied to both economic and political life.

The Political System

There are at least five important elements in the American view of the political system:

- *Liberty:* Americans are preoccupied with their rights. They believe they should be free to do pretty much as they please, with some exceptions, so long as they don't hurt other people.

- *Equality:* Americans believe everybody should have an equal vote and an equal chance to participate and succeed.

- *Democracy:* Americans think government officials should be accountable to the people.

- *Civic duty:* Americans generally feel people ought to take community affairs seriously and help out when they can.[4]

- *Individual responsibility:* A characteristically American view is that, barring some disability, individuals are responsible for their own actions and well-being.

The Meaning of Political Culture

A political culture is a patterned set of ways of thinking about how politics and governing ought to be carried out. A nation, if it is made up of people who are quite similar to one another, may have a single political culture, part of what is sometimes referred to as a "national character." Most nations are not homogeneous, however, being made up instead of distinctive regions, religions, and ethnic groups. Each of these parts may have a distinctive political subculture. The American South, for example, has a political culture that differs in important ways from that of the Northeast.

Because a political culture consists of our fundamental assumptions about how the political process should operate, we often take it for granted or are completely unaware of how important these assumptions are. For instance, we assume that a person who loses an election should not try to prevent the winner from taking office, that it is wrong to use public office to enrich oneself or one's family, and that nobody should have a greater claim to political authority simply because he or she comes from a rich or wellborn family. In many other societies these are not widely shared assumptions, and in some societies the opposite is often believed.

A political culture is not the same as a **political ideology**. The concept of ideology will be explained in Chapter 5. As used there, it will refer to more or less consistent sets of views concerning the policies government ought to pursue. A doctrinaire conservative, liberal, or radical has an ideology. Up to a point people can disagree on ideology (what government should do) but still share a common political culture and viewpoint about how government ought to be operated. Some ideologies, however, are so critical of the existing state of affairs that they require a fundamental change in the way politics is carried on, and thus they embody a different political culture as well.

America has both a shared political culture and some distinctive subcultures associated with various ethnic and religious groups.

At the height of immigration to this country there was a striking emphasis on creating a shared political culture. Schoolchildren, whatever their national origin, were taught to salute this country's flag.

By vast majorities Americans believe that every citizen should have an equal chance to influence government policy and to hold public office, and they oppose the idea of letting people have titles, such as "Lord" or "Duke," as in England. By somewhat smaller majorities they believe that people should be allowed to vote even if they can't read or write or vote intelligently.[5] Though Americans recognize that people differ in their abilities, they overwhelmingly agree with the statement that "teaching children that all people are really equal recognizes that all people are equally worthy and deserve equal treatment."[6]

At least three questions can be raised about this political culture. First, how do we know that the American people share these beliefs? For most of our history there were no public opinion polls, and even after they became commonplace, they were rather crude tools for measuring the existence and meaning of complex, abstract ideas. There is in fact no way to prove that such values as those listed above are important to Americans. But neither is there good reason for dismissing the list out of hand. One can infer, as have many scholars, the existence of certain values by a close study of the kinds of books Americans read, the speeches they hear, the slogans to which they respond, and the political

choices they make, as well as by noting the observations of insightful foreign visitors. Personality tests as well as opinion polls, particularly those asking similar questions in different countries, also supply useful evidence, some of which will be reviewed in the following paragraphs.

Second, if these values are important to Americans, how can we explain the existence in our society of behavior that is obviously inconsistent with them? For example, if white Americans believe in equality of opportunity, why did so many of them for so long deny that equality to black Americans? That people act contrary to their professed beliefs is an everyday fact of life: people believe in honesty, yet they steal from their employers and sometimes underreport their taxable income. Besides values, self-interest and social circumstances also shape behavior. Gunnar Myrdal, a Swedish observer of American society, described race relations in this country as "an American dilemma" resulting from the conflict between the "American creed" (a belief in equality of opportunity) and American behavior (denying blacks full citizenship).[7] But the creed remains important because it is a source of change: as more and more persons become aware of the inconsistency between their values and their behavior, that behavior slowly changes.[8] Race relations in this country would take a very different course if instead of an abstract but widespread belief in equality there were an equally widespread belief that one race is inherently inferior to another. (No doubt some Americans believe that, but most do not.)

Third, if there is agreement among Americans on certain political values, why has there been so much political conflict in our history? How could a people who agree on such fundamentals fight a bloody civil war, engage in violent labor-management disputes, take to the streets in riots and demonstrations, and sue each other in countless court battles? Conflict, even violent struggles, can occur over specific policies even among those who share, at some level of abstraction, common beliefs. Many political values may be irrelevant to specific controversies: there is no abstract value, for example, that would settle the question of whether steelworkers ought to organize unions. More important, much of our conflict has occurred precisely because we have strong beliefs that happen, as each of us interprets them, to be in conflict. Equality of opportunity seems an attractive idea, but sometimes it can be pursued only by curtailing personal liberty, another attractive idea. The states went to war in 1861 over one aspect of that conflict—the rights of slaves versus the rights of slaveowners.

Indeed, the Civil War illustrates the way certain fundamental beliefs about how a democratic regime ought to be organized have persisted despite bitter conflict over the policies adopted by particular governments. When the southern states seceded from the Union, they formed not a wholly different government but one modeled, despite some important differences, on the United States Constitution. Even some of the language of the Constitution was duplicated, suggesting that the southern states believed not that a new form of government or a different political culture ought to be created but that the South was the true repository of the existing constitutional and cultural order.[9]

Perhaps the most frequently encountered evidence that Americans believe themselves bound by common values and common hopes has been the persistence of the word *Americanism* in our political vocabulary. Throughout the nineteenth and most of the twentieth centuries, *Americanism* and *American*

When in the 1950s a committee of the House of Representatives investigated alleged subversion, it was called the committee on *"Un-American"* activities—a term that seemed strange to nations that did not understand the great appeal of the concept of "Americanism."

way of life were familiar terms not only in Fourth of July speeches but also in everyday discourse. For many years the House of Representatives had a committee called the House Un-American Activities Committee. There is hardly any example to be found abroad of such a way of thinking: there is no "Britishism" or "Frenchism," and when Britons and French people become worried about subversion, they call it a problem of internal security, not a manifestation of "un-British" or "un-French" activities.

The Economic System

Americans judge the economic system using many of the same standards by which they judge the political one, albeit with some very important differences. As it is in American politics, liberty is important in the U.S. economy. Thus Americans support the idea of a free-enterprise economic system, calling the nation's economy "generally fair and efficient" and denying that it "survives by keeping the poor down."[10] However, there are limits to how much freedom they think should exist in the marketplace. People support government regulation of business in order to keep some firms from becoming too powerful and to correct specific abuses.[11]

Americans are more willing to tolerate economic inequality than political inequality. They believe in maintaining "equality of opportunity" in the economy but not "equality of results." If everyone has an equal opportunity to get ahead, then it is all right for people with more ability to earn higher salaries, and it is all right for wages to be set based on how hard people work rather than on their economic needs.[12] Although Americans are quite willing to support education and training programs to help disadvantaged people get ahead, they are strongly opposed to anything that looks like preferential treatment (for example, hiring quotas) in the workplace.[13]

The leaders of very liberal political groups, such as civil rights and feminist organizations, are more willing than the average American to support preferential treatment in the hiring and promoting of minorities and women. They do so because, unlike most citizens, they believe that whatever disadvantages blacks and women face are the result of failures of the economic system rather than the fault of individuals.[14] Even so, these leaders strongly support the idea that earnings should be based on ability and oppose the idea of having any top limit on what people can earn.[15]

This popular commitment to economic individualism and personal responsibility may help explain how Americans think about particular public policies, such as welfare and civil rights. Polls show that Americans are willing to help people "truly in need" (this includes the elderly and the disabled) but not those deemed "able to take care of themselves" (this includes, in the public's mind, people "on welfare"). Also, Americans dislike preferential hiring programs and the use of quotas to deal with racial inequality.

At the core of these policy attitudes is a widely (but not universally) shared commitment to economic individualism and personal responsibility. Some scholars, among them Donald Kinder and David Sears, interpret these individualistic values as "symbolic racism"—a kind of plausible camouflage for antiblack attitudes.[16] But other scholars, such as Paul M. Sniderman and Michael Gray Hagen, argue that these views are not a smoke screen for bigotry or insensitivity but a genuine commitment to the ethic of self-reliance.[17] Since there are many Americans on both sides of this issue, debates about welfare and civil rights tend to be especially intense. What is striking about the American political culture is that in this country the individualist view of social policy is by far the most popular.[18]

Views about specific economic policies change. Americans now are much more inclined than they once were to believe that the government should help the needy and regulate business. But the commitment to certain underlying principles has been remarkably enduring. In 1924 most of the high school students in Muncie, Indiana, said that "it is entirely the fault of the man himself if he cannot succeed" and disagreed with the view that differences in wealth showed that the system was unjust. In 1977, over half a century later, the students in this same high school were asked the same questions again, with the same results (see Table 4.1)[19]

TABLE 4.1   **Responsibility for Success or Failure**

Statement	Percentage of High School Students Agreeing	
	1924	1977
It is entirely the fault of the man himself if he cannot succeed.	47%	47%
The fact that some men [in 1977: people] have so much more money than others shows there is an unjust condition in this country that ought to be changed.	30	34

SOURCE: Theodore Caplow and Howard M. Bahr, "Half a Century of Change in Adolescent Attitudes: Replication of a Middletown Survey by the Lynds," *Public Opinion Quarterly* 43 (Spring 1979): 1–17, Table 1. Copyright © 1979, reprinted by permission of University of Chicago Press.

Comparing America with Other Nations

The best way to learn what is distinctive about the American political culture is to compare it with that of other nations. This comparison shows that Americans have somewhat different beliefs about the political system, the economic system, and religion.

Political System

Sweden has a well-developed democratic government, with a constitution, free speech, an elected legislature, competing political parties, and a reasonably honest and nonpartisan bureaucracy. But the Swedish political culture is significantly different from ours; it is more deferential than participatory. Though almost all adult Swedes vote in national elections, few participate in politics in any other way. They defer to the decisions of experts and specialists who work for the government, rarely challenge governmental decisions in court, believe leaders and legislators ought to decide issues on the basis of "what is best" more than on "what the people want," and value equality as much as (or more than) liberty.[20] Whereas Americans are contentious, Swedes value harmony; while Americans tend to assert their rights, Swedes tend to observe their obligations.

The contrast in political cultures is even greater when one looks at a nation, such as Japan, with a wholly different history and set of traditions. One study compared the values expressed by a small number of upper-status Japanese with those of some similarly situated Americans. Whereas the Americans emphasized the virtues of individualism, competition, and equality in their political, economic, and social relations, the Japanese attached greater value to maintaining good relations with colleagues, having decisions made by groups, preserving social harmony, and displaying respect for hierarchy. Americans were more concerned than the Japanese with rules and with treating others fairly but impersonally, with due regard for their rights. The Japanese, on the other hand, stressed the importance of being sensitive to the personal needs of others, avoiding conflict, and reaching decisions through discussion rather than the application of rules.[21] These cultural differences affect in profound but hard-to-measure ways the workings of the political and economic systems of the two countries, making them function quite differently despite the fact that both are industrialized, capitalist nations.

It is easy to become carried away by the more obvious differences among national cultures and to overgeneralize from them. Thinking in stereotypes about the typical American, the typical Swede, or the typical Japanese is as risky as thinking of the typical white or the typical black American. This can be especially misleading in nations, such as the United States and Canada, that have been settled by a variety of ethnic and religious groups (English-speaking versus French-speaking Canadians, for example, or Jewish, Protestant, and Catholic Americans). But it is equally misleading to suppose that the operation of a political system can be understood entirely from the nation's objective features—its laws, economy, or physical terrain.

In 1959–1960 Gabriel Almond and Sidney Verba published a study of political culture in five nations. In general they found that Americans, and to a lesser degree citizens of Great Britain, had a stronger sense of **civic duty** (a belief that one has an obligation to participate in civic and political affairs) and a stronger sense of **civic competence** (a belief that one can affect government policies) than did the citizens of Germany, Italy, or Mexico. Over half of all Americans and a third of all Britons believed that the average citizen ought to "be active in one's community," compared to only a tenth in Italy and a fifth in Germany. Moreover, many more Americans and Britons than Germans, Italians, or Mexicans believed that they could "do something" about an unjust national law or local regulation.[22] Since 1960 nobody has asked people in these five countries the same questions, and hence we do not know whether these views have changed in recent years. But in a 1995 study of citizen participation in politics, Verba and others reported that while America lagged behind Austria, the Netherlands, West Germany, and the United Kingdom in voter participation, when it came to campaigning, attending political meetings, becoming active in the local community, and contacting government officials, Americans were as active—or substantially more active—than citizens elsewhere.[23]

Nevertheless, today the American people have less trust in government than they once did. But even so, popular confidence in political institutions remains higher here than in many places abroad. In 1987 a survey in the United States and four European nations showed that Americans and Britons were much more likely than people in West Germany, France, or Spain to say that they had a "great deal of" or "some" confidence in their country's armed forces, police, and legislature. With respect to the nation's judicial system and labor

TABLE 4.2   Popular Confidence in Institutions in Europe and America, 1987

| Institution | *Percentage Saying They Have a "Great Deal of" or "Some" Confidence* | | | | |
	U.S.	Great Britain	West Germany	France	Spain
Armed forces	86%	79%	69%	59%	36%
Police	88	80	80	72	44
Congress (Parliament)	83	52	64	55	30
Schools	82	53	82	82	59
Church	85	56	66	53	38
Business	84	55	44	30	26
Press / media / TV	69	38	41	48	46
Labor unions	52	29	43	36	26
Judicial system	77	56	72	62	35

SOURCE: Laurence Parisot, "Attitudes About the Media: A Five-Country Comparison," *Public Opinion* (January–February 1988): 18. Reprinted with the permission of the American Enterprise Institute for Public Policy Research, Washington, D.C.

unions, Americans displayed less confidence but still more than did Europeans (see Table 4.2).[24]

By the same token, Americans were more likely to say that they were "very proud" of their national identity and that, if a war came, they would be "willing to fight" for their country (see Table 4.3).[25] Of course Americans know that their country has a lot of faults. But even the most disaffected voters believe the United States needs to change only certain policies, not its system of government.[26]

A television picture of a U.S. serviceman captured by the enemy (here, Michael Durant, a prisoner of war in Somalia) powerfully unites the nation.

Economic System

The political culture of Sweden is not only more deferential than ours but also more inclined to favor equality of results over equality of opportunity. Sidney Verba and Gary Orren compared the views of Swedish and American trade union and political party leaders on a variety of economic issues. In both countries the leaders were chosen from either blue-collar unions or the major liberal political party (the Democrats in the United States, the Social Democrats in Sweden).

The results (as you can see in Table 4.4) are quite striking. By margins of four or five to one, the Swedish leaders were more likely to believe in giving workers equal pay than were their American counterparts. Moreover, by margins of at least three to one, the Swedes were more likely than the Americans to favor putting a top limit on incomes.[27]

Just what these differences in beliefs mean in dollars-and-cents terms was revealed by the answers to another question. Each group was asked what should be the ratio between the income of an executive and that of a menial worker (a dishwasher in Sweden, an elevator operator in the United States). The Swedish leaders said the ratio should be a little over two to one. That is, if the dishwasher earned $200 a week, the executive should earn no more than $440 to $480 a week. But the American leaders were ready to let the executive earn between $2,260

TABLE 4.3   Patriotism in America and Europe, 1991

Statement	Percentage Agreeing				
	U.S.	Germany	Great Britain	Italy	France
I am very patriotic.	88%	77%	72%	69%	64%
We should all be willing to fight for our country whether it is right or wrong.	55	28	56	39	37

SOURCE: Adapted from *The Public Perspective* (November/December 1991): 6. Reprinted by permission of *The Public Perspective*, a publication of the Roper Center for Public Opinion Research, University of Connecticut.

and $3,040 per week when the elevator operator was earning $200.

Americans, compared to people in many other countries, are more likely to think that freedom is more important than equality and less likely to think that hard work goes unrewarded or that the government should guarantee citizens a basic standard of living (see Table 4.5, page 94). These cultural differences make a difference in politics. In fact there is less income inequality in Sweden than in the United States—the government sees to that.

The Role of Religion

In the 1830s Tocqueville was amazed at how religious Americans were in comparison to his fellow Europeans. As political sociologist Seymour Martin Lipset has observed, "from the early nineteenth century down to the present, the United States has been among the most religious countries in the world."[28] The average American is more likely than the average European to believe in God, to pray on a daily basis, and to acknowledge clear standards of right and wrong (see Table 4.6, page 94). Surveys in forty-five countries conducted from 1990 to 1993 revealed that America was the only industrial nation in which over 80 percent of citizens identified themselves as religious. Only 1 percent of Americans claimed they were atheist (see Table 4.7, page 95).

Religious beliefs have always played a significant role in American politics. The religious revivalist movement of the late 1730s and early 1740s (known as the First Great Awakening) transformed the political life of the American colonies. Religious ideas fueled the break with England, for violating, in the words of the Declaration of Independence, "the laws of nature and nature's God." Religious leaders were central to the struggle over slavery in the nineteenth century and the temperance movement of the early twentieth century.

Both liberals and conservatives have used the pulpit to promote political change. The civil rights

TABLE 4.4   Commitment to Income Equity in Sweden and the United States

	Political-Party Leaders		Blue-Collar Union Leaders	
	Sweden (Social Democrats)	U.S. (Democrats)	Sweden	U.S.
Favor equality of results (%)	21%	9%	14%	4%
Favor equal pay (%)	58	12	68	11
Favor top limit on income (%)	44	17	51	13
Fair income ratio of executive to menial worker[a]	2 : 1	15 : 1	2 : 1	11 : 1

[a] In Sweden, menial worker was a dishwasher; in U.S., menial worker was an elevator operator.
SOURCE: Reprinted by permission of the publisher from *Equality in America: The View from the Top* by Sidney Verba and Gary R. Orren, Cambridge, Mass.: Harvard University Press, Copyright © 1985 by the Presidents and Fellows of Harvard College.

TABLE 4.5   Attitudes Toward Economic Equality in America and Europe, 1991

Statement	*Percentage Agreeing*				
	U.S.	Great Britain	Germany	Italy	France
It is government's responsibility to take care of the very poor who can't take care of themselves.	23%	62%	50%	66%	62%
Hard work guarantees success.	63	46	38	51	46
Government should *not* guarantee every citizen food and basic shelter.	34	9	13	14	10

SOURCE: Adapted from *The Public Perspective* (November/December 1991): 5, 7. Reprinted by permission of *The Public Perspective,* a publication of the Roper Center for Public Opinion Research, University of Connecticut.

movement of the 1950s and 1960s was led mainly by black religious leaders, most prominently Martin Luther King, Jr. In the 1980s, a conservative religious group known as the Moral Majority advocated constitutional amendments that would allow prayer in public schools and ban abortion. In the 1990s, another conservative religious group, the Christian Coalition, attracted an enormous amount of media attention and became a prominent force in many national, state, and local elections. If history is any guide, religious beliefs will continue to shape American political culture well into the next century.

The Sources of Political Culture

That Americans bring a distinctive way of thinking to their political life is easier to demonstrate than to explain. But even a brief, and necessarily superficial, effort to understand the sources of our political culture can help make its significance clearer.

The American Revolution, as we discussed in Chapter 2, was essentially a war fought over liberty: an assertion by the colonists of what they took to be their rights. Though the Constitution, produced eleven years after the Revolution, had to deal with other issues as well, its animating spirit reflected the effort to reconcile personal liberty with the needs of social control. These founding experiences, and the political disputes that followed, have given to American political thought and culture a preoccupation with the assertion and maintenance of rights. This tradition has imbued the daily conduct of U.S. politics with a kind of adversarial spirit quite foreign to the political life of countries that did not undergo a libertarian revolution or that were formed out of an interest in other goals, such as social equality, national independence, or ethnic supremacy.

The adversarial spirit of the American political culture reflects not only our preoccupation with rights but also our long-standing distrust of authority and of people wielding power. The colonies' ex-

TABLE 4.6   Religious Belief in America and Europe, 1991

Statement	*Percentage Agreeing*				
	U.S.	Great Britain	Germany	Italy	France
I never doubt the existence of God.	60%	31%	20%	56%	29%
Prayer is an important part of my daily life.	77	37	44	69	32
There are clear guidelines about what is good and evil.	79	65	54	56	64

SOURCE: Adapted from *The Public Perspective* (November/December 1991): 5, 8. Reprinted by permission of *The Public Perspective,* a publication of the Roper Center for Public Opinion Research, University of Connecticut.

TABLE 4.7   Religion in Industrial Nations, 1990–1993

Statement	U.S.	Sweden	France	W. Germany	Britian	Spain	Canada	Mexico
				Percentage Answering Yes				
Would you say you are . . .								
A religious person?	82	29	48	54	55	64	69	72
Not a religious person?	15	56	36	27	37	27	26	22
A convinced atheist?	1	7	11	2	4	4	3	2
Not sure	2	9	5	17	4	5	2	4

SOURCE: Adapted from *The Public Perspective*, reporting data from surveys conducted from 1990 to 1993 by the Inter-University Consortium for Political and Social Research. *The Public Perspective* (Storrs, CT: The Roper Center for Public Opinion Research, University of CT), April/May 1995, p. 2. © The Public Perspective. Reprinted by permission.

periences with British rule was one source of that distrust. But another, older source was the religious belief of many Americans, which saw human nature as fundamentally depraved. To the colonists, all of mankind suffered from original sin, symbolized by Adam and Eve eating the forbidden fruit in the Garden of Eden. Since no one was born innocent, no one could be trusted with power. Thus, the Constitution had to be designed in such a way as to curb the darker side of human nature. Otherwise, everyone's rights would be in jeopardy.

The contentiousness of a people animated by a suspicion of government and devoted to individualism could easily have made democratic politics so tumultuous as to be impossible. After all, one must be willing to trust others with power if there is to be any kind of democratic government, and sometimes those others will be people not of one's own choosing. The first great test case took place around 1800 in a battle between the Federalists, led by John Adams and Alexander Hamilton, and the Democratic-Republicans, led by Thomas Jefferson and James Madison. The two factions deeply distrusted each other: the Federalists had passed laws designed to suppress Jeffersonian journalists; Jefferson suspected the Federalists were out to subvert the Constitution; and the Federalists believed Jefferson intended to sell out the country to France. But as we shall see in Chapter 7, the threat of civil war never materialized, and the Jeffersonians came to power peacefully. Within a few years the role of an opposition party became legitimate, and people abandoned the idea of making serious efforts to suppress their opponents. By happy circumstance people came to accept

that liberty and orderly political change could coexist.

The Constitution, by creating a federal system and dividing political authority among competing institutions, provided ample opportunity for widespread—though hardly universal—participation in politics. The election of Jefferson in 1800 produced no political catastrophe, and those who had predicted one were, to a degree, discredited. But other, more fundamental features of American life contributed to the same end. One of the most important of these was religious diversity.

Religion plays a larger role in the lives of Americans than it does in the lives of the citizens of most other Western countries.

The absence of an established or official religion for the nation as a whole, reinforced by a constitutional prohibition of such an establishment and by the migration to this country of people with different religious backgrounds, meant that religious diversity was inevitable. Since there could be no orthodox or official religion, it became difficult for a corresponding political orthodoxy to emerge. Moreover, the conflict between the Puritan tradition, with its emphasis on faith and good works, and the Catholic church, with its devotion to the sacraments and priestly authority, provided a recurrent source of cleavage in American public life. The differences in values between these two groups showed up not only in their religious practices but also in areas involving the regulation of manners and morals, and even in people's choice of political party. For more than a century candidates for state and national office were deeply divided over whether the sale of liquor should be prohibited, a question that arose ultimately out of competing religious doctrines.

Even though there was no established church, there was certainly a dominant religious tradition—Protestantism, and especially Puritanism. The Protestant churches provided people with both a set of beliefs and an organizational experience that had profound effects on American political culture. Those beliefs encouraged, or even required, a life of personal achievement as well as religious conviction: a believer had an obligation to work, save money, obey the secular law, and do good works. Max Weber explained the rise of capitalism in part by what he called the Protestant ethic—what we now sometimes call the **work ethic**.[29] Such values had political consequences, as people holding them were motivated to engage in civic and communal action.

Churches offered ready opportunities for developing and practicing civic and political skills. Since most Protestant churches were organized along congregational lines—that is, the church was controlled by its members, who put up the building, hired the preacher, and supervised the finances—they were, in effect, miniature political systems, with leaders and committees, conflict and consensus. Developing a participatory political culture was undoubtedly made easier by the existence of a participatory religious culture. Even some Catholic churches in early America were under a degree of lay control.

Parishioners owned the church property, negotiated with priests, and conducted church business.

All aspects of culture, including the political, are preserved and transmitted to new generations primarily by the family. Though some believe that the weakening of the family unit has eroded the extent to which it transmits anything, particularly culture, and has enlarged the power of other sources of values—the mass media and the world of friends and fashion, leisure and entertainment—there is still little doubt that the ways in which we think about the world are largely acquired within the family. In Chapter 5 we shall see that the family is the primary source of one kind of political attitude—identification with one or another political party. Even more important, the family shapes in subtle ways how we think and act on political matters. Erik Erikson, the psychologist, noted certain traits that are more characteristic of American than of European families—the greater freedom enjoyed by children, for example, and the larger measure of equality among family members. These familial characteristics promote a belief, carried through life, that every person has rights deserving protection and that a variety of interests have a legitimate claim to consideration when decisions are made.[30]

The combined effect of religious and ethnic diversity, an individualistic philosophy, fragmented political authority, and the relatively egalitarian American family can be seen in the absence of a high degree of **class consciousness** among Americans. Class consciousness means thinking of oneself as a worker whose interests are in opposition to those of management, or vice versa. In this country most people, whatever their jobs, think of themselves as "middle class."

If any group of Americans were likely to think and act in terms of their economic class, one would suppose it would be the unemployed. Nonetheless, a careful study in 1976 showed that, though unemployed people feel deprived, the great majority do not identify with other unemployed persons or think that their interests as a class are in opposition to those of management. The political views of the unemployed do not seem to differ much from those of the employed, and even when the former think in class terms, their political views do not seem to be affected. Moreover, we know that even in the late 1930s, when the country was in the grip of a massive

The changing American family. At the top is an extended
family in Black River Falls, Wisconsin, around 1900;
on the lower left a single-parent family; on the lower right
a nuclear family in contemporary America.

depression, only a small minority of the unemployed expressed a strong sense of class consciousness.[31]

Though the writings of Horatio Alger are no longer popular, Americans still seem to believe in the message of those stories—that the opportunity for success is available to people who work hard. This may help explain why the United States is the only large industrial democracy without a significant socialist party and why the nation has been slow to adopt certain welfare programs.

The Culture War

Almost all Americans share some elements of a common political culture. Why, then, is there so much cultural conflict in American politics? For many years, the most explosive political issues have included abortion, gay rights, drug use, school prayer, and pornography. Viewed from a Marxist perspective, politics in the United States is utterly baffling: instead of two economic classes engaged in a bitter struggle over wealth, we have two cultural classes locked in a war over values.

As chancellor of the New York City public school system, Joseph Fernandez supported condom distribution and a curriculum that recognized nontraditional families. His contract was not renewed.

To say that there are two cultural classes is, of course, an oversimplification, but to say that there is a culture war is not an exaggeration.[32] Groups supporting and opposing the right to abortion have had many angry confrontations in recent years. The latter have been arrested while attempting to block access to abortion clinics; some clinics have been fire-bombed; and at least one physician has been killed. A controversy over what schoolchildren should be taught about homosexuals was responsible, in part, for the firing of the head of the New York City school system; in other states there have been fierce arguments in state legislatures and before the courts over whether gay and lesbian couples should be allowed to adopt children. Although most Americans want to keep heroin, cocaine, and other drugs illegal, a significant number of people want to legalize (or at least decriminalize) their use. The Supreme Court has ruled that children cannot pray in public schools, but this has not stopped many parents and school authorities from trying to reinstate school prayer, or at least prayerlike moments of silence. The discovery that a federal agency, the National Endowment for the Arts, had given money to support exhibitions and performances that many people thought were obscene led to a furious congressional struggle over the future of the agency. The 1992 presidential election centered, in part, on a passionate argument over which candidate best exemplified "family values."

The culture war differs from other political disputes (over such matters as taxes, business regulations, and foreign policy) in several ways: money is not at stake, compromises are almost impossible to arrange, and the conflict is more profound. It is animated by deep differences in people's beliefs about private and public morality—that is, about the standards that ought to govern individual behavior and social arrangements. It is about what kind of country we ought to live in, not just about what kinds of policies our government ought to adopt.

To simplify, there are two opposed camps, the **orthodox** and the **progressive.** On the orthodox side are people who believe that morality is as important as, or more important than, self-expression and that moral rules derive from the commands of God or the laws of nature—commands and laws that are relatively clear, unchanging, and independent of individual preferences. On the progressive side are people who think that personal freedom is as important as, or more important than, certain traditional moral rules and that those rules must be evaluated in light of the circumstances of modern life—circumstances that are quite complex, changeable, and dependent on individual preferences.

Most conspicuous among the orthodox are fundamentalist Protestants and born-again Christians, and so critics who dislike orthodox views often dismiss them as the fanatical expressions of "the Religious Right." But many people who hold orthodox views are not fanatical or deeply religious or right-wing on most issues; they simply have strong views about drugs, pornography, and sexual morality. Similarly, the progressive side often includes members of liberal Protestant denominations (for example, Episcopalians and Unitarians) and people with no strong religious beliefs, and so their critics often denounce them as immoral, anti-Christian radicals who have embraced the ideology of secular humanism, the belief that moral standards do not require religious justification. But in all likelihood few progressives are immoral or anti-Christian, and most do not regard secular humanism as their defining ideology.

Moreover, the culture war is occurring not just between different religious denominations but also within them. Catholic, Protestant, and Jewish leaders with an orthodox perspective tend to assign great importance to two-parent families, condemn pornography, denounce homosexuality, oppose ratification of the Equal Rights Amendment to the Constitution, and think the United States is in general a force for good in the world. Leaders of the same faiths who have a progressive outlook are more likely to say that many legitimate alternatives to the traditional two-parent family exist, that pornography and homosexuality are private matters protected by individual rights, and that the United States has been at best a neutral and at worst a bad force in world affairs.[33] This conflict between the orthodox and progressive view of American culture is similar to, and has many of the same causes, as the cleavage (described in Chapter 5) between the traditional middle class and the new middle class.

American history has always had conflicts of this sort, but they have acquired special importance today as a result of two major changes in American society. The first is the great increase in the proportion of people who consider themselves progressive. Once almost everyone was religiously orthodox, even if politically liberal; today fewer are. The second factor is the rise of media (such as television and direct-mail advertising) that make it easy to wage a cultural war on a large scale. In the past, preachers, writers, and lecturers could reach at most a few hundred people at a time; today, television evangelists, radio talk-show hosts, and the authors of direct-mail messages can wage a furious war of words reaching tens of millions of people and recruiting hundreds of thousands of followers. A cultural war that once enlisted only a few activists can now mobilize mass armies.

The tensions generated by the culture war affect our views as to how well our government works, how much influence ordinary people can have over it, and how large a measure of freedom we ought to grant to our opponents. Trust in government, a sense of political efficacy, and tolerance for views we dislike are always fragile under the best of circumstances. Have the cultural tensions of recent decades made matters worse? In the rest of this chapter we shall try to answer these questions.

Mistrust of Government

In 1979 President Jimmy Carter, taking note of numerous public opinion polls that showed a dramatic decline in the proportion of Americans who said they had a great deal of confidence in our system, made a nationwide television address on the subject of "the American malaise," which he defined as a crisis of confidence evident in Americans' "growing disrespect" for government, schools, churches, and other institutions.

Though it probably wasn't a politically astute speech—Americans don't like to be told they suffer from a malaise, and the following year they voted against Carter and for a man, Ronald Reagan, who offered a much more upbeat assessment of the American condition—it was based on some solid factual evidence. As can be seen in Figure 4.1, various measures of mistrust in government rose steadily for about fifteen years beginning in the mid-1960s. By 1976 nearly twice as many Americans as in 1958 thought that there were "quite a few" crooks in

FIGURE 4.1   The Growth of Mistrust of Government

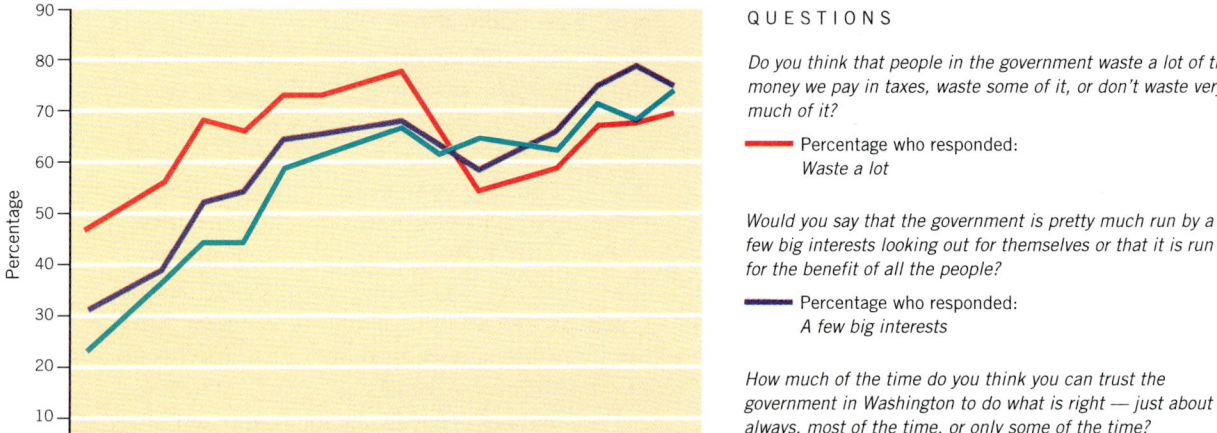

QUESTIONS

Do you think that people in the government waste a lot of the money we pay in taxes, waste some of it, or don't waste very much of it?

—— Percentage who responded:
   Waste a lot

Would you say that the government is pretty much run by a few big interests looking out for themselves or that it is run for the benefit of all the people?

—— Percentage who responded:
   A few big interests

How much of the time do you think you can trust the government in Washington to do what is right — just about always, most of the time, or only some of the time?

—— Percentage who responded:
   Only some of the time

SOURCES: Survey Research Center, University of Michigan. Supplied by the SRC/CPS American National Election Studies, University of Michigan. 1990, 1992, and 1994 figures supplied by ICPSR American National Election Studies, University of Michigan.

The trust and confidence that Americans felt in their government was especially high in the 1950s, during the period Eisenhower was president.

government, that government was run for the benefit of a "few big interests," that "a lot" of tax money was wasted, and that we can expect government to do the right thing only "some of the time."[34]

In part this decline in trust was the result of some dramatic events. The largest single increase in mistrust occurred between 1972 and 1974—the time of the Watergate scandal, when close aides to President Nixon authorized a burglary of the Democratic party headquarters and the president himself participated in the cover-up of the bungled break-in. But the decline began long before Watergate (or the war in Vietnam) and continued after both events were history.

This rising mistrust is worrisome, but it should be viewed in context. There is evidence that the mistrust is chiefly aimed not at our *system* of government but at specific leaders and policies.[35] We have already seen that Americans have more confidence in their governmental institutions than do citizens of many other countries. Even in 1972–1974, when distrust of government was especially high, 86 percent of those interviewed in a national survey agreed with the following statement: "I am proud of many things about our form of government."[36]

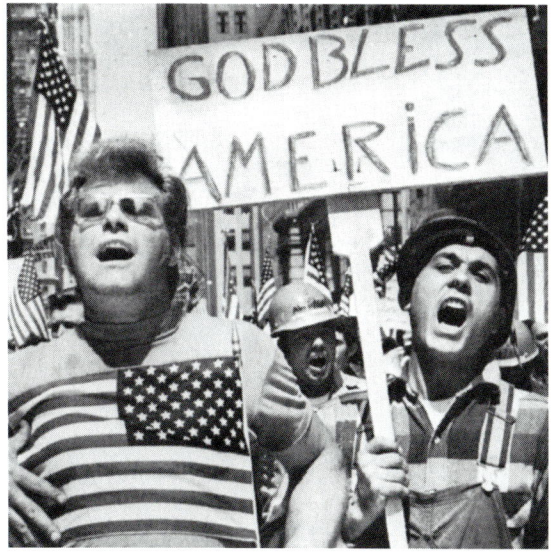

The impassioned conflict over American involvement in Vietnam brought out protesters on both sides, each side seeking to associate important symbols ("peace" and "patriotism") with its cause.

Moreover, there are reasons for thinking that the current level of trust in government is close to the historical norm and that the much higher levels of trust of the late 1950s and early 1960s were unusual. Though polling was then in its infancy, there is evidence that Americans in the 1930s were not much more trustful of their government than they are

now.[37] Between the 1930s and the 1960s this nation overcame an economic depression and won World War II, events that gave to citizens an unusually high degree of confidence in the capacity of their government. The 1960s and 1970s, when that confidence weakened, were years of great turmoil—the civil rights movement, the war in Vietnam, a sharp rise in

TABLE 4.8 Confidence in People Running American Institutions, 1966–1996

Institution	Percentage saying they have "a great deal of confidence" in "people in charge of running" various institutions				
	1966	1971–1979	1980–1989	1990–1996	Change 1966–1996
Congress	42%	16%	19%	10%	55%
U.S. Supreme Court	50	29	29	28	76
Federal bureaucracy	41	19	20	12	70
The press	29	23	18	16	44
Major companies	55	22	18	18	69

SOURCE: Calculated from survey data compiled by Louis Harris and Associates, 1966–1996.

Intense press coverage of scandals has deepened popular distrust of government. Here, special counsel Kenneth Starr talks about his investigation of the Whitewater affair.

crime rates, the assassination of various leaders, urban riots and campus demonstrations, and economic inflation. Small wonder that people thought that things were getting out of hand and that political leaders ought to take some of the blame.

The decline in popular confidence in government that began in the 1960s was part and parcel of a general loss of confidence in almost all institutions. As we can see in Table 4.8 on page 101, the percentage of Americans saying they had "a great deal of confidence in" the people running major companies and the press also declined sharply between 1966 and the early 1990s.

There was a brief and small improvement in trust during the early Reagan years,[38] but that gain was washed out, and then some, by a big drop in the early 1990s. Owing to the combined effects of an economic recession, political scandals (such as the revelation that members of the House of Representatives were writing checks without having money in the House bank to cover them), and the continued growth in such problems as crime, drug abuse, and the federal debt, Americans in record numbers expressed disgust at politics and politicians. Ross Perot, the Texas businessman who ran for president in 1992 as an independent, tried to capitalize on that anger. But there was no sign of a popular revolt against the system of government laid out in the Constitution.

In sum, Americans have not lost confidence in themselves or in their governmental system, but they no longer so readily give to political leaders and their policies the kind of support they gave in the less troubled years of the 1950s.

Political Efficacy

Perhaps the most worrisome aspect of recent changes in the American political culture is the decline in the extent to which citizens feel that the political system will respond to their needs and beliefs. These changes are in what scholars call a citizen's sense of **political efficacy,** by which they mean a citizen's capacity to understand and influence political events.

This sense of efficacy has two parts—**internal efficacy** (the ability to understand and take part in political affairs) and **external efficacy** (the ability to make the system respond to the citizenry). Since the mid-1960s there has been a fairly sharp drop in the sense of external efficacy (or system responsiveness) but not much change in the sense of internal efficacy (personal competence).

As we can see in Figure 4.2, people today are not much different from people in 1952 with respect to whether they can understand what is going on in government (most find it too complicated to fathom) and whether they have much say in what the government does. But there has been a big change in how responsive people think the government is to their interests. In 1980 people were twice as likely as they were in the late 1950s to say that public officials don't "care much what people like me think." And in 1980 they were much more likely than they had been

FIGURE 4.2 Changes in the Sense of Political Efficacy

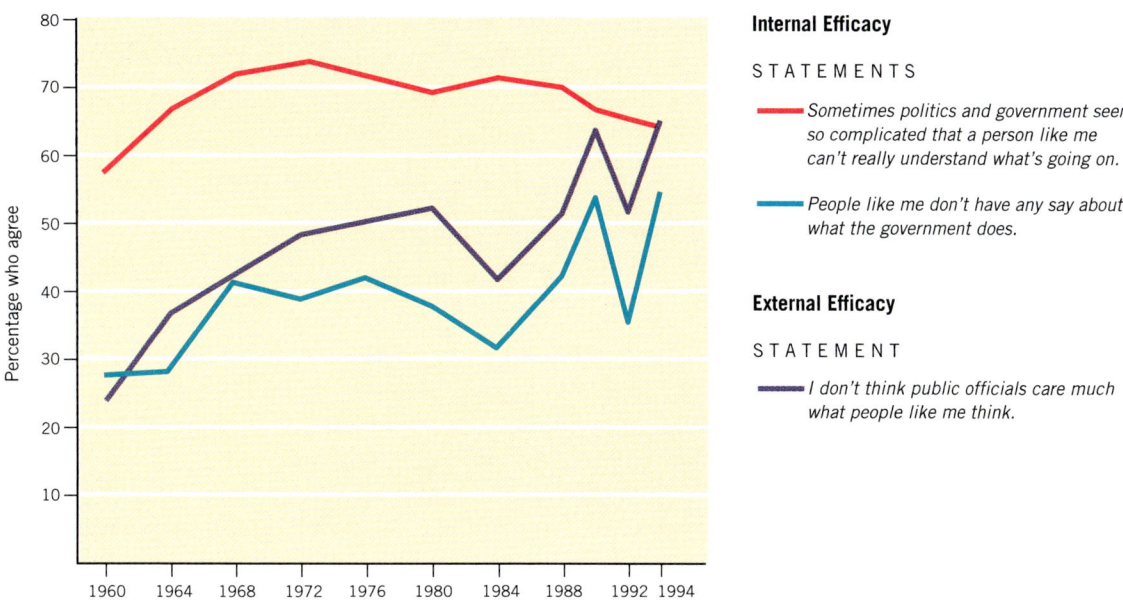

Internal Efficacy

STATEMENTS

—— *Sometimes politics and government seem so complicated that a person like me can't really understand what's going on.*

—— *People like me don't have any say about what the government does.*

External Efficacy

STATEMENT

—— *I don't think public officials care much what people like me think.*

SOURCES: Center for Political Studies, University of Michigan, as reported in Seymour Martin Lipset and William Schneider, *The Confidence Gap: Business, Labor, and Government in the Public Mind* (New York: Free Press, 1983); 1990, 1992, and 1994 figures supplied by ICPSR American National Election Studies, University of Michigan.

(even as recently as 1968) to say "those we elect to Congress in Washington lose touch with the people pretty quickly" and "parties are only interested in people's votes, not their opinions."[39]

Unlike the increase in the mistrust of government, the increase in the feeling that government was unresponsive was not shaped by any particular events; the sense of external efficacy dropped more or less steadily throughout the 1960s and 1970s. What seems to have happened is that Americans gradually have come to the view that government has become too big and pervasive for it to be sensitive to citizen preferences. In 1964 less than a third of Americans thought the federal government was too powerful; in 1976 half did.[40]

Though Americans may feel less effective as citizens than they once did, their sense of efficacy remains much higher than it is among Europeans. In 1974 a poll taken in five nations found that the average American scored significantly higher on the efficacy scale than the average person in Austria, Germany, Great Britain, or the Netherlands. More-

over, Americans were much more likely than Europeans to say that they regularly discussed politics, signed petitions, and worked to solve community problems.[41] Though Americans are less likely to vote than Europeans, they are more likely to do the harder chores that make up democratic politics.

Because Americans are less likely than they once were to hold their leaders in high esteem, to have confidence in government policies, and to believe the system will be responsive to popular wishes, some observers like to say that Americans today are more "alienated" from politics. It probably would be better to say that they are simply more realistic.

Political Tolerance

Democratic politics depends crucially on citizens' being reasonably tolerant of the opinions and actions of others. If unpopular speakers were always shouted down, if government efforts to censor newspapers were usually met with popular support or even public indifference, if peaceful demonstrations were regularly broken up by hostile mobs, if the losing candidates in an election refused to allow their victorious opponents to take office, then the essential elements of a democratic political culture would be missing, and democracy would fail. Democracy does not require perfect tolerance; if it did, the passions of human nature would make democracy forever impossible. But at a minimum citizens must have a political culture that allows the discussion of ideas and the selection of rulers in an atmosphere reasonably free of oppression.

Public opinion surveys show that the overwhelming majority of Americans agree with such concepts as freedom of speech, majority rule, and the right to circulate petitions—at least in the abstract.[42]

But when we get down to concrete cases, a good many Americans are not very tolerant of groups they dislike. Suppose you must decide which groups will be permitted to espouse their causes at meetings held in your community's civic auditorium. Which of these groups would *you* allow to run such a meeting?

1. Protestants holding a revival meeting

2. Right-to-life groups opposing abortion

3. People protesting a nuclear power plant

4. Feminists organizing a march for the Equal Rights Amendment

5. Gays organizing for homosexual rights

6. Atheists preaching against God

7. Students organizing a sit-in to shut down city hall

In a national opinion poll conducted by Herbert McClosky and Alida Brill in 1978–1979, a majority of Americans would have allowed the first four groups to hold their meetings but would have refused to allow the last three. (Similar findings from another opinion survey are shown in Figure 4.3.) Leaders in the communities where this survey was performed would have allowed the first five groups to meet. Lawyers and judges in these communities would have allowed all seven to meet.[43]

Clearly community leaders, and especially lawyers and judges, are more tolerant of specific political activities than are most citizens. But two things need to be said on behalf of the average citizen.

First, Americans are willing to allow many people with whom they disagree to do a great deal politically. In the McClosky-Brill study, for example, the general public supported the right of the movie industry to make movies on any subjects it chooses, upheld the right of reporters to keep confidential their sources of information, defended the right of newspapers and television stations to hire "radical reporters," believed that college officials should allow nonviolent protest demonstrations by students, and supported freedom of worship even for extremist religious groups.[44]

Second, Americans have become more tolerant over the last few decades. For instance, in the 1970s people were much more willing to allow communists, socialists, and atheists to meet and disseminate their views than they were in the early 1950s, even though Americans in the 1970s were probably no more sympathetic to these causes than they were in the 1950s.[45] Similarly, there has been a general increase in the willingness of citizens to say that they would vote for a Catholic, Jew, black, or woman for president (see Figure 4.4, page 106).

Americans may not vote at as high a rate as citizens in European countries, but they probably sign more petitions than any other people anywhere.

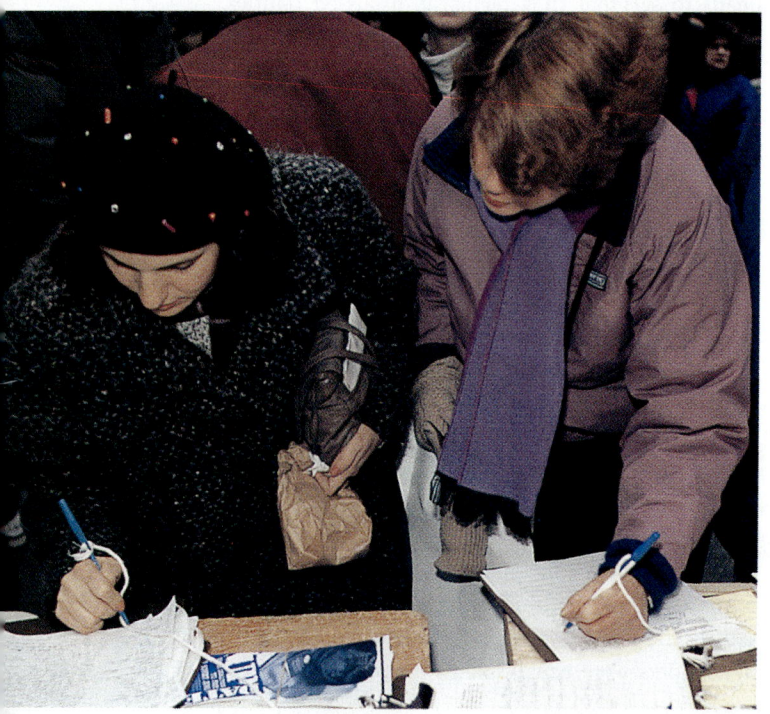

FIGURE 4.3 Public Tolerance for Advocates of Unpopular Ideas, 1954–1993

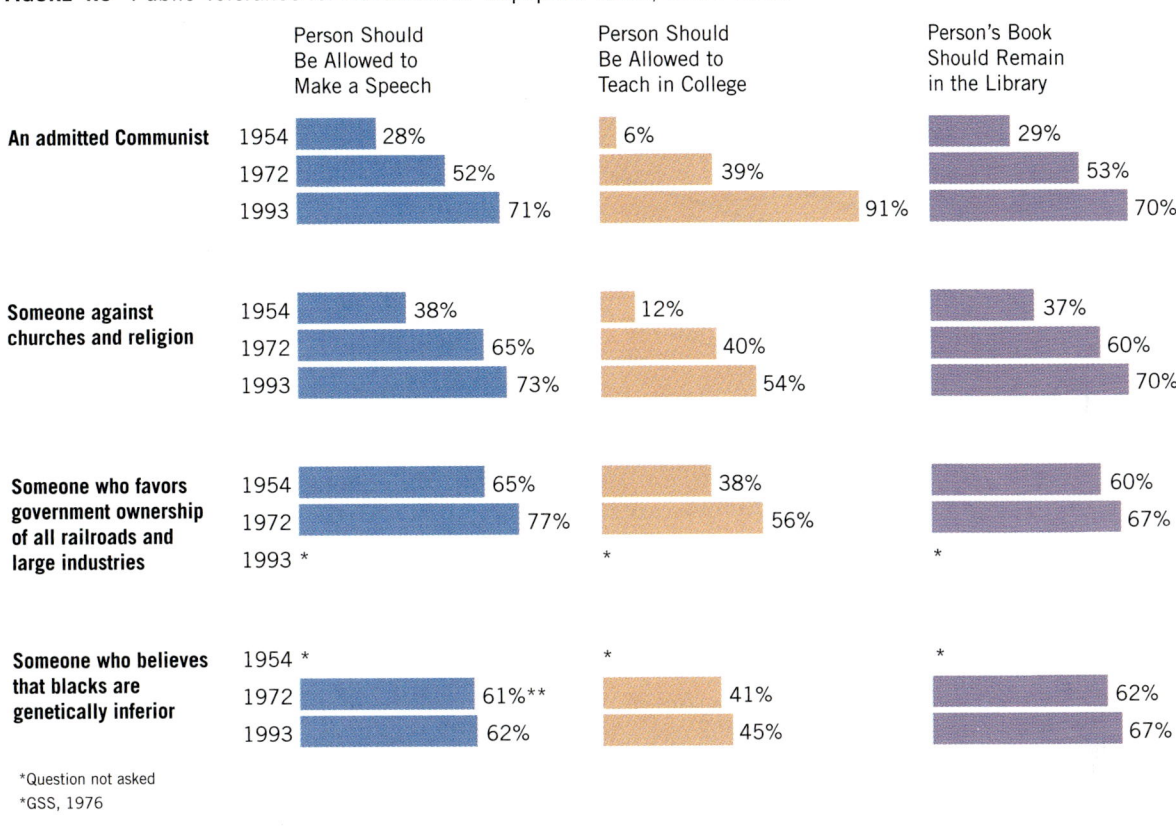

	Person Should Be Allowed to Make a Speech	Person Should Be Allowed to Teach in College	Person's Book Should Remain in the Library
An admitted Communist			
1954	28%	6%	29%
1972	52%	39%	53%
1993	71%	91%	70%
Someone against churches and religion			
1954	38%	12%	37%
1972	65%	40%	60%
1993	73%	54%	70%
Someone who favors government ownership of all railroads and large industries			
1954	65%	38%	60%
1972	77%	56%	67%
1993	*	*	*
Someone who believes that blacks are genetically inferior			
1954	*	*	*
1972	61%**	41%	62%
1993	62%	45%	67%

*Question not asked
*GSS, 1976

SOURCE: Adapted from Robert S. Erickson and Kent L. Tedin, *American Public Opinion*, 5th ed. Copyright © 1995 by Allyn and Bacon. Reprinted by permission.

Nonetheless, this majority tolerance for many causes should not blind us to the fact that for most of us there is some group or cause from which we are willing to withhold political liberties—even though we endorse those liberties in the abstract.

If most people dislike one or another group strongly enough to deny it certain political rights that we usually take for granted, how is it that such groups (and such rights) survive? The answer, in part, is that most of us don't act on our beliefs. We rarely take the trouble—or have the chance—to block another person from making a speech or teaching school. And among people who are in a position to deny other people rights—officeholders and political activists, for example—the level of political tolerance is somewhat greater than among the public at large.[46]

But another reason may be just as important. Most of us are ready to deny *some* group its rights, but we usually can't agree on which group that should be. Sometimes we can agree, and then the disliked group may be in for real trouble. There have been times (1919–1920, and again in the early 1950s) when socialists or communists were disliked by most people in the United States. The government on each occasion took strong actions against them. Today fewer people agree that these left-wing groups are a major domestic threat, and so their rights are now more secure.

Finally, the courts are sufficiently insulated from public opinion that they can act against majority sentiments and enforce constitutional protections (see Chapter 14). Most of us are not willing to give all rights to all groups, but most of us are not judges.

FIGURE 4.4 Changes in Levels of Political Tolerance

QUESTION

There's always much discussion about the qualifications of presidential candidates — their education, age, race, religion, and the like. If your party nominated a generally well-qualified person for president who happened to be a (name of group), would you vote for that person?

— Catholic
— Jew
— Woman
— Black
— Atheist
— Homosexual

SOURCE: Gallup poll data, various years, as compiled by Professor John Zaller, Department of Political Science, UCLA.

These facts should be a sober reminder that political liberty cannot be taken for granted. Men and women are not, it would seem, born with an inclination to live and let live, at least politically, and many—possibly most—never acquire that inclination. Liberty must be learned and protected. Happily the United States during much of its recent history has not been consumed by a revulsion for any one group that has been strong enough to place the group's rights in jeopardy.

Nor should any part of society pretend that it is always more tolerant than another. In the 1950s, for example, ultraconservatives outside the universities were attacking the rights of professors to say and teach certain things. In the 1960s and 1970s ultraliberal students and professors inside the universities were attacking the rights of other students and professors to say certain things.

SUMMARY

The American system of government is supported by a political culture that fosters a sense of civic duty, takes pride in the nation's constitutional arrangements, and provides support for the exercise of essential civil liberties (albeit out of indifference

or diversity more than principle at times). In recent decades mistrust of government officials (though not of the system itself) has increased, and confidence in their responsiveness to popular feelings has declined.

Although Americans value liberty in both the political system and the economy, they believe equality is important only in the political realm. In economic affairs they wish to see equality of opportunity but accept inequality of results.

Not only is our culture generally supportive of democratic rule, it also has certain distinctive features that make our way of governing different from what one finds in other democracies. Americans are preoccupied with their rights, and this fact, combined with a political system that (as we shall see) encourages the vigorous exercise of rights and claims, gives to our political life an *adversarial* style. Unlike Swedes or Japanese, we do not generally reach political decisions by consensus, and we often do not defer to the authority of administrative agencies. American politics, more than that of many other nations, is shot through at every stage with protracted conflict.

But as we shall learn in the next chapter, that conflict is not easily described as always pitting liberals against conservatives. Not only do we have a lot of conflict, it is often messy conflict, a kind of political Tower of Babel. Foreign observers sometimes ask how we stand the confusion. The answer, of course, is that we have been doing it for over two hundred years. Maybe our Constitution is two centuries old not in spite of this confusion but because of it. We shall see.

KEY TERMS

political culture   *p. 86*

political ideology   *p. 87*

civic duty   *p. 91*

civic competence   *p. 91*

work ethic   *p. 96*

class consciousness   *p. 96*

orthodox   *p. 98*

progressive   *p. 98*

political efficacy   *p. 102*

internal efficacy   *p. 102*

external efficacy   *p. 102*

SUGGESTED READINGS

Almond, Gabriel, and Sidney Verba. *The Civic Culture.* Princeton, N.J.: Princeton University Press, 1963. A survey of the political cultures of five nations—the United States, Germany, Great Britain, Italy, and Mexico—as they were in 1959.

Devine, Donald J. *The Political Culture of the United States.* Boston: Little, Brown, 1972. Useful summary of several studies of American political values.

Hartz, Louis. *The Liberal Tradition in America.* New York: Harcourt Brace Jovanovich, 1955. A stimulating interpretation of American political thought since the Founding, emphasizing the notion of a liberal consensus.

Hochschild, Jennifer L. *What's Fair? American Beliefs About Distributive Justice.* Cambridge, Mass.: Harvard University Press, 1981. Revealing, in-depth interviews that compare the attitudes of rich and poor people toward inequality.

Lipset, Seymour Martin. *The First New Nation.* Rev. ed. New York: Norton, 1979. How the origins of American society gave rise to the partially competing values of equality and achievement and the ways in which these values shape political institutions.

McClosky, Herbert, and Alida Brill. *Dimensions of Tolerance: What Americans Believe About Civil Liberties.* New York: Russell Sage Foundation, 1983. How—and whether—different kinds of Americans learn political tolerance.

McClosky, Herbert, and John Zaller. *The American Ethos: Public Attitudes Toward Capitalism and Democracy.* Cambridge, Mass.: Harvard University Press, 1984. Study of the ways in which Americans evaluate political and economic arrangements.

Tocqueville, Alexis de. *Democracy in America.* Edited by Phillips Bradley. 2 vols. New York: Knopf, 1951. First published in 1835–1840, this was and remains the greatest single interpretation of American political culture.

Verba, Sidney, and Gary R. Orren. *Equality in America: The View from the Top.* Cambridge, Mass.: Harvard University Press, 1985. Elite views on political and economic equality.

Wald, Kenneth. *Religion and Politics in the United States,* 2nd ed. Washington, D.C.: Congressional Quarterly Press, 1992. A thoughtful look at how religious beliefs and organizations shape American politics.

PART TWO

Opinions, Interests, and Organizations

"The latent causes of faction are thus sown in the nature of man; and we see them everywhere brought into different degrees of activity, according to the different circumstances of civil society."

— FEDERALIST NO. 10

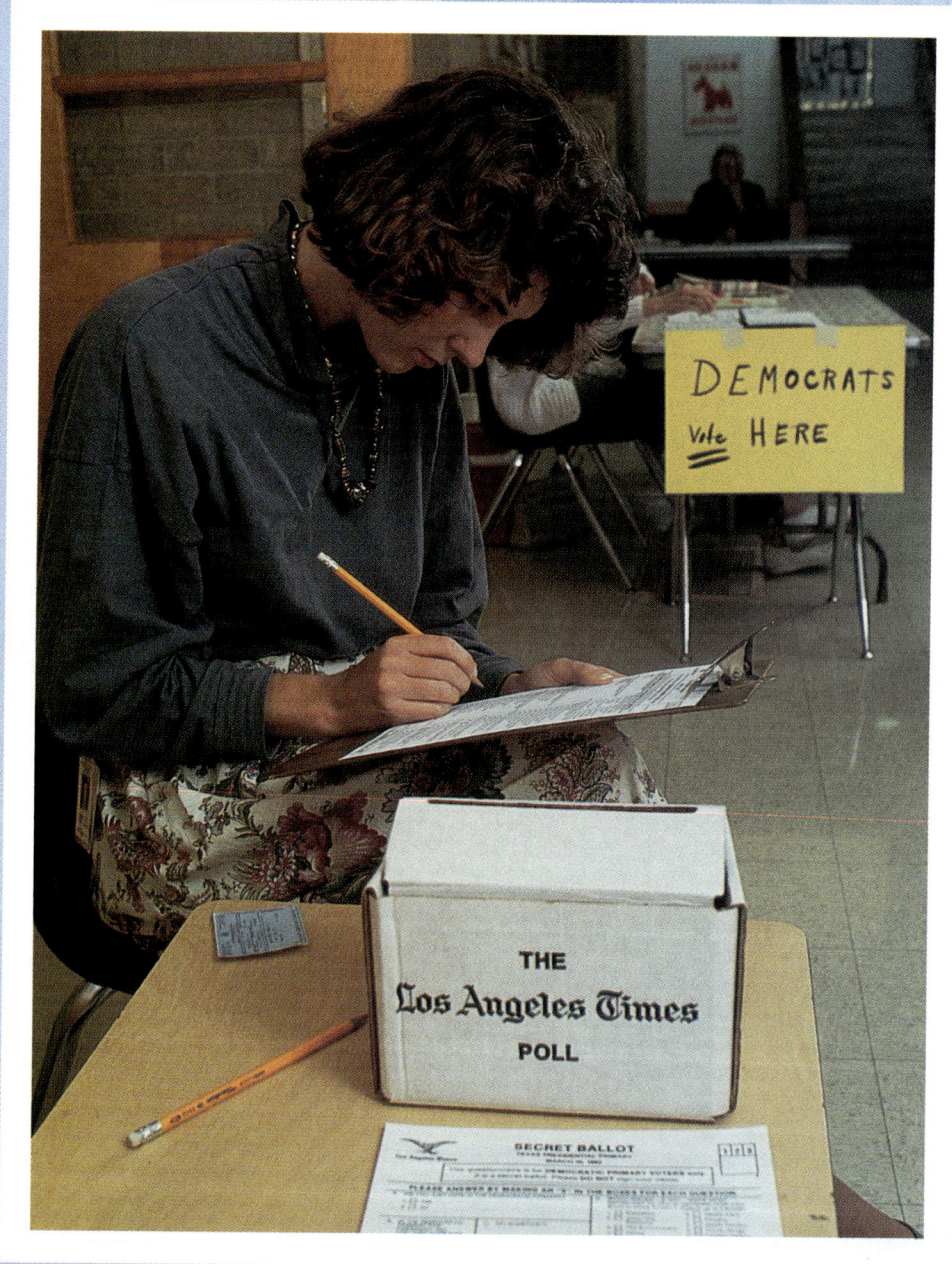

5

Public Opinion

★ Democracy and public opinion

★ Acquiring party identification from parents

★ Influence of religion, gender, and college on opinion

★ Conducting polls

★ Cleavages in public opinion

★ Liberal and conservative ideology

★ Activists and elite opinion

In the Gettysburg Address Abraham Lincoln said that the United States has a government "of the people, by the people, and for the people." That suggests that the government should do what the people want. If that is the case, it is puzzling that

- The federal government has had a large budget deficit, but the people want a balanced budget.
- Courts have ordered that children be bused in order to balance the schools racially, but the people opposed busing.
- The Equal Rights Amendment to the Constitution was not ratified, but polls showed that most people supported it.
- President Reagan sent aid to Nicaraguans fighting against the Marxist government there, but the people said they did not think our government should do this.
- Most people believe that there should be a limit on the number of terms to which U.S. senators and members of the U.S. House of Representatives can be elected, but Congress has not approved on term limits.

Some people, reflecting on the many gaps between what the government does and what the people want, may become cynical and think our system is democratic in name only. That would be a mistake. There are several very good reasons why government policy will often appear to be at odds with public opinion.

First, the Framers of the Constitution did not try to create a government that would do from day to day "what the people want." They created a government for the purpose of achieving certain substantive goals. The preamble to the Constitution lists six of these: "to form a more perfect union, establish justice, ensure domestic tranquility, provide for the common defense, promote the general welfare, and secure the blessings of liberty."

One means of achieving these goals was popular rule, as provided for by the right of the people to vote for members of the House of Representatives (and later for senators and presidential electors). But other means were provided as well: representative

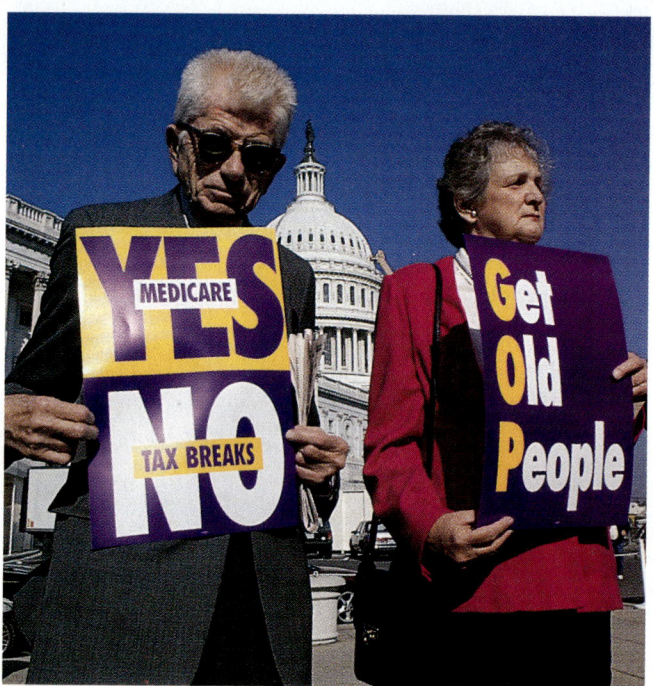

Elderly Americans express—vocally—their opinions about Medicare benefits.

ions carry in governmental circles. For most of us, politics ranks way down on the list of things to think about, well below our families, jobs, health, sweethearts, entertainment, and sports. Some people, however, are political activists, and so come to know as much about politics as the rest of us know about batting averages, soap operas, and car repair. Not only do these activists, or political elites, *know more* about politics than the rest of us, they *think differently* about it—they have different views and beliefs. The government attends more to the elite views than to popular views, at least on many matters.

In this chapter we shall take a close look at what "public opinion" is, how it is formed, the major cleavages in public opinion, and, especially, how political elites differ from ordinary citizens. In later chapters we shall examine the workings of political parties, interest groups, and government institutions and consider what impact they have on whether public opinion affects government policy.

What Is Public Opinion?

A few years ago some researchers at the University of Cincinnati asked twelve hundred local residents whether they favored passage of the Monetary Control Bill of 1983. About 21 percent said that they favored the bill, 25 percent said that they opposed it, and the rest said that they hadn't thought much about the matter or didn't know.

The members of Congress from Cincinnati would have been surprised to learn of this expression of public opinion from their constituents, for there was no such thing as the Monetary Control Bill. The researchers had made it up. Nor is there anything unusual about people in Cincinnati. A few years earlier, about 26 percent of the people questioned in a national survey also expressed opinions on the same nonexistent piece of legislation.[1]

Such ignorance (or the inclination to pretend that one is informed) is apparent not only when people are questioned about arcane bits of legislation. In 1986 a national survey found that only a third of the people polled could identify Caspar Weinberger (he was then the secretary of defense), and only 14 percent knew who William Rehnquist was (the chief justice of the United States Supreme Court). Robert Dole was running for president (and

government, federalism, the separation of powers, a Bill of Rights, and an independent judiciary. These were all intended to be checks on public opinion. In addition, the Framers knew that in a nation as large and diverse as the United States there would rarely be any such thing as "public opinion"; rather, there would be many "publics" (that is, factions), holding many opinions. The Framers hoped that the struggle among these many publics would protect liberty (no one "public" would dominate) while at the same time permitting the adoption of reasonable policies that commanded the support of many factions.

Second, it is not as easy as one may suppose to know what the public thinks. We are so inundated these days with public opinion polls that we may imagine that they tell us what the public believes. That may be true on a few rather simple, clear-cut, and widely discussed issues, but it is not true with respect to most matters on which the government must act. The best pollsters know the limits of their methods, and the citizen should know them as well.

Third, the more people are active in and knowledgeable about politics, the more weight their opinaccording to some polls, doing reasonably well), but only 12 percent of the people could identify him accurately.[2] Given this low level of name recognition, how much confidence should we place in polls that presumably tell us "what the American people think" about our defense policy, the posture of the Supreme Court, and presidential candidates?

Even if people have heard of a given person or issue, how a pollster words a question can dramatically affect the answer he or she gets. Suppose we want to know whether the public believes that the federal government should provide housing for people. In Table 5.1 we see the results obtained from asking that question in three different ways. In the first example people are asked whether they agree or disagree with a one-sided statement ("The federal government should see to it that all people have adequate housing"). A majority agree. In the second example we give people a choice between two statements, one favoring a federal housing policy (mentioned first) and the other favoring individual responsibility ("each person should provide for his own housing"). Given this choice, a small majority now opposes federal housing programs. In the third example the question is repeated, but this time with the individual responsibility option mentioned first. Now over 70 percent of the respondents oppose fed-

John Q. Public/ Middle America/ Silent Majority

John Q. Public is the average man or woman in the street, often portrayed by cartoonists as bespectacled and befuddled. The "little guy," the "common man" (or woman), John Doe or Jane Doe. John Q. Public is sometimes confused with James Q. Wilson, to whom he is only distantly related.

Middle America is a phrase coined by the late Joseph Kraft in 1968 to refer to Americans who have moved out of poverty but are not yet affluent and who cherish the traditional middle-class values.

The **silent majority** consists of those people, whatever their economic status, who uphold traditional values, especially against the counter-culture of the 1960s.

SOURCE: Adapted from *Safire's Political Dictionary* by William Safire. Copyright © 1968, 1972, 1978 by William Safire. Reprinted by permission of Random House, Inc. and the author.

TABLE 5.1   **The Effects of Question Wording: The Issue of Public Housing**

One-sided question		
Do you agree or disagree with the following statement: The federal government should see to it that all people have adequate housing.	Agree: government responsible Disagree: government not responsible	55.0% 45.0%
Two-sided question, government option first		
Some people feel that the federal government should see to it that all people have adequate housing, while others feel each person should provide for his own housing. Which comes *closest* to how you feel about this?	Government responsible Government not responsible	44.6% 55.4%
Two-sided question, government option second		
Some people feel that each person should provide for his own housing, while others feel the federal government should see to it that all people have adequate housing. Which comes *closest* to how you feel about this?	Government responsible Government not responsible	29.5% 70.5%

SOURCE: Howard Schuman and Stanley Presser, *Questions and Answers in Attitude Surveys* (New York: Academic Press, 1981), 70–71.

eral housing programs. Obviously just altering the order in which people are presented with options affects which option they choose and, in this case, changes what "public opinion" is on housing programs.

Moreover, opinions on public issues may not be stable—that is, they may not be firmly held. In a study conducted in 1980, the same people were asked the same questions in January and again in June of the same year. The first had to do with how tough we should be in dealing with the Soviet Union, the second with whether spending should be cut on things like health and education programs. As Table 5.2 shows, many people gave one opinion in January and then a different one in June. Of those who said in January that we should cooperate more with the Soviets, only one-quarter said in June that we should get together with them. Of those who said in January that the government should cut the services it provides, more than one-quarter said in June that they wanted to keep those services at the same level or expressed a middle-of-the-road position.

In sum, public opinion on many matters suffers from ignorance, instability, and sensitivity to the way questions are worded in polls. This does not mean that the American people are ignorant, unstable, or gullible, only that most Americans do not find it worth their while to spend the amount of time thinking about politics that they spend on their jobs, families, and friends. Moreover, just because people do not think much about politics does not mean that democracy is impossible, only that it can work best when people are given relatively simple, clear-cut choices—like the choice between Democrats and Republicans or between one presidential candidate and another.

Furthermore, our specific attitudes about particular matters may be much less important for the health of society than our underlying political culture—our commitment, discussed in Chapter 4, to liberty, equality, individualism, and civic duty. As we shall see, different people give different weight to the various parts of this culture, producing what can be described as a political ideology.

TABLE 5.2 **Response Stability over Repeated Interviews: Two Examples**

AMERICAN RELATIONS WITH RUSSIA[a]
Some people feel it is important for us to try very hard to get along with Russia. Others feel it is a big mistake to try too hard to get along with Russia. Where would you place yourself on this scale, or haven't you thought about this?

Attitudes in **June** 1980	Attitudes in **January** 1980			
	Cooperate	Middle	Tougher	Unsure
Cooperate	**52%**	25%	13%	19%
Middle	14	**24**	17	16
Tougher	23	41	**60**	18
Unsure	10	11	11	**47**
Number	338	153	266	74

LEVEL OF GOVERNMENT SERVICES[b]
Some people think the government should provide fewer services, even in areas such as health and education, in order to reduce spending. Other people feel it is important for the government to continue the services it now provides even if it means no reduction in spending. Where would you place yourself on this scale, or haven't you thought about this?

Attitudes in **June** 1980	Attitudes in **January** 1980			
	Cut	Middle	Keep Same	Unsure
Cut	**54%**	38%	18%	34%
Middle	18	**24**	10	10
Keep same	11	25	**59**	15
Unsure	17	14	13	**41**
Number	362	122	208	138

[a] Respondents were asked to place themselves on a seven-point scale. In this table, points 1, 2, and 3 have been counted as "cooperate"; 4 is counted as "middle"; 5, 6, and 7 have been counted as "tougher." [b] Points 1, 2, and 3 have been counted as "cut"; 4 is counted as "middle"; 5, 6, and 7 have been counted as "keep same." SOURCE: National Election Studies, 1980 panel study. Reprinted from The American Enterprise, a Washington-based magazine of politics, business, and culture.

The Origins of Political Attitudes

Because our attitudes are often unstable or uninformed, some critics of American society have argued that we are brainwashed—duped by television or demagogic leaders into thinking one way or another. Often we are told that presidential candidates are "sold," as if they were boxes of soap flakes. Naturally these critics never say that *they* are brainwashed, only the rest of us.

However shallow their analysis, the argument is a serious one. If the government (or the media) were able to manipulate our political attitudes, then democracy would be a joke. It is akin to what would happen in the marketplace if automobile dealers were able to "brainwash" us into buying Chevrolets, Fords, Chryslers, or Toyotas. The car manufacturers would no longer have to strive to achieve greater efficiency and produce better products; they would only have to "persuade" us what to like. We would be happy not because we owned a good car but because Madison Avenue *told* us we owned a good car.

Of course, advertising does affect our choice of candidates and policies, just as it affects our choice of automobiles. Otherwise, why would companies and politicians spend so much money on advertising? But there are real and important limits to the impact of that advertising. Those limits exist because we have learned, independently of government and the market, some things that help us make our own choices.

The Role of the Family

The best-studied (though not necessarily the most important) case of opinion formation is that of party identification. The majority of young people identify with their parents' political party. A study of high school seniors showed that, of these young men and women, almost all (91 percent) knew accurately the presidential preference of their parents, the great majority (71 percent) knew accurately their parents' party identification, and most shared that identification (only 9 percent identified with the party opposite to that of their parents).[3] (See Table 5.3.) This process begins fairly early in life: by the time they are in the fifth grade (age eleven), over half of all schoolchildren identify with one party or the other, and another fifth claim to be independents.[4]

Naturally, as people grow older they become more independent of their parents in many ways, including politically, but there nonetheless remains a great deal of continuity between youthful partisanship, learned from one's parents, and adult partisanship. One study of adults found that around 60 percent still had the party identification—Democrat, Republican, or independent—of their parents.

"Yes, son, we're Republicans."

Drawing by Richter; © 1991 The *New Yorker* Magazine, Inc.

Of those who differ with their parents, the overwhelming majority do so not by identifying with the opposite party but by describing themselves as "independents."[5]

The ability of the family to inculcate a strong sense of party identification has declined in recent years. The proportion of citizens who say they consider themselves to be Democrats or Republicans has become steadily smaller since the early 1950s. This drop has been greatest among those who *strongly* identify with one party or another. In 1952, fully 22 percent of voters said they were strong

TABLE 5.3   **Parent and Child Agreement in Party Identification**

Child	Parents		
	Democrat	Independent	Republican
Democrat	**66%**	29%	13%
Independent	27	**53**	36
Republican	7	17	**51**
Number	914	442	495

SOURCE: M. Kent Jennings and Richard G. Niemi, *The Political Character of Adolescence: The Influence of Families and Schools* (Princeton, N.J.: Princeton University Press, 1974), 41. Copyright © 1974 by Princeton University Press. Reprinted by permission.

Democrats and 13 percent said they were strong Republicans; by 1976 only 15 percent claimed to be strong Democrats and 9 percent to be strong Republicans. Accompanying this decline in partisanship has been a sharp rise in the proportion of citizens describing themselves as independents.

Part of this change results from the fact that young voters have always had a weaker sense of partisanship than older ones, and today there are proportionally a larger number of young voters than there were thirty years ago. But the youthfulness of the population cannot explain all the changes, for the decline in partisanship has occurred at all age levels. Moreover, those who reached voting age in the 1960s were less apt than those who matured in the 1950s to keep the party identification of their parents.[6]

Though we still tend to acquire some measure of partisanship from our parents, the meaning of that identification is far from clear. There are, after all, liberal and conservative Democrats, as well as liberal and conservative Republicans. So far the evidence suggests that children are more independent of their parents in policy preferences than in party identification. The correlation of children's attitudes with parental attitudes on issues involving civil liberties and racial questions is much lower than the correlation in their party identification. This may be because issues change from one generation to the next, because children are more idealistic than their parents, or because most parents do not communicate to their children clear, consistent positions on a range of political issues. The family dinner table is not a seminar in political philosophy but a place where people discuss jobs, school, dates, and chores.

In some families, however, the dinner table is a political classroom. Fairly clear political ideologies (a term we shall define in a later section) seem to be communicated to that small proportion of children raised in families where politics is a dominant topic of conversation and political views are strongly held. Studies of the participants in various student radical movements in the 1960s suggested that college radicals were often the sons and daughters of people who had themselves been young radicals; some commentators dubbed them the "red-diaper babies." Presumably, deeply conservative people come disproportionately from families that were also deeply conservative. This transfer of political beliefs from one generation to the next does not appear in large

TABLE 5.4 Religious Orientation

Political Opinion	Secular	In Between	Fundamentalist
Increase domestic spending	48%	41%	32%
Institute national health insurance	63	56	38
Guarantee good standard of living	38	23	21
Permit all abortions	70	50	14
Prohibit mandatory school prayers	67	60	51
Allow gays in the military	68	59	32
Encourage equal role for women	99	93	71
Fund more AIDS research	63	52	46
Cut defense spending	77	70	42
Oppose Gulf War	17	11	10
Increase aid to Russia	35	33	24
Percent Democratic (of party identifiers)	41	40	30
Percent liberal (of ideological identifiers)	48	38	7
Percent for Clinton (1992)	57	49	23

SOURCE: From Robert S. Erikson and Kent L. Tedin, *American Public Opinion*, 5th ed. Copyright © 1995 by Allyn and Bacon. Reprinted by permission.

national studies, because such a small proportion of the population is at either the far left or the far right of the political spectrum.

Religion

One way in which the family forms and transmits political beliefs is by its religious tradition. In general, Catholic families are somewhat more liberal on economic issues than white Protestant ones, while Jewish families are much more liberal on both economic and social issues than families of either Catholics or Protestants.[7]

There are two theories as to why this should be so. The first has to do with the **social status** of religious groups in America. When they immigrated to this country, Catholics and Jews were often poor and the object of discrimination. As a result they often affiliated themselves with whichever party and social doctrine seemed most sympathetic to their plight. In many places the Democratic party and a liberal social doctrine seemed to offer the most support. Today Catholics and Jews enjoy greater economic prosperity and face much less discrimination, and so their support for Democrats and liberal candidates has weakened.

The status explanation cannot be the whole story, for if it were simply a matter of low status and discrimination, born-again Christians, many of whom are poor and all of whom are treated with contempt by the national media, would be liberal Democrats.

The second theory emphasizes the content of the **religious tradition** more than the social status of its adherents. In this view the Jewish religion has always emphasized social justice as much as personal rectitude. By contrast evangelical Protestant denominations emphasize personal salvation (becoming "born again") more than questions of social policy. This difference in teachings has led Jews to be disproportionately liberal and fundamentalist Protestants to be disproportionately conservative on many social issues.

Whatever the reason, religious differences make for political differences. In Table 5.4 we can see how the religious beliefs of white voters affected their policy preferences in 1992. Fundamentalists believe that the Bible is God's word and literally true. They are more likely than those who doubt that the Bible

The Christian Coalition was for many years headed by Ralph Reed.

is inspired by God to oppose cuts in defense spending, to want cuts in domestic spending, to oppose abortions, and to favor prayer in schools. (These differences remain essentially the same even after you divide the respondents between those who have a lot of political information and those who have rather little.)

Interestingly, there are no significant differences in how people holding differing views of the Bible feel about economic issues, as opposed to social or foreign policy issues. Fundamentalists and nonfundamentalists have about the same opinion on government job guarantees and spending on government services. This suggests that both social status and religious tradition help explain the effect of religion on politics: the poor status of many fundamentalists inclines them to back liberal government economic policies, but the religious tradition of this group leads them to take a conservative position on social and foreign policy matters.

In the early 1990s a broad-based political movement arose to represent the views of conservative evangelical Christians. The movement was spearheaded by the Christian Coalition, an activist organ-

TABLE 5.5   **The Gender Gap: Differences in Political Views of Men and Women**

Issue	Men	Women
Federal spending for welfare programs should be increased.	13%	20%
Abortion should be permitted by law.	65	60
Sexual harassment is a very serious problem in the workplace.	24	38
This country would be better off if we just stayed home and did not concern ourselves with problems in other parts of the world.	21	33
The United States did the right thing in sending military forces to the Persian Gulf.	83	71
All things considered, the Persian Gulf War was worth it.	66	47
I voted for Clinton in 1992.	41	53
Generally speaking, I think of myself as a Democrat.	30	39
The United States should increase defense spending.	22	18
The United States should increase spending on solving the problems of the homeless.	66	78
Over the past year, America's ability to compete in the world economy has gotten better.	18	11

SOURCE: ICPSR American National Election Survey, 1992: Pre- and Post-Election Surveys.

ization founded by Pat Robertson and led by Ralph Reed. Unlike the older Moral Majority, the Christian Coalition took seriously the task of entering politics at the grassroots and recognized the need to build working alliances with mainstream politicians. Within a short time, people allied with the Christian Coalition have won power in many local Republican party organizations, and its national conferences have become important places for Republican presidential candidates to appear. Although the Christian Coalition is strongest in the South, Midwest, and West, it is unmistakably a national force in American politics. During the 1994 elections, for example, it distributed some 30 million voter guides nationwide, and affiliated local organizations may have distributed several million more. Recent opinion surveys show that since 1960, evangelical Christians

have become more attached to Republican presidential candidates (except in 1976, when Jimmy Carter ran), while Jews and those without a religious orientation have been consistently supportive of the Democratic party.

The Gender Gap

In recent elections much has been made of the **gender gap**—that is, the differences in political views between women and men. In fact, such differences have existed for as long as we have records. What has changed about the gender gap is which party benefits from it.

During the 1950s women were more likely to be Republicans than men; since the late 1960s they have been more likely to be Democrats. The reason for the shift is that the political parties have changed their positions on the kinds of issues to which women respond differently than men—certain social questions (such as prohibition and gun control) and foreign policy (especially the threat of war). For example, in the 1930s and 1940s more women than men wanted to ban the sale of liquor and keep the country out of war; this helped the Republicans, who were then more sympathetic to such policies than the Democrats. In 1980 the aversion that women felt to any policy that might increase the risk of war hurt the Republicans, whom they saw being led by a candidate (Reagan) who was ready to send troops into combat (even so, in 1984 a clear majority of women voted for Reagan).[8]

The gender gap tends to disappear during years in which gender-sensitive policies—war, gun control, or pornography—are not in the limelight and to reemerge during those years in which these topics become hotly partisan. As we see in Table 5.5, the biggest male-female differences are over the use of force and in confidence in the future. The gender gap is not unique to the United States; it can be found throughout the world.

Analysts disagree about the electoral significance of the gender gap. One unresolved question is whether, other things being equal, female voters are more likely than male voters to support female candidates. For example, in 1992 there were ten U.S. Senate races with female candidates. As we see in Table 5.6, women gave a higher fraction of their

TABLE 5.6 **The Gender Gap in Selected U.S. Senate Races, 1992**

		Men	Women	Gender Gap[a]
Selected Senate races involving women				
California	Barbara Boxer (D)	43%	57%	28%
	Bruce Herschensohn (R)	51	37	
	Dianne Feinstein (D)	50	64	27
	John Seymour (R)	46	33	
Illinios	Carol Moseley Braun (D)	50	57	14
	Richard Williamson (R)	47	40	
Missouri	Geri Rothman-Serot (D)	39	48	17
	Christopher Bond (R)	58	50	
Pennsylvania	Lynn Yeakel (D)	42	52	19
	Arlen Specter (R)	54	45	
Selected Senate races not involving women				
Georgia	Wyche Fowler (D)	47	54	14
	Paul Coverdell (R)	53	46	
New York	Robert Abrams (D)	43	52	18
	Alfonse D'Amato (R)	54	45	
Oregon	Les AuCoin (D)	39	55	31
	Robert Packwood (R)	58	43	

a The gender gap is the difference between the margin of support women gave women (or Democratic) candidates and their opponents and the margin of support men gave women (or Democratic) candidates and their opponents.
SOURCE: Reprinted from *The American Enterprise*, a Washington-based magazine of politics, business, and culture (January/February 1993): 100.

votes to female candidates than did men in all of these races. But the size of the gender gap varied from race to race, and the gender gap was also a party gap. A hard-to-specify fraction of the gender gap in voting reflects the tendency of women to identify more strongly than men with the Democratic party.[9]

Schooling and Information

Studies going back over half a century seem to show that attending college has a big impact on political attitudes, usually making them more liberal. College students are more liberal than the population generally, and students at the most prestigious or selective colleges are the most liberal of all.[10] For example, the undergraduates at Harvard College in 1984 preferred Mondale to Reagan 61 percent to 28 percent, while the country at large favored Reagan over Mondale 59 percent to 41 percent.[11] Moreover, the longer students stay in college, the more liberal they are, with seniors more liberal than freshmen and graduate students more liberal than undergraduates.[12] Harvard seniors were more supportive of Mondale than were Harvard freshmen. Students studying the social sciences tend to be more liberal than those studying engineering or the physical sciences.[13] As we shall see in the next chapter, having gone to college increases the rate at which people participate in politics.

Why schooling should have this effect on attitudes is not clear. One possibility is that it has nothing to do with schooling but rather with the individual traits typically possessed by people who go to college and beyond. Some combination of temperament, intelligence, and family background may lead to greater liberalism, with the contents of a college education playing no role at all.

A second possibility is that college and postgraduate schooling expose people to more information

TABLE 5.7   Automobiles and Ideology: Kinds of Automobiles Owned by College Faculty Members Who Have Differing Political Ideologies (in percentages)

| | *Political Ideology* | | | | |
| | liberal | ← | | → | conservative |
Automobile	1	2	3	4	5
GM	12%	18%	18%	23%	29%
Ford	15	19	20	22	24
Chrysler	19	22	18	21	20
AMC	21	17	12	23	26
Japanese	22	22	17	20	18
Volkswagen	26	26	16	17	15
Fiat	27	18	30	11	13
Mercedes-Benz	32	19	21	17	11
Volvo	32	19	18	18	14
No car	31	28	23	11	7

NOTE: The more liberal the faculty member, the more likely he or she is to own no car or an imported car, especially a Volvo or a Mercedes-Benz. The more conservative the faculty member, the more likely he or she is to own an American car, especially a General Motors product.
SOURCE: Data from survey of faculty opinion by Everett Carll Ladd, Jr., and Seymour Martin Lipset, 1975. B. Bruce-Briggs, *The War against the Automobile* (New York: Dutton, 1977), 184.

about politics from all sources. College graduates, compared to high school graduates, read more newspapers and periodicals, join more organizations and social movements, and participate in more election campaigns and lobbying efforts. Their political beliefs may be shaped by these experiences as much as, or more than, by what they learn in the college classroom. In addition, evidence collected by John Zaller shows that the level of political information one has is the best single predictor of being liberal on some kinds of issues, such as civil liberties and civil rights.[14] Information on these matters, he suggests, is today produced by a predominantly liberal cultural elite (see Chapter 10). The longer you stay in school, the more you are exposed to the views of that elite.

The third possibility is that college somehow teaches liberalism. We know that professors are more liberal than members of other occupations, that professors at the most prestigious schools are more liberal than those at the less-celebrated ones, that professors in the social sciences are more liberal than those in engineering or business, and that younger faculty members are more liberal than older ones.[15]

(College faculty members often develop a lifestyle that reveals their political convictions. As shown in Table 5.7, a professor who drives a Volvo or Mercedes tends to be politically more liberal than one who drives a Chevrolet or Ford.)

The political disposition of professors is in part the result of the kinds of people who become college teachers, but it is also the result of the nature of intellectual work. Intellectuals require freedom to explore new or unpopular ideas and thus tend to be strong supporters of civil liberties. Intellectuals work with words and numbers to develop general or abstract ideas; frequently they do not take personal responsibility for practical matters. Thus they are often critical of people who do take such responsibility and who, in the management of complex human affairs, inevitably make compromises. Intellectuals are by training and profession skeptical of common opinions, and thus they are often critical of accepted values and existing institutions. They are interested in ideas and the ideal and thus are sometimes disdainful of the interests and institutions of society.

At one time the liberalizing effect of college had only a small impact on national politics, because so few persons were college graduates. In 1900 only 6 percent of Americans seventeen years of age had even graduated from high school, and less than 1 percent of twenty-three-year-olds were college graduates. By 1982, fully 71 percent of all Americans ages twenty-five and over were high school graduates, and 18 percent of those ages twenty-five and over were college graduates.[16] College, or the exposure to ideas and movements that one encounters there, has become, along with the family, an important source of political opinion for the American electorate.

Some people believe that college students today are more conservative than students were ten or twenty years ago. That is partly true and partly false. As indicated in Table 5.8, contemporary college freshmen are less likely to favor legalizing marijuana or abortion but more willing to support busing to integrate schools. Their opinions about government-sponsored environmental protection measures are unchanged.

How long the liberalizing effect of college persists depends on a number of factors. One study found that former college students still described themselves as more liberal than their parents seven years after graduation.[17] Another study found that students who changed in college from being conservative to being liberal tended to maintain that liberalism for at least twenty years if they acquired, after graduation, liberal friends and spouses.[18] College graduates who go on to get a postgraduate degree—say, a law degree or a Ph.D.—tend to become decidedly more liberal than those who stop with just a B.A. degree.[19] A scholar who tracked students graduating from college in 1969 found that those who had taken part in protests remained very liberal well into the 1980s, while nonprotesters became somewhat more conservative over the years.[20]

Cleavages in Public Opinion

The way in which political opinions are formed helps explain the cleavages that exist among these opinions and why these cleavages do not follow any single political principle but instead overlap and crosscut in bewildering complexity. If, for example, the United States lacked regional differences and was composed almost entirely of white Protestants who had never attended college there would still be plenty of political conflict—the rich would have different views from the poor; workers would have different views from farmers—but that conflict would be much simpler to describe and explain. It might even lead to political parties that were more clearly aligned with competing political philosophies than those we now have. In fact, some democratic nations in the world today do have a population very much like the one we have asked you to imagine, and the United States itself, during the first half of the nineteenth century, was overwhelmingly white, Protestant, and without much formal schooling.

Today, however, there are crosscutting cleavages based on race, ethnicity, religion, region, and education, in addition to those created by income and occupation. To the extent that politics is sensitive to public opinion, it is sensitive to a variety of different and even competing publics. Not all these publics have influence proportionate to their numbers or even to their numbers adjusted for the intensity of their feelings. As will be described later, a filtering process occurs that makes the opinions of some publics more influential than those of others.

TABLE 5.8 **The Changing College Student**

Since the 1970s college freshmen have become more conservative on some issues and more liberal on others.

Issue	Percentage Agreeing	
	1970s[a]	1993
Abolish death penalty	33%	22%
Legalize abortion	83	62
Legalize marijuana	47	28
Increase military spending	39	23
Criminals have too many rights	52	68
Government not doing enough to:		
Control pollution	91	84
Protect consumers	77	72

NOTE: We have no comparable figures for college seniors. Freshmen may change their opinions on these matters while in school.

[a] Exact year the question was asked in 1970s varies between 1970 and 1976, depending on the question.

SOURCE: Richard C. Braungart and Margaret M. Braungart, "Black Colleges: Freshmen Attitudes," *Public Opinion* (May–June 1989): 14. Reprinted with the permission of the American Enterprise Institute for Public Policy Research, Washington, D.C. Updated to 1993 from Alexander W. Astin, William S. Korn, and Ellyne R. Riggs, *The American Freshman* (Los Angeles, CA: UCLA Graduate School of Education, 1993), p. 25.

Whatever this state of affairs may mean for democracy, it creates a messy situation for political scientists. It would be so much easier if everyone's opinion on political affairs reflected some single feature of his or her life, such as income, occupation, age, race, or sex. Of course, some writers have argued that political opinion is a reflection of one such feature, social class, usually defined in terms of income or occupation, but that view, though containing some truth, is beset with inconsistencies: poor blacks and poor whites disagree sharply on many issues involving race; well-to-do Jews and well-to-do Protestants often have opposing opinions on social welfare policy; and low-income elderly people are much more worried about crime than are low-income graduate students. Plumbers and professors may have similar incomes, but they rarely have similar views, and businesspeople in New York City often take a very different view of government than businesspeople in Houston or Birmingham.

In some other democracies a single factor such as class may explain more of the differences in political attitudes than it does in the more socially heterogeneous United States. Most blue-collar workers

The Art of Public-Opinion Polling

A survey of public opinion—popularly called a **poll**—can provide us with a reasonably accurate measure of how people think, provided certain conditions are met. There are five key criteria that must be met in designing and interpreting surveys.

1. **The persons interviewed must be a random sample of the entire population.** In a **random sample** poll any given person, or any given voter or adult, has an equal chance of being interviewed. Most national surveys draw a sample of between a thousand and fifteen hundred persons by a process called stratified or multistage area sampling. The pollster makes a list of all the geographical units in the country (say, all the counties) and groups (or "stratifies") them by the size of their population. The pollster then selects at random units from each group or stratum in proportion to its total population. For example, if one stratum's total population is 10 percent of the national population, then 10 perent of the counties in the sample will be drawn from this stratum. Within each selected county, smaller and smaller geographical units (cities, towns, census tracts, blocks) are chosen, and then, within the smallest unit, individuals are selected at random (by, for example, choosing the occupant of every fifth house). The key is to stick to the sample and not let people volunteer to be interviewed—volunteers often have views different from those who do not volunteer.

2. **The questions must be comprehensible.** The questions must ask people about things they have some knowledge of and some basis for forming an opinion about. Most people know, at least at election time, whom they would prefer as president; most people also have views about what they think the most important national problems are. But relatively few voters will have any opinion about our policy toward El Salvador (if indeed they have even heard of it) or about the investment tax credit. If everybody refused to answer questions about which they are poorly informed, no problem would arise, but unfortunately many of us like to pretend that we know things that in fact we don't or to be "helpful" to interviewers by inventing opinions on the spur of the moment.

3. **The questions must be asked fairly.** They should be worded in clear language, without the use of "loaded" or "emotional" words. They must give no indication of what the "right" answer is but offer a reasonable explanation, where necessary, of the consequences of each possible answer. For example, in 1971 a Gallup poll asked people whether they favored a proposal "to bring home all U.S. troops [from Vietnam] before the end of the year." Two-thirds of the public agreed with that. Then the question was asked in a different way: Do you agree or disagree with a proposal to withdraw all U.S. troops by the end of the year "regardless of what happens there [in Vietnam] after U.S. troops leave"? In this form, substantially less than half the public agreed.

4. **The answer categories offered to a person must be carefully considered.** This is no problem when there are only two candidates for office—say, Bill Clinton and Bob Dole—and you want only to know which one the voters prefer. But it can be a big problem when you want more complex information. For example, if you ask people (as does George Gallup) whether they "approve" or "disapprove" of how the president is handling his job, you will get one kind of answer—let us say that 55 percent approve and 45 percent disapprove. On the other hand, if you ask them (as does Louis Harris) how they rate the job the president is doing, "excellent, pretty good, only fair, or poor," you will get very different results. It is quite possible that only 46 percent will pick such positive answers as "excellent" or "pretty good," and the rest will pick the negative answers, "only fair" and

"poor." If you are president, you can choose to believe Mr. Gallup (and feel pleased) or Mr. Harris (and be worried). The differences in the two polls do not arise from the competence of the two pollsters but entirely from the choice of answers that they include with their questions.

5. **Not every difference in answers is a significant difference.** A survey is based on a sample of people. Select another sample, by equally randomized methods, and you might get slightly different results. This difference is called a **sampling error,** and its likely size can be computed mathematically. In general, the bigger the sample and the bigger the differences between the percentage of people giving one answer and the percentage giving another, the smaller the sampling error. If a poll of fifteen hundred voters reveals that 47 percent favor Bill Clinton, we can be 95 percent certain that the actual proportion of all voters favoring Clinton is within three percentage points of this figure—that is, it lies somewhere between 44 and 50 percent. In a close race an error of this size could be quite important. It could be reduced by using a bigger sample, but the cost of interviewing a sample big enough to make the error much smaller is huge.

As a result of sampling error and for other reasons, it is very hard for pollsters to predict the winner in a close election. Since 1952 every major national poll has in fact picked the winner of the presidential election, but there may have been some luck involved in such close races as the 1960 Kennedy-Nixon and the 1976 Carter-Ford contests. In 1980 the polls greatly underestimated the Reagan vote, partly because many voters made up their minds at the last minute and partly because a bigger percentage of Carter supporters decided not to vote at all. In contrast, pollsters did remarkably well in forecasting the results of the 1992 presidential election, a volatile three-way race between Bill Clinton, George Bush, and Ross Perot. Although they tended to overestimate Clinton's margin and to underestimate Perot's, twenty of the most frequently cited national polls came close to predicting the actual results. Polling is not an exact science, but done right, it is a highly skilled art.

in America think of themselves as being "middle-class," whereas most such workers in Britain and France describe themselves as "working-class." In England the working class prefers the Labour party by a margin of three to one, while in the United States workers prefer the Democratic party by less than two to one, and in 1980 and 1984 they gave most of their votes to Ronald Reagan.[21]

Social Class

Americans speak of "social class" with embarrassment. The norm of equality tugs at our conscience, urging us to judge people as individuals, not as parts of some social group (such as "the lower class"). Social scientists speak of "class" with confusion. They know it exists but quarrel constantly about how to define it: By income? Occupation? Wealth? Schooling? Prestige? Personality?

Let's face up to the embarrassment and skip over the confusion. Truck drivers and investment bankers look different, talk different, and vote different. There is nothing wrong with saying that the first group consists of "working-class" (or "blue-collar") people and the latter of "upper-class" (or "management") people. Moreover, though different definitions of class produce slightly different groupings of people, most definitions overlap to such an extent that it does not matter too much which we use.

However defined, public opinion and voting have been less determined by class in the United States than in Europe, and the extent of class cleavage has declined in the last few decades in both the United States and Europe. In the 1950s V. O. Key, Jr., found that differences in political opinion were closely associated with occupation. He noted that people holding managerial or professional jobs had distinctly more conservative views on social welfare policy and more internationalist views on foreign policy than did manual workers.[22]

During the next decade this pattern changed greatly. Opinion surveys done in the late 1960s showed that business and professional people had views quite similar to those of manual workers on such matters as the poverty program, health insurance, American policy in Vietnam, and government efforts to create jobs.[23]

The voting patterns of different social classes have also become somewhat more similar. Class vot-

ing has declined sharply since the late 1940s in the United States, France, Great Britain, and West Germany and declined moderately in Sweden.

Class differences remain, of course. Unskilled workers are more likely than affluent white-collar workers to be Democrats and to have liberal views on economic policy. And when economic issues pinch—for example, when farmers are hurting or steelworkers are being laid off—the importance of economic interests in differentiating the opinions of various groups rises sharply. Moreover, there is some evidence that during the Reagan administration, income once again began to make a large difference in the party affiliation of voters.

Why should social class, defined along income lines, have become less important over the long term? One reason has to do largely with schooling. At one time the income of people did not depend so heavily as it now does on having educational credentials. Most people had only a high school education, whatever their job might be, and only a small minority had a college or postgraduate degree. Today access to higher-paying jobs (outside of sports and entertainment) is increasingly restricted to people with extensive schooling. Since, as we have seen, college and (especially) postgraduate education tends to make people more liberal than they would otherwise be, the arrival of millions of college graduates, lawyers, and Ph.D.'s into the ranks of the financially affluent has brought into the upper classes a more liberal political outlook than once was the case.

Another reason is that the issues that now lead us to choose which party to support and that determine whether we think of ourselves as liberals or conservatives have increasingly become noneconomic issues. In recent years our political posture has been shaped by the positions we take on race relations, abortion, school prayer, arms control, and environmentalism, issues that do not clearly affect the rich differently from the poor (or at least do not affect them as differently as do the union movement, the minimum wage, and unemployment). Moral, symbolic, and foreign policy matters do not divide rich and poor in the same way as economic ones. Thus we have many well-off people who think of themselves as liberals because they take liberal positions on these noneconomic matters, and many not-so-well-off people who think of themselves as conservatives because that is the position they take on these issues.

Race and Ethnicity

If class has become a less clear-cut source of political cleavage, race has become more of one. Whites and blacks differ profoundly over whether children should be bused to achieve racially balanced schools and whether a person should be able to sell his or her home to anyone, even if it means refusing to sell it to a black. The differences extend to nonracial matters as well. Whites are more likely than blacks to support the death penalty for murder and to favor increased spending on national defense; they are less likely to endorse national health insurance. In the 1960s blacks were more opposed than whites to the war in Vietnam. An issue that divides blacks and whites in the 1990s is how to remedy the effects of past racial discrimination. As Seymour Martin Lipset has observed, "every national survey still shows that a sizable majority of whites is opposed to remedying the effects of past discrimination by giving special consideration to the less formally qualified with respect to hiring or school admissions."[24] For example, a 1991 Gallup poll asked, "Do you believe that because of past discrimination against black people, qualified blacks should receive preference over equally qualified whites in such matters as getting into college or getting jobs?" Only 19 percent of whites, compared to 48 percent of blacks, responded positively.[25] More generally, a 1996 report by the Center for New Black Leadership documented wide and persistent differences of opinion between blacks and whites on a number of important public policy issues. For example, blacks have long been more in favor of welfare expenditures and school prayer, and less in favor of the death penalty, than whites.[26]

There are, however, many issues on which the two races feel pretty much the same, such as allowing the police to search the homes of known drug dealers without a warrant, opposing a woman's right to abortion on demand, and opposing the legalization of marijuana. And despite broad differences over how to remedy the effects of past discrimination, majorities of both blacks and whites oppose policies requiring specific quotas and numerical goals for integration.[27] Finally, between 1974 and

TABLE 5.9	Changes in Race and Public Opinion			
	Whites		Blacks	
	1974	1992	1974	1992
Government should help blacks	25%	19%	63%	42%
Unsure	26	26	25	24
Blacks should help themselves	50	54	12	33
	101%	100%	100%	100%

SOURCE: From Robert S. Erikson and Kent L. Tedin, *American Public Opinion*, 5th ed. Copyright © 1995 by Allyn and Bacon. Reprinted by permission.

1992 the gap between black and white views on the government's responsibility to help blacks narrowed somewhat (see Table 5.9).

Blacks have become the most consistently liberal group within the Democratic party.[28] Nevertheless, a majority of blacks believe they are as a group better off today than they were ten years ago and that their children's opportunities will be better yet.[29]

There appears to be less class cleavage among blacks than among whites—that is, the differences in opinion between poor and better-off blacks is less than it is between poor and better-off whites.[30] This means that at every income level blacks are more liberal than whites.* However, there is a significant gap between the leaders of black organizations and black people generally. A 1985 survey of over one hundred black leaders and six hundred black citizens found that the leaders were much more likely than the rank and file to favor abortions, school busing, affirmative action, and forcing U.S. corporations to pull out of South Africa. Most black leaders

* One problem in interpreting opinion polls on race issues is that responses will differ depending on whether the interviewee is being questioned by a person of the same or a different race. In 1986 a *New York Times*/CBS poll found that 56 percent of all blacks said that they approved of how Reagan was handling the presidency, but a *Washington Post*/ABC poll, asking the same question at about the same time, found that only 23 percent of all blacks said that they approved of Reagan as president. One major difference: the *Washington Post*/ABC poll used only black interviewers to question blacks, and they prefaced their questions by saying that they were doing a survey of blacks only, perhaps inducing respondents to "think black." There is no way to know which responses were the "right" ones.

TABLE 5.10 Party Identification and Political Attitudes of Ethnic Groups in California (1984)

	Anglo-White	Black	Latino	Asian-American
Party Identification				
Democrat	37%	78%	54%	35%
Republican	35	3	20	38
In between, other	28	18	26	27
Political attitude				
Favor increased military spending	32	18	28	38
Favor increased welfare spending	59	84	73	66
Favor prayer in public schools	50	62	53	46
Favor death penalty for murder	75	47	57	73
Favor abortion on demand	60	47	40	53
Favor bilingual education programs	41	63	69	51
Number	409	335	593	305

SOURCE: Bruce Cain and Roderick Kiewit, "California's Coming Minority Majority," *Public Opinion* (February–March 1986): 50–52. Reprinted with permission of American Enterprise Institute for Public Policy Research.

deny that blacks are making progress, while most black citizens think they are.[31] This cleavage between the black political elite and black voters should not surprise us; as we shall see, there are similar cleavages between white political elites and white voters.

Though there are an estimated 20 million Hispanics and 7 million Asian-Americans in this country, they tend to be concentrated in a few locations, and so not enough appear in the usual national opinion polls to permit us to say much about their views.

However, a survey of ethnic groups in California, a state where fully one-third of all recent immigrants to this country live, gives us some knowledge of how Latinos and Asian-Americans feel about political parties and issues. As you can see in Table 5.10, Latinos identify themselves as Democrats, but much less so than do blacks, and Asian-Americans are even more identified with the Republican party than Anglo-whites. On such issues as spending on the military and welfare programs, prayer in the public schools, and the imposition of the death penalty for murder, Asian-American views are much more like those of Anglo-whites than either blacks or Hispanics. Latinos are somewhat more liberal than Anglos or Asian-Americans, but much less lib-

eral than blacks, except with respect to bilingual education programs.[32]

These figures conceal important differences within these ethnic groups. For example, Japanese-Americans are among the more conservative of Asian-Americans, whereas Korean-Americans (perhaps because they are among the most recent immigrants) are more liberal. Similarly, Latinos, the fastest-growing ethnic group in the United States, are a diverse mix of Cuban-Americans, Mexican-Americans, Central Americans, and Puerto Ricans, each with distinct political views. A study of Latino voting in the 1988 presidential election found that Mexican-Americans were the most Democratic, Cuban-Americans were the most Republican, and Puerto Ricans were in between the other two groups.[33]

Region

It is widely believed that geographic region affects political attitudes and in particular that southerners and northerners disagree significantly on many policy questions. As we will see, southern members of Congress tend to vote differently—and more conservatively—than northern ones, and it should stand to reason that this is because their constituents, southern voters, expect them to vote differently. At one time white southerners were conspicuously less liberal than easterners, midwesterners, or westerners on such questions as aid to minorities, legalizing marijuana, school busing, and enlarging the rights of those accused of crimes. Although more conservative on these issues, they held views on economic issues similar to those of whites in other regions of the country. This helps to explain why the South was for so long a part of the Democratic party coalition: on national economic and social welfare policies, southerners expressed views not very different from northerners. That coalition was always threatened, however, by the divisiveness produced by issues of race and liberty.

Today the political views of white southerners are less distinct from those of whites living in other parts of the country. As Table 5.11 illustrates, the proportion of white Protestants in the South who gave liberal answers to questions regarding both civil liberties/civil rights issues and economic/welfare issues in 1992 was only somewhat different from that of white Protestants in other regions. (The

Recently, immigrants have been applying for American citizenship in record numbers.

TABLE 5.11   **Does the South Differ?**

Percentage giving "liberal" response among white Protestants living in different regions, 1992.

Issue	Northeast[a]	North Central[b]	South[c]	West[d]
Economic and welfare issues				
More government services	26.4	27.4	28.8	26.5
More government job guarantees	23.0	19.2	20.7	21.2
Increase social security	55.1	39.7	43.8	42.0
Cut defense spending	47.3	36.4	37.0	44.4
Civil rights and civil liberties issues				
Government aid to black citizens	10.4	13.8	12.0	21.7
Laws to protect homosexuals against job discrimination	61.1	45.8	50.3	56.8
Women's equality	72.5	66.8	72.1	75.8
Right to abortion	50.0	40.6	34.7	53.8
Average percentage liberal, all issues	43.2	36.2	37.4	42.8

[a] Northeast: Connecticut, Massachusetts, New Hampshire, New Jersey, New York, Pennsylvania
[b] North Central: Illinois, Indiana, Iowa, Kansas, Michigan, Minnesota, Missouri, Nebraska, Ohio, Wisconsin
[c] South: Alabama, Arkansas, Deleware, District of Columbia, Florida, Georgia, Louisiana, Maryland, North Carolina, Tennessee, Texas, Virginia, West Virginia
[d] West: Arizona, California, Colorado, Oregon, Washington, Wyoming
SOURCE: Compiled by Meenekshi Bose, using data from the ICPSR *1992 American National Election Survey,* University of Michigan.

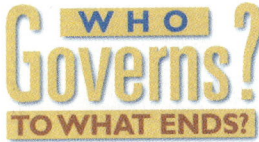

Public Opinion on Immigration

Just as it has been from the earliest days of the Republic, today America is a land —*the* land—of immigrants. About 1.1 million foreigners now come here to live each year, roughly seven hundred thousand as legal immigrants, one hundred thousand as refugees, and three hundred thousand without authorization. Compared to many other democracies, the United States has long had one of the most generous immigration policies in the world. (Just try immigrating to Japan!) In 1990, the number of immigrants in the United States climbed to 19.8 million, or roughly 7.9 percent of the total U.S. population—higher than in 1960, but still small by historic standards (see the accompanying pie charts). Earlier in the century, most foreign-born Americans came from Europe. Today, most foreign-born Americans come from non-European nations such as Mexico, the Philippines, Cuba, Vietnam, India, Guyana, and Iran.

Over the last decade, a debate has raged about restricting legal immigration below its present level and redoubling efforts to keep illegal aliens and their children out. This debate has given rise to lots of new federal laws, but the matter is far from settled.

Likewise, many states have acted on immigration. California, for example, is home to an estimated 40 percent of the nation's approximately 4 million illegal immigrants. In 1994, California voters approved Proposition 187, a ballot initiative to cut off most state and local benefits, including nonemergency medical services and public education, for unlawful immigrants. A federal judge has ruled that much of the law is unconstitutional.

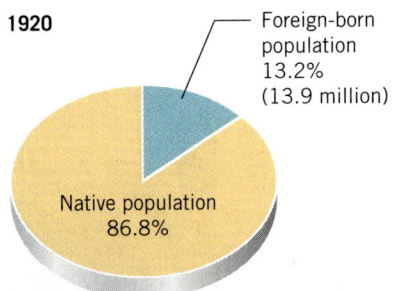

1920 Foreign-born population 13.2% (13.9 million) / Native population 86.8%

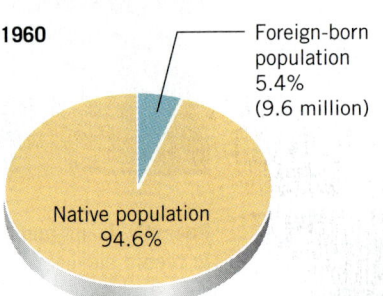

1960 Foreign-born population 5.4% (9.6 million) / Native population 94.6%

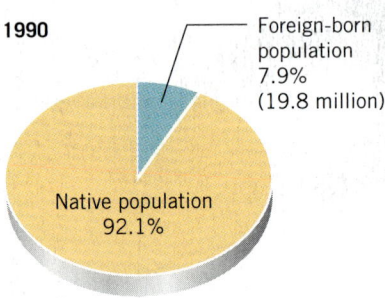

1990 Foreign-born population 7.9% (19.8 million) / Native population 92.1%

SOURCE: *The Public Perspective*, August/September 1995, p. 13.

Trying to figure out who governs on immigration and to what ends is no easy task. Contributors to immigration law and policy include the following:

Congress: In 1986 Congress passed a law barring the employment of illegal aliens. But then in 1990 it expanded legal immigration quotas to bring in more skilled workers. Between 1994 and 1996 members of Congress considered nearly a dozen proposals to overhaul U.S. policy on legal and illegal immigration, but they could agree on only a few major provisions.

The Courts: For decades the courts have shaped immigration policy. In 1948, for example, the U.S. Supreme Court struck down a California law denying commercial fishing rights to legal aliens who were ineligible to become naturalized citizens. In 1976 the Court ruled that Congress has the power to restrict federal health benefits to legal aliens. Today, California's Proposition 187 is facing various challenges in the courts.

The Bureaucracy: Congress's decisions on immigration are carried out by a much-criticized federal bureaucracy, the Immigration and Naturalization Service (INS). In addition to patrolling the border, the INS is responsible for enforcing an incredibly complicated array of laws and regulations governing the conditions under which foreigners may enter (or must leave) the country, determining the legal employability of various categories of immigrants, administering detention facilities for some nine thousand aliens, and much more.

Affected Groups: Business leaders, researchers, and spokespersons for various ethnic and religious groups also play a role. But here, too, there are differences of opinion and clashing interests. For instance, some business leaders want to import foreign workers with special high-tech job skills; others are more concerned about obtaining low-skill workers; and still others have no real stake in the issue. Spokespersons for diverse ethnic and religious groups occasionally speak with one voice on immigration (they did so during the 1996 debate in Congress, when they criticized proposed across-the-board cuts in family reunification visas and a possible cap on refugee admissions). But often they compete with one another to get their fellow nationals and believers in at the expense of individuals from other lands or of different religions (especially their historic ethnic or religious rivals).

Public Opinion: Since the mid-1980s, most polls have shown that a majority of Americans favor some cuts in legal immigration and strongly support measures to curtail illegal immigration and deport unlawful residents. In 1994, over 60 percent favored decreases in legal immigration, and nearly 60 percent favored having a law in their state similar to California's Proposition 187. Thus, as they debate whether and how to restrict immigration, lawmakers in most states must balance the general public sentiment in favor of cuts against concerted opposition from affected groups. Especially in high-immigration states such as California, politicians must contend with increasingly powerful currents of mass support for restricting the flow of foreigners, legal and illegal.

It is hard to know precisely how, if at all, public opinion on immigration would change if most people knew more about

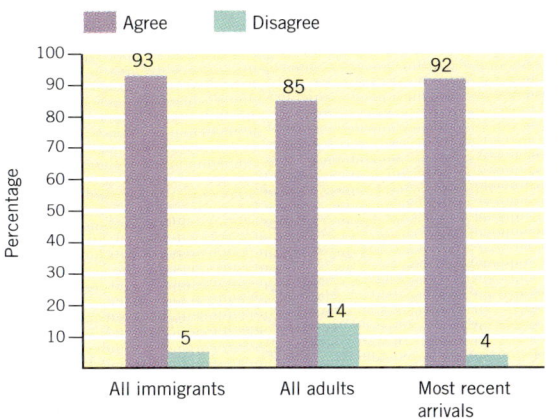

QUESTION

[Do you agree or disagree that] people who work hard to better themselves can get ahead in this country?

SOURCE: *The Public Perspective*, August/September 1995, p. 15.

it. For example, many people believe that today's immigrants are poor and poorly educated. In 1990, however, foreign-born Americans approximated native-born Americans in terms of education (20 percent of U.S.-born and foreign-born Americans held a bachelor's degree or higher), average annual household income (about $30,000 for native-born households, versus $28,000 for foreign-born ones), and careers (27 percent of native-born and 22 percent of foreign-born workers held managerial or professional jobs).

Likewise, many people have come to believe that today's immigrants resist learning English, are against "blending into" American culture, and don't believe in the American dream. But a 1995 survey found that for 69 percent of all immigrants, and 81 percent of those who arrived over two decades ago, English was the language used most often at home. As the graph above suggests, today's immigrants, including the most recent arrivals, remain dedicated to the "melting pot" ideal and the belief that America is the "land of opportunity." Moreover, despite the sometimes harsh rhetoric that has characterized the immigration debate, when asked whether they felt welcome in America, over 90 percent

of all immigrants, including the newest ones, said they felt welcome when they first arrived, and still do. Like most native-born Americans, their main complaints about America concern crime in the streets and an erosion in the moral values of society.

Where does public opinion on immigration fall in your home state? Does it differ by race, ethnic background, region, or religion? What, if any, changes in immigration policy have been made in your state since 1990, and how would you characterize these changes? Who has figured prominently in the debate? The governor? Members of Congress? Business leaders? And what have they advocated? Did they lead public opinion or follow it? Would you be inclined to support or oppose further restrictions on immigration, and why? If you were in charge of immigration policy in the United States, how would you govern, and to what ends?

SOURCES: Dick Kirschten, "Second Thoughts on Immigration," *National Journal*, January 21, 1995, pp. 150–155; Jeffrey Rosen, "The War on Immigrants," *The New Republic*, January 30, 1995, pp. 22–26; *The American Enterprise*, March/April 1995, p. 104; "The Immigration Story," *The Public Perspective*, August/September 1995, pp. 13–17; Holly Idelson, "Economic Anxieties Bring Debate on Immigration to a Boil," *Congressional Quarterly Weekly*, March 16, 1996, pp. 697–701.

table is limited to white Protestants to eliminate the effect of the very different proportions of Catholics, Jews, blacks, and other ethnic groups living in various regions.)

The southern lifestyle is in fact different from that of other regions of the country. The South has, on the whole, been more accommodating to business enterprise and less so to organized labor than, for example, the Northeast; it gave greater support to the third-party candidacy of George Wallace in 1968, which was a protest against big government and the growth of national political power as well as against civil rights; and it was in the South that the greatest opposition arose to income-redistribution plans such as the Family Assistance Plan of 1969. Moreover, there is some evidence that white southerners became by the 1970s more conservative than they had been in the 1950s, at least when compared to white northerners.[34] Finally, white southerners have become less attached to the Democratic party: whereas over three-fourths described themselves as Democrats in 1952, only a third did by 1992 (see Figure 5.1).

These changes in the South can have great significance, as we shall see in the next three chapters when we consider how elections are fought. It is enough for now to remember that, without the votes of the southern states, no Democrat except Lyndon Johnson in 1964 would have been elected president from 1940 through 1976. (Without the South, Roosevelt would have lost in 1944, Truman in 1948, Kennedy in 1960, and Carter in 1976. And even though Carter carried the South, he did not win a majority of white southern votes.) Clinton won in 1992 and 1996 without carrying the South, but those were three-man races.

Political Ideology

Up to now the words **liberal** and **conservative** have been used here as if everyone agreed on what they meant and as if they accurately described general sets of political beliefs held by large segments of the population. Neither of these assumptions is correct. Like many useful words—*love, justice, happiness*—they are as vague as they are indispensable.

FIGURE 5.1 Whites in the South Leaving the Democrats

Percentage of southern white registered voters who identified with each party

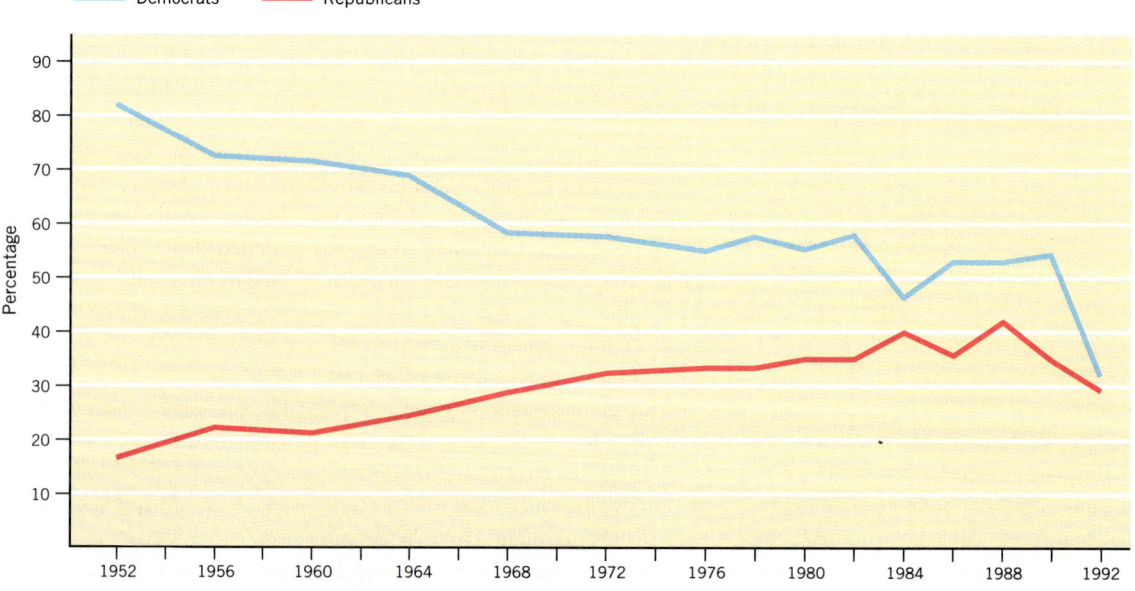

SOURCE: ICPSR National Election Studies, Cumulative Data File, 1952–1990.

When we refer to people as liberals, conservatives, socialists, or radicals, we are implying that they have a patterned set of beliefs about how government and other important institutions in fact operate and how they ought to operate, and in particular about what kinds of policies government ought to pursue. They are said to display to some degree a **political ideology**—that is, a coherent and consistent set of beliefs about who ought to rule, what principles rulers ought to obey, and what policies rulers ought to pursue. Political scientists measure the extent to which people have a political ideology in two ways: first, by seeing how frequently people use broad political categories (such as "liberal," "conservative," "radical") to describe their own views or to justify their preferences for various candidates and policies, and second, by seeing to what extent the policy preferences of a citizen are consistent over time or are based at any one time on consistent principles.

This second method involves a simple mathematical procedure: measuring how accurately one can predict a person's view on a subject at one time based on his or her view on that subject at an earlier time, or measuring how accurately one can predict a person's view on one issue based on his or her view on a different issue. The higher the accuracy of such predictions (or correlations), the more we say a person's political opinions display "constraint," or ideology. Despite annual fluctuations, ideological self-identification surveys typically find that moderates are the largest group among American voters, conservatives the second-largest, and liberals the smallest (see Figure 5.2).

Except when asked by pollsters, most Americans do not actually employ the words *liberal* or *conservative* in explaining or justifying their preferences for candidates or policies, and not many more than half can give plausible definitions of these terms. Furthermore, there are relatively low correlations among the answers to similar questions asked by pollsters at different times and to comparable questions asked at the same time. From this, many scholars have concluded that the great majority of Americans do not think about politics in an ideological or even in a very coherent manner and that they make little use of such concepts, so dear to political commentators and professors alike, as "liberal" and "conservative."[35]

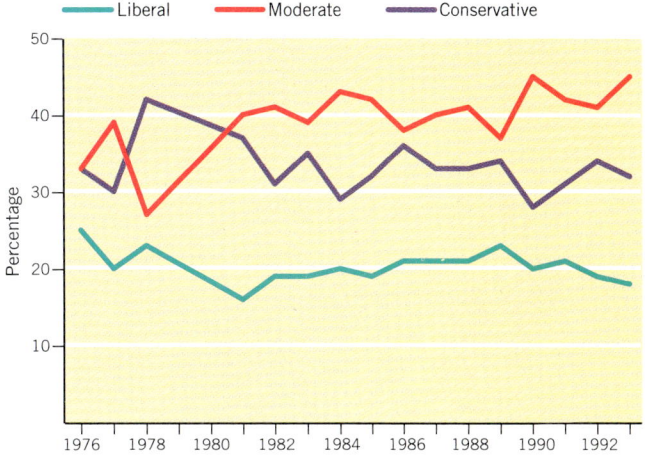

FIGURE 5.2 Ideological Self-Identification, 1976–1993

QUESTION

How would you describe your views on most political matters? Generally, do you think of yourself as a liberal, moderate, or conservative?

SOURCE: *The American Enterprise* (March/April 1993): 84, citing surveys by CBS/*New York Times*.

Consistent Attitudes

This does not settle the question entirely, however. Critics of the view that Americans are nonideological have argued that people can have general, and strongly felt, political predispositions even though they are not able to use such terms as *liberal* correctly. Moreover, public opinion polls must of necessity ask rather simple questions, and the apparent "inconsistency" in the answers people give at different times may mean only that the nature of the problem and the wording of the question have changed in ways not obvious to the people analyzing the surveys.[36]

People can have an ideology without using the words *liberal* or *conservative* and without having beliefs that line up neatly along the conventional liberal-versus-conservative dimension. We saw in Chapter 4 that most Americans share in a distinctive political culture—a belief in freedom, equality (of political condition and economic opportunity), and civic duty. They also attach a great deal of importance to "Americanism." Though these words may be vague, they are not trivial—at some level they are an ideology.

Scholars regularly discover that people have what some would consider "inconsistent" opinions. For example, a voter may want the government to spend more on education and the environment and at the same time favor a bigger military budget and a tough posture toward unfriendly nations. These

views are "inconsistent" only in the sense that they violate a political rule of thumb, common in the media and in national policy debates, that expects people who favor a bigger welfare state to favor a smaller military establishment as well. That is the conventional "liberal" view. Similarly, the rule of thumb in the media is that people who support a strong military posture are also going to favor prayer in the schools and oppose abortion on demand. That is the conventional "conservative" position. But of course many citizens violate these rules of thumb, picking and choosing their positions without regard to the conventional definitions of liberalism and conservatism.

What Do *Liberalism* and *Conservatism* Mean?

Just because most people are not consistent liberals or consistent conservatives does not prove that these terms are meaningless. As we shall see, they are very meaningful for political elites. And they even have meaning for ordinary citizens, but this meaning is a complicated one that requires careful analysis.

The definition of these words has changed since they first came into use in the early nineteenth century. At that time a liberal was a person who favored personal and economic liberty—that is, freedom from the controls and powers of the state. An economic liberal, for example, supported the free market and opposed government regulation of trade. A conservative was originally a person who opposed the excesses of the French Revolution and its emphasis on personal freedom and favored instead a restoration of the power of the state, the church, and the aristocracy.

Beginning around the time of Franklin Roosevelt and the New Deal, the meaning of these terms began to change. Roosevelt used the term *liberal* to refer to his political program—one that called for an active national government that would intervene in the economy, create social welfare programs, and help certain groups (such as organized labor) acquire greater bargaining power. In time the opponents of an activist national government began using the term *conservative* to describe themselves. (Barry Goldwater, in 1964, was the first major U.S.

Politically SPEAKING

Ideology: You Versus Your Enemies

A political ideology is a coherent set of political rules for explaining how the world works and prescribing how it ought to work.

Liberals describe

- *themselves* as "caring," "committed," "an activist," or "progressive";
- *their enemies* as "reactionary," "right-wing," and "extremist."

Conservatives describe

- *themselves* as "moderate," "responsible," "prudent," or "mainstream";
- *their enemies* as "crackpot," "knee-jerk," "left-wing," or "bleeding-heart."

An easy way to tell whether a politician, newspaper, or magazine is liberal or conservative is to see whether, in describing liberals or conservatives, it uses terms from the "nice" (themselves) list or the "hostile" (their enemies) list.

politician to proclaim himself a conservative.) In general a conservative favored a free market rather than a regulated one, states' rights over national supremacy, and greater reliance on individual choice in economic affairs.

Though the meaning of these terms changed, it did not in the process become more precise. Two persons may describe themselves as liberals even though the first favors both the welfare state and a strong national defense and the second favors the welfare state but wants a sharp reduction in military spending. Similarly, one conservative may favor enforcement of laws against drug abuse, and another may believe that the government should let people decide for themselves what drugs to take. Once, liberals favored laws guaranteeing equality of opportunity among the races; now some liberals favor "affirmative action" plans involving racial quotas or goals. Once, conservatives opposed American intervention abroad; today many conservatives believe the United States should play an active role in foreign affairs.

In view of this confusion one is tempted to throw up one's hands in disgust and consign words like *liberal* and *conservative* to the garbage can. While understandable, such a reaction would be a mistake, because in spite of their ambiguities, these words remain in general use, convey some significant meaning, and point to real differences between, for example, the liberal and conservative wings of the Democratic and Republican parties. Our task is to clarify these differences by showing the particular meanings these words have. One way to do this is by considering how self-described liberals and conservatives differ in their opinions on prominent issues, such as those listed in Table 5.12.

Various Categories

We can imagine certain broad categories of opinion to which different people subscribe. These categories are found by analyzing the answers people give to dozens of questions about political issues. Different analysts come up with slightly different categories,

TABLE 5.12 How Liberals and Conservatives Differ

Belief	Support Among Self-Declared Liberals	Support Among Self-Declared Conservatives
The government should provide "more services even if it means an increase in spending."	73%	32%
The government should guarantee "that every person has a job and a good standard of living."	55	21
Favor "government insurance plan which would cover all medical and hospital expenses for everyone."	82	27
The government "should make every effort to improve the social and economic position of blacks."	55	18
The U.S. "should spend less on defense."	85	65
"Aid to [Russia] should be increased."	36	32
"Women should have an equal role in running business, industry, and government."	96	81
The United States should always permit abortion "as a matter of personal choice."	72	36
"Homosexuals should be allowed to serve in U.S. Armed Forces."	70	45
"Oppose death penalty for persons convicted of murder."	35	15

SOURCE: Robert S. Erikson and Kent L. Tedin, *American Public Opinion*, 5th ed. (Boston: Allyn and Bacon, 1995), p. 69.

Thinking CRITICAL

Public Opinion on Homosexuality: Liberal, Conservative, or Neither?

When President Clinton announced his plan to end the U.S. military's ban on homosexuals, leaders on both sides of the issue claimed that the people were on their side. But numerous surveys indicate that public opinion is much more complicated than such assertions imply.

In sixteen national surveys conducted between 1973 and 1991, an average of about 70 percent of all Americans agreed with the statement "homosexual relations between adults are always wrong." But by 1996, the number had dropped to 61 percent, and Americans became more likely to agree that "homosexuality should be considered an acceptable lifestyle." Whether people agree that homosexuality is acceptable depends somewhat on their sex, age, party affiliation, and schooling. Men, older persons, Republicans, and those without a high school education are least tolerant; women, younger persons, Democrats, and people with a postgraduate education are most tolerant. But even with all of these differences, most people in every group think homosexuality is wrong.

Opinion on the issue of allowing homosexuals in the military is much more closely divided than is opinion on the morality of homosexuality. In 1992, half of Americans supported the ban, while 43 percent were in favor of lifting it. The strongest opposition came from within the military: 74 percent of enlisted personnel supported the ban; only 18 percent wanted it ended.

However, attitudes toward gays and lesbians in the military are not the same as feelings about them in other occupations. In 1992 large majorities felt that it was all right to hire homosexuals as salespersons, doctors, high school teachers, and members of the president's cabinet. In 1993 the public was evenly split as to whether "civil rights laws" should be extended to "include homosexuals."

Clearly, public opinion on this matter is complicated and changing. Labels such as *liberal* and *conservative* are not very precise.

SOURCES: *The American Enterprise* (March/April 1993): 82, 83; the National Opinion Research Center; the Gallup Organization; *The Gallup Poll Monthly* (April 1993): 33.

but on the whole there is a substantial amount of agreement. Three categories in particular have proved useful.

The first category involves questions about government policy with regard to the *economy*. We will describe as liberal those persons who favor government efforts to ensure that everyone has a job, to spend more money on medical and educational programs, and to increase rates of taxation for well-to-do persons.

The second involves questions about *civil rights* and race relations. We will describe as liberal those who favor strong federal action to desegregate schools, to increase hiring opportunities for minorities, to provide compensatory programs for minorities, and to enforce civil rights laws strictly.

The third involves questions about public and political *conduct*. We will describe as liberal those who are tolerant of protest demonstrations, who favor legalizing marijuana and in other ways wish to "decriminalize" so-called victimless crimes, who emphasize protecting the rights of the accused over punishing criminals, and who see the solution to crime in eliminating its causes rather than in getting tough with offenders.

Analyzing Consistency

Now, it is obvious that people can take a liberal position on one of these issues and a conservative position on another without feeling in the slightest degree "inconsistent." Several studies, such as those by Herbert McClosky and John Zaller and by Seymour Martin Lipset and Earl Raab, show that this is exactly what most people do.[37]

This fact does not mean that people are unideological but that we need more than two labels to describe their ideology. If we considered all possible combinations of the three sets of views described above, we would have nine categories of opinion; if people always stuck with whichever category they were in, we would need nine different ideological labels to describe those people.

To invent those labels and describe the people who have those views would take countless pages and bore the reader to tears. To avoid all that pain

and suffering, let's use just two sets of views—those on economic policy and those on personal conduct—and describe the kinds of people that have each of the four combinations (liberal or conservative on each set). The data are from a study by William S. Maddox and Stuart A. Lilie.

1. ***Pure liberals:***[38] These people are liberal on both economic policy and personal conduct. They want the government to reduce economic inequality, regulate business, tax the rich heavily, cure the (presumably) economic causes of crime, allow abortions, protect the rights of the accused, and guarantee the broadest possible freedoms of speech and press.

Number: In 1994 about 17 percent of the population were pure liberals.

Traits: Pure liberals are more likely than the average citizen to be young, college-educated, and either Jewish or nonreligious. They voted heavily against Ronald Reagan.

2. ***Pure conservatives:*** These people are conservative on both economic and conduct issues. They want the government to cut back on the welfare state, allow the market to allocate goods and services, keep taxes low, lock up criminals, and curb forms of conduct they regard as antisocial.

Number: In 1994 about 28 percent of the population were pure conservatives.

Traits: Pure conservatives are more likely than the average citizen to be older, to have higher incomes, to be white, and to live in the Midwest. They voted overwhelmingly for Ronald Reagan.

3. ***Libertarians:*** These people are conservative on economic matters and liberal on social ones. The common theme is that they want a small, weak government—one that has little control over either the economy or the personal lives of citizens.

Number: In 1994 about 21 percent of the population were libertarians.

Traits: Libertarians are more likely than the average citizen to be young, college-educated,

Thinking

*Public Opinion on Abortion:
Liberal, Conservative, or Neither?*

The media often depict abortion as a hotly divisive issue that pits pro-choice liberals against pro-life conservatives. But numerous surveys indicate that public opinion on abortion transcends conventional ideological definitions. The politics of abortion are complex because most people's ideas and feelings about abortion are complex. For example:

• Between 1975 and 1996 the majority of Americans believed that abortion should be legal "only under certain circumstances." There were no national majorities either for the position that abortion should be "legal under any circumstances" or for the position that it should be "illegal in all circumstances."[a]

• Between 1973 and 1989 most Americans *favored* a woman's right to obtain a legal abortion if her health was seriously endangered by the pregnancy, if she became pregnant as the result of rape, or if there was a strong chance of a serious defect in the baby.[b]

• Over the same years most Americans *opposed* a woman's right to obtain a legal abortion for any of the following reasons: she had a low income (or was unable to afford more children), she was unmarried and did not want to marry the child's father, or she was married but did not want to have any more children.[b]

• Democratic leaders and activists tend to be strongly pro-choice; their

Republican counterparts tend to be strongly pro-life. But rank-and-file members of the two parties hold strikingly similar views on the issue. In surveys taken from 1984 through 1988, of those who identified themselves as strongly committed Democrats, 34 percent said they favored abortion for any reason and 66 percent opposed abortion on demand. Among strong Republicans the distribution was identical—34 percent in favor, 66 percent opposed.[c]

• Jewish voters, women with postgraduate degrees, and persons with no religion are the most consistently pro-choice; born-again Christian vot-

ers, Asian-Americans, and persons who did not graduate from high school are the most strongly pro-life.[d] However, even among these groups there are many individual differences of opinion.

SOURCES: (a) *The American Enterprise* (May/June 1992), p. 99, citing surveys by the Gallup Organization. (b) *Public Opinion* (May/June 1989), p. 37, citing surveys by NORC (1975–1988) and the *Los Angeles Times* (1989). (c) Everett Carll Ladd, "The Partisan Consequences," *Public Opinion* (May/June 1989): 6, analyzing and citing data from NORC surveys (1984–1988). (d) *The American Enterprise* (January/February 1993): 103, citing 1992 surveys by the Voter Research & Surveys Consortium.

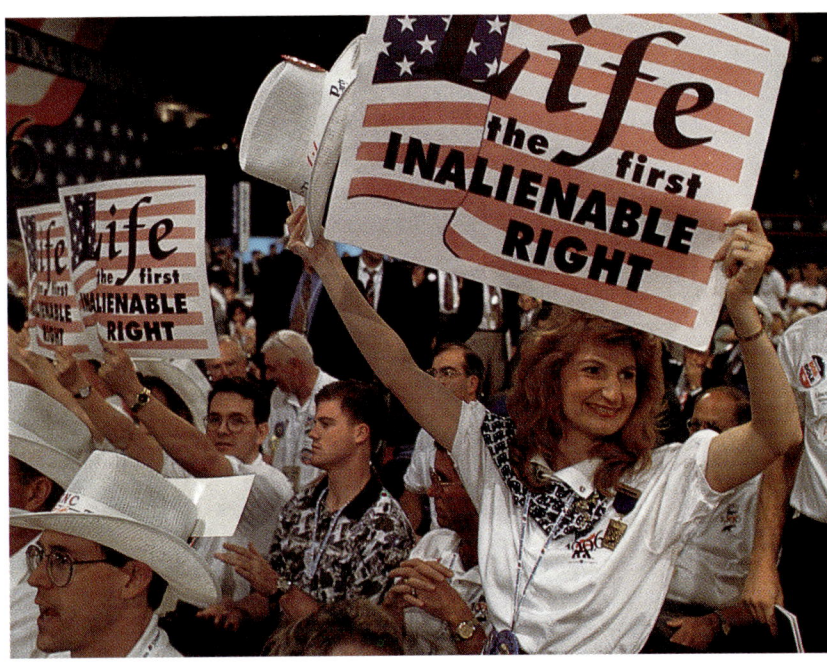

Activists tend to take political ideology more seriously than do most voters.

and white, to have higher incomes and no religion, and to live in the West. They voted for Ronald Reagan, but many also supported the third-party ticket of John Anderson.

4. *Populists:* These people are liberal on economic matters and conservative on social ones. They want a government that will reduce economic inequality and control business, but they also want it to regulate personal conduct, lock up criminals, and permit school prayer.

Number: In 1994 about 24 percent of the population were populists.

Traits: Populists are more likely than the average citizen to be older, poorly educated, low-income, religious, and female and to live in the South or Midwest. In 1980 they voted for Jimmy Carter, but in 1984 they voted for Reagan.[39]

Obviously this classification is an oversimplification. There are many exceptions, and the number of people in each category changes from time to time. Moreover, this categorization leaves out about one-seventh of the population—their views do not fit any of these categories. Nonetheless, it is a useful way to explain how complex are the political ideologies in this country and why such terms as *liberal* and *conservative,* in their "pure" form, only describe the views of relatively few people.

Political Elites

There is one group that can be classified as liberals or conservatives in a pure sense, and it is made up of people who are in the **political elite**. By "elite" we do not mean people who are "better" than others. *Elite* is a technical term used by social scientists to refer to people who have a disproportionate amount of some valued resource—money, schooling, prestige, athletic ability, political power, or whatever. Every society, capitalist or communist, has an elite, because in every society government officials will have more power than ordinary folk, some persons will make more money than others, and some people will be more popular than others. (In the former Soviet Union they even had an official name for the political elite—the *nomenklatura*.)

In this country we often refer to the political elite as "activists"—people who hold office, run for office, work in campaigns or on newspapers, lead interest groups and social movements, and speak out on public issues. Being an activist is not an all-or-nothing proposition; people display differing degrees of activism, from full-time politicians to persons who occasionally get involved in a campaign (see Chapter 6). But the more a person is an activist, the more likely he or she will display ideological consistency on the conventional liberal-conservative spectrum.

The reasons for this greater consistency seem to be information and peers. First, information: in general, the better informed people are about politics and the more interest they take in politics, the more likely they are to have consistently liberal or conservative views.[40] This higher level of information and interest may lead them to find relationships among issues that others don't see and to learn from the media and elsewhere what are the "right" things to believe. This does not mean that there are no differences within liberal elites (or within conservative ones), only that the differences occur within a liberal (or conservative) consensus that is more well defined, more consistent, and more important to those who share it than would be the case among ordinary citizens.

Second, peers: politics does not make strange bedfellows. On the contrary, politics is a process of likes attracting likes. The more active you are in politics, the more you will associate with people who agree with you on some issues; and the more time you spend with those people, the more your other views will shift to match theirs.

The greater ideological consistency of political elites can be seen in Congress. As we shall note in Chapter 11, Democratic members of Congress tend to be consistently liberal, and Republican members of Congress tend to be consistently conservative—

far more consistently than Democratic voters and Republican voters. By the same token, we shall see in Chapter 7 that the delegates to presidential nominating conventions are far more ideological (liberal in the Democratic convention, conservative in the Republican one) than is true of voters who identify with the Democratic or Republican parties.

Is There a "New Class"?

Some writers have speculated that political elites now represent a "new class" in American politics. The old classes were those who owned the means of production (the capitalists) and those who were employed by those owners (the workers). The "new class" consists of people who possess certain advantages conferred not by the power, resources, and growth of business but by the power, resources, and growth of government.[41]

Politicians, bureaucrats, members of the media, interest-group leaders—these people and others like them have, it is claimed, a stake in the growth of government. Because of that, they often have liberal (that is, progovernment) views even though they also have high incomes. The emergence of the new class helps explain, in this theory, why affluent people are not as consistently conservative as they were in the 1940s and 1950s.

It is true, as we have already seen, that many well-off people are liberals. That these people benefit from big government may be one explanation for this fact. But there is another explanation: the spread of higher education.

High levels of schooling, especially at the postgraduate level, tend to make people more liberal. This was not always the case. For example, in the 1940s and 1950s a clear majority of Harvard students, and probably of most college students, preferred Republican candidates for president.[42] For whatever reason, things are different now. Some people with law degrees and Ph.D.'s may favor government because they get grants and jobs from it, but most people probably favor it because they have acquired an ideology that is consistent with a more activist government.

In any event, it is striking how strongly postgraduate education affects political preferences. John McAdams has analyzed the voting results for several presidential, gubernatorial, and senatorial elections and for various state referenda elections on issues such as the death penalty, school busing, nuclear energy, gun control, environmental protection, and the Equal Rights Amendment. In each and every case he discovered that those with a postgraduate education were much more likely to take a liberal position, even after holding constant age, race, and income.[43]

On the basis of his findings, McAdams suggests that the middle class in the United States has been split in two—one part he calls the "traditional middle class," and the other he calls the "new class" (though it might more appropriately be called the "liberal middle class").[44] The traditional middle class consists of people who often have gone to college but not graduate school and who live in the suburbs, go to church, are well disposed toward business, have conservative views on social issues, and usually vote Republican. The liberal middle class is more likely to consist of people who have a postgraduate education, live in or near big cities, are critical of business, have liberal views on social issues, and usually vote Democratic. The cleavage between the traditional and the liberal middle class has many of the same causes as the growing rift between orthodox and progressive ideologies discussed in Chapter 4.

As we shall see in Chapter 7, the strain within the middle class has been particularly felt by the Democratic party. That strain has made it harder to hold together the coalition (often called the New Deal coalition) that once made that party so strong, a coalition among blue-collar workers, southerners, blacks, and intellectuals. Increasingly the workers and white southerners have displayed conservatism on social issues, while members of the liberal middle class have displayed liberalism on these issues. Each side has a label for the other: the workers in the Democratic party call the members of the liberal middle class the "cheese and white wine set," while the people in the liberal middle class call the workers "Joe Six-Pack."

Political Elites, Public Opinion, and Public Policy

Though the elites and the public see politics in very different ways, and though there are often intense antagonisms between the two groups, the elites influence public opinion in at least two important ways.

First, elites, especially those in or having access to the media (see Chapter 10), raise and frame political issues. At one time environmentalism was not on the political agenda; at a later time not only was it on the agenda, it was up near the top of government concerns. At some times the country had little interest in what we should do in South Africa or Central America; at other times the government was preoccupied with these matters. Though world events help shape the political agenda, so also do political elites. A path-breaking study by John Zaller shows in fact that elite views shape mass views by influencing both what issues capture the public's attention and how those issues are debated and decided.[45]

Second, elites state the norms by which issues should be settled. (A **norm** is a standard of right or proper conduct.) By doing this, they help determine the range of acceptable and unacceptable policy options. For example, elites have for a long time emphasized that racism is wrong. Of late they have emphasized that sexism is wrong. Over a long period, the steady repetition of views condemning racism and sexism will at least intimidate, and perhaps convince, those of us who are racist and sexist.

A recent example of this process has been the public discussion of AIDS and its relationship to homosexuality. The initial public reaction to AIDS was one of fear and loathing. But efforts to quarantine people infected with AIDS were met with firm resistance from the medical community and from other policy elites. The elites even managed to persuade some legislatures to bar insurance companies from testing insurance applicants for the disease.

There are limits to how much influence elites can have on the public. For instance, elites do not define economic problems—people can see for themselves that there is or is not unemployment, that there is or is not raging inflation, that there are or are not high interest rates. Elite opinion may shape the policies, but it does not define the problem. Similarly, elite opinion has little influence on whether we think there is a crime or drug problem; it is, after all, *our* purses being snatched, cars being stolen, and children being drugged. On the other hand, elite opinion does define the problem as well as the policy options with respect to most aspects of foreign affairs; the public has little firsthand experience with which to judge what is going on in Panama or Iraq.

Because elites affect how we see some issues and determine how other issues get resolved, it is important to study the differences between elite and public opinion. But it is wrong to suppose that there is one elite, unified in its interests and opinions. Just as there are many publics, and hence many public opinions, there are many elites, and hence many different elite opinions. Whether there is enough variety of opinion and influence among elites to justify calling our politics "pluralist" is one of the central issues confronting any student of government.

SUMMARY

"Public opinion" is a slippery notion, partly because there are many publics, with many different opinions, and partly because opinion on all but relatively simple matters tends to be uninformed, unstable, and sensitive to different ways of asking poll questions.

The chief sources of political opinion are the family, religion, information, and schooling. Once, occupation (or income) was a central determinant of opinion, but with the spread of higher education, the connection between occupational status (or income) and opinion is no longer quite as close.

The chief source of cleavages in opinion are race and ethnicity, class (in which schooling is an important component), and region.

Americans are divided by their political ideologies but not along a single liberal-conservative di-

mension. There are several kinds of issues on which people may take "liberal" or "conservative" positions, and they often do not take the same position on all issues. Just using two kinds of issues—economic and social—it is possible to define four kinds of ideologies: pure liberal, pure conservative, libertarian, and populist.

Political elites are much more likely to display a consistently liberal or consistently conservative ideology. Elites are important because they have a disproportionate influence on public policy and even an influence on mass opinion (through the dissemination of information and the evocation of political norms).

KEY TERMS

John Q. Public   *p. 113*

middle America   *p. 113*

silent majority   *p. 113*

social status   *p. 117*

religious tradition   *p. 117*

gender gap   *p. 118*

poll   *p. 122*

random sample   *p. 122*

sampling error   *p. 123*

liberal   *p. 132*

conservative   *p. 132*

political ideology   *p. 131*

libertarians   *p. 135*

populists   *p. 137*

political elite   *p. 137*

norm   *p. 139*

SUGGESTED READINGS

Dionne, E. J. *Why Americans Hate Politics.* New York: Simon and Schuster, 1991. Misnamed, this book actually describes the emergence of various elite ideologies since the 1960s and why, in the author's view, none is relevant to actually solving problems.

Erikson, Robert S., and Kent L. Tedin. *American Public Opinion.* 5th ed. Boston: Allyn and Bacon, 1995. An excellent summary of how opinion is measured, what it shows, and how it affects politics.

Jennings, M. Kent, and Richard G. Niemi. *The Political Character of Adolescence: The Influence of Families and Schools.* Princeton, N.J.: Princeton University Press, 1974. A study of political attitudes among high school students.

——. *Generations and Politics.* Princeton, N.J.: Princeton University Press, 1981. A study of persistence and change in the political views of young adults and their parents.

Key, V. O., Jr. *The Responsible Electorate.* Cambridge, Mass.: Harvard University Press, 1966. An argument, with evidence, that American voters are not fools.

Lipset, Seymour Martin. *Political Man: The Social Bases of Politics.* Garden City, N.Y.: Doubleday, 1959. An exploration of the relationship between society, opinion, and democracy in America and abroad.

Nie, Norman H., Sidney Verba, and John R. Petrocik. *The Changing American Voter.* Cambridge, Mass.: Harvard University Press, 1976. Traces shifts in American voter attitudes since 1960.

Zaller, John. *The Nature and Origins of Mass Opinion.* Cambridge, England: Cambridge University Press, 1992. A pathbreaking study of how the public forms an opinion, illustrating the ways in which elite views help shape mass views.

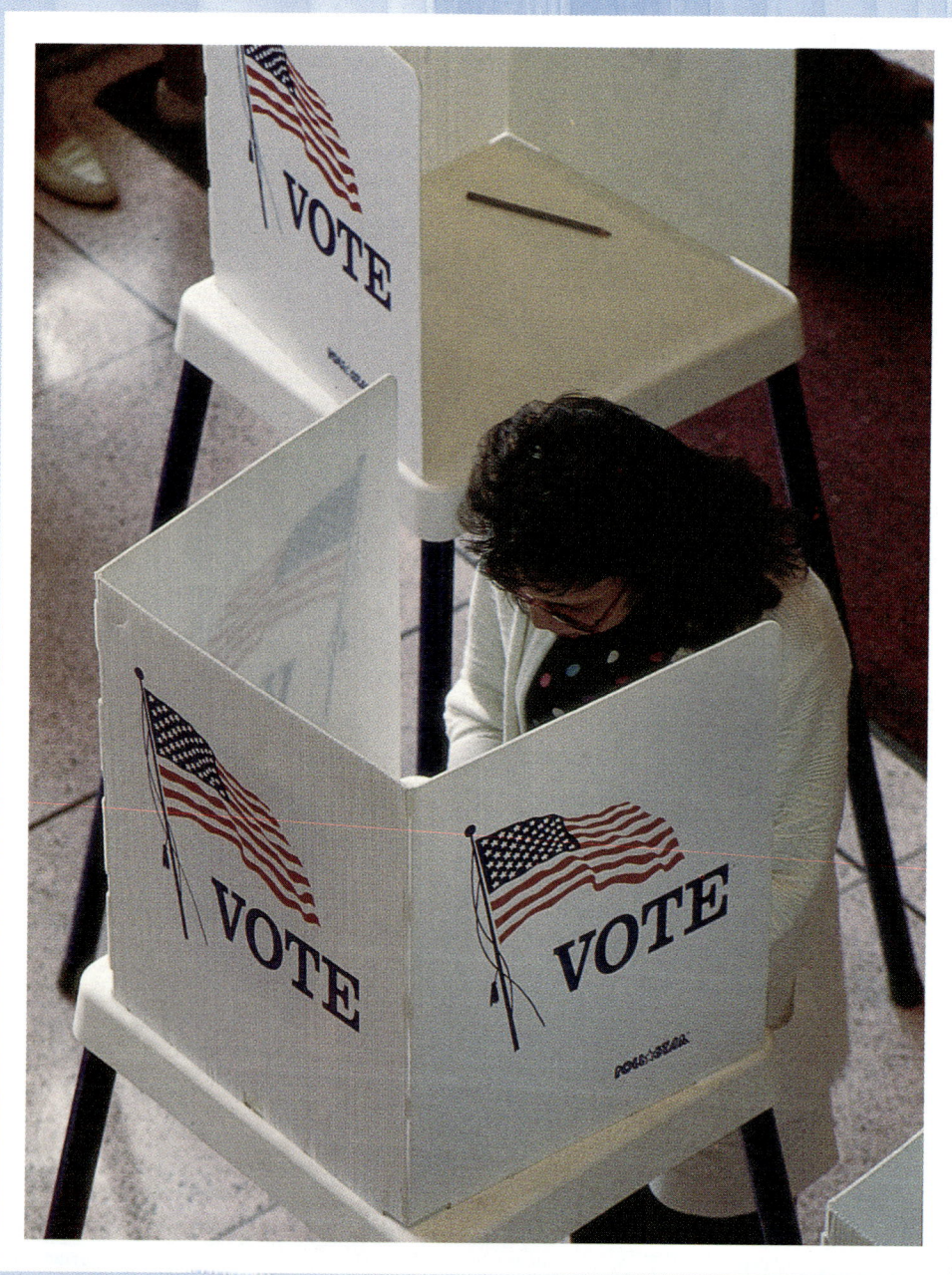

6

Political Participation

★ The problem of nonvoting

★ The rise of the American electorate

★ Voter turnout

★ Who participates?

★ Different forms of participation

★ Causes of participation

Americans are often embarrassed by their low rate of participation in national elections. Data such as those shown in Figure 6.1 on page 144 are frequently used to make the point: whereas well over 80 percent of the people vote in many European elections, only about half of the people vote in American presidential elections (and a much smaller percentage vote in congressional contests). Many observers blame this low turnout on voter apathy and urge the government and private groups to mount campaigns to get out the vote.

There are only three things wrong with this view. First, it is a misleading description of the problem; second, it is an incorrect explanation of the problem; and third, it proposes a remedy that won't work.

A Closer Look at Nonvoting

First, let's look at how best to describe the problem. The conventional data on voter turnout here and abroad are misleading, because they compute participation rates by two different measures. Figure 6.1 shows what proportion of the **registered voters** in various European nations went to the polls, but it shows what percentage of the **voting-age population** in the United States went to the polls. In this country only two-thirds of the voting-age population is registered to vote. To understand what this means, look at Table 6.1 on page 144. In column A are several countries ranked in terms of the percentage of the voting-age population that voted in the 1984 national election. As you can see, the United States, where 52.6 percent voted, ranked near the bottom; only Switzerland was lower. Now look at column B, where the same countries are ranked in terms of the percentage of registered voters who participated in the last national election. The United States, where almost 87 percent of registered voters turned out at the polls, is now up in the middle of the pack.[1]

Second, let's consider a better explanation for the problem. Apathy on election day is clearly not the source of the problem. Of those who are regis-

143

tered, the overwhelming majority vote. The real source of the participation problem in the United States is that a relatively low percentage of the adult population is registered to vote.

Third, let's look at how to cure the problem. Mounting a get-out-the-vote drive wouldn't make much difference. What would make a difference is a plan that would get more people to register to vote. But doing that does not necessarily involve overcoming the "apathy" of unregistered voters. Some people may not register because they don't care about politics or their duty as citizens. But there are other explanations for being unregistered. In this country the entire burden of registering to vote falls on the individual voters. They must learn how and when and where to register; they must take the time and trouble to go someplace and fill out a registration form; and they must reregister in a new county

or state if they happen to move. In most European nations registration is done for you, automatically, by the government. Since it is costly to register in this country and costless to register in other countries, it should not be surprising that fewer people are registered here than abroad.

In 1993 Congress passed a law designed to make it easier to register to vote. Known as the **motor-voter bill**, the law requires states to allow people to register to vote when applying for driver's licenses and to provide registration through the mail and at some state offices that serve the disabled or provide public assistance (such as welfare checks). As we can see in Figure 6.2, some 49 million voting-age people who were not registered to vote had driver's licenses or state-issued identification cards. The motor-voter bill took effect in 1995. In just two months, 630,000 new voters signed up in twenty-seven states. It ap-

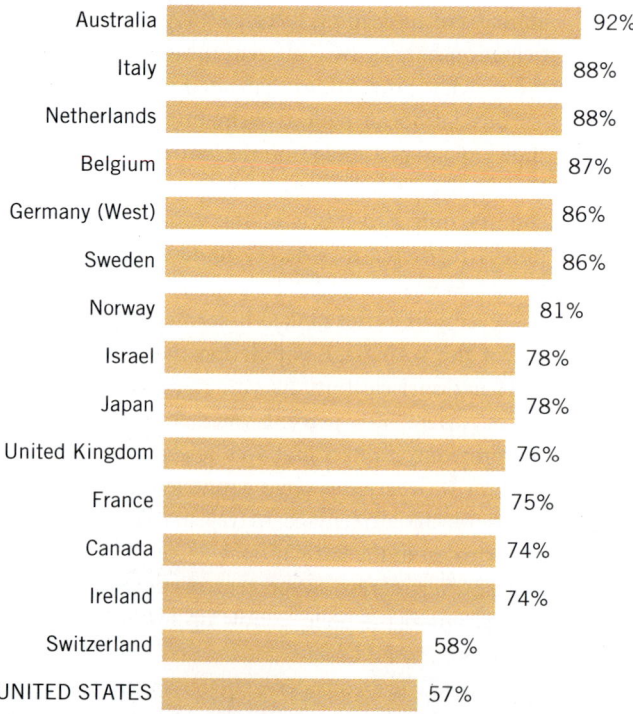

FIGURE 6.1   Average Voter Turnout from the 1950s to 1980s

Country	Turnout
Australia	92%
Italy	88%
Netherlands	88%
Belgium	87%
Germany (West)	86%
Sweden	86%
Norway	81%
Israel	78%
Japan	78%
United Kingdom	76%
France	75%
Canada	74%
Ireland	74%
Switzerland	58%
UNITED STATES	57%

SOURCE: Russell J. Dalton and Martin P. Wattenberg, "The Not So Simple Act of Voting," in *Political Science: The State of the Discipline,* ed. Ada Finifter, 2nd ed. (Washington, D.C.: APSA, 1993), 210. Reprinted by permission of American Political Science Review.

TABLE 6.1   **Two Ways of Calculating Voting Turnout**

A — Turnout as Percentage of Voting-Age Population		B — Turnout as Percentage of Registered Voters	
Austria	89.3%	Belgium	94.6%
Belgium	88.7	Australia	94.5
Sweden	86.8	Austria	91.6
Netherlands	84.7	Sweden	90.7
Australia	83.1	New Zealand	89.0
Denmark	82.1	West Germany	88.6
Norway	81.8	Netherlands	87.0
West Germany	81.1	UNITED STATES	86.8
New Zealand	78.5	France	85.9
France	78.0	Denmark	83.2
United Kingdom	76.0	Norway	82.0
Japan	74.4	United Kingdom	76.3
Canada	67.4	Japan	74.5
Finland	63.0	Canada	69.3
UNITED STATES	52.6	Finland	64.3
Switzerland	39.4	Switzerland	48.3

SOURCE: Adapted from tables in David Glass, Peverill Squire, and Raymond Wolfinger, "Voter Turnout: An International Comparison," *Public Opinion* (December–January 1984); 50, 52. Reprinted with permission of American Enterprise Institute for Public Policy Research.

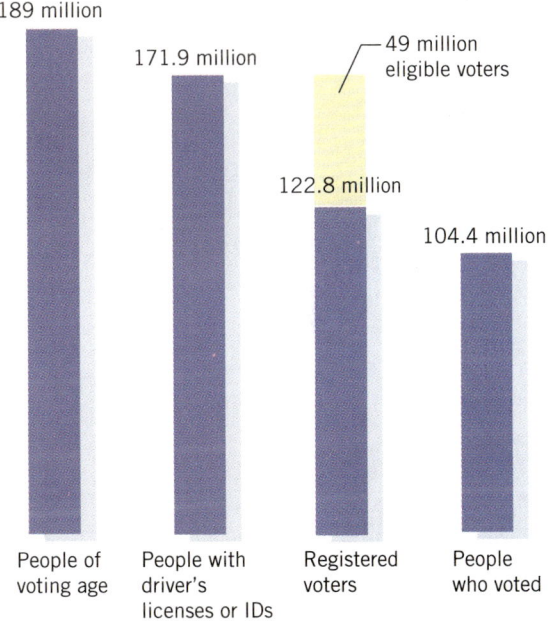

MOTOR VOTER
REGISTRATION INSTRUCTIONS

You must complete steps 1-3. Failure to provide this information may jeopardize your registration.

BOX 1 — **Print** your name on the line in box # 1.

BOX 2 — Please read the oath and then sign your name in the grey shaded area next to the RED X. This signature attests that you meet the qualifications of the oath.

BOX 3 — Enter your daytime phone number, and date of birth.

BOX 4 — If you are changing your address, or name, or have been registered to vote before, please write the name and address at which you were previously registered in box 4.

BOX 5 — Do you want to be registered at the address on your current license or I.D. card?
 - If Yes, skip box #5.
 - If No, please write the address where you live in box #5. (You may not use a work address as your residence address.)

BOX 6 — If your mailing address is different from the address where you live please write your mailing address in box #6. (You may not use a work address for mailing purposes.)

BOX 7 — Please sign your name next to the RED X on the lower half of the form.

BOX 8 — Please print your name.

OATH

"I declare that the facts relating to my qualifications as a voter recorded on this voter registration form are true. I am a citizen of the United States, I am not presently denied my civil rights as a result of being convicted of an infamous crime, I will have lived in this state, county, and precinct for thirty days immediately preceding the next election at which I offer to vote, and I will be at least eighteen years of age at the time of voting."

When you apply for a driver's license in the state of Washington, you are given this form so that you can register to vote at the same time. This "motor-voter" idea became the basis of a federal law passed in 1993.

pears that the measure has increased voter registration throughout the country. In many states, the party breakdown among motor-voters has been about even. But some analysts stress that record numbers of new voters have been registering in the South, with the gains concentrated in fast-growing Republican suburbs. Only future elections will tell, but if the motor-voter law does end up helping Republicans more than Democrats, it will be a testimony to our national lawmakers' limited powers of political prognostication: in 1993 the bill was opposed by nearly 90 percent of all congressional Republicans and supported by over 95 percent of all congressional Democrats.

A final point: voting is only one way of participating in politics. It is important (we could hardly be considered a democracy if nobody voted), but it is not all-important. Joining civic associations, supporting social movements, writing to legislators, fighting city hall—all these and other activities are ways of participating in politics. It is possible that,

FIGURE 6.2 The Motor-Voter Bill, 1992

189 million / 171.9 million / 49 million eligible voters / 122.8 million / 104.4 million

People of voting age / People with driver's licenses or IDs / Registered voters / People who voted

NOTE: The voting-age figure includes 11 million illegal aliens and 600,000 convicted felons who are not eligible to vote. It does not include about 600,000 Americans overseas who are eligible to vote.
SOURCE: Richard Sammon, "Senate Filibuster Kills Threat, Clears 'Motor-Voter' Bill," *Congressional Quarterly* (May 15, 1993): 1221.

by these measures, Americans participate in politics *more* than most Europeans—or anybody else, for that matter. Moreover, it is possible that low rates of registration indicate that people are reasonably well satisfied with how the country is governed. If 100 percent of all adult Americans registered and voted (especially under a system that makes registering relatively difficult), it could mean that people are deeply upset about how things are run. In short, it is not at all clear whether low voter turnout is a symptom of political disease or a sign of political good health.

The important question about participation is not how much participation there is but how different kinds of participation affect the kind of government we get. This question cannot be answered just by looking at voter turnout, the subject of this chapter; it also requires us to look at the composition and activities of political parties, interest groups, and the media (the subjects of later chapters).

Nonetheless, voting is important. To understand why participation in American elections takes the form that it does, we must first understand how laws have determined who shall vote and under what circumstances.

The Rise of the American Electorate

It is ironic that relatively few citizens vote in American elections, since it was in this country that the mass of people first became eligible to vote. At the time the Constitution was ratified, the vote was limited to property owners or taxpayers, but by the administration of Andrew Jackson it had been broadened to include virtually all white male adults. Only in a few states did property restrictions persist: they were not abolished in New Jersey until 1844 or in North Carolina until 1856. And, of course, black males could not vote in many states, in the North as well as the South, even if they were not slaves. Women could not vote in most states until the twentieth century; Chinese-Americans were widely denied the vote; and being in prison is grounds for losing the franchise even today. Aliens, on the other hand, were often allowed to vote if they had at least begun the process of becoming a citizen. By 1880 only an estimated 14 percent of all adult males in the United States could not vote; in England in the same period about 40 percent of adult males were disfranchised.[2]

In the first years of the republic, voting was frequently restricted to male property owners.

From State to Federal Control

Initially it was left entirely to the states to decide who could vote and for what offices. The Constitution gave to Congress only the right to pick the day on which presidential electors would gather and to alter state regulations regarding congressional elections. The only provision of the Constitution requiring a popular election was the clause in Article I stating that members of the House of Representatives be chosen by the "people of the several states."

Because of this permissiveness, early federal elections varied greatly. Several states picked their members of the House at large (that is, statewide) rather than by district; others used districts but elected more than one representative from each. Still others had their elections in odd-numbered years, and some even required that a congressional candidate win a majority, rather than simply a plurality, of votes to be elected (when that requirement was in effect, runoff elections—in one case as many as twelve—were necessary). Furthermore, presidential electors were at first picked by state legislatures rather than by the voters directly.

Congress, by law and constitutional amendment, has steadily reduced state prerogatives in these matters. In 1842 a federal law required that all members of the House be elected by districts; other laws over the years required that all federal elections be held in even-numbered years on the Tuesday following the first Monday in November.

The most important changes in elections have been those that extended the suffrage to women, blacks, and eighteen-year-olds and made mandatory the direct popular election of United States senators. The Fifteenth Amendment, adopted in 1870, said that the "right of citizens of the United States to vote shall not be denied or abridged by the United States or by any state on account of race, color, or previous condition of servitude." Reading those words today,

After the Civil War, while Union forces were still in control, blacks began to vote in the South, as here in Richmond, Virginia, in 1871.

When Reconstruction ended in 1876, black voting shrank under the attack of white supremacists.

TABLE 6.2   **Voter Registration in the South**

						Percentage of Voting-Age Population That Is Registered							
		Ala.	Ark.	Fla.	Ga.	La.	Miss.	N.C.	S.C.	Tenn.	Tex.	Va.	Total
1960	White	63.6	60.9	69.3	56.8	76.9	63.9	92.1	57.1	73.0	42.5	46.1	61.1
	Black*	13.7	38.0	39.4	29.3	31.1	5.2	39.1	13.7	59.1	35.5	23.1	29.1
1970	White	85.0	74.1	65.5	71.7	77.0	82.1	68.1	62.3	78.5	62.0	64.5	62.9
	Black	66.0	82.3	55.3	57.2	57.4	71.0	51.3	56.1	71.6	72.6	57.0	62.0
1986	White	77.5	67.2	66.9	62.3	67.8	91.6	67.4	53.4	70.0	79.0	60.3	69.9
	Black	68.9	57.9	58.2	52.8	60.6	70.8	58.4	52.5	65.3	68.0	56.2	60.8

* Includes other minority races.

SOURCE: Voter Education Project, Inc., of Atlanta, Georgia, as reported in *Statistical Abstract of the United States, 1990,* 264.

one would assume that they gave blacks the right to vote. That is not what the Supreme Court during the 1870s thought that they meant. By a series of decisions, it held that the Fifteenth Amendment did not necessarily confer the right to vote on anybody; it merely asserted that if someone was denied that right, the denial could not be explicitly on the grounds of race. And the burden of proving that it was race that led to the denial fell on the black who was turned away at the polls.[3]

This interpretation opened the door to all manner of state stratagems to keep blacks from voting. One was a **literacy test** (a large proportion of former slaves were illiterate); another was a requirement that a **poll tax** be paid (most former slaves were poor); a third was the practice of keeping blacks from voting in primary elections (in the one-party South the only meaningful election was the Democratic primary). To allow whites who were illiterate or poor to vote, a **grandfather clause** was added to the law, saying that you could vote, even though you did not meet the legal requirements, if you or your ancestors voted before 1867 (blacks, of course, could not vote before 1867). When all else failed, blacks were intimidated, threatened, or harassed if they showed up at the polls.

There began a long, slow legal process of challenging in court each of these restrictions in turn. One by one, the Supreme Court set most of them aside. The grandfather clause was declared unconsti-

tutional in 1915,[4] and the **white primary** finally fell in 1944.[5] Some of the more blatantly discriminatory literacy tests were also overturned.[6] The practical result of these rulings was slight: only a small proportion of voting-age blacks were able to register and vote in the South, and they were found mostly in the larger cities. A dramatic change did not begin until 1965, with the passage of the Voting Rights Act. This act suspended the use of literacy tests and authorized the appointment of federal examiners who could order the registration of blacks in states and counties (mostly in the South) where fewer than 50 percent of the voting-age population were registered or had voted in the last presidential election. It also provided criminal penalties for interfering with the right to vote.

Though implementation in some places was slow, the number of blacks voting rose sharply throughout the South. For example, in Mississippi the proportion of voting-age blacks who registered rose from 5 percent to over 70 percent in just ten years (see Table 6.2). These changes had a profound effect on the behavior of many white southern politicians: Governor George Wallace stopped making prosegregation speeches and began courting the black vote.

Women were kept from the polls by law more than by intimidation, and when the laws changed, women almost immediately began to vote in large numbers. By 1915 several states, mostly in the West, had begun to permit women to vote. But it was not until the Nineteenth Amendment to the Constitution was ratified in 1920, after a struggle lasting many decades, that women generally were allowed to vote. At one stroke the size of the eligible voting population almost doubled. Contrary to the hopes of some and the fears of others, no dramatic changes occurred in the conduct of elections, the identity of the winners, or the substance of public policy. Initially, at least, women voted more or less in the same manner as men, though not quite as frequently.

The political impact of the youth vote was also less than expected. The Voting Rights Act of 1970 gave eighteen-year-olds the right to vote in federal elections, beginning January 1, 1971. It also contained a provision lowering the voting age to eighteen in state elections, but the Supreme Court declared this unconstitutional. As a result a constitutional amendment, the Twenty-sixth, was proposed by Congress and ratified by the states in 1971. The 1972 elections became the first in which all people between the ages of eighteen and twenty-one could cast ballots (before then, four states had allowed those under twenty-one to vote). About 25 million people suddenly became eligible to participate in elections, but their turnout was lower than for the population as a whole, and they did not flock to any particular party or candidate. George McGovern, the Democratic candidate for president in 1972, counted heavily on attracting the youth vote but did not succeed. Most young voters supported Nixon (though college students favored McGovern).[7]

National standards now govern almost every aspect of voter eligibility. All persons eighteen years of age and older may vote; there may be no literacy test or poll tax; states may not require residency of more than thirty days in that state before a person may vote; areas with significant numbers of citizens not speaking English must give those people ballots written in their own language; and federal voter registrars and poll watchers may be sent into areas where less than 50 percent of the voting-age population participates in a presidential election. Before 1961 residents of the District of Columbia could not vote in presidential elections; the Twenty-third Amendment to the Constitution gave them this right.

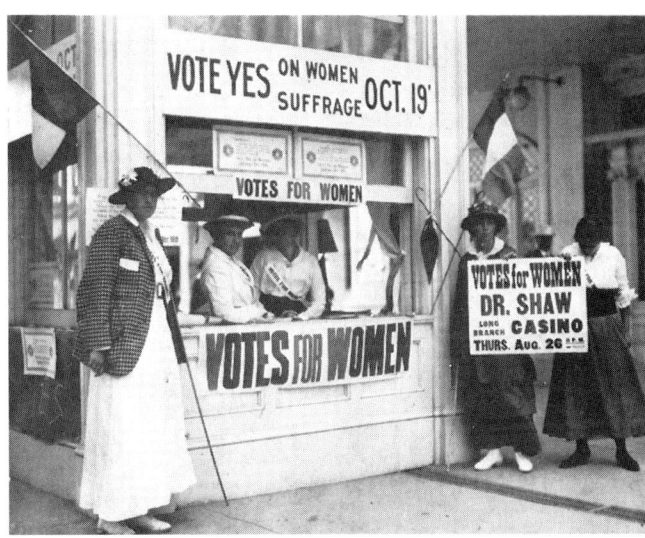

The campaign to win the vote for women nationwide succeeded with the adoption of the Nineteenth Amendment in 1920.

Voting Turnout

Given all these legal safeguards, one might expect that participation in elections would have risen sharply. In fact the proportion of the voting-age population that has gone to the polls in presidential elections has remained about the same—between 50 percent and 60 percent of those eligible—at least since 1932 and appears today to be much smaller than it was in the latter part of the nineteenth century (see Figure 6.3, page 150). In every presidential election between 1860 and 1900, at least 70 percent of the eligible population apparently went to the polls, and in some years (1860 and 1876) over 80 percent seem to have voted. Since 1900 not a single presidential election turnout has reached 70 percent, and on two occasions (1920 and 1924) it did not even reach 50 percent.[8] Even outside the South (where efforts to disfranchise blacks make data on voting turnout especially hard to interpret) turnout seems to have declined: over 84 percent of the voting-age population participated in presidential elections in nonsouthern states between 1884 and 1900, but only 68 percent participated between 1936 and 1960, and even fewer have done so since 1960.[9]

Scholars have vigorously debated the meaning of these figures. One view is that this decline in turn-

FIGURE 6.3   Voter Participation in Presidential Elections, 1860–1996

NOTE: Several southern states did not participate in the 1864 and 1868 elections.
SOURCES: For 1860–1928: Bureau of the Census, *Historical Statistics of the United States, Colonial Times to 1970*, Pt. 2, 1071; 1932–1992: *Statistical Abstract of the United States, 1992*, 517.

out, even allowing for the shaky data on which the estimates are based, has been real and is the result of a decline of popular interest in elections and a weakening of the competitiveness of the two major parties. During the nineteenth century, according to this theory, the parties fought hard, worked strenuously to get as many voters as possible to the polls, afforded the mass of voters a chance to participate in party politics through caucuses and conventions, kept the legal barriers to participation (such as complex registration procedures) low, and looked forward to close, exciting elections. After 1896, by which time the South had become a one-party Democratic region and the North heavily Republican, both parties became more conservative, national elections usually resulted in lopsided victories for the Republicans, and citizens began to lose interest in politics because it no longer seemed relevant to their needs. The parties ceased functioning as organizations to mobilize the mass of voters and fell under the control of leaders, mostly conservative, who resisted mass participation.[10]

There is another view, however. It argues that the decline in voter turnout has been more apparent than real. Though elections were certainly more of a popular sport in the nineteenth century than they are

today, the parties were no more democratic then than now, and voters then may have been more easily manipulated. Until around the beginning of the twentieth century, voting fraud was commonplace because it was easy to pull off. The political parties, not the government, printed the ballots; they were often cast in public, not private, voting booths; there were few serious efforts to decide who was eligible to vote, and the rules that did operate were easily evaded.

Under these circumstances it was easy for a person to vote more than once, and the party machines made heavy use of these "floaters," or repeaters. "Vote early and often" was not a joke but a fact. "Big Tim" Sullivan, a boss in New York's old Tammany Hall, once had his party's ballots soaked in perfume so that he could use scent as well as sight to ensure that his voters put the right ballot in the right box.[11] The parties often controlled the counting of votes, padding the totals whenever they feared losing. As a result of these machinations, the number of votes counted was often larger than the number cast, and the number cast was in turn often larger than the number of individuals eligible to vote. For example, in 1888 West Virginia officially claimed that there were 147,408 persons in the state eligible to vote, but mysteriously 159,440 votes were cast in the

CRITICAL Thinking

Voter Turnout: Some Myths and Realities

MYTH	REALITY
Turnout is declining because the poor are dropping out of politics.	Turnout is declining because *all* groups—the poor, the middle class, and the rich—have become less likely to vote.
Today's voters see no differences between Democrats and Republicans.	More voters see more important differences between the parties today than they did in the 1960s.
Nonvoters don't vote because the policies they prefer haven't been debated or adopted.	Voters and nonvoters differ very little in their policy preferences.
Many elections are decided by levels of voter turnout.	Levels of turnout do not, as a rule, make much of a difference in election outcomes.
Registration reform (for example, the "motor-voter" bill, Figure 6.2 on page 145) would definitely help the Democrats and hurt the Republicans.	Nobody really knows, but surveys suggest that the political leanings of voters and nonvoters do not differ enough for the addition of even millions of nonvoters to make much of a partisan impact.

SOURCE: Adapted from Ruy A. Teixeira, "Voter Turnout in America," *The Brookings Review* (Fall 1992): 28–31. Reprinted with permission of the Brookings Institution.

---

presidential election, for a "voter turnout" of 108 percent![12]

Around 1890 the states began adopting the **Australian ballot.** This was a government-printed ballot of uniform size and shape that was cast in secret, created to replace the old party-printed ballots cast in public. By 1910 only three states were without the Australian ballot. Its use cut back on (but certainly did not eliminate) vote buying and fraudulent vote counts.

In short, if votes had been legally cast and honestly counted in the nineteenth century, the statistics on election turnout might well be much lower than the inflated figures we now have.[13] To the extent that this is true, we may not have had a decline in voter participation as great as some have suggested. Nevertheless, most scholars believe that turnout probably did actually decline somewhat after the 1890s. One reason was that voter-registration regulations became more burdensome: there were longer residency requirements; aliens who had begun but not completed the process of becoming citizens could no longer vote in most states; it became harder for

blacks to vote; educational qualifications for voting were adopted by several states; and voters had to register long in advance of the elections. These changes, designed to purify the electoral process, were aspects of the Progressive reform impulse (described in Chapter 7) and served to cut back on the number of persons who could participate in elections.

Strict voter-registration procedures tended, like most reforms in American politics, to have unintended as well as intended consequences. These changes not only reduced fraudulent voting but also reduced voting generally, because they made it more difficult for certain groups of perfectly honest voters—those with little education, for example, or those who had recently moved—to register and vote. This was not the first time, and it will not be the last, that a reform designed to cure one problem created another.

Even after all the legal changes are taken into account, there has still been a decline in citizen participation in elections. Between 1960 and 1980 the proportion of voting-age people casting a ballot in presidential elections fell by about 10 percentage points, a drop that cannot be explained by how ballots were printed or how registration rules were rewritten. By the same token, these factors cannot explain the 5 percent increase in turnout from the 1988 to the 1992 presidential election (from 50 to 55 percent).

Who Participates in Politics?

To understand better why voting turnout declined and what, if anything, that decline may mean, we must first look at who participates in politics.

Forms of Participation

Voting is by far the most common form of political participation, while giving money to a candidate and being a member of a political organization are the least common. Many Americans exaggerate how frequently they vote or how active they are in politics. In a study by Sidney Verba and Norman Nie, 72 percent of those interviewed said that they vote "regularly" in presidential elections. Yet we know that since 1960, on average only 56 percent of the

FIGURE 6.4 Nonpolitical Voluntary Activity Among Citizens

Activity	Percent active
Affiliated with non-political organization	68%
Attend meeting of non-political organization	37%
Attend church services once a month or more	57%
Attend church services weekly	32%
Give time to church work	25%
Church contribution	62%
Give time to charitable work	36%
Charitable contribution	66%

Percent active

voting-age population has actually cast presidential ballots. Careful studies of this discrepancy suggest that 8 to 10 percent of Americans interviewed misreport their voting habits: they claim to have voted when in fact they have not. Young, low-income, less-educated, and nonwhite people are most likely to misreport than others.[14] If people misreport their voting behavior, it is likely that they also misreport—that is, exaggerate—the extent to which they participate in other ways.

Indeed, most research shows that "politics is not at the heart of the day-to-day life of the American people."[15] Work, family, church, and other voluntary activities come first, both in terms of how Americans spend their time and in terms of the money they donate. For example, a recent study by Verba and others found that a higher proportion of citizens take part in nonpolitical than political activities: "More citizens reported giving time to church-related or charitable activities than indicated contacting a government official or working informally on a community problem, two of the most frequent forms of political participation beyond the vote"[16] (see Figure 6.4).

In an earlier study, Verba and Nie analyzed the ways in which people participate in politics and came up with six forms of participation that are characteristic of six different kinds of U.S. citizens. About one-fifth (22 percent) of the population is completely inactive: they rarely vote, they do not get involved in organizations, and they probably do not even talk about politics very much. These inactives typically have little education and low incomes and are relatively young. Many of them are black. At the opposite extreme are the complete **activists,** constituting about one-ninth of the population (11 percent). These people are highly educated, have high incomes, and tend to be middle-aged rather than young or old. They tend to participate in all forms of politics.

Between these extremes are four categories of limited forms of participation. The voting specialists are people who vote but do little else; they tend not to have much schooling or income and to be substantially older than the average person. Campaigners not only vote but also like to get involved in campaign activities. They are better educated than the average voter, but what seems to distinguish

FIGURE 6.5   Voter Turnout in Presidential Elections, by Age, Schooling, and Race, 1964–1992

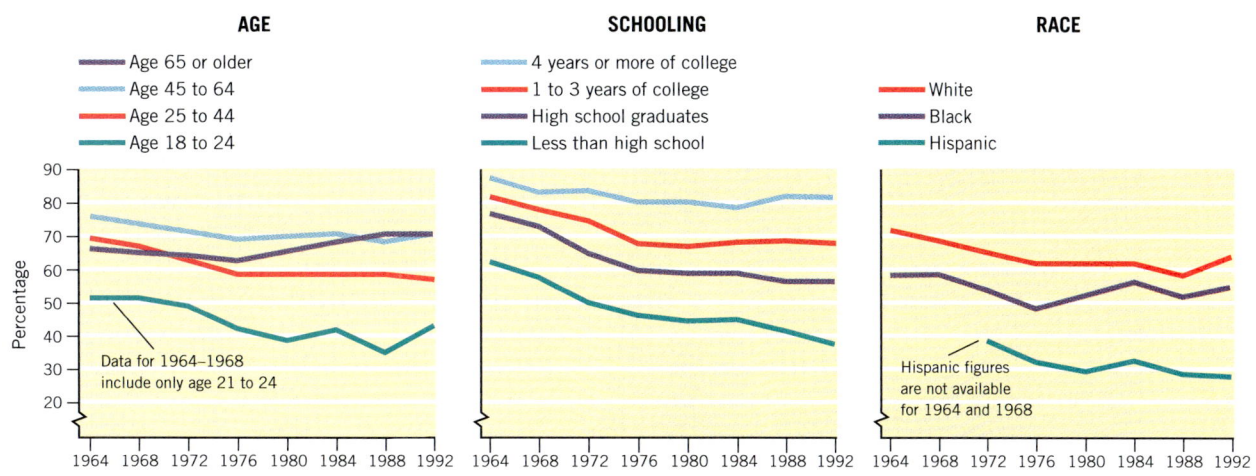

AGE

- Age 65 or older
- Age 45 to 64
- Age 25 to 44
- Age 18 to 24

Data for 1964–1968 include only age 21 to 24

SCHOOLING

- 4 years or more of college
- 1 to 3 years of college
- High school graduates
- Less than high school

RACE

- White
- Black
- Hispanic

Hispanic figures are not available for 1964 and 1968

SOURCE: Gary R. Orren, "The Linkage of Policy to Participation," in *Presidential Selection,* ed. Alexander Heard and Michael Nelson (Durham, N.C.: Duke University Press, 1987) and tabulated by Daron Shaw; data for 1992 are from *Statistical Abstract of the United States, 1993,* 283.

them most is their interest in the conflicts, passions, and struggle of politics, their clear identification with a political party, and their willingness to take strong positions. Communalists are much like campaigners in social background but have a very different temperament: they do not like the conflict and tension of partisan campaigns. They tend to reserve their energies for community activities of a more nonpartisan nature—forming and joining organizations to deal with local problems and contacting local officials about these problems. Finally, there are some parochial participants who do not vote and stay out of election campaigns and civic associations but are willing to contact local officials about specific, often personal, problems.[17]

The Causes of Participation

Whether participation takes the form of voting or being a complete activist, it is higher among persons who have gone to college than among persons who have not and higher among persons who are over thirty-five years of age than among persons who are under thirty-five. (The differences in voting rates for these groups are shown in Figure 6.5.) Even after controlling for differences in income and occupation, the more schooling one has, the more likely

one is to vote. Of course it may not be schooling itself that causes participation but something that is strongly correlated with schooling, such as high levels of political information.[18]

In fact the differences in participation that are associated with schooling (or its correlates) are probably even greater than reported in this figure, since we have already seen that less-educated persons exaggerate how frequently they vote. An excellent study of turnout concludes that people are more likely to vote when they have those personal qualities that "make learning about politics easier and more gratifying."[19]

Religious involvement also increases political participation. If you are a regular churchgoer who takes your faith seriously, the chances are that you will be more likely to vote and otherwise take part in politics than if you are a person of the same age, sex, income, and educational level who does not go to church. Church involvement leads to social connectedness, teaches organizational skills, increases one's awareness of larger issues, and puts one in contact with like-minded people.[20]

Men and women vote at about the same rate, but blacks and whites do not. Although at one time that difference was largely the result of discrimination, today it can be explained mostly by differences

In the 1840 presidential campaign, political parties strove to increase political participation with slogans ("Tippecanoe and Tyler Too!") and less subtle appeals (free hard cider).

in social class—blacks are poorer and have less schooling, on average, than whites. However, among people of the same socioeconomic status—that is, having roughly the same level of income and schooling—blacks tend to participate *more* than whites.[21]

Because the population has become younger (due to the baby boom of the 1960s and 1970s) and because blacks have increased in numbers faster than whites, one might suppose that these demographic changes would explain why the turnout in presidential elections has gone down a bit since the early 1960s. And they do—up to a point. But there is another factor that ought to make turnout go *up*—schooling. Since college graduates are much

likely to vote than those with less educational experience, and since the college-graduate proportion of the population has gone up sharply, turnout should have risen. But it has not. What is going on here?

Perhaps turnout has declined despite the higher levels of schooling due to the rising level of distrust of government. We saw in Chapter 4 that, well into the 1990s, more and more people were telling pollsters that they lacked confidence in political leaders. Rising distrust seems a plausible explanation for declining turnout, until one looks at the facts. The data show that there is *no correlation* between expressing distrust of political leaders and not voting.[22] People who are cynical about our leaders are just as likely to vote as people who are not.

As we have seen, turnout is powerfully affected by the number of people who have registered to vote; perhaps in recent years it has become harder to register. But in fact exactly the opposite is true. Since 1970 federal law has prohibited residency requirements longer than thirty days for presidential elections, and a Supreme Court decision in 1972 held that requirements much in excess of this were invalid for state and local elections.[23] By 1982 twenty-one states and the District of Columbia, containing about half the nation's population, had adopted laws permitting voters to register by mail. In four states—Maine, Minnesota, Oregon, and Wisconsin—voters can register and vote on the same day, all at once.

What is left? Several small things. First, the greater youthfulness of the population, together with the presence of growing numbers of blacks and other minorities, has pushed down the percentage of voters who are registered and vote.

Second, political parties today are no longer as effective as they once were in mobilizing voters, ensuring that they are registered, and getting them to the polls. As we shall see in Chapter 7, the parties once were grassroots organizations with which many people strongly identified. Today the parties are somewhat distant, national bureaucracies with which most of us do not identify very strongly.

Third, the remaining impediments to registration exert some influence. One study estimated that if every state had registration requirements as easy as the most permissive states, turnout in a presidential election would be about 9 percent higher.[24] The experience of the four states where you can register and vote on the same day is consistent with this: in 1976, when same-day registration first went into effect, three of the four states that had it saw their turnout go up by 3 or 4 percent, while those states that did not have it saw their turnout go down.[25] If an even bolder plan were adopted, such as the Canadian system of universal enrollment, whereby the government automatically puts on the voter list every eligible citizen, there would probably be some additional gain in turnout.[26]

Fourth, if *not* voting is costless, then there will be more nonvoting. Several nations with higher turnouts than ours make voting compulsory. For example, in Italy a person who does not vote has his or her government identification papers stamped *"DID NOT VOTE."*[27] In Australia and other countries fines can be levied on nonvoters. As a practical matter such fines are rarely imposed, but just the threat of them probably induces more people to register and vote.

Finally, voting (and before that, registering) will go down if people do not feel that elections matter much. There has been a decline in the proportion of people who feel that elections matter a lot, corresponding to the decrease in those who do participate in elections.

In short there are a number of reasons why we register and vote less frequently here than do citizens of other countries. Two careful studies of all these factors found that almost all of the differences in turnout among twenty-four democratic nations, including the United States, could be explained by party strength, automatic registration, and compulsory voting laws.[28]

The presence of these reasons does not necessarily mean that somebody ought to do something about them. We could make registration automatic—but that might open the way to voter fraud, since here people move around and change names often enough to enable some of them, if they wanted to, to vote more than once. We could make voting compulsory, but Americans have an aversion to government compulsion in any form and probably would object strenuously to any plan for making citizens carry identification papers that the government would stamp.

Democrats and Republicans fight over various measures designed to increase registration and voting because one party (usually the Democrats)

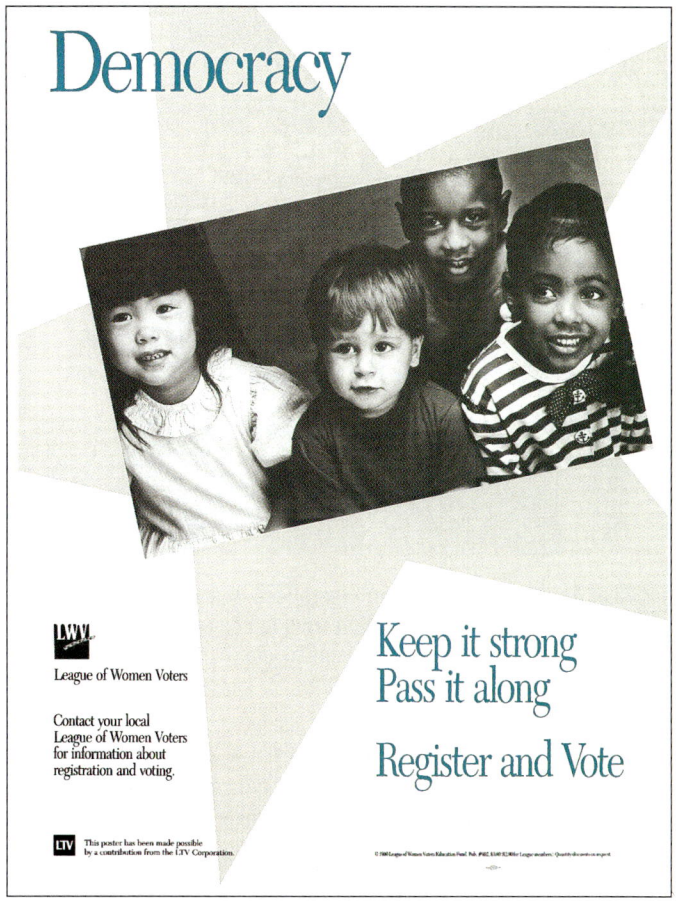

Registering to vote will become easier now that the "motor-voter" law has been passed.

thinks that higher turnout will help them and the other (usually the Republicans) fears that higher turnout will hurt them. In fact no one really knows whether either party would be helped or hurt by higher voter turnout.

Nonvoters are more likely than voters to be poor, black or Hispanic, or uneducated. However, the proportion of nonvoters with some college education rose from 7 percent in 1960 to 18 percent in 1980. In addition, the percentage of nonvoters who held white-collar jobs rose from 33 percent to 50 percent in the same period. Many of these better-off nonvoters might well have voted Republican had they gone to the polls. And even if the turnout rates only of blacks and Hispanics had increased, there would not have been enough votes added to the Democratic column to affect the outcome of the 1984 or 1988 presidential elections.[29]

Latino Americans tend to participate less frequently in elections than other groups. This billboard tries to change that: "Don't leave yourself out. Arm yourself. Register to vote."

Both political parties try to get a larger turnout among voters likely to be sympathetic to them, but it is hard to be sure that these efforts will produce real gains. If one party works hard to get its nonvoters to the polls, the other party will work just as hard to get its people there. For example, when Jesse Jackson ran for the presidency in 1984, registration of southern blacks increased, but registration of southern whites increased even more.

The Meaning of Participation Rates

Americans may be voting less, but there is evidence that they are participating more. As Table 6.3 shows, between 1967 and 1987 the percentage of Americans who voted regularly in presidential and local elections dropped, but the percentage who participated increased for ten out of twelve other political activities, steeply in some cases. Thus, although Americans are going to the polls less, they are campaigning, contacting government officials, and working on community issues more. And while the proportion of the population that votes is lower in the United States than in many other democracies, the percentage of Americans who engage in one or more political activities beyond voting is higher (see Table 6.4).

Public demonstrations such as sit-ins and protest marches have become much more common in recent decades than they once were. By one count there were only 6 demonstrations per year between 1950 and 1959 but over 140 per year between 1960 and 1967. Though the demonstrations of the 1960s began with civil rights and antiwar activists, public protests were later employed by farmers demanding government aid, truckers denouncing the national speed limit, disabled persons seeking to dramatize their needs, parents objecting to busing to achieve racial balance in the schools, conservationists hoping to block nuclear power plants, and construction workers urging that nuclear power *not* be blocked.[30]

Although we vote at lower rates here than people do abroad, the meaning of our voting is different. For one thing, we elect far more public officials than do the citizens of any other nation. One scholar has estimated that there are 521,000 elective offices in the United States and that almost every week of the year there is an election going on somewhere in this country.[31]

A citizen of Massachusetts, for example, votes not only for the U.S. president but also for two senators, the state governor, the member of the House of Representatives for his or her district, a state representative, a state senator, the state attorney general, the state auditor, the state treasurer, the secretary of state, a county commissioner, a sheriff, and clerks of various courts, as well as (in the cities) for the mayor, the city councillor, and school committee members and (in towns) for selectmen, town-meeting members, a town moderator, library trustees, health board members, assessors, water commissioners, the town clerk, housing authority members, the tree warden, and the commissioner of the public burial ground. (There are probably others that we have forgotten.)

In many European nations, by contrast, the voters get to make just one choice once every four or five years: they can vote for or against a member of parliament. When there is only one election for one office every several years, that election is bound to assume more importance to the voter than many elections for scores of offices. But one election for one office probably has less effect on how the nation is governed than many elections for thousands of offices. Americans may not vote at high rates, but

TABLE 6.3 **How Citizens Participate**

Specific Activity	Percentage Engaging in Fourteen Acts of Participation, 1967 and 1987		
	1967	1987	Absolute Change
VOTING			
Regularly vote in presidential elections	66%	58%	−8%
Always vote in local elections	47	35	−12
CAMPAIGNING			
Persuade others how to vote	28	32	+4
Actively work for party or candidate	26	27	+1
Attend political meetings or rallies	19	19	0
Contribute money to a party or candidate	13	23	+10
Participate in a political club	8	4	−4
CONTACTING GOVERNMENT			
Contact local officials: issue-based	14	24	+10
Contact state or national officials: issue-based	11	22	+11
Contact local officials: particularized	7	10	+3
Contact state or national officials: particularized	6	7	+1
TAKING ACTION IN THE COMMUNITY			
Work with others on a local problem	30	34	+4
Actively participate in community problem-solving organization	31	34	+3
Form group to help solve local problem	14	17	+3

SOURCE: Reprinted by permission of the publisher from *Voice and Equality: Civic Voluntarism in American Politics* by Sidney Verba, Kay Lehman Scholzman and Henry A. Brady, Cambridge, Mass.: Harvard University Press, Copyright © 1995 by the Presidents and Fellows of Harvard College. Data from p. 72.

TABLE 6.4 **Participation Beyond Voting in Fourteen Democracies**

Percentage of adult population who engaged in some form of political participation beyond voting in 1990

Britain	77%	Italy	56
Sweden	74	Iceland	55
Norway	68	Netherlands	54
UNITED STATES	66	Belgium	51
Denmark	59	Ireland	46
France	57	Finland	38
West Germany	57	Spain	32

SOURCES: U.S. percentage calculated from Sidney Verba et al., *Voice and Equality: Civic Voluntarism in American Politics* (Cambridge, Mass.: Harvard University Press, 1995), 83; other percentages calculated from Max Kaase and Kenneth Newton, *Beliefs in Government*, vol. 5 (New York: Oxford University Press, 1995), 51.

FIGURE 6.6   Voter Turnout in National Elections in Three Countries, by Occupation

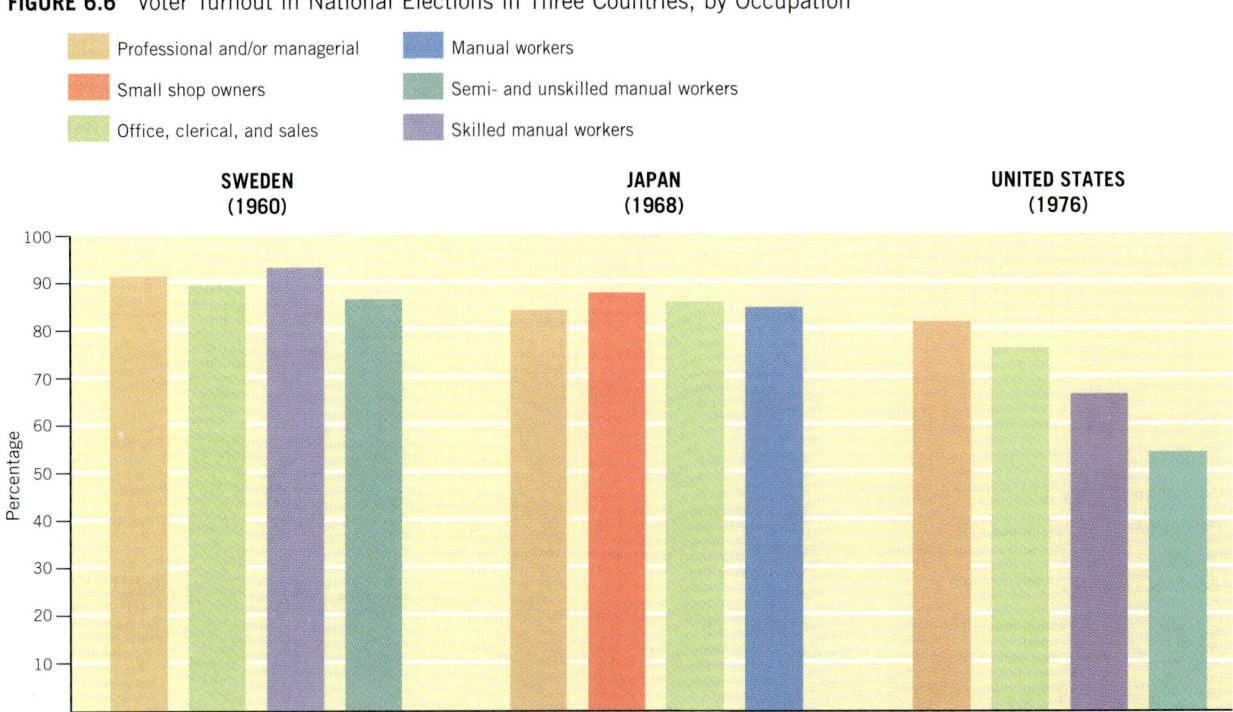

SOURCES: For Japan: The Society for Promotion of Clean Elections, Survey of 34th General Election, 1976. Reprinted from an unpublished paper by Gary Orren, "Political Participation and Public Policy: The Case for Institutional Reform" (Cambridge, Mass., November 1985), 16A. Data on U.S. and Sweden from *No Easy Choice* by Samuel P. Huntington and Joan M. Nelson (Cambridge, Mass.: Harvard University Press, 1976), 88.

voting affects a far greater part of the political system here than abroad.

The kinds of people who vote here are also different from those who vote abroad. Since almost everybody votes in many other democracies, the votes cast there mirror almost exactly the social composition of those nations. Since only slightly over half of the voting-age population turns out even for presidential elections here, the votes cast in the United States may not truly reflect the country.

That is in fact the case. Figure 6.6 shows the proportion of each major occupational group that usually votes in Japan, Sweden, and the United States. Each occupational group—or, if you prefer, social class—votes at about the same rate in Japan and Sweden. But in the United States the turnout is heavily skewed toward higher-status persons: those in professional, managerial, and other white-collar occupations are overrepresented among the voters.

Although nonwhites and Latinos are the fastest-growing segment of the population, they tend to be the most underrepresented groups among American

voters. Little is known about the relationship between political participation and such variables as command of the language and involvement in non-political institutions that provide information or impart skills relevant to politics (such as workplaces and voluntary associations). However, such factors could be quite important in explaining differences in political participation rates among poor and minority citizens. As we can see in Figure 6.7, although less involved than whites, blacks participate in voting and political activities at higher rates than do Latino citizens. One excellent study suggests that these differences are due in part to the fact that blacks are more likely than Latinos to be members of churches that stimulate political interest, activity, and mobilization.[32] Language barriers also make it harder for many Latinos to get in touch with a public official, serve on local governing boards, and engage in other forms of political participation in which command of English is an asset. The lower participation rates of minority citizens are likely compounded by their being disproportionately of

FIGURE 6.7 Electoral and Nonelectoral Political Participation Among Anglo-Whites, African-Americans, and Latinos

Each bar shows the percentage of an ethnic group that:

- Anglo-whites
- African-Americans
- Latinos

Votes
- 76.8%
- 69.1%
- 53.5%

Works on campaigns
- 8.3%
- 11.6%
- 7.4%

Contributes to campaigns
- 15.5%
- 9.8%
- 6.9%

Gets involved in community issues
- 20.2%
- 23.1%
- 17.2%

Serves on a community governing board
- 3.2%
- 2.3%
- 4.1%

Contacts public officials
- 36.9%
- 22.8%
- 15.1%

Protests
- 5.2%
- 9.3%
- 3.8%

NOTE: "Community activists" were defined as persons who got "involved informally on local community issues"; "board members" were defined as persons who served in an "unpaid capacity on a local community governing board, for example, a school or zoning board"; "contactors" were defined as persons who contacted public officials; and "protesters" were defined as persons who attended "protests or other demonstrations." "Latinos" includes Latino citizens plus Latino noncitizens living in the U.S.
SOURCE: Adapted from Sidney Verba, Kay Lehman Scholzman, Henry Brady, and Norman H. Nie, "Race, Ethnicity, and the Resources for Participation: the Role of Religion," paper delivered at the 1992 Annual Meeting of the American Political Science Association, September 3–6, 1992. Reprinted by permission.

low socioeconomic status compared to white Americans.

Exactly what these differences in participation mean in terms of how the government is run is not entirely clear. But since we know from evidence presented in the last chapter that upper-status persons are more likely to have an ideological view of politics, it may suggest that governance here is a bit more sensitive not only to the interests of upper-status white people but also to their (conflicting) ideologies.

SUMMARY

The popular view that Americans don't vote as a result of apathy is not quite right. The correct view is that we don't register to vote (but once registered, we do vote) and that there are many factors having nothing to do with apathy that shape our participation rates—age, race, party organization, the barriers to registration, and popular views about the significance of elections.

The most powerful determinants of participation are schooling and information; the next most powerful is age. Race makes a difference, but black participation rates approximate white rates once you control for socioeconomic status.

Compared to other nations, Americans vote at lower rates but more frequently and for many more offices, so elections make a bigger difference in the conduct of public affairs here than abroad. We also engage somewhat more frequently than do people abroad in various nonelectoral forms of participation.

Civic Participation: Is America "Bowling Alone"?

In *Democracy in America*, Alexis de Tocqueville marveled at the extent to which the Americans of the 1830s participated in all sorts of civic associations. "Americans of all ages, all stations in life, and all types of disposition," the Frenchman famously observed, "are forever forming associations. There are not only commercial and industrial associations in which all take part, but others of a thousand different types—religious, moral, serious, futile, general or restricted, immensely large or very minute.... Nothing, in my view, deserves more attention than the intellectual and moral associations in America." Tocqueville warned that if Americans ever lost "the principle of association," they would both lose their freedom and enervate democracy. For the less associations do, the more government does, and the more government "stands in the place of associations, the more will individuals, losing the notion of combining together, require its assistance.... The morals and the intelligence of a democratic people would be as much endangered as its business and manufactures if the government ever wholly usurped the place" of civic associations.

As we have explained in this chapter, turnout in national elections has de-

clined somewhat in this century. But has this decline in political participation been matched by a decline in civic associations? Whatever the state of political participation in America, don't Americans continue to form, join, and participate in "a thousand different types" of private associations?

In an essay published in the January 1995 issue of *The Journal of Democracy*, political scientist Robert D. Putnam argued that fewer and fewer Americans were joining clubs, associations, and other groups that promote civic trust and cooperation. He depicted contemporary America as being in a state of "democratic disarray" due to "a broad and continuing erosion of civic engagement that began a quarter century ago." Data from the National Opinion Research Center (NORC), he argued, showed a 25 percent membership drop in all types of groups (fraternal groups, sports clubs, literary clubs, church-related associations, and so on) since 1974. As a metaphor for the broader decline of civic participation which he believed he had uncovered, he highlighted the fact that since 1980, league bowling had dropped by 40 percent. Americans, once a nation of joiners, were now "bowling alone."

Putnam's "bowling alone" thesis at-

tracted a tremendous amount of media attention. President Clinton and a number of Republican leaders invoked it. Numerous journalists and others have cited it as evidence that the vigorously civic-minded America that persisted from the days of Tocqueville through the end of the Second World War was gone for good. And many have written and spoken with great alarm about the ostensible deterioration in the country's civic participation.

Are they right? How might one test the evidence that civic participation in America is in a steep and steady decline?

First, look at the NORC data. At right are the participation rates for various types of groups for 1974 and 1994.

In seven of the areas measured by NORC, group or club participation was down, but often by only a slight margin. In six cases participation was up. More people might have been bowling alone, but more people were also participating in other sporting activities—like, for example, the tens of millions of people associated with the country's 261,000 teams registered in softball leagues, up from only 19,000 teams in 1967.

The single biggest decline in civic participation reported by NORC was in church attendance. This decline in par-

---

KEY TERMS

registered voters   *p. 143*

voting-age population   *p. 143*

motor-voter bill   *p. 144*

literacy test   *p. 148*

poll tax   *p. 148*

grandfather clause   *p. 148*

white primary   *p. 148*

Australian ballot   *p. 151*

activists   *p. 152*

SUGGESTED READINGS

Burnham, Walter Dean. *Critical Elections and the Mainsprings of American Politics.* New York: Norton, 1970. An argument about the decline of voter participation, linking it to changes in the economic system.

Conway, M. Margaret. *Political Participation in the United* ticipation is offset, however, by the fact that the number of Americans who claim membership in a church or synagogue has nonetheless remained between 65 and 75 percent of the population since 1937 (in 1995 it was 70 percent). And nearly 60 percent of Americans still attend church services once a month or more. Moreover, today many of the country's fastest-growing religious groups are loosely organized evangelical denominations that often do not have stable memberships or a large, formal network of churches.

Group/Club	Participation Rates	
	1974	1994
Veterans	9.0%	7.8%
Labor	16.5	11.8
Political	4.5	4.7
Sports	17.9	21.8
School	17.7	16.1
Hobby	9.8	9.2
Service	9.0	10.1
Nationality	3.6	3.5
Farm	4.3	3.7
Church	42.1	33.4
Literary/Art	9.4	9.8
Professional	13.2	18.7
Other	10.4	10.7

Next, remember that membership and participation in organizations can fluctuate for many different reasons. For example, what about participation in such civic organizations as the Parent-Teacher Association (PTA)? Putnam reported a 56 percent decline in PTA membership from the early 1960s through the early 1980s and gloomily concluded that the drop represented a decrease of "parental involvement in the educational process" and the loss of "a particularly valuable form of social capital." But, in fact, PTA membership increased by 28 percent between 1982 and 1994. Moreover, the ups and downs in PTA membership partly reflect changes in the size of the school-age population. Also, as many different surveys have shown, parental involvement in education in America is high. And if anything, it has been increasing of late. For example, the percentage of parents who attended school board meetings in 1995 (39 percent) was more than twice the percentage that did so in 1969 (16 percent).

Have you bowled alone lately? Find Putnam's essay in your school's library. Read it. Compare and contrast his data and arguments about civic participation with those of the authors cited in the source note below. Do you agree with Putnam that "by almost every measure, American's direct engagement in politics and government has fallen steadily and sharply over the last generation"? What is the evidence for and against his conclusion that every "year over the last decade or two, millions more have withdrawn from the affairs of their communities"? To what, if any, groups, clubs, or other associations do you belong? Should one count, say, Internet users' groups as "civic associations"? How important are religious, political, literary, sporting, or other associations in your own life, and how do you judge their importance to your community? Do you suppose that "the principle of association" has proven as vital to the health of American democracy as Tocqueville supposed it would be?

SOURCES: Alexis de Tocqueville, *Democracy in America* (New York: Vintage Books, 1990), vol. I, especially pp. 191–192, and vol. II, especially pp. 106–108; Robert D. Putnam, "Bowling Alone: America's Declining Social Capital," *The Journal of Democracy* (January 1995), pp. 65–78; Robert J. Samuelson, "Bowling Alone Is Bunk," *Washington Post* (April 10, 1996), sec. A., p. 19; Everett C. Ladd, "The Data Just Don't Show Erosion of America's 'Social Capital,'" *The Public Perspective* (June/July 1996), pp. 1, 5–22; *The Gallup Monthly Poll* (January 1996), p. 22; *The Gallup Monthly Poll* (January 1995), p. 20.

States. 2d ed. Washington, D.C.: *Congressional Quarterly Press,* 1991. Good brief summary of what we need to know about who participates in politics and why.

Orren, Gary R. "The Linkage of Policy to Participation." In *Presidential Selection,* edited by Alexander Heard and Michael Nelson. Durham, N.C.: Duke University Press, 1987. Carefully evaluates various proposals for increasing electoral turnout in the United States.

Teixeira, Ruy. *Why Americans Don't Vote.* Westport, Conn.: Greenwood Press, 1987. Good summary of what we know about nonvoting.

Verba, Sidney, et al. *Voice and Equality: Civic Voluntarism in American Politics.* Cambridge, Mass.: Harvard University Press, 1995.

Verba, Sidney, Norman H. Nie, and Jae-on Kim. *Participation and Political Equality.* Cambridge, England: Cambridge University Press, 1978. Comparative study of political participation in seven nations.

Wolfinger, Raymond E., and Steven R. Rosenstone. *Who Votes?* New Haven, Conn.: Yale University Press, 1980. Excellent analysis of what factors determine turnout.

7

Political Parties

★ Function of parties

★ Comparison with European parties

★ Party history

★ Party structure today

★ Convention delegates: how they are selected and their policy views

★ How parties operate at the local level

★ The two-party system

★ Minor parties

★ Nominating a presidential candidate and the importance of primaries

★ Democrats and Republicans versus the voters

One of the reasons why voter turnout is higher abroad than in this country is that political parties in other democratic nations are more effective at mobilizing voters than here. The sense of being a party member and the inclination to vote the party ticket are greater in France, Italy, or Sweden than in the United States. From this fact you might suppose that political parties here are recent inventions with little experience at organizing and no history of attracting voter identification.

Quite the contrary. American political parties are the oldest in the world, and at one time being a Democrat or a Republican was a serious commitment that people did not make lightly or abandon easily. In those days it would have been hard to find anything in Europe that could match the vote-getting power of such party organizations as those in Chicago, New York, and Philadelphia.

Parties in the United States are relatively weak today, not because they are old but because the laws and rules under which they operate have taken away much of their power at the same time that many voters have lost their sense of commitment to party identification. This weakening has proceeded unevenly, however, because our constitutional system has produced a decentralized party system just as it has produced a decentralized governmental system, with the result that parties in some places are strong and in other places almost nonexistent.

Parties—Here and Abroad

A **political party** is a group that seeks to elect candidates to public office by supplying them with a label—a "party identification"—by which they are known to the electorate.[1] This definition is purposefully broad so that it will include both familiar parties (Democratic, Republican) and unfamiliar ones (Whig, Libertarian, Socialist Worker) and will cover periods in which a party is very strong (having an elaborate and well-disciplined organization that provides money and workers to its candidates) as well as periods in which it is quite weak (supplying nothing but the label to candidates). The label by which a candidate is known may or may not actually be printed on the ballot opposite the candidate's name: in the United States it does appear on the ballot in all national elections but in only a minority of municipal ones; in Australia and Israel (and in Great Britain before 1969) it never appears on the ballot at all.

This definition suggests the three political arenas within which parties may be found. A party exists as a *label* in the minds of the voters, as an *organization* that recruits and campaigns for candidates, and as a *set of leaders* who try to organize and control the legislative and executive branches of government. A powerful party is one whose label has a strong appeal for the voters, whose organization can decide who will be candidates and how their campaigns will be managed, and whose leaders can dominate one or all branches of government.

American parties have become weaker in all three arenas. As a *label* with which voters identify, the parties are probably much weaker than they were in the nineteenth century but only somewhat weaker than they were thirty years ago (see Figure 7.1). In 1952, a total of 22 percent of the voters de-

scribed themselves as "strong" Democrats; by 1992 only 18 percent did. In 1952, a total of 13 percent said that they were "strong" Republicans; in 1992, only 11 percent did. There has been an increase in the proportion of people saying that they either are "independent" or have no preference between the two major parties. (Many of the "independents," of course, lean more to one party than the other, and many of the "no preference" voters simply don't care about politics, period.) After 1980 the number of Republicans increased, owing, apparently, to the popularity of President Reagan; however, scholars are not sure that this increase will last. But the best evidence of weakening party identification is what voters *do*. As we shall see in the next chapter, they increasingly have been voting split tickets—that is, supporting a president from one party and members of Congress from the other.

As a *set of leaders* who organize government, especially Congress, political parties remain somewhat strong in ways that will be described in Chapter 11. As *organizations* that nominate and elect candidates, parties have become dramatically weaker just since the 1960s. In most states parties have very little control over who gets nominated to office. The causes

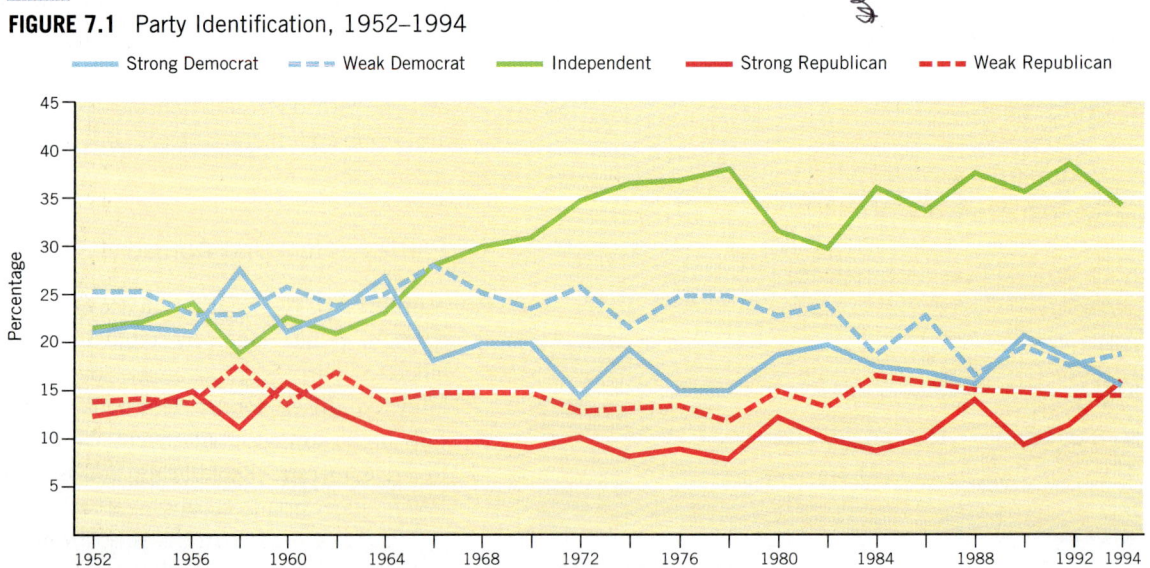

FIGURE 7.1 Party Identification, 1952–1994

SOURCES: For 1952–1987: University of Michigan Survey Research Center (1952–1982) and University of Chicago National Opinion Research Center (1984–1987) as reported in *National Journal* (November 14, 1987), 2866, updated by Daron Shaw; for 1990–1994: ICPSR American National Election Studies, University of Michigan.

Party means more in Italy than in the United States, as is evident from this party rally.

and consequences of that change are the subject of this chapter.

In Europe things are very different. Almost the only way a person can become a candidate for elective office is to be nominated by party leaders. Campaigns are run by the party, using party funds and workers, not by the candidate. Once in office, the elected officials are expected to vote and act together with other members of their party. The principal criterion by which voters choose among candidates is their party identification or label. This has been changing somewhat of late: European parties, like American ones, have not been able to count as heavily as in the past on party loyalty among the voters.

Several factors explain the striking differences between American and European political parties. First, the federal system of government in the United States decentralizes political authority and thus decentralizes political party organizations. For nearly two centuries most of the important governmental decisions were made at the state and local levels—decisions regarding education, land use,

business regulation, and public welfare—and thus it was at the state and local levels that the important struggles over power and policy occurred. Moreover, most people with political jobs—either elective or appointive—worked for state and local government, and thus a party's interest in obtaining these jobs for its followers meant that it had to focus attention on who controlled city hall, the county courthouse, and the state capitol. Federalism, in short, meant that political parties would acquire jobs and money from local sources and fight local contests. This, in turn, meant that the national political parties would be coalitions of local parties, and though these coalitions would have a keen interest in capturing the presidency (with it, after all, went control of large numbers of federal jobs), the national party leaders rarely had as much power as the local ones. The Republican leader of Cuyahoga County, Ohio, for example, could often ignore the decisions of the Republican national chairman and even of the Ohio state chairman.

Political authority in the United States has of late come to be far more centralized: the federal government now makes decisions affecting almost all aspects of our lives, including those—such as schooling and welfare—once left entirely in local hands. Yet the political parties have not become more centralized as a result. If anything, they have become even weaker and more decentralized. One reason for this apparent paradox is that in the United States, unlike in most other democratic nations, political parties are closely regulated by state and federal laws, and these regulations have had the effect of weakening the power of parties substantially. Perhaps the most important of these regulations are those that prescribe how a party's candidates are to be selected.

In the great majority of American states, the party leaders do not select people to run for office; by law those people are chosen by the voters in primary elections. Though sometimes the party can influence who will win a primary contest, in general people running for state or national office in this country owe little to party leaders. In Europe, by contrast, there is no such thing as a primary election—the only way to become a candidate for office is to persuade party leaders to put your name on the ballot. In a later section of this chapter, the impact of the direct primary will be discussed in more detail; for now, it is enough to note that its use removes from the hands of the party leadership its most important source of power over officeholders.

Furthermore, if an American political party wins control of Congress, it does not—as in most European nations with a parliamentary system of government—also win the right to select the chief executive of the government. The American president, as we have seen, is independently elected, and this means that he will choose his principal subordinates not from among members of Congress but from among persons out of Congress. Should he pick a representative or senator for his cabinet, the Constitution requires that person to resign from Congress in order to accept the job. Thus an opportunity to be a cabinet secretary is not an important reward for members of Congress, and so the president cannot use the prospect of that reward as a way of controlling congressional action. All this weakens the significance and power of parties in terms of organizing the government and conducting its business.

Political Culture

The attitudes and traditions of American voters reinforce the institutional and legal factors that make American parties relatively weak. Political parties in this country have rarely played an important part in the life of the average citizen; indeed, one does not usually "join" a party here except by voting for its candidates. In many European nations, on the other hand, large numbers of citizens will join a party, pay dues, and attend regular meetings. Furthermore, in countries such as France, Austria, and Italy, the political parties sponsor a wide range of activities and dominate a variety of associations to which a person may belong—labor unions, youth groups, educational programs, even chess clubs.

In the United States we tend to keep parties separate from other aspects of our lives. As Democrats or Republicans, we may become excited by a presidential campaign, and a few of us may even participate in helping elect a member of Congress or state senator. Our social, business, working, and cultural lives, however, are almost entirely nonpartisan. Indeed, most Americans, unlike many Europeans, would resent partisanship's becoming a conspicuous feature of other organizations to which they belong. All this is a way of saying that American parties play a segmental, rather than comprehensive, role in our lives and that even this role is diminishing as more and more of us proclaim ourselves to be "independents."

The Rise and Decline of the Political Party

Our nation began without parties, and today's parties, though far from extinct, are about as weak as at any time in our history. In between the Founding and the present, however, parties arose and became powerful. We can see this process in four broad periods of party history: when political parties were created (roughly from the Founding to the 1820s); when the more or less stable two-party system emerged (roughly from the time of President Jackson to the Civil War); when parties developed a comprehensive organizational form and appeal (roughly from the Civil War to the 1930s); and fi-

The weakening of parties can be seen in these campaign buttons—they mention the candidates but not the parties.

Two Views of Parties

President George Washington, in his 1796 Farewell Address: "Let me warn you in the most solemn manner against the baneful effects of the spirit of party generally. This spirit . . . exists under different shapes in all government, more or less stifled, controlled, or repressed; but in those of the popular form it is seen in its greatest rankness and is truly their worst enemy."

Political scientist E. E. Schattschneider, in a 1942 book: "Political parties created democracy and . . . modern democracy is unthinkable save in terms of the parties."

Hamilton's policies, it seemed to Hamilton and *his* followers that Jefferson was opposing not just a policy or a leader but also the very concept of a national government. Jefferson, for his part, thought that Hamilton was not simply pursuing bad policies but was subverting the Constitution itself. Before political parties could become legitimate, it was necessary for people to be able to separate in their minds quarrels over policies and elections from disputes over the legitimacy of the new government itself. The ability to make that distinction was slow in coming, and thus parties were objects of profound suspicion, defended, at first, only as temporary expedients.

The first organized political party in American history was made up of the followers of Jefferson, who, beginning in the 1790s, called themselves *Republicans* (hoping to suggest thereby that their opponents were secret monarchists).* The followers of Hamilton kept the label, *Federalist,* that once had been used to refer to all supporters of the new Constitution (hoping to imply that their opponents were "Antifederalists," or enemies of the Constitution).

These parties were loose caucuses of political notables in various localities, with New England being strongly Federalist and much of the South

nally when party "reform" began to alter the party system (beginning in the early 1900s but taking effect chiefly since the New Deal).

The Founding

The Founders disliked parties, thinking of them as "factions" motivated by ambition and self-interest. George Washington, dismayed by the quarreling between Hamilton and Jefferson in his cabinet, devoted much of his Farewell Address to condemning parties. This hostility to party was understandable: the legitimacy and success of the newly created federal government were still very much in doubt. When Jefferson organized his followers to oppose

*The Jeffersonian Republicans were not the party that today we call Republican. In fact, present-day Democrats consider Jefferson to be their founder.

passionately Republican. Jefferson and his ally James Madison thought that their Republican party was a temporary arrangement designed to defeat John Adams, a Federalist, in his bid to succeed Washington in 1796. (Adams narrowly defeated Jefferson, who, under the system then in effect, became vice president because he had the second most electoral votes.) In 1800 Adams's bid to succeed himself intensified party activity even more, but this time Jefferson won and the Republicans assumed office. The Federalists feared that Jefferson would dismantle the Constitution, but Jefferson adopted a conciliatory posture, saying in his inaugural address that "we are all Republicans, we are all Federalists."[2] It was not true, of course: the Federalists detested Jefferson, and some were planning to have New England secede from the Union. But it was good politics, expressive of the need that every president has to persuade the public that, despite partisan politics, the presidency exists to serve all the people.

So successful were the Republicans that the Federalists virtually ceased to exist as a party. Jefferson was reelected in 1804 with almost no opposition; Madison easily won two terms; James Monroe carried sixteen out of nineteen states in 1816 and was reelected without opposition in 1820. Political parties had seemingly disappeared, just as Jefferson had hoped. The weakness of this so-called first party system can be explained by the fact that it was the first: nobody had been born a Federalist or a Republican; there was no ancestral party loyalty to defend; the earliest political leaders did not think of themselves as professional politicians; and the Federalist party had such a limited sectional and class base that it could not compete effectively in national elections. The parties that existed in these early years were essentially small groups of local notables. Political participation was limited, and nominations for most local offices were arranged rather casually.

Even in this early period, the parties, though they had very different views on economic policy and somewhat different class bases, did not represent clear, homogeneous economic interests. Farmers in Virginia were Republicans, but farmers in Delaware were Federalists; the commercial interests of Boston were firmly Federalist, but commercial leaders in urban Connecticut were most likely to be Republican.

When Andrew Jackson ran for president in 1828, over a million votes were cast for the first time in American history. This poster, from the 1832 election, was part of the emergence of truly mass political participation.

From the beginning to the present, elections have created heterogeneous coalitions as Madison had anticipated.

The Jacksonians

What is often called the second party system emerged around 1824 with Andrew Jackson's first run for the presidency and lasted until the Civil War became inevitable. Its distinctive feature was that political participation became a mass phenomenon. For one thing, the number of voters to be reached had become quite large. Only about 365,000 popular votes were cast in 1824. But as a result of laws that enlarged the number of people eligible to vote and of an increase in the population, by 1828 well over a million votes were tallied. By 1840 the figure was well over 2 million. (In England at this time there were only 650,000 eligible voters.) In addition, by 1832 presidential electors were selected by popular vote in virtually every state. (As late as 1816 electors were chosen by the state legislatures, rather than by the people, in about half the states.) Presidential politics had become a truly national, genuinely popular activity; indeed, in many communities election campaigns had become the principal public spectacle.

The party system of the Jacksonian era was built from the bottom up rather than—as during the period of the Founding—from the top down. No change better illustrates this transformation than the abandonment of the system of having caucuses composed of members of Congress nominate presidential candidates. The caucus system was an effort to unite the legislative and executive branches by giving the former some degree of control over who would have a chance to capture the latter. The caucus system became unpopular when the caucus candidate for president in 1824 ran third in a field of four in the general election, and it was completely discredited that same year when Congress denied the presidency to Jackson, the candidate with the greatest share of the popular vote.

To replace the caucus, the party convention was invented. The first convention in American history was that of the Anti-Masonic party in 1831; the first convention of a major political party was that of the anti-Jackson Republicans later that year (it nominated Henry Clay for president). The Democrats held a convention in 1832 that ratified Jackson's nomination for reelection and picked Martin Van Buren as his running mate. The first convention to select a man who would be elected president and who was not already the incumbent president was held by the Democrats in 1836; it chose Van Buren.

Considering the many efforts made in recent years to curtail or even abolish the national nominating convention, it is worth remembering that the convention system was first developed in part as a reform—a way of allowing for some measure of local control over the nominating process. Virtually no other nation adopted this method, just as no other nation was later to adopt the direct primary after the convention system became the object of criticism. It is interesting, but perhaps futile, to speculate on how American government would have evolved if the legislative caucus had remained the method for nominating presidents.

The Civil War and Sectionalism

Though the party system created in the Jacksonian period was the first truly national system, with Democrats (followers of Jackson) and Whigs (opponents of Jackson) fairly evenly balanced in most regions, it could not withstand the deep split in opinion created by the agitation over slavery. Both

The Donkey and the Elephant

Since 1874, when Thomas Nast published political cartoons using these figures, the elephant has been the symbol of the Republican party and the donkey (originally the jackass) the symbol of the Democratic party.

The association of the Democrats with donkeys may have begun with a remark by Ignatius Donnelly, a Republican in the Minnesota legislature, who said that the "Democratic party is like a mule—without pride of ancestry or hope of posterity." An equally uncharitable explanation for the link between Republicans and elephants was offered by Democratic presidential

candidate Adlai Stevenson, who in the 1950s made the observation that "the elephant has a thick skin, a head full of ivory, and as everyone who has seen a circus parade knows, proceeds best by grasping the tail of its predecessor."

SOURCE: Adapted from *Safire's Political Dictionary* by William Safire. Copyright © 1968, 1972, 1978 by William Safire. Reprinted by permission of Random House, Inc. and the author.

Old-Style Party Loyalties

*T*oday we take party loyalties rather lightly. In the latter part of the nineteenth century and well into the twentieth, however, such loyalties were deep and powerful. Brand Whitlock recalls what it meant to be a Republican in Ohio during his youth:

> *In the Ohio of those days it was natural to be a Republican; it was more than that, it was inevitable that one should be a Republican; it was not a matter of intellectual choice, it was a process of biological selection. The Republican party was not a faction, not a group, not a wing, it was an institution, . . . rooted like oak-trees. . . . It was elemental, like gravity, the sun, the stars, the ocean. . . . One became, in Urbana and Ohio for many years, a Republican just as the Eskimo dons fur clothes. It was inconceivable that any self-respecting person should be a Democrat.**

By changing the place to Georgia, the same could have been written about what it meant to be a Democrat.

* From Brand Whitlock, *Forty Years of It* (New York: Appleton, 1914), 27. Quoted in James L. Sundquist, *Dynamics of the Party System* (Washington, D.C.: Brookings Institution, 1973), 91.

In 1968, older party leaders were still to be seen at national conventions, but they were already being replaced by younger activists.

parties tried, naturally, to straddle the issue, since neither wanted to divide its followers and thus lose the election to its rival. But slavery and sectionalism were issues that could not be straddled. The old parties divided and new ones emerged. The modern Republican party (not the old Democratic-Republican party of Thomas Jefferson) began as a third party. As a result of the Civil War, it came to be a major party (the only third party ever to gain major-party status) and to dominate national politics, with only occasional interruptions, for three-quarters of a century.

Republican control of the White House, and to a lesser extent of Congress, was in large measure the result of two events that gave to Republicans a marked advantage in the competition for the loyalties of voters. The first of these was the Civil War. This bitter, searing crisis deeply polarized popular attitudes. Those who supported the Union side became, for generations, Republicans; those who supported the Confederacy, or who had opposed the war, became Democrats.

As it turned out, this partisan division was, for a while, nearly even: though the Republicans usually won the presidency and the Senate, they often lost control of the House. There were many northern Democrats. In 1896, however, another event—the presidential candidacy of William Jennings Bryan—further strengthened the Republican party. Bryan, a Democrat, alienated many voters in the populous northeastern states while attracting voters in the South and Midwest. The result was to confirm and deepen the split in the country, especially North versus South, begun by the Civil War. From 1896 to the 1930s, with rare exceptions, northern states were solidly Republican, southern ones solidly Democratic.

This split had a profound effect on the organization of political parties, for it meant that most states were now one-party states. As a result, competition for office at the state level had to go on *within* a single dominant party (the Republican party in Massachusetts, New York, Pennsylvania, Wisconsin, and elsewhere; the Democratic party in Georgia, Mississippi, South Carolina, and elsewhere). Consequently there emerged two major factions within each party, but especially within the Republican party. One was composed of the party regulars—the professional politicians, the "stalwarts," the Old Guard. They were preoccupied with building up the party machinery, developing party loyalty, and acquiring and dispensing patronage—jobs and other favors—for themselves and their faithful followers. Their great skills were in organization, negotiation, bargaining, and compromise; their great interest was in winning.

The other faction, variously called **mugwumps** or **progressives** (or "reformers"), was opposed to the heavy emphasis on patronage; disliked the party machinery, because it only permitted bland candidates to rise to the top; was fearful of the heavy influx of immigrants into American cities and of the ability of the party regulars to organize them into "machines"; and wanted to see the party take unpopular positions on certain issues (such as free trade). Their great skills lay in the areas of advocacy and articulation; their great interest was in principle.

At first the mugwumps tried to play a balance-of-power role, sometimes siding with the Republican party of which they were members, at other times defecting to the Democrats (as when they bolted the Republican party to support Grover Cleveland, the Democratic nominee, in 1884). But later, as the Republican strength in the nation grew, progressives within that party became less and less able to play a balance-of-power role, especially at the state level. Wisconsin, Michigan, Ohio, and Iowa were solidly Republican; Georgia, the Carolinas, and the rest of the Old South had by 1880 become so heavily Democratic that the Republican party in many areas had virtually ceased to exist. If the progressives were to have any power, it would require, they came to believe, an attack on the very concept of partisanship itself.

The Era of Reform

Progressives began to espouse measures to curtail or even abolish political parties. They favored primary elections to replace nominating conventions, because the latter were viewed as being manipulated by party bosses; they favored nonpartisan elections at the city level and in some cases at the state level as well; they argued against corrupt alliances between parties and businesses. They wanted strict voter-registration requirements that would reduce voting fraud (but would also, as it turned out, keep ordinary citizens who found the requirements cumber-

This was Tammany Hall in its heyday as Democratic party headquarters in Manhattan.

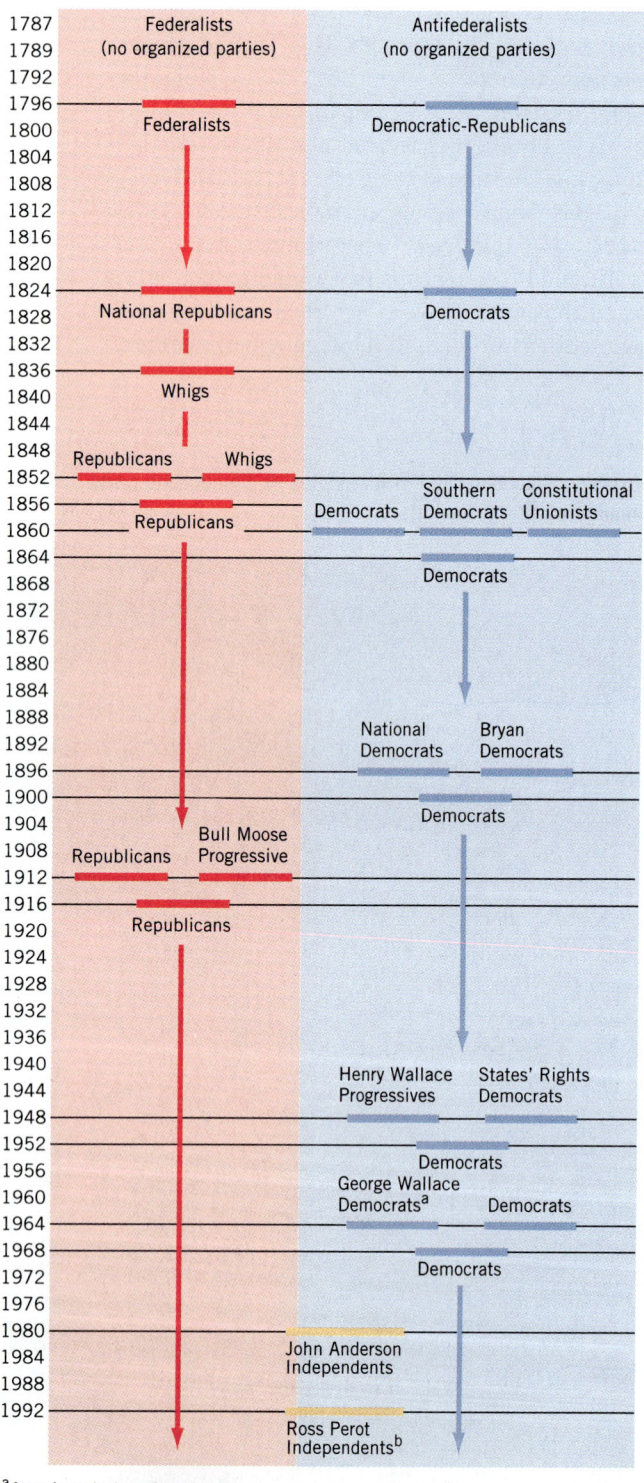

FIGURE 7.2 Cleavages and Continuity in the Two-Party System

ªAmerican Independent party.

ᵇUnited We Stand America or Reform Party.

some from voting); they pressed for civil-service reform to eliminate patronage; and they made heavy use of the mass media as a way of attacking the abuses of partisanship and of promoting their own ideas and candidacies.

The progressives were more successful in some places than in others. In California, for example, progressives led by Governor Hiram Johnson in 1910–1911 were able to institute the direct primary and to adopt procedures—called the *initiative* and the *referendum*—so that citizens could vote directly on proposed legislation, thereby bypassing the state legislature. Governor Robert La Follette brought about similar changes in Wisconsin.

The effect of these changes was to reduce substantially the worst forms of political corruption and ultimately to make boss rule in politics difficult if not impossible. But they also had the effect of making political parties, whether led by bosses or by statesmen, weaker, less able to hold officeholders accountable, and less able to assemble the power necessary for governing the fragmented political institutions created by the Constitution. In Congress party lines began to grow fainter, as did the power of congressional leadership. Above all, the progressives did not have an answer to the problem first faced by Jefferson: if there is not a strong political party, by what other means will candidates for office be found, recruited, and supported? Political candidacies, like people, are not the products of a virgin birth. Some group or organization must arrange a candidacy, and if that group is not a party, then it can only be another kind of interest group, the mass media, or the personal supporters and family of the candidate. These alternatives are best seen by looking at the forms of party structure now operating.

The National Party Structure Today

Since political parties exist at the national, state, and local levels, you might suppose that they are arranged like a big corporation, with a national board of directors giving orders to state managers, who in turn direct the activities of rank-and-file workers at the county and city level.

Nothing could be further from the truth. At each level a separate and almost entirely independent or-

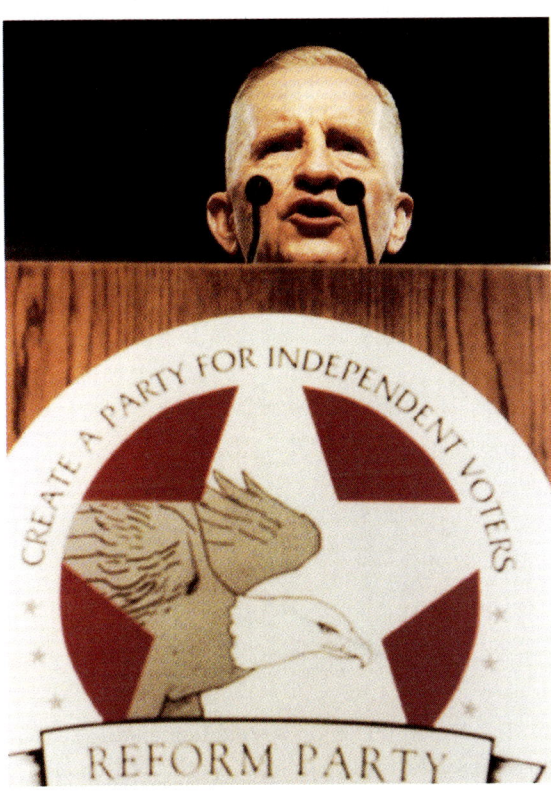

Ross Perot ran for president in 1996 not only as an independent candidate but also as a symbol of popular opposition to political parties.

ganization exists that does pretty much what it wants, and in many counties and cities there is virtually no organization at all.

On paper the national Democratic and Republican parties look quite similar. In both parties ultimate authority is in the hands of the **national convention** that meets every four years to nominate a presidential candidate. Between these conventions party affairs are managed by a **national committee,** made up of delegates from each state and territory. In Congress each party has a **congressional campaign committee** that helps members of Congress who are running for reelection or would-be members running for an open seat or challenging a candidate from the opposition party. The day-to-day work of the party is managed by a full-time, paid **national chairman** who is elected by the committee.

For a long time the two national parties were alike in behavior as well as description. The national

chairman, if his party held the White House, would help decide who among the party faithful would get federal jobs. Otherwise the parties did very little.

But beginning in the late 1960s and early 1970s, the Republicans began to convert their national party into a well-financed, highly staffed organization devoted to finding and electing Republican candidates, especially to Congress. At about the same time, the Democrats began changing the rules governing how presidential candidates are nominated in ways that profoundly altered the distribution of power within the party. As a consequence the Republicans became a bureaucratized party and the Democrats became a factionalized one. After the Republicans won four out of five presidential elections from 1968 to 1984 and briefly took control of the Senate, the Democrats began to suspect that maybe an efficient bureaucracy was better than a collection of warring factions, and so they made an effort to emulate the Republicans.

What the Republicans had done was to take advantage of a new bit of technology—computerized mailings. They built up a huge file of names of people who had given or might give money to the party, usually in small amounts, and used that list to raise a big budget for the national party. In 1983 the Republican National Committee (RNC) raised $35 million from over 1.7 million individual donors; by the time of the 1994 election, the Republican Party committees—the National Committee, the Senatorial Committee, and the Congressional Committee—had raised $246 million from 2.8 million donors.

The RNC used this money to run, in effect, a national political consulting firm. Money went to recruit and train Republican candidates, give them legal and financial advice, study issues and analyze voting trends, and conduct national advertising campaigns on behalf of the party as a whole. No one can be sure how much political success this money bought (after all, the Republicans lost control of the Senate in 1986), but many observers believed that Republican losses in Congress in 1982 and 1986 would have been even greater if the RNC had not worked so vigorously on behalf of its candidates.

When the Democratic National Committee (DNC) decided to play catch-up, it followed the RNC strategy. Using the same computerized direct-mail techniques, the Democratic party committees—

In the Democrats' determination to raise party money, President Clinton allowed many large contributors to spend the night in the White House's Lincoln Bedroom.

the National Committee, Senatorial Committee, and Congressional Committee—raised $131 million from 2.2 million contributors, about half of what the Republican equivalents had raised. This was a great improvement over what it had managed to do just ten years earlier. The Democrats, like the Republicans, ship a lot of their national party money to state organizations to finance television ads supporting their parties. By doing this, the national parties sidestep a restriction on how their money can be used. By law, the national parties can only spend $12 million each directly on their presidential candidates. But by sending money to state parties to spend, they can get around this limitation.

A lot of RNC money goes to commission public opinion polls, not only to find out which candidate is likely to win an election but also, more importantly, to find out what issues are troubling the voters, how different segments of the population respond to different kinds of issues and news stories, and how people react to the campaign efforts of specific candidates. During the Reagan administration the RNC's principal pollster, Richard Wirthlin, was taking polls at least monthly, and sometimes daily.[3] For reasons explained in Chapter 5, these polls can take you just so far; they are helpful, but they are not a sure-fire guide to public opinion or how to change it.

In 1996 both Democrats and Republicans redoubled their efforts to raise what is called *soft money*— that is, funds to aid parties (and their ads and polls). The Republican money advantage almost disappeared. The Republicans raised $138 million, the Democrats $124 million. Both totals were two or three times larger than the soft money raised in 1992. Afterwards, a Senate investigating committee found evidence that illegal foreign contributions were funneled through intermediaries into both parties, that President Clinton and Vice President Gore made many White House phone calls to raise funds, and that big donors were invited to spend the night in the White House's Lincoln Bedroom.

National Conventions

The national committee selects the time and place of the next national convention and issues a "call" for the convention that sets forth the number of delegates each state and territory is to have and also the rules under which delegates must be chosen. The number of delegates and their manner of selection can significantly influence the chances of various presidential candidates, and considerable attention is thus devoted to these matters. In the Democratic party, for example, a long struggle took place between those who wished to see southern states receive a large share of delegates to the convention, in

The national nominating convention was created to broaden political participation, but by 1880, when the Republicans met in Chicago, the convention was often under the control of party bosses. Today the bosses are gone, but the spectacle endures.

recognition of their firm support of Democratic candidates in presidential elections, and those who preferred to see a larger share of delegates allotted to northern and western states that, though less solidly Democratic, were larger or more liberal. A similar conflict within the Republican party has pitted conservative Republican leaders in the Midwest against liberal ones in the East.

A compromise formula is usually chosen; nevertheless, over the years these formulas have gradually changed, shifting voting strength in the Democratic convention away from the South and toward the North and West and in the Republican convention away from the East and toward the South and Southwest. These delegate allocation formulas are but one sign (others will be mentioned later in this chapter) of the tendency of the two parties' conventions to move in opposite ideological directions—Democrats more to the left, Republicans more to the right.

The exact formula for apportioning delegates is extremely complex. For the Democrats it takes into account the vote each state cast for Democratic can-

No longer functioning as deliberative bodies, party conventions have become arenas for made-for-television hoopla.

TRIVIA

Political Parties

First national political convention	*Anti-Masonic party, 1831, in Baltimore*
First time incumbent governors were nominated for president	*Rutherford B. Hayes of Ohio (by Republicans in 1876) Samuel J. Tilden of New York (by Democrats in 1876)*
First black to receive a vote at a national party convention	*Frederick Douglass (at Republican convention in 1888)*
First year in which women attended conventions as delegates	*1900 (one woman at both Democratic and Republican conventions)*
Most ballots needed to choose a presidential nominee	*103, by Democrats in 1924 to select John W. Davis*
Closest vote in convention history	*543 $\frac{3}{20}$ to 542 $\frac{7}{20}$, defeating a motion to condemn the Ku Klux Klan at 1924 Democratic convention*
First Catholic nominated for president by major party	*Al Smith, by Democrats in 1928*
Only person nominated for president four times by major political party	*Franklin D. Roosevelt (by Democrats in 1932, 1936, 1940, and 1944)*
First presidential nominee to make an acceptance speech at the party convention	*Franklin D. Roosevelt*

Franklin D. Roosevelt

Frederick Douglass

didates in past elections and the number of electoral votes of each state; for the Republicans it takes into account the number of representatives in Congress and whether the state in past elections cast its electoral votes for the Republican presidential candidate and elected Republicans to the Senate, the House, and the governorship. Thus the Democrats give extra delegates to large states while the Republicans give extra ones to loyal states.

The way in which delegates are chosen can be even more important than their allocation. The Democrats, beginning in 1972, have developed an elaborate set of rules designed to weaken the control over delegates by local party leaders and to increase the proportion of women, young people, blacks, and Native Americans attending the convention. These rules were first drafted by a party commission chaired by Senator George McGovern (who was later to make skillful use of these new procedures in his successful bid for the Democratic presidential nomination). They were revised in 1974 by another commission chaired by Barbara Mikulski, whose decisions were ratified by the 1974 midterm convention. After the 1976 election yet a third commission, chaired by Morley Winograd, produced still another revision of the rules, which took effect in 1980. Then a fourth commission, chaired by North Carolina Governor James B. Hunt, recommended in 1981 yet another set of rules, which became effective with the 1984 convention.

The general thrust of the work of the first three rules commissions was to broaden the antiparty changes started by the progressives at the beginning of this century. Whereas the earlier reformers had tried to minimize the role of parties in the election process, those of the 1970s sought to weaken the influence of leaders within the party. In short, the newer reforms were aimed at creating *intra*party democracy as well as *inter*party democracy. This was done by rules that, for the 1980 convention, required

- Equal division of delegates between men and women

- Establishment of "goals" for the representation of blacks, Hispanics, and other groups in proportion to their presence in a state's Democratic electorate

- Open delegate selection procedures, with advance publicity and written rules

- Selection of 75 percent of the delegates at the level of the congressional district or lower

- No "unit rule" that would require all delegates to vote with the majority of their state delegation

- Restrictions on the number of party leaders and elected officials who could vote at the convention

- A requirement that all delegates pledged to a candidate vote for that candidate

In 1981 the Hunt Commission changed some of these rules—in particular, the last two—in order to increase the influence of elected officials and to make the convention a somewhat more deliberative body. The commission reserved about 14 percent of the delegate seats for party leaders and elected officials, who would not have to commit themselves in advance to a presidential candidate, and it repealed the rule requiring that delegates pledged to a candidate vote for that candidate.

Rules have consequences. Whereas in 1980 only one-seventh of the Democratic senators and representatives got to be delegates to the national convention, in 1984 more than half were delegates. In the 1984 presidential primaries, Walter Mondale was the chief beneficiary of the delegate selection rules. He won the support of the overwhelming majority of elected officials—the so-called **superdelegates**—and he did especially well in those states that held winner-take-all primaries. Had different rules been in effect (if, for example, the delegates had been allocated strictly in proportion to the primary votes that the candidates won), Mondale probably would not have entered the Democratic convention with an assured majority.

But the "reform" of the parties, especially the Democratic party, has had far more profound consequences than merely helping one candidate or another. Before 1968 the Republican party represented, essentially, white-collar voters and the Democratic party represented blue-collar ones. After a decade of "reform," the Republican and the Democratic parties each represented two ideologically different sets of upper-middle-class voters (see Table 7.1). In the terminology of Chapter 5, the Republicans came to represent the more conservative wing of the traditional middle class and the Democrats the more leftist wing of the liberal middle class (or the "new class").

TABLE 7.1   Who Are the Party Delegates?

Characteristics of delegates to Democratic and Republican national conventions in 1988

	Democrats	Republicans
Women	52%	37%
Blacks	21	3
Under age 30	4	4
Religion		
Catholic	30	24
Jewish	6	2
Protestant	51	70
Education		
College degree or beyond	73	68
Postgraduate degree	52	42
Occupation		
Lawyer	16	17
Teacher	14	5
Union member	25	3
Hold elective office	26	28

SOURCE: *New York Times* (August 14, 1988): Copyright © 1988 by the New York Times Company. Reprinted by permission.

This was more troubling to the Democrats than to the Republicans, because the traditional middle class is somewhat closer to the opinions of most citizens than is the liberal middle class (and thus the Republican national convention more closely reflected public opinion than did the Democratic national convention). And for whatever reason, the Republicans won five out of six presidential races between 1968 and 1988.

Before the 1988 convention the Democrats took a long, hard look at their party procedures. Under the leadership of DNC chairman Paul Kirk, they decided against making any major changes, especially ones that would increase the power of grassroots activists at the expense of elected officials and party leaders. The number of such officials (or superdelegates) to be given delegate seats was increased. For example, 80 percent of the Democratic members of Congress and all Democratic governors were automatically made convention delegates in 1988. The official status of some special-interest caucuses (such as those organized to represent blacks, homosexuals, and various ethnic groups) was reduced in order to lessen the perception that the Democrats were simply a party of factions.

The surface harmony was a bit misleading, however, as some activists, notably supporters of Jesse Jackson, protested that the rules made it harder for candidates like Jackson to win delegates in proportion to their share of the primary vote. (In 1984 Jackson got 18 percent of the primary votes but only 12 percent of the delegates.) The DNC responded by changing the rules for the 1992 campaign. Former DNC chairman Ronald H. Brown (later President Clinton's secretary of commerce) won approval for three important requirements:

- The winner-reward systems of delegate distribution, which gave the winner of a primary or caucus extra delegates, were banned. (In 1988 fifteen states used winner-reward systems, including such vote-rich states as Florida, Illinois, New Jersey, and Pennsylvania.)

- The proportional representation system was put into use. This system divides a state's publicly elected delegates among candidates who receive at least 15 percent of the vote.

- States that violate the rules are now penalized with the loss of 25 percent of their national convention delegates.

Even though the Democrats have retreated a bit from the reforms of the 1960s and 1970s, the conventions of both parties have changed fundamentally, and probably permanently. Delegates once selected by party leaders are now chosen by primary elections and grassroots caucuses. As a result the national party conventions are no longer places where party leaders meet to bargain over the selection of their presidential candidates; they are instead places where delegates come together to ratify choices already made by party activists and primary voters.

Most Americans dislike bosses, deals, and manipulation and prefer democracy, reform, and openness. These are commendable instincts. But such instincts, unless carefully tested against practice, may mislead us into supposing that anything carried out in the name of reform is a good idea. Rules must be judged by their practical results as well as by their conformity to some principle of fairness. Rules affect the distribution of power: they help some people win and others lose. Later in this chapter we

shall try to assess delegate selection rules by looking more closely at how they affect who attends conventions and which presidential candidates are selected there.

State and Local Parties

While the national party structures have changed, the grassroots organizations have withered. In between, state party systems have struggled to redefine their roles.

In every state there is a Democratic and Republican state party organized under state law. Typically each will consist of a state central committee, below which will be found county committees and sometimes city, town, or even precinct committees. The members of these committees are chosen in a variety of ways—sometimes in primary elections, sometimes by conventions, sometimes by a building-block process whereby people elected to serve on precinct or town committees choose the members of county committees, who in turn choose state committee members.

Knowing these formal arrangements is much less helpful than knowing the actual distribution of power in each state party. In a few places strong party bosses handpick the members of these committees; in other places powerful elected officials—key state legislators, county sheriffs, or judges—control the committees. And in many places no one is in charge, so that either the party structure is largely meaningless or it is made up of the representatives of various local factions.

To understand how power is distributed in a party, we must first know what *incentives* motivate people in a particular state or locality to become active in a party organization. Different incentives lead to different ways of organizing parties.

The Machine

A **political machine** is a party organization that recruits its members by the use of tangible incentives—money, political jobs, an opportunity to get favors from government—and that is characterized by a high degree of leadership control over member activity. At one time many local party organizations were machines, and the struggle over political jobs—patronage—was the chief concern of their members. Though Tammany Hall in New York City began as a caucus of well-to-do notables in the local Democratic party, by the late nineteenth century it had become a machine organized on the basis of political clubs in each assembly district. These clubs were composed of party workers whose job it was to get out the straight party vote in their election districts and who hoped for a tangible reward if they were successful.

And there were abundant rewards to hope for. During the 1870s it was estimated that one out of every eight voters in New York City had a federal, state, or city job.[4] The federal bureaucracy was one important source of those jobs. The New York Custom House alone employed thousands of people, virtually all of whom were replaced if their party lost the presidential election. The postal system was another source, and it was frankly recognized as such. When James N. Tyner became postmaster general in 1876, he was "appointed not to see that the mails were carried, but to see that Indiana was carried."[5] Elections and conventions were so frequent and the intensity of party competition so great that being a party worker was for many a full-time paid occupation.

Well before the arrival of vast numbers of poor immigrants from Ireland, Italy, and elsewhere, old-stock Americans had perfected the machine, run up the cost of government, and systematized voting fraud. Kickbacks on contracts, payments extracted from officeholders, and funds raised from business-people made some politicians rich but also paid the huge bills of the elaborate party organization. When the immigrants began flooding the eastern cities, the party machines were there to provide them with all manner of services in exchange for their support at the polls: the machines were a vast welfare organization operating before the creation of the welfare state.

The abuses of the machine were well known and gradually curtailed. Stricter voter registration laws reduced fraud, civil service reforms cut down the number of patronage jobs, and competitive-bidding laws made it harder to award overpriced contracts to favored businesses. The Hatch Act (passed by Congress in 1939) made it illegal for federal civil service employees to take an active part in political management or political campaigns by serving as party officers, soliciting campaign funds, running for partisan office, working in a partisan campaign, endorsing partisan candidates, taking voters to the polls, counting ballots, circulating nominating petitions, or being delegates to a party convention. (They may still vote and make campaign contributions.)

These restrictions gradually took federal employees out of machine politics, but they did not end

Ex-Senator George Washington Plunkitt of Tammany Hall explains machine politics from atop the bootblack stand in front of the New York County Court House, around 1905.

A powerful conservative group is the Christian Coalition, founded by evangelist Pat Robertson (center).

the machines. In many cities—Chicago, Philadelphia, and Albany—ways were found to maintain the machine even though city employees were technically under the civil service. Far more important than the various progressive reforms that weakened machines were changes among voters. As voters grew in education, income, and sophistication, they depended less and less on the advice and leadership of local party officials. And as the federal government created a bureaucratic welfare system, the parties' welfare systems declined in value.

It is easy either to scorn the political party machine as a venal and self-serving organization or to romanticize it as an informal welfare system. In truth it was a little of both. Above all it was a frank recognition of the fact that politics requires organization; the machine was the supreme expression of the value of organization. Even allowing for voting fraud, in elections where party machines were active, voter turnout was huge: more people participated in politics when mobilized by a party machine

than when appealed to by television or good-government associations.[6] Moreover, because the party machines were interested in winning, they would subordinate any other consideration to that end. This has meant that the machines were usually willing to support the presidential candidate with the best chance of winning, regardless of his policy views (provided, of course, that he was not determined to wreck the machines once in office). Republican machines helped elect Abraham Lincoln as well as Warren G. Harding; Democratic machines were of crucial importance in electing Franklin D. Roosevelt and John F. Kennedy.

The old-style machine is almost extinct, though important examples still can be found in the Democratic organization in Cook County (Chicago) and the Republican organization in Nassau County (New York). But a new-style machine has emerged in a few places. It is a machine in the sense that it uses money to knit together many politicians, but it is new in that the money comes not from patronage and contracts but from campaign contributions supplied by wealthy individuals and the proceeds of direct-mail campaigns.

The political organization headed by Democratic congressmen Henry A. Waxman and Howard L. Berman on the west side of Los Angeles is one such new-style machine. By the astute use of campaign funds, the "Waxman-Berman organization" builds loyalties to it among a variety of elected officials at all levels of government. Moreover, this new-style machine, unlike the old ones, has a strong interest in issues, especially at the national level. In this sense it is not a machine at all, but a cross between a machine and an ideological party.

Ideological Parties

At the opposite extreme from the machine is the **ideological party.** Where the machine values winning above all else, the ideological party values principle above all else. Where the former depends on money incentives, the latter spurns them. Where the former is hierarchical and disciplined, the latter is usually contentious and factionalized.

The most firmly ideological parties have been independent "third parties," such as the Socialist, Socialist Workers, Libertarian, and Right-to-Life parties. But there have been ideological factions

Political parties have come increasingly to consist of social movements. People opposing abortion are well represented in the Republican party; those supporting it are well represented in the Democratic party.

within the Democratic and Republican parties as well, and in some places these ideological groups have taken over the regular parties.

In the 1950s and 1960s these ideological groups were "reform clubs" within local Democratic and Republican parties. In Los Angeles, New York, and many parts of Wisconsin and Minnesota, issue-oriented activists fought to take over the party from election-oriented regulars. Democratic reform clubs managed to defeat the head of Tammany Hall in Manhattan; similar activist groups became the dominant force in California state politics.[7] The Democratic club leaders were more liberal than rank-and-file Democrats, and Republican club leaders were often more conservative than rank-and-file Republicans.

The 1960s and 1970s saw these "reform" movements replaced by more focused social movements. The "reform" movement was based on a generalized sense of liberalism (among Democrats) or conservatism (among Republicans). With the advent of social movements concerned with civil rights, peace, feminism, environmentalism, libertarianism, and abortion, the generalized ideology of the clubs was replaced by the specific ideological demands of single-issue activists.

Today, for example, the Christian Coalition is an active group within the Republican party. Strongly pro-life and conservative on social issues, in the early 1990s these religiously oriented Republican party activists were influential in everything from local school board races to congressional races.

The result is that in many places the party has become a collection of people drawn from various social movements. For a candidate to win the party's support, he or she often has to satisfy the "litmus-test" demands of the ideological activists in the party. Democratic Senator Barbara Mikulski put it this way: "The social movements are now our farm clubs."

With social movements as their farm clubs, the big-league teams—the Democrats and Republicans at the state level—behave very differently than they did when political machines were the farm clubs. Internal factionalism is more intense, and the freedom of action of the party leader (say, the chairperson of the state committee) has been greatly reduced. A leader who demands too little or gives up too much, or who says the wrong thing on a key issue, is quickly accused of having "sold out." Under these circumstances many "leaders" are that in name only.

Solidary Groups

Many people who participate in state and local politics do so not in order to earn money or vindicate some cause, but simply because they find it fun. They enjoy the game, they meet interesting people, and they like the sense of being "in the know" and rubbing shoulders with the powerful. When people get together out of gregarious or game-loving instincts, we say that they are responding to **solidary incentives;** if they form an organization, it is a solidary association.

Some of these associations were once machines. When a machine loses its patronage, some of its members—especially the older ones—may continue to serve in the organization out of a desire for camaraderie. In other cases precinct, ward, and district committees are built up on the basis of friendship networks. One study of political activists in Detroit found that most of them mentioned friendships and a liking for politics, rather than an interest in issues, as their reasons for joining the party organization.[8] Members of ward and town organizations in St. Louis County gave the same answers when asked why they joined.[9] Since patronage has declined in value and since the appeals of ideology are limited to a minority of citizens, the motivations for participating in politics have become very much like those for joining a bowling league or a bridge club.

The advantage of such groups is that they are neither corrupt nor inflexible; the disadvantage is that they often do not work very hard. Knocking on doors on a rainy November evening to try to talk people into voting for your candidate is a chore under the best of circumstances; it is especially unappealing if you joined the party primarily because you like to attend meetings or drink coffee with your friends.[10]

Sponsored Parties

Sometimes a relatively strong party organization can be created among volunteers without heavy reliance on money or ideology and without depending entirely on people's finding the work fun. This type of **sponsored party** occurs when another organization exists in the community that can create, or at least sponsor, a local party structure. The clearest example of this is the Democratic party in and around Detroit, which has been developed, led, and to a degree financed by the political-action arm of the United Auto Workers union. The UAW has had a long tradition of rank-and-file activism, stemming from its formative struggles in the 1930s, and since the city is virtually a one-industry town, it was not hard to transfer some of this activism from union organizing to voter organizing.

By the mid-1950s union members and leaders made up over three-fourths of all the Democratic party district leaders within the city.[11] On election day union funds were available for paying workers to canvass voters; between elections political work on an unpaid basis was expected of union leaders. Though the UAW–Democratic party alliance in Detroit has not always been successful in city elections (the city is nonpartisan), it has been quite successful in carrying the city for the Democratic party in state and national elections.

Not many areas have organizations as effective or as dominant as the UAW that can bolster, sponsor, or even take over the weak formal party structure. Thus sponsored local parties are not common in the United States.

Personal Following

Because most candidates can no longer count on the backing of a machine, because sponsored parties are limited to a few unionized areas, and because solidary groups are not always productive, a person wanting to get elected will often try to form a **personal following** that will work for him or her during a campaign and then disband until the next election rolls around. Sometimes a candidate tries to meld a personal following with an ideological group, especially during the primary election campaign, when candidates need the kind of financial backing and hard work that only highly motivated activists are likely to supply.

To form a personal following, the candidate must have an appealing personality, a lot of friends, or a big bank account. The Kennedy family has all three, and the electoral success of the personal followings of John F. Kennedy, Edward M. Kennedy, Robert Kennedy, and Joseph P. Kennedy II are legendary.

Southern politicians who have to operate in one-party states with few, if any, machines have become

The Kennedy family succeeded in developing strong political followings for three of its members—John F. Kennedy (center, standing), Robert F. Kennedy (to the right of John), and Edward M. Kennedy (seated, right).

grand masters at building personal followings, such as those of the Talmadge family in Georgia, the Long family in Louisiana, and the Byrd family in Virginia. But the strategy is increasingly followed wherever party organization is weak. The key asset is to have a known political name. That has helped the electoral victories of the son of Hubert Humphrey in Minnesota, the son and daughter of Pat Brown in California, the son of Birch Bayh in Indiana, the son of George Wallace in Alabama, and the son and grandson of Robert La Follette in Wisconsin.

The traditional party organization—one that is hierarchical, lasting, based on material incentives, and capable of influencing who gets nominated for office—exists today, according to political scientist David Mayhew, in only about eight states, mostly the older states of the Northeast. Another five states, he feels, have faction-ridden versions of the traditional party organization.[12] The states in the rest of the country display the weak party system of solidary clubs, personal followings, ideological groups, and sponsored parties. What that means can be seen in the composition of recent Democratic national conventions. More than half of the delegates have been drawn from the ranks of the AFL-CIO, the National Education Association, and the National Organization for Women.[13]

The Two-Party System

With so many different varieties of local party organizations (or nonorganizations), and with such a great range of opinion found within each party, it is remarkable that we have had only two major political parties for most of our history. In the world at large a **two-party system** is a rarity; by one estimate only fifteen nations have it.[14] Most European democracies are multiparty systems. We have only two parties with any chance of winning nationally, and these parties have been, over time, rather evenly balanced—between 1888 and 1992, the Republicans won fifteen presidential elections and the Democrats twelve. Furthermore, whenever one party has achieved a temporary ascendancy and its rival been pronounced dead (as were the Democrats in the first third of this century and the Republicans during the 1930s and the 1960s), the "dead" party has displayed remarkable powers of recuperation, coming back to win important victories.

At the state and congressional district levels, however, the parties are not evenly balanced. For a long time the South was so heavily Democratic at all levels of government as to be a one-party area, while upper New England and the Dakotas were strongly

Republican. All regions are more competitive today than once was the case, but even now one party tends to enjoy a substantial advantage in at least half the states and in perhaps two-thirds of the congressional districts. Nevertheless, though the parties are not as competitive in state elections as they are in presidential ones, states have rarely had, at least for any extended period, political parties other than the Democratic and Republican (see Table 7.2).

Scholars do not entirely agree on why the two-party system should be so permanent a feature of American political life, but two explanations are of major importance. The first has to do with the system of elections, the second with the distribution of public opinion.

Elections at every level of government are based on the plurality, winner-take-all method. The **plurality system** means that in all elections for representative, senator, governor, or president, and in almost all elections for state legislator, mayor, or city councillor, the winner is that person who gets the *most* votes, even if he or she does not get a *majority* of all votes cast. We are so familiar with this system that we sometimes forget that there are other ways of running an election. For example, one could require that the winner get a majority of the votes, thus producing runoff elections if nobody got a majority on the first try. France does this in choosing its national legislature. In the first election candidates for parliament who win an absolute majority of the

TABLE 7.2   The Rise of Republican Politics in the South, 1956–1996

Year	Number of Representatives		Number of Senators		Number of Governors		Number of States Voting for Presidential Nominee	
	Dem.	Rep.	Dem.	Rep.	Dem.	Rep.	Dem.	Rep.
1956	99	7	22	0	11	0	6	5
1958	99	7	22	0	11	0		
1960	99	7	22	0	11	0	8[a]	2
1962	95	11	21	1	11	0		
1964	89	17	21	1	11	0	6	5
1966	83	23	19	3	9	2		
1968	80	26	18	4	9	2	1	5[b]
1970	79	27	16 (1)[c]	5	9	2		
1972	74	34	14 (1)[c]	7	8	3	0	11
1974	81	27	15 (1)[c]	6	8	3		
1976	82	26	16 (1)[c]	5	9	2	10	1
1978	77	31	15 (1)[c]	6	8	3		
1980	55	53	11 (1)[c]	10	6	5	1	10
1982	80	33	11	11	11	0		
1984	72	41	11	11	10	1	0	11
1986	77	39	16	6	6	5		
1988	80	36	15	7	6	5	0	11
1990	77	39	15	7	8	3		
1992	82	43	14	8	8	3	4	7
1994	61	64	9	13	5	6		
1996	54	71	9	13	4	7	4	7

[a] Eight Mississippi electors voted for Harry Byrd.
[b] George Wallace won five states on the American Independent ticket.
[c] Harry Byrd, Jr., was elected in Virginia in 1970 and 1976 as an independent.

votes cast are declared elected. A week later, remaining candidates who received at least one-eighth but less than one-half of the vote go into a runoff election; those who then win an absolute majority are also declared elected.

The French method encourages many political parties to form, each hoping to win at least one-eighth of the vote in the first election and then to enter into an alliance with its ideologically nearest rival in order to win the runoff. In the United States the plurality system means that a party must make all the alliances it can before the first election—there is no second chance. Hence every party must be as broadly based as possible; a narrow, minor party has no hope of winning.

The winner-take-all feature of American elections has the same effect. Only one member of Congress is elected from each district. In many European countries the elections are based on proportional representation. Each party submits a list of candidates for parliament, ranked in order of preference by the party leaders. The nation votes. A party winning 37 percent of the vote gets 37 percent of the seats in parliament; a party winning 2 percent of the vote gets 2 percent of the seats. Since even the smallest parties have a chance of winning something, minor parties have an incentive to organize.

The most dramatic example of the winner-take-all principle is the electoral college (see pages 368–371). In every state but Maine and Nebraska, the candidate who wins the most popular votes in a state wins *all* of that state's electoral votes. In 1992, for example, Bill Clinton won only 45 percent of the popular vote in Missouri, but he got all of Missouri's eleven electoral votes because his two rivals (George Bush and Ross Perot) each got fewer popular votes. Minor parties cannot compete under this system. Voters are often reluctant to "waste" their vote on a minor-party candidate who cannot win.

The United States has experimented with other electoral systems. Proportional representation was used for municipal elections in New York City at one time and is still in use for that purpose in Cambridge, Massachusetts. Many states have elected more than one state legislator from each district. In Illinois, for example, three legislators have been elected from each district, with each voter allowed to cast two votes, thus virtually guaranteeing that the minority party will be able to win one of the three

United We Stand America: A New Third Party?

*I*n the 1992 presidential election Ross Perot captured 19 percent of the popular vote, an impressive showing for a third-party candidate. Then in 1996 Perot was back, this time as the candidate of the Reform party. But as in 1992, Perot won no states in the electoral college and arguably did not affect the outcome of the election.

Most third-party candidates soon fade from the scene. After the defeat of his Bull Moose party candidacy in 1912, Theodore Roosevelt left America to study the flora and fauna of Brazil. John Anderson forswore electoral politics and became a television commentator in Chicago following his unsuccessful independent bid in 1980.

But after the 1992 election Ross Perot took to the airwaves with campaign-style programs on the nation's deficit and trade problems and testified frequently before Congress, continuing to make headlines. In January of 1993 Perot announced the formation of United We Stand America (UWSA), an advocacy group for governmental and political reform. In the first few months of UWSA's existence, Perot visited thirty-seven cities in fourteen states. UWSA soon boasted 1 million members, each of whom paid at least $15 in annual dues. Between 1992 and 1996, UWSA evolved into the Reform party, complete with organized state chapters and a presidential nominating convention. The 1996 Reform party presidential contest pitted Perot against former Democratic governor Richard Lamm of Colorado, who intimated that "Ross the Boss" had denied his supporters an equal opportunity to be heard and to vote. Perot won the nomination but in the election got only 9 percent of the vote.

Will the Reform party develop into a viable third party? And will it outlive Perot's involvement? Stay tuned.

SOURCE: James A. Barnes, "Still on the Trail," *National Journal* (April 10, 1993): 863–864.

seats. But none of these experiments has altered the national two-party system, probably because of the existence of a directly elected president chosen by a winner-take-all electoral college.

The presidency is the great prize of American politics; to win it, you must form a party with as broad appeal as possible. As a practical matter, that means there will be, in most cases, only two serious parties—one made up of those who support the party already in power, and the other made up of everybody else. Only one third party ever won the presidency—the Republicans in 1860—and it had by then pretty much supplanted the Whig party.

The second explanation for the persistence of the two-party system is to be found in the opinions of the voters. Though there have been periods of bitter dissent, most of the time most citizens have agreed enough to permit them to come together into two broad coalitions. There has not been a massive and persistent body of opinion that has rejected the prevailing economic system (and thus we have not had a Marxist party with mass appeal); there has not been in our history an aristocracy or monarchy (and thus there has been no party that has sought to restore aristocrats or monarchs to power). Churches and religion have almost always been regarded as matters of private choice that lie outside politics (and thus there has not been a party seeking to create or abolish special government privileges for one church or another). In some European nations the organization of the economy, the prerogatives of the monarchy, and the role of the church have been major issues with long and bloody histories. So divisive have these issues been that they have helped prevent the formation of broad coalition parties.

But Americans have had other deep divisions— between white and black, for example, and between North and South—and yet the two-party system has endured. This suggests that our electoral procedures are of great importance—the winner-take-all, plurality election rules have made it useless for anyone to attempt to create an all-white or an all-black national party except as an act of momentary defiance or in the hope of taking enough votes away from the two major parties to force the presidential election into the House of Representatives. (That may have been George Wallace's strategy in 1968.)

For many years there was an additional reason for the two-party system: the laws of many states made it difficult, if not impossible, for third parties to get on the ballot. In 1968, for example, the American Independent party of George Wallace found that it would have to collect 433,000 signatures (15 percent of the votes cast in the last statewide election) in order to get on the presidential ballot in Ohio. Wallace took the issue to the Supreme Court, which ruled, six to three, that such a restriction was an unconstitutional violation of the equal-protection clause of the Fourteenth Amendment.[15] Wallace got on the ballot. In 1980 John Anderson, running as an independent, was able to get on the ballot in all fifty states; in 1992 Ross Perot did the same. But for the reasons already indicated, the two-party system will probably persist even without the aid of legal restrictions.

Minor Parties

The electoral system may prevent minor parties from winning, but it does not prevent them from forming. Minor parties—usually called, erroneously, "third parties"—have been a permanent feature of American political life. Four major kinds of minor parties, with examples of each, are described in the box on page 187.

The minor parties that have endured have been the ideological ones. Their members feel themselves to be outside the mainstream of American political life and sometimes, as in the case of various Marxist parties, look forward to a time when a revolution or some other dramatic change in the political system will vindicate them. They are usually not interested in immediate electoral success and thus persist despite their poor showing at the polls. One such party, however, the Socialist party of Eugene Debs, won nearly 6 percent of the popular vote in the 1912 presidential election and during its heyday elected some twelve hundred candidates to local offices, including seventy-nine mayors. Part of the Socialist appeal arose from its opposition to municipal corruption, part from its opposition to American entry into World War I, and part from its critique of American society. No ideological party has ever carried a state in a presidential election.

Apart from the Republicans, who quickly became a major party, the only minor parties to carry states and thus win electoral votes were one party of economic protest (the Populists, who carried five states in 1892) and several factional parties (most recently, the States' Rights Democrats in 1948 and the American Independent party of George Wallace in 1968). Though factional parties may hope to cause the defeat of the party from which they split, they have not always been able to achieve this. Harry Truman was elected in 1948 despite the defections of both the leftist progressives, led by Henry Wallace, and the right-wing Dixiecrats, led by J. Strom Thurmond. In 1968 it seems likely that Hubert

Humphrey would have lost even if George Wallace had not been in the race (Wallace voters would probably have switched to Nixon rather than to Humphrey, though of course one cannot be certain). It is quite possible, on the other hand, that a Republican might have beaten Woodrow Wilson in 1912 if the Republican party had not split in two (the regulars supporting William Howard Taft, the progressives supporting Theodore Roosevelt).

What is striking is not that we have had so many minor parties but that we have not had more. There have been several major political movements that did not produce a significant third party: the civil rights movement of the 1960s, the antiwar movement of the same decade, and, most important, the labor movement in this century. Blacks were part of the Republican party after the Civil War and part of the Democratic party after the New Deal (even though the southern wing of that party for a long time kept them from voting). The antiwar movement found candidates with whom it could identify within the Democratic party (Eugene McCarthy, Robert F. Kennedy, George McGovern), even though it was a Democratic president, Lyndon B. Johnson, who was chiefly responsible for our commitment in Vietnam. After Johnson only narrowly won the 1968 New Hampshire primary, he withdrew from the race. Unions in this century have not tried to create a labor party—indeed, they were for a long time opposed to almost any kind of national political activity. Since labor became a major political force in the 1930s, the largest industrial unions have been content to operate as a part (and a very large part) of the Democratic party.

One reason why some potential sources of minor parties never formed such parties, in addition to the dim chance of success, is that the direct primary and the national convention have made it possible for dissident elements of a major party, unless they become completely disaffected, to remain in the party and influence the choice of candidates and policies. The antiwar movement had a profound effect on the Democratic conventions of 1968 and 1972; blacks have played a growing role in the Democratic party, especially with the candidacy of Jesse Jackson in 1984 and 1988; only in 1972 did the unions feel that the Democrats nominated a presidential candidate (McGovern) unacceptable to them.

Types of Minor Parties

Ideological parties: Parties professing a comprehensive view of American society and government that is radically different from that of the established parties. Most have been Marxist in outlook, but some are quite the opposite, such as the Libertarian party.

Examples:
Socialist party (1901 to 1960s)
Socialist Labor party (1888 to present)
Socialist Workers party (1938 to present)
Communist party (1920s to present)
Libertarian party (1972 to present)

One-issue parties: Parties seeking a single policy, usually revealed by their names, and avoiding other issues.

Examples:
Free Soil party—to prevent the spread of slavery (1848–1852)
American or "Know-Nothing" party—to oppose immigration and Catholics (1856)
Prohibition party—to ban the sale of liquor (1869 to present)
Woman's party—to obtain the right to vote for women (1913–1920)

Economic-protest parties: Parties, usually based in a particular region, especially involving farmers, that protest against depressed economic conditions. These tend to disappear as conditions improve.

Examples:
Greenback party (1876–1884)
Populist party (1892–1908)

Factional parties: Parties that are created by a split in a major party, usually over the identity and philosophy of the major party's presidential candidate.

Examples:
Split off from the Republican party:
    "Bull Moose" Progressive party (1912)
    La Follette Progressive party (1924)
Split off from the Democratic party:
    States' Rights ("Dixiecrat") party (1948)
    Henry Wallace Progressive party (1948)
    American Independent (George Wallace) party (1968)
Split off from both Democrats and Republicans:
    Reform party (Ross Perot)

The Socialist party and the Progressive party were both minor parties, but their origins were different. The Socialist party was an ideological party; the "Bull Moose" Progressive party split off from the Republicans to support Theodore Roosevelt.

The impact of minor parties on American politics is hard to judge. One bit of conventional wisdom holds that minor parties develop ideas that the major parties later come to adopt. The Socialist party, for example, is supposed to have called for major social and economic policies that the Democrats under Roosevelt later embraced and termed the New Deal. It is possible that the Democrats did steal the thunder of the Socialists, but it hardly seems likely that they did it because the Socialists had proposed these things or proved them popular. (In 1932 the Socialists got only 2 percent of the vote and in 1936 less than one-half of 1 percent.) Roosevelt probably adopted the policies he did in part because he thought them correct and in part because dissident elements within his *own* party—leaders such as Huey Long of Louisiana—were threatening to bolt the Democratic party if it did not move to the left. Even Prohibition was adopted more as a result of the efforts of interest groups such as the Anti-Saloon League than as the consequence of its endorsement by the Prohibition party.

The minor parties that have probably had the greatest influence on public policy have been the factional parties. Mugwumps and liberal Republicans, by bolting the regular party, may have made that party more sensitive to the issue of civil service reform; the Bull Moose and La Follette progressive parties probably helped encourage the major parties to pay more attention to issues of business regulation and party reform; the Dixiecrat and Wallace movements probably strengthened the hands of those who wished to go slow on desegregation. The threat of a factional split is a risk that both major parties must face, and it is in the efforts that each makes to avoid such splits that one finds the greatest impact, at least in this century, of minor parties.

In 1992 and again in 1996, Ross Perot led the most successful recent third-party movement. Begun as United We Stand America and later renamed the

Reform party, Perot's appeal seemed to reflect a growing American dissatisfaction with the existing political parties and a heightened demand for bringing in a leader who would "run the government without politics." Of course, it is no more possible to take politics out of governing than it is to take churches out of religion. Though unrealistic, people seem to want policies without bargaining.

Nominating a President

The major parties face, as we have seen, two contrary forces: one, generated by the desire to win the presidency, pushes them in the direction of nominating a candidate who can appeal to the majority of voters and who will thus have essentially middle-of-the-road views. The other, produced by the need to keep dissident elements in the party from bolting and forming a third party, leads them to compromise with dissidents or extremists in ways that may damage the party's standing with the voters.

The Democrats and Republicans have always faced these conflicting pressures, but of late they have become especially acute. When the presidential nomination was made by a party convention that was heavily influenced, if not controlled, by party leaders and elected officials, it was relatively easy to ignore dissident factions and pick candidates on the basis of who could win. The *electoral* objectives of the party were predominant. The result was that often a faction left the party and ran a separate ticket—as in 1912, 1924, 1948, 1968, and 1980. Today the power of party leaders and elected officials within the parties is greatly diminished, with most delegates now selected by primary elections. A larger proportion of the delegates is likely to be more interested in issues and to be less amenable to compromise over those issues than formerly. In these circumstances the *policy* interests of the party activists are likely to be important.

Are the Delegates Representative of the Voters?

There would be no conflict between the electoral and policy interests of a political party if the delegates to its nominating convention had the same policy views as most voters, or at least as most party

supporters. In fact this is not the case: in parties, as in many organizations, the activists and leaders tend to have views different from those of the rank and file.[16] In American political parties in recent years, this difference has become very great.

In 1964 the Republican party nominated the highly conservative Barry Goldwater for president. We have no opinion data for delegates to that convention as detailed and comprehensive as those available for subsequent conventions, but it seems clear that the Republican delegates selected as their nominee a person who was not the most popular candidate among voters at large and thus not the candidate most likely to win.

At every Democratic national convention since 1972, the delegates have had views on a variety of important issues that were vastly different from those of rank-and-file Democrats. On welfare, military policy, school desegregation, crime, and abortion, Democratic delegates expressed opinions almost diametrically opposed to those of most Democrats. The delegates to the 1980, 1984, and (to a lesser extent) 1988 and 1992 conventions were ideologically very different from the voters at large. The Democratic delegates were more liberal than the Democratic voters, and the Republican delegates were more conservative than the Republican voters (see Table 7.3).[17]

What accounts for the sharp disparity between delegate opinion (and often delegate candidate preference) and voter attitudes? Some blame the discrepancy on the rules, described earlier in this

TABLE 7.3 How Party Delegates and Party Voters Differ in Liberal Ideology

Liberal Ideology	1984	1988	1992
Democrats			
Delegates	66%	39%	47%
Voters	31	25	28
Republicans			
Delegates	2	1	1
Voters	15	12	12

SOURCES: For 1984: *Los Angeles Times* (August 19, 1984); for 1988: *New York Times*/CBS News poll, in *New York Times* (August 14, 1988); for 1992: *New York Times* (July 13, and August 17, 1992) and unpublished CBS news poll, "The 1992 Republican Convention Delegates."

Popular Preferences and Convention Nominations

Usually the presidential candidate nominated by a party's convention is the person who has the most support in opinion polls of the party rank and file. There are exceptions, however. In 1952 and 1972 the Democrats nominated someone other than the most popular Democrat, and in 1964 the Republicans nominated a man who was tied with his rival in voter popularity.

Election Year		Candidate Preferred by Party Voters	Candidate Nominated by Party Conversion
1948	Democrats	Truman	Truman
	Republicans	Dewey	Dewey
1952	**Democrats**	**Kefauver**	**Stevenson**
	Republicans	Eisenhower	Eisenhower
1956	Democrats	Stevenson	Stevenson
	Republicans	Eisenhower	Eisenhower
1960	Democrats	Kennedy	Kennedy
	Republicans	Nixon	Nixon
1964	Democrats	Johnson	Johnson
	Republicans	**Goldwater or Nixon** (tie)	**Goldwater**
1968	Democrats	Humphrey	Humphrey
	Republicans	Nixon	Nixon
1972	**Democrats**	**Humphrey or Wallace** (tie)	**McGovern**
	Republicans	Nixon	Nixon
1976	Democrats	Carter	Carter
	Republicans	Ford	Ford
1980	Democrats	Carter	Carter
	Republicans	Reagan	Reagan
1984	Democrats	Mondale	Mondale
	Republicans	Reagan	Reagan
1988	Democrats	Dukakis	Dukakis
	Republicans	Bush	Bush
1992	Democrats	Clinton	Clinton
	Republicans	Bush	Bush
1996	Democrats	Clinton	Clinton
	Republicans	Dole	Dole

NOTE: Poll data are from last poll taken before convention.

SOURCE: Reprinted by permission of Elsevier North Holland, Inc. from James R. Beniger, "Winning the Presidential Nomination: National Polls and State Primary Elections, 1936–1972," *Public Opinion Quarterly* 40:27. Copyright © 1976 by The Trustees of Columbia University. 1976, 1980, 1984, 1988, and 1992 entries based on Gallup poll data.

chapter, under which Democratic delegates are chosen, especially those that require increased representation for women, minorities, and the young. Close examination suggests that this is not a complete explanation. For one thing, it does not explain why the Republicans nominated Goldwater in 1964 (and almost nominated Ronald Reagan instead of Gerald Ford in 1976). For another, women, minorities, and youth have among them all shades of opinions: there are many middle-of-the-road women and young people, as well as very liberal or very conservative ones. (There are not many very conservative blacks, at least on race issues, but there are certainly plenty who are moderate on race and conservative on other issues.) The question is why only *certain* elements of these groups are heavily represented at the conventions.

Who Votes in Primaries?

Maybe delegates are unrepresentative of the party rank and file because they are chosen in caucuses and primary elections whose participants are unrepresentative. Before 1972 most delegates were picked by party leaders; primaries were relatively unimportant, and voter caucuses were almost unheard of. Adlai Stevenson in 1952 and Hubert Humphrey in 1968 won the Democratic presidential nominations without even entering a primary. Harry Truman once described primaries as "eyewash."[18]

After 1972 they were no longer eyewash. The vast majority of delegates were selected in primaries and caucuses. In 1992 forty states and territories held primaries, and twenty held caucuses (some places had both primaries and caucuses).

Only about half as many people vote in primaries as in general elections. If these primary voters have more extreme political views than do the rank-and-file party followers, then they might support presidential delegates who also have extreme views. However, there is not much evidence that such is the case. Studies comparing the ideological orientations of primary voters with those of rank-and-file party voters show few strong differences.[19]

Caucuses are a different matter. A **caucus** is a meeting of party followers, often lasting for hours and held in the dead of winter in a schoolhouse miles from home, in which party delegates are picked. Only the most dedicated partisans attend.

For the Democrats, these have been liberals; for the Republicans, conservatives. In 1988 the most liberal Democratic candidate, Jesse Jackson, got more delegates in the Alaska, Delaware, Michigan, and Vermont caucuses than did Michael Dukakis, the eventual nominee. Republican evangelist Pat Robertson did not win any primary, but he won the caucuses in Alaska, Hawaii, and Washington.

Who Are the New Delegates?

However delegates are chosen, they are a different breed today than they once were. Whether picked by caucuses or primaries, and whatever their sex and race, a far larger proportion of convention delegates, both Republican and Democratic, are issue-oriented activists—people with an "amateur" or "purist" view of politics. Far fewer delegates are in it for the money (there is no longer much patronage to pass around) or to help their own reelection prospects. For example, in 1980 only 14 percent of the Democratic senators and 15 percent of the Democratic members of the House were delegates to the national convention. In 1956, by contrast, 90 percent of the senators and 33 percent of the representatives were delegates.[20]

Party activists, especially those who work without pay and who are in politics out of an interest in issues, are not likely to resemble the average citizen, for whom politics is merely an object of observation, discussion, and occasional voting. In 1972 such activists at the Democratic convention were most likely to support one of the two candidates with the strongest ideological appeal—McGovern or Wallace—and least likely to support those candidates that represented party regularity (Edmund Muskie or Hubert Humphrey).[21] It seems likely that the same thing was true at the Republican conventions of 1964, 1976, and 1980; the activists favored the more ideological candidates.

The changing incentives for participation in party work, in addition to the effects of the primary system, have contributed to the development of a national presidential nominating system different from that which once existed. The advantage of the new system is that it increases the opportunity for those with strong policy preferences to play a role in the party and thus reduces the chance that they will bolt the party and form a factional minor party. The disadvantage of the system is that it increases the chances that one or both parties may nominate presidential candidates who are not appealing to the average voter or even to a party's rank and file.

In sum, presidential nominating conventions are now heavily influenced by ideologically motivated activists. Democratic conventions have heavy representation from organized feminists, unionized school teachers, and abortion rights activists; Republican conventions have large numbers of anti-abortion activists, Christian conservatives, and small-government libertarians. As a result, the presidential nominating system is now fundamentally different from what it was as late as the mid-1960s.

Parties versus Voters

Since 1968 the Democratic party has had no trouble winning congressional elections but great difficulty winning presidential contests. Except for 1980–1986 and since 1994, the Democrats have controlled both houses of Congress; except for 1976, 1992, and 1996, they have lost every presidential election. The Republican party has had the opposite problem: though it won five out of seven presidential elections between 1968 and 1992, it did not control Congress for the forty years preceding its big win in 1994.

There are many reasons for this odd state of affairs, most of which will be discussed later. But one requires attention here. The difficulty the Democrats have had in competing for the presidency is in part because their candidates for the presidency have had, on certain issues—chiefly social and taxation issues—views very different from those of the average voter. That disparity to a large degree mirrors (and may be caused by) the gulf that separates the opinions of delegates to Democratic nominating conventions from the opinions of most citizens.

The Republicans have not been immune to this problem. In 1964 they nominated a candidate, Barry Goldwater, whose beliefs placed him well to the right of most voters. Not surprisingly, he lost. And the delegates to recent Republican conventions have held opinions on some matters that continue to be very different from most people's. Still, the problem has been more acute for the Democrats.

The problem can be seen in Table 7.4 on page 192. A lot of information is shown there; to under-

TABLE 7.4   **Political Opinions of Delegates and Voters, 1996**

	Delegates and Voters, 1996		
	Democratic Delegates	Voters	Republican Delegates
Who They Are			
Male	47%	46%	64%
Female	53	54	36
White	71	84	91
Black	17	11	3
Income over $75,000	46	11	47
What They Think			
Abortion should be permitted in all cases.	61	27	11
Government should do more to solve national problems.	76	36	4
Trade restrictions are necessary to protect domestic industries.	54	60	31
Government should protect traditional values.	27	42	56
Laws are necessary to protect racial minorities.	88	51	30
There should be a nationwide ban on assault weapons.	91	72	34
Most affirmative action programs should be continued.	81	45	9
Children of illegal immigrants should be allowed to attend public schools.	79	54	26

SOURCE: *New York Times*/CBS News polls, as reported in *New York Times* (August 12 and August 26, 1996).

stand it, study the table step by step. First, look at the middle column, which summarizes the views of voters in 1996. (Because there are about the same number of Democratic and Republican voters, the opinion of the average voter is about halfway between those of the followers of the two parties.) Now look at the columns on the far left and the far right. These show the views of delegates to the 1996 Democratic and Republican conventions. On almost every issue, the delegates are in sharp disagreement. There were hardly any conservatives at the Democratic convention or liberals at the Republican convention. On every social issue and every tax or spending issue, the delegates were at opposite ends of the spectrum.

Still, either party can win *if* its delegates nominate a candidate whose views put him or her closer to the average citizen than to the average delegate or if the campaign is fought out over issues on which the delegates and the voters agree. For example, if the election turned on what to do about an economic recession, the delegates, the voters, and the candidate would probably all agree: do whatever is necessary to end the recession. Exactly that happened in 1992, and the Democrats won.

Of course, even without a scandal, recession, or some other unifying issue, the need to win an election will lead all candidates to move toward the middle of the road. That is where the votes are. But this creates a dilemma for a candidate of either party. The stance one takes to win support from party activists in the caucuses and primaries will often be quite different from the stance one should take to win votes from the general public. In the next chapter we shall look more closely at how politicians try to cope with that dilemma.

SUMMARY

A political party exists in three arenas: among the voters who psychologically identify with it, as a grassroots organization staffed and led by activists, and as a group of elected officials who follow its lead in lawmaking. In this chapter we have looked at the party primarily as an organization and seen the various forms it takes at the local level—the machine, the ideological party, the solidary group, the sponsored party, and the personal following.

Nationally the parties are weak, decentralized coalitions of these local forms. As organizations that influence the political systems, parties are getting weaker. Voters no longer strongly identify with one of the major parties as they once did. The spread of the direct primary has made it harder for parties to control who is nominated for elective office, thus making it harder for the parties to influence the behavior of these people once elected. Delegate selection rules, especially in the Democratic party, have helped shift the center of power in the national nominating convention. Because of the changes in rules, power has moved away from officeholders and party regulars and toward the more ideological wings of the parties.

Minor parties have arisen from time to time, but the only ones that have affected the outcome of presidential elections have been those that represented a splinter group within one of the major parties (such as the Bull Moose Progressives). The two-party system is maintained, and minor parties are discouraged, by an election system (winner-take-all, plurality elections) that makes voters reluctant to waste a vote on a minor party and by the ability of potential minor parties to wield influence within a major party by means of the primary system.

In the next chapter we shall look at the role of parties in shaping voter attitudes, and in Chapter 11 we shall look at the role of parties in Congress. In each of these areas we will find more evidence of party decay.

KEY TERMS

political party   *p. 163*

mugwumps or progressives   *p. 171*

national convention   *p. 173*

national committee   *p. 173*

congressional campaign committee   *p. 173*

national chairman   *p. 173*

superdelegates   *p. 177*

political machine   *p. 178*

ideological party   *p. 180*

solidary incentives   *p. 182*

sponsored party   *p. 182*

personal following   *p. 182*

two-party system   *p. 183*

plurality system   *p. 184*

caucus   *p. 190*

SUGGESTED READINGS

Chambers, William Nisbet, and Walter Dean Burnham, eds. *The American Party Systems: Stages of Political Development.* 2d ed. New York: Oxford University Press, 1975. Essays tracing the rise of the party system since the Founding.

Goldwin, Robert A., ed. *Political Parties in the Eighties.* Washington, D.C.: American Enterprise Institute, 1980. Essays evaluating parties and efforts at reform.

Kayden, Xandra, and Eddie Mahe, Jr. *The Party Goes On.* New York: Basic Books, 1985. How the two major parties have adjusted to new political conditions.

Key, V. O., Jr. *Southern Politics.* New York: Knopf, 1949. A classic account of the one-party South.

Mayhew, David R. *Placing Parties in American Politics.* Princeton, N.J.: Princeton University Press, 1986. A state-by-state description of state party organizations.

Polsby, Nelson W. *Consequences of Party Reform.* New York: Oxford University Press, 1983. Fine analysis of how changed party rules have affected the parties and the government.

Ranney, Austin. *Curing the Mischiefs of Faction: Party Reform in America.* Berkeley: University of California Press, 1975. History and analysis of party "reforms," with special attention to the 1972 changes in the Democratic party rules.

Riordan, William L. *Plunkitt of Tammany Hall.* New York: Knopf, 1948 (first published in 1905). Insightful account of how an old-style party boss operated.

Schattschneider, E. E. *Party Government.* New York: Holt, Rinehart and Winston, 1942. An argument for a more disciplined and centralized two-party system.

Shafer, Byron E. *Quiet Revolution: The Struggle for the Democratic Party and the Shaping of Post-Reform Politics.* New York: Russell Sage Foundation, 1983. Detailed, insightful history of how the Democratic party came to be reformed.

Sundquist, James L. *Dynamics of the Party System.* Rev. ed. Washington, D.C.: Brookings Institution, 1983. History of the party system, emphasizing the impact of issues on voting.

Wilson, James Q. *The Amateur Democrat.* Chicago: University of Chicago Press, 1962. Analysis of the issue-oriented political clubs that rose in the 1950s and 1960s.

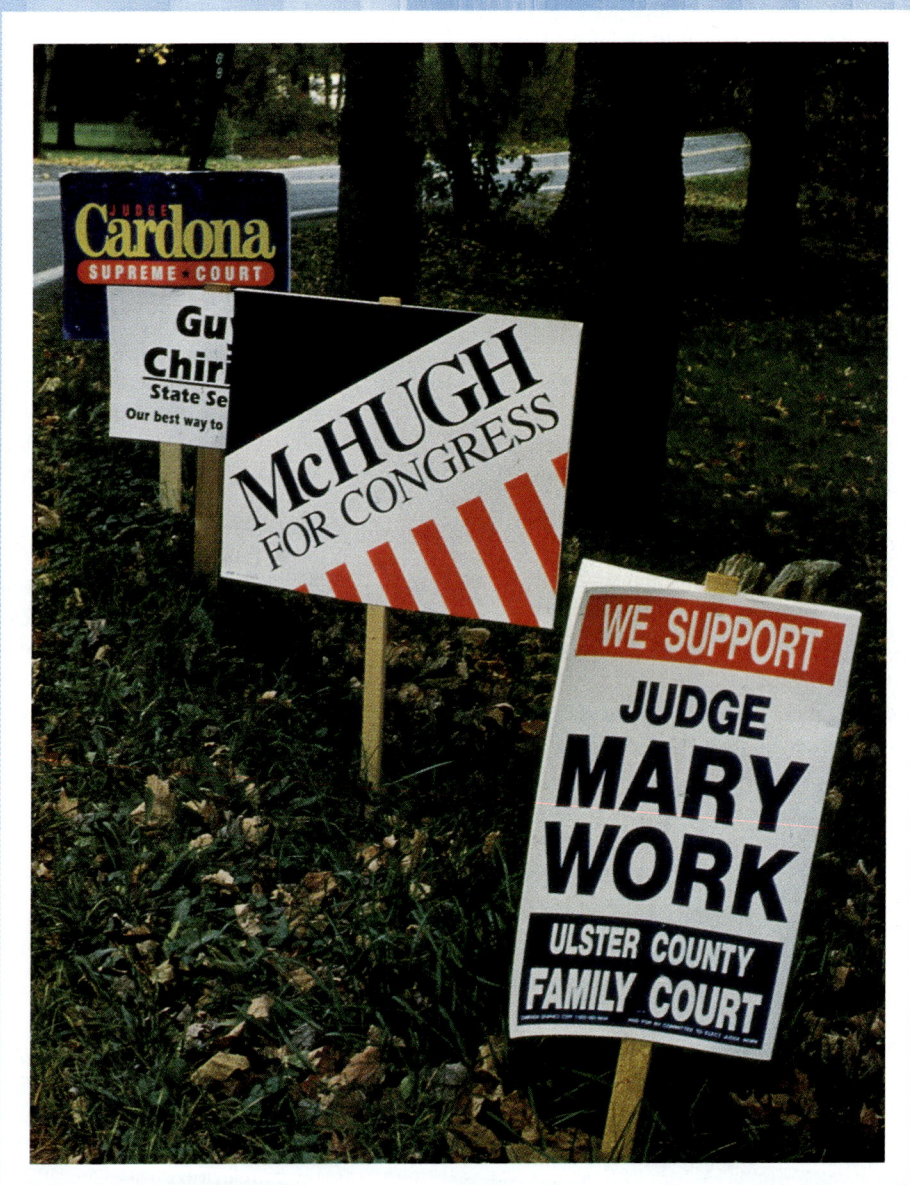

8

Elections and Campaigns

★ **Presidential versus congressional elections**

★ **Designing a campaign strategy**

★ **Primary versus general elections**

★ **Use of the media**

★ **Financing the campaigns**

★ **Campaign finance reform**

★ **Effects of campaigns**

★ **Analyzing election results**

★ **Party realignments**

★ **Changes in balloting**

★ **Elections and policy change**

I f you want to be elected to Congress or to the presidency, you must develop a game plan that is in tune with the unique legal, political, and financial realities of American politics. A plan that will work here would be useless in almost any other democratic nation; one that would work abroad would be useless here.

Elections have two crucial phases—getting nominated and getting elected. Getting nominated means getting your name on the ballot. In the great majority of states, winning your party's nomination for either the presidency or Congress requires an *individual* effort—*you* decide to run, *you* raise money, *you* and your friends collect signatures to get your name on the ballot, and *you* appeal to voters in primary elections on the basis of your personality and your definition of the issues. In most European nations, winning your party's nomination for parliament involves an *organizational* decision—*the party* looks you over, *the party* decides whether to allow you to run, and *the party* puts your name on its list of candidates.

American political parties do play a role in determining the outcome of the final election, but even that role involves parties more as labels in the voters' minds than as organizations that get out the vote. By contrast, many other democratic nations conduct campaigns that are almost entirely a contest between parties as organizations. In Israel and the Netherlands the names of the candidates for the legislature do not even appear on the ballot; only the party names are listed there. And even where candidate names are listed, as in Great Britain, the voters tend to vote "Conservative" or "Labour" more than they vote for Smith or Jones. European nations (except France) do not have a directly elected president; instead the head of the government—the prime minister—is selected by the party that has won the most seats in parliament.

At one time parties played a much larger role in elections in the United States than they do now. Until well into this century they determined, or powerfully influenced, who got nominated. In the early nineteenth century the members of Congress from a given party would meet in a caucus to pick their presidential candidate. After these caucuses were replaced by national nominating conventions, the real power over presidential nominations was wielded by local party leaders, who came together (sometimes in the legendary "smoke-filled rooms") to choose the candidate, whom the rest of the delegates would then endorse.

Congressional candidates were often handpicked by powerful local party bosses. In the past people were much more likely to vote a straight party ticket than they are today.

Chapter 7 described the factors that weakened the parties' ability to control nominations. There is little chance that they will ever regain that control. Thus candidates are now pretty much on their own. So if you want to be a candidate, what do you do?

Presidential versus Congressional Campaigns

Presidential and congressional races differ in important ways. The most obvious, of course, is size: more voters participate in the former than the latter contest, and so presidential candidates must work harder and spend more. But there are some less obvious differences that are equally important.

First, presidential races are more competitive than those for the House of Representatives. In the thirty-three elections from 1932 to 1996, the Republicans won control of the House only four times (12.5 percent of the time); in the seventeen presidential elections during the same period, the Republicans won the White House on seven occasions (41 percent of the time). In the typical presidential race, the winner gets less than 55 percent of the two-party vote; in the typical House race, the **incumbent** wins with over 60 percent of the vote. A president cannot serve more than two terms, so at least once every eight years you have a chance of running against a nonincumbent; members of Congress can serve for an unlimited number of terms, and so the chances are you will run against an incumbent. If you do, the odds are very much against you. Most years over 90 percent of all House incumbents who stand for reelection are reelected; in 1986 and 1988 *over 98 percent* retained their seats.

Second, a much smaller proportion of people vote in congressional races during off years (that is, when there is no presidential contest) than vote for president. This lower turnout (around 36 percent of the voting-age population) means that candidates in congressional races must be appealing to the more motivated and partisan voter.

Third, members of Congress can do things for their constituents that a president cannot do. They take credit—sometimes deserved, sometimes not—for every grant, contract, bridge, canal, and highway that the federal government provides the district or state. They send letters (at the government's expense) to a large fraction of their constituents and visit their district every weekend. Presidents get little credit for district improvements and must rely on the mass media to communicate with voters.

Fourth, a candidate for Congress can deny that he or she is responsible for "the mess in Washington," even when the candidate is an incumbent. As we shall see in Chapter 11, incumbents tend to run as individuals, even to the point of denouncing the very Congress of which they are a part. An incumbent president can't get away with this; rightly or wrongly, he is often held responsible for whatever has gone wrong, not only in the government but in the nation as a whole.

These last three factors—low voter turnout, services to constituents, and the ability to duck responsibility—probably help explain why so high a percentage of congressional incumbents get reelected.

But they do not enjoy a completely free ride. Members of Congress who belong to the same party as the president often feel voters' anger about national affairs, particularly economic conditions. When the economy turns sour and a Republican is in the White House, Republican congressional candidates lose votes; if a Democrat is in the White House, Democratic congressional candidates lose votes.

At one time the **coattails** of a popular presidential candidate could help congressional candidates in his own party. But there has been a sharp decline in the value of presidential coattails; indeed, some scholars doubt that they still exist.

The net effect of all these factors is that, to a substantial degree, congressional elections have become independent of presidential ones. Though economic factors may still link the fate of a president and some members of his party, by and large the incumbent members of Congress enjoy enough of a cushion to protect them against whatever political storms engulf an unpopular president. This fact further reduces the meaning of party—members of Congress can get reelected even though their party's "leader" in the White House has lost popular support, and nonincumbent candidates for Congress may lose despite the fact that a very popular president from their party is in the White House.

Running for President

The first task facing anyone who wishes to be president is to get "mentioned" as someone who is of "presidential caliber." No one is quite sure why some people are mentioned and others are not. The journalist David Broder has suggested that somewhere there is "The Great Mentioner," who announces from time to time who is of presidential caliber (and only The Great Mentioner knows how big that caliber is).

But if The Great Mentioner turns out to be as unreal as the Easter bunny, you have to figure out for yourself how to get mentioned. One way is to let it be known to reporters, "off the record," that you are thinking about running for president. Another is to travel around the country making speeches (Ronald Reagan, while working for General Electric, made a dozen or more speeches *a day* to audiences all over the country). Another way is to already have a famous name (John Glenn, the former astronaut, was in the public eye long before he declared for the presidency in 1984). Another way to get mentioned is to be identified with a major piece of legislation. Senator Bill Bradley of New Jersey was known as an architect of the Tax Reform Act of 1986; Representative Richard Gephardt of Missouri was known as an author of a bill designed to reduce foreign imports. Still another way is to be the governor of a big state. New York governors, such as Mario Cuomo, are often viewed as presidential prospects, partly because New York City is the headquarters of the television and publishing industries.

Once mentioned, it is wise to set aside a lot of time to run, especially if you are only "mentioned" as opposed to being really well known. Ronald Reagan devoted the better part of six years to run-

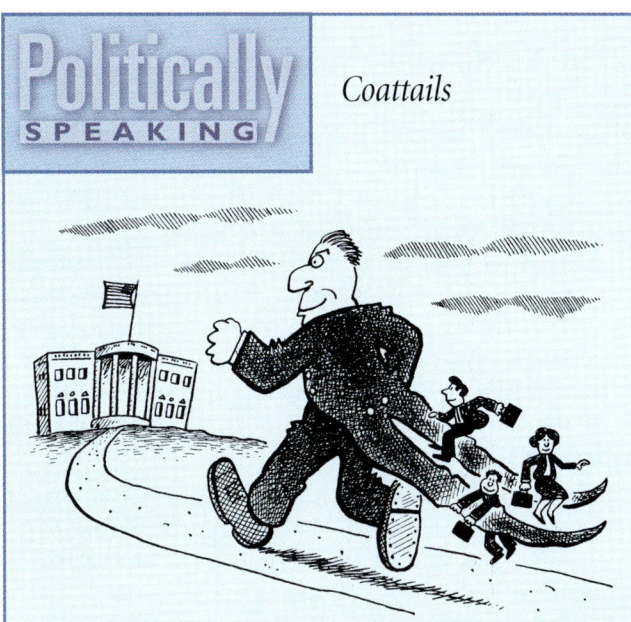

Politically SPEAKING — *Coattails*

Today the word is used in the sense of riding into office on the coattails of a better-known or more popular candidate for office. The political carrying power of coattails depends on the voters' casting a straight-ticket ballot so that their support for a popular presidential candidate is translated into support for lesser candidates on the same party ticket. Scholars are skeptical that such a coattail effect exists today.

The word first came into popular usage in 1848, when Abraham Lincoln defended the Whig party's effort to take shelter under the military coattail of that party's presidential candidate, General Zachary Taylor. Lincoln argued that in the past the Democrats had run under the coattail of General Andrew Jackson.

Later the military connotation of *coattail* fell by the wayside, and the term came to mean any effort to obtain straight-ticket voting.

SOURCE: Adapted from *Safire's Political Dictionary* by William Safire. Copyright © 1968, 1972, 1978 by William Safire. Reprinted by permission of Random House, Inc. and the author.

ning; Walter Mondale spent four years campaigning; Howard Baker resigned from the Senate in 1984 to prepare to run in 1988 (he finally dropped out of the race). However, most 1988 and 1992 candidates—George Bush; Senators Bob Dole, Al Gore, Tom Harkin, Bob Kerrey, and Paul Simon; Governors Michael Dukakis and Bill Clinton; and House members Richard Gephardt and Jack Kemp—made the run while holding elective office.

Mobilization Politics in the Nineteenth Century

Politics was a national sport during much of the nineteenth century. Torch-light parades, massive rallies, colorful banners, and public orations were commonplace then; today they have been replaced with television interviews and sedate meetings in auditoriums.

Morton Keller notes that in 1888 twenty-five possible presidential candidates were pictured on cards placed in packages of Honest Long Cut Tobacco. The cards were collected and traded as if they were pictures of baseball players.*

The very language of politics emphasized the warlike nature of the effort to mobilize voters, as suggested by this pastiche of typical phrases:

*From the **opening gun** of the **campaign** the **standard bearer,** along with other **war-horses** fielded by the party, **rallied** the **rank and file** around the party **standard,** the **bloody shirt,** and other **slogans.** Precinct **captains** aligned their **phalanxes** shoulder-to-shoulder to **mobilize** votes for the **Old Guard.** . . . Finally the **well-drilled fuglemen** in the **last ditch** closed **ranks,** overwhelmed the enemy **camp,** and divided the **spoils** of victory.†*

PRESIDENTIAL POSSIBILITIES
JOHN M. PALMER, OF ILLINOIS.

* Morton Keller, *Affairs of State* (Cambridge, Mass.: Harvard University Press, 1977), 535.
† Richard Jensen, *The Winning of the Midwest* (Chicago: University of Chicago Press, 1971), 11.

Money One reason why running takes so much time is that it takes so long to raise the necessary money and build up an organization of personal followers. As we shall see later in this chapter, federal law restricts the amount that any single individual can give a candidate to $1,000 in each election. (A **political action committee,** or PAC, which is a committee set up by and representing a corporation, labor union, or other special interest group, can give up to $5,000.) Moreover, to be eligible for federal matching grants to pay for your primary campaign, you must first raise at least $5,000, in individual contributions of $250 or less, in each of twenty states.

Organization Raising and accounting for this money requires a staff of fund-raisers, lawyers, and accountants. You also need a press secretary, a travel scheduler, an advertising specialist, a direct-mail company, and a pollster, all of whom must be paid, plus a large number of volunteers in at least those states that hold early primary elections or party caucuses.

These volunteers will brief you on the facts of each state, try to line up endorsements from local politicians and celebrities, and put together a group of people who will knock on doors, make telephone calls, organize receptions and meetings, and try to keep you from mispronouncing the name of the town in which you are speaking. Finally you have to assemble advisers on the issues. These advisers will write "position papers" for you on all sorts of things that you are supposed to know about (but probably don't). Because a campaign is usually waged around a few broad themes, these position papers rarely get used or even read. The papers exist so that you can show important interest groups that you have taken "sound" positions, so that you can be prepared to answer tough questions, and so that journalists can look up your views on matters that may become topical.

Strategy and Themes Every candidate picks a strategy for the campaign. In choosing one, much depends on whether you are the incumbent.

Incumbents must defend their record, like it or not. (An incumbent ran for president in 1964, 1972, 1976, 1980, 1984, 1992, and 1996.) The challenger attacks the incumbent. When there is no incumbent (as in 1960, 1968, and 1988), both candidates can announce their own programs; however, the candidate from the party that holds the White House must take, whether he thinks he deserves it or not, some of the blame for whatever has gone wrong in the preceding four years. Within these limits, a strategy consists of the answer to questions about tone, theme, timing, and targets:

- What *tone* should the campaign have? Should it be a positive (build-me-up) or negative (attack-the-opponent) campaign? In 1988 George Bush began with a negative campaign; Michael Dukakis followed suit.

- What *theme* can I develop? A theme is a simple, appealing idea that can be repeated over and over again. For Jimmy Carter in 1976 it was "trust"; for Ronald Reagan in 1980 it was "competence," and in 1984 it was "it's morning again in America"; for Bush in 1988 it was "stay the course"; for Clinton in 1992 it was "we need to change."

- What should be the *timing* of the campaign? If you are relatively unknown, you will have to put everything into the early primaries and caucuses, try to emerge a front-runner, and then hope for the best. If you are already the front-runner, you may either go for broke early (and try to drive out all your opponents) or hold back some reserves for a long fight.

- Whom should you *target*? Only a small percentage of voters change their vote from one election to the next. Who is likely to change this time—unemployed steelworkers? Unhappy farmers? People upset by inflation?

Primary versus General Campaigns

These four strategic decisions are not easily made, however, because you are (you hope) entering two elections, not just one. The first consists of primary elections and caucuses, which select the nominees; the second is the general election, which decides who wins the office. Each election attracts a different

The Road to the Nomination

A campaign for the presidential nomination must begin early. Among the key steps are these:

Create an organization: A campaign manager, fund-raiser, pollster, and several lawyers and accountants must be hired early—two or even three years before the election. Money cannot legally be raised until an organization exists to receive and account for it.

Start raising money: To be eligible for federal matching dollars for your primary-election campaign, you must raise $250 from each of at least twenty donors in each of twenty states. You cannot receive more than $1,000 from any individual or $5,000 from any PAC. There are national and state-by-state limits on what you can spend.

Prepare for the early primaries and caucuses: To show that you are a serious contender and have "momentum," you should enter the early primaries and caucuses. In 1996 some key early ones were

- February 12: Iowa caucus
- February 20: New Hampshire primary
- March 12: "Super Tuesday" (primaries in six states, mostly in the South)
- March 19: "Big 10 Tuesday" (primaries in the Midwest)

To win a primary you must campaign hard and often; to win a caucus you must have an organization that can get your supporters to attend and vote at the local caucuses.

Pick a strategy: If you are relatively unknown, you must campaign heavily in the early primaries (this is called a "front-loaded" campaign). But then you risk running out of money before the later primaries in the big states. If you are the front-runner you are in better shape, but then you must worry about losing even one primary (as did Dole to Buchanan in New Hampshire in 1996), thereby tarnishing your "unbeatable" image.

Control the convention: If you win the most delegates in the primaries and caucuses, you will be nominated. (From 1956 through 1996 the winning candidate was nominated on the first ballot at the Democratic and Republican conventions.) Then your problem is to control everything else that goes on at the convention—the platform, the speeches, the vice presidential nomination—so nothing happens that will embarrass you.

Presidential campaigns, such as this by Steve Forbes, start off as retail politics in small meetings.

mix of voters, workers, and media attention. What works in the primary election may not work in the general one, and vice versa.

To win the nomination you must mobilize political activists who will give money, do volunteer work, and attend local caucuses. As we saw in Chapters 5 and 6, activists are more ideologically stringent than the voters at large. To motivate these activists you must be more liberal (if you are a Democrat) in your tone and theme than are rank-and-file Democrats, or more conservative (if you are a Republican) than are rank-and-file Republicans.

Consider the caucuses held in Iowa in early February of a presidential election year. This is the first real test of the candidates vying for the nomination. Anyone who does poorly here is at a disadvantage, in terms of media attention and contributor interest, for the rest of the campaign.

The several thousand Iowans who participate in their party caucuses are not representative of the followers of their party in the state, much less nationally. In 1988 Senator Robert Dole came in first and evangelist Pat Robertson came in second in the Iowa Republican caucus, with Vice President George Bush finishing third. As it turned out, there was little support for Dole or Robertson in the rest of the country.

Democrats who participate in the Iowa caucuses tend to be more liberal than Democrats generally.[1] Moreover, the way the caucuses are run is a far cry from how most elections are held. To vote in the Republican caucus, you need not prove you are a

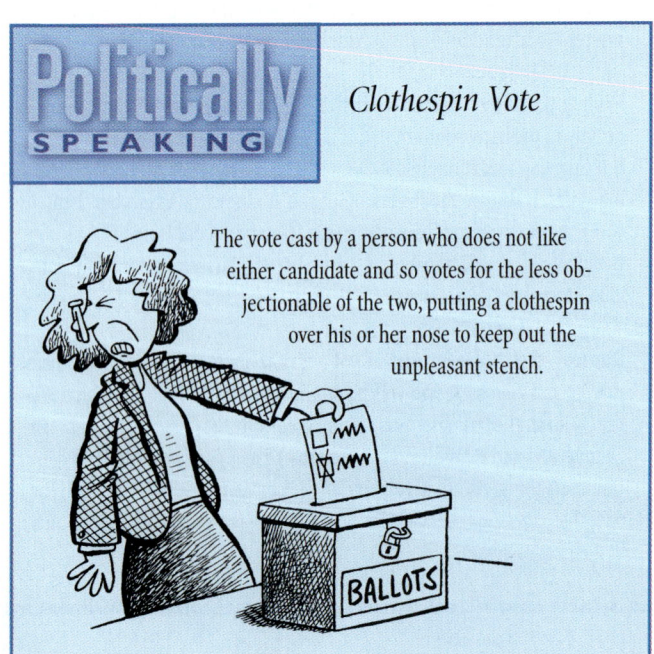

Politically SPEAKING

Clothespin Vote

The vote cast by a person who does not like either candidate and so votes for the less objectionable of the two, putting a clothespin over his or her nose to keep out the unpleasant stench.

Republican or even a voter. The Democratic caucus is not an election at all; instead, a person supporting a certain candidate stands in one corner of the room with people who also support him, while those supporting other candidates stand in other corners with other groups. There is a lot of calling back and forth, intended to persuade people to leave one group and join another. No group with fewer than 15 percent of the people in attendance gets to choose any delegates, so people in these small groups then go to other, larger ones. It is a cross between musical chairs and fraternity pledge week.

Suppose you are a Democrat running for president and you do well in the Iowa caucuses. Suppose you go on to win your party's nomination. Now you have to go back to Iowa to campaign for votes in the general election. Since 1940 Iowa has voted Republican in every presidential election but four (1948, 1964, 1988, and 1996). Your Republican opponent is not going to let you forget all of the liberal slogans you uttered nine months before. The Republican candidate faces the mirror image of this problem—sounding very conservative to get support from Republican activists in states such as Massachusetts and New York and then having to defend those speeches when running against his Democratic opponent in those states.

The problem is not limited to Iowa but exists in every state where activists are more ideologically polarized than the average voter. To get activist support for the nomination candidates move to the ideological extremes; to win the general election they try to move back to the ideological center. The typical voter looks at the results and often decides that neither candidate appeals to him or her very much, and so casts a "clothespin vote" (see the box on page 200).

Occasionally even the voters in the primary elections will be more extreme ideologically than are the general-election voters. This certainly happened in 1972. George McGovern won the Democratic nomination with the support of voters who were well to the left of the public at large (and even of rank-and-file Democratic voters) on such issues as U.S. policy in Vietnam, amnesty for draft resisters, decriminalizing marijuana, and helping minorities.[2] His general-election opponent, Richard Nixon, was able to take advantage of this by portraying McGovern as a leftist. But even when primary voters are not too dif-

TRIVIA

Elections

Only two men to have been elected president by the House of Representatives after failing to win a majority in the Electoral College	*Thomas Jefferson (1800) and John Quincy Adams (1824)*
Only Democratic senator to be the running mate of a Republican presidential candidate	*Andrew Johnson (1864)*
The candidate for president who received more popular votes than his opponent but was not elected	*Grover Cleveland got more popular votes but fewer electoral votes than Benjamin Harrison in 1888*
President who won the largest percentage of the popular vote	*Lyndon B. Johnson, 61.7 percent (1964)*
Only person to serve as vice president and president without having been elected to either post	*Gerald Ford (1973–1976)*
President who won the most electoral votes	*Ronald Reagan (525 in 1984)*
First woman to run for national office on a major-party ticket	*Geraldine Ferraro (Democratic candidate for vice president, 1984)*

Geraldine Ferraro

Kinds of Elections

There are two kinds of elections in the United States: general and primary. A **general election** is used to fill an elective office. A **primary election** is used to select a party's candidates for an elective office, though in fact those who vote in a primary election may not consider themselves party members. Some primaries are closed. In a **closed primary** you must declare in advance (sometimes several weeks in advance) that you are a registered member of the political party in whose primary you wish to vote. About forty states have closed primaries.

Other primaries are open. In an **open primary** you can decide when you enter the voting booth which party's primary you wish to participate in. You are given every party's ballot; you may vote on one. Idaho, Michigan, Minnesota, Montana, North Dakota, Utah, Vermont, and Wisconsin have open primaries. A variant on the open primary is the **blanket** (or "free love") **primary**—in the voting booth you mark a ballot that lists the candidates of all the parties, and thus you can help select the Democratic candidate for one office and the Republican candidate for another. Alaska and Washington have blanket primaries.

The ballots from a state with an "open" primary election.

The differences among these kinds of primaries should not be exaggerated, for even the closed primary does not create any great barrier for a voter who wishes to vote in the Democratic primary in one election and the Republican in another. Some states also have a **runoff primary:** if no candidate gets a majority of the votes, there is a runoff between the two with the most votes. Runoff primaries are common in the South.

A special kind of primary, a **presidential primary,** is that used to pick delegates to the presidential nominating conventions of the major parties. Presidential primaries come in a bewildering variety. A simplified list looks like this:

- **Delegate selection only** Only the names of prospective delegates to the convention appear on the ballot. They may or may not indicate their presidential preference.

- **Delegate selection with advisory presidential preference** Voters pick delegates and indicate their

preferences among presidential candidates. The delegates are not legally bound to observe these preferences.

- **Binding presidential preference** Voters indicate their preferred presidential candidate. Delegates must observe these preferences, at least for a certain number of convention ballots. The delegates may be chosen in the primary or by a party convention.

In 1981 the Supreme Court ruled that political parties, not state legislatures, have the right to decide how delegates to national conventions are selected. Thus Wisconsin could not retain an "open" primary if the national Democratic party objected (*Democratic Party* v. *La Follette,* 101 Sup. Ct. 1010, 1981). Now the parties can insist that only voters who declare themselves Democrats or Republicans can vote in presidential primaries. The Supreme Court's ruling may have relatively little practical effect, however, since the "declaration" might occur only an hour or a day before the election.

OFFICIAL BALLOT FOR PRESIDENTIAL PREFERENCE VOTE

REPUBLI

NOTICE TO ELECTORS: THIS BALLO
INITIALED BY 2 ELECTION INSPECT
BALLOT, THE BALLOT MUST BEAR
CLERK OR DEPUTY CLERK.

IN THE PRESIDENTIAL PREFEREN
BALLOT OF ONLY

MARK THIS BALLOT IN ONE SPAC

Express your preference for o
printed on this ballot (in that
at the RIGHT of that person's

Vote for an uninstructed dele
national convention of the Re
a cross (X) in the square at th

Write in the name of another
candidate of the Republican
name into the space followin

Lamar Alexander . . . . . .

Robert K. Dornan . . . . . .

Richard Lugar . . . .

OFFICIAL BALLOT FOR PRESIDENTIAL PREFERENCE VOTE

DEMOCRATIC PARTY

NOTICE TO ELECTORS: THIS BALLOT MAY BE INVALID UNLESS
INITIALED BY 2 ELECTION INSPECTORS. IF CAST AS AN ABSENTEE
BALLOT, THE BALLOT MUST BEAR THE INITIALS OF THE MUNICIPAL
CLERK OR DEPUTY CLERK.

IN THE PRESIDENTIAL PREFERENCE PRIMARY, YOU MAY VOTE ON THE
BALLOT OF ONLY ONE POLITICAL PARTY.

MARK THIS BALLOT IN ONE SPACE ONLY. YOU HAVE ONE OF 3 CHOICES:

Express your preference for the person whose name is printed on
this ballot (in that case, make a cross (X) in the square at the
RIGHT of that person's name); or

Vote for an uninstructed delegation from Wisconsin to the
national convention of the Democratic party (in that case, make
a cross (X) in the square at the RIGHT of "Uninstructed delegation"); or

Write in the name of another person to become the presidential
candidate of the Democratic party (in that case, write that
person's name into the space following "Write i

ferent from general-election voters, the activists who contribute the time, money, and effort to mount a campaign are very different from the voters—in both parties.

Television, Debates, and Direct Mail

Once campaigns mostly involved parades, big rallies, "whistle-stop" train tours, and shaking hands outside factory gates and near shopping centers. All of this still goes on, but increasingly presidential and senatorial candidates (and those House candidates with television stations in their districts) use broadcasting.

There are two ways to use television—by running paid advertisements and by getting on the nightly news broadcasts. In the language of campaigners, short television ads are called *spots,* and a campaign activity that appears on a news broadcast is called a *visual.* Much has been written about the preparation of spots, usually under titles such as "the selling of the president" or "packaging the candidate" (and mostly by advertising executives, who are not especially known for underestimating their own influence). No doubt spots can have an important effect in some cases. A little-known candidate can increase his or her visibility by frequent use of spots (this is what Jimmy Carter did in the 1976 presidential primaries). Sometimes a complete unknown can win a primary by clever use of television, as allegedly happened when Mike Gravel became the Democratic nominee for senator from Alaska in 1968 and Milton Shapp became the Democratic nominee for governor of Pennsylvania in 1966.

The effect of television advertising on general elections is probably a good deal less than its effect on primaries; indeed, as we shall see in Chapter 10, most scientific studies of television's influence on voting decisions have shown that either it has no effect or the effect is subtle and hard to detect. Nor is it surprising that this should be the case. In a general election, especially one for a high-visibility office (such as president or governor), the average voter has many sources of information—his or her own party or ideological preference, various kinds of advertising, the opinions of friends and family, and newspaper and magazine stories. Furthermore, both sides will use TV spots; if well done, they are likely to cancel each other out. In short, it is not yet clear

that a gullible public is being sold a bill of goods by slick Madison Avenue advertisers, whether the goods are automobiles or politicians.

Visuals are a vital part of any major campaign effort because, unlike spots, they cost the campaign little and, as "news," they may have greater credibility with the viewer. A visual is a brief filmed episode showing the candidate doing something that a reporter thinks is newsworthy. Simply making a speech, unless the speech contains important new facts or charges, is often thought by TV editors to be uninteresting: television viewers are not attracted by pictures of "talking heads," and in the highly competitive world of TV, audience reactions are all-important determinants of what gets on the air. Knowing this, campaign managers will strive to have their candidates do something visually interesting every day, no later than 3:00 P.M. (if the visual is to be on the 6:00 P.M. news)—talk to elderly folks in a nursing home, shake hands with people waiting in an unemployment line, or sniff the waters of a polluted lake. Obviously all these efforts are for nought if a TV camera crew is not around; great pains are therefore taken to schedule these visuals at times

In the 1888 presidential campaign, supporters of Benjamin Harrison rolled a huge ball covered with campaign slogans across the country. The gimmick, first used in 1840, gave rise to the phrase "keep the ball rolling."

Candidates first made phonographic recordings of their speeches in 1908. Warren G. Harding is shown here recording a speech during the 1920 campaign.

Urbanization and the movement of people to big cities made railroad tours of small towns an increasingly inefficient way to meet voters. Thus the motorcade through city streets began to take its place, such as this one in 1968 where the public greeted Robert F. Kennedy.

and in places that make it easy for the photographers to be present.

Ironically, visuals—and television newscasts generally—may give the viewer less information than commercial spots. This, of course, is the exact opposite of what many people believe. It is commonplace to deplore political advertising, especially the short spot, on the grounds that it is either devoid of information or manipulative, and to praise television news programs, especially longer debates and interviews, because they are informative and balanced. In fact, the best research we have so far suggests that the reverse is true: news programs covering elections tend to convey very little information (they often show scenes of crowds cheering or candidates shouting slogans) and make little or no impression on viewers, if indeed they are watched at all. Paid commercials, on the other hand, especially the shorter spots, often contain a good deal of information that is seen, remembered, and evaluated by a public that is quite capable of distinguishing between fact and humbug.[3]

A special kind of television campaigning is the campaign debate. Incumbents or well-known candidates have little incentive to debate their opponents; by so doing, they only give more publicity to lesser-

"Whistle-stop" tours were popular in the railroad era; in 1992, Bill Clinton and Al Gore substituted a bus tour.

known rivals. Despite the general rule among politicians never to help an opponent, Vice President Nixon debated the less-well-known John Kennedy in 1960, and President Gerald Ford debated the less-well-known Jimmy Carter in 1976. Nixon and Ford lost. Lyndon Johnson would not debate Barry Goldwater in 1964, nor would Nixon debate Humphrey in 1968 or McGovern in 1972. Johnson and Nixon won. Carter debated the equally well known Reagan in 1980 (but refused to join in a three-way debate with Reagan and John Anderson). Carter lost. It is hard to know what effect TV debates have on election outcomes, but poll data suggest that in 1980 voters who watched the debates were reassured by Reagan's performances; after the second debate with Carter, he took a lead in the polls that he never relinquished.[4] In 1984 most people thought that Mondale did better than Reagan in the first debate, but there is little evidence that the debate affected the outcome of the election. In 1992 and 1996, Clinton was probably the better debater, but he most likely would have won even if he had stumbled.

In 1988 the televised debate became a major activity during—and even before—the primary elec-

tions. The half dozen or so contenders for both the Democratic and the Republican presidential nominations participated in so many debates that one journalist was led to compare the campaign to a political version of the television program "The Dating Game," with the candidates, like bachelors trying to impress a woman, describing, over and over again, all their good qualities. Other than providing free television exposure (and probably boring the candidates to tears), it is hard to see what this accomplished.

Though TV visuals and debates are free, they are also risky. The risk is the slip of the tongue. You may have spent thirty years of your life in unblemished public service, you may have thought through your position on the issues with great care, you may have rehearsed your speeches until your dog starts to howl, but just make one verbal blunder and suddenly the whole campaign focuses on your misstep. In 1976 President Ford erroneously implied that Poland was not part of the Soviet bloc. For days the press dwelt on this slip. His opponent, Jimmy Carter, admitted in a *Playboy* interview that he had sometimes had lust in his heart. It is hard to imagine anyone who has not, but apparently presidents are supposed to be above that sort of thing. In 1980 Ronald Reagan said that trees cause pollution—oops, here we go again.

Because of the fear of a slip, because the voters do not want to hear long, fact-filled speeches about complex issues, and because general-election campaigns are fights to attract the centrist voter, the candidates will rely on a stock speech that sets out the campaign theme as well as on their ability to string together several proven applause-getting lines. For reporters covering the candidate every day, it can be a mind-numbing experience. Nelson Rockefeller spoke so often of the "brotherhood of man and the fatherhood of God" that the reporters started referring to it as his BOMFOG speech. Occasionally this pattern is interrupted by a "major" address—that is, a carefully composed talk on some critical issue, usually delivered before a live audience and designed to provide issue-related stories for the reporters to write.

If you dislike campaign oratory, put yourself in the candidate's shoes for a moment. Every word you say will be scrutinized, especially for slips of the tongue. Interest group leaders and party activists

The first televised presidential campaign debate occurred in 1960 between John F. Kennedy and Richard M. Nixon.

will react sharply to any phrase that departs from their preferred policies. Your opponent stands ready to pounce on any error of fact or judgment. You must give countless speeches every day. The rational reaction to this state of affairs is to avoid controversy, stick to prepared texts and tested phrases, and

In 1992 and 1996 Ross Perot bought "infomercials"—half-hour television broadcasts devoted to his discussion of national issues.

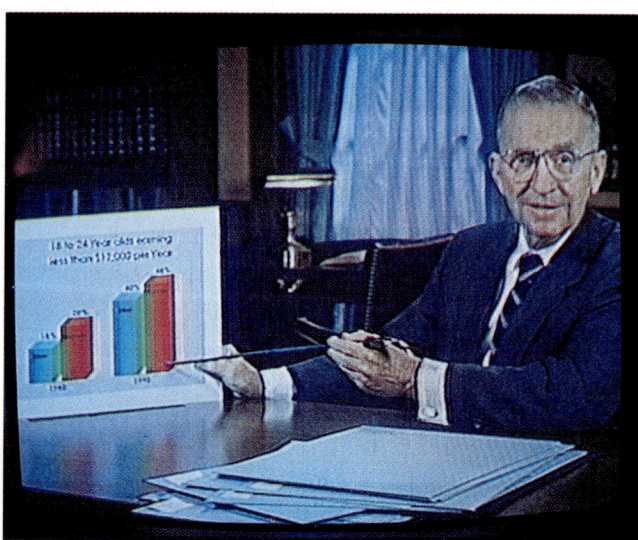

shun anything that sounds original (and hence untested). You therefore wind up trying to sell yourself as much as or more than your ideas. Voters may *say* that they admire a blunt, outspoken person, but in a tough political campaign they would probably find such bluntness a little unnerving.

Television is the most visible example of modern technology's effect on campaigns. Since 1960 presidential elections have been contested largely through television. Without television, the campaign waged in 1992 by independent candidate Ross Perot might not have happened at all. Perot launched his candidacy with successive appearances on Cable News Network's call-in program "Larry King Live," and he bought several half-hour chunks of television time to air his views on the federal budget deficit. In early October, before the first of three televised debates featuring Perot, Republican incumbent George Bush, and Democratic challenger Bill Clinton, most national polls showed Perot with only 10 percent of the vote. But after the debates Perot's support in the polls doubled, and he ended up with about 19 percent of the votes cast on election day.

In 1996 the big television networks agreed to make some free television time available to the major presidential candidates. The Federal Communications Commission approved the plan to limit the free TV to "major" candidates, thus denying it to minor third-party nominees.

Less visible than television but perhaps just as important is the computer. The computer makes possible sophisticated direct-mail campaigning, and this in turn makes it possible for a candidate to address specific appeals to particular voters easily and rapidly solicit campaign contributions.

Whereas television is heard by everybody—and thus leads the candidate using it to speak in generalities to avoid offending anyone—direct mail is aimed at particular groups (college students, Native Americans, bankers, auto workers), to whom specific views can be expressed with much less risk of offending someone. So important are the lists of names of potential contributors to whom a computer may send appeals that a prized resource of any candidate, guarded as if it were a military secret, is "The List." Novices in politics must slowly develop their own lists or beg sympathetic incumbents for a peek at theirs.

The Clinton-Dole TV debate in 1996 continued a tradition begun in 1960.

The chief consequence of the new style of campaigning is not, as some think, that it is more manipulative than old-style campaigning (picnics with free beer and $5 bills handed to voters can be just as manipulative as TV ads); rather, it is that running campaigns has become divorced from the process of governing. Previously, the party leaders who ran the campaigns would take part in the government once it was elected, and since they were *party* leaders, they had to worry about getting their candidate reelected. Modern political consultants take no responsibility for governing, and by the time the next election rolls around, they may be working for someone else.

Money

All these consultants, TV ads, and computerized mailings cost money—lots of it (see Figure 8.1). A powerful California politician once observed that "money is the mother's milk of politics," and many people think that our democracy is drowning in it.

The 1992 presidential election cost $286 million, up from $177 million in 1988. The 1992 congres-

sional races cost another $364 million. In total the candidates, parties, and taxpayers had to come up with $650 million to pick our national leaders. When that kind of money is spent, many people will cynically conclude that elections are being bought and sold. Clever television producers are being paid huge sums, so the theory goes, to put on TV ads that sell candidates as if they were boxes of soap.

But matters are a good deal more complicated and less sinister than the popular theory supposes. Money is important in politics as in everything else, but it is not obvious that the candidates with the most money always win or that the donors of the money buy big favors in exchange for their big bucks. In Chapter 9 we will consider what, if anything, interest groups get for the money they give to politicians, and in Chapter 10 we shall summarize what we know about the effects of television adver-

FIGURE 8.1   The Cost of Winning

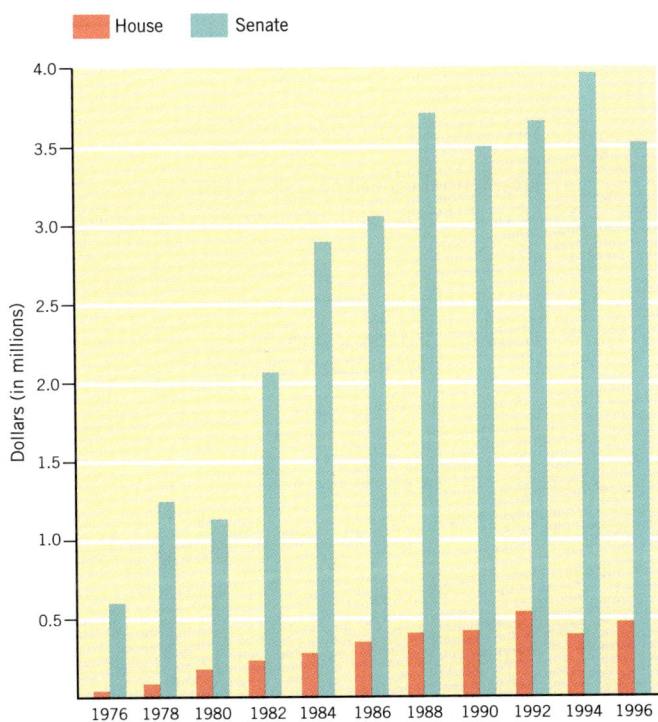

SOURCES: For 1976–1988: *New York Times* (March 20, 1990): A10, reporting data from the Federal Election Commission. Copyright © 1990 by the New York Times Company. Reprinted by permission. For 1990–1992: Federal Election Commission Report, March 4, 1993.

FIGURE 8.2   Where the Money Comes From: Sources of Campaign Funds of All House and Senate Candidates, 1982 and 1990

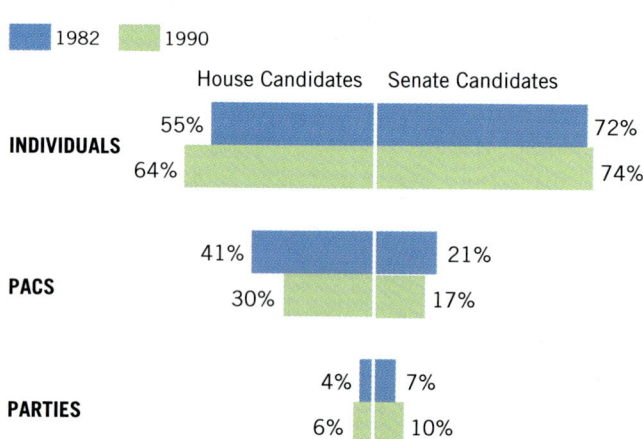

SOURCE: Michael J. Malbin, "Fixing the Race: Dollars and Sense in Campaigns," *The American Enterprise,* November/December 1991, 65. Reprinted with permission.

tising on elections. Here let us try to answer four questions: Where does campaign money come from? What rules govern how it is raised and spent? What has been the effect of campaign finance reform? What does campaign spending buy?

The Sources of Campaign Money

Presidential candidates get part of their money from private donors and part from the federal govern-

ment; congressional candidates get all of their money from private sources. In the presidential primaries, candidates raise money from private citizens and interest groups. The federal government will provide matching funds, dollar for dollar, for all monies raised from individual donors who contribute no more than $250. Since every candidate wants as much of this "free" federal money as possible, each has an incentive to raise money from small, individual givers. (To prove they are serious candidates, they must first raise $5,000 in each of twenty states from such small contributors.) The government also gives a lump-sum grant to each political party to help pay the costs of its nominating convention. In the general election the government pays all the costs of each candidate, up to a limit set by law (in 1996 that limit was $61.8 million for each major candidate and $29 million for Perot).

Congressional candidates get no government funds; all their money must come out of their own pockets or be raised from individuals, interest groups (PACs), or the political parties. Contrary to what many people think, most of that money comes—and has always come—from individual donors (see Figure 8.2). Because the rules sharply limit how much any individual can give, these donors tend not to be fat cats but people of modest means who contribute $100 or $200 per person.

Since the typical individual contribution is very small (and in no case larger than $1,000), some candidates have turned to rock bands and movie stars

TABLE 8.1   **Sources of Campaign Funds: All House and Senate Candidates in 1991–1992 by Incumbents, Challengers, and Open**

	Incumbents		Challengers		Open	
	Sum (millions)	Percent	Sum	Percent	Sum	Percent
Individuals	$151.7	50.5%	$107.0	58.5%	$96.6	55.1%
PACs	126.7	42.2	21.4	11.7	32.4	18.5
Candidates	1.0	0.3	10.5	5.7	6.8	3.9
Loans	9.6	3.2	37.0	20.2	33.6	19.2
Other	11.3	3.8	6.9	3.8	6.0	3.4
Totals	$300.3		$182.8		$175.4	

NOTE: The data on candidates' contributions are especially messy. They include direct personal contributions and loans to the campaign, but the campaign committees often repay loans from previous elections. In the end, loans from incumbents are almost always repaid by campaign committees, and direct contributions by candidates amount to a trace of the incumbents' totals.
SOURCE: *Federal Election Commission Report* (March 4, 1993).

to put on benefit performances. If five thousand people will each pay $25 for a performance by Slipped Disc, a lot of money can be raised in a hurry.

The most a PAC can give a candidate in any election is $5,000, but the typical PAC does not donate anything approaching the maximum amount; usually it gives a few hundred dollars to each candidate it supports.

These figures conceal some important differences among kinds of candidates, however. As Table 8.1 shows, incumbent members of Congress running for reelection get over a third of their money from PACs and spend next to nothing out of their own pockets. Their challengers, by contrast, spend only half as much as the incumbent and are able to get only one-sixth of that from PACs. Challengers have to put up much more of their own money. As we shall see in the next section, these money problems weaken the ability of challengers to mount effective campaigns.

Campaign Finance Rules

During the 1972 presidential election, men hired by President Nixon's campaign staff broke into the headquarters of the Democratic National Committee in the Watergate office building. They were caught by an alert security guard. The subsequent investigation disclosed that the Nixon people had engaged in dubious or illegal money-raising schemes, including taking large sums from wealthy contributors in exchange for appointing them to ambassadorships. Many individuals and corporations were indicted for making illegal donations (since 1925 it had been against the law for corporations or labor unions to contribute money to candidates, but the law had been unenforceable). Some of the accused had given money to Democratic candidates as well as to Nixon.

To prevent these abuses, in 1974 Congress passed a new federal campaign finance reform law. It created a six-person Federal Election Commission (FEC) charged with enforcing a new, tougher set of restrictions on political spending as well as a system of public financing of presidential campaigns. The key provisions of this law are summarized in the accompanying box.

If you want to run for Congress today, you must report to the FEC every contribution you receive of

Major Federal Campaign-Finance Rules

General

- All federal election contributions and expenditures are reported to the six-person Federal Election Commission, which has the power to investigate and prosecute violators.

- All contributions over $100 must be disclosed, with name, address, and occupation of contributor.

- No cash contributions over $100, no foreign contributions.

- No ceiling on amount a candidate or campaign may spend (unless a presidential candidate accepts federal funding).

Individual Contributions

- May not exceed $1,000 to any candidate in any election per year.

- May not exceed $20,000 per year to a national party committee or $5,000 to a political action committee.

- No limit on expenditures for "independent advertising."

Political Action Committees (PACs)

- A corporation, union, or other association may each establish one PAC.

- A PAC must register six months in advance, have at least fifty contributors, and give to at least five candidates.

- PAC contributions to a candidate may not exceed $5,000 per election, or to a national party, $15,000 per year.

Presidential Primaries

- Federal matching funds, dollar for dollar, are available for all money raised by candidates from individual donors giving $250 or less.

- To be eligible, a candidate must raise $5,000 in each of twenty states, in contributions of $250 or less.

Presidential Election

- Federal government will pay all campaign costs of major-party candidates and part of the cost of minor-party candidates (those winning between 5 percent and 25 percent of the vote).

$100 or more, and you cannot accept more than $1,000 from any individual during any election. (If you run in both the primary and the general election, you can take up to $1,000 in each campaign from the same person.) The law against taking money from corporations or labor unions was reaffirmed, but such organizations were allowed to form PACs that could raise money in voluntary contributions from their employees or members. (Trade associations, professional societies, and other groups were also allowed to form PACs.) No PAC can give more than $5,000 to any candidate in any election, with the primary and the general contest counted as separate elections.

Initially the law also set limits on how much an individual candidate could spend on his or her own campaign, but the Supreme Court ruled that this was an unconstitutional infringement of the First Amendment's guarantee of free speech.[5] The right to run for office and to express your views includes the right to spend your own money on the effort. However, the Court let stand a limit of $50,000 on how much a presidential candidate could spend out of his pocket on his own campaign if he accepted federal financing. They reasoned that anybody taking the taxpayers' money was getting plenty of help in exercising his First Amendment rights, and so it

was not unreasonable to restrict his own spending on that cause.

The law sets no limits on how much individuals or organizations can spend for "independent" political advertising on behalf of a candidate. To be considered independent, an expenditure cannot be made at the request of or in cooperation or consultation with the candidate or the candidate's campaign organization. These independent expenditures are typically made by ideologically oriented PACs and sometimes take the form of "negative ads"— that is, advertisements attacking an opposing candidate for his or her position on the environment, abortion, or whatever.

No law regulating a powerful human desire, such as ambition for office, can ever be entirely successful, and campaign finance rules are no exception. Though the law has ended many of the worst abuses, it leaves a number of loopholes that candidates can exploit. Among them are these:

• The political parties can solicit unlimited funds from individuals, corporations, and unions, provided that they spend the money on local party activities such as voter registration campaigns and get-out-the-vote drives and not on behalf of specific candidates. But of course a successful cam-

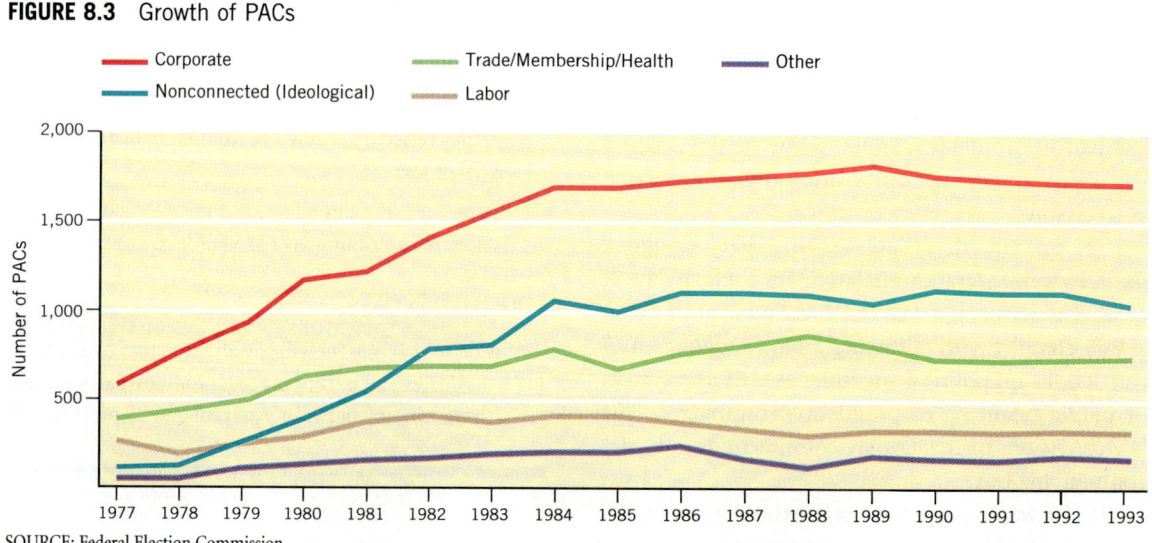

FIGURE 8.3 Growth of PACs

SOURCE: Federal Election Commission.

paign by a party to get voters to the polls will tend to help the candidate of that party. The funds are called **soft money,** as opposed to the hard money that must be reported to the FEC. In 1996, political parties raised huge amounts of soft money, leading to new demand for another law to change campaign finance.

• Many small contributions from different individuals or PACs can be bundled together and delivered at one time in order to increase the impact of the contributions on the campaign and, presumably, better promote the interests of the contributors before those of the candidate.

The Effects of Reform

The intent of the reform was to get political fundraising out in the open and subject to clearly understood rules that would minimize the chance of some fat cat's buying a pet politician. By and large the law has succeeded at that.

But the reform has also had some unintended effects. First, by authorizing PACs to raise money, the law made possible a vast increase in the amount of money spent on elections by special interests. Figure 8.3 shows how PACs have grown from just a few hundred in 1977 to over four thousand in 1993. During that same period their contributions to federal candidates rose from about $25 million to nearly $190 million.

Second, the reform has shifted the control of campaign money away from the political parties and toward individual candidates, thus further weakening the power of the parties. Some people might think this is a good thing, but there is another side to the story. To the extent that people vote for parties rather than for individuals (and many people still do), the party ought to have some way of influencing the selection and behavior of its candidates. It is harder for this to occur when parties play so small a role in financing campaigns.

Third, the reforms provide an advantage to wealthy challengers. If you want to take on a well-entrenched incumbent and have no money of your own, you will find that the rules make raising the necessary funds a slow and painful process involving endless appeals to countless individuals to obtain small donations. It can easily take half a million dollars to mount a credible congressional campaign;

that adds up to a lot of phone calls and coffee parties. But if you can write a check for half a million dollars, you can spare yourself all the trouble.

Fourth, the reforms give an advantage to candidates with strong ideological appeal. Unless you are rich, the easiest way to get money from lots of small donors is to use direct-mail pieces that evoke powerful emotions such as feelings for or against abortion, gun control, school prayer, or the death penalty. Never mind whether these are the most important issues—they generate cash.

Fifth, the reforms penalize people who start late in a campaign. Fund-raising takes a lot of time; if you decide at the last minute to run, you may discover you have no chance of raising the money you need before it is too late. Incumbents know this, so many of them spend their time in office raising huge war chests well in advance of the election in order to scare off would-be challengers.

Do American Elections Really Cost So Much?

Many people worry that elections in the United States are too costly. But compared to what? One way to answer that question is to see how our elections stack up against those held abroad. The data are hard to find and even harder to compare, but Howard Penniman has produced these estimates of the cost of a national election per eligible voter:

United Kingdom	$0.50
West Germany	3.20
UNITED STATES	3.25
(Congressional, $1.51)	
(Presidential, $1.74)	
Ireland	3.93
Israel	4.34

Elections are inexpensive in the United Kingdom, in part because campaigns are limited to three weeks. But the United States compares favorably to West Germany, Ireland, and Israel.

SOURCE: Howard Penniman, "U.S. Elections: Really a Bargain?" *Public Opinion* (June–July 1984): 51ff. Reprinted with permission of the American Enterprise Institute for Public Policy Research.

The 1996 Election

The things that made it possible for Bill Clinton to win the presidency in 1992 were the things that made it possible for him to win reelection in 1996.

In 1992 Clinton ran against George Bush, whose presidency was mired in a national economic recession. In 1996 Clinton ran as president when the economy was in good shape, with more jobs and low unemployment.

In 1992 Clinton ran as a moderate Democrat who said things that appealed to voters—for example, that he would "end welfare as we know it." In 1996 Clinton said he had signed a bill to change welfare radically.

In 1992 there were allegations of sexual misconduct and draft evasion directed at Clinton. The voters decided they didn't matter. The attacks persisted in 1996, with more added—the Whitewater real estate fiasco, alleged misuse of FBI files by the White House, and the firing of the White House travel staff early in the administration. The voters again decided these things didn't matter.

In short, the 1996 election showed again that a president who is in office when the economy is sound and has centrist views on social issues will usually win the election.

Against these odds, the Republican candidate, Bob Dole, had little hope, especially since he was for a while unwilling to raise the issue of Clinton's supposed character flaws. He was reluctant to do that for two reasons: First, he did not like talking about personalities and had generally avoided doing so during his long political career. Second, polls showed that character attacks irritated women voters, making them even more likely to support Clinton.

Women voters were an important part of the election. They were much more supportive of Clinton than of Dole. The effort by Democrats to keep them loyal and by Republicans to woo them back became known as the campaign to reach "soccer moms"—suburban women with children.

WINNING THE NOMINATION

Clinton, unlike the last Democratic incumbent, Jimmy Carter, was unopposed for renomination. The money he raised during the primary season could be spent not on his rivals but on attacking Republicans.

During the primaries, Bob Dole, then a senator, had to campaign against several rivals—Lamar Alexander, Pat Buchanan, Robert Dornan, Steve Forbes, Phil Gramm, Alan Keyes, and Dick Lugar. After a shaky win in the Iowa caucuses and a loss in the New Hampshire primary, it became apparent that Dole's real opponents were Buchanan, a conservative columnist, and Alexander, the former governor of Tennessee. Forbes, a wealthy publisher who paid for his own race, drew attention but was never a real factor. By March, however, when primaries were being held in many states, it was clear that Dole was on his way to securing the nomination. Buchanan could not expand his conservative support, and Alexander could not win enough moderate Republican votes to defeat Dole.

In June Dole resigned from the Senate in order to run for president full time (Trent Lott took over Dole's leadership position). Just before his party's convention Dole announced that former congressman Jack Kemp would be his vice-presidential candidate.

WINNING THE GENERAL ELECTION

Like most presidential candidates throughout history, Clinton and Dole campaigned for the political center. There were many divisive issues in the country—abortion, affirmative action, gun control, school prayer—but these did not play much of a role in the contest. And for good reason: they were "hot button" issues that split the country. The candidates wanted to avoid dividing their supporters, so they said relatively little about such hot buttons.

Finally, the reforms help incumbents and hurt challengers. Incumbents find it easier to raise money from PACs, regardless of the incumbent's party and of the type of PAC. As we shall see in Chapter 9, corporate PACs are more likely to support incumbents of either party than they are to support challengers.

Money and Winning

Money doesn't make much difference in presidential contests, because in the general election both candidates have the same amount (not counting money spent by the parties—soft money—which is about equally divided between the two parties).

The race might have been different if it had been held in 1994 instead of 1996. Clinton had run as a centrist in 1992 but had governed like a liberal in 1993 and 1994. He had raised taxes, cut defense spending, proposed a vast new government health plan, and tried to get the military to admit homosexuals. In 1994 the Democratic party lost control of both houses of Congress, and Clinton's approval rating in the polls was near rock bottom.

Faced with this situation, Clinton changed course. He decided to become a centrist again and made speeches endorsing curfews and school uniforms for children, condemning crime and drug abuse, and worrying about teenage pregnancies. He sent troops to maintain the peace in Bosnia. His approval ratings rose dramatically.

With the economy strong, the nation at peace, and Clinton again running as a centrist, the race didn't leave Bob Dole much to talk about. He and Kemp developed a tax cut plan that would reduce everyone's taxes by 15 percent. They defended it as a way to reduce government influence and encourage economic growth, but with the economy strong most voters were not attracted to the idea. Polls showed that voters preferred further cuts in the deficit to tax reductions.

From the first, the election-year polls showed Clinton ahead. All he had to do was avoid making mistakes. He made none, and he won.

THE DECLINE OF ROSS PEROT

In 1992 Ross Perot won 19 percent of the presidential vote. He reorganized his supporters into the Reform Party and announced that it would pick a presidential candidate. Dick Lamm, former governor of Colorado, ran for the nomination, but—to no one's surprise—the party wanted Perot back.

But this time his standing in the polls was low. The commission managing the presidential debates decided to exclude him. He complained, but to no avail. The nation's flirtation with Perot was over. He won less than 9 percent of the vote, half of his 1992 total.

THE PRESIDENTIAL RESULT

Clinton won by carrying the Northeast, the industrial areas of the Midwest, and the West Coast. He received 379 electoral votes. He did not achieve his goal—of getting more than half the popular vote, however; he won 49.2 percent of it, thus remaining a president whom more people had voted against than for.

Dole won most of the South and the farm and mountain states of the Midwest, earning 159 electoral votes. Perot, of course, got no electoral votes.

THE CONGRESSIONAL RACE

The Republicans retained their control of Congress, winning two more Senate seats and losing only a half dozen or so House seats. The congressional contests continued to show that the two political parties had very different regional bases. Republican control of the South grew, with the Republicans winning Senate seats in Alabama and Arkansas and more House seats in Alabama, Arkansas, Louisiana, Mississippi, Oklahoma, and Texas. The Democrats won back some of the House seats they had lost two years earlier in places such as California, Iowa, Washington, and Wisconsin, and they also gained some seats in Florida and North Carolina.

GOVERNORS

There was no big change: the Republicans lost one governorship (New Hampshire) but won a new one (West Virginia), so the party count remained the same—thirty-two Republican governors and seventeen Democratic governors.

In congressional races it is another matter. Scholars are not entirely agreed on the facts, but in general it seems that money does make a difference. There is strong evidence that how much the challenger spends is most important, because the challenger usually must become known to the public. Buying name recognition is expensive. Gary Jacobson has shown that, other things being equal, in every congressional election since 1972, challengers who spent more money did better than those who spent less.[6] Jacobson also suggested that how much the incumbents spent was not very im-

What Other Countries Do

	Public Financing	Limits on Fund-Raising or Spending	Television
Britain	No	Yes	Free time, allocated according to party's strength in previous election
Denmark	Allowance to parties, based on strength in previous election	No	Parties given equal and free time on public stations
France	Reimbursement to candidates, according to votes received	Yes	Free and equal time to candidates
Italy	Reimbursement to candidates, according to votes received	No	Free and equal time to candidates on state-run stations, but parties control major private stations
Israel	No	Yes	Parties given equal and free time on public stations
Japan	No	Yes	Candidates given some free time for speeches: no negative advertising
Germany	Reimbursement to parties, according to votes received	No	Free time to candidates on public stations

SOURCE: *New York Times* (March 21, 1990): A12. Copyright © 1990 by the New York Times Company. Reprinted by permission.

portant, presumably because they already had all the name recognition they needed (as well as the other benefits of holding office, such as free mail and travel). But other scholars, applying different statistical methods to the same facts, have come to different conclusions. It now seems that, other things being equal, high-spending incumbents do better than low-spending ones.[7]

That money makes a difference does not mean it makes the only difference. In 1986 and 1988, Republican challengers for Senate seats spent more money than the Democratic incumbents to whom they lost. Political party, incumbency, and issues affect the outcome, along with spending.

Incumbents find it easier to raise money than do challengers; incumbents provide services to their districts that challengers cannot; incumbents regularly send free ("franked") mail to their constituents while challengers must pay for their mailings; incumbents can get free publicity by sponsoring legislation or conducting an investigation. Thus it is hardly surprising that incumbents who run for election win in the overwhelming majority of races.

Many people think the campaign finance system should be reformed once again—this time, to undo some of the effects of the 1974 reforms. It will be very difficult for Congress to agree on any significant changes, however, because no matter what is done it will help some politicians and hurt others. Moreover, campaigning—whether by licking envelopes, making speeches, or giving money—is a valued and constitutionally protected right.

Some people would like to have public financing of congressional as well as presidential races. But since incumbent members of Congress already enjoy an enormous advantage, it would be difficult to design a public-financing law that did not perpetuate and even increase that advantage. For example, giving incumbents and challengers equal amounts of money might keep challengers at a disadvantage, since they often must spend more than the incumbent to overcome the latter's advantages.

Other people would like to restrict or even abolish campaign contributions from PACs. But even if that were constitutional, money for elections must come from somewhere. If not from PACs, then from whom? One answer is individuals, but that would require increasing the present $1,000 limit on what each person can give. Otherwise, with PAC spending banned, we would be back to the days before 1974, when money flowed into politics invisibly through hard-to-trace or even illegal channels.

Yet another way is to lower the cost of elections by shortening the campaign season, reducing the number of presidential primaries, or providing free or low-cost television for campaign speeches. Most Americans no doubt think that campaigns are far too long, but they should remember that shorter ones might well make it even harder for challengers to defeat incumbents.

There are no easy answers, especially since it is almost impossible to think up a plan that will not appear to help one party and hurt the other.

What Decides the Election?

To the voter it all seems quite simple—he or she votes for "the best person" or maybe "the least-bad person." To scholars it is all a bit mysterious. How do voters decide who the best person is? What does "best" mean, anyway?

Party

One answer to these questions is party identification. People may say that they are voting for the "best person," but for many people the best person is always a Democrat or a Republican. Moreover, we have seen in Chapter 5 that many people know rather little about the details of political issues. They

may not even know what position their favored candidate has taken on issues that the voters care about. Given these facts, many scholars have argued that party identification is the principal determinant of how people vote.[8]

If it were only a matter of party identification, though, the Democrats would always win the presidency, since more people identify with the Democratic than the Republican party (that gap narrowed, however, in the early 1980s). But we know that the Democrats lost five of the seven presidential elections between 1968 and 1992. There are at least three reasons for this.

First, those people who consider themselves Democrats are less firmly wedded to their party than are Republicans. Table 8.2 shows how people identifying themselves as Democrats, Republicans, or

TABLE 8.2 Percentage of Popular Vote by Groups in Presidential Elections, 1960–1996

		National	Republicans	Democrats	Independents
1960	Kennedy	50%	5%	84%	43%
	Nixon	50	95	16	57
1964	Johnson	61	20	87	56
	Goldwater	39	80	13	44
1968	Humphrey	43	9	74	31
	Nixon	43	86	12	44
	Wallace	14	5	14	25
1972	McGovern	38	5	67	31
	Nixon	62	95	33	69
1976	Carter	51	11	80	48
	Ford	49	89	20	52
1980[a]	Carter	41	11	66	30
	Reagan	51	84	26	54
	Anderson	7	4	6	12
1984	Mondale	41	7	73	35
	Reagan	59	92	26	63
1988	Dukakis	46	8	82	43
	Bush	54	91	17	55
1992	Clinton	43	10	77	38
	Bush	38	73	10	32
	Perot	19	17	13	30
1996	Clinton	49	13	84	43
	Dole	41	80	10	35
	Perot	8	6	5	17

[a] The 1980 figures fail to add up to 100 percent because of missing data.
SOURCE: Gallup poll data, compiled by Robert D. Cantor, *Voting Behavior and Presidential Elections* (Itasca, Ill.: F. E. Peacock, 1975), 35; Gerald M. Pomper, *The Election of 1976* (New York: David McKay, 1977), 61; Gerald M. Pomper, *The Election of 1980* (Chatham, N.J.: Chatham House, 1981), 71; *New York Times*/CBS Poll, November 5, 1992.

The Earthquake Election

Since 1934, every president has seen his party lose seats in Congress in midterm elections. No doubt President Clinton expected to take some losses too, but nothing could have prepared him for the electoral earthquake that hit on November 8, 1994. The Democrats lost fifty-two seats in the House and eight in the Senate, giving the Republicans control of both houses of Congress for the first time since 1954. To add insult to injury, one Democratic senator—Richard Shelby of Alabama—announced after the election that he was switching to the Republican party.

What happened? Explaining the 1994 election is a lot like explaining an earthquake—you feel the ground shake, you know something slipped, but the cause lies so deep in the earth you can't be sure why it moved. Here are some leading possibilities:

1. *The Economy.* Voters usually punish the president's party when the economy is bad. In 1994 voters who said that their standard of living had declined voted against the Democrats. But during the 1982 recession, when Ronald Reagan was in office, the Republicans lost only twenty-six seats in the House and actually gained one in the Senate. During the 1994 recovery, President Clinton's party lost twice as many House seats and eight in the Senate. Why the difference? Perhaps it was because the voters had lost confidence in the ability of the Democrats to manage the economy and had lost confidence in the president as a leader.

2. *Crime.* Rising rates of juvenile violence—gang killings, drive-by shootings, senseless murders to get a pair of Nike or Reebok sneakers—terrified people and convinced them that the country was on the wrong track. There is in fact not much the federal government can do about that, but whatever it can do, the people became convinced that the Republicans could do it better.

3. *The Southern Conversion.* The South was once solidly Democratic. Beginning in 1964, it started to give more support to Republican presidential candidates. Except for its support of Jimmy Carter in 1976, the South went Republican in every election after 1964.* But for a long time this shift of white Southerners to the Republican party took place mostly in presidential elections. In 1954, the last time the Republicans controlled the House before their 1994 victory, there were only seven Republican representatives from the states of the old Confederacy. By 1994 that had changed dramatically—there were sixty-three Republican representatives from the South. The

*In 1968 the South backed George Wallace, a conservative independent. It amounted to the same thing as voting Republican.

Independents voted in presidential elections from 1960 to 1996. At least 80 percent of Republican voters supported the Republican candidate in each election; indeed, if we omit the unusual 1964 election, when Goldwater was the candidate, at least 84 percent of Republican identifiers regularly voted Republican. By contrast, there have been more defections among Democratic voters—in 1972, a third of Democrats supported Nixon, and in 1984, some 26 percent supported Reagan.

The second reason, also clear from Table 8.2, is that the Republicans do much better than the Democrats among the self-described "independent" voters. In every election since 1952 (except 1964 and 1992 and 1996), the Republican candidate has won a larger percentage of the independent vote than the Democratic nominee; in fact the Republicans usually got a majority of the independents, who tend to be younger whites.

Finally, a higher percentage of Republicans than Democrats vote in elections. In every presidential contest in the last thirty years, those describing themselves as "strongly Republican" have been much more likely to vote than those describing themselves as "strongly Democratic."

Issues, Especially the Economy

Even though voters may not know a lot about the issues, that does not mean that issues play no role in elections or that voters respond irrationally to them. For example, V. O. Key, Jr., looked at those change had been occurring gradually, but in 1994 it accelerated sharply, with Republicans picking up nineteen new Southern seats.

4. *"The Mess in Washington."* In his press conference the day after the election, President Clinton said that people were watching how Washington did business and didn't like what they saw. But for some reason that is not yet clear, the voters held the Democrats more responsible for that than they did the Republicans. Maybe it is because the voters equated messy government with big government and so decided to vote against both the mess and the bigness—and the Democrats had been labeled the party of big government. Or maybe it was because the Democrats, who controlled Congress, seemed to be the chief beneficiaries of the Washington mess, and so they became the chief victims of the voter backlash.

5. *The Quality of Candidates.* Veteran observers from both parties noted that in 1994 the Republicans fielded more experienced and more appealing candidates than they had in the past.

Even so, it is important to keep things in perspective. Though the Democrats suffered heavy losses, roughly nine out of every ten incumbent members of the House who stood for reelection were reelected. Many of the Republican gains came in races for open seats.

The defeat of the Democrats in Congress was only part of the story, however. The Republicans also won a majority of the governorships and increased their power in state legislatures. The number of Republican governors rose from nineteen to thirty, and the Republicans gained control of fifteen more state legislatures, without losing any.

In the Senate, Robert Dole (R., Kansas) became majority leader; in the House, Newt Gingrich (R., Georgia) became Speaker. During the campaign Gingrich had persuaded several hundred Republican candidates to sign a "Contract with America," in which they pledged to vote for ten major proposals within the first hundred days of the 104th Congress. These included constitutional amendments requiring a balanced budget and imposing term limits on members of Congress and bills reforming welfare, strengthening the military, fighting crime, and cutting certain taxes.

The House voted for almost all of these measures, but the Senate did not.

voters who switched from one party to another between elections and found that most of them switched in a direction consistent with their own interests. As Key put it, the voters are not fools.[9]

Moreover, voters may know a lot more than we suppose about issues that really matter to them. They may have hazy, even erroneous, views about monetary policy, Central America, and the trade deficit, but they are likely to have a very good idea about whether unemployment is up or down, prices at the supermarket are stable or rising, or crime is a problem in their neighborhoods. And on some issues—such as abortion, school prayer, and race relations—they are likely to have some strong principles that they want to see politicians obey.

Contrary to what we learn in our civics lessons, representative government does not require voters to be well informed on the issues. If it were our duty as citizens to have accurate facts and sensible ideas about how best to negotiate with foreign adversaries, stabilize the value of the dollar, revitalize failing industries, and keep farmers prosperous, we might as well forget about citizenship and head for the beach. It would be a full-time job, and then some, to be a citizen. Politics would take on far more importance in our lives than most of us would want, given our need to earn a living and our belief in the virtues of limited government.

To see why our system can function without well-informed citizens, we must understand the difference between two ways in which issues can affect elections.

Prospective Voting *Prospective* means "forward-looking"; we vote prospectively when we examine the views that the rival candidates have on the issues of the day and then cast our ballot for the person we think has the best ideas for handling these matters. **Prospective voting** requires a lot of information about issues and candidates. Some of us do vote prospectively. Those who do tend to be political junkies. They are either willing to spend a lot of time learning about issues or are so concerned about some big issue (abortion, school busing, nuclear energy) that all they care about is how a candidate stands on that question.

Prospective voting is more common among people who are political activists, have a political ideology that governs their voting decision, or are involved in interest groups with a big stake in the election. They are a minority of all voters, though (as we saw in Chapters 5 and 6) they are more influential than their numbers would suggest. Some prospective voters (by no means all) are organized into single-issue groups, to be discussed below.

Retrospective Voting *Retrospective* means "backward-looking"; **retrospective voting** involves looking at how things have gone in the recent past and then voting for the party that controls the White House if we like what has happened and voting against that party if we don't like what has happened. Retrospective voting does not require us to have a lot of information—we only need know whether things have, in our view, gotten better or worse.

Elections are decided by retrospective voters.[10] In 1980 they decided to vote against Jimmy Carter because inflation was rampant, interest rates were high, and we seemed to be getting the worst of things overseas. The evidence suggests rather clearly that they did not vote *for* Ronald Reagan; they voted for *an alternative* to Jimmy Carter. (Some people did vote for Reagan and his philosophy; they were voting prospectively, but they were in the minority.) In 1984 people voted for Ronald Reagan because unemployment, inflation, and interest rates were down and because we no longer seemed to be getting pushed around overseas. In 1980 retrospective voters wanted change; in 1984 they wanted continuity. In 1988 there was no incumbent running, but Bush

portrayed himself as the candidate who would continue the policies that led to prosperity and depicted Dukakis as a "closet liberal" who would change those policies. In 1992 the economy had once again turned sour, and so voters turned away from Bush and toward his rivals, Clinton and Perot.

Though most incumbent members of Congress get reelected, those who lose do so, it appears, largely because they are the victims of retrospective voting. After Reagan was first elected, the economy went into a recession in 1981–1982. As a result Republican members of Congress were penalized by the voters, and Democratic challengers helped. But it is not just the economy that can hurt congressional candidates. Since 1860 every midterm election but one (1934) has witnessed a loss of congressional seats by the party holding the White House. Just why this should be is not entirely clear, but it probably has something to do with the tendency of some voters to change their opinions of the presidential party once that party has had a chance to govern—which is to say, a chance to make some mistakes, disappoint some supporters, and irritate some interests.

Some scholars believe that retrospective voting is based largely on economic conditions. Figure 8.4 certainly provides support for this view. Each dot represents a presidential election (thirteen of them, from 1948 to 1996). The horizontal axis is the percentage increase or decrease in per capita income (adjusted for inflation) during the election year. The vertical axis is the percentage of the two-party vote won by the party already occupying the White House. You can see that, as per capita income goes up (as you move to the right on the horizontal axis), the incumbent political party tends to win a bigger share of the vote.

Other scholars feel that matters are more complicated than this. As a result a small industry has grown up consisting of people who use different techniques to forecast the outcome of elections. If you know how the president stands in the opinion polls several months before the election and how well the economy is performing, you can make a pretty good guess as to who is going to win the presidency. For congressional races predicting is a lot tougher, because so many local factors affect these contests. Election forecasting remains an inexact science. As one study of the performance of presidential election forecasting models and the 1992 election concluded, "models may be no improvement over pundits."[11]

The Campaign

If party loyalty and national economic conditions play so large a role in elections, is the campaign just sound and fury, signifying nothing?

No. Campaigns can make a difference in three ways. First, they reawaken the partisan loyalties of voters. Right after a party's nominating convention selects a presidential candidate, that person's standing with voters of both parties goes way up in the polls. The reason is that the just-nominated candidate has received a lot of media attention during the summer months, when not much else is happening. When the campaign gets under way, however, both candidates get publicity, and voters return to their normal Democratic or Republican affiliations.[12]

Second, campaigns give voters a chance to watch how the candidates handle pressure, and they give candidates a chance to apply that pressure. The two rivals, after promising to conduct a campaign "on the issues" without mudslinging, immediately start searching each other's personal history and records to find acts, statements, or congressional votes that can be shown in the worst possible light in newspaper or television ads. In 1988 George Bush asserted that as governor Michael Dukakis had vetoed a bill to make the Pledge of Allegiance mandatory in the Massachusetts schools; Dukakis retaliated by saying that Bush had to accept responsibility for some of the scandals of the Reagan administration, because "a fish rots from the head." Many voters don't like these "negative ads"—but they work. As a result, every politician constantly worries about how an opponent might portray his or her past record, a fact that helps explain why so many politicians never do or say anything that can't be explained in a thirty-second television spot.

Third, campaigns allow voters an opportunity to judge the character and core values of the candidates. Most voters don't study in detail a candidate's position on issues; even if they had the time, they know that you can't predict how politicians will behave just from knowing what a campaign manager has written

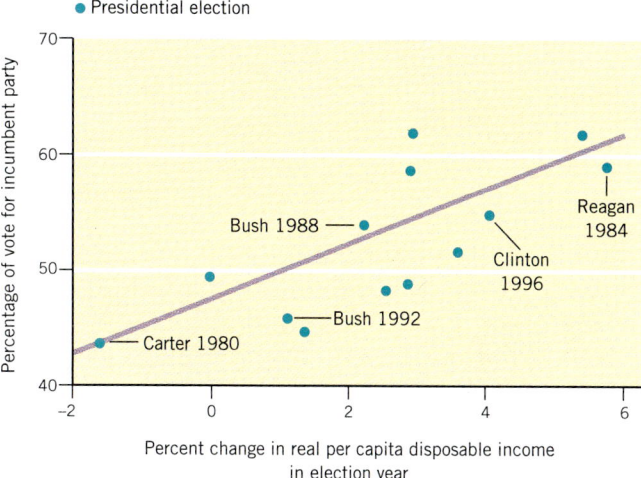

FIGURE 8.4 Economic Performance and Vote for the Incumbent President's Party

● Presidential election

[Scatter plot: y-axis "Percentage of vote for incumbent party" from 40 to 70; x-axis "Percent change in real per capita disposable income in election year" from −2 to 6. Labeled points: Bush 1988, Clinton 1996, Reagan 1984, Bush 1992, Carter 1980.]

NOTE: Each dot represents a presidential election showing the popular vote received by the incumbent president's party. 1992 data do not include votes for independent candidate H. Ross Perot.
SOURCE: Robert S. Erikson and Kent L. Tedin, *American Public Opinion*, 5th ed. (Boston: Allyn and Bacon, 1995), 271.

in a position paper. The voters want some guidance as to how a candidate will behave once elected. They get that guidance by listening not to the details of what a candidate says but to the themes and tone of those statements. Is the candidate tough on crime and drugs? Are his or her statements about the environment sincere or perfunctory? Does the candidate favor having a strong military? Does the candidate care more about not raising taxes or more about helping the homeless?

The desire of voters to discern character, combined with the mechanics of modern campaigning—short radio and television ads and computer-targeted direct mail—lend themselves to an emphasis on themes at the expense of details. This tendency is reinforced by the expectations of ideological party activists and single-issue groups.

Thematic campaigning, negative ads, and the demands of single-issue groups are not new; they are as old as the republic. In the nineteenth century the theme was slavery and the single-issue groups were abolitionists and their opponents; their negative ads make the ones we have today sound like Sunday-school sermons. At the turn of the century

The Hispanic Vote

Some people call the Hispanic vote the "sleeping giant." In 1990 there were an estimated 22 million people of Hispanic origin in the United States, making them a potentially powerful voting bloc. But two things reduce this power considerably.

First, only about 2 million Hispanics voted in the 1980 and 1984 presidential elections. And in 1992, although they were about 9 percent of the population, they cast only 3 percent of the votes. The main reason for this low turnout is that many Hispanic citizens are not registered to vote. In addition, about one-third of all Hispanics are resident aliens and hence not entitled to register.

Second, the Hispanic vote is not homogeneous. Cuban-Americans, many of them concentrated in the Miami area, tend to be strongly Republican, while Mexican-Americans are strongly Democratic.

However, because the Hispanic vote is chiefly located in a few key states—California, Texas, and New York—any presidential candidate who can succeed in getting Hispanic voters to the polls could enjoy a big advantage. These three states have 119 electoral votes, almost half of the total number needed to win the presidency. Moreover, in 1990 there were nineteen Hispanic-majority congressional districts—seven in Texas, six in California, two each in New York and Florida, and one each in Arizona and Illinois. In these districts the Hispanic vote has already become crucial to winning election to Congress; it remains to be seen how or when the Hispanic vote will take on the same importance on the national level.

SOURCES: *National Journal* (November 19, 1983): 2410–2416; *New York Times* (July 18, 1986); *New York Times* (August 3, 1992): A14; 1993 World Almanac: 73, 383.

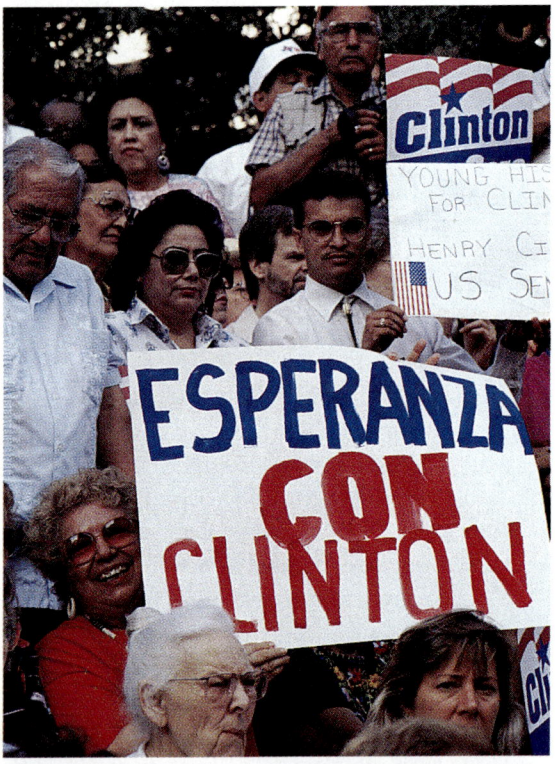

Both parties are trying to mobilize the potentially large Latino vote. Here, the Clinton campaign appeals to Mexican-Americans in Austin, Texas.

---

the themes were temperance and votes for women; both issues led to no-holds-barred, rough-and-tumble campaigning. In the 1970s and 1980s new themes were advanced by fundamentalist Christians and by pro- and anti-abortion groups.

What has changed is not the tone of campaigning but the advent of primary elections. Once, political parties picked candidates out of a desire to win elections. Today activists and single-issue groups influence the selection of candidates, sometimes out of a belief that it is better to lose with the "right" candidate than to win with the wrong one. In a five-candidate primary, only 21 percent of the voters can pick the winner. Single-issue groups can make a big

difference under these conditions, even though they may not have much influence in the general election.

Finding a Winning Coalition

Putting together a winning electoral coalition means holding on to your base among committed partisans and attracting the swing voters who cast their ballots in response to issues (retrospectively or prospectively) and personalities.

There are two ways to examine the nature of the parties' voting coalitions. One is to ask what percentage of various identifiable groups in the popula-

Do "Angry White Males" and "Soccer Moms" Decide National Elections?

Following the Republican victory in the midterm congressional elections of 1994, numerous media commentators and political analysts confidently attributed the results to the sudden growth of a new and powerful bloc of voters—namely, "angry white males." According to the pundits, these voters were angry about many things, not least among them government affirmative action policies that favor blacks and women over economically strapped white males. How might one test such a bit of instant political wisdom?

Berkeley political scientist Jack Citrin tested it by looking carefully at credible national and state survey research findings. He discovered that nationally between 1986 and 1994, men and women, blacks and whites, Democrats, Independents, and Republicans had all become less supportive of certain affirmative action policies. Blacks were more in favor of such policies than whites, but the divide between blacks and whites did not widen between 1986 and 1994. Moreover, he found that differences between white males and white females had diminished. In 1986, a total of 66 percent

of white males were strongly opposed to racial preferences in hiring, compared to 58 percent of white females; in 1994 the figures had narrowed to 70 percent and 67 percent, respectively. Likewise, Citrin found no statistically significant difference between white males and white females concerning preferential treatment based on gender: big majorities of each group favored banning such gender-conscious policies. "The angry white male," he concluded, "is a straw man."

Following the 1996 election there was hardly any mention of "angry white males," but there was much media hype about "soccer moms"— married suburban white women with children. According to the newest bit of instant political wisdom, the moms had decided the presidential race by supporting Bill Clinton and the Democrats over Bob Dole and the Republicans in big numbers. Ostensibly they favored Clinton over Dole because they favored Clinton's pro-choice view over Dole's pro-life stand.

But there are at least two reasons to doubt seriously that "soccer moms" returned President Clinton to the White House. First is the fact, revealed by voter

exit surveys, that although married suburban white women with children supported Clinton over Dole, they did so in almost exactly the same proportion as the general electorate (49 to 42 percent); furthermore, they strongly favored congressional Republicans (55 to 45 percent). Second, Dole's well-publicized position on abortion—namely, that abortion should not be legal in all cases but should be permitted in cases of rape, incest, or a threat to the mother's life— was in fact the majority position; only 27 percent of those who voted in 1996 favored abortion on demand. Moreover, several pro-choice Republicans lost bids for the Senate in 1996.

Just because a particular interpretation of a political event or trend is hyped by the media does not mean that it is wrong. But get in the habit of submitting any news and commentary you hear to your critical faculties before joining the pundits' chorus.

SOURCES: Jack Citrin, "The Angry White Male Is a Straw Man," *Public Affairs Report* (January 1996): vol. 37, no. 1; *New York Times*/CBS News Polls, as reported in *New York Times* (August 12 and August 26, 1996).

tion supported the Democratic or Republican candidate for president. The other is to ask what proportion of a party's total vote came from each of these groups. The answer to the first question tells us how *loyal* blacks, farmers, union members, and others are to the Democratic or Republican party or candidate; the answer to the second question tells us how *important* each group is to a candidate or party.

For the Democratic coalition, blacks are the most loyal voters. In every election but one since 1952, two-thirds or more of all blacks voted Democratic; since 1964 four-fifths have gone Democratic. At one time Jewish voters were almost as solidly Democratic, but in 1980 only a minority supported Jimmy Carter (the rest split their votes between Reagan and John Anderson). Most His-

Union members were once heavily Democratic, but since Ronald Reagan began winning white union votes in 1980, these votes have been up for grabs.

panics have been Democrats, though the label "Hispanic" conceals differences among Cuban-Americans (who often vote Republican) and Mexican-Americans and Puerto Ricans (who are strongly Democratic). The turnout among most Hispanic groups has been quite low (many are not yet citizens), so their political power is not equivalent to their numbers.

The Democrats have lost their once strong hold on Catholics, southerners, and union members. In 1960 Catholics supported John F. Kennedy (a fellow Catholic), but they also have voted for Republicans Eisenhower, Nixon, and Reagan. Union members deserted the Democrats in 1968 and 1972, came back in 1980 and 1988, and divided about evenly between the two parties in 1952, 1956, and 1980. White southerners have voted Republican in national elections but Democratic in many local ones (see Table 8.3).

The Republican party is often described as the party of business and professional people. The loyalty of these groups to Republicans is in fact strong:

only in 1964 did they desert the Republican candidate, to support Lyndon Johnson. Farmers have usually been Republican, but they are a volatile group, highly sensitive to the level of farm prices—and thus quick to change parties. They abandoned the Republicans in 1948 and 1964. Contrary to popular wisdom, the Republican party usually wins a majority of the votes of poor people (defined as those earning less than roughly $5,000 a year). Only in 1964 did most poor people support the Democratic candidate. This can be explained by the fact that the poor include quite different elements—low-income blacks (who are Democrats) and many elderly, retired persons (who usually vote Republican).

In sum, the loyalty of most identifiable groups of voters to either party is not overwhelming. Only blacks, businesspeople, and Jews usually give two-thirds or more of their votes to one party or the other; other groups display tendencies, but none that cannot be overcome.

The contribution that each of these groups makes to the party coalitions is a different matter. Though blacks are overwhelmingly and persistently Democratic, they make up so small a portion of the total electorate that only in recent years have they accounted for as much as one-fifth of the total Democratic vote (see Table 8.4). The groups that make up the largest part of the Democratic vote—Catholics, union members, southerners—are also the least dependable parts of that coalition.[13]

When representatives of various segments of society make demands on party leaders and presidential candidates, they usually stress their numbers or their loyalty, but rarely both. Black leaders, for example, sometimes describe the black vote as being of decisive importance to Democrats and thus deserving of special consideration from a Democratic president. But blacks are so loyal that a Democratic candidate can almost take their votes for granted, and in any event they are not as numerous as other groups. Union leaders emphasize how many union voters there are, but a president will know that union leaders cannot "deliver" the union vote and that this vote may go to the president's opponent, whatever the leaders say. For any presidential candidate a winning coalition must be put together anew for each election. Only a few voters can be taken for granted or written off as a lost cause.

TABLE 8.3	Who Likes the Democrats?

Percentage of Various Groups Saying That They Voted for the Democratic Presidential Candidate, 1964–1996

		1964	1968[a]	1972	1976	1980[c]	1984	1988	1992[d]	1996
Sex	Men	60%	41%	37%	53%	37%	37%	41%	41%	43%
	Women	62	45	38	48	45	42	49	46	54
Race	White	59	38	32	46	36	34	40	39	43
	Nonwhite	94	85	87	85	82	90	86	82	84
Education	College	52	37	37	42	35	40	43	44	47
	Grad school	66	52	49	58	43	49	56	55	52
Occupation	Professional and business	54	34	31	42	33	37	40	NA	NA
	Blue-collar	71	50	43	58	46	46	50	NA	NA
Age	Under 30	64	47	48	53	43	41	47	44	53
	50 and over	59	41	36	52	41[e]	39	49	50	48[g]
Religion	Protestant	55	35	30	46	NA	NA	33[f]	33	36
	Catholic	76	59	48	57	40	44	47	44	53
	Jewish[b]	89	85	66	68	45	66	64	78	78
Southerners		52	31	29	54	47	36	41	42	46

[a] 1968 election had three major candidates (Humphrey, Nixon, and Wallace). [b] Jewish vote estimated from various sources; since the number of Jewish persons interviewed is often less than 100, the error in this figure, as well as that for nonwhites, may be large. [c] 1980 election had three major candidates (Carter, Reagan, and Anderson). [d] 1992 election had three major candidates (Clinton, Bush, and Perot). [e] For 1980–1992, refers to age 60 and over. [f] For 1988, white Protestants only. [g] For 1996, refers to age 45 and over.
SOURCES: Gallup poll data, as tabulated in Jeane J. Kirkpatrick, "Changing Patterns of Electoral Competition," in *The New American Political System,* ed. Anthony King (Washington, D.C.: American Enterprise Institute, 1978), 264–256. Copyright © 1978 by the American Enterprise Institute. Reprinted by permission. 1980, 1984, 1988, and 1992 data from *New York Times*/CBS News exit polls.

TABLE 8.4	The Contribution Made to Democratic Vote Totals by Various Groups, 1952–1992[a]

	1956	1960	1964	1968	1972	1976	1980	1984	1988	1992
Poor (income under $3,000 before 1980, $5,000 in 1990)	19%	16%	15%	12%	10%	7%	5%	8%	5%	5%
Black (and nonwhite)	5	7	12	19	22	16	22	24	15	23
Union member (or union member in family)	36	31	32	28	32	33	32	32	27	21
Catholic (and other non-Protestant)	38	47	36	40	34	35	32	47	43	46
South (including border states)	23	27	21	24	25	36	39	29	24	33
Central cities (12 largest metropolitain areas)	19	19	15	14	14	11	12	12	14	NA

[a] The figures shown represent the percentage of the party's vote in any specific election attributable to the group in question.
SOURCES: Extracted from figures presented by Robert Axelrod, "Communications," *American Political Science Review* (June 1981). Updated by Daron Shaw; ICPSR American National Election Study, 1992, Pre- and Post-Election Surveys.

FIGURE 8.5 Partisan Division of the Presidential Vote in the Nation, 1824–1996

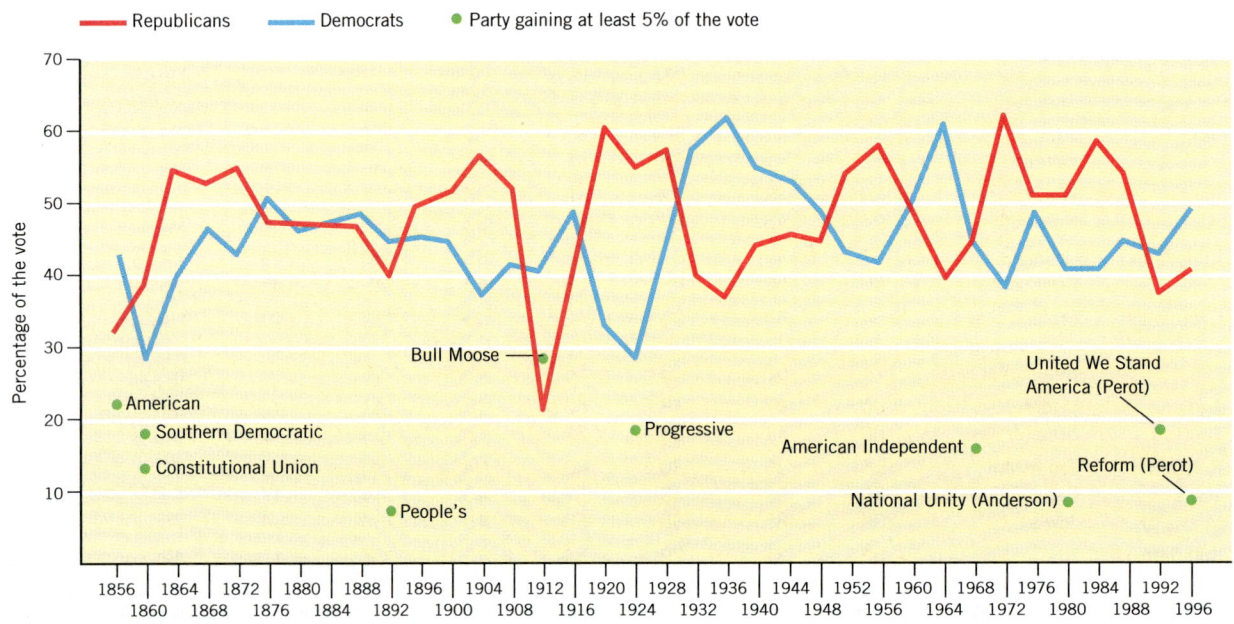

SOURCES: For 1824–1988: Historical Data Archive, Inter-University Consortium for Political Research, as reported in William H. Flanigan and Nancy H. Zingale, *Political Behavior of the American Electorate*, 3d ed., 32. Copyright © 1975 by Allyn and Bacon, Inc., Boston. Reprinted with permission of William C. Brown Publishers, Dubuque, Iowa. For 1992: Reprinted with permission from *The World Almanac and Book of Facts 1994*: 73. Copyright ©1993 K-III Reference Corporation. All rights reserved.

Election Outcomes

To the candidates, and perhaps to the voters, the only interesting outcome of an election is who won. To a political scientist the interesting outcomes are the broad trends in winning and losing and what they imply about the attitudes of voters, the operation of the electoral system, the fate of political parties, and the direction of public policy.

Figure 8.5 shows the trend in the popular vote for president since before the Civil War. From 1876 to 1896 the Democrats and Republicans were hotly competitive. The Republicans won three times, the Democrats twice in close contests. Beginning in 1896, the Republicans became the dominant party, and except for 1912 and 1916, when Woodrow Wilson, a Democrat, was able to win owing to a split in the Republican party, the Republicans carried every presidential election until 1932. Then Franklin Roosevelt put together what has since become known as the "New Deal coalition," and the

Democrats became the dominant party. They won every election until 1952, when Eisenhower, a Republican and a popular military hero, was elected for the first of his two terms.

Party Realignments

There have clearly been important turning points in the strength of the major parties, especially in the twentieth century, when for long periods we have not so much had close competition between two parties as we have had an alternation of dominance by one party and then another. To help explain these major shifts in the tides of politics, scholars have developed the theory of **critical** or **realigning periods.** During such periods a sharp, lasting shift occurs in the popular coalition supporting one or both parties. The issues that separate the two parties change, and so the kinds of voters supporting each party change. This shift may occur at the time of the election or just after, as the new administration draws in new supporters.[14] There seem to have been five re-alignments so far, during or just after these elections: 1800 (when the Jeffersonian Republicans defeated the Federalists), 1828 (when the Jacksonian Democrats, came to power), 1860 (when the Whig party collapsed and the Republicans under Lincoln came to power), 1896 (when the Republicans defeated William Jennings Bryan), and 1932 (when the Democrats under Roosevelt came into office). Some observers noting that these realignments have occurred with marked regularity every twenty-eight to thirty-six years, have speculated on whether they are the result of inevitable cycles in American political life.

Such speculations need not concern us, for what is more important is to understand why a realignment occurs at all. That is not entirely clear. For one thing there are at least two kinds of realignments—one, in which a major party is so badly defeated that it disappears and a new party emerges to take its place (this happened to the Federalists in 1800 and to the Whigs in 1856–1860), and another, in which the two existing parties continue but voters shift their support from one to the other (this happened in 1896 and 1932). Furthermore, not all critical elections have been carefully studied.

The three clearest cases seem to be 1860, 1896, and 1932. By 1860 the existing parties could no longer straddle the fence on the slavery issue. The Republican party was formed in 1856 on the basis of clear-cut opposition to slavery; the Democratic party split in half in 1860, with one part (led by Stephen A. Douglas and based in the North) trying to waffle on the issue and the other (led by John C. Breckinridge and drawing its support from the South) categorically denying that any government had any right to outlaw slavery. The remnants of the Whig party, renamed the Constitutional Union party, tried to unite the nation by writing no platform at all, thus remaining silent on slavery. Lincoln and the antislavery Republicans won in 1860; Breckinridge and the proslavery Southern Democrats came in second. From that moment on, the two major political parties had acquired different sources of support and stood (at least for a decade) for different principles. The parties that had tried to straddle the fence were eliminated. The Civil War fixed these new party loyalties deeply into the popular mind, and the structure of party competition was set for nearly forty years.

THE ELECTION OF 1828

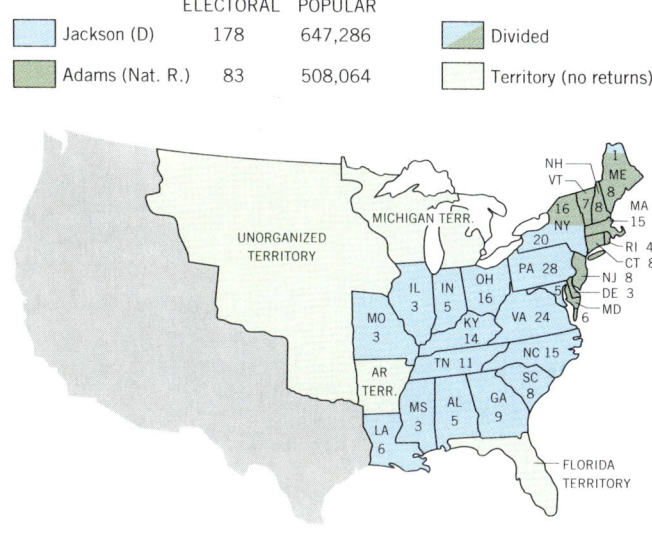

	ELECTORAL	POPULAR
Jackson (D)	178	647,286
Adams (Nat. R.)	83	508,064

Divided

Territory (no returns)

THE ELECTION OF 1860

	ELECTORAL	POPULAR
Lincoln (R)	180	1,866,452
Douglas (No. D)	12	1,375,157
Breckenridge (So. D)	76	847,953
Bell (Const. Union)	39	590,631

Divided

Territory (no returns)

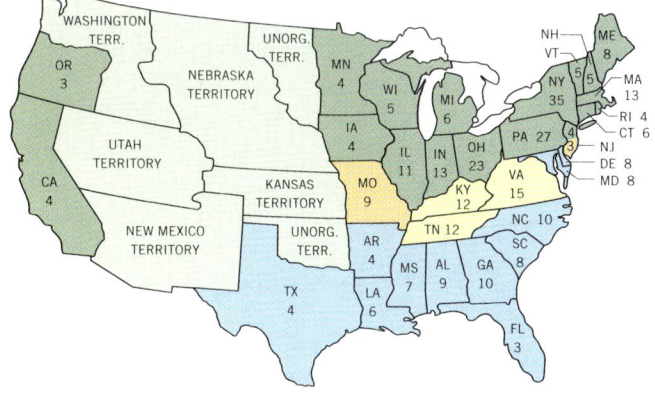

In 1896 a different kind of realignment occurred. Economics rather than slavery was at issue. A series of depressions during the 1880s and 1890s fell especially hard on farmers in the Midwest and parts of the South. The prices paid to farmers for their commodities had been falling more or less

THE ELECTION OF 1896

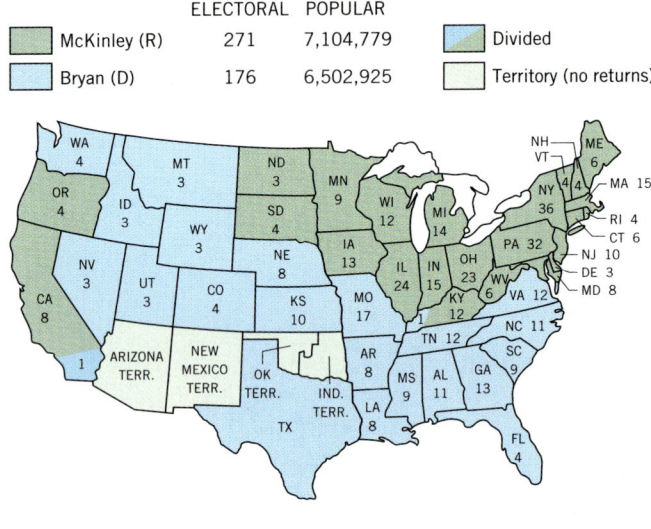

	ELECTORAL	POPULAR		
McKinley (R)	271	7,104,779		Divided
Bryan (D)	176	6,502,925		Territory (no returns)

THE ELECTION OF 1932

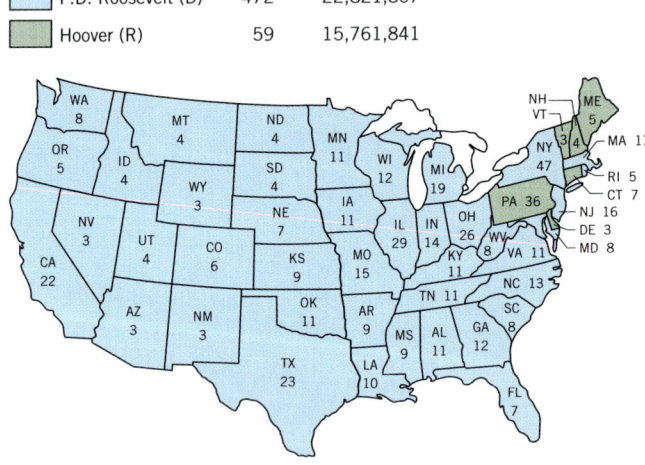

	ELECTORAL	POPULAR
F.D. Roosevelt (D)	472	22,821,857
Hoover (R)	59	15,761,841

Matters came to a head in 1896 when William Jennings Bryan captured the Democratic nomination for president and saw to it that the party adopted a populist platform. The existing Populist party endorsed the Bryan candidacy. In the election anti-Bryan Democrats deserted the party in droves to support the Republican candidate, William McKinley. Once again a real issue divided the two parties: the Republicans stood for industry, business, hard money, protective tariffs, and urban interests; the Democrats, for farmers, small towns, low tariffs, and rural interests. The Republicans won, carrying the cities, workers and businesspeople alike; the Democrats lost, carrying most of the southern and midwestern farm states. The old split between North and South that resulted from the Civil War was now replaced in part by an East versus West, city versus farm split.[15] It was not, however, only an economic cleavage—the Republicans had been able to appeal to Catholics and Lutherans, who disliked fundamentalism and its hostility to liquor and immigrants.

This alignment persisted until 1932. Again change was triggered by an economic depression; again more than economic issues were involved. The New Deal coalition that emerged was based on bringing together into the Democratic party urban workers, northern blacks, southern whites, and Jewish voters. Unlike 1860 and 1896, it was not preceded by any third-party movement; it occurred suddenly (though some groups had begun to shift their allegiance in 1928) and gathered momentum throughout the 1930s. The Democrats, isolated since 1896 as a southern and midwestern sectional party, had now become the majority party by finding a candidate and a cause that could lure urban workers, blacks, and Jews away from the Republican party, where they had been for decades. It was obviously a delicate coalition—blacks and southern whites disagreed on practically everything except their liking for Roosevelt; Jews and the Irish bosses of the big-city machines also had little in common. But the federal government under Roosevelt was able to supply enough benefits to each of these disparate groups to keep them loyal members of the coalition and to provide a new basis for party identification.

These critical elections may have involved not converting existing voters to new party loyalties but recruiting into the dominant party new voters—

steadily since the Civil War, making it increasingly difficult for them to pay their bills. A bitter reaction against the two major parties, which were straddling this issue as they had straddled slavery, spread like a prairie fire, leading to the formation of parties of economic protest—the Greenbackers and the Populists. Reinforcing the economic cleavages were cultural ones: populists tended to be fundamentalist Protestants; urban voters were increasingly Catholic.

The 1896 election was a watershed in American politics—a "realigning election" that brought together new party coalitions. It pitted William McKinley, the Republican defender of the gold standard (left), against William Jennings Bryan, a fiery midwestern champion of strict religion and easy money (right).

young people just coming of voting age, immigrants just receiving their citizenship papers, and blacks just receiving, in some places, the right to vote. But there were also genuine conversions—northern blacks, for example, had been heavily Republican before Roosevelt but became heavily Democratic after his election.

In short, an electoral realignment occurs when a new issue of utmost importance to the voters (slavery, the economy) cuts across existing party divisions and replaces old issues that were formerly the basis of party identification. Some observers have speculated that we are due for a new party realignment as the tensions within the New Deal coalition become more evident. As the memory of Roosevelt and the Great Depression fades and as new voters come of age, the ability of the Democrats to hold onto both people who are liberal and those who are conservative on social issues may decline.

Some people wondered whether the election of 1980, since it brought into power the most conserv-

ative administration in half a century, signaled a new realignment. Many of President Reagan's supporters began talking of their having a "mandate" to adopt major new policies in keeping with the views of the "new majority." But Reagan won in 1980 less because of what he stood for than because he was not Jimmy Carter, and he was reelected in 1984 primarily because people were satisfied with how the country was doing, especially economically.[16]

Just because we have had periods of one-party dominance in the past does not mean that we will have them in the future. Reagan's election could not have been a traditional realignment, because it left Congress in the hands of the Democratic party. Moreover, some scholars are beginning to question the theory of critical elections, or at least the theory that they occur with some regularity.

Nevertheless, one major change has occurred of late—the shift in the presidential voting patterns of the South. From 1972 through 1996 the South was more Republican than the nation as a whole. The

Franklin Roosevelt greets Dr. George Washington Carver at Tuskegee Institute in Alabama. Blacks had long voted Republican; during the New Deal they shifted to the Democratic party. This change was part of the political realignment that occurred in the elections of 1932 and 1936.

proportion of white southerners describing themselves to pollsters as "strongly Democratic" fell from more than one-third in 1952 to about one-seventh in 1984. There has been a corresponding increase in "independents." As it turns out, southern white independents have voted overwhelmingly Republican in recent presidential elections.[17] If you lump independents together with the parties for which they actually vote, the party alignment among white southerners has gone from six-to-one Democratic in 1952 to about fifty-fifty Democrats and Republicans. If this continues, it will constitute a major realignment in a region of the country that is growing rapidly in population and political clout.

In general, however, the kind of dramatic realignment that occurred in the 1860s or after 1932 may not occur again, because party labels have lost their meaning for a growing number of voters. For these people politics may *de*align rather than *re*align.

Party Decline

The evidence that the parties are decaying, not realigning, is of several sorts. We have already noted (Chapter 7) that the proportion of people identifying with one or the other party declined between 1960 and 1980. Simultaneously, the proportion of those voting a **split ticket** (as opposed to a **straight ticket**) increased. Figure 8.6, for example, shows the steep increase in the percentage of congressional districts carried by one party for the presidency and by the other for Congress. Whereas in the 1940s one party would carry a given district for both its presidential and congressional candidates, today more than a third of the districts split their votes between one party's presidential candidate and the other's congressional candidate.

In 1988 more than *half* of all House Democrats were elected in districts that voted for Republican George Bush as president. This ticket splitting was greatest in the South, but it was common everywhere. If every district that voted for Bush had also elected a Republican to Congress, the Republican party would have held a two-to-one majority in the House of Representatives. Ticket splitting creates divided government—the White House and Congress are controlled by different parties (see Chapter 12). Ticket splitting helped the Democrats keep control of the House of Representatives from 1954 to 1994.

Ticket splitting was almost unheard of in the nineteenth century, and for a very good reason. In those days the voter was either given a ballot by the party of his choice and he dropped it, intact, into the ballot box (thereby voting for everybody listed on the ballot), or he was given a government-printed ballot that listed in columns all the candidates of

FIGURE 8.6 Trends in Split-Ticket Voting for President and Congress, 1920–1996

NOTE: The figure is the percentage of congressional districts carried by presidential and congressional candidates of different parties in each election year.

each party. All the voter had to do was mark the top of one column in order to vote for every candidate in that column. (When voting machines came along, they provided a single lever that, when pulled, cast votes for all the candidates of a particular party.) Progressives around the turn of the century began to persuade states to adopt the **office-bloc** (or "Massachusetts") **ballot** in place of the **party-column** (or "Indiana") **ballot.** The office-bloc ballot lists all candidates by office; there is no way to vote a straight party ticket by making one mark. Not surprisingly, states using the office-bloc ballot show much more ticket splitting than those without it.[18]

The Effects of Elections on Policy

Cynics complain that elections are meaningless: no matter who wins, crooks, incompetents, or self-serving politicians still hold office. The more charitable argue that elected officials are usually decent enough but that public policy remains more or less the same no matter which official or party is in office.

There is no brief and simple response to this latter view. Much depends on which office or policy you examine. One reason it is so hard to generalize about the policy effects of elections is that the offices to be filled by the voters are so numerous and the ability of the political parties to unite these office-holders behind a common policy is so weak that any policy proposal must run a gauntlet of potential opponents. Though we have but two major parties, and though only one party can win the presidency, each party is a weak coalition of diverse elements that reflect the many divisions in public opinion. The proponents of a new law must put together a majority coalition almost from scratch, and a winning coalition on one issue tends to be somewhat different—quite often dramatically different—from a winning coalition on another issue.

In a parliamentary system with strong parties, such as that in Great Britain, an election can often have a major effect on public policy. When the Labour party won office in 1945, it put several major industries under public ownership and launched a comprehensive set of social services, including a nationalized health-care plan. Its ambitious and controversial campaign platform was converted, almost item by item, into law. When the Conservative party returned to power in 1951, it accepted some of these changes but rejected others (for example, it denationalized the steel industry).

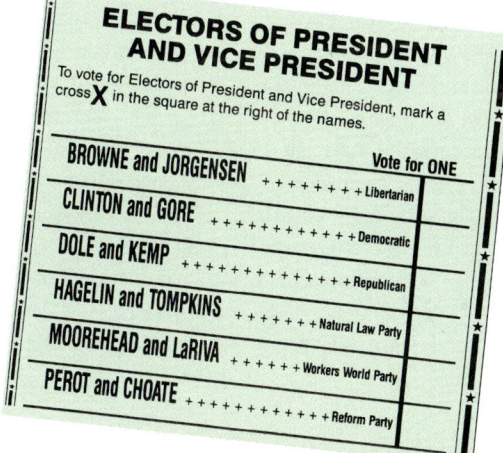

SAMPLE BALLOTS
The party-column or "Indiana" ballot lists all candidates of one party under the party name or emblem, making it easier to vote a straight party ticket by putting an X in the emblem (or pulling the party lever on a voting machine). The office-bloc or "Massachusetts" ballot groups candidates of all parties by office, thereby making it harder to cast a straight party vote.

Two Kinds of Campaign Issues: Position and Valence

There are at least two distinct kinds of campaign issues that have figured prominently in American elections. A **position issue** is one on which the rival parties or candidates reach out for the support of the electorate by taking different positions on a policy question that divides the electorate. Position issues have punctuated the history of presidential elections. Each of the great party realignments from 1860 onward was rooted in position issues. The party alignment that emerged from the Civil War was formed from a position issue of extraordinary power—should black Americans be enslaved or free? In the realignment of the 1890s the Republicans drew support from those who favored high rather than low tariffs on manufactured goods. In the 1930s the Democrats drew support from those who wanted to protect the interests of the poor and working class rather than those of the more affluent in American society. In the 1960s the New Deal coalition began to unravel around another position issue that divided the electorate along racial and regional lines—should there be laws to protect civil rights? And in the 1980s rivals for the presidency reached out for the support of the electorate in part by staking out different positions on yet another issue that sharply polarized voters—should women have legal access to abortion?

But some of the issues that powerfully move the electorate do not present two alternative positions that divide support for the two major parties and their candidates. There are issues on which voters choose parties and candidates not by their real or perceived differences on policy questions but by the degree to which they are linked in the voters' minds with conditions, goals, or symbols that are almost universally approved or disapproved by the electorate. The economy is a prime example of such a **valence issue.** We do not have one party advocating economic prosperity and the other advocating economic bad times—there is no constituency for economic distress. The issue of economic prosperity acquires its power as a valence issue from the fact that the parties or candidates may be very unequally linked in the public's mind with the universally approved condition of good times or the universally disapproved condition of bad times. The difference between electoral success and disaster may turn on each contender's ability to strengthen or weaken these perceptual bonds, or *valences,* in the public's mind.

Examples abound of valence issues that have powerfully moved the electorate. Corruption is a valence issue with a deep historical resonance in American politics. Many times in American political history—indeed, as recently as the House of Representatives' check-kiting scandal in 1992—there have been calls to "throw the rascals out." It should be obvious, however, that the impact of the corruption issue does not depend on what position the campaign rivals take: no party or candidate avowedly favors bribery. It depends, rather, on how closely the rival parties or candidates are linked in the public's mind with the universally approved value of honesty or the universally disapproved value of corruption. There is as little constituency for corruption as there is for economic bad times—or for a variety of other negative symbols that are staples of valence campaigns: irresolute leadership, unpatriotic beliefs, weak national defense, wasted tax dollars, and failure itself.

There are innumerable examples of valence campaigns in modern presidential elections. The valence issue of economic prosperity cost Martin Van Buren the presidency in 1840, when the electorate held him responsible for the misery that followed the panic of 1837. In 1964 the Democratic campaign was largely a valence campaign, in which voters were encouraged to link a vote for the Republican candidate, Arizona senator Barry Goldwater, with negative symbols such as nuclear annihilation and a vote for President Lyndon B. Johnson with positive symbols such as carrying on the work of a beloved fallen president, John F. Kennedy. Four years later Richard Nixon made law and order a valence issue. In the shadow of Watergate, Jimmy Carter made honesty in government a valence issue in 1976. In 1980 Carter was the victim of a valence campaign that linked a vote for him with symbols of abject failure, from long gas lines to pictures of American hostages in Teheran. Ronald Reagan's campaign in 1984 was carefully designed to encourage voters to link the president with such positive symbols as patriotism, peace, and prosperity— "morning in America." Likewise, in 1988 the Bush campaign encouraged voters to link Bush with positive symbols such as respect for the American flag and his rival, Michael S. Dukakis, with negative symbols such as disrespect for the flag, water pollution, and fawning treatment of violent and remorseless criminals.

Presidential campaigns have always involved a mix of position and valence issues, but the relative importance of valence issues has risen as the party alignments rooted in the powerful position issues of the past have weakened and as modern image-making, image-carrying technologies such as television have proliferated.

THE VALENCE VICTORIES OF 1992 AND 1996

Certainly the valence strategy, tactics, and tempos of the 1992 presidential campaign was consistent with the trend. The Clinton campaign was battered with charges of marital infidelity, draft dodging, and pot smoking. At their convention, the Republicans depicted Clinton as "Slick Willie" and his wife as a power-hungry radical feminist who equated marriage with slavery, encouraged children to sue their parents, and eschewed family values. In the televised debates and up to election day, the Bush campaign, with some help from Ross Perot's televised appeals, attempted to make Clinton over as an unpatriotic, indecisive, fast-talking, failed governor of a small and insignificant state.

But Clinton's campaign strategists took a public relations hose to these valence fires. While continuing to stress the positive valences of change and better economic times, the Clinton campaign responded with what the *New York Times* termed "one of the most ambitious campaigns of political rehabilitation ever attempted. They proposed the construction of a new image for Mr. and Mrs. Clinton: an honest, plain-folks idealist and his warm and loving wife." As the paper explained, "Retooling the image of a couple who had been already in the public eye for five battering months required a campaign of behavior modification and media manipulation so elaborate that its outline ran to fourteen single-spaced pages."*

Known within the Clinton campaign as the General Election Project, the plan called for the candidate to depict himself as the "agent of change." The message was to be delivered in town-hall style forums, on live television talk shows, and in a series of speeches challenging specific special interests. The candidate was to appear on television playing the saxophone and poking fun at himself for saying he had tried marijuana but "didn't inhale." The plan also orchestrated events where the Clintons would "seem more warm and cuddly: 'events where Bill and Hillary can go on dates with the American people.'" It even called for staging an event where "Bill and Chelsea surprise Hillary on Mother's Day" and "joint appearances with her friends where Hillary can laugh, cry, do her mimickry."†

The Clinton campaign of 1996 was run almost purely in valence terms. About a year before election day, ads hit the television airwaves depicting the president as tough on crime and crediting him for "putting one hundred thousand police officers on the streets." In subsequent ads and speeches the Clinton campaign painted Republican presidential challenger Bob Dole as the candidate of "extremists" who wanted to abolish Medicare (the major government health program for the elderly), slash college loans, and outlaw all abortions. The Clinton campaign also took symbolic swipes at Dole's advanced age, thanking him for his "long, long" record of public service while contrasting his "bridge to the past" with the baby-boomer incumbent's "bridge to the future."

The Dole campaign responded with valence appeals of its own, characterizing Clinton as generally untrustworthy, up to his neck in scandals, morally indifferent to teenage drug abuse, and a radical liberal dressed in centrist clothing. But these efforts proved consistently unsuccessful, and Dole could not even get much political mileage from position issues on which a clear, bipartisan majority of the electorate sided with him over Clinton (for example, concerning Clinton's veto of a bill banning partial-birth abortion),

Clinton won 54 percent of the female vote, versus 38 percent for Dole. Some analysts believe that Clinton's valence tactics were especially successful among female voters, who, as postelection surveys showed, had on average less knowledge of each candidate's stance on position issues than did male voters. Other analysts acknowledge the gender gap but believe that the valence deck was simply too stacked against Dole for him to overcome the incumbent. They could be right. In this connection, perhaps the most revealing poll of the 1996 presidential election season was one that asked voters whether they would rather have Clinton or Dole "responsible for raising your children" if "something happened to you or your spouse." A clear majority favored Clinton as substitute parent. But another survey asked, "Who would you rather have your child grow up to be more like?" A clear majority favored Dole. An electorate that would prefer that its children be raised by Clinton but turn out like Dole is an electorate to give valence campaign strategists fits and political pundits much to debate and ponder.

---

*Michael Kelley, "The Making of a First Family: A Blueprint," *New York Times* (November 14, 1992): 1.
†Ibid., 9.
SOURCE: Adapted from Donald E. Stokes and John J. DiIulio, Jr., "The Setting: Valence Politics in Modern Elections," in Michael J. Nelson, ed., *The 1992 Elections* (Washington, D.C.: Congressional Quarterly Press, 1993), 6–9, 14–15, 19. *The American Enterprise,* November/December 1996, p. 102, reporting data from *The Washington Post* and Princeton Survey Research Associates.

American elections, unless accompanied by a national crisis such as a war or a depression, rarely produce changes of the magnitude of those that occurred in Britain in 1945. The constitutional system within which our elections take place was designed to moderate the pace of change—to make it neither easy nor impossible to adopt radical proposals. But the fact that the system is intended to moderate the rate of change does not mean that it will always work that way.

The election of 1860 brought to national power a party committed to opposing the extension of slavery and southern secession; it took a bloody war to vindicate that policy. The election of 1896 led to the dominance of a party committed to high tariffs, a strong currency, urban growth, and business prosperity—a commitment that was not significantly altered until 1932. The election of that year led to the New Deal, which produced the greatest single enlargement of federal authority since 1860. The election of 1964 gave the Democrats such a large majority in Congress (as well as control of the presidency) that there began to issue forth an extraordinary number of new policies of sweeping significance—Medicare and Medicaid, federal aid to education and to local law enforcement, two dozen environmental and consumer-protection laws, the Voting Rights Act of 1965, a revision of the immigration laws, and a new cabinet-level Department of Housing and Urban Development.

The election of 1980 brought into office an administration determined to reverse the direction of policy over the preceding half century. Reagan's administration succeeded in obtaining large tax cuts, significant reductions in spending (or in the rate of increase of spending) on some domestic programs, and changes in the policies of some regulatory agencies. The election of 1982, in which the Democrats made gains in the House of Representatives, stiffened congressional resistance to further spending cuts and stimulated renewed interest in tax increases as a way of reducing the deficit. Following the election of 1984 a major tax-reform plan was passed. After the 1996 election, Clinton and Republican congressional leaders agreed on a plan to balance the budget.

In view of all these developments it is hard to argue that the pace of change in our government is always slow or that elections never make a difference. Studies by scholars confirm that elections are often significant, despite the difficulty of getting laws passed. One analysis of about fourteen hundred promises made between 1944 and 1964 in the platforms of the two major parties revealed that 72 percent were put into effect.[19]

Another study examined the party platforms of the Democrats and Republicans from 1844 to 1968 and all the laws passed by Congress between 1789 and 1968. By a complex statistical method, the author of the study was able to show that during certain periods the differences between the platforms of the two parties were especially large (1856, 1880, 1896, 1932) and that there was at about the same time a high rate of change in the kinds of laws being passed.[20] This study supports the general impression conveyed by history that elections can often be central to important policy changes.

Why then do we so often think that elections make little difference? It is because public opinion and the political parties enter a phase of consolidation and continuity between periods of rapid change. During this phase the changes are, so to speak, digested, and party leaders adjust to the new popular consensus, which may (or may not) evolve around the merits of these changes. During the 1870s and 1880s Democratic politicians had to come to terms with the failure of the southern secessionist movement and the abolition of slavery; during the 1900s the Democrats had to adjust again, this time to the fact that national economic policy was going to support industrialization and urbanization, not farming; during the 1940s and 1950s the Republicans had to learn to accept the popularity of the New Deal.

Elections in ordinary times are not "critical"—they do not produce any major party realignment, they are not fought out over a dominant issue, and they provide the winners with no clear mandate. In most cases an election is little more than a retrospective judgment on the record of the incumbent president and the existing congressional majority. If times are good, incumbents win easily; if times are bad, incumbents may lose even though their opponents may have no clear plans for change. But even a "normal" election can produce dramatic results if the winner is a person such as Ronald Reagan, who helped give his party a distinctive political philosophy.

SUMMARY

Political campaigns have increasingly become personalized, with little or no connection to formal party organizations, as a result of the decay of parties, the rise of the direct primary and the electronic media, and campaign finance laws. Candidates face the problem of creating a temporary organization that can raise money from large numbers of small donors, mobilize enthusiastic supporters, and win a nomination in a way that will not harm their ability to appeal to a broader, more diverse constituency in the general election. Campaigning has an uncertain effect on election outcomes, but election outcomes can have important effects on public policy, especially at those times—during critical or "realigning" elections—when new voters are coming into the electorate in large numbers, old party loyalties are weakening, or a major issue is splitting the majority party. Most people vote retrospectively rather than prospectively.

KEY TERMS

incumbent   *p. 196*

coattails   *p. 196*

political action committee   *p. 198*

general election   *p. 202*

primary election   *p. 202*

closed primary   *p. 202*

open primary   *p. 202*

blanket primary   *p. 202*

runoff primary   *p. 202*

presidential primary   *p. 202*

soft money   *p. 211*

prospective voting   *p. 218*

retrospective voting   *p. 218*

critical or realigning periods   *p. 224*

split ticket   *p. 228*

straight ticket   *p. 228*

office-bloc ballot   *p. 229*

party-column ballot   *p. 229*

position issue   *p. 230*

valence issue   *p. 230*

SUGGESTED READINGS

Asher, Herbert. *Presidential Elections and American Politics.* 5th ed. Pacific Grove, Calif.: Brooks/Cole, 1992. A useful, brief analysis of how Americans have voted.

Burnham, Walter Dean. *Critical Elections and the Mainsprings of American Politics.* New York: Norton, 1970. An argument about the decline in voting participation and the significance of the realigning election of 1896.

Jacobson, Gary C. *The Politics of Congressional Elections.* 2d ed. Boston: Little, Brown, 1987. Careful analysis of how people get elected to Congress.

Kayden, Xandra. *Campaign Organization.* Lexington, Mass.: D. C. Heath, 1978. A close look at how political campaigns are organized, staffed, and led at the state level.

Malbin, Michael J., ed. *Money and Politics in the United States: Financing Elections in the 1980s.* Chatham, N.J.: Chatham House, 1984. Articles on the sources and uses of campaign money, with special attention to political parties and political action committees.

Page, Benjamin I. *Choices and Echoes in Presidential Elections.* Chicago: University of Chicago Press, 1978. Analyzes the interaction between the behavior of candidates and of voters in American elections.

Sorauf, Frank. *Money in American Elections.* Glenview, Ill.: Scott Foresman, 1988. The best summary of what we know about the sources and effects of campaign spending.

Sundquist, James L. *Dynamics of the Party System: Alignment and Realignment of Political Parties in the United States.* Rev. ed. Washington, D.C.: Brookings Institution, 1983. Historical analysis of realigning elections from 1860 to the nonrealignment of 1980.

9

Interest Groups

★ Reasons for proliferation of interest groups

★ Rise of interest groups

★ Kinds of interest groups

★ Role of staff

★ Responding to social movements

★ Raising money

★ The problem of bias

★ Wielding influence

★ Spending money

★ Government regulation

Almost every tourist arriving in Washington will visit the White House and the Capitol. Many will look at the Supreme Court building. But hardly any will walk down K Street, where much of the political life of the country occurs.

K Street? From the sidewalk it is just a row of office buildings, no different from what one might find in downtown Seattle or Kansas City. What's to see? But in these buildings, and in similar ones lining nearby streets, are the offices of the nearly seven thousand organizations that are represented in Washington.

It is doubtful whether there is any other nation in which so many organizations are represented in its capital. They are there to participate in politics. They are **interest groups,** or, if you prefer, lobbies.

Explaining Proliferation

There are at least three reasons why interest groups are so common in this country. First, the more cleavages there are in a society, the greater the variety of interests that will exist. In addition to divisions along lines of income and occupation found in any society, America is a nation of countless immigrants and many races. There are at least eighty-five religions that claim fifty thousand members or more. Americans are scattered over a vast land made up of many regions with distinctive traditions and cultures. These social facts make for a great variety of interests and opinions; as James Madison said in *Federalist* No. 10, "The latent causes of faction are thus sown in the nature of man."

Second, the American constitutional system contributes to the number of interest groups by multiplying the points at which such groups can gain access to the government. In a nation such as Great Britain, where most political authority is lodged in a single official such as the prime minister, there are only a few places where important decisions are made—and thus only a few opportunities for affecting those decisions. But when political authority is shared by the president, the courts, and

Congress (and within Congress among two houses and countless committees and subcommittees), there are plenty of places where one can argue one's case. And the more chances there are to influence policy, the more organizations there will be that seek to exercise that influence.

This fact helps explain why in Great Britain there is often only one organization representing a

given interest, whereas in the United States there are several. In London only one major association represents farmers, one represents industry, one represents veterans, and one represents doctors. In the United States, by contrast, at least three organizations represent farmers (the American Farm Bureau Federation, the National Farmers' Union, and the Grange); and each of these is made up of state and county branches, many of which act quite independently of national headquarters. Though there is one major American labor organization, the AFL-CIO, it is in fact a loose coalition of independent unions (plumbers, steelworkers, coal miners), and some large unions, such as the Teamsters, were for many years not part of the AFL-CIO at all.

Third, the weakness of political parties in this country may help explain the number and strength of our interest groups. Where parties are strong, interests work through the parties; where parties are weak, interests operate directly on the government. That at least is the theory. Though scholars are not certain of its validity, it is a plausible theory and can be illustrated by differences among American cities. In cities such as Chicago where a party (in this case, the Democrats) has historically been very strong, labor unions, business associations, and citizens' groups have had to work with the party, and on its terms. But in cities such as Boston or Los Angeles where the parties are very weak, interest groups proliferate and play a large role in making policy.[1]

In Austria, France, and Italy, many if not most interest groups are closely linked to one or another political party. In Italy, for example, each party—Socialist, Communist, and Christian Democrat—has a cluster of labor unions, professional associations, and social clubs allied with it.[2] Though American interest groups often support one party (the AFL-CIO, for example, almost always backs Democratic candidates for office), the relationship between party and interest group here is not as close as it is in Europe.

The Birth of Interest Groups

The number of interest groups has grown rapidly since 1960. A study of Washington-based political associations revealed that roughly 70 percent of them established their Washington offices after

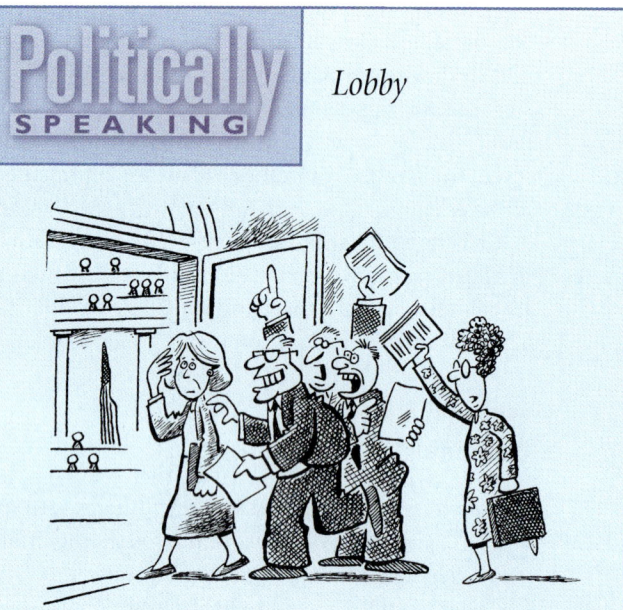

Politically SPEAKING

Lobby

To **lobby** means to attempt to influence governmental decisions, especially legislation. A lobby is a group organized for this purpose, and a **lobbyist** is an individual who engages in lobbying.

The term came into vogue in the mid-seventeenth century to refer to a large anteroom near the English House of Commons, wherein members of Parliament could be approached by people pleading their cases.

In the United States, lobbyists were people who met members of Congress just outside the chambers of the House or Senate to argue their cause. In the nineteenth century *lobbyist* became synonymous with *vote buyer*, because of the widespread belief that lobbyists were using money to corrupt legislators.

Today lobbying is no longer regarded as an inevitably corrupt activity, and lobbyists in Washington are no longer embarrassed to refer to themselves by this term.

SOURCE: Adapted from *Safire's Political Dictionary* by William Safire. Copyright © 1968, 1972, 1978 by William Safire. Reprinted by permission of Random House, Inc. and the author.

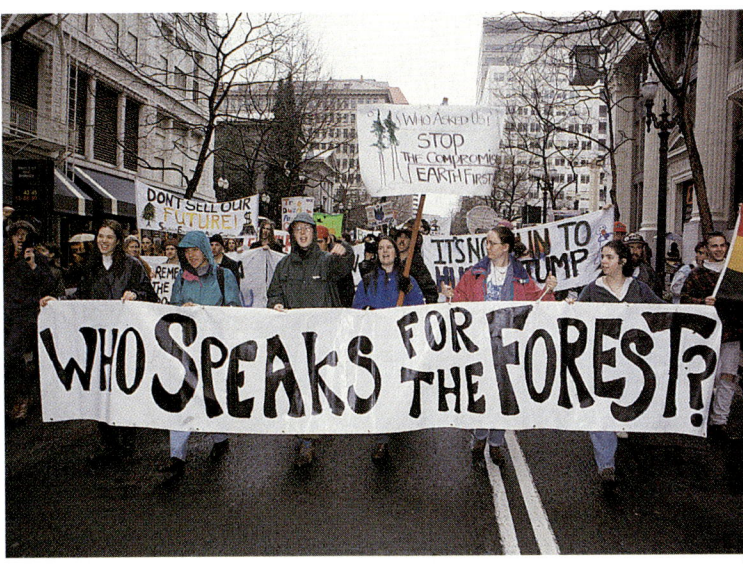

The greater the activity of government—for example, in regulating the timber industry—the greater the number of interest groups.

1960, and nearly half have opened their doors since 1970.[3]

The 1960s and 1970s were boom years for interest groups, but there have been other periods in our history when political associations were created in especially large numbers. During the 1770s many groups arose to agitate for American independence; during the 1830s and 1840s the number of religious associations increased sharply and the antislavery movement began. In the 1860s trade unions based on crafts emerged in significant numbers, farmers formed the Grange, and various fraternal organizations were born. In the 1880s and 1890s business associations proliferated. The great era of organization building, however, was in the first two decades of the twentieth century. Within this twenty-year period, many of the best-known and largest associations with an interest in national politics were formed: the Chamber of Commerce, the National Association of Manufacturers, the American Medical Association, the NAACP, the Urban League, the American Farm Bureau, the Farmers' Union, the National Catholic Welfare Conference, the American Jewish Committee, and the Anti-Defamation League. The wave of interest group formation that occurred in the 1960s led to the emergence of environmental, con-sumer, and political reform organizations such as those sponsored by consumer activist Ralph Nader.

The fact that associations in general, and political interest groups in particular, are created more rapidly in some periods than in others suggests that these groups do not arise inevitably out of natural social processes. There have always been farmers in this country, but there were no national farm organizations until the latter part of the nineteenth century. Blacks had been victimized by various white-supremacy policies from the end of the Civil War on, but the NAACP did not emerge until 1910. Men and women worked in factories for decades before industrial unions were formed.

At least four factors help explain the rise of interest groups. The first consists of broad economic developments that create new interests and redefine old ones. Farmers had little reason to become organized for political activity so long as most of them consumed what they produced. The importance of regular political activity became evident only after most farmers began to produce cash crops for sale in markets that were unstable or affected by forces (the weather, the railroads, foreign competition) that farmers could not control. Similarly, for many decades most workers were craftspeople working

Almost any group today is prepared to stage a demonstration. Here, a group of senior citizens gather in front of the Capitol.

alone or in small groups. Such unions as existed were little more than craft guilds interested in protecting their jobs and in training apprentices. The reason for large, mass-membership unions did not exist until there arose mass-production industry operated by large corporations.

Second, government policy itself helped create interest groups. Wars create veterans, who in turn demand pensions and other benefits. The first large veterans' organization, the Grand Army of the Republic, was made up of Union veterans of the Civil War. By the 1920s these men were receiving about a quarter of a billion dollars a year from the government, and naturally they created organizations to watch over the distribution of this money. The federal government encouraged the formation of the American Farm Bureau Federation (AFBF) by paying for county agents who would serve the needs of farmers under the supervision of local farm organizations; these county bureaus eventually came together as the AFBF. The Chamber of Commerce was launched at a conference attended by President William Howard Taft.

Professional societies, such as those made up of lawyers and doctors, became important in part because state governments gave to such groups the authority to decide who was qualified to become a lawyer or a doctor. Workers had a difficult time organizing so long as the government, by the use of

injunctions enforced by the police and by the army, prevented strikes. Unions, especially those in mass-production industries, began to flourish after Congress passed laws in the 1930s that prohibited the use of injunctions in private labor disputes, that required employers to bargain with unions, and that allowed a union representing a majority of the workers in a plant to require all workers to join it.[4]

Third, political organizations do not emerge automatically, even when government policy permits them and social circumstances seem to require them. Somebody must exercise leadership, often at substantial personal cost. These organizational entrepreneurs are found in greater numbers at certain times than at others. They are often young, caught up in a **social movement,** drawn to the need for change, and inspired by some political or religious doctrine. Antislavery organizations were created in the 1830s and 1840s by enthusiastic young people influenced by a religious revival then sweeping the country. The period from 1890 to 1920, when so many national organizations were created, was a time when the college-educated middle class was growing rapidly. (The number of men and women who received college degrees each year tripled between 1890 and 1920.)[5] During this era natural science and fundamentalist Christianity were locked in a bitter contest, with the Gospels and Darwinism offering competing ideas about personal salvation and social progress. The 1960s, when many new organizations were born, was a decade in which young people were powerfully influenced by the civil rights and antiwar movements and when college enrollments more than doubled.

Finally, the more activities government undertakes, the more organized groups there will be that are interested in those activities. As can be seen from Table 9.1, most Washington offices representing corporations, labor unions, and trade and professional associations were established before 1960—in some cases many decades before—because it was during the 1930s or even earlier that the government began making policies important to business and labor. The great majority of "public-interest" lobbies (those concerned with the environment or consumer protection), social welfare associations, and organizations concerned with civil rights, the elderly, and the handicapped established offices in Washington after 1960. Policies of interest to these groups, such as the major civil rights and environmental laws, were adopted after that date. In fact, over half the "public-interest" lobbies opened their doors after 1970.

Kinds of Organizations

An **interest group** is any organization that seeks to influence public policy. When we think of an organization, we usually think of something like the Boy Scouts or the League of Women Voters—a group consisting of individual members. In Washington, however, many organizations do not have individual members at all but are offices—corporations, law firms, public relations firms, or "letterhead" organizations that get most of their money from foundations or from the government—out of which a staff operates. It is important to understand the differences between the two kinds of interest groups—"institutional" and "membership" interests.[6]

Institutional Interests

Institutional interests are individuals or organizations representing other organizations. General Motors, for example, has a Washington representative. Over five hundred firms have such representatives in the capital, most of which have opened their

TABLE 9.1 Dates of Founding of Organizations Having Washington Offices

Organization	Percentage Founded	
	After 1960	After 1970
Corporations	14%	6%
Unions	21	14
Professional	30	14
Trade	38	23
Civil rights	56	46
Women/elderly/disabled	56	46
"Public interest"	76	57
Social welfare	79	51

SOURCE: Kay Lehman Schlozman and John T. Tierney, *Organized Interests and American Democracy* (New York: Harper & Row, 1986), 76. Copyright © 1986 by Kay Lehman Schlozman and John T. Tierney. Reprinted by permission of Addison-Wesley Educational Publishers, Inc.

offices since 1970.[7] Firms that do not want to place their own full-time representative in Washington can hire a Washington lawyer or public relations expert on a part-time basis. Between 1970 and 1980 the number of lawyers in Washington more than tripled; Washington now has more lawyers (over 38,000) than Los Angeles, a city three times its size.[8] Another kind of institutional interest is the trade or governmental association, such as the National Independent Retail Jewelers or the National Association of Counties.

Individuals or organizations that represent other organizations tend to be interested in bread-and-butter issues of vital concern to their clients. Some of the people who specialize in this work can earn very large fees—top public relations experts and Washington lawyers can charge $250 an hour or more for their time. Since they earn a lot, they are expected to deliver a lot.

Just what they are expected to deliver, however, varies with the diversity of the groups making up the organization. The American Cotton Manufacturers Institute represents southern textile mills. Those mills are few enough in number and similar enough in outlook to allow the institute to carry out clear policies squarely based on the business interests of its clients. For example, the institute works hard to get the federal government to adopt laws and rules that will keep foreign-made textiles from competing too easily with American-made goods.

Sometimes the institute is successful, sometimes not, but it is never hard to explain what it is doing.

By contrast, the United States Chamber of Commerce represents thousands of different businesses in hundreds of different communities. Its membership is so large and diverse that the Chamber in Washington can speak out clearly and forcefully on only those relatively few matters in which all, or most, businesses take the same position. Since all businesses would like lower taxes, the Chamber favors that. On the other hand, since some businesses (those that import goods) want low tariffs and other businesses (those that face competition from imported goods) want higher tariffs, the Chamber says little or nothing about tariffs.

Institutional interests do not just represent business firms; they also represent governments, foundations, and universities. For example, the American Council on Education claims to speak for most institutions of higher education, the American Public Transit Association represents local mass-transit systems, and the National Association of Counties argues on behalf of county governments.

Membership Interests

It is often said that Americans are a nation of joiners, and so we take for granted the many organizations around us supported by the activities and

W. E. B. Du Bois was one of the founders of the NAACP in 1910 and the editor of its magazine, *The Crisis.*

contributions of individual citizens. But we should not take this multiplicity of organizations for granted; in fact their existence is something of a puzzle.

Americans join only certain kinds of organizations more frequently than do citizens of other democratic countries. We are no more likely than the British, for example, to join social, business, professional, veterans', or charitable organizations, and we are *less* likely to join labor unions. Our reputation as a nation of joiners arises chiefly out of our unusually high tendency to join religious and civic or political associations. About three times as many Americans as Britons say that they are members of a civic or political organization.[9]

This proclivity of Americans to get together with other citizens to engage in civic or political action reflects, apparently, a greater sense of political efficacy and a stronger sense of civic duty in this country. When Gabriel Almond and Sidney Verba asked citizens of five nations what they would do to protest an unjust local regulation, 56 percent of the Americans—but only 34 percent of the British and 13 percent of the Germans—said that they would try to organize their neighbors to write letters, sign petitions, or otherwise act in concert.[10] Americans are also more likely than Europeans to think that organized activity is an effective way to influence the national government, remote as that institution may seem. And this willingness to form civic or political groups is not a product of higher levels of education in this country; Americans of every level of schooling are political joiners.[11]

But explaining the American willingness to join politically active groups by saying that Americans feel a "sense of political efficacy" is not much of an explanation; we might as well say that people vote because they think that their vote makes a difference. But one vote clearly makes no difference at all in almost any election; similarly, one member, more or less, in the Sierra Club, the Christian Coalition, or the National Association for the Advancement of Colored People (NAACP) clearly will make no difference in the success of those organizations.

And in fact most people who are sympathetic to the aims of a mass-membership interest group do not join it. The NAACP, for example, enrolls as members only a tiny fraction of all blacks. This is not because people are selfish or apathetic but because they are rational and numerous. A single black, for example, knows that he or she can make no difference in the success of the NAACP, just as a single nature enthusiast knows that he or she cannot enhance the power of the Sierra Club. Moreover, if the NAACP or the Sierra Club succeeds, blacks and nature lovers will benefit even if they are not members. Therefore rational people who value their time and money would no more join such organizations than they would attempt to empty a lake with a cup—unless they get something out of joining.

Incentives to Join

To get people to join mass-membership organizations, they must be offered an **incentive**—something of value they cannot get without joining. There are three kinds of these incentives.

Solidary incentives are the sense of pleasure, status, or companionship that arises out of meeting together in small groups. Such rewards are extremely important, but because they tend to be available only from face-to-face contact, national interest groups offering them often have to organize themselves as coalitions of small local units. For example, the League of Women Voters, the Parent-Teachers Association, the NAACP, the Rotary Club, and the American Legion all consist of small local chapters that support a national staff. It is the task of the local chapters to lure members and obtain funds from them; the state or national staff can then pursue political objectives by using these funds. Forming organizations made up of small local chapters is probably easier in the United States than in Europe because of the great importance of local government in our federal system. There is plenty for a PTA, an NAACP, or a League of Women Voters to do in its own community, and so its members can be kept busy with local affairs while the national staff pursues larger goals.

A second kind of incentive consists of **material incentives**—that is, money, or things and services readily valued in monetary terms. Farm organizations have recruited many members by offering a wide range of services. The Illinois Farm Bureau, for example, offers to its members—and *only* to its members—a chance to buy farm supplies at discount prices, to market their products through cooperatives, and to purchase low-cost insurance.

Bumper stickers are a sign of how many groups and causes Americans join.

These material incentives help explain why the Illinois Farm Bureau has been able to enroll nearly every farmer in the state as well as many nonfarmers who also value these rewards.[12]

Similarly, the American Association of Retired Persons (AARP) has recruited over 30 million members by supplying them with everything from low-cost life insurance and mail-order discount drugs to

Among the services the American Association of Retired Persons provides the elderly is free assistance in preparing tax returns.

The Nader Network

tax advice and group travel plans. About 45 percent of the nation's population that is fifty and older—one out of every four registered voters—belongs to the AARP. With an annual operating budget of over $200 million and a cash flow estimated at a whopping $10 billion, the AARP seeks to influence public poiicy in many areas, from health and housing to taxes and transportation.

The third—and most difficult—kind of incentive is the *purpose* of the organization. Many associations rely chiefly on this **purposive incentive**—the appeal of their stated goals—to recruit members. If the attainment of those goals will also benefit people who do not join, individuals who do join will have to be those who feel passionately about the goal, who have a strong sense of duty (or who cannot say no to a friend who asks them to join), or for whom the cost of joining is so small that they are indifferent to joining or not. Organizations that attract members by appealing to their interest in a coherent set of (usually) controversial principles are sometimes called **ideological interest groups.**

When the purpose of the organization, if attained, will principally benefit nonmembers, it is customary to call the group a **public-interest lobby**. (Whether the public at large will really benefit, of course, is a matter of opinion, but at least the group members think that they are working selflessly for the common good.)

Though some public-interest lobbies may pursue relatively noncontroversial goals (for example, persuading people to vote or raising money to house orphans), the most visible of such organizations are highly controversial. It is precisely the controversy that attracts the members, or at least those members who support one side of the issue. Many of these groups can be described as markedly liberal or decidedly conservative in outlook.

Perhaps the best known of the liberal public-interest groups are those founded by or associated with Ralph Nader. Nader became a popular figure in the mid-1960s after General Motors made a clumsy attempt to investigate and discredit his background at a time when he was testifying in favor of an auto-safety bill. Nader won a large out-of-court settlement against General Motors, his books began to earn royalties, and he was able to command substantial lecture fees. Most of this money was turned over to various organizations he created that dealt with matters of interest to consumers. In addition, he founded a group called Public Citizen that raised money by direct-mail solicitation from thousands of small contributors and sought foundation grants. Finally, he helped create Public Interest Research Groups (PIRGs) in a number of states, supported by donations from college students (voluntary at some colleges, a compulsory assessment levied on all students at others) and concerned with organizing student activists to work on local projects.

Recently, cracks have begun to appear in the Nader movement. When Hawaii and California considered plans to develop no-fault automobile insurance, some former allies of Nader led the effort to reduce auto insurance prices by adopting a no-fault system. Nader himself denounced this effort and urged Hawaii's governor to veto the no-fault bill. Each side criticized the other.

Conservatives, though slow to get started, have also adopted the public-interest organizational strategy. As with such associations run by liberals, they are of two kinds: those that engage in research and lobbying and those that bring lawsuits designed to advance their cause. The box on this page and the box on page 244 list some examples of public-interest organizations that support liberal or conservative causes.

Membership organizations that rely on purposive incentives, especially appeals to deeply controversial purposes, tend to be shaped by the mood of the times. When an issue is hot—in the media or with the public—such organizations can grow rapidly. When the spotlight fades, the organization may lose support. Thus such organizations have a powerful motive to stay in the public eye. To remain visible, public-interest lobbies devote a lot of attention to generating publicity by developing good contacts with the media and issuing dramatic press releases about crises and scandals.

Because of their need to take advantage of a crisis atmosphere, public-interest lobbies often do best when the government is in the hands of an administration that is *hostile*, not sympathetic, to their views. Environmentalist organizations could mobilize more resources when James Watt, an opponent of much of the environmental movement, was secretary of the interior than they could when Cecil D. Andrus, his proenvironment predecessor, was in office. By the same token, many conservative interest groups were able to raise more money with the rela-

Public-Interest Law Firms

A special kind of public-interest lobby is an organization that advances its cause by bringing lawsuits to challenge existing practices or proposed regulations. A public-interest law firm will act in one of two ways: First, it will find someone who has been harmed by some public or private policy and bring suit on his or her behalf. Second, it will file a brief with a court supporting somebody else's lawsuit (this is called an amicus curiae brief; it is explained in Chapter 14).

Here are some examples of liberal and conservative public-interest law firms:

Liberal	Conservative
American Civil Liberties Union	Atlantic Legal Foundation
Asian-American Legal Defense Fund	The Center for Individual Rights
Lawyers' Committee for Civil Rights	Criminal Justice Legal Foundation
Mexican-American Legal Defense Fund	Landmark Legal Foundation
NAACP Legal Defense and Education Fund	Mountain States Legal Foundation
Natural Resources Defense Council	Pacific Legal Foundation
Women's Legal Defense Fund	Washington Legal Foundation

tively liberal Jimmy Carter or Bill Clinton in the White House than with the conservative Ronald Reagan.

The Influence of the Staff

We often make the mistake of assuming that what an interest group does politically is simply to exert influence on behalf of its members. That is indeed the case when all the members have a clear and similar stake in an issue. But many issues affect different members differently. In fact, if the members joined to obtain solidary or material benefits, they may not care at all about many of the issues with which the organization gets involved. In such cases what the interest group does may reflect more what the staff wants than what the members believe.

Quiz

What do the following interest groups have in common?

Amateur Softball Association

Barbecue Industry Association

Candy Wholesalers Association

Chocolate Manufacturers Association

Retinitis Pigmentosa Foundation

Sporting Goods Manufacturers Association

Hint: They were all in favor of the passage of the same law. What was that law? Answer on page 245.

Think Tanks in Washington

*T*hink tanks are public-interest organizations that do research on policy questions and disseminate their findings in books, articles, conferences, op-ed essays for newspapers, and (occasionally) testimony before Congress. Some are nonpartisan and ideologically more or less neutral, but others—and many of the most important ones—are aligned with liberal or conservative causes. Here are some examples of each:

Liberal	*Conservative*
Center on Budget and Policy Priorities	American Enterprise Institute
Center for Defense Information	Cato Institute
Children's Defense Fund	Center for Strategic and International Studies
Economic Policy Institute	Competitive Enterprise Institute
Institute for Policy Studies	
Joint Center for Political and Economic Studies	Ethics and Public Policy Center
Progressive Policy Institute	Free Congress Foundation
	Heritage Foundation

Note that the labels "liberal" and "conservative," while generally accurate, conceal important differences among the think tanks in each list.

For example, a survey of the white members of a large labor union showed that one-third of them believed that the desegregation of schools, housing, and job opportunities had gone too fast; only one-fifth thought that it had gone too slowly. But among the staff members of the union, *none* thought that desegregation had gone too fast, and over two-thirds thought that it had gone too slowly.[13] As a result the union staff aggressively lobbied Congress for the passage of tougher civil rights laws, even though most of the union's members did not feel that they were needed. The members stayed in the union for reasons unrelated to civil rights, giving the staff freedom to pursue its own goals.

The National Council of the Churches of Christ (NCC), an organization of various Protestant denominations claiming several million members, has spoken out frequently on political questions, generally by taking a strongly liberal position. But opinion surveys show that most white Protestants are relatively conservative, especially those in the South. Thus it is quite likely that the staff of the NCC does not, on many political questions, actually represent the majority of the churchgoers for whom it claims to speak.[14] It can ignore them because people join churches, by and large, for reasons other than how staff members in New York or Washington think.

Interest Groups and Social Movements

Because it is difficult to attract people with purposive incentives, interest groups employing them tend to arise out of social movements. A **social movement** is a widely shared demand for change in some aspect of the social or political order. The civil rights movement of the 1960s was such an event, as was the environmentalist movement of the 1970s. A social movement need not have liberal goals. In the nineteenth century, for example, there were various nativist movements that sought to reduce immigration to this country or to keep Catholics or Masons out of public office. Broad-based religious revivals are social movements.

No one is quite certain why social movements arise. At one moment people are largely indifferent to some issue; at another moment many of these same people care passionately about religion, civil rights, immigration, or conservation. A social movement may be triggered by a scandal (an oil spill on the Santa Barbara beaches helped launch the environmental movement), the dramatic and widely publicized activities of a few leaders (lunch counter sit-ins helped stimulate the civil rights movement), or by the coming of age of a new generation that takes up a cause advocated by eloquent writers, teachers, or evangelists.

The Environmental Movement

Whatever its origin, the effect of a social movement is to increase the value some people attach to purposive incentives. As a consequence, new interest groups are formed that rely on these incentives. In the box on page 246 are some examples. In the 1890s, as a result of the emergence of conservation as a major issue, the Sierra Club was organized. In the 1930s conservation once again became popular, and the Wilderness Society and the National Wildlife Federation took form. In the 1960s and 1970s environmental issues again came to the fore, and we see the emergence of the Environmental Defense Fund and Environmental Action.

This box contains the results of a survey of the members of these organizations. Note that the smallest organizations (Environmental Action and the Environmental Defense Fund) tended, at the time of this survey, to have the most liberal members. This is often the case with social movements. A movement will spawn many organizations (there are many more environmental organizations than those listed in this box). The most passionately aroused people will be the fewest in number, and they will gravitate toward the organizations that take the most extreme positions; as a result these organizations are small but vociferous. The more numerous and less passionate people will gravitate toward more moderate, less vociferous organizations, which will tend to be larger.

The Feminist Movement

There have been several feminist social movements in this country's history—in the 1830s, in the 1890s, in the 1920s, and in the 1960s. Each period has

Answer to Quiz

*T*hese organizations were all members of the National Daylight Saving Coalition.

For years the coalition lobbied Congress to lengthen the number of days during which daylight saving time would be in effect. In 1986 it was successful: Congress added three weeks to daylight saving, so that beginning in 1987 people in most states set their clocks ahead one hour on the first Sunday in April rather than the last Sunday, as previously.

Why did these interest groups join the coalition?

The businesses making sporting goods and barbecue equipment wanted more daylight saving so that they could sell more things for people to use outdoors in the evening.

The softball players wanted to start playing evening games earlier in the year so that they could get more games in during the season.

The Retinitis Pigmentosa Foundation is concerned about people who suffer from night blindness. With more daylight hours available during which to drive home from work, these people would not have to worry so much about night blindness.

The chocolate manufacturers and the candy wholesalers joined the coalition in hopes of getting daylight saving time extended *later* in the year, not begun earlier. If daylight saving included Halloween, then it would stay light longer on that day; hence more parents would let their children go out trick-or-treating. This would result in the sale of more candy. These two organizations were unhappy that Congress decided to start daylight saving earlier instead of ending it later.

Some farm groups don't like daylight saving because it means that when farmers get up in the morning to milk cows, it is still dark out. Some western states don't like it either, and so (with congressional permission) Arizona, Hawaii, and most of Indiana don't observe the new law.

The point of the story: There is almost nothing that will not attract interest group activity.

brought into being new organizations, some of which have endured to the present. For example, the League of Women Voters was founded in 1920 to educate and organize women for the purpose of using effectively their newly won right to vote.

Though a strong sense of purpose may lead to the creation of organizations, each will strive to find some incentive that will sustain it over the long haul.

Profile of Five Environmental Organizations

"Environmentalists" are not all alike. There are well over a dozen major national environmentalist organizations. They differ in their goals, tactics, membership, and political ideology. Here are profiles of five such groups, ranging from (roughly) the most liberal to the most conservative:

	Environmental Action	Environmental Defense Fund	Sierra Club	Wilderness Society	National Wildlife Federation
Founded	1970	1967	1892	1935	1936
Membership	7,500	250,000	560,000	302,000	4,700,000
Budget	$1.2 million	$22 million	$38 million	$16.2 million	$100 million
Self-described ideology of members:					
Radical	10%	7%	4%	2%	2%
Liberal	72	67	57	51	21
Moderate	10	13	16	18	31
Conservative	9	13	23	29	47
Schooling of members:					
High school	7%	6%	7%	9%	34%
College	41	31	41	41	45
Postgraduate	52	63	53	50	22
Membership beliefs:					
Favor closing nuclear plants	40%	31%	22%	23%	10%
Government should redistribute income	72	63	53	55	42
Membership who were:					
Hunters	6%	5%	12%	13%	31%
Fishermen	22	22	33	34	53

SOURCE: Membership and budget figures as of January 1994, as reported by spokesperson for each organization. Membership characteristics and beliefs from a 1978 survey by Resources for the Future. Tabulations from John McAdams, Marquette University.

These permanent incentives will affect how the organization participates in politics.

There are at least three kinds of feminist organizations. First there are those that rely chiefly on solidary incentives, enroll middle-class women with relatively high levels of schooling, and tend to support those causes that command the widest support among women generally. The League of Women Voters and the Federation of Business and Professional Women are examples. Both supported the campaign to ratify the Equal Rights Amendment (ERA), but as Jane Mansbridge has observed in her history of the ERA, they were uneasy with the kind of intense, partisan fighting displayed by some other women's organizations and with the tendency of more militant groups to link the ERA to other issues, such as abortion. The reason for their uneasiness is clear: to the extent to which they relied on solidary incentives, they had a stake in avoiding issues and tactics that would divide their membership or reduce the extent to which membership provided camaraderie and professional contacts.[15]

Second, there are women's organizations that attract members with purposive incentives. The National Organization for Women (NOW) and the National Abortion Rights Action League (NARAL) are two of the largest such groups, though there are many smaller ones. Because they rely on purposes, these organizations must take strong positions, tackle divisive issues, and employ militant tactics. Anything less would turn off the committed feminists who make up the rank and file and contribute the funds. But because these groups take controversial stands, they are constantly embroiled in internal quarrels between those who think that they have gone too far and those who think that they have not gone far enough, between women who want NOW or NARAL to join with lesbian and socialist organizations and those who want them to steer clear. Moreover, as Mansbridge showed, purposive organizations often cannot make their decisions stick on the local level (local chapters will do pretty much as they please).[16]

The third kind of women's organization is the caucus that takes on specific issues that have some material benefit to women. The Women's Equity Action League (WEAL) is one such group. Rather than relying on membership dues for financial support, it obtains grants from foundations and government agencies. Freed of the necessity of satisfying a large rank-and-file membership, WEAL has concentrated its efforts on bringing lawsuits aimed at enforcing or enlarging the legal rights of women in higher education and other institutions. In electoral politics, the National Women's Political Caucus (officially nonpartisan, but generally liberal and Democratic) and the National Federation of Republican Women (openly supportive of the Republican party) work to get more women active in politics and more women elected or appointed to office.

The feminist movement has, of course, spawned an antifeminist movement, and thus feminist organizations have their antifeminist counterparts. The campaign by NOW for the ERA was attacked by a women's group called STOP ERA; the proabortion position of NARAL has been challenged by the various organizations associated with the right-to-life movement. These opposition groups have their own tactical problems, which arise in large part from their reliance on different kinds of incentives. In the chapter on civil rights we shall see how the conflict between these opposing groups shaped the debate over the ERA.

The Union Movement

When social movements run out of steam, they leave behind organizations that continue the fight. But with the movement dead or dormant, the organizations often must struggle to stay alive. This has happened to labor unions.

The major union movement in this country occurred in the 1930s, when the Great Depression, popular support, and a sympathetic administration in Washington led to a rapid growth in union membership. In 1945 union membership peaked; at that time nearly 36 percent of all nonfarm workers were union members.

Since then union membership has fallen more or less steadily, so that by 1984 fewer than 19 percent of all workers were unionized (see Figure 9.1, page 248). This decline has been caused by several factors. There has been a shift in the nation's economic life away from industrial production (where unions have traditionally been concentrated) and toward service delivery (where unions have usually been weak). But accompanying this decline, and perhaps contributing to it, has been a decline in popular approval of unions. Approval has moved down side by side with a decline in membership and declines in union victories in elections held to see whether workers in a plant want to join a union. The social movement that supported unionism has faded.

But unions will persist, because most can rely on incentives other than purposive ones to keep them going. In many industries they can require workers to join if they wish to keep their jobs, and in other industries workers believe that they get sufficient benefits from the union to make even voluntary membership worthwhile. And in a few industries, such as teaching and government, there has been a growth in membership, as some white-collar workers have turned to unions to advance their interests.

FIGURE 9.1   The Decline in Union Membership

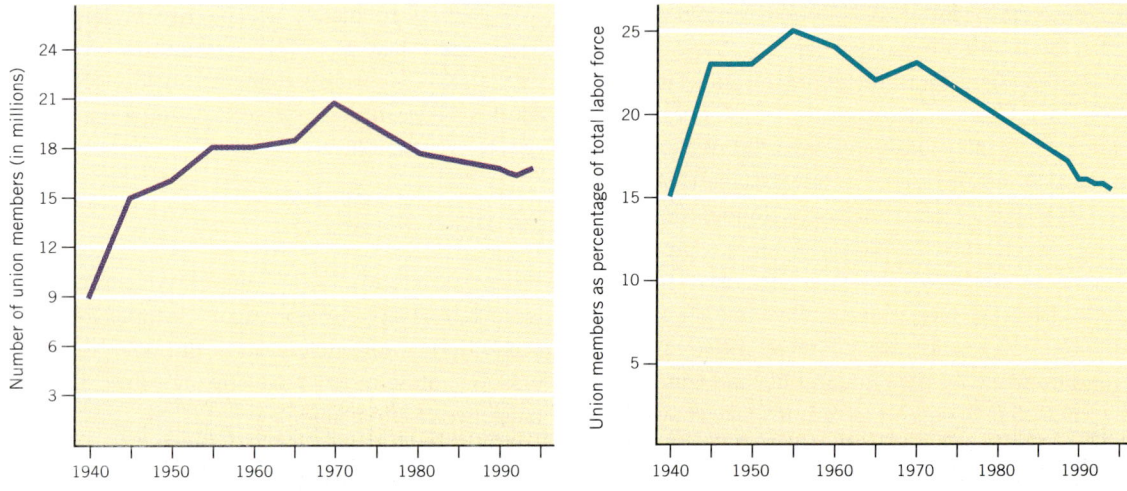

SOURCE: *Historical Statistics of the United States*, vol. 1, 178; *Statistical Abstract of the United States, 1990*, 419; *Statistical Abstract of the United States, 1992*, 422; and *Statistical Abstract of the United States, 1994*, p. 443.

Unions composed of government workers are becoming the most important part of the union movement. They are almost the only part that is growing in size. For example, from 1983 to 1994 the number of private sector union members fell from 11.9 million to 9.6 million, a 19 percent drop. Over the same period, however, the number of public sector union members rose from 5.7 to 7 million, a 22 percent increase. Especially significant has been the membership growth in certain government employee unions affiliated with the AFL-CIO (see Table 9.2). These unions have gained new members and

Unions of government employees have become the most rapidly growing part of the labor movement.

TABLE 9.2   **The Rise in Four Government Employee Unions**

Name of Union	Number of Members by Year		
	1979	1983	1993
National Association of Letter Carriers	151,000	201,000	210,000
Postal Workers	245,000	213,999	249,000
American Federation of Teachers	423,000	544,000	574,000
American Federation of State and County Municipal Employees	889,000	1 million	1.16 million

Four-Union Total 1979: 1.70 million
Four-Union Total 1993: 2.19 million
Percent Change, 1979–1993: +22.3%

SOURCE: *Statistical Abstract of the United States, 1994*, table 696, p. 443.

political clout at a time when almost every industrial union was losing both.

Funds for Interest Groups

All interest groups have some trouble raising money, but membership organizations have more trouble than most, especially membership organizations relying on appeals to purpose—to accomplishing stated goals. As a result the Washington office of a public-interest lobbying group is likely to be small, stark, and crowded, whereas that of an institutional lobby, such as the AFL-CIO or the American Council on Education, will be rather lavish.

To raise more money than members supply in dues, lobbying organizations have turned to three sources that have become important in recent years: foundation grants, government grants, and direct-mail solicitation.

Foundation Grants

One study of eighty-three (primarily liberal) public-interest lobbying groups found that one-third of them received half or more of all their funds from foundation grants; one-tenth received over 90 percent from such sources.[17] Between 1970 and 1980 the Ford Foundation alone contributed about $21 million to liberal public-interest groups. Many of these organizations were law firms that, other than

 Who Gets the Money?

*I*f you give money in response to a direct-mail solicitation, don't assume that the money will go to support the cause in which you believe. It may just go to support the people who are in the business of producing direct-mail solicitations.

Representative Edward Markey of Massachusetts sent an emotional letter to people asking them to give money to support a freeze on nuclear weapons. Eula McNabb of Dallas, Texas, was impressed and sent in a $100 check, thinking that the money would help elect a nuclear freeze candidate. But that's not what happened. According to the *Washington Monthly*, the Markey organization (the U.S. Committee Against Nuclear War) raised $1.3 million from people like Ms. McNabb but spent only $40,000—just 3 percent of the total—on candidates. The rest went to pay for the mailing and to build up a mailing list of interested people to whom Markey could turn for money when he wanted to run for office.

This practice is not limited to liberal Democrats such as Markey. Conservatives, such as the Committee for the Survival of a Free Congress, have in the past given no more than 10 percent or 11 percent of what they raised to help political candidates; the rest went to overhead—offices, salaries, and the cost of direct-mail advertising.

SOURCE: Steven Waldman, "The Hiroshima Hustle," *Washington Monthly* (October 1986): 35–40; and Tina Rosenberg, "Diminishing Returns: The False Promise of Direct Mail," *Washington Monthly* (June 1983): 32–38.

the staff lawyers, really had no members at all. The Environmental Defense Fund is supported almost entirely by grants from such foundations as the Rockefeller Family Fund. The more conservative Scaife foundations gave $1.8 million to a conservative public-interest group, the National Legal Center for the Public Interest.[18]

Federal Grants and Contracts

The expansion of federal grants during the 1960s and 1970s benefited interest groups as well as cities and states; the cutbacks in those grants during the early 1980s hurt interest groups even more than they hurt local governments. Of course the federal government usually does not give the money to support lobbying itself; it is given instead to support some project that the organization has undertaken. For example, the National Alliance of Business received $20 million in 1980 from Washington, much of it for summer youth job programs and the like. But money for a project helps support the organization as a whole and thus enables the organization to press Congress for policies it favors (including, of course, policies that will supply it with more grants and contracts).

Before running for president in 1984, the Reverend Jesse Jackson had been heavily supported for several years by federal grants to his community-development organization, PUSH. Between 1978 and 1982 PUSH received in excess of $5 million from various federal agencies.

Since most public-interest groups pursue liberal policies, the Reagan administration became interested in saving money by reducing grants to interest groups and was particularly interested in cutting back on money being spent to lobby for liberal causes. Some writers called this an effort to "de-fund the left."

Direct Mail

If there is any one technique that is unique to the modern interest group, it is the sophistication with which mailings are used both to raise money and to mobilize supporters. By using computers, membership interest groups can mail directly to specialized audiences identified from lists developed by the staff or purchased from other organizations. Letters can be tailor-made, for example, to appeal to upper-income residents of Oregon who belong to the Sierra Club, live near the Columbia River, own four-wheel-drive vehicles, and thus might be interested in maintaining a local wilderness area.

A classic example of an interest group that was created and maintained by direct-mail solicitation is Common Cause, a liberal organization founded in 1970. Its creator, John Gardner, sent letters to tens of thousands of people selected from mailing lists it had acquired, urging them to join the organization and to send in money. Over two hundred thousand members were obtained in this way, each of whom mailed in dues (initially $15 a year) in return for nothing more than the satisfaction of belonging.

But raising money by mail costs money—lots of money. To bring in more money than it spends, the interest group must write a letter that will galvanize enough readers to send in a check. "Enough" usually amounts to at least 2 percent of the names on the list. Techniques include:

- Put a "teaser" on the outside of the envelope so that it won't be thrown out as "junk mail." If the letter is going to blacks, put a picture of some members of the Ku Klux Klan on the envelope.

- Arouse emotions, preferably by portraying the threat posed by some "devil." To environmentalists, a typical devil would be former Secretary of the Interior James Watt; to civil libertarians, former Moral Majority leader Jerry Falwell; to conservatives, Senator Ted Kennedy.

- Have the endorsement of a famous name; for liberals it is often Senator Kennedy; for conservatives it may be Ronald Reagan.

- Personalize the letter by instructing the computer to insert the recipient's name into the text of the letter to create the impression that it was written personally to him or her.

The Problem of Bias

Many observers believe that the interest groups active in Washington reflect an upper-class bias. There are two reasons for this belief: first, well-off people

How Political Mail Piles Up

One day Daniel Aaron Schlozman of Massachusetts joined eight interest groups, four liberal and four conservative.

Over the next eighteen months, he received 248 pieces of mail, weighing a total of *eighteen pounds.* Included were 135 separate appeals for money.

Of the total, 63 pieces of mail were from organizations that he had not joined but that, apparently, had bought or borrowed mailing lists from organizations that he had joined. The conservative organizations allowed their mailing list to be used by other conservatives; the liberal organizations, by other liberals.

For example, by joining the National Conservative Caucus, he found himself on the mailing lists of Young Americans for Freedom, the Committee for the Survival of a Free Congress, the National Tax Limitation Committee, and the Senator Orrin Hatch Election Committee.

By joining Common Cause, he found himself on the mailing lists of the NAACP, the League of Women Voters, the National Organization for Women, the Campaign to Save the Massachusetts Bottle Bill, and the Union of Concerned Scientists.

But it didn't do any of these organizations much good. Daniel Schlozman was only four months old. His mother, Professor Kay Schlozman, a political scientist at Boston College, had enrolled him just to find out who shares mailing lists.

SOURCE: Adapted from Kay Lehman Schlozman and John T. Tierney, *Organized Interests and American Democracy* (New York: Harper & Row, 1986), 94–95.

---

are more likely than poor people to join and be active in interest groups, and second, interest groups representing business and the professions are much more numerous and better financed than organizations representing minorities, consumers, or the disadvantaged.

Doubtless both these facts are true. As we can see from Table 9.3 on page 252, a survey of citizens done in 1976 shows that those with higher incomes, those whose schooling went through college or beyond, and those in professional or managerial jobs are much more likely to belong to a voluntary association than people with the opposite characteristics. Just as we would expect, higher-income people can afford more organizational memberships than lower-income ones; people in business and the professions find it both easier to attend meetings (they have more control over their own work schedules) and more necessary to do so than people in blue-collar jobs; and people with college degrees often have a wider range of interests than those without.

Of the nearly seven thousand groups that are represented in Washington, over half are corpora-

tions, and another third are professional and trade associations. Only 4 percent are public-interest groups; fewer than 2 percent are civil rights or minority groups.[19] About 170 organizations represented in Washington are concerned just with the oil industry.

But the question of an upper-class bias cannot be settled by these two facts taken alone. In the first place, they only describe certain *inputs* into the political system; they say nothing about the *outputs*—that is, who wins and who loses on particular issues. Even if 170 interest groups are trying to protect the oil industry, this is important only if the oil industry in fact gets protected. Sometimes it does, sometimes it does not. At one time, when oil prices were low, oil companies were able to get Congress to pass a law that sharply restricted the importation of foreign oil; a few years later, after oil prices had risen and people were worried about energy issues, these restrictions were ended.

In the second place, business-oriented interest groups are often divided among themselves. Take one kind of business: farming. Once, farm organiza-

TABLE 9.3   Organizational Membership and Social Class

	Percentage Who Are Members of an Organization or a Union, or Both
Total	53%
Education	
Grade school	35
Some high school	43
High school graduate	44
Some college	49
College graduate	60
Graduate school	80
Occupation	
Sales	39
Service	40
Clerical	41
Operative	48
Manager/administrator	51
Laborer	56
Crafts	64
Professional/technical	70
Income	
Under $6,000	29
$6,000–10,999	42
$11,000–15,999	52
$16,000 and over	65

SOURCE: 1976 Metropolitan Work Force Survey, as reported in Kay Lehman Schlozman and John T. Tierney, *Organized Interests and American Democracy* (New York: Harper & Row, 1986), 60. Copyright © 1986 by Kay Lehman Schlozman and John T. Tierney. Reprinted by permission of Addison-Wesley Educational Publishers Inc.

tions seemed so powerful in Washington that scholars spoke of an irresistible "farm bloc" in Congress that could get its way on almost anything. Today dozens of agricultural organizations operate in the capital, with some (such as the Farm Bureau) attempting to speak for all farmers and others (such as the Tobacco Institute and Mid-America Dairymen) representing particular commodities and regions.

Farmers still have a great deal of influence, especially when it comes to blocking a bill that they oppose. But it is proving difficult for them to get a bill that they want passed by Congress. In part this po-

litical weakness reflects the decline in the number of farmers and thus in the number of legislators who must take their interests into account. (Only 2.5 percent of all Americans live on farms—just one-sixth of the number who lived there thirty years ago.) In part their political weakness reflects splits among the farmers themselves, with southern cotton growers often seeing things differently from midwestern wheat growers or New England dairy farmers. And to some extent it reflects the context within which interest group politics must operate. In the 1950s few people thought that providing subsidies for farmers was too expensive—if indeed they knew of such programs at all. But in the 1980s consumers are acutely aware of food prices, and their legislators are keenly aware of the cost of farm-support programs.[20]

Whenever American politics is described as having an upper-class bias, it is important to ask exactly what this bias is. Most of the major conflicts in American politics—over foreign policy, economic affairs, environmental protection, or equal rights for women—are conflicts *within* the upper-middle-class; they are conflicts, that is, among politically active elites. As we saw in Chapter 5, there are profound cleavages of opinion among these elites. Interest group activity reflects these cleavages.

Nonetheless, it would be a mistake to ignore the overrepresentation of business in Washington. A student of politics should always take differences in the availability of political resources as an important clue to possible differences in the outcomes of political conflicts. But they are only clues, not conclusions.

The Activities of Interest Groups

Size and wealth are no longer entirely accurate measures of an interest group's influence—if indeed they ever were. Depending on the issue, the key to political influence may be the ability to generate a dramatic newspaper headline, mobilize a big letter-writing campaign, stage a protest demonstration, file a suit in federal court to block (or compel) some government action, or quietly supply information to key legislators. All of these things require organization, but only some of them require big or expensive organizations.

Farmers once had great influence in Congress and could get their way with a few telephone calls. Today they often must use mass protest methods.

Information

Of all these tactics, the single most important one—in the eyes of virtually every lobbyist and every academic student of lobbying—is supplying credible information. The reason why information is so valuable is that, to busy legislators and bureaucrats, information is in short supply. Legislators in particular must take positions on a staggering number of issues about which they cannot possibly become expert.

Though there are nonpolitical sources of information, such as encyclopedias, they often do not provide the kind of detailed, specific, and up-to-date information that politicians need. This kind of information will ordinarily be gathered only by a group that has a strong interest in some issue. Lobbyists, for the most part, are not flamboyant, party-giving arm twisters; they are specialists who gather information (favorable to their client, naturally) and present it in as organized, persuasive, and factual a manner as possible. All lobbyists no doubt exaggerate, but few can afford to misrepresent the facts or mislead a legislator, and for a very simple reason: almost every lobbyist must develop and maintain the confidence of a legislator over the long term, with an eye on tomorrow's issues as well as today's. Misrepresentation or bad advice can embar-

rass a legislator who accepts it or repel one who detects it, leading to distrust of the lobbyist. Maintaining contacts and channels of communication is vital; to that end, maintaining trust is essential.

The value of the information provided by a lobbyist is often greatest when the issue is fairly narrow, involving only a few interest groups or a complex economic or technical problem. The value of information, and thus the power of the lobbyist, is likely to be least when the issue is one of broad and highly visible national policy.

Sometimes the nature of an issue or the governmental process by which an issue is resolved gives a great advantage to the suppliers of certain information and imposes a great burden on would-be suppliers of contrary information. This is an example of what is called "client politics." For example, the Civil Aeronautics Board (CAB) once set airline fares and decided what airlines would fly to what cities. Historically the only organizations with any incentive to appear before the CAB and supply the necessary information were, naturally, the airlines. Until the CAB began to deregulate civil aviation, CAB decisions often tended to favor the established airlines.

For a long time only radio and television broadcasters had any incentive (or could afford) to appear before the Federal Communications Commission (FCC), which decides what broadcasters shall be licensed and on what terms. Owing to changes in the industry (such as the rise of cable and satellite television) and to the growth of consumer groups, FCC hearings are now often hotly contested. When the Federal Energy Administration (FEA) was trying to allocate scarce oil and gasoline supplies among competing users, it discovered that the information it needed was possessed only by the oil companies. (It later took steps to develop its own sources of data.)

Public officials not only want technical information; they also want political cues. A **political cue** is a signal telling the official what values are at stake in an issue—who is for, who against a proposal—and how that issue fits into his or her own set of political beliefs. Some legislators feel comfortable when they are on the liberal side of an issue, and others feel comfortable when they are on the conservative side, especially when they are not familiar with the details of the issue. A liberal legislator will look to see whether the AFL-CIO, the NAACP, the Americans for Democratic Action, the Farmers' Union, and various consumer organizations favor a proposal; if so, that is often all he or she has to know. If these liberal groups are split, then the legislator will worry about the matter and try to look into it more closely.

Political news, including cues for voters and legislators, is now rapidly distributed via computer on World Wide Web pages.

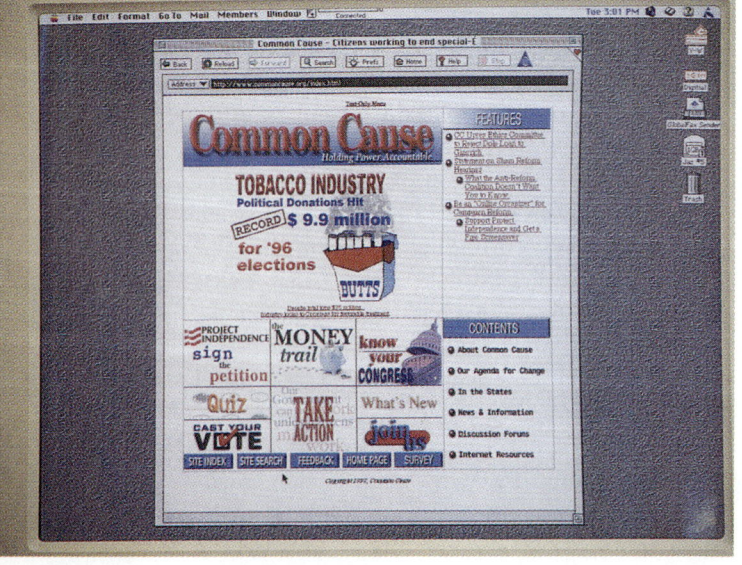

Similarly, a conservative legislator will feel comfortable taking a stand on an issue if the Chamber of Commerce, the Christian Coalition, the American Medical Association, various business associations, and Americans for Constitutional Action are in agreement about it; he or she will feel less comfortable if such conservative groups are divided. As a result of this process lobbyists often work together in informal coalitions based on general political ideology.

One important way in which these cues are made known is by **ratings** that interest groups make of legislators. These are regularly compiled by the AFL-CIO (on who is prolabor), by the Americans for Democratic Action (on who is liberal), by the Americans for Constitutional Action (on who is conservative), by the Consumer Federation of America (on who is proconsumer), and by the League of Conservation Voters (on who is proenvironment). These ratings are designed to generate public support for (or opposition to) various legislators. They can be helpful sources of information, but they are sometimes biased by the arbitrary determination of what constitutes a liberal or a proconsumer or a conservative vote.

Both political information and political cues now arrive in the offices of politicians at a faster rate than ever before, thanks to fax machines. Many interest groups and political activists have banks of computer-operated fax machines that can get a short, snappy document into the hands of every legislator within minutes. William Kristol, a Republican activist, used this technique to good effect in 1993 when he bombarded Republican members of Congress with arguments concerning why they should oppose President Clinton's health care plan. Many credit him with having played a major role in the defeat of that plan.

Public Support: The Rise of the New Politics

Once upon a time, when the government was small, Congress was less individualistic, and television was nonexistent, lobbyists mainly used an *insider strategy*: they worked closely with a few key members of Congress, meeting them privately to exchange information and (sometimes) favors. Matters of mutual interest could be discussed at a leisurely pace, over dinner or while playing golf. Public opinion was important on some highly visible issues, but there were not many of these.

Following an insider strategy is still valuable, but increasingly interest groups have turned to an *outsider strategy*. The newly individualistic nature of Congress has made this tactic useful, and modern technology has made it possible. Radio, fax machines, and the Internet can now get news out almost immediately. Satellite television can be used to link interested citizens in various locations across the country. Toll-free phone numbers can be publicized, enabling voters to call the offices of their members of Congress without charge. Public opinion polls can be done by telephone, virtually overnight, to measure (and help generate) support for or opposition to proposed legislation. Mail can be directed by computers to people already known to have an interest in a particular matter.

This kind of *grass-roots lobbying* is central to the outsider strategy. It is designed to generate public pressure directly on government officials. The "public" that exerts this pressure is not every voter or even most voters; it is that part of the public (sometimes called an *issue public*) that is directly affected by or deeply concerned with a government policy. What modern technology has made possible is the overnight mobilization of specific issue publics.

Not every issue lends itself to an outsider strategy: it is hard to get many people excited about, for example, complex tax legislation affecting only a few firms. But as the government does more and more, its policies affect more and more people, and so more and more will join in grassroots lobbying efforts over such matters as abortion, Medicare, Social Security, environmental protection, and affirmative action.

Undoubtedly, the new politics spells new conflicts. Since conflict is the essence of politics, it may seem strange that politicians dislike controversy. But they do, and for perfectly human reasons: no one enjoys dealing with people who are upset or who find one's viewpoint objectionable or unworthy. Consequently, most legislators tend to hear what they want to hear and to deal with interest groups that agree with them.[21] Two senators from the same state may choose to listen to very different con-

stituencies in that state and to take very different policy positions. Neither senator may feel "pressured" or "lobbied," because each has heard mostly from groups or persons who share his or her views. (Politicians define "pressure" as arguments and inducements supplied by somebody with whom they disagree.)

Members of an interest group will also tend to work primarily with legislators with whom they agree; lobbyists do not like to argue with people who are suspicious of them or who are unlikely to change their mind no matter what is said. For the lobbyist the key target is the undecided or wavering legislator or bureaucrat. Sometimes lobbyists will make a major effort to persuade the undecided legislator that public opinion is strongly inclined in one direction. A lobbyist will do this by commissioning public opinion polls, by stimulating local citizens to write letters or send telegrams, by arranging for constituents to pay personal visits to the legislator, or by getting newspapers to run editorials supporting the lobbyist's position.

Lobbyists don't confine their efforts to the lobby of the Capitol; here, one makes his case outside on the steps.

National Rifle Association: The Lobby That Can't Be Beat?

*T*he National Rifle Association (NRA) was founded in 1871 as a group dedicated to providing shooting instruction. But in the 1960s and early 1970s, the NRA became a lobby dedicated primarily to opposing public policies that would restrict or abolish citizens' rights to own and use firearms for sporting and other legal purposes. By the 1980s the NRA's membership had increased from one million to nearly three million. Its members receive magazines, decals, and other direct benefits.

Throughout its lobbying history, the NRA has invoked the symbolic and legal authority of the last clause of the Constitution's Second Amendment: "the right of the people to keep and bear Arms, shall not be infringed." In 1986 the NRA achieved one of its greatest lobbying victories when Congress passed the Firearm Owners Protection Act, which abolished the 1968 ban on interstate rifle and shotgun sales. The NRA's lobbying arm, the Institute for Legislative Action, has a budget that many other interest groups only dream of—$29 million in 1992. From 1983 to 1992 the NRA spent $8 million on congressional races in both direct contributions to their favored candidates and in independent expenditures supporting or opposing various candidates.

With millions of members, a big budget, and demonstrated political clout, the NRA has typified a lobby that can't be beat. However, in the 1992 congressional races the NRA spent millions to defeat incumbents who had sponsored strict gun-control measures, but the incumbents won handily despite the NRA's efforts. At the state level, the NRA lost a major battle to repeal New Jersey's ban on semiautomatic assault weapons and lost similar battles in Connecticut, Virginia, and other states. In 1992 the NRA's membership hovered around 2.6 million, down from its peak in the 1980s.

Why this apparent weakening in the NRA's political influence? Like any lobby, the NRA's influence depends not only on the size of its membership and financial clout but also on its consonance with public opinion and the strength of opposition lobbying groups. A 1992 poll found that 86 percent of the American public and 82 percent of the gun-owning public favored a national law that would require a seven-day waiting period between the time a person applies to buy a handgun and the time it is sold. The same poll found that 79 percent of the general public and 76 percent of the gun-owning public favored a ban on assault weapons (semiautomatic military-style rifles that

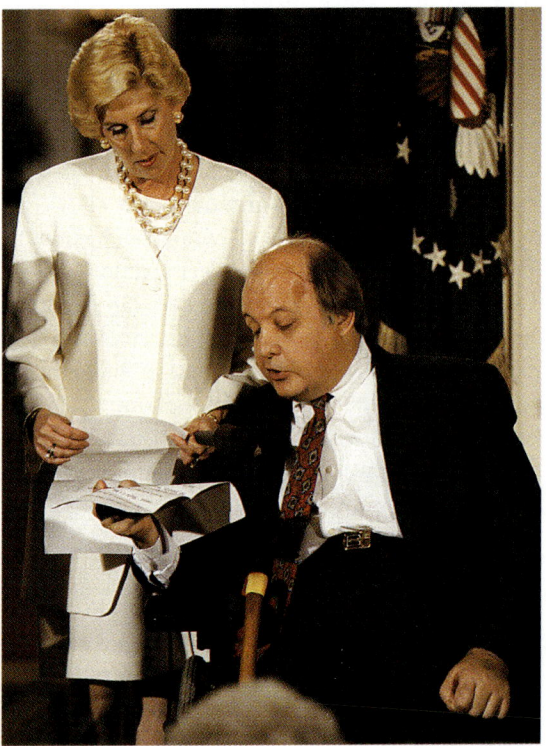

After Jim Brady was shot during an attempt to assassinate President Reagan, he (shown here with his wife, Sarah) became a symbol to and a leader of gun-control advocates. The 1993 bill was named after him.

can hold up to thirty bullets). These are precisely the types of gun-control measures that the NRA *opposes*. Given this discrepancy between the NRA and public opinion, it's not surprising that only 27 percent of the general public and 42 percent of gun owners expressed a favorable opinion of the NRA. At the same time, law enforcement groups like the Fraternal Order of Police and pro-gun-control lobbies such as Handgun Control, Inc., have joined forces to offset the influence of the NRA. With the force of public opinion behind them, these groups are beginning to undermine the impact of the NRA's anti-gun-control lobby.

As the NRA's recent history helps to illustrate, no lobby is all-powerful.

SOURCE: Peter H. Stone, "Under the Gun," *The National Journal* (June 5, 1993), 1334-1338; *New York Times*/CBS News poll, January 22–25, 1992, as presented in the *New York Times* (March 12, 1992), D21.

Though most lobbying organizations cultivate the goodwill of government officials, there are important exceptions. Some groups, especially those that use an ideological appeal to attract supporters or that depend for their maintenance and influence on media publicity, will deliberately attack actual or potential allies in government in order to embarrass them. Ralph Nader is as likely to denounce as to praise those officials who tend to agree with him, if their agreement is not sufficiently close or public. He did this with Senator Edmund Muskie, the author of the Clean Air Act, and with William Haddon, Jr., an early administrator of the National Highway Traffic Safety Administration. The head of the Fund for Animals is not reluctant to attack those officials in the Forest Service and the Interior Department on whose cooperation the fund must rely if it is to achieve its goals.[22] Sometimes, as we shall see in a later section, the use of threats instead of rewards extends to physical confrontations.

It is not clear how often public pressure works. Members of Congress are skilled at recognizing and discounting organized mail campaigns and feel that they can occasionally afford to go against even legitimate expressions of hostile public opinion. Only a few issues of great symbolic significance and high visibility are so important that a member of Congress would think that to ignore public opinion would mean losing the next election. In 1978 the proposed Panama Canal treaties were one such case; since the 1980s abortion has been another. Issues such as these can make or break a member of Congress.

Of late, interest groups have placed great emphasis on developing grassroots support. Sometimes it is impossible to develop such support, as when a complicated tax regulation of interest to only a few firms is being changed. But sometimes a proposed bill touches a public nerve such that even businesses can help generate an outpouring of mail: when the Food and Drug Administration announced it was going to ban saccharin on the grounds that it caused cancer in laboratory animals, the Calorie Control Council (closely tied to the Coca-Cola Company, a big user of saccharin in such soft drinks as Tab) ran newspaper ads denouncing the policy. The public, worried about losing access to an artificial sweetener important to dieters, responded with an avalanche of mail to Congress, which promptly passed a law reversing the ban.

Usually, however, the public at large doesn't care that much about an issue, and so interest groups will try by direct-mail campaigns to arouse a small but passionate group to write letters or vote (or not

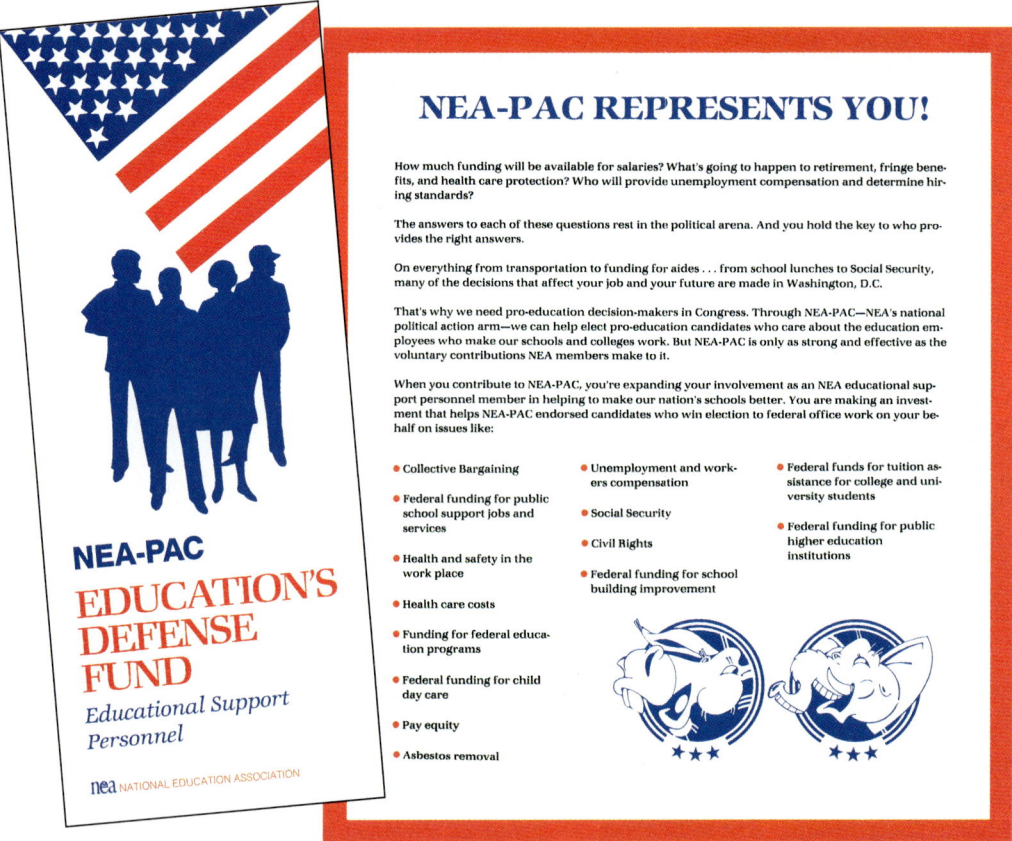

The political action committee of the National Education Association—a teachers' union—is one of the biggest in the nation.

vote) for specified candidates. Beginning in 1970, Environmental Action designated certain members of the House of Representatives as the "Dirty Dozen" because of their votes against bills that the lobbying group claimed were necessary to protect the environment. Of the thirty-one members of Congress so listed in various elections, only seven survived in office. Many members of Congress believe that the "Dirty Dozen" label hurts them with proenvironment voters in their districts, and though they are angry over what they feel is the unfair use of that label, they strive to avoid it if at all possible.

Money and PACs

Contrary to popular suspicions, money is probably one of the less effective ways by which interest groups advance their causes. That was not always the case. Only a few decades ago, powerful interests used their bulging wallets to buy influence in Congress. The passage of the campaign finance reform law in 1973 changed that. The law had two effects. First, it sharply restricted the amount that any interest could give to a candidate for federal office (see Chapter 8). Second, it made it legal for corporations and labor unions to form political action committees (PACs) that could make political contributions.

The effect of the second change was to encourage the rapid growth of PACs. By 1993 some 4,200 PACs existed, over six times the number that existed in 1975. In 1991–1992 they gave nearly $180 million to congressional candidates. Some people worry that the existence of all this political money has resulted in our having, as Senator Edward Kennedy put it, "the finest Congress that money can buy." More likely the increase in the number of PACs has had just the opposite effect. The reason is simple: with PACs so numerous and so easy to form, it is now probable that there will be money available on every side of almost every conceivable issue. As a result, members of Congress can take money and still decide for themselves how to vote. As we shall see, there is not much scholarly evidence that money buys votes in Congress.

Indeed, some members of Congress tell PACs what to do rather than take orders from them. Members will frequently inform PACs that they "expect" money from them; grumbling PAC officials feel that they have no choice but to contribute for fear of alienating the members. Moreover, some members have created their *own* PACs—organizations set up to raise money from individual donors that is then given to favored political allies in and out of Congress or used to advance the members' own political ambitions. When Charles Rangel, congressman from New York, was hoping to be elected whip of the Democratic party in the House, he set up a PAC that made campaign contributions to fellow representatives in hopes that they might vote for him as whip. There are many other examples from both sides of the aisle. An ironic consequence of this is that a conservative Republican may give money to a PAC set up by a moderate Democrat, who then gives the money to a liberal Democrat (or vice versa), with the result that the original donor winds up having his or her money go to somebody that he or she profoundly dislikes.

Almost any kind of organization—corporation, labor union, trade association, public-interest lobby, citizens group—can form a PAC. Over half of all PACs are sponsored by corporations, about a tenth by labor unions, and the rest by various groups, including ideological ones.

The rise of ideological PACs has been the most remarkable development in interest group activity in recent years. They have increased in number at a faster rate than business or labor PACs, and in the 1980 and 1982 elections they raised more money than either business or labor. In the 1992 election there were more than one thousand ideological PACs; about one-third were liberal, about two-thirds conservative.[23]

Though the ideological PACs raised more money than business or labor ones, they spent less on campaigns and gave less to candidates. The reason for this anomaly is that an ideological PAC usually has to raise its money by means of massive direct-mail solicitations, expensive efforts that can

TABLE 9.4 **Spending by Political Action Committees (PACs), 1994**

Ten largest PAC contributors to federal candidates during the 1994 election.

Committee	Contribution
United Parcel Service	$2,647,113
State, County, and Municipal Employees	2,529,682
Voter Education Committee	2,487,152
American Medical Association	2,386,947
National Education Association	2,260,850
Trial Lawyers Association	2,164,035
United Auto Workers	2,147,190
National Rifle Association	1,853,038
Realtors Association	1,851,978
Automobile Dealers' Association	1,832,570

SOURCE: Federal Election Commission, press release, March 31, 1995.

consume all the money raised, and more. By contrast, a typical business or labor PAC solicits money from within a single corporation or union. Even a well-run ideological PAC must spend fifty cents to raise a dollar; some spend much more than that.[24]

As Table 9.4 shows, of the ten PACs that gave the most money to candidates in the 1994 election, most were labor unions, business organizations, and groups that represented doctors, lawyers, accountants, and retirees. Except for the National Rifle Association, none was an ideological PAC. There have been many proposals to cut the amount that PACs can give to candidates for federal office from a maximum of $5,000 to $2,500 per election. The table shows the total amount that the top ten PACs would have been able to give under each of these proposed limits. (If the $2,500 limit had been in effect in 1992, the ten PACs that gave the most money to congressional candidates would have been prohibited from giving $6.4 million, or 29 percent of their contributions; if the $1,000 limit had been in effect, it would have prohibited $14.9 million, or two-thirds of their contributions.)

Table 9.5 on page 260 shows that, as we learned in Chapter 8, incumbents received more PAC money than challengers and that, whereas labor PACs gave almost exclusively to Democrats, business PACs divided their contributions between Democrats and

TABLE 9.5	How the PACs Spent Their Money in 1994

During the 1994 campaign, more than three thousand PACs divided up their contributions as follows (in millions of dollars):

PAC sponsor	House					Senate				
	Dem.	Rep.	Incumbent	Challenger	Open	Dem.	Rep.	Incumbent	Challenger	Open
Corporate	$24.8	$20.4	$37.9	$3.1	$4.3	$9.2	$15.1	$15.2	$2.0	$7.1
Trade/Professional	22.7	17.1	31.0	3.4	5.4	5.6	7.4	8.3	1.1	3.5
Labor	32.5	1.4	24.2	4.2	5.6	7.4	0.3	4.0	1.7	1.9
Nonconnected	7.5	4.4	7.6	1.9	2.4	3.3	2.8	3.6	0.8	1.7

SOURCE: Harold W. Stanley and Richard G. Niemi, *Vital Statistics on American Politics*, 5th ed. (Washington, D.C.: CQ Press, 1995), p. 169.

Republicans. The result of this pattern of spending is that, though business raises more political money than labor, Democratic candidates often receive more PAC funds than do Republicans.

The popular image of rich PACs stuffing huge sums into political campaigns and thereby buying the attention and possibly the favors of the grateful candidates is a bit overdrawn. For one thing, the typical PAC contribution is rather small. The average PAC donation to a House candidate is only a few hundred dollars and accounts for less than 1 percent of the candidate's total receipts. Most PACs spread small sums of money over many candidates, and despite their great growth in numbers and expenditures, PACs still provide only about one-third of all the money spent by candidates for the House.[25]

Moreover, scholars have yet to find systematic evidence that PAC contributions generally affect how members of Congress vote. On most issues, how legislators vote can be explained primarily by their general ideological outlook and the characteristics of their constituents; how much PAC money they have received turns out to be a small factor. On the other hand, when an issue arises in which most of their constituents have no interest and ideology provides little guidance, there is a slight statistical correlation between PAC contributions and votes. But even here the correlation may be misleading. The same groups that give money also wage intensive lobbying campaigns, flooding representatives with information, press releases, and letters from interested constituents. What these studies may be measuring is the effect of persuasive arguments, not dollars; no one can be certain.[26]

It is possible that money affects legislative behavior in ways that will never appear in studies of roll-call votes in Congress. Members of Congress may be more willing to set aside time in their busy schedules for a group that has given money than for a group that has not. What the money has bought is access: it has helped open the door. Or contributions might influence how legislators behave on the committees on which they serve, subtly shaping the way in which they respond to arguments and the facts on which they rely. No one knows, because the research has not been done.

In any event, if interest group money makes a difference at all, it probably makes it on certain kinds of issues more than others. In Chapter 15 we define the kind of issues—we call them "client politics"—on which a given interest group is likely to be especially influential, whether by means of arguments, money, or both. After reading that chapter and considering the examples given there, it will be easier to put the present discussion of PAC money into context.

The "Revolving Door"

Every year, hundreds of people leave important jobs in the federal government to take more lucrative positions in private industry. Some go to work as lobbyists, others as consultants to business, still others as key executives in corporations, foundations, and universities. Many people worry that this "revolving door" may give private interests a way of improperly influencing government decisions. If a federal official uses his or her government position to do something for a corporation in exchange for a cushy job after leaving government, or if a person who has left government uses his or her personal contacts in Washington to get favors for private parties, then the public interest may suffer.

From time to time there are incidents that seem to confirm these fears. Michael K. Deaver, once the deputy chief of staff in the Reagan White House, was convicted of perjury in connection with a grand jury investigation of his having used his former government contacts to help the clients of his public relations firm. Lyn Nofziger, a former Reagan White House aide, was convicted of violating the Ethics in Government Act (see the accompanying box) by lobbying the White House, soon after he left it, on behalf of various businesses and labor unions.

In 1988 federal investigators revealed evidence of corrupt dealings between some Defense Department officials and industry executives. Contractors and their consultants, many of whom were former Pentagon personnel, obtained favors from procurement officials, gaining an edge on their competitors.

How systematic is this pattern of abuse? We don't know. Studies of the revolving door in federal regulatory agencies have found no clear pattern of officials' tilting their decisions in hopes of landing a lucrative business job.[27]

Agencies differ in their vulnerability to outside influences. If the Food and Drug Administration is not vigilant, people in that agency who help decide whether a new drug should be placed on the market may have their judgment affected somewhat by the possibility that, if they approve the drug, the pharmaceutical company that makes it will later offer them a lucrative position.

On the other hand, lawyers in the Federal Trade Commission who prosecute businesses that violate the antitrust laws may decide that their chances for getting a good job with a private law firm later on will increase if they are particularly vigorous and effective prosecutors. The firm, after all, wants to hire competent people, and winning a case is a good test of competence.[28]

Trouble

Public displays and disruptive tactics—protest marches, sit-ins, picketing, and violence—have always been a part of American politics. Indeed, they were among

Conflict of Interest

*I*n 1978 a new federal law, the Ethics in Government Act, codified and broadened the rules governing possible conflicts of interest among senior members of the executive branch. The key provisions were these:

The president, vice president, and top-ranking (GS-16 and above) executive branch employees must each year file a public financial disclosure report that lists

- The source and amount of all earned income as well as income from stocks, bonds, and property; the worth of any investments or large debts; and the source of a spouse's income, if any

- Any position held in business, labor, or certain nonprofit organizations

Employment after government service is restricted. Former executive branch employees may *not*

- Represent anyone before their former agencies in connection with any matter that the former employees had been involved in before leaving the government

- Appear before an agency, for two years after leaving government service, on matters that came within the former employees' official sphere of responsibility, even if they were not personally involved in the matter

- Represent anyone on any matter before their former agency, for one year after leaving it, even if the former employees had no connection with the matter while in the government

In addition, another law prohibits bribery—it is illegal to ask for, solicit, or receive anything of value in return for being influenced in the performance of one's duties.

Finally, an executive order forbids outside employment—an official may not hold a job or take a fee, even for lecturing or writing, if such employment or income might create a conflict of interest or an apparent conflict of interest.

SOURCES: *National Journal* (November 19, 1977): 1796–1803; and *Congressional Quarterly Weekly Report* (October 28, 1978): 3121–3127.

the favorite tactics of the American colonists seeking independence in 1776.

Both ends of the political spectrum have used display, disruption, and violence. On the left, feminists, antislavery agitators, coal miners, auto workers, welfare mothers, blacks, antinuclear power groups, public housing tenants, the American Indian Movement, the Students for a Democratic Society, and the Weather Underground have created "trouble" ranging from peaceful sit-ins at segregated lunch counters to bombings and shootings. On the right, the Ku Klux Klan has used terror, intimidation, and murder; parents opposed to forced busing of schoolchildren have demonstrated; business firms have used strong-arm squads against workers; right-to-life groups have blockaded abortion clinics; and an endless array of "anti-" groups (anti-Catholics, anti-Masons, anti-Jews, anti-immigrants, antisaloons, antiblacks, antiprotesters, and probably even anti-antis) have taken their disruptive turns on stage. These various activities are not morally the same—a sit-in demonstration is quite different from a lynching—but politically they constitute a similar problem for a government official.

An explanation of why and under what circumstances disruption occurs is beyond the scope of this book. To understand interest group politics, however, it is important to remember that making trouble has since the 1960s become a quite conventional political resource and is no longer simply the last resort of extremist groups. Making trouble is now an accepted political tactic of ordinary middle-class citizens as well as the disadvantaged or disreputable.

There is of course a long history of the use of disruptive methods by "proper" people. In a movement that began in England at the turn of the century and then spread here, feminists would chain themselves to lampposts or engage in what we now call "sit-ins" as part of a campaign to win the vote for women. The object then was much the same as the object of similar tactics today: to disrupt the workings of some institution so that it is forced to negotiate with you, or, failing that, to enlist the sympathies of third parties (the media, other interest groups) who will come to your aid and press your target to negotiate with you, or, failing that, to goad the police into making attacks and arrests so that martyrs are created.

The civil rights and antiwar movements of the 1960s gave experience in these methods to thousands of young people and persuaded others of the effectiveness of such methods under certain conditions. Though these movements have abated or disappeared, their veterans and emulators have put such tactics to new uses—trying to block the construction of the Seabrook, New Hampshire, nuclear power plant, for example, or occupying the office of a cabinet secretary to obtain concessions for the handicapped.

Government officials dread this kind of trouble. They usually find themselves in a no-win situation. If they ignore the disruption, they are accused of being "insensitive," "unresponsive," or "arrogant." If they give in to the demonstrators, they encourage more demonstrations by proving that this is a useful tactic. If they call the police, they run the risk of violence and injuries, followed not only by bad publicity but by lawsuits. (When mass arrests were made during an antiwar demonstration in Washington, D.C., subsequent lawsuits were filed that were decided in favor of the protesters, and millions of dollars in damages had to be paid.)

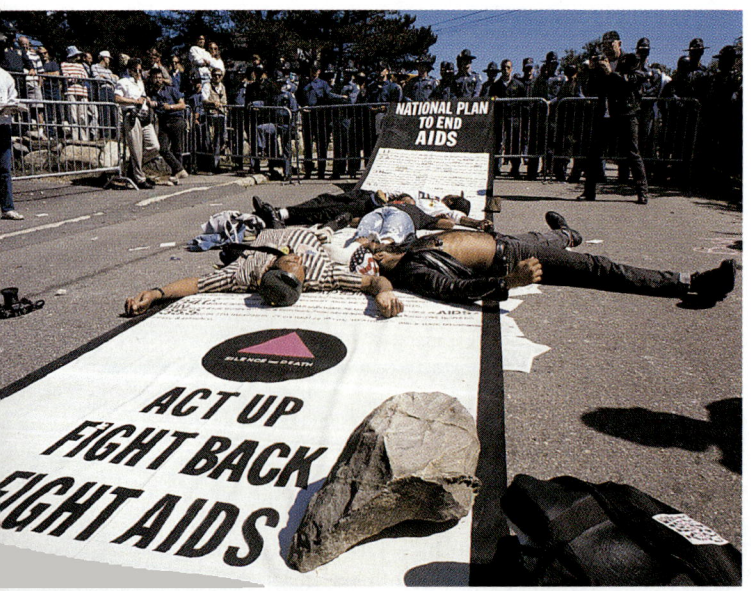

Disruptive tactics have been a part of American politics since the Boston Tea Party. These gay-rights activists are blocking a road near then-president George Bush's Maine home.

Regulating Interest Groups

Interest group activity is a form of political speech protected by the First Amendment to the Constitution: it cannot lawfully be abolished or even much curtailed. In 1946 Congress passed the Federal

Regulation of Lobbying Act, which requires groups and individuals seeking to influence legislation to register with the secretary of the Senate and the clerk of the House and to file quarterly financial reports. The Supreme Court upheld the law but restricted its application to lobbying efforts involving direct contacts with members of Congress.[29] More general "grassroots" interest group activity may not be restricted by the government. The 1946 law had little practical effect. Not all lobbyists took the trouble to register, and there was no guarantee that the financial statements were accurate. There was no staff in charge of enforcing the law.

After years of growing popular dissatisfaction with Congress, prompted in large measure by the (exaggerated) view that legislators were the pawns of powerful special interests, Congress in late 1995 unanimously passed a bill that tightened up the registration and disclosure requirements. Signed by the president, the law restates the obligation of lobbyists to register with the House and Senate, but it broadens the definition of a lobbyist to include

- People who spend at least 20 percent of their time lobbying

- People who are paid at least $5,000 in any six-month period to lobby

- Corporations and other groups that spend more than $20,000 in any six-month period on their own lobbying staffs

The law covers people and groups who lobby the executive branch and congressional staffers as well as elected members of Congress, and it includes law firms that represent clients before the government. Twice a year, all registered lobbyists must report

- The names of their clients

- Their income and expenditures

- The issues on which they worked

The registration and reporting requirements do not, however, extend to so-called grassroots organizations—that is, campaigns (sometimes led by volunteers, sometimes by hired professionals) to mobilize citizens to write or call the government about some issue. Nor is any new enforcement organization created, although congressional officials may refer violations to the Justice Department for investigation.

Fines for breaking the law could amount to $50,000. In addition, the law bars tax-exempt, nonprofit advocacy groups that lobby from getting federal grants, a provision aimed at such organizations as the American Association of Retired Persons (AARP).

The most significant legal constraints on interest groups come not from the current federal lobbying law (though that may change) but from the tax code and the campaign finance laws. A nonprofit organization—which includes not only charitable groups but almost all voluntary associations that have an interest in politics—need not pay income taxes, and financial contributions to it can be deducted on the donor's income tax return, provided that the organization does not devote a "substantial part" of its activities to "attempting to influence legislation."[30] Many tax-exempt organizations do take public positions on political questions and testify before congressional committees. If the organization does any serious lobbying, however, it will lose its tax-exempt status (and thus find it harder to solicit donations and more expensive to operate). Exactly this happened to the Sierra Club in 1968 when the Internal Revenue Service revoked its tax-exempt status because of its extensive lobbying activities. Some voluntary associations try to deal with this problem by setting up separate organizations to collect tax-exempt money—for example, the NAACP, which lobbies, must pay taxes, but the NAACP Legal Defense and Education Fund, which does not lobby, is tax-exempt.

Finally, the campaign finance laws, described in detail in Chapter 8, limit to $5,000 the amount any political action committee can spend on a given candidate in a given election. These laws have sharply curtailed the extent to which any *single* group can give money, though they have increased the *total* amount that different groups are providing.

Beyond making bribery or other manifestly corrupt forms of behavior illegal and restricting the sums that campaign contributors can donate, there is probably no system for controlling interest groups that would both make a useful difference and leave important constitutional and political rights unimpaired. Ultimately the only remedy for imbalances or inadequacies in interest group representation is to devise and sustain a political system that gives all affected parties a reasonable chance to be heard on

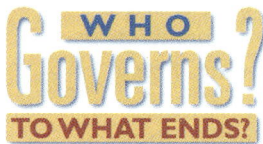

Outlawing PAC Contributions

In 1996 Congress considered but shelved a bipartisan bill to outlaw campaign contributions from PACs. The bill also would have rewarded candidates who met voluntary campaign spending limits with free television broadcast time, required candidates to raise 60 percent of their campaign funds in their own state, relaxed contribution limits for candidates facing self-funded opponents, and prohibited incumbents from sending franked mailings to their constituents during an election year. The failed bill's supporters included such diverse groups as Public Citizen, the League of Women Voters, Common Cause, United We Stand America, and the American Association of Retired Persons. Supporters argued that since the last major overhaul of the campaign finance laws, in 1974, Washington had become a haven for free-spending lobbyists.

• *Soft money.* These largely unregulated contributions amounted to more than $30 million in the first half of 1995 alone. In 1991–1992, the Republicans and President Bush collected nearly $50 million in soft money, while the Democrats and Bill Clinton collected about $35 million.

• *Bundling.* The practice of delivering a bunch of "individual" campaign contributions in a single big check. In 1991–1992, twenty-nine members of Congress received bundled donations greater than $20,000 from individuals

at a single company. The biggest recipient of bundled funds was the House Democratic majority leader at the time, Richard Gephardt, who received $43,350 bundled from Anheuser-Busch Cos., Inc., and $20,000 or more bundled from individuals at four other big firms.

• *Leadership PACs.* These are political action committees led by politicians. One was GOPAC, formerly chaired by House Republican leader Newt Gingrich. Because they are not officially tied to the national party committees, these PACs can maintain "nonfederal" accounts—worth millions—that are not clearly subject to the disclosure regulations of the Federal Election Commission (FEC). (In 1996 the FEC sued GOPAC for allegedly failing to disclose more than $500,000 in election-related donations from 1989–1991.) In 1995, after stepping down as GOPAC's chairman, Gingrich formed another Leadership PAC called Monday Morning. This new PAC held fund-raising breakfasts for lobbyists and raised $325,000 in a few months.

Polls show that most Americans favor banning PAC contributions. So, apparently, do many newspaper editors: the no-more-PAC-money bill was endorsed by over 260 newspapers nationwide.

But as we have explained, it is by no means clear that PAC money has a big effect on how members of Congress vote. PACs are not an incumbency-pro-

tection system, and they do not single-handedly determine election outcomes (refer back to Chapter 8). Also, a PAC-money ban is almost certainly unconstitutional. Among other relevant precedents, it violates the Supreme Court's 1976 ruling in *Buckley* v. *Valeo* that giving candidates money is a form of protected speech under the First Amendment.

Still, campaign finance practices are bound to draw future calls for far-reaching reform, and not just in Washington. In 1996 over two dozen states were considering various reform measures, including some that would pay for state campaigns entirely from the public treasury. For example, in 1996 reformers in Maine pushed for a "clean election" initiative that would provide generous public financing for candidates who wanted it. The initiative's supporters gathered 65,000 signatures in just fourteen hours.

You now know as much or more about the issue of campaign finance reform as most of those who hold strong opinions about it. Would you favor outlawing PAC contributions? Are you troubled by soft money and related "loopholes"? Is there any case to be made for reforms that remove rather than toughen limits on campaign contributions and spending? Has the issue come up in your home state? If so, what has been debated, and has anything major been decided?

matters of public policy. That, of course, is exactly what the Founders thought that they were doing. Whether they succeeded or not is a question to which we shall return at the end of this book.

SUMMARY

Interest groups in the United States are more numerous and more fragmented than those in nations such as Great Britain, where the political system is more centralized. The goals and tactics of interest groups reflect not only the interests of their members but also the size of the groups, the incentives with which they attract supporters, and the role of their professional staffs. Because of the difficulty of organizing large numbers of people, a group purporting to speak for mass constituencies will often have to provide material benefits to members or acquire an affluent sponsor (such as a foundation). The chief source of interest group influence is information; public support, money, and the ability to create "trouble" are also important. The right to lobby is protected by the Constitution, but the tax and campaign finance laws impose significant restrictions on how money may be used.

KEY TERMS

interest group   *p. 235*

lobby   *p. 236*

lobbyist   *p. 236*

social movement   *p. 238*

incentive   *p. 241*

solidary incentive   *p. 241*

material incentive   *p. 241*

purposive incentive   *p. 242*

ideological interest group   *p.242*

public-interest lobby   *p. 242*

cue (political)   *p. 254*

ratings   *p. 254*

SUGGESTED READINGS

Bauer, Raymond A., Ithiel de Sola Pool, and Lewis A. Dexter. *American Business and Public Policy.* New York: Atherton, 1963. A classic study of how business groups tried to shape foreign-trade legislation, set in a broad analysis of pressure groups and Congress.

Berry, Jeffrey M. *Lobbying for the People.* Princeton, N.J.: Princeton University Press, 1977. Analyzes more than eighty "public-interest" lobbies, with a detailed discussion of two.

Cigler, Allan J., and Burdett A. Loomis, eds. *Interest Group Politics.* 3d ed. Washington, D.C.: Congressional Quarterly Press, 1991. Essays on several interest groups active in Washington.

Lowi, Theodore J. *The End of Liberalism.* New York: Norton, 1969. A critique of the role of interest groups in American government.

Malbin, Michael J. *Money and Politics in the United States.* Chatham, N.J.: Chatham House, 1984. Excellent studies of PACs and of the influence of money in elections.

Mansbridge, Jane J. *Why We Lost the ERA.* Chicago: University of Chicago Press, 1986. Insightful analysis of the relationship between organizational incentives and tactics in the ERA campaign.

Olson, Mancur. *The Logic of Collective Action.* Cambridge, Mass.: Harvard University Press, 1965. An economic analysis of interest groups, especially the "free-rider" problem.

Sabato, Larry. *PAC Power.* New York: Norton, 1985. A full discussion of the nature and activities of political-action committees.

Schlozman, Kay Lehman, and John T. Tierney. *Organized Interests and American Democracy.* New York: Harper & Row, 1985. Comprehensive treatise on interest groups based on original research.

Truman, David B. *The Governmental Process.* 2d ed. New York: Knopf, 1971. First published in 1951, this was the classic analysis—and defense—of interest-group pluralism.

Wilson, James Q. *Political Organizations.* Rev. ed. Princeton, N.J.: Princeton University Press, 1995. A theory of interest groups emphasizing the incentives they use to attract members.

10

The Media

★ Early partisan sponsorship of the press

★ Emergence of mass newspapers

★ National magazines of opinion

★ Electronic journalism

★ Local versus national orientation of the media

★ Regulation of radio and TV and nonregulation of newspapers

★ Effects of the media on politics

★ Attempts by government to shape public opinion

★ Is the news slanted?

★ News leaks

All public officials have a love-hate relationship with newspapers, television, and the other media of mass communication. They depend on the media for the advancement of their careers and policies but fear the media's power to criticize, expose, and destroy. As political parties have declined—especially, strong local party organizations—politicians have become increasingly dependent on the media. Their efforts to woo the press have become ever greater, and their expressions of rage and dismay when that courtship is spurned, ever stronger. At the same time, the media have been changing, especially in regard to the kinds of people who have been attracted to leading positions in journalism and the attitudes they have brought with them. There has always been an adversarial relationship between those who govern and those who write, but events of recent decades have, as we shall see, made that conflict especially keen.

The relationships between government and the media in this country are shaped by laws and understandings that accord the media a degree of freedom greater than that found in almost any other nation. Though many public officials secretly might like to control the media, and though no medium of communication in the United States or elsewhere is totally free of government influence, the press in this country is among the freest in the world. A study of ninety-four countries found only sixteen in which the press enjoyed a high degree of freedom; the United States was one of these.[1] Some democratic nations, such as France and Great Britain, place more restrictions on the communications media than are found here. The laws governing libel in England are so strict that public figures frequently sue newspapers for printing statements that tend to defame or ridicule them—and they collect. In the United States, as will be explained, the law of libel is loose enough to permit intense and even inaccurate criticism of anybody in the public eye. England also has an Official Secrets Act that can be used to punish any present or past public official who divulges to the press private government business.[2] In this

HOW SLOWLY NEWS TRAVELED, 1790

SOURCE: *Atlas of Early American History* (1976), 69. Adapted from map in Allan R. Pred, *Urban Growth and the Circulation of Information: The United States System of Cities, 1790–1840,* 37. By permission of Princeton University Press and Harvard University Press. Copyright © 1973 by the President and Fellows of Harvard College.

This map marks the average lag, in days, between the occurrence of an event in an outlying place and the published report of that event in the Philadelphia newspapers. The shaded areas show places with similar lag times. For example, it took over ten days in 1790 for news of an event in Boston to be published in Philadelphia. The numbers give lag times for locations beyond twenty days.

country, by contrast, the Freedom of Information Act, together with a long tradition of leaking inside stories and writing memoirs of one's public service, virtually guarantees that very little can be kept secret for very long.

Almost all American radio and television stations are privately owned, though they require government licenses (issued for seven- and five-year terms, respectively) to operate. In France broadcasting is operated by a government agency (Radio-diffusion-Télévision Française) under the control of the minister of information, who is not averse to using that control to protect the government's image. Until recently the French government had the power to ban the showing of any motion picture that was thought likely to "disturb the public order" or for other "reasons of state."[3] A French newspaper editor was heavily fined by a court for having written an article critical of the president of France.[4] While the federal government does impose rules on American broadcasters, it does not have the power to censor or dictate the contents of particular stories. As we shall see, though, its power to license broadcasters has been used, on occasion, to harass station owners who were out of favor with the White House.

The freedom from government control that comes with the private ownership of the media of mass communication has a price, of course: newspapers, magazines, and broadcast stations are businesses that must earn a profit. Some critics believe that the need for profit leads publishers and station owners to distort the news coverage of politics to satisfy the desires of advertisers, the pecuniary interests of stockholders, or the private ideology of the managers. This is much too simple a view, however. Every owner of a communications medium must satisfy the often competing interests of a number of distinct constituencies—advertisers, readers or viewers, editors and reporters, and organized external pressure groups. How each newspaper or broadcaster balances the preferences of these groups varies from case to case. Moreover, the relative strength of these groups has changed over time. In general the history of American journalism, at least among newspapers, has been the history of the growing power and autonomy of editors and reporters.

Journalism in American Political History

Important changes in the nature of American politics have gone hand in hand with major changes in the organization and technology of the press. It is the nature of politics, being essentially a form of communication, to respond to changes in how communications are carried on. This can be seen by considering four important periods in journalistic history.

The Party Press

In the early years of the Republic, politicians of various factions and parties created, sponsored, and controlled newspapers to further their interests. This was possible because circulation was of necessity small (newspapers could not easily be distributed to large audiences, owing to poor transportation) and newspapers were expensive (the type was set by hand and the presses printed copies slowly). Furthermore, there were few large advertisers to pay the bills. These newspapers circulated chiefly among the political and commercial elites, who could afford the high subscription prices. Even with high prices, the newspapers, to exist, often required subsidies. That money frequently came from the government or from a political party.

During the Washington administration the Federalists, led by Alexander Hamilton, created the *Gazette of the United States.* The Republicans, led by Thomas Jefferson, retaliated by creating the *National Gazette* and made its editor, Philip Freneau, "clerk for foreign languages" in the State Department at $250 a year to help support him. After Jefferson became president, he induced another publisher, Samuel Harrison Smith, to start the *National Intelligencer,* subsidizing him by giving him a contract to print government documents. Andrew Jackson, when he became president, aided in the creation of the *Washington Globe.* By some estimates there were over fifty journalists on the government payroll during this era.[5] Naturally these newspapers were relentlessly partisan in their views. Citizens could choose among different party papers, but only rarely could they find a paper that presented both sides of an issue.

The National Gazette, edited by Philip Freneau, supported the Thomas Jefferson faction in national politics. Jefferson, as secretary of state, helped Freneau by giving him a job in the State Department. **The Gazette of the United States,** published by John Fenno, supported Jefferson's rival, Alexander Hamilton.

Two New York newspapers report on the stock market crash of October 19, 1987. The facts in both stories were essentially the same, but the use of photos and headlines made the *Times* coverage seem like a textbook, while that of the *Daily News* looked like a soap opera.

The Popular Press

Changes in society and technology made possible the rise of a self-supporting, mass-readership daily newspaper. The development of the high-speed rotary press enabled publishers to print thousands of copies of a newspaper cheaply and quickly. The invention of the telegraph in the 1840s meant that news from Washington could be flashed almost immediately to New York, Boston, Philadelphia, and Charleston, thus providing local papers with access to information that once only the Washington papers enjoyed. The creation in 1848 of the Associated Press allowed telegraphic dissemination of information to newspaper editors on a systematic basis. Since the AP provided stories that had to be brief and that went to newspapers of every political hue, it could not afford to be partisan or biased; to attract as many subscribers as possible, it had to present the facts objectively. Meanwhile the nation was becoming more urbanized, with large numbers of people brought together in densely settled areas. These people could support a daily newspaper by paying only a penny per copy and by patronizing merchants who advertised in its pages. Newspapers no longer needed political patronage to prosper, and soon such subsidies began to dry up. In 1860 the Government Printing Office was established, thereby putting an end to most of the printing contracts that Washington newspapers had once enjoyed.

The mass-readership newspaper was scarcely nonpartisan, but the partisanship it displayed arose from the convictions of its publishers and editors rather than from the influence of its party sponsors. And these convictions blended political beliefs with economic interest. The way to attract a large readership was with sensationalism: violence, romance, and patriotism, coupled with exposés of government, politics, business, and society. As practiced by Joseph Pulitzer and William Randolph Hearst, founders of large newspaper empires, this editorial policy had great appeal for the average citizen and especially for the immigrants flooding into the large cities.

Strong willed publishers could often become powerful political forces. Hearst used his papers to agitate for war with Spain when the Cubans rebelled against Spanish rule. Conservative Republican political leaders were opposed to the war, but a steady diet of newspaper stories about real and imagined Spanish brutalities whipped up public opinion in favor of intervention. At one point Hearst sent the noted artist Frederic Remington to Cuba to supply paintings of the conflict. Remington cabled back: "Everything is quiet.... There will be no war." Hearst supposedly replied: "Please remain. You furnish the pictures and I'll furnish the war."[6] When the battleship USS *Maine* blew up in Havana harbor, President William McKinley felt helpless to resist popular pressure, and war was declared in 1898.

For all their excesses, the mass-readership newspapers began to create a common national culture, to establish the feasibility of a press free of government control or subsidy, and to demonstrate how exciting (and profitable) could be the criticism of public policy and the revelation of public scandal.

Magazines of Opinion

The growing middle class was often repelled by what it called "yellow journalism" and was developing, around the turn of the century, a taste for political reform and a belief in the doctrines of the progressive movement. To satisfy this market, a variety of national magazines appeared that, unlike those devoted to manners and literature, discussed issues of public policy. Among the first of these were the *Nation,* the *Atlantic Monthly,* and *Harper's,* founded in the 1850s and 1860s; later there came the more broadly based mass-circulation magazines such as *McClure's, Scribner's,* and *Cosmopolitan.* They provided the means for developing a national constituency for certain issues, such as regulating business (or in the language of the times, "trust busting"), purifying municipal politics, and reforming the civil service system. Lincoln Steffens and other so-called muckrakers were frequent contributors to the magazines, setting a pattern for what we now call "investigative reporting."

The national magazines of opinion provided an opportunity for individual writers to gain a nationwide following. The popular press, though initially under the heavy influence of founder-publishers, made the names of certain reporters and columnists household words. In time the great circulation wars between the big-city daily newspapers started to

Muckraker

A **muckraker** is a journalist who searches through the activities of public officials and organizations, especially business firms, seeking to expose conduct contrary to the public interest.

Anyone who has been around stables knows that *muck* means manure; by extension it can refer to anything that is filthy or disgusting.

The word was first used in a political sense by President Theodore Roosevelt, who warned in a 1906 speech that antibusiness journalism could go too far. He said that "the men with the muckrakes are often indispensable to the well-being of society; but only if they know when to stop raking the muck, and to look upward to the celestial crown above them, to the crown of worthy endeavor."

Roosevelt was referring to a character named the Man with the Muck Rake in John Bunyan's book *Pilgrim's Progress;* this fellow was so preoccupied with raking the muck on the stable floor that he could never look any way but down.

SOURCE: Adapted from *Safire's Political Dictionary* by William Safire. Copyright © 1968, 1972, 1978 by William Safire. Reprinted by permission of Random House, Inc. and the author.

wane, as the more successful papers bought up or otherwise eliminated their competition. This reduced the need for the more extreme forms of sensationalism, a change that was reinforced by the growing sophistication and education of America's

FIGURE 10.1   Subject Areas of New Magazines Established in 1991

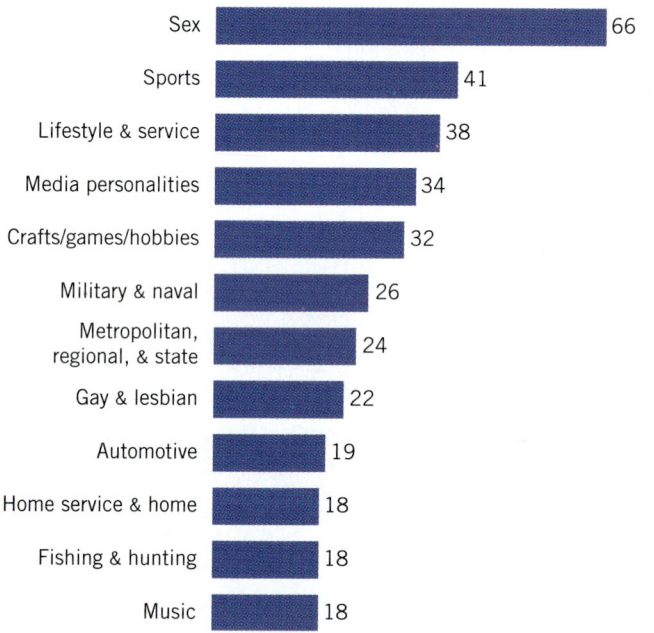

Subject	Count
Sex	66
Sports	41
Lifestyle & service	38
Media personalities	34
Crafts/games/hobbies	32
Military & naval	26
Metropolitan, regional, & state	24
Gay & lesbian	22
Automotive	19
Home service & home	18
Fishing & hunting	18
Music	18

SOURCE: *The Public Perspective* (September/October 1992): 7, reporting data from *The Magazine Handbook* 64 (1992–1993). Reprinted by permission of *The Public Perspective*, a publication of the Roper Center for Public Opinion Research, University of Connecticut.

readers. And the founding publishers were gradually replaced by less flamboyant managers. All of these changes—in circulation needs, in audience interests, in managerial style, in the emergence of nationally known writers—helped increase the power of editors and reporters and make them a force to be reckoned with.

Although politics dominated the pages of most national magazines in the late nineteenth century, today national magazines that focus mainly on politics and government affairs account for only a small and declining fraction of the national magazine market (see Figure 10.1). Over five hundred new consumer magazines were established in 1991, but only a few of these covered the political scene. Among all magazines in circulation today, only a fraction focus on politics—the majority of today's magazines focus on popular entertainment and leisure activities.

The Internet and the World Wide Web have become increasingly significant sources of political information and debate. In 1996 there were computers in an estimated 30 million American homes (about half of them capable of linking up with an information service) and some two thousand politics-related Web sites. Still, relatively few Americans (as low as 3 percent by some estimates) have ever signed on to the Web to get political news or for any other purpose. Many more Americans read newspapers and public affairs magazines than surf the Net or browse the Web. But that may be slowly changing. One sign of the times: Michael Kinsley, a well-known former editor of *The New Republic* magazine and the cohost of CNN's "Crossfire," left Washington, D.C., for Washington State to launch a new political magazine in cyberspace.

Electronic Journalism

Radio came on the national scene in the 1920s, television in the late 1940s. They represented a major change in the way news was gathered and disseminated, though few politicians at first understood the importance of this change. A broadcast permits public officials to speak directly to audiences without their remarks being filtered through editors and reporters. This was obviously an advantage to politicians, provided they were skilled enough to use it: they could in theory reach the voters directly on a national scale without the services of political parties, interest groups, or friendly editors.

But there was an offsetting disadvantage—people could easily ignore a speech broadcast on a radio or television station, either by not listening at all or by tuning to a different station. By contrast, the views of at least some public figures would receive prominent and often unavoidable display in newspapers, and in a growing number of cities there was only one daily paper. Moreover, space in a newspaper is cheap compared to time on a television broadcast. Adding one more story, or one more name to an existing story, costs the newspaper little. By contrast, less news can be carried on radio or television, and each news segment must be quite brief to avoid boring the audience. As a result, the number of political personalities that can be covered by radio and television news is much smaller than is the case with newspapers, and the cost (to the station) of making a news item or broadcast longer is often prohibitively large.

Thus, to obtain the advantages of electronic media coverage, public officials must do something sufficiently bold or colorful to gain free access to radio and television news—or they must find the money to purchase radio and television time. The president of the United States, of course, is routinely covered by radio and television and can ordinarily get free time to speak to the nation on matters of importance. All other officials must struggle for access to the electronic media by making controversial statements, acquiring a national reputation, or purchasing expensive time.

As we discussed in Chapter 8, the rise of the talk show as a political forum has increased politicians' access to the electronic media, as has the televised "town meeting." But such developments need to be understood as part of a larger story.

Until recently, the "big three" television networks (ABC, CBS, and NBC) together claimed 80 percent or more of all viewers (see Table 10.1, page 274). Their evening newscasts dominated electronic media coverage of politics and government affairs. When it came to presidential campaigns, for example, the three networks were the only television

News moves in a fast and focused way on the Internet, where not only can you stay up to date, you can be in contact with like-minded people.

In 1933 White House press conferences were informal affairs, as when reporters gathered around Franklin Roosevelt's desk in the Oval Office. Today they are huge gatherings held either in a special conference room or (as here) outside in the Rose Garden.

TABLE 10.1 Decline in Viewership of the Three Major Television Networks—ABC, CBS, and NBC

"Big Three" Networks: Average Shares of Prime-Time Viewing Audience

Year	Share
1961–1962	94%
1971–1972	91
1981–1982	83
1991–1992	63

Average Number of Households Tuned into the "Big Three" and Other Television Networks[a] During Prime Time, 1992

Network	Number (in thousands)
CBS	11,328
NBC	10,776
ABC	10,223
Fox	6,908
Independents	4,881
PBS	1,934
HBO	1,474
USA	1,382
TBS	1,289
ESPN	1,197
TNT	1,013
CNN	665
LIF	553
SHO	553
CMX	461
MTV	368

[a] Ten other networks not listed also had audiences of at least 100,000 households. Approximately 130 others together were viewed by about 2.7 million households.

SOURCE: Adapted from *The Public Perspective* (September/October 1992): 6, reporting data provided by Nielsen Media Research and NBC. Used by permission of *The Public Perspective,* a publication of the Roper Center for Public Opinion Research, University of Connecticut.

games in town—they reported on the primaries, broadcast the party conventions, and covered the general election campaigns, including any presidential debates. But over the last twenty-five years, the networks' evening newscasts changed in ways that made it harder for candidates to use them to get their messages across. For instance, the average **sound bite**—a video clip of a presidential contender

speaking—dropped from about 42 seconds in 1968 to less than ten seconds in 1988.[7]

Today politicians have sources other than the network news for sustained and personalized television exposure. Cable television, early-morning news and entertainment programs, and prime-time "news magazine" shows have greatly increased and diversified politicians' access to the electronic media. One of the most memorable moments of the 1992 presidential campaign—Ross Perot's declaring his willingness to run for president on CNN's "Larry King Live"—occurred on cable television. And while the networks' evening news programs feature only small sound bites, their early-morning programs and news magazine shows feature lengthy interviews with candidates.

Naturally, many politicians favor the call-in format, town-meeting setups, lengthy human interest interviews, and casual appearances on entertainment shows to televised confrontations on policy issues with seasoned network journalists who push, probe, and criticize. And naturally they favor being a part of visually interesting programs rather than traditional "talking heads" news shows. But what is preferable to candidates is not necessarily helpful to the selection process that voters must go through in choosing a candidate. No one has yet systematically analyzed what, if any, positive or negative consequences these recent changes in politicians' access to the electronic media hold for campaigns, elections, or governance. Nor, for that matter, is there yet any significant research on the broader societal consequences of so-called narrowcasting—the proliferation of television and radio stations that target highly segmented listening and viewing audiences, and the relative decline of electronic and print media that reach large and heterogeneous populations.

One thing is clear: most politicians crave the media spotlight, both on the campaign trail and in office. The efforts made by political candidates to get "visuals"—filmed stories—on television continue after they are elected. Since the president is always news, a politician wishing to make news is well advised to attack the president. Even better, attack him with the aid of a photogenic prop: when the late Senator John Heinz III of Pennsylvania wanted to criticize President Carter's bridge-repair program, Heinz had himself filmed making the attack not in his office but standing on a bridge.

In their effort to bring their message to the public directly without going through reporters, presidential candidates make increasing use of talk shows. Here, Bob and Elizabeth Dole are interviewed by Larry King in 1996.

In sum, the transformations in the nature of journalism have altered significantly the way in which public officials and candidates can use communications. In the early era of the party press only a small number of better-off citizens regularly read newspapers, and those they read were typically highly partisan. This was a period in which politics consisted of competition among relatively small groups of notables and in which presidential candidates were nominated by legislators. The era of the mass-circulation newspaper made easier the emergence of mass politics: national conventions, the mobilization of voters at election time by broad appeals, mass rallies, and the development of strong party loyalties. The emergence of national magazines of opinion facilitated the development (discussed in Chapter 9) of national interest groups organized around policy questions and gave voice to the middle-class "reform" movement that agitated for a reduction in the role and power of political parties. Electronic journalism made it possible for politicians to develop personal followings independent of party structure, perhaps contributing to the decline of party loyalties and organization. Recent changes in the nature of politicians' access to the electronic media, many of them linked to the development of cable television and the diminishing im-

portance of the "big three" networks, have ushered in a new era of electronic journalism.

The Structure of the Media

The relationship between journalism and politics is a two-way street: though politicians take advantage as best they can of the media of communication available to them, these media in turn attempt to use politics and politicians as a way of both entertaining and informing their audiences. The mass media, whatever their disclaimers, are not simply a mirror held up to reality or a messenger that carries the news. There is inevitably a process of selection, of editing, and of emphasis, and this process reflects, to some degree, the way in which the media are organized, the kinds of audiences they seek to serve, and the preferences and opinions of the members of the media.

Degree of Competition

Contrary to popular belief, there has not been any significant decline in the number of daily newspapers in this country. There has been a decline, however, in the number of cities in which there are competing daily papers. There were competing newspapers in 60 percent of American cities in 1900 but in only 4 percent by 1972. The largest cities—New York, Chicago, Detroit, Philadelphia, Los Angeles, Washington, Atlanta, Boston—have at least two central-city newspapers, but most other cities have just one. This is partially offset by the fact that in many metropolitan areas, two or more neighboring cities will each have a newspaper whose readership overlaps. Residents of Manchester, New Hampshire, for example, can easily obtain the *Manchester Union Leader,* the *Boston Globe,* and the *Boston Herald.*

Radio and television, by contrast, are intensely competitive and becoming more so. Almost every American home has a radio and a television set. Though there are only five major television networks, there are over one thousand television stations, each of which has its own news programs. Local stations affiliated with a network are free to accept or reject network programs. There are more than eleven thousand cable TV systems, serving over fifty million people (and a typical cable can carry dozens of channels). In addition, there are nearly ten thousand radio stations; some broadcast nothing but news, and others develop a specialized following among blacks, Hispanics, or other minorities. Magazines exist for every conceivable interest. The number of news sources available to an American is vast—more than even dedicated readers and viewers can keep up with.

To a degree that would astonish most foreigners, the American press—radio, television, and newspapers—is made up of locally owned and managed enterprises. In Britain, France, Germany, Japan, Sweden, and elsewhere, the media are owned and operated with a national audience in mind. The *Times* of London may be published in that city, but it is read throughout Great Britain, as are the *Guardian,* the *Daily Telegraph,* and the *Daily Mirror.* Radio and television broadcasts are centrally planned and nationally aired.

The American newspaper, however, is primarily oriented to its local market and local audience, and there is typically more local than national news in it. Radio and television stations accept network programming, but the early- and late-evening news programs provide a heavy diet of local political, social, and sports news. Government regulations developed by the Federal Communications Commission (FCC) are in part responsible for this. In general no one, including the networks, may own and operate more than one newspaper, one AM radio station, one FM radio station, or one television station in a given market. (In June 1993 the FCC granted its first waiver to this regulation when it permitted Rupert Murdoch to own and operate both WNYW-TV and the *New York Post* in New York. It did so on the grounds that New York City has three other large-circulation dailies and dozens of smaller newspapers—making it unlikely that the *Post* could monopolize the city's readership—and because closing the newspaper would have cost hundreds of jobs.) Nationally no one may own more than twelve television stations and twelve AM and twelve FM radio stations; and the networks may not compel a local affiliate to accept any particular broadcast. (In fact almost all network news programs are carried by the affiliates.) The result has been the development of a decentralized broadcast industry. A recently enacted law, the Telecommunications Act of 1996, gives broadcasters greater freedom to enter new businesses and purchase more television and radio stations (see box, opposite). Whether this law will further competition and decentralization in the broadcast industry remains to be seen.

The National Media

The local orientation of much of the American communications media is partially offset, however, by the emergence of certain publications and broadcast services that constitute a kind of national press. The wire services—the Associated Press and United Press International—supply most of the national news that local papers publish. Certain news magazines—*Time, Newsweek, U.S. News & World Report*—have a national readership. The network evening news broadcasts produced by ABC, CBS, and NBC are carried by most television stations with a network affiliation. CNN—the Cable News Network—broadcasts national news around the clock. There are only three truly national newspapers, the *Wall Street Journal,* the *Christian Science Monitor,* and *USA Today,* but the *New York Times* and the *Washington Post* have acquired national influence because

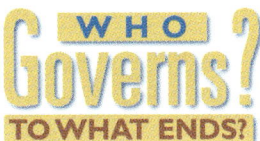

Deregulating Telecommunications

On February 8, 1996, President Clinton signed the Telecommunications Act of 1996. It was the first major rewrite of telecommunications legislation in sixty-two years. Many observers also viewed the bill as the culmination of a series of political and judicial decisions that began in 1974 when the U.S. Justice Department filed an antitrust suit against AT&T, leading to the breakup of the old monopoly and the creation in 1984 of the seven regional telephone companies (the "Baby Bells"). As Clinton signed the bill into law, a TV screen showed comedienne Lily Tomlin playing her telephone company operator, Ernestine, saying "one gigabyte" instead of "one ringie-dingie."

But the long and incredibly complicated bill is no joke. Basically, the law removed regulatory restrictions that have prevented local and long-distance phone companies from competing against each another. It also opened the door to greater competition in the cable television industry and gave broadcasters freedom to enter new businesses and purchase more television and radio stations. In addition, it required that a "V-chip" be installed in most new television sets, which would allow parents to lock out programs rated too violent or otherwise inappropriate for children. It also criminalized the distribution of "indecent material" over the Internet, establishing jail terms as the punishment for persons convicted of doing so.

After the bill was passed, the Supreme Court decided that punishing people for sending out "indecent material" was unconstitutional.

Of this bill, the political process that produced it, and the ways in which it is likely to be interpreted and carried out in the future, one can truly say, "Only in America." Here are a few of the confusing aspects of this legislation:

- *The States.* In many nations, the national government owns and operates the telephone, telegraph, and postal services. The United States is the only Western democracy with a dual regulatory structure for telephone service— the national government, via the Federal Communications Commission (FCC), regulates the interstate telephone services, while the states regulate local and interstate service. Thus any question about "who governs" telecommunications policy in America must consider a wide variety of federal and state officials, both elected (the president, Congress, governors, state legislators) and appointed (FCC employees, state public utility commission regulators).

  The new law further complicates this dual regulatory system. On the one hand, it leaves to the states an enormous number of decisions about how to deregulate the industry while still enforcing a battery of regulations governing sales of TV stations and cable systems, telecommunications firm mergers and acquisitions, and the affordability of telecommunications products. On the other hand, it admonishes the states to follow "specific, predictable, and sufficient mechanisms," as defined by the FCC.

- *The Companies.* The bill's enactment unleashed a flurry of big business activity, including two "Baby Bell" phone company mergers. Within a year of the bill's passage, two new all-news networks owned by parent networks (MSNBC of NBC, and Fox News of Fox Television) went on the air. Many of the industry's telephone, television, and cable companies played a major role in shaping the bill. They have a big financial stake in how certain provisions of it get implemented and interpreted.

- *Other Groups.* Also involved in the bill's passage were various religious, pro-family, and other groups that expressed little interest in its technical provisions but powerful interest in its clauses relating to "cyberporn" and the like.

- *Public Opinion.* Few average citizens have a ready opinion on deregulating telecommunications. The debate over the bill was not about whether the government should see to it that consumers enjoy the best telecommunications systems at the lowest prices (everybody agreed on that point) but about how best to change the laws so as to achieve that goal while preserving "the best telecommunications systems in the world" (respected experts could not agree on how). On the other hand, most citizens do have a ready opinion on such issues as banning the dissemination of "indecent material"—they're for it. Thus some members of Congress saw a vote for the act as a vote for "jailing purveyors of kiddie porn" and "giving concerned parents the V-chip," with little or no concern for the bill's major deregulation provisions.

To find out more about who was responsible for the bill, what they hoped to achieve, and what's happened since, you can begin by looking up the sources below.

SOURCES: Thomas W. Bonnet, *Telewars in the States* (Washington, D.C.: Council of Governor's Policy Advisors, 1996); Dan Carney, "Congress Fires Its First Shot in Information Revolution," *Congressional Quarterly Weekly* (February 3, 1996): 289–294; Mike Mills, "Ushering in a New Age in Communications," *The Washington Post* (February 9, 1996): C1.

The national press wields great influence because it is read by presidents and virtually every other top government official. President Lyndon Johnson surveys his daily collection of newspapers in the Oval Office.

they are read daily by virtually every important official in Washington (and thus have become an important channel by which these officials keep track of one another) and because the television networks and many local newspapers use the stories that the *Times* and the *Post* print. In fact, one study found that the front page of the morning *Times* significantly shapes the contents of each network's evening news broadcasts.[8]

The existence of a national press is important for two reasons: First, government officials in Washington pay great attention to what these media say about them and their programs. They pay much less attention to what local papers and broadcasters say (if, indeed, they even know about their comments). Politicians read and worry about newspaper editorials, something that the average citizen rarely does. Second, reporters and editors for the national press tend to differ from those who work for the local press. They are usually better paid than most other journalists, they have often graduated from the most prestigious colleges and universities, and in general they have more liberal political views.[9] Above all they seek—and frequently obtain—the opportunity

to write stories that are not accounts of a particular news event but "background," investigative, or interpretive stories about issues and policies.[10]

The national press plays the role of gatekeeper, scorekeeper, and watchdog for the federal government.

Gatekeeper As gatekeeper it can influence what subjects become national political issues, and for how long. Automobile safety, water pollution, and the quality of prescription drugs were not major political issues before the national press began giving substantial attention to these matters and thus helped place them on the political agenda. When crime rates rose in the early 1960s, the subject was given little political attention in Washington, in part because the media did not cover it extensively. Media attention to crime increased in the late 1960s and early 1970s, slackened in the late 1970s, and rose again in the 1980s and 1990s. Throughout most of these years crime went up. In short, *reality* did not change during this time; only the focus of media and political attention shifted. Elite opinion about the war in Vietnam also changed significantly as the attitude toward the war expressed by the national media changed.

Scorekeeper As scorekeepers the national media keep track of and help make political reputations, note who is being "mentioned" as a presidential candidate, and help decide who is winning and losing in Washington politics. When Jimmy Carter, then a virtually unknown former governor of Georgia, was planning his campaign to get the Democratic nomination for president, he understood clearly the importance of being "mentioned." So successful was he in cultivating members of the national press that between November 1975 and February 1976, before the first primary election was held, he was the subject of more stories in the *New York Times,* the *Washington Post,* and the *Columbus Dispatch* than any other potential Democratic presidential candidate, even though the others (Henry Jackson, Hubert Humphrey, and George Wallace) were much better known. He did almost as well in getting mentioned on the three television networks.

The scorekeeper role of the media often leads the press to cover presidential elections as if they were horse races rather than choices among policies. Consider the enormous attention the media give to the Iowa caucuses and the New Hampshire primary election, despite the fact that these states produce only a tiny fraction of the delegates to either party's nominating convention and that neither state is representative of the nation as a whole. The results of the Iowa caucus, the first in the nation, are given great importance by the press. In 1988 the Iowa caucus received twice as much television coverage as did all the primaries and caucuses in the twenty "Super Tuesday" states put together, even though the Super Tuesday states chose over twenty times as many delegates as did Iowa. Consequently the coverage received by a candidate who does well in Iowa constitutes a tremendous amount of free publicity that can help him or her in the New Hampshire primary election. Doing well in that primary results in even more media attention, thus boosting the candidate for the next primaries. And so on.

For example, in 1984 Gary Hart won 15 percent of the vote in the Iowa caucuses. Not many, you may think. But it placed him second, after Walter Mondale (who got a whopping 45 percent). The television networks "discovered" Hart, increasing their (free) news coverage of him by a factor of more than five. A "horse race" that once was portrayed as having a "clear leader" followed by several "also-rans" was now described as a "two-man race." Hart won the New Hampshire primary (to the surprise of almost everybody). The press increased its attention to Hart even more.[11]

There are other examples. In 1972 the press decided that George McGovern was the "man to watch" after he *lost* the New Hampshire primary to Edmund Muskie (McGovern came in second). In 1968 Eugene McCarthy was described as having won a "moral victory" after losing to Lyndon Johnson in New Hampshire.

Watchdog But once the scorekeepers decide that you are the person to watch, they adopt their watchdog role. Before his New Hampshire victory in 1984, Hart's background went largely unexamined; after he had been declared a "front-runner," stories began appearing about how he had changed his name and altered his birth date by a year. In 1987, when Hart was already the front-runner for the 1988 Democratic presidential nomination, the press played its watchdog role right from the start. When rumors circulated that he was unfaithful to his wife, the *Miami Herald* staked out his apartment in Washington, D.C., and discovered that he had spent several evening hours there with an attractive young woman, Donna Rice. Soon there appeared other stories about his having taken Ms. Rice on a boat trip to Bimini. Not long thereafter, Hart dropped out of the presidential race, accusing the press of unfair treatment. Then, in late 1987, Hart reentered the race only to drop out again after getting little popular support.

This close scrutiny is natural. The media have an instinctive—and profitable—desire to investigate personalities and expose scandals. To some degree all reporters probably share H. L. Mencken's belief that the role of the press is to "comfort the afflicted and afflict the comfortable." They tend to be tolerant of underdogs, tough on front-runners. Though some reporters develop close relations with powerful personages, many—especially younger ones—find the discovery of wrongdoing both more absorbing and more lucrative. Bob Woodward and Carl Bernstein, who wrote most of the Watergate stories for the *Washington Post,* simultaneously performed an important public service, received the accolades of their colleagues, and earned a lot of money.

Newspapers and television stations play these three roles in somewhat different ways. A newspaper can cover more stories in greater depth than a TV station and faces less competition from other papers than TV stations face from other broadcasters. A TV station faces brutal competition, must select its programs in part for their visual impact, and must keep its stories short and punchy. As a result newspaper reporters have more freedom to develop their own stories, but they earn less money than television news broadcasters. The latter have little freedom (the fear of losing their audience is keen), but they can make a lot of money (if they are attractive personalities who photograph well).

Rules Governing the Media

Ironically, the least competitive media outlets—the big-city newspapers—are almost entirely free from government regulation, while the most competitive ones—radio and television stations—must have a government license to operate and must adhere to a variety of government regulations.

Newspapers and magazines need no license to publish, their freedom to publish may not be restrained in advance, and they are liable for punishment for what they do publish only under certain highly restricted circumstances. The First Amendment to the Constitution has been interpreted as meaning that no government, federal or state, can place "prior restraints" (that is, censorship) on the press except under very narrowly defined circumstances.[12] When the federal government sought to prevent the *New York Times* from publishing the Pentagon Papers, a set of secret government documents stolen by an antiwar activist, the Court held that the paper was free to publish them.[13]

Once something is published, a newspaper or magazine may be sued or prosecuted if the material is libelous or obscene or if it incites someone to commit an illegal act. But these are usually not very

serious restrictions, because the courts have defined *libelous, obscene,* and *incitement* so narrowly as to make it more difficult here than in any other nation to find the press guilty of such conduct. For example, for a paper to be found guilty of libeling a public official or other prominent person, the person must not only show that what was printed was wrong and damaging but must also show, with "clear and convincing evidence," that it was printed maliciously—that is, with "reckless disregard" for its truth or falsity.[14] When in 1984 Israeli General Ariel Sharon sued *Time* magazine for libel, the jury decided that the story that *Time* had printed was false and defamatory but that *Time* had not published it as the result of malice, and so Sharon did not collect any damages.

There are also laws intended to protect the privacy of citizens, but they do not really inhibit newspapers. In general, your name and picture can be printed without your consent if they are part of a news story of some conceivable public interest. And if a paper attacks you in print, the paper has no legal obligation to give you space for a reply.[15]

It is illegal to use printed words to advocate the violent overthrow of the government if by your advocacy you incite others to action, but this rule has been applied to newspapers only rarely, and in recent years, never.[16]

Confidentiality of Sources

Reporters believe that they should have the right to keep confidential the sources of their stories. Some states agree and have passed laws to that effect. Most states and the federal government do not agree, so the courts must decide in each case whether the need of a journalist to protect confidential sources does or does not outweigh the interest of the government in gathering evidence in a criminal investigation. In general the Supreme Court has upheld the right of the government to compel reporters to divulge information as part of a properly conducted criminal investigation, if it bears on the commission of a crime.[17]

This conflict arises not only between reporters and law enforcement agencies but also between reporters and persons accused of committing a crime. Myron Farber, a reporter for the *New York Times,* wrote a series of stories that led to the indictment

Reporter Susan Wornick in Boston was arrested when she refused to divulge the name of a person who told her that police officers had broken into a drugstore. Eventually, the source revealed himself and the charges against her were dropped.

Thinking CRITICAL

How to Read a Newspaper

Newspapers don't simply report the news, they report somebody's idea of what is news, written in language intended to *persuade* as well as inform. To read a newspaper intelligently, look for three things: what is covered, who are the sources, and how language is used.

Coverage Every newspaper will cover a big story, such as a flood, fire, or presidential trip, but newspapers can pick and choose among lesser stories. One paper will select stories about the environment, business fraud, and civil rights; another will prefer stories about crime, drug dealers, and "welfare cheats." What do these choices tell you about the beliefs of the editors and reporters working for these two papers? What do these people want you to believe are the important issues?

Sources For some stories, the source is obvious: "The Supreme Court decided . . . ," "Congress voted . . . ," or "the president said . . . ." For others, the source is not so obvious. There are two kinds of sources you should beware of. The first is an anonymous source. When you read phrases such as "a high official said today . . ." or "White House sources revealed that . . ." always ask yourself this question: Why does the source want

me to know this? The answer usually will be this: Because if I believe what he or she said, it will advance his or her interests. This can happen in one of three ways. First, the source may support a policy or appointment and want to test public reaction to it. This is called floating a **trial balloon.** Second, the source may oppose a policy or appointment and hope that by leaking word of it, the idea will be killed. Third, the source may want to take credit for something good that happened or shift blame on to somebody else for something bad that happened. When you read a story that is based on anonymous sources, ask yourself these questions: Judging from the tone of the story, is this leak designed to support or kill an idea? Is it designed to take credit or shift blame? In whose interest is it to accomplish these things? By asking these questions, you often can make a pretty good guess as to the identity of the anonymous source.

Some stories depend on the reader's believing a key fact, previously unknown. For example: "The world's climate is getting hotter because of man-made pollution," "drug abuse is soaring," "the death penalty will prevent murder," "husbands are more likely to beat up on their wives on Super Bowl Sunday." Each of these "facts" is either

wrong, grossly exaggerated, or stated with excessive confidence. But each comes from an advocate organization that wants you to believe it, because if you do you will take that organization's solution more seriously. Be skeptical of key facts if they come from an advocacy source. Don't be misled by the tendency of many advocacy organizations to take neutral or scholarly names like "Center for the Public Interest" or "Institute for Policy Research." Some of these really are neutral or scholarly, but many aren't.

Language Everybody uses words so as to persuade people of something without actually making a clear argument for it. This is called using **loaded language.** For example: if you like a politician, call him "Senator Smith"; if you don't like him, refer to him as "right-wing (or left-wing) senators such as Smith." If you like an idea proposed by a professor, call her "respected"; if you don't like the idea, call her "controversial." If you favor abortion, call somebody who agrees with you "pro-choice" ("choice" is valued by most people); if you oppose abortion, call those who agree with you "pro-life" ("life," like "choice," is a good thing). Recognizing loaded language in a newspaper article can give you important clues to the writer's own point of view.

and trial of a physician on charges that he had murdered five patients. The judge ordered Farber to show him his notes to determine whether they should be given to the defense lawyers. Farber refused, arguing that revealing his notes would infringe upon the confidentiality that he had promised to his sources. Farber was sent to jail for contempt of court. On appeal, the New Jersey Supreme Court

and the United States Supreme Court decided against Farber, holding that the accused person's right to a fair trial includes the right to compel the production of evidence, even from reporters.

In another case the Supreme Court upheld the right of the police to search newspaper offices, so long as they have a warrant. But Congress then passed a law forbidding such searches (except in special cases), requiring instead that the police sub-poena the desired documents.[18]

Regulating Broadcasting

Although newspapers and magazines by and large are not regulated, broadcasting is regulated by the government. No one may operate a radio or television station without a license from the Federal Communications Commission, renewable every seven years for radio and every five for television stations. An application for renewal is rarely refused, but until recently the FCC required the broadcaster to submit detailed information about its programming and how it planned to serve "community needs" in order to get a renewal. Based on this information or on the complaints of some group, the FCC could use its powers of renewal to influence what the station puts on the air. For example, it could induce stations to reduce the amount of violence shown, increase the proportion of "public service" programs on the air, or alter the way it portrays various ethnic groups.

Of late a movement has arisen to deregulate broadcasting, on the grounds that so many stations are now on the air that competition should be allowed to determine how each station defines and serves community needs. In this view citizens can choose what they want to hear or see without the government's shaping the content of each station's programming. For example, since the early 1980s a station can simply submit a postcard requesting that its license be renewed, a request automatically granted unless some group formally opposes the renewal. In that case the FCC holds a hearing. As a result some of the old rules—for instance, that each hour on TV could contain only sixteen minutes of commercials—are no longer rigidly enforced.

The content of radio and television is still regulated in ways that newspapers and magazines are not. These include the following:

- **Equal time rule:** If a station sells time to one candidate for office, it must be willing to sell equal time to opposing candidates.

- **Right-of-reply rule:** If a person is attacked on a broadcast (other than in a regular news program), that person has the right to reply over that same station.

- **Political editorializing rule:** If a broadcaster endorses a candidate, the opposing candidate has a right to reply.

For many years there was also in place the **fairness doctrine,** which required broadcasters to give time to opposing views if they broadcast a program giving one side of a controversial issue. In 1987 the FCC, believing that the doctrine inhibited the free discussion of issues, abolished it; Congress has tried to pass a law to reinstate it (so far without success). Most broadcasters still follow the rule voluntarily.

Campaigning

When candidates wish to campaign on radio or television, the equal time rule applies. A broadcaster must provide equal access to candidates for office and charge them rates no higher than the cheapest rate applicable to commercial advertisers for comparable time.

At one time this rule meant that a station or network could not broadcast a debate between the Democratic and Republican candidates for an office without inviting all other candidates as well—Libertarian, Prohibitionist, or whatever. Thus a presidential debate in 1980 could be limited to the major candidates, Reagan and Carter (or Reagan and Anderson), only by having the League of Women Voters sponsor it and then allowing radio and TV to cover it as a "news event." Now stations and networks can themselves sponsor debates limited to major candidates.

Though laws guarantee that candidates can buy time at favorable rates on television, not all candidates take advantage of this. The reason is that television is not always an efficient way to reach voters. A television message is literally "broad cast"—spread out to a mass audience without regard to the boundaries of the district in which a candidate is running. Presidential candidates, of course, always use television, because their constituency is the whole nation. Candidates for senator or representative, however, may or may not use television, depending on whether the boundaries of their state or district conform well to the boundaries of a television market.

A **market** is an area easily reached by a television signal; there are about two hundred such markets in

Why Doesn't the Press Let Candidates Talk?

The next time you're watching television news coverage of a political campaign, look at who's talking. Chances are it won't be the candidates. In 1968 the average televised news program allowed candidates for office to speak an average of forty-two seconds each. By 1988 that number had fallen to nine seconds and by 1992 to eight seconds. Defenders of television say that it is a competitive business in which long speeches turn off audiences and that TV newscasters do a fine job of summarizing what the candidates say anyway. Critics reply that newscasters are often biased (for example, most evaluative comments by newscasters about any of the Republican candidates in the 1996 primary were negative).

Moreover, what newscasters really talk about is not what the candidates have to say but how well they are doing in the contest (so-called horse-race reporting). Does it make a difference whether we hear from the candidates themselves, or only from newscasters who summarize their views? What do you think?

---

the country. Congressman Tim Roemer comes from a district in Indiana centered on the city of South Bend, which is also the hub of a distinct TV market. Roemer can use television effectively and relatively cheaply (in terms of dollars per viewer reached). By contrast, when Adam K. Levin ran for a congressional seat in New Jersey in 1982, he spent large sums on television ads on the only stations—those in New York City—that reach his district. But just 4 percent of the viewers of these stations live in Levin's district, and so most of the money was wasted. As a more experienced politician commented, he "might as well give the money away at a bus station." Because of these factors, a far higher proportion of Senate than of House candidates buy television ads.[19]

The Effects of the Media on Politics

Everyone believes that the media have a profound effect, for better or for worse, on politics. A small but growing body of research indicates that what appears in print or on the air probably does have an effect on how citizens think and what they think about—what they cite as "important problems," how they attribute responsibility for problems, what policy preferences they hold—and what policymakers do.[20] But there is as of yet relatively little scholarly evidence that enables us to know precisely how large that effect is or under what conditions it exists.

The reason for this gap between what everyone knows and what no one can prove is probably that until recently scholars have chiefly tried to measure the effect of the media on election outcomes. But as we have seen (Chapter 8), elections—especially those for important, highly visible offices—are occasions when the voter is bombarded with all manner of cues from friends, family, interest groups, candidates, memories, and loyalties, as well as radio, television, and newspapers. It would be surprising if the effect of the media were very strong, or at least very apparent, under these circumstances.

Efforts to determine whether voters who watch a lot of television or who see candidates on television frequently vote differently from those who do not watch television at all (or who watch only nonpolitical messages) have generally proved unavailing.[21] This is quite consistent with studies of political propaganda generally. At least in the short run, television and radio suffer from processes called **selective attention** (the citizen sees and hears only what he or she wants) and mental tune-out (the citizen simply ignores or gets irritated by messages that do not accord with existing beliefs). Radio and television may tend to reinforce existing beliefs, but it not clear that they change them.[22]

But if this is true, why do companies spend millions of dollars advertising deodorants and frozen pizza? And if advertising can sell these products, why can't it sell candidates? The answer is quite simple: citizens are not idiots. They can tell the

The Maxims of Media Relations

The importance of the national media to politicians has given rise to some shared understandings among officeholders about how one deals with the media. Some of these are caught in the following maxims:

- All secrets become public knowledge. The more important the secret, the sooner it becomes known.

- All stories written about me are inaccurate; all stories written about you are entirely accurate.

- The rosier the news, the higher-ranking the official who announces it.

- Always release bad news on Saturday night. Fewer people notice it.

- Never argue with a person who buys ink by the barrel.

difference between a deodorant and a Democrat, between a pizza and a Republican. If an ad persuades them to try a deodorant or a pizza, they will do so, knowing that not much is at stake, the costs are small, and if they do not like it, they can change brands in an instant. But they know that government is a more serious business, that one is stuck with the winning candidate for two, four, or even six years, and that as citizens they have accumulated a lot of information about the past behavior of the two major parties and their principal figures.

Local newspapers have generally endorsed Republican candidates for president throughout this century. Indeed, only in 1964 did more newspapers endorse the Democrat (Johnson) than the Republican (Goldwater). Since the Democrats won eight of the fourteen presidential elections between 1932 and 1984, you might think that newspaper endorsements are worthless. They may have some value, however. A careful study of the effect of such endorsements on the 1964 presidential election found that, at least in the North, a newspaper endorsement may have added about five percentage points to what the Democratic candidate would otherwise have obtained.[23]

There are some elections, however, in which voters have few sources of information beyond what the media provide. Primary elections involving political unknowns and general elections for low-visibility offices (for example, tax assessor or superior court judge) may make voters dependent on newspaper and broadcast ads for information. Skillful ads may have a big effect on the results of these contests.

The major effects of the media, however, probably have much less to do with how people vote in an election and much more to do with how politics is conducted, how candidates are perceived, and how policies are formulated. National nominating conventions have been changed to fit the needs of television broadcasters. Some candidates have found it possible to win their party's nomination for senator or governor with expensive advertising campaigns that bypass the parties and ultimately weaken them. Unknown politicians can acquire a national reputation overnight by being shrewd enough—or lucky enough—to be at the center of an event heavily covered by the press.

In 1950 Estes Kefauver was a little-known senator from Tennessee. Then he chaired a special Senate investigating committee that brought before it various figures in organized crime. When these dramatic hearings were televised to audiences numbering in the millions, Kefauver became a household word, and in 1952 he became a leading contender for the Democratic nomination for president. He was a strong vote getter in the primaries and actually led on the first ballot at the Chicago convention, only to lose to Adlai Stevenson.

The lesson was not lost on other politicians. From that time on, developing through the media a recognized name and a national constituency became important to many senators. It also became a strategy whereby a variety of issues could be placed on the national agenda and pressed on Congress. Environmental and consumer issues benefited especially from the attention given them by the national press.

A survey of public opinion in North Carolina found that the issues that citizens believed to be important politically were very similar to the issues that newspapers and television newscasts had featured. Experiments conducted in New Haven, Connecticut, also showed that watching television news programs affected the importance people attached to various issues. TV influenced the political agenda.[24] On the other hand, people are much less likely to take their cues from the media on matters that affect them personally. Everybody who is unemployed, the victim of crime, or worried about high food prices will identify these matters as issues whether or not the media emphasize them.[25] In short, the media help set the political agenda on matters with which citizens have little personal experience, but they have much less influence over how people react to things that touch their lives directly.

The media also affect how we perceive certain issues and candidates. A study of the differences between voters who get their news primarily from television and those who get it chiefly from newspapers found that the two groups did not view political matters the same way. On a variety of issues, newspaper readers thought that Gerald Ford was more conservative and Jimmy Carter more liberal than did television viewers. This difference persisted even after taking into account the fact that newspaper readers tend to have more schooling than do television viewers. Put another way, newspaper readers saw bigger differences between the 1976 presidential candidates than did television viewers.[26]

Another study found that television news stories affect the popularity of presidents and that television "commentary"—that is, the expression by newscasters of their personal opinions—tends to have a large effect, at least in the short run.[27] This will not come as a surprise to White House officials, who spend almost every waking moment trying to get the television networks to say something nice about the president. The data support much anecdotal evidence on this score, such as Lyndon Johnson's belief that his war policy in Vietnam was doomed when Walter Cronkite, in his heavily watched CBS News programs, turned against the war.

Government and the News

Every government agency, every public official, spends a great deal of time trying to shape public opinion. From time to time somebody publishes an exposé of the efforts of the Pentagon, the White

Senator Estes Kefauver pioneered the televised Senate investigation with hearings into organized crime and (pictured here) teenage drug addiction.

House, or some bureau to "sell" itself to the people, but in a government of separated powers, weak parties, and a decentralized legislature, any government agency that fails to cultivate public opinion will sooner or later find itself weak, without allies, and in trouble.

Prominence of the President

Theodore Roosevelt was the first president to raise the systematic cultivation of the press to an art form. From the day he took office he made it clear that he would give inside stories to friendly reporters and withhold them from hostile ones. He made sure that scarcely a day passed without the president's doing something newsworthy. In 1902 he built the West Wing of the White House and included in it, for the first time, a special room for reporters near his office, and he invited the press to become fascinated by the antics of his children. In return the reporters adored him. Teddy's nephew, Franklin Roosevelt, institutionalized this system by making his press secretary (a job created by Herbert Hoover) a major instrument for cultivating and managing, as well as informing, the press.[28]

When President Theodore Roosevelt cultivated the media, reporters were usually unknown and poorly paid.

All this effort is directed primarily at the White House press corps, a group of men and women who have a lounge in the White House itself where they wait for a story to break, attend the daily press briefing, or take advantage of a "photo op"— an opportunity to photograph the president with some newsworthy person.

No other nation in the world has brought the press into such close physical proximity to the head of its government. The result is that the actions of our government are personalized to a degree not found in most other democracies. Whether the president rides a horse, comes down with a cold, greets a Boy Scout, or takes a trip in his airplane, the press is there. The prime minister of Great Britain does not share his home with the press or expect to have his every sneeze recorded for posterity.

Coverage of Congress

Congress has watched all this with irritation and envy. It resents the attention given the president, but it is not certain how it can compete. The 435 members of the House are so numerous and play such specialized roles that they do not get much individualized press attention. In the past the House was quite restrictive about television or radio coverage of its proceedings. Until 1978 it prohibited television cameras on the floor except on purely ceremonial

Today the press secretary heads a large staff that meets with reporters, briefs the president on questions he is likely to be asked, attempts to control the flow of news from cabinet departments to the press, and arranges briefings for out-of-town editors (to bypass what many presidents think are the biases of the White House press corps).

Every presidential action is a media event, as when Bill Clinton plays miniature golf.

occasions (such as the annual State of the Union message delivered by the president). From 1952 to 1970 the House would not even allow electronic coverage of its committee hearings (except for a few occasions during those periods when the Republicans were in the majority). Significant live coverage of committee hearings began in 1974 when the House Judiciary Committee was discussing the possible impeachment of President Nixon.[29] Since 1979 cable TV (C-SPAN) has provided gavel-to-gavel coverage of speeches on the House floor.

The Senate has used television much more fully, heightening the already substantial advantage that senators have over representatives in getting the public eye. Although radio and television coverage of the Senate floor was not allowed until 1978 (when the debates on the Panama Canal treaties were broadcast live), Senate committee hearings have frequently been televised for either news films or live broadcasts ever since Estes Kefauver demonstrated the power of this medium in 1950. Since 1986 the Senate has allowed live television coverage of its sessions.

Senatorial use of televised committee hearings has helped turn the Senate into the incubator for presidential candidates. At least in most states, if you are a governor, you are located far from network television news cameras; the best you can hope for is that some disaster—a flood or a blizzard—will bring the cameras to you and focus them on your leadership. But senators all work in Washington, a city filled with cameras. No disaster is necessary to get on the air; only an investigation, a scandal, a major political conflict, or an articulate and telegenic personality is needed.

Interpreting Political News

News stories, especially those about events of which we have no firsthand knowledge, are apt to be accepted without question. This may be particularly true of television news stories, since they enable us to judge not only what is said but how it is said.

Americans tell pollsters that they get most of their news from television, not newspapers, and that they regard TV as more reliable than the printed press. Though in general the public has a favorable view of the media, there has been a sharp increase of

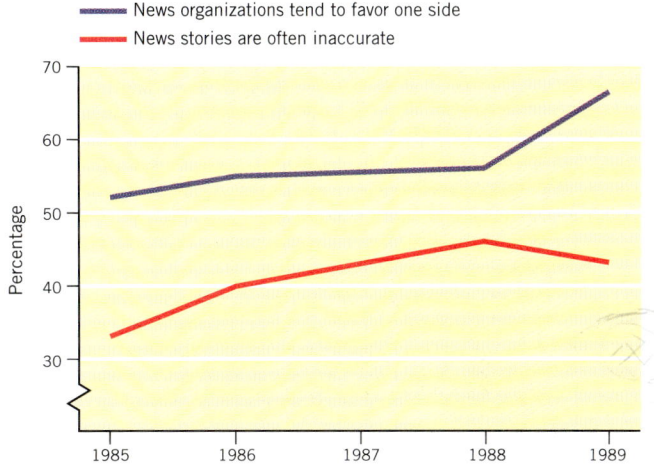

FIGURE 10.2 Public Perception of Bias and Accuracy in the Media

SOURCE: "The People and the Press," Part 5, *Los Angeles Times* (November, 1989): 13–14. Copyright © 1989, Los Angeles Times. Reprinted by permission.

late in the proportion of Americans who think the media tend to favor one side of a story—from 53 percent in 1985 to 68 percent in 1989—and in the percentage who think stories are inaccurate (see Figure 10.2). This is in sharp contrast to how the press sees itself. Two-thirds of all journalists think that the press deals fairly with all sides of political and social questions. Among the biggest losers in public confidence were Dan Rather and Ted Koppel; the biggest gainer was CNN (Cable News Network).

Bias is difficult to define and harder to measure, but in general the popular worry is that editors and reporters allow their personal political beliefs to influence the stories that they choose to run and to color the way in which they report them.

We do know that journalists are much more liberal than the public at large and that journalists working in the national media are the most liberal of all. In Table 10.2 on page 288, we can see how the beliefs of some 2,700 journalists from around the country compare with those of about three thousand ordinary citizens. On most issues the journalists are more liberal. In Table 10.3 we see the views of the members of the "elite" or "national" media. Unfortunately this survey did not ask the same questions of the public as it did of the journalists. Nonetheless, on such questions as abortion and

TABLE 10.2   Journalist Opinion versus Public Opinion

	Journalists	The Public
Self-described ideology:		
Liberal	55%	23%
Conservative	17	29
Favor government regulation of business	49	22
U.S. should withdraw investments from South Africa	62	31
Allow women to have abortions	82	49
Allow prayer in public schools	25	74
Favor "affirmative action"	81	56
Favor death penalty for murder	47	75
Want stricter controls on handguns	78	50
Increase defense budget	15	38
Favor hiring homosexuals	89	55

SOURCES: *Los Angeles Times* poll of about 3,000 citizens and 2,700 journalists nationwide, as reported in William Schneider and I. A. Lewis, "Views on the News," *Public Opinion* (August–September 1985): 7. Reprinted with permission of American Enterprise Institute for Public Policy Research.

TABLE 10.3   The Political Attitudes of the Media Elite

	Percentage Agree
People with ability should earn more.	86%
Less regulation of business is good for the United States.	63
Government should reduce the income gap.	68
There should be a strong affirmative-action program for blacks.	80
A woman has a right to decide on an abortion.	90
Homosexuality is wrong.	25
The United States exploits the Third World and causes poverty.	56
U.S. use of resources is immoral.	57
The CIA should sometimes undermine hostile governments.	45

SOURCES: Survey of 240 journalists and broadcasters employed by the national media, reported in S. Robert Lichter and Stanley Rothman, "Media and Business Elites," *Public Opinion* (October–November 1981): 44.

affirmative action there is little doubt that the media elite are significantly to the left of the public. This is confirmed by a comparison of their voting patterns. In 1972, for example, when 61 percent of the American people voted for Richard Nixon, only 19 percent of persons in the national media voted for him.[30] Likewise, in 1992 over 80 percent of media leaders in Washington, D.C., versus 43 percent of the public, voted for Bill Clinton.[31] And as can be seen in Table 10.4, members of the media, especially those who work in television, are more likely than the members of many other professions to identify themselves as politically liberal.

Are News Stories Slanted?

The fact that reporters tend to have liberal views does not mean that their stories will inevitably have a liberal slant. Other factors influence how stories are written, including the need to meet an urgent deadline, the desire to attract an audience, a professional obligation to be fair and to tell the truth, and the need to develop sources among people holding different views. For example, whatever their views, the national media gave, according to a careful study, quite evenhanded treatment to both the Republican and Democratic presidential candidates during the 1980 campaign, although they gave quite decidedly anti-Reagan coverage during the 1984 campaign and appeared to have been consistently tougher on George Bush than on his 1992 campaign rivals, especially in the primaries (see Table 10.5).[32]

Still, it would be astonishing if strongly held beliefs had *no* effect on what is written or broadcast. To understand the circumstances under which a reporter's or editor's opinion is more or less likely to affect a story—and thus to be able to interpret intelligently what we read and hear—we must distinguish among these three *kinds* of stories:

1. **Routine stories:** These are public events regularly covered by reporters, involving relatively simple, easily described acts or statements. For example, the president takes a trip, a bill passes Congress, the Supreme Court rules on an important case.

2. **Feature stories:** These are public events knowable to any reporter who cares to inquire, but involving acts and statements not routinely

covered by a group of reporters. Thus a reporter must take the initiative and select a particular event as newsworthy, decide to write about it, and persuade an editor to run it. Examples: an obscure agency issues a controversial ruling, an unknown member of Congress conducts an investigation, an interest group works for the passage of a bill.

3. **Insider stories:** Information not usually made public becomes public because someone with inside knowledge tells a reporter. The reporter may have worked hard to learn these facts, in which case we say it is "investigative reporting," or some official may have wanted a story to get out, in which case we call it a "leak."

Routine stories are covered in almost exactly the same way by almost all the media, differing only in their length, the kinds of headlines written, and the position the story occupies on the pages or the evening news. The wire services—AP and UPI—supply routine stories immediately to practically every daily newspaper in America. (The headlines and placement, however, can make a big difference in how the same story is perceived.) The political opinions of journalists have the least effect on these stories, especially if several competing journalists are covering the same story over a protracted period of time.

Even a routine news story can be incorrectly reported, however, if something dramatic or unique occurs. For example, toward the end of the Vietnam War the North Vietnamese army launched a massive, all-out attack on cities held by the South Vietnamese and their American allies. The attack failed—it was repulsed, and there were heavy North Vietnamese casualties. But the news stories reported exactly the opposite: the North Vietnamese could move and fight at will, and the Americans were helpless to defend the cities or even their own fortified positions. Peter Braestrup, who later analyzed the Tet Offensive and its journalistic coverage, painstakingly described the errors and omissions that led to the misleading versions published. He did not conclude that the political views of reporters explained the mistakes, and surely it would be difficult for any reporters, however fair, to grasp quickly and accurately an event as complex, dramatic, and violent as a major military struggle. But it is also proba-

TABLE 10.4 **Self-Identified Ideology Among American Elites**

	Percentages		
	Liberal	Conservative	Moderate
Television	75	14	12
Labor	73	6	20
Bureaucrats	56	27	17
Media	55	17	28
Judges	54	23	22
Lawyers	47	32	22
Business	14	63	17
Military	14	75	12

SOURCE: Table adapted from Robert Lerner et al., *American Elites*, Yale University Press, 1996, p. 50, table 3.2. Reprinted by permission of Yale University Press.

TABLE 10.5 **Negative Coverage in the 1992 Presidential Campaign**

Percentages of Negative Remarks About the Candidates' Ability to Govern, Proposals, and Actions from All Interviews Aired on the Evening News Broadcasts of ABC, CBS, and NBC.

	Bush	Clinton	Perot
Primaries (January 1–June 2)	78%	59%	36%
Conventions (June 3–September 6)	62	55	60
General Election (September 7–November 2)	69	63	54

SOURCE: Adapted from Elizabeth Kolbet, "Maybe the Media Did Treat Bush Harshly," *The New York Times* (November 22, 1992): E3, reporting data from the Center for Media and Public Affairs.

bly the case that the antiwar attitudes of most reporters reinforced the interpretation of Tet that they wrote.[33]

Feature and insider stories must be selected, and thus someone must do the selecting. The grounds on which the selections are made include not only the intrinsic interest of a story but also the reporter's or editor's beliefs about what *ought* to be interesting. Among these beliefs are the political ideologies of the journalists. A liberal paper may well select for coverage stories about white-collar crime, consumerism, the problems of minorities, and environmentalism; a conservative paper might instead select

The hostility between the press and the executive branch has been intensified by scandals: Watergate in the 1970s, the Iran-contra affair in 1988. Here, Lieutenant Colonel Oliver North testifies before Congress. In 1994 he was a candidate for the Senate from Virginia.

stories about street crime, the decline of a city's central business district, and the need for family values.

Nor are selected stories rare. In order to compete with television, newspapers increasingly print feature stories, thereby becoming more like a magazine, with something for everybody. As a result, a large part of a newspaper consists of precisely the kinds of stories that are most likely to be influenced by the ideological attitudes of reporters.

In one of the few studies of the effect of journalistic opinions on news stories, the authors found that in two examples of selected stories—articles concerning nuclear power and stories on the use of busing to integrate schools—the coverage provided by the national press reflected more the views of the press than those of experts or the public. But different segments of the media differed in how much slant they gave to their stories.

On nuclear power plants the vast majority of the stories in the *New York Times* gave a balanced view of the issue; the national news magazines (especially *Time* and *Newsweek*) and network television news programs, however, gave a predominately antinuclear slant to their stories. Moreover, though the great majority of scientists and engineers working in the field favor the rapid development of nuclear

power plants, very few of the experts quoted on this subject by the national press favored nuclear power.[34] On school busing the majority of the stories run by the *New York Times,* the *Washington Post, Time,* and CBS News had a probusing slant.

If a nonroutine story is a major, complex, somewhat unique event, such as the congressional investigation of Irangate in 1987, all the media will cover it, but each will choose what themes to emphasize and what questions to raise. Almost inevitably the media will put some "spin" on the story. (For example, was the star witness, Lieutenant Colonel Oliver North, a "hero," a "loose cannon," or a "Rambo"? It depended on whom you read or listened to.) If it is an offbeat story, it will be covered by one newspaper or TV station but not others; the very act of selection usually involves some political perspective. In evaluating feature and insider stories, every reader or viewer should keep these questions in mind:

- What beliefs or opinions led the editors to run this story?

- How representative of expert and popular opinion are the views of the people quoted in the story?

- What adjectives are being used to color the story?

Insider stories raise the most difficult questions of all—those of motive. When somebody inside government with private or confidential information gives a story to a reporter, that somebody must have a reason for doing so. But the motives of those who leak information are almost never reported. Sometimes the reporter does not know the motives. More often, one suspects, the reporter is dependent on his or her "highly placed source" and is reluctant to compromise it.

The reliance on the insider leak is as old as the Republic. At one time reporters were grateful for "background briefings" at which top government officials tried to put themselves in the best possible light while explaining the inner meaning of American policy. In the aftermath of Vietnam and Watergate, which weakened the credibility of "the Establishment," many reporters became even more interested in the leaks from insiders critical of top officials. In neither case were the motives of the sources discussed, leaving the reader or viewer to accept at face value whatever remarks are attributed to unnamed "highly placed sources" or "well-informed observers."

Why Do We Have So Many News Leaks?

American government is the leakiest in the world. The bureaucracy, members of Congress, and the White House staff regularly leak stories favorable to their interests. Of late the leaks have become geysers, gushing forth torrents of insider stories. Many people in and out of government find it depressing that our government seems unable to keep anything secret for long. Others think that the public has a right to know even more and that there are still too many secrets.

However you view leaks, you should understand why we have so many. The answer is found in the Constitution. Because we have separate institutions that must share power, each branch of government competes with the others to get power. One way to compete is to try to use the press to advance your pet projects and to make the other side look bad. There are far fewer leaks in other democratic nations in part because power is centralized in the hands of a prime minister, who does not need to leak in order to get the upper hand over the legislature, and because the legislature has too little infor-

On Background

When politicians talk to the press, they set certain ground rules that the press (usually) observes. These rules specify who, if anyone, is quoted as the source of the story.

On the record. The official is quoted by name. For example: "I say that water runs downhill, and you can quote me on that."

Off the record. What the official says cannot be printed. For example: "Off the record, the head of my party is a complete wacko."

On background. What the official says can be printed, but it may not be attributed to him or her by name. For example: "A well-placed source said today that the sun will continue to rise in the East."

On deep background. What the official says can be printed, but it cannot be attributed to anybody. The reporter must say it on his or her own authority. For example: "In my opinion this administration secretly believes that two plus two equals five."

mation to be a good source of leaks. In addition we have no Official Secrets Act of the kind that exists in England; except for a few matters, it is not against the law for the press to receive and print government secrets.

Even if the press and the politicians loved each other, the competition between the various branches of government would guarantee plenty of news leaks. But since the Vietnam War, the Watergate scandal, and the Iran-contra affair, the press and the politicians have come to distrust one another. As a result, journalists today are far less willing to accept at face value the statements of elected officials and are far more likely to try to find somebody who will leak "the real story." We have come, in short, to have

Young People and the News

Most Americans seem to care less and less about the news, especially televised news. In 1993 a total of 60 percent of adults said they watched a nightly network TV newscast. By 1996 that had fallen to 42 percent.

But young Americans watch and read even less. From 1995 to 1996 the percentage of people under the age of thirty who watched a regular TV newscast dropped from 36 to 22. In 1967 two-thirds of people under the age of thirty-five said they read a newspaper yesterday. By 1990 only a quarter of that group said the same thing.

What young people know has also declined. Between 1941 and 1975 young Americans knew as much about public affairs as older ones. By 1990 young people were much less informed than their elders on almost every issue except abortion.

For example, between 1940 and the 1970s people under age thirty knew as much as those over age fifty about Senator Joseph McCarthy, German Chancellor Helmut Schmidt, the threatened war over Quemoy and Matsu, the fighting in Vietnam, and the Watergate scandal. But by 1990 young people were much less likely than older ones to identify House Speaker Jim Wright, to know that the United States was going to give up control of the Panama Canal, to be aware of the fall of the Iron Curtain, or to have heard of Michael Dukakis.

This big drop in what young people know has occurred despite big increases in the proportion of young people going to college.

SOURCES: Times Mirror Center for The People and The Press, "The Age of Indifference: A Study of Young Americans and How They View the News" (June 28, 1990); Pew Research Center, "Fall Off Greater for Young Adults and Computer Users."

an **adversarial press**—that is, one that (at least at the national level) is suspicious of officialdom and eager to break an embarrassing story that will win for its author honor, prestige, and (in some cases) a lot of money.

This cynicism and distrust of government and elected officials have led to an era of attack journalism—seizing upon any bit of information or rumor that might call into question the qualifications or character of a public official. Media coverage of gaffes—misspoken words, misstated ideas, clumsy moves—has become a staple of political journalism. At one time, such "events" as President Ford slipping down some stairs, Governor Dukakis dropping the ball while playing catch with a Boston Red Sox player, or Vice President Quayle misspelling the

word *potato* would have been ignored, but now they are hot news items. (In fact, one publication, the *Quayle Quarterly,* was devoted entirely to covering the gaffes of one man, Vice President Dan Quayle.) Attacking public figures has become a professional norm, where once it was a professional taboo.

During the 1992 election, most of the national press clearly supported Bill Clinton. The love affair between Clinton and reporters lasted for several months after his inauguration. But when stories began to appear about Whitewater (an Arkansas real estate deal in which the Clintons were once involved), Clinton's alleged sexual escapades while governor, and Hillary Rodham Clinton's profits in commodities trading, the press went into a feeding frenzy. The Clintons learned the hard way the truth of an old adage: if you want a friend in Washington, buy a dog.

Many people do not like this type of journalism, and the media's rising cynicism about the government is mirrored by the public's increasing cynicism about the media. As Figure 10.3 shows, most Americans have less confidence in the news media today than they did when they first began paying attention to the news. Most people also believe that the press slants its coverage, has too much influence over events, and abuses its constitutional protections.

Furthermore, the public's confidence in big business has eroded along with its confidence in government, and the media are increasingly big business. As noted earlier in this chapter, network television has become a highly competitive industry. Under these circumstances, every contribution to "market share" is vitally important, and the newsroom is no exception. In a highly competitive environment that is rich in information, those who aspire to reach a mass market must find a mass theme into which they can tap with visually dramatic, quick-tempo messages. In politics the theme is obvious: politics is a corrupt, self-serving enterprise. Many people include the profit-driven press in their antipolitical sentiments.

Given their experiences with Watergate and Irangate, given the highly competitive nature of national news gathering, and given their political ideology (which tends to put them to the left of the administration in power), American editors and reporters, at least at the national level, are likely to

FIGURE 10.3   Decline in Public Trust of the Media

QUESTION

Do you have more or less or about the same amount of confidence in the news media today as you did when you first began paying attention to news and current events?

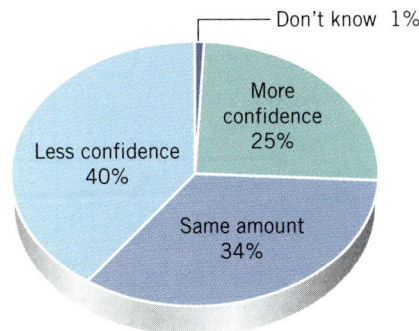

QUESTION

Do you agree or disagree with this statement: "The news media give more coverage to stories that support their own point of view than to those that don't"?

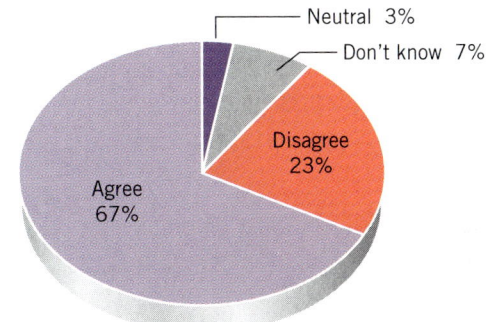

QUESTION

Generally speaking, do you feel that the news media have too much or too little or the right amount of influence over what happens today?

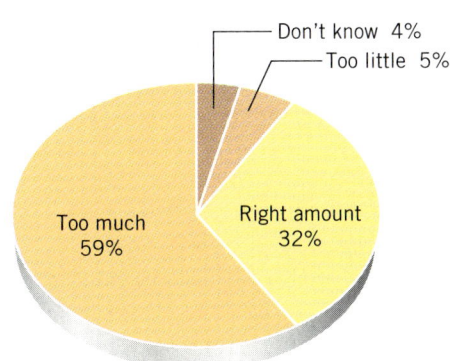

QUESTION

The Bill of Rights of the U.S. Constitution guarantees freedom of the press so that the news media can be a watchdog over the government and other powerful institutions. And the courts have ruled that the news media should be protected even in some cases when they have been unfair or inaccurate. Do you think the news media are careful to use this power responsibly?

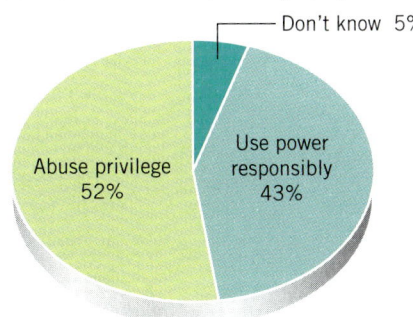

SOURCE: David Shaw, "Trust In Media Is on Decline," *Los Angeles Times* (March 31, 1993): A16, reporting data from a Times Poll conducted March 6–9, 1993. Copyright © 1993, Los Angeles Times. Reprinted by permission.

have an adversarial relationship with government for a long time to come. Given our constitutional system, there will always be plenty of people in government eager to help them with leaks hostile to one faction or another.

One side effect of the increasingly adversarial nature of the press is the increased prevalence of negative campaign advertising—that is, of ads that lambaste opponents and attack them on a personal level. Adversarial media coverage has helped make these types of ads more socially acceptable. The reason candidates use attack ads is simple: they work. A good negative ad will change the preferences of some voters. But this change is purchased at a price. Research shows that a negative ad not only changes voter preferences, it reduces voter turnout. Negative advertising may help a candidate win, but only by turning other people against elections.

Tensions Mount Between U.S. and Ruritania

U.S. 6th Fleet Maneuvering near African Nation

* * *

WASHINGTON, D.C. FEBRUARY 23— The State Department today denied Ruritanian claims that the United States is planning military action against Ruritania in the wake of Ruritanian-sponsored terrorist actions. . .

What Would You Do?

MEMORANDUM

TO: Editor in chief, Washington Post
FROM: Foreign news editor
SUBJECT: Ruritania

One of our best reporters has information that the United States plans to invade Ruritania three days from now. His source is a top military official who has been reliable in the past. As of now we do not think that any other newspaper has this story. As you know, opinion in the government is deeply divided over the wisdom of any action against Ruritania. So far all official sources in the White House and the State Department have denied that anything is afoot. But we all know that the president is deeply upset by the continuation of Ruritanian-sponsored terrorism against U.S. personnel overseas. Your options are:

1. Print the story in tomorrow's edition.

Advantages: (a) This is important news, and we have an obligation to publish news. (b) We get a major scoop that no other newspaper can match. (c) In our editorials we have said that we think an invasion of Ruritania would be a mistake. This story, if printed now, may lead to a cancellation of the military action.

Disadvantages: (a) There is a small chance that we could be wrong and no invasion is planned. (b) We will be criticized for leaking military secrets. (c) If the invasion takes place despite our story, the United States may lose the element of surprise, and this may affect the outcome and cause additional casualties.

2. Do not print the story.

Advantages: (a) We avoid charges that we are leaking military secrets. (b) If an invasion occurs, we will not have alerted the enemy.

Disadvantages: (a) There is the possibility that another newspaper may learn of this story in the next two days; if we don't publish now, they may publish later and we will look foolish. (b) We will be failing in our duty to inform the people about the activities of their government. (c) The Ruritanians may already know of the planned invasion, and so our story will not have alerted them.

Your decision: Option 1 _____ Option 2 _____

Government Constraints on Journalists

An important factor works against the influence of ideology and antiofficial attitudes on reporters—the need every reporter has for access to key officials. A reporter is only as good as his or her sources, and it is difficult to cultivate good sources if you regularly antagonize them. Thus Washington reporters must constantly strike a balance between expressing their own views (and risk losing a valuable source) and keeping a source (and risk becoming its mouthpiece).

The great increase in the number of congressional staff members has made striking this balance easier than it once was. Since it is almost impossible to keep anything secret from Congress, the existence of fifteen to twenty thousand congressional staffers means that there is a potential source for every conceivable issue and cause. Congress has become a gold mine for reporters. If a story annoys one congressional source, another source can easily be found.

The government is not without means to fight back. The number of press officers on the payroll of the White House, Congress, and the executive agencies has grown sharply in recent decades. Obviously these people have a stake in putting out news stories that reflect favorably on their elected superiors. They can try to do this with press releases, but adversarial journalists are suspicious of "canned news" (although they use it nonetheless). Or the press officers can try to win journalistic friends by offering leaks and supplying background stories to favored reporters. (A **background story** is one that purportedly explains current policy and is given on condition that the source not be identified by name.) Finally, the press officers can try to bypass the national press and directly reach the local press—the hometown newspapers and radio stations. Members of the local press are less likely to feel an adversarial attitude toward official Washington and perhaps are more likely to have a political ideology akin to that of the national administration.

The ultimate weapon in the government's effort to shape the press to its liking is the president's rewarding of reporters and editors who treat him well and his punishing of those who treat him badly. President Kennedy regularly called in offending reporters for brutal tongue lashings and favored friendly reporters with tips and inside stories. Johnson did the same, with special attention to television reporters. Nixon made the mistake of attacking the press publicly, thereby allowing it to defend itself with appeals to the First Amendment. (Kennedy's and Johnson's manipulative skills were used privately.) Probably every president tries to use the press with whatever means are at his disposal, but in the long run it is the press, not the president, who wins. Johnson decided not to run again in 1968 in part because of press hostility to him; Nixon was exposed by the press; Carter came to be disliked by national reporters. The press and the president need but do not trust one another; it is inevitably a stormy relationship.

SUMMARY

Changes in the nature of American politics have been accompanied by—and influenced by—changes in the nature of the mass media. The rise of strong national political party organizations was facilitated by the emergence of mass-circulation daily newspapers. Political reform movements depended in part on the development of national magazines catering to middle-class opinion. The weakening of political parties was accelerated by the ability of candidates to speak directly to constituents by radio and television.

The role of journalists in a democratic society poses an inevitable dilemma: if they are to serve well their functions as information gatherer, gatekeeper, scorekeeper, and watchdog, they must be free of government controls. But to the extent that they are free of such controls, they are also free to act in their own interests, whether political or economic. In the United States a competitive press largely free of government controls (except in the area of broadcast licenses) has produced both a substantial diversity of opinion and a general (though not unanimous) commitment to the goal of fairness in news reporting. The national media are in general more liberal than the local media, but the extent to which a reporter's beliefs affect reporting varies greatly with the kind of story—routine, feature, or insider.

KEY TERMS

muckraker   *p. 271*

sound bite   *p. 274*

trial balloon   *p. 281*

loaded language   *p. 281*

equal time rule   *p. 282*

right-of-reply rule   *p. 282*

political editorializing rule   *p. 282*

fairness doctrine   *p. 282*

market (television)   *p. 282*

selective attention   *p. 283*

routine stories   *p. 288*

feature stories   *p. 288*

insider stories   *p. 289*

adversarial press   *p. 292*

background story (news)   *p. 295*

SUGGESTED READINGS

Braestrup, Peter. *Big Story: How the American Press and Television Reported and Interpreted the Crises of Tet 1968 in Vietnam and Washington.* Boulder, Col.: Westview, 1977. 2 vols. A massive, detailed account of how the press reported one critical event; the factual accuracy or inaccuracy of each story is carefully checked.

Crouse, Timothy. *The Boys on the Bus.* New York: Random House, 1973. A lively, irreverent account by a participant of how reporters cover a presidential campaign.

Epstein, Edward J. *Between Fact and Fiction: The Problem of Journalism.* New York: Random House, 1975. Essays by a perceptive student of the press on media coverage of Watergate, the Pentagon Papers, the deaths of Black Panthers, and other major stories.

———. *News from Nowhere.* New York: Random House, 1973. Analysis of how television network news programs are produced and shaped.

Garment, Suzanne. *Scandal.* New York: Random House, 1991. A careful look at the role of the media (and others) in fostering the "culture of mistrust."

Graber, Doris A. *Mass Media and American Politics.* 3d ed. Washington, D.C.: Congressional Quarterly Press, 1989. A good summary of what we know about the press and politics.

Grossman, Michael Baruch, and Martha Joynt Kumar. *Portraying the President: The White House and the News Media.* Baltimore: Johns Hopkins University Press, 1981. How the White House is organized to handle the press and how the press is organized to cover the president.

Iyengar, Shanto, and Donald R. Kinder. *News That Matters.* Chicago: University of Chicago Press, 1987. The report of experiments testing the effect of television news on public perceptions of politics.

Lichter, S. Robert, Stanley Rothman, and Linda S. Lichter. *The Media Elite.* Bethesda, Md.: Adler & Adler, 1986. A study of the political beliefs of "elite" journalists and how those beliefs influence what we read and hear.

Linsky, Martin. *Impact: How the Press Affects Federal Policymaking.* New York: Norton, 1986. Study of how the national press affects the way in which federal officials make, discuss, and leak policy.

Patterson, Thomas W. *The Mass Media Election.* New York: Praeger, 1980. Analyzes what effect, if any, the media had on the 1976 election.

Robinson, Michael J., and Margaret A. Sheehan. *Over the Wire and on TV.* New York: Russell Sage Foundation, 1983. Analyzes how CBS News and United Press International covered the 1980 election.

PART THREE

Institutions of Government

"But the great security against a gradual concentration of the several powers in the same department consists in giving to those who administer each department the necessary constitutional means and personal motives to resist encroachments of the others."

— Federalist no. 51

11

Congress

★ **Difference between a congress and a parliament**

★ **Intent of the Framers**

★ **Power of the early House**

★ **Rise of the Senate**

★ **Composition of Congress**

★ **Determining fair representation**

★ **Congressional organization**

★ **Party leadership**

★ **Party votes**

★ **Ideological views**

★ **Committees**

★ **Decentralization of Congress**

★ **Effect of the staff**

★ **How laws get made**

★ **Methods of voting**

★ **How members of Congress vote**

★ **Congress and reform**

Senator Daniel Patrick Moynihan of New York once remarked that the United States is the only democratic government that has a legislative branch. Of course, lots of democracies have parliaments that pass laws. What he meant is that among the large democracies of the world, only the United States Congress has great powers that it can exercise independently of the executive branch. To see why this is the case, we must understand the difference between a congress and a parliament.

The United States (along with most Latin American nations) has a congress; Great Britain (along with most Western European nations) has a parliament. A hint as to the difference between the two kinds of legislatures can be found in the original meanings of the words: *Congress* derives from a Latin term that means "a coming together," a meeting, as of representatives from various places. *Parliament* comes from a French word, *parler,* that means "to talk."

There is of course plenty of talking—some critics say that there is nothing *but* talking—in the United States Congress, and certainly members of a parliament represent to a degree their local districts. But the differences implied by the names of the lawmaking groups are real ones, with profound significance for how laws are made and how the government is run. These differences affect two important aspects of lawmaking bodies: how one becomes a member and what one does as a member.

Ordinarily a person becomes a member of a parliament (such as the British House of Commons) by persuading a political party to put his or her name on the ballot. Though usually a local party committee selects a person to be its candidate, that committee often takes suggestions from national party headquarters. In any case the local group selects as its candidate someone willing to support the national party program and leadership. In the election, voters in the district choose not between two or three personalities running for office but between two or three national parties.

By contrast a person becomes a candidate for representative or senator in the United States Con-

299

gress by running in a primary election. Except in a very few places, political parties exercise little control over the choice of who is nominated to run for congressional office. (This is the case even though the person who wins the primary will describe himself or herself in the general election as a Democrat or a Republican.) Voters select candidates in the primaries because of their personalities, positions on issues, or overall reputation; even in the general election, where the party label affects who votes for whom, many citizens vote "for the man" (or for the woman), not for the party. As a result of these different systems, a parliament tends to be made up of people loyal to the national party leadership who meet to debate and vote on party issues. A congress, on the other hand, tends to be made up of people who think of themselves as independent representatives of their districts or states and who, while willing to support their party on many matters, expect to vote as their (or their constituents') beliefs and interests require.

Once they are in the legislature, members of a parliament discover that they can make only one

The work of Congress takes place in committees with members of both parties—here Senators Orrin Hatch (R., Utah) and Patrick Leahy (D., Vermont).

important decision—whether or not to support the government. The government in a parliamentary system such as Britain's consists of a prime minister and various cabinet officers selected from the party that has the most seats in parliament. As long as the members of that party vote together, that government will remain in power (until the next election). Should members of a party in power in parliament decide to vote against their leaders, the leaders lose office and a new government must be formed. With so much at stake, the leaders of a party in parliament have a powerful incentive to keep their followers in line. They insist that all members of the party vote together on almost all issues; if someone refuses, the penalty is often drastic: the party does not renominate the offending member in the next election.

Members of the United States Congress do not select the head of the executive branch of government—that is done by the voters when they choose a president. Far from making members of Congress less powerful, this makes them more powerful. Representatives and senators can vote on proposed laws without worrying that their votes will cause the government to collapse and without fearing that a failure to support their party will lead to their removal from the ballot in the next election. Congress has independent powers, defined by the Constitution, that it can exercise without regard to presidential preferences. Political parties do not control nominations for office, and thus they cannot discipline members of Congress who fail to support the party leadership. Because Congress is constitutionally independent of the president and because its members are not tightly disciplined by a party leadership, individual members of Congress are free to express their views and vote as they wish. They are also free to become involved in the most minute details of lawmaking, budget making, and supervision of the administration of laws. They do this through an elaborate set of committees and subcommittees.

During the first months of the 104th Congress (1994–1996), it appeared that parliamentary governance of a sort had at last come to Capitol Hill. For the first time in four decades, Republicans controlled both houses of Congress. On January 4, 1995, their very first day in power, the members of the House adopted procedural changes that enhanced the powers of the Speaker to control the legislative agenda. Mindful of these changes, a reporter declared that the "mini-universe known as Capitol Hill turned upside down January 4."[1] For a while at least, those words seemed prophetic. For example, the new Republican leadership proved so cohesive that it was able to pass a budget resolution promising tax cuts, deep spending cuts, and a balanced budget. Only one House Republican broke ranks on the resolution, and none did so in the Senate. It was not long, however, before congressional Republicans fought among themselves and with their leadership on funding for the B-2 bomber, Medicare, the National Endowment for the Arts, abortion policy, and environmental issues. In late September, disaffected House Republicans joined Democrats to defeat the Republican leadership on certain defense and appropriations bills. Meanwhile, President Clinton and congressional Democrats blocked or stalled many of the Republican leadership's major proposals. By the end of the first session of the 104th Congress, only 67 bills had been enacted (the previous post-1950 low was 145, in 1981), and any notion that parliamentary governance had come to Washington was laid to rest.

A real parliament, such as that in Britain, is an assembly of party representatives who choose a government and discuss major national issues. The principal daily work of a parliament is debate. A congress, such as that in the United States, is a meeting place of the representatives of local constituencies—districts and states. Members of the U.S. Congress can initiate, modify, approve, or reject laws, and they share with the president supervision of the administrative agencies of the government. The principal work of a congress is representation and action, most of which takes place in committees.

What this means in practical terms to the typical legislator is easy to see. Since members of the British House of Commons have little independent power, they get rather little in return. They are poorly paid, may have no offices of their own and virtually no staff, are allowed only small sums to buy stationery, and can make a few free local telephone calls. Each is given a desk, a filing cabinet, and a telephone, but not always in the same place.

By contrast, a member of the United States House of Representatives, even a junior one, has power and is rewarded accordingly. For example, in 1995 each member earned a substantial salary ($133,600) and was entitled to an annual office (or "clerk-hire") allowance of nearly $570,000, to pay for as many as twenty-two staffers. Each member also received individual allowances for travel,

Every member of Congress, like Rep. Constance Morella (R., MD) has a large staff.

The Powers of Congress

*T*he powers of Congress are found in Article I, section 8, of the Constitution.

- To lay and collect taxes, duties, imposts, and excises.
- To borrow money.
- To regulate commerce with foreign nations and among the states.
- To establish rules for naturalization (that is, becoming a citizen) and bankruptcy.
- To coin money, set its value, and punish counterfeiting.
- To fix the standard of weights and measures.
- To establish a post office and post roads.
- To issue patents and copyrights by inventors and authors.
- To create courts inferior to (that is, below) the Supreme Court.
- To define and punish piracies, felonies on the high seas, and crimes against the law of nations.
- To declare war.
- To raise and support an army and navy and make rules for their governance.
- To provide for a militia (reserving to the states the right to appoint militia officers and to train the militia under congressional rules).
- To exercise exclusive legislative powers over the seat of government (that is, the District of Columbia) and other places purchased to be federal facilities (forts, arsenals, dockyards, and "other needful buildings").
- To "make all laws which shall be necessary and proper for carrying into execution the foregoing powers, and all other powers vested by this Constitution in the government of the United States." (*Note:* This "necessary and proper," or "elastic" clause has been generously interpreted by the Supreme Court, as explained in Chapter 14.)

computer services, and the like, averaging $193,000. In addition, each member could mail newsletters and certain other documents to constituents for free using the "franking privilege." Senators, and representatives with seniority, received even larger bene-

fits. In 1995 each senator was entitled to an office budget and legislative assistance allowance totaling over $2 million and was free to hire as many staff as he or she wished with that money. These examples are not given to suggest that members of Congress are overrewarded but only that their importance, as individuals, in our political system can be inferred from the resources that they command.

The Evolution of Congress

The Framers chose to place legislative powers in the hands of a congress rather than a parliament for philosophical and practical reasons. They did not want to have all powers concentrated in a single governmental institution, even one that was popularly elected, because they feared that such a concentration could lead to rule by an oppressive or impassioned majority. At the same time they knew that the states were jealous of their independence and would never consent to a national constitution if it did not protect their interests and strike a reasonable balance between large and small states. Hence they created a **bicameral** (two-chamber) **legislature**—with a House of Representatives, to be elected directly by the people, and a Senate, consisting of two members from each state, to be chosen by the legislatures of each state. Though "all legislative powers" were to be vested in Congress, those powers would be shared with the president (who could veto acts of Congress), limited to powers explicitly conferred on the federal government, and, as it turned out, subject to the power of the Supreme Court to declare acts of Congress unconstitutional.

Although they designed these checks and balances to prevent legislative tyranny, the Framers nonetheless expected that Congress would be the dominant institution in the national government. And for at least a century and a half it was, except for a few brief periods when activist presidents (such as Andrew Jackson, Abraham Lincoln, Theodore Roosevelt, and Woodrow Wilson) were able to challenge congressional supremacy. Until the twentieth century, and during some periods since, the major struggles for national political power have been *within* Congress, over the rules and leadership of that body, rather than between Congress and the president.

The struggles within Congress were generally over issues of great national significance—slavery, the admission of new states, the development of internal improvements, tariffs against foreign goods, and the regulation of business—but cutting across most of these substantive issues was a conflict over the distribution of power within Congress itself. Two competing values were at stake: centralization versus decentralization. If Congress were to act quickly and decisively as a body, then there must be strong central leadership, restrictions on debate, few opportunities for stalling tactics, and minimal committee interference. If, on the other hand, the interests of individual members—and the constituencies that they represent—were to be protected or enhanced, then there must be weak leadership, rules allowing for delay and discussion, and many opportunities for committee activity.

Though there have been periods of strong central leadership in Congress, the general trend, especially in this century, has been toward decentralizing decision making and enhancing the power of the individual member at the expense of the congressional leadership. This decentralization may not have been inevitable. Most American states have constitutional systems quite similar to the federal one, yet in many state legislatures, such as those in New York, Massachusetts, and Indiana, the leadership is quite powerful. In part the position of these strong state legislative leaders may be the result of the greater strength of political parties in some states than in the nation as a whole. In large measure, however, it is a consequence of permitting state legislative leaders to decide who shall chair what committee and who shall receive what favors.

The House of Representatives, though always powerful, has often changed the way in which it is organized and led. In some periods it has given its leader, the Speaker, a lot of power; in other periods it has given much of that power to the chairmen of the House committees; and in still other periods it has allowed individual members to acquire great influence. In the 1990s it seemed for a while that the Speaker would permanently reclaim powers previously given away to individual members, but it is too early to tell whether that change will endure. To simplify a complicated story, here are six snapshots of how the House operated at six different periods in our history.

Phase One: The Powerful House

During the first three administrations—of George Washington, John Adams, and Thomas Jefferson—leadership in Congress was often supplied by the president or his cabinet officers. Alexander Hamilton, as secretary of the treasury, acted as Washington's leader in Congress, even though he was not a member of that body. Albert Gallatin, Jefferson's secretary of the treasury, performed essentially the same function, working through intermediaries.

Rather quickly, however, Congress began to assert its independence and to develop its own leadership. The House of Representatives was the preeminent institution, overshadowing the tiny Senate. It originated most legislation. Henry Clay, as Speaker of the House, was a powerful leader who appointed the members and chairmen of the committees and kept his party, the Democratic-Republicans, under reasonable control. The party caucus, dominated by Clay, was often influential in shaping policy

One of the most powerful Speakers of the House, Henry Clay, is shown here addressing the United States Senate around 1850.

questions before they were debated on the floor of the House. Indeed, during these early years, the caucus selected its party's candidate for president. For example, the Democratic-Republican caucus nominated Jefferson in 1804, James Madison in 1808 and again in 1812, and James Monroe in 1816. The caucus system of nomination enhanced the power of the House, for it meant that the president of the United States, though not elected by Congress, was nominated for that office by important members of Congress. This political fact of life helped make the presidents quite sensitive to congressional desires.

Phase Two: A Divided House

In the late 1820s the preeminence of the House began to wane. Andrew Jackson asserted the power of the presidency by vetoing legislation that he did not like. The caucus system of nominations had fallen into disrepute and was replaced (as we saw in Chapter 7) with a system of national nominating conventions. Most important, the party unity necessary for a Speaker, or any other leader, to control the House was shattered by the issue of slavery. So divided were the parties over this question that the choice of a Speaker became a protracted struggle; one contest in 1856 took 133 ballots before the outcome was decided. A Speaker chosen under these circumstances could hardly wield much power.

The Civil War led to the end of slavery, and hence to the end of the argument in the House over that issue. Of course, representatives from the South did not attend during the war, and their seats remained vacant for several years after it ended. This meant that a group called the "Radical Republicans," led by men such as Thaddeus Stevens of Pennsylvania, could produce strong majorities for measures aimed at punishing the defeated South. The House even voted to impeach President Andrew Johnson for being too soft on the South. (The Senate, by a margin of one vote, failed to convict Johnson on the impeachment.) But such measures were driven more by shared beliefs among the representatives than by people in powerful leadership positions. As time passed, the hot passions the war had generated began to cool, and it became clear that the leadership of the House remained weak.

Phase Three: The Rise of a Powerful Speaker

Toward the end of the nineteenth century, the Speaker of the House gained power. When Thomas B. Reed of Maine became Speaker in 1889, he obtained by vote of the Republican majority more authority than any of his predecessors. He had the right to select the chairmen and members of all committees, and he used this power to reward friends and punish enemies. He chaired the Rules Committee and had the authority to decide what business would come up for a vote and what the limitations on debate would be. He decided who would be allowed to speak and who would not, which allowed him to thwart the delaying tactics of other members. While he was in power, Reed produced a great deal of party unity in the House.

Not long after Reed resigned in 1899, another powerful man became Speaker, Joseph G. Cannon of Illinois. He sought to maintain the Reed tradition, but by now circumstances had changed. Whereas Reed had political views quite similar to those of most Republicans, Cannon was distinctly more conservative than many Republicans around the turn of the century. Moreover, the desire of individual members to act independently was becoming more pronounced. Within a few years the revolt came.

Phase Four: The Revolt Against the Speaker

In 1910–1911 the House revolted against Cannon, voting to strip the Speaker of his right to appoint committee members and chairmen and to remove him from membership on the powerful Rules Committee. What power Cannon lost did not flow immediately into the hands of individual members, however. Instead, three other sources of power emerged.

One was the party caucus. For a time the members of each political party in the House, meeting in their caucuses, would take positions on issues coming before the House and induce each member to support them. On occasion the leader of a caucus was an especially influential or respected figure, and the caucus was strong. But the caucuses lacked any real authority, and soon their influence waned.

Three powerful Speakers of the House: Thomas B. Reed (1889–1891, 1895–1899) (left), Joseph G. Cannon (1903–1911) (center), and Sam Rayburn (1941–1947, 1949–1953, 1955–1961) (right). Reed put an end to the filibuster in the House by refusing to allow dilatory motions and by counting as "present"—for purposes of a quorum—members in the House, even though they were not voting. Cannon further enlarged the Speaker's power by refusing to recognize members who wished to speak without Cannon's approval and increased the power of the Rules Committee, over which he presided. Cannon was stripped of much of his power in 1910. Rayburn's influence rested more on his ability to persuade than on his formal powers.

Individual members increasingly discovered that they could defy them without penalty.

A second was the Rules Committee. Though the Speaker was no longer a member, the committee still decided what bills would come up for a vote and in what order, and it still set restrictions on the length of debate and on members' ability to offer amendments.

Third, the power of the chairmen of the standing committees rose as the power of the Speaker fell. Until the 1970s these chairmen had substantial ability to decide what business the committees they chaired would take up, what bills would be sent out of the committees to the full House, and even what some of these bills would contain. In the days when these chairmen were chosen by the Speaker, they often used their power to follow his leadership or that of the party as a whole. But once the Speaker no longer appointed them, they acquired office strictly on the basis of seniority.

Phase Five: The Empowerment of Individual Members

In the 1960s and 1970s, the House struck out against almost all forms of leadership. The defining issue was civil rights. Newly elected Democrats could not get the House to vote on a meaningful civil rights bill until 1965 because powerful committee chairmen, most of them from the South, kept such legislation bottled up. To make certain that never happened again, Democrats changed the rules so that chairmen lost much of their authority. Beginning in the 1970s, committee chairmen would no longer be selected simply on the basis of seniority; they had to be elected by the members of the majority party. Committees without subcommittees had to create them and allow their members to choose subcommittee chairmen. Chairmen could no longer refuse to call committee meetings, and most meetings had to be public. Individual members' staffs were greatly enlarged.

Individual members of the House became more powerful. Each member could introduce bills, and half of all majority party members were chairman of at least one committee or subcommittee. There was no way old-style committee chairmen could block legislation any longer.

Phase Six: The Return of Leadership

The new individualistic system had its costs, of course. Since every member had power, it was harder for the House to get anything done. By slow steps, culminating in some sweeping changes made in 1995, there were efforts to restore some of the power the Speaker had once had. In the late 1970s and early 1980s the Speaker acquired the power to choose a majority of the members of the Rules Committee (which still schedules legislation for a vote) and of the committee that chooses which members will serve on which committees. He also acquired the authority to assign a bill to several different committees for consideration.

When the Republicans took control of the House after the 1994 election, they retained many of the changes the Democrats had made during the 1970s and added several of their own, many designed to ensure more open debate. Some of the changes they introduced, such as a decision that no one could chair a committee for more than six years, seem to weaken leadership. But other changes strengthened it. The number of committees and subcommittees was reduced, thus reducing the chance for a member to become a chairman. They continued the policy of ignoring seniority in the selection of some committee chairmen. Speaker Newt Gingrich dominated the choice of committee chairmen, often passing over more senior members for more agreeable junior ones. The Speaker set the agenda for the House— and got it to vote on every item on the "Contract with America" within the first few months of 1995. In many of these votes, virtually every Republican voted with his party leadership, while most Democrats opposed.

The Future?

All of these changes suggest that the House has trouble deciding once and for all how to run itself.

Sometimes it has a strong Speaker, sometimes a weak one; sometimes committee chairmen are selected by seniority, sometimes by the Speaker, and sometimes by party vote.

These fluctuations reveal the fundamental problem the House faces: it wants to be both big (it has 435 members) and powerful, and its members want to be powerful both as individuals and as a group. But being big makes it hard for the House to be powerful unless some small group is given the authority to run it. If a group runs the place, however, the individual members lack much power. Individuals can gain power, but only at the price of making the House harder to run and thus reducing its collective power in government. There is no lasting solution to these dilemmas, and so the House will always be undergoing changes.

The Evolution of the Senate

None of these problems face the Senate. It is small enough (100 members) that it can be run without giving much authority to any small group of leaders. In addition, it has escaped some of the problems the House once faced. During the period leading up to the Civil War, it was carefully balanced so that the number of senators from slave-owning states exactly equaled the number from free states. Hence, fights over slavery rarely arose in the Senate.

From the first, the Senate was small enough that no time limits had to be placed on how long a senator could speak. This meant that there never was anything like a Rules Committee that controlled the amount of debate.

Finally, senators were not elected by the voters until this century. Prior to that, they were picked instead by state legislatures. Thus senators were often the leaders of local party organizations, with an interest in funneling jobs and contracts back to their states.

The big changes in the Senate came not from any fight about how to run it (nobody ever really ran it) but from a dispute over how its members should be chosen. For more than a century after the Founding, members of the Senate were chosen by state legislatures. Though often these legislatures picked popular local figures to be senators, just as often there was intense political maneuvering among the leaders of various factions, each struggling to win (and sometimes buy) the votes necessary to become senator. By the end of the nineteenth century, the Senate was known as the "Millionaires' Club," because of the number of wealthy party leaders and businessmen in it. There arose a demand for the direct, popular election of senators.

Naturally the Senate resisted, and without its approval the necessary constitutional amendment could not pass Congress. When some states threatened to demand a new constitutional convention, the Senate feared that such a convention would change more than just the way in which senators were chosen. A protracted struggle ensued, during which many state legislatures devised ways to ensure that the senators they picked would already have won a popular election. The Senate finally agreed to a constitutional amendment that required the popular election of its members, and in 1913 the Seventeenth Amendment was approved by the necessary three-fourths of the states. Ironically, given the intensity of the struggle over this question, no great change in the composition of the Senate resulted; most of those members who had first been chosen by state legislatures managed to win reelection by popular vote.

The other major issue in the development of the Senate was the filibuster. A **filibuster** is a prolonged speech, or series of speeches, made to delay action in a legislative assembly. It had become a common—and unpopular—feature of Senate life by the end of the nineteenth century. It was used by liberals and conservatives alike and for lofty as well as self-serving purposes. The first serious effort to restrict the filibuster came in 1917, after an important foreign policy measure submitted by President Wilson had been talked to death by, as Wilson put it, "eleven willful men." Rule 22 was adopted by a Senate fearful of tying a president's hands during a wartime crisis. The rule provided that debate could be cut off if two-thirds of the senators present and voting agreed to a "cloture" motion (it has since been revised to allow sixty senators to cut off debate). Two years later it was first invoked successfully when the Senate voted cloture to end, after fifty-five days, the debate over the Treaty of Versailles. Despite the existence of Rule 22, the tradition of unlimited debate remains strong in the Senate.

A cartoon from *Puck* in 1890 expressed popular resentment over the "Millionaires' Club," as the Senate had become known.

Who Is in Congress?

With power so decentralized in Congress, the kind of person elected to it is especially important. Since each member exercises some influence, the beliefs and interests of each individual affect policy. Viewed simplistically, most members of Congress seem the same: the typical representative or senator is a middle-aged white Protestant male lawyer. If all such persons usually thought and voted alike, that would be an interesting fact, but they do not, and so it is necessary to explore the great diversity of views among seemingly similar people.

Sex and Race

Congress has gradually become less male and less white. Between 1950 and 1997, the number of

Politically SPEAKING

Filibuster

A filibuster is a technique by which a small number of senators attempts to defeat a measure by talking it to death—that is, by speaking continuously and at such length as to induce the supporters of the measure to drop it in order to get on with the Senate's business.

The right to filibuster is governed by the Senate's Rule 22, which allows for unlimited debate unless at least sixty senators agree to a motion to cut it off.

Originally *filibusterers* were sixteenth-century English and French pirates and buccaneers who raided Spanish treasure ships. The term came from a Dutch word, *vrijbuiter*, meaning "freebooter," which was converted into the English word *filibuster.*

The word came into use in America as a term for "continuous talking" in the mid–nineteenth century. One of its first appearances was in 1854, when a group of senators tried to talk to death the Kansas-Nebraska Act.

SOURCE: From *Safire's Political Dictionary* by William Safire. Copyright © 1968, 1972, 1978 by William Safire. Reprinted by permission of Random House, Inc. and the author.

tion there were no blacks and only two women in the Senate. But in 1992 four more women, including one black, Carol Mosely Braun of Illinois, were elected. Two more were elected in 1994. And a Native American, Ben Nighthorse Campbell of Colorado, became a senator.

The relatively small number of blacks and Hispanics in the House understates their influence, at least when the Democrats are in the majority. In 1994 four House committees were chaired by blacks and three by Hispanics. In the same year, however, no woman chaired a committee. The reason for this difference in power is that the former tend to come from safe districts and thus to have more seniority than the latter. Republican control of the House in 1995 reduced minority influence.

Incumbency

The most important change that has occurred in the composition of Congress has been so gradual that most people have not noticed it. In the nineteenth century a large fraction—often a majority—of congressmen served only one term. In 1869, for example, more than half the members of the House were serving their first term in Congress. Being a congressman in those days was not regarded as a career. This was in part because the federal government was not very important (most of the interesting political decisions were made by the states); in part because travel to Washington, D.C., was difficult and the city was not a pleasant place in which to live; and in part because being a congressman did not pay well. Furthermore, many congressional districts were highly competitive, with the two political parties fairly evenly balanced in each.

By the 1950s, however, serving in Congress had become a career. Between 1863 and 1969 the proportion of first-termers in the House fell from 58 percent to 8 percent (see Figure 11.1, page 310).[2] As the public took note of this shift, people began to complain about "professional politicians" being "out of touch with the people." A movement to impose term limits was started. In 1995 the House approved a constitutional amendment to do just that, but it died in the Senate. Then the Supreme Court struck down an effort by a state to impose term limits on its own members of Congress.

women in the House increased from nine to fifty-one and the number of blacks from two to thirty-seven. There are also eighteen Hispanic members.

Until recently the Senate has changed much more slowly (see Table 11.1). Before the 1992 elec-

As it turned out, natural political forces were already doing what the term limits amendment was supposed to do. The 1992 and 1994 elections brought scores of new members to the House, with the result that by 1995 the proportion of members who were serving their first or second term had risen sharply. Three things were responsible for this change. First, when congressional district lines were redrawn after the 1990 census, a lot of incumbents found themselves running in new districts that they couldn't carry. Second, voter disgust at a variety of Washington political scandals made them receptive to appeals from candidates who could describe themselves as "outsiders." And third, the Republican victory in 1994—made possible in part by the conversion of the South from a Democratic bastion to a Republican stronghold—brought a lot of new faces to the Capitol.

This influx of freshman members should not obscure the fact that incumbents still enjoy enormous advantages in congressional elections.[3] Even in 1994, when thirty-five incumbent Democrats lost to Republicans, over 90 percent of all House members who ran for reelection were reelected. In the Senate, 92 percent of incumbents who ran again were reelected. In 1996, over 90 percent of House incumbents were reelected, and only one in twenty Senate incumbents who stood for reelection was defeated.

The arrival of scores of new faces in the 1990s should not obscure the fact that most House members still win big in their districts. Political scientists call districts that have close elections (when the winner gets less than 55 percent of the vote) **marginal districts** and districts where incumbents win by wide margins (55 percent or more) **safe districts**. The proportion of House incumbents who have won reelection with at least 60 percent of the vote increased from about three-fifths in the 1950s and early 1960s to three-quarters in the 1970s and almost nine-tenths in the late 1980s (see Figure 11.2, page 310). Even as this trend began to change in 1990, most House districts remained safe. Senators remained less secure: the rule, to which the period from 1980 to 1990 is the exception, is that fewer than half of Senate incumbents win with as much as 60 percent of the vote (see Table 11.2, page 311).

TABLE 11.1   Blacks and Women in Congress, 1951–1998

Congress	Senate		House	
	Blacks	Women	Blacks	Women
105th (1997–1998)	1	9	37	51
104th	1	8	38	48
103d	1	6	38	47
102d	0	2	26	29
101st	0	2	24	25
100th	0	2	23	23
99th	0	2	20	22
98th	0	2	21	22
97th	0	2	17	19
96th	0	1	16	16
95th	1	2	16	18
94th	1	0	15	19
93d	1	0	15	14
92d	1	2	12	13
91st	1	1	9	10
90th	1	1	5	11
89th	0	2	6	10
88th	0	2	5	11
87th	0	2	4	17
86th	0	1	4	16
85th	0	1	4	15
84th	0	1	3	16
83d	0	3	2	12
82d (1951–1952)	0	1	2	10

SOURCE: *Congressional Quarterly Almanac*, various years.

Why congressional seats have become less marginal—that is, safer—is a matter on which scholars are not entirely in agreement. Some feel that it is the result of television and other ways of reaching the voters through the media. But challengers can go on television, too, so why should this benefit incumbents? Another possibility is that voters are becoming less and less likely to automatically support whatever candidate wins the nomination of their own party. They are more likely, in short, to vote for the person rather than the party. And they are more likely to have heard of a person who is an incum-

FIGURE 11.1 Changing Percentage of First-Term Members in Congress

House   Senate

NOTES: 1989 freshman class in the House was the smallest in history. 1993 freshman class in the House was the largest since 1949.
SOURCES: Data for 90th through 103rd Congresses are from *Congressional Quarterly Weekly Reports.* Data for 69th through 89th Congresses are adapted from Nelson W. Polsby, "The Institutionalization of the U.S. House of Representatives," *American Political Science Review* (March 1968), 146. Data for 1st through 68th Congresses are from Stuart A. Rice, *Quantitative Methods in Politics* (New York: Knopf, 1928), 296–297, as reported in Polsby, 146. Data for Senate are from N. J. Ornstein, T. J. Mann, and M. J. Malbin, *Vital Statistics on Congress, 1989–1990* (Washington, D.C.: CQ Press, 1990), 56–57, 59–60.

FIGURE 11.2 Percentage of Incumbents Reelected to Congress

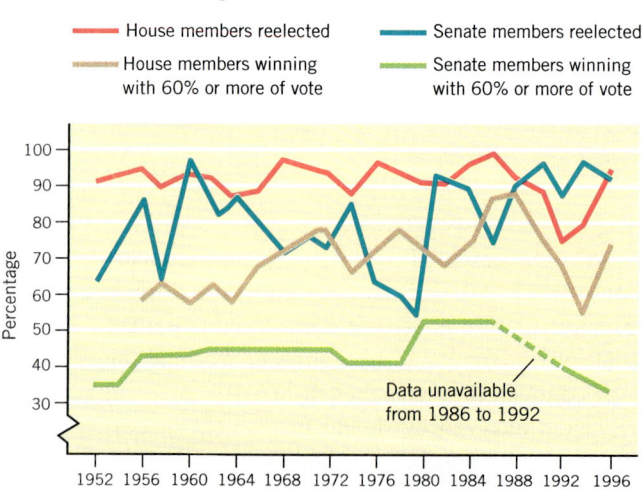

House members reelected   Senate members reelected
House members winning with 60% or more of vote   Senate members winning with 60% or more of vote

Data unavailable from 1986 to 1992

SOURCES: N. J. Ornstein, T. E. Mann, and M. J. Malbin, *Vital Statistics on Congress, 1989–1990* (Washington, D.C.: CQ Press, 1990), 56–57, 59–60; *Congressional Quarterly Weekly Reports* (March 4, 1993).

bent: incumbents can deluge the voter with free mailings, they can travel frequently (and at public expense) to meet constituents, and they can get their name in the newspaper by sponsoring bills or conducting investigations. Simply having a familiar name is important in getting elected, and incumbents find it easier than challengers to make their name known.

Finally, some scholars argue that incumbents can use their powers to get programs passed or funds spent to benefit their districts—and thereby to benefit themselves. They can help keep an army base open, support the building of a new highway (or block the building of an unpopular one), take credit for federal grants to local schools and hospitals, make certain that a particular industry or labor union is protected by tariffs against foreign competition, and so on.[4]

Probably all of these factors make some difference. Whatever the explanation, the tendency of vot-

TABLE 11.2   Incumbents in Congress Reelected by 60 Percent or More

House, 1956–1996

Year	Number of incumbents running in general election	Percentage of incumbents reelected with at least 60 percent of the vote
1956	403	59.1
1958	390	63.1
1960	400	58.9
1962	376	63.6
1964	388	58.5
1966	401	67.7
1968	397	72.2
1970	389	77.3
1972	373	77.8
1974	383	66.4
1976	381	71.9
1978	377	78.0
1980	392	72.9
1982	383	68.9
1984	406	74.6
1986	391	86.4
1988	407	88.5
1990	406	76.4
1992	349	65.6
1994	383	64.5
1996	383	73.6

Senate, 1944–1994

Election period	Number of incumbents running in general election	Percentage of incumbents reelected with at least 60 percent of the vote
1944–1948	61	39.3
1950–1954	76	35.5
1956–1960	84	42.9
1962–1966	86	44.2
1968–1972	74	44.6
1974–1978	70	41.4
1980–1984	84	54.1
1986–1990	87	57.5
1992–1994	53	43.4
1996	20	31.6

SOURCE: Norman J. Ornstein, Thomas E. Mann, and Michael J. Malbin, *Vital Statistics on Congress, 1995–1996* (Washington, D.C.: CQ Press, 1996), pp. 67–68.

ers to return incumbents to office means that in ordinary times no one should expect any dramatic
changes in the composition of Congress.

Party

From 1933 to 1994 thirty-one Congresses convened
(a new Congress convenes every two years). Democrats controlled both houses in twenty-five of these
thirty-one Congresses and at least one house in
twenty-eight of them. Scholars differ in their explanations of why the Democrats have so thoroughly
dominated Congress. Most of the research on the
subject has focused on the reasons for Democratic
control of the House.

As Table 11.3 shows, in every election from 1968
to 1992 the percentage of the popular vote for
Republican candidates to the House was higher than
the percentage of House seats that actually went to
Republicans. For example, in 1976 the Republicans
won 42.1 percent of the vote but received only 32.9
percent of the seats. Some have argued that this gap
between votes and seats has occurred because

Democratic-controlled state legislatures have redrawn congressional district maps in ways that
make it hard for Republicans to win House seats.
There is some striking anecdotal evidence to support this conclusion. For example, following the
1990 census, the Democratic-controlled Texas legislature crafted a new congressional district map
clearly designed to benefit Democrats. In 1992
Republicans won 48 percent of the House vote in
Texas but received only 30 percent of the seats.
Similarly, in 1984 Democrats in California won nine
more congressional seats than did Republicans, even
though the latter received about one hundred thousand more votes statewide. After 1990 California's
congressional map was redrawn by a state court, and
in 1992 Republican House candidates won 41 percent of the statewide vote and 42 percent of the
seats.[5] Only in 1994, with the historic election of
the first Republican majorities in Congress in four
decades, did the gap close.

Partisan tinkering with district maps and other
structural features of House elections is not a sufficient explanation of why Democrats dominated the
House until 1994. As one recent study concluded,
"virtually all the political science evidence to date
indicates that the electoral system has little or no
partisan bias, and that the net gains nationally from
redistricting for one party over another are very
small."[6] To control the redistricting process, one
party must control both houses of the legislature,
the governor's office, and, where necessary, the state
courts. These conditions simply do not exist in most
states. And even if district lines were consistently
drawn with scrupulous fairness, the Democrats
would still win control of the House, because they
win more votes. The Republican vote-seat gap is accounted for in part by the fact that the Democrats
tend to do exceptionally well in low-turnout districts such as minority-dominated inner cities, while
the Republicans tend to do better in high-turnout
districts such as affluent white suburbs (see Figure
11.3).

In 1994, however, the year the gap closed,
Republican candidates for the House ran especially
strong in the roughly half of all districts that have
predominantly suburban constituencies. Thus even
though only 19 percent of eligible voters cast a vote
for a Republican, it was enough to best the Dem-

TABLE 11.3   **Republican Vote-Seat Gap, 1968–1994**

Year	Percentage of Popular Vote for Republican House Candidates	Percentage of House Seats Held by Republicans
1968	48.2%	44.1%
1970	44.5	41.4
1972	46.4	44.2
1974	40.5	33.1
1976	42.1	32.9
1978	44.7	36.3
1980	48.0	44.1
1982	43.3	38.2
1984	47.0	41.8
1986	44.6	40.7
1988	45.5	40.2
1990	45.0	38.4
1992	45.6	40.5
1994	52.4	52.9

SOURCE: "House Republicans Scored A Quiet Victory in '92," *Congressional Quarterly* (April 17, 1993): 965, 966.

ocrats, who won the votes of only 16.6 percent of all eligible voters.

Congressional incumbents have come to enjoy certain built-in electoral advantages over challengers, and the Democrats were in the majority as the advantages of incumbency grew. Studies suggest that the incumbency advantage was worth about two percentage points prior to the 1960s but has grown to six to eight points today.

But as political scientist Gary C. Jacobson has observed, the historical Democratic dominance of the House cannot be explained simply by reference to incumbency advantages. Instead, Jacobson argues that "Democrats' continued dominance of the House (as well as of other lower offices) despite a string of Republican presidential victories is a consequence of electoral politics."[7] In comparison with the Republicans, the Democrats, he finds, generally have fielded better, more experienced congressional candidates, have more closely reflected district-level voters' policy preferences, and have been able to fashion winning, district-level coalitions from among national Democratic constituencies such as organized labor, civil rights activists, feminists, and environmentalists. This implies that more than mere changes in the structural features of House elections (incumbency advantages, partisan redistricting) would be necessary to keep the GOP's vote-seat gap closed.

It is important to remember that from time to time major electoral convulsions do alter the membership patterns in Congress. For example, in the election of 1938 the Democrats lost seventy seats in the House; in 1942 they lost fifty; in 1950 they lost twenty-nine; and in 1966 they lost forty-eight. Despite these big losses, the Democrats retained a majority in the House in each of these years. Not so, however, in 1994, when the Democrats lost fifty-two House seats (the largest loss by either party since the Republicans lost seventy-five seats in 1948), and Republicans gained majorities in both the House and the Senate.

Just as it is not easy to explain why Democrats dominated Congress for half a century, so it is not easy to explain why that domination ended when and as it did. Several reasons, however, stand out. By the 1990s the advantages of incumbency had turned into disadvantages: voters increasingly came to dis-

FIGURE 11.3 Results of 1992 House Election by Turnout

SOURCE: "House Republicans Scored a Quiet Victory in '92," *Congressional Quarterly* (April 17, 1993): 967.

like "professional politicians," whom they held responsible for "the mess in Washington." Just what "the mess" was varied according to which voter you asked, but it included chronic budget deficits, the congressional habit of exempting itself from laws that affected everybody else, constant bickering between Congress and the White House, and various congressional scandals. During the 1980s about forty members of Congress were charged with misconduct ranging from having sex with minors to accepting illegal gifts. When it was disclosed that the House had its own bank that would cash checks even for members who (temporarily) had no funds in their accounts, public indignation exploded, even though almost no taxpayer money was lost. Public respect for Congress, as measured by the polls, plummeted.

The Democrats had the misfortune of being the majority party in Congress when all of this happened. The anti-incumbent mood, coupled with the effects of redistricting after the 1990 census and the shift of the South to the Republican party, brought the Republicans into power in the House and Senate in the 1994 elections.

In the past the Democratic party was more deeply divided than the Republicans, because of the presence in Congress of conservative Democrats from the South. Often these southern Democrats would vote with the Republicans in the House or Senate, thereby forming what came to be called the **conservative coalition**. During the 1960s and 1970s that coalition came together in about one-fifth of all roll-call votes. When it did, it usually won, defeating

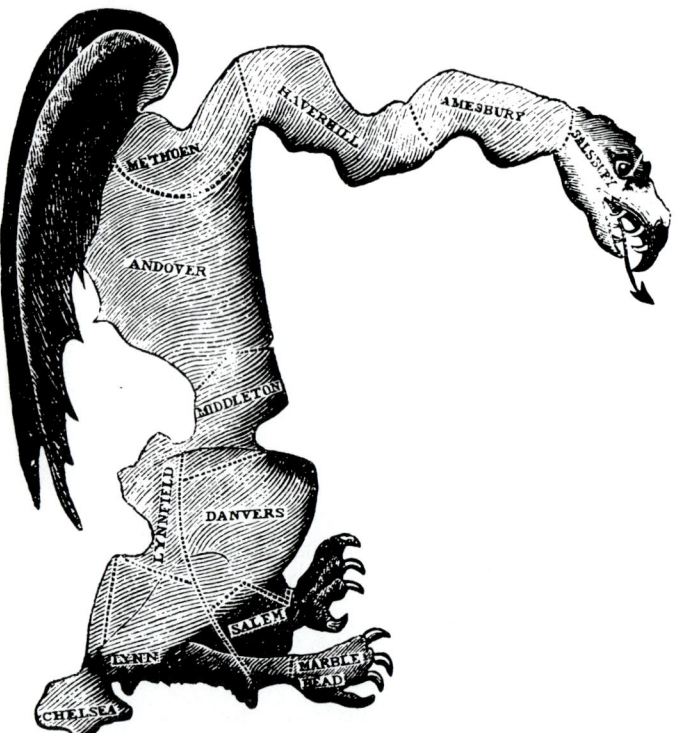

The original Gerrymander: Elbridge Gerry had this Massachusetts district drawn to ensure the election of a Republican. Cartoonist Elkanah Tinsdale in 1812 compared the district to a salamander and termed it a "Gerry-Mander."

northern Democrats. But since the 1980s, and especially since the watershed election of 1994, the conservative coalition has become much less important. The reason is simple: many southern Democrats in Congress have been replaced by southern Republicans, and the southern Democrats who remain (many of them blacks) are as liberal as northern Democrats. The effect of this change is to make Congress, and especially the House, more ideologically partisan—Democrats are liberals, Republicans are conservatives—and this in turn helps explain why there is more party unity in voting.

Getting Elected to Congress

Who serves in Congress, and what interests are represented there, is affected by the mechanisms by which its members are elected. Each state is entitled to two senators, who serve six-year terms, and at least one representative, who serves a two-year term. How many more representatives a state has depends on its population; what local groups these representatives speak for depends in part on how the district lines are drawn.

The Constitution says very little about how representatives will be selected except to require that they be inhabitants of the states from which they are chosen. It says nothing about districts and originally left it up to the states to decide who would be eligible to vote for representatives. The size of the first House was set by the Constitution at sixty-five members, and the apportionment of the seats among the states was spelled out in Article I, section 2. From that point on it has been up to Congress to decide how many representatives each state would have (provided that each had at least one).

Determining Fair Representation

Initially some states did not create congressional districts; all their representatives were elected at large. Others elected them from multimember as well as single-member districts. In time all states with more than one representative elected each from a single-member district. How those district boundaries were drawn, however, could profoundly affect the outcomes of elections. There were two problems. One was **malapportionment,** which results from having districts of very unequal sizes. If one district is twice as populous as another, twice as many votes are needed in the larger district to elect a representative. Thus a citizen's vote in the smaller district is worth twice as much as a vote in the larger.

The other problem was **gerrymandering,** which means drawing a district boundary in some bizarre or unusual shape to make it easy for the candidate of one party to win election in that district. In a state entitled to ten representatives, where half the voters are Democrats and half are Republicans, district lines could be drawn so that eight districts would have a slight majority of citizens from one party and two districts would have lopsided majorities from the other. Thus it can be made easy for one party to win eight of the ten seats.

Malapportionment and gerrymandering have been conspicuous features of American congressional politics. In 1962, for example, one district in Texas had nearly a million residents while another had less than a quarter million. In California, Democrats in control of the state legislature drew district lines in the early 1960s so that two pockets of Republican strength in Los Angeles separated by many miles were connected by a thin strip of coastline. In this way most Republican voters were thrown into one district while Democratic voters were spread more evenly over several.

Hence there are four problems to solve in deciding who gets represented in the House:

1. establishing the total size of the House

2. allocating seats in the House among the states

3. determining the size of congressional districts within states

4. determining the shape of those districts

By and large Congress has decided the first two questions, and the states have decided the last two—but under some rather strict Supreme Court rules.

In 1911 Congress decided that the House had become large enough and voted to fix its size at 435 members. There it has remained ever since (except for a brief period when it had 437 members owing to the admission of Alaska and Hawaii to the union in 1959). Once the size was decided upon, it was necessary to find a formula for performing the painful task of apportioning seats among the states as they gained and lost population. The Constitution requires such reapportionment every ten years. A more or less automatic method was selected in 1929 based on a complex statistical system that has withstood decades of political and scientific testing. Under this system many states—such as New York, Ohio, Pennsylvania, and Illinois—have lost representation in the House as other states grew more rapidly in population. The largest gainers have been California, Florida, and Texas (see Table 11.4). The average congressional district in 1990 had about 575,000 residents.

The states did little about malapportionment and gerrymandering until ordered to do so by the Supreme Court. In 1964 the Court ruled that the Constitution requires that districts be drawn so that, as nearly as possible, one person's vote would be worth as much as another's.[8] The Court rule, "one person, one vote," seems clear, but in fact leaves a host of questions unanswered. How much deviation

TABLE 11.4 Changes in State Representation in the House of Representatives after the 1990 Census

States	Before Census	After Census	Change	Party Control of State, 1991
Gaining seats				
Arizona	5	6	+1	Split
California	45	52	+7	Split
Florida	19	23	+4	Democrats
Georgia	10	11	+1	Democrats
North Carolina	11	12	+1	Democrats
Texas	27	30	+3	Democrats
Virginia	10	11	+1	Democrats
Washington	8	9	+1	Split
Losing seats				
Illinois	22	20	−2	Split
Iowa	6	5	−1	Split
Kansas	5	4	−1	Split
Kentucky	7	6	−1	Democrats
Louisiana	8	7	−1	Democrats
Massachusetts	11	10	−1	Split
Michigan	18	16	−2	Split
Montana	2	1	−1	Split
New Jersey	14	13	−1	Democrats
New York	34	31	−3	Split
Ohio	21	19	−2	Split
Pennsylvania	23	21	−2	Split
West Virginia	4	3	−1	Democrats

NOTE: "Split" means that the same party does not control the governorship, House and Senate in that state.
SOURCE: U.S. Bureau of the Census.

from equal size is allowable? Should other factors be considered besides population? (For example, a state legislature might want to draw district lines to make it easier for blacks—or Italian-Americans or farmers or some other group with a distinct interest—to elect a representative; the requirement of exactly equal districts might make this impossible.) And the gerrymandering problem remains: districts of the same size can be drawn to favor one party or another. The courts have struggled to find answers to these questions, but they remain far from settled.

DISTRICTS 1 AND 12 IN NORTH CAROLINA

1st District

12th District

SOURCE: *Congressional Quarterly* (May 22, 1993): 1323.

Majority-Minority Districts

Perhaps the most vexing legal questions concern **majority-minority districts**—congressional districts designed to make it easier for minority citizens to elect minority representatives. For many years geographically concentrated communities of blacks in the South and in many big cities throughout the country were carved up in ways that kept black politicians out of power. Even as recently as 1991, blacks constituted about 25 percent of the southern population but held barely 4 percent of the congressional seats in the South. In response, some southern states created majority-minority districts. For example, in 1991 the North Carolina General Assembly created two majority-black districts (shown on the map). One of these districts, the twelfth, was a 160-mile path no wider at some points than the interstate highway it traced.[9] The redistricting paid off. In 1992 Democratic Representatives Melvin Watt and Eva Clayton became the first blacks to represent North Carolina in Congress since 1901.[10] Similarly, New York City's X-shaped twelfth district snakes through a dozen different school districts and police precincts and is only a block wide at one point. It was designed to pool Hispanic voters in Manhattan, Queens, and Brooklyn.[11] In the 1992 Democratic primary in this district, a Hispanic challenger, Nydia M. Velasquez, defeated a Jewish incumbent, Stephen Solarz, and went on to win a House seat.

The constitutionality of majority-minority redistricting efforts has been called into question. In a 5-4 decision issued on June 28, 1993, in the case of *Shaw* v. *Reno,* the U.S. Supreme Court reinstated a suit by five white North Carolinians who maintained that the state's congressional map violated their Fourteenth Amendment right to "equal protection under the law."[12] The *Shaw* decision sent the case back to the lower courts for review, telling them that race could be a factor in drawing congressional district lines only if there was a "compelling governmental interest" in doing so. The states took a fresh look, but when the issue came back to the Supreme Court the justices were not persuaded that such a compelling interest had been established. In two 5-4 decisions the Court said that race had been used so heavily and with so little justification in drawing the lines of districts like North Carolina's twelfth that they were unlawful "racial gerrymanders."[13] Since the Court did not spell out the meaning of a "compelling governmental interest" that might justify using race as the main factor in drawing districts, we can expect that it will have to hear a lot more cases like these.

In 1993 there were twenty Hispanic-majority districts and thirty-two black-majority districts nationwide. Not all are drawn as oddly as the ones the Court rejected (in North Carolina and Texas), and so they will likely survive. In any case, blacks were elected even from districts that were redrawn to conform to Supreme Court opinions. But it seems clear that the current Court majority will want to take a hard look at any new districts that use race in a way that makes for bizarre-appearing districts.

It is important to recognize that two conceptions of representation are at odds in the debate over majority-minority districts. The political theorist Hannah F. Pitkin has distinguished between **descriptive representation,** the statistical correspondence of the demographic characteristics of representatives with those of their constituents, and **substantive representation,** the correspondence between representatives' opinions and those of their constituents.[14]

To those who favor descriptive (also sometimes referred to as categorical) representation, majority-minority districts are desirable for their own sake, and creating them is a legitimate way of ensuring that citizens of a given racial or ethnic background are represented by persons of the same background. To those who favor substantive representation, however, the key question is whether representatives work to support the interests and opinions of the voters in their districts.

One challenging question is whether the substantive interests of minority voters are adequately represented by nonminority representatives in Congress. In a sophisticated analysis, political scientist Carol M. Swain has explored this question by studying the constituency relations and roll-call votes of black members of Congress from a variety of districts (historically black, newly black, heterogeneous, and primarily white) and of white members from districts with either a black majority or a significant black minority. Among other things, she found that liberal white members of Congress represented black interests as strongly as did black representatives (their voting records on key economic and other issues of import to the black community were virtually the same) and that "creating newly black districts will not significantly increase black substantive representation."[15]

Winning the Primary

Once the district lines are set, the other major procedural arrangement that affects the election of a candidate has to do with the system for getting one's name on the ballot. At one time the political parties nominated candidates and even printed ballots with the party slates listed on them. All the voter had to do was take the ballot of the preferred party and put it in the ballot box. Today, with rare exceptions, a candidate wins a party's nomination by gathering enough voter signatures to get on the ballot in a primary election, the outcome of which is often beyond the ability of political parties to influence. Candidates tend to form organizations of personal followings and win "their party's" nomination simply by getting more primary votes than the next candidate. It is quite unusual for an incumbent to lose a primary: from 1946 to 1988 only 6 percent of incumbent senators and fewer than 2 percent of incumbent representatives seeking reelection failed to win renomination in primaries. These statistics suggest how little opportunity parties have to control or punish their congressional members.

Nor are the voters much inclined to punish their members of Congress. We have already seen that

TRIVIA

Congress

First woman in Congress	*Jeannette Rankin (Mont., 1916)*
First black in Congress	*Joseph H. Rainey (S.C., 1870)*
Longest session of Congress	*366 days (75th Congress, meeting from Jan. 3, 1940, to Jan. 3, 1941)*
Shortest length of time for states to ratify a constitutional amendment	*3 months, 7 days—26th Amendment*
Longest period of time to ratify an amendment	*203 years—27th Amendment*
Longest service in Congress by one member	*57 years, Carl Hayden of Arizona (15 years in House, 42 years in Senate), 1912–1969*
First member of the House to be elected president	*James Madison*
First member of the Senate to be elected president	*James Monroe*
The only woman to serve in the House at the same time as her son	*Frances Bolton, whose son was Oliver Bolton (served together 1953–1957, 1963–1965)*
Longest speech ever made in the Senate	*24 hours, 18 minutes, made on August 28–29, 1957, by Senator J. Strom Thurmond (D, S.C.), seeking to block a civil-rights bill*
First woman elected to the Senate for a full term who was not preceded in office by her husband	*Nancy Landon Kassebaum, elected in 1978 from Kansas*

Jeannette Rankin

Qualifications for Entering Congress and Privileges of Being in Congress

QUALIFICATIONS

Representative

- Must be twenty-five years of age (when seated, not when elected).
- Must have been a citizen of the United States for seven years.
- Must be an inhabitant of the state from which elected. (*Note:* custom, but *not* the Constitution, requires that a representative live in the district that he or she represents.)

Senator

- Must be thirty years of age (when seated, not when elected).
- Must have been a citizen of the United States for nine years.
- Must be an inhabitant of the state from which elected.

JUDGING QUALIFICATIONS

Each house is the judge of the "elections, returns, and qualifications" of its members. Thus Congress alone can decide disputed congressional elections. On occasion it has excluded a person from taking a seat on grounds that the election was improper.

Either house can punish a member—by reprimand, for example—or, by a two-thirds vote, expel a member.

PRIVILEGES

Members of Congress have certain privileges, the most important of which, conferred by the Constitution, is that "for any speech or debate in either house they shall not be questioned in any other place." This doctrine of "privileged speech" has been interpreted by the Supreme Court to mean that members of Congress cannot be sued or prosecuted for anything that they say or write in connection with their legislative duties.

When Senator Mike Gravel read the Pentagon Papers—some then-secret government documents about the Vietnam War—into the *Congressional Record* in defiance of a court order restraining their publication, the Court held that this was "privileged speech" and beyond challenge [*Gravel* v. *United States,* 408 U.S. 606 (1972)]. But when Senator William Proxmire issued a press release critical of a scientist doing research on monkeys, the Court decided that the scientist could sue him for libel because a press release was not part of the legislative process [*Hutchinson* v. *Proxmire,* 443, U.S. 111 (1979)].

typically over 90 percent of incumbent House members are reelected. Most newly elected members become strong in their districts very quickly; this is called the **sophomore surge.** It is the difference between the votes candidates get the first time they are elected (and thus become freshman members) and the votes they get when they run for reelection (in hopes of becoming sophomore members). Before the 1960s House candidates did not do much better the second time they ran than the first. Beginning then, however, the sophomore surge kicked in, so that today freshman candidates running for reelection will get 8 percent to 10 percent more votes than when they were first elected. Senate candidates also benefit now from a sophomore surge, though to a lesser degree.

The reason for this surge is that members of Congress have figured out how to use their offices to run *personal* rather than party campaigns. They make use of free ("franked") mail, frequent trips home, radio and television broadcasts, and the distribution of services to their districts to develop among their constituents a good opinion of *themselves,* not their party. They also cater to their constituents' distrust of the federal government by promising to "clean things up" if reelected. They run *for* Congress by running *against* it.[16]

To the extent that they succeed, they enjoy great freedom in voting on particular issues and have less need to explain away votes that their constituents might not like. If, however, any single-issue groups are actively working in their districts for or against abortion, gun control, nuclear energy, or tax cuts, muting the candidates' voting record may not be possible.

The way people get elected to Congress has two important effects. First, it produces legislators who are closely tied to local concerns (their districts, their states), and second, it ensures that party leaders will have relatively weak influence over them (because those leaders cannot determine who gets nominated for office).

The local orientation of legislators has some important effects on how policy is made. For example:

- Every member of Congress organizes his or her office to do as much as possible for people back home.
- If your representative serves on the House Transportation and Infrastructure Committee, your state has a much better chance of getting a new bridge or canal than if you do not have a representative on this committee.[17]
- If your representative serves on the House Appropriations Committee, your district is more likely to get approval for a federal grant to improve your water and sewage-treatment programs than if your representative does not serve on that committee.[18]

Former House Speaker Thomas P. "Tip" O'Neill had this in mind when he said, "All politics is local." Some people think that this localism is wrong; in their view members of Congress should do what is best for "the nation as a whole." This argument is about the role of legislators: are they supposed to be *delegates* who do what their district wants or *trustees* who use their best judgment on issues without regard to the preferences of their district?

Naturally most members are some combination of delegate and trustee, with the exact mix depending on the nature of the issue. But some, as we shall see, definitely lean one way or the other. All members want to be reelected, but "delegates" tend to value this over every other consideration and so seek out committee assignments and projects that will produce benefits for their districts. On the other hand, "trustees" will seek out committee assignments that give them a chance to address large questions, such as foreign affairs, that may have no implications at all for their districts.

The Organization of Congress: Parties and Caucuses

Congress is not a single organization; it is a vast and complex collection of organizations by which the business of the legislative branch is carried on and through which its members form alliances. If we were to look inside the British House of Commons, we would find only one kind of organization of any importance—the political party. Though party organization is important in the United States Congress, it is only one of many important elements. In fact, other organizations have grown in number as the influence of the parties has declined.

The Democrats and Republicans in the House and the Senate are organized by party leaders. The key leaders in turn are elected by the full party membership within the House and Senate. The description that follows is confined to the essential positions.

Party Organization of the Senate

The majority party (in 1997, the Republicans) chooses one of its members—usually the person with the greatest seniority—to be president pro tempore of the Senate. It is largely an honorific position, required by the Constitution so that the Senate will have a presiding officer in the absence of the vice president of the United States (who is also, according to the Constitution, the president of the Senate). In fact presiding over the Senate is a tedious chore that neither the vice president nor the president pro tem relishes, and so the actual task of presiding is usually assigned to some junior senator.

The real leadership is in the hands of the **majority leader** (chosen by the senators of the majority party) and the **minority leader** (chosen by the senators of the other party). In addition, the senators of each party elect a whip. The principal task of the majority leader is to schedule the business of the Senate, usually in consultation with the minority leader. The majority leader has the right to be recognized first in any floor debate. A majority leader with a strong personality who is skilled at political bargaining may do much more. Lyndon Johnson, who was Senate majority leader for the Democrats

Politically SPEAKING

Whip

A whip is a party leader who makes certain that party members are present for a vote and vote the way the party wishes. In the British House of Commons, the whips produce strong party votes; in the U.S. Congress, whips are a lot less successful.

The word comes from *whipper-in,* a term from fox hunting denoting the person whose job it was to keep the hounds from straying off the trail. It became a political term in England in the eighteenth century, and from there came to the United States.

SOURCE: From *Safire's Political Dictionary* by William Safire. Copyright © 1968, 1972, 1978 by William Safire. Reprinted by permission of Random House, Inc. and the author.

during much of the 1950s, used his prodigious ability to serve the needs of fellow senators. He helped them with everything from obtaining extra office space to getting choice committee assignments, and in this way he acquired substantial influence over the substance as well as the schedule of Senate business. Johnson's successor, Mike Mansfield, was a less assertive majority leader and had less influence.

The **whip** is a senator who helps the party leader stay informed about what party members are thinking, rounds up members when important votes are to be taken, and attempts to keep a nose count on how the voting on a controversial issue is likely to go. The whip has several senators who assist him or her in this task.

Each party in the Senate also chooses a Policy Committee composed of a dozen or so senators who help the party leader schedule Senate business, choosing what bills are to be given major attention and in what order.

From the point of view of individual senators, however, the key party organization is the group that assigns senators to the standing committees of the Senate. The Democrats have a Steering Committee that does this; the Republicans have a Committee on Committees. These assignments are especially important for newly elected senators: their political careers, their opportunities for favorable publicity, and their chances for helping their states and their supporters depend in great part on the committees to which they are assigned. For example, when Daniel Patrick Moynihan was elected to the Senate from New York in 1976, he waged an intensive and successful effort to get appointed to the Finance Committee. That body handles bills providing aid to cities and welfare recipients—two concerns of great importance to the big urban areas in Moynihan's state. When Lloyd Bentsen of Texas left the Senate to become the Clinton administration's secretary of the treasury, Moynihan succeeded him as chairman of the Finance Committee. During the 1960s many new senators fought to get on the Foreign Relations Committee because of the controversy surrounding the war in Vietnam and the highly visible role of members of that committee in criticizing or defending American policy.

The key—and delicate—aspect of selecting party leaders, of making up the important party committees, and of assigning freshman senators to Senate committees is achieving ideological and regional balance. Liberals and conservatives in each party will fight over the choice of majority and minority leader, but factors in addition to ideology play a part in the choice. These include personal popularity, the ability of the leader to make an effective television appearance, and who owes whom what favors.

Party Structure in the House

Though the titles of various posts are different, the party structure is essentially the same in the House as in the Senate. But leadership carries more power in the House than in the Senate because of the House rules. Being so large (435 members), the

Newt Gingrich (R., Georgia) is not only Speaker of the House but also head of his party in that chamber.

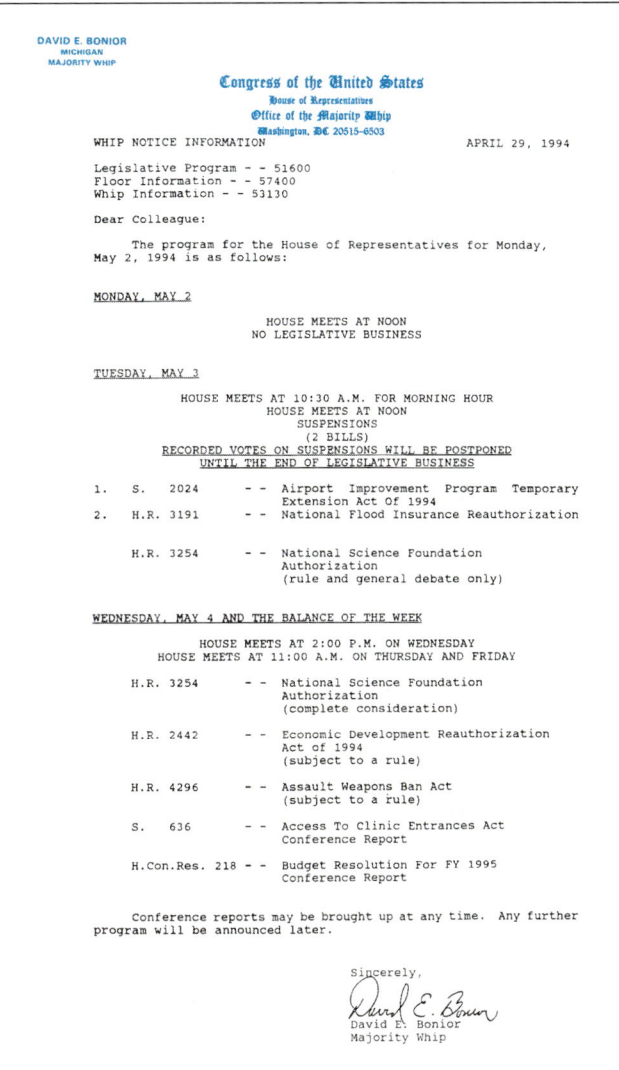

This Whip Notice was issued by David Bonior (D., Mich.), majority whip of the 103rd Congress, to inform party members and round up votes.

House must restrict debate and schedule its business with great care; thus leaders who do the scheduling and who determine how the rules shall be applied usually have substantial influence.

The Speaker is the most important person in the House. He is elected by whichever party has a majority, and he presides over all House meetings. Unlike the president pro tem of the Senate, however, his position is anything but honorific. He is the principal leader of the majority party as well as the presiding officer of the entire House. Though Speakers-as-presiders are expected to be fair, Speakers-as-party-leaders are expected to use their powers to help pass legislation favored by their party.

In helping his party, the Speaker has some important formal powers at his disposal: he decides who shall be recognized to speak on the floor of the House; he rules whether a motion is relevant and germane to the business at hand; and he decides (subject to certain rules) the committees to which new bills shall be assigned. He influences what bills are brought up for a vote and appoints the members of special and select committees (to be explained on pages 330–331). Since 1975 the Speaker has been able to nominate the majority-party members of the Rules Committee. He also has some informal powers: he controls some patronage jobs in the Capitol building and the assignment of extra office space. Even though he is far less powerful than in the days of Clay, Reed, and Cannon, the Speaker is still an important person to have on one's side. Sam Rayburn of Texas exercised great influence as

Party Leadership Structure

SENATE

President Pro Tempore Selected by majority party

Democrats

Majority Leader Leads the party

Majority Whip Assists the leader, rounds up votes, heads group of deputy whips

Chairman of the Conference Presides over meetings of all Senate Democrats

Policy Committee Schedules legislation

Steering Committee Assigns Democratic senators to committees

Democratic Senatorial Campaign Committee Provides funds, assistance to Democratic candidates for the Senate

Republicans

Minority Leader Leads the party

Assistant Minority Leader Assists the leader, rounds up votes

Chairman of the Conference Presides over meetings of all Senate Republicans

Policy Committee Makes recommendations on party policy

Committee on Committees Assigns Republican senators to committees

Republican Senatorial Committee Provides funds, advice to Republican candidates for the Senate

HOUSE

Speaker of the House Selected by majority party

Democrats

Majority Leader Leads the party

Majority Whip Assists the leader, rounds up votes, heads group of deputy and assistant whips

Chairman of the Caucus Presides over meetings of all House Democrats

Steering and Policy Committee Schedules legislation, assigns Democratic representatives to committees

Democratic Congressional Campaign Committee Provides funds, advice to Democratic candidates for the House

Republicans

Minority Leader Leads the party

Minority Whip Assists the leader, rounds up votes, heads large group of deputy and assistant whips

Chairman of the Conference Presides over meetings of all House Republicans

Committee on Committees Assigns Republican representatives to committees

Policy Committee Advises on party policy

National Republican Congressional Committee Provides funds, advice to Republican candidates for the House

Research Committee On request, provides information about issues

---

Speaker, and Tip O'Neill, Jim Wright, Tom Foley, and Newt Gingrich have tried to do the same.

In the House, as in the Senate, the majority party elects a floor leader, called the majority leader. The other party also chooses a leader—the minority leader. Traditionally the majority leader becomes Speaker when the person in that position dies or retires—provided, of course, that the departing Speaker's party is still in the majority. Each party also has a whip, with several assistant whips in charge of rounding up votes from various state delegations. Committee assignments are made and the scheduling of legislation is discussed, by the Democrats, in a Steering and Policy Committee, chaired by the Speaker. The Republicans have divided committee assignments and policy discussions, with the former task assigned to a Committee on Committees and the latter to a Policy Committee. Each party also has a congressional campaign committee to provide funds and other assistance to party members running for election or reelection to the House.

The Strength of Party Structures

One important measure of the strength of the parties in Congress is the ability of party leaders to get their members to vote together on the rules and structure of Congress. When Newt Gingrich became Speaker of the Republican-controlled House in 1995, he proposed sweeping changes in House rules, many not popular with some Republican members. For example, he wanted no one to serve as a committee chairman for more than six years, for three committees to be abolished, and for other committees to lose either functions or members. He also

wanted to pass over some senior members in picking committee chairmen. Though these moves adversely affected some Republican representatives, they all voted in favor of the new rules.[19] Of course, Gingrich would have not made these proposals unless he was certain he could get them adopted. But it was a measure of his influence and of his support among newly elected Republicans that even major changes in congressional procedures would get unanimous party support.[20] Getting support on proposed legislation is a harder task.

The Senate, however, is another matter. As Barbara Sinclair has argued, in the last few decades

THE UNITED STATES CONGRESS

HOUSE OF REPRESENTATIVES
1. House Minority Whip
2. Lobby
3. House chamber
4. Cloakrooms
5. Speaker of the House
6. Ways and Means Committee
7. House Minority Leader

SENATE
8. Senate Minority Leader
9. Office of the Secretary
10. Senate chamber
11. Cloakrooms
12. Senate Majority Leader
13. Vice President

The House and Senate meet at opposite ends of the Capitol building. When there is a joint session of Congress—for example, to hear the president's State of the Union address—the senators sit with the representatives in the House chamber. Though the most important work of Congress goes on in committee meetings, which are held in office buildings behind the Capitol, some important political negotiations occur in the offices surrounding the chambers—especially in the cloakrooms (actually, lounges) and the offices of the majority and minority leaders, the Speaker and the vice president, and the secretary of the Senate.

| TABLE 11.5 | Party Unity Votes in Congress, 1953–1994 (percentage of all votes) |

Year	House	Senate	Year	House	Senate
1953	52	n.a.	1974	29	44
1954	38	47	1975	48	48
1955	41	30	1976	36	37
1956	44	53	1977	42	42
1957	59	36	1978	33	45
1958	40	44	1979	47	47
1959	55	48	1980	38	46
1960	53	37	1981	37	48
1961	50	62	1982	36	43
1962	46	41	1983	56	44
1963	49	47	1984	47	40
1964	55	36	1985	61	50
1965	52	42	1986	57	52
1966	41	50	1987	64	41
1967	36	35	1988	47	42
1968	35	32	1989	55	35
1969	31	36	1990	49	54
1970	27	35	1991	55	49
1971	38	42	1992	64	53
1972	27	36	1993	65	67
1973	42	40	1994	62	52

SOURCE: Norman J. Ornstein, Thomas E. Mann, and Michael J. Malbin, *Vital Statistics on Congress, 1995–1996* (Wash. D.C.: CQ Press, 1996), p. 208.

the Senate has been transformed by changes in norms (informal understandings governing how members ought to behave toward their colleagues), without any far-reaching changes in the written Senate rules.[21] Compared to the Senate of the 1950s and 1960s, today's Senate is less party-centered, less leader-oriented, more hospitable to freshmen (who no longer have to "pay their dues" before assuming major roles as legislators), more heavily staffed, and more subcommittee-oriented.

Party Unity

The strength of Congress's elaborate party machinery can also be measured by the extent to which members of a party vote together in the House and Senate. A **party unity vote** is defined as a vote in which a majority of voting Democrats oppose a majority of voting Republicans. In seven of the twelve years from 1953 to 1965, over half of all House votes pitted a majority of voting Democrats against a majority of voting Republicans (see Table 11.5). But in 1966 the number dropped to 41 percent, and it was not until 1983 that voting in the House once again took on a distinctively partisan cast. By the 1990s party unity voting was the norm in both the House and the Senate. A kindred measure of party strength is the cohesion of the parties on votes that elicit a party split. By this measure, between 1991 and 1994 over 80 percent of all House and Senate Democrats voted with a majority of their party on party unity votes, as did over 80 percent of House and Senate Republicans (see Table 11.6).

As these recent trends make plain, party unity in Congress is hardly a thing of the past. Specific issues can trigger an extraordinary degree of party cohesion. For example, in 1993 every single Republican in both the House and Senate voted against the Clinton budget plan, the first budget offered by a Democratic president since Jimmy Carter left office in 1980. This may be an extreme example, but it reflects the increasingly adversarial relationship between Democrats and Republicans, especially in the House.

Still, it is worth remembering that even today's Congress is less divided along party lines than many of its predecessors were. During the years 1890–1910, for example, two-thirds of all votes evoked a party split, and in several sessions more than half the roll calls found 90 percent of each party's members opposing the other party.[22] Whereas the party splits of the past often reflected the routine operations of highly disciplined parties interested mainly in winning elections, dispensing patronage, and keeping power, today's party splits often reflect sharp ideological differences between the parties (or at least between their respective leaders).

The party unity of today's Congress poses something of a puzzle. Given that the parties do not tightly control legislators' ability to get elected and that members of both parties are far more interested in getting reelected than in scoring ideological points debating their colleagues across the aisle, why do the members of one party ever vote en masse against the other party? There are several reasons. First, members of Congress do not randomly decide to be Democrats or Republicans; these choices reflect some broad ideological orientation, at least for most members. Democrats vote alike in part because they are ideologically alike.

Several interest groups tabulate the votes of legislators on important issues to see who is most and least sympathetic to their positions. By combining the scores given by many such organizations—including Americans for Democratic Action (liberal), Americans for Constitutional Action (conservative), the AFL-CIO, and the Chamber of Commerce—it is possible to rank each member of Congress from most to least liberal in three policy areas: economic

TABLE 11.6　**Party Unity Scores in Congressional Voting, 1954–1994 (percent)**

Year	House		Senate	
	Dem	Rep	Dem	Rep
1954	80	84	77	89
1955	84	78	82	82
1956	80	78	80	80
1957	79	75	79	81
1958	77	73	82	74
1959	85	85	76	80
1960	75	77	73	74
1961	n.a	n.a.	n.a.	n.a.
1962	81	80	80	81
1963	85	84	79	79
1964	82	81	73	75
1965	80	81	75	78
1966	78	82	73	78
1967	77	82	75	73
1968	73	76	71	74
1969	71	71	74	72
1970	71	72	71	71
1971	72	76	74	75
1972	70	76	72	73
1973	75	74	79	74
1974	72	71	72	68
1975	75	78	76	71
1976	75	75	74	72
1977	74	77	72	75
1978	71	77	75	66
1979	75	79	76	73
1980	78	79	76	74
1981	75	80	77	85
1982	77	76	76	80
1983	82	80	76	79
1984	81	77	75	83
1985	86	80	79	81
1986	86	76	74	80
1987	88	79	85	78
1988	88	80	85	74
1989	86	76	79	79
1990	86	78	82	77
1991	86	81	83	83
1992	86	84	82	83
1993	88	87	87	86
1994	88	87	86	81

SOURCE: Norman J. Ornstein, Thomas E. Mann, and Michael J. Malbin, *Vital Statistics on Congress, 1995–1996* (Washington, D.C.: CQ Press, 1996), pp. 209–210.

Politically SPEAKING

Caucus

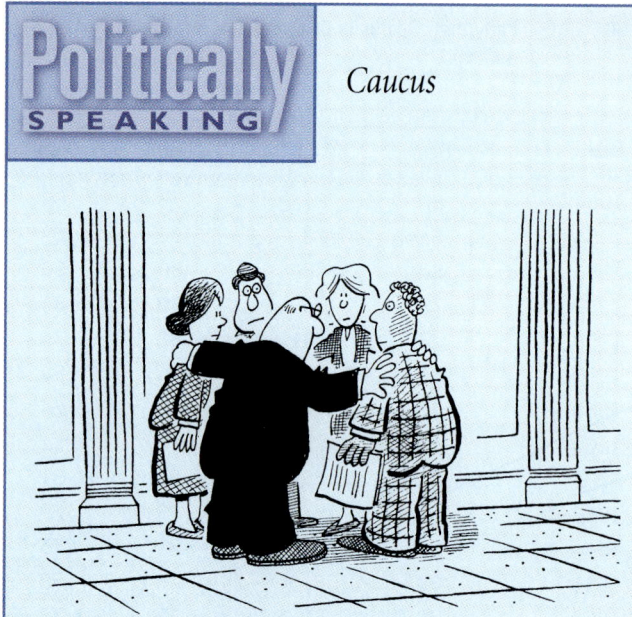

A *caucus* is a closed meeting of the members of a political party, either to select a candidate for office or to agree on a legislative position.

The term is from an American Indian word meaning "elder" or "counselor." It quickly entered political usage in the United States, there being a Caucus Club in Boston as early as 1763.

The first national political caucuses were in Congress, where legislators would gather to select their party's candidate for president. Persons who did not get a caucus endorsement soon began denouncing the entire procedure, referring contemptuously to the "decrees of King Caucus." Popular resentment led in the 1830s to the creation of the nominating convention as a way of choosing presidential candidates.

Today congressional caucuses are organizations of legislators from a single party (Democrats or Republicans), with a common background (for example, women, blacks, Hispanics), sharing a particular ideology (liberals or conservatives), or having an interest in a single issue (such as mushrooms, steel mills, or the environment).

SOURCE: From *Safire's Political Dictionary* by William Safire. Copyright © 1968, 1972, 1978 by William Safire. Reprinted by permission of Random House, Inc. and the author.

ideological differences between the parties that, even allowing for the existence of conservative southern Democrats, the average southern Democrat in the House is more liberal than the average northern Republican.

In addition to their personal views, members of Congress have other reasons for supporting their party's position at least some of the time. On many matters that come to a vote, members have little information and no opinion. They have no chance of becoming personally familiar with more than a small fraction of the hundreds of items with which Congress deals each session. They must get advice on how to vote, and it is only natural that Democrats look to Democratic leaders and fellow partisans for that advice, and Republicans look to Republicans.

Furthermore, supporting the party position can work to the long-term advantage of a member interested in rising in status and influence in Congress. As a number of recent studies have shown, though party leaders are weaker today than in the past, they are hardly powerless.[23] If you are a member of Congress who wants to get a committee assignment, obtain a favorable hearing for a bill, become chairman of an important subcommittee, or be taken seriously by other members in the party caucus, it pays not to insult, ignore, or challenge party leaders. Sam Rayburn, who served as Speaker for seventeen years (in the 1940s and 1950s), reputedly told freshman members of Congress that "if you want to get along, go along." That is less true today, but it's still good advice.

In short, party *does* make a difference in Congress—not as much as it once did, and not nearly as much as it does in a parliamentary system, but party affiliation is still the most important thing to know about a member of Congress. Knowing whether a member is a Democrat or a Republican will not tell you everything about the member, but it will tell you more than any other single fact.

Caucuses

Congressional caucuses are a growing rival to the parties as a source of policy leadership. A **caucus** is an association of members of Congress created to advocate a political ideology or a regional or economic interest. In 1959 there were only four cau-

affairs (taxes, job programs, and so forth), social questions (abortion, civil rights, school prayer), and foreign affairs (defense spending, support for military intervention). Democrats in the House and Senate have been much more liberal than Republicans in most recent years. So pronounced are the cuses; by the late 1980s, over one hundred.

As Congress expert Susan Webb Hammond has observed, "The pace of caucus formation accelerated rapidly during the 1970s as members, operating with increased and more equitably distributed resources within a decentralized institution, sought to respond to increased external demands. . . . Members derive benefits—gaining information, being identified as a 'leader,' symbolically showing that they care about an issue of importance to constituents—from caucus activities."[24] In January 1995, at the beginning of the Republican-led 104th Congress, it was widely reported that the House of Representatives would "abolish" congressional caucuses. Yet as of January 1996 there were 129 congressional caucuses—111 from the 103rd Congress and 18 new ones established by the 104th. What the Republicans did do was to adopt a rule making operation of caucuses more difficult. All aides working on caucus matters must be housed in members' offices. Therefore, aides are often scattered among several offices and coordination becomes more difficult. Some caucuses responded by spinning off informational functions to new outside groups. Clearly, the death of the caucuses was greatly exaggerated.

The caucuses are alive, well, and changing. Hammond has identified six types, four of which are constituency-based (see Table 11.7, page 328). Intraparty caucuses are formed by groups whose members share a similar ideology; for example, the Democratic Study Group was established by liberal Democrats. Personal-interest caucuses form around a common interest in an issue—for example, the environment, the arts, or human rights. Constituency caucuses are established to represent certain groups (blacks, women, Vietnam-era veterans), regions (New England, the western states), or both (in states or congressional districts with diffuse constituents, such as different ethnic populations or family and corporate farms).

One long-established national constituency caucus is the Congressional Black Caucus (CBC). Founded in 1970, its membership increased from nine members that year to forty in the 104th Congress. Most CBC members have been liberal House Democrats, but in recent Congresses the CBC has become both bicameral (with the election of Senator Carol Mosley Braun of Illinois) and bipartisan (with the election of Republican Gary Franks of Connecticut and Delegate Victor Frazer of the Virgin Islands, in 1992 and 1994). J. C. Watts, a black Republican from Oklahoma, was elected in 1994 but refused to join the CBC. In the Democratic-controlled 103rd Congress, CBC members chaired three standing committees and eighteen subcommittees. The CBC was influential on crime prevention, gun control, and economic issues, including empowerment zones. The votes of the thirty-eight members of

Speaking is Maxine Waters (D., Calif.), the chairwoman of the Congressional Black Caucus in 1997.

Standing Committees of the Senate

Major committees

No senator is supposed to serve on more than two.*

Agriculture, Nutrition, and Forestry
Appropriations
Armed Services
Banking, Housing, and Urban Affairs
Budget
Commerce, Science, and Transportation
Energy and Natural Resources
Environment and Public Works
Finance
Foreign Relations
Governmental Affairs
Judiciary
Labor and Human Resources

Minor committees

No senator is supposed to serve on more than one.*

Indian Affairs
Rules and Administration
Small Business
Veterans' Affairs

Select committees

Aging
Ethics
Intelligence

TABLE 11.7   Congressional Caucuses, by Type

Type	Typical Examples
Intra-Party	The Coalition
	The Conservative Opportunity Society
	Democratic Study Group
	Tuesday Lunch Bunch
	Wednesday Groups
	Class Clubs
Personal Interest	Arts Caucuses
	Constitutional Caucus
	Constitutional Forum
	Congressional Family Caucus
	Senate Children's Caucus
	Human Rights Caucuses
	Military Reform Caucus
	Population and Development Coalition
Constituency Concerns, National	Congressional Black Caucus
	Congressional Hispanic Caucus
	Congressional Caucus for Women's Issues
	Vietnam Veterans Caucus
Constituency Concerns, Regional	Congressional Border Caucus
	Northeast-Midwest Congressional Coalition
	Congressional Sunbelt Council
	Tennessee Valley Authority Caucus
	Western Caucus
	Western States Senate Coalition
Constituency Concerns, State/District	Congressional Caucus on American Issues
	Export Caucus
	Task Force on Industrial Innovation & Productivity
	Irish Caucuses
	Rural Caucus
	Suburban Caucus
Constituency Concerns, Industry	Automotive Caucus
	Boating Caucus
	Depot Caucus
	Steel Caucuses
	Textile Caucus
	Travel and Tourism Caucus

SOURCE: *Congress Reconsidered* by Lawrence Dodd and Bruce Oppenheimer, eds. (Washington, D.C.: Congressional Quarterly Inc., 1997), table 12-1 by Susan Hammond. Reprinted by permission of the author and the publisher.

the CBC in 1993 were crucial to House passage of President Clinton's budget bill.

But in the Republican-controlled 104th Congress, CBC committee leaders became ranking minority members, and some caucus Democrats lost their seats on major House committees—Appropriations, Ways and Means, and Rules. Moreover, the CBC grew less unified as liberal Democratic members from northern districts were forced to share power with more centrist members representing southern rural and suburban districts. The CBC suffered other blows, too. One of the group's stars, Representative Kwiese Mfume, resigned from the House to head the NAACP, and two other CBC members resigned from Congress. As the Republican-led 105th Congress convened, the CBC was in a defensive posture, limited to affecting policy mainly by opposing funding cuts from programs critical to caucus members' national constituency and modifying legislative proposals that its members opposed.

In contrast, other caucuses (and not only Republican ones), have fared better in recent years. For example, an intraparty caucus of "Blue Dog Democrats" known as the Coalition was born in February 1995. The Coalition's two dozen moderate-to-conservative members favor "middle-of-the-road" policies, especially on welfare and budget issues. For example, in 1995 the Coalition introduced its own welfare and budget bills, and although neither proposal was enacted, certain provisions of each strongly influenced final House deliberations. As Hammond has concluded, although the political fortunes of the CBC, the Coalition, and other caucuses may change from year to year, caucuses will continue and thrive as congressional institutions "because they help members to achieve personal goals of policy, representation, or power."[25]

The Organization of Congress: Committees

The most important organizational feature of Congress is the set of legislative committees of the House and Senate. It is there that the real work of Congress is done, and it is in the chairmanships of

Standing Committees of the House

Exclusive committees
(members may not serve on any other committee, except Budget)

Appropriations
Rules
Ways and Means

Major committees
(members may serve on only one major committee)

Agriculture
Banking and Financial Services
Commerce
Economic Opportunity
International Relations
Judiciary
National Security
Transportation and Infrastructure

Nonmajor committees
(members may serve on one major and one nonmajor committee, or on two nonmajor committees)

Budget
Government Reform and Oversight
Public Lands and Resources
Technology and Competitiveness
Small Business
Standards of Official Conduct
Veterans' Affairs

Select committee

Intelligence

NOTE: In 1995 the House Republican majority abolished three committees—District of Columbia, Post Office and Civil Service, and Merchant Marine and Fisheries—and gave their duties to other standing committees.

these committees and their subcommittees that most of the power in Congress is found. The number and jurisdiction of these committees are of the greatest interest to members of Congress, since decisions on these subjects determine what group of members, with what political views, will pass on legislative proposals, oversee the workings of agencies in the executive branch, and conduct investigations.

There are three kinds of committees: **standing committees** (more or less permanent bodies with specified legislative responsibilities), **select committees** (groups appointed for a limited purpose and usually lasting for only a few congresses), and **joint committees** (those on which both representatives and senators serve). An especially important kind of joint committee is the **conference committee,** made up of representatives and senators appointed to resolve differences in the Senate and House versions of the same piece of legislation before final passage.

From the 90th Congress (1967–1968) to the 103rd Congress (1993–1994), the total number of House and Senate committees and subcommittees (including select, special, and joint subcommittees) ranged from a high of 385 in the 94th Congress (1975–1976) to a low of 252 in the 103rd Congress. Periodically efforts have been made to cut the number of committees in order to give each a broader jurisdiction and reduce conflict between committees over a single bill. One such effort was the Legislative Reorganization Act of 1946. But as the number of committees declined, the number of subcommittees rose, leaving matters about as they once were.

The 104th Congress (1995–1996), however, proved an exception to this rule. Led by Speaker Newt Gingrich, the new Republican majority reduced the number of committees as part of its larger plan to reform House operations. Similar efforts were made in the Senate. When the dust settled on Capitol Hill, the total number of House and Senate committees had fallen from 252 in the previous Congress to 198, a smaller total even than the 242 committees of the 84th Congress (1955–1956). The House went from 22 to 19 standing committees and from 115 to 84 subcommittees of standing committees. The Senate maintained 17 committees but reduced the number of subcommittees of standing committees from 86 to 68.

Though members of the majority party could, in theory, occupy all the seats on all the committees, in

practice they take the majority of the seats on each committee, name the chairmen, and allow the minority party to have the remainder of the seats. The number of seats varies with the committee, from about six to over fifty. Usually the ratio of Democrats to Republicans on a committee roughly corresponds to their ratio in that house of Congress. In 1981 the Democrats held 56 percent of the House seats but tried to keep a two-to-one majority on key committees. After the Republicans complained, a compromise still left the Democrats overrepresented (with 66 percent of the seats on Ways and Means, 60 percent on Appropriations and Budget). A similar quarrel occurred in 1985.

Standing committees are the important ones, because, with a few exceptions, they are the only ones that can propose legislation by reporting a bill out to the full House or Senate. Each member of the House usually serves on two standing committees, unless he or she is on an "exclusive" committee—Appropriations, Rules, or Ways and Means. In such a case the representative is limited to one. Each senator may serve on two "major" committees and one "minor" committee.

When party leaders were strong, as under Speakers Reed and Cannon, committee chairmen were picked on the basis of loyalty to the leader. Now that this leadership has been weakened, seniority on the committee governs the selection of chairmen. Of late, however, even seniority has been under attack. In 1971 House Democrats decided in their caucus to elect committee chairmen by secret ballot. From then through 1991 they used that procedure to remove six committee chairmen. In 1975 three were deposed, in 1985 another, and in 1992 two more. When the Republicans took control of the House in 1995, they could have returned to the strict seniority rule, but they did not. House Speaker Gingrich passed over three senior representatives in favor of more junior ones as committee chairmen. Though most chairmen still get and hold their posts through seniority, these changes have made all chairmen worry about pleasing their rank-and-file members and the party leaders.

Traditionally the committees of Congress were dominated by the chairmen. They often did their most important work behind closed doors (though their hearings and reports were almost always published in full). In the early 1970s Congress further decentralized and democratized its operations by a series of changes that some members regarded as a "bill of rights" for representatives and senators, especially those with relatively little seniority. These changes were by and large made by the Democratic Caucus, but since the Democrats were in the majority, the changes, in effect, became the rules of Congress. The more important were as follows.

House

- Committee chairmen to be elected by secret ballot in party caucus.
- No member to chair more than one committee.
- All committees with more than twenty members to have at least four subcommittees (at the time, Ways and Means had no subcommittees).
- Committee and personal staffs to be increased in size.
- Committee meetings to be public unless members vote to close them.

Senate

- Committee meetings to be public unless members vote to close them.
- Committee chairmen to be selected by secret ballot at request of one-fifth of the party caucus.
- Committees to have larger staffs.
- No senator to chair more than one committee.

The effect of these changes, especially in the House, was to give greater power to individual members and to lessen the power of party leaders and committee chairmen. The decentralization of the House meant that it was much harder for chairmen to block legislation they did not like or to discourage junior members from playing a large role. House members were quick to take advantage of these enlarged opportunities. In the 1980s they proposed three times as many amendments to bills as they had in the 1950s.[26]

There was a cost to be paid, however, for this empowerment of the membership. The 435 members of the House could not get much done if everyone talked as much as they liked and introduced as many amendments as they wished. And with the big increase in the number of subcommittees, many subcommittee meetings were attended by (and thus controlled by) only one person, the chairman. To deal with this, the Democratic leaders began re-

How Should Committee Chairmen Be Picked?

*T*here are essentially three methods by which committee chairmen can be selected in a legislature such as Congress. Each has its advantages and disadvantages.

Seniority
Let the person with the most seniority on a committee chair it.

Advantages:

- Eliminates fights over selection.
- Makes it easier for legislators with unpopular views and for blacks and other minorities with tenure to become chairmen.

Disadvantages:

- May result in incompetent people's chairing committees.
- Chairmen will be independent of party leadership.

Election by caucus
Let the party members in the legislature elect committee chairmen.

Advantages:

- Chairmen will reflect views of party members.
- Autocratic chairmen can be replaced.

Disadvantages:

- Encourages bruising fights for chairmanships that can divide party.
- Committee chairmen not loyal to party leaders.

Appointment by party leaders
Let party leaders (Speaker, majority leader, or minority leader) choose chairmen.

Advantages:

- Increases party discipline and accountability.
- Makes it easier for party program to be enacted.

Disadvantages:

- Makes party leaders very powerful.
- Can deny chairmanships to people out of favor with leaders.

claiming some of their lost power. They made greater use of restrictive rules that sharply limited debate and the introduction of amendments. Committee chairmen began casting proxy votes. (A proxy is a written authorization to cast another person's vote.) In this way a chairman could control the results of committee deliberations by casting the proxies of absent members.

Republican House members were angered by all of this. They suspected that restrictive rules and proxy voting were designed to keep them from having any voice in House affairs. When they took control of the House in 1995, they announced some changes:

- They banned proxy voting.
- They limited committee and subcommittee chairmen's tenure to three terms (six years) and the Speaker's to four terms (eight years).
- They allowed more frequent floor debate under open rules.
- They reduced the number of committees and subcommittees.
- They authorized committee chairmen to hire subcommittee staffs.

The endless arguments about rules illustrate a fundamental problem that the House faces. Closed rules, proxy voting, powerful committee chairmen, and strong Speakers make it easier for business to get done; they put the House in a good bargaining position with the president and the Senate; and they make it easier to reduce the number of special-interest groups with legislative power. But this system also keeps individual members weak. The opposite arrangements—open rules, weak chairmen, many subcommittees, meetings open to the public—help individual members be heard and increase the amount of daylight shining on congressional processes. But if everyone is heard, no one is heard, because the noise is deafening and the speeches endless. And though open meetings and easy amending processes may be intended to open up the system to "the people," the real beneficiaries are the lobbyists.

The House Republican rules of 1995 gave back some power to chairmen (for example, by letting them pick all staff members) but further reduced it in other ways (for example, by imposing term limits

and banning proxy voting). The commitment to public meetings remained.

In the Senate there have been fewer changes, in part because individual members of the Senate have always had more power than their counterparts in the House. Two important changes made by the Republicans in 1995 were

- A six-year term limit on all committee chairmen (no limit on the majority leader's term, however)
- A requirement that committee members select their chairmen by secret ballot

Despite these new rules, the committees remain the place where the real work of Congress is done. The different types of committees tend to attract different kinds of members. Some, such as the committees that draft tax legislation (the Senate Finance Committee and the House Ways and Means Committee) or that oversee foreign affairs (the Senate Foreign Relations Committee and the House International Relations Committee) are attractive to members who want to shape public policy, become an expert on important issues, or have influence with their colleagues. Others, such as the House and Senate committees dealing with public lands, small business, and veterans' affairs, are attractive to members who want to serve particular constituents.[27]

The Organization of Congress: Staffs and Specialized Offices

In 1900 representatives had no personal staff, and senators averaged fewer than one staff member each. As recently as 1935 the typical representative had but two aides. In 1994 the average representative had seventeen assistants and the average senator forty. To the more than ten thousand individuals who served on the personal staffs of members of the 103rd Congress must be added three thousand more who worked for congressional committees and yet another three thousand employed by various congressional research agencies. Until the 1990s, Congress had the most rapidly growing bureaucracy in Washington—the personal staffs of legislators increased more than fivefold from 1947 to 1991, then leveled off and declined slightly[28] (see Figure 11.4). Though some staffers perform routine chores, many help draft legislation, handle constituents, and otherwise shape policy and politics.

Tasks of Staff Members

Staff members assigned to a senator or representative spend most of their time servicing requests from constituents—answering mail, handling problems, sending out newsletters, and meeting with voters. In short, a major function of a member of Congress's staff is to help constituents solve problems and thereby help that member get reelected. Indeed, over the last two decades a larger and larger portion of congressional staffs—now about one-third—work in the local (district or state) office of the member of Congress rather than in Washington. Almost all members of Congress have such offices on a full-time basis; about half maintain two or more offices in their constituencies. Some scholars believe that this growth in constituency-serving staff helps explain why it is so hard to defeat an incumbent representative or senator.[29]

The legislative function of congressional staff members is also important. With each senator serving on an average of more than two committees and seven subcommittees and each representative serving on an average of six committees and subcommittees, it is virtually impossible for members of Congress to become familiar in detail with all the proposals that come before them or to write all the bills that they feel ought to be introduced.[30] As the workload of Congress has grown (over six thousand bills are introduced, about six hundred public laws are passed, and uncounted hearings and meetings are held during a typical Congress), the role of staff members in devising proposals, negotiating agreements, organizing hearings, writing questions for members of Congress to ask of witnesses, drafting reports, and meeting with lobbyists and administrators has grown correspondingly.

Those who work for individual members of Congress, as opposed to committees, see themselves entirely as advocates for their bosses. As the mass media have supplanted political parties as ways of communicating with voters, the advocacy role of staff members had led them to find and promote legislation for which a representative or senator can take credit. This is the entrepreneurial function of

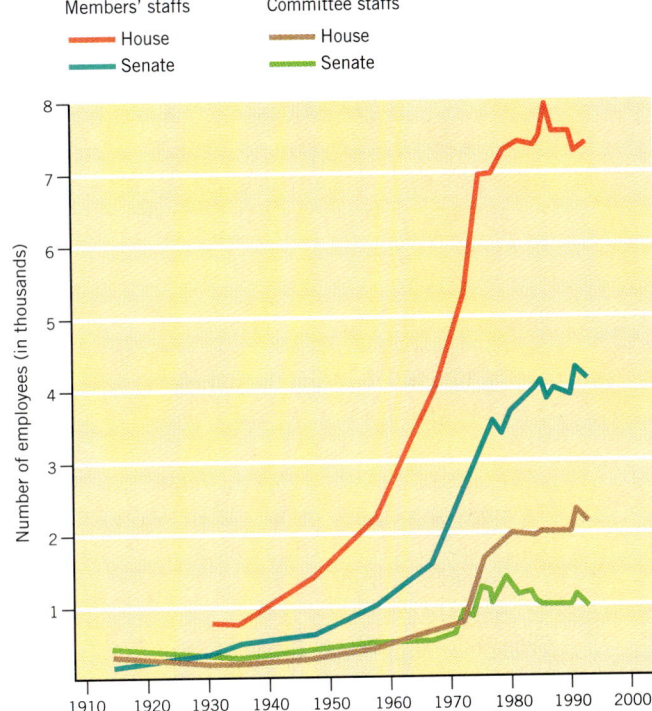

FIGURE 11.4   The Growth in Staff of Members and Committees in Congress, 1891–1993

SOURCES: Ornstein et al., *Vital Statistics on Congress* (Washington, D.C.: American Enterprise Institute, 1984 and 1996) from David C. Kozak and John D. Macartney, eds., *Congress and Public Policy,* 2d ed. (Chicago: Dorsey Press, 1987), 95; *Statistical Abstract of the United States* (1992): 264.

the staff. While it is sometimes performed under the close supervision of the member of Congress, just as often a staff member takes the initiative, finds a policy, and then "sells" it to his or her employer. Lobbyists and reporters understand this completely and therefore spend a lot of time cultivating congressional staffers, both as sources of information and as consumers of ideas.

One reason for the rapid growth in the size and importance of congressional staffs is that a large staff creates conditions that seem to require an even larger staff. As the staff grows in size, it generates more legislative work. Subcommittees proliferate to handle all the issues with which legislators are concerned. But as the workload increases, legislators complain that they cannot keep up and need more help.

The increased reliance on staff has changed Congress, not because staffers do things against the wishes of their elected masters but because the staff has altered the environment within which Congress does its work. In addition to their role as entrepreneurs promoting new policies, staffers act as negotiators. As a result, members of Congress today are more likely to deal with one another through staff intermediaries than personally. Congress has thereby become less collegial, more individualistic, and less of a deliberative body.[31]

Staff Agencies

In addition to increasing the number of staff members, Congress has also created a set of staff agencies that work for Congress as a whole. These staff agencies have come into being in large part to give Congress specialized knowledge equivalent to what the president has by virtue of his position as chief of the executive branch.

Congressional Research Service (CRS)   Formerly the Legislative Reference Service, the CRS is part of the Library of Congress. Since 1914 it has responded to congressional requests for information and now employs nearly nine hundred people, many with advanced academic training, to respond to more than a quarter of a million questions each year. As a politically neutral body, it does not recommend policy, but it will look up facts and indicate the arguments for and against a proposed policy. CRS also keeps track of the status of every major bill before Congress and produces a summary of each bill introduced. This information is instantly available to legislators via computer terminals located in almost all Senate and most House offices.

General Accounting Office (GAO)   Created in 1921, this agency once performed primarily routine financial audits of the money spent by executive-branch departments. Today it also investigates agencies and policies and makes recommendations on almost every aspect of government—defense contracting, drug enforcement policies, the domestic security investigations of the FBI, Medicare and Medicaid programs, water-pollution programs, and so forth. Though the head of the GAO—the comptroller general—is appointed by the president (with

the consent of the Senate), he or she serves for a fifteen-year term and is very much the servant of Congress rather than of the president. The GAO employs about five thousand people, many of whom are permanently assigned to work with various congressional committees. Between 1992 and 1994 the GAO's budget was cut, and in 1995 Congress made plans to downsize the agency further.

Office of Technology Assessment (OTA)   Established in 1972 to study and evaluate policies and programs with a significant use of or impact on technology, the OTA had a staff of more than one hundred. Staff members looked into such matters as a plan to build a pipeline to transport coal slurry. The agency had little impact and was abolished in 1995.

Congressional Budget Office (CBO)   Created in 1974, the CBO advises Congress on the likely economic effect of different spending programs and provides information on the cost of proposed policies. This latter task has been more useful to Congress than the more difficult job of estimating future economic trends. The CBO prepares analyses of the president's budget and economic projections that often come to conclusions different from those of the administration, thus giving members of Congress arguments to use in the budget debates.

How a Bill Becomes Law

Some bills zip through Congress; others make their way slowly and painfully. Congress, an English observer once remarked, is like a crowd, moving either sluggishly or with great speed.

Bills that have sped through on the fast track include ones to reduce drug abuse, reform Defense Department procurement procedures, end the mandatory retirement age, and help the disabled. Those that have plodded through on the slow track include ones dealing with health care, tax laws, energy conservation, and foreign trade, as well as several appropriations bills.

Why the difference? Studying the list above gives some clues. Bills to spend a lot of money move slowly, especially during times (such as the 1980s and early 1990s) when the government is running up big deficits. Bills to tax or regulate businesses move slowly because so many different interests have to be heard and accommodated. On the other hand, bills that seem to embody a clear, appealing idea ("stop drugs," "help old folks," "end scandal") gather momentum quickly, especially if the government doesn't have to spend a lot of its money (as opposed to requiring other people to spend *their* money) on the idea.

In the following account of how a bill becomes law, keep in mind the central fact that the complexity of these procedures ordinarily gives a powerful advantage to the opposition. There are many points at which action can be blocked. This does not mean

Union Calendar No. 115

105TH CONGRESS
1ST SESSION

H. R. 2169

[Report No. 105–188]

Making appropriations for the Department of Transportation and related agencies for the fiscal year ending September 30, 1998, and for other purposes.

IN THE HOUSE OF REPRESENTATIVES

JULY 16, 1997

Mr. WOLF, from the Committee on Appropriations, reported the following bill; which was committed to the Committee of the Whole House on the State of the Union and ordered to be printed

---

A BILL

Making appropriations for the Department of Transportation and related agencies for the fiscal year ending September 30, 1998, and for other purposes.

1   *Be it enacted by the Senate and House of Representa-*
2   *tives of the United States of America in Congress assembled,*
3   That the following sums are appropriated, out of any
4   money in the Treasury not otherwise appropriated, for the
5   fiscal year ending September 30, 1998, and for other pur-
6   poses, namely:

A bill (H.R. 2169) as it looks after being introduced in the House.

that nothing gets done but that, to get something done, a member of Congress must *either* assemble a majority coalition slowly and painstakingly *or* take advantage of temporary enthusiasm for some new cause that sweeps away the normal obstacles.

Introducing a Bill

Any member of Congress may introduce a bill—in the House simply by handing it to a clerk or dropping it in a box (the "hopper"), in the Senate by being recognized by the presiding officer and announcing the bill's introduction. Bills are numbered and sent to the printer: a House bill bears the prefix

H.R., a Senate bill the prefix *S.* A bill can be either a **public bill** (pertaining to public affairs generally) or a **private bill** (pertaining to a particular individual, such as a person pressing a financial claim against the government or seeking special permission to become a naturalized citizen). Private bills were once very numerous; today many such matters have been delegated to administrative agencies or the courts. If a bill is not passed by both houses and signed by the president within the life of one Congress, it is dead and must be reintroduced again during the next Congress. Pending legislation does not carry over from one Congress to the next. (A new Congress is organized every two years.)

We often hear that legislation is initiated by the president and enacted by Congress—the former proposes, the latter disposes. The reality is more complicated. Congress frequently initiates legislation; in fact, most of the consumer and environmental-protection legislation passed since 1966 began in Congress, not in the executive branch. And even laws formally proposed by the president often represent presidential versions of proposals that have incubated in Congress. This was the case, for example, with some civil rights laws and with the proposal that eventually became Medicare. Even when the president is the principal author of a bill, he usually submits it (if he is prudent) only after careful consultation with key congressional leaders. In any case, the president cannot himself introduce legislation; he must get a member of Congress to do it for him.

One study showed that of ninety major laws passed between 1880 and 1945, seventy-seven were introduced without presidential sponsorship. In shaping the final contents, congressional influence was dominant in thirty-five cases, presidential influence dominated in nineteen, and influence was mixed in the remaining thirty-six. Another study, covering the period 1940 to 1967, found that Congress was the major contributor to the contents of about half of all laws passed.[32]

In addition to bills, Congress can pass resolutions. A **simple resolution** (passed by either the House or the Senate) is used for such matters as establishing the rules under which each body will operate. A **concurrent resolution** settles housekeeping and procedural matters that affect both houses. Simple and concurrent resolutions are not signed by the president and do not have the force of law. A

The House is a collection of powerful committees, none more influential than the Ways and Means Committee.

joint resolution requires the approval of both houses and the signature of the president; it is essentially the same as a law. A joint resolution is also used to propose a constitutional amendment; in this case it must be approved by a two-thirds vote of each house, but it does not require the signature of the president.

Study by Committees

A bill is referred to a committee for consideration by either the Speaker of the House or the presiding officer of the Senate. Rules govern which committee will get which bill, but sometimes a choice is possible; in the House the right of the Speaker to make such choices is an important component of his power. (His decisions can be appealed to the full House.) In 1963 a civil rights bill was referred by the presiding officer of the Senate to the Commerce Committee in order to keep it out of the hands of the chairman of the Judiciary Committee, who was hostile to the bill. In the House the same piece of legislation was referred by the Speaker to the Judiciary Committee in order to keep it out of the grasp of the hostile chairman of the Interstate and Foreign Commerce Committee.

The Constitution requires that "all bills for raising revenue shall originate in the House of Repre-

sentatives." The Senate can and does amend such bills, but only after the House has first acted. Bills that are not for raising revenue—that is, bills that do not change the tax laws—can originate in either house. In practice the House also originates appropriations bills—that is, bills directing how money shall be spent. Because of the House's special position on revenue legislation, the committee that handles those bills—the Ways and Means Committee—is particularly powerful.

Most bills die in committee. They are often introduced only to get publicity for the member of Congress or to enable the member to say to constituents or pressure groups that he or she "did something" on a matter concerning them. Bills of general interest—many of which will have been drafted in the executive branch even though introduced by a member of Congress—are assigned to a subcommittee for a hearing, where witnesses appear, evidence is taken, and questions are asked. These hearings are used to inform members of Congress, to permit interest groups to speak out (whether or not they have anything helpful to say), and to build public support for a measure favored by the majority on the committee.

Though committee hearings are necessary and valuable, they also fragment the process of considering bills dealing with complex matters. Both power and information are dispersed in Congress, and thus

Congressional Calendars

HOUSE

Union Calendar Bills to raise revenue or spend money
　　Example: an appropriations bill
House Calendar Nonmoney bills of major importance
　　Example: a civil-rights bill
Private Calendar Private bills
　　Example: a bill to waive the immigration laws so that a
　　Philadelphia woman could be joined by her Italian husband
Consent Calendar Noncontroversial bills
　　Example: a resolution creating National Stenographers' Week
Discharge Calendar Discharge petitions

SENATE

Executive Calendar Presidential nominations, proposed treaties
Calendar of Business All legislation

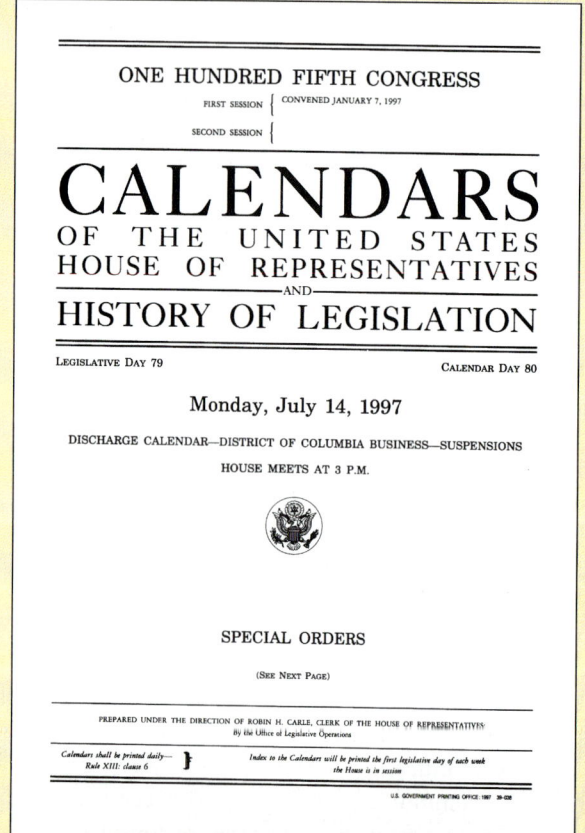

it is difficult to take a comprehensive view of matters cutting across committee boundaries.

To deal with this problem, Congress has established a process whereby a bill may now be referred to several committees that simultaneously consider it in whole or in part. This process, called **multiple referral,** was used in 1977 to send President Carter's energy proposals to six different committees in both the House and Senate. An even bigger multiple referral was used for the 1988 trade bill, which was considered by fourteen committees in the House and nine in the Senate. The advantage of this procedure is that all views have a chance to be heard; the disadvantage is that it takes a lot of time and gives opponents a greater chance to kill or modify the bill. And if the different committees disagree about the bill, their members have to come together in a gargantuan joint meeting to iron out their differences. In these cases the advantages of the committee system—providing expert knowledge and careful deliberation—are often lost. Before the practice was abolished in 1995, about a quarter of all House bills and resolutions went through multiple referrals. Under the new rules, the Speaker is allowed to send a bill to a second committee after the first is finished acting, or he may refer parts of a bill to separate committees. This process, called **sequential referral,** did not noticeably slow down the pace of legislative activity in the 104th Congress.

After the hearings the committee or subcommittee will "mark up" the bill—that is, make revisions and additions, some of which are extensive. These changes do not become part of the bill unless they are approved by the house of which the committee is a part. If a majority of the committee votes to report a bill out to the House or Senate, it goes forward. It is accompanied by a report that explains why the committee favors the bill and why it wishes to see its amendments, if any, adopted. Committee members who oppose the bill have an opportunity to include their dissenting opinions in the report.

If the committee does not report the bill out favorably, that ordinarily kills it. There is a procedure whereby the full House or Senate can get a bill that is stalled in committee out and onto the floor, but it is rarely used. In the House a **discharge petition** must be signed by 218 members; if the petition is approved by a vote of the House, the bill comes before it directly. In the Senate a member can move to

TABLE 11.8   **Frequency of Open, Restrictive, and Closed Rules**

			Congress			
Type of Rule	94th ('75–'76)	95th ('77–'78)	96th ('79–'80)	97th ('81–'82)	98th ('83–'84)	99th ('85–'86)
All measures						
Open	84.3%	83.9%	68.9%	71.2%	64.0%	55.4%
Restrictive	11.3	12.4	20.0	22.1	22.4	33.7
Closed	4.4	3.8	11.1	6.7	13.6	10.9
Number	248	186	180	104	125	101
Key vote measures						
Open	63.3%	70.6%	52.0%	23.5%	31.8%	13.6%
Restrictive	31.8	23.5	40.0	64.7	63.6	72.7
Closed	4.5	5.9	8.0	11.8	4.5	13.6
Number	22	17	25	17	22	22

SOURCES: Stanley Boch and Steven S. Smith, *Managing Uncertainty in the House of Representatives* (Washington, D.C.: Brookings Institution, 1988), 57. Reprinted with permission of the Brookings Institution. Richard E. Cohen, "Challenging the House's Traffic Cop," *The National Journal* (April 4, 1993): 1002.

discharge a committee of any bill, and if the motion passes, the bill comes before the Senate. During this century there have been over eight hundred efforts in the House to use discharge petitions; only two dozen have succeeded. Discharge is rarely tried in the Senate, in part because Senate rules permit almost any proposal to get to the floor as an amendment to another bill.

For a bill to come before either house, it must first be placed on a calendar. There are five such calendars in the House and two in the Senate (see the box opposite).

Though the bill goes onto a calendar, it is not necessarily considered in chronological order or even considered at all. In the House the Rules Committee reviews most bills and adopts a rule that governs the procedures under which they will be considered by the House. A **closed rule** sets a strict time limit on debate and forbids the introduction of any amendments from the floor, or forbids amendments except those offered by the sponsoring committee. Obviously such a rule can make it very difficult for opponents to do anything but vote yes or no on the measure. An **open rule** permits amendments from the floor. A **restrictive rule** permits some amendments but not others.

In the early 1970s most bills were debated under open rules. In the 1980s the Rules Committee—which is controlled by the Speaker—increasingly introduced bills for consideration under closed or restrictive rules in an effort to reduce the number of amendments from the floor (and, the Republicans claimed, to reduce Republican influence). By the end of the 1980s roughly half of all bills, and nearly three-fourths of all important ones, were debated under restrictive or closed rules (see Table 11.8). In 1992 only one-third of all bills were considered under an open rule.[33] In 1995 the Republicans allowed more debate under open rules.

The House has at least three ways of bypassing the Rules Committee: (1) a member can move that the rules be suspended, which requires a two-thirds vote; (2) a discharge petition, as explained above, can be filed; or (3) the House can use the "Calendar Wednesday" procedure.* These methods are not

---

* On Wednesdays the list of committees of the House is called more or less in alphabetical order, and any committee can bring up for action a bill of its own already on a calendar. Action on a bill brought to the floor on Calendar Wednesday must be completed that day, or the bill goes back to committee. Since major bills rarely can be voted on in one day, this procedure is not often used.

Riders and Christmas Trees

A **rider** is a provision added to a piece of legislation that is not germane to the bill's purpose. The goal is usually to achieve one of two outcomes: either to get the president (or governor) to sign an otherwise objectionable bill by attaching to it, as an amendment, a provision that the chief executive desperately wants to see enacted, or to get the president to veto a bill that he would otherwise sign by attaching to it, as an amendment, a provision that the chief executive strongly dislikes.

A rider is a convenient way for a legislator to get a pet project approved that might not be approved if it had to be voted on by itself. The term can be traced back to seventeenth-century England.

When a bill has lots of riders, it becomes a **Christmas-tree bill.** In 1966, for example, the Foreign Investors Act, a bill designed to solve the balance-of-payments problem, had added to it riders giving assistance to hearse owners, the mineral ore business, importers of scotch whiskey, and presidential candidates.

SOURCE: From *Safire's Political Dictionary* by William Safire. Copyright © 1968, 1972, 1978 by William Safire. Reprinted by permission of Random House, Inc. and the author.

used very often, but they are available if the Rules Committee departs too far from the sentiments of the House.

In theory, few such barriers to floor consideration exist in the Senate. There bills may be considered in any order at any time whenever a majority of the Senate chooses. The majority leader, in consultation with the minority leader, schedules bills for consideration. In practice, however, getting proposals to the Senate floor is far more complicated. Whereas the House normally plows through its legislative schedule, ignoring individual members' complaints in favor of getting its work done, the

Senate Majority Leader must accommodate the interests of individual senators before proceeding with the Senate's business.

Floor Debate—The House

Once on the floor, the bills are debated. In the House all revenue and most other bills are discussed by the "Committee of the Whole," which is nothing more than whoever happens to be on the floor at the time. The **quorum,** or minimum number of members who must be present for business to be conducted, is only 100 members for the Committee of the Whole; obviously, this number is easier to assemble than a quorum for the House itself, which the Constitution specifies as a majority, or 218 members. The Speaker does not preside but chooses another person to wield the gavel. The Committee of the Whole debates, amends, and generally decides the final shape of the bill, but technically cannot pass it. To do that, the Committee of the Whole reports the bill back to the House (that is, to itself!), which takes final action. During the debate in the Committee of the Whole, the committee sponsoring the bill guides the discussion, divides the time equally between proponents and opponents, and decides how long each member will be permitted to speak. If amendments are allowed under the rule, they must be germane to the purpose of the bill—extraneous matters (riders) are not allowed—and no one may speak for more than five minutes on an amendment. During this process people wishing to take time out to huddle about strategy or to delay action can demand a **quorum call**—a calling of the roll to find out whether the necessary minimum number of members is present. If a quorum is not present, the House must either adjourn or dispatch the sergeant at arms to round up missing members. The sponsoring committee almost always wins; its bill, as amended by it, usually is the version that the House passes.

Floor Debate—The Senate

Things are a good deal more casual in the Senate. Short of cloture (discussed below), there is no rule limiting debate, and members can speak for as long as they can stay on their feet. A senator's remarks need not be relevant to the matter under consideration (some senators have read aloud from the Washington telephone directory), and anyone can offer an amendment at any time. There is no Committee of the Whole. Amendments need not be germane to the purpose of the bill, and thus the Senate often attaches riders to bills.

In fact, the opportunity to offer nongermane amendments gives a senator a chance to get a bill onto the floor without regard to the calendar or the schedule of the majority leader: he or she need only offer a pet bill as an "amendment" to a bill already under discussion. (This cannot be done to an appropriations bill.) Indeed, the entire committee hearing process can be bypassed in the Senate if the House has already passed the bill. In that case a senator can get the House-passed measure put directly onto the Senate calendar without committee action. In 1957 and again in 1964 this was done with House-passed civil rights bills to make certain that they would not be bottled up in the conservative Senate Judiciary Committee.

A Senate filibuster is difficult to break. The current **cloture rule** requires that sixteen senators sign a petition to move cloture. The motion is voted on two days after the petition is introduced; to pass, three-fifths of the entire Senate membership (sixty senators if there are no vacancies) must vote for it. If it passes, each senator is thereafter limited to one hour of debate on the bill under consideration. The total debate, including roll calls and the introduction of amendments, cannot exceed one hundred hours.

In recent years, both filibusters and cloture votes have become more common. The filibuster occurs more frequently because it is now easier to stage one. Often it consists not of a senator's making a long speech but of endless requests for the clerk to call the roll. More filibusters means more cloture votes, which are now easier to win since the 1975 change lowering the required number of supporters from two-thirds to three-fifths of all senators. During the 100th Congress (1987–1988) there were almost as many cloture votes—forty-three—as there had been in the half century after the procedure was invented. Since 1975, about 40 percent of all cloture votes have succeeded in cutting off debate.

Conservatives have used the filibuster to try to block civil rights laws; liberals have used it to try to block decontrol of gas prices. Since both factions have found the filibuster useful, it seems most unlikely that it will ever be abolished, though it has been somewhat curtailed. One way to keep the Senate going during a filibuster is **double-tracking,** whereby the disputed bill is shelved temporarily so that the Senate can get on with other business. Because double-tracking permits the Senate to discuss and vote on matters other than the bill that is being filibustered, it is less costly to individual senators to stage a filibuster. In the past, before double-tracking, a senator and his allies had to keep talking around the clock to keep their filibuster alive. If they stopped talking, the Senate was free to take up other business. Opponents of the filibuster would bring cots and blankets to the Senate so that they could sleep and eat there, ready to take the floor the moment the filibuster faltered. But with double-tracking other business can go on while the stalled bill is temporarily set aside. As a result, the number of filibusters has skyrocketed. In the words of two expert Senate watchers, the "Senate has become increasingly unmanageable as filibusters have become virtually commonplace on both major and minor pieces of legislation, raising the standard for passage of even routine bills from fifty to sixty votes and resulting in frequent delays in scheduling, stop-and-go patterns of floor debate," and the use of other procedures "that make the institution hostage to the whims of individual senators."[34]

What the threat of a filibuster means in practice is this: neither political party can control the Senate unless it has at least sixty votes. Neither party has had that many Senate seats since 1979, and so for the Senate to act there must be a bipartisan majority.

Methods of Voting

Some observers of Congress make the mistake of deciding who was for and who was against a bill by the final vote. This can be misleading—often a member of Congress will vote for final passage of a bill after having supported amendments that, if they had passed, would have made the bill totally different. To keep track of various members' voting records, therefore, it is often more important to know how they voted on key amendments than to know how they voted on the bill itself.

Finding that out is not always easy, though it has become more so in recent years. There are four pro-

The electronic voting system in the House of Representatives displays each member's name on the wall of the chamber. By inserting a plastic card in a box fastened to the chairs, a member can vote "yea," "nay," or "present," and the result is shown opposite his or her name.

cedures for voting in the House. A **voice vote** consists of the members' shouting "yea" or "nay"; a **division** (or standing) **vote** involves the members' standing and being counted. In neither a voice nor a standing vote are the names of members recorded as having voted one way or the other.

To learn how an individual votes, there must be either a recorded teller vote or a roll call. In a **teller vote** the members pass between two tellers, the yeas first and then the nays. Since 1971 a teller vote can be "recorded," which means that, at the request of twenty members, clerks write down the names of those favoring or opposing a bill as they pass the tellers. Since teller votes but not roll calls may be taken in the Committee of the Whole, the use of a recorded teller vote enables observers to find out how members voted in those important deliberations.

A **roll-call vote,** of course, consists of people's answering "yea" or "nay" to their names. It can be done at the request of one-fifth of the representatives present in the House. When roll calls were handled orally, it was a time-consuming process, since the clerk had to drone though 435 names. Since 1973 an electronic voting system has been in operation that permits each member, by inserting a plastic card into a slot, to record his or her own vote and to learn the total automatically. Owing to the use of

recorded teller votes and the advent of electronic roll-call votes, the number of recorded votes has gone up sharply in the House. There were only seventy-three House roll calls in 1955; twenty years later there were over eight times as many. Voting in the Senate is much the same, only simpler: there is no such thing as a teller vote, and no electronic counters are used.

If a bill passes the House and Senate in different forms, the differences must be reconciled if the bill is to become law. If they are minor, the last house to act may simply refer the bill back to the other house, which then accepts the alterations. If the differences are major, it is often necessary to appoint a conference committee to iron them out. Only a minority of bills require a conference. Each house must vote to form such a committee. The members are picked by the chairmen of the House and Senate standing committees that have been handling the legislation, with representation given to the minority as well as the majority party. There are usually between three and fifteen members from each house. No decision can be made unless approved by a majority of *each* delegation.

Bargaining is long and hard; in the past it was also secret. Now some conference sessions are open to the public. Often—as with President Carter's energy bill—the legislation is substantially rewritten in

House-Senate Differences: A Summary

House	Senate
435 members serving two-year terms.	100 members serving rotating six-year terms.
House members have only one major committee assignment, thus tend to be policy specialists.	Senators have two or more major committee assignments, tend to be policy generalists.
Speaker's referral of bills to committee is hard to challenge.	Referral decisions easy to challenge.
Committees almost always consider legislation first.	Committee consideration easily bypassed.
Scheduling and rules controlled by majority party.	Scheduling and rules generally agreed to by majority and minority leaders.
Rules Committee powerful; controls time of debate, admissibility of amendments.	Rules Committee weak; few limits on debate or amendments.
Debate usually limited to one hour.	Unlimited debate unless shortened by unanimous consent or by invoking cloture.
Nongermane amendments may not be introduced from floor.	Nongermane amendments may be introduced.

conference. Complex bills can lead to enormous conference committees. The 1988 trade bill went before a conference committee of two hundred members. Theoretically the conferees are not supposed to change anything already agreed to by both the House and Senate, but in the inevitable give-and-take even matters already approved may be changed.

In most cases the conference reports tend to favor, slightly, the Senate version of the bill. Several studies have suggested that the Senate wins in from 57 percent to 65 percent of cases.[35] Whoever wins (and both sides always claim that they got everything out of the bargaining that they possibly could have), conferees report their agreement back to their respective houses, which usually consider the report immediately. The report can be accepted or rejected; it cannot be amended. In the great majority of cases it is accepted: the alternative is to have no bill at all, at least for that Congress. The bill, now in final form, goes to the president for signature or veto. If a veto is cast, the bill returns to the house of origin. There an effort can be made to override the veto.

This requires that two-thirds of those present (provided that there is a quorum) must vote to override; this vote must be a roll call. If both houses override in this manner, the bill becomes law without the president's approval.

How Members of Congress Vote

Voting on bills is not the only thing that a member of Congress does, but it is among the more important and is probably the most visible. Since leaders in Congress are not nearly so powerful as those in a typical parliament, since political parties have been declining in influence, and since Congress has gone to great lengths to protect the independence and power of the individual members, it is by no means obvious what factors will lead a representative or senator to vote for or against a bill or amendment.

There are at least three kinds of explanations: representational, organizational, and attitudinal. A *representational* explanation is based on the reasonable assumption that members want to get reelected, and therefore they vote to please their constituents. The *organizational* explanation is based on the equally reasonable assumption that since most constituents do not know how their legislator has voted, it is not essential to please them. But it is important to please fellow members of Congress, whose goodwill is valuable in getting things done and in acquiring status and power in Congress. The *attitudinal* explanation is based on the assumption that there are so many conflicting pressures on members of Congress that they cancel one another out, leaving them virtually free to vote on the basis of their own beliefs.

Political scientists have studied, tested, and argued about these (and other) explanations for decades, and nothing like a consensus has emerged. Some facts have been established, however.

Representational View

The representational view has some merit under certain circumstances—namely, when constituents have a clear view on some issue and a legislator's vote on that issue is likely to attract their attention. Such is often the case for civil rights laws: representatives with significant numbers of black voters in their districts are not likely to oppose civil rights bills; representatives with few blacks in their districts are comparatively free to oppose such bills. (Until the late 1960s, many southern representatives were able to oppose civil rights measures because the blacks in their districts were prevented from voting; on the other hand, many representatives without black constituents have supported civil rights bills, partly out of personal belief and partly, perhaps, because certain white groups in their districts—organized liberals, for example—insisted on such support.)

One study of congressional roll-call votes and constituency opinion showed that the correlation between the two was quite strong on civil rights bills. There was also a positive (though not as strong) correlation between roll-call votes and constituency opinion on social welfare measures. Scarcely any correlation, however, was found between congressional votes and hometown opinion on foreign policy measures.[36] Foreign policy is generally remote from the daily interests of most Americans, and public opinion about such matters can change rapidly. It is

not surprising, therefore, that congressional votes and constituent opinion should be different on such questions.

From time to time an issue arouses deep passions among the voters, and legislators cannot escape the need either to vote as their constituents want, whatever their personal views, or to anguish at length about which side of a divided constituency to support. Gun control has been one such question, the ratification of the Panama Canal treaties another, and the use of federal money to pay for abortions a third. Some fortunate members of Congress get unambiguous cues from their constituents on these matters, and no hard decision is necessary; others get conflicting views, and they know that whichever way they vote, it may cost them dearly in the next election. Occasionally members of Congress in this fix will try to be out of town when the matter comes up for a vote. One careful study found that constituency influences were an important factor in Senate votes,[37] but no comparable study has been done for the House.

You might think that members of Congress who won a close race in the last election—who come from a "marginal" district—would be especially eager to vote the way that their constituents want. Research so far has shown that is not generally the case. There seem to be about as many independent-minded members of Congress from marginal as from safe districts. Perhaps it is because opinion is so divided in a marginal seat that one cannot please everybody; as a result the representative votes on other grounds.

In general the problem with the representational explanation is that public opinion is not strong and clear on most measures on which Congress must vote. Many representatives and senators face constituencies that are divided on key issues. Some constituents go to special pains to make their views known (these interest groups were discussed in Chapter 9). But as we indicated, the power of interest groups to affect congressional votes depends, among other things, on whether a legislator sees them as united and powerful or as disorganized and marginal.

This does not mean that constituents rarely have a direct influence on voting. The influence that they have probably comes from the fact that legislators risk defeat should they steadfastly vote in ways that can be held against them by a rival in the next election. Though most congressional votes are not known to most citizens, blunders (real or alleged) quickly become known when an electoral opponent exploits them.

Still any member of Congress can choose the positions that he or she takes on most roll-call votes (and on all voice or standing votes, where names are not recorded). And even a series of recorded votes that are against constituency opinion need not be fatal: a member of Congress can win votes in other ways—for example, by doing services for constituents or by appealing to the party loyalty of the voters.

Organizational View

When voting on matters where constituency interests or opinions are not vitally at stake, members of Congress respond primarily to cues provided by their colleagues. This is the organizational explanation of their votes. The principal cue is party; as already noted, what party a member of Congress belongs to explains more about his or her voting record than any other single factor. Additional organizational cues come from the opinions of colleagues with whom the member of Congress feels a close ideological affinity: for liberals in the House it is the Democratic Study Group; for conservatives it has often been the Republican Study Committee or the Wednesday Club. But party and other organizations do not have clear positions on all matters. For the scores of votes that do not involve the "big questions," a representative or senator is especially likely to be influenced by the members of his or her party on the sponsoring committee.

It is easy to understand why. Suppose you are a Democratic representative from Michigan who is summoned to the floor of the House to vote on a bill to authorize a new weapons system. You haven't the faintest idea what issues might be at stake. There is no obvious liberal or conservative position on this matter. How do you vote? Simple. You take your cue from several Democrats on the House Armed Services Committee that handled the bill. Some are liberal (such as Ron Dellums of California), others are conservative (such as Owen Pickett of Virginia). If Dellums and Pickett both support the bill, you vote for it unhesitatingly. If Dellums and Pickett dis-

agree, you vote with whichever Democrat is generally closest to your own political ideology. If the matter is one that affects your state, you can take your cue from members of your state's delegation to Congress.

Attitudinal View

Finally, there is evidence that the ideology of a member of Congress affects how he or she votes. We have seen that Democratic and Republican legislators differ sharply on a liberal-versus-conservative scale. On both domestic and foreign policy issues, many tend to be consistently liberal or conservative.[38]

This consistency isn't surprising; as we saw in Chapter 5, political elites think more ideologically than the public generally.

On many issues the average member of the House has opinions close to those of the average voter, as seen in Figure 11.5 (see page 346). Senators, by contrast, are often less in tune with public opinion. In the 1970s they were much more liberal than voters; in the early 1980s, more conservative. Two senators from the same state often mobilize quite different bases of support. The result is that many states, such as California, Delaware, and New York, have been represented by senators with almost diametrically opposed views.

Of late the Senate has gone through three phases. In the first, during the 1950s and early 1960s, it was a cautious, conservative institution dominated by southern senators and displaying many of the features of a "club" that welcomed members into its inner circle only after they had displayed loyalty to its gentlemanly (and, in effect, conservative) customs. This was the era when the Senate was the graveyard of civil rights bills.

The second period began in the mid-1960s as liberal senators rose steadily in number, seniority, and influence, helped along by the Johnson reforms, which made it easier for junior senators to gain chairmanships. The decentralization of the Senate gave more power to individual senators, including liberals. In 1972 there were about twenty-four liberal senators, but among them they held forty subcommittee chairmanships.[39]

The third period began in the late 1970s and became most visible after the 1980 elections, when many liberals lost their seats to conservative Repub-

FIGURE 11.5   Comparison of Public and Congressional Opinion on Policy Issues, 1978

◼ Public   ◼ House members

Defense: Favor more money for national defense

Public: 23%
House members: 26%

Arms control: Favor Strategic Arms Limitation Talks (SALT)

Public: 67%
House members: 74%

Health insurance: Favor national health insurance fully paid for by the government

Public: 47%
House members: 45%

Tax cut: Oppose a "large" federal income-tax cut

Public: 53%
House members: 51%

Abortion: Favor government paying for abortions for the poor

Public: 41%
House members: 35%

SOURCE: CBS–*New York Times* poll, as reported in Robert S. Erikson, Norman R. Luttbeg, and Kent L. Tedin, *American Public Opinion*, 2d ed. (New York: Wiley, 1980), 240.

licans. The conservatism of the present Senate is based more on ideology than on the rules of the southern "club" that characterized it in the 1950s.

The Democratic party is more deeply divided than the Republican. There are only a few liberal Republicans, but there are many more conservative Democrats from the South and West. Southern Democrats often team up with Republicans to form a conservative coalition. In a typical year a majority of Republicans and southern Democrats will vote together against a majority of northen Democrats about 20 to 25 percent of the time. When the conservative coalition does form, it usually wins: between 1970 and 1982 it won about two thirds of the votes on which it held together. After the Reagan victory and the Republican gain of thirty seats in the House in 1981, the conservative coalition became even more effective, dominating key votes on the Reagan budget and tax plans. It has declined during the 1990s, as many Democrats were replaced by Republicans in the South.

Reforming Congress

Most citizens are less interested in why members of Congress vote the way they do than they are in whether Congress as an institution serves the public interest and fulfills its mission as a democratic body. In recent years a number of proposals have been made to reform Congress—term limitations, new ethics and campaign finance laws, and organizational changes intended to reduce the power and perks of members while making it easier for Congress to pass needed legislation in a timely fashion.

It is important to recognize that the kind of reform proposed depends not only on what is feasible but also on an underlying idea of what Congress ought to be. For example, which of the two conceptions of democracy discussed in Chapter 1—direct or representative—should Congress embody? What definition of "the public interest" should Congress favor? And by what criteria should one decide whether a given piece of legislation is so badly needed that a failure to pass it promptly constitutes a failure of Congress?

Representative or Direct Democracy?

The Framers of the Constitution believed that representatives should refine, not reflect, public wishes. Today, however, many believe that elected officials should mirror, not mediate, the majority's views. Some would go so far as to bypass Congress entirely. A survey conducted in 1993 found that two-thirds of Americans favored having binding national referenda on policy questions and about half favored selecting members of Congress randomly from lists of eligible voters. (One in six even supported the idea of auctioning seats in Congress to the highest bidders as a way of retiring the national debt.)[40] A more moderate vision of direct democracy in Congress would have citizen legislators serving short terms as the people's delegates (voting as a majority of their constituents want them to vote), with small staffs and no perks. In contrast, representative democracy in Congress would mean professional legislators serving as the people's trustees (consulting their constituents' views but voting their consciences), with expert staffs, no term limits, and such work-related perks (travel allowances, mailing privileges) as they required to fulfill their duties.

Any reforms that move Congress away from representative democracy and toward direct democracy could have far-reaching consequences. For example, consider how the House of Representatives voted on June 21, 1990. On that day the House defeated a proposed constitutional amendment on protection of the American flag. Ten days before the House vote, the U.S. Supreme Court had struck down a Texas law against flag desecration. The public reaction to this ruling, which was widely interpreted as legalizing and legitimizing flag burning, was intensely negative. On the eve of the House vote, pollster George Gallup, Jr., reported that the "will of the public on making flag burning illegal appears to be both straightforward and remarkably stable."[41] Nevertheless, the House voted against the amendment. One study found that 87 percent of the legislators who voted against the amendment represented constituencies who supported it. This study also found that those who voted against the amendment were not punished by the voters for doing so in the 1992 congressional elections.[42]

Proper Guardians of the Public Weal?

Everyone agrees that Congress should serve the public interest, but what is the public interest? In *Federalist* No. 10 James Madison offered one answer. To him, the public interest— "the permanent and aggregate interests of the community"—was to be expressed concretely in national laws that transcended "local prejudices" and frustrated the "sinister designs" of factions.

In Madison's view the public interest was not the simple sum of whatever societal interests demanded from government. Instead, members of Congress were to be "proper guardians of the public weal," representatives who served "the great and aggregate interests" of the country. To Madison, the art of the public-spirited legislator was to know the true ends of the body politic and to effect reasonable compro-

mises among competing societal interests via the legislative process. He held that "the regulation of these various and interfering interests" was the "principal task" of representatives, and he argued that a Congress fashioned institutionally as a representative body, rather than one that carried out direct democracy, would be best able to balance contending societal interests without succumbing to the demands of factions.

Madison's conception of the public interest lives on in contemporary calls for reforming Congress to make the body less captive of so-called special interests, our modern term for factions. Some people believe that by outlawing political action committees, fine-tuning congressional ethics regulations, or taking related measures Congress would become less accessible to special interests and more solicitous of the public interest.

The difficulty, however, is that one person's special-interest group is often another's professional association, trade group, or public-interest lobby. If you were a member of Congress, would you listen to the views of the National Abortion Federation, the U.S. Catholic Conference, both, or neither? Would you view the interests of the Meat Importers' Council of America as more or less important than the interests of the American Institute of Certified Public Accountants, the Bituminous Coal Operators Association, the Cement Kiln Recycling Association, or the American Political Science Association? Might you view the Southern Governors' Association as a faction but the National Governors' Association as a public-interest lobby? And what, as a committed "proper guardian of the public weal," would you make of the National Rifle Association or the American Association of Retired Persons?

A Decisive Congress or a Deliberative One?

Madison and the other Framers recognized that Congress, as a representative body designed to protect the public interest while balancing the competing views and interests of the citizenry, would normally proceed slowly. Congress was designed for deliberative, not decisive, action. It was intended to check and balance strong leaders in the executive branch, not automatically cede its authority to them. Its institutional mission was more to block or delay popular legislative action than it was to speed it along.

But many contemporary critics of Congress do not share the Framers' vision of what Congress ought to be. During the 1992 presidential campaign, for example, there was a great deal of talk about policy gridlock in Washington, D.C. Almost everyone agreed that the federal budget deficit needed to be reduced, but national policymakers could not agree on how to do it. Everyone admitted that the nation's health care system needed to be reformed, but no single plan gained widespread acceptance. And everyone insisted that America needed to strengthen its international trading position, but disagreements were rife over just how, if at all, this could be accomplished in our increasingly complex global economy.

Many wish to reform Congress in ways that might end "policy gridlock" by making Congress capable of speedily adopting sweeping changes in national policies. They see a need to reduce separation-of-powers barriers to joint executive-legislative action and to adopt other changes that would make the American political system more closely resemble a parliamentary system. The problem, however, is that a Congress capable of doing much good quickly would also be capable of doing much bad quickly. A Congress that could move decisively to adopt wise budget, health, or trade policies could also move decisively to adopt unwise ones, and a Congress that could suddenly endorse and enact popular laws could do the same for unpopular ones. This is true whatever the subject—toxic waste disposal or civil service reform, environmental protection or mass transportation, juvenile justice or national defense.

As the reformers argue, there are costs associated with having congressional machinery that runs slowly on the precious fuel of political consensus. But there are benefits as well, not least among them the chance to identify competing interests, consider opposing ideas, weigh alternative approaches, and resist pressures to act where action may be premature, unwarranted, overly expensive, or socially divisive.

Imposing Term Limits

As explained in Chapter 2, the Antifederalists (those who opposed the new Constitution in the late 1780s) believed that a strong national government

would grow corrupt, distant from the people, and contemptuous of states' rights. Among other measures to check the national government's power and ensure its responsiveness to the popular will, many Antifederalists believed that members of Congress should stand for election annually, and that no citizen should serve more than a few terms in Congress.

Today there are many Americans who have come to the view that the Antifederalists were right about the need for some type of term limits in Congress. When upwards of 95 percent of House incumbents are reelected, people worry that popular control of Congress has weakened, while state and local officials complain that there is no room for them to move up the political ladder. A 1992 survey showed that about 80 percent of Americans felt there should be a limit on the number of terms to which a senator or member of the House can be elected.[43]

The contemporary term-limit movement began in the fall of 1990, when term-limit measures passed in three statewide initiatives (California, Colorado, and Oklahoma). In 1991 voters in the state of Washington, home of former Speaker of the House Thomas Foley, also considered a term-limit initiative, but Foley and others waged a successful campaign against the measure, which failed by a vote of 54 to 46 percent. The movement gained speed again in 1992, however. By 1994 twenty-two states had voted, in most places by large majorities, to impose limits on the number of years their representatives could serve in Congress.

The effects of term limits on Congress would vary according to which type of term limits applied.[44] Proposals that would place a lifetime limit on legislative service would result in an amateur legislature. Let us assume, as many supporters of these measures do, that amateurs in Congress would act out of personal conviction rather than from the desire to be reelected. Reelection-minded professional politicians must be concerned about what their constituents think and want; principled amateur legislators need not be. Would a Congress composed of such legislators be good or bad, better or worse? The answer, of course, depends largely on whether you favor representative or direct democracy.

But whichever you favor, do not suppose that amateur legislators would eliminate policy gridlock: people who act out of conviction are more prone to disagree and less apt to compromise than people

Thinking CRITICAL

Limit Terms or Enlarge Congress?

Article I, section 2 of the Constitution allows no more than one representative for every thirty thousand inhabitants. The Antifederalists warned that such a low ratio of representatives to constituents would make the House a barony dominated by a few leaders out of touch with the people. The first House had 65 members. Since 1913 the House has had 435 members; that number was fixed by law in 1929. But the nation's population has roughly doubled over the last seven decades. As a result, in 1992 each member of the House represented about six hundred thousand persons. That ratio would have horrified the Antifederalists, and it probably would have given the Framers of the Constitution second thoughts as well. It is also way out of line with the ratios in most other modern democracies, such as Japan (1:238,600), Germany (1:120,000), France (1:96,300), and Great Britain (1:87,500).

To return to the Framers' original ratio would require a House with over eight thousand members. So far no one has advocated doing that, but Michael Merrill and Sean Wilentz propose a return to the 1929 baseline, doubling the House to 870 members so that each member would represent about three hundred thousand rather than six hundred thousand citizens. Enlarging Congress, they argue, would "reduce the crushing load of constituent service for each member, encourage less expensive campaigns, and mitigate the distracting and corrupting pursuit of PAC financing. Doubling the membership would make life all the more difficult (and costly) for special interests that lack a significant popular base among the citizenry."

Which strategy—limiting terms or enlarging Congress—do you favor? Which do you think is more likely to win popular support and be enacted into law? Which do you think stands a better chance of passing muster on constitutional terms? What are the likely drawbacks of each proposal? Short of such far-reaching reforms, what do you think can and should be done to change Congress?

SOURCE: Michael Merrill and Sean Wilentz, "The Big House: An Alternative to Term Limits," *The New Republic* (November 16, 1992): 16–17.

whose profession it is to practice the ABC's of democratic politics—making *a*lliances, striking *b*argains, and forging *c*ompromises.[45] In a diverse, pluralistic, and multicultural society, a politics of unbending principle can be a recipe for political stalemate—or worse.

By the same token, do not suppose that all the amateur legislators would be true political novices. As should be obvious, the typical American is simply not well positioned to quit work in order to spend a year or two in Washington, D.C. But there are people for whom such a brief tour of duty in Congress would be both feasible and desirable. With lifetime term limits, many of tomorrow's citizen-legislators on Capitol Hill could well be yesterday's lawyer-lobbyists from K Street.

On the other hand, were term limits to take the form of limiting continuous service in one legislative branch without restricting eligibility for other elected offices, the probable result would be a Congress of office-hopping political professionals who must constantly prepare to run for the other chamber or some other office. In a Congress dominated by members who played electoral "musical chairs," it is probable that seniority would fade as the basis for distributing committee assignments, party leadership would change hands every few years, and individual members would probably keep one eye fixed on their next constituencies (local, regional, statewide, or national) and would have every incentive to act in ways that bring them public attention rather than work behind the scenes to get things done.

Some analysts believe that, despite its popularity, the term limits movement is fading. In 1995 Congress failed to approve resolutions proposing a constitutional amendment limiting the terms of members in both chambers to twelve years of service. The Supreme Court narrowly ruled that term limits cannot constitutionally be imposed on Con-

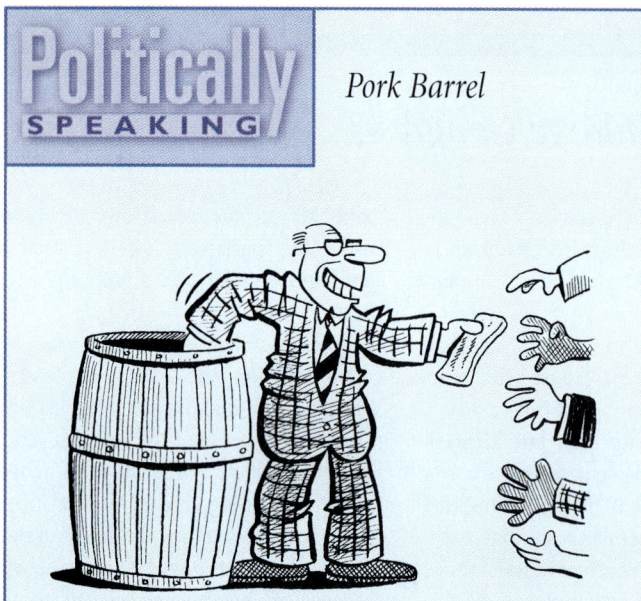

Politically SPEAKING   *Pork Barrel*

Before the Civil War it was the custom to take salt pork from barrels and distribute it to the slaves. Often the eagerness of the slaves to get the food would result in a rush on the barrels, with each slave trying to get as much as possible.

By the 1870s members of Congress were using the term *pork* to refer to benefits for their districts and *pork barrel* to mean the piece of legislation containing those benefits.

Today the classic example of pork-barrel legislation is the rivers and harbors bill, which provides appropriations for countless dams, bridges, and canals to be built in congressional districts all over the country.

SOURCE: From *Safire's Political Dictionary* by William Safire. Copyright © 1968, 1972, 1978 by William Safire. Reprinted by permission of Random House, Inc. and the author.

Reducing Powers and Perks

To many term-limitation enthusiasts and other would-be reformers, Congress is grossly overstaffed and self-indulgent. It is quick to impose new laws on states, cities, businesses, and average citizens but slow to apply those same laws to itself and its members. It is quick to pass **pork-barrel legislation**—bills that give tangible benefits (highways, dams, post offices) to constituents in the hope of winning their votes in return—but slow to tackle complex and controversial questions of national policy. The reformers' image of Congress is unflattering, but is it wholly unwarranted? Which calls to reduce congressional powers and perks amount to mere Congress-bashing and which come closer to being reasonable criticisms of a body that has lost its way as a representative institution?

Banning Legal Bribes   As any baseball fan knows, tickets to an All-Star game are always hard to come by. But it was harder than usual to get a ticket to the 1993 All-Star game. Only ten thousand of the forty-six thousand seats at Orioles Park at Camden Yards in Baltimore were available to the public. But Congress was well represented in the bleachers. Major league baseball owners gave members of Congress a special opportunity to purchase tickets for themselves and others. Over half of the 535 representatives and senators took the tickets, despite the fact that Congress was in the midst of deciding whether major league baseball's long-standing exemption from federal antitrust laws should be rescinded. One member who did not take the tickets was Representative Jim Bunning of Kentucky. Bunning, a former All-Star player who threw a perfect game for the Philadelphia Phillies in 1964, wrote "No bribe" on the solicitation and sent it back.[46]

Reformers were generally pleased in November 1995 when new House rules, adopted on a 422-6 vote, prohibited lawmakers from accepting any gifts—baseball tickets, lobbyist-financed vacations, fruit baskets, free hair-care products—except from family and friends. (Gifts from friends valued at more than $250 require a waiver from the House ethics committee.) Likewise, the Senate put a limit of $50 on any gift, including meals and entertainment, and a $100-per-year limit on gifts from any

gress by state action. The Court held that limiting the number of terms representatives and senators can serve is tantamount to adding an additional qualification to the three (age, citizenship, and residency in the particular state) that the Constitution establishes. But the 5-4 majority met with a vigorous dissent by Justice Clarence Thomas, and the issue will undoubtedly come up again in the courts—and at the ballot boxes.

single source, unless the gift-givers are family or "close personal friends." In both chambers the rules now ban members from taking free travel to mostly recreational events and forbid them from accepting gifts from lobbyists for charities that members control. Given the prices charged for good food in Washington restaurants, the $50-per-meal allowance probably has senators eating in fast-food outlets.

Still, critics complain that these new rules stop short of banning "legal bribes." They stress that members in both the House and Senate are still permitted to accept campaign donations and expense-paid travel with their spouses for "fact-finding" trips (including seven-day international trips) and other "official duties," such as flying to a private group's convention to "speak on Congress." Also, the House Committee on Standards of Official Conduct is able to grant members waivers from the new rules in any cases it judges to be "unusual." There has been no word as of yet on how many House members, if any, have exploited such ostensible loopholes in the gift-ban rules.

Fencing in the Frank No perk is more treasured by members of Congress than the frank. Members of Congress are allowed by law to send material through the mail free of charge by substituting their facsimile signature (*frank*) for postage. But rather than using this **franking privilege** to keep their constituents informed about their government, most members use franked newsletters and questionnaires as campaign literature. That is why use of the frank soars in the months before an election. For example, more than 30 million newsletters were sent out in March 1992, the last month in which members facing June primaries could send franked mailings.[47] And two of the top three users of the frank during the first quarter of 1993 were both running at the time to fill the Senate seat vacated when Lloyd Bentsen became the Clinton administration's secretary of the treasury.[48]

Thus, the frank amounts to a taxpayer subsidy of members' campaigns, a perk that bolsters the electoral fortunes of incumbents. Some reformers do not believe that it is possible to fence in congressional use of the frank for public education or other legitimate purposes, and so they propose abolishing it outright. Other reformers, however, argue that the

frank can be fenced in by prohibiting mailings just before primaries and general elections (to dilute any electoral impact) and by placing a prominent notice, "Paid For at Taxpayer Expense," on the front of every franked piece of mail.[49] Such measures could well discourage members from abusing their franking privilege. Reformers cheered in 1995 when the House resolved to limit the use of the frank and to prevent members from using the frank as a campaign tool. The House Oversight Committee voted to cut franking authorization by one-third of the 1994 level. It remains to be seen just how much less franked mail of various kinds will result from the changes.

Placing Congress Under the Law For years Congress routinely exempted itself from many of the laws it passed. In defense of this practice, members said that if members of Congress were subject to, for example, the minimum wage laws, the executive branch, charged with enforcing these laws, would acquire excessive power over Congress. This would violate the separation of powers. But as public criticism of Congress grew and confidence in government declined, more and more people demanded that Congress subject itself to the laws that applied to everybody else. In 1995 the 104th Congress did this by passing a bill that obliges Congress to obey eleven important laws governing such things as civil rights, occupational safety, fair labor standards, and family leave. The bipartisan Congressional Accountability Act of 1995 had to solve a key problem: under the constitutional doctrine of separated powers, it would have been unwise and perhaps unconstitutional for the executive branch to enforce congressional compliance with executive branch regulations. So Congress created the independent Office of Compliance and an employee grievance procedure to deal with implementation. Now Congress too must obey such laws as the Civil Rights Act, the Equal Pay Act, the Age Discrimination Act, and the Family and Medical Care Leave Act. Whatever effect the law will have on the people who work for Congress, it has at least addressed a source of public anger. And it may already be teaching Capitol Hill dwellers valuable lessons about how certain well-intentioned federal laws and regulations affect average citizens and businesses. In 1996 many Capitol Hill veterans complained loudly about having to drop everything in order to deal with compliance monitors from the Occupational Safety and Health Administration.

Trimming the Pork   Reformers are not alone in believing that Congress spends money on wasteful projects designed solely to win votes in home districts. Bills containing money for local dams, bridges, roads, and monuments are referred to disparagingly as pork-barrel legislation. Reformers complain that when members act to "bring home the bacon," Congress misallocates tax dollars by supporting projects with trivial social benefits in order to bolster their reelection prospects. And now that the federal budget deficit has grown to such staggering dimensions, a favorite reform for restoring fiscal sanity is to "cut the pork."

No one can doubt the value of trimming unnecessary spending, but pork is not necessarily the villain it is made out to be. For example, the main cause of the budget deficit is the increase in spending on entitlement programs (like health care and interest on the national debt) without a corresponding increase in taxes. Spending on pork is a small fraction of spending on entitlements, and most categories of pork spending have decreased in the last ten or fifteen years. Furthermore, one person's pork is another person's necessity. No doubt some congressional districts get an unnecessary bridge or highway, but others get bridges and highways that are long overdue. The notion that every bridge or road a member of Congress gets for his or her district is wasteful pork is tantamount to saying that no member attaches any importance to merit. Opponents of pork assume that bridges and roads that are built as the result of a central plan (a plan drawn up in the executive branch) are inherently superior to bridges and roads built as a result of political bargaining. That may be true sometimes, but there is no reason to think it is always true.

Even if all pork were bad, it would still be necessary. Congress is an independent branch of government, and each member is, by constitutional design, the advocate of his or her district or state. No member's vote can be won by coercion, and few can be had by mere appeals to party loyalty or presidential needs. Pork is a way of obtaining consent. The only alternative is bribery, but bribery, besides being

wrong, would benefit only the member, whereas pork usually benefits voters in the member's district. If you want to eliminate pork, you must eliminate Congress, by converting it into a parliament under the control of a powerful party leader or prime minister. In a tightly controlled parliament, no votes need be bought; they can be commanded. But members of such a parliament can do little to help their constituents cope with government or to defend them against bureaucratic abuses, nor can they investigate the conduct of the executive branch. The price of a citizen-oriented Congress is a pork-oriented Congress.

Cutting Committees   Congress is supposed to organize itself in ways that enable its members to deliberate, debate, and decide matters of national policy in the public interest. Instead, it often appears that Congress is organized mainly to afford each member a spot in numerous political feifdoms (committees) while keeping thousands of staff gainfully employed.

It is clear that congressional organization has been increasing in both size and complexity (see Table 11.9). The overall number of seats on House committees and subcommittees grew from 2,511 in 1982 to 3,177 in 1992, and the average number of member assignments grew during this period from 5.7 to 7.2. In the Senate in 1993 members averaged more than eleven committee and subcommittee assignments.[50] As two experts on the Congress, Thomas E. Mann and Norman J. Ornstein, have observed,

> *As the basic structure for a division of labor, the committee system serves several functions. It allows for simultaneous consideration of many important substantive matters without having to use shortcuts because of lack of time. . . . It allows multiple points of access for interests and individuals in society to approach Congress with their concerns. It enables Congress to legislate, investigate, and oversee executive behavior. . . . The ballooning number of committee assignments of members, leading to increasing conflicts in scheduling, a frenetic pace of legislative life, and a shorter attention span for members, accompanied by decreasing attendance at committee and subcommittee meetings and hearings and less real focus on important problems, has*

TABLE 11.9	Membership of House Standing Committees, 1983 and 1993		
Committee	1983	1993	Percent Change
Agriculture	41	45	+10%
Appropriations	57	60	+5
Armed Services	44	55	+25
Banking	46	51	+11
Budget	31	43	+39
District of Columbia	11	11	None
Education and Labor	31	39	+26
Energy and Commerce	42	44	+5
Foreign Affairs	37	44	+19
Government Operations	39	42	+8
House Administration	19	19	None
Judiciary	31	35	+13
Merchant Marine	39	46	+18
Natural Resources	40	39	−3
Post Office	24	23	−4
Public Works	48	61	+27
Rules	13	13	None
Science and Technology	41	55	+34
Small Business	41	45	+10
Standards	12	14	+17
Veterans Affairs	33	35	+6
Ways and Means	35	38	+9

SOURCE: Thomas E. Mann and Norman J. Ornstein, *Renewing Congress: A Second Report* (Washington, D.C.: Brookings Institution and American Enterprise Institute, 1993), 18. Reprinted with permission of the Brookings Institution.

been one of the clearest and deepest problems we have seen emerge and grow.[51]

To deal with these problems, Mann and Ornstein recommended strict limitations on committee assignments for members in both chambers: no representative would be allowed to serve on more than two committees (one if exclusive) and four subcommittees, and no senator could serve on more than two major committees, one minor committee, and four subcommittees, with exceptions only for the Ethics Committee and temporary investigative panels. Except for Appropriations, no committee would be allowed more than six subcommittees. Under their plan, most select and joint committees would be abolished.[52]

As explained earlier in this chapter, the 104th Congress did initiate a reduction in the number of committees. The total number of House committees was cut by 25 percent, and for the first time since 1955 the House reduced the number of standing committees (from 22 to 19). The new reforms stipulated that, with the exception of three committees, no committee could have more than five subcommittees. As in the House, the number of Senate committees dropped, but not by as much. Likewise, the House limited most members to two standing committees and four subcommittee assignments, bringing the average number of assignments down to five, the lowest average since the 92nd Congress (1971–1972). But "assignment inflation" remained a problem in the Senate, as the average number of assignments stuck at about eleven. Even with the dramatic cuts, senators are averaging more than twice as many assignments as their House counterparts.

Most reformers who advocate cutting committees also believe in downsizing staff. During the 1992 presidential campaign, Bill Clinton called for a 25 percent across-the-board cut in congressional staff, while George Bush called for a 33 percent cut. Most staff growth occurred in the 1960s and 1970s, a time when the White House was dramatically increasing its own staff. Congressional staff sizes in the early 1990s were roughly equal to what they were in the early 1980s.[53] Staffers provide Congress with its own independent base of information and expertise, and the capacity to process mail and establish contacts with constituents. Thus it is likely that a large across-the-board cut in congressional staff would make Congress more dependent on the executive branch and on interest groups for information and policy expertise and less able to process constituent demands. As Mann and Ornstein conclude, any such "cut in staff would be a penny-wise, pound-foolish approach" to reform.[54] In any case, today's congressional staffs, personal and committee, are about the same size as they were in the mid-1980s, with a slight decline in the past few years and plans for further cuts on Congress's drawing board. Nearly half of the personal staffs of representatives and over a third of those of senators now work in district or state offices, not inside the beltway. If and when big staff cuts take effect, it will be interesting to see how they are distributed between Capitol Hill staff and congressional staff working in offices back home.

Ethics and Congress

Most contemporary proposals to reform Congress are motivated at least in part by a belief that "congressional ethics" has become an oxymoron.* The Framers of the Constitution hoped that members of Congress would be virtuous citizens, but they feared that some would not. They had, as stated earlier, a rather sober view of human nature and designed the system of checks and balances in part to minimize the chance that anybody, by gaining undue influence over one part of the government, would be able to tyrannize over the other parts.

It could be argued that this very separation of powers made corruption more, rather than less, likely. If power were concentrated in one set of hands—say, those of a prime minister—nobody would have any incentive to bribe or even influence any other political figure; there is little that subordinate officials could do for that person. And though a favor seeker might try to influence the prime minister, few could pay the price of bribing someone with

---

*An oxymoron is a phrase that combines contradictory terms ("deafening silence").

so much power. When bits and pieces of power are placed in many different hands, as in the United States, there are many opportunities to exercise influence: lots of officials have something that they could sell, and at a price that many favor seekers could afford.

For example, the appointive power is shared by the president and the Senate. Since the Senate will not confirm anybody for appointment to federal office who is personally obnoxious to either senator from the candidate's state (the rule of "senatorial courtesy"), the opportunity exists for an office seeker to try to influence a senator to get the desired appointment. The stage is also set for a senator, who may want the president to nominate a certain person, to delay some piece of presidential legislation until the nomination is made, or for the president to try to get a piece of legislation passed by offering to appoint the senator's campaign manager, brother-in-law, or law partner to a lucrative federal post.

Some of these attempts at influence may involve money, some may not. The point is that divided power means divided responsibility, and divided responsibility creates the possibility for evaded responsibility. It also creates the need to use influence to assemble enough power to get anything done. What the Constitution has separated, individuals must pull together; sometimes the pulling together involves mere persuasion, sometimes an exchange of favors, occasionally the payment of money.

Though the moral climate of American politics has improved in the last century, scandals continue. From 1941 to 1989 nearly fifty members of Congress faced criminal charges; most were convicted. From 1978 to 1992 Congress considered charges involving sixty-three members; thirty-one were sanctioned or convicted, and sixteen resigned or announced their intention to retire.[55] Charges of congressional misconduct included misuse of funds, having sex with minors, failing to disclose income, and accepting illegal gifts. The two most dramatic events were the 1980–1981 Abscam investigation and the 1989 Jim Wright hearings. In the former, six House members and one senator were convicted of having accepted money from an FBI agent posing as a wealthy Arab seeking political favors. In the latter, House Speaker Wright was found by the House Ethics Committee to have broken rules against taking certain gifts and exceeding limits on outside income. The Speaker resigned. In 1995 Senator Robert Packwood (R., Oregon) was forced to resign from Congress after the Ethics Committee recommended that he be expelled for having sexually harassed various women and for refusing to be completely cooperative with the ethics investigation. In 1997, Speaker Gingrich was fined $300,000 for having improperly raised money.

Rules on Congressional Ethics

Senate

Gifts: No gifts (in money, meals, or things) totaling $100 or more from anyone except spouse or personal friends.

Lobbyists may not pay for gifts, official travel, legal defense funds, or charitable contributions to groups controlled by senators.

Fees: No fees for lectures or writing ("honoraria"), except that fees of up to $2,000 may go to a senator-designated charity.

Outside earned income may not exceed 15 percent of a senator's salary.

Ex-senators may not try to influence members of Congress for one year after leaving the Senate.

Mass mailings: no senator may receive more than $50,000 from the Senate to send out a mailing to constituents.

House

Gifts: Members may not accept any gift of whatever value, even a meal, except from family or personal friends, and must get House approval for gifts from friends that exceed $250.

Lobbyists may not offer gifts or pay for travel, even if lobbyist is a spouse or personal friend.

Travel: House members may travel at the expense of others if travel is for officially connected meetings.

Fees: No honoraria for House members.

Ex-House members may not lobby Congress for one year after leaving office.

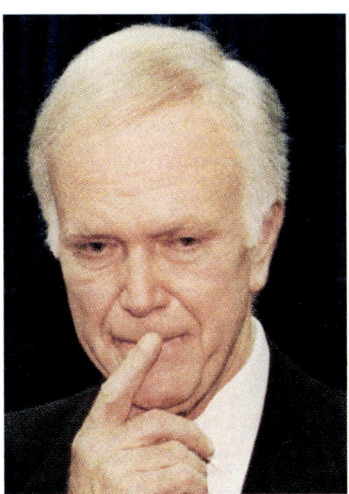

Senator Robert Packwood

These scandals, together with the large amount of PAC money given to legislators, have led many people to conclude that "we have the best Congress money can buy." No doubt there are moral failings, as there would be among any group of 535 powerful men and women, but it is not clear that Congress is inherently corrupt. Ethics codes and related reforms enacted in 1978, 1989, and 1995 have placed members of Congress under tight rules governing financial disclosure, accepting gifts, and other practices that were already regulated, while also prohibiting numerous practices (such as the use of office ac-

How Congress Raises Its Pay

*F*or over two hundred years Congress has tried to find a politically painless way to raise its own pay. It has managed to vote itself a pay increase twenty-three times in those two centuries, but usually at the price of a hostile public reaction. Twice during the nineteenth century a pay raise led to a massacre of incumbents in the next election.

Knowing this, Congress has invented various ways to get a raise without actually appearing to vote for it. These have included the following:

- Voting for a tax deduction for expenses incurred as a result of living in Washington

- Creating a citizens' commission that could recommend a pay increase that would take effect automatically provided Congress did not vote *against* it

- Linking increases in pay to decreases in honoraria (that is, speaking fees)

In 1989 a commission recommended a congressional pay raise of over 50 percent (from $89,500 to $135,000) and a ban on honoraria. The House planned to let it take effect automatically. But the public wouldn't have it, demanding that Congress vote on the raise—and vote it down. It did.

Embarrassed by its maneuvering, Congress retreated. At the end of 1989 it voted itself (as well as most top executive and judicial branch members) a small pay increase (7.9 percent for representatives, 9.9 percent for senators) that also provided for automatic cost-of-living adjustments (up to 5 percent a year) in the future. But the automatic adjustments in congressional pay have been rejected every year in recorded roll-call votes. Apparently, nobody in Congress wants to be accused of "getting rich" at the taxpayers' expense.

counts for campaign purposes) that had been unregulated. There "are more rules than there used to be and more rules than in any other political system. A comparative study of twenty-five countries with the most developed ethics rules for national legislators found that regulations in the United States are clearly the most restrictive."[56]

The more difficult issues are much deeper than brazen corruption:

- Members of Congress are elected to look out for their constituents. What limits, if any, should exist on how they go about this job?

- Congress has the right to judge and discipline its own members but insists that ethics cases in the executive branch be turned over to an independent special prosecutor. Shouldn't the same rules apply to both branches?

- Election campaigns are expensive, and somebody must pay the bill. If private fund-raising is outlawed or even sharply restricted, this could add to the already heavy burden that challengers must shoulder in running against incumbents. How can campaigns be paid for in ways that are both fair *and* honest?

The 104th Congress adopted new ethics rules for itself. They differ somewhat between the House and Senate (under the Constitution, each chamber can set its own rules). They include the rules listed in the box on page 355.

Other laws had already restricted the amount of money that any individual may contribute to a congressional election campaign and set rules for how those funds are to be handled (see Chapter 8).

Each successive wave of ethics laws has been predicated on the assumption that improper influence is associated with financial transactions, yet obviously that is not always the case. Many members of Congress who in the past earned substantial incomes from speaking and writing did not have their votes corrupted by such activities; other members of Congress who rarely take such fees may be heavily influenced, perhaps unduly so, by personal friendships and political alliances that have no direct monetary value at all. And no ethics code can address the bargaining among members of Congress, or between members of Congress and the president, involving the exchange of favors and votes.

Moreover, the ethics rules seem to favor people with inherited wealth or those who earned large sums before entering Congress. When the Senate voted in 1990 to limit the outside income its members could earn (mostly by writing and speaking) to 15 percent of their Senate salary, Senator Daniel Patrick Moynihan, who can earn a lot from writing and speaking, proposed an amendment to limit what senators could receive from their "unearned income" (that is, their investments and inherited wealth) to 15 percent of their Senate salaries. It passed. Had the bill become law (which it did not, lacking presidential approval), it would have meant that the many Senate millionaires would have had either to leave their money to charity or leave the Senate. Moynihan reasoned that calling senators unethical if they made too much money by working, while calling them ethical if they did no work more arduous than collecting dividends, made no sense.

It might not have made sense to the Framers, either. Their object was not to create a simon-pure Congress but to create one that was powerful, one that would be composed of representatives who (at least in the lower house) could be closely checked by the voters, and one that would offer manifold opportunities for competing interests and opinions to check one another. Their goal was liberty more than morality, though they knew that in the long run the latter was essential to the former.

SUMMARY:
THE OLD AND THE NEW CONGRESS

Over the last half century or so, Congress, especially the House, has evolved through three stages. The modern Congress is an uneasy combination of stages two and three.

During the first stage, lasting from the end of World War I until the early 1960s, the House was dominated by powerful committee chairmen who controlled the agenda, decided which members would get what services for their constituents, and tended to follow the leadership of the Speaker. Newer members were expected to be seen but not heard; power and prominence came only after a long apprenticeship. Congressional staffs were small, and so members dealt with each other face to face. In dealing with other members, it helped to have a southern accent: half of all committee chairmen in both the House and the Senate were from the South. Not many laws were passed over their objections.

The second stage emerged in the early 1970s, in part as the result of trends already under way (for example, the steady growth in the number of staffers assigned to each member) and in part as a result of changes in procedures and organization brought

How to Look Up Facts About Congress

To find out how Congress is organized, staffed, and run:
Congressional Quarterly, *Guide to Congress.* 3d ed. Washington, D.C.: Congressional Quarterly, 1982. One volume that covers almost everything.
Congressional Directory (published annually by Congress). Lists members of Congress, committee assignments, telephone numbers, maps of districts.
Congressional Staff Directory. Lists all staffers and gives biographical sketches.

To find out about the political inclinations and constituency characteristics of members of Congress:
Michael Barone et al. *The Almanac of American Politics.* Revised every two years, this is a candid description of districts, states, members of Congress, and how they vote.
Congressional District Data Book. Published by the Census Bureau, it compiles all relevant census data by congressional district.

To find out what is going on in Congress currently:
Congressional Quarterly Weekly Report. A weekly summary of issues, votes, politics. Commercially published.
Congressional Record. The official, verbatim account of what is said (after being revised by members of Congress who do the saying). Published daily by the Government Printing Office while Congress is in session.

To find out what Congress did in the past:
Congressional Quarterly Almanac. Published each year as a summary of issues, votes, and politics.
Congressional Quarterly: Congress and the Nation. 8 volumes, 1945–1992. Convenient compilation of past Almanacs.

To find out the exact wording of bills and laws:
United States Statutes at Large. Published by the Government Printing Office; the laws and volumes are chronologically arranged.
Digest of Public Bills. Published by Congressional Research Service.

CRITICAL Thinking

Constituent Service or Political Corruption?

Constituent service. To me, it's very important.... If I think there is a cause where the government has mistreated a constituent, I'm going to do all I can, within the bounds of ethical conduct, to see that government responds to this constituent.

Thus explained Senator Dennis DeConcini (D., Arizona) in his opening statement to the Senate ethics committee during the hearings in the case of the "Keating Five." The case involved DeConcini and four other senators—Alan Cranston (D., California), John Glenn (D., Ohio), Donald Riegle (D., Mich.), and John McCain (R., Arizona).

As described in a recent study of ethics in Congress by political philosopher Dennis F. Thompson, Charles Keating, Jr., was a successful real estate financier and developer who operated in several states. Among his companies was Lincoln Savings and Loan in California, which he bought in 1984. For a half decade he and his lawyers battled state regulators who insisted that Lincoln was in violation of many laws governing investment practices and financial disclo-

sure. The state regulators were joined by Edwin Gray, the head of the three-member Federal Home Loan Bank Board that regulated the industry. In 1989 Lincoln went bankrupt, wiping out the savings of twenty-three thousand uninsured depositors, most of them elderly people. The Lincoln collapse cost federal taxpayers $2 billion and came to epitomize the country's "Savings and Loan Crisis."

On April 2, 1987, DeConcini summoned Gray to his office. Three of the four other senators joined DeConcini (Riegle, who helped arrange the meeting, was expected to attend but did not). The senators asked Gray why the investigation of Lincoln and their "friend" Keating was being pursued so doggedly. A week later, all five senators met in DeConcini's office, this time with four California bank regulators from San Francisco. The senators complained that the government was harassing a constituent whose companies had boosted their respective regional economies. Then the state regulators revealed that they were about to make a criminal referral against Lincoln. The meeting ended there.

McCain and Riegle had no fur dealings with Keating. Glenn had a b lunch with Keating the follow January. Cranston and DeConcini, h ever, continued to act on Keating's half. During a two-month period 1989, Cranston approached regulator least six times. DeConcini continue press Keating's case with state and fed regulators.

In assessing the ethics of the Kea Five, Professor Thompson wei DeConcini's claim that what he and fellow senators did for Keating was s ply an instance of good old-fashio constituent service, the customary pr tice of "providing help to individu groups, and localities in coping with federal government." As Thomp frames the issue, the "Keating Five, es cially DeConcini and Cranston, certai provided this constituent with go service. Because corruption typically volves an exchange of some kind, should ask, what did the senators get return?" The answer is $1.3 million campaign funds and contributions.

But the amounts and the timing the exchanges varied. McCain and Gle

about by younger, especially northern, members. Dissatisfied with southern resistance to civil rights bills and emboldened by a sharp increase in the number of liberals who had been elected in the Johnson landslide of 1964, the House Democratic caucus adopted rules that allowed the caucus to select committee chairmen without regard to seniority, dramatically increased the number and staffs of subcommittees (for the first time, the Ways and Means Committee was required to have subcommittees), authorized individual committee members

(instead of the chairman) to choose the chairmen of these subcommittees, ended the ability of chairmen to refuse to call meetings, and made it much harder for those meetings to be closed to the public. The installation of electronic voting made it easier to require recorded votes, and so the number of times each member had to go on record rose sharply. The Rules Committee was instructed to issue more rules that would allow floor amendments.

At the same time, the number of southern Democrats in leadership positions began to decline, received their money years before Keating enlisted their help with the bank regulators. Riegle and DeConcini solicited contributions while intervening for Keating. Cranston received the lion's share of the money (almost $1 million) when he was actively intervening for Keating. Still, most of the money Cranston received went to voter registration groups, the largest portion to the Center for Participation in Democracy, headed by Cranston's son. In fact, none of the senators put a penny in their own pockets.

In February 1991 the ethics committee lightly rebuked McCain and Glenn, severely rebuked DeConcini and Riegle, and formally reprimanded Cranston. All but McCain and Glenn announced that they would not seek reelection.

Thompson recounts that Cranston, like DeConcini, claimed "that he had done nothing worse than most of his Senate colleagues had done," namely, aggressive constituent service. But Thompson is unpersuaded: "Cranston's defense exemplifies in a cynical form the dynamics of corruption conversion. The accused member seeks to sanitize his own conduct by showing that it is a legitimate institutional practice. He represents his conduct as part of a normal competitive process in which all politicians are encouraged by the political system to solicit support and bestow favors in order to win elections. What he is doing is not only not individually corrupt, but institutionally required. If permitted to run its course, this dynamic results in either exonerating the member completely—he did only what had to be done to get reelected—or condemning the entire institution as corrupt—he is just one of the 'Keating 535.'"

What do you think? For his part in this affair, the high-living Keating made a fortune but was convicted of mismanagement in a court of law. Should it matter that none of the Keating Five sought to line his own pockets or used his public office to secure a personal (as opposed to a political) gain? Should it matter whether or not the senators involved had given Keating no special favors and would do the same for any constituent—rich or poor, powerful or powerless—who had such a problem with the government? Putting questions of favoritism aside, should this brand of constituent service be practiced at all?

Who should judge where constituent service ends and political corruption begins? Members of Congress (inevitably some of them friends and political allies of the accused, others foes and political enemies)? Bipartisan panels of distinguished ex-members of Congress? Who?

Finally, how should one define ethics rules and regulations? Should the aim of such laws be mainly to increase the chances that corrupt members will be caught and punished, or to prevent or deter members from getting into trouble in the first place?

Ponder these questions in relation to the other things you have learned so far about Congress and the American political system. Learn to raise such questions in your own mind the next time you hear a news flash about some instance of corruption in high places. We encourage you to think critically about these issues, for as Thompson wisely concludes, "No reforms alone can restore public confidence or promote legislative independence and fairness unless both citizens and their representatives come to understand better the nature and importance of ethics in the modern Congress."

SOURCE: Dennis F. Thompson, *Ethics in Congress: From Individual to Institutional Corruption* (Washington, D.C.: Brookings Institution, 1995).

and the conservatism of the remaining ones began to lessen. (In 1990 southerners held only a quarter of committee chairmanships in the House and none of the major party leadership posts.) Moreover, northern and southern Democrats began to vote together a bit more frequently (though the conservative Boll Weevils remained a significant—and often swing—group).

These changes created a House ideally suited to serve the reelection needs of its members. Each representative could be an individual political entrepreneur, seeking publicity, claiming credit, introducing bills, holding subcommittee hearings, and assigning staffers to work on constituents' problems. There was no need to defer to powerful party leaders or committee chairmen. But because representatives in each party were becoming more alike ideologically, there was a rise in party voting. Congress became a career attractive to men and women skilled in these techniques, and these people entered Congress in large numbers. Their skill was manifest in the growth of the sophomore surge—the increase in their winning percentage during their first reelection campaign.

Even junior members could now make their mark on legislation. In the House more floor amendments were offered and were passed; in the Senate filibusters became more commonplace. Owing to multiple referrals and overlapping subcommittee jurisdictions, more members could participate in writing bills and overseeing government agencies.

But lurking within the changes that defined the second stage were others, less noticed at the time, that created the beginnings of a new phase. The third stage was an effort in the House to strengthen and centralize party leadership. The Speaker acquired the power to appoint a majority of the members of the Rules Committee. That body, worried by the flood of floor amendments, began issuing more restrictive rules. By the mid-1980s this had reached the point where Republicans were complaining that they were being gagged. The Speaker also got control of the Democratic Steering and Policy Committee (it assigns new members to committees) and was given the power to refer bills to several committees simultaneously.

These opportunities for becoming a powerful Speaker were not noticed while the affable Tip O'Neill of Massachusetts held that post, but when Jim Wright of Texas replaced O'Neill, he began making full use of those powers. Perhaps if he had not stumbled over his ethical problems, Wright might have succeeded in becoming the policy leader of the House, setting the agenda and getting much of it adopted. The replacement of Wright by Tom Foley of Washington signaled a return to a more accommodative leadership style. Foley's replacement, Republican Newt Gingrich, is a more assertive policy leader. The evolution of the House remains an incomplete story; it is not yet clear whether it will remain in stage two or find some way of moving decisively into stage three. For now it has elements of both.

Meanwhile the Senate remains as individualistic and decentralized as ever—a place where it has always been difficult to exercise strong leadership.

Though its members may complain that Congress is collectively weak, to any visitor from abroad it seems extraordinarily powerful, probably the most powerful legislative body in the world. Congress has always been jealous of its constitutional independence and authority. Three compelling events led to Congress's reasserting its authority: the increasingly unpopular war in Vietnam; the Watergate scandals, which revealed a White House meddling illegally in the electoral process; and the advent of divided governments—with one party in control of the presidency and the other in control of Congress.

In 1973 Congress passed, over a presidential veto, the War Powers Act, giving it a greater voice in the use of American forces abroad. The following year it passed the Congressional Budget and Impoundment Control Act, which denied the president the right to refuse to spend money appropriated by Congress and allowed Congress to play a greater role in the budget process. It passed more laws to provide a legislative veto over proposed presidential actions, especially with respect to the sale of arms abroad. Not all these steps have withstood the tests of time or Supreme Court review, but taken together they symbolize the resurgence of congressional authority and helped set the stage for sharper conflicts between Congress and the presidency.

Claims that Congress became weak as the president grew stronger are a bit overdrawn. As we shall see in the next chapter, the view from the White House is quite different. Recent presidents have complained bitterly of their inability to get Congress even to act on, much less approve, many of their key proposals and have resented what they regard as congressional interference in the management of executive-branch agencies and the conduct of foreign affairs.

KEY TERMS

bicameral legislature   *p. 302*

filibuster   *p. 307*

marginal district   *p. 309*

safe district   *p. 309*

conservative coalition   *p. 313*

malapportionment   *p. 314*

gerrymandering   *p. 314*

majority-minority districts   *p. 316*

descriptive representation   *p. 316*

substantive representation   *p. 316*

sophomore surge   *p. 318*

majority leader   *p. 319*

minority leader   *p. 319*

whip   *p. 320*

party unity vote   *p. 324*

caucus (congressional)   *p. 326*

standing committees   *p. 330*

select committees   *p. 330*

joint committees   *p. 330*

conference committees   *p. 330*

public bill   *p. 336*

private bill   *p. 336*

simple resolution   *p. 336*

concurrent resolution   *p. 336*

joint resolution   *p. 337*

multiple referral   *p. 338*

sequential referral   *p. 338*

discharge petition   *p. 338*

closed rule   *p. 339*

open rule   *p. 339*

restrictive rule   *p. 339*

quorum   *p. 340*

quorum call   *p. 340*

rider   *p. 340*

Christmas-tree bill   *p. 340*

cloture rule   *p. 341*

double-tracking   *p. 341*

voice vote   *p. 342*

division vote   *p. 342*

teller vote   *p. 342*

roll-call vote   *p. 342*

pork-barrel legislation   *p. 350*

franking privilege   *p. 351*

SUGGESTED READINGS

Davidson, Roger H., and Walter J. Oleszek. *Congress and Its Members.* 3d ed. Washington, D.C.: Congressional Quarterly Press, 1990. Complete and authoritative account of who is in Congress and how it operates.

Dodd, Lawrence C., and Bruce I. Oppenheimer, eds. *Congress Reconsidered.* 4th ed. Washington, D.C.: Congressional Quarterly Press, 1989. Recent studies of congressional politics.

Fenno, Richard F., Jr. *Congressmen in Committees.* Boston: Little, Brown, 1973. Study of the styles of twelve standing committees.

Maass, Arthur. *Congress and the Common Good.* New York: Basic Books, 1984. Insightful account of congressional operations, especially those involving legislative-executive relations.

Malbin, Michael J. *Unelected Representatives.* New York: Basic Books, 1980. Study of the influence of congressional staff members.

Malbin, Michael J., and Gerald Ginsberg, eds. *Limiting Legislative Terms.* Washington, D.C.: Congressional Quarterly, 1992. Good collection of essays on term limits.

Mann, Thomas E., and Norman J. Ornstein. *Renewing Congress.* 2 vols. Washington, D.C.: Brookings Institution and American Enterprise Institute, 1993. Superb, up-to-date overview of what's really wrong with Congress and how to fix it.

Mayhew, David R. *Congress: The Electoral Connection.* New Haven, Conn.: Yale University Press, 1974. Argues that a member of Congress's desire to win reelection shapes his or her legislative behavior.

Smith, Steven S., and Christopher J. Deering. *Committees in Congress.* Washington, D.C.: Congressional Quarterly, 1984. Analysis of how different kinds of congressional committees operate.

Sundquist, James L. *The Decline and Resurgence of Congress.* Washington, D.C.: Brookings Institution, 1981. A history of the fall and, after 1973, the rise of congressional power vis-à-vis the president.

12

The Presidency

★ Comparison of presidents and prime ministers

★ Government gridlock

★ Concerns of the Founders

★ The electoral college

★ Legitimacy of the office

★ Relationship to Congress

★ Presidential appointments

★ Character of the president

★ Communication with the electorate

★ Effect of the president's personal popularity

★ Veto power

★ Executive privilege

★ Impoundment of funds

★ Formulation of a program

★ Presidential transition

★ The vice president

★ Impeachment

Professor Jones speaks to his political science class: "The president of the United States occupies one of the most powerful offices in the world. Presidents Kennedy and Johnson sent American troops to Vietnam, and President Bush sent them to Panama and to Saudi Arabia, all without war being declared by Congress. President Nixon imposed wage and price controls on the country. Between them, presidents Carter and Reagan selected most of the federal judges now on the bench; thus the political philosophies of these two men were stamped on the courts. No wonder people talk about our having an 'imperial presidency.'"

A few doors down the hall, Professor Smith speaks to her class: "The president, compared to the prime ministers of other democratic nations, is one of the weakest chief executives anywhere. President Carter signed an arms-limitation treaty with the Soviets, but the Senate wouldn't ratify it. President Reagan was not allowed even to test antisatellite weapons, and in 1986 Congress rejected his budget before the ink was dry. President Clinton's health care plan was ignored. Regularly, subordinates who are supposed to be loyal to the president leak his views to the press and undercut his programs before Congress. No wonder people call the U.S. president a 'pitiful, helpless giant.'"

Can Professors Jones and Smith be talking about the same office? Who is right? In fact they are both right. The American presidency is a unique office, with elements of great strength *and* profound weakness built into it by its constitutional origins.

Presidents and Prime Ministers

The popularly elected president is an American invention. Of the roughly five dozen countries in which there is some degree of party competition and thus, presumably, some measure of free choice for the voters, only sixteen have a directly elected president, and thirteen of these are nations of North and South America. The democratic alternative is for the chief executive to be a prime minister, chosen

363

by and responsible to the parliament. This system prevails in most Western European countries as well as in Israel and Japan. There is no nation with a purely presidential political system in Europe; France combines a directly elected president with a prime minister and parliament.[1]

In a parliamentary system the prime minister is the chief executive. The prime minister is chosen not by the voters but by the legislature, and he or she in turn selects the other ministers from the members of parliament. If the parliament has only two major parties, the ministers will usually be chosen from the majority party; if there are many parties (as in Italy), several parties may participate in a coalition cabinet. The prime minister remains in power as long as his or her party has a majority of the seats in the legislature or as long as the coalition he or she has assembled holds together. The voters choose who is to be a member of parliament—usually by voting for one or another party—but cannot choose who is to be the chief executive officer.

Whether a nation has a presidential or a parliamentary system makes a big difference in the identity and powers of the chief executive.

Presidents are often outsiders   People become president by winning elections, and sometimes winning is easier if you can show the voters that you are not part of "the mess in Washington." Prime ministers are selected from among people already in parliament, and so they are always insiders.

Jimmy Carter, Ronald Reagan, and Bill Clinton did not hold national office before becoming president. Franklin Roosevelt had been assistant secretary of the navy, but his real political experience was as governor of New York. Dwight Eisenhower was a general, not a politician. John F. Kennedy, Lyndon Johnson, and Richard Nixon had been in Congress, but only Nixon had had top-level experience in the executive branch (he had been vice president). George Bush had had a great deal of executive experience in Washington—as vice president, director of the CIA, and representative to China, whereas Bill Clinton's executive experience was as governor of Arkansas.

The prime minister of Great Britain may or may not have any real personal following at the time he or she is appointed. Winston Churchill was immensely popular in the country before he became

the British prime minister in 1939, but Margaret Thatcher was largely unknown to the country when she became prime minister in 1979. But all British prime ministers have a lot of political experience.

Presidents choose cabinet members from outside Congress   Under the Constitution, no sitting member of Congress can hold office in the executive branch. The persons chosen by a prime minister to be in the cabinet are almost always members of parliament.

Of the fourteen heads of the cabinet-level government departments in the first Clinton administration, only three had been members of Congress. The rest, as is customary with most presidents, were close personal friends or campaign aides, representatives of important constituencies (for example, farmers, blacks, or women), experts on various policy issues, or some combination of all three.

The prime minister of Great Britain, by contrast, picks all of his or her cabinet ministers from among members of Parliament. This is one way by which the prime minister exercises control over the legislature. If you were an ambitious member of Parliament, eager to become prime minister yourself some day, and if you knew that your main chance of realizing that ambition was to be appointed to a series of ever-more-important cabinet posts, then you would not be likely to antagonize the person doing the appointing.

Presidents have no guaranteed majority in the legislature   A prime minister's party (or coalition) always has a majority in parliament; if it did not, somebody else would be prime minister. A president's party often does not have a congressional majority; instead, Congress is often controlled by the opposite party, creating a divided government. Divided government means that cooperation between the two branches, hard to achieve under the best of circumstances, is often further reduced by partisan bickering.

Even when one party controls both the White House and Congress, the two branches often work at cross purposes. The U.S. Constitution created a system of separate branches sharing powers. The authors of the document expected that there would be conflict between the branches, and they have not been disappointed.

When Kennedy was president, his party, the Democrats, held a big majority in the House and the Senate. Yet Kennedy was frustrated by his inability to get Congress to approve proposals to enlarge civil rights, supply federal aid for school construction, create a Department of Urban Affairs and Housing, or establish a program of subsidized medical care for the elderly. During his last year in office, Congress passed only about one-fourth of his proposals. Carter did not fare much better; even though the Democrats controlled Congress, many of his most important proposals were defeated or greatly modified. Only Franklin Roosevelt (1933–1945) and Lyndon Johnson (1963–1969) had even brief success in leading Congress, and for Roosevelt most of that success was confined to his first term or to wartime.

Divided Government

In the forty-four years between 1952 and 1996 there were twenty-two congressional or presidential elections. Fifteen of the twenty-two produced **divided government**—that is, a government in which one party controls the White House and a different party controls one or both houses of Congress. When Bill Clinton became president in 1992, it was the first time since 1981 (and only the second time since 1969) that the same party was in charge of both the presidency and Congress, creating a **unified government.** And it only lasted two years.

Americans say they don't like divided government. They, or at least the pundits who claim to speak for them, think divided government produces partisan bickering, political paralysis, and policy gridlock. During the 1990 battle between President Bush and a Democratic Congress, one magazine compared it to a movie featuring the Keystone Kops, characters from the silent movies who wildly chased each other around while accomplishing nothing.[2] In the 1992 campaign, Bush, Clinton, and Ross Perot bemoaned the "stalemate" that had developed in Washington. When Clinton was sworn in as president, many commentators spoke approvingly of the "end of gridlock."

There are two things wrong with these complaints. First, it is not clear that divided government produces a gridlock that is any worse than that which exists with unified government. Second, it is

British Prime Minister Tony Blair, unlike the president of the United States, knows that almost any bill he submits to his legislature will be approved.

not clear that, even if gridlock does exist, it is always, or even usually, a bad thing for the country.

Does Gridlock Matter?

Despite the well-publicized stories about presidential budget proposals being ignored by Congress (Democrats used to describe Reagan's and Bush's budgets as being "dead on arrival"), it is not easy to tell whether divided governments produce fewer or worse policies than unified ones. The scholars who have looked closely at the matter have, in general, concluded that divided governments do about as well as unified ones in passing important laws, conducting important investigations, and ratifying significant treaties.[3] Political scientist David Mayhew studied 267 important laws that were enacted between 1946 and 1990. These laws were as likely to be passed when different parties controlled the White House and Congress as when the same party controlled both branches.[4] For example, divided governments produced the 1946 Marshall Plan to rebuild war-torn Europe and the 1986 Tax Reform Act.

Why do divided governments produce about as much important legislation as unified ones? The main reason is that "unified government" is something of a myth. Just because the Democrats control both the presidency and Congress does not mean that the Democratic president and the Democratic senators and representatives will see things the same way. For one thing, Democrats are themselves divided between conservatives (mainly from the South) and liberals (mainly from the Northeast and the West). They disagree about policy almost as much as Republicans and Democrats disagree. For another thing, the Constitution ensures that the president and Congress will be rivals for power and thus rivals in policy making. That's what the separation of powers and checks and balances are all about.

As a result, periods of unified government often turn out not to be so unified. Democratic President Lyndon Johnson could not get many Democratic members of Congress to support his war policy in Vietnam. Democratic President Jimmy Carter could not get the Democratic-controlled Senate to ratify his strategic arms limitation treaty. Democratic President Bill Clinton could not get the Democratic Congress to go along with his policy on gays in the military or his health proposals; and when the heavily revised Clinton budget did pass in 1993, it was by just one vote.

The only time there really is a unified government is when not just the same party but the same *ideological wing* of that party is in effective control of both branches of government. This was true in 1933 when Franklin Roosevelt was president and change-oriented Democrats controlled Congress, and it was true again in 1965 when Lyndon Johnson and liberal Democrats dominated Congress. Both were periods when many major policy initiatives became law: Social Security, business regulations, Medicare, and civil rights legislation. But these periods of ideologically unified government are very rare.

Is Policy Gridlock Bad?

An American president has less ability to decide what laws get passed than does a British prime minister. If you think that the job of a president is to "lead the country," that weakness will worry you. The only cure for that weakness is either to change the Constitution so that our government resembles the parliamentary system in effect in Great Britain

or always to vote into office members of Congress who not only are of the same party as the president but also agree with him on policy issues.

We suspect that even Americans who hate gridlock and want more leadership aren't ready to make sweeping constitutional changes or to stop voting for presidents and members of Congress from different parties. This unwillingness suggests that they like the idea of somebody being able to block a policy they don't like. Since all of us don't like something, we all have an interest in some degree of gridlock.

And we seem to protect that interest. In a typical presidential election, about one-fourth of all voters will vote for one party's candidate for president and the other party's candidate for Congress. As a result, about one-third of all congressional districts will be represented in the House by a person who does not belong to the party of the president who carried that district. Some scholars believe that voters split tickets deliberately in order to create divided government and thus magnify the effects of the checks and balances built into our system, but the evidence supporting this belief is not conclusive.

Gridlock, to the extent that it exists, is a necessary consequence of a system of **representative democracy.** Such a system causes delays, intensifies deliberations, forces compromises, and requires the creation of broad-based coalitions to support most new policies. This system is the opposite of **direct democracy.** If you believe in direct democracy, you believe that what the people want on some issue should become law with as little fuss and bother as possible. Political gridlocks are like traffic gridlocks—people get overheated, things boil over, nothing moves, and nobody wins except journalists who write about the mess and lobbyists who charge big fees to steer their clients around the tie-up. In a direct democracy, the president would be a traffic cop with broad powers to decide in what direction the traffic should move and to make sure that it moves that way.

Gridlock in History

The debate between advocates of direct and representative democracy has gone on since the founding of the republic. What is new is the greater frequency of divided government. Between 1900 and 1952, unified government was common (twenty-two out of twenty-six elections gave control over the White House and Congress to the same party). Since 1952, as we have seen, unified government has become a rarity and divided government has become common.

But if unified governments are not really unified—if in fact they are split by ideological differences within each party and by the institutional rivalries between the president and Congress—then this change is less important than it may seem. What *is* important is the relative power of the president and Congress. That has changed greatly.

The Evolution of the Presidency

In 1787 few issues inspired as much debate or concern among the Framers as the problem of defining the chief executive. The delegates feared anarchy and monarchy in about equal measure. When the Constitutional Convention met, the existing state constitutions gave most, if not all, power to the legislatures. In eight states the governor was actually chosen by the legislature, and in ten states the governor could not serve more than one year. Only in New York, Massachusetts, and Connecticut did governors have much power or serve for any length of time.

Some of the Framers proposed a plural national executive (that is, several people would each hold the executive power in different areas, or they would exercise the power as a committee). Others wanted the executive power checked, as it was in Massachusetts, by a council that would have to approve many of the chief executive's actions. Alexander Hamilton strongly urged the exact opposite: in a five-hour speech he called for something very much like an elective monarchy, patterned in some respects after the British kind. No one paid much attention to this plan or even, at first, to the more modest (and ultimately successful) suggestion of James Wilson for a single, elected president.

In time those won out who believed that the governing of a large nation, especially one threatened by foreign enemies, required a single president with significant powers. Their cause was aided, no doubt, by the fact that everybody assumed that George Washington would be the first president,

The first cabinet: left to right, Secretary of War Henry Knox, Secretary of State Thomas Jefferson, Attorney General Edmund Randolph, Secretary of the Treasury Alexander Hamilton, and President George Washington.

and confidence in him—and in his sense of self-restraint—was widely shared. Even so, several delegates feared that the presidency would become, in the words of Edmund Randolph of Virginia, "the fœtus of monarchy."

Concerns of the Founders

The delegates in Philadelphia, and later the critics of the new Constitution during the debate over its ratification, worried about aspects of the presidency that were quite different from those that concern us today. In 1787–1789 some Americans suspected that the president, by being able to command the state militia, would use the militia to overpower state governments. Others were worried that, if the president were allowed to share treaty-making power with the Senate, he would be "directed by minions and favorites" and become a "tool of the Senate."

But the most frequent concern was over the possibility of presidential reelection: Americans in the late eighteenth century were sufficiently suspicious of human nature and sufficiently experienced in the arts of mischievous government to believe that a president, once elected, would arrange to stay in office in perpetuity by resorting to bribery, intrigue, and force. This might happen, for example, every time the presidential election was thrown into the House of Representatives because no candidate had received a majority of the votes in the electoral college, a situation that most people expected to happen frequently.

In retrospect these concerns seem misplaced, even foolish. The power over the militia has had little significance; the election has gone to the House only twice (1800 and 1824); and though the Senate dominated the presidency off and on during the second half of the nineteenth century, it has not done so recently. The real sources of the expansion of presidential power—the president's role in foreign affairs, his ability to shape public opinion, his position as head of the executive branch, and his claims to have certain "inherent" powers by virtue of his office—were hardly predictable in 1787. And not surprisingly. There was nowhere in the world at that time, nor had there been at any time in history, an example of an American-style presidency. It was a unique and unprecedented institution, and the Framers and their critics can easily be forgiven for not predicting accurately how it would evolve. At a more general level, however, they understood the issue quite clearly. Gouverneur Morris of Pennsylvania put the problem of the presidency this way: "Make him too weak: the Legislature will usurp his powers. Make him too strong: he will usurp on the Legislature."

The Framers knew very well that the relations between the president and Congress and the manner in which the president is elected were of profound importance, and they debated both at great length. The first plan was for Congress to elect the president—in short, for the system to be quasi-parliamentary. But if that were done, some delegates pointed out, the Congress could dominate an honest or lazy president while a corrupt or scheming president might dominate Congress.

After much discussion it was decided that the president should be chosen directly by voters. But by which voters? The emerging nation was large and diverse. It seemed unlikely that every citizen would be familiar enough with the candidates to cast an informed vote for a president directly. Worse, a direct popular election would give inordinate weight to the large, populous states, and no plan with that outcome had any chance of adoption by the smaller states.

The Electoral College

Thus the electoral college was invented, whereby each of the states would select electors in whatever manner it wished. The electors would then meet in each state capital and vote for president and vice president. Many Framers expected that this procedure would lead to each state's electors' voting for a favorite son, and thus no candidate would win a majority of the popular vote. In this event, it was decided, the House of Representatives should make the choice, with each state delegation casting one vote.

The plan seemed to meet every test: large states would have their say, but small states would be protected by having a minimum of three electoral votes no matter how tiny their population. The small states together could wield considerable influence in the House, where, it was widely expected, most presidential elections would ultimately be decided. Of course it did not work out quite this way: the Framers did not foresee the role that political parties would play in producing nationwide support for a slate of national candidates.

Once the manner of electing the president was settled, the question of his powers was much easier to decide. After all, if you believe that the procedures are fair and balanced, then you are more confident in assigning larger powers to the president within this system. Accordingly, the right to make treaties and the right to appoint lesser officials, originally reserved for the Senate, were given to the president "with the advice and consent of the Senate."

The President's Term of Office

Another issue was put to rest soon thereafter. George Washington, the unanimous choice of the electoral college to be the first president, firmly limited himself to two terms in office (1789–1797), and no president until Franklin D. Roosevelt (1933–

The Evolution of the Presidency

Corazon Aquino became president of the Philippines only after popular demonstrations and military support forced her predecessor, Ferdinand Marcos, to leave office amidst charges that he had presided over a rigged election. Free elections and peaceful transfers of power are rare in the world.

1945) dared to run for more (though Ulysses S. Grant tried). In 1951 the Twenty-second Amendment to the Constitution was ratified, formally limiting all subsequent presidents to two terms. The remaining issues concerning the nature of the presidency, and especially the relations between the president and Congress, have been the subject of continuing dispute. The pattern of relationships that we see today is the result of an evolutionary process that has extended over more than two centuries.

The first problem was to establish the legitimacy of the presidency itself: that is, to ensure, if possible, public acceptance of the office, its incumbent, and its powers and to establish an orderly transfer of power from one incumbent to the next.

Today we take this for granted. When Bill Clinton was inaugurated in January 1993 as our forty-second president, George Bush, the forty-first president, quietly left the White House and went home. In the world today such an uneventful

America has witnessed peaceful transfers of power not only between leaders of different parties (such as Woodrow Wilson and William Howard Taft in 1913) but also after a popular leader is assassinated (Lyndon Johnson is sworn in after Kennedy's death).

The Electoral College

Each state is allotted by the Constitution as many electoral votes as it has senators and representatives in Congress. Thus no state has fewer than three electoral votes. (The District of Columbia also gets three, even though it has no members of Congress.)

In each state each party runs a slate of electors pledged to that party's presidential and vice presidential candidates. The names of these electors usually do not appear on the ballots. The slate whose candidate wins more popular votes than any other is authorized to cast all the votes of that state in the electoral college.

This results in a "winner-take-all" effect. Since it is up to the state legislatures to decide how electors are chosen, they could devise systems that would produce a split in the state's electoral votes. Maine and Nebraska are the only states that have done this. In these two states, one electoral vote goes to the winner of the popular vote in each district, and two electoral votes go to the top vote-getter statewide.

The winning slates of electors assemble in their state capitals about six weeks after the election to cast their ballots. Ordinarily this is a pure formality. Occasionally, however, an elector will vote for a presidential candidate other than the one who carried the state. Such "faithless electors" have appeared in nine elections since 1796. The most recent case was in 1988, when a West Virginia elector pledged to Michael Dukakis voted instead for Lloyd Bentsen.

The state electoral ballots are opened and counted before a joint session of Congress during the first week of January. The candidate with a majority of votes is declared elected.

If no candidate wins a majority, the House of Representatives chooses the president from among the three leading candidates, with each state casting one vote. By House rule, each state's vote is allotted to the candidate preferred by a majority of the state's House delegation. If there is a tie within a delegation, that state's vote is not counted.

The House has had to decide two presidential contests. In 1800 Thomas Jefferson and Aaron Burr tied in the electoral college because of a defect in the language of the Constitution—each state cast two electoral votes, without indicating which was for president and which for vice president. (Burr was supposed to be vice president and after much maneuvering, he was.) This problem was corrected by the Twelfth Amendment, ratified in 1804. The only House decision under the modern system was in 1824, when it chose John Quincy Adams over Andrew Jackson and William H. Crawford, even though Jackson had more electoral votes (and probably more popular votes) than his rivals.

The chief political effects of the electoral college are these: The winner-take-all system probably discourages the emergence of serious third parties. The system encourages candidates to focus their campaigns on states, especially states whose vote may be in doubt. It especially encourages candidates to emphasize large, doubtful states. A candi-

succession is unusual. In many nations a new chief executive comes to power with the aid of military force or as a result of political intrigue; his predecessor often leaves office disgraced, exiled, or dead. At the time that the Constitution was written, the Founders could only hope that an orderly transfer of power from one president to the next would occur. France had just undergone a bloody revolution; England in the not-too-distant past had beheaded a king; and in Poland the ruler was elected by a process so manifestly corrupt and so open to intrigue that Thomas Jefferson, in what may be the first example of ethnic humor in American politics,

was led to refer to the proposed American presidency as a "bad edition of a Polish king."

Yet by the time Abraham Lincoln found himself at the helm of a nation plunged into a bitter, bloody civil war, fifteen presidents had been elected, served their time, and left office without a hint of force being used to facilitate the process and with the people accepting the process—if not admiring all the presidents. This orderly transfer of authority occurred despite passionate opposition and deeply divisive elections (such as that which brought Jefferson to power). And it did not happen by accident.

ELECTORAL VOTES PER STATE FOR 1992 ELECTION

ND 3
SD 3
MT 3
WY 3
WA 11
OR 7
ID 4
NE 5
MN 10
IA 7
WI 11
MI 18
IL 22
IN 12
OH 21
PA 23
NY 33
ME 4
NH 4
VT 3
MA 12
CT 8
RI 4
NJ 15
DC 3
DE 3
MD 10
NV 4
UT 5
CO 8
KS 6
MO 11
KY 8
WV 5
VA 13
NC 14
CA 54
NM 5
OK 8
AR 6
TN 11
SC 8
AZ 8
TX 32
LA 9
MS. 7
AL 9
GA 13
FL 25

HAWAII 4
ALASKA 3

Note: States drawn in proportion to number of electoral votes. Total electoral votes: 538

each state's electoral votes in proportion to the popular vote received by each candidate in that state; to have electors chosen by congressional district rather than at large; and to retain the electoral system but abolish the office of elector and thus the chance of a faithless elector.

The issues and arguments are complex. Those who want to preserve the electoral college believe that it is important for the states to have a role in choosing the president and for the president to have an electoral reason to attend to state interests. Moreover, the electoral college helps maintain the two-party system. Those favoring direct popular election argue that the states are irrelevant in presidential elections and that each person's vote should count the same as every other person's, regardless of where he or she lives.

date who carries the ten largest states wins 254 electoral votes, only 16 short of a majority. These states tend to be the most urbanized, industrialized, and politically competitive ones. A president seeking reelection has reason to be attentive to the needs of such states.

Proposals to alter or abolish the electoral college have been made, but none has come close to adoption. Among these are plans to elect the president by direct, national, popular vote; to divide

The First Presidents

Those who first served as president were among the most prominent men in the new nation, all active either in the movement for independence or in the Founding or in both. Of the first five presidents, four (all but John Adams) served two full terms. Washington and Monroe were not even opposed. The first administration had at the highest levels the leading spokesmen for all of the major viewpoints: Alexander Hamilton was Washington's secretary of the treasury (and was sympathetic to the urban commercial interests), and Thomas Jefferson was secretary of state (and more inclined toward rural, small-town, and farming views). Washington spoke out strongly against political parties, and though parties soon emerged, there was a stigma attached to them: many people believed that it was wrong to take advantage of divisions in the country, to organize deliberately to acquire political office, or to make legislation depend upon party advantage. As it turned out, this hostility to party (or "faction," as it was more commonly called) was unrealistic: parties are as natural to democracy as churches are to religion.

Establishing the legitimacy of the presidency in the early years was made easier by the fact that the national government had relatively little to do. It had, of course, to establish a sound currency and to settle the debt accrued during the Revolutionary War. The Treasury Department inevitably became the principal federal office, especially under the strong leadership of Hamilton. Relations with England and France were important—and difficult—but otherwise government took little time and few resources.

In appointing people to federal office, a general rule of "fitness" emerged: those appointed should have some standing in their communities and be well thought of by their neighbors. Appointments based on partisanship soon arose, but community stature could not be neglected.

The presidency was kept modest. Washington clearly had not sought the office and did not relish the exercise of its then modest powers. He traveled widely so that as many people as possible could see their new president. His efforts to establish a semiregal court etiquette were quickly rebuffed; the presidency was to be kept simple. Congress decided that not until after a president was dead might his likeness appear on a coin or on currency; no president until Eisenhower was given a pension on his retirement.

The president's relations with Congress were correct but not close. Washington appeared before the Senate to ask its advice on a proposed treaty with some Indian tribes. He got none, and instead was politely told that the Senate would like to consider the matter in private. He declared that he would be "damned if he ever went there again," and he never did. Thus ended the responsibility of the Senate to "advise" the president. Vetoes were sometimes cast by the president, but sparingly, and only when the president believed that the law was not simply unwise but unconstitutional. Washington cast only two vetoes; Jefferson and Adams cast none.

The Jacksonians

At a time roughly corresponding to the presidency of Andrew Jackson (1829–1837), broad changes began to occur in American politics. These changes, together with the personality of Jackson himself, altered the relations between president and Congress and the nature of presidential leadership. As so often happens, few people at the time Jackson took office had much sense of what his presidency would be like. Though he had been a member of the House of Representatives and of the Senate, he was elected as a military hero—and an apparently doddering one at that. Sixty-one years old and seemingly frail, he

President Andrew Jackson thought of himself as the "Tribune of the People," and he symbolized this by throwing a White House party that anyone could attend. Hundreds of people showed up and ate or carried away most of a 1,400-pound block of cheese.

nonetheless used the powers of his office as no one before him had.

Jackson vetoed twelve acts of Congress, more than all his predecessors combined and more than any subsequent president until Andrew Johnson thirty years later. His vetoes were not simply on constitutional grounds but on policy ones: as the only official elected by the entire voting citizenry, he saw himself as the "Tribune of the People." None of his vetoes were overridden. He did not initiate many new policies, but he struck out against the ones that he did not like. He did so at a time when the size of the electorate was increasing rapidly, and new states, especially in the West, had entered the Union. (There were then twenty-four states in the Union, nearly twice the original number.)

Jackson demonstrated what could be done by a popular president. He did not shrink from conflict with Congress, and the tension between the two branches of government that was intended by the Framers became intensified by the personalities of those in government: Jackson in the White House, and Henry Clay, Daniel Webster, and John Calhoun in Congress. These powerful figures walked the political stage at a time when bitter sectional conflicts—over slavery and commercial policies—were beginning to split the country. Jackson, though he was opposed to a large and powerful federal government and wished to return somehow to the agrarian simplicities of Jefferson's time, was nonetheless a believer in a strong and independent presidency. This view, though obscured by nearly a century of subsequent congressional dominance of national politics, was ultimately to triumph—for better or for worse.

The Reemergence of Congress

With the end of Jackson's second term, Congress quickly reestablished its power, and except for the wartime presidency of Lincoln and brief flashes of presidential power under James Polk (1845–1849) and Grover Cleveland (1885–1889, 1893–1897), the presidency for a hundred years was the subordinate branch of the national government. Of the eight presidents who succeeded Jackson, two (William H. Harrison and Zachary Taylor) died in office, and none of the others served more than one term. Schoolchildren, trying to memorize the list of American presidents, always stumble in this era of the "no-name" presidents. This is hardly a coincidence: Congress was the leading institution, struggling, unsuccessfully, with slavery and sectionalism.

It was also an intensely partisan era, a legacy of Jackson that lasted well into the twentieth century. Public opinion was closely divided. In nine of the seventeen presidential elections between the end of Jackson's term in 1837 and Theodore Roosevelt's election in 1904, the winning candidate received less than half the popular vote. Only two candidates (Lincoln in 1864 and Ulysses S. Grant in 1872) received more than 55 percent of the popular vote.

During this long period of congressional—and usually senatorial—dominance of national government, only Lincoln broke new ground for presidential power. Lincoln's expansive use of that power, like Jackson's, was totally unexpected. He was first elected in 1860 as a minority president, receiving less than 40 percent of the popular vote in a field of four candidates. Though a member of the new Republican party, he had been a member of the Whig party, a group that had stood for limiting presidential power. He had opposed America's entry into the Mexican War and had been critical of Jackson's use of executive authority. But as president during the Civil War, he made unprecedented use of the vague gift of powers in Article II of the Constitution, especially those that he felt were "implied" or "inherent" in the phrase "take care that the laws be faithfully executed" and in the express authorization for him to act as commander in chief. Lincoln raised an army, spent money, blockaded southern ports, temporarily suspended the writ of habeas corpus, and issued the Emancipation Proclamation to free the slaves—all without prior congressional approval. He justified this, as most Americans probably would have, by the emergency conditions created by civil war. In this he acted little differently from Thomas Jefferson, who while president waged undeclared war against various North African pirates.

After Lincoln, Congress reasserted its power and became, during Reconstruction and for many decades thereafter, the principal federal institution. But it had become abundantly clear that a national emergency could equip the president with great powers and that a popular and strong-willed president could expand his powers even without an emergency.

Except for the administrations of Theodore Roosevelt (1901–1909) and Woodrow Wilson (1913–1921), the president was, until the New Deal, at best a negative force—a source of opposition to Congress, not a source of initiative and leadership for it. Grover Cleveland was a strong personality, but for all his efforts he was able to do little more than veto bills that he did not like. He cast 414 vetoes—more than any other president until Franklin Roosevelt. A frequent target of his vetoes were bills to confer special pensions on Civil War veterans.

Today we are accustomed to thinking that the president formulates a legislative program to which Congress then responds, but until the 1930s the opposite was more the case. Congress ignored the initiatives of such presidents as Grover Cleveland, Rutherford Hayes, Chester Arthur, and Calvin Coolidge. Woodrow Wilson in 1913 was the first president since John Adams to deliver personally the State of the Union address, and he was one of the first to develop and argue for a presidential legislative program.

Our popular conception of the president as the central figure of national government, devising a legislative program and commanding a large staff of advisers, is very much a product of the modern era and of the enlarged role of government. In the past the presidency only became powerful during a national crisis (the Civil War, World War I) or because of an extraordinary personality (Andrew Jackson, Theodore Roosevelt, Woodrow Wilson). Since the 1930s, however, the presidency has been powerful no matter who occupied the office and whether or not there was a crisis. Because government now plays such an active role in our national life, the president is the natural focus of attention and the titular head of a huge federal administrative system (whether he is the real boss is another matter).

But the popular conception of the president as the central figure of national government belies the realities of present-day legislative-executive relations. In a thorough analysis of national policy-making from the Eisenhower years through the Reagan administration, Mark A. Peterson demonstrated that Congress, not the president, often took the lead in setting the legislative agenda.[5] For example, the 1990 Clean Air Act, like the 1970 Clean Air Act before it, was born and bred mainly by congres-sional, not presidential, action. Indeed, administration officials played almost no role in the legislative process that culminated in these laws.[6] When President Bush signed the 1990 bill at a stately ceremony in the East Room of the White House, he quipped, "Mission defined. Mission accomplished," but it is clear that it was members of Congress who had actually proposed and drafted "the several-inch stack of legislation" that Bush signed.[7] Likewise, although presidents dominated budget policy making from the 1920s into the early 1970s, they no longer do. Instead, the "imperatives of the budgetary process have pushed congressional leaders to center stage."[8] Thus, as often as not, the Congress proposes, the president disposes, and legislative-executive relations involve hard bargaining and struggle between these two branches of government.

The Powers of the President

Though the president, unlike a prime minister, cannot command an automatic majority in the legislature, he does have some formidable, albeit vaguely defined, powers. These are mostly set forth in Article II of the Constitution and are of two sorts: those he can exercise in his own right without formal legislative approval, and those that require the consent of the Senate or of Congress as a whole.

Powers of the President Alone

- Serve as commander in chief of the armed forces
- Commission officers of the armed forces
- Grant reprieves and pardons for federal offenses (except impeachment)
- Convene Congress in special sessions
- Receive ambassadors
- Take care that the laws be faithfully executed
- Wield the "executive power"
- Appoint officials to lesser offices

Powers of the President That Are Shared with the Senate

- Make treaties
- Appoint ambassadors, judges, and high officials

Powers of the President That Are Shared with Congress as a Whole

- Approve legislation

An Army officer carrying what the White House calls "the football"—the briefcase containing the secret codes the president can use to launch a nuclear attack.

Taken alone and interpreted narrowly, this list of powers is not very impressive. Obviously the president's authority as commander in chief is important, but literally construed, most of the other constitutional grants seem to provide for little more than a president who is chief clerk of the country. A hundred years after the Founding, that is about how matters appeared to even the most astute observers. In 1884 Woodrow Wilson wrote a book about American politics entitled *Congressional Government,* in which he described the business of the president as "usually not much above routine," mostly "*mere* administration." The president might as well be an officer of the civil service. To succeed, he need only obey Congress and stay alive.[9]

But even as Wilson wrote, he was overlooking some examples of enormously powerful presidents, such as Lincoln, and was not sufficiently attentive to the potential for presidential power to be found in the more ambiguous clauses of the Constitution as well as in the political realities of American life. The president's authority as commander in chief has grown—especially, but not only, in wartime—to encompass not simply the direction of the military forces but also the management of the economy and the direction of foreign affairs as well. A quietly dramatic reminder of the awesome implications of the president's military powers occurs at the precise instant that a new president assumes office. An army officer carrying a locked briefcase moves from the side of the outgoing president to the side of the new one. In the briefcase are the secret codes and orders that permit the president to authorize the launching of American nuclear weapons.

The president's duty to "take care that the laws be faithfully executed" has become one of the most elastic phrases in the Constitution. By interpreting this broadly, Grover Cleveland was able to use federal troops to break a labor strike in the 1890s, and Dwight Eisenhower was able to send troops to help integrate a public school in Little Rock, Arkansas, in 1957.

The greatest source of presidential power, however, is not found in the Constitution at all but in politics and public opinion. Increasingly since the 1930s, Congress has passed laws that confer on the executive branch broad grants of authority to achieve some general goals, leaving it up to the

The President: Qualifications and Benefits

Qualifications

- A natural-born citizen (can be born abroad of parents who are American citizens)
- Thirty-five years of age
- A resident of the United States for at least fourteen years (but not necessarily the fourteen years just preceding the election)

Benefits

- A nice house
- A salary of $200,000 per year (taxable)
- Expense account of $50,000 per year (taxable)
- Travel expenses of $100,000 per year (tax-free)
- Pension, on retirement, equal to the pay of a cabinet member (taxable)
- Staff support and Secret Service protection on leaving the presidency
- A White House staff of 400–500 persons
- A place in the country—Camp David
- A personal airplane—Air Force One
- A fine chef

president and his deputies to define the regulations and programs that will actually be put into effect. In Chapter 13 we shall see how this delegation of legislative power to the president has contributed to the growth of the bureaucracy. Moreover, the American people—always in times of crisis, but increasingly as an everyday matter—look to the president for leadership and hold him responsible for a large and growing portion of our national affairs. The public thinks, wrongly, that the presidency is the "first branch" of government.

The Office of the President

It was not until 1857 that the president was allowed to have a private secretary paid for with public funds, and it was not until after the assassination of President McKinley in 1901 that the president was given a Secret Service bodyguard. He was not able to submit a single presidential budget until after 1921, when the Budget and Accounting Act was passed and the Bureau of the Budget (now called the Office of Management and Budget) was created. Grover Cleveland personally answered the White House telephone, and Abraham Lincoln often answered his own mail.

Today, of course, the president has hundreds of people assisting him, and the trappings of power—helicopters, guards, limousines—are plainly visible. The White House staff has grown enormously. (Just how big the staff is, no one knows. Presidents like to pretend that the White House is not the large bureaucracy that it in fact has become.) Add to this the opportunities for presidential appointments to the cabinet, the courts, and various agencies, and the resources at the disposal of the president would appear to be awesome. That conclusion is partly true and partly false, or at least misleading, and for a simple reason. If the president was once helpless for lack of assistance, he now confronts an army of assistants so large that it constitutes a bureaucracy that he has difficulty controlling (see Figure 12.1).

The ability of a presidential assistant to affect the president is governed by the rule of propinquity: in general, power is wielded by people who are in the room when a decision is made. Presidential appointments can thus be classified in terms of their proximity, physical and political, to the president. There are three degrees of propinquity: the White House Office, the Executive Office, and the cabinet.

The White House Office

The president's closest assistants have offices in the White House, usually in the West Wing of that building. Their titles often do not reveal the functions that they actually perform: "counsel," "counsellor," "assistant to the president," "special assistant," "special consultant," and so forth. The actual titles vary from one administration to another, but in general the men and women who hold them oversee the political and policy interests of the president. As part of the president's personal staff, these aides do not have to be confirmed by the Senate; the president can hire and fire them at will. In 1993 the Clinton White House had five hundred staff members and a budget of $35.4 million.

There are essentially three ways in which a president can organize his personal staff—the "pyramid," "circular," and "ad hoc" methods. In a **pyramid structure,** used by Eisenhower, Nixon, Reagan, and Bush, most assistants report through a hierarchy to a chief of staff, who then deals directly with the president. In a **circular structure,** used by Carter, cabinet secretaries and assistants report directly to the president. In an **ad hoc structure,** used for a while by President Clinton, task forces, committees, and informal groups of friends and advisers deal directly with the president. For example, the Clinton administration's health-care policy planning was spearheaded not by Health and Human Services secretary Donna E. Shalala but by First Lady Hillary Rodham Clinton and a White House adviser, Ira Magaziner. Likewise, its initiative to reform the federal bureaucracy (the National Performance Review) was led not by Office of Management and Budget director Leon E. Panetta but by an adviser to Vice President Gore, Elaine Kamarck.[10]

It is common for presidents to mix methods; for example, Franklin Roosevelt alternated between the circular and ad hoc methods in the conduct of his domestic policy and sometimes employed a pyramidal structure when dealing with foreign affairs and military policy. Taken individually, each method of organization has advantages and disadvantages. A

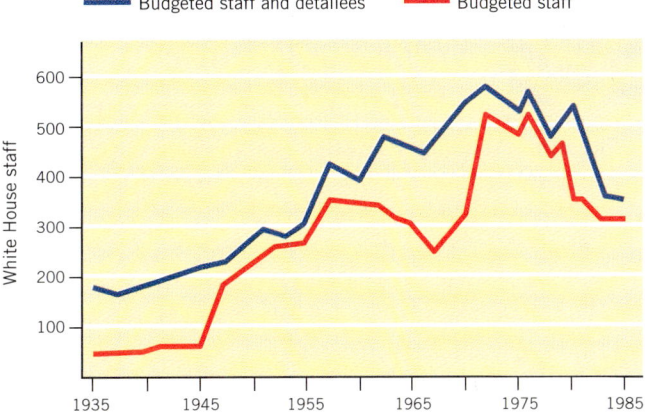

FIGURE 12.1 Growth of the White House Office, 1935–1985

NOTE: Detailees are people who are employed by and paid by another federal agency but are assigned to work in the White House. Number of detailees for 1981 unavailable.

SOURCES: For 1935–1977: *Congressional Record* (April 13, 1978), 10111; for 1979–1985: annual reports filed by the White House with the House of Representatives Committee on Post Office and Civil Service, entitled "Aggregate Report on Personnel; Pursuant to Title 3, United States Code, Section 113"; and *Budget of the United States Government.* Reproduced from Samuel Kernell and Samuel Popkin, eds., *Chief of Staff,* University of California Press, 1986, p. 201. Reprinted by permission of the publisher.

pyramid structure provides for an orderly flow of information and decisions but does so at the risk of isolating or misinforming the president. The circular method has the virtue of giving the president a great deal of information, but at the price of confusion and conflict among cabinet secretaries and assistants. An ad hoc structure allows great flexibility, minimizes bureaucratic inertia, and generates ideas and information from disparate channels, but it risks cutting the president off from the government officials who are ultimately responsible for translating presidential decisions into policy proposals and administrative action.

All presidents claim that they are open to many sources of advice, and some presidents try to guarantee that openness by using the circular method of staff organization. President Carter liked to describe his office as a wheel with himself as the hub and his several assistants as spokes. But most presidents discover, as did Carter, that the difficulty of managing the large White House bureaucracy and of conserving their own limited supply of time and energy makes it necessary for them to rely heavily on one or

The Myth and Reality of the White House Office

The myth   The White House Office was created in the 1930s following recommendations made by the President's Commission on Administrative Management. The principles underlying those recommendations have been endorsed by almost every presidential chief of staff since then. The key ones are:

1. *Small is beautiful.* The presidential staff should be small. At first there were only six assistants.

2. *A passion for anonymity.* The president's personal assistants should stay out of the limelight.

3. *Honest brokers.* The presidential staff should not make decisions for the president; it should only coordinate the flow of information to the president.

The reality   Increasingly the operations of the White House Office seem to reflect almost the exact opposite of these principles.

1. *Big is better.* The White House staff has grown enormously in size. Hundreds now work there.

2. *Get out front.* Key White House staffers have become household words—Henry Kissinger (under Nixon and Ford), H. R. Haldeman (under Nixon), Hamilton Jordan (under Carter), Donald Regan and Howard Baker (under Reagan), George Stephanopoulos (under Clinton).

3. *Be in charge.* Cabinet officers regularly complain that White House staffers are shutting them out and making all the important decisions. Congressional investigations have revealed the power of such White House aides as Haldeman, John Poindexter, and Lieutenant Colonel Oliver North.

Why the gap between myth and reality?   The answer is—the people and the government. The people expect much more from presidents today; no president can afford to say, "We're too busy here to worry about that." The government is much more complex, and so leadership requires more resources. Even conservatives such as Ronald Reagan have been activist presidents.

SOURCE: Adapted from Samuel Kernell and Samuel L. Popkin, eds., *Chief of Staff* (Berkeley: University of California Press, 1986), 193–232.

two key subordinates. Carter, in July 1979, dramatically altered the White House staff organization by elevating Hamilton Jordan to the post of chief of staff, with the job of coordinating the work of the other staff assistants.

At first President Reagan adopted a compromise between the circle and the pyramid, putting the White House under the direction of three key aides. At the beginning of his second term in 1985, however, the president shifted to a pyramid, placing all his assistants under a single chief of staff (see Figure 12.2). Clinton began with an ad hoc system and then changed to one more like a pyramid. Each assistant has, of course, others working for him or her, sometimes a large number. There are, at a slightly lower level of status, "special assistants to the president" for various purposes. (Being "special" means, paradoxically, being less important.)

Typically senior White House staff members are drawn from the ranks of the president's campaign staff—longtime associates in whom he has confidence. A few members, however, will be experts brought in after the campaign: such was the case, for example, with Henry Kissinger, a former Harvard professor who became President Nixon's assistant for national security affairs. The offices that these men and women occupy are often small and crowded (Kissinger's was not much bigger than the one that he had while a professor at Harvard), but their occupants willingly put up with any discomfort in exchange for the privilege (and the power) of being *in* the White House. The arrangement of offices—their size, and especially their proximity to the president's Oval Office—is a good measure of the relative influence of the people in them.

To an outsider, the amount of jockeying among the top staff for access to the president may seem comical or even perverse. The staff attaches enormous significance to whose office is closest to the president's, who can see him on a daily as opposed to a weekly basis, who can get an appointment with the president and who cannot, and who has a right to see documents and memoranda just before they go to the Oval Office. To be sure, there is ample grist here for Washington political novels. But there is also something important at stake: it is not simply a question of power plays and ego trips. Who can see the president and who sees and "signs off" on memoranda going to the president affect in important ways who influences policy and thus whose goals and beliefs become embedded in policy.

For example, if a memo from a secretary of the treasury who believes in free trade can go directly to the president, the president may be more likely to support free trade (low tariffs). On the other hand, if that memo must be routed through the office of the assistant to the president for political affairs, who is worried about the adverse effects of foreign competition on jobs in the American steel industry because the votes of steelworkers are important to the president's reelection campaign, then the president may be led to support higher tariffs.

Executive Office of the President

Agencies in the Executive Office report directly to the president and perform staff services for him but are not located in the White House itself. Their members may or may not enjoy intimate contact with him; some agencies are rather large bureaucracies. The top positions in these organizations are filled by presidential appointment, but unlike the White House staff positions, these appointments must be confirmed by the Senate.

The principal agencies in the Executive Office are

- Office of Management and Budget (OMB)
- Central Intelligence Agency (CIA)
- Council of Economic Advisers (CEA)
- Office of Personnel Management (OPM)
- Office of the U.S. Trade Representative

Of all the agencies in the Executive Office of the President, perhaps the most important in terms of the president's need for assistance in administering the federal government is the Office of Management and Budget. First called the Bureau of the Budget when it was created in 1921, it became OMB in 1970 to reflect its broader responsibilities. Today it does considerably more than assemble and analyze the figures that go each year into the national budget that the president submits to Congress. It also studies the organization and operations of the executive branch, devises plans for reorganizing various departments and agencies, develops ways of getting better information about government programs,

FIGURE 12.2 The Changing White House Office

played a major role in advocating policies rather than merely analyzing them. David Stockman, President Reagan's OMB director, was the primary architect of the 1981 and 1985 budget cuts that were proposed by the president and enacted by Congress. Stockman's proposals were often adopted over the objections of the affected department heads.

The Cabinet

The **cabinet** is a product of tradition and hope. At one time the heads of the federal departments met regularly with the president to discuss matters, and some people, especially those critical of strong presidents, would like to see this kind of collegial decision making reestablished. But in fact this role of the cabinet is largely a fiction. Indeed the Constitution does not even mention the cabinet (though the Twenty-fifth Amendment implicitly defines it as consisting of "the principal offices of the executive departments"). When Washington tried to get his cabinet members to work together, its two strongest members—Alexander Hamilton and Thomas Jefferson—spent most of their time feuding. The cabinet, as a presidential committee, did not work any better for John Adams or Abraham Lincoln, for Franklin Roosevelt or John Kennedy. Dwight Eisenhower is almost the only modern president who came close to making the cabinet a truly deliberative body: he gave it a large staff, held regular meetings, and listened to opinions expressed there. But even under Eisenhower, the cabinet did not have much influence over presidential decisions, nor did it help him gain more power over the government.

By custom, cabinet officers are the heads of the fourteen major executive departments. These departments, together with the dates of their creation and the approximate number of their employees, are given in Table 12.1. The order of their creation is unimportant except in terms of protocol: where one sits at cabinet meetings is determined by the age of the department that one heads. Thus the secretary of state sits next to the president on one side and the secretary of the treasury next to him on the other. Down at the foot of the table are found the heads of the newer departments.

Though the president appoints, with the consent of the Senate, the heads of these cabinet depart-

and reviews proposals that cabinet departments want included in the president's legislative program.

OMB has a staff of over five hundred people, almost all career civil servants, many of high professional skill and substantial experience. Traditionally OMB has been a nonpartisan agency—experts serving all presidents, without regard to party or ideology. In recent administrations, however, OMB has ments, the power he obtains over them is sharply limited. One reason is that he cannot appoint more than a tiny fraction of all of a department's employees. In only one small department, the Department of Education, can the president appoint at his discretion more than 3 percent of the employees. Table 12.2 shows the number of employees (and the percentage of all employees) presidentially chosen in each cabinet department. Even this number of presidential positions is an exaggeration, since many of the posts exempted from civil service are scientific or professional in nature and are occupied by persons who are not replaced by a new administration. A British prime minister has far fewer political appointments to make than an American president, but then a prime minister does not need so many, because he or she does not have to compete with an independent Congress for influence over the bureaucracy.

But the main reason why the cabinet is a weak entity is that its members are heads of vast organizations that they seek to defend, explain, and enlarge. The secretary of Housing and Urban Development (HUD), for example, spends 99 percent of his or her time on departmental business and perhaps 1 percent (or even less) of the time speaking to the president about his business. It is hardly surprising that the HUD secretary is more of a representative of HUD *to* the president than his representative to HUD. Under these circumstances the HUD secretary is not especially interested in discussing policy at cabinet meetings with the secretary of the treasury: the latter probably wants the president to do things that are very different from what the former would like him or her to do.

Independent Agencies, Commissions, and Judgeships

The president also appoints people to four dozen or so agencies and commissions that are not considered part of the cabinet and that by law often have a quasi-independent status. The difference between an "executive" and an "independent" agency is not precise. In general it means that the heads of executive agencies serve at the pleasure of the president and can be removed at his discretion. On the other hand, the heads of many independent agencies serve for

TABLE 12.1   The Cabinet Departments

Department	Created	Approximate Employment (1994)
State	1789	25,600
Treasury	1789	156,400
Defense[a]	1947	879,600
Justice	1789	97,900
Interior	1849	80,700
Agriculture[b]	1889	119,600
Commerce	1913	37,600
Labor	1913	16,700
Health and Human Services[c]	1953	128,200
Housing and Urban Development	1965	13,200
Transportation	1966	64,900
Energy	1977	19,900
Education	1979	4,800
Veterans Affairs	1989	262,400

[a] Formerly the War Department, created in 1789. Figures are for civilians only.
[b] Agriculture Department created in 1862; made part of cabinet in 1889.
[c] Originally Health, Education and Welfare; reorganized in 1979.
SOURCE: *Statistical Abstract of the United States, 1994*, p. 350.

TABLE 12.2   Number of Non–Civil Service Positions in Cabinet Departments, 1992

Department	Number of Non–Civil Service Positions	Percentage of All Positions in Each Department
State	454	1.70%
Treasury	287	0.17
Defense (civilians)	853	0.08
Justice	543	0.56
Interior	311	0.37
Agriculture	501	0.38
Commerce	399	1.10
Labor	214	1.20
Health and Human Services	541	0.40
Housing and Urban Development	188	1.40
Transportation	429	0.60
Energy	503	2.40
Education	252	4.90
Veterans Affairs	364	0.14

SOURCES: *United States Government Policy and Supporting Positions*, 1992, and *Federal Civilian Workforce Statistics, Employment, and Trends as of July 1992*.

Federal Agencies

Classified by Whether President Has Unlimited or Limited Right of Removal

"Executive" Agencies   *Head can be removed at any time*

Action
Arms Control and Disarmament Agency
Commission on Civil Rights
Energy Research and Development Agency
Environmental Protection Agency
Federal Mediation and Conciliation Service
General Services Administration
National Aeronautics and Space Administration
Postal Service
Small Business Administration
All cabinet departments
Executive Office of the President

"Independent" or "Quasi-Independent" Agencies
Member serves for a fixed term

Federal Reserve Board (14 years)
Consumer Product Safety Commission (6 years)
Equal Employment Opportunity Commission (5 years)
Federal Communications Commission (7 years)
Federal Deposit Insurance Corporation (6 years)
Federal Energy Regulatory Commission (5 years)
Federal Maritime Commission (5 years)
Federal Trade Commission (7 years)
National Labor Relations Board (5 years)
National Science Foundation (6 years)
Securities and Exchange Commission (5 years)
Tennessee Valley Authority (9 years)

fixed terms of office and can be removed only "for cause."

The president can also appoint federal judges, subject to the consent of the Senate. Judges serve for life unless they are removed by impeachment and conviction. The reason for the special barriers to the removal of judges is that they represent an independent branch of government as defined by the Constitution, and limits on presidential removal powers are necessary to preserve that independence.

Who Gets Appointed

As we have seen, a president can make relatively few appointments; furthermore, he rarely knows more than a few of the people whom he does appoint.

Unlike cabinet members in a parliamentary system, the president's cabinet officers and their principal deputies usually have not served with the chief executive in the legislature. Instead they come from private business, universities, "think tanks," foundations, law firms, labor unions, and the ranks of former and present members of Congress as well as past state and local government officials. A president is fortunate if most cabinet members turn out to agree with him on major policy questions. President Reagan made a special effort to ensure that his cabinet members were ideologically in tune with him, but even so Secretary of State Alexander Haig soon got into a series of quarrels with senior members of the White House staff and had to resign.

The men and women appointed to the cabinet and to the "subcabinet" (a loose term for those holding posts as deputy secretary or assistant secretary in the cabinet departments) will usually have had some prior federal experience. One study of over a thousand such appointments made by five presidents (Franklin Roosevelt through Lyndon Johnson) found that about 85 percent of the cabinet, subcabinet, and independent-agency appointees had some prior federal experience. In fact most were in government service (at the federal, state, or local levels) just before they received their cabinet or subcabinet appointment.[11] Clearly the executive branch is not, in general, run by novices.

Many of these appointees are what Richard Neustadt has called "in-and-outers": people who alternate between jobs in the federal government and ones in the private sector, especially in law firms and in universities. Cyrus Vance, before becoming secretary of state to President Carter, had been general counsel in the Defense Department, secretary of the army, and deputy secretary of defense under President Johnson. Before and after these federal jobs he was a member of a large Wall Street law

Secretary of Labor Frances Perkins (left), appointed by President Franklin Roosevelt, was the first woman cabinet member. When Robert Weaver (right) was made Secretary of Housing and Urban Development by President Johnson, he became the first black to hold a cabinet post.

firm. This pattern is quite different from that of parliamentary systems, where all the cabinet officers come from the legislature and are typically full-time career politicians.

At one time the cabinet had in it many people with strong political followings of their own—former senators and governors and powerful local party leaders. Under Franklin Roosevelt, Truman, and Kennedy, the postmaster general was the president's campaign manager. George Washington, Abraham Lincoln, and other presidents had to contend with cabinet members who were powerful figures in their own right: Alexander Hamilton and Thomas Jefferson worked with Washington; Simon Cameron (a Pennsylvania political boss) and Salmon P. Chase (formerly a governor of Ohio) worked for—and against—Lincoln. Before 1824 the post of secretary of state was regarded as a stepping-stone to the presidency; and after that at least ten persons ran for president who had been either secretary of state or ambassador to a foreign country.[12]

Of late, however, a tendency has developed for presidents to place in their cabinets people known for their expertise or administrative experience rather than for their political following. This is in part because political parties are now so weak that party leaders can no longer demand a place in the cabinet and in part because presidents want (or think they want) "experts." A remarkable illustration of this is the number of people with Ph.D.'s who have entered the cabinet. President Nixon, who supposedly did not like Harvard professors, appointed two—Henry Kissinger and Daniel Patrick Moynihan—to important posts; Gerald Ford added a third, John Dunlop.

A president's desire to appoint experts who do not have independent political power is modified—but not supplanted—by his need to recognize various politically important groups, regions, and organizations. Since Robert Weaver became the first black to serve in the cabinet (as secretary of HUD under President Johnson), it is clear that it would be quite costly for a president *not* to have one or more blacks in his cabinet. The secretary of labor must be acceptable to the AFL-CIO, the secretary of agriculture to at least some organized farmers. Women have

TRIVIA

Presidents

Only divorced president	*Ronald Reagan*
Only bachelor president	*James Buchanan*
Three presidents who died on the Fourth of July	*Thomas Jefferson (1826) John Adams (1826) James Monroe (1831)*
The shortest presidential term	*William Henry Harrison (one month)*
The longest presidential term	*Franklin D. Roosevelt (12 years and 1 month)*
The youngest president when inaugurated	*Theodore Roosevelt (42)*
The oldest president when first inaugurated	*Ronald Reagan (69)*
First president born in a hospital	*Jimmy Carter*
First presidential automobile	*Owned by William Howard Taft*
Only former presidents elected to Congress	*John Quincy Adams (to House) and Andrew Johnson (to Senate)*
Only president who never attended school	*Andrew Johnson*

John Adams

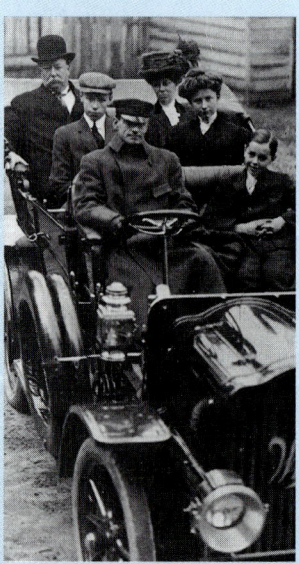

William Howard Taft and family

been in several cabinets since Franklin Roosevelt's; with the growing importance of the feminist movement, it is now essential that they be in every cabinet. Traditionally the interior secretary comes from the resource- and land-conscious West. And so on and on.

Because political considerations must be taken into account in making cabinet and agency appointments and because any head of a large organization will tend to adopt the perspective of that organization, there is an inevitable tension—even a rivalry—between the White House staff and the department heads. Staff members see themselves as extensions of the president's personality and policies; department heads see themselves as repositories of expert knowledge (often knowledge of why something will not work as the president hopes). White House staffers, many of them young men and women in their twenties or early thirties with little executive experience, will call department heads, often persons in their fifties with substantial executive experience, and tell them that "the president wants" this or that or that "the president asked me to tell you" one thing or another. Department heads try to conceal their irritation and then maneuver for some delay so that they can develop their own counterproposals. On the other hand, when department heads call a White House staff person and ask to see the president, unless they are one of the privileged few in whom the president has special confidence, they are often told that "the president can't be bothered with that" or that "the president doesn't have time to see you."

Presidential Character

Every president brings to the White House a distinctive personality; the way the White House is organized and run will reflect that personality. Moreover, the public will judge the president not only in terms of what he accomplished but also in terms of its perception of his character. Thus personality plays a more important role in explaining the presidency than it does in explaining Congress.

DWIGHT EISENHOWER brought an orderly, military style to the White House. He was accustomed to delegating authority and to having careful and complete staff work done for him by trained specialists.

Though critics often accused him of having a bumbling, incoherent manner of speaking, in fact much of that was a public disguise—a strategy for avoiding being pinned down in public on matters where he wished to retain freedom of action. His private papers reveal a very different Eisenhower—sharp, precise, deliberate.

JOHN KENNEDY brought a very different style to the presidency. He projected the image of a bold, articulate, and amusing leader who liked to surround himself with talented amateurs. Instead of clear, hierarchical lines of authority, there was a pattern of personal rule and an atmosphere of improvisation. Kennedy did not hesitate to call very junior subordinates directly and tell them what to do, bypassing the chain of command.

LYNDON JOHNSON was a master legislative strategist who had risen to be majority leader of the Senate on the strength of his ability to persuade other politicians in face-to-face encounters. He was a consummate deal maker who, having been in Washington for thirty years before becoming president, knew everybody and everything. As a result he tried to make every decision himself. But the style that served him well in political negotiations did not serve him well in speaking to the country at large, especially when trying to retain public support for the war in Vietnam.

RICHARD NIXON was a highly intelligent man with a deep knowledge of and interest in foreign policy, coupled with a deep suspicion of the media, his political rivals, and the federal bureaucracy. In contrast to Johnson, he disliked personal confrontations and tended to shield himself behind an elaborate staff system. Distrustful of the cabinet agencies, he tried first to centralize power in the White House and then to put into key cabinet posts former White House aides loyal to him. Like Johnson, his personality made it difficult for him to mobilize popular support. Eventually he was forced to resign under the threat of impeachment arising out of his role in the Watergate scandal.

GERALD FORD, before being appointed vice president, had spent his political life in Congress and was at home with the give-and-take, discussion-oriented procedures of that body. He was also a genial man who liked talking to people. Thus he preferred the circular to the pyramid system of White House organization. But this meant that many decisions were

Three presidents—George Bush, Bill Clinton, and Jimmy Carter—at a summit to encourage volunteer activity.

made in a disorganized fashion in which key people—and sometimes key problems—were not taken into account.

JIMMY CARTER was an outsider to Washington, and boasted of it. A former Georgia governor, he was determined not to be "captured" by Washington insiders. He also was a voracious reader with a wide range of interests and an appetite for detail. These dispositions led him to try to do many things and to do them personally. Like Ford, he began with a circular structure; unlike Ford, he based his decisions on reading countless memos and asking detailed questions. His advisers finally decided that he was trying to do too much in too great detail, and toward the end of his term he shifted to a pyramid structure.

RONALD REAGAN was also an outsider, a former governor of California. But unlike Carter, he wanted to set the broad directions of his administration and leave the details to others. He gave wide latitude to

Lyndon Johnson's great political skill was not his ability to make speeches but his knack for dealing effectively with people singly or in small groups. Left, he relaxes while talking informally with reporters in the White House; right, his face shows the strain of making a public address.

subordinates and to cabinet officers, within the framework of an emphasis on lower taxes, less domestic spending, a military buildup, and a tough line with the Soviet Union. He was a superb leader of public opinion, earning the nickname of "The Great Communicator."

GEORGE BUSH lacked Reagan's speaking skills but was much more of a hands-on manager. Drawing on his extensive experience in the federal government (he had been vice president, director of the CIA, ambassador to the United Nations, representative to China, and a member of the House), Bush made decisions on the basis of personal contacts with key foreign leaders and Washington officials.

BILL CLINTON is much like Carter in the attention he pays to the details of policy and his preference for informal, ad hoc organizational arrangements. Unlike Carter, he is an effective speaker who uses those skills to try to get support for his policies. And unlike Reagan and Bush, he took office with little apparent interest in foreign affairs.

Professor James David Barber has attempted to study presidential personality systematically and use the results to predict presidential performance in office. Scholars are divided over whether this approach

works, but none disputes the fact that personality affects how the White House is run.[13]

The Power to Persuade

The sketchy constitutional powers given the president, combined with the lack of an assured legislative majority, mean that he must rely heavily on persuasion if he is to accomplish much. Here the Constitution gives him some advantages: he and the vice president are the only officials elected by the whole nation, and he is the ceremonial head of state as well as the chief executive of the government. The president can use his national constituency and ceremonial duties to enlarge his power, but he must do so quickly: the second half of his first term in office will be devoted to running for reelection, especially if he faces opposition for his own party's nomination (as was the case with Carter and Ford).

The Three Audiences

The president's persuasive powers are aimed at three audiences. The first, and often the most important, is his Washington, D.C., audience of fellow politicians and leaders. As Richard Neustadt points out in his book *Presidential Power,* a president's reputation among his Washington colleagues is of very great importance in affecting how much deference his views receive and thus how much power he can wield.[14] If a president is thought to be "smart," "sure of himself," "cool," "on top of things," or "shrewd," and thus "effective," he *will* be effective. Franklin Roosevelt had that reputation, and so did Lyndon Johnson, at least for his first few years in office. Truman, Ford, and Carter often did not have that reputation, and they lost ground accordingly. Power, like beauty, exists largely in the eye of the beholder.

A second audience is composed of party activists and officeholders outside Washington—the partisan grassroots. These persons want the president to exemplify their principles, trumpet their slogans, appeal to their fears and hopes, and help them get reelected. Since, as we explained in Chapter 7, partisan activists increasingly have an ideological orientation toward national politics, these people will expect "their" president to make fire-and-brimstone speeches that confirm in them a shared sense of purpose and, incidentally, help them raise money from contributors to state and local campaigns.

The third audience is "the public." But of course that audience is really many publics, each with a different view or set of interests. A president on the campaign trail speaks boldly of what he will accomplish; a president in office speaks quietly of the problems that must be overcome. Citizens are often irritated at the apparent tendency of officeholders, including the president, to sound mealy-mouthed and equivocal. But it is easy to criticize the cooking when you haven't been the cook. A president learns quickly that his every utterance will be scrutinized closely by the media and by organized groups here and abroad, and his errors of fact, judgment, timing, or even inflection will be immediately and forcefully pointed out. Given the risks of saying too much, it is a wonder that presidents say anything at all.

In general presidents have made fewer and fewer impromptu remarks in the years since Franklin Roosevelt and have relied more and more on prepared addresses (from which errors can be culled in advance). The box above and Figure 12.3 (page 388) show how press conferences have declined and how other ways of reaching the public have grown.

How Presidents Go to the People

*T*he three graphs in Figure 12.3 show how presidents have changed the way in which they "go public." The first graph shows the increase in public appearances by the president, from a dozen or so per year by Roosevelt to nearly a hundred per year by Bush, Reagan, Carter, and Nixon.

The number of presidential trips and broadcast addresses has also increased. The second graph shows that the number of radio and television speeches grew from a dozen or so per year by Roosevelt to more than a hundred per year by Bush (combining major and minor addresses).

Offsetting this increase has been the decline in the number of press conferences held per month. The third graph indicates that the number of press conferences held per month has decreased from a peak of almost seven when Franklin Roosevelt was in office to a low of less than one when Nixon, Carter, Reagan, and Bush were in office.

The reason? Broadcast speeches and public appearances allow the president to talk to the people *directly;* press conferences filter the president's words through the media.

SOURCE: Samuel Kernell, *Going Public* (Washington, D.C.: Congressional Quarterly Press, 1986), 69, 86, and 94. President Ford is omitted because he served so briefly in office.

Popularity and Influence

The object of all this talk is to convert personal popularity into congressional support for the president's legislative programs (and improved chances for reelection). It is not obvious, of course, why Congress should care about a president's popularity. After all, as we saw in Chapter 11, most members of Congress are secure in their seats, and few need fear any "party bosses" who might deny them renomination. Moreover, the president cannot ordinarily provide credible electoral rewards or penalties to members of Congress. By working for their defeat in the 1938 congressional election, President Roosevelt attempted to "purge" members of Congress who opposed his program, but he failed. Nor does presidential support help a particular member of Congress: most

FIGURE 12.3 Public Appearances, Addresses, and Press Conferences by Presidents

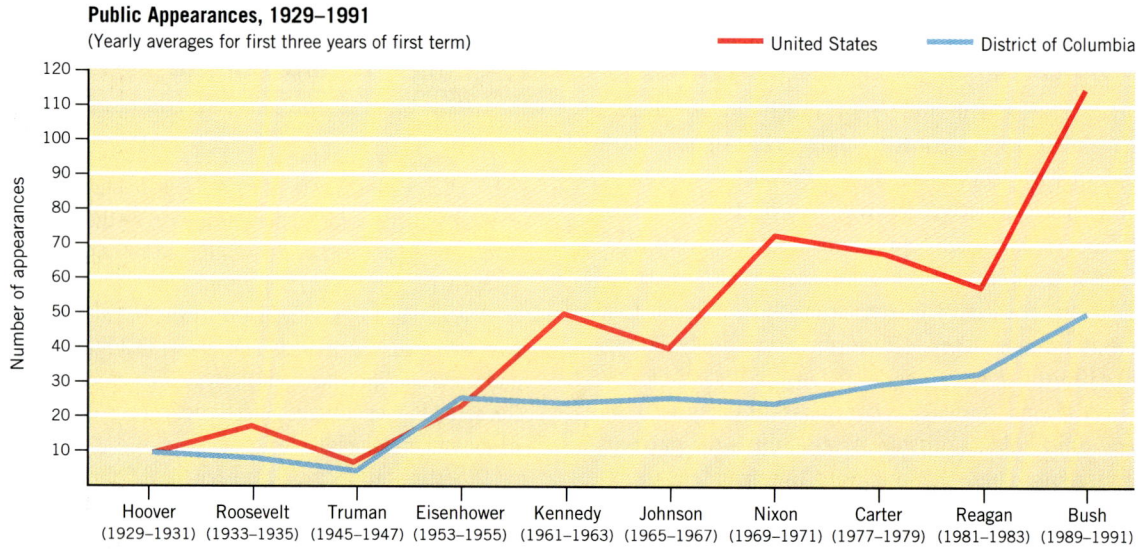

Public Appearances, 1929–1991
(Yearly averages for first three years of first term)

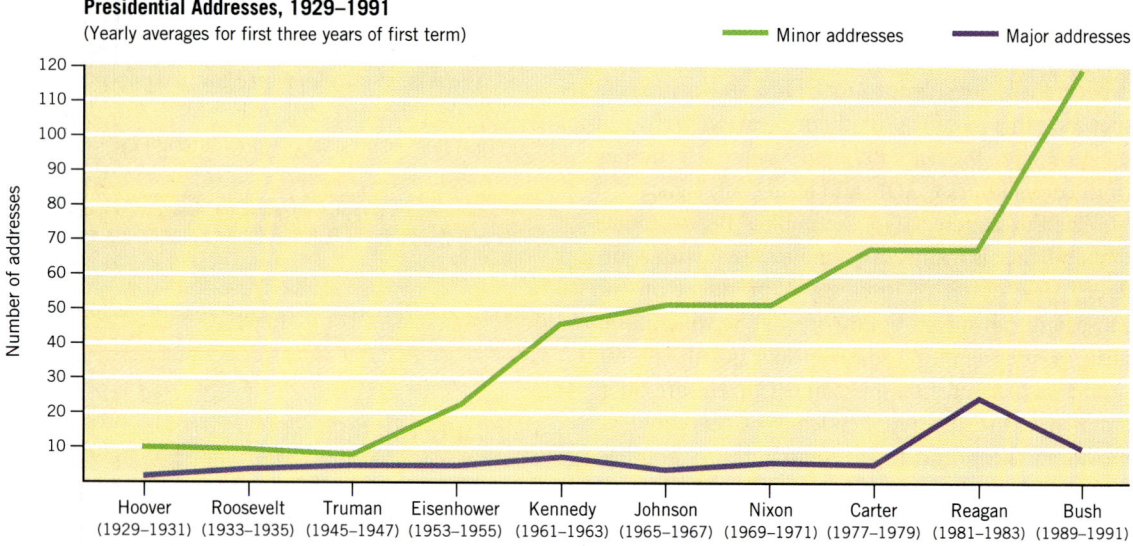

Presidential Addresses, 1929–1991
(Yearly averages for first three years of first term)

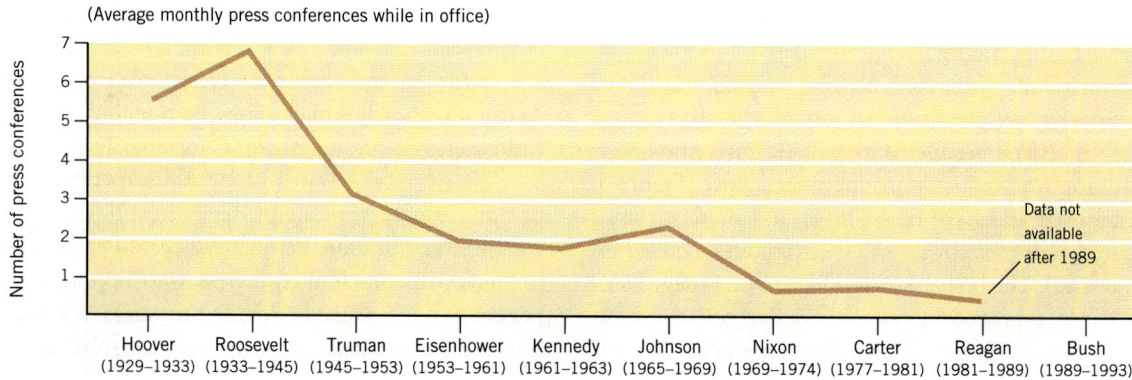

Press Conferences, 1929–1989
(Average monthly press conferences while in office)

TABLE 12.3 Partisan Gains or Losses in Congress in Presidential Election Years

Year	President	Party	Gains or Losses of President's Party in	
			House	Senate
1932	Roosevelt	Dem.	+90	+9
1936	Roosevelt	Dem.	+12	+7
1940	Roosevelt	Dem.	+7	−3
1944	Roosevelt	Dem.	+24	−2
1948	Truman	Dem.	+75	+9
1952	Eisenhower	Rep.	+22	+1
1956	Eisenhower	Rep.	−3	−1
1960	Kennedy	Dem.	−20	+1
1964	Johnson	Dem.	+37	+1
1968	Nixon	Rep.	+5	+7
1972	Nixon	Rep.	+12	−2
1976	Carter	Dem.	+1	+1
1980	Reagan	Rep.	+33	+12
1984	Reagan	Rep.	+16	−2
1988	Bush	Rep.	−3	−1
1992	Clinton	Dem.	−9	+1
1996	Clinton	Dem.	+9	−2

SOURCES: Updated from Congressional Quarterly, *Guide to U.S. Elections*, 928; and *Congress and the Nation*, vol. IV (1973–1976), 28.

representatives win reelection anyway, and the few who are in trouble are rarely saved by presidential intervention. When President Reagan campaigned hard for Republican senatorial candidates in 1986, he, too, failed to have much impact.

For a while scholars thought that congressional candidates might benefit from the president's coattails: they might ride into office on the strength of the popularity of a president of their own party. It is true, as can be seen from Table 12.3, that a winning president will find that his party's strength in Congress increases.

But there are good reasons to doubt whether the pattern observed in Table 12.3 is the result of presidential coattails. For one thing, there are some exceptions. Eisenhower won 57.4 percent of the vote in 1956, but the Republicans lost seats in the House and Senate. Kennedy won in 1960, but the Democrats lost seats in the House and gained but one in the Senate. When Nixon was reelected in 1972 with

one of the largest majorities in history, the Republicans lost seats in the Senate.

Careful studies of voter attitudes and of how presidential and congressional candidates fare in the same districts suggest that, whatever may once have been the influence of coattails, their effect has declined in recent years and is quite small today. The weakening of party loyalty and of party organizations, combined with the enhanced ability of members of Congress to build secure relations with their constituents, has tended to insulate congressional elections from presidential ones. When voters choose as members of Congress people of the same party as an incoming president, they probably do so out of a desire for a general change and as an adverse judgment about the outgoing party's performance as a whole, not because they want to supply the new president with members of Congress favorable to him.[15] The big increase in Republican senators and representatives that accompanied the election of

FIGURE 12.4 Presidential Popularity

NOTE: Popularity was measured by asking every few months, "Do you approve of the way _____ is handling his job as president?"

SOURCE: Thomas E. Cronin, *The State of the Presidency* (Boston: Little, Brown, 1975), 110–111. Copyright © 1975 by Little, Brown and Company, Inc. Reprinted by permission. Updated with Gallup poll data, 1976–1993. Reprinted by permission of the Gallup Poll News Service.

Ronald Reagan in 1980 was probably as much a result of the unpopularity of the outgoing president and the circumstances of various local races as it was of Reagan's coattails.

Nonetheless, a president's personal popularity may have a significant effect on how much of his program Congress passes, even if it does not affect the reelection chances of those members of Congress. Though they do not fear a president who threatens to campaign against them (or cherish one who promises to support them), members of Congress do have a sense that it is risky to oppose too adamantly the policies of a popular president. Politicians share a sense of a common fate: they tend to rise or fall together. Statistically a president's popularity, as measured by the Gallup poll (see Figure 12.4), is associated with the proportion of his legislative proposals that are approved by Congress (see Figure 12.5). Other things being equal, the more popular the president, the higher the proportion of his bills that Congress will pass.[16]

The Decline in Popularity

Though presidential popularity is an asset, its value tends inexorably to decline. As can be seen from Figure 12.4, every president except Eisenhower lost popular support between his inauguration and the time that he left office, except when his reelection gave him a brief burst of renewed popularity. Truman was hurt by improprieties among his subordinates and by the protracted Korean War; Johnson was crippled by the increasing unpopularity of the Vietnam War; Nixon was severely damaged by the Watergate scandal; Ford was hurt by having pardoned Nixon for his part in Watergate; Carter was weakened by continuing inflation, staff irregularities, and the Iranian kidnapping of American hostages; Bush was harmed by a protracted economic recession.

Because a president's popularity tends to be highest right after an election, political commentators like to speak of a "honeymoon," during which,

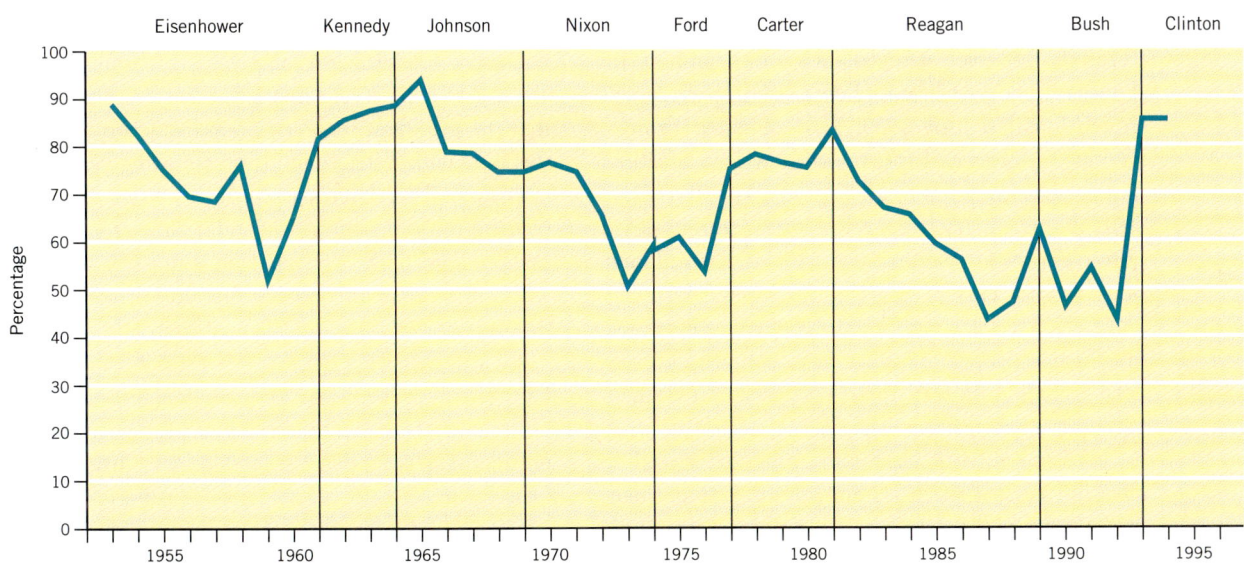

FIGURE 12.5 Presidential Victories on Votes in Congress, 1953–1994

Note: Percentages indicate number of congressional votes supporting the president
divided by the total number of votes on which the president has taken a position.

SOURCE: Figure taken from Norman J. Ornstein, Thomas E. Mann and Michael J. Malbin, *Vital Statistics on Congress*, 1995–1996, Congressional Quarterly Inc., 1996: 205. Reprinted with permission.

TABLE 12.4   Partisan Gains or Losses in Congress in Off-Year Elections

Year	President	Party	Gains or Losses of President's Party in	
			House	Senate
1934	Roosevelt	Dem.	+9	+9
1938	Roosevelt	Dem.	−70	−7
1942	Roosevelt	Dem.	−50	−8
1946	Truman	Dem.	−54	−11
1950	Truman	Dem.	−29	−5
1954	Eisenhower	Rep.	−18	−1
1958	Eisenhower	Rep.	−47	−13
1962	Kennedy	Dem.	−5	+2
1966	Johnson	Dem.	−48	−4
1970	Nixon	Rep.	−12	+1
1974	Ford	Rep.	−48	−5
1978	Carter	Dem.	−12	−3
1982	Reagan	Rep.	−26	0
1986	Reagan	Rep.	−5	−8
1990	Bush	Rep.	−9	−1
1994	Clinton	Dem.	−52	−9

SOURCES: Updated from Congressional Quarterly, *Guide to U.S. Elections*, 928; and *Congress and the Nation*, vol. IV (1973–1976), 28.

presumably, the president's love affair with the people and with Congress can be consummated. Certainly Roosevelt enjoyed such a honeymoon. In the legendary "first hundred days" of his presidency, from March to June 1933, FDR obtained from a willing Congress a vast array of new laws creating new agencies and authorizing new powers. But those were extraordinary times: the most serious economic depression of this century had put millions out of work, closed banks, impoverished farmers, and ruined the stock market. It would have been political suicide for Congress to have blocked, or even delayed, action on measures that appeared designed to help the nation out of the crisis.

Other presidents, serving in more normal times, have not enjoyed such a honeymoon. Truman had little success with what he proposed; Eisenhower proposed little. Kennedy, Nixon, Ford, and Carter had some victories in their first year in office, but nothing that could be called a honeymoon. Only Lyndon Johnson enjoyed a highly productive relationship with Congress; until the Vietnam War

sapped his strength, he rarely lost. Reagan began his administration with important victories in his effort to cut expenditures and taxes, but in his second year in office he ran into trouble.

The decay in the reputation of the president and his party in midterm is evident in Table 12.4. Since 1934, in every off-year election the president's party has lost seats in one or both houses of Congress. The ability of the president to persuade is important but limited. However, he also has a powerful bargaining chip to play: the ability to say no.

The Power to Say No

The Constitution gives the president the power to veto legislation. In addition most presidents have asserted the right of "executive privilege," or the right to withhold information that Congress may want to obtain from the president or his subordinates, and some presidents have tried to impound funds appropriated by Congress. These efforts by the president to say no are not only a way of blocking action but also a way of forcing Congress to bargain with him over the substance of policies.

Veto

If a president disapproves of a bill passed by both houses of Congress, he may veto it in one of two ways. One is by a **veto message.** This is a statement that the president sends to Congress accompanying the bill, within ten days (not counting Sundays) after the bill has been passed. In it he sets forth his reasons for not signing the bill. The other is the **pocket veto.** If the president does not sign the bill within ten days *and* Congress has adjourned within that time, then the bill will not become law. Obviously a pocket veto can only be used during a certain time of the year—just before Congress adjourns at the end of its second session. At times, however, presidents have pocket-vetoed a bill just before Congress recessed for a summer vacation or to permit its members to campaign during an off-year election. In 1972 Senator Edward M. Kennedy of Massachusetts protested that this was unconstitutional, since a recess is not the same thing as an adjournment. In a case brought to federal court, Kennedy was upheld, and it is now understood that the pocket veto can only be used just before the life of a given Congress expires.

A bill that is not signed or vetoed within ten days while Congress is still in session becomes law automatically, without the president's approval. A bill that has been returned to Congress with a veto message can be passed over the president's objections if at least two-thirds of each house votes to override the veto. A bill that has received a pocket veto cannot be brought back to life by Congress (since Congress has adjourned), nor does such a bill carry over to the next session of Congress. If Congress wants to press the matter, it will have to start all over again by passing the bill anew in its next session, and then hope that the president will sign it or, if he does not, that they can override his veto.

Until 1996 the president had to either accept or reject the entire bill. Presidents did not have the power, possessed by most governors, to exercise a **line-item veto,** with which the chief executive can approve some provisions of a bill and disapprove others. Congress could take advantage of this by putting items the president did not like into a bill he otherwise favored, forcing him to approve those provisions along with the rest of the bill or reject the whole thing. But in 1996 Congress passed a bill, which the president signed into law, that gives the president the power of "enhanced rescission." This means the president can cancel parts of a spending bill passed by Congress without vetoing the entire bill. The president has five days after signing a bill to send a message to Congress rescinding some parts of what he has signed. These rescissions take effect unless Congress, by a two-thirds vote, overturns them. Congress can choose which parts of the president's cancellations it wants to overturn. The law has a lot of complications—for example, some kinds of spending are excluded from presidential cancellation, and any money saved by such cancellations must go to reduce the deficit. But the biggest problem is that a federal court has decided that this law is unconstitutional. The Constitution gives the president no such power to carve up a bill: he must either sign the whole bill, veto the whole bill, or allow it to become law without his signature. The Supreme Court may eventually act on this.

Nevertheless, the veto power is a substantial one, because Congress rarely has the votes to override it.

TABLE 12.5 Presidential Vetoes, 1789–1994

	Regular Vetoes	Pocket Vetoes	Total Vetoes	Vetoes Overridden
Washington	2	—	2	—
Madison	5	2	7	—
Monroe	1	—	1	—
Jackson	5	7	12	—
Tyler	6	3	9	1
Polk	2	1	3	—
Pierce	9	—	9	5
Buchanan	4	3	7	—
Lincoln	2	4	6	—
A. Johnson	21	8	29	15
Grant	45	49	94	4
Hayes	12	1	13	1
Arthur	4	8	12	1
Cleveland	304	109	413	2
Harrison	19	25	44	1
Cleveland	43	127	170	5
McKinley	6	36	42	—
T. Roosevelt	42	40	82	1
Taft	30	9	39	1
Wilson	33	11	44	6
Harding	5	1	6	—
Coolidge	20	30	50	4
Hoover	21	16	37	3
F. Roosevelt	372	263	635	9
Truman	180	70	250	12
Eisenhower	73	108	181	2
Kennedy	12	9	21	—
L. Johnson	16	14	30	—
Nixon	24	18	42	6
Ford	53	19	72	12
Carter	13	18	31	2
Reagan	39	39	78	9
Bush	14	6	20	1
Clinton	0	0	0	0

SOURCES: *Statistical Abstract of the United States,* 1987, 235; Senate Library, *Presidential Vetoes* (Washington, DC: Government Printing Office, 1960), 199. Clinton figures through December 1994.

From George Washington to George Bush, over 2,400 presidential vetoes were cast; less than 4 percent were overridden (see Table 12.5). Cleveland, Franklin Roosevelt, Truman, and Eisenhower made the most extensive use of vetoes, accounting for 70 percent of all vetoes ever cast. Often the vetoed legislation is revised by Congress and passed in a form suitable to the president. There is no tally of how often this happens, but it is frequent enough so that both branches of government recognize that the veto, or even the threat of it, is part of an elaborate process of political negotiation in which the president has substantial powers.

Executive Privilege

The Constitution says nothing about whether the president is obliged to divulge private communications between himself and his principal advisers, but presidents have acted as if they did have that privilege of confidentiality. The presidential claim is based on two grounds. First, the doctrine of the separation of powers means that one branch of government does not have the right to inquire into the internal workings of another branch headed by constitutionally named officers. Second, the principles of statecraft and of prudent administration require that the president have the right to obtain confidential and candid advice from subordinates; such advice could not be obtained if it would quickly be exposed to public scrutiny.

For almost two hundred years there was no serious challenge to the claim of presidential confidentiality. The Supreme Court did not require the disclosure of confidential communications to or from the president.[17] Congress was never happy with this claim but until 1973 did not seriously dispute it. Indeed, in 1962 a Senate committee explicitly accepted a claim by President Kennedy that his secretary of defense, Robert S. McNamara, was not obliged to divulge the identity of Defense Department officials who had censored certain speeches by generals and admirals.

In 1973 the Supreme Court for the first time met the issue directly. A federal special prosecutor sought tape recordings of White House conversations between President Nixon and his advisers as part of his investigation of the Watergate scandal. In the case of *United States* v. *Nixon,* the Supreme Court, by a vote of eight to zero, held that while there may be a sound basis for the claim of executive privilege, especially where sensitive military or diplomatic matters are involved, there is no "absolute unqualified Presidential privilege of immunity from judicial process under all circumstances."[18] To admit otherwise would be to block the constitutionally defined function of the federal courts to decide criminal cases.

Thus Nixon was ordered to hand over the disputed tapes and papers to a federal judge so that the judge could decide which were relevant to the case at hand and allow those to be introduced into evidence. In the future another president may well persuade the Court that a different set of records or papers is so sensitive as to require protection, especially if there is no allegation of criminal misconduct requiring the production of evidence in court. As a practical matter it seems likely that presidential advisers will be able, except in unusual cases such as Watergate, to continue to give private advice to the president.

President Nixon justified his refusal to disclose tapes of conversations in the Oval Office by the argument that a president must have the private and candid views of his advisers, such as John Ehrlichman and Henry Kissinger (standing) and H. R. Haldeman (seated). The Supreme Court recognized this need but decided that tapes containing evidence bearing on possible criminal violations must be handed over to a judge.

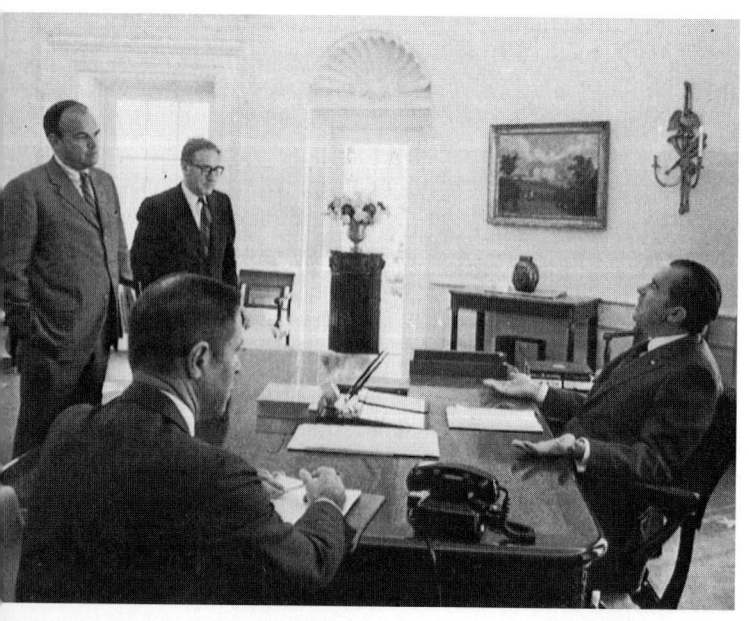

In 1997 the Supreme Court also decided that a president (in this case, Clinton) could be sued by a private person. (Clinton was being sued by Paula Jones over an alleged case of sexual harassment.) The Court's action did not bear on executive privilege, but it did make clear that in civil law the president is pretty much like everybody else.

Impoundment of Funds

From time to time presidents have refused to spend money appropriated by Congress. Truman did not spend all that Congress wanted spent on the armed forces, and Johnson did not spend all that Congress made available for highway construction. Kennedy refused to spend money appropriated for new weapons systems that he did not like. Indeed the precedent for impounding funds goes back at least to the administration of Thomas Jefferson.

But what has precedent is not thereby constitutional. The Constitution is silent on whether the president *must* spend the money that Congress appropriates; all it says is that the president cannot spend money that Congress has *not* appropriated. The major test of presidential power in this respect occurred during the Nixon administration. Nixon wished to reduce federal spending. He proposed in 1972 that Congress give him the power to reduce federal spending so that it would not exceed $250 billion for the coming year. Congress, under Democratic control, refused. Nixon responded by pocket-vetoing twelve spending bills and then impounding funds appropriated under other laws that he had not vetoed.

Congress in turn responded by passing the Budget Reform Act of 1974, which, among other things, requires the president to spend all appropriated funds unless he first tells Congress what funds he wishes not to spend and Congress, within forty-five days, agrees to delete the items. If he wishes simply to delay spending the money, he need only inform Congress, but Congress then can refuse the delay by passing a resolution requiring the immediate release of the money. Federal courts have upheld the rule that the president must spend, without delay for policy reasons, money that Congress has appropriated.

The President's Program

Imagine that you have just spent three or four years running for president, during which time you have given essentially the same speech over and over again. You have had no time to study the issues in any depth. To reach a large television audience, you have couched your ideas largely in rather simple—if not simple-minded—slogans. Your principal advisers are political aides, not legislative specialists.

You win. You are inaugurated. Now you must *be* a president instead of just talking about it. You must fill hundreds of appointive posts, but you know personally only a handful of the candidates. You must deliver a State of the Union message to Congress only two or three weeks after you are sworn in. It is quite possible that you have never read, much less written, such a message before. You must submit a new budget; the old one is hundreds of pages long, much of it comprehensible only to experts. Foreign governments, as well as the stock market, hang on your every word, interpreting many of your remarks in ways that totally surprise you. What will you do?

The Constitution is not much help. It directs you to report on the state of the union and to recommend "such measures" as you shall judge "necessary and expedient." Beyond that you are charged to "take care that the laws be faithfully executed."

At one time, of course, the demands placed on a newly elected president were not very great, because the president was not expected to do very much. The president, on assuming office, might speak of the tariff, or relations with England, or the value of veterans' pensions, or the need for civil service reform, but he was not expected to have something to say (and offer) to everybody. Today he is.

Putting Together a Program

To develop policies on short notice, a president will draw on several sources, each with particular strengths and weaknesses:

• Interest groups

  Strength: Will have specific plans and ideas.

  Weakness: Will have narrow view of the public interest.

- Aides and campaign advisers

  Strength: Will test new ideas for their political soundness.

  Weakness: Will not have many ideas to test, being inexperienced in government.

- Federal bureaus and agencies

  Strength: Will know what is feasible in terms of governmental realities.

  Weakness: Will propose plans that promote own agencies and will not have good information on whether plans will work.

- Outside, academic, and other specialists and experts

  Strength: Will have many general ideas and criticisms of existing programs.

  Weakness: Will not know the details of policy or have good judgment as to what is feasible.

There are essentially two ways for a president to develop a program. One, exemplified by President Carter, is to have a policy on almost everything. To do this Carter worked endless hours and studied countless documents, trying to learn something

In 1997, the budget was passed after negotiations among President Bill Clinton, House Speaker Newt Gingrich, and Senate Majority Leader Trent Lott.

about, and then state his positions on, a large number of issues. The other method, illustrated by President Reagan, is to concentrate on three or four major initiatives or themes, and leave everything else to subordinates.

But even when a president has a governing philosophy, as did Reagan, he cannot risk plunging ahead on his own. He must judge public and congressional reaction to this program before he commits himself fully to it. Therefore he will often allow parts of his program to be "leaked" to the press, or to be "floated" as a trial balloon. Reagan's commitment to a 30 percent tax cut and larger military expenditures was so well known that it required no leaking, but he did have to float his ideas on Social Security and certain budget cuts to test popular reaction. His opponents in the bureaucracy did exactly the same thing, hoping for the opposite effect. They leaked controversial parts of the program in an effort to discredit the whole policy. This process of testing the winds by a president and his critics helps explain why so many news stories coming from Washington mention no person by name but only an anonymous "highly placed source."

In addition to the risks of adverse reaction, the president faces three other constraints on his ability to plan a program. One is the sheer limit of his time and attention span. Every president works harder than he has ever worked before. A ninety-hour week is typical. Even so, he has great difficulty keeping up with all the things that he is supposed to know and make decisions about. For example, Congress during an average year passes between four hundred and six hundred bills, each of which the president must sign, veto, or allow to take effect without his signature. Scores of people wish to see him. Hundreds of phone calls must be made to members of Congress and others in order to ask for help, to soothe ruffled feathers, or to get information. He must receive all newly appointed ambassadors and visiting heads of state and in addition have his picture taken with countless people, from a Nobel Prize winner to a child whose likeness will appear on the Easter Seal.

The second constraint is the unexpected crisis. Franklin Roosevelt obviously had to respond to a depression and to the mounting risks of world war. But most presidents get their crises when they least expect them.

Truman

- Major strikes in the auto, steel, coal, railroad, and shipping industries
- Civil wars in Greece and Palestine
- South Korea invaded by North Korea
- Berlin put under siege by Soviet troops
- Truman's military aide charged with accepting improper gifts

Eisenhower

- Egypt seizes Suez Canal
- Revolts against communist rule in East Berlin, Poland, and Hungary
- Supreme Court outlaws school segregation
- USSR launches *Sputnik* satellite
- Presidential aide accused of accepting improper gifts

Kennedy

- Failure of Bay of Pigs invasion of Cuba
- Soviets put missiles in Cuba
- China invades India
- Federal troops sent to the South to protect blacks

Johnson

- Vietnam War
- Black riots in major cities
- War between India and Pakistan
- Civil war in Dominican Republic
- Arab-Israeli war
- Civil rights workers murdered in South

Nixon

- Watergate scandal
- Arab-Israeli war
- Value of dollar falls in foreign trade
- Arabs raise the price of oil

Carter

- OMB Director Bert Lance accused of improprieties
- Lengthy coal strike
- Seizure of American hostages in Iran
- Soviet invasion of Afghanistan

Reagan

- Poland suppresses Solidarity movement
- U.S. troops sent to Lebanon
- U.S. hostages held in Lebanon
- Civil war in Nicaragua
- Iran-contra crisis

Bush

- Soviet Union dissolves
- Iraq invades Kuwait
- China suppresses student rebellion in Tiananmen Square, Beijing

Clinton

- Murderous civil war continues in Bosnia and other parts of the former Yugoslavia
- North Korea resists inspections designed to detect possible manufacture of nuclear weapons
- Investigation of possible wrongdoing of President and Mrs. Clinton in Whitewater real estate development
- Charges of sexual harassment made against Clinton

The third constraint is the fact that the federal government and most federal programs, as well as the federal budget, can only be changed marginally, except in special circumstances. The vast bulk of federal expenditures are beyond control in any given year: the money must be spent whether the president likes it or not. Many federal programs have such strong congressional or public support that they must be left intact or modified only slightly. And this means that most federal employees can count on being secure in their jobs, whatever a president's views on reducing the bureaucracy.

The result of these constraints is that the president, at least in ordinary times, has to be selective about what he wants. He can be thought of as having a stock of influence and prestige the way that he might have a supply of money. If he wants to get the most "return" on his resources, he must "invest" that influence and prestige carefully in enterprises that promise substantial gains—in public benefits and political support—at reasonable costs. Each president tends to speak in terms of changing everything at once, calling his approach a "New Deal," a "New Frontier," a "Great Society," or the "New Federalism." But beneath the rhetoric he must identify a few spe-

CRITICAL Thinking

Measuring Presidential Success in Congress

Everyone has a favorite president. But how do you measure presidential success?

Modern political scientists have developed ways, most especially in relation to presidential victories in Congress. One of the most popular is calculated by taking the number of congressional votes supporting the president on bills for which the president has taken a definite public position and dividing that number by the total number of votes cast on those bills. Following that method, the line in Figure 12.5 (see page 391) charts presidential victories on votes in Congress for the period 1953–1994. Journalists and others often rely on such summary statistics when assessing presidential performance.

But whenever you encounter simple numerical measures of complex political or other realities, stop, look, and do some critical thinking. In this case, what does the figure really tell you about presidential success? Clearly it offers a rough approximation of how successful various presidents have been in getting their way in Congress. But just how rough is that approximation? How much do the numbers actually tell you about either the

quality of presidential leadership or the state of legislative-executive relations at any given point in time?

For starters, note that this measure of presidential success does not distinguish between victories on major and highly controversial bills and victories on minor or "motherhood and apple pie" bills. Next, observe that (surprise, surprise) success is most common for presidents whose party controls Congress: from 1953 to 1994, in years when the president's party controlled both chambers of Congress, the president won 75 percent of the time, but in periods of divided government, success rates averaged well below that level. Also, notice that in most cases presidential success erodes over time.

Dig even deeper, and you will discover that there is a story behind each score. For example, what's behind the scores of Presidents Carter and Eisenhower? President Carter's success rate averaged 76.8 percent. But during his third year in office, President Carter made his position known on only 22 percent of all recorded House votes and only 19 percent of

Senate votes. The comparable figures for President Eisenhower's third year in office were 56 percent in the House and 59 percent in the Senate. President Carter, a Democrat, had a Democratic Congress during his four years in office. President Eisenhower, a Republican, had a Republican Congress during his first two years and a Democratic Congress for his next six. President Carter had a big congressional liaison staff and dealt with an increasingly independent and resurgent Congress. President Eisenhower had no such army of legislative liaisons, and the Congress with which he dealt was still dominated by each party's leaders. Upon leaving office, most presidency watchers rated Eisenhower a flop with Congress; but today most experts hold exactly the opposite view of Ike's relationship with legislators. When President Carter left office, many analysts regarded his presidency as a textbook example of how not to handle Congress—an opinion that has yet to be revised in his favor.

Or consider the more recent case of President Clinton, a Democrat who began his first term with a Democratic

cific proposals on which he wishes to bet his resources, mindful of the need to leave a substantial stock of resources in reserve to handle the inevitable crises and emergencies. In recent decades events have required every president to devote much of his time and resources to two key issues: the state of the economy and foreign affairs. What he manages to do in addition to this will depend on his personal views and his sense of what the nation, as well as his re-election, requires.

Attempts to Reorganize

One item on the presidential agenda has been the same for almost every president since Herbert Hoover: reorganizing the executive branch of government. With few exceptions every president since 1928 has tried to change the structure of the staff, departments, and agencies that are theoretically subordinate to him. Every president has been appalled by the number of agencies that report to him and by

Congress. During his first two years in office he achieved a success score of 86.4 percent. In his first year in office he won a number of real legislative battles on Capitol Hill. But in his second year, his score remained high only because most of his key legislation was bottled up in Congress and never even reached a vote. Then, in 1994, President Clinton suffered a dramatic loss of party support in Congress (see table).

Now, how would you measure President Clinton's performance in dealing with Congress? Shortly after the midterm elections of 1994, one of the country's leading scholars of legislative-executive relations, Professor Charles O. Jones, wrote an article in which he counseled President Clinton that there were four basic approaches to congressional relations:

- *Partisan.* A no-compromise strategy in which the president relies on the veto to situate his position and build his record.

- *Copartisan.* A strategy in which the president proposes alternatives to congressional initiatives and sticks with those alternatives to the point

Dramatic Congressional Losses for First-Term, Elected Presidents, 1901–1995

President	Election	Net Loss in House	Net Loss in Senate	Loss of Majority?
Taft	1910	57	10	House only
Wilson	1914	59	—	No
Harding	1922	75	8	No
Hoover	1930	49	8	House only
Johnson	1966	47	4	No
Clinton	1994	52	9	Both houses

SOURCE: Charles O. Jones, "Bill Clinton and the GOP Congress," *The Brookings Review,* Spring 1995, p. 33. Reprinted by permission of the publisher.

where compromise is essential to save the legislation.

- *Cross-partisan.* A strategy directed at gaining support from the other party on certain key issues.

- *Bipartisan.* A strategy in which the president works with opposition party leaders in Congress from start to finish.

Which of these strategies did President Clinton most often employ in dealing with the 104th Congress? On issues ranging from crime and welfare to the budget and trade, how often did he lose legislative battles only to win legislative wars? Explore these questions, and decide for yourself what criteria (and which, if any, summary statistics) should be used in measuring presidential success in dealing with Congress.

SOURCES: Norman J. Ornstein, Thomas E. Mann, and Michael J. Malbin, *Vital Statistics on Congress, 1995–1996* (Washington, DC: CQ Press, 1996), pp. 196–198; Charles O. Jones, "Bill Clinton and the GOP Congress," *The Brookings Review,* Spring 1995, pp. 26–33.

the apparently helter-skelter manner in which they have grown up. But this is only one—and often not the most important—reason for wanting to reorganize. If a president wants to get something done, or put new people in charge of a program, or recapture political support for a policy, it often proves easier to do so by creating a new agency or reorganizing an old one than by abolishing a program, firing a subordinate, or passing a new law. Reorganization serves many objectives and thus is a recurring theme.

Between 1948 and 1961 the agency in charge of foreign aid was reorganized eight times. Between 1968 and 1973 the federal agency charged with enforcing narcotics laws was reorganized twice; in 1981 it was reorganized again and placed under the FBI. Truman and Eisenhower each created a national commission to recommend wholesale reorganizations of the executive branch, both chaired by former President Hoover. President Franklin Roosevelt appointed a commission on administrative management; over thirty years later President

Nixon created another one. President Carter made reorganization a priority concern of his staff. From 1949 to 1977 one hundred and fourteen separate reorganization plans, some calling for small changes, some for large ones, were sent to Congress. About three-fourths were approved, many only after hard-fought battles. In modern times Presidents Johnson, Nixon, and Carter have been the most determined advocates of reorganization, though not necessarily the most successful.

Legally the president can reorganize his personal White House staff any time that he wishes. To reorganize in any important way the larger Executive Office of the President or any of the executive departments or agencies, however, Congress must first be consulted. For over forty years this consultation usually took the form of submitting to Congress a reorganization plan that would take effect provided that neither the House nor the Senate passed, within sixty days, a concurrent resolution disapproving the plan (such a resolution was called a **legislative veto**). This procedure, first authorized by the Reorganization Act of 1939, could be used to change, but not create or abolish, an executive agency. In 1981 authority under that act expired, and Congress did not renew it. Two years later the Supreme Court declared that all legislative vetoes were unconstitutional (see Chapter 13), and so today any presidential reorganization plan would have to take the form of a regular law, passed by Congress and signed by the president.

There have been many bitter fights over reorganization plans. At stake are differing beliefs as to what an agency should do, who should head it, and what congressional committee should have power over it. The Department of Health, Education and Welfare was created by a reorganization plan in 1953, but to get the plan accepted, President Eisenhower had to promise to leave the Public Health Service and the Office of Education, nominally part of the new department, relatively autonomous. The first efforts to create a Department of Urban Affairs were blocked because key members of Congress objected to the prospect of a black's heading the agency (it was later created, and a black did head it). The law designed to create a Department of Transportation, which finally passed in 1966, involved one of the most difficult legislative struggles of President Johnson's administration: his chief domestic policy aide later wrote that it took 15

percent of the aide's time and required daily presidential attention, and even then fell well short of a thorough restructuring of transportation agencies.[19]

What has been said so far may well give the reader the impression that the president is virtually helpless. That is not the case. The *actual* power of the president can only be measured in terms of what he can accomplish. What this chapter has described so far is the office as the president finds it—the burdens, restraints, demands, complexities, and resources that he encounters on entering the Oval Office for the first time. Every president since Truman has commented feelingly on how limited the powers of the president seem from the inside compared to what they appear to be from the outside. Franklin Roosevelt compared his struggles with the bureaucracy to punching a featherbed; Truman wrote that the power of the president was chiefly the power to persuade people to do what they ought to do anyway. After being in office a year or so, Kennedy spoke to interviewers about how much more complex the world appeared than he had first supposed. Johnson and Nixon were broken by the office and the events that happened there.

Yet Franklin Roosevelt helped create the modern presidency, with its vast organizational reach, and directed a massive war effort. Truman ordered two atomic bombs dropped on Japanese cities. Eisenhower sent American troops to Lebanon; Kennedy supported an effort to invade Cuba. Johnson sent troops to the Dominican Republic and to Vietnam; Nixon ordered an invasion of Cambodia; Reagan launched an invasion of Grenada and sponsored an antigovernment insurgent group in Nicaragua; Bush invaded Panama and sent troops to the Persian Gulf to fight Iraq; Clinton sent troops to Haiti and Bosnia. Obviously, Europeans, Russians, Vietnamese, Cambodians, Dominicans, Panamanians, and Iraqis do not think of the American president as "helpless."

Presidential Transition

No president but Franklin Roosevelt has ever served more than two terms, and since the ratification of the Twenty-second Amendment in 1951, no president will ever again have the chance. But more than tradition or the Constitution escorts presidents from office. Only fourteen of the forty-one presidents since George Washington have been elected to a second term. Of the twenty-seven not reelected, four died in office during their first term. But the remainder either did not seek, or (more usually) could not obtain reelection.

Of the eight presidents who died in office, four were assassinated: Lincoln, Garfield, McKinley, and Kennedy. At least six other presidents were the objects of unsuccessful assassination attempts: Jackson, Theodore Roosevelt, Franklin Roosevelt, Truman, Ford, and Reagan. (There may have been attempts on other presidents that never came to public notice; the attempts mentioned here involved public efforts to fire weapons at presidents.)

The presidents who served two or more terms fall into certain periods, such as the Founding (Washington, Jefferson, Madison, Monroe) or wartime (Lincoln, Wilson, Roosevelt), or they happened to be in office during especially tranquil times (Monroe, McKinley, Eisenhower), or some combination of the above. When the country was deeply divided, as during the years just before the Civil War and during the period of Reconstruction after it, it was the rare president who was reelected.

The Vice President

Eight times a vice president has become president because of the death of his predecessor. It first happened to John Tyler, who became president in 1841 when William Henry Harrison died peacefully after only one month in office. The question for Tyler and for the country was substantial: was Tyler simply to be the acting president and a kind of caretaker until a new president was elected, or was he to be *president* in every sense of the word? Despite criticism and despite what might have been the contrary intention of the Framers of the Constitution, Tyler decided on the latter course and was confirmed in that opinion by a decision of Congress. Ever since, the vice president has automatically become president, in title and in powers, when the occupant of the White House has died or resigned.

But if vice presidents frequently acquire office because of death, they rarely acquire it by election. Since the earliest period of the Founding, when John Adams and Thomas Jefferson were each elected president after having first served as vice president

President Reagan, moments before he was shot on March 30, 1981, by a would-be assassin.

under their predecessors, there have only been three occasions when a vice president was later able to win the presidency without his president's having died in office. One was in 1836, when Martin Van Buren was elected president after having served as Andrew Jackson's vice president; the second was in 1968, when Richard Nixon became president after having served as Eisenhower's vice president eight years earlier; the third was in 1988 when Bush succeeded Reagan. Many vice presidents who enter the Oval Office because their predecessors died are subsequently elected to terms in their own right—as happened to Theodore Roosevelt, Calvin Coolidge, Harry Truman, and Lyndon Johnson. But no one who wishes to become president should assume that to become vice president first is the best way to get there.

The vice presidency is just what so many vice presidents have complained about its being: a rather empty job. John Adams described it as "the most insignificant office that ever the invention of man contrived or his imagination conceived," and most of his successors would have agreed. Thomas Jefferson, almost alone, had a good word to say for it: "The second office of the government is honorable and

Six-Year Term for President

Delegates Divided on Big Issue

＊ ＊ ＊

EUDORA, KANS. OCTOBER 15—Here at the convention called to propose amendments to the United States Constitution, the major issue facing the delegates is the proposal to limit the president to a single six-year term. Proponents of the measure claim . . .

What Would You Do?

MEMORANDUM

TO: Delegate James Nagle
FROM: Robert Gilbert, legal staff
SUBJECT: Six-year presidential term

The proposal to give the president a single six-year term is perhaps the most popular amendment now before the convention. Polls suggest that it is supported by a sizable percentage of the American people.

Arguments for:

1. Today a president no sooner learns the ropes after being elected for the first time than he or she has to start preparing for the next election. A six-year term will give the president a chance to govern for several years after learning how to be president. This will lessen the extent to which political pressures dictate what the president does.

2. Limited to a single term, the president need not cater to special-interest groups or the media in deciding on policy. He or she can concentrate on what is good for the country.

3. Many states have limited their governors to a single term.

Arguments against:

1. It is the need to win reelection that keeps the president (like any politician) attentive to what the people want. A president unable to succeed himself or herself will be tempted to ignore public opinion.

2. Limiting a president to a single term will not free him or her from the need to play to the media or special-interest groups, since the formal powers of the presidency are too weak to permit the incumbent to govern without the aid of Congress and the press.

3. There is no evidence that presidents (such as Dwight Eisenhower) who served a second term knowing that they could not run for reelection did a better or less "political" job in the second term than in the first.

Your decision: Favor amendment ___ Oppose amendment ___

easy, the first is but a splendid misery."[20] Daniel Webster rejected a vice presidential nomination in 1848 with the phrase, "I do not choose to be buried until I am really dead."[21] (Had he taken the job, he would have become president after Zachary Taylor died in office, thereby achieving a remarkable secular resurrection.) For all the good and bad jokes about the vice presidency, however, candidates still struggle mightily for it. John Nance Garner gave up the speakership of the House to become Franklin Roosevelt's vice president (a job he valued as "not worth a pitcher of warm spit"*), and Lyndon Johnson gave up the majority leadership of the Senate to become Kennedy's. Truman, Nixon, Humphrey, Mondale, and Gore all left reasonably secure Senate seats for the vice presidency.

The only official task of the vice president is to preside over the Senate and to vote in case of a tie. Even this is scarcely time-consuming, as the Senate chooses from among its members a president pro tempore, as required by the Constitution, who (along with others) presides in the absence of the vice president. The vice president's leadership powers in the Senate are weak, especially when the vice president is of a different party from the majority of the senators. Presidents have from time to time found tasks for their vice presidents—attending the funerals of world figures, being the chairman of governmental commissions, and the like—but all in all the vice president can do little more than endorse whatever the president does, and wait. And if they should run for president after their former boss retires (as George Bush did in 1988), they have to walk the fine line between appearing loyal to the president and having opinions of their own. It isn't easy.

Problems of Succession

If the president should die in office, the right of the vice president to assume that office has been clear since the time of John Tyler. But two questions remain: What if the president falls seriously ill but does not die? And if the vice president steps up, who then becomes the new vice president?

The first problem has arisen on a number of occasions. After President James A. Garfield was shot

* The word he actually used was a good deal stronger than spit, but historians are decorous.

When President Woodrow Wilson suffered a stroke in 1919, his wife, Edith Galt Wilson, became the power behind the scenes. The Twenty-fifth Amendment is intended to solve the problem of presidential disability by providing for an orderly transfer of power to the vice president.

in 1881, he lingered through the summer before he died. President Woodrow Wilson collapsed from a stroke and was a virtual recluse for seven months in 1919 and an invalid for the rest of his term. Eisenhower had three serious illnesses while in office; Reagan was shot during his first term and hospitalized during his second.

The second problem has arisen on eight occasions when the vice president became president owing to the death of the incumbent. In these cases no elected person was available to succeed the new president should he die in office. For many decades the problem was handled by law. The Succession Act of 1886, for example, designated the secretary of state as next in line for the presidency should the vice president die, followed by the other cabinet offi-

Politically SPEAKING

Lame Duck

A **lame duck** is a politician whose power has diminished because he or she is about to leave office as a result of electoral defeat or statutory limitation (for example, the president can serve no more than two terms).

The expression was first used in eighteenth-century England, where it meant a "bankrupt businessman." Soon it was used to refer to "bankrupt" politicians. Perhaps they were called "lame ducks" because they had been shot on the wing and, though still alive, could no longer fly.

A lame duck is not to be confused with a "sitting duck" (somebody who is an easy target).

SOURCE: From *Safire's Political Dictionary* by William Safire. Copyright © 1968, 1972, 1978 by William Safire. Reprinted by permission of Random House, Inc. and the author.

cers in order of seniority. But this meant that a vice president who becomes president could pick his own successor by choosing his own secretary of state. In 1947 the law was changed to make the Speaker of the House and then the president pro tempore of the Senate next in line for the presidency. But that created still other problems: a Speaker or a president pro tempore is likely to be chosen because of his seniority, not his executive skill, and in any event might well be of the party opposite to that occupying the White House.

Both problems were addressed in 1967 by the Twenty-fifth Amendment to the Constitution. It deals with the disability problem by allowing the vice president to serve as "acting president" whenever the president declares that he is unable to discharge the powers and duties of his office or whenever the vice president and a majority of the cabinet declare that the president is incapacitated. If the president disagrees with the opinion of his vice president and a majority of the cabinet, then Congress decides the issue. A two-thirds majority is necessary to confirm that the president is unable to serve.

The amendment deals with the succession problem by requiring a vice president who assumes the presidency (after a vacancy is created by death or resignation) to nominate a new vice president. This person takes office if the nomination is confirmed by a majority vote of both houses of Congress. When there is no vice president, then the 1947 law governs: next in line are the Speaker, the Senate president, and the fourteen cabinet officers, beginning with the secretary of state.

The disability problem has not arisen since the adoption of the amendment, but the succession problem has. In 1973 Vice President Spiro Agnew resigned, having pleaded no contest to criminal charges. President Nixon nominated Gerald Ford as vice president, and after extensive hearings he was confirmed by both houses of Congress and sworn in. Then on August 9, 1974, Nixon resigned the presidency—the first man to do so—and Ford became president. He nominated as his vice president Nelson Rockefeller, who was confirmed by both houses of Congress—again, after extensive hearings—and was sworn in on December 19, 1974. For the first time in history, the nation had as its two principal executive officers men who had not been elected to either the presidency or the vice presidency. It is a measure of the legitimacy of the Constitution that this arrangement caused no crisis in public opinion.

Impeachment

There is one other way—besides death, disability, or resignation—by which a president can leave office before his term expires, and that is by impeachment. Not only the president and vice president but also all "civil officers of the United States" can be removed by being impeached and convicted. As a practical matter civil officers—cabinet secretaries, bureau chiefs, and the like—will not be subject to impeachment, because the president can remove them at any time and usually will if their behavior makes them a serious political liability. Federal judges, who serve during good behavior and who are constitutionally independent of the president and Congress, have been the most frequent objects of impeachment.

An **impeachment** is like an indictment in a criminal trial: a set of charges against somebody, voted by (in this case) the House of Representatives. To be removed from office, the impeached officer must be convicted by a two-thirds vote of the Senate, which sits as a court, hears the evidence, and makes its decision under whatever rules it wishes to adopt. Fifteen persons have been impeached by the House, and seven have been convicted by the Senate. The last conviction was in 1989, when two federal judges were removed from office.

Only one president has been impeached—Andrew Johnson in 1868—but Richard Nixon almost surely would have been had he not first resigned. Johnson was not convicted on the impeachment, the effort to do so falling one vote short of the necessary two-thirds majority. Many historians feel that the effort to remove Johnson was entirely partisan and ideological in nature, for he was not charged with anything that they would regard as "high crimes and misdemeanors" within the meaning of the Constitution. The Congress detested Johnson's "soft" policy toward the defeated South after the Civil War and was determined to use any pretext to remove him. The charges against Nixon were far graver: allegations of illegal acts arising from his efforts to cover up his subordinates' involvement in the burglary of the Democratic National Committee headquarters in the Watergate building.

Some Founders may have thought that impeachment would frequently be used against presidents, but as a practical matter it is so complex and serious an undertaking that we can probably expect it to be reserved in the future only for the gravest forms of presidential misconduct. No one quite knows what a high crime or misdemeanor is, but most scholars agree that the charge must involve something illegal or unconstitutional, not just unpopular. Unless a president or vice president is first impeached and convicted, many experts believe that he is not liable to prosecution as would be an ordinary citizen. (No one is certain, because the question has never arisen.) President Ford's pardon of Richard Nixon meant that he could not be prosecuted under federal law for things that he may have done while in office.

Students may find the occasions of misconduct or disability remote and the details of succession or impeachment tedious. But the problem is not remote—succession has occurred nine times and disability at least twice—and what may appear tedious goes, in fact, to the heart of the presidency. The first and fundamental problem is to make the office legitimate. That was the great task George Washington set himself, and that was the substantial accomplishment of his successors. Despite bitter and sometimes violent partisan and sectional strife, beginning almost immediately after Washington stepped down, presidential succession has always occurred peacefully, without a military coup or a political plot. For centuries, in the bygone times of kings as well as in the present times of dictators and juntas, peaceful succession has been a rare phenomenon among the nations of the world. Many of the critics of the Constitution believed, in 1787, that peaceful succession would not happen in the United States either: somehow the president would connive to hold office for life or to handpick his successor. Their predictions were wrong, though their fears were understandable.

How Powerful Is the President?

Just as members of Congress bemoan their loss of power, so presidents bemoan theirs. Can both be right?

In fact they can. If Congress is less able to control events than it once was, it does not mean that the president is thereby more able to exercise control. The federal government *as a whole* has become more constrained so that it is less able to act decisively. The chief source of this constraint is the greater complexity of the issues with which Washington must deal.

It was one thing to pass a Social Security Act in 1935; it is quite another thing to keep the Social Security system adequately funded. It was one thing for the nation to defend itself when attacked in 1941; it is quite another to maintain a constant military preparedness while simultaneously exploring possibilities for arms control. It was not hard to give pensions to veterans; it seems almost impossible today to find the cure for drug abuse or juvenile crime.

In the face of modern problems, all branches of government, including the presidency, seem both big and ineffectual. Add to this the much closer and more critical scrutiny of the media and the proliferation of interest groups, and it is small wonder that both presidents and members of Congress feel that they have lost power.

Presidents have come to acquire certain rules of thumb for dealing with their political problems. Among them are these:

- *Move it or lose it.* A president who wants to get something done should do it early in his term, before his political influence erodes.
- *Avoid details.* President Carter's lieutenants regret having tried to do too much. Better to have three or four top priorities and forget the rest.
- *Cabinets don't get much accomplished; people do.* Find capable White House subordinates and give them well-defined responsibility; then watch them closely.[22]

SUMMARY

A president, chosen by the people and with powers derived from a written constitution, has less power than does a British prime minister, even though the latter depends entirely on the support of his or her party in Parliament. The separation of powers between the executive and legislative branches, the distinguishing feature of the American system, means that the president must deal with a competitor— Congress—in setting policy and even in managing executive agencies.

Presidential power, though still sharply limited, has grown from its constitutional origins as a result of congressional delegation, the increased importance of foreign affairs, and public expectations. But if the president today has more power, more is also demanded of him. As a result how effective he is de-

pends not on any general grant of authority but on the nature of the issue that he confronts and the extent to which he can mobilize informal sources of power (public opinion, congressional support).

Though the president seemingly controls a vast executive-branch apparatus, in fact he appoints but a small portion of the officials, and the behavior of even these is often beyond his easy control. Moreover, public support, high at the beginning of any new presidency, usually declines as the term proceeds. Consequently each president must conserve his power (and his energy and time), concentrating these scarce resources to deal with a few matters of major importance. Virtually every president since Franklin Roosevelt has tried to enlarge his ability to manage the executive branch—by reorganization, by appointing White House aides, by creating specialized staff agencies—but no president has been satisfied with the results.

The president, in dealing with Congress, can rely to some degree on party loyalty; thus presidents whose party controls Congress tend to have more of their proposals approved. But such loyalty is insufficient; every president must in addition cajole, award favors, and threaten vetoes to influence legislation. Few presidents can count on a honeymoon; most discover that their own plans are at the mercy of unexpected crises.

The extent to which a president will be weak or powerful will vary with the kind of issue and the circumstances of the moment. It is a mistake to speak of an "imperial presidency" or of an ineffectual one. A president's power is better assessed by considering how he behaves in regard to specific issues.

KEY TERMS

divided government   *p. 365*

unified government   *p. 365*

representative democracy   *p. 366*

direct democracy   *p. 366*

pyramid structure   *p. 377*

circular structure   *p. 377*

ad hoc structure *p. 377*

perks *p. 380*

cabinet *p. 380*

veto message *p. 392*

pocket veto *p. 392*

line-item veto *p. 393*

legislative veto *p. 400*

lame duck *p. 404*

impeachment *p. 405*

SUGGESTED READINGS

General

Barber, James David. *The Presidential Character.* 3d ed. Englewood Cliffs, N.J.: Prentice-Hall, 1985. How a president's personality evolves and shapes his conduct in office.

Corwin, Edward S. *The President: Office and Powers.* 5th ed. New York: New York University Press, 1985. Historical, constitutional, and legal development of the office.

Cunliffe, Marcus. *American Presidents and the Presidency.* New York: American Heritage Press/McGraw-Hill, 1972. Readable history of the presidency, with shrewd insights and ample anecdotes.

Kernell, Samuel. *Going Public: New Strategies of Presidential Leadership.* Washington, D.C.: Congressional Quarterly Press, 1986. How presidents try to enlarge their power by taking their case to the public.

Neustadt, Richard E. *Presidential Power: The Politics of Leadership.* Rev. ed. New York: Wiley, 1976. How presidents try to acquire and hold political power in the competitive world of official Washington, by a man who has been both a scholar and an insider.

Peterson, Mark A. *Legislating Together: The White House and Congress from Eisenhower to Reagan.* Cambridge: Harvard University Press, 1990. Challenges the conventional view that "the president proposes, Congress disposes." Contains many excellent examples of bargaining and cooperation between Congress and the executive branch.

On Franklin D. Roosevelt

Burns, James MacGregor. *Roosevelt: The Lion and the Fox.* New York: Harcourt Brace, 1956.

Leuchtenberg, William E. *Franklin D. Roosevelt and the New Deal, 1932–1940.* New York: Harper & Row, 1963.

On Harry S Truman

Hamby, A. L. *Beyond the New Deal: Harry S Truman and American Liberalism.* New York: Columbia University Press, 1973.

Truman, Harry S *Memoirs.* 2 vols. Garden City, N.Y.: Doubleday, 1958.

On Dwight D. Eisenhower

Greenstein, Fred I. *The Hidden-Hand Presidency: Eisenhower as Leader.* New York: Basic Books, 1982.

On John F. Kennedy

Paper, Lewis J. *The Promise and the Performance: The Leadership of John F. Kennedy.* New York: Crown, 1975.

Sorenson, Theodore M. *Kennedy.* New York: Harper & Row, 1965.

On Lyndon B. Johnson

Kearns, Doris. *Lyndon Johnson and the American Dream.* New York: Harper & Row, 1976.

Evans, Rowland, and Robert Novak. *Lyndon B. Johnson: The Exercise of Power.* New York: New American Library, 1968.

On Richard M. Nixon

Ambrose, Stephen E. *Nixon—The Education of a Politician, 1913–1962.* New York: Simon and Schuster, 1987.

13

The Bureaucracy

★ Comparison with other countries

★ Growth of the bureaucracy

★ Change in role

★ Scope of power

★ Hiring and firing

★ Agency point of view

★ A bureaucratic personality?

★ Constraints

★ Agency–interest group relations

★ Relationship to Congress and the president

★ The problems of bureaucracy

★ Bureaucratic reform

There is probably not a man or woman in the United States who has not, at some time or other, complained about "the bureaucracy." Your letter was slow in getting to Aunt Minnie? The Internal Revenue Service took months to send you your tax refund? The Defense Department paid $400 for a hammer? The Occupational Safety and Health Administration told you that you installed the wrong kind of portable toilet for your farm workers? The "bureaucracy" is to blame.

For most people and politicians *bureaucracy* is a pejorative word implying waste, confusion, red tape, and rigidity. But for scholars—and for bureaucrats themselves—*bureaucracy* is a word with a neutral, technical meaning. A **bureaucracy** is a large, complex organization composed of appointed officials. By *complex* we mean that authority is divided among several managers; no one person is able to make all the decisions (see the box on this subject, page 410). A large corporation is a bureaucracy; so also are a big university and a government agency. With its sizable staff, even Congress has become, to some degree, a bureaucracy.

What is it about complex organizations in general, and government agencies in particular, that leads so many people to complain about them? In part the answer is to be found in their very size and complexity. But in large measure the answer is to be found in the political context within which such agencies must operate. If we examine that context carefully, we will discover that many of the problems that we blame on "the bureaucracy" are in fact the result of what Congress, the courts, and the president do.

Distinctiveness of the American Bureaucracy

Bureaucratic government has become an obvious feature of all modern societies, democratic and non-democratic. In the United States, however, three aspects of our constitutional system and political traditions give to the bureaucracy a distinctive char-

409

Fifty-Two Layers of Bureaucracy at the Top

In 1960 only three cabinet departments had deputy secretaries. By 1994 all fourteen had them. In addition, today more agencies have principal deputy secretaries, deputy associate administrators, office directors, division chiefs, bureau heads, assistant bureau heads, and more. When you pile them up one on top of the other, you get fifty-two layers of executive management at the top of the federal bureaucracy—and scores more below it. And while there are more layers below, there's definitely more room at the top. In 1996 as in 1960 there were about 2 million federal civil servants. But from 1960 to 1962 the number of top political appointees in the agencies rose from 451 to 2,393, an increase of 430 percent.

	Number of Positions	
	Kennedy	Clinton
Secretary	10	14
Deputy Secretary	6	21
Under Secretary	14	32
Assistant Secretary	81	212
Deputy Assistant Secretary	77	507
Deputy Administrator	52	190

SOURCE: From Paul C. Light, *Thickening Government: Federal Hierarchy and the Diffusion of Accountability* (Washington, DC: Brookings Institution, 1995). Reprinted by permission of the publisher.

acter. First, political authority over the bureaucracy is not in one set of hands but is shared among several institutions. In a parliamentary regime, such as in Great Britain, the appointed officials of the national government work for the cabinet ministers, who are in turn dominated by the prime minister. In theory, and to a considerable extent in practice, British bureaucrats report to and take orders from the ministers in charge of their departments, do not deal directly with Parliament, and rarely give interviews to the press. In the United States the Constitution permits both the president and Congress to exercise authority over the bureaucracy. Every senior appointed official has at least two masters: one in the executive branch and the other in the legislative. Often there are many more than two: Congress, after all, is not a single organization but a collection of committees, subcommittees, and individuals. This divided authority encourages bureaucrats to play one branch of government off against the other and to make heavy use of the media.

Second, most of the agencies of the federal government share their functions with related agencies in state and local government. Though some federal agencies deal directly with American citizens—the Internal Revenue Service collects taxes from them, the Federal Bureau of Investigation looks into crimes for them, the Postal Service delivers mail to them—many agencies work with other organizations at other levels of government. For example: the Department of Education gives money to local school systems; the Health Care Financing Administration in the Department of Health and Human Services reimburses states for money spent on health care for the poor; the Department of Housing and Urban Development gives grants to cities for community development; and the Employment and Training Administration in the Department of Labor supplies funds to local governments so that they can run job-training programs. In France, by contrast, government programs dealing with education, health, housing, and employment are centrally run, with little or no control exercised by local governments.

Third, the institutions and traditions of American life have contributed to the growth of what was called in Chapter 4 an "adversary culture," in which the definition and expansion of personal rights, and the defense of rights and claims through lawsuits as well as political action, are given central importance. A government agency in this country operates under closer public scrutiny and with a greater prospect of court challenges to its authority than in almost any other nation. Virtually every important decision of the Occupational Safety and Health Administration or of the Environmental Protection Agency is likely to be challenged in the courts or attacked by an affected party; in Sweden the decisions of similar agencies go largely uncontested.

The scope as well as the style of bureaucratic government differs. In most Western European nations the government owns and operates large parts of the economy: the French government operates the railroads and owns companies that make automobiles and cigarettes, and the Italian government owns many similar enterprises and also the nation's oil refineries. In just about every large nation except the United States, the telephone system is owned by the government. Publicly operated enterprises account for about 12 percent of all employment in France but less than 3 percent in the United States.[1] The United States government regulates privately owned enterprises to a degree not found in many other countries, however. Why we should have preferred regulation to ownership as the proper government role is an interesting question to which we shall return.

The Growth of the Bureaucracy

The Constitution made scarcely any provision for an administrative system other than to allow the president to appoint, with the advice and consent of the Senate, "ambassadors, other public ministers and consuls, judges of the Supreme Court, and all other officers of the United States whose appointments are not herein otherwise provided for, and which shall be established by law."[2] Departments and bureaus were not mentioned.

In the first Congress, in 1789, James Madison introduced a bill to create a Department of State to assist the new secretary of state, Thomas Jefferson, in carrying out his duties. People appointed to this department were to be nominated by the president and approved by the Senate, but they were "to be removable by the president" alone. These six words, which would confer the right to fire government officials, occasioned six days of debate in the House. At stake was the locus of power over what was to become the bureaucracy. Madison's opponents argued that the Senate should consent to the removal of officials as well as their appointment. Madison responded that, without the unfettered right of removal, the president would not be able to control his subordinates, and without this control he would not be able to discharge his constitutional obligation to "take care that the laws be faithfully executed."[3] Madison won, twenty-nine votes to twenty-two. When the issue went to the Senate, another debate resulted in a tie vote, broken in favor of the president by Vice President John Adams. The Department of State, and all cabinet departments subsequently created, would be run by people removable only by the president.

That decision did not resolve the question of who would really control the bureaucracy, however. Congress retained the right to appropriate money, to investigate the administration, and to shape the laws that would be executed by that administration—more than ample power to challenge any president who claimed to have sole authority over his subordinates. And many members of Congress expected that the cabinet departments, even though headed by people removable by the president, would report to Congress.

The government in Washington was at first minuscule. The State Department started with only nine employees; the War Department did not have eighty civilian employees until 1801. Only the Treasury Department, concerned with collecting taxes and finding ways to pay the public debt, had much power, and only the Post Office Department provided any significant service.

The Appointment of Officials

Small as the bureaucracy was, people struggled, often bitterly, over who would be appointed to it. From George Washington's day to modern times, presidents have found appointment to be one of their most important and difficult tasks. The officials that they select affect how the laws are interpreted (thus the political ideology of the job holders is important), what tone the administration will display (thus personal character is important), how effectively the public business is discharged (thus competence is important), and how strong will be the political party or faction in power (and thus party affiliation is important). Presidents trying to balance the competing needs of ideology, character, fitness, and partisanship have rarely pleased most people. As John Adams remarked, every appointment creates one ingrate and ten enemies.

Because Congress, during most of the nineteenth and twentieth centuries, was the dominant branch of government, congressional preferences often controlled the appointment of officials. And since Congress was, in turn, a collection of people who represented local interests, appointments were made with an eye to rewarding the local supporters of members of Congress or building up local party organizations. These appointments made on the basis of political considerations—patronage—were

Politically SPEAKING

Spoils System

The **spoils system** is another phrase for *political patronage*—that is, the practice of giving the fruits of a party's victory, such as jobs and contracts, to the loyal members of that party.

Spoils became a famous word when it was used in 1832 by Senator William Marcy of New York in a speech that he made defending the decision of President Andrew Jackson to appoint one of his supporters, Martin Van Buren, as ambassador to Great Britain. New York politicians, he said, "boldly preach what they practice.... If they are successful, they claim, as a matter of right, the advantages of success. They see nothing wrong in the rule, that to the victor belong the spoils of the enemy."

In fact both the word and the practice are much older than Marcy and Jackson. Thomas Jefferson had appointed his partisans to office when he won the presidency from John Adams. Though Jackson is remembered as a heavy user of spoils, in fact he only replaced about 20 percent of all the officeholders that he inherited from his predecessor.

By the late nineteenth century the spoils system was both more extensively used and sharply criticized. Ending the system and replacing it with appointments based on merit was a major goal of the progressive movement around the turn of the century.

Today most federal appointments are based on merit, but in many state governments there continues to be a heavy reliance on patronage.

SOURCE: From *Safire's Political Dictionary* by William Safire. Copyright © 1968, 1972, 1978 by William Safire. Reprinted by permission of Random House, Inc. and the author.

later to become a major issue. They galvanized various reform efforts that sought to purify politics and to raise the level of competence of the public service. Many of the abuses that the reformers complained about were real enough, but patronage served some useful purposes as well. It gave the president a way to ensure that his subordinates were reasonably supportive of his policies; it provided a reward that the president could use to induce recalcitrant members of Congress to vote for his programs; and it enabled party organizations to be built up to perform the necessary functions of nominating candidates and getting out the vote.

Though at first there were not many jobs to fight over, by the middle of the nineteenth century there were a lot. From 1816 to 1861 the number of federal employees increased eightfold. This expansion was not, however, the result of the government's taking on new functions but simply a result of the increased demands on its traditional functions. The Post Office alone accounted for 86 percent of this growth.[4]

The Civil War was a great watershed in bureaucratic development. Fighting the war led, naturally, to hiring many new officials and creating many new offices. Just as important, the Civil War revealed the administrative weakness of the federal government and led to demands by the civil service reform movement for an improvement in the quality and organization of federal employees. And finally, the war was followed by a period of rapid industrialization and the emergence of a national economy. The effects of these developments could no longer be managed by state governments acting alone. With the creation of a nationwide network of railroads, commerce among the states became increasingly important. The constitutional powers of the federal government to regulate interstate commerce, long dormant for want of much commerce to regulate, now became an important source of controversy.

A Service Role

From 1861 to 1901 new agencies were created, many to deal with particular sectors of society and the economy. Over two hundred thousand new federal employees were added, with only about half of this increase in the Post Office. The rapidly growing

The Hollerith machine (left) was invented by Herman Hollerith (1860–1929) to help the government take the census. It analyzed statistical data by sorting and counting punched paper cards. Today, high-speed computers (right) read data optically and analyze them electronically.

Pension Office began paying benefits to Civil War veterans; the Department of Agriculture was created in 1862 to help farmers; the Department of Labor was founded in 1882 to serve workers; and the Department of Commerce was organized in 1903 to assist businesspeople. Many more specialized agencies, such as the National Bureau of Standards, also came into being.

These agencies had one thing in common: their role was primarily to serve, not to regulate. Most did research, gathered statistics, dispensed federal lands, or passed out benefits. Not until the Interstate Commerce Commission (ICC) was created in 1887 did the federal government begin to regulate the economy (other than by managing the currency) in any large way. Even the ICC had, at first, relatively few powers.

There were several reasons why federal officials primarily performed a service role. The values that had shaped the Constitution were still strong: these included a belief in limited government, the importance of states' rights, and the fear of concentrated discretionary power. The proper role of government in the economy was to promote, not to regulate; and

a commitment to **laissez-faire**—a freely competitive economy—was strongly held. But just as important, the Constitution said nothing about giving any regulatory powers to bureaucrats. It gave to *Congress* the power to regulate commerce among the states. Now, obviously Congress could not make the necessary day-to-day decisions to regulate, for example, the rates that interstate railroads charged to farmers and other shippers. Some agency or commission composed of appointed officials and experts would have to be created to do that. For a long time, however, the prevailing interpretation of the Constitution was that no such agency could exercise such regulatory powers unless Congress first set down clear standards that would govern the agency's decisions. As late as 1935 the Supreme Court held that a regulatory agency could not make rules on its own; it could only apply the standards enacted by Congress.[5] The Court's view was that the legislature may not delegate its powers to the president or to an administrative agency.[6]

These restrictions on what administrators could do were set aside in wartime. During World War I, for example, President Woodrow Wilson was authorized by Congress to fix prices, operate the railroads, manage the communications system, and even control the distribution of food.[7] This kind of extraordinary grant of power usually ended with the war.

Some changes in the bureaucracy did not end with the war. During the Civil War, World War I, World War II, the Korean War, and the war in Vietnam, the number of civilian (as well as military) employees of the government rose sharply. These increases were not simply in the number of civilians needed to help serve the war effort; many of the additional people were hired by agencies, such as the Treasury Department, not obviously connected with the war. Furthermore, the number of federal officials did not return to prewar levels after each war. Though there was some reduction, each war left the number of federal employees larger than before.[8]

It is not hard to understand how this happens. During wartime almost every government agency argues that its activities have *some* relation to the war effort, and few legislators want to be caught voting against something that may help that effort. Hence in 1944 the Reindeer Service in Alaska, an agency of the Interior Department, asked for more employees because reindeer are "a valued asset in military planning."

A Change in Role

Today's bureaucracy is largely a product of two events: the Depression of the 1930s (and the concomitant New Deal program of President Roosevelt) and World War II. Though many agencies have been added since then, the basic features of the bureaucracy were set mainly as a result of changes in public attitudes and in constitutional interpretation that occurred during these periods. The government was now expected to play an active role in dealing with economic and social problems. In the late 1930s, the Supreme Court reversed its earlier decisions (see Chapter 14) on the question of delegating legislative powers to administrative agencies and upheld laws by which Congress merely instructs agencies to make decisions that serve "the public interest" in some area.[9] As a result it was possible for President Nixon to set up in 1971 a system of price and wage controls based on a statute that simply authorized the president "to issue such orders and regulations as he may deem appropriate to stabilize prices, rents,

wages, and salaries."[10] The Cost of Living Council and other agencies that Nixon established to carry out this order were run by appointed officials who had the legal authority to make sweeping decisions based on general statutory language.

World War II was the first occasion during which the government made heavy use of federal income taxes—on individuals and corporations—to finance its activities. Between 1940 and 1945 total federal tax collections increased from about $5 billion to nearly $44 billion. The end of the war brought no substantial tax reduction: the country believed that a high level of military preparedness continued to be necessary and that various social programs begun before the war should enjoy the heavy funding made possible by wartime taxes. Tax receipts continued, by and large, to grow. Before 1913, when the Sixteenth Amendment to the Constitution was passed, the federal government could not collect income taxes at all (it financed itself largely from customs duties and excise taxes). From 1913 to 1940 income taxes were small (in 1940 the average American paid only $7 in federal incomes taxes). World War II created the first great financial boom for the government, permitting the sustained expansion of a wide variety of programs and thus entrenching a large number of administrators in Washington.[11]

The Federal Bureaucracy Today

No president wants to admit that he has increased the size of the bureaucracy. He can avoid saying this by pointing out that the number of civilians working for the federal government has not increased significantly in recent years and is about the same today (3.2 million persons) as it was in 1970, and less than it was during World War II.[12] This explanation is true but misleading, for it neglects the large and growing number of people who work *indirectly* for Washington as employees of private firms and state or local agencies that are largely, if not entirely, supported by federal funds. No one knows for certain, but there may be as many as four persons earning their living indirectly from the federal government for every one earning it directly. While federal employment has remained quite stable, employment among federal contractors and consultants and in state and local governments has mushroomed.

The power of the federal bureaucracy cannot be measured by the number of employees, however. A bureaucracy of 5 million persons would have little power if each employee did nothing but type letters or file documents, whereas a bureaucracy of only one hundred persons would have awesome power if each member were able to make arbitrary life-and-death decisions affecting the rest of us. The power of the bureaucracy depends on the extent to which appointed officials have **discretionary authority**—that is, the ability to choose courses of action and to make policies that are not spelled out in advance by laws. In Figure 13.1 we see how the volume of regulations issued and the amount of money spent have risen much faster than the number of federal employees who write the regulations and spend the money.

By this test the power of the federal bureaucracy has grown enormously. Congress has delegated substantial authority to administrative agencies in three areas: (1) paying subsidies to particular groups and organizations in society (farmers, veterans, scientists, schools, universities, hospitals); (2) transferring money from the federal government to state and local governments (the grant-in-aid programs described in Chapter 3); and (3) devising and enforcing regulations for various sectors of society and the economy. Some of these administrative functions, such as grants-in-aid to states, are closely monitored by Congress; others, such as the regulatory programs, usually operate with a greater degree of independence. These delegations of power, especially in the areas of paying subsidies and regulating the economy, did not become commonplace until the 1930s, and then only after the Supreme Court decided that such delegations were constitutional. Today, by contrast, appointed officials can decide, within rather broad limits, who shall own a television station, what safety features automobiles shall have, what kinds of scientific research shall be specially encouraged, what drugs shall appear on the market, which dissident groups shall be investigated, what fumes an industrial smokestack may emit, which corporate mergers shall be allowed, what use shall be made of national forests, and what price crop and dairy farmers shall receive for their products.

If appointed officials have this kind of power, then how they use it is of paramount importance in understanding modern government. There are,

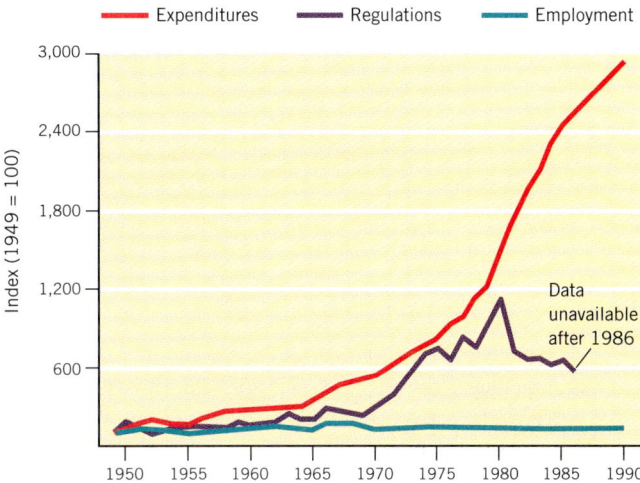

FIGURE 13.1 Federal Government Growth: Money, Rules, and People

— Expenditures — Regulations — Employment

Data unavailable after 1986

SOURCES: Hugh Heclo, "Issue Networks and the Executive Establishment," in *The New American Political System*, ed. Anthony King (Washington, D.C.: American Enterprise Institute, 1978), 90. Copyright © 1978 by the American Enterprise Institute. Reprinted by permission. Updated with the *Federal Register* and *Statistical Abstract of the United States*.

broadly, four factors that may explain the behavior of these officials:

1. The manner in which they are recruited and rewarded

2. Their personal attributes, such as their socioeconomic backgrounds and their political attitudes

3. The nature of their jobs

4. The constraints that outside forces—political superiors, legislators, interest groups, journalists—impose on their agencies

Recruitment and Retention

The federal civil service system was designed to recruit qualified people on the basis of merit, not political patronage, and to retain and promote employees on the basis of performance, not political favoritism. Many appointed federal officials belong to the **competitive service**. This means that they are appointed only after they have passed a written examination administered by the Office of Personnel

Management (OPM) or met certain selection criteria (such as training, educational attainments, or prior experience) devised by the hiring agency and approved by OPM. Where competition for a job exists and candidates can be ranked by their scores or records, the agency must usually appoint one of the three top-ranking candidates.

In recent years the competitive service system has become ever more decentralized, and increasing numbers of federal workers have been recruited in nontraditional ways. Today only about 56 percent of all appointed federal government workers are part of the competitive service, a dramatic decline from the peak of 86.4 percent in 1960. Federal intelligence agencies, the Federal Aviation Administration, the Postal Service, and others have obtained congressional approval to develop agency-specific recruitment policies and procedures. In fiscal year 1994, for example, the federal government hired 37,898 full-time career employees: 36 percent through the excepted service ("excepted" from special qualifying exams and not strictly governed by OPM personnel selection rules), 17 percent through OPM examinations, 12 percent through agency-specific examinations or other agency-based selection processes, 13 percent through special hiring authority, and 27 percent through other routes. There are now nearly forty different ways to hire a temporary employee. Students with excellent undergraduate records may be hired without any examination whatsoever.

Thus it is wrong to suppose that a standardized, centralized system governs the federal service. As one recent study concluded, today much of the "real responsibility for recruiting, testing, and hiring has shifted to the agencies from OPM and its central system."[13]

Moreover, the kinds of workers being recruited into the federal civil service have changed. For example, blue-collar employment fell from 26 percent of the federal work force in 1973 to 16 percent in 1993. Meanwhile, the federal government's white-collar work force has become more diverse occupationally. Between 1960 and 1980 the number of engineers on the federal payroll increased by 50 percent, and the number of computer specialists rose by 600 percent. As one writer on civil service reform noted, the "need to recruit and retain physicists, biologists, oceanographers, nurses, statisticians, botanists, and epidemiologists, as well as large numbers

Federal employees aren't just paper shufflers; many, such as this biologist, perform skilled professional tasks.

of engineers, lawyers, and accountants, now preoccupies federal personnel managers."[14]

It is clear that the federal government's recruitment and retention practices have been changing. But the OPM has not kept careful records on the issue since the late 1980s, and no one has yet made a detailed study of how the more decentralized hiring system is functioning.

Some excepted employees—probably no more than 3 percent—are appointed on grounds other than or in addition to merit, narrowly defined. These legal exceptions exist to permit the president and his staff to select, for policy-making and politically sensitive posts, people who are in agreement with their policy views. These appointees are generally of three kinds:

1. Presidential appointments authorized by statute (cabinet and subcabinet officers, judges, U.S. marshals and U.S. attorneys, ambassadors, and members of various boards and commissions).

2. "Schedule C" jobs, which are described as having a "confidential or policy-determining character"

below the level of cabinet or subcabinet posts (including executive assistants, special aides, and confidential secretaries).

3. Noncareer executive assignments (NEA jobs) given to high-ranking members of the regular competitive civil service, or to persons brought into the civil service at these high levels, who are deeply involved in the advocacy of presidential programs or who participate in policy-making.

These three groups of excepted appointments constitute the patronage available to a president and his administration. In the nineteenth century practically every job was a patronage job. For example, when Grover Cleveland, a Democrat, became president in 1885, he replaced some forty thousand Republican postal employees with Democrats. In 1883, with the passage of the Pendleton Act, there began a slow but steady transfer of federal jobs from the patronage to the merit system. It may seem strange that a political party in power should be willing to relinquish its patronage in favor of a merit-based appointment system. Two factors made it easier for the Republicans in 1883 to pass the Pendleton Act: (1) public outrage over the abuses of the spoils system, highlighted by the assassination of President James Garfield by a man always described in the history books as a "disappointed office seeker" (*lunatic* would be a more accurate term); and (2) the fear that if the Democrats came to power on a wave of antispoils sentiment, existing Republican officeholders would be fired. (The Democrats won anyway.)

The merit system spread to encompass most of the federal bureaucracy, generally with presidential support. Though presidents may have liked in theory the idea of hiring and firing subordinates at will, most felt that the demands for patronage were impossible either to satisfy or to ignore. Furthermore, by increasing the coverage of the merit system a president could "blanket in" patronage appointees already holding office, thus making it difficult or impossible for the next administration to fire them.

The Buddy System The actual recruitment of civil servants, especially in middle- and upper-level jobs, is somewhat more complicated, and slightly more political, than the laws and rules might suggest. Though many people enter the federal bureaucracy

A Day in the Life of a Bureaucrat

Here is how the Commissioner of the Social Security Administration (SSA), a high-level bureaucrat, spent a typical day:

5:45 A.M.	Arise.
6:50 A.M.	Leave for the office.
7:30 A.M.	Read newspapers.
8:00 A.M.	Meeting with deputy commissioner.
8:30 A.M.	Brief cabinet secretary on Social Security data.*
9:45 A.M.	Decide how to respond to press criticisms.
10:05 A.M.	Leave for meeting in another building.
11:30 A.M.	Meet with top staff.
1:00 P.M.	Meet with bureau chiefs on half a dozen issues.
2:45 P.M.	Meet with a deputy to discuss next year's budget.
3:30 P.M.	Meet with business executive about use of computers in SSA.
4:30 P.M.	Meet with deputy in charge of Medicare to discuss plan for national health insurance.
5:10 P.M.	Catch up on phone calls; meet with committee concerned with drug abuse.
6:10 P.M.	Leave for home. Get out of attending a dinner meeting in Washington.

As is obvious, high-level bureaucrats spend most of their time discussing things in meetings. It is in such meetings that government policy is made.

---

* SSA was a part of the Department of Health and Human Services, but no longer is.

SOURCE: Adapted from "A Day in the Life of a Government Executive," in *Inside the System*, 4th ed., ed. Charles Peters and Nicholas Leamann (New York: Holt, Rinehart and Winston, 1979), 205–213.

by learning of a job, filling out an application, perhaps taking a test, and being hired, many also enter on a "name-request" basis. A **name-request job** is one that is filled by a person whom an agency has already identified. In this respect the federal government is not so different from private business. A person learns of a job from somebody who already has one, or the head of a bureau decides in advance whom he or she wishes to hire. The agency must still send a form describing the job to the OPM, but

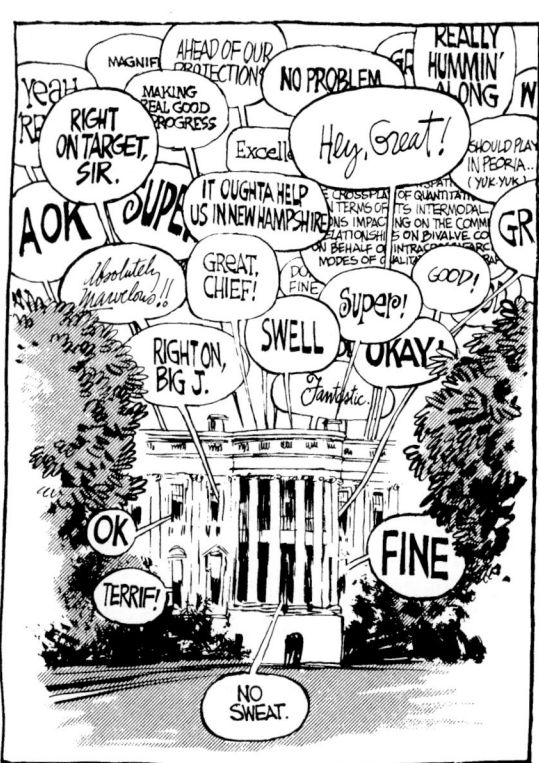

One barrier to improving presidential control of the federal bureaucracy is that even the White House has become a large bureaucracy.

it also names the person whom the agency wants to appoint. Sometimes the job is even described in such a way that the person named is the only one who can qualify for it. Occasionally this tailor-made, name-request job is offered to a person at the insistence of a member of Congress who wants a political supporter taken care of; more often it is made available because the bureaucracy itself knows whom it wishes to hire and wants to circumvent an elaborate search. This is the "buddy system."

The buddy system does not necessarily produce poor employees. Indeed, it is frequently a way of hiring people known to the agency as being capable of handling the position. It also opens up the possibility of hiring people whose policy views are congenial to those already in office. Such networking is based on shared policy views, not (as once was the case) on narrow partisan affiliations. For example, bureaucrats in consumer-protection agencies, recruit new staff from private groups with an interest in consumer protection, such as the various organi-

zations associated with Ralph Nader, or from academics who have a proconsumer inclination.

There has always been an informal "old boys' network" among those who move in and out of high-level government posts; with the increasing appointment of women to these jobs, there has begun to emerge an old girls' network as well.[15] In a later section we will consider whether, or in what ways, these recruitment patterns make a difference.

Firing a Bureaucrat   The great majority of bureaucrats who are part of the civil service and who do not hold presidential appointments have jobs that are, for all practical purposes, beyond reach. An executive must go through elaborate steps to fire, demote, or suspend a civil servant. Realistically this means that no one is fired or demoted unless his or her superior is prepared to invest a great deal of time and effort in the attempt. In 1987 about 2,600 employees who had completed their probationary period were fired for misconduct or poor performance. That is about one-tenth of 1 percent of all federal employees. It is hard to believe that a large private company would fire only one-tenth of 1 percent of its workers in a given year. It's also impossible to believe that, as is often the case in Washington, it would take a year to fire anyone. To cope with this problem, federal executives have devised a number of stratagems for bypassing or forcing out civil servants with whom they cannot work—denying them promotions, transferring them to undesirable locations, or assigning them to meaningless work.

With the passage of the Civil Service Reform Act of 1978, Congress recognized that many high-level positions in the civil service have important policymaking responsibilities and that the president and his cabinet officers ought to have more flexibility in recruiting, assigning, and paying such people. Accordingly, the act created the Senior Executive Service (SES), about eight thousand top federal managers who can (in theory) be hired, fired, and transferred more easily than ordinary civil servants. Moreover, the act stipulated that members of the SES would be eligible for substantial cash bonuses if they performed their duties well. (To protect the rights of SES members, anyone who is removed from the SES is guaranteed a job elsewhere in the government.)

Things did not work out quite as the sponsors of the SES had hoped. Though most eligible civil servants joined it, there was only a modest increase in the proportion of higher-ranking positions in agencies that were filled by transfer from another agency; the cash bonuses did not prove to be an important incentive (perhaps because the base salaries of top bureaucrats did not keep up with inflation); and hardly any member of the SES was actually fired. Two years after the SES was created, less than one-half of 1 percent of its members had received an unsatisfactory rating, and none had been fired. Nor does the SES give the president a large opportunity to make political appointments: only 10 percent of the SES can be selected from outside the existing civil service. And no SES member can be transferred involuntarily.

The Agency's Point of View   When one realizes that most agencies are staffed by people who were recruited by those agencies, sometimes on a name-

Firing a Bureaucrat

*T*o fire or demote a member of the competitive civil service, these procedures must be followed:

1. The employee must be given written notice at least thirty days in advance that he or she is to be fired or demoted for incompetence or misconduct.

2. The written notice must contain a statement of reasons, including specific examples of unacceptable performance.

3. The employee has the right to an attorney and to reply, orally or in writing, to the charges.

4. The employee has the right to appeal any adverse action to the Merit Systems Protection Board (MSPB), a three-person, bipartisan body appointed by the president with the consent of the Senate.

5. The MSPB must grant the employee a hearing, at which the employee has the right to have an attorney present.

6. The employee has the right to appeal the MSPB decision to the United States Court of Appeals, which can hold new hear-

request basis, and who are virtually immune from dismissal, it becomes clear that the recruitment and retention policies of the civil service work to ensure that most bureaucrats will have an "agency" point of view. Even with the encouragement for transfers created by the SES, very few persons appointed to the top three civil-service grades in a given agency come from other agencies.[16]

The Senior Executive Service may in time change this pattern, but for now most government agencies are dominated by people who have not served in any other agency and who have been in government service most of their lives. This fact has some advantages: it means that most bureaucrats are expert in the procedures and policies of their agencies and that there will be a substantial degree of continuity in agency behavior no matter which political party happens to be in power.

But the agency point of view has its costs as well. A political executive entering an agency with responsibility for shaping its direction will discover that he or she must carefully win the support of career subordinates. A subordinate has an infinite capacity for discreet sabotage and can make life miserable for a political superior by delaying action, withholding information, following the rule book with literal exactness, or making an "end run" around a superior to mobilize members of Congress who are sympathetic to the bureaucrat's point of view. For instance, when one political executive wanted to downgrade a bureau in his department, he found, naturally, that the bureau chief was opposed. The bureau chief spoke to some friendly lobbyists and a key member of Congress. When the political executive asked the congressman whether he had any problem with the contemplated reorganization, the congressman replied, "No, you have the problem, because if you touch that bureau, I'll cut your job out of the budget."[17]

Personal Attributes

A second factor that might shape the way bureaucrats use their power is their personal attributes. These include their social class, education, and personal political beliefs. The federal civil service as a whole looks very much like a cross section of American society in the education, sex, race, and social origins of its members (see Figure 13.2). But as with many other employers, blacks, other minorities, and women are most likely to be heavily represented in the lowest grade levels and tend to be underrepresented at the executive level (see Table 13.1). At the higher-ranking levels, where the most power is found—say, in the supergrade ranks of GS-16 through GS-18—the typical civil servant is a middle-aged white male with a college degree whose father was somewhat more advantaged than the average

FIGURE 13.2   Characteristics of Federal Civilian Employees, 1960 and 1994

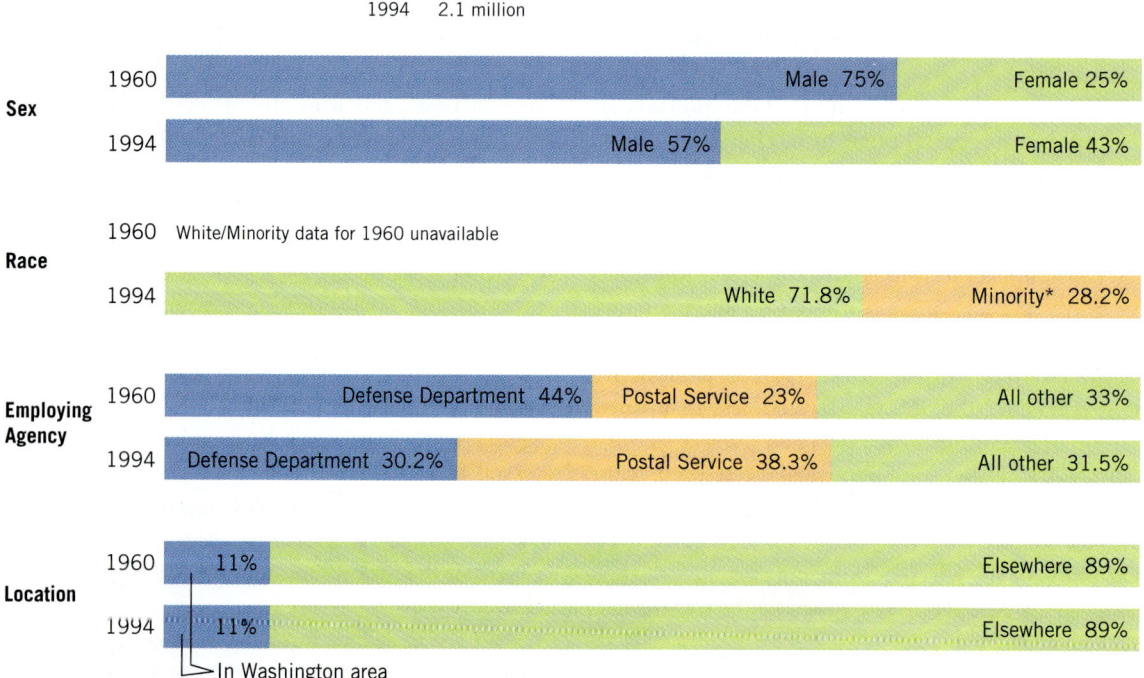

Total number of employees   1960   2.2 million
1994   2.1 million

Sex
1960   Male 75%   Female 25%
1994   Male 57%   Female 43%

Race
1960   White/Minority data for 1960 unavailable
1994   White 71.8%   Minority* 28.2%

Employing Agency
1960   Defense Department 44%   Postal Service 23%   All other 33%
1994   Defense Department 30.2%   Postal Service 38.3%   All other 31.5%

Location
1960   11%   Elsewhere 89%
1994   11%   Elsewhere 89%
In Washington area

*Blacks, Native Americans, Hispanics, Asians, and Pacific Islanders

SOURCES: *Statistical Abstract of the United States, 1961,* 392–394; *Statistical Abstract of the United States, 1992,* 330–331.

TABLE 13.1 Percentage of Female, Black, and Total Minority Employment in the Federal Bureaucracy, by Rank, 1989–1990

Grade	Female (1989)	Black (1990)	All Minorities (1990)[a]
Lowest	74.8% (GS 1-6)	28.5% (GS 1-4)	42.1% (GS 1-4)
Moderate Low	53.5 (GS 7-10)	22.7 (GS 5-8)	33.3 (GS 5-8)
Moderate	32.9 (GS 11-12)	11.6 (GS 9-12)	21.3 (GS 9-12)
Moderate High	17.0 (GS 13-15)	6.4 (GS 13-15)	12.7 (GS 13-15)
Highest	9.1 (GS 16-18)	5.0 (Executive)	7.9 (Executive)
Totals	(NA)	16.6	27.3

[a] "All minorities" includes blacks, Hispanics, American Indians, Alaska natives, Asians, and Pacific Islanders.

SOURCE: *Statistical Abstract of the United States, 1992,* 330, 333.

citizen. In the great majority of cases this individual is in fact very different from the typical American in both background and personal beliefs.

Because the higher civil service is unrepresentative of the average American, some critics speculate that people holding these top jobs think and act in ways very different from most Americans. Depending on their politics, these critics have concluded that the bureaucracy is either more conservative or more liberal than the country it helps govern. Some critics believe that the upper-middle-class bureaucrats defend their class privileges.[18] Other critics, such as former President Nixon, have argued that since many members of the higher civil service were appointed by Democratic presidents and trained by liberal faculty members in prestigious universities, the civil service favors liberal or leftist causes.[19]

A survey of the attitudes of some two hundred top-level, nonpolitical federal bureaucrats suggests that they are, in fact, somewhat more liberal than the average American voter but considerably less liberal than key members of the media (see Chapter 10). As we can see in Table 13.2 (see page 422), about 56 percent of those interviewed in 1982 described themselves as liberal and said that they had voted for the Democratic candidate for president in 1968, 1972, 1976, and 1980. By contrast, a much smaller proportion of average voters think of themselves as liberals, and most voted for the Republican presidential candidate in 1968, 1972, and 1980. But on most specific policy questions, bureaucrats do not have extreme positions. For example, they don't

think that the government should take over the big corporations, they support some amount of business deregulation, and a majority (by a slim margin) don't think that the goal of U.S. foreign policy has been to protect business.[20]

We can also see, however, that the kind of agency for which a bureaucrat works makes a difference. Those employed in "activist" agencies, such as the Federal Trade Commission, Environmental Protection Agency, and Food and Drug Administration, have much more liberal views than those who work for the more "traditional" agencies, such as the departments of Agriculture, Commerce, and the Treasury.

This association between attitudes and kind of agency has been confirmed by other studies. Even when the bureaucrats come from roughly the same social backgrounds, their policy views seem to reflect the type of government work that they do. For example, people holding foreign service jobs in the State Department tended to be more liberal than those coming from similar family backgrounds and performing similar tasks (such as working on foreign affairs) in the Defense Department.[21] It is not clear whether these differences in attitudes were produced by the jobs that they held or whether certain jobs attract people with certain beliefs. Probably both forces were at work.

Whatever the mechanism involved, there seems little doubt that different agencies display different political ideologies. A study done in 1976 revealed that Democrats and people with liberal views tended

TABLE 13.2   Political Attitudes of High-Level Federal Bureaucrats

Attitude	*Percentage Agreeing*		
	All Bureaucrats	"Traditional" Agencies	"Activist" Agencies
I am a liberal.	56%	48%	63%
I voted for:			
Humphrey (1968)	72	67	76
McGovern (1972)	57	47	65
Carter (1976)	71	65	76
Carter (1980)	45	34	55
Less regulation of business is good for the U.S.	61	66	57
U.S. military should be the strongest in the world, regardless of cost.	25	31	19
Women should get preference in hiring.	34	28	40
Blacks should get preference in hiring.	44	35	53
Homosexuality is wrong.	47	54	40
Nuclear plants are safe.	52	58	46

SOURCE: Stanley Rothman and S. Robert Lichter, "How Liberal Are Bureaucrats?" Reprinted with permission from *Regulation* (November–December 1983). Copyright© 1983 by American Enterprise Institute.

to be overrepresented in social service agencies, whereas Republicans and people with conservative views tend to be overrepresented in defense agencies.[22]

Do Bureaucrats Sabotage Their Political Bosses?

Because it is so hard to fire career bureaucrats, it is often said that these people will sabotage any actions by their political superiors with which they disagree. And since civil servants tend to have liberal views, it has been conservative presidents and cabinet secretaries who have usually expressed this worry.

There is no doubt that some bureaucrats will drag their heels if they don't like their bosses, and a few will block actions they oppose. However, most bureaucrats try to carry out the policies of their superiors even when they personally disagree with them. When David Stockman was director of the Office of Management and Budget (OMB), he set out to make sharp cuts in government spending programs in accordance with the wishes of his boss, President Reagan. He later published a book complaining about all the people in the White House

and Congress who worked against him.[23] But nowhere in the book is there any major criticism of the civil servants at OMB. It appears that whatever these people thought about Stockman and Reagan, they loyally tried to carry out the Stockman policies.

Bureaucrats tend to be loyal to political superiors who deal with them cooperatively and constructively. An agency head who tries to ignore or discredit them can be in for a tough time, however. The powers of obstruction available to aggrieved bureaucrats are formidable. Such people can leak embarrassing stories to Congress or to the media, help interest groups mobilize against the agency head, and discover a thousand procedural reasons why a new course of action won't work.

The exercise of some of those bureaucratic powers is protected by the Whistle Blower Protection Act. Passed in 1989, the law creates an Office of Special Counsel charged with investigating complaints from bureaucrats that they were punished after reporting to Congress about waste, fraud, or abuse in their agencies.

It may seem odd that bureaucrats, who have great job security, would not always act in accordance with their personal beliefs instead of in accordance with the wishes of their bosses. Bureaucratic sabotage, in this view, ought to be very common. But bureaucratic cooperation with superiors is not odd, once you take into account the nature of a bureaucrat's job.

If you are a voter at the polls, your beliefs will clearly affect how you vote (see Chapter 5). But if you are the second baseman for the Boston Red Sox, your political beliefs, social background, and education will have nothing to do with how you field ground balls. Sociologists like to call the different things that people do in their lives "roles" and to distinguish between roles that are loosely structured (such as the role of voter) and those that are highly structured (such as that of second baseman). Personal attitudes greatly affect loosely structured roles and only slightly affect highly structured ones. Applied to the federal bureaucracy, this suggests that civil servants performing tasks that are routinized (such as filling out forms), tasks that are closely defined by laws and rules (such as issuing welfare checks), or tasks that are closely monitored by others (supervisors, special interest groups, the media) will probably perform them in ways that can only partially be explained, if at all, by their personal attitudes. Civil servants performing complex, loosely defined tasks that are not closely monitored may carry out their work in ways powerfully influenced by their attitudes.

Among the loosely defined tasks are those performed by professionals, and so the values of these people may influence how they behave. An increasing number of lawyers, economists, engineers, and physicians are hired to work in federal agencies. These men and women have received extensive training that produces not only a set of skills but also a set of attitudes as to what is important and valuable. For example, the Federal Trade Commission (FTC), charged with preventing unfair methods of competition among businesses, employs two kinds of professionals—lawyers, organized into a Bureau of Competition, and economists, organized into a Bureau of Economics. Lawyers are trained to draw up briefs and argue cases in court and are taught the legal standards by which they will know whether they have a chance of winning a case or not. Economists are trained to analyze how a competitive economy works and what costs consumers must bear if the goods and services are produced by a mo-

TRIVIA

Famous Bureaucrats

The federal government has employed as bureaucrats people who were later to become famous in other careers.

Clara Barton, founder of the American Red Cross	*Clerk in the U.S. Patent Office, 1854–1861*
Alexander Graham Bell, inventor of the telephone	*Special agent of the U.S. Census Bureau, 1890*
Nathaniel Hawthorne, author	*Weigher in the Boston Custom House, 1839–1841, and surveyor of the Port of Salem, Massachusetts, 1845–1849*
Washington Irving, author	*U.S. foreign service*
Abraham Lincoln, president	*Postmaster of New Salem, Illinois, 1833–1836*
Knute Rockne, football coach	*Clerk in Chicago Post Office, 1907–1910*
James Thurber, humorist	*Code clerk in State Department*
James Whistler, painter	*Draftsman, U.S. Coast Survey, 1854–1855*
Walt Whitman, poet	*Clerk, U.S. Department of the Interior, 1865*

Clara Barton

Nathaniel Hawthorne

How to Get Rid of a Career Civil Servant Without Going Through the System

The frontal assault   Tell him that he is no longer wanted and that if he quits, he will get a nice letter of recommendation and a farewell luncheon. If he won't quit but later wants to leave for a better job, he will get a nasty letter of recommendation.

The transfer technique   Find out where in the country the civil servant does *not* want to live, and threaten to transfer her there. Send Bostonians to Texas and Texans to Maine.

The special-assignment technique   Useful for a family person who does not like to travel. Tell him that to keep his job he must inspect all the agency's offices in cities with a population under twenty thousand and stay in bad motels. Even if he doesn't quit, at least you will have him out of the office.

The layering technique   Put loyal subordinates in charge of disloyal ones, or put the objectionable civil servant into an out-of-the-way post where you can ignore her.

SOURCE: Adapted from the "Federal Political Personnel Manual," printed in "Presidential Campaign Activities of 1972," Hearings before the Select Committee on Presidential Campaign Activities, Ninety-third Congress, 2d Session, vol. 19 (1974). This manual was produced by members of the Nixon administration, but in some version its principles have been applied by all administrations.

nopoly (one firm controlling the market) or an oligopoly (a small number of firms dominating the market).

Because of their training and attitudes, lawyers in the FTC prefer to bring cases against a business firm that has done something clearly illegal, such as attending secret meetings with competitors to rig the prices that will be charged to a purchaser. These cases appeal to lawyers because there is usually a victim (the purchaser or a rival company) who complains to the government, the illegal behavior can be proved in a court of law, and the case can be completed rather quickly.

Economists, on the other hand, are trained to measure the value of a case not by how quickly it can be proved in court but by whether the illegal practice imposes large or small costs on the consumer. FTC economists often dislike the cases that appeal to lawyers. The economists feel that the amount of money that such cases save the consumer is often small and that the cases are a distraction from the major issues—such as whether IBM unfairly dominates the computer business or whether General Motors is too large to be efficient. Lawyers, in turn, are leery of big cases, because the facts are hard to prove and they may take forever to decide (one blockbuster case can drag through the courts for ten years). In many federal agencies divergent professional values such as these help explain how power is used.

Culture and Careers

Unlike the lawyers and economists working in the FTC, the government bureaucrats in a typical agency don't have a lot of freedom to choose a course of action. Their jobs are spelled out not only by the laws, rules, and routines of their agency but also by the informal understandings among fellow employees as to how they are supposed to act. These understandings are the *culture* of the agency.[24]

If you belong to the air force you can do a lot of things, but only one thing really counts: flying airplanes, especially advanced jet fighters and bombers. The culture of the air force is a pilots' culture. If you belong to the navy you have more choices: fly jet aircraft or operate nuclear submarines. Both jobs provide status and a chance for promotion to the highest ranks. By contrast, sailing minesweepers or transport ships (or worse, having a desk job and not sailing anything at all) is not a very rewarding job. The culture of the CIA emphasizes working overseas as a clandestine agent; staying in Washington as a report writer is not as good for your career. The culture of the State Department rewards skill in political negotiations; being an expert on international economics or embassy security is much less rewarding.

You can usually tell what kind of culture an agency has by asking an employee, "If you want to get ahead here, what sort of jobs should you take?" The jobs that are career enhancing are part of the culture; the jobs that are "not career enhancing" ("NCE" in bureaucratic lingo) are not part of it.

Being part of a strong culture is good—up to a point. It motivates employees to work hard in order to win the respect of their coworkers as well as the approval of their bosses. But a strong culture also makes it hard to change an agency. FBI agents for many years resisted getting involved in civil rights or organized crime cases, and diplomats in the State Department didn't pay much attention to embassy security. These important jobs were not a career-enhancing part of the culture.

Constraints

The biggest difference between a government agency and a private organization is the vastly greater number of constraints on the agency. Unlike a business firm, the typical government bureau cannot hire, fire, build, or sell without going through procedures set down in laws. How much money it pays its members is determined by statute, not by the market. Not only the goals of an agency but often its exact procedures are spelled out by Congress.

At one time the Soil Conservation Service was required by law to employ at least 14,177 full-time workers. The State Department is forbidden by law from opening a diplomatic post in Antigua or Barbuda but forbidden from closing a post anywhere else. The Agency for International Development (which administers our foreign-aid program) has been given by Congress thirty-three objectives and seventy-five priorities and must send to Congress 288 reports each year. When it buys military supplies, the Defense Department must give a "fair proportion" of its contracts to small businesses,

---

Learning Bureaucratese

A few simple rules, if remembered, will enable you to speak and write in the style of a government official.

- **Use nouns as if they were verbs.** Don't say, "We must set priorities"; say instead, "We must prioritize."

- **Use adjectives as if they were verbs.** Don't say, "We put the report in final form"; say instead, "We finalized the report."

- **Use several words where one word would do.** Don't say, "now"; say instead, "at this point in time."

- **Never use ordinary words where unusual ones can be found.** Don't say that you "made a choice"; say that you "selected an option."

- **No matter what subject you are discussing, employ the language of sports and war.** Never say, "progress"; say, "breakthrough." Never speak of a "compromise"; instead consider "adopting a fallback position."

- **Avoid active verbs.** Never say, "Study the problem"; say instead, "It is felt that the problem should be subjected to further study."

So You Want a Big Job in Washington . . . *

*T*he White House or a cabinet secretary has just called to ask you to become an assistant secretary of defense.

Wow! you say. A title, power, status, and a chance to do good! Before you call your mother to let her know how important you have become, think about what accepting that job involves.

Say you are an engineer working for a middle-sized company that does business with the Pentagon. This means that you know what needs to be done in Washington. You want to do a good job. You are honest and hard-working. Now here's what happens:

1. You will take a big pay cut.

2. Conflict-of-interest laws will require you to sell your stock in your present company and drop out of its pension plan. This will cost you a bundle.

3. You will have to pay your own moving expenses to Washington—the government won't pay, and it is against the law for your company to pay.

4. Since you will have to be confirmed by the Senate, your life will be put under a microscope. Every detail of your personal and professional affairs will become fair game for congressional

staffers and newspaper reporters. If anybody has anything against you, the hearings could drag on for weeks.

5. Once in office you will discover that there are hundreds of rules telling you what you *can't* do and dozens of committees telling you what you *should* do.

6. Members of Congress will call asking favors, old friends will turn their backs on you for not doing them favors, the White House will demand party loyalty, and the press will leap on your every mistake—real or imagined.

7. When you get ready to leave government and go back to your company (assuming your old job is still open), you will by law be barred for life from lobbying the executive branch on matters in which you were personally and substantially involved while in office and barred for two years from lobbying the executive branch on matters that were under your official responsibility.

You won't be sure whether you will be allowed to have *any* conversations with people in government for at least two years. Under these circumstances your old company may not want you back. Now what do you do?

*With thanks to Dr. John S. Foster, Jr., who has gone through this.

---

especially those operated by "socially and economically disadvantaged individuals" and must buy from American firms even if, in some cases, buying abroad would be cheaper. Some of the more general constraints include the following:

- Administrative Procedure Act (1946). Before adopting a new rule or policy, an agency must give notice, solicit comments, and (often) hold hearings.
- Freedom of Information Act (1966). Citizens have the right to inspect all government records except those containing military, intelligence, or trade secrets or revealing private personnel actions.
- National Environmental Policy Act (1969). Before undertaking any major action affecting the envi-

ronment, an agency must issue an environmental impact statement.
- Privacy Act (1974). Government files about individuals, such as Social Security and tax records, must be kept confidential.
- Open Meeting Law (1976). Every part of every agency meeting must be open to the public unless certain matters (for example, military or trade secrets) are being discussed.

One of the biggest constraints on bureaucratic action is that Congress rarely gives any job to a single agency. Stopping drug trafficking is the task of the Customs Services, the FBI, the Drug Enforcement Administration, the Border Patrol, and the Defense Department (among others). Disposing of the assets of failed savings-and-loan associations is the job of the Resolution Funding Corporation, Resolution Trust Corporation, Federal Housing Finance Board, Office of Thrift Supervision in the Treasury Department, Federal Deposit Insurance Corporation, Federal Reserve Board, and Justice Department (among others).

The effects of these constraints on agency behavior are not surprising.

- The government will often act slowly. (The more constraints that must be satisfied, the longer it will take to get anything done.)
- The government will sometimes act inconsistently. (What is done to meet one constraint—for example, freedom of information—may endanger another constraint—for example, privacy.)
- It will be easier to block action than to take action. (The constraints ensure that lots of voices will be heard; the more voices that are heard, the more they may cancel each other out.)
- Lower-ranking employees will be reluctant to make decisions on their own. (Having many constraints means having many ways to get into trouble; to avoid trouble, let your boss make the decision.)
- Citizens will complain of red tape. (The more constraints to serve, the more forms to fill out.)

These constraints do not mean that government bureaucracy is powerless, only that, however great its power, it tends to be clumsy. That clumsiness arises not from the fact that the people who work for agencies are dull or incompetent but from the complicated political environment in which that work must be done.

The moral of the story: The next time you get mad at a bureaucrat, ask yourself, Why would a rational, intelligent person behave that way? Chances are you will discover that there are good reasons for that action. You would probably behave the same way if you were working for the same organization.

Why So Many Constraints? Government agencies behave as they do in large part because of the many different goals they must pursue and the complex rules they must follow. Where does all this red tape come from?

From us. From us, the people.

"Laws" of Bureaucratic Procedure

Acheson's Rule   A memorandum is written not to inform the reader but to protect the writer.

Boren's Laws
When in doubt, mumble.
When in trouble, delegate.
When in charge, ponder.

Chapman's Rules of Committees
Never arrive on time, or you will be stamped a beginner.
Don't say anything until the meeting is half over; this stamps you as being wise.
Be as vague as possible; this prevents irritating others.
When in doubt, suggest that a subcommittee be appointed.

Meskimen's Law   There's never time to do it right but always time to do it over.

Murphy's Law   If anything can go wrong, it will.

O'Toole's Corollary to Murphy's Law   Murphy was an optimist.

Parkinson's First Law   Work expands to fill the time available for its completion.

Parkinson's Second Law   Expenditure rises to meet income.

Peter Principle   In every hierarchy, each employee tends to rise to his level of incompetence; thus, every post tends to be filled by an incompetent employee.

Robertson's Rule   The more directives you issue to solve a problem, the worse it gets.

Smith's Principle   Never do anything for the first time.

Every goal, every constraint, every bit of red tape, was put in place by Congress, the courts, the White House, or the agency itself responding to the demands of some influential faction. Civil rights groups want every agency to hire and buy from women and minorities. Environmental groups want every agency to file environmental impact statements. Industries being regulated want every new agency policy to be formulated only after a lengthy public hearing with lots of lawyers present. Labor unions also want those hearings so that they can argue against industry lawyers. Everybody who sells something to the government wants a "fair chance" to make the sale, and so everybody insists that government contracts be awarded only after complex procedures are followed. A lot of people don't trust the government, and so they insist that everything it does be done in the sunshine—no secrets, no closed meetings, no hidden files.

If we want agencies to pursue their main goal with more vigor and less encumbering red tape, we would have to ask Congress, the courts, or the White House to repeal some of these constraints. In other words, we would have to be willing to give up something we want in order to get something else we want even more But politics does not encourage people to make these trade-offs; instead it encourages us to expect to get everything—efficiency, fairness, help for minorities—all at once.

Agency Allies

Despite these constraints, government bureaucracies are not powerless. In fact, some of them actively seek certain constraints. They do so because it is a way of cementing a useful relationship with a congressional committee or an interest group.

At one time scholars described the relationship among an agency, a committee, and an interest group as an **iron triangle**. For example, the Department of Veterans Affairs, the House and Senate committees on veterans affairs, and veterans' organizations (such as the American Legion) would form a tight, mutually advantageous alliance. The department would do what the committees wanted and in return get political support and budget appropriations; the committee members would do what the veterans' groups wanted and in return get votes and campaign contributions. Iron triangles are examples of what are called *client politics.*

Many agencies still have important allies in Congress and the private sector, especially those bureaus that serve the needs of specific sectors of the economy or regions of the country. The Department of Agriculture works closely with farm organizations, the Department of the Interior with groups interested in obtaining low-cost irrigation or grazing rights, and the Department of Housing and Urban Development with mayors and real-estate developers.

Sometimes these allies are so strong that they can defeat a popular president. For years President Reagan tried to abolish the Small Business Administration (SBA), arguing that its program of loans to small firms was wasteful and ridden with favoritism. But Congress, reacting to pressures from small-business groups, rallied to the SBA's defense. As a result Reagan had to oversee an agency that he didn't want.

But iron triangles are much less common today than once was the case. Politics of late has become far more complicated. For one thing, the number and variety of interest groups has increased so much in recent years that there is scarcely any agency that is not subject to pressures from several competing interests instead of only from one powerful interest. For another, the growth of subcommittees in Congress has meant that most agencies are subject to control by many different legislative groups, often with very different concerns. Finally, the courts have made it much easier for all kinds of individuals and interests to intervene in agency affairs.

As a result, nowadays government agencies face a bewildering variety of competing groups and legislative subcommittees that constitute not a loyal group of allies but a fiercely contentious collection of critics. The Environmental Protection Agency is caught between the demands of environmentalists and of industry organizations, the Occupational Safety and Health Administration between the pressures of labor and of business, and the Federal Communications Commission between the desires of broadcasters and of cable television companies. Even the Department of Agriculture faces not a unified group of farmers but many different farmers split into rival groups, depending on the crops they raise, the regions in which they live, and the attitudes they have toward the relative merits of farm subsidies or free markets.

Political scientist Hugh Heclo has described the typical government agency today as being embedded not in an iron triangle but in an **issue network**.[25] These issue networks consist of people in Washington-based interest groups, on congressional staffs, in universities and think tanks, and in the mass media who regularly debate government policy on a certain subject—say, health care or auto safety. The networks are contentious, split along political, ideological, and economic lines. When a president takes office, he often recruits key agency officials from those members of the issue network who are most sympathetic to his views.

When Jimmy Carter, a Democrat, became president, he appointed to key posts in consumer agencies people who were from that part of the consumerist issue network associated with Ralph Nader. Ronald Reagan, a conservative Republican, filled these same jobs with people who were from that part of the issue network holding free market or antiregulation views. When George Bush, a more centrist Republican, took office, he filled these posts with more centrist members of the issue network. Bill Clinton brought back the consumer activists.

Congressional Oversight

The main reason why some interest groups are important to agencies is that they are important to Congress. Not every interest group in the country has substantial access to Congress, but those that do and that are taken seriously by the relevant committees or subcommittees must also be taken seriously by the agency. Furthermore, even apart from interest groups, members of Congress have constitutional powers over agencies and policy interests in how agencies function.

Congressional supervision of the bureaucracy takes several forms. First, no agency may exist (except for a few presidential offices and commissions) without congressional approval. Congress influences—and sometimes determines precisely—agency behavior by the statutes it enacts.

Second, no money may be spent unless it has first been authorized by Congress. **Authorization legislation** originates in a legislative committee (such as Agriculture, Education and Labor, or Public Works) and states the maximum amount of money that an agency may spend on a given program. This authorization may be permanent, it may be for a fixed number of years, or it may be annual (that is, it must be renewed each year or the program or agency goes out of business).

Third, even funds that have been authorized by Congress cannot be spent unless (in most cases) they are also appropriated. Appropriations are usually made annually, and they originate not with the legislative committees but with the House Appropriations Committee and its various (and influential) subcommittees. An **appropriation** (money formally set aside for a specific use) may be, and often is, for less than the amount authorized. The Appropriations Committee's action thus tends to have a budget-cutting effect. There are some funds that can be spent without an appropriation, but in virtually every part of the bureaucracy each agency is keenly sensitive to congressional concerns at the time that the annual appropriations process is going on.

The Appropriations Committee and Legislative Committees

The fact that an agency budget must be both authorized and appropriated means that each agency serves not one congressional master but several, and that these masters may be in conflict. The real power over an agency's budget is exercised by the Appropriations Committee; the legislative committees are especially important when a substantive law is first passed or an agency first created or when an agency is subject to annual authorization.

In the past the power of the Appropriations Committee was rarely challenged: from 1947 through 1962, fully 90 percent of the House Appropriations Committee's recommendations on expenditures were approved by the full House without change.[26] Furthermore, the Appropriations Committee tends to recommend less money than an agency requests (though some specially favored agencies, such as the FBI, the Soil Conservation Service, and the Forest Service, have tended to get almost everything that they have asked for). Finally, the process of "marking up" (revising, amending, and approving) an agency's budget request gives to the Appropriations Committee, or one of its subcommittees, substantial influence over the policies that the agency follows.

Of late the appropriations committees have lost some of their great power over government agencies. This has happened in three ways:

First, Congress has created trust funds to pay for the benefits many people receive. The Social

Security trust fund is the largest of these. In 1990 it took in about $260 billion in Social Security taxes and paid out about $220 billion in old-age benefits. There are several other trust funds as well. **Trust funds** operate outside the regular government budget, and the appropriations committees have no control over these expenditures. They are automatic.

Second, Congress has changed the authorization of many programs from permanent or multiyear to **annual authorizations.** This means that every year the legislative committees, as part of the reauthorization process, get to set limits on what these agencies can spend. This limits the ability of the appropriations committees to determine the spending limits. Before 1959 most authorizations were permanent or multiyear. Now a long list of agencies must be reauthorized every year—the State Department, NASA, military procurement programs of the Defense Department, the Justice Department, the Energy Department, and parts or all of many other agencies.

Third, the existence of huge budget deficits during the 1980s and early 1990s has meant that much of Congress's time has been taken up with trying (usually not very successfully) to keep spending down. As a result there has rarely been much time to discuss the merits of various programs or how much ought to be spent on them; instead attention has been focused on meeting a target spending limit. In 1981 the budget resolution passed by Congress mandated cuts in several programs before the appropriations committees had even completed their work.[27]

In addition to the power of the purse, there are informal ways by which Congress can control the bureaucracy. An individual member of Congress can call an agency head on behalf of a constituent. Most such calls merely seek information, but some result in, or attempt to second, special privileges for particular people. Congressional committees may also obtain the right to pass on certain agency decisions. This is called **committee clearance,** and though it is usually not legally binding on the agency, few agency heads will ignore the expressed wish of a committee chairman that he or she be consulted before certain actions (such as transferring funds) are taken.

The Legislative Veto

For many decades Congress made frequent use of the legislative veto to control bureaucratic or presidential actions. A **legislative veto** is a requirement that an executive decision must lie before Congress for a specified period (usually thirty or ninety days) before it takes effect. Congress could then veto the decision if a resolution of disapproval were passed by either house (a "one-house veto") or both houses (a "two-house veto"). Unlike laws, such resolutions were not signed by the president. Between 1932 and 1980 about two hundred laws were passed providing for a legislative veto, many of them involving presidential proposals to sell arms abroad.

But in June 1983 the Supreme Court declared the legislative veto to be unconstitutional. In the *Chadha* case the Court held that the Constitution clearly requires in Article I that "every order, resolution, or vote to which the concurrence of the Senate and House of Representatives may be necessary" (with certain minor exceptions) "shall be presented to the President of the United States," who must either approve it or return it with his veto attached. In short, Congress cannot take any action that has the force of law unless the president concurs in that action.[28] At a stroke of the pen parts of some two hundred laws suddenly became invalid.

At least that happened in theory. In fact, since the *Chadha* decision Congress has passed a number of laws that contain legislative vetoes, despite the Supreme Court's having ruled against them! (Someone will have to go to court to test the constitutionality of these new provisions.)

Opponents of the legislative veto hope that future Congresses will have to pass laws that state much more clearly than before what an agency may or may not do. But it is just as likely that Congress will continue to pass laws stated in general terms and require that agencies implementing those laws report their plans to Congress so that it will have a chance to enact and send to the president a regular bill disapproving the proposed action. Or Congress may rely on informal (but scarcely weak) means of persuasion, including threats to reduce the appropriations of an agency that does not abide by congressional preferences.

Abbreviations for Federal Government Agencies

ACDA	Arms Control and Disarmament Agency	INS	Immigration and Naturalization Service
BIA	Bureau of Indian Affairs	IRS	Internal Revenue Service
CEA	Council of Economic Advisers	NASA	National Aeronautics and Space Administration
CIA	Central Intelligence Agency	NHTSA	National Highway Traffic Safety Administration
DEA	Drug Enforcement Administration	NIH	National Institutes of Health
DOD	Department of Defense	NIJ	National Institute of Justice
DOJ	Department of Justice	NLRB	National Labor Relations Board
DOL	Department of Labor	NRC	Nuclear Regulatory Commission
DOT	Department of Transportation	NSC	National Security Council
EEOC	Equal Employment Opportunity Commission	NSF	National Science Foundation
EOP	Executive Office of the President	OMB	Office of Management and Budget
EPA	Environmental Protection Agency	OPM	Office of Personnel Management
FAA	Federal Aviation Administration	OSHA	Occupational Safety and Health Administration
FBI	Federal Bureau of Investigation	SBA	Small Business Administration
FCC	Federal Communications Commission	SEC	Securities and Exchange Commission
FDA	Food and Drug Administration	TVA	Tennessee Valley Authority
FDIC	Federal Deposit Insurance Corporation	USA	United States Army
FEC	Federal Election Commission	USAF	United States Air Force
FRB	Federal Reserve Board	USCG	United States Coast Guard
FTC	Federal Trade Commission	USDA	United States Department of Agriculture
GAO	General Accounting Office	USMC	United States Marine Corps
GSA	General Services Administration	USN	United States Navy
HHS	Department of Health and Human Services	USPS	United States Postal Service
HUD	Department of Housing and Urban Development	WHO	White House Office

Congressional Investigations

Perhaps the most visible and dramatic form of congressional supervision of an agency is the investigation. Since 1792, when Congress investigated an army defeat by a Native American tribe, congressional investigations of the bureaucracy have been a regular feature—sometimes constructive, sometimes destructive—of legislative-executive relations. The investigative power is not mentioned in the Constitution but has been inferred from the power to legislate. The Supreme Court has consistently upheld this interpretation, though it has also said that such investigations should not be solely for the purpose of exposing the purely personal affairs of private individuals and must not operate to deprive citizens of their basic rights.[29] Congress may compel a person to attend an investigation by issuing a subpoena;

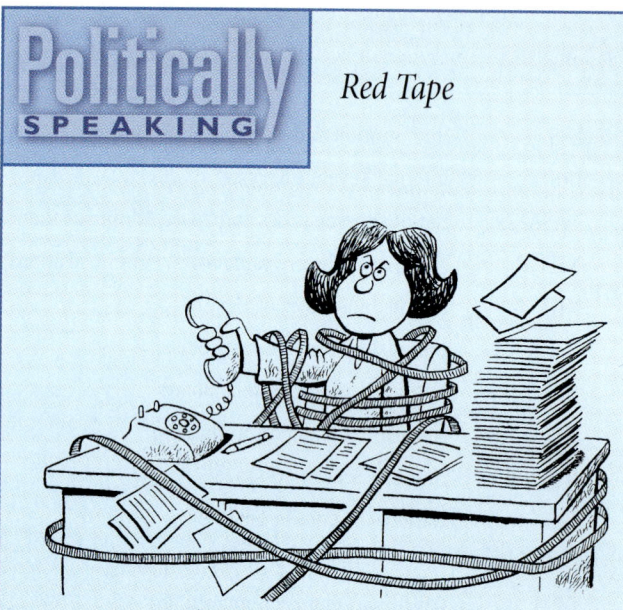

Politically SPEAKING

Red Tape

As early as the seventh century, legal and government documents in England were bound together with a tape of pinkish red color. In the 1850s historian Thomas Carlyle described a British politician as "little other than a red tape Talking Machine," and later the American writer Washington Irving said of an American figure that "his brain was little better than red tape and parchment."

Since then *red tape* has come to mean "bureaucratic delay or confusion," especially that accompanied by unnecessary paperwork.

SOURCE: From *Safire's Political Dictionary* by William Safire. Copyright © 1968, 1972, 1978 by William Safire. Reprinted by permission of Random House, Inc. and the author.

anyone who ignores the subpoena may be punished for contempt. Congress can vote to send the person to jail or can refer the matter to a court for further action. As explained in Chapter 12, the president and his principal subordinates have refused to answer certain congressional inquiries on grounds of "executive privilege."

Although many areas of congressional oversight—budgetary review, personnel controls, investigations—are designed to control the exercise of bureaucratic discretion, other areas are intended to ensure the freedom of certain agencies from effective control, especially by the president. In dozens of cases Congress has authorized department heads and bureau chiefs to operate independently of presidential preferences. Congress has resisted, for example, presidential efforts to ensure that policies to regulate pollution do not impose excessive costs on the economy, and interest groups have brought suit to prevent presidential coordination of various regulatory agencies. If the bureaucracy sometimes works at cross-purposes, it is usually because Congress—or competing committees in Congress—wants it that way.

Bureaucratic "Pathologies"

Everyone complains about bureaucracy in general (though rarely about bureaucratic agencies that everyone believes are desirable). This chapter should persuade you that it is difficult to say anything about bureaucracy "in general"; there are too many different kinds of agencies, kinds of bureaucrats, and kinds of programs to label the entire enterprise with some single adjective. Nevertheless, many people who recognize the enormous variety among government agencies still believe that they all have some general features in common and suffer from certain shared problems or pathologies.

This is true enough, but the reasons for it—and the solutions, if any—are not often understood. There are five major (or at least frequently mentioned) problems with bureaucracies: red tape, conflict, duplication, imperialism, and waste. **Red tape** refers to the complex rules and procedures that must be followed to get something done. *Conflict* exists because some agencies seem to be working at cross-purposes with other agencies. (For example, the Agricultural Research Service tells farmers how to grow crops more efficiently, while the Agricultural Stabilization and Conservation Service pays farmers to grow fewer crops or to produce less.) *Duplication* (usually called "wasteful duplication") occurs when two government agencies seem to be doing the same thing, as when the Customs Service and the Drug Enforcement Administration both attempt to intercept illegal drugs being smuggled into the country. *Imperialism* refers to the tendency of agencies to grow without regard to the benefits that their programs confer or the costs that they entail.

Waste means spending more than is necessary to buy some product or service.

These problems all exist, but they do not necessarily exist because bureaucrats are incompetent or power-hungry. Most exist because of the very nature of government itself. Take red tape: partly we encounter cumbersome rules and procedures because any large organization, governmental or not, must have some way of ensuring that one part of the organization does not operate out of step with another. Business corporations have red tape also; it is to a certain extent a consequence of bigness. But a great amount of governmental red tape is also the result of the need to satisfy legal and political requirements. Government agencies must hire on the basis of "merit," must observe strict accounting rules, must supply Congress with detailed information on their programs, and must allow for citizen access in countless ways. Meeting each need requires rules; enforcing the rules requires forms.

Or take conflict and duplication: they do not occur because bureaucrats enjoy conflict or duplication. (Quite the contrary!) They exist because Congress, in setting up agencies and programs, often wants to achieve a number of different, partially inconsistent goals or finds that it cannot decide which goal it values the most. Congress has 535 members and little strong leadership; it should not be surprising that 535 people will want different things and will sometimes succeed in getting them.

Imperialism results in large measure from government agencies' seeking goals that are so vague and so difficult to measure that it is hard to tell when they have been attained. When Congress is unclear as to exactly what an agency is supposed to do, the agency will often convert that legislative vagueness into bureaucratic imperialism by taking the largest possible view of its powers. It may do this on its own; more often it does so because interest groups and judges rush in to fill the vacuum left by Congress. As we saw in Chapter 3, the 1973 Rehabilitation Act was passed with a provision barring discrimination against the disabled in any program receiving federal aid. Under pressure from the disabled, that lofty but vague goal was converted by the Department of Transportation into a requirement that virtually every big-city bus have a device installed to lift people in wheelchairs on board.

Waste is probably the biggest criticism that people have of the bureaucracy. Everybody has heard stories of the Pentagon's paying $91 for screws that cost 3 cents in the hardware store. President Reagan's "Private Sector Survey on Cost Control," generally known as the Grace Commission (after its chairman, J. Peter Grace), publicized these and other tales in a 1984 report.

No doubt there is waste in government. After all, unlike a business firm worried about maximizing profits, in a government agency there are only weak incentives to keep costs down. If a business employee cuts costs, he or she often receives a bonus or raise, and the firm gets to add the savings to its profits. If a government official cuts costs, he or she receives no reward, and the agency cannot keep the savings—they go back to the Treasury.

But many of the horror stories are either exaggerations or unusual occurrences.[30] Most of the screws, hammers, and light bulbs purchased by the government are obtained at low cost by means of competitive bidding among several suppliers. When the government does pay outlandish amounts, the

These long lines of cars at the border between the United States and Mexico may be a symbol of "bureaucratic red tape" to some travelers, but they are a sign of "effective law enforcement" to people who want to cut off the flow of drugs and illegal immigrants.

Reforming the Federal Bureaucracy, 1905–1993

Keep Commission (1905–1909) Personnel management, government contracting, information management.

President's Commission on Economy and Efficiency (1910–1913) Recommended creating a national executive budget.

Joint Committee on Reorganization (1921–1924) Proposed ways of distributing executive functions among the departments.

President's Committee on Administrative Management (1936–1937) Known as the Brownlow Commission, after its chairman, Louis Brownlow. Recommended creation of the Executive Office of the President. Famous conclusion: "The president needs help."

First Hoover Commission (1947–1949) Comprehensive review of the executive branch.

Second Hoover Commission (1953–1955) Follow-up to the first Hoover commission; focused mainly on policy problems rather than organizational structure.

Study commission on executive reorganization (1953–1968) Series of low-key reforms that produced small but significant changes.

Ash Council (1969–1971) Proposed creation of new "super departments" to encompass existing departments.

Carter reorganization effort (1977–1979) Attempted to reorganize agencies from the bottom up; new cabinet departments created independently of effort.

Grace Commission (1982–1984) Large-scale, politically contentious effort to determine how government could be operated for less money.

National Performance Review (1993–present) Attempt to "reinvent" government to improve its performance.

SOURCE: Adapted from Ronald C. Moe, *Reorganizing the Executive Branch in the Twentieth Century* (Congressional Research Service, March 1992).

buying what it needs. The reason is red tape—the rules and procedures designed to ensure that when the government buys something, it will do so in a way that serves the interests of many groups. For example, it must often buy from American rather than foreign suppliers, even if the latter charge a lower price; it must make use of contractors that employ minorities; it must hire only union laborers and pay them the "prevailing" (that is, the highest) wage; it must allow public inspection of its records; it frequently is required to choose contractors favored by influential members of Congress; and so on. Private firms do not have to comply with all these rules and thus can buy for less.

From this discussion it should be easy to see why these five basic bureaucratic problems are so hard to correct. To end conflicts and duplication, Congress would have to make some policy choices and set some clear priorities, but with all the competing demands that it faces, Congress finds it difficult to do that. You make more friends by helping people than by hurting them, and so Congress is more inclined to add new programs than to cut old ones, whether or not the new programs are in conflict with existing ones. To check imperialism, some way would have to be found to measure the benefits of government, but that is often impossible; government exists in part to achieve precisely those goals—such as national defense—that are least measurable. Furthermore, what might be done to remedy some problems would make other problems worse: if you simplify rules and procedures to cut red tape, you are likely also to reduce the coordination among agencies and thus to increase the extent to which there is duplication or conflict. If you want to reduce waste, you will have to have more rules and inspectors—in short, more red tape. The problem of bureaucracy is inseparable from the problem of government generally.

Just as people are likely to say that they dislike Congress but like their own member of Congress, they are also inclined to express hostility toward "the bureaucracy" but goodwill for that part of the bureaucracy with which they have dealt personally. In 1973 a survey of Americans found that over half had had some contact with one or more kinds of government agencies, most of which were either run directly or funded indirectly by the federal government. The great majority of people were satisfied with these contacts and felt that they had been

reason typically is that it is purchasing a new or one-of-a-kind item not available at your neighborhood hardware store—for example, a new bomber or missile.

Even when the government is not overcharged, it still may spend more money than a private firm in treated fairly and given useful assistance. When these people were asked their feelings about government officials in general, however, they expressed much less favorable attitudes. Whereas about 80 percent liked the officials with whom they had dealt, only 42 percent liked officials in general.[31] This finding helps explain why government agencies are rarely reduced in size or budget: whatever the popular feelings about the bureaucracy, any given agency tends to have many friends.

Reforming the Bureaucracy

The history of American bureaucracy has been punctuated with countless efforts to make it work better and cost less. There have been eleven major attempts in this century alone (see the box at left). The latest was the National Performance Review (NPR)—popularly called the plan to "reinvent government"—led by Vice President Al Gore. The results of the review were published in 1993.

The NPR differed from many of the preceding reform efforts in one important way. Most of the earlier ones suggested ways of increasing central (that is, presidential) control of government agencies: the Brownlow Commission (1936–1937) recommended giving the president more assistants, the Hoover Commission (1947–1949) suggested ways of improving top-level management, and the Ash Council (1969–1971) called for consolidating existing agencies into a few big "super departments." The intent was to make it easier for the president and his cabinet secretaries to run the bureaucracy. The key ideas were efficiency, accountability, and consistent policies.

The NPR, by contrast, emphasized customer satisfaction (the "customers" in this case being the citizens who come into contact with federal agencies). To the authors of the NPR report, the main problem with the bureaucracy was that it had become too centralized, too rule-bound, too little concerned with making programs work, and too much concerned with avoiding scandal. The NPR report contained many horror stories about useless red tape, excessive regulations, and cumbersome procurement systems that make it next to impossible for agencies to do what they were created to do. (For example, before it could buy an ashtray the General Services Administration issued a nine-page document that described an ashtray and specified how many pieces it must break into should it be hit with a hammer.)[32] To solve these problems, the NPR called for less centralized management and more employee initiative, fewer detailed rules and more emphasis on customer satisfaction. It sought to create a new kind of organizational culture in government agencies, one more like that found in the more innovative, quality-conscious American corporations.

But making these changes is easier said than done. Most of the rules and red tape that make it hard for agency heads to do a good job are the result either of the struggle between the White House and Congress for control over the agencies or of the agencies' desire to avoid irritating influential voters. Silly as the rules for ashtrays may sound, they were written so that the government could say it had an "objective" standard for buying ashtrays. If it simply went out and bought ashtrays at a department store the way ordinary people do, it would risk being accused by the Acme Ashtray Company of buying trays from its competitor, the A-1 Ashtray Company, because of political favoritism.

The rivalry between the president and Congress for control of the bureaucracy makes bureaucrats nervous about irritating either branch, and so they issue rules designed to avoid getting into trouble, even if these rules make it hard to do their job. Matters become even worse during periods of divided government when different parties control the White House and Congress. As we saw in Chapter 12, divided government may not have much effect on *making* policy, but it can have a big effect on *implementing* it. Republican presidents have tried to increase political control over the bureaucracy ("executive micromanagement"), and Democratic Congresses have responded by increasing the number of investigations and detailed rule-making ("legislative micromanagement"). Divided government intensifies the cross-fire between the executive and legislative branches, making bureaucrats dig into even deeper layers of red tape to avoid getting hurt.

This does not mean that reform is impossible, only that it is very difficult. Everyone in the White House and Congress is in favor of reform in principle; the trick is finding a practical solution that everyone can agree on. It might be easier to make

Reforming How Bureaucrats Buy

*I*f you are like most people, when you go shopping you want to buy the best products or services at the lowest prices, and you probably favor merchants who have served you well in the past over ones who have not (especially known "rip-off artists"). But until quite recently the government's rules on procurement, which control what government agencies buy and how they buy it, not only discouraged but in many cases prohibited federal bureaucrats from behaving that way on the job. The rules were intended to ensure fairness to all competitors for government business. Over time, however, the rules just grew . . . and grew . . . and grew. Federal acquisition regulations and the armed services procurement regulations filled tens of thousands of pages. They allowed procurement officers little discretion. The military specification for fruitcake, adopted in 1980, ran to eighteen pages. It defined, among other things, the size of the nuts and the procedures for soaking the raisins.

The desire to avoid political favoritism in awarding government contracts resulted in a compartmentalized bidding process that most Americans (including the companies doing the bidding!) found ludicrous. Successful past performance by a contractor was rarely considered, let alone rewarded, when competitive bids for new government work were assessed. In 1990 a public management expert, Professor Steven Kelman of Harvard, lamented that "Public officials cannot use common sense and good judgement in ways that would promote better vendor performance." The system, he argued, "should be significantly deregulated to allow public officials greater discretion."

In 1993 Professor Kelman became the head of the federal government's procurement office. In 1994 Congress passed the Federal Acquisition Streamlining Act. Since then, many changes have been made in what and how federal bureaucrats buy. While the rules governing procurement are still many, cumbersome, and often counterproductive, as a result of the act and related reforms it is now far easier for federal bureaucrats to shop around, take past vendor performance into account, and let contracts go to the best (not just the lowest) bidder. Small purchases (generally defined as under $25,000) can now be made without having to go through a complicated process or being authorized by a half dozen or more top procurement officials.

Most bureaucrats like the more flexible rules. Martin Lieb, a veteran defense procurement officer in Philadelphia who purchased food for the military during the Gulf War, summed it up this way: "I can now usually buy what's needed—the best products at the best prices—get the job done in a timely way, serve my customers well, and save taxpayers money." By some estimates, the rule changes will save federal taxpayers as much as $22.5 billion by 1999.

SOURCES: Donald F. Kettl and John J. DiIulio, Jr., eds., *Inside the Reinvention Machine: Appraising Governmental Reform* (Washington, D.C.: Brookings Institution, 1995); Steven Kelman, *Procurement and Public Management: The Fear of Discretion* (Washington, D.C.: American Enterprise Institute, 1990).

---

desirable changes if the bureaucracy were accountable to but one master—say the president—instead of to several. But that situation, which exists in many parliamentary democracies, creates its own problems. When the bureaucracy has but one master, it often ends up having none: it becomes so powerful that it controls the prime minister and no longer listens to citizen complaints. A weak, divided bureaucracy, such as exists in the United States, may strike us as inefficient, but that very inefficiency may help protect our liberties.

SUMMARY

Bureaucracy is characteristic of almost all aspects of modern life, not simply the government. Government bureaucracies, however, pose special problems because they are subject to competing sources of political authority, must function in a constitutional system of divided powers and federalism, have vague goals, and lack incentive systems that will encourage efficiency. The power of a bureaucracy should be measured by its discretionary authority, not by the number of its employees or the size of its budget.

War and depression have been the principal sources of bureaucratic growth, aided by important changes in constitutional interpretation in the 1930s that permitted Congress to delegate broad grants of authority to administrative agencies. With only partial success, Congress seeks to check or recover those grants by controlling budgets, personnel, and policy decisions and by the exercise of legislative vetoes. The uses to which bureaucrats put their authority can be explained in part by their recruitment and security (they have an agency orientation), their personal political views, and the nature of the tasks that their agencies are performing.

Many of the popular solutions for the problems of bureaucratic rule—red tape, duplication, conflict, agency imperialism, and waste—fail to take into account that these problems are to a degree inherent in any government that serves competing goals and is supervised by rival elected officials. Nevertheless, some reform efforts have succeeded in making government work better and cost less to operate.

KEY TERMS

bureaucracy   *p. 409*

spoils system   *p. 412*

laissez-faire   *p. 413*

discretionary authority   *p. 415*

competitive service   *p. 415*

name-request job   *p. 417*

iron triangle   *p. 428*

issue network   *p. 428*

authorization legislation   *p. 429*

appropriation   *p. 429*

trust funds   *p. 430*

annual authorizations   *p. 430*

committee clearance   *p. 430*

legislative veto   *p. 430*

red tape   *p. 432*

SUGGESTED READINGS

Burke, John P. *Bureaucratic Responsibility.* Baltimore: Johns Hopkins University Press, 1986. Examines the problem of individual responsibility—for example, when to be a "whistle blower"—in government agencies.

DiIulio, John J., ed. *Deregulating the Public Service: Can Government Be Improved?* Washington, D.C.: Brookings Institution Press, 1994. Essays by leading academics, public administrators, and journalists on how government personnel and procurement practices can be improved.

DiIulio, John J., Gerald Garvey, and Donald F. Kettl. *Improving Government Performance: An Owner's Manual.* Washington, D.C.: Brookings Institution Press, 1993. A concise overview of the history of federal bureaucracy and ideas about how to reform it.

Downs, Anthony. *Inside Bureaucracy.* Boston: Little, Brown, 1967. An economist's explanation of why bureaucrats and bureaus behave as they do.

Halperin, Morton H. *Bureaucratic Politics and Foreign Policy.* Washington, D.C.: Brookings Institution, 1974. Insightful account of the strategies by which diplomatic and military bureaucracies defend their interests.

Heclo, Hugh. *A Government of Strangers.* Washington, D.C.: Brookings Institution, 1977. Analyzes how political appointees attempt to gain control of the Washington bureaucracy and how bureaucrats resist those efforts.

Howard, Philip K. *The Death of Common Sense.* New York: Random House, 1994. A brief but spirited criticism of how bureaucratic regulations get in the way of achieving desirable goals.

Moore, Mark H. *Creating Public Value: Strategic Management in Government.* Cambridge: Harvard University Press, 1995. A thoughtful account of how wise bureaucrats can make government work better.

Parkinson, C. Northcote. *Parkinson's Law.* Boston: Houghton Mifflin, 1957. Half-serious, half-joking explanation of why government agencies tend to grow.

Seidman, Harold, and Robert Gilmour. *Politics, Position, and Power.* 4th ed. New York: Oxford University Press, 1986. Perceptive account by a former insider of relations between the White House and the bureaucracy.

Wilson, James Q. *Bureaucracy: What Government Agencies Do and Why They Do It.* New York: Basic Books, 1989. A comprehensive review of what we know about bureaucratic behavior in the United States.

14

The Judiciary

★ "Strict-constructionist" versus "activist" judges

★ Framers' view of the Supreme Court

★ *Marbury* v. *Madison*

★ Marshall's leadership

★ Taney and the *Dred Scott* decision

★ Protecting private property and personal liberties

★ Structure of the federal courts

★ Presidential appointments

★ Jurisdiction

★ How cases get to the Supreme Court

★ Standing

★ Class-action suits

★ How the Supreme Court operates

★ Influences on the justices

★ Courts' role in making policy

★ Checks on judicial power

President Bush nominated Clarence Thomas to the Supreme Court on July 1, 1991. He was confirmed by a Senate vote of 52 to 48 on October 15. Thomas's margin of confirmation was the closest in more than one hundred years, and the second closest in U.S. history. His hearings were dominated by allegations of sexual harassment lodged against him by Anita F. Hill, a former subordinate during his tenure at the Equal Employment Opportunity Commission and later a University of Oklahoma law professor. Thomas became the sixth justice named by either Reagan or Bush, including the elevation of Justice Rehnquist to chief justice in 1986, and thus represented the arrival of a conservative lock on the high court. Apart from the sexual harassment allegations, which both sides estimated cost him about ten votes, opponents of his confirmation claimed that his judicial philosophy was outside the mainstream, while supporters claimed he would be sensitive to the rights of the disadvantaged, having himself risen from childhood poverty.

Only in the United States would the selection of a judge produce so dramatic and bitter a conflict. The reason is simple: only in the United States do judges play so large a role in making public policy.

One aspect of this power is **judicial review**—the right of the federal courts to declare laws of Congress and acts of the executive branch void and unenforceable if they are judged to be in conflict with the Constitution. Since 1789 the Supreme Court has declared over one hundred federal laws to be unconstitutional. In Britain, by contrast, Parliament is supreme, and no court may strike down a law that it passes. As the second Earl of Pembroke is supposed to have said, "A parliament can do anything but make a man a woman and a woman a man." All that prevents Parliament from acting contrary to the (unwritten) constitution of Britain are the consciences of its members and the opinion of the citizens. About sixty nations do have something resembling judicial review, but in only a few cases does this power mean much in practice. Where it means something—in Australia, Canada, Germany, India, and some other nations—one finds a stable, federal system of government with a strong tradition of an independent judiciary.[1] (Some other nations—France, for example—have special councils, rather than courts, that can under certain circumstances decide that a law is not authorized by the constitution.)

Judicial review is the federal courts' chief weapon in the system of checks and balances on which the American government is based. Today few people would deny to the courts the right to decide that a legislative or executive act is unconstitutional, though once that right was controversial. What remains controversial is the method by which such review is conducted.

There are two competing views, each ardently pressed during the Bork fight (and later in the fight to confirm Clarence Thomas). The first holds that judges should only judge—that is, they should confine themselves to applying those rules that are stated in or clearly implied by the language of the Constitution. This is often called the **strict-constructionist approach.** The other argues that judges should discover the general principles underlying the Constitution and its often vague language,

amplify those principles on the basis of some moral or economic philosophy, and apply them to cases. This is sometimes called the **activist approach.**

Note that the difference between activist and strict-constructionist judges is not necessarily the same as the difference between liberals and conservatives. Judges can be political liberals and still believe that they are bound by the language of the Constitution. A liberal justice, Hugo Black, once voted to uphold a state law banning birth control because nothing in the Constitution prohibited such a law. Or judges can be conservative and still think that they have the duty to use their best judgment in deciding what is good public policy. Rufus Peckham, one such conservative, voted to overturn a state law setting maximum hours of work because he believed that the Fourteenth Amendment guaranteed something called "freedom of contract," even though those words are not in the amendment.

Fifty years ago judicial activists tended to be conservatives and strict constructionist judges tended to be liberals; today the opposite is usually the case.

TABLE 14.1   Chief Justices of the United States

Chief Justice	Appointed by President	Years of Service
John Jay	Washington	1789–1795
Oliver Ellsworth	Washington	1796–1800
John Marshall	Adams	1801–1835
Roger B. Taney	Jackson	1836–1864
Salmon P. Chase	Lincoln	1864–1873
Morrison R. Waite	Grant	1874–1888
Melville W. Fuller	Cleveland	1888–1910
Edward D. White	Taft	1910–1921
William Howard Taft	Harding	1921–1930
Charles Evans Hughes	Hoover	1930–1941
Harlan Fiske Stone	F. Roosevelt	1941–1946
Fred M. Vinson	Truman	1946–1953
Earl Warren	Eisenhower	1953–1969
Warren E. Burger	Nixon	1969–1986
William H. Rehnquist	Reagan	1986–present

NOTE: Omitted is John Rutledge, who served for only a few months in 1795 and who was not confirmed by the Senate.

Chief Justice William H. Rehnquist

The Development of the Federal Courts

Most of the Founders probably expected the Supreme Court to have the power of judicial review (though they did not say that in so many words in the Constitution), but they did not expect federal courts to play so large a role in making public policy. The traditional view of civil courts was that they judged disputes between people who had direct dealings with each other—they had entered into a contract, for example, or one had dropped a load of bricks on the other's toe—and decided which of the two parties was right. The court then supplied relief to the wronged party, usually by requiring the other person to pay him or her money ("damages").

This traditional understanding was based on the belief that judges would find and apply existing law. The purpose of a court case was not to learn what the judge believes but what the law requires. The later rise of judicial activism occurred when judges questioned this traditional view and argued instead that judges do not merely find the law, they make the law.

The view that judges interpret the law and do not make policy made it easy for the Founders to justify the power of judicial review and led them to predict that the courts would play a relatively neutral, even passive, role in public affairs. Alexander Hamilton, writing in *Federalist* No. 78, described the judiciary as the branch "least dangerous" to political rights. The president is commander in chief and thus holds the "sword of the community"; Congress appropriates money and thus "commands the purse" as well as decides what laws shall govern. But the judiciary "has no influence over either the sword or the purse" and "can take no active resolution whatever." It has "neither force nor will but merely judgment," and thus is "beyond comparison the weakest of the three departments of power." As a result, "liberty can have nothing to fear from the judiciary alone." Hamilton went on to state clearly that the Constitution intended to give to the courts the right to decide whether a law is contrary to the Constitution. But this authority, he explained, was designed not to enlarge the power of the courts but to confine that of the legislature.

Obviously things have changed since Hamilton's time. The evolution of the federal courts, especially the Supreme Court, toward the present level of activism and influence has been shaped by the political, economic, and ideological forces of three historical eras. From 1787 to 1865 nation building, the legitimacy of the federal government, and slavery were the great issues; from 1865 to 1937 the dominant issue was the relationship between the government and the economy; from 1938 to the present the major issues confronting the Court have involved personal liberty and social equality and the potential conflict between the two. In the first period the Court asserted the supremacy of the federal government; in the second it placed important restrictions on the powers of that government; and in the third it enlarged the scope of personal freedom and narrowed that of economic freedom.

National Supremacy and Slavery

"From 1789 until the Civil War, the dominant interest of the Supreme Court was in that greatest of all the questions left unresolved by the Founders—the nation-state relationship."[2] The answer that the Court gave, under the leadership of Chief Justice John Marshall, was that national law was in all instances the dominant law, with state law having to give way, and that the Supreme Court had the power to decide what the Constitution meant. In two cases of enormous importance—*Marbury* v. *Madison* in 1803 and *McCulloch* v. *Maryland* in 1819—the Court, in decisions written by Marshall, held that the Supreme Court could declare an act of Congress unconstitutional; that the power granted by the Constitution to the federal government flows from the people and thus should be generously construed (and thus any federal laws that are "necessary and proper" to the attainment of constitutional ends are permissible); and that federal law is supreme over state law, even to the point that a state may not tax an enterprise (such as a bank) created by the federal government.[3]

The supremacy of the federal government was reaffirmed by other decisions as well. In 1816 the Supreme Court rejected the claim of the Virginia courts that the Supreme Court could not review the decisions of state courts. The Virginia courts were

Marbury v. Madison

*T*he story of *Marbury* v. *Madison* is often told, but it deserves another telling because it illustrates so many features of the role of the Supreme Court—how apparently small cases can have large results, how the power of the Court depends not simply on its constitutional authority but also on its acting in ways that avoid a clear confrontation with other branches of government, and how the climate of opinion affects how the Court goes about its task.

When President John Adams lost his bid for reelection to Thomas Jefferson in 1800, he—and all members of his party, the Federalists—feared that Jefferson and the Republicans would weaken the federal government and turn its powers to what the Federalists believed were wrong ends (states' rights, an alliance with the French, hostility to business). Feverishly, as his hours in office came to an end, Adams worked to pack the judiciary with fifty-nine loyal Federalists by giving them so-called midnight appointments before Jefferson took office.

John Marshall, as Adams's secretary of state, had the task of certifying and delivering these new judicial commissions. In the press of business he delivered all but seventeen; these he left on his desk for the incoming secretary of state,

James Madison, to send out. Jefferson and Madison, however, were furious at Adams's behavior and refused to deliver the seventeen. William Marbury and three other Federalists who had been promised these commissions hired a lawyer and brought suit against Madison to force him to produce the documents. The suit requested the Supreme Court to issue a writ of mandamus (from the Latin, "we command") ordering Madison to do his duty. The right to issue such writs had been given to the Court by the Judiciary Act of 1789.

Marshall, the man who had failed to deliver the commissions to Marbury and his friends in the first place, had become the chief justice and was now in a position to decide the case. These days a justice who had been involved in an issue before it came to the Court would probably disqualify himself or herself, but Marshall had no intention of letting others decide this question. He faced, however, not simply a partisan dispute over jobs but what was nearly a constitutional crisis. If he ordered the commission delivered, Madison might still refuse, and the Court had no way—if Madison was determined to resist—to compel him. The Court had no police force, whereas Madison had the support of the

president of the United States. And if the order were given, whether or not Madison complied, the Jeffersonian Republicans in Congress would probably try to impeach Marshall. On the other hand, if Marshall allowed Madison to do as he wished, the power of the Supreme Court would be seriously reduced.

Marshall's solution was ingenious. Speaking for a unanimous Court, he announced that Madison was wrong to withhold the commissions, that courts could issue writs to compel public officials to do their prescribed duty—*but* that the Supreme Court had no power to issue such writs in this case because the law (the Judiciary Act of 1789) giving it that power was unconstitutional. The law said that the Supreme Court could issue such writs as part of its "original jurisdiction"—that is, persons seeking such writs could go *directly* to the Supreme Court with their request (rather than go first to a lower federal court and then, if dissatisfied, appeal to the Supreme Court). Article III of the Constitution, Marshall pointed out, spelled out precisely the Supreme Court's original jurisdiction; it did not mention issuing writs of this sort and plainly indicated that on all matters not mentioned in the Constitution, the Court would have only appellate jurisdiction. Congress may not change what the Constitution says; hence the part of the Judiciary Act attempting to do this was null and void.

The result was that a show-down with the Jeffersonians was avoided—Madison was not ordered to deliver the commissions—but the power of the Supreme Court was unmistakably clarified and enlarged. As Marshall wrote, "It is emphatically the province and duty of the judicial department to say what the law is." Furthermore, "a law repugnant to the Constitution is void."

James Madison

John Adams

Roger B. Taney, chief justice from 1836 to 1864, wrote the *Dred Scott* decision, which asserted that blacks were not citizens of the United States. Dred Scott claimed that when his master brought him north to a free state, he ceased to be a slave. The public outcry against the decision was intense, at least in the North, as is evident from this poster announcing a mass meeting "to consider the atrocious decision."

ready to acknowledge the supremacy of the United States Constitution but believed that they had as much right as the United States Supreme Court to decide what the Constitution meant. The Supreme Court felt otherwise, and in this case and another like it the Court asserted its own broad powers to review any state court decision if that decision seemed to violate federal law or the federal Constitution.[4]

The power of the federal government to regulate commerce among the states was also established. When New York gave to Robert Fulton, the inventor of the steamboat, the monopoly right to operate his steamboats on the rivers of that state, the Marshall Court overturned the license because the rivers connected New York and New Jersey and thus trade on those rivers would involve *inter*state commerce, and federal law in that area was supreme. Since there was a conflicting federal law on the books, the state law was void.[5]

All of this may sound rather obvious to us today, when the supremacy of the federal government is largely unquestioned. In the early nineteenth century, however, these were almost revolutionary decisions. The Jeffersonian Republicans were in power and had become increasingly devoted to states'

rights; they were aghast at the Marshall decisions. President Andrew Jackson attacked the Court bitterly for defending the right of the federal government to create a national bank and for siding with the Cherokee Indians in a dispute with Georgia. In speaking of the latter case, Jackson is supposed to have remarked, "John Marshall has made his decision; now let him enforce it!"[6]

Though Marshall seemed to have secured the supremacy of the federal government over the state governments, another even more divisive issue had arisen; that, of course, was slavery. Roger B. Taney succeeded Marshall as chief justice in 1836. He was deliberately chosen by President Jackson because he was an advocate of states' rights, and he began to chip away at federal supremacy, upholding state claims that Marshall would have set aside. But the decision for which he is famous—or infamous— came in 1857, when in the *Dred Scott* case he wrote perhaps the most disastrous judicial opinion ever issued. A slave, Dred Scott, had been taken by his owner to a territory (near what is now St. Paul, Minnesota) where slavery was illegal under federal law. Scott claimed that since he had resided in a free territory, he was now a free man. Taney held that

Negroes were not citizens of the United States and
could not become so, and that the federal law—
the Missouri Compromise—prohibiting slavery in
northern territories was unconstitutional.[7] The public outcry against this view was enormous, and the
Court and Taney were discredited in the North, at
least. The Civil War was ultimately fought over what
the Court mistakenly had assumed was a purely
legal question.

Government and the Economy

The supremacy of the federal government may have
been established by John Marshall and the Civil War,
but the scope of the powers of that government or
even of the state governments was still to be defined.
During the period from the end of the Civil War to
the early years of the New Deal, the dominant issue
the Supreme Court faced was deciding when the
economy would be regulated by the states and when
by the nation.

The Court revealed a strong though not inflexible attachment to private property. In fact that attachment had always been there: the Founders
thought that political and property rights were inextricably linked, and Marshall certainly supported the
sanctity of contracts. But now, with the muting of
the federal supremacy issue and the rise of a national economy with important unanticipated effects, the property question became the dominant
one. In general the Court developed the view that
the Fourteenth Amendment, adopted in 1868 primarily to protect black claims to citizenship from
hostile state action, also protected private property
and the corporation from unreasonable state action.
The crucial phrase was this: no state shall "deprive
any person of life, liberty, or property, without due
process of law." Once it became clear that a "person"
could be a firm or a corporation as well as an individual, business and industry began to flood the
courts with cases challenging various government
regulations.

The Court quickly found itself in a thicket: it
began ruling on the constitutionality of virtually
every effort by any government to regulate any aspect of business or labor, and its work load rose
sharply. Judicial activism was born in the 1880s and
1890s as the Court set itself up as the arbiter of what
kind of regulation was permissible. In the first

seventy-five years of this country's history, only 2
federal laws were held to be unconstitutional; in the
next seventy-five years, 71 were.[8] Of the roughly 900
state laws held to be in conflict with the federal
Constitution since 1789, about 800 were overturned
after 1870. In one decade alone—the 1880s—5 federal and 48 state laws were declared unconstitutional.

Many of these decisions provided clear evidence
of the Court's desire to protect private property: it
upheld the use of injunctions to prevent labor
strikes,[9] struck down the federal income tax,[10]
sharply limited the reach of the antitrust law,[11] restricted the powers of the Interstate Commerce
Commission to set railroad rates,[12] prohibited the
federal government from eliminating child labor,[13]
and prevented the states from setting maximum
hours of work.[14] In 184 cases between 1899 and
1937, the Supreme Court struck down state laws for
violating the Fourteenth Amendment, usually by
economic regulation.[15]

But the Court also rendered decisions that authorized various kinds of regulation. It allowed
states to regulate businesses "affected with a public
interest,"[16] changed its mind about the Interstate
Commerce Commission and allowed it to regulate
railroad rates,[17] upheld rules requiring railroads to
improve their safety,[18] approved state antiliquor
laws,[19] approved state mine safety laws,[20] supported
state workers' compensation laws,[21] allowed states to
regulate fire-insurance rates,[22] and in time upheld a
number of state laws regulating wages and hours.
Indeed, between 1887 and 1910, in 558 cases involving the Fourteenth Amendment, the Supreme Court
upheld state regulations over 80 percent of the
time.[23]

To characterize the Court as probusiness or antiregulation is both simplistic and inexact. More accurate, perhaps, is to characterize it as supportive of
the rights of private property but unsure how to
draw the lines that distinguish "reasonable" from
"unreasonable" regulation. Nothing in the Constitution clearly differentiates reasonable from unreasonable regulation, and the Court has been able to
invent no consistent principle of its own to make
this determination. For example, what kinds of businesses are "affected with a public interest"? Grain
elevators and railroads are, but are bakeries? Sugar
refiners? Saloons? And how much of commerce is

"interstate"—anything that moves? Or only something that actually crosses a state line? The Court found itself trying to make detailed judgments that it was not always competent to make and to invent legal rules where no clear legal rules were possible.

In one area, however, the Supreme Court's judgments were clear: the Fourteenth and Fifteenth Amendments were construed so narrowly as to give blacks only the most limited benefits of their provisions. In a long series of decisions the Court upheld segregation in schools and on railroad cars and permitted blacks to be excluded from voting in many states.

Government and Political Liberty

After 1936 the Supreme Court stopped imposing any serious restrictions on state or federal power to regulate the economy, leaving such matters in the hands of the legislatures. From 1937 to 1974 the Supreme Court did not overturn a single federal law designed to regulate business but did overturn thirty-six congressional enactments that violated personal political liberties. It voided as unconstitutional laws that restricted freedom of speech,[24] denied passports to communists,[25] permitted the government to revoke a person's citizenship,[26] withheld a person's mail,[27] or restricted the availability of government benefits.[28]

This new direction began when one justice changed his mind, and it continued as the composition of the Court changed. At the outset of the New Deal the Court was, by a narrow margin, dominated by justices who opposed the welfare state and federal regulation based on broad grants of discretionary authority to administrative agencies. President Franklin Roosevelt, who was determined to get just such legislation implemented, found himself powerless to alter the composition of the Court during his first term (1933–1937): because no justice died or retired, he had no vacancies to fill. After his overwhelming reelection in 1936, he moved to remedy this problem by "packing" the Court.

Roosevelt proposed a bill that would have allowed him to appoint one new justice for each one over the age of seventy who refused to retire, up to a total membership of fifteen. Since there were six men in this category then on the Supreme Court, he would have been able to appoint six new justices, enough to ensure a comfortable majority supportive of his economic policies. A bitter controversy ensued, but before the bill could be voted on, the Supreme Court, perhaps reacting to Roosevelt's big win in the 1936 elections, changed its mind. Whereas it had been striking down several New Deal measures by votes of five to four, now it started approving them by the same vote. One justice, Owen Roberts, had switched his position—the famous "switch in time that saved nine."

The "court-packing" bill was not passed, but it was no longer necessary. Justice Roberts had yielded before public opinion in a way that Chief Justice Taney a century earlier had not, thus forestalling an assault on the Court by the other branches of government. Shortly thereafter several justices stepped

The "nine old men": the Supreme Court in 1937, not long after President Franklin D. Roosevelt tried, unsuccessfully, to "pack" it by appointing six additional justices who would have supported his New Deal legislation. Justice Owen J. Roberts (standing at the left) changed his vote on these matters, and the Court ceased to be a barrier to the delegation of power to the bureaucracy.

U.S. DISTRICT AND APPELLATE COURTS

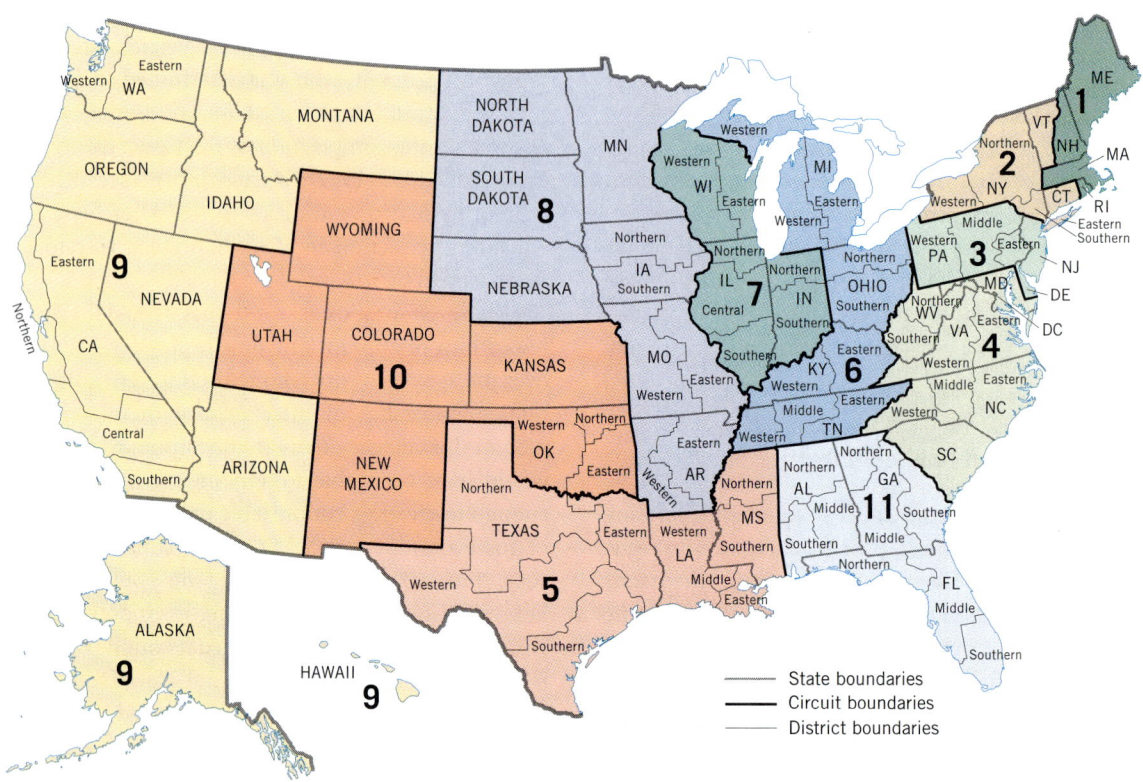

NOTE: Washington, D.C., is in a separate court. Puerto Rico is in the first circuit; the Virgin Islands are in the third; Guam and the Northern Mariana Islands are in the ninth.

SOURCE: Administrative Office of the United States Courts (January 1983).

down, and Roosevelt was able to make his own appointments (he made nine in all during his four terms in office). From then on the Court turned its attention to new issues—political liberties and, in time, civil rights.

With the arrival in office of Chief Justice Earl Warren in 1953, the Court began its most active period yet. Activism now arose to redefine the relationship of citizens to the government and especially to protect the rights and liberties of citizens from governmental trespass. Although the Court has always seen itself as protecting citizens from arbitrary government, before 1937 that protection was of a sort that conservatives preferred; after 1937 it was of a kind that liberals preferred.

The history of the Supreme Court seems to support the view that the federal government can pass almost any law authorized by the Constitution re-

gardless of what rights the states once thought they had. But in recent years there have been hints that the Court has not entirely abandoned the idea that states have some constitutional power to resist federal authority. In 1990 Congress passed the Gun-Free School Zones Act, which forbade anybody from carrying a gun near a school. When a boy was arrested for breaking this law, the Supreme Court held that Congress's power to regulate interstate commerce does not give it the right to decide whether a gun can be carried near a school. And so the law was declared unconstitutional.[29] This was the first time in over half a century that the Court had taken a restrictive view of Congress's power to regulate interstate commerce. A year later, in 1991, the Court overruled a federal law that gave Indians the right to sue state governments, saying that this violated the protection states enjoyed under the Eleventh

Amendment.[30] The supremacy of federal power over commerce may seem secure, but there are, apparently, still a few loose ends.

The Structure of the Federal Courts

The only federal court that the Constitution requires is the Supreme Court, as specified in Article III. All other federal courts and their jurisdictions are creations of Congress. Nor does the Constitution indicate how many justices shall be on the Supreme Court (there were originally six, now there are nine) nor what its appellate jurisdiction shall be.

Congress has created two kinds of lower federal courts to handle cases that need not be decided by the Supreme Court: constitutional and legislative courts. A **constitutional court** is one exercising the judicial powers found in Article III of the Constitution, and therefore its judges are given constitutional protection: they may not be fired (they serve during "good behavior"), nor may their salaries be reduced while they are in office. The most important of the constitutional courts are the **district courts** (a total of ninety-four, with at least one in each state, the District of Columbia, and the commonwealth of Puerto Rico) and the **courts of appeals** (one in each of eleven regions, or circuits, plus one in the District of Columbia). There are also certain specialized courts having constitutional status, such as the Court of International Trade, but we shall not be concerned with them.

A **legislative court** is one set up by Congress for some specialized purpose and staffed with people who have fixed terms of office and can be removed or have their salaries reduced. Legislative courts include the Court of Military Appeals and the territorial courts.

Selecting Judges

Since the judges on the constitutional courts serve for life and have the power of judicial review, how they are selected and what attitudes they bring to the bench are obviously important. All are nominated by the president and confirmed by the Senate. Almost invariably the president nominates a member of his own political party.

How Partisanship Affects Judicial Attitudes

*I*n 1984 over one hundred federal judges were interviewed, to learn about their background and attitudes. There were about equal numbers of Democrats and Republicans, and they were quite similar in social background. The overwhelming majority were white males; their average age was sixty. Most had attended a prestigious college. Despite these similarities, they expressed quite different political views and applied quite different judicial philosophies.

	Judges Appointed by	
Attitudes	Democrats	Republicans
Political ideology		
Liberal	75%	28%
Conservative	11	37
Policy Positions		
Favor less government regulation of business	54	85
Government should reduce income gap between rich and poor	78	44
Special preference should be given to blacks in hiring	62	41
Special preference should be given to women in hiring	47	22
A woman has right to decide on abortion	81	80
Judicial philosophy		
Courts show too much concern for criminals	16	44
Judges should just apply the law, leave the rest to legislators	51	69
Judges need to supervise public bureaucracies	81	64

SOURCE: Althea K. Nagai, Stanley Rothman, and S. Robert Lichter, "The Verdict of Federal Judges," *Public Opinion* (November–December 1987): 52–56. Reprinted with the permission of the American Enterprise Institute for Public Policy Research, Washington, D.C.

FIGURE 14.1 Female and Minority Judicial Appointments, 1963–1991

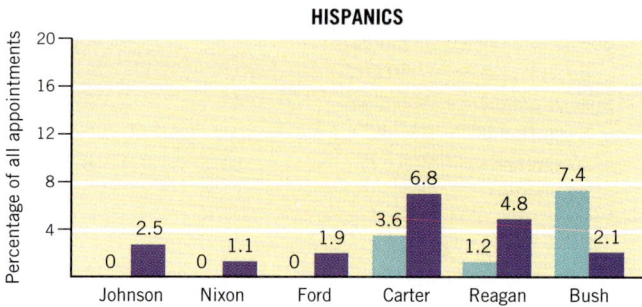

SOURCE: *Congressional Quarterly Weekly Report* (January 18, 1992): 112, reporting data gathered by Sheldon Goldman of University of Massachusetts (Johnson, Nixon, Ford) and Justice Department, Senate Judiciary Committee (Carter, Reagan, Bush).

Party background does have some effect on how judges behave. A study by Robert A. Carp and C. K. Rowland of over twenty-seven thousand district court cases decided between 1933 and 1977 revealed that Democratic judges took somewhat more liberal positions than Republican ones. The biggest differences were in cases alleging discrimination based on race or sex and in those involving the rights of the accused in criminal prosecutions. In these matters Democratic judges reached a "liberal" decision 13 to

18 percent more frequently than Republican ones. Comparable findings have come from studies of appeals court and Supreme Court justices.[31] This is consistent with what we have already learned about public opinion: within political elites partisanship is associated with ideology, and this affects behavior.

But ideology does not determine behavior. So many other things shape court decisions—the facts of the case, prior rulings by other courts, the arguments presented by lawyers—that there is no reliable way of predicting how judges will behave in all matters. Presidents often make the mistake of thinking that they know how their appointees will behave, only to be surprised by the facts. Theodore Roosevelt appointed Oliver Wendell Holmes to the Supreme Court, only to remark later, after Holmes had voted in a way that Roosevelt did not like, that "I could carve out of a banana a judge with more backbone than that!" Holmes, who had plenty of backbone, said that he did not "give a damn" what Roosevelt thought. Richard Nixon, an ardent foe of court-ordered school busing, appointed Warren Burger to be chief justice. Burger promptly sat down and wrote the opinion upholding busing. Another Nixon appointee, Harry Blackmun, wrote the opinion declaring the right to an abortion to be constitutionally protected.

Senatorial Courtesy   In theory, the president nominates a "qualified" person to be a judge, and the Senate approves or rejects the nomination based on those "qualifications." In fact, the tradition of *senatorial courtesy* gives heavy weight to the preferences of the senators from the state where a federal district judge is to serve. Ordinarily the Senate will not confirm a district court judge if the senior senator from the state where the district is located objects (if he is of the president's party). The senator can exercise this veto power by means of the "blue slip"—a blue piece of paper on which the senator is asked to record his or her views on the nominee. A negative opinion, or even failure to return the blue slip, usually kills the nomination. This means that as a practical matter the president nominates only persons recommended to him by that key senator. Someone once suggested that, at least with respect to district judges, the Constitution has been turned on its head. To reflect reality, he said, Article II, section 2, ought to read: "The senators shall nominate, and by and with the consent of the President, shall appoint" federal judges.

The "Litmus Test" Of late, presidents have tried to exercise more influence on the selection of federal district and appellate court judges by getting the Justice Department to find candidates that not only are supported by their party's senators but also reflect the political and judicial philosophy of the president. President Carter sought out liberal, activist judges; President Reagan sought out conservative, strict-constructionist ones.

As far as we can tell, they succeeded. (See Figure 14.1.) Carter appointed more blacks and women than Reagan (though Reagan appointed the second-highest percentage of women in history). We have no systematic data on the ideological differences between Carter and Reagan appointees, but every bit of impressionistic evidence suggests that Carter's were liberal and Reagan's conservative.*

This has led some to worry about the use of a political **litmus test**—a test of ideological purity—for judges. When conservatives are out of power (as they were under Carter), they complain about liberals' using a litmus test; when liberals are out of power (as they were under Reagan), they complain about conservatives' using it. People who are neither conservatives nor liberals wish that judges could be picked purely on the basis of "professional qualifications," without reference to ideology, but the courts are now so deeply involved in political issues that it is hard to imagine what a politically neutral set of professional qualifications might be.

The litmus-test issue is of greatest importance in selecting Supreme Court justices. Here there is no tradition of senatorial courtesy. The president takes a keen personal interest in the choices and, of late, has sought to find nominees who share his philosophy. In the Reagan administration there were bruising fights in the Senate over the nomination of William Rehnquist to be chief justice (he won) and Robert Bork to be an associate justice (he lost), with liberals pitted against conservatives. When President

Politically SPEAKING

Litmus Test

In chemistry a litmus test is a way of finding out whether a liquid is acid or alkaline. It involves exposing the fluid to an organic dye that turns red in acids, blue in alkalines.

The term is used in politics to mean a test of ideological purity, a way of finding out whether a person is a dyed-in-the-wool liberal or conservative. For liberals a litmus-test issue might be support for abortion or opposition to school prayer; for conservatives it might be holding the opposite of these views, or perhaps favoring tax cuts.

SOURCE: From *Safire's Political Dictionary* by William Safire. Copyright © 1968, 1972, 1978 by William Safire. Reprinted by permission of Random House, Inc. and the author.

Bush nominated David Souter, there were lengthy hearings as liberal senators tried to pin down Souter's views on issues such as abortion. Souter refused to discuss matters on which he might later have to judge, however. Clarence Thomas, another Bush nominee, also tried to avoid the litmus test by saying that he had not formed an opinion on prominent abortion cases. In his case, however, the litmus-test issue was overshadowed by sensational allegations from a former employee, Anita Hill, that Thomas had sexually harassed her.

Of the roughly 140 Supreme Court nominees presented to it, the Senate has rejected 27. Only 5 of these were in the twentieth century.[32] (These five cases are described in Table 14.2 on page 450.) The reasons for rejecting a Supreme Court nominee are complex—each senator may have a different reason—but have involved such matters as the nominee's alleged hostility to civil rights, questionable personal financial dealings, a poor record as a lower-court judge, and Senate opposition to the nominee's

* A survey of federal judges found that 75 percent of the Democrats, but only 28 percent of the Republicans, considered themselves to be liberals. See Althea K. Nagai, Stanley Rothman, and S. Robert Lichter, "The Verdict on Federal Judges," *Public Opinion* (November–December, 1987): 52.

President Reagan's nomination of Robert H. Bork (left) was rejected by the Senate; that of Anthony Kennedy (right) was confirmed. Whether the two men actually differed in their judicial philosophy is unclear, but Bork, a former Yale Law School professor, had published many articles stating his commitment to a jurisprudence based on original intent, and this gave his Senate critics ample ammunition. Kennedy's record was not as easily targeted.

political or legal philosophy. Nominations of district court judges are rarely defeated, because typically no nomination is made unless the key senators approve in advance.

There are exceptions, however. Some district court nominees have been controversial, and senators who have displeased their constituents by their vote have paid a price. Senator Slade Gorton of Washington lost his 1986 reelection bid in part, it appears, because he had supported an unpopular court nominee.

TABLE 14.2	Senate Rejections of Supreme Court Nominations in This Century		
Nominee	Year	President	Action
John J. Parker	1930	Hoover	Rejected
Abe Fortas[a]	1968	Johnson	Withdrawn
Clement F. Haynsworth, Jr.	1969	Nixon	Rejected
G. Harold Carswell	1970	Nixon	Rejected
Robert Bork	1987	Reagan	Rejected

[a] Already on the Supreme Court, Fortas was nominated to be chief justice; when his nomination was blocked by a Senate filibuster, he resigned from the Court.

The Jurisdiction of the Federal Courts

We have a dual court system—one state, one federal—and this complicates enormously the task of describing what kinds of cases federal courts may hear and how cases beginning in the state courts may end up before the Supreme Court. The Constitution lists the kinds of cases over which federal courts have jurisdiction (in Article III and the Eleventh Amendment); by implication all other matters are left to state courts. Federal courts can hear all cases "arising under the Constitution, the laws of the United States, and treaties" (these are **federal-question cases**), and cases involving citizens of different states (called **diversity cases**).

Some kinds of cases can be heard in either federal or state courts. For example, if citizens of different states wish to sue one another and the matter involves more than $50,000, they can do so in either a federal or a state court. Similarly, if someone robs a federally insured bank, he or she has broken both state and federal law and thus can be prosecuted in state or federal courts, or both. Lawyers have become quite sophisticated in deciding whether, in a

The Jurisdiction of the Federal Courts

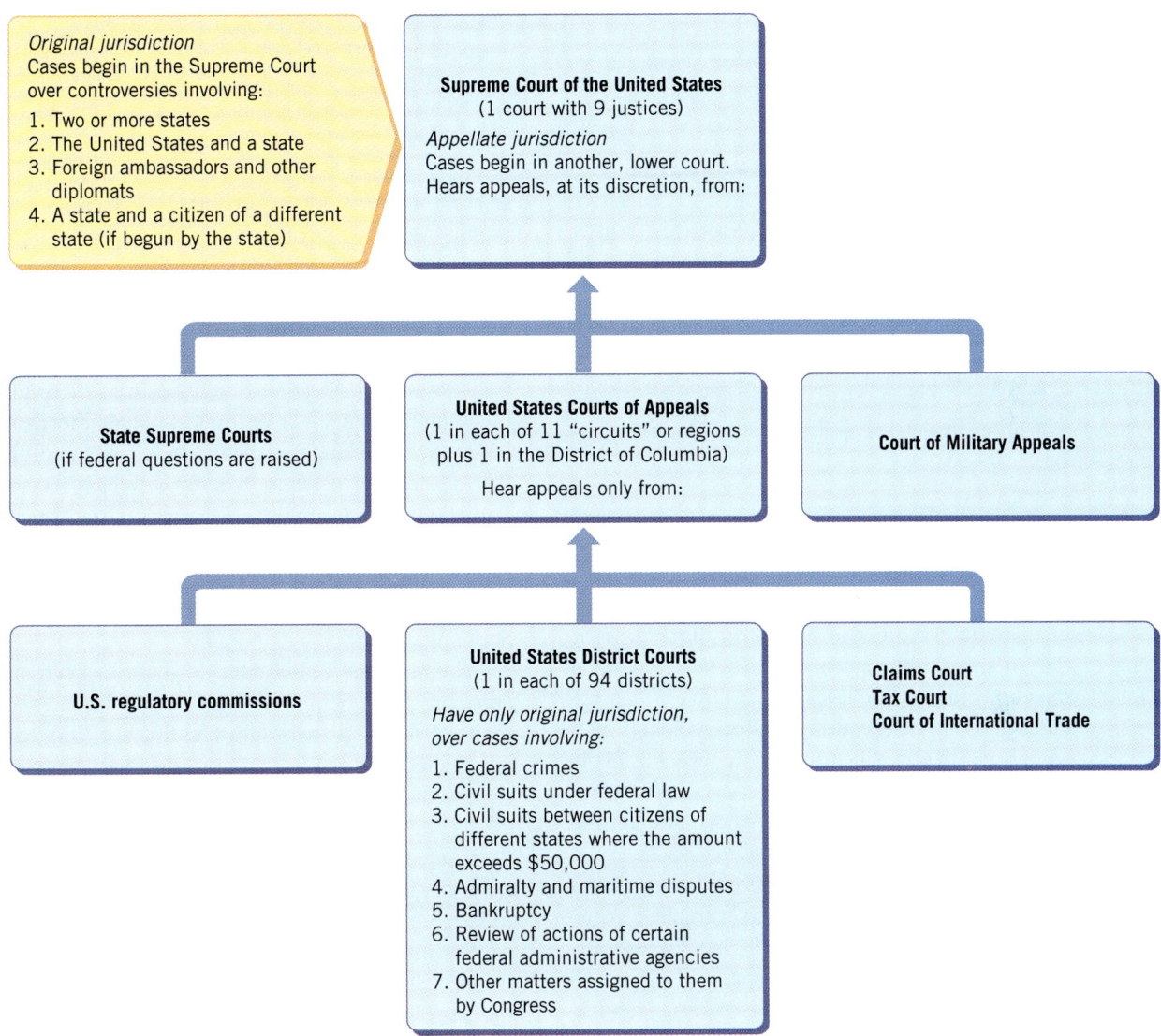

Original jurisdiction
Cases begin in the Supreme Court over controversies involving:
1. Two or more states
2. The United States and a state
3. Foreign ambassadors and other diplomats
4. A state and a citizen of a different state (if begun by the state)

Supreme Court of the United States
(1 court with 9 justices)
Appellate jurisdiction
Cases begin in another, lower court. Hears appeals, at its discretion, from:

State Supreme Courts
(if federal questions are raised)

United States Courts of Appeals
(1 in each of 11 "circuits" or regions plus 1 in the District of Columbia)
Hear appeals only from:

Court of Military Appeals

U.S. regulatory commissions

United States District Courts
(1 in each of 94 districts)
Have only original jurisdiction, over cases involving:
1. Federal crimes
2. Civil suits under federal law
3. Civil suits between citizens of different states where the amount exceeds $50,000
4. Admiralty and maritime disputes
5. Bankruptcy
6. Review of actions of certain federal administrative agencies
7. Other matters assigned to them by Congress

Claims Court
Tax Court
Court of International Trade

given civil case, their clients will get better treatment in a state or federal court. Prosecutors often send a person who has broken both federal and state law to whichever court system is likelier to give the toughest penalty.

Sometimes defendants may be tried in both state and federal courts for the same offense. In 1992 four Los Angeles police officers accused of beating Rodney King were tried in a California state court and acquitted of assault charges. They were then prosecuted in federal court for violating King's civil

rights. This time two of the four were convicted. Under the dual sovereignty doctrine, state and federal authorities can prosecute the same person for the same conduct. The Supreme Court has upheld this doctrine on two grounds: First, each level of government has the right to enact laws serving its own purposes.[33] As a result, federal civil rights charges could have been brought against the officers even if they had already been convicted of assault in state court (though as a practical matter this would have been unlikely). Second, neither level of govern-

Kinds of Law

*T*he differences between *civil* and *criminal* law are not precise. Generally speaking,

- **Civil law** is the body of rules defining relationships among private citizens. It consists of both statutes and the accumulated customary law embodied in judicial decisions (the "common law").

- **Criminal law** is the body of rules defining offenses that, though they harm an individual (such as murder, rape, robbery), are considered to be offenses against society as a whole and thus warrant punishment by and in the name of society.

You can go to prison if convicted of a crime but not if you lose a civil suit.

ment wants the other to be able to block prosecution of an accused person who has the sympathy of the authorities at one level. For example, when certain southern state courts were in sympathy with whites who had lynched blacks, the absence of the dual sovereignty doctrine would have meant that a trumped-up acquittal in state court would have barred federal prosecution.

Furthermore, a matter that is exclusively within the province of a state court—for example, a criminal case in which the defendant is charged with violating only a state law—can be appealed to the U.S. Supreme Court under certain circumstances (described below). Thus federal judges can overturn state court rulings even when they had no jurisdiction over the original matter. Under what circumstances this should occur has been the subject of long-standing controversy between the state and federal courts.

Some matters, however, are exclusively under the jurisdiction of federal courts. When a federal criminal law is broken—but not a state one—the case is heard in federal district court. If you wish to appeal the decision of a federal regulatory agency, such as the Federal Communications Commission, you can do so only before a federal court of appeals. And if you wish to declare bankruptcy, you do so in federal

court. If there is a controversy between two state governments—say, California and Arizona sue each other over which state is to use how much water from the Colorado River—the case can be heard only by the Supreme Court.

The vast majority of all cases heard by federal courts begin in the district courts. The volume of business there is huge. In 1990 the five hundred or so district court judges received 218,000 civil cases (about 415 per judge) and 49,000 criminal ones (about 93 per judge). Most of the cases heard in federal courts involve rather straightforward applications of law; few lead to the making of new public policy. Cases that do affect how the law or the Constitution is interpreted can begin with seemingly minor events. For example, a major broadening of the Bill of Rights—requiring for the first time that all accused persons in *state* as well as federal criminal trials be supplied with a lawyer, free if necessary—began when impoverished Clarence Earl Gideon, imprisoned in Florida, wrote an appeal in pencil on prison stationery and sent it to the Supreme Court.[34]

The Supreme Court does not have to hear any appeal it does not want to hear. At one time it was required to listen to certain appeals, but Congress has changed the law so that now the Court can pick the cases it wants to consider.

It does this by issuing a **writ of certiorari**. *Certiorari* is a Latin word meaning, roughly, "made more certain"; lawyers and judges have abbreviated it to *cert*. It works this way: The Court considers all the petitions it receives to review lower court decisions. If four justices agree to hear a case, cert is issued and the case is scheduled for a hearing.

In deciding whether to grant certiorari, the Court tries to reserve its time for cases decided by lower federal courts or by the highest state courts in which a significant federal or constitutional question has been raised. For example, the Court will often grant certiorari when one or both of the following is true:

- Two or more federal circuit courts of appeal have decided the same issue in different ways.

- The highest court in a state has held a federal or state law to be in violation of the Constitution or has upheld a state law against the claim that it is in violation of the Constitution.

In a typical year the Court may consider over seven thousand petitions asking it to review decisions of lower or state courts. It rarely accepts more than 3 or 4 percent of them (in 1992–1993, it accepted only 1 percent). This still leaves it with about two hundred appeals it must hear. (The Court's original jurisdiction may produce another dozen or so cases.)

In exercising its discretion in granting certiorari, the Supreme Court is on the horns of a dilemma. If it grants it frequently, it will be inundated with cases. As it is, the Court's workload has quintupled in the last fifty years. If, on the other hand, the Court grants certiorari only rarely, then the federal courts of appeals have the last word on the interpretation of the Constitution and federal laws, and since there are twelve of these, staffed by about 168 judges, they may well be in disagreement. In fact this has already happened: because the Supreme Court reviews only about 1 or 2 percent of appeals court cases, applicable federal law may be different in different parts of the country.[35] One proposal to deal with this dilemma is to devote the Supreme Court's time entirely to major questions of constitutional interpretation and to create a national court of appeals that would ensure that the twelve circuit courts of appeals are producing uniform decisions.[36]

Clarence Earl Gideon studied law books while in prison so that he could write an appeal to the Supreme Court. His handwritten appeal asked that his conviction be set aside because he had not been provided with an attorney. His appeal was granted.

Getting to Court

In theory the courts are the great equalizer in the federal government. To use the courts to settle a question, or even to alter fundamentally the accepted interpretation of the Constitution, one need not be elected to any office, have access to the mass media, be a member of an interest group, or be otherwise powerful or rich. Once the contending parties are before the courts, they are legally equal.

It is too easy to believe this theory uncritically or to dismiss it cynically. In fact it is hard to get before the Supreme Court: it rejects over 96 percent of the applications for certiorari that it receives. And the costs involved in getting to the Court can be high. To apply for certiorari costs only $300 (plus forty copies of the petition), but if certiorari is granted and the case heard, the costs—for lawyers and for copies of the lower-court records in the case—can be very large. And by then one has already paid for the cost of the first hearing in the district court and probably one appeal to the circuit court of appeals. Furthermore, the time it takes to settle a matter in federal court can be quite long.

But there are ways to make these costs lower. If you are indigent—without funds—you can file and be heard as a pauper for nothing; about half the petitions arriving before the Supreme Court are **in forma pauperis** (such as the one from Gideon, described earlier). If your case began as a criminal trial in the district courts and you are poor, the government will supply you with a lawyer at no charge. If the matter is not a criminal case and you cannot afford to hire a lawyer, interest groups representing a wide spectrum of opinion sometimes are willing to take up the cause if the issue in the case seems sufficiently important. The American Civil Liberties Union (ACLU), a liberal group, represents some people who believe that their freedom of speech has been abridged or that their constitutional rights in criminal proceedings have been violated. The Center for Individual Rights, a conservative group, represents some people who feel that they were victimized by racial quotas.

But interest groups do much more than just help people pay their bills. Many of the most important cases decided by the Court got there because an interest group organized the case, found the plaintiffs, chose the legal strategy, and mobilized legal allies. The NAACP has brought many key civil rights cases on behalf of individuals. Although in the past most such cases were brought by liberal interest groups, of late conservative interest groups have entered the courtroom on behalf of individuals. One helped sue CBS for televising a program that allegedly libeled General William Westmoreland, once the American commander in Vietnam. (Westmoreland lost the case.) And many important issues are raised by attorneys representing state and local governments. Several price-fixing cases have been won by state attorneys general on behalf of consumers in their states.

Fee Shifting

Unlike what happens in most of Europe, each party to a lawsuit in this country must pay its own way. (In England, by contrast, if you sue someone and lose, you pay the winner's costs as well as your own.) But various laws have made it easier to get someone else to pay. **Fee shifting,** as it is called, enables the **plaintiff** (the party that initiates the suit) to collect its costs from the defendant if the defendant loses, at least in certain kinds of cases. For example, if a corporation is found to have violated the antitrust laws, it must pay the legal fees of the winner. If an environmentalist group sues the Environmental Protection Agency, it can get the EPA to pay the group's legal costs. Even more important to individuals, Section 1983 of the *United States Code* allows a citizen to sue a state or local government official—say, a police officer or a school superintendent—who has deprived the citizen of some constitutional right or withheld some benefit to which the citizen is entitled. If the citizen wins, he or she can collect money damages and lawyers' fees from the government. Citizens, more aware of their legal rights, have become more litigious, and a flood of such "Section 1983" suits has burdened the courts. The Supreme Court has restricted fee shifting to cases authorized by statute,[37] but it is clear that the drift of policy has made it cheaper to go to court—at least for some cases.

Standing

There is, in addition, a nonfinancial restriction on getting into federal court. To sue, one must have **standing,** a legal concept that refers to who is entitled to bring a case. It is especially important in determining who can challenge the laws or actions of the government itself. A complex and changing set of rules governs standings; some of the more important ones are these:

- There must be an actual controversy between real adversaries. (You cannot bring a "friendly" suit against someone, hoping to lose in order to prove your friend right. You cannot ask a federal court for an opinion on a hypothetical or imaginary case or ask it to render an advisory opinion.)

- You must show that you have been harmed by the law or practice about which you are complaining. (It is not enough to dislike what the government or a corporation or a labor union does; you must show that you were actually harmed by that action.)

- Merely being a taxpayer does not ordinarily entitle you to challenge the constitutionality of a federal governmental action. (You may not want your tax money to be spent in certain ways, but your remedy is to vote against the politicians doing the spending; the federal courts will generally require that you show some other personal harm before you can sue.)

Congress and the courts have recently made it easier to acquire standing. It has always been the rule that a citizen could ask the courts to order federal officials to carry out some act that they were under a legal obligation to perform or to refrain from some action that was contrary to law. A citizen can also sue a government official personally in order to collect damages if the official acted contrary to law. For example, it was for long the case that if an FBI agent broke into your office without a search warrant, you could sue the agent and, if you won, collect money. However, you cannot sue the government itself without its consent. This is the doctrine of **sovereign immunity.** For instance, if the army accidentally kills your cow while testing a new cannon, you cannot sue the government to recover the cost of the cow unless the government agrees to be sued. (Since testing cannons is legal, you cannot sue the army officer who fired the cannon.) By statute Congress has given its consent for the government to be sued in many cases involving a dispute over a contract or damage done as a result of negligence (for example, the dead cow). Over the years these statutes have made it easier to take the government into court as a defendant.

Even some of the oldest rules defining standing have been liberalized. The rule that merely being a taxpayer does not entitle you to challenge in court a government decision has been relaxed where the citizen claims that a right guaranteed under the First Amendment is being violated. The Supreme Court allowed a taxpayer to challenge a federal law that would have given financial aid to parochial (or church-related) schools on the grounds that this aid violated the constitutional requirement of separation between church and state. On the other hand, another taxpayer suit to force the CIA to make public its budget failed because the Court decided that the taxpayer did not have standing in matters of this sort.[38]

Class-Action Suits

Under certain circumstances a citizen can benefit directly from a court decision, even though the citizen

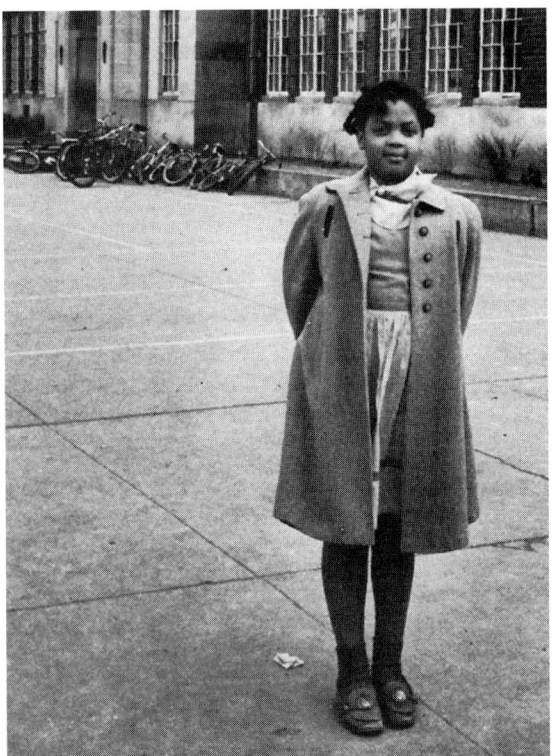

Linda Brown was refused admission to a white elementary school in Topeka, Kansas. On her behalf the NAACP brought a class-action suit that resulted in the 1954 landmark Supreme Court decision, *Brown* v. *Board of Education.*

himself or herself has not gone into court. This can happen by means of a **class-action suit:** a case brought into court by a person on behalf not only of himself or herself but of all other persons in similar circumstances. Among the most famous of these was the 1954 case in which the Supreme Court found that Linda Brown, a black girl attending the fifth grade in the Topeka, Kansas, public schools, was denied the equal protection of the laws (guaranteed under the Fourteenth Amendment) because the schools in Topeka were segregated. The Court did not limit its decision to Linda Brown's right to attend an unsegregated school but extended it—as Brown's lawyers from the NAACP had asked—to cover all "others similarly situated."[39] It was not easy to design a court order that would eliminate segregation in the schools, but the principle was clearly established in this class action.

Since the *Brown* case, many other groups have been quick to take advantage of the opportunity created by class-action suits. By this means the courts could be used to give relief not simply to a particular person but to all those represented in the suit. A landmark class-action case was that which challenged the malapportionment of state legislative districts (see Chapter 11).[40] In 1980 there were seven thousand class-action suits in the federal courts involving civil rights, the rights of prisoners, antitrust suits against corporations, and other matters. These suits became more common partly because people were beginning to have new concerns that were not being met by Congress and partly because some class-action suits became quite profitable. The NAACP got no money from Linda Brown or from the Topeka Board of Education in compensation for its long and expensive labors, but beginning in the 1960s court rules were changed to make it financially attractive for lawyers to bring certain kinds of class-action suits.

Suppose, for example, that you think your telephone company overcharged you by $75. You could try to hire a lawyer to get a refund, but not many lawyers would take the case, because there would be no money in it. Even if you were to win, the lawyer would stand to earn no more than perhaps one-third of the settlement, or $25. Now suppose that you bring a class action against the company on behalf of everybody who was overcharged. Millions of dollars might be at stake; lawyers would line up eagerly to take the case, because their share of the settlement, if they won, would be huge. The opportunity to win profitable class-action suits, combined with the possibility of having the loser pay the attorneys' fees, led to a proliferation of such cases.

In response to the increase in its workload, the Supreme Court decided in 1974 to tighten drastically the rules governing these suits. It held that it would no longer hear (except in certain cases defined by Congress, such as civil rights matters) class-action suits seeking monetary damages unless each and every ascertainable member of the class was individually notified of the case. To do this is often prohibitively expensive (imagine trying to find and send a letter to every customer that may have been overcharged by the telephone company!), and so the number of such cases declined and the number of lawyers seeking them out dropped.[41]

In sum, getting into court depends on having standing and having resources. The rules governing standing are complex and changing, but generally they have been broadened to make it easier to enter the federal courts, especially for the purpose of challenging the actions of the government. Obtaining the resources is not easy but has become easier because laws in some cases now provide for fee shifting, private interest groups are willing to finance cases, and it is sometimes possible to bring a class-action suit that lawyers find lucrative.

TABLE 14.3   Supreme Court Justices in Order of Seniority, 1994

Name (Birthdate)	Home State	Prior Experience	Appointed by (Year)
William H. Rehnquist, Chief Justice (1924)	Arizona	Justice: Assistant attorney general	Reagan (1986) as chief; Nixon (1971) as justice
John Paul Stevens (1916)	Illinois	Federal judge	Ford (1975)
Sandra Day O'Connor (1930)	Arizona	State judge	Reagan (1981)
Antonin Scalia (1936)	New York	Federal judge	Reagan (1986)
Anthony Kennedy (1936)	California	Federal judge	Reagan (1988)
David Souter (1939)	New Hampshire	State judge	Bush (1990)
Clarence Thomas (1948)	Georgia	Federal judge	Bush (1991)
Ruth Bader Ginsburg (1933)	New York	Federal judge	Clinton (1993)
Stephen Breyer (1938)	Massachusetts	Federal judge	Clinton (1994)

This photo of the Supreme Court in session on February 8, 1932, may be the only one ever taken while the justices were actually hearing a case.

The Supreme Court in Action

If your case should find its way to the Supreme Court—and of course the odds are that it will not—you will be able to participate in one of the more impressive, sometimes dramatic ceremonies of American public life. The Court is in session in its white marble building for thirty-six weeks out of each year, from early October until the end of June. The nine justices read briefs in their individual offices, hear oral arguments in the stately courtroom, and discuss their decisions with one another in a conference room where no outsider is ever allowed.

Most cases, as we have seen, come to the Court on a writ of certiorari. The lawyers for each side may then submit their briefs. A **brief** is a document that sets forth the facts of the case, summarizes the lower-court decision, gives the arguments for the side represented by the lawyer that wrote the brief, and discusses the other cases that the Court has decided bear on the issue. Then the lawyers are allowed to present their oral arguments in open court. They usually summarize their briefs or emphasize particular points in them, and they are strictly limited in

time—usually to no more than a half hour. (The lawyer speaks from a lectern that has two lights on it. When the white light goes on, the attorney has five minutes remaining; when the red flashes, he or she must stop—instantly.) The oral arguments give the justices a chance to question the lawyers, sometimes searchingly.

Since the federal government is a party—as either plaintiff or defendant—to about half the cases that the Supreme Court hears, the government's top trial lawyer, the solicitor general of the United States, appears frequently before the Court. The solicitor general is the third-ranking officer of the Department of Justice, right after the attorney general and deputy attorney general. The solicitor general decides what cases the government will appeal from lower courts and personally approves every case the government presents to the Supreme Court. In recent years the solicitor general has often been selected from the ranks of distinguished law school professors.

In addition to the arguments made by lawyers for the two sides in a case, written briefs and even oral arguments may also be offered by "a friend of the court," or **amicus curiae.** An amicus brief is from an interested party not directly involved in the suit. For example, when Allan Bakke complained that he had been the victim of "reverse discrimination" when he was denied admission to a University of California medical school, fifty-eight amicus briefs were filed supporting or opposing his position. Before such briefs can be filed, both parties must agree or the Court must grant permission. Though these briefs sometimes offer new arguments, they are really a kind of polite lobbying of the Court that declare what interest groups are on which side. The ACLU, the NAACP, the AFL-CIO, and the United States government itself have been among the leading sources of such briefs.

These briefs are not the only source of influence on the justices' views. Legal periodicals such as the *Harvard Law Review* and the *Yale Law Journal* are frequently consulted, and citations to them often appear in the Court's decisions. Thus the outside world of lawyers and law professors can help shape, or at least supply arguments for, the conclusions of the justices.

The justices retire every Friday to their conference room, where in complete secrecy they debate the cases they have heard. The chief justice speaks first, followed by the other justices in order of seniority. After the arguments they vote, traditionally in reverse order of seniority: the newest justice votes first, the chief justice last. By this process an able chief justice can exercise considerable influence—in guiding or limiting debate, in setting forth the issues, and in handling sometimes temperamental personalities. In deciding a case, a majority of the justices must be in agreement: if there is a tie, the lower-court decision is left standing. (There can be a tie among nine justices if one is ill or disqualifies himself or herself because of prior involvement in the case.)

Though the vote is what counts, by tradition the Court usually issues a written opinion explaining its decision. Sometimes the opinion is brief and unsigned (called a **per curiam opinion**); sometimes it is quite long and signed by the justices agreeing with it. If the chief justice is in the majority, he will either write the opinion or assign the task to a justice who agrees with him. If he is in the minority, the senior justice on the winning side will decide who writes the Court's opinion. There are three kinds of opinions—an **opinion of the Court** (reflecting the ma-

jority's view), a **concurring opinion** (an opinion by one or more justices who agree with the majority's conclusion but for different reasons that they wish to express), and a **dissenting opinion** (the opinion of the justices on the losing side). Each justice has three or four law clerks (bright recent graduates of leading law schools) to help him or her review the many petitions the Court receives, study cases, and write opinions.

Voting Patterns of the Court

Scholars have made elaborate and ingenious efforts to explain the voting patterns of Supreme Court justices. The intricacies of these inquiries are best left to specialists, but the results can be summarized in general terms. They show that justices, like any group of men or women in politics, tend to take more or less consistent positions on public issues. They have a political philosophy. When the Court must decide a case that raises philosophical issues (and that occurs only part of the time), we should not be surprised to see rather clear voting blocs emerge.

During the 1970s and 1980s there were often three such blocs: a liberal/activist bloc (led by former justice William Brennan and including former justice Thurgood Marshall and sometimes former justices Harry Blackmun and Lewis Powell), a conservative/strict-constructionist bloc (consisting of former chief justice Burger, Justice Rehnquist, and Justice O'Connor), and a swing bloc (composed of former justice White and Justice Stevens).[42] The liberal bloc was usually in the minority but sometimes picked up enough swing votes to decide the issue.[43]

With the retirement of Blackmun, Brennan, Burger, Marshall, Powell, and White, observers assumed that the Court's orientation would change markedly. Three Reagan appointees (Sandra Day O'Connor, Antonin Scalia, and Anthony Kennedy) and two Bush appointees (David Souter and Clarence Thomas) were expected to join Chief Justice Rehnquist in forming a solid six-justice conservative/strict-constructionist bloc. It did not work out quite that way. On many issues, Kennedy and Souter have been unwilling to side with Rehnquist, Scalia, and Thomas, joining instead with one Ford appointee, Stevens, and two Clinton appointees, Ruth Bader Ginsburg and Stephen Breyer. The Supreme

The members of the United States Supreme Court in 1997: from left to right, Sandra Day O'Connor, Anthony Kennedy, Antonin Scalia, William H. Rehnquist (Chief Justice), David Souter, Ruth Bader Ginsburg, Clarence Thomas, Stephen Breyer, John Paul Stevens.

Court remains deeply divided, with different blocs forming on different issues.

These voting blocs are important, but they are not the whole story and often not even a significant factor. During the 1995 Court term, 38.7 percent of all the opinions of the Court were unanimous. Even two justices who are as different philosophically as Scalia and Ginsburg voted the same way on 55 percent of the cases in 1995.

The differing judicial philosophies of the justices, though important, do not prevent them from agreeing a lot of the time. The reason is that many cases have no "liberal" or "conservative" side, and even in those that do the justices must take into account the language of the law or the Constitution, the prior decisions (precedents) they have issued, and the facts of the case. And when philosophy plays a role, unexpected cleavages may develop, as when O'Connor and Kennedy broke ranks with Rehnquist and Scalia on the abortion question.

And in evaluating the Court's actions, the student should remember that it is not the *results*,

whether liberal or conservative, that ought to count; what should count is the *quality* of the justices' reasoning.

The Power of the Federal Courts

The great majority of the cases heard in the federal courts have little or nothing to do with changes in public policy: people accused of bank robbery are tried, disputes over contracts are settled, personal-injury cases are heard, and the patent law is applied. In most instances the courts are simply applying a relatively settled body of law to a specific controversy.

The Power to Make Policy

The courts make policy whenever they reinterpret the law or the Constitution in significant ways, extend the reach of existing laws to cover matters not previously thought to be covered by them, or design remedies for problems that involve the judges' acting in administrative or legislative ways. By any of these tests the courts have become exceptionally powerful.

One measure of that power is the fact that more than 120 federal laws have been declared unconstitutional, although since 1937 relatively few of these have had broad national significance. And as we shall see, on matters where Congress feels strongly, it can often get its way by passing slightly revised versions of the voided law.

Another measure, and perhaps a more revealing one, is the frequency with which the Court changes its mind. An informal rule of judicial decision making has been **stare decisis,** meaning "let the decision stand." It is the principle of precedent: a court case today should be settled in accordance with prior decisions on similar cases. (What constitutes a similar case is not always clear; lawyers are especially gifted at finding ways of showing that two cases are different in some relevant way.) There are two reasons why precedent is important. The practical reason should be obvious: if the meaning of the law continually changes, if the decisions of judges become wholly unpredictable, then human affairs affected by those laws and decisions become chaotic. A contract signed today might be invalid tomorrow. The other reason is at least as important: if the principle of equal justice means anything, it means that similar cases should be decided in a similar manner. On the other hand, times change, and the Court can make mistakes. As Justice Felix Frankfurter once said, "Wisdom too often never comes, and so one ought not to reject it merely because it comes late."[44]

However compelling the arguments for flexibility, the pace of change can become dizzying. By one count the Court has overruled its own previous decisions in over 140 cases since 1810.[45] In fact it may have done it more often, because sometimes the Court does not say that it is abandoning a precedent, claiming instead that it is merely distinguishing the present case from a previous one.

A third measure of judicial power is the degree to which courts are willing to handle matters once left to the legislature. For example, the Court refused for a long time to hear a case about the size of congressional districts, no matter how unequal their populations.[46] The determination of congressional district boundaries was regarded as a **political ques-**

tion—that is, as a matter that the Constitution left entirely to another branch of government (in this case, Congress) to decide for itself. Then in 1962 the Court decided that it was competent after all to handle this matter, and the notion of a "political question" became a much less important (but by no means absent) barrier to judicial power.[47]

By all odds the most powerful indicator of judicial power can be found in the kinds of remedies that the courts will impose. A **remedy** is a judicial order setting forth what must be done to correct a situation that a judge believes to be wrong. In ordinary cases, such as when one person sues another, the remedy is straightforward: the loser must pay the winner for some injury that he or she has caused, or the loser must agree to abide by the terms of a contract he or she has broken, or the loser must promise not to do some unpleasant thing (such as dumping garbage on a neighbor's lawn). Today, however, judges design remedies that go far beyond what is required to do justice to the individual parties who actually appear in court. The remedies now imposed often apply to large groups and affect the circumstances under which thousands or even millions of people work, study, or live. For example, when a federal district judge in Alabama heard a case brought by a prison inmate in that state, he issued an order not simply to improve the lot of that prisoner but to revamp the administration of the entire prison system. The result was an improvement in the living conditions of many prisoners, at a cost to the state of an estimated $40 million a year. Similarly, a person who feels entitled to welfare payments that have been denied him or her may sue in court to get the money, and the court order will in all likelihood affect all welfare recipients. In one case certain court orders made an additional one hundred thousand people eligible for welfare.[48]

The basis for sweeping court orders can sometimes be found in the Constitution; the Alabama prison decision, for example, was based on the judge's interpretation of the Eighth Amendment, which prohibits "cruel and unusual punishments."[49] Others are based on court interpretations of federal laws. The Civil Rights Act of 1964 forbids discrimination on grounds of "race, color, or national origin" in any program receiving federal financial assistance. The Supreme Court interpreted that as meaning that the San Francisco school system was obliged to teach English to Chinese students unable to speak it.[50] Since a Supreme Court decision is the law of the land, the impact of that ruling was not limited to San Francisco. Local courts and legislatures elsewhere decided that that decision meant that classes must be taught in Spanish for Hispanic children. What Congress meant by the Civil Rights Act is not clear; it may or may not have believed that teaching Hispanic children in English rather than Spanish was a form of discrimination. What is important is that it was the Court, not Congress, that decided what Congress meant.

Views of Judicial Activism

Judicial activism has, of course, been controversial. Those who support it argue that the federal courts must correct injustices when the other branches of the federal government, or the states, refuse to do so. The courts are the institution of last resort for those without the votes or the influence to obtain new laws, and especially for the poor and powerless. After all, Congress and the state legislatures tolerated segregated public schools for decades. If the Supreme Court had not declared segregation unconstitutional in 1954, it might still be law today.

Those who criticize judicial activism rejoin that judges usually have no special expertise in matters of school administration, prison management, environmental protection, and so on; they are lawyers, expert in defining rights and duties but not in designing and managing complex institutions. Furthermore, however desirable court-declared rights and principles may be, implementing those principles means balancing the conflicting needs of various interest groups, raising and spending tax monies, and assessing the costs and benefits of complicated alternatives. Finally, judges are not elected; they are appointed and are thus immune to popular control. As a result, if they depart from their traditional role of making careful and cautious interpretations of what a law or the Constitution means and instead begin formulating wholly new policies, they become unelected legislators.

Some people think that we have activist courts because we have so many lawyers. The more we take matters to courts for resolution, the more likely it is

The activism of federal courts is exemplified by the sweeping orders they have issued designed to correct such problems as overcrowded prisons.

that the courts will become powerful. It is true that we have more lawyers in proportion to our population than most other nations. In 1982 there was one lawyer for every 400 Americans but only one for every 1,600 Britons, every 3,400 French, and every 7,000 Japanese.[51] But that may well be a symptom, not a cause, of court activity. As we suggested in Chapter 4, we have an adversary culture based on an emphasis on individual rights and an implicit antagonism between the people and the government. Generally speaking, lawyers do not create cases; contending interests do, thereby generating a demand for lawyers. Furthermore, we had more lawyers in relation to our population in 1900 than in 1970, yet the courts seventy years ago were far less active in

0123456789

A Debate: Constitutional Interpretation

Imagine that you are at a debate between two people with opposed views on how judges should interpret the Constitution (and its amendments). Study carefully the words that these two persons use in explaining their views, and then try to imagine how they would answer the questions given below. Finally, try to decide which theory you favor and how you would answer those questions.

On the basis of *original intent*

A jurisprudence of original intent . . . is not difficult to describe. Where the language of the Constitution is specific, it must be obeyed. Where there is a demonstrable consensus among the framers and ratifiers as to a principle stated or implied by the Constitution, it should be followed. Where there is ambiguity as to the precise meaning or reach of a constitutional provision, it should be interpreted and applied in a manner so as to at least not contradict the text of the Constitution itself.

—Edwin Meese III, former attorney general of the United States (1985)

How do you think Mr. Meese would answer the following questions? How would you?

1. How do we discover what the Framers of the Constitution and its amendments really intended? What if the supporters of, say, the First Amendment disagreed as to its meaning?

2. What if the intentions of the Framers profoundly offend our sense of justice? For example, the authors of the Fourteenth Amendment did not intend for it to outlaw racially segregated schools, yet most people today believe that such schools should be regarded as an unconstitutional violation of that amendment).

On the basis of *contemporary meaning*

[T]he genius of the Constitution rests not in any static meaning it might have had in a world that is dead and gone, but in the adaptability of its great principles to cope with current problems and current needs. What the constitutional fundamentals meant to the wisdom of other times cannot be their measure to the vision of our times.

—William J. Brennan, Jr., former justice of the Supreme Court (1985)

How do you think Justice Brennan would answer the following questions? How would you?

1. Why should judges, who are not elected, decide what the "contemporary meaning" of the Constitution is? Shouldn't these questions be decided by elected legislators or by the people, through the amendment process?

2. What is the "vision of our times" that judges should follow? Should judges be free to pick *any* "vision"? Or only liberal ones? Or conservative ones?

---

public affairs. In fact, in 1932 there were more court cases per 100,000 people than there were in 1972.[52]

A more plausible reason for activist courts has been the developments discussed earlier in this chapter that have made it easier for people to get standing in the courts, to pay for the costs of litigation, and to bring class-action suits. The courts and Congress have gone a long way toward allowing private citizens to become "private attorneys general." Making it easier to get into court increases the number of cases being heard. For example, in 1961 civil rights cases, prisoners' rights cases, and cases under the Social Security laws were relatively uncommon in federal court. Between 1961 and 1990 the increase in the number of such matters was phenomenal:

civil rights cases rose over sixtyfold and prisoners' petitions over fortyfold (see Figure 14.2). Such matters are the fastest-growing portion of the courts' civil workload.

Legislation and the Courts

An increase in cases will not by itself lead to sweeping remedies. For that to occur, the law must be sufficiently vague to permit judges wide latitude in interpreting it, and the judges must want to exercise that opportunity to the fullest. The Constitution is filled with words of seemingly ambiguous meaning—"due process of law," the "equal protection of the laws," the "privileges or immunities of citizens."

Such phrases may have been clear to the Framers, but to the Court they have become equivocal or elastic. How the Court has chosen to interpret such phrases has changed greatly over the last two centuries in ways that can be explained in part by the personal political beliefs of the justices.

Increasingly Congress has passed laws that also contain vague language, thereby adding immeasurably to the courts' opportunities for designing remedies. Various civil rights acts outlaw discrimination but do not say how one is to know whether discrimination has occurred or what should be done to correct it if it does occur. That is left to the courts and the bureaucracy. Various regulatory laws empower administrative agencies to do what the "public interest" requires but say little about how the public interest is to be defined. Laws intended to alleviate poverty or rebuild neighborhoods speak of "citizen participation" or "maximum feasible participation" but do not explain who the citizens are that should participate, or how much power they should have.

In addition to laws that require interpretation, other laws induce litigation. Almost every agency that regulates business will make decisions that cause the agency to be challenged in court—by business firms if the regulations go too far, by consumer or labor organizations if they do not go far enough. In 1988 the federal courts of appeals heard over three thousand cases in which they had to review the decision of a regulatory agency. In two-thirds of them the agency's position was supported; in the other third the agency was overruled.[53] Perhaps one-fifth of these cases arose out of agencies or programs that did not even exist in 1960. The federal government today is much more likely to be on the defensive in court than it was twenty or thirty years ago.

Finally, the attitudes of the judges powerfully affect what they will do, especially when the law gives them wide latitude. There have been very few studies of the attitudes of federal judges, but their decisions and opinions have been extensively analyzed—well enough, at least, to know that different judges often decide the same case in different ways. Conservative southern federal judges in the 1950s, for example, often resisted plans to desegregate public schools while judges with a different background authorized bold plans.[54] Some of the greatest disparities in judicial behavior can be found in the area of sentencing criminals.[55]

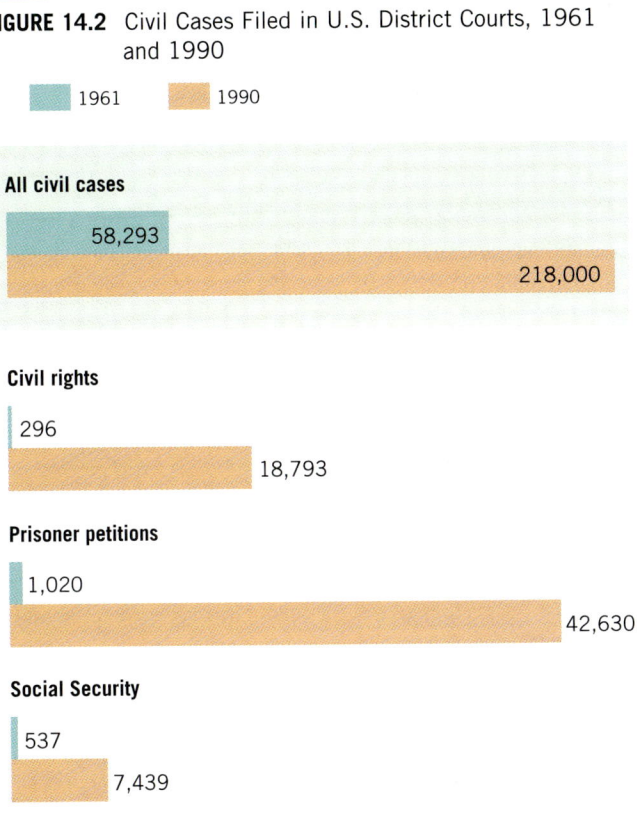

FIGURE 14.2 Civil Cases Filed in U.S. District Courts, 1961 and 1990

SOURCES: *Annual Report of the Director of the Administrative Office of the United States Courts,* 1975, Table 17. Updated by author.

Checks on Judicial Power

No institution of government, including the courts, operates without restraint. The fact that judges are not elected does not make them immune to public opinion or to the views of the other branches of government. How important these restraints are varies from case to case, but in the broad course of history they have been significant.

One restraint exists because of the very nature of courts. A judge has no police force or army; decisions that he or she makes can sometimes be resisted or ignored, *if* the person or organization resisting is not highly visible and is willing to run the risk of being caught and charged with contempt of court. For example, long after the Supreme Court had decided that praying and Bible reading could not take place in public schools,[56] schools all over the country were still allowing prayers and Bible reading.[57] Years

TRIVIA

The Supreme Court

Supreme Court justice who served the longest	*William O. Douglas: 36 years (1939–1975)*
Only Supreme Court justice to run for president	*Charles Evans Hughes (resigned from Court in 1916 to seek presidency; lost to Woodrow Wilson)*
Only president to become Supreme Court justice	*William Howard Taft (president, 1909–1913; chief justice of the United States, 1921–1930)*
First Catholic Supreme Court justice	*Roger B. Taney (1836–1864)*
First Jewish Supreme Court justice	*Louis Brandeis (1916–1939)*
First black Supreme Court justice	*Thurgood Marshall (1967–1991)*
First woman Supreme Court justice	*Sandra Day O'Connor (1981 to present)*
Only Supreme Court justice to have been impeached	*Samuel Chase (impeached by House in 1804; acquitted by Senate)*
Only Supreme Court justice whose grandson also served on the Court	*John Harlan (1877–1911), whose grandson, John Harlan, served from 1954 to 1971*

Charles Evans Hughes

Sandra Day O'Connor

after the Court declared segregated schools to be unconstitutional, scores of school systems remained segregated. On the other hand, when a failure to comply is easily detected and punished, the courts' power is usually unchallenged. When the Supreme Court declared the income tax to be unconstitutional in 1895, income tax collections promptly ceased. When the Court in 1952 declared illegal President Truman's effort to seize the steel mills in order to stop a strike, the management of the mills was immediately returned to their owners.

Congress and the Courts

Congress has a number of ways of checking the judiciary. It can gradually alter the composition of the judiciary by the kinds of appointments that the Senate is willing to confirm, or it can impeach judges that it does not like. Fifteen federal judges have been the object of impeachment proceedings in our history, and nine others have resigned when such proceedings seemed likely. Of the fifteen who were impeached, seven were acquitted, four were convicted, and one resigned. The most recent convictions were those of Alcee Hastings of Florida and Walter Nixon of Mississippi, both in 1989.[58] In practice, however, confirmation and impeachment proceedings do not make much of an impact on the federal courts because simple policy disagreements are not generally regarded as adequate grounds for voting against a judicial nominee or for starting an impeachment effort.

Congress can alter the number of judges, though; and by increasing the number sharply, it can give a president a chance to appoint judges to his liking. As described above, a "court-packing" plan was proposed (unsuccessfully) by Franklin Roosevelt in 1937 specifically to change the political persuasion of the Supreme Court. In 1978 Congress passed a bill creating 152 new federal district and appellate judges, to help ease the workload of the federal judiciary. This bill gave President Carter a chance to appoint over 40 percent of the federal bench. In 1984 an additional eighty-four judgeships were created; by 1988 President Reagan had appointed about half of all federal judges. In 1990 an additional seventy-two judges were authorized.

During and after the Civil War, Congress may have been trying to influence Supreme Court deci-

When the States Go Beyond the Supreme Court

*A*s the U.S. Supreme Court increasingly becomes a less activist body, interests as different as the abortion-rights movement and the National Rifle Association are looking to state courts and state constitutions for help. In many instances, the states have obliged by going beyond Supreme Court rulings. Here are some examples.

SOURCE: *National Journal* (October 5, 1991): 2400. Copyright © 1991 by National Journal, Inc. All rights reserved. Reprinted by permission.

[Map of the United States with colored dots indicating states and categories]

- **Abortion**
  Allowed state medicaid financing of abortions

- **Criminal Law**
  Rejected good-faith exception to the exclusionary rule

- **Death Penalty**
  Barred execution of the mentally incompetent

- **Education**
  Required equal spending in all school districts

- **Freedom of the Press**
  Held that opinion is protected from libel suits under state constitution

- **Gay Rights**
  Overturned state sodomy statutes (20 other states have done the same through legislation)

- **Gun Control**
  Found a constitutional right to own a handgun

sions when it changed the size of the Court three times in six years (raising it from nine to ten in 1863, lowering it again from ten to seven in 1866, and raising it again from seven to nine in 1869).

Congress and the states can also undo a Supreme Court decision interpreting the Constitution by amending that document. This happens, but rarely: the Eleventh Amendment was ratified to prevent a citizen from suing a state in federal court; the Thirteenth, Fourteenth, and Fifteenth were ratified to undo the *Dred Scott* decision regarding slavery; the Sixteenth was added to make it constitutional for Congress to pass an income tax; and the Twenty-sixth to give the vote to eighteen-year-olds in state elections. In 1983 a proposed amendment to authorize prayer in public schools failed to get the necessary two-thirds vote of the Senate. In 1997, an amendment to ban flag-burning passed the House and awaits action in the Republican Senate.

On over thirty occasions Congress has merely repassed a law that the Court has declared unconstitutional. In one case a bill to aid farmers, voided in 1935, was accepted by the Court in slightly revised form three years later.[59] (In the meantime, of course, the Court had changed its collective mind about the New Deal.)

One of the most powerful potential sources of control over the federal courts, however, is the authority of Congress to decide what the entire jurisdiction of the lower courts and the appellate jurisdiction of the Supreme Court shall be. In theory Congress could prevent matters on which it did not want federal courts to act from ever coming before the courts. In 1868 just this happened. A Mississippi newspaper editor named McCardle was jailed by federal military authorities who had occupied the defeated South. McCardle asked the federal district court for a writ of habeas corpus to get him out of custody; when the district court rejected his plea, he appealed to the Supreme Court. Congress at that

Police escorting black students being bused to a once all-white high school in Boston.

time was fearful that the Court might find the laws on which its Reconstruction policy was based (and under which McCardle was in jail) unconstitutional. To prevent that from happening, it passed a bill withdrawing from the Supreme Court appellate jurisdiction in cases of this sort. The Court conceded that Congress could do this and thus dismissed the case because it no longer had jurisdiction.[60]

Congress has threatened to withdraw jurisdiction on other occasions, and the mere existence of the threat may have influenced the nature of Court decisions. In the 1950s, for example, congressional opinion was hostile to Court decisions in the field of civil liberties and civil rights, and legislation was proposed that would have curtailed the Court's jurisdiction in these areas. It did not pass, but the Court may have allowed the threat to temper its decisions.[61] On the other hand, as congressional resistance to the Roosevelt court-packing plan shows, the Supreme Court enjoys a good deal of prestige in the nation, even among people who disagree with some of its decisions, and so passing laws that would frontally attack it would not be easy except perhaps in times of national crisis.

Furthermore, laws narrowing jurisdiction or restricting the kinds of remedies that a court can impose are often blunt instruments that might not achieve the purposes of their proponents. Suppose that you, as a member of Congress, would like to prevent the federal courts from ordering schoolchildren to be bused for the purpose of achieving racial balance in the schools. If you denied the Supreme Court appellate jurisdiction in this matter, you would leave the lower federal courts and all state courts free to do as they wish, and many of them would go on ordering busing. If you wanted to attack that problem, you could propose a law that would deny to all federal courts the right to order busing as a remedy for racial imbalance. But the courts would still be free to order busing (and of course a lot of busing goes on even without court orders), provided that they did not say that it was for the purpose of achieving racial balance. (It could be for the purpose of "facilitating desegregation" or making possible "redistricting.") Naturally you could always make it illegal for children to enter a school bus for any reason, but then many children would not be able to get to school at all. Finally, the Supreme Court might well decide that if busing is essential to achieve a constitutional right, then any congressional law prohibiting such busing would itself be unconstitutional. Trying to think through how *that* dilemma would be resolved is like trying to visualize two kangaroos simultaneously jumping into each other's pouches.

Public Opinion and the Courts

Though they are not elected, judges read the same newspapers as members of Congress, and thus they, too, are aware of public opinion, especially elite opinion. Though it may be going too far to say that the Supreme Court follows the election returns, it is nonetheless true that the Court is sensitive to certain bodies of opinion, especially of those elites—liberal or conservative—to which its members happen to be attuned. The justices will keep in mind historical cases in which their predecessors, by blatantly disregarding public opinion, very nearly destroyed the legitimacy of the Court itself. This was the case with the *Dred Scott* decision, which infuriated the North and was widely disobeyed. No such crisis exists today, but it is altogether possible that changing political moods affect the kinds of remedies that judges will think appropriate.

Opinion not only restrains the courts; it may also energize them. The most activist periods in Supreme Court history have coincided with times when the political system was undergoing profound and lasting changes. The assertion by the Supreme Court, under John Marshall's leadership, of the principles of national supremacy and judicial review occurred at the time when the Jeffersonian Republicans were coming to power and their opponents, the Federalists, were collapsing as an organized party. The proslavery decisions of the Taney Court came when the nation was so divided along sectional and ideological lines as to make almost any Court decision on this matter unpopular. Supreme Court review of economic regulation in the 1890s and 1900s came at a time when the political parties were realigning and the Republicans were acquiring dominance that was to last for several decades. The Court decisions of the 1930s corresponded to another period of partisan realignment. (The meaning of a realigning election was discussed in Chapter 8.)

Since 1966 pollsters have been measuring how much confidence the public has in the Supreme Court. The results are shown in Figure 14.3. The percentage of people saying that they have a "great deal of confidence" in the Court rose sharply from

FIGURE 14.3 Patterns of Public Confidence in the Court, 1974–1996

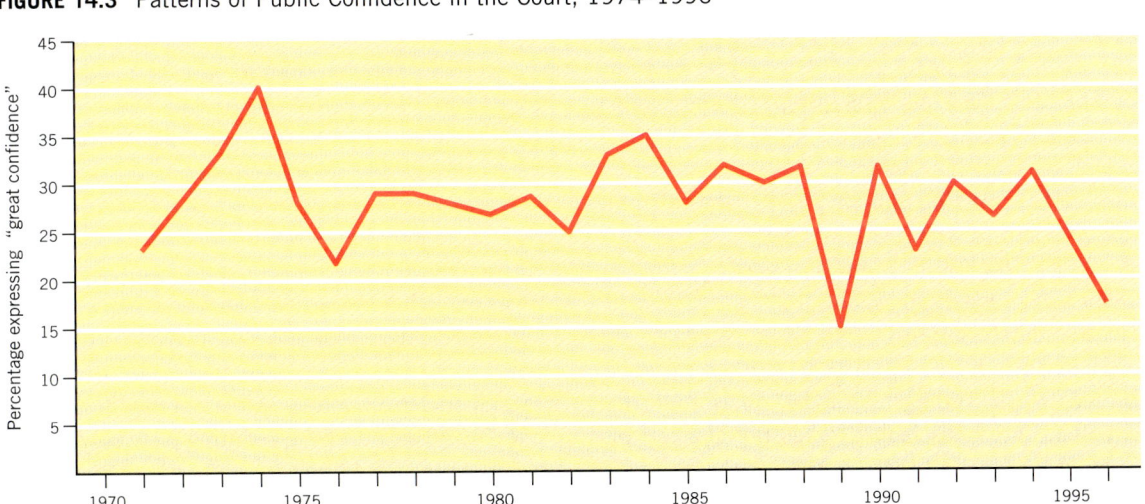

SOURCES: For 1966–1984: Gregory A. Caldeira, "Neither the Purse Nor the Sword: Dynamics of Public Confidence in the Supreme Court," *American Political Science Review* 80 (1988): 1213; for 1987–1991: *The Gallup Poll: Public Opinion 1991* (Wilmington, Del.: Scholarly Resources, Inc., 1992), 213. Reprinted by permission of American Political Science Review.

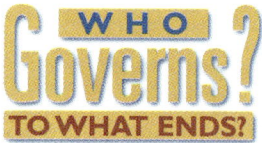

The Courts, the People, and School Prayer

Since the early 1960s the federal judiciary, led by the U.S. Supreme Court, has issued numerous decisions limiting the freedom of children to pray in public schools. In August 1995 the Clinton administration sent to all fifteen thousand U.S. public school superintendents guidelines on the do's and don'ts of school prayer, based on Supreme Court decisions and existing statutes. But the courts are far from having determined precisely how, when, or even whether school prayer is permitted.

One thing is increasingly clear, however: many Americans, arguably most, oppose some or all of the existing court-mandated restrictions on school prayer. For example, a 1995 opinion survey found that by a margin of 71 to 25 percent, Americans favor an amendment to the U.S. Constitution that would permit prayers to be spoken in public schools. About 46 percent of Americans are "very strongly" in favor of such an amendment, and only 14 percent are "very strongly opposed."

To most Americans, "school prayer" does not necessarily mean either spoken prayer or Christian prayer. Some four out of five Americans believe that any prayers spoken in school should not reflect only Christian beliefs and values. Rather, most Americans believe that in addition to spoken Christian prayer, spoken Jewish, Muslim, and Hindu prayers should be allowed. If given the choice, 70 percent of Americans would prefer that public schools favor silent contemplation over spoken prayer. And while three-quarters of Americans believe that allowing spoken prayer in local public schools would be offensive to more than a tiny percentage of students' parents, 55 percent say such prayers should not be allowed if spoken prayer were to offend a large number of parents.

How much, if at all, should the apparent gap between court doctrine and public opinion on school prayer be closed? Who should decide, and at what level of government? For instance, whatever your personal view on the issue, do you think the matter would be best left to the judicial process, referred to the state legislatures, or put to the test nationwide by attempting to enact a constitutional amendment? If the issue were to be decided by state legislatures, do you think it likely that the resulting laws and procedures governing school prayer would mirror public opinion? Or do you think well-organized groups on one side of the issue or the other would dominate the debate? Has there been any effort to limit the restrictions on school prayer in your home state, and if so, what was the result? How have recent school prayer amendment efforts within Congress fared? Find out.

SOURCE: Gallup Organization July 1995 Newsletter Archive, vol. 60, no. 11, July 20, 1995.

1971 to 1974, fell again until 1976, seesawed up and down until 1989, took a sharp dip and then recovered from 1989 to 1991, and again seesawed before declining in 1996. These movements seem to reflect the public's reaction not only to what the Court does but also to what the government as a whole is doing. The decline in popular support in the late 1960s was probably the result of a spate of controversial Court decisions enlarging the rights of the accused; the upturn in the early 1970s was probably caused by the Watergate scandal, an episode that simultaneously discredited the presidency and boosted the stock of those institutions (such as the courts) that seemed to be checking the abuses of the White House. The gradual upturn in the 1980s may have reflected a general restoration of public confidence in government during that decade.[62]

Though popular support is now relatively low for the Supreme Court, this decline has so far not resulted in any legal checks being placed on it. In the 1970s and 1980s several bills were introduced in Congress that would have restricted the jurisdiction of federal courts over busing for purposes of racial integration or altered the Supreme Court's decisions regarding school prayer and abortion. None passed.

The changes that have occurred in the Court have been caused by changes in its personnel. Presidents Nixon and Reagan attempted to produce a less activist Court by appointing justices who were more inclined to be strict constructionists and conservatives. To some extent they succeeded: Justices Kennedy, O'Connor, Rehnquist, and Scalia were certainly less inclined than Justice Thurgood Marshall to find new rights in the Constitution or to overturn the decisions of state legislatures. But as of yet there has been no wholesale retreat from the positions staked out by the Warren Court. As noted above, a Nixon appointee, Justice Blackmun, wrote the decision making antiabortion laws unconstitutional; and another Nixon appointee, Chief Justice Burger, wrote the opinion upholding court-ordered school busing to achieve racial integration. A Reagan appointee, Justice O'Connor, voted to uphold a right to an abortion. The Supreme Court has become somewhat less willing to impose restraints on police practices, and it has not blocked the use of the death penalty. But in general the major features of Court activism and liberalism during the Warren years—school integration, sharper limits on police practice, greater freedom of expression—have remained intact.

The reasons for the growth in court activism are clear. One is the sheer growth in the size and scope of the government as a whole. The courts have come to play a larger role in our lives because Congress, the bureaucracy, and the president have come to play larger ones. In 1890 hardly anybody would have thought of asking Congress—much less the courts—to make rules governing the participation of women in college sports or the district boundaries of state legislatures. Today such rules are commonplace, and the courts are inevitably drawn into interpreting them.

The other reason for increased activism is the acceptance by a large number of judges, conservative as well as liberal, of the legislative, or activist, view of the function of the courts. If courts once existed solely to "settle disputes," today they also exist in the eyes of their members to "solve problems."

SUMMARY

An independent judiciary with the power of judicial review—the right to decide the constitutionality of acts of Congress, the executive branch, and state governments—can be a potent political force in American life. That influence has been realized from the earliest days of the nation, when Marshall and Taney put the Supreme Court at the center of the most important issues of the time. From 1787 to 1865 the Supreme Court was preoccupied with the establishment of national supremacy. From 1865 to

1937 it struggled with defining the scope of political power over the economy. In the present era it has sought to expand personal liberties.

The scope of the courts' political influence has increasingly widened as various groups and interests have acquired access to the courts, as the judges serving on them have developed a more activist stance, and as Congress has passed more laws containing vague or equivocal language. Whereas in other political arenas (the electorate, Congress, the bureaucracy) the influence of contending groups is largely dependent on their size, intensity, prestige, and political resources, the influence of contending groups before the courts depends chiefly on their arguments and the attitudes of the judges.

Though the Supreme Court is the pinnacle of the federal judiciary, most decisions, including many important ones, are made by the twelve courts of appeals and the ninety-four district courts. The Supreme Court can control its own workload by deciding when to grant certiorari. It has become easier for citizens and groups to gain access to the federal courts (through class-action suits, by amicus curiae briefs, by laws that require government agencies to pay legal fees, and because of the activities of private groups such as the NAACP and the ACLU).

At the same time, the courts have widened the reach of their decisions by issuing orders that cover whole classes of citizens or affect the management of major public and private institutions. However, the courts can overstep the bounds of their authority and bring upon themselves a counterattack from both the public and Congress. Congress has the right to control much of the courts' jurisdiction, but it rarely does so. As a result the ability of judges to make law is only infrequently challenged directly.

KEY TERMS

judicial review   *p. 439*

strict-constructionist approach   *p. 440*

activist approach   *p. 440*

constitutional court   *p. 447*

district courts   *p. 447*

courts of appeals   *p. 447*

legislative court   *p. 447*

litmus test   *p. 449*

federal-question cases   *p. 450*

diversity cases   *p. 450*

civil law   *p. 452*

criminal law   *p. 452*

writ of certiorari   *p. 452*

in forma pauperis   *p. 454*

fee shifting   *p. 454*

plaintiff   *p. 454*

standing   *p. 454*

sovereign immunity   *p. 455*

class-action suit   *p. 455*

brief   *p. 457*

amicus curiae   *p. 457*

per curiam opinion   *p. 458*

opinion of the Court   *p. 458*

concurring opinion   *p. 458*

dissenting opinion   *p. 458*

stare decisis   *p. 460*

political question   *p. 460*

remedy   *p. 460*

SUGGESTED READINGS

Abraham, Henry J. *The Judicial Process.* 6th ed. New York: Oxford University Press, 1993. An excellent, comprehensive survey of how the federal courts are organized and function.

Cardozo, Benjamin N. *The Nature of the Judicial Process.* New Haven, Conn.: Yale University Press, 1921. Important statement of how judges make decisions, by a former Supreme Court justice.

Carp, Robert A., and Ronald Stidham. *The Federal Courts.* Washington, D.C.: Congressional Quarterly Press, 1985. Excellent summary of the workings of the lower federal courts.

Ely, John Hart. *Democracy and Distrust.* Cambridge, Mass.: Harvard University Press, 1980. Effort to create a theory of judicial review that is neither strict-constructionist nor activist.

Hall, Kermit L., ed. *The Oxford Companion to the Supreme Court of the United States.* New York: Oxford University Press, 1992. Everything you ever wanted to know about the Supreme Court, its justices, and its major decisions, arranged in more than one thousand alphabetical entries.

Lasser, William. *The Limits of Judicial Power.* Chapel Hill, N.C.: University of North Carolina Press, 1988. Shows how the Court through history has withstood the political storms created by its more controversial decisions.

Lewis, Anthony. *Gideon's Trumpet.* New York: Random House, 1964. Fascinating account of how a pauper in jail persuaded the Supreme Court to change the rules governing criminal trials.

McCloskey, Robert G. *The American Supreme Court.* 2nd ed. Edited by Sanford Levinson. Chicago: University of Chicago Press, 1994. Superb brief history of the Supreme Court, updated by one of McCloskey's former students who now teaches law at the University of Texas.

O'Brien, David M. *Storm Center: The Supreme Court and American Politics.* New York: Norton, 1986. Insightful survey of the workings of the Supreme Court.

Rabkin, Jeremy. *Judicial Compulsions.* New York: Basic Books, 1989. Explains (and argues against) the extensive Court intervention in the work of administrative agencies.

Wolfe, Christopher. *The Rise of Modern Judicial Review.* New York: Basic Books, 1986. An excellent history of judicial review from 1787 to the present.

PART FOUR

The Politics of Public Policy

"In the extended republic of the United States, and among the great variety of interests, parties, and sects which it embraces, a coalition of a majority of the whole society could seldom take place on any other principles than those of justice and the general good."

— FEDERALIST NO. 51

472

15

The Policy-Making Process

★ Deciding what goes on the political agenda

★ A model for explaining the politics of different policy issues

★ Perceived costs and benefits of programs

★ The case of business regulation

★ Perception of policy costs and benefits

If our political system handled all issues in the same way, this study of American government would be at an end. Now that we have seen how Congress, the presidency, the courts, the parties, the mass media, and other interest groups operate, we should be able to explain how policies get made (or not made). Some observers do argue that the system always operates more or less the same way—to serve corporate interests (the Marxist view), to manage conflict among organized groups (the pluralist view), to sustain the dominance of a pervasive bureaucracy (the Weberian view), and so on. In this part we shall look at how policies are actually made to see whether any of these generalizations are correct.

Consider some outcomes that need to be explained if we are to understand the political influence wielded by just one kind of institution—the business corporation. Certain oil companies were once able to persuade the government to restrict sharply the amount of foreign oil imported into the United States, to give them preferential tax treatment, and to permit them to drill for new oil just about anywhere they liked. Today the restrictions on foreign oil imports have ended, the tax breaks the oil companies enjoy have been reduced considerably (though they still exist), and their freedom to drill in certain places, particularly offshore locations, has been restricted.

Automobile manufacturers once faced virtually no federal controls on the products they manufactured; now they face many. In the past some corporations have been regulated in ways that have increased their profitability (the airlines), reduced it (the railroads), or had no appreciable effect one way or the other (electric utilities). These outcomes of government action or inaction are complicated. To understand why they happen, we need some theory of policy-making. This chapter will provide one; subsequent chapters will apply it.

Setting the Agenda

The most important decision that affects policy-making is also the least noticed one: deciding what to make policy *about,* or in the language of political science, deciding what belongs on the **political agenda.** We take for granted that politics is about certain familiar issues such as taxes, energy, welfare, and civil rights. We forget that there is nothing inevitable about having these issues—rather than some other ones—on the nation's agenda. At one time it was unconstitutional for the federal government to levy income taxes; energy was a nonissue because everybody (or at least everybody who could chop down trees for a fireplace) had enough; welfare was something for cities and towns to handle; and civil rights were supposed to be a matter of private choice rather than government action. Until the 1930s the national political agenda was quite short, and even in the 1950s many people would have been astonished or upset to be told that the federal government was supposed to worry about the environment, consumerism, or civil rights.

"He who decides what politics is about runs the country."[1] This is a statement of profound significance, though it exaggerates the extent to which somebody—some person—actually "decides" what politics is all about. The statement correctly suggests that at any given time certain shared beliefs determine what is legitimate (proper, right) for the government to do. This legitimacy is affected by several forces:

- Shared political values—for example, if many people believe that poverty is the result of individual failure rather than social forces, then there is no reason for a government program to combat poverty.

- The weight of custom and tradition—people will usually accept what the government has customarily done, even if they are leery of what it proposes to do.

- The impact of events—wars, depressions, and the like alter our sense of the proper role of government.

- Changes in the way political elites think and talk about politics.

The Legitimate Scope of Government Action

Because many people believe that whatever the government now does it ought to continue doing, and because changes in attitudes and the impact of events tend to increase the number of things that government does, the scope of legitimate government action is always getting larger. As a result the scope of what it is illegitimate for the government to do steadily gets smaller. This means that today we hear far fewer debates about the legitimacy of a proposed government policy than we heard in the 1920s or the 1930s. The existence of "big government" is sustained by these expanded beliefs about legitimacy and is not the consequence of some sinister power grab by politicians or bureaucrats. When President Gerald Ford, a Republican, ran for election in 1976, a favorite slogan of his was that a government big enough to give you everything you want is also big enough to take away everything you have. No doubt he thought that he was criticizing liberal Democrats. But it was his immediate predecessor, President Nixon, also a Republican, who had imposed peacetime wage and price controls and proposed a guaranteed annual income for every family, working or not working. It was another Republican president, Dwight Eisenhower, who had sent federal troops to Little Rock, Arkansas, to enforce a school-desegregation order. And it was yet another Republican president, Ronald Reagan, who was in office when federal payments to farmers grew to be six times larger than they had been in the 1970s. For better or worse, the expansion of government has been the result, fundamentally, of a nonpartisan process.

Popular views on the legitimate scope of government action, and thus on the kinds of issues that ought to be on the political agenda, are changed by the impact of events. During wartime, especially during a war in which the United States has been attacked, the people expect the government to do whatever is necessary to win, whether or not such actions are clearly authorized by the Constitution. (As we saw in Chapter 13, the federal bureaucracy enjoys its most rapid growth in wartime.) A depression, such as the one that began in 1929, also leads people to expect the government to do something. As we shall see in Chapter 17, public opinion favored federal action to deal with the problems of the unemployed, the elderly, and the poor well in advance of the actual decisions of the government to take action. A coal-mine disaster leads to an enlarged role for the government in promoting mine safety. A series of airplane hijackings leads to a change in public opinion so great that what once would have been unthinkable—requiring all passengers at airports to be searched before boarding their flights—becomes routine. Most citizens probably oppose rationing; but let there be a sharp increase in gasoline prices, and the demands for rationing become loud.

But sometimes the government enlarges its agenda of policy issues, often dramatically, without any crisis or widespread public demand. This may happen even at a time when the conditions at which a policy is directed are improving. There was no public demand for government action to make automobiles safer before 1966, when a law was passed imposing safety standards on cars. Though the number of auto fatalities (per 100 million miles driven) had gone up slightly just before the law was passed, the long-term trend in highway deaths had been more or less steadily downward. The Occupational Safety and Health Act was passed in 1970 at a time when the number of industrial deaths (per 100,000 workers) had been steadily dropping for almost twenty years.[2] Programs to combat urban poverty and unemployment were adopted in the mid-1960s at a time when the number of persons, black as well as white, living below the poverty line was declining and when the adult unemployment rate—for blacks as well as whites—was lower than it had been at any time in the preceding ten years.[3]

It is not easy to explain why the government adds new issues to its agenda and adopts new programs when there is little public demand and when, in fact, there has been an improvement in the conditions to which the policies are addressed. In general the explanation may be found in the behavior of groups, the workings of institutions, and the opinions of political elites.

Groups Many policies are the result of small groups of people enlarging the scope of government by their demands. Sometimes these are organized interests (for example, corporations or unions); sometimes they are intense but unorganized groups (urban minorities). The organized groups often

An oil spill on a beach is one event that changed the political agenda.

work quietly, behind the scenes; the intense, unorganized ones may take their causes to the streets.

Organized labor favored a tough federal safety law governing factories and other workplaces not because it was unaware that factory conditions had been improving but because the standards by which union leaders and members judged working conditions had risen even faster. As people became better off, conditions that once were thought normal suddenly became intolerable. When Alexis de Tocqueville sought to explain the French Revolution, he observed that citizens are most restless and easily aroused not when they are living in abject poverty or under grinding repression but when they have started to become better off.[4] Social scientists sometimes refer to this as a sense of "relative deprivation."

On occasion a group expresses in violent ways its dissatisfaction with what it judges to be intolerable conditions. The black riots in American cities during the mid-1960s had a variety of causes, and people participated out of a variety of motives. For many, rioting was a way of expressing pent-up anger at what they regarded as an unresponsive and unfair society. This sense of relative deprivation—of being worse off than one thinks one *ought* to be—helps explain why so large a proportion of the rioters were not uneducated, unemployed recent migrants to the city, but rather young men and women born in the North, educated in its schools, and employed in its factories.[5] Life under these conditions turned out to be not what they had come to expect or what they were prepared to tolerate.

The new demands of such groups need not result in an enlarged political agenda, and they do not when society and its governing institutions are confident of the rightness of the existing state of affairs. Unions could have been voted down on the occupational safety bill; rioting blacks could have been jailed and ignored. At one time exactly this would have happened. But society itself had changed: many people who were not workers sympathized with the plight of the injured worker and distrusted the good intentions of business in this matter. Many whites felt that a constructive as well as a punitive response to the urban riots was required and thus urged the formation of commissions to study—and the passage of laws to deal with—the problems of inner-city life. Such changes in the values and beliefs of people generally—or at least of people in key government positions—are an essential part of any explanation of why policies not demanded by public opinion nonetheless become part of the political agenda.

Institutions Among the institutions whose influence on agenda-setting has become especially important are the courts, the bureaucracy, and the Senate.

The courts can make decisions that force the hand of the other branches of government. When in 1954 the Supreme Court ordered schools desegregated, Congress and the White House could no longer ignore the issue. Local resistance to implementing the order led President Eisenhower to send troops to Little Rock, Arkansas, despite his dislike for using force against local governments. When the Supreme Court ruled in 1973 that the states could not ban abortions during the first trimester of pregnancy, abortion suddenly became a national political issue. Right-to-life activists campaigned to reverse the Court decision or, failing that, to prevent federal funds from being used to pay for abortions. Pro-choice activists fought to prevent the Court from changing its mind and to get federal funding for abortions. In these and many other cases the courts act like tripwires: when activated, they set off a chain reaction of events that alters the political agenda and creates a new constellation of political forces.

The bureaucracy has acquired a new significance in American politics not simply because of its size or power but also because it is now a source of political innovation. At one time the federal government *reacted* to events in society and to demands from segments of society; ordinarily it did not itself propose changes and new ideas. Today the bureaucracy is so large, and includes within it so great a variety of experts and advocates, that it has become a *source* of policy proposals as well as an implementer of those that become law. Daniel Patrick Moynihan called this the "professionalization of reform," by which he meant, in part, that the government bureaucracy had begun to think up problems for government to solve rather than simply to respond to the problems identified by others.[6] In the 1930s many of the key elements of the New Deal—Social Security, unemployment compensation, public housing, old-age benefits—were ideas devised by nongovernment experts and intellectuals here and abroad and then, as the crisis of the depression deepened, taken up by the federal government. In the 1960s, by contrast, most of the measures that became known as part of Lyndon Johnson's "Great Society"—federal aid to education, manpower development and training, Medicare and Medicaid, the "War on Poverty," the "safe-streets" act providing federal aid to local law-enforcement agencies—were developed, designed, and advocated by government officials, bureaucrats, and their political allies.

Chief among these political allies are United States senators and their staffs. Once the Senate was best described as a club that moved slowly, debated endlessly, and resisted, under the leadership of conservative southern Democrats, the plans of liberal presidents. With the collapse of the one-party South and the increase in the number of liberal activist senators, the Senate became in the 1960s an incubator for developing new policies and building national constituencies.[7] As the Senate became more conservative in the 1980s, it retained the initiative, but now on behalf of reversing some of the changes wrought earlier. The Senate has thus become one of the sources of political change rather than, as the Founders intended, a balance wheel designed to moderate change.[8] That senators are tempted to run for president magnifies this tendency. When senators such as Edward M. Kennedy, George McGovern, Robert Dole, Gary Hart, Edmund Muskie, Joseph Biden, Albert Gore, and Paul Simon decide to try for the presidency, they have an incentive to seek out new issues and raise new proposals as a way of attracting attention.

Media   Finally, the national press can either help place new matters on the agenda or publicize those matters placed there by others. There was a close correlation between the political attention given in the Senate to proposals for new safety standards for industry, coal mines, and automobiles and the amount of space devoted to these questions in the pages of the *New York Times.* Newspaper interest in the matter, low before the issue was placed on the agenda, peaked at about the time that the bill was passed.[9] It is hard, of course, to decide which is cause and which effect. The press may have stimulated congressional interest in the matter or merely reported on what Congress had already decided to pursue. Nonetheless, the press must choose which of thousands of proposals it will cover. The beliefs of editors and reporters led it to select the safety issue. In later chapters we shall discuss the kinds of issues for which the national press is important.

In short, the political agenda can change because of changes in popular attitudes, elite interest, critical events, or government actions. An overly simple but essentially correct generalization might be this: popular attitudes usually change slowly, often in response to critical events; elite attitudes and government actions are more volatile and interdependent and thus change more quickly, often in response to each other.

Making a Decision

Once an issue is on the political agenda, its nature affects the kind of politicking that ensues. Some issues provoke intense interest group conflict; others allow one group to prevail almost unchallenged. Some issues involve ideological appeals to broad national constituencies; others involve quiet bargaining in congressional offices. We all know that private groups try to influence government policies; we often forget that the nature of the issues with which government is dealing influences the kinds of groups that become politically active.

One way to understand how an issue affects the distribution of political power among groups and institutions is to examine what appear to be the costs and benefits of the proposed policy. The **cost** is any burden, monetary or nonmonetary, that some people must bear, or think that they must bear, if the policy is adopted. The costs of a government spending program are the taxes that it entails; the costs of a school-desegregation plan may include the need to have children bused to schools away from home; the cost of a foreign policy initiative may be the in-

Crises, such as midwestern floods, require presidential action.

creased chance of having the nation drawn into war. The **benefit** is any satisfaction, monetary or non-monetary, that people believe that they will enjoy if the policy is adopted. The benefits of a government spending program are the payments, subsidies, or contracts received by some people; the benefits of a school-desegregation plan include any improvement in educational opportunity, attainment, or motivation; the benefits of a foreign policy initiative may include the enhanced security of the nation, the protection of a valued ally, or the vindication of some important principle such as human rights.

Two aspects of these costs and benefits should be borne in mind. First, it is the *perception* of costs and benefits that affects politics. People may think that the cost of an auto-emission-control system is paid by the manufacturer, when it is actually passed on to the consumer in the form of higher prices and reduced performance. Political conflict over pollution control will take one form when people think that Ford and GM pay the costs and another form when they think that the consumers pay.

Second, people take into account not only who benefits but also whether it is *legitimate* for that group to benefit. When programs providing financial assistance to women with dependent children were first developed in the early part of this century, they were relatively noncontroversial because people saw the money as going to widows and orphans who deserved such aid. Later on giving aid to mothers

with dependent children became controversial because some people now perceived the recipients not as deserving widows but as sexually loose women who had never married. Whatever the truth of the matter, the program had lost some of its legitimacy because the beneficiaries were no longer seen as "deserving." By the same token, groups once thought undeserving, such as men out of work, were later thought to be entitled to aid, and thus the unemployment compensation program acquired a legitimacy that it once lacked.

Politics is in large measure a process of raising and settling disputes over who *will* benefit or pay for a program and who *ought* to benefit or pay. Since beliefs about the results of a program and the rightness of those results are matters of opinion, it is evident that ideas are at least as important as interests in shaping politics. In recent years ideas have become especially important with the rise of issues whose consequences are largely intangible, such as abortion, school prayer, and racial integration.

Though perceptions about costs and benefits change, most people most of the time prefer government programs that provide substantial benefits to them at low cost. This rather obvious fact can have important implications for how politics is carried out. In a political system based on some measure of popular rule, public officials have a strong incentive to offer programs that confer—or appear to confer—benefits on people with costs that are either

Highway safety was always a problem, but it did not become an issue on the national political agenda until after politicians and policy entrepreneurs found a way to dramatize it.

FIGURE 15.1 A Way of Classifying and Explaining the Politics of Different Policy Issues

PERCEIVED COSTS

	Distributed	Concentrated
Distributed	**Majoritarian Politics**	**Entrepreneurial Politics**
Concentrated	**Client Politics**	**Interest-group Politics**

PERCEIVED BENEFITS

small in amount, remote in time, or borne by "somebody else." Policies that seem to impose high, immediate costs in return for small or remote benefits will be avoided, or enacted with a minimum of publicity, or proposed only in response to a real or apparent crisis.

Ordinarily no president would propose a policy that would immediately raise the cost of fuel, even if he were convinced that future supplies of oil and gasoline were likely to be exhausted unless higher prices reduced current consumption. But when a crisis occurs, such as the Arab oil cartel's price increases beginning in 1973, it becomes possible for the president to offer such proposals—as did Nixon, Ford, and Carter in varying ways. Even then, however, people are reluctant to bear increased costs, and thus many are led to dispute the president's claim that an emergency actually exists. Walter Mondale probably lost votes when he promised in 1984 that, if elected, he would raise taxes in order to cut the deficit.

These entirely human responses to the perceived costs and benefits of proposed policies can be organized into a simple theory of politics.[10] It is based on the observation that the costs and benefits of a policy may be *widely distributed* (spread over many, most, or even all citizens) or *narrowly concentrated* (limited to a relatively small number of citizens or to some identifiable, organized group). For instance, a widely distributed cost would include an income tax, a Social Security tax, or a high rate of crime; a widely distributed benefit might include retirement benefits for all citizens, clean air, national security, or low crime rates. Examples of narrowly concentrated costs include the expenditures by a factory to reduce its pollution, government regulations im-

posed on doctors and hospitals participating in the Medicare program, or restrictions on freedom of speech imposed on a dissident political group. Examples of narrowly concentrated benefits include subsidies to farmers or merchant ship companies, the enlarged freedom to speak and protest afforded a dissident group, or protection against competition given to an industry because of favorable government regulation.

The perceived distribution of costs and benefits shapes the *kinds of political coalitions that will form*— but it will not necessarily determine *who wins*. A given popular majority, interest group, client, or entrepreneur may win or lose depending on its influence and the temper of the times.

In the remainder of this chapter we shall describe the politics of four kinds of policies and then illustrate each kind with examples drawn from government efforts to regulate business.

Majoritarian Politics: Distributed Benefits, Distributed Costs

Some policies promise benefits to large numbers of people at a cost that large numbers of people will have to bear (see Figure 15.1). For example, almost everybody will sooner or later receive Social Security benefits, and almost everybody who works has to pay Social Security taxes. Similarly, defending the nation against military attack benefits everyone, and every taxpayer contributes to its cost. If government-sponsored research to find cures for cancer and heart disease is successful, a large proportion of the citizenry will benefit from a program that all taxpayers have been obliged to support.

Majoritarian politics: widespread bank failures in the 1930s helped pave the way for laws regulating and insuring financial institutions.

Such **majoritarian politics** are usually not dominated by pulling and hauling among rival interest groups; instead they involve making appeals to large blocs of voters and their representatives in hopes of finding a majority. The reason why interest groups are not so important in majoritarian politics is that, as we saw in Chapter 9, citizens rarely will have much incentive to join an interest group if the policy that such a group supports will benefit everybody, whether or not they are members of the group. This is the "free-rider" problem. Why join the Committee to Increase (or Decrease) the Defense Budget when what you personally contribute to that committee makes little difference in the outcome and when you will enjoy the benefits of more (or less) national defense even if you have stayed on the sidelines?

Majoritarian politics may be controversial, but the controversy is usually over matters of cost or ideology, not between rival interest groups. In the 1980s Congress passed three laws to reduce drug use. This was a majoritarian issue (that is, there were no interest groups active on behalf of drug dealers). The arguments were over such matters as the desirability of the death penalty for big traffickers. The military budget went up during the early 1980s and down in the late 1980s; the changes reflected different views on how much we should spend and the relationship between military spending and arms-control negotiations.

Interest Group Politics: Concentrated Benefits, Concentrated Costs

In this second case, **interest group politics,** a proposed policy will confer benefits on some relatively small, identifiable group and impose costs on another small, equally identifiable group. For example, when Congress in 1988 passed a bill requiring companies to give sixty days' notice of a plant closing or a large-scale layoff, labor unions (whose members would benefit) backed the bill, and many business firms (which would pay the costs) opposed it.

Issues of this kind tend to be fought out by organized interest groups. Each side will be so powerfully affected by the outcome that it has a strong incentive to mobilize: union members who worry about layoffs will have a personal stake in favoring the notice bill; business leaders who fear government control of investment decisions will have an economic stake in opposing it.

Though many issues of this type involve monetary costs and benefits, they can also involve intangible considerations. If the American Nazi party wants to march through a predominantly Jewish neighborhood carrying flags with swastikas on them, the community may organize itself to resist out of revulsion against the disgraceful treatment of Jews by Nazi Germany. Each side hires lawyers who debate the issue before the city council and in the courts.

Client Politics: Concentrated Benefits, Distributed Costs

With **client politics** some identifiable, often small group will benefit, but everybody—or at least a large part of society—will pay the costs. Because the benefits are concentrated, the group that is to receive those benefits has an incentive to organize and work to get them. But because the costs are widely distributed, affecting many people only slightly, those who pay the costs may be either unaware of any costs or indifferent to them, because per capita they are so small.

This situation gives rise to client politics (sometimes called "clientele politics"); the beneficiary of the policy is the "client" of the government. For example, many farmers benefit substantially from agricultural price supports; each consumer, however, pays only a small amount of these subsidies, in the form of higher taxes and higher food prices. Moreover, the average consumer is unaware of how much higher his or her grocery bill is as a result of the government's paying certain farmers to produce

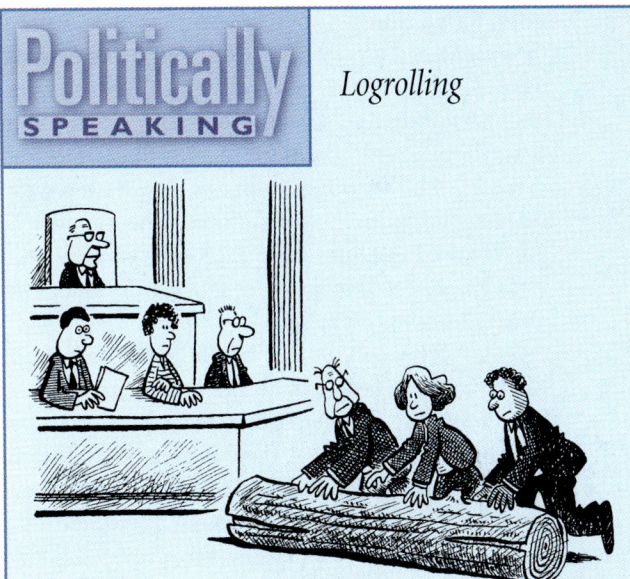

Politically SPEAKING

Logrolling

Among settlers in the American wilderness it was often necessary to cooperate in order to move logs off a piece of property that was to be farmed.

By the early nineteenth century *logrolling* had come to mean mutual aid among politicians, whereby one legislator supported another's pet project in return for the latter's support of his. Congressman B. F. Butler put it this way in 1870: "If you will vote for my interest, I will vote for yours. That is how these low tariffs are log rolled through."

Logrolling is the equivalent of the saying "You scratch my back and I'll scratch yours."

SOURCE: From *Safire's Political Dictionary* by William Safire. Copyright © 1968, 1972, 1978 by William Safire. Reprinted by permission of Random House, Inc. and the author.

less food than they otherwise would. In the same way, airlines for a long time benefited from the higher prices that they were able to charge on certain routes as a result of government regulations that restricted competition over prices. But the average passenger was either unaware that his or her costs were higher or did not think that the higher prices were worth making a fuss about.

Not all clients are economic interests. Localities can also benefit as clients when, for example, a city or county obtains a new dam, a better harbor, or an improved irrigation system. Some of these projects may be worthwhile, others may not; by custom, however, they are referred to as **pork-barrel projects.** Usually several pieces of "pork" are put into one barrel—that is, several projects are approved in a single piece of legislation, such as the "rivers and harbors" bill that Congress passes almost every year. Trading votes in this way attracts the support of members of Congress from each affected area; with enough projects a majority coalition is formed. This process is called **logrolling.**

Not every group that wants something from government at little cost to the average citizen will get it. Welfare recipients cost the typical taxpayer about $190 per year; yet there is great resistance to increasing these benefits. The homeless have not organized themselves to get benefits; indeed, most do not even vote. Yet benefits are being provided (albeit in modest amounts so far). These examples illustrate the importance of popular views concerning the legitimacy of client claims as a factor in determining the success of client demands. As we shall see in Chapter 17, welfare recipients have never enjoyed much legitimacy in the public's eye, and so programs to increase their benefits have been hard to sell to Congress. The plight of the homeless, on the other hand, has aroused a good deal of sympathy and produced bipartisan agreement in 1987 on a bill providing emergency aid. Moreover, that agreement seems to have persisted.

By the same token, groups can lose legitimacy that they once had. Farmers who grow tobacco once were supported simply because they were farmers, and were thus seen as both "deserving" and politically important. But when people began worrying about the health risks associated with using tobacco, farmers who produce tobacco lost some legitimacy compared to those who produce corn or cotton. As a result it became harder to get votes for maintaining tobacco price supports and easier to slap higher taxes on cigarettes.

Entrepreneurial Politics:
Distributed Benefits, Concentrated Costs

In **entrepreneurial politics** society as a whole or some large part of it benefits from a policy that imposes substantial costs on some small, identifiable

segment of society. The antipollution and safety requirements for automobiles were proposed as ways of improving the health and well-being of all people at the expense (at least initially) of automobile manufacturers. Some members of Congress would like to reduce or end subsidies for farmers, to cut the deficit or to lower food prices. Others would like to abolish laws that require construction workers working on federal projects to be paid more than what the market would pay.

It is remarkable that policies of this sort are ever adopted, and in fact many are not. After all, the American political system creates many opportunities for checking and blocking the actions of others. The Founders deliberately arranged things so that it would be difficult to pass a new law; a determined minority therefore has an excellent chance of blocking a new policy. And any organized group that fears the loss of some privilege or the imposition of some burden will become a very determined minority indeed. The opponent has every incentive to work hard; the large group of prospective beneficiaries may be unconvinced of the benefit or regard it as too small to be worth fighting for.

Nonetheless, policies with distributed benefits and concentrated costs are in fact adopted, and in recent decades they have been adopted with increasing frequency. A key element in the adoption of such policies has been the work of people who act on behalf of the unorganized or indifferent majority. Such people, called **policy entrepreneurs,** are those both in and out of government who find ways of pulling together a legislative majority on behalf of interests that are not well represented in the government.

These policy entrepreneurs may or may not represent the interests and wishes of the public at large, but they do have the ability to dramatize an issue in a convincing manner. Ralph Nader is perhaps the best-known example of a policy entrepreneur, or as he might describe himself, a "consumer advocate." But there are other examples from both ends of the political spectrum, conservative as well as liberal.

Entrepreneurial politics can occur without the leadership of a policy entrepreneur if voters or legislators in large numbers suddenly become disgruntled by the high cost of some benefit that a group is receiving (or become convinced of the urgent need for a new policy to impose such costs). For example, voters may not care about government programs that benefit the oil industry when gasoline costs only 50 cents a gallon, but they might care very much when the price rises to $2.00 a gallon, even if the government benefits had nothing to do with the price increase. By the same token, legislators may not worry much about the effects of smog in the air until a lot of people develop burning eyes and runny noses during an especially severe smog attack.

Likewise, most legislators did not worry very much about toxic or hazardous wastes until 1977, when the Love Canal dump site near Buffalo, New York, spilled some of its toxic waste into the backyards of an adjacent residential neighborhood and people were forced to leave their homes. Five years later, anyone who had forgotten about Love Canal was reminded of it when the town of Times Beach, Missouri, had to be permanently evacuated because it had become contaminated with the chemical dioxin. Only then did it become at all widely known that there were more than thirty thousand toxic waste sites nationwide that posed public safety risks. Although researchers have yet to find any conclusive evidence of health damage at either site, the Superfund program was born in 1980 of the political pressure that developed in the wake of these and other highly publicized tales of toxic waste dangers. Superfund was intended to force industries to clean up their own toxic waste sites. It also authorized the Environmental Protection Agency to act speedily, with or without cooperation from industries, in identifying and cleaning up any sites that posed a large or imminent danger.

Superfund has suffered a number of political and administrative problems, and only a few of the 1,300 sites initially targeted by the EPA have actually been cleaned up since the program went into effect.[11] However, Superfund is a good illustration of entrepreneurial politics in action. Special taxes on once largely unregulated oil and chemical companies have funded the program. Previously these companies enjoyed special tax privileges as beneficiaries of client politics; today they face special tax burdens as the targets of entrepreneurial politics.

For many reasons—including the enlarged political role of the media, the decentralization of Congress, and a change in the attitudes of many citizens—entrepreneurial politics has become more

A policy entrepreneur in action: Howard Jarvis celebrating the passage of Proposition 13 to cut local property taxes in California (June 1978).

common and policy entrepreneurs more visible in recent decades.

The Case of Business Regulation

Efforts by government to regulate business not only illustrate these four kinds of policy-making processes but also shed light on an issue that many people think is central to the study of politics—namely, the relationship between wealth and power.

To some observers the very existence of large corporations is a threat to popular rule. Economic power will dominate political power, they believe, for one or more of three reasons: first, because wealth can be used to buy influence; second, because politicians and business leaders have similar class backgrounds and thus similar beliefs about public policy; and third, because elected officials must defer to the preferences of business so as to induce corporations to keep the economy healthy and growing. Karl Marx, of course, proposed the most sweeping version of the view that economics controls politics; for him the state in a capitalist society was nothing more than the executive committee of the propertied classes.[12] But there are other non-Marxist or neo-Marxist versions of the same concern.[13]

To other observers politics, far from being subordinate to economic power, is a threat to the very existence of a market economy and the values—economic growth, private property, personal freedom—that they believe such an economy protects. In this view politicians will find it in their interest, in their struggle for votes, to take the side of the non-business majority against that of the business minority. The heads of large corporations, few in number but great in wealth, fear that they will be portrayed as a sinister elite on whom politicians can blame war, inflation, unemployment, and pollution. Defenders of business worry that corporations will be taxed excessively to pay for social programs that in turn will produce more votes for politicians. Just as bad, in this view, is the tendency of universities (on which corporations must rely for technical experts) to inculcate antibusiness values in their students.[14]

The theory of the policy-making process presented earlier in this chapter should suggest that neither of these two extreme views of business-government relations is entirely correct. These relations depend on many things, including the *kind* of policy being proposed. Instead of clenching our fists and shouting pro- or anti-business slogans at each other, we should be able, after applying this theory to the available facts, to make more careful and exact statements of the following sort: "If certain conditions exist, then business-government relations will take certain forms."

Majoritarian Politics

Not all efforts to regulate business pit one group against another. From time to time laws are passed that reflect the views of a majority of voters that is neither imposing its will on a hostile business community nor acceding to the desires of a privileged industry.

Much of the antitrust legislation passed in this country, including the Sherman Act (1890) and parts of the Federal Trade Commission Act (1914) and the Clayton Act (1914), has been the result of majoritarian politics. Toward the end of the nineteenth century there arose a broadly based criticism of business monopolies (then called "trusts") and, to a lesser extent, of large corporations, whether or not they monopolized trade. The Grange, an organization of farmers, was especially outspoken in its criticism, and popular opinion generally—insofar as we can know it in an era without pollsters—seems to have been indignant about trusts and in favor of "trust busting." Newspaper editorials and magazine articles frequently dwelt on the problem.[15]

But though antitrust feeling was strong, it was also relatively unfocused: no single industry was the special target of this criticism (the oil industry, and especially the Standard Oil Company, came as close as any), and no specific regulation was proposed. In fact there was no general agreement about how to define the problem: for some it was monopoly; for others, sheer bigness; and for still others, the legal basis of the modern corporation. The bill proposed by Senator John Sherman did not clarify matters much: while it made it a crime to "restrain" or "monopolize" trade, it did not define these terms, nor did it create any new regulatory agency charged with enforcing the law.[16]

No doubt some large corporations worried about what all this would mean for them, but few felt sufficiently threatened to try very hard to defeat the bill. It passed the Senate by a voice vote and the House by a vote of 242 to 0.

Laws are not self-executing, and vague laws are especially likely to lie dormant unless political leaders work hard at bringing them to life. For the first decade or so after 1890, only one or two antitrust cases a year were filed in the courts. In 1904 President Theodore Roosevelt persuaded Congress to provide enough money to hire five full-time lawyers, and soon the number of prosecutions increased to about seven a year. Then in 1938 President Franklin Roosevelt appointed as head of the Antitrust Division of the Justice Department a vigorous lawyer named Thurman Arnold, who began bringing an average of fifty cases a year.[17] Today over four hundred lawyers in the division sift through complaints alleging monopolistic or other unfair business practices. Though controversy exists over the kinds of cases that should be brought, there is no serious effort among either politicians or business leaders to abandon the commitment to a firm antitrust policy, the strongest such policy to be found in any industrial nation.

The antitrust laws were strengthened in 1914 by bills that created the Federal Trade Commission and made (via the Clayton Act) certain specific practices, such as price discrimination, illegal. As with the earlier Sherman Act, the advocates of these measures had a variety of motives. Some proponents favored these laws because they would presumably help consumers (by preventing unfair business practices); other proponents supported them because they might help business (by protecting firms against certain tactics that competitors might employ).

President Woodrow Wilson endorsed both of these bills and helped create a broad coalition on behalf of the legislation; the Federal Trade Commission Act and the Clayton Act passed Congress by lopsided majorities.[18]

As with the Sherman Act, there has been continual controversy about how these laws should be administered. But this controversy, like the debate over the initial passage of the laws, has not been dominated by interest groups.[19] The reason for the relative absence of interest group activity is that these laws do not divide society into permanent and identifiable blocs of proponents and opponents. Any given business firm can be either helped or hurt by the enforcement of the antitrust laws. One year the XYZ Widget Company may be sued by the government to prevent it from unfairly advertising its widgets, and the next year the same XYZ Company may ask the government to prosecute its competitor for trying to drive XYZ out of business by selling widgets at prices below cost.

The amount of money that the federal government devotes to antitrust enforcement and the direction that those enforcement efforts take are determined more by the political ideology and personal convictions of the administration in power than by interest group pressures. For example, in 1982 the Reagan administration decided that the benefits of trying to break up IBM were not worth the costs, and thus it ended its antitrust prosecution of the giant computer firm. At the same time, however, it decided that it was desirable to break up American Telephone and Telegraph, making the local phone companies independent of AT&T and

The Grange sought to warn farmers of the dangers of a railroad monopoly.

forcing AT&T to compete with other long-distance service providers.

In sum, as with most majoritarian policies, antitrust regulation tends to reflect broad philosophies of governance more than interest group activity.

Interest Group Politics

Organized interest groups are very powerful, however, when the regulatory policies confer benefits on a particular group and costs on another, equally distinct group.

In 1935 labor unions sought government protection for their right to organize, to bargain collectively with industry, and to compel workers in unionized industries to join the unions. Business firms opposed these plans. The struggle was fought out in Congress, where the unions won. The Wagner Act, passed that year, created the National Labor

Politically SPEAKING

Boycott

In 1880 an Irish landowner, Captain Boycott, was the target of an effort by the Irish Land League to get people to refuse to do business with him.

Today the term **boycott** refers to any concerted effort to get people to stop buying goods and services from a merchant or farmer in order to punish that person or to coerce him or her into changing policies.

The boycott has become a favored tool of interest group politics. The Reverend Jesse Jackson has, in recent years, tried to get blacks to boycott certain businesses that had not, in his judgment, hired a sufficient number of black employees.

Relations Board (NLRB) to regulate the conduct of union organizing drives and to hear complaints of unfair labor practices brought by workers against management.

But the struggle was far from over. In 1947 management sought to reverse some of the gains won by unions by pressing for a law (the Taft-Hartley Act) that would make illegal certain union practices (such as the closed shop and secondary boycotts) and would authorize the president to obtain a court order blocking for up to eighty days any strike that imperiled the "national health or safety." Business won.

Business and labor fought round three in 1959 over a bill (the Landrum-Griffin Act) intended to prevent corruption in unions, to change the way in which organizing drives were carried out, and to prohibit certain kinds of strikes and picketing. Business won.

In each of these cases the struggle was highly publicized. The winners and losers were determined by the partisan composition of Congress (Republicans and southern Democrats tended to support business, northern Democrats to support labor) and by the existence of economic conditions (a depression in 1935, revelations of labor racketeering in 1959) that affected public opinion on the issue.

But the interest group struggle did not end with the passage of the laws; it continued throughout their administration. The National Labor Relations Board, composed of five members appointed by the president, had to adjudicate countless disputes between labor and management over the interpretation of these laws. The losing party often appealed the NLRB decision to the courts, where the issue was fought out again. Moreover, each president has sought to tilt the NLRB in one direction or another by means of whom he appoints to it. Democratic presidents favor labor and thus tend to appoint prounion board members; Republican presidents favor business and thus tend to appoint promanagement members. Since NLRB members serve five-year terms, a new president cannot immediately appoint all of the board's members; thus there is often a split on the board between two factions.

A similar pattern of interest group influence is revealed by the history of the Occupational Safety and Health Act, passed in 1970. Labor unions wanted a strict bill with tough standards set by a single administrator; business organizations wanted a more flexible bill with standards set by a commission that would include some business representatives. After a long struggle labor won, and the Occupational Safety and Health Administration (OSHA), headed by a single administrator, was set up inside the Department of Labor.

As with the NLRB, conflict did not end with the passage of the law, and OSHA decisions were frequently appealed to the courts. The politics swirling about OSHA were all the more contentious because of the vast mandate of the agency: it is supposed to determine the safe limits for worker exposure to hundreds of chemicals and to inspect tens of thousands of workplaces to see whether they should be cited for violating any standards. During the Carter administration an OSHA administrator was appointed who was sympathetic to the labor view and thus set many standards and issued many citations; during the Reagan administration an administrator was selected who was admired by business because he set fewer standards and issued fewer citations.

Client Politics

Many people suppose that when government sets out to regulate business, the firms that are supposed to be regulated will in fact "capture" the agency that is supposed to do the regulating. But as we have already seen, certain kinds of policies—those that give rise to majoritarian and interest group politics—do not usually lead to capture, because the agency either faces no well-organized, enduring opponent (as with majoritarian politics) or is caught in a crossfire of competing forces (as with interest group politics).

But when a policy confers a benefit on one group at the expense of many other people, client politics arises, and so agency "capture" is likely. More precisely, nothing needs to be captured at all, since the agency will have been created from the outset to serve the interests of the favored group. We sometimes think that regulations are always resisted. But a regulation need not be a burden; it can be a great benefit.

How this works can be seen close to home. State and city laws regulate the practice of law and medicine as well as a host of other occupations—barbers, beauticians, plumbers, dry cleaners, taxi drivers, and undertakers. These regulations are sometimes designed and always defended as ways of preventing fraud, malpractice, and safety hazards. But they also have the effect of restricting entry into the regulated occupation, thereby enabling its members to charge higher prices than they otherwise might.[20] Ordinarily citizens do not object to this, in part because they believe, rightly or wrongly, that the regulations in fact protect them, and in part because the higher prices are spread over so many customers as to be unnoticed.

Much the same thing can be found at the national level. In the early 1930s the American dairy industry was suffering from rapidly declining prices

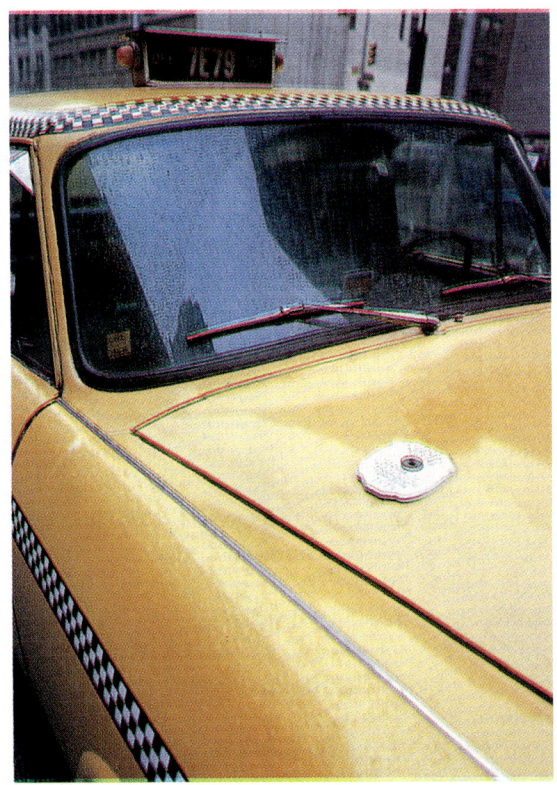

Client politics: to operate a New York taxi, the owner must have a medallion bolted to the hood. The number of medallions (and thus of taxis) is limited. This keeps competition down and prices up.

for milk. As the farmers' incomes fell, many could no longer pay their bills and were forced out of business. Congress responded with the Agricultural Adjustment Act, which authorized an agency of the Department of Agriculture to regulate the milk industry. This agency, the Dairy Division of the Agricultural Marketing Service, would issue "market orders" that had the effect of preventing price competition among dairy farmers and thus kept the price of milk up. If this guaranteed minimum price leads to the production of more milk than people want to drink, then another part of the Agriculture Department—the Commodity Credit Corporation—stands ready to buy up the surplus with tax dollars.[21]

Consumers wind up paying more for milk than they otherwise would, but they have no way of knowing the difference between the regulated and unregulated price of milk (economists estimate that it amounts to between five and twenty-one cents per gallon).[22] Consumers have little incentive to organize politically to do much about it. The total cost, however, can be very high; in the 1980s it was $2 billion to $3 billion a year.

A similar system works with sugar. Sugar produced abroad, in countries such as Brazil and the Philippines, costs much less than sugar produced here, in states such as Louisiana. To keep the incomes of U.S. sugar producers high, Congress decided to restrict the importation of cheap foreign sugar by imposing quotas. This costs the consumer money—maybe as much as $3 billion a year—but the extra cost per pound of sugar is not noticeable.[23]

From time to time various officials attempt to change the regulations that benefit a client group. But they must confront some sobering political facts. Dairy farmers are found scattered through scores of congressional districts; sugar-beet growers are concentrated in southern states that are important in any presidential election. Efforts have been made in Congress to cut milk subsidies and sugar quotas, but with only limited success.

In 1996 Congress passed and the president signed a bill that will, at least for wheat and corn crops, begin to phase out the practice of paying farmers the difference between what they can sell their crops for and what the government thinks the crops ought to be worth. It will replace these crop subsidies with direct cash payments to farmers that they can use for anything, including not farming. (The law as it applies to cotton, rice, sugar, and peanuts is more complex.) If the bill stays in effect for several years (and this is a big *if*), it would help end the idea of having the government pay people to grow things for which there is no market. If that happens, it would be a revolution. But despite being relatively few in number today, farmers are not politically impotent. If things don't go well, they may well demand a return to the old system.

Farmers are not the only group to enjoy a client relationship with a federal regulatory agency. Originally the Civil Aeronautics Board, established in 1938, regulated airlines in ways that prevented competition over prices and discouraged the creation of new airlines. (That has now changed.) The Federal Maritime Commission regulates the prices charged by American merchant ships engaged in international commerce in ways that tend to keep those prices higher than they would be in the absence of regulation.

Entrepreneurial Politics

During the 1960s and 1970s some two dozen consumer- and environmental-protection laws were passed, including laws that regulated the automobile industry, oil companies, toy manufacturers, poultry producers, the chemical industry, and pharmaceutical companies.[*]

When measures such as these become law, it is often because a policy entrepreneur has dramatized an issue, galvanized public opinion, and mobilized congressional support. Sometimes that entrepreneur is in the government (a senator or an outspoken bureaucrat); sometimes that entrepreneur is a private person (the best known, of course, is Ralph Nader). The motives of such entrepreneurs can be either self-serving or public-spirited; the policies that they embrace may be either good or bad. (Just because someone succeeds in regulating business does not mean that the public will necessarily benefit; by the same token, just because business claims that a new regulation will be excessively costly does not mean that business will in fact have to pay those costs.)

An early example of a policy entrepreneur inside the government was Dr. Harvey Wiley, a chemist in the Department of Agriculture, who actively campaigned for what was to become the Pure Food and Drug Act of 1906. Later Senator Estes Kefauver held hearings that built support for the 1962 drug laws (and incidentally for his presidential bid), and Senator Edmund Muskie called attention to the need for air- and water-pollution-control legislation (and incidentally to his own 1972 presidential aspirations).

When a policy entrepreneur is outside the government, he or she will need a sympathetic ear within it. Occasionally the policy needs of the entrepreneur and the political needs of an elected official

---

[*] The Motor Vehicle Air Pollution Control Act of 1965, the National Traffic and Motor Vehicle Safety Act of 1966, the Clean Air Act of 1970, the Water Quality Improvement Act of 1970, the Children's Protection and Toy Safety Act of 1969, the Wholesome Poultry Act of 1968, the Toxic Substances Control Act of 1976, and the 1962 amendments to the Pure Food and Drug Act.

Entrepreneurial politics: Upton Sinclair's book *The Jungle,* published in 1906, shocked readers about conditions in the meat-packing industry and helped bring about passage of the Meat Inspection Act of 1906.

coincide. When Ralph Nader was walking the corridors of the Capitol looking for someone interested in auto safety, he found Senators Abraham Ribicoff and Warren Magnuson, who themselves were looking for an issue with which they could be identified.[24]

The task of the policy entrepreneur is made easier when a crisis or scandal focuses public attention on a problem. Upton Sinclair's book *The Jungle*[25] dramatized the frightful conditions in meat-packing plants at the turn of the century and helped pave the way for the Meat Inspection Act of 1906. The stock market collapse of 1929 helped develop support for the Securities and Exchange Act. When some people who had taken a patent medicine (elixir of sulfanilamide) died as a result, the passage of the 1938 drug laws became easier. Oil spilled on the beaches of Santa Barbara, California, drew attention to problems addressed by the Water Quality Improvement Act of 1970.

The dramatic event need not be an actual crisis; in some cases a political scandal will do. Highway fatalities were not a matter of great concern to most citizens when Congress began considering the auto-safety act in 1965–1966, but support for the bill grew when it was revealed that General Motors had hired a private detective who made a clumsy effort to collect (or manufacture) gossip harmful to Ralph Nader, whose book *Unsafe at Any Speed* had criticized the safety of certain GM cars.

In some cases no dramatic event at all is required for entrepreneurial politics to succeed. Most of the air- and water-pollution-control bills were passed despite the absence of any environmental catastrophe.[26] Support for such measures was developed by holding carefully planned committee hearings that were closely followed by the media. For example, by drawing attention to the profits of the pharmaceutical companies, Senator Kefauver was able to convince many people that these firms were insensitive to public needs. By drawing on information made available to him by environmentalists, Senator Muskie was able to capitalize on and help further a growing perception in the country during the early 1970s that nature was in danger.

Because political resistance must be overcome without the aid of a powerful economic interest group, policy entrepreneurs seeking to regulate an industry often adopt a moralistic tone, with their opponents portrayed as devils, their allies viewed

Agencies created by the use of entrepreneurial politics, such as those controlling the disposal of toxic wastes, must be wary of capture by the interests they are supposed to regulate.

with suspicion, and compromises fiercely resisted. When Senator Muskie was drafting an air pollution bill, Ralph Nader issued a highly publicized report *attacking* Muskie, his nominal ally, for not being tough enough. This strategy forced Muskie—who wanted acclaim, not criticism, for his efforts—to revise the bill so that it imposed even more stringent standards.[27] Other allies of Nader, such as Dr. William Haddon, Jr., and Joan Claybrook, got the same treatment when they later became administrators of the National Highway Traffic Safety Administration. They came under attack not only from the auto industry, for designing rules that the companies thought were too strict, but also from Nader, for devising rules that he thought were not strict enough.

Once a policy entrepreneur manages to defeat an industry that is resisting regulation, he or she creates—at least for a while—a strong impetus for additional legislation of the same kind. A successful innovator produces imitators, in politics as in rock music. After the auto-safety law was passed in 1966, it became easier to pass a coal-mine-safety bill in 1969 and an occupational-safety-and-health bill in 1970.

The great risk faced by policy entrepreneurs is not that their hard-won legislative victories will later be reversed but that the agency created to do the regulating will be captured by the industry that it is supposed to regulate. The Food and Drug Administration (FDA), which regulates the pharmaceutical industry, has fallen victim during much of its history to precisely this kind of capture. Once the enthusiasm of its founders had waned and public attention had turned elsewhere, the FDA seemed to develop a cozy and rather uncritical attitude toward the drug companies. (In 1958 the head of the FDA received an award from the Pharmaceutical Manufacturers' Association.)[28] In the mid-1960s, under the spur of renewed congressional and White House attention, the agency was revitalized. During the Reagan administration environmentalists worried that the leadership of the Environmental Protection Agency had been turned over to persons who were unduly sympathetic to polluters.

There are at least five reasons, however, why the newer consumer- and environmental-protection agencies may not be as vulnerable to capture as some critics contend. First, these agencies often enforce laws that impose specific standards in accordance with strict timetables, and so they have relatively little discretion. (The Environmental Protection Agency, for example, is required by law to reduce certain pollutants by a fixed percentage within a stated number of years.) Second, the newer agencies, unlike the FDA, usually regulate many different industries and so do not confront a single, unified opponent. The Occupational Safety and Health Administration, for example, deals with virtually every industry. Third, the very existence of these agencies has helped strengthen the hand of the "public interest" lobbies that initially demanded their creation. Fourth, these lobbies can now call upon many sympathetic allies in the media who will attack agencies that are thought to have a pro-business bias (witness the heavy criticism directed at James Watt, President Reagan's first secretary of the interior).

Finally, as explained in Chapter 14, it has become easier for groups to use the federal courts to put pressure on the regulatory agencies. These groups do not have to be large or broadly representative of the public; all they need are the services of one or two able lawyers. If the Environmental

Protection Agency (EPA) issues a rule disliked by a chemical company, the company will promptly sue the EPA; if it issues a ruling that pleases the company, the Environmental Defense Fund or some similar group will sue.

Perceptions, Beliefs, Interests, and Values

The politics of business regulation provides a good illustration of the theory of policy-making offered in this book, but the reader should not be misled by a discussion of costs and benefits into thinking that all or even most of politics is about getting or losing money or that it is an easy matter to classify the costs and benefits of a policy and thus put it into the correct pigeonhole.

For one thing, what constitutes a cost or a benefit is a matter of opinion, and opinions change. We have already said that it is the *perception* of costs and benefits that affects politics. If people think that laws requiring factories to install devices to remove from their smokestacks chemicals that contribute to acid rain can be implemented in ways that make the companies but not the consumers pay the bills, they will favor such measures, and the affected industries will oppose them. But if people believe that the cost of preventing acid rain will be borne by them—in the form of fewer jobs or higher prices—then these citizens may be less enthusiastic about such measures.

Some people favor having the government regulate the price of natural gas, and others oppose it. One reason for the conflict, obviously, is that people who use natural gas in their homes want to buy it cheaply, whereas people who work in the natural gas industry want gas prices to go up so that they can earn more. Interests are clearly in conflict.

Yet some users may oppose regulating the price of gas because they believe that keeping the price of gas artificially low now will discourage exploration for new gas fields, thereby creating shortages—and much higher prices—in the future. Thus *beliefs* are also in conflict; in this case some users believe that it is more important to take the long view and worry about gas shortages ten years from now, while others believe that what counts is how much you have to pay for natural gas today.

A political conflict is in large measure a struggle to make one definition of the costs and benefits of a proposal prevail over others; that is, it is a struggle to alter perceptions and beliefs. Material interests do play a part in all this: the more you stand to gain or lose in hard cash from a proposal, the harder it will be for someone else to change your mind about your position. But many, perhaps most, government proposals will not have an immediate, unambiguous impact on your pocketbook, and so your perceptions and beliefs about what will happen in the future become the prize for which political activists compete.

In that competition certain arguments enjoy a natural advantage over others. One might be called the *here-and-now* argument. What happens now or in the near future is more important to most people than what happens in the distant future. (Economists refer to this as the human tendency to "discount the future.") Thus most users of natural gas probably care more about present prices than future shortages, and so many will tend to favor price regulation today.

Another political tactic that enjoys a natural advantage might be called the *cost* argument. People seem to react more sharply to what they will lose if a policy is adopted than to what they may gain. Thus there will usually be strong opposition to putting a tax on imported oil, even if the benefit gained will be to reduce our dependence on foreign oil.

Politicians know the value of the here-and-now and the cost arguments and so try to present their proposals in ways that take advantage of these sentiments. Regulations aimed at new drugs, for example, will emphasize the harm that will be prevented now from keeping dangerous drugs off the market, not the harm that may come later if life-saving drugs with some dangerous side effects are kept off the market. Plans to solve the problems of our Social Security system stress keeping intact the benefits now received by people already retired, postponing into the future the tax increases necessary to pay for these benefits.

Policies are affected not only by our perceptions and beliefs about where our interests lie but also by our *values*—that is, by our conceptions of what is good for the country or for our community. Many whites, for example, want to see opportunities increased for blacks, not because such opportunities

The Savings-and-Loan Mess

Savings and loans (sometimes called "thrifts" or "S&Ls") were created primarily to help the average person borrow money to buy a house. Until the 1960s the president of an S&L followed the "3–6–3 Rule"; he paid depositors 3 percent interest, he lent money at 6 percent interest, and he played golf every day at three o'clock.

To prevent competition, the government limited by law the amount of interest an S&L could pay to a depositor. To protect the depositors, the federal government guaranteed their deposits up to some limit; in 1979 it was $40,000 per account.

This worked fine so long as interest rates did not go up very fast. But starting in the 1960s, other financial institutions began paying people higher interest on their savings than the S&Ls were allowed to pay. As a result people took their money out of the S&Ls and put it into money-market funds or certificates of deposit. The S&Ls were losing money, and so they went to Congress for help. They got it: they were allowed to pay higher interest in order to attract deposits.

But this competition for deposits only made matters worse. An S&L's income came from the interest it earned on the mortgage loans it had made. These mortgages, however, were often for twenty-five years. Many had been written in the low-interest days of the 1950s and

paid the S&L only 6 percent. When the S&L began paying depositors 9 percent or 10 percent interest, it started to lose money. So the S&Ls went back to Congress and asked for permission to invest in things that would earn them a higher return than a home mortgage. Again Congress went along. Now the S&Ls could invest their depositors' money not just in home mortgages but in shopping malls, farmland, and high-yield junk bonds. At the same time, federal regulators eased up on the S&Ls. Finally, Congress increased the size of the deposits guaranteed by the federal government from $40,000 to $100,000. One person or business could open accounts in any number of S&Ls and get the $100,000 guarantee on each account.

Many S&Ls started paying sky-high interest rates to get new depositors. To earn enough money to pay this interest, they invested in high-risk deals—deals that would pay off handsomely *if* they worked out but would cause big losses if they didn't. Many didn't.

Why didn't the S&Ls worry that they might not make enough on their investments to pay off their depositors? Simple: the government had promised to pay off these depositors if anything went wrong. In effect the S&Ls were playing with free money. It was a recipe for disaster. Or, if you were an unscrupulous S&L owner, it was party time.

Starting in the early 1980s, more and more S&Ls went bankrupt—they couldn't earn enough from their loans to pay what they owed their depositors. And so the federal government had to take over these failed thrifts and pay off the depositors. Soon there were hundreds of bankrupt thrifts, many concentrated in the Southwest. Some of these, such as Lincoln Savings and Loan, made big contributions to politicians to get them to persuade federal regulators not to declare these S&Ls insolvent. (The head of Lincoln, Charles Keating, was later convicted for mismanagement of his S&L, and the Senate Ethics Committee launched an investigation into the conduct of five senators whom Keating had approached.) But political influence could cover up the mess for only so long. As the federal regulators ran out of money with which to pay the depositors, Congress could no longer ignore the problem.

In 1989 Congress passed a law to bail out the system by paying $50 billion to close insolvent institutions and pay off the depositors. (The law also reorganized and tightened federal regulation of the thrifts.) But by 1990 it was clear that much more money would be needed. It could cost each taxpayer $2,000 to clean up the mess—the biggest single bill ever presented to the American public.

will make whites better off but because they think that it is the right thing to do. Many citizens worry about political conditions in Central America, not because they fear having to fight a war there or because they work for a company that does business there but because they wish a better life for people

who live in that region and want them to be free of both right-wing and Marxist dictatorships. Some citizens oppose restrictions on the sale of obscene magazines and others favor those restrictions; neither group stands to benefit—those who oppose censorship usually don't plan to read the publications, and those who favor it would not thereby have their own lives improved—yet both groups often advocate their opposing views with great passion.

All this may seem obvious, but the reader should recall how often he or she assumes that people are only "looking out for themselves" and so politics is only about "who gets what." We all have a tendency to be a bit cynical about government—that is, to impute self-seeking motives to whoever is involved. Since there is plenty of self-interest in politics, this assumption is often a pretty good one. But following it blindly can lead us to ignore those cases in which ideas—beliefs, perceptions, and values—are the decisive forces in political conflict.

There are many examples of the power of ideas, even in conflicts that involve money interests. One—the Tax Reform Act of 1986—will be described in Chapter 16. Here, two other examples are noted: the deregulation of certain industries and the ending of certain taxpayer-financed agricultural subsidies.

Deregulation

In the 1980s several industries were deregulated over the objections of those industries. Airline fares were once set by the Civil Aeronautics Board. The airlines liked it that way—it kept competition down and prices up. But today airline fares are set by the market, with the result that in some (but not all) areas fares are lower than they once were. Not only did most airlines fight tooth and nail to prevent this deregulation from occurring, some couldn't adjust to the new era of competition and, like Eastern Airlines, went bankrupt.

Long-distance telephone services were once provided on a monopoly basis by AT&T; its prices were set by the Federal Communications Commission. Today there are several long-distance telephone systems—MCI, Sprint, AT&T—and prices are heavily influenced by competition. AT&T was not eager to have this happen, but it couldn't prevent it.

Once, the number of trucking companies and the prices they charged were set by the Interstate Commerce Commission (ICC). The trucking companies and the Teamsters Union favored this pattern of regulation—as with the airlines, the system kept competition down and prices up. But then Congress

changed the law, and in January 1996 the ICC was abolished.

People who think that politics is simply the result of deals struck between certain favored industries and friendly or "captured" agencies would have a hard time explaining this period of deregulation. Client politics—the cozy relationship (or "iron triangle") between a private client, a government agency, and a supportive Congress—was ended. How did it happen?

Martha Derthick and Paul Quirk, two political scientists, answered the question in their book *The Politics of Deregulation*.[29] The key to that answer is the power of ideas. Academic economists were in agreement that regulating prices in industries that were competitive, or could easily be made so, was a bad idea; the regulations hurt consumers by keeping prices artificially high. But academic ideas by themselves are powerless. In the three cases described above, key political leaders—Presidents Carter, Ford, and Reagan, and Senators Edward Kennedy and Howard Cannon—accepted and acted on these ideas, albeit for very different reasons. The regulatory commissions—the Civil Aeronatics Board (CAB), the Federal Communications Commission (FCC), the ICC—were led by people who wanted to deregulate. In one case, the breakup of AT&T, a federal judge made many of the key decisions. The public did not support deregulation, but it was concerned about inflation, and deregulation could be defended as a way of bringing prices down. Finally, the industries that fought to save their client relationships with government—the airlines, the trucking companies, the phone company—were not wildly popular businesses; once they were subjected to political criticism, they found that they had relatively few allies.

Reducing Subsidies

At one time the taxpayer shelled out a lot of money to help tobacco growers make money. Under that system, tobacco farmers who could not sell all the tobacco they were entitled to grow under a federal license could get a federal loan, using their unsold tobacco as collateral. If they did not pay back the loan, they got to keep the money, and the government was stuck with the bill.

Deregulation: Legislative Milestones

Act	Year	Key Elements
Railroad Revitalization and Regulatory Reform Act	1976	Allowed railroads limited rate-setting autonomy; was the first piece of deregulation legislation on the recent wave
Airline Deregulation Act	1978	Instructed the Civil Aeronautics Board to place maximum reliance on competition in its regulation of passenger service; provided that the board's authority over domestic fares and mergers end January 1, 1983, and that the CAB be abolished January 1, 1985
Staggers Rail Act	1980	Limited the Interstate Commerce Commission's jurisdiction over rates to those markets where railroads exercised market dominance; introduced price competition
Motor Carrier Act	1980	Allowed truckers to form subsidiaries and expand into additional regional markets; ended necessity of demonstrating public need; placed fewer restrictions on certain industry hauling practices; eased entry and introduced price competition
Depository Institution Deregulation and Monetary Control Act	1980	Allowed mutual savings banks to make commercial, corporate, and business loans equal to 5 percent of their assets; allowed payment of interest on demand deposits; removed interest-rate ceilings
Bus Deregulatory Reform Act	1982	Allowed companies to obtain operating authority without applying to ICC in many circumstances
Thrift Institutions Restructuring Act	1982	Authorized savings and loans to make commercial loans equal to 10 percent of their assets; allowed investments in nonresidential personal property and small-business investment companies
Interstate Commerce Commission Termination Act of 1995	1995	Abolished the Interstate Commerce Commission effective January 1, 1996

SOURCE: *Business Economics* magazine. Reprinted by permission of the National Association of Business Economists.

Since tobacco farming is a key industry in certain states (such as Kentucky and North Carolina), the members of Congress from those states had a big stake in making certain that the subsidy program kept going. Since the program did not cost the average taxpayer too much (and since, in any case, the public had no idea of how much money went to pay for the program), most people had no incentive to organize to end the favored treatment of tobacco farmers.

They didn't, that is, until smoking became a well-publicized national health problem. Then many members of Congress from nontobacco states became upset about spending money to grow crops that contributed to cancer, heart disease, and emphysema. In 1982, when the tobacco-subsidy program was up for renewal, its congressional backers realized that they had to make concessions if the

program were to survive. They did this by agreeing to a system in which the subsidies to the farmers would be paid for by the farmers themselves (in the form of mandatory contributions to a fund set up to pay for crop loans). The principle was to be "no net cost to the taxpayer" (except for administrative expenses).

Client politics was weakened when larger concerns (in this case, antismoking groups) were activated. Widely held beliefs ("smoking is bad for you") significantly reduced the influence of narrowly distributed benefits. The tobacco lobby lost again when the ban on smoking on all domestic airline flights was enacted in 1987.

In 1997, under the threat of losing expensive lawsuits brought by state governments, the tobacco industry began negotiating with the attorneys general of these states to change tobacco marketing practices. The tobacco companies would make a big cash payment to the governments in return for a cap on the size of any future lawsuit settlements.

Since the mid-1970s every president has put in place machinery to bring government regulation of industry under more central review. President Ford in 1974 ordered all regulatory agencies to assess the inflationary impact of their decisions. President Carter in 1978 directed each agency to consider alternative ways of achieving the goals of regulation. President Reagan in 1981 created a Task Force on Regulatory Relief and instructed those agencies under his control not to issue a regulation if, in the judgment of the Office of Management and Budget, its potential benefits to society did not outweigh its costs.[30] President Bush essentially continued the Reagan system.

Deregulation is opposed, of course, by groups that benefit from it. But it is controversial in at least two other ways. First, some members of the public do not like the results, especially if the world becomes more complicated as a result of relying on the market. Many people liked CAB control of the airlines, for example, because the higher prices kept the number of air travelers down, and so airports were less congested. Second, some people who favor deregulating *prices* oppose deregulating *processes*. **Process regulation** (sometimes called "social regulation") includes rules aimed at improving consumer or worker safety and reducing environmental damage. There are good and bad ways of achieving these goals, and much of the dispute about regulation concerns the question of means, not ends. The intensity of that dispute shows how important perceptions and beliefs are even when economic interests are at stake.

The Limits of Ideas

Ideas can be powerful, but there are limits to their power. There are many forms of client politics that persist—some because people agree that the client deserves to benefit, others because the conditions do not exist for mounting an effective challenge to the client.

Tobacco subsidies no longer are paid for by taxpayers, but dairy and other agricultural price supports still are. Regulations that increased above market levels the prices charged by airlines and

trucking companies were successfully challenged; regulations that increased above market levels the prices charged by ocean-going freighters were not. The wages paid to airline pilots and truck drivers are no longer protected by federal rules; the wages paid to merchant seamen and construction workers employed on federal projects still are.

It is not entirely clear why it is easier to challenge client politics in some industries and occupations than in others. We can say, however, why it is generally harder to maintain client politics free of challenge today than once was the case. That we shall do in Chapter 23, where we summarize what can be learned in the next few chapters about the politics of public policy.

SUMMARY

Policy-making involves two stages—placing an issue on the governmental agenda and deciding what to do about that issue once it is on the agenda. The agenda steadily expands as the result of historical crises, interest group activity, the competition for votes, and the operation of key institutions, especially the courts, the bureaucracy, and the mass media.

Decision making requires that a majority coalition be formed. The kinds of coalitions that form will depend in large measure on the nature of the issue, especially the perceived distribution of costs and benefits. We have identified four kinds of coalitions, or distinctive political processes: majoritarian, client, interest group, and entrepreneurial.

Government regulation of business illustrates the relationship between these four kinds of policies and the sorts of coalitions that will form in each instance. These case studies make clear that there is no single, simple answer to the question of how much influence business has over government (or vice versa).

The outcome of these political struggles will depend not only on who gains and who loses but also on the perceptions, beliefs, and values of key political actors. The example of airline deregulation shows that changes in how people think can make a big difference even in the case of policies where money interests are at stake.

KEY TERMS

political agenda   *p. 474*

cost   *p. 477*

benefit   *p. 478*

majoritarian politics   *p. 480*

interest group politics   *p. 480*

client politics   *p. 481*

pork-barrel projects   *p. 482*

logrolling   *p. 482*

entrepreneurial politics   *p. 482*

policy entrepreneurs   *p. 482*

boycott   *p. 486*

process regulation   *p. 495*

SUGGESTED READINGS

Derthick, Martha, and Paul J. Quirk. *The Politics of Deregulation.* Washington, D.C.: Brookings Institution, 1985. A brilliant analysis of how three industries—airlines, trucking, and telecommunications—were deregulated, often in the teeth of industry opposition.

Kingdon, John W. *Agendas, Alternatives, and Public Policies.* Boston: Little, Brown, 1984. An insightful account of how issues, especially those involving health and transportation, get on (or drop off) the federal agenda.

Lowi, Theodore J. "American Business, Public Policy, Case Studies, and Political Theory." *World Politics* 16 (July 1964). A theory of policy-making somewhat different from that offered in this book.

Nadel, Mark V. *The Politics of Consumer Protection.* 2d ed. Indianapolis, Ind.: Bobbs-Merrill, 1975. An analysis of the sources and uses of political influence in consumer legislation.

Noll, Roger G. *Reforming Regulation.* Washington, D.C.: Brookings Institution, 1971. A useful summary of the criticisms that economists make of many regulatory laws.

Polsby, Nelson W. *Political Innovation in America.* New Haven, Conn.: Yale University Press, 1984. Explains how eight policy innovations were adopted by the federal government.

Wilson, James Q., ed. *The Politics of Regulation.* New York: Basic Books, 1980. Analyzes regulatory politics in nine agencies and provides a fuller statement of the theory presented in this text.

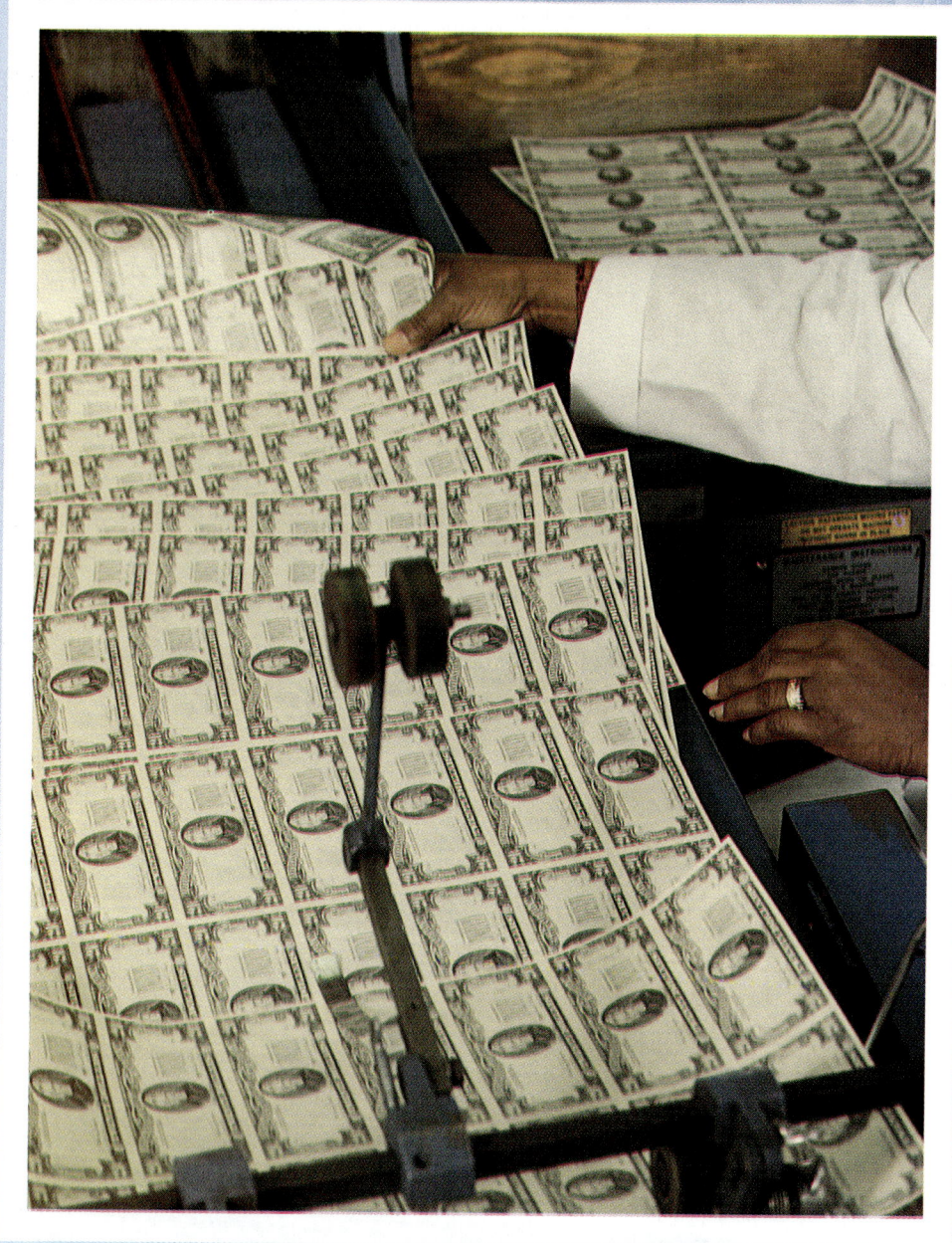

16

Economic Policy

★ Voters and the economy

★ Economic theories

★ Making economic policy

★ The budget

★ Taxes and tax reform

For decades the Republicans complained that the Democrats were big spenders. But when a conservative Republican, Ronald Reagan, entered the White House in 1981, he cut taxes and allowed spending to increase. The government spent more money than it took in. Yet in 1986 the Democrats, who had long complained that corporations and rich people didn't pay enough in taxes, voted for a tax reform bill that cut tax rates. In addition, politicians who had always looked for new tax loopholes to let people escape some taxes voted to close many existing loopholes.

For a decade or so, the politics of economic policy making was turned upside down. People who were supposed to hate deficits voted to create them; people who were supposed to want high taxes voted to lower them; and people who loved tax loopholes voted to close them. It made it hard to write a chapter like this one.

By the 1990s, however, order had been restored. A Republican president (George Bush) unhappily went along with tax increases, and a Democratic president (Bill Clinton) happily signed a bill to increase them even more. The national deficit began to decline—but not because spending had been cut, only because taxes had been raised.

By the mid-1990s cutting the deficit had become a joint endeavor of both President Clinton and a Republican-led Congress. They had a lot of arguments, but mostly over who was cutting the budget faster. Things got so testy that at one point Congress would not pass spending bills the president would sign, and so the federal government was partially shut down for a few days because there was no money to pay many government workers. In 1997, Clinton and the Republican congressional leaders agreed on a deficit reduction plan.

How do we explain all of these gyrations? The answer lies in ourselves, the American people. In the early 1980s voters thought taxes were too high, and so the government cut them. As the deficit shot up voters objected, and so politicians looked for ways (higher taxes, mostly) to cut it.

From a political point of view there are three

FIGURE 16.1 Federal Outlays as a Percentage of Gross
National Product, 1869–1990

SOURCE: *Budget of the United States Government, Fiscal Year 1991*, A–332.

kinds of economic realities: the general health of the nation (as measured by employment, inflation, and growth in incomes), the level and distribution of taxes, and the amount and kind of government spending. Voters and interest groups judge the government on the basis of how well the economy is doing, how much they are paying in taxes, and how much they are getting from government spending programs. Economists may tell us that these three realities are closely intertwined, so that a change in taxes or spending will affect inflation or unemployment, and vice versa. But voters are not very interested in these relationships and theories; they are interested in results. They want economic growth, low taxes, high levels of government spending on most programs, and no budget deficit. This confronts the government with a problem: it may be impossible to achieve all of these results simultaneously. To see why, we shall look at these three economic realities.

Economic Health

Disputes about the economic well-being of the nation tend to produce majoritarian politics. This may seem strange, since each individual presumably cares most about his or her own material comfort. If that were the case, we would expect each voter to support politicians who offer programs to make that voter better off, regardless of what those programs

would or would not do for other voters. In fact, though, people see connections between their own conditions and the economic health of the nation and tend to hold politicians responsible for those national conditions.

Everybody knows that just before an election politicians worry about the *pocketbook issue.* We have seen in Chapter 8 that economic conditions are strongly associated with how much success the incumbent party has in holding on to the White House and to the seats held by the White House's party in Congress. But whose pocketbook are voters worried about?

In part, of course, it is their own. We know that low-income people are more likely to worry about unemployment and to vote Democratic, and higher-income people are more likely to worry about inflation and to vote Republican.[1] We also know that people who tell pollsters that their families' finances have gotten worse are more likely than other people to vote against the incumbent president.[2] In 1980 about two-thirds of those who said that they had become worse off economically voted for Ronald Reagan, the challenger, while over half of those who felt that they had become better off voted for Jimmy Carter, the incumbent.[3] In 1992 people who felt economically pinched were more likely to vote for Clinton than for Bush. Clinton campaign aides often reminded each other, "It's the economy, stupid!"

But people do not simply vote their own pocketbooks. In any recession the vast majority of people will still have jobs; nevertheless, these people will say that unemployment is the nation's biggest problem, and many of them will vote accordingly—against the incumbent during whose watch unemployment went up.[4] Why should employed people worry about other people's unemployment?

By the same token, younger voters, whose incomes tend to go up each year, often worry more about inflation than do retired people living on fixed incomes, the purchasing power of which goes down with inflation.[5] In presidential elections those people who think that national economic trends are bad are much more likely to vote against the incumbent, *even when* their own personal finances have not worsened.[6]

In technical language, voting behavior and economic conditions are strongly correlated at the national level but not at the individual level, and this is true both in the United States and in Europe.[7] Such voters are behaving in an "other-regarding" or "sociotropic" way. In ordinary language, voters seem to respond more to the condition of the national economy than to their own personal finances.

It is not hard to understand why this might be true. Part of the explanation is that people understand what government can and cannot be held accountable for. If you lose your job at the aircraft plant because the government has not renewed the plant's contract, you will be more likely to hold the government responsible than if you lose your job because you were always showing up drunk or because the plant moved out of town.

And part of the explanation is that people see general economic conditions as having indirect effects on them even when they are still doing pretty well. They may not be unemployed, but they may have friends who are, and they may worry that if unemployment grows worse, they will be the next to lose their jobs.

What Politicians Try to Do

Elected officials, who have to run for reelection every few years, are strongly tempted to take a short-run view of the economy and to adopt those policies that will best satisfy the self-regarding voter. They would dearly love to produce low unemployment rates and rising family incomes just before an election. Some scholars think that they do just this.

Since the nineteenth century the government has used money to affect elections. At first this mostly took the form of patronage passed out to the party faithful and money benefits given to important blocs of voters. The massive system of Civil War pensions for Union army veterans was run in a way that did no harm to the political fortunes of the Republican party. After the Social Security system was established, Congress voted to increase the benefits in virtually every year in which there was an election (see Chapter 17).

But it is by no means clear that the federal government can or will do whatever is necessary to reduce unemployment, cut inflation, lower interest rates, and increase incomes just to win an election. For one thing, the government does not know how to produce all these desirable outcomes. Moreover, doing one of these things may often be possible only

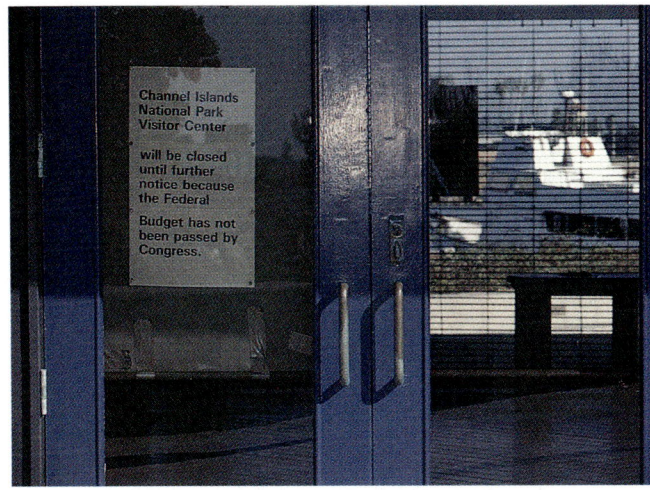

Congress can only push the president so far. If it fails to appropriate money, he can close down the government and blame Congress.

at the cost of not doing another. For example, reducing inflation can, in many cases, require the government to raise interest rates, and this in turn can slow down the economy by making it harder to sell houses, automobiles, and other things that are purchased with borrowed money.

If it were easy to stimulate the economy just before an election, practically every president would serve two full terms. But because of the uncertainties and complexities of the economy, presidents can lose elections over economic issues that they do not manage to the satisfaction of voters. Ford lost in 1976, Carter in 1980, and Bush in 1992. In all cases economic conditions played a major role.

All this means that politicians must make choices about economic policy, choices that are affected by uncertainty and ignorance. Those choices are shaped significantly by the ideological differences between the two political parties over what ought to be the principal goal of economic policy. Democrats and Republicans alike would prefer to have both low unemployment and no inflation, but if they must choose (and choose they must), then the Democrats attempt first to reduce unemployment and the Republicans attempt to reduce inflation.[8] This is no hard-and-fast rule; some say that Jimmy Carter, a Democrat, tried so hard to cut inflation in 1980 that he lost the support of many liberal Democrats, such as Edward Kennedy, who thought

America—Land of Economic Opportunity or Income Inequality?

Look at Chart A below. What does it tell you? Clearly it tells you that income growth in the United States has been un-equally distributed since 1973. But does it also tell you that income inequality in America is growing or that America is rapidly becoming a society of haves and have-nots? Some experts think so. But what other data might you need to test this grim conclusion, and what other interpretations are possible? Here are just three of many possible leads: factoring in economic mobility, defining "family income," and measuring the size of the middle class.

1. *Economic Mobility.* Today you are a student earning little or nothing. Upon graduation, you will almost certainly earn more. Likewise, today's prosperous farmer is a crop failure away from being next year's poor farmer. And last year's penniless computer programmer could be the next decade's millionaire computer software entrepreneur. As these examples suggest, while the distribution of income among people may be unequal in any given year, most individuals move up and down the economic ladder over their lifetime. Urban Institute scholars Daniel P. McMurrer and Isabel Sawhill have found that as much as 40 percent of the American population moves up or down into a new income quintile each year. As Chart B suggests, college graduates enjoyed more family income growth in the 1980s than they did in the 1970s, while all others enjoyed considerably less. And as Chart C indicates, economic mobility rates in the United States have not changed much over the last quarter century. As McMurrer and Sawhill conclude, "Americans continue to move up and down in the income distribution at the same rate as they did in the past." Thus America is not becoming an economically "bifurcated society."

CHART A Income Growth, 1973–1994

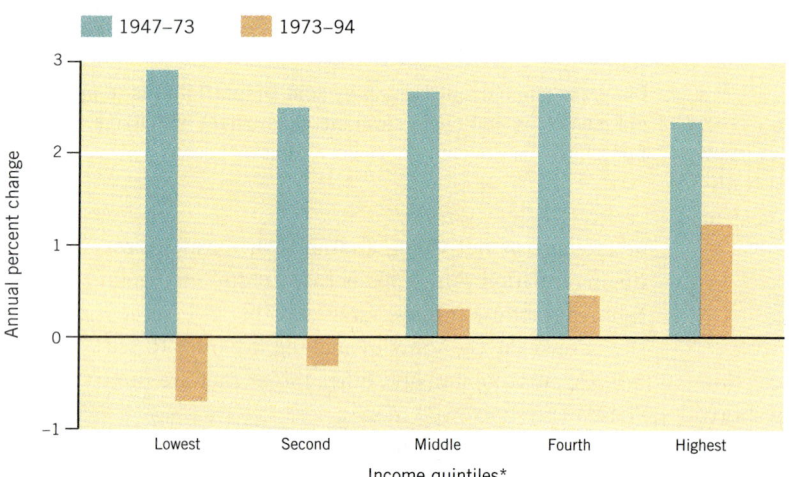

SOURCE: Mishel and Bernstein, *The State of Working America 1996-97* (Washington, D.C.: Economic Policy Institute, 1996).

*The lowest income quintile consists of the 20 percent of all families with the lowest income as measured by the Census Bureau. The second quintile consists of the second poorest 20 percent, and so forth.

CHART B Income Growth Among College Graduates, 1970s and 1980s

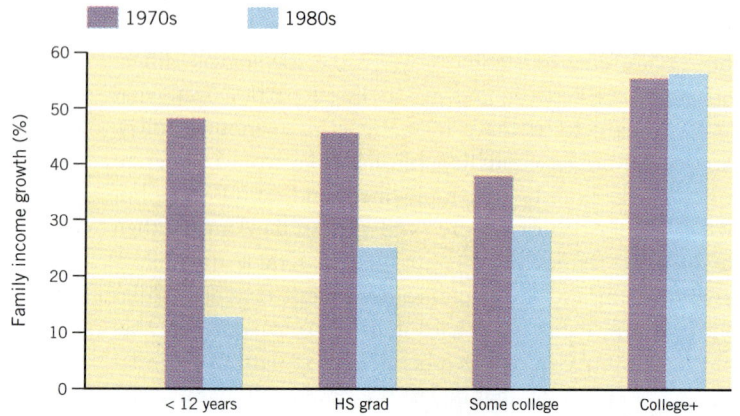

2. *Family Income.* Say a two-earner, $40,000-a-year couple with dependent children gets divorced: one family with $40,000 a year in income becomes two "households" with $20,000 each, and the parent with the children is now classified as living in a low-income household. In 1993 about 17.5 percent of all families were headed by a woman with no husband present, up from 10.8 percent in 1973. As economic analyst Alan Reynolds has observed, "when a rising percentage of 'families' consists of women with children, this naturally holds down median family income for *all* families. The resulting dilution of median income does not mean that some 'average' or typical family has had little or no increase in income. Instead, it means that 'family' income two decades ago cannot properly be compared with 'family' income today, when some families are so differently constituted." In fact, as Chart D shows, median family income in the United States (measured in constant dollars) has been fairly stable over the last quarter century.

3. *The Middle Class.* First the "bad" news: from 1979 to 1989, the percentage of families earning between $15,000 and $50,000 a year (in constant 1992 dollars) shrank from 61 percent to 49 percent of all families. Now, however, the good news: all of that loss in the middle is fully accounted for by an increase in the number of families earning over $50,000 a year. As Reynolds notes, the "fact that a rising percentage of U.S. families earned over $50,000 in the eighties" does not mean that "the rich got richer. Actually, the middle got richer."

What other data might help you to decide whether or not America, long heralded as the land of economic oppor-

tunity, has become or is rapidly becoming a land of income inequality? Think about the normative issues involved. For example, do you think corporate executives should be allowed to earn fifty or more times what the lowest-earning employee of the corporation makes? What about super highly paid professional athletes? And what do you suppose the Founders would say about income inequality? (Hint: take another look at *Federalist* No. 10.)

In any case, be on guard against negative-sounding statements about U.S. in-

come inequality like this one, made by a journalist and overheard at a conference: "Half of all households in the U.S. today are below the median household income." This dour-sounding statement is of course quite true—by definition of the word *median*.

SOURCES: Daniel P. McMurrer and Isabel V. Sawhill, *How Much Do Americans Move Up and Down the Economic Ladder?* The Urban Institute Opportunity in America Series, No. 3 (Washington, D.C.: The Urban Institute), November 1996; Alan Reynolds, "Economic Foundations of the American Dream," in L. Alexander and C. E. Finn, *The New Promise of American Life* Indianapolis, Ind.: (The Hudson Institute), chapter 12.

CHART C Mobility Rates, 1970s and 1980s

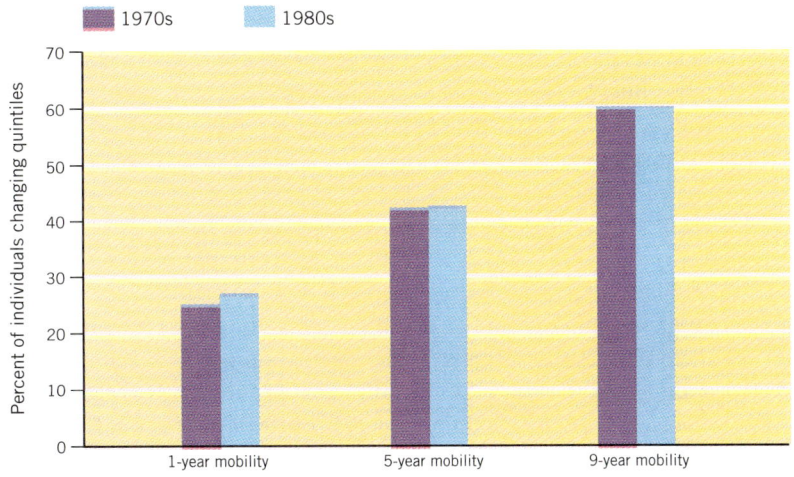

CHART D Median Family Income, 1970–1993 (Constant 1991 Dollars)

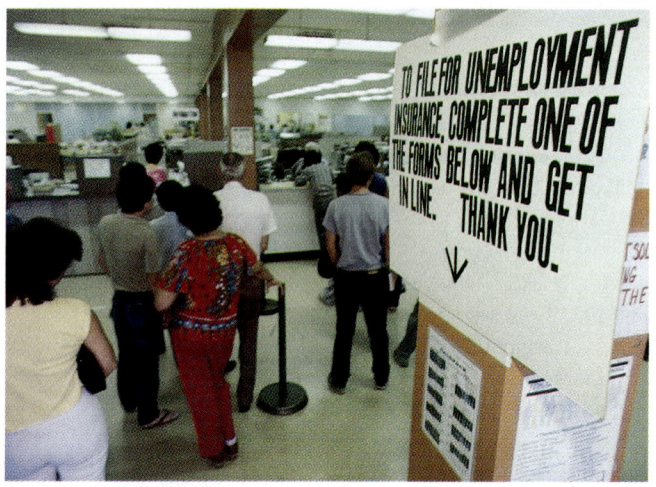

When there are long lines at the unemployment office (as here in Detroit), the political party of the incumbent president is in trouble.

that he should be worrying more about creating jobs. But the general tendency seems clear: the Democratic party worries more about unemployment, the Republican party about inflation.

This tendency mirrors to some degree what Democratic and Republican voters want their parties to do. Polls regularly show that those who think of themselves as Democrats are much more worried about unemployment than those who think of themselves as Republicans.[9] (There is not as much of a difference between Democratic and Republican voters in worrying about inflation.) Because of these beliefs, voters concerned about unemployment not only are more likely to vote against the incumbent but also are more likely to vote Democratic.

Economic Theories and Political Needs

Policies aimed at improving the economy as a whole are examples of majoritarian politics. Benefits and costs are widely distributed, because a healthy economy benefits almost everybody and a stagnant one hurts almost everybody. As with most majoritarian issues, the president takes the lead and is held responsible for the results. But as we have seen, presidents do not always know what to do. The economy is an extraordinarily complex, poorly understood set of interrelationships. Nations that have tried to run this machine by central commands have not done very well. Presidents thus become very dependent on the advice of experts who claim to have an idea about how best to nudge the machine in the right direction. For better or worse, presidents (and governments) choose among competing economic theories.

There are at least four major theories about how best to manage the economy. Each theory, if fully stated, would be quite complicated; moreover, many experts combine parts of one theory with parts of another. What follows is a highly simplified account of these theories that highlights their differences.

Monetarism

A monetarist, such as economist Milton Friedman, believes that inflation occurs when there is too much money chasing too few goods. The federal government has the power to create money (in ways to be described on page 508); according to monetarists, inflation occurs when it prints too much money. When inflation becomes rampant and government tries to do something about it, it often cuts back sharply on the amount of money in circulation. Then a recession will occur, with slowed economic growth and an increase in unemployment. Since the government does not understand that economic problems result from its own start-and-stop habit of issuing new money, it will try to cure some of these problems by policies that make matters worse—such as having an unbalanced budget or creating new welfare programs. **Monetarism** suggests that the proper thing for government to do is to have a steady, predictable increase in the money supply at a rate about equal to the growth in the economy's productivity; beyond that it should leave matters alone and let the free market operate.

Keynesianism

John Maynard Keynes, an English economist who died in 1946, believed that the market will not automatically operate at a full-employment, low-inflation level. Its health will depend on what fraction of their incomes people save or spend. If they save too much, there will be too little demand, production will decline, and unemployment will rise. If they spend too much, demand will rise too fast, prices will go up, and shortages will develop. According to **Keynesianism,** the key is to create the right level of demand. This is the task of government. When demand is too little, the government should pump more money into the economy (by spending more than it takes in in taxes and by creating public-works programs). When demand is too great, the government should take money out of the economy (by increasing taxes or cutting federal expenditures). There is no need for the government's budget to be balanced on a year-to-year basis; what counts is the performance of the economy. Keynesians, unlike monetarists, tend to favor an activist government.

Planning

Some economists have too little faith in the workings of the free market to be pure Keynesians, much less monetarists. They believe that the government should plan, in varying ways, some part of the country's economic activity. One form of **economic planning** is **price and wage controls,** as advocated by John Kenneth Galbraith and others. In this view big corporations can raise prices because the forces of competition are too weak to restrain them, and labor unions can force up wages because management finds it easy to pass the increases along to consumers in the form of higher prices. Thus during inflationary times the government should regulate the maximum prices that can be charged and wages that can be paid, at least in the larger industries.

In the mid-1980s inflation was not the problem that it once had been, however; instead the automakers were cutting car prices and labor unions were accepting wage reductions. This shift drew attention to a different form of economic planning. Called an **industrial policy,** it reflected the public's concern for the declining health of certain basic industries such as steel and automobile manufacturing. People thought that these "smokestack" industries would not recover through market forces; what was needed instead was for the government somehow to direct or plan investments so that either these industries would recover or new and better industries would take their places. Advocates of this form of planning, such as Robert Reich (who became secretary of labor in the Clinton administration), often

 ## Are Economists Ever Right?

*T*he jokes about them are endless. George Meany, a labor leader, once said that economics is the only profession in which you can rise to eminence without ever being right. Rudolph Penner, one-time head of the Congressional Budget Office (and himself an economist), quipped that economists can't even predict what happened in the past. What Paul Samuelson, a Nobel-prize-winning economist, once said about the stock market could also be said about economists: they have predicted nine of the last five recessions.

It is true that economists have not done a very good job of predicting which way the economy would move in the years ahead. In 1986, for example, the forecasts, made one year in advance by fifteen leading economic forecasters (two in the government, thirteen in the private sector), were in error by 25 percent in forecasting growth in the gross national product, by nearly 99 percent in forecasting price levels (that is, inflation), and by 19 percent in forecasting key interest rates.[1]

The government forecasters are the Office of Management and Budget (OMB), part of the executive branch, and the Congressional Budget Office (CBO), part of Congress. Both tend to make overly optimistic predictions. For example, both thought that economic growth in 1986 would be higher than it was by an average of 44 percent.[2]

Does all this make economics useless? Not at all, any more than meteorology is useless despite the inability of meteorologists to predict the weather one year (or even one week) in advance. Today economists measure, with growing accuracy, what the economy is doing at any given moment. By contrast, when Herbert Hoover was president, we had no reliable information on how many people were unemployed or how much money workers were making.

Moreover, economics reminds us of some sensible propositions that we forget at our peril: for example, that everything has a cost, or in popular parlance that there is no such thing as a free lunch. Finally, economists can use their concepts of price and cost to explain (and even predict) how parts of the economy will respond to specific changes in certain conditions. For instance, higher interest rates will cause less housing to be built.

SOURCES: [1]Charles Wolf, Jr., "Scoring the Economic Forecasters," *The Public Interest* (Summer 1987): 48–55, and Stephen K. McNees and John Ries, "The Track Record of Macroeconomic Forecasts," *New England Economic Review* (November–December 1983): 5–18. [2]Mark S. Kamlet, David C. Mowrey, and Tsai-Tsu Su, "Whom Do You Trust? An Analysis of Executive and Congressional Economic Forecasts," *Journal of Policy Analysis and Management* 6 (Spring 1987): 365–384, and *National Journal* (March 7, 1987): 552.

point to Japan as an example of a country in which the government does direct industrial investments.

Supply-Side Tax Cuts

Exactly the opposite remedy for declining American productivity is suggested by people who call themselves "supply siders." The view of economists such as Arthur Laffer and Paul Craig Roberts is that the market, far from having failed, has not been given an adequate chance. According to **supply-side theory,** what is needed is not more planning but less government interference. In particular, sharply cutting taxes will increase people's incentive to work, save, and invest. Greater investments will then lead to more jobs, and if the earnings from these investments and jobs are taxed less, it will lessen the tendency of many individuals to shelter their earnings from the tax collector by taking advantage of various tax loopholes or cheating on their income tax returns. The greater productivity of the economy will produce more tax revenue for the government. Even though tax *rates* will be lower, the total national income to which these rates are applied will be higher.

Ideology and Theory

Each economic theory has clear political consequences, and so it is no accident that people embrace one theory or another in part because of their political beliefs. If you are a conservative, monetarism or supply-side tax cuts will appeal to you, because both imply that the government will be smaller and less intrusive. If you are a liberal, Keynesian economics will appeal to you, because it permits (or even requires) the federal government to carry on a wide range of social welfare programs. And if you are a socialist, economic planning will appeal to you, because it is an alternative to the free market and the private management of economic resources.

Of course there are many exceptions to these patterns. Many advocates of so-called industrial policy are not socialists; some liberals have become skeptical of Keynesian economics; and quite a few conservatives think that supply-side economics is unrealistic. But in general one's economic theory tends to be consistent with one's political convictions.

"Reaganomics"

When Ronald Reagan became president in 1981, he set in motion changes in federal economic policies that were soon called **Reaganomics.** These changes were not dictated by any single economic theory but by a combination of monetarism, supply-side tax cuts, and domestic budget cutting. The president wanted to achieve several goals simultaneously—reduce the size of the federal government, stimulate economic growth, and increase American military strength. As it turned out for him (as for most presidents), the things that he wanted were not entirely consistent.

Milton Friedman

John Maynard Keynes

John Kenneth Galbraith

Arthur B. Laffer

Spending on some domestic programs was reduced. These reductions slowed the rate of growth of federal spending on these programs but did not actually decrease the spending. Military spending was sharply increased (see Chapter 21). The money supply was held under control in order to combat inflation (at the price of allowing interest rates to rise). Finally, and most important, there were sharp across-the-board cuts in personal income taxes, but for many people these cuts were more than offset by increases in Social Security taxes.

The effect of lowering taxes while increasing spending was to stimulate the economy (by pumping more money into it) and to create large deficits. The stimulated economy resulted in a drop in the unemployment rate and a rise in business activity. The large deficits increased dramatically the size of the national debt. The effects of the tax cuts on productivity and investment were hard to estimate and remain a matter of controversy.

John Maynard Keynes, had he been alive, would have been startled. A conservative president (aided, of course, by Congress) created a massive budget deficit that helped reduce unemployment—just as Keynes, a liberal, might have recommended. The Democrats, taken aback, began for the first time to argue against large budget deficits. In 1984 the Democratic presidential candidate, Walter Mondale, called for raising taxes to balance the budget—just as a traditional conservative might once have done. In 1996, another Democrat, Bill Clinton, committed himself to eliminating the annual budget deficit.

The Machinery of Economic Policy Making

Even if the president knew exactly the right thing to do, he would still have to find some way of doing it. In our government that is no easy task. The machinery for making decisions about economic matters is complex and not under the president's full control. Within the executive branch three people other than the president are of special importance. Sometimes called the "troika,"* these are the chairman of the Council of Economic Advisers (CEA), the director

* From the Russian word for a carriage pulled by three horses.

Defining Some Economic Terms

Fiscal policy An attempt to use taxes and expenditures to affect the economy. A **budget deficit** means that the government spends more than it takes in, thus pumping more money into the economy. A **budget surplus** means that the government takes in more than it spends, thus draining money out of the economy.

Monetary policy An attempt to use the amount of money and bank deposits and the price of money (the interest rate) to affect the economy.

Fiscal year (FY) October 1 to September 30, the period of time for which federal government appropriations are made and federal books are kept. A fiscal year is named after the year in which it *ends*—thus "fiscal 1995" (or "FY 95") means the twelve-month period ending September 30, 1995.

At one time every U.S. dollar could be exchanged for gold. Today the dollar is backed chiefly by public confidence rather than by a precious metal.

The Federal Reserve Board

The Tools by Which the Fed Implements Its Monetary Policy

1. **Buying and selling federal government securities** (bonds, Treasury notes, and other pieces of paper that constitute government IOUs). When the Fed buys securities, it in effect puts more money into circulation and takes securities out of circulation. With more money around, interest rates tend to drop, and more money is borrowed and spent. When the Fed sells government securities, it in effect takes money out of circulation, causing interest rates to rise and making borrowing more difficult.

2. **Regulating the amount of money that a member bank must keep in hand as reserves** to back up the customer deposits it is holding. A bank lends out most of the money deposited with it. If the Fed says that it must keep in reserve a larger fraction of its deposits, then the amount that it can lend drops, loans become harder to obtain, and interest rates rise.

3. **Changing the interest charged banks** that want to borrow money from the Federal Reserve System. Banks borrow from the Fed to cover short-term needs. The interest that the Fed charges for this is called the *discount* rate. The Fed can raise or lower that rate; this will have an effect, though usually rather small, on how much money the banks will lend.

Federal Reserve Board (7 members)

- Determines how many government securities will be bought or sold by regional and member banks.

- Determines interest rates to be charged by regional banks and amount of money member banks must keep in reserve in regional banks.

Regional Federal Reserve Banks (12)

- Buy and sell government securities.
- Loan money to member banks.
- Keep percentage of holdings for member banks.

Member Banks (6,000)

- Buy and sell government securities.
- May borrow money from regional banks.
- Must keep percentage of holdings in regional banks.
- Interest rates paid to regional banks determine interest rates charged for business and personal loans and influence all bank interest rates.

of the Office of Management and Budget (OMB), and the secretary of the treasury.

The CEA, composed of three professional economists plus a small staff, has existed since 1946. In theory it is an impartial group of experts responsible for forecasting economic trends, analyzing economic issues, and helping prepare the economic report that the president submits to Congress each year. Though quite professional in tone, the CEA is not exactly impartial in practice, since each president picks members sympathetic to his point of view. Kennedy picked Keynesians; Reagan picked supply-siders and monetarists. But whatever its philosophical tilt, the CEA is seen by other executive agencies as the advocate of the opinion of professional economists, who despite their differences generally tend to favor reliance on the market.

OMB was originally the Bureau of the Budget, which was created in 1921 and made part of the executive office of the president in 1939; in 1970 it was renamed the Office of Management and Budget. Its chief function is to prepare estimates of the amount that will be spent by federal agencies, to negotiate with other departments over the size of their budgets, and to make certain (insofar as it can) that the legislative proposals of these other departments are in accord with the president's program. Of late it has acquired something of a split personality: it is in part an expert, nonpartisan agency that analyzes spending and budget patterns and in part an activist, partisan organization that tries to get the president's wishes carried out by the bureaucracy. Under President Reagan's appointee David Stockman it became the device for making deep budget cuts in domestic spending.

The secretary of the treasury is often close to or drawn from the world of business and finance and is expected to argue the point of view of the financial community. (Since its members do not always agree, this is not always easy.) The secretary provides estimates of the revenue that the government can expect from existing taxes and what will be the result of changing tax laws, and he or she represents the United States in its dealings with the top bankers and finance ministers of other nations.

A good deal of pulling and hauling takes place among members of the troika, but if that were the extent of the problem, presidential leadership would be fairly easy. The problem is far more complex. In 1978 one study found 132 separate government bureaus engaged in formulating economic policy. They regulate business, make loans, and supply subsidies. For example, as foreign trade becomes increasingly important to this country, the secretary of state (among many others) acquires an interest in economic policy. One-third of corporate profits come from overseas investments, and one-fourth of farm output is sold abroad.

The Fed Among the most important of these other agencies is the board of governors of the Federal Reserve System (the "Fed"). Its seven members are appointed by the president, with the consent of the Senate, for fourteen-year, nonrenewable terms and may not be removed except for cause. (No member has ever been removed since it was created in 1913.) The chairman serves for four years. In theory, and to some degree in practice, the Fed is independent of both the president and Congress. Its most important function is to regulate, insofar as it can, the supply of money (both in circulation and in bank deposits) and the price of money (in the form of interest rates). In the box at left are shown the means employed by the Fed to achieve this, and the structure of the Federal Reserve System over which it presides.

Just how independent the Fed is can be a matter of dispute. During the 1980 election Fed policies helped keep interest rates at a high level, a circumstance that did not benefit President Carter's reelection bid. On the other hand, whenever a president is determined to change monetary policy, he usually can do so. For example, the term of Fed chairman Arthur F. Burns, appointed by President Nixon, came up for renewal in 1978. President Carter, seeking to influence Burns's decisions, held out the prospect of reappointing him chairman. When Burns balked, he was passed over, and G. William Miller was appointed in his stead. Presidents Truman, Johnson, and Nixon were all able to obtain changes in monetary policy. However, inducing the Fed to change its policy requires influence, of which no president has an unlimited supply.

Congress The most important part of the economic policy–making machinery, of course, is Con-

Alan Greenspan, chairman of the Federal Reserve Board.

gress. It must approve all taxes and almost all expenditures; there can be no wage or price controls without its consent; and it has the ability to alter the policy of the nominally independent Federal Reserve Board by threatening to pass laws that would reduce its powers. And Congress itself is fragmented, with great influence wielded by the members of key committees, especially the House and Senate Budget Committees, the House and Senate Appropriations Committees, the House Ways and Means Committee, and the Senate Finance Committee.

In sum, no matter what economic theory the president may have, if he is to put that theory into effect he needs the assistance of (1) many agencies within the executive branch, (2) such independent agencies as the Federal Reserve Board, and (3) the various committees of Congress. Though members of the executive and legislative branches are united by their common desire to get reelected (and thus have a common interest in producing sound economic growth), each part of this system may also be influenced by different economic theories and will be motivated by the claims of interest groups.

The effect of these interest group claims is clearly shown in the debate over trade restriction. Usually the economic health of the nation affects everyone in pretty much the same way—we are all hurt by inflation or helped by stable prices; the incomes of all of us tend to grow (or remain stagnant) together. In these circumstances the politics of economic health is majoritarian.

Now suppose, however, that most of us are doing pretty well but that the people in a few industries or occupations are suffering. That is exactly what happened in the 1980s when various forces combined to hurt such basic U.S. industries as steel and such important occupations as farming. Although economists differ over exactly what went wrong, in general these sectors of the economy were hurt by foreign competition (that is, foreign nations found it easy to sell things here), the rising value of the dollar (as a result U.S. companies and farmers found it hard to sell their products abroad), and overexpansion (many companies and farmers had gone heavily into debt to expand production beyond what the market would support).

Under these conditions the politics of economic health will pit one part of the country against another. People who want to buy things made abroad—German automobiles, Japanese computers, Taiwanese shoes—will oppose placing any restrictions on their ability to import these things. By contrast, people who make American automobiles, American computers, and American shoes will favor heavy restrictions (such as quotas or tariffs). Economic health becomes subject to interest group politics.

In 1988 Congress responded to these competing pressures by passing a trade bill that put enough restrictions on foreign imports to satisfy the protectionists but not so many as to outrage the advocates of free trade. In the 1988 presidential election the worth of this legislation was a big issue, not only between the Democratic and Republican candidates but among the primary candidates within each party.

Spending Money

If only the economic health of the nation mattered, then majoritarian politics would dominate, and so the president and Congress would both work to improve economic conditions. Although they still might work at cross-purposes because they held to different economic theories, the goal would be the same.

But the government must also respond to the demands of voters and interest groups. The trade bill was an example of that. While these demands are no less legitimate than the voters' general interest in economic health, they produce not majoritarian but client and interest group politics.

The sources of this conflict can be seen in public opinion polls. Voters consistently say that they want a balanced budget and lower government spending. They believe that the government spends too much and that if it wanted to, it could cut spending. When the government runs a deficit, the reason in the voters' eyes is that it is spending too much, not that it is taxing too little. But these same polls show that the voters believe that the government should spend more on education, homelessness, child care, crime control, and almost anything else that one can think of (except welfare and food stamps) (see Figure 16.2).

The voters are not irrational, thinking that they can have more spending and less spending simultaneously. Nor are they hypocrites, pretending to want less spending overall but more spending for particular programs. They are simply expressing a variety of concerns and a theory about spending. They want a limited government with no deficit; they also want good schools, cleaner air, better health care, and less crime. They believe that a frugal government could deliver what they want by cutting out waste. They may by wrong about that belief, but it is not obviously silly.

What this means for the government is easy to imagine. Politicians have an incentive to make two kinds of appeals: The first is, "Vote for me and I will keep government spending down and cut the deficit." The second is, "Vote for me and I will make certain that your favorite program gets more money." Some people will vote for the candidate be-

cause of the first appeal, some will vote for him or her because of the second. But acting on these two appeals is clearly going to lead to inconsistent policies. Where those inconsistencies become evident is in the budget.

FIGURE 16.2 Do People Want More for Less?

The average citizen thinks that government spends too much. Most people don't want their taxes raised. But when asked about whether government should spend more, less, or about the same on various programs, the great majority favors spending the same or even more:

SOURCE: On taxes, space program, and the military: ABC-*Washington Post* survey as reported in *National Journal* (April 18, 1987): 924, and (February 21, 1987): 444; on other programs: 1992 NES Pre/Post-Election Study.

The Budget

A **budget** is a document that announces how much the government will collect in taxes and spend in revenues and how those expenditures will be allocated among various programs. In theory the federal budget should be based on *first* deciding how much money the government is going to spend and *then* allocating that money among different programs and agencies. That is the way a household makes up its budget: "We have this much in the paycheck, and so we will spend *X* dollars on rent, *Y* dollars on food, and *Z* dollars on clothing, and what's left over on entertainment. If the amount of the paycheck goes down, we will cut something out—probably entertainment."

In fact, the federal budget is a list of everything the government is going to spend money on, with only slight regard (sometimes no regard) for how much money is available to be spent. Instead of being a way of *allocating* money to be spent on various purposes, it is a way of *adding up* what is in fact being spent.

Indeed, there was no federal budget at all before 1921, and there was no unified presidential budget until the 1930s. Even after the president began submitting a single budget, the committees of Congress acted on it separately, adding to or subtracting from the amounts he proposed. (Usually they followed his lead, but they were certainly free to depart from it as they wished.) If one committee wanted to spend more on housing, no effort was made to take that amount away from the committee that was spending money on health (in fact, there was no machinery for making such an effort).

The Congressional Budget Act of 1974 changed this somewhat. Now after the president submits his budget in January, two budget committees—one in the House, one in the Senate—study the president's overall package and obtain an analysis of it from the Congressional Budget Office (CBO). Each committee then submits to its house a **budget resolution** that proposes a total budget ceiling and a ceiling for each of several spending areas (such as health or defense). Each May Congress adopts, with some modifications, these budget resolutions, intending them to be targets to guide the work of each legislative committee as it decides what should be spent in its area. During the summer Congress then takes up the specific appropriations bills, informing its members as it goes along whether or not the spending proposed in these bills conforms to the May budget res-

FIGURE 16.3 Trends in the National Debt

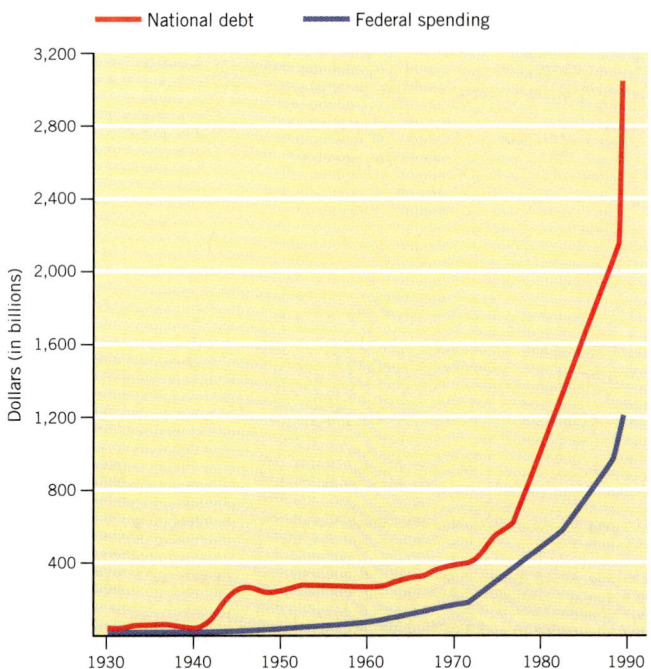

SOURCE: *Economic Reports of the President,* various years.

olution. The object, obviously, is to impose some discipline on the various committees. After all the individual appropriations are decided, Congress then adopts a second budget resolution that "reconciles" the overall budget ceiling with the total resulting from the individual appropriations bills.

The loophole in this process is very large: there is nothing to prevent Congress from ignoring its first budget resolution, passed in May, and thereby making its second resolution, passed in September, simply reflect the total of all the individual spending bills that it has adopted. And sometimes Congress does just that. But the existence of this formal budget process has made a difference, despite the loophole: Congress is now conscious of how its spending decisions match up with an overall total that, for reasons of economic theory and practical politics, it wants to maintain.

When President Reagan took office, he and his allies in Congress took advantage of the Congressional Budget Act to start the controversial process of cutting federal spending. The House and Senate budget committees, with the president's support, used the first budget resolution in May 1981 not simply to set a budget ceiling that, as in the past, looked pretty much like the previous year's budget but to direct each committee of Congress to make *cuts*—sometimes deep cuts—in the programs for which it was responsible. These cuts were to be made in the authorization legislation (see Chapter 13) as well as in the appropriations.

The object was to get members of Congress to vote for a total package of cuts before they could vote on any particular cut. Republican control of the Senate and an alliance between Republicans and conservative southern Democrats in the House allowed this strategy to succeed. The first budget resolution ordered Senate and House committees to reduce federal spending during fiscal 1982 by about $36 billion—less than the president had first asked, but a large sum nonetheless. Then the individual committees set to work trying to find ways of making these cuts.

Note how the *procedures* used by Congress can affect the *policies* adopted by Congress. If the Reagan plan had been submitted in the old piecemeal way, it is unlikely that cuts of this size would have occurred in so short a time, or at all. The reason is not that Congress would have wanted to ignore the president but that, then as now, Congress reflects public opinion on economic policy. As stated at the beginning of the chapter, the public wants less total federal spending but more money spent on specific federal programs. Thus, if you allow the public or Congress to vote first on specific programs, spending is bound to rise. But if you require Congress to vote first on a budget ceiling, then (unless it changes its mind as it goes along) total spending will go down, and tough choices will have to be made about the component parts of the budget.

That, at least, is the theory. It worked once, in 1981, but it did not work very well thereafter. During the rest of the Reagan years the budget process broke down in the warfare between the president and Congress. President Reagan represented the part of public opinion that wanted less government spending in general; most members of Congress represented the part of public opinion that wanted more spending on particular programs. The result was a stalemate. In 1984 the budget resolution was not passed until late September (four months late); in 1985, not until August (three months late). The amount being spent every year (see Figure 16.3) was far in excess of the amount coming in from tax revenues. Part of this gap existed because taxes had been sharply cut in 1981. The responsibility was bipartisan—a Republican president had proposed the tax cut and signed the spending bills, and a majority of Senate Democrats had voted for the tax cut and the spending bills.

The deficit grew to the point that even politicians eager to please their constituents' demand for more services began to worry that the economy's health might be in peril. Accordingly, in 1985 Congress changed the budget process once again by passing the Gramm-Rudman Balanced Budget Act (named after two of its sponsors, Senators Phil Gramm [R., Texas] and Warren Rudman [R., New Hampshire]).

Signed by President Reagan, the law created a plan whereby the budget would automatically be cut until there was no longer a deficit. Each year between 1986 and 1991 the deficit could not exceed a specified, declining amount. If Congress and the president could not agree on a spending plan within those targets, there would be automatic, across-the-board percentage cuts—called a **sequester**—in federal programs except for certain exempt programs.* No one liked the idea of automatic budget cuts. Senator Rudman called it "a bad idea whose time has come."

In 1988 George Bush campaigned for the presidency on the slogan "Read my lips—no new taxes." But by 1990 it had become clear that the White House and Congress could not agree on spending cuts sufficient to meet the Gramm-Rudman limits for that year. As a result, Washington faced the prospect of a sequester of close to $100 billion. Everybody's favorite ox was going to be gored. The president and congressional leaders hastily called a summit meeting. After much shadowboxing the president's lips moved again, but this time they said that there would have to be "increased tax revenues."

The first summit agreement was rejected by Congress (one more measure of how little power congressional leaders have). After more back-room bargaining, a budget agreement was finally passed that increased taxes, cut defense spending, and put

---

* The exempt programs were Social Security, interest on the federal debt, veterans' benefits, food stamps, and various other welfare programs.

Budget Reforms

Hardly anyone is satisfied with how the federal government makes spending decisions. It is a complex, cumbersome, and time-consuming process, and in the end it does not produce a true budget but merely a list of appropriations only loosely related to how much money the government has to spend.

Two kinds of reforms have been proposed—procedural and constitutional. In general liberals have preferred the procedural changes and conservatives the constitutional ones, but there are many exceptions.

Procedural Changes

1. Have Congress vote on a budget and pass appropriations bills only once every two years. This would unclog the process and lighten the workload.

2. Combine appropriations and authorization bills. At present separate committees must approve the authorization for a program and the appropriation for that program.

Constitutional Changes

1. Amend the Constitution to require a balanced budget. As of 1988 thirty-two states had passed resolutions asking Congress to call a constitutional convention to consider a balanced-budget amendment. This is only two states short of the number needed to force Congress to call such a convention, which would be the first since 1787. The amendment would allow an unbalanced budget in wartime or whenever an extraordinary majority in Congress voted for it. One version of the amendment would also limit increases in federal spending to some percentage of the increase in national income.

2. Amend the Constitution to give the president a line-item veto, now possessed by the governors of forty-three states. This would make it possible for the president to veto a specific item in a bill without vetoing the whole bill. A mild version of a line-item veto has been authorized by legislation, but the courts may declare it unconstitutional.

---

in place new budgeting procedures. The top tax rate went up from 28 percent to 31 percent, gasoline taxes were raised by ten cents a gallon, tax deductions were limited, and alcohol and tobacco taxes were increased. Hardly any domestic spending pro-

Major Provisions of the 1993 Budget Reconciliation Act

Individuals

- Created a fourth tax bracket, increasing the effective top rate from 36 percent to 39.6 percent for upper-income taxpayers.
- Phased out the personal exemption for upper-income taxpayers.
- Raised the portion of Social Security benefits subject to taxation from 50 percent to 85 percent for individuals making more than $34,000 a year and couples making more than $44,000 a year.
- Eliminated deductions for dues in any club organized for business, pleasure, recreation, or other social purposes.

Corporations

- Increased top tax rate from 25 percent to 34 percent.
- Reduced deductions for

  Business meals.

  Moving expenses.

  Travel expenses.
- Eliminated deductions for lobbying expenses.

Minimum Tax

- Increased the minimum tax on individuals by creating a two-tiered rate structure: a 26 percent rate for the first $175,000 of a taxpayer's income and a 28 percent rate for income above $175,000.
- Relaxed the minimum tax on business by changing the formula by which it is calculated.

to calm the raging debate over tax increases versus spending cuts as the best means of reducing the deficit. That debate exploded into all-out partisan warfare in 1993 when the newly elected Democratic president, Bill Clinton, offered a new plan to achieve substantial deficit reduction.

The Clinton administration claimed that its first budget, approved in August 1993, would reduce the deficit by an estimated $505 billion over five years, about half through spending cuts ($255 billion) and the other half through tax increases ($250 billion). By comparison, tax increases accounted for only about one-third of the deficit reduction achieved by the 1990 budget agreement. Among the key provisions of the 1993 budget bill are the following:

- An increase in the top tax rate from 31 percent to over 39 percent
- An increase in the portion of Social Security benefits subject to taxation from 50 percent to 85 percent for upper-income retirees
- About one-quarter of all spending cuts ($56 billion) to come from Medicare
- About $21 billion added to expand the earned income tax credit, which goes to poor, working families
- A 4.3¢ increase in the 14.1¢ per gallon federal gasoline tax

Politically, the most significant feature of the 1993 budget bill mirrors that of the 1990 budget agreement—namely, caps on appropriations that mandate area-specific cuts to finance new expenditures. The 1993 bill also capped discretionary spending at $539 billion in fiscal 1994 and allows such spending to increase to only $549 billion by 1998.

In the early 1990s, following the collapse of the Soviet Union, there was much talk of a **peace dividend**—vast sums of money for domestic spending freed up by cuts in post–Cold War defense spending. By most estimates, however, the defense cuts in the 1993 bill were not even enough to let existing domestic programs grow at the rate of inflation between 1994 and 1998, let alone to finance new programs. Thus the 1990 and 1993 caps on domestic spending constituted a "hard freeze," meaning that any new domestic programs must be paid for by

grams were cut; indeed, even after the defense cuts, total spending was scheduled to go up by almost 5 percent.[10]

The 1990 budget agreement was designed to permit the Democratic Congress and the Republican White House to get through the 1992 elections without having to make immediate spending cuts. The agreement did little either to cut the deficit or cost-saving reforms or the elimination of existing programs.

To say that Clinton had difficulty in getting the 1993 budget bill passed is an understatement. The final bill was hammered out in a grueling summer of negotiations. The president was forced to give ground on several major provisions of his original plan, including his call for a broad-based, $72 billion energy tax. During the often heated debate, Republicans insisted that the bill relied too much on taxes and not enough on spending cuts, while Democrats worried about the domestic spending caps and argued that the bill was not generous enough with the poor. Some members of both parties complained that even if the plan's economic projections proved to be exactly on target, it would slow the deficit only temporarily through 1997; then the deficit would start galloping again.

When the political dust settled, the bill passed in the House on August 5 by a vote of 218–216. Not a single Republican voted for the package, and forty-one Democrats voted against it. The next day, the Senate adopted the bill by a razor-thin margin of 51–50, with Vice President Al Gore casting the tie-breaking vote. Once again not a single Republican voted for the bill. (It was the first time since 1945 that the majority party in Congress had passed major legislation without a single vote from the minority party.)

In 1997, Clinton had an easier time getting the budget agreement. He persuaded Republican congressional leaders to support a plan that would eliminate the annual budget deficit by the year 2002. In return for this, he got them to agree to several new spending programs. They, in turn, got him to agree to certain tax cuts. What made it possible to claim that the deficit would disappear even though spending increased was the productivity of the American economy. There was a new increase in tax revenues that resulted from prosperity. In short, few hard choices had to be made.

Under any circumstances, cutting spending is no easy matter. Strong pressures support every government program, and a large part of the federal budget consists of expenditures that represent past commitments that, politically and sometimes legally, cannot be altered. Politicians speak of these as "uncontrollable" expenditures because they involve contracts

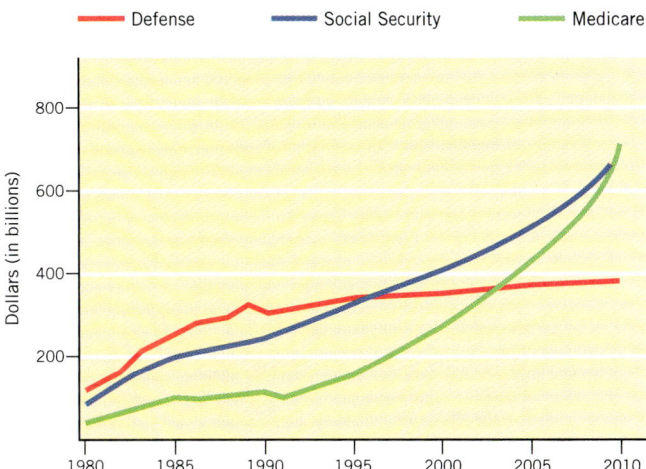

FIGURE 16.4 Where Will the Crunch Come? Projections of the Growth in Federal Spending

NOTE: Outyear defense projections are extrapolations of FY 1991–1995 presidential policy, which could change.

SOURCE: *Budget of the United States Government, Fiscal Year 1991*, 187.

already signed, payments (such as Social Security) that are guaranteed by law, and interest on the national debt that must be paid if the government is to stay in business. In Figure 16.4 we see how rapidly spending on Social Security and Medicare has grown. Projections of the growth of federal spending suggest that Medicare expenditures will in time exceed those for Social Security and defense.

In 1985, a typical year, these relatively uncontrollable expenditures accounted for about *three-fourths* of all federal outlays. Of course some (such as Social Security) can be controlled if one is willing to reduce benefits promised to individuals, but such an action is quite risky. Most of the easily controllable expenditures are concentrated in the national defense area, a fact that helps explain why there is greater variation from year to year in spending on defense than in spending on nondefense programs.

Just how difficult it is to cut federal spending is underscored by the fact that one year after President Reagan was inaugurated, the federal government was spending *more* than it had been before he was elected. Although planned expenditures were cut, significantly affecting some domestic programs, this cut did not reduce total federal spending, or even total non-defense spending—it simply slowed the rate of increase.

FIGURE 16.5   Tax Burdens in Twenty-two Democratic Nations

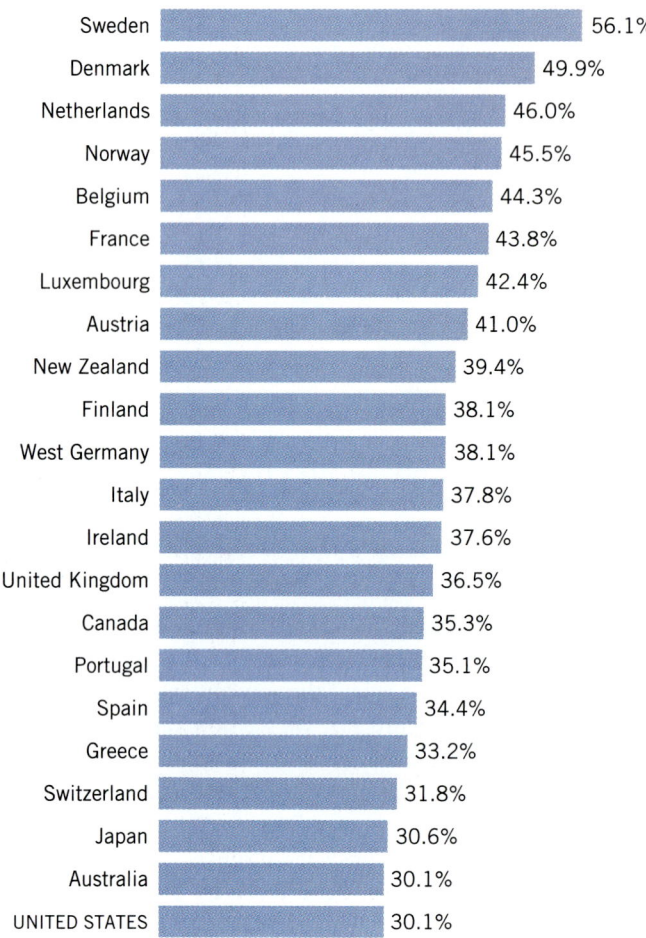

Sweden	56.1%
Denmark	49.9%
Netherlands	46.0%
Norway	45.5%
Belgium	44.3%
France	43.8%
Luxembourg	42.4%
Austria	41.0%
New Zealand	39.4%
Finland	38.1%
West Germany	38.1%
Italy	37.8%
Ireland	37.6%
United Kingdom	36.5%
Canada	35.3%
Portugal	35.1%
Spain	34.4%
Greece	33.2%
Switzerland	31.8%
Japan	30.6%
Australia	30.1%
UNITED STATES	30.1%

SOURCE: *Statistical Abstract of the United States,* 1992, 836.

Indeed, it is almost impossible for any president to know by how much he *has* cut the budget. Federal programs contain countless provisions that automatically cause spending to increase or decrease depending on economic conditions that cannot be foreseen. For example, it has been estimated that a 1 percent increase in the unemployment rate will cause the government to spend $7 billion more than it had planned (in the form of unemployment and welfare benefits) and to take in $12 billion less than it had hoped (because people out of work do not pay taxes). In short, a small change in unemploy-

ment can cause a $19 billion swing in the government's budget. As someone has said, much of the government budget is on automatic pilot.

Levying Taxes

Tax policy reflects a various mixture of majoritarian politics ("What is a 'fair' tax law?") and client politics ("How much is in it for me?"). In the United States a fair tax law has generally been viewed as one that keeps the overall tax burden rather low, requires everyone to pay something, and requires the better-off to pay at a higher rate than the less-well-off. The law, in short, was viewed as good if it imposed modest burdens, prevented cheating, and was mildly progressive.

Americans have had their first goal satisfied. The tax burden in the United States is lower than it is in most other democratic nations (see Figure 16.5). There is some evidence that they have also had their second goal met—there is reason to believe that Americans evade their income taxes less than do citizens of, say, France or Italy. (That is one reason why many nations rely more on sales taxes than we do—they are harder to evade.) Just how progressive our tax rates are is a matter of dispute; to determine whether the rich really pay at higher rates than the poor, one has to know not only the official rates but also the effect of deductions, exemptions, and exclusions (that is, of loopholes).

Keeping the burden low and the cheating at a minimum are examples of majoritarian politics: most people benefit, most people pay. The loopholes, however, are another matter—all manner of special interests can get some special benefit from the tax law that the rest of us must pay for but, given the complexity of the law, rarely notice. Loopholes are client politics, par excellence.

Because of that, hardly any scholars believed that tax reform (dramatically reducing the loopholes) was politically possible. Every interest that benefited from a loophole—and these included not just corporations but universities, museums, states, cities, and investors—would lobby vigorously to protect it.

Nevertheless, in 1986 a sweeping tax reform act was passed. Many of the most cherished loopholes

FIGURE 16.6 Federal Taxes on Income, Top Percentage
Rates, 1913–1993

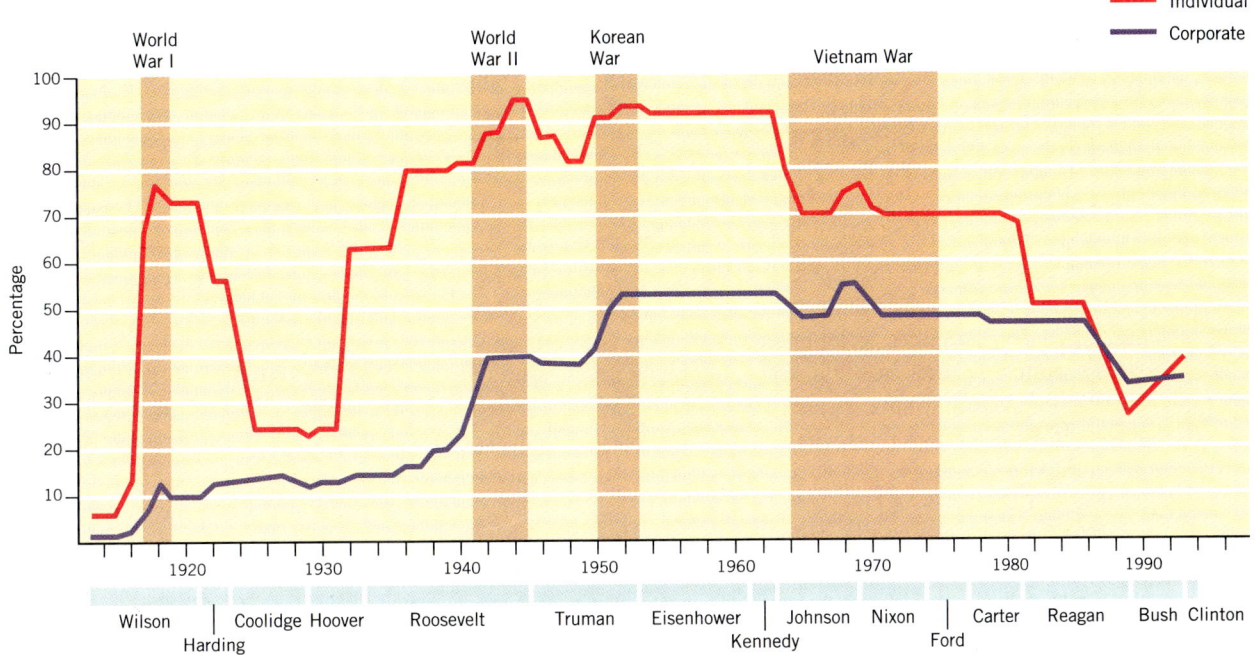

SOURCE: *Wall Street Journal* (August 18, 1986): 10. Reprinted by permission of the
Wall Street Journal, ©1982 Dow Jones & Company, Inc. All rights reserved worldwide.
Congressional Quarterly Weekly Report (September 18, 1993): 2488.

were closed or reduced. What happened? It is as if
scientists who had proved that a bumblebee could
not fly got stung by a flying bumblebee.

The Rise of the Income Tax

To understand what happened in 1986, one must
first understand the political history of taxation in
the United States. Until almost the end of the nineteenth century, there was no federal income tax (except for a brief period during the Civil War). The
money that the government needed came mostly
from tariffs (that is, taxes on goods imported into
this country). And when Congress did enact a
peacetime income tax, the Supreme Court in 1895
struck it down as unconstitutional.[11] To change this,
Congress proposed, and in 1913 the states ratified,
the Sixteenth Amendment, which authorized such a
tax.

For the next forty years or so tax rates tended to
go up during wartime and down during peacetime
(see Figure 16.6). The rates were progressive—that
is, the wealthiest individuals paid at a higher rate
than the less affluent. For example, during World
War II incomes in the highest bracket were taxed at
a rate of 94 percent. (The tax rate in the highest
bracket is called by economists the "marginal rate."
This is the percentage of the last dollar that you earn
that must be paid out in taxes.)

An income tax offers the opportunity for majoritarian politics to become class politics. The majority of the citizenry earn average incomes and
control most of the votes. In theory there is nothing
to prevent the mass of people from voting for legislators who will tax only the rich, who as a minority
will always be outvoted. During the early decades of
this century, that is exactly what the rich feared
would happen. Since the highest marginal tax rate

was 94 percent, you might think that that is in fact what did happen.

You would be wrong. Offsetting the high rates were the deductions, exemptions, and exclusions by which people could shelter some of their income from taxation. These loopholes were available for everyone, but they particularly helped the well-off. In effect a political compromise was reached during the first half of this century. The terms were these: the well-off, generally represented by the Republican party, would drop their bitter opposition to high marginal rates provided that the less-well-off, generally represented by the Democratic party, would support a large number of loopholes. The Democrats (or more accurately, the liberals) were willing to accept this compromise because they feared that if they insisted on high rates with no loopholes, the economy would suffer as people and businesses lost their incentive to save and invest.

For at least thirty years after the adoption of the income tax in 1913, only a small number of high-income people paid any significant amount in federal income taxes. The average citizen paid very little in such taxes until World War II. After the war, taxes did not fall to their prewar levels.

Most people did not complain too much, because they, too, benefited greatly from the loopholes. They could deduct from their taxable income the interest they paid on their home mortgages, the state and local taxes they paid, much of what they paid in medical insurance premiums, and the interest they paid on consumer loans (such as those used to buy automobiles). On the eve of the Tax Reform Act of 1986, an opinion poll showed that more people favored small cuts in tax rates coupled with many large deductions than favored big cuts in tax rates coupled with fewer and smaller deductions.[12]

Interest groups organized around each loophole. Home builders organized to support the mortgage-interest deduction; universities supported the charitable-contribution deduction; insurance companies supported the deduction for medical insurance premiums; and automakers supported the deduction for interest on consumer loans.

In addition to these well-known loopholes there were countless others, not so well known and involving much less money, that were defended and enlarged through the efforts of other interest groups:

for instance, oil companies supported the deduction for drilling costs, heavy industry supported the investment tax credit, and real estate developers supported special tax write-offs for apartment and office buildings.

Until 1986 the typical tax fight was less about rates than about deductions. Rates were important, but not as important as tax loopholes. "Loophole politics" was client politics. When client groups pressed for benefits, they could take advantage of the decentralized structure of Congress to find well-placed advocates who could advance these interests through low-visibility bargaining. In effect these groups were getting a subsidy from the federal government equal to the amount of the tax break. However, the tax break was even better than a subsidy, because it did not have to be voted on every year as part of an appropriations bill: once part of the tax code, it lasted for a long time, and given the length and complexity of that code, scarcely anyone would notice it was there.

Many of these loopholes could be justified by arguments about economic growth. Especially low tax rates on a certain kind of investment encouraged more investment of that kind. Deductions for mortgage interest and property taxes encouraged people to own their own homes and boosted the construction industry.

Then the Tax Reform Act of 1986 turned the decades-old compromise on its head: instead of high rates with big deductions, we got low rates with much smaller deductions. The big gainers were individuals; the big losers were businesses. What happened?

The Politics of Tax Reform

What happened, in essence, is that majoritarian politics resurfaced in the form of a demand for fairness. The old system of loophole politics had created a situation in which some policy entrepreneurs could point to both real and imagined scandals that enabled them to mobilize majorities supporting change.

There were several kinds of entrepreneurs. Some were professional economists who had been writing for years about the inequities and inefficiencies of the old tax code. They complained that high tax rates discouraged investment and risk taking by people who could not take advantage of any existing loopholes. They argued that many business decisions were being made not on the basis of what was economically efficient but on the basis of what worked under the tax law. Over time the weight of this professional opinion on taxes was beginning to make itself felt, just as the weight of such opinion against regulation of the airlines had made itself felt in the events leading up to deregulation in 1978 (see Chapter 15). In the government these economists found allies in the Treasury Department, the Council of Economic Advisers, and the Congress.

Another kind of entrepreneur included people who had an ideological commitment to supply-side economics. Then-Representative Jack Kemp was a leader of this group, whose members argued that low tax rates would spur economic growth. They won an initial victory in 1981 when the Reagan tax cut, which they endorsed, was enacted by Congress (it cut the average tax rate by about 23 percent). The 1986 legislation was seen as another step in that direction.

Still other entrepreneurs were those publicists and journalists who liked to produce stories about "tax cheats." These often took the form of lists of wealthy individuals or big corporations that had not paid anything in taxes that year. Usually they had paid no taxes for perfectly legal reasons—their deductions and exemptions were so large as to leave them owing no tax. The people supported the idea of deductions, but not when the system lets somebody get off owing nothing. Opinion polls showed that a clear majority of the public thought that the existing tax laws were "unfair."

For policy entrepreneurs to succeed, they must be able to motivate key politicians. In 1986 the motives were there. Representatives Kemp and Gephardt had presidential ambitions, and so they were willing to take up the cause in order to advance their candidacies. The chairman of the House Ways and Means Committee, Representative Dan Rostenkowski, wanted to be Speaker of the House and saw in support for comprehensive tax reform a way of becoming a stronger candidate for that job (as it turned out, he lost to Representative Jim Wright). The chairman of the Senate Finance Committee, Senator Bob Packwood, had been chagrined by press attacks labeling him "Senator

Major Provisions of the 1986 Tax Reform Act

Individuals

- Eliminated more than a dozen tax brackets, replacing them with two basic brackets: 15 percent and 28 percent. (Previously, the highest bracket was 50 percent.)

- Removed several million poor persons from the tax rolls altogether.

- Increased the size of the personal exemption and standard deduction for individuals and couples.

- Retained deductions for

  Home mortgage interest.

  State and local taxes.

  Itemized charitable contributions.

- Eliminated deductions for

  Interest on consumer loans.

  Sales taxes.

  Many tax shelters.

  Contributions to Individual Retirement Accounts (depending on income and whether covered by employer pension).

- Made tax on capital gains same as tax on other income.

Corporations

- Lowered top tax rate from 46 percent to 34 percent.

- Repealed the investment tax credit.

- Eliminated many tax loopholes.

- Stipulated that only 80 percent of business meals and entertainment can be deducted.

Minimum Tax

- Stipulated that both individuals and corporations would have to pay a minimum tax, even when their deductions and exemptions would otherwise entitle them to pay no tax.

Hackwood" for his prior support of various tax loopholes. The Democratic leadership in Congress wanted to overcome the adverse effect on public opinion created by the support that their 1984 presidential candidate, Walter Mondale, had given to raising taxes; tax reform seemed a good way of making people forget tax increases.

What may have sealed the victory was the behavior of the client groups who fought to keep their favorite loopholes. At congressional hearings on the bill they would sometimes applaud when, in the early negotiations, some pet loophole survived intact. Members of the Senate Finance Committee finally rebelled at this, tore up the bill that they had been considering, and voted overwhelmingly for a new bill that eliminated many loopholes and cut rates. Within a few months the bill was passed and signed (for its provisions, see the box on page 519).

Tax politics had come full circle. The original 1913 tax law had been the product of majoritarian politics. Then, as the fight over rates intensified, subsequent versions of the law became more the product of client politics. In 1986 majoritarian politics reemerged to dominate the proceedings. As with airline deregulation, civil rights, and (as we shall see) foreign policy, ideas sometimes are more important than interests. But in time, the old system began to

reassert itself. Tax rates were slowly increased from where the 1986 law had left them, and more and more tax deductions were added to the law. By the mid-1990s, many people were complaining that the tax law had become so complex that the average person could no longer figure out his or her own taxes.

SUMMARY

There are three economic factors that make a difference to voters; the policies for each are formulated by a distinctive type of policy-making. The first is the economic health of the nation, the second the amount and kinds of government spending, and the third the level and distribution of taxes.

National economic health has powerful effects on the outcome of elections, as much through people's perception of national conditions as from their worries about their own finances. The politics of inflation, unemployment, and economic growth tend to be majoritarian. The president is held responsible for national conditions. But he must meet that responsibility by using imperfect economic theories to manage clumsy government tools controlled by divided political authorities.

When economic ill health occurs in some industries and places but not others (as a result of such forces as foreign competition), the politics of economic health are shaped by interest group politics. Firms that import foreign products or sell to foreign nations try to avoid trade restrictions, while firms and unions hurt by foreign competition try to impose such restrictions.

The amount of spending is theoretically determined by the budget, but in fact the nation has no meaningful budget. Instead the president and Congress struggle over particular spending bills whose amounts reflect interest group and client pressures. In the 1980s those pressures, coupled with a large tax cut, led to a sharp increase in the size of the federal debt.

The general shape of federal tax legislation is determined by majoritarian politics, but the specific provisions (especially the deductions, exemptions, and exclusions) are the result of client-group politics. The Tax Reform Act of 1986 was a remarkable example of the reassertion of majoritarian politics over client-group pressures made possible by policy entrepreneurs and political incentives.

KEY TERMS

monetarism   *p. 504*

Keynesianism   *p. 505*

economic planning   *p. 505*

price and wage controls   *p. 505*

industrial policy   *p. 505*

supply-side theory   *p. 506*

Reaganomics   *p. 506*

fiscal policy   *p. 507*

budget deficit   *p. 507*

budget surplus   *p. 507*

monetary policy   *p. 507*

fiscal year (FY)   *p. 507*

budget   *p. 511*

budget resolution   *p. 511*

sequester   *p. 513*

peace dividend   *p. 514*

SUGGESTED READINGS

Birnbaum, Jeffrey H., and Alan S. Murray. *Showdown at Gucci Gulch.* New York: Random House, 1987. Lively journalistic account of the passage of the Tax Reform Act of 1986.

Kiewiet, D. Roderick. *Macroeconomics and Micropolitics.* Chicago: University of Chicago Press, 1983. Argues that citizens vote on the basis of their estimate of national economic conditions as well as their own financial circumstances.

Samuelson, Robert J. *The Good Life and Its Discontents.* New York: Times Books/Random House, 1995. A readable, intelligent account of American economic life since the Second World War.

Schick, Allen. *The Capacity to Budget.* Washington, D.C.: Urban Institute, 1990. Analysis of federal budget and spending policies.

Stein, Herbert. *Presidential Economics: The Making of Economic Policy from Hoover to Reagan and Beyond.* New York: Simon & Schuster, 1984. History, by a knowledgeable insider, of how economists participate in making federal economic policy, with special emphasis on the period since 1968.

Stein, Herbert, and Murray Foss. *The New Illustrated Guide to the American Economy*, 2nd ed. Washington, D.C.: American Enterprise Institute, 1995. A vivid collection of graphs, all clearly explained, that describes the American economy and government spending from the 1950s through the early 1990s.

Tufte, Edward R. *Political Control of the Economy.* Princeton, N.J.: Princeton University Press, 1978. Argues that there is a "political business cycle" caused by politicians' trying to stimulate the economy just before an election.

17

Social Welfare

* How Americans view welfare programs

* Social Security Act of 1935

* Medicare Act of 1965

* Majoritarian and client-oriented politics

* Welfare reform

There are two kinds of welfare programs in the United States: those that benefit most or all of the people and those that help only a small number of them. In the first category are Social Security and Medicare, programs that provide retirement benefits or medical assistance to almost every citizen who has reached a certain age. In the second are programs such as Medicaid and Food Stamps that offer help only to people with low incomes.

Legally, the difference between the two kinds of programs is that the first have no *means test* (that is, they are available to everyone without regard to income) while the second are *means tested* (that is, you must fall below a certain income level to enjoy them). Politically, the programs differ in how they get money from the government. The first kind of welfare programs represent **majoritarian politics:** nearly everyone benefits, nearly everyone pays. The second kind represent **client politics:** a (relatively) few number of people benefit, but almost everyone pays.

This political difference has a huge impact on how the government acts in regard to these programs. Social Security and Medicare are sacrosanct. The thought of making any changes that might lower the benefits these programs pay is so politically risky that most politicians never even discuss the possibility. When programs such as these run into trouble because of rising expenses (Medicare is in deep trouble today, and Social Security will be in even deeper trouble in a few decades), politicians scramble to look for ways of maintaining benefits while hiding the rising costs or postponing dealing with them. As we shall see later in this chapter, there has been a sharp growth in the proportion of people who are retired and are thus entitled to Social Security and Medicare. To keep benefits flowing to these individuals, people who are not retired will have to pay more and more in taxes. No politician wants to raise taxes or cut benefits, so they adopt a variety of halfhearted measures (like slowly increasing the age at which people can get these benefits) designed to postpone the tough decisions until they are out of office.

Client-based welfare programs—those that are means tested—are a very different matter. Like many other client-based programs, their political appeal changes as popular opinion about them changes. Take the old Aid to Families with Dependent Children (AFDC) program. When it was started in 1935, people thought of it as a way of helping poor women whose husbands had been killed in war or had died in mining accidents. The goal was to help these women support their children, who had been made fatherless by death or disaster. Most people thought of these women as the innocent victims of a tragedy. No one thought that they would take AFDC for very long. It was a program to help smooth things over for them until they could remarry.

About thirty years later, however, the public's opinion of AFDC had begun to change. People started to think that AFDC was paying money to women who had never married and had no intention of marrying. The government, according to this view, was subsidizing single-parent families, encouraging out-of-wedlock births, and creating social dependency. Moreover, some people thought that black Americans were taking undue advantage of the program. (In fact, when this opinion emerged, blacks were still a minority among AFDC recipients.) From the mid-1960s through the mid-1990s these views became stronger. AFDC had lost the legitimacy it needed, as a client program, to survive politically.

Whenever a client program loses political legitimacy, the program is in trouble. AFDC recipients were in much the same fix as tobacco farmers. Once, government subsidies to tobacco growers were a routine feature of political life. Tobacco farmers were just farmers, like those who produced corn or wheat. Very few citizens knew or cared how much money it cost to support this program, and even if they had known, the amount was so small that they wouldn't have had a strong incentive to organize and fight the program. But then the harmful effects of smoking began to become widely known. The surgeon general condemned smoking. Scores of scientific studies criticized it. Labels appeared on cigarette packages and in tobacco advertisements telling users that the product was dangerous. Many people began to give up the smoking habit. As a result, gov-

ernment subsidies to tobacco growers were in political trouble. The program was cut back, sharply.

Client politics, in short, depends on the beneficiaries' being thought of as legitimate. Almost any means-tested program risks losing its political legitimacy, because some people will always wonder whether the program itself causes people to avoid working in order to claim the benefits. Some people think that about Food Stamps, the program that gives low-income people free stamps that they can exchange for food. There have been a few publicized cases of people using food stamps to buy luxury items. But no powerful opposition to the program has developed, because in general the only thing the beneficiaries have in common is that they have low incomes. Many Americans can imagine becoming poor, and so they probably are willing to allow such a program to operate as part of a government-supplied safety net that might, someday, help them.

But AFDC was a different matter. Having to accept AFDC was not something the typical taxpayer thought would ever happen to him or her. Moreover, the beneficiaries weren't just poor; some of them did things—such as having babies without getting married—that most Americans thought were simply wrong. The legitimacy of AFDC was thus in jeopardy, because it either made possible or actually encouraged behavior that most Americans found improper.

In this chapter we provide examples of both majoritarian and client welfare programs and describe how they have changed over the years. There are far too many social welfare programs to describe them all here; rather, the main purpose of this chapter is to explain the key features of the two main kinds of these programs.

Social Welfare in the United States

Before analyzing how these programs came into being, it is first necessary to understand that social welfare policy in the United States is shaped by three factors that make it different from what exists in many other nations. First, Americans have generally taken a more restrictive view of who is entitled to government assistance. Second, America has been slower than other countries to embrace the welfare state. And third, we have insisted that the states (and to a degree private enterprise) play a large role in running welfare programs.

The first distinctive feature of the American welfare state involves who benefits. To Americans, who benefits has been a question of who *deserves* to benefit. We have usually insisted that public support be given only to those who cannot help themselves. But what does it mean to say that a person cannot help himself or herself? Surely a disabled, blind, elderly woman deserted by her family cannot do much to help herself, but would she still be deserving of public aid were she merely disabled? Or merely elderly? And to what extent should we require that her family support her? As we shall see, American welfare policy since the 1930s has been fundamentally shaped by a slow but steady change in how we have separated the "deserving" from the "undeserving" poor.

That we have always thought this way may make us forget that there are other ways of thinking about welfare. The major alternative view is to ask not who deserves help but what each person's "fair share" of the national income is. Seen this way, the role of government is to take money from those who have a lot and give it to those who have only a little, until each person has, if not the same amount, then at least a fair share. But defining a "fair share" is even more difficult than defining the "deserving poor."

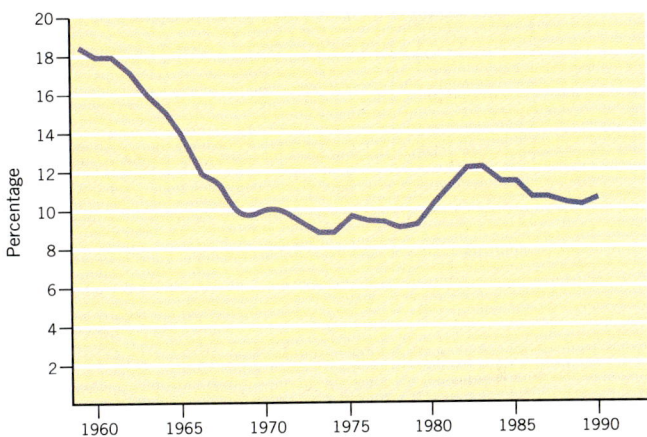

FIGURE 17.1   Family Poverty Rate, 1960–1990

Percentage of U.S. families living below the poverty line

SOURCE: Poll data from *Los Angeles Times* survey, as reported in *Public Opinion* (June–July 1985): 25; poverty data from *Statistical Abstract, 1987*, 442, 444.

TABLE 17.1   Beneficiaries of Major Government Transfer Programs, Selected Years, 1960–1990

Program	Number of Recipients (in millions)			
	1960	1970	1980	1990 (estimated)
Social Security	14.3	25.8	35.4	39.5
Medicare	0	19.9	27.5	33.2
Medicaid	0	14.5	21.6	25.8
School Lunch	13.6	22.4	26.6	25.0
Food Stamps[a]	4.3	8.5	19.3	25.4
Assisted Housing	1.6	3.5	10.6	14.0
Aid to Families with Dependent Children	3.0	7.4	10.6	10.9
Supplemental Security Income	2.8	2.9	3.7	4.2
Women, Infants, and Children Nutrition Program[a]	0	0.1	2.0	3.8
Veterans' Payments	4.0	4.7	4.7	3.6
Unemployment Insurance[b]	2.1	2.1	3.8	2.4[c]

[a]Predecessor programs included. [b]Weekly average insured unemployment. [c]1987 data.
NOTE: Because some persons received benefits from two or more programs, the number of beneficiaries cannot be added up to determine the total number of persons receiving transfer payments.
SOURCE: The Urban Institute, 1990.

Moreover, Americans have generally felt that giving money to people who are already working, or who could work if they chose to, is unfair. In some nations—Sweden is an example—government policy is aimed at redistributing income from better-off to not-so-well-off persons, without regard to who "deserves" the money.

Thus Americans base welfare policy on the concept of "help for the deserving poor" rather than "redistribution to produce fair shares."[1] They have done so, one suspects, because they believe that citizens should be encouraged to be self-reliant, that people who work hard will get what they deserve, and that giving money to people who could help themselves will produce a class of "welfare chiselers." If Americans believed that success at work was a matter of luck rather than effort or was dictated by forces over which they had no control, they might support a different concept of welfare.

Moreover, we have always been a bit uneasy about giving money to people. Though we recognize that many people through no fault of their own cannot buy groceries and thus need funds, we would prefer that, to the extent possible, people who deserve help be given *services* (education, training, medical care) rather than money. Throughout much of our history our welfare policies have reflected a general philosophical disposition in favor of providing services to deserving persons.

The second striking fact about American welfare policy is how late in our history it arrived (at least at the national level) compared to other nations. By 1935, when Congress passed the Social Security Act, at least twenty-two European nations already had similar programs, as did Australia and Japan.[2] Germany was the first to create a nationwide social security program when it developed sickness and maternity insurance in 1883. Six years later it added old-age insurance and in 1927 unemployment insurance.

England offers perhaps the clearest contrast with the United States. In 1908 a national system of old-age pensions was set up, followed three years later by a plan for nationwide health and unemployment insurance.[3] England had a parliamentary regime in which a political party with liberal sentiments and a large majority had come to power. With authority concentrated in the hands of the prime minister and his cabinet, there was virtually no obstacle to insti-

tuting measures, such as welfare programs, that commended themselves to party leaders on grounds of either principle or party advantage. Furthermore, the British Labour party was then beginning to emerge. Though the party was still small (it had only thirty seats in Parliament in 1908), its leaders included people who had been influential in formulating welfare programs that the leaders of the dominant Liberal party backed. And once these programs were approved, they were in almost all cases nationally run: there were no state governments to which authority had to be delegated or whose different experiences had to be accommodated.

Moreover, the British in 1908 were beginning to think in terms of social classes, to accept the notion of an activist government, and to make welfare the central political issue. Americans at that time also had an activist leader, Theodore Roosevelt; there was a progressive movement; and labor was well along in its organizing drives. But the issues were defined differently in the United States. Progressives, or at least most of them, emphasized the reform of the political process—by eliminating corruption, by weakening the parties, and by improving the civil service—and attacked bigness by breaking up industrial trusts. Though some progressives favored the creation of a welfare state, they were a distinct minority. They had few allies in organized labor (which was skeptical of public welfare programs) and could not overcome the general distrust of big government and the strong preference for leaving matters of welfare in state hands. In sum, what ordinary politics brought to England in 1908–1911, only the crisis politics of 1935 would bring to the United States. But once started, the programs grew. By 1983, almost one-third of all Americans received benefits from one or more social welfare programs.

The third factor involves the degree to which federalism has shaped national welfare policy. Since the Constitution was silent on whether Congress had the power to spend money on welfare and since powers not delegated to Congress were reserved to the states, it was not until the constitutional reinterpretation of the 1930s (see Chapter 14) that it became clear that the federal government could do anything in the area of social policy. At the same time, federalism meant that any state so inclined could experiment with welfare programs. Between 1923 and 1933 thirty states enacted some form of an old-age pension. By 1935 all but two states had adopted a "mother's pension"—a program whereby a widow with children was given financial assistance, provided that she was a "fit mother" who ran a "suitable home." The poor were given small doles by local governments, helped by private charities, or placed in almshouses. Only one state, Wisconsin, had an unemployment insurance program.

Politically the state programs had a double-edged effect: they provided opponents of a federal welfare system with an argument (the states were already providing welfare assistance), but they also supplied a lobby for federal financial assistance (state authorities would campaign for national legislation to help them out). Some were later to say that the states were the laboratories for experimentation in welfare policy. When the federal government entered the field in 1935, it did so in part by spending money through the states, thereby encouraging the formation in the states of a strong welfare bureaucracy whose later claims would be difficult to ignore.

Majoritarian Welfare Programs: Social Security and Medicare

At the time the Great Depression began, in 1929, the job of providing relief to needy people fell to state and local governments or to private charities, and even these sources were primarily concerned with widows, orphans, and the elderly.[4] Hardly any state had a systematic program for supporting the unemployed, though many states provided some kind of help if it was clear that the person was out of work through no fault of his or her own. When the economy suddenly ground to a near standstill and the unemployment rate rose to include one-fourth of the work force, private charities and city relief programs nearly went bankrupt.

The election of 1932 produced an overwhelming congressional majority for the Democrats and placed Franklin D. Roosevelt in the White House. Almost immediately a number of emergency measures were adopted to cope with the depression by supplying federal cash to bail out state and local relief agencies and by creating public works jobs under federal auspices. These measures were recognized as temporary expedients, however, and were unsatisfactory to those who believed that the federal government had a permanent and major responsi-

Major Social Welfare Programs

INSURANCE, OR "CONTRIBUTORY," PROGRAMS

Old Age, Survivors, and Disability Insurance (OASDI)
Monthly payments to retired or disabled people and to surviving members of their families. This program, popularly called Social Security, is paid for by a payroll tax on employers and employees. *No means test.*

Medicare Federal government pays for part of the cost of hospital care for retired or disabled people covered by Social Security. Paid for by payroll taxes on employees and employers. *No means test.*

ASSISTANCE, OR "NONCONTRIBUTORY," PROGRAMS

Unemployment Insurance (UI) Weekly payments to workers who have been laid off and cannot find work. Benefits and requirements determined by states. Paid for by taxes on employers. *No means test.*

Temporary Assistance for Needy Families (TANF). Payments to needy families with children. Replaced the old AFDC program. Partially paid for by block grants from the federal government to the states. *Means test.*

Supplemental Security Income (SSI) Cash payments to aged, blind, or disabled people whose income is below a certain amount. Paid for from general federal revenues. *Means test.*

Food Stamps Vouchers, given to people whose income is below a certain level, that can be used to buy food at grocery stores. Paid for out of general federal revenues. *Means test.*

Medicaid Pays medical expenses of persons receiving TANF or SSI payments. *Means test.*

Earned Income Tax Credit Pays a cash subsidy (or tax credit) to poor working families. *Means test.*

The Great Depression: a bread line forms on a New York City street in December 1931.

bility for welfare. Roosevelt created the Cabinet Committee on Economic Security to consider long-term policies. The committee drew heavily on the experience of European nations and on the ideas of various American scholars and social workers, but it understood that it would have to adapt these proposals to the realities of American politics. Chief among these was the widespread belief that any direct federal welfare program might be unconstitutional. The Constitution nowhere explicitly gave to Congress the authority to set up an unemployment compensation or old-age retirement program. And even if a welfare program were constitutional, many believed, it would be wrong because it violated the individualistic creed that people should help themselves unless they were physically unable to do so.

But failure by the Roosevelt administration to produce a comprehensive social security program, his supporters felt, might make the president vulnerable in the 1936 election to the leaders of various radical social movements. Huey Long of Louisiana was proposing a "Share Our Wealth" plan; Upton Sinclair was running for governor of California on a platform calling for programs to "End Poverty in California"; and Dr. Francis E. Townsend was leading an organization of hundreds of thousands of elderly people on whose behalf he demanded government pensions of $200 a month.

The plan that emerged from the cabinet committee was carefully designed to meet popular demands within the framework of popular beliefs and constitutional understandings. It called for two kinds of programs: (1) an **insurance program** for the unemployed and elderly, to which workers would contribute and from which they would benefit when they became unemployed or retired; and (2) an **assistance program** for the blind, dependent children, and the aged. (Giving assistance as well as providing "insurance" for the aged was necessary because for the first few years the insurance program would not pay out any benefits.) The federal government would use its power to tax to provide the funds, but all of the programs (except for old-age insurance) would be administered by the states. Everybody, rich or poor, would be eligible for the insurance programs. Only the poor, as measured by a **means test** (a measure to determine that incomes are below a certain level), would be eligible for the assistance programs. Though bitterly opposed by some, the resulting Social Security Act passed swiftly and virtually unchanged through Congress. It was introduced in January 1935 and signed by President Roosevelt in August of that year.

The idea of having the government pay the medical and hospital bills of the elderly and the poor had been discussed in Washington since the drafting of the Social Security Act. President Roosevelt and his Committee on Economic Security sensed that medical care would be very controversial, and so health programs were left out of the 1935 bill in order not to jeopardize its chances of passage.[5]

The proponents of the idea did not abandon it, however. Working mostly within the executive branch, they continued to press, sometimes publicly, sometimes behind the scenes, for a national health care plan. Democratic presidents, including Truman, Kennedy, and Johnson, favored it; Republican president Eisenhower opposed it; Congress was deeply

Senator Huey P. Long of Louisiana formed the "Share Our Wealth" movement, threatening the unity of the Democratic party. Left, in May 1935 he greets supporters of his effort to override President Roosevelt's veto of a veterans' bonus. Right, President Roosevelt meets with members of the Civilian Conservation Corps, which put unemployed young men to work; he feared that Long might challenge him in the 1936 election.

divided on it. The American Medical Association attacked it as "socialized medicine." For thirty years key policy entrepreneurs, such as Wilbur Cohen, worked to find a formula that would produce a congressional majority.

The first and highest hurdle to overcome, however, was not Congress as a whole but the House Ways and Means Committee, especially its powerful chairman from 1958 to 1975, Wilbur Mills of Arkansas. A majority of the committee members opposed a national health care program. Some members believed it wrong in principle; others feared that adding a costly health component to the Social Security system would jeopardize the financial solvency and administrative integrity of one of the most popular government programs. By the early 1960s a majority of the House favored a health care plan, but without the approval of Ways and Means it would never reach the floor.

The 1964 elections changed all that. The Johnson landslide produced such large Democratic majorities in Congress that the composition of the committees changed. In particular the membership of the Ways and Means Committee was altered. Whereas before it had three Democrats for every two Republicans, after 1964 it had two Democrats for every one Republican. The House leadership saw to it that the new Democrats on the committee were strongly committed to a health care program. Suddenly the committee had a majority favorable to such a plan, and Mills, realizing that a bill would pass and wanting to help shape its form, changed his position and became a supporter of what was to become Medicare.

The policy entrepreneurs in and out of the government who drafted the Medicare plan attempted to anticipate the major objections to it. First, the bill would apply only to the aged—those eligible for Social Security retirement benefits. This would reassure legislators worried about the cost of providing tax-supported health care for everybody. Second, the plan would cover only hospital expenses, not doctors' bills. Since doctors were not to be paid by the government, they would not be regulated by it; thus,

President Lyndon Johnson signs the Medicare Act in 1965 in the company of Vice President Hubert Humphrey (standing) and former President Harry S. Truman (seated).

FIGURE 17.2   AFDC Benefits versus Poverty Line

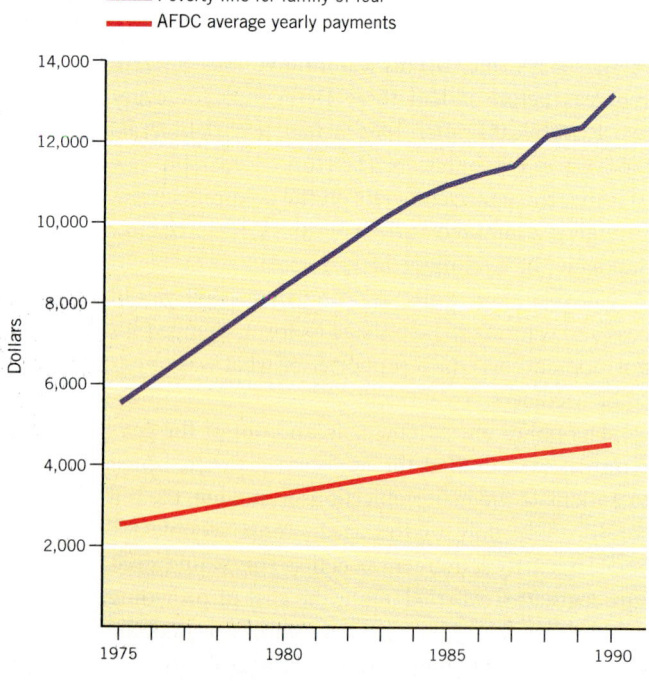

▬▬ Poverty line for family of four
▬▬ AFDC average yearly payments

NOTE: AFDC figures converted from monthly to yearly payments.
SOURCE: *Statistical Abstract of the United States, 1992*, 370, 427.

presumably, the opposition of the American Medical Association would be blunted.

Unexpectedly, however, the Ways and Means Committee broadened the coverage of the plan beyond what the administration had thought was politically feasible. It added sections providing medical assistance, called Medicaid, for the poor (defined as those already getting public assistance payments) and payment of doctors' bills for the aged (a new part of Medicare). The new, much-enlarged bill passed both houses of Congress with ease. The key votes pitted a majority of the Democrats against a majority of the Republicans.

Client Welfare Programs: Aid to Families with Dependent Children

One part of the Social Security Act of 1935 created what came to be called Aid to Families with Dependent Children (AFDC). It was scarcely noticed at the time. The federal government, in response to the Depression crisis, promised to provide aid to states that were, in many cases, already running programs to help poor children who lacked a father.

Because AFDC involved giving federal aid to existing state programs, it allowed the states to define what constitutes "need," to set benefit levels, and to administer the program. Washington did set—(and over the years, continued to increase) a number of rules governing how the program would work, however. Washington told the states how to calculate applicants' income and required the states to give Medicaid to AFDC recipients. The states had to establish mandatory job-training programs for many AFDC recipients and to provide child care programs for working AFDC parents. Washington also required that women on AFDC identify their children's fathers.

In addition to the growing list of requirements, Washington also created new programs for which AFDC recipients were eligible, such as Food Stamps, the **Earned Income Credit** (a cash grant to poor parents who are working), free school meals, various forms of housing assistance, and certain other benefits. But while all this was happening, public opinion moved against the AFDC program.

The combination of souring public opinion, increasing federal regulations, and a growing roster of benefits produced a program that irritated almost everyone. The states disliked having to conform to a growing list of federal regulations, but critics complained that the states offered very different levels of benefits. The public hated the program because they thought it was weakening the family by encouraging out-of-wedlock births (since AFDC recipients received additional benefits for each new child). But some scholars denied that this was happening. The public worried that AFDC recipients were working covertly on the side; the data proved that this was true of at least half of them in several large cities. AFDC recipients saw that the actual (that is, inflation-adjusted) value of their AFDC checks was going down. Critics countered that if you added together all the benefits they were receiving (food stamps, Medicaid, housing assistance, and so on), benefit levels were actually going up. Politicians complained that healthy parents were living off AFDC instead of working. Other politicians rejoined that AFDC mothers needed to stay home with their young children or to get day care so they could work. The AFDC law was revised many times, but never in a way that satisfied all, or even most, of

Aid to Families with Dependent Children (AFDC) became controversial as Americans began to see it as a program that chiefly aided unmarried black mothers.

its critics. Though AFDC recipients were only a small fraction of all Americans, they had become a large political problem.

What made matters worse was that the composition of the people in the program had changed. In 1970 about half of the mothers on AFDC were there

A food stamp. Over 25 million people use them to help pay the cost of food.

because their husband had died or divorced them; only a quarter had never been married.[6] By 1994 the situation had changed dramatically: only about a quarter of AFDC mothers were widowed or divorced, and over half had never been married at all. And though most women on AFDC for the *first* time got off it after just a few years, almost two-thirds of the women on AFDC at any given moment had been on it for eight years or more.

These facts, combined with the increased proportion of out-of-wedlock births in the country as a whole, made it virtually impossible to sustain political support for what had begun as a noncontroversial client program.

Two Kinds of Welfare Politics

The programs just described illustrate two patterns of policy-making. The old-age pensions created by the Social Security Act of 1935 and the health care benefits created by the Medicare Act of 1965 are examples of majoritarian politics: almost everybody benefits, and almost everybody pays. The AFDC program is an example of client politics: a relatively few people benefit, but everybody pays.

Majoritarian Politics

When both the benefits and the costs of a proposed program are widely distributed, the proposal will be adopted *if* the beneficiaries believe that their benefits will exceed their costs *and* if political elites believe that it is legitimate for the federal government to adopt the program.

Initially, the benefits people received from the retirement program greatly exceeded its costs to them. Older people were able to get an old-age pension or health care even though they had paid in taxes only a small fraction of what these benefits cost. Social Security and Medicare seemed initially like the nearest thing to a free lunch. There were several reasons for this. First, the retirement benefits were initially set at a relatively low level, and so the taxes needed to pay for them were relatively small. (In 1937, a worker had to pay only 1 percent of his wages in Social Security—or FICA—taxes.) Second, the population was young enough that lots of employed workers were available to pay for the benefits

received by a relatively small number of retired persons. In 1950 there were fourteen workers paying Social Security taxes for every retired person. Even as late as 1960 there were five workers paying for every person collecting. Third, people supporting Medicare vastly underestimated the actual costs of the program. One proponent said in 1965 that it would never cost more than $8 billion a year. Today the actual cost is more than thirteen times that.

The big debate in 1935 and in 1965 was not over whether the people wanted these programs—the polls showed that they did—but over whether it was legitimate for the federal government to provide them.[7] In 1935 conservatives argued that as desirable as Social Security might be, nothing in the Constitution authorized the federal government to spend money for this purpose; welfare, they said, was a policy area reserved to the states. Liberals rejoined that the federal government had an obligation to help people avoid poverty in their old age. Besides, they said, as an "insurance" program, retirement benefits were not really a federal expenditure at all: Washington was merely collecting payments and holding them in a trust fund until the people who paid them were ready to retire. In the midst of the Great Depression and at a time when liberals had large majorities in Congress, it was an easy argument to make, and so the Social Security bill readily crossed over the legitimacy barrier.

In 1965 the same issues were raised. Conservatives argued that medical care was a private, not a governmental, matter and that any federal involvement would subject doctors and hospitals to endless red tape and harm the quality of the doctor-patient relationship. Liberals rejoined that the elderly had health needs that they could not meet without help and that only the federal government had the resources to provide that assistance. Because the 1964 elections, when Lyndon Johnson defeated Barry Goldwater, had swept into the House and Senate large majorities of liberal Democrats, there was no chance that a conservative coalition of Republicans and southern Democrats could defeat Medicare, and so it passed.

As can be seen in Table 17.2, the votes in Congress on Social Security and Medicare followed party lines. Since the Democratic opponents of these bills were typically conservative southerners, the vote followed ideological lines even more closely.

Once the ideological issue had been settled and the benefits began to flow, it quickly became good politics to support frequent increases in the scope of the program and the size of the benefits. From 1950 to 1975 there was only one period (1959–1965) when Congress allowed more than two years to pass without either increasing retirement benefits or broadening the kinds of workers covered by the plan.[8]

It is not hard to see why. The House comes up for reelection every two years. Though some members no doubt voted to increase benefits out of a sincere conviction that the elderly needed more help, every member knew that it was a political asset to be able to say that he or she had voted to provide more benefits. By 1954 Social Security was so well established that a Republican president proposed to a Republican-controlled Congress that benefits be increased. The vote in the House was 356 in favor, 8 opposed.

Majoritarian politics remains good politics unless the costs to the voters begin to exceed their benefits. Though Social Security and Medicare were supposed to be insurance programs, in fact they are not. What a retired person takes out in benefits bears little relationship to what he or she has previously paid in taxes. These programs are in fact devices whereby people now working are taxed to provide benefits for people now retired.

Three things began to change the politics of these programs. First, Congress raised retirement benefits to the point where tax increases were necessary to pay for them. A tax that had taken only 1 percent of a worker's salary in 1935 was taking over 7.5 percent of it by 1990. Second, older people began to live longer, and so the number of retired people who had to be supported increased. By 1975 only about three workers were paying taxes for every one person who was retired; early in the next century the ratio will fall to about two to one. Third, the cost of health care began to shoot up. By 1985 the price of a hospital room was almost five times greater than it had been in 1970.

By 1977 Congress for the first time had to raise Social Security taxes without raising benefits. The bill carried the House by only twenty-six votes, a far cry from the nearly unanimous votes by which retirement bills had once passed. The days of easy votes on Social Security had come to an end.[9]

TABLE 17.2   **Key Votes on Major Welfare Proposals in the House**

Proposals	Democrats	Republicans
Social Security (1935)		
For	252	1
Against	45	95
Economic Opportunity (1964)		
For	204	22
Against	40	145
Medicare (1965)		
For	226	10
Against	63	128
Family Assistance Plan (1970)		
For	141	102
Against	83	72

Client Politics

When the benefits of a proposal are to go to a relatively small group, but the public at large pays, we have client politics. Proposals to benefit clients will pass *if* the cost to the public at large is not perceived to be great *and* if the client receiving the benefit is thought to be "deserving."

AFDC did not cost much. In 1995 the federal government spent less than $14 billion on AFDC, less than half what it spent on veterans' benefits and only a tenth of what it spent on Medicare. The politics of these programs centers less on their cost than on the legitimacy of their beneficiaries.

As noted above, when it was first enacted AFDC was relatively noncontroversial. Originally it seemed intended to help deserving people. In 1935 the typical welfare mother was perceived to be a woman living in a small town, whose husband had been killed in a mining accident. Who could object to giving some modest help to a person who was the victim of circumstances?

Right or wrong, American values on this subject are quite clear. As can be seen in Table 17.3 on page 535, both poor and nonpoor people believe that "welfare encourages husbands to avoid family responsibilities" and "poor young women often have babies so they can collect welfare." These poll data also indicate that Americans prefer to see poor people helped by

FIGURE 17.3 The Perception and Reality of Poverty

Perception	Reality

Has the percentage of Americans living in poverty been going up?

65% of the public thinks it has.

In fact, the percentage of persons living in poverty as defined by the Census Bureau declined sharply from 1960 to 1970 and then has leveled off.

Percentage of persons living in poverty

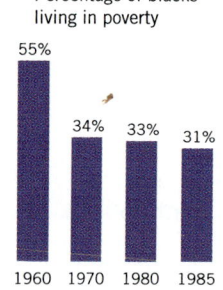

22% 13% 13% 14%
1960 1970 1980 1985

Has the percentage of black Americans living in poverty been going up?

44% of the public thinks it has; 30% thinks it has been staying about the same.

In fact, the percentage of black persons living in poverty declined sharply from 1960 to 1970 and more gradually thereafter.

Percentage of blacks living in poverty

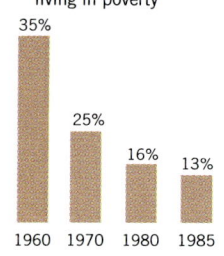

55% 34% 33% 31%
1960 1970 1980 1985

Has the percentage of elderly Americans living in poverty been going up?

66% of the public thinks it has.

In fact, the percentage of persons aged 65 and over living in poverty fell sharply from 1960 to 1980 and more gradually thereafter.

Percentage of elderly living in poverty

35% 25% 16% 13%
1960 1970 1980 1985

SOURCE: *Congressional Quarterly Weekly* (January 18, 1992): 110, reporting data from the Joint Economic Committee.

giving them job training or even creating government jobs for them. This **service strategy** (providing training and education) is strongly preferred to an **income strategy** (giving people money)—unless, of course, the income can be called "insurance."[10]

Indeed, some critics of welfare, such as Charles Murray, have argued that AFDC actually increases the number of people living in poverty. Murray claimed that high welfare benefits made it more attractive for some people to go on welfare than to look for a job and more attractive for some women to have babies than to get married. This kept them poor. Other scholars have criticized Murray's thesis. They argued that there is no direct evidence that welfare encourages family breakup and suggested that the rise in the number of illegitimate children occurred during a period (the 1970s) when welfare benefits, in real (that is, inflation-adjusted) dollars, were going down.[11]

In short, the clients of these programs never acquired in the public's mind the legitimacy necessary for their programs to prosper. As a result, whereas for forty years it was thought to be good politics to increase old-age benefits, it increasingly became considered bad politics to do anything but attack, investigate, and curtail the "welfare" programs.

Toward a New Welfare Politics

The biggest problem facing majoritarian welfare programs is their cost: who will pay, and how much will they pay? The biggest problem facing client-oriented welfare programs is their legitimacy: who should benefit, and how should they be served?

Costs

The supporters of Social Security and Medicare have spent most of their time since the mid-1970s trying to devise politically painless ways of maintaining existing benefits or providing new ones. It hasn't been easy.

By 1981 many people in Washington feared that the Social Security system was about to run out of money, especially since, beginning in 1972, the amount paid to each retired person automatically went up with inflation (that is, the payments were "indexed" to inflation). Liberals wanted to solve this problem by raising taxes; conservatives wanted to solve it by cutting benefits. After many false starts the two sides agreed to turn the matter over to a bipartisan commission. Its plan, adopted by Congress in 1983, both raised taxes and reduced (slightly) benefits for future retirees, mostly by gradually increasing the age at which people would become eligible for retirement benefits, from sixty-five to sixty-seven.[12]

Medicare was a far tougher problem. It was politically impossible either to increase taxes enough to pay for the rapidly escalating health costs of retired people or to cut their benefits enough to make up for the shortfall.

The strategy Congress has followed is to try to control costs by imposing ever-greater restrictions on what doctors and hospitals can charge. Doctors and hospitals don't like this, of course, and many economists warn that price controls won't work—one way or another, people will find a way to buy what they want and doctors to charge what they want. Nevertheless, Congress works on the assumption that irritating physicians and economists is a lot better than outraging retired persons on Medicare.

The essence of the price-control system, adopted in 1983, is to replace the traditional way of paying hospitals (sending them a check to cover their customary costs) with a new policy of paying a flat fee for each particular treatment, from broken bones to brain tumors, regardless of what they cost. Doctors and hospitals that couldn't deliver the service for what the government would pay would have to swallow the extra cost themselves; if they could treat the patient for less, they could pocket the difference. Sounds good, but there is a hitch: some hospitals reacted to the price controls not by becoming more efficient but by scrimping on services and discharging patients "quicker but sicker."[13]

Despite the anguish of having to figure out how to deliver the greatest benefits for the least tax dollars, Congress and the White House could not resist trying to create an entirely new health benefit. The law was called the Medicare Catastrophic Coverage Act of 1988. It should have been called the Politically Catastrophic Act of 1988.

The idea was simple enough: elderly people are especially worried about having to pay for some medical catastrophe, such as cancer, a stroke, or Alzheimer's disease. These illnesses can quickly consume almost anyone's savings. Under the existing Medicare plan, the government would pay your hospital bills for only 150 days in any given year. The catastrophic illness bill dealt with this by guaranteeing that the government would pay your hospital bills for the whole year, every year, after you had paid a deductible. The cost of this additional coverage was to be paid for largely by the elderly them-

selves, with the increase in fees to be greatest for the more affluent.

Though the idea was simple, the problem was that the beneficiaries didn't think the new law provided any real benefit, certainly not one they wanted to pay for. They expressed their feelings in a tidal wave of opposition, and within eighteen months Congress was forced to back down and repeal the Medicare Catastrophic Coverage Act. The House vote to pass the act in 1988 had been 302 to 127; the House vote to repeal it in 1989 was 352 to 63. It was

TABLE 17.3   Attitudes Toward Poverty and Welfare

There is a remarkable similarity between the views of poor and non-poor Americans on the nature of poverty, the government's obligation to help, and the likely causes of failure.

Question	Percentage Agreeing	
	Poor	Nonpoor
Most poor people:		
Prefer to stay on welfare	20%	25%
Prefer to earn own living	68	62
Poor young women often have babies so they can collect welfare	60	61
Welfare often encourages husbands to avoid family responsibilities	60	61
Antipoverty programs worked:		
Often	31	33
Seldom	56	59
Welfare benefits:		
Give poor people a chance to get started again	31	16
Encourage people to stay poor	43	61
Poor people find:		
It's very hard to get work	59	39
There are jobs available for anyone willing to work	31	59
Best thing to do about poverty is to:		
Give poor money	3	0
Provide services	6	6
Create government jobs	32	19
Provide job training	56	73

SOURCE: *Los Angeles Times* poll, as reported in I. A. Lewis and William Schneider, "Hard Times: The Public on Poverty," *Public Opinion* (June–July 1985): 6, 7, 59.

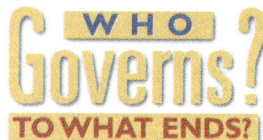

Why a Health Care Bill Did Not Become Law

In September 1993 President Bill Clinton gave a speech to Congress in which he called for radical changes in federal health care policy. At the time of the speech, and in the year after the president's health care bill was formally introduced on November 20, 1993, many leading health care policy experts—not least among them the dozens of experts who were part of the special health care policy task force headed by First Lady Hillary Rodham Clinton—argued strongly in favor of bold federal government action to insure citizens who had no health coverage. In his January 1994 State of the Union Address, the president himself declared:

> *I am open, as I have said repeatedly, to the best ideas of concerned members of both parties. I have no special brief for any approach, even in our own bill, except this: If you send me legislation that does not guarantee every American private health insurance that can never be taken away, you will force me to take this pen, veto the legislation, and we'll come right back here and start all over again.*

But the president never got to use his veto pen. Before the end of 1994, his 1,342-page health care reform bill was dead. Not only did Congress not "start all over again" and give the president what he demanded, by the end of 1996 Congress had submitted, and the president had signed, a package of minor health care reform measures that fell far

short of the president's demands for universal coverage, employer-funded insurance (so-called employer mandates), and more.

Why didn't the president's health care bill become law? Many complicated answers are possible, but the best answer can be seen in the "How a Bill Becomes Law" diagram on page 335 of Chapter 11. As Congress-watcher Allen Schick has argued, the president's bill failed in 1994 "because it did not have the votes—not in Congress and not in the country, not when Bill Clinton announced his plan and not when the legislative effort collapsed. . . . No post-mortems, what-ifs, or finger-pointing can change the fact that the overhaul of the nation's health care system lacked majority support with the American people and in Congress." Schick's straightforward explanation for the bill's failure is supported by such facts as the following:

- Less than 40 percent of all House Democrats cosponsored Clinton's bill when it was formally introduced.

- The number of Senate sponsors never reached a third of that body.

- Right from the start, key Democratic sponsors of the bill, including Representative Pete Starck, chairman of the Subcommittee on Health of the House Committee on Ways and Means, and Senator Daniel Patrick Moynihan, chairman of the Senate Finance Committee, were openly critical of the bill and expressed grave reservations about it.

- At every turn in the legislative and lobbying battles over the bill, Republicans were more united against it than Democrats were for it.

- Powerful interest groups lined up on each side of the debate; several shifted their positions, but the administration's efforts to make allies of major opponents such as the American Medical Association, the Chamber of Commerce, and the insurance companies were invariably too little, too late, and poorly executed.

- About four out of five Americans favored universal health insurance that could never be lost or canceled for any reason, but most citizens doubted the president's plan would work, feared it would adversely affect their own existing coverage, and believed it would cost too much and hurt small businesses.

- The president's veto threat served mainly to rule out incremental steps of the sort considered by a mainstream coalition of Democratic and Republican senators in the final weeks of the 1994 session.

As this example of "How a Bill Did Not Become Law" suggests, when it comes to major changes in public policy, no president can govern without building a broad consensus within Congress and a sustainable majority among the American people.

SOURCE: Allen Schick, "How a Bill Did Not Become Law," in Thomas E. Mann and Norman J. Ornstein, eds., *Intensive Care* (Washington, D.C.: Brookings Institution, 1996).

the most dramatic reversal in the history of welfare legislation.

In the 1996 election, Clinton and Dole agreed that perhaps a bipartisan commission should be formed to debate the future of Medicare. But everybody still handled the subject with kid gloves, and a commission that might have produced some positive results was never formed. President Clinton and congressional Republicans had already suggested postponing the Medicare crisis by cutting the amount of money going to doctors and hospitals. They disagreed only on how big the cut should be. Cutting payments to hospitals, however, does not seem a viable solution to the problem because hospitals must make up for such cuts either by reducing services or by charging paying customers more money.

At least for Social Security the tactic of turning to a commission had already been tried. In 1996 a second advisory commission on Social Security produced three reports but no clear majority opinion about what should be done to maintain the program. The most challenging recommendation was that the system be revised to allow people to put some fraction of their Social Security taxes into the stock market. There they could earn much higher returns than what is typical of federal bonds, where the Social Security trust fund is currently invested. Younger workers seemed to like the idea, because many don't think Social Security will be there for them when they retire. Older workers and retirees didn't like the idea, because it entails a certain amount of risk to current benefit levels.

When costs rise, majoritarian politics no longer looks so easy.

Public Support

Aid to the Poor   By contrast, client politics get easier when the legitimacy of its beneficiaries declines. After many efforts to reform AFDC, the 104th Congress passed and President Clinton signed a law that turns the program back to the states. The law that created AFDC—Title IV of the Social Security Act—was abolished.

The Personal Responsibility and Work Opportunity Reconciliation Act of 1996 was designed to do several things. First, it lets the states run welfare pro-

grams for the poor as they see fit, without tight federal regulation. Each state will get a fixed federal block grant to help pay for what is now called Temporary Assistance for Needy Families (TANF). The block grants are fixed in size; they won't go up automatically, though states that achieve certain goals—such as reducing out-of-wedlock births or increasing welfare recipients who work—will be eligible for extra benefits. Second, the new law requires that most welfare recipients find work, by placing limits on how long they can get benefits. Third, the bill denies food stamps for legal aliens and denies TANF for illegal aliens.

The work requirements are at the heart of the bill. To keep receiving their block grants, the states must ensure that all adults who receive benefits are working within two years of receiving a TANF grant. Furthermore, federal money cannot be used to support any adult for more than five years, and mothers will have their TANF grants reduced if they do not identify the fathers of their children. New machinery has been put into place to track down "deadbeat dads." Unmarried mothers under the age of eighteen will qualify for a TANF grant only if they live with a parent (or in an adult-supervised setting) and attend school.

Food Stamps, Medicaid, the Earned Income Credit, child nutrition and child care grants, and Supplementary Security Income (SSI) continue to be available to TANF recipients, though in some cases under stricter limits.

Many state governors supported the bill (they may be wondering why now that they have full responsibility for administering TANF). Many liberal Democrats and childrens' advocates denounced the bill, but it passed both houses of Congress by large majorities. At the time he signed the bill, President Clinton said he disagreed with some of its provisions and planned to offer legislation to change these items. Whatever happens on this front, it is clear that unmarried moms have lost their status as a legitimate client group.

Aid to the Homeless   No issue better illustrates the tensions within American social welfare politics than the problem of the homeless. The streets and parks of many cities are filled with homeless people. That much is clear. Everything else is in dispute.

Thinking CRITICAL

The 1996 Welfare Reform Act: Shredding the Social Safety Net?

In August 1996 the 104th Congress passed and President Clinton signed the Personal Responsibility and Work Opportunity Act. The law gave the states more responsibility for providing cash assistance to low-income families; placed limits on how long people can receive federally financed aid; imposed stricter work requirements on nonaged, nondisabled recipients of food stamps and cash assistance; and eliminated benefits for most legal aliens. Leading critics of the act (and not a few leading supporters) claimed that it significantly reduced the government's spending for the poor.

But did it? It is certainly true that the poor will shoulder the bulk of the budget

reductions enacted in 1995 and 1996. Indeed, one study found that programs for low-income families and individuals absorbed 93 percent of all cuts to entitlement programs. Programs for people with low incomes accounted for 23 percent of the federal budget outside of defense but bore 53 percent of the reductions in nondefense programs.

Still, as detailed in a 1997 study by the Brookings Institution and other recent research, there are two main strands of the safety net, each of them woven of many different antipoverty programs.

One strand consists of "cash programs" that distribute money and other resources directly to poor and nearly

poor children and their parents. [O]ne such program—Aid to Families [with] Dependent Children (AFDC)—wa[s eli]minated by the 1996 reform. U[nder] AFDC, the federal government o[ffered] states grants for low-income fam[ilies.] The states were required to match [these] grants and spend the money on [cash] welfare payments to needy children [and] their adult caretakers. At the same [time,] however, the states were free to esta[blish] basic benefit levels and determine [eligi]bility pretty much as they wished. [As a] result, the basic monthly cash pay[ment] for a three-person AFDC family ra[nged] from a low of $120 a month [in] Mississippi to a high of $923 a mont[h in] Alaska, with the median benefit a[bout] $370 a month. The new law elimin[ated] AFDC, but it did not end federal spe[nd]ing on cash assistance to the p[oor.] Rather, in place of AFDC the new law [es]tablished a block grant program [(see] Chapter 3) that allocates funds to [the] states based largely on historical fund[ing] levels for AFDC.

Other programs woven into the [fab]ric of federal cash assistance incl[ude] Supplemental Security Income (SSI) [and] the Earned Income Tax Credit (EIT[C).] SSI provides federal benefits to aged, [dis]abled, or blind adults and children w[ith] low or no household incomes. M[ost] states supplement federal SSI payme[nts,] which in 1995 totaled over $24 billi[on,] compared to $17 billion for AFDC ([see] table). Likewise, the $15-billion-a-y[ear] EITC goes only to low-income peo[ple] who work. In 1996 the EITC provide[d]

In 1996 President Clinton signed into law a welfare reform act that mainly reflected Republican views in Congress as to how the old AFDC system should be changed.

Federal Spending on Major Programs for the Poor, 1965–1995

	Expenditures (in billions of 1995 dollars)						
	1965	1970	1975	1980	1985	1990	1995
Cash Programs							
Aid to Families with Dependent Children	12.5	15.4	14.2	13.7	13.1	14.1	17.1
Supplemental Security Income	7.9	7.5	11.9	10.7	12.4	13.3	24.5
Earned Income Tax Credit	. . .	. . .	. . .	2.4	1.6	5.1	15.2
In-Kind Programs							
Food and nutrition	1.3	3.8	18.3	24.6	23.7	24.6	33.5
Housing assistance	1.0	1.8	5.8	10.2	15.9	18.4	25.5
Medicaid	1.3	10.1	18.9	26.3	32.3	47.5	89.1
Total	24.0	38.6	69.1	87.9	99.0	123.0	204.9
Total as Percent of Gross Domestic Product	0.8	1.0	1.6	1.8	1.8	1.9	2.9

SOURCE: Gary Burtless et al., "The Future of the Social Safety Net," in Robert D. Reischauer, ed., *Setting Budget Priorities* (Washington, DC: Brookings Institution, 1997), p. 79. Reprinted by permission of the publisher.

much as $3,556 in refundable income tax credits to a working but low-income adult with two or more dependents.

The second strand of the safety net consists of in-kind programs, which provide poor people with food (through food stamps and subsidized school lunches), housing (through public housing projects and rent and home-ownership subsidies), and medical care (mainly via the Medicaid program). In 1995 the federal government spent a total of nearly $150 billion on these in-kind assistance programs for the poor and a total of over $55 billion on AFDC, SSI, and the EITC. In addition, state and local governments spent about $70 billion on Medicaid and about $12 billion on AFDC (about 45 percent of the total cost of these two safety net programs).

Between 1965 and 1995 federal spending on major cash programs and in-kind programs increased nearly ninefold in real (inflation-adjusted) dollars, rising from under 1 percent to nearly 3 percent of the nation's gross domestic product. As the authors of the aforementioned Brookings Institution study concluded, the 1996 welfare reform made "a decisive break with the past," but it is too soon to tell whether the social safety net will be shredded, shrunk, or merely restitched by the states.

SOURCES: Center on Budget and Policy Priorities, *Poor Bearing Budget Burden?* Washington, D.C.: November 26, 1996; Richard P. Nathan, "Overview Essay on Federalism and Social Policy," Rockefeller Institute, Albany, New York, December 10, 1996; Gary Burtless et al., "The Future of the Social Safety Net," in Robert D. Reischauer, ed., *Setting Budget Priorities* (Washington, D.C.: Brookings Institution, 1997), chapter 3.

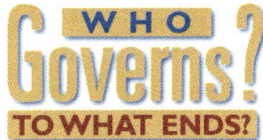

Public Opinion, Policy Intellectuals, and Welfare Reform

As we discussed in Chapter 5, under certain conditions public opinion can play a major role in shaping what the government does. But there is often a gap between public opinion (what most citizens say they want) and public policy (the laws enacted or preserved by elected representatives). And sometimes there is a big lag between changes in majority preferences and commensurate changes in public laws.

So it was until recently with welfare spending. The mass popularity of welfare spending began its decline in 1960. Between 1961 and 1973, the proportion of Americans supporting more welfare spending fell from about 60 percent to around 20 percent. Over this period, the percentage of Americans who believed that the government was spending too much on welfare increased nearly eightfold. Public support for welfare spending continued to erode in the 1980s and into the early 1990s. Surveys showed that large proportions of average Americans had come to identify "loose morals" and "lack of effort" as "very important" explanations for poverty and welfare dependency.

But while public opinion progressively hardened against welfare, well into the 1980s most leading social policy intellectuals—professors at major research universities and professional researchers at think tanks and other institutions—remained highly supportive of welfare spending and explained poverty largely in terms of poor economic conditions rather than poor individual behavior or cultural norms that legitimated welfare dependency.

Even in the 1960s, however, there were some notable—and highly controversial—exceptions. For example, political scientist Edward C. Banfield's 1966 book *The Unheavenly City* identified urban poverty and welfare dependency with "lower class culture," a culture of people who are "present-oriented" and "therefore radically improvident" and prone to poor work habits, impulsive violence, poor health, and other problems.

In a 1996 study of Aid to Families with Dependent Children (AFDC), Steven Teles describes how conservative intellectuals, beginning with Banfield, eventually came to dominate the welfare reform debate among policy elites, pointing to welfare's role in perpetuating the "undeserving poor" and the "voluntarily unemployed." A number of writers—political scientist Lawrence Mead, sociologist Nathan Glazer, and national magazine editor Myron Magnet, to cite just three—wrote books and articles that reinforced Banfield's behavioral analysis of poverty and welfare.

Meanwhile, other conservative thinkers paved a somewhat different intellectual path to the same welfare reform destination that the public had long since reached. Following the lead of economist Milton Friedman, they argued that welfare spending had created disincentives for work. In his much-publicized and much-debated 1984 book *Losing Ground*, political scientist Charles Murray argued that in the "absence of countervailing influences, people will avoid work and be amoral." Likewise, economist George Gilder concluded, "In order to succeed, the poor need most of all the spur of their own poverty."

Although what Teles terms the "ideological dissensus" among welfare policy intellectuals remains very much alive, by the late 1980s and early 1990s a number of liberal scholars—for example, sociologist William Julius Wilson, economist David Ellwood, and human services commissioner Mary Jo Bane—had written books and articles echoing the idea that welfare creates work disincentives and is at least partially implicated in the behavioral pathologies commonly (even if wrongly) associated with the "underclass."

Teles argues that reports of public antagonism toward "welfare" mask public support for "assistance to the poor." He blames policy intellectuals, both liberals and conservatives, for failing to debate the issue in ways that bolster the more positive currents in public sentiment about welfare spending and images of the poor. In contrast, others insist that even with the enactment of the Personal Responsibility and Work Opportunity Act of 1996, the level of public spending on cash assistance, housing, and other programs for the poor remains inexplicably high in relation to most valid measures of public opinion on welfare.

Whichever side is more correct, the historic welfare reform bill of 1996 can be seen at least in part as an example of what happens when the critical mass of intellectual opinion catches up to and combines with the governing force of public opinion. In deciding who governs and to what ends, ideas matter.

SOURCE: Steven M. Teles, *Whose Welfare? AFDC and Elite Politics* (Lawrence: University Press of Kansas, 1996).

People disagree concerning how many people are homeless, why they are homeless, and what should be done about it. Many liberals argue that there are millions of homeless people, that most of them are the victims of high housing costs or cuts in social services, and that the government should (at a minimum) not harass them and (at a maximum) provide them with shelter. Many conservatives, by contrast, argue that there are relatively few homeless people, that most of them are mentally ill or drug-dependent, and that the government should use the criminal justice and mental health systems to get them off the streets and into institutions.

When government is faced with a problem over which there is such profound disagreement, no one should be surprised to discover that it adopts a policy that satisfies neither group. In many cities the police enforce laws against public disorder but not against sleeping on the streets; local agencies supply shelters, but only during cold weather; health organizations offer treatment to mentally ill or drug-dependent people, but they do not require it.

The federal government has so far limited its role to supplying money to the states and cities to help pay for the variety of local programs. Beginning in 1987, Congress has authorized spending money for emergency food, shelter, and health care for the homeless.

Aid to Immigrants The political controversies surrounding homelessness pale in comparison to the present and potential political battles over immigration. In the early 1990s an estimated 1.25 million immigrants entered the country each year. Most entered legally, but some unknown fraction entered illegally (so-called undocumented aliens). Not since the early decades of this century has the United States experienced anything like this level of immigration.

The majority of these new immigrants are from Mexico, China, and Haiti, and they are different in both culture and appearance from the descendants of European immigrants who make up the majority of Americans. While many Americans of European ancestry cherish their grandparents' tales of how they came to this country, today's immigrants face a very different set of circumstances. Rather than landing on Ellis Island and spreading out across many states, an estimated 90 percent of today's immi-

Immigration has become a major political issue with the continued influx of undocumented aliens, such as these Mexicans waiting for a chance to slip through the fence into California near Tijuana.

grants are concentrated in six states: California, Florida, Illinois, New Jersey, New York, and Texas. California alone was the final destination of about half of all immigrants to the United States in the 1980s.

Most studies by economists indicate that the impact of immigration on the wages and unemployment rate of less-skilled workers is virtually nil. This holds even in such dramatic cases as the 1980 influx of some 125,000 Cubans into Miami, Florida. Although the Cuban immigration increased the city's labor force by almost 8 percent, it had virtually no deleterious economic effects on the city's less-skilled workers. Nevertheless, many Americans believe that immigration harms American workers and that immigrants who do not find jobs drain the public coffers of billions of tax dollars. Especially with respect to illegal aliens, many Americans are not inclined to number immigrants among the "deserving poor" nor to favor social welfare policies that benefit immigrants at the expense of all taxpayers.

Research findings on the economic effects of immigration are mixed. Some studies contradict the view that immigrants take jobs from native-born workers and depress wages, but others estimate that a large fraction (by some estimates as much as one-third) of the decline in the earnings of low-skilled, native-born workers in the 1980s resulted from competition from low-skilled immigrants. Likewise, some studies show that immigrants pay more in taxes than they receive in government services, but others reach the opposite conclusion.[14] In any case, research alone will not decide the coming national debate over immigration and social welfare policy. There are two historic oversimplifications in American thinking about immigrants—the "pitiable, huddled masses" view versus the "job-stealing aliens" view. It remains to be seen which view will prevail in government policy on immigrants, but the Welfare Reform Act of 1996 provided an early clue in its goals of cutting benefit to aliens, especially illegal ones.

SUMMARY

We can explain the politics of social welfare policy in America principally in terms of two factors: who benefits and who pays, and the beliefs citizens have about social justice. Neither factor is static: gainers and losers vary as the composition of society and the workings of the economy change, and beliefs about who deserves what are modified as attitudes toward work, the family, and the obligations of government change.

The benefits and costs of the policies help explain the popularity of two social welfare programs and the controversy surrounding others. Social Security and Medicare provide widely distributed benefits and impose widely distributed costs. The politics surrounding their enactment and expansion have been majoritarian. The Aid to Families with Dependent Children (AFDC) program provided benefits to some at a cost to many. As a form of client politics, it was made especially controversial by the public's perception of the program as one that helped an "undeserving" group. It became so controversial that it lost its political legitimacy and was repealed. Debates over health care reform are essentially arguments about who should pay and who should benefit.

The congressional (as opposed to the parliamentary) system of government means that greater political effort and more time are required for the adoption of a new welfare policy. Federalism means that the states will play a large role in determining how any welfare program is administered and at what level benefits are set.

KEY TERMS

majoritarian politics   *p. 523*

client politics   *p. 523*

insurance program   *p. 528*

assistance program   *p. 528*

means test   *p. 528*

Earned Income Tax Credit   *p. 531*

service strategy   *p. 534*

income strategy   *p. 534*

SUGGESTED READINGS

Derthick, Martha. *Policymaking for Social Security.* Washington, D.C.: Brookings Institution, 1979. A detailed analysis of how the Social Security program grew.

Heclo, Hugh. *Modern Social Politics in Britain and Sweden.* New Haven, Conn.: Yale University Press, 1974. Comparative analysis of how social-welfare programs came to Britain and Sweden.

Mead, Lawrence. *Beyond Entitlement: The Social Obligations of Citizenship.* New York: Free Press, 1986. Argument for "workfare," a requirement that able-bodied people work as a condition of receiving welfare.

Moynihan, Daniel Patrick. *Family and Nation.* New York: Harcourt Brace Jovanovich, 1986. Argument for the importance of federal policy to aid families. Disputes the Murray thesis.

Murray, Charles. *Losing Ground: American Social Policy, 1950–1980.* New York: Basic Books, 1984. An argument that federal spending on the poor actually increased poverty during the 1960s and 1970s.

Wilson, William J. *The Truly Disadvantaged.* Chicago: University of Chicago Press, 1987. Disputes Murray's explanation, arguing instead that ghetto poverty is the result of the movement of jobs out of cities.

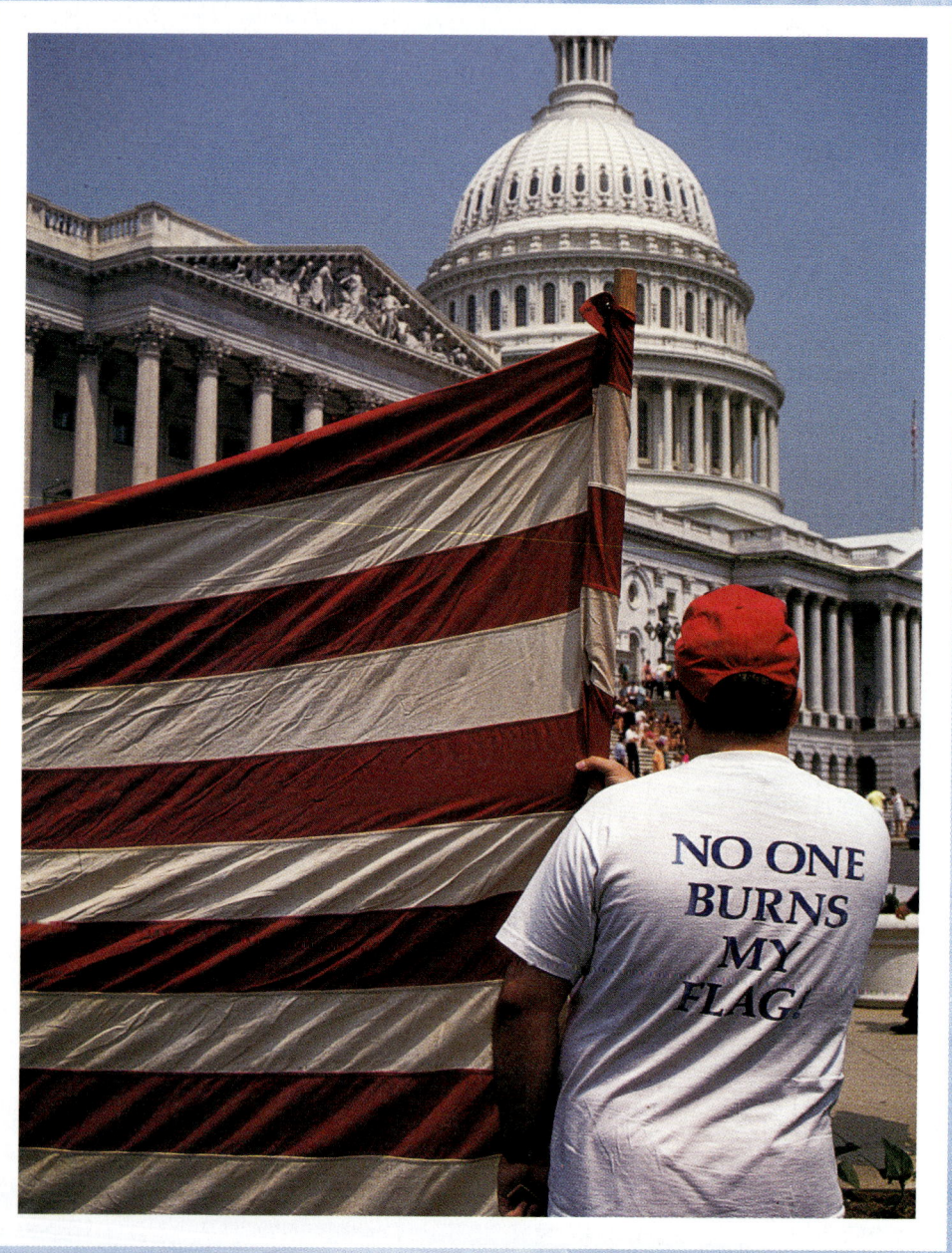

18

Civil Liberties

★ **Purpose of the Bill of Rights**

★ **Competing rights**

★ **Freedom of expression**

★ **Restrictions on free speech**

★ **The "clear-and-present-danger" test**

★ **The states and the Bill of Rights**

★ **What kinds of expression are not protected**

★ **Church and state**

★ **Crime and due process**

★ **The exclusionary rule**

Dogs trained to sniff out drugs go down your high school corridors and detect marijuana in some lockers. The school authorities open and search your locker without permission or a court order. You are expelled from the school without any hearing. Have your liberties been violated?

Angry at what you consider unfair treatment, you decide to wear a cloth American flag sewn to the seat of your pants, and your fellow students decide to wear black armbands to class to protest how you were treated. The police arrest you for wearing a flag on your seat, and the school punishes your classmates for wearing armbands contrary to school regulations. Have your liberties, or theirs, been violated?

You go into federal court to find out. We cannot be certain how the court would decide the issues in this particular case, but in similar cases in the past the courts have held that school authorities can use dogs to detect drugs in schools and that these officials can conduct a "reasonable" search of you and your effects if they have a "reasonable suspicion" that you are violating a school rule. But they cannot punish your classmates for wearing black armbands, they cannot expel you without a hearing, and the state cannot make it illegal to treat the flag "contemptuously" (by sewing it to the seat of your pants, for example).[1]

Your claim that these actions violated your constitutional rights would have astonished the Framers of the Constitution. They thought that they had written a document that stated what the federal government *could* do, not one that specified what state governments (such as school systems) *could not* do. And they thought that they had created a national government of such limited powers that it was not even necessary to add a list—a Bill of Rights—stating what that government was forbidden from doing. It would be enough, for example, that the Constitution did not authorize the federal government to censor newspapers; an amendment prohibiting censorship would be superfluous.

The people who gathered in the state ratifying conventions weren't so optimistic. They suspected—rightly, as it turned out—that the federal government might well try to do things that it was not authorized to do, and so they insisted that the Bill of Rights be added to the Constitution. But even they never imagined that the Bill of Rights would affect what *state* governments could do. Each state would decide that for itself, in its own constitution. And if by chance the Bill of Rights did apply to the states, surely its guarantees of free speech and freedom from unreasonable searches and seizures would apply to big issues—the freedom to attack the government in a newspaper editorial, for example, or to keep the police from breaking down the door of your home without a warrant. The courts would not be deciding who can wear what kinds of armbands or under what circumstances a school can expel a student.

To understand the nature of civil liberties today, it is necessary to understand why the liberties mentioned in the Bill of Rights were thought to be important, how they came to apply to the states, and why they have grown in scope and meaning.

Politics, Culture, and Civil Liberties

The Bill of Rights is an important limitation on popular rule. It says that there are things that a government cannot do even if a majority wants them done. But why would the government, to say nothing of a popular majority, ever want to do these things? In our review of the politics of policy-making, we have repeatedly observed the ability of small but intensely motivated minorities to block action that would impose heavy costs on them. Milk producers for a long time resisted efforts that would reduce government subsidies for their products, and ship owners and merchant seamen have been able to block efforts to introduce more competition (and presumably lower prices) into their industry. The political system has facilitated this kind of client politics.

If a largely indifferent public permits various economic, occupational, or professional minorities to safeguard their own interests, why should other kinds of minorities—religious or ideological ones—require special constitutional protection? Just as the average citizen bears only slight costs created by the advantages enjoyed by milk producers or truck drivers, presumably the average citizen bears only slight (if any) costs from the publication of a Communist

party newspaper or from the refusal of a member of the Jehovah's Witnesses to recite the pledge of allegiance to the flag. If costs are small and widely distributed, then one would expect that political activity to reduce those costs would be infrequent and often ineffective. Moreover, some of these "costs"—such as the consequences of people's reading a Communist party newspaper—will occur in the distant future, if at all. Ordinarily people are not politically sensitive to such distant or hypothetical burdens.

So why do the liberties claimed by some people ever become a major issue? There are three reasons. In two of the three the politics surrounding civil liberties are similar to those around any other issue. First, there may be rights in conflict (in which case we have interest group politics). Second, passions may be inflamed by a skilled policy entrepreneur (in which case we have entrepreneurial politics). But the third reason makes the politics of civil liberties different from that of most issues: the political culture of the United States, described in Chapter 4, contains principles that are in conflict with one another. Most Americans accept that culture and thus accept the contradictions built into it. From time to time we tend to favor one part of that culture (say, a belief in "Americanism") over another part (say, a belief in personal freedom). When that happens, we find ourselves fighting over matters such as flag-burning with an intensity that seems out of proportion to what is actually at stake.

Rights in Conflict

We often think of "civil liberties" as a set of principles that protect the freedoms of all of us all of the time. That is true—up to a point. But in fact the Constitution and the Bill of Rights contain a list of *competing* rights and duties. That competition becomes obvious when one person asserts one constitutional right or duty and another person asserts a different one. For example:

• Dr. Samuel H. Sheppard of Cleveland, Ohio, asserted his right to have a fair trial on the charge of having murdered his wife. Bob Considine and Walter Winchell, two radio commentators, as well as other reporters, asserted their right to broadcast whatever facts and rumors they heard about Dr. Sheppard and his love life. Two rights in conflict.

- The United States government has an obligation to "provide for the common defense" and, in pursuit of that duty, has claimed the right to keep secret certain military and diplomatic information. The *New York Times* claimed the right to publish such secrets as the "Pentagon Papers" without censorship, citing the Constitution's guarantee of freedom of the press. A duty and a right in conflict.

- Carl Jacob Kunz delivered inflammatory anti-Jewish speeches on the street corners of a Jewish neighborhood in New York City, suggesting, among other things, that Jews be "burnt in incinerators." The Jewish people living in that area were outraged. The New York police commissioner revoked Kunz's license to hold public meetings on the streets. When he continued to air his views on the public streets, Kunz was arrested for speaking without a permit. Freedom of speech versus the preservation of public order.

Even a disruptive high school student's right not to be a victim of arbitrary or unjustifiable expulsion is in partial conflict with the school's obligation to maintain an orderly environment in which learning can take place.

Political struggles over civil liberties follow much the same pattern as interest group politics involving economic issues, even though the claims in question are made by individuals. Indeed, there are formal, organized interest groups concerned with civil liberties. The Fraternal Order of the Police complains about restrictions on police powers, whereas the American Civil Liberties Union defends and seeks to enlarge those restrictions. Catholics have pressed for public support of parochial schools; Protestants and Jews have argued against it. Sometimes the opposed groups are entirely private; sometimes one or both are government agencies. Often their clashes end up in the courts. (When the Supreme Court decided the cases given earlier, Sheppard, the *New York Times*, and Kunz all won.[2])

Policy Entrepreneurs

Just as a skilled policy entrepreneur can sometimes arouse legislators to act against the normally undisputed claims of an interest group, so also can such an entrepreneur sometimes arouse people to take action against the rights and liberties claimed by political or religious dissidents. The success of entrepreneurial politics, whether involving money interests or civil liberties, often depends on the existence of a crisis.

War has usually been the crisis that has facilitated entrepreneurial politics aimed at restricting the liberty of some minority. For example:

- The Sedition Act was passed in 1798, making it a crime to write, utter, or publish "any false, scandalous, and malicious writing" with the intention of defaming the president, Congress, or the government or of exciting against the government "the hatred of the people." The occasion was a kind of half-war between the United States and France, stimulated by fear in this country of the violence following the French Revolution of 1789. The policy entrepreneurs were Federalist politicians who believed that Thomas Jefferson and his followers were supporters of the French Revolution and would, if they came to power, encourage here the kind of anarchy that seemed to be occurring in France.

- The Espionage and Sedition Acts were passed in 1917–1918, making it a crime to utter false statements that would interfere with the American

A 1919 cartoon expresses popular fears of "reds" (that is, leftist radicals) threatening American institutions.

Politically SPEAKING   *McCarthyism*

In 1950 Senator Joseph R. McCarthy of Wisconsin began making a long series of charges, usually unsubstantiated, that people working for various government agencies were communists. Since then anyone making a charge that unfairly impugns the motives, attacks the patriotism, or violates the rights of individuals is often criticized for engaging in **McCarthyism.** The word has become a synonym for "character assassination." Senator McCarthy was a conservative, and so liberals today are often quick to denounce conservative attacks on them as "McCarthyism." But increasingly conservatives have used the term against liberals, usually by modifying it to read "McCarthyism of the left."

SOURCE: From *Safire's Political Dictionary* by William Safire. Copyright © 1968, 1972, 1978 by William Safire. Reprinted by permission of Random House, Inc. and the author.

- The Smith Act was passed in 1940, the Internal Security Act in 1950, and the Communist Control Act in 1954. These laws made it illegal to advocate the overthrow of the U.S. government by force or violence (Smith Act), required members of the Communist party to register with the government (Internal Security Act), and declared the Communist party to be part of a conspiracy to overthrow the government (Communist Control Act). The occasion was World War II and the Korean War, which, like earlier wars, inspired fears that foreign agents (Nazi and Soviet) were trying to subvert the government. For the latter two laws the policy entrepreneur was Senator Joseph McCarthy, who attracted a great deal of attention with his repeated (and sometimes inaccurate) claims that Soviet agents were working inside the U.S. government.

- In 1968 a law was passed making it a federal crime to cross state lines or use interstate commerce in order to incite or organize a riot. The occasion was the wave of ghetto riots that had swept the country in the mid-1960s and the fear that some of the opponents of the war in Vietnam were going underground to organize violent attacks on governmental and other institutions. In this case there was no policy entrepreneur.

These laws had in common an effort to protect the nation from threats, real and imagined, posed by people who claimed to be exercising their freedom to speak, publish, organize, and assemble. In each case a real threat (a war or a riot) led the government to narrow the limits of permissible speech and activity. Almost every time such restrictions were imposed, the Supreme Court was called upon to decide whether Congress (or sometimes state legislatures) had drawn those limits properly. In most instances the Court tended to uphold the legislatures. But as time passed and the war or crisis ended, popular passions abated and many of the laws proved to be unimportant.

Though it is uncommon, some use is still made of the sedition laws. In the 1980s various white supremacists and Puerto Rican nationalists were charged with sedition. In each case the government alleged that the accused had not only spoken in favor of overthrowing the government, they had actually engaged in violent actions such as bombings.

military, to send through the mails material "advocating or urging treason, insurrection, or forcible resistance to any law of the United States," or to utter or write any disloyal, profane, scurrilous, or abusive language intended to incite resistance to the United States or to curtail war production. The occasion was World War I; the impetus was the fear that Germans in this country were spies and that radicals were seeking to overthrow the government. Under these laws more than two thousand persons were prosecuted (about half were convicted), and thousands of aliens were rounded up and deported. The policy entrepreneur leading this massive crackdown (the so-called Red Scare) was Attorney General A. Mitchell Palmer.

FIGURE 18.1 Annual Immigration, 1840–1990

NOTE: Figures for 1989 and 1990 include persons who were granted permanent residence under the legalization program of the Immigration and Reform and Control Act of 1986.

SOURCES: For 1985–1990: *Statistical Abstract of the United States, 1992,* 10.

Later in this chapter we shall see how the Court has increasingly restricted the power of Congress and state legislatures to outlaw political speech; to be found guilty of sedition now it is usually necessary to do something more serious than just talk about it.

Cultural Conflicts

In the main the United States was originally the creation of white European Protestants. Blacks were, in most cases, slaves, and American Indians were not citizens. Catholics and Jews in the colonies composed a small minority, and often a persecuted one. The early schools tended to be religious—that is, Protestant—ones, many of them receiving state aid. It is not surprising that under these circumstances a view of America arose that equated "Americanism" with the values and habits of white Anglo-Saxon Protestants.

But immigration to this country brought a flood of new settlers, many of them coming from very different backgrounds (see Figure 18.1). In the mid–nineteenth century the potato famine led millions of

Irish Catholics to migrate here. At the turn of the century religious persecution and economic disadvantage brought more millions of people, many Catholic or Jewish, from southern and eastern Europe.

In recent decades political conflict and economic want have led Hispanics (mostly from Mexico but increasingly from all parts of Latin America), Caribbeans, Africans, Middle Easterners, Southeast Asians, and Asians to cross our borders—some legally, some illegally (see Figure 18.2, page 550). Among them have been Buddhists, Catholics, Muslims, and the members of many other religious and cultural groups.

Ethnic, religious, and cultural differences have given rise to different views as to the meaning and scope of certain constitutionally protected freedoms. For example:

- Many Jewish groups find it offensive for a crèche (that is, a scene depicting the birth of Christ in a manger) to be displayed in front of a government building such as city hall at Christmastime, while many Catholics and Protestants regard such displays as an important part of our cultural

FIGURE 18.2 Changing Composition of U.S. Immigration, 1901–1990

1901–1920

Mexico 2.0%
Asia 4.3%
Central America 0.2%
Africa 0.1%
Europe 93.4%

1921–1940

Central America 0.6%
Mexico 13.9%
Asia 3.7%
Africa 0.2%
Europe 81.6%

1941–1960

Central America 2.6%
Mexico 14.0%
Asia 7.1%
Africa 0.8%
Europe 75.5%

1961–1980

Central America 4.4%
Mexico 20.3%
Africa 2.0%
Europe 35.8%
Asia 37.5%

1981–1990

Central America 5.4%
Mexico 16.8%
Africa 2.7%
Other 15.8%
South America 6.4%
Europe 10.2%
Asia 42.7%

SOURCES: For 1901–1980: Associated Press, adapted from a *Boston Globe* graphic by Steven Nelson. Reprinted courtesy of the *Boston Globe*. For 1981–1989: *Statistical Abstract of the United States, 1992*, 11.

heritage. Does a religious display on public property violate the First Amendment requirement that the government pass no law "respecting an establishment of religion"?

- Many English-speaking people believe that the public schools ought to teach all students to speak and write English, because the language is part of our nation's cultural heritage. Some Hispanic groups argue that the schools should teach pupils in both English and Spanish, since Spanish is part of the Hispanic cultural heritage. Is bilingual education constitutionally required?

Even within a given cultural tradition there are important differences of opinion as to the balance between community sensitivities and personal self-expression. To some people the sight of a store carrying pornographic books or a theater showing a pornographic movie is deeply offensive; to others pornography is offensive but such establishments ought to be tolerated to ensure that laws restricting them do not also restrict politically or artistically important forms of speech; to still others pornography itself is not especially offensive. What forms of expression are entitled to constitutional protection?

Interpreting and Applying the First Amendment

The First Amendment contains the language that has been at issue in most of the cases to which we have thus far referred. It has roughly two parts: one protecting **freedom of expression** ("Congress shall make no law . . . abridging the freedom of speech, or of the press, or the right of people peaceably to assemble, and to petition the government for a redress of grievances") and the other protecting **freedom of religion** ("Congress shall make no law respecting an establishment of religion; or abridging the free exercise thereof"). In this section we shall discuss freedom of expression and in the next, freedom of religion.

Speech and National Security

The traditional view of free speech and a free press was expressed by William Blackstone, the great English jurist, in his *Commentaries*, published in

1765. A free press is essential to a free state, he wrote, but the freedom that the press should enjoy is the freedom from **prior restraint**—that is, freedom from censorship, or rules telling a newspaper in advance what it can publish. Once a newspaper has published an article or a person has delivered a speech, that paper or speaker has to take the consequences if what was written or said proves to be "improper, mischievous, or illegal."[3]

The U.S. Sedition Act of 1798 was in keeping with traditional English law. Like it, the act imposed no prior restraint on publishers; it did, however, make them liable to punishment after the fact. The act was an improvement over the English law, however, because unlike the British model it entrusted the decision to a jury, not a judge, and allowed the defendant to be acquitted if he or she could prove the truth of what had been published. Although several newspaper publishers were convicted under the act, none of these cases reached the Supreme Court. When Jefferson became president in 1801, he pardoned everyone who had been convicted under the Sedition Act. Though Jeffersonians objected vehemently to the law, their principal objection was not to the idea of holding newspapers accountable for what they published but to letting the *federal* government do this. Jefferson was perfectly prepared to have the *states* punish what he called the "overwhelming torrent of slander" by means of "a few prosecutions of the most prominent offenders."[4]

It was not for another century that the federal government would attempt to define the limits of free speech and writing. Perhaps recalling the widespread opposition to the sweep of the 1798 act, Congress in 1917–1918 placed restrictions not on publications that were critical of the government but only on those that advocated "treason, insurrection, or forcible resistance" to federal laws or attempted to foment disloyalty or mutiny in the armed services.

In 1919 this new law was examined by the Supreme Court when it heard the case of Charles T. Schenck, who had been convicted of violating the Espionage Act because he had mailed circulars to men eligible for the draft, urging them to resist. At issue was the constitutionality of the Espionage Act and, more broadly, the scope of Congress's power to control speech. One view held that the First Amendment prevented Congress from passing *any*

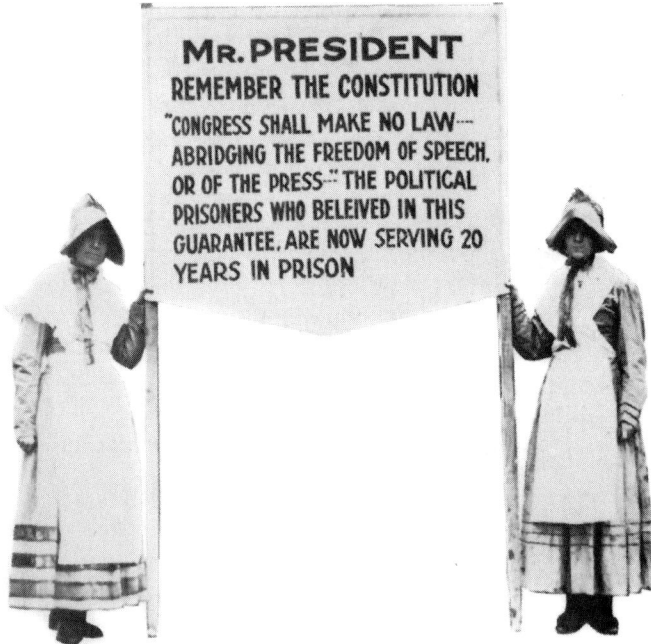

Women picketed in front of the White House, urging President Warren Harding to release political radicals arrested during his administration.

law restricting speech; the other held that Congress could punish dangerous speech. For a unanimous Supreme Court, Justice Oliver Wendell Holmes announced a rule by which to settle the matter. It soon became known as the **clear-and-present-danger test:**

The question in every case is whether the words used are used in such circumstances and are of such a nature as to create a clear and present danger that they will bring about the substantive evils that Congress has a right to prevent.[5]

The Court held that Schenck's leaflets did create such a danger, and so his conviction was upheld. In explaining why, Holmes said that not even the Constitution protects a person who has been "falsely shouting fire in a theatre and causing a panic." In this case things that might safely be said in peacetime may be punished in wartime.

The clear-and-present-danger test may have clarified the law, but it kept no one out of jail. Schenck went, and so did the defendants in five other cases in the period 1919–1927, even though during this time Holmes, the author of the test, shifted his position and began writing dissenting opinions in which he urged that the test had not been met and so the defendant should go free.

During the same period the Court for the first time came to grips with the power of state governments to punish speech. As we saw in Chapter 2, the Bill of Rights was originally intended only to limit the powers of the *federal* government. The adoption in 1868 of the Fourteenth Amendment, however, brought into the Constitution language that for the first time created the possibility that some or all of the Bill of Rights might now restrict the states' actions. The key phrase was the **due-process clause:**

No state shall . . . deprive any person of life, liberty or property, without due process of law.

For over half a century after 1868, the Supreme Court steadfastly denied that the due-process clause made the Bill of Rights applicable to the states. Therefore, state legislatures could pass sedition laws or antiobscenity laws without fear of having them overturned by the Supreme Court.

Then in 1925 Benjamin Gitlow was convicted of violating New York's sedition law—a law similar to the federal Sedition Act of 1918—by passing out some leaflets. The Supreme Court upheld his conviction but added a statement that changed constitutional history: freedom of speech and of the press were now among the "fundamental personal rights" protected by the due-process clause of the Fourteenth Amendment from infringements by *state* action.[6] Thereafter state laws involving speech, the press, and peaceful assembly were struck down by the Supreme Court for being in violation of the freedom-of-expression guarantees of the First Amendment, made applicable to the states by the Fourteenth Amendment.[7]

The clear-and-present-danger test was a way of balancing the competing demands of free expression and national security. As the memory of World War I and the ensuing Red Scare evaporated, the Court began to develop other tests, ones that shifted the balance more toward free expression. Some of these tests are listed in the box on page 554.

But when a crisis reappears, as it did in World War II and the Korean conflict, the Court has tended to defer, up to a point, to legislative judgments about the need to protect national security. For ex-

ample, it upheld the conviction of eleven leaders of the Communist party for having advocated the violent overthrow of the United States government, a violation of the Smith Act of 1940.

This conviction once again raised the hard question of the circumstances under which words can be punished. Hardly anybody would deny that actually *trying* to overthrow the government is a crime; the question is whether *advocating* its overthrow is a crime. In the case of the eleven communist leaders, the Court said that the government did not have to wait to protect itself until "the *putsch* [rebellion] is about to be executed, the plans have been laid and the signal is awaited." Even if the communists were not likely to be successful in their effort, the Court held that specifically advocating violent overthrow could be punished. "In each case," the opinion read, the courts "must ask whether the gravity of the 'evil,' discounted by its improbability, justifies such invasion of free speech as is necessary to avoid the danger."[8]

But as the popular worries about communists began to subside and the membership of the Supreme Court changed, the Court began to tip the balance even farther toward free expression. By 1957 the Court made it clear that for advocacy to be punished, the government would have to show not just that a person believed in the overthrow of the government but also that he or she was using words "calculated to incite" that overthrow.[9]

By 1969 the pendulum had swung to the point where the speech would have to be judged likely to incite "imminent" unlawful action. In this case Clarence Brandenburg, a leader of the Ku Klux Klan in Ohio, staged a cross-burning rally during which he reviled blacks and Jews. The police told him to clear the street; as he left, he said, "We'll take the [expletive] street later." He was convicted of attempting to incite lawless mob action. The Supreme Court overturned the conviction, holding that any speech that does not call for illegal action is protected, and even speech that *does* call for illegal action is protected if the action is not "imminent" or there is reason to believe that the listeners will not take action.[10]

This means that no matter how offensive or provocative some forms of expression may be, this expression has powerful constitutional protections. In 1977 a group of American Nazis wanted to parade through the streets of Skokie, Illinois, a community with a large Jewish population. The residents, outraged, sought to ban the march. Many feared violence if it occurred. But the lower courts, under prodding from the Supreme Court, held that, noxious and provocative as the anti-Semitic slogans of the Nazis may be, the Nazi party had a constitutional right to speak and parade peacefully.[11]

Similar reasoning led the Supreme Court in 1992 to overturn a Minnesota statute that made it a crime to display symbols or objects, such as a Nazi swastika or a burning cross, that are likely to cause alarm or resentment among an ethnic or racial group, such as Jews or blacks.[12] On the other hand, if you are convicted of actually hurting someone, you may be given a tougher sentence if it can be shown that you were motivated to assault them by racial or ethnic hatred.[13] To be punished for such a hate crime, your bigotry must result in some direct and physical harm and not just the display of an odious symbol.

What Is Speech?

If most political speaking or writing is permissible, save that which actually incites someone to take illegal actions, what *kinds* of speaking and writing qualify for this broad protection? Though the Constitution says that the legislature may make "no law" abridging freedom of speech or the press, and although some justices have argued that this means literally *no* law, the Court has held that there are at least four forms of speaking and writing that are not automatically granted full constitutional protection: libel, obscenity, symbolic speech, and false advertising.

Libel

A **libel** is a written statement that defames the character of another person. (If the statement is oral, it is called a slander.) In some countries, such as England, it is easy to sue another person for libel and to collect. In this country it is much harder. For one thing, you must show that the libelous statement was false. If it was true, you cannot collect no matter how badly it harmed you.

A beauty contest winner was awarded $14 million (later reduced on appeal) when she proved that

Even hateful symbols, such as this burning cross lit by members of the Ku Klux Klan, enjoy constitutional protection.

Penthouse magazine had libeled her. The actress Carol Burnett collected a large sum from a libel suit brought against a gossip newspaper. But when Theodore Roosevelt sued a newspaper for falsely claiming that he was a drunk, the jury awarded him damages of only six cents.[14]

If you are a public figure, it is much harder to win a libel suit. A public figure such as an elected official, an army general, or a well-known celebrity must prove not only that the publication was false and damaging but also that the words were published with "actual malice"—that is, with reckless disregard for their truth or falsity or with knowledge that they were false.[15] As we saw in Chapter 10, that is not easily done. General Ariel Sharon was able to prove that the statements made about him by *Time* magazine were false and damaging but not that they were the result of "actual malice."

Testing Restrictions on Expression

*T*he Supreme Court has employed various standards and tests to decide whether a restriction on freedom of expression is constitutionally permissible.

1. **Preferred position** The right of free expression, though not absolute, occupies a higher, or more preferred, position than many other constitutional rights, such as property rights. This is still a controversial rule; nonetheless, the Court always approaches a restriction on expression skeptically.

2. **Prior restraint** With scarcely any exceptions, the Court will not tolerate a prior restraint on expression, such as censorship, even when it will allow subsequent punishment of improper expressions (such as libel).

3. **Imminent danger** Punishment for uttering inflammatory sentiments will be allowed only if there is an imminent danger that the utterances will incite an unlawful act.

4. **Neutrality** Any restriction on speech, such as a requirement that parades or demonstrations not disrupt other people in the exercise of their rights, must be neutral—that is, it must not favor one group more than another.

5. **Clarity** If you must obtain a permit to hold a parade, the law must set forth clear (as well as neutral) standards to guide administrators in issuing that permit. Similarly, a law punishing obscenity must contain a clear definition of obscenity.

6. **Least-restrictive means** If it is necessary to restrict the exercise of one right to protect the exercise of another, the restriction should employ the least-restrictive means to achieve its end. For example, if press coverage threatens a person's right to a fair trial, the judge may only do what is minimally necessary to that end, such as transferring the case to another town rather than issuing a "gag order."

Cases cited, by item: (1) *United States* v. *Carolene Products*, 304 U.S. 144 (1938). (2) *Near* v. *Minnesota*, 283 U.S. 697 (1931). (3) *Brandenburg* v. *Ohio*, 395 U.S. 444 (1969). (4) *Kunz* v. *New York*, 340 U.S. 290 (1951). (5) *Hynes* v. *Mayor and Council of Oradell*, 425 U.S. 610 (1976). (6) *Nebraska Press Association* v. *Stuart*, 427 U.S. 539 (1976).

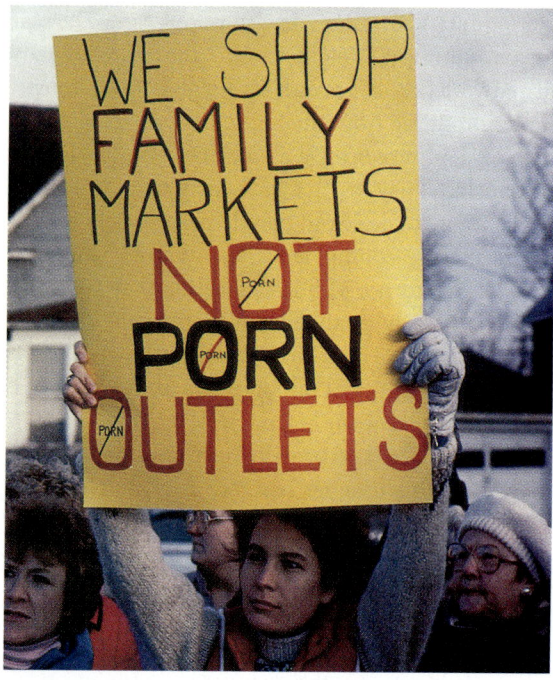

Rights in conflict: some people object to pornographic books and videos being sold in their neighborhood; others think people have a right to patronize such stores.

Obscenity

Obscenity is not protected by the First Amendment. The Court has always held that obscene materials, because they have no redeeming social value and are calculated chiefly to appeal to one's sexual rather than political or literary interests, can be regulated by the state. The problem, of course, arises with the meaning of *obscene*. In the eleven-year period from 1957 to 1968 the Court decided thirteen major cases involving the definition of obscenity, which resulted in fifty-five separate opinions.[16] Some justices, such as Hugo Black, believed that the First Amendment protected all publications, even wholly obscene ones. Others believed that obscenity deserved no protection and struggled heroically to define the term. Still others shared the view of former Justice Potter Stewart, who objected to "hard-core pornography" but admitted that the best definition he could offer was "I know it when I see it."[17]

It is unnecessary to review in detail the many attempts by the Court at defining obscenity. The justices have made it clear that nudity and sex are not, by definition, obscene and that they will provide First Amendment protection to anything that has political, literary, or artistic merit, allowing the government to punish only the distribution of "hard-core pornography." Their most recent (1973) definition of this is as follows: to be obscene, the work, taken as a whole, must be judged by "the average person applying contemporary community standards" to appeal to the "prurient interest" or to depict "in a patently offensive way, sexual conduct specifically defined by applicable state law" and to lack "serious literary, artistic, political, or scientific value."[18]

After Albany, Georgia, decided that the movie *Carnal Knowledge* was obscene by contemporary local standards, the Supreme Court overturned the distributor's conviction on the grounds that the authorities in Albany failed to show that the film depicted "patently offensive hard-core sexual conduct."[19]

It is easy to make sport of the problems the Court has faced in trying to decide obscenity cases (one conjures up images of black-robed justices leafing through the pages of *Hustler* magazine, taking notes), but these problems reveal, as do other civil liberties cases, the continuing problem of balancing competing claims. One part of the community wants to read or see whatever it wishes; another part wants to protect private acts from public degradation. The first part cherishes liberty above all; the second values decency above liberty. The former fears that *any* restriction on literature will lead to *pervasive* restrictions; the latter believes that reasonable people can distinguish (or reasonable laws can require them to distinguish) between patently offensive and artistically serious work.

Anyone strolling today through an "adult" bookstore must suppose that no restrictions at all exist on the distribution of pornographic works. This condition does not arise simply from the doctrines of the Court. Other factors operate as well, including the priorities of local law enforcement officials, the political climate of the community, the procedures that must be followed to bring a viable court case, the clarity and workability of state and local laws on the subject, and the difficulty of changing the behavior of many people by prosecuting one person. The current view of the Court is that localities can decide for themselves whether to tolerate hard-core

pornography; but if they choose not to, they must meet some fairly strict constitutional tests.

The protections given by the Court to expressions of sexual or erotic interest have not been limited to books, magazines, or films. Almost any form of visual or auditory communication can be considered "speech" and thus protected by the First Amendment. In one case even nude dancing was given protection as a form of "speech,"[20] although in 1991 the Court held that nude dancing was only "marginally" within the purview of First Amendment protections, and so it upheld an Indiana statute that banned *totally* nude dancing.[21]

Of late some feminist organizations have attacked pornography on the grounds that it exploits and degrades women. They persuaded Indianapolis to pass an ordinance that defined pornography as portrayals of the "graphic, sexually explicit subordination of women" and allowed people to sue the producers of such material. Sexually explicit portrayals of women in positions of equality were not defined as pornography. The Court disagreed. In 1986 it affirmed a lower court ruling that such an ordinance was a violation of the First Amendment because it represented a legislative preference for one form of expression (women in positions of equality) over another (women in positions of subordination).[22]

"Symbolic speech": when young men burned their draft cards during the 1960s to protest the Vietnam War, the Supreme Court ruled that it was an illegal act for which they could be punished.

The toughest test of our commitment to political liberties is our willingness to tolerate the activities of groups that we find repellent.

One constitutionally permissible way to limit the spread of pornographic materials has been to establish rules governing where in a city they can be sold. When one city adopted a zoning ordinance prohibiting an "adult" movie theater from locating within one thousand feet of any church, school, park, or residential area, the Court upheld the ordinance, noting that the purpose of the law was not to regulate speech but to regulate the use of land. And in any case the adult theaters still had much of the city's land area in which to find a location.[23]

With the advent of the Internet it has become more difficult for the government to regulate obscenity. The Internet spans the entire globe. It offers an amazing variety of materials—some educational, some entertaining, some sexually explicit. But it is difficult to apply the Supreme Court's standard for judging whether sexual material is obscene—the "average person" applying "contemporary community standards"—to the Internet, because there is no easy way to tell what "the community" is. Is it the

place where the recipient lives or the place where the material originates? And since no one is in charge of the Internet, who can be held responsible for controlling offensive material? Since anybody can send anything to anybody else without knowing the age or location of the recipient, how can the Internet protect children? When Congress tried to ban obscene, indecent, or "patently offensive" materials from the Internet, the Supreme Court struck it down as unconstitutional.[24]

Symbolic Speech

You cannot ordinarily claim that an illegal act should be protected because that action is meant to convey a political message. For example, if you burn your draft card in protest against the foreign policy of the United States, you can be punished for the illegal act (burning the card), even if your intent was to communicate your beliefs. The Court reasoned that giving such **symbolic speech** the same protection as real speech would open the door to permitting all manner of illegal actions—murder, arson, rape—if the perpetrator meant thereby to send a message.[25]

On the other hand, a statute that makes it illegal to burn the American flag is an unconstitutional infringement of free speech.[26] Why is there a difference between a draft card and the flag? The Court argues that the government has a right to run a military draft and so can protect draft cards, even if this incidentally restricts speech. But the only motive that the government has in banning flag burning is to restrict this form of speech, and that would make such a restriction improper. In 1989–1990 Congress refused to endorse a proposed constitutional amendment that, if ratified, would have reversed this Court ruling. It did pass a bill making flag-burning a crime, but the Supreme Court, consistent with its decision in an earlier Texas case, held that this law was an unconstitutional infringement of free speech.[27]

Who Is a Person?

If people have a right to speak and publish, do corporations, interest groups, and children have the same right? By and large the answer is yes, though there are some exceptions.

When the attorney general of Massachusetts tried to prevent the First National Bank of Boston from spending money to influence votes in a local election, the Court stepped in and blocked him. The Court held that a corporation, like a person, has certain First Amendment rights.[28]

Similarly, when the federal government tried to limit the spending of a group called Massachusetts Citizens for Life (an antiabortion organization), the Court held that such organizations have First Amendment rights. The Court has also barred states from forbidding liquor dealers from advertising their prices.[29]

When the California Public Utility Commission tried to compel one of the utilities that it regulates, the Pacific Gas and Electric Company, to enclose in its monthly bills to customers statements written by groups attacking the utility, the Supreme Court blocked the agency, saying that forcing it to disseminate political statements violated the firm's free-speech rights. "The identity of the speaker is not decisive in determining whether speech is protected," the Court said. "Corporations and other associations, like individuals, contribute to the 'discussion, debate, and the dissemination of information and ideas' that the First Amendment seeks to foster." In this case the right to speak includes the choice of what *not* to say.[30]

Even though corporations have some First Amendment rights, the government can place more limits on commercial than on noncommercial speech. The legislature can place restrictions on advertisements for cigarettes, liquor, and gambling; it can even regulate advertising for some less harmful products provided that the regulations are narrowly tailored and serve a substantial public interest.[31] If the regulations are too broad or do not serve a clear interest, then ads are entitled to some constitutional protection. For example, the states cannot bar lawyers from advertising or accountants from personally soliciting clients.[32]

Under certain circumstances, young people may have less freedom of expression than adults. In 1988 the Supreme Court held that the principal of a high school could censor articles appearing in the student-edited newspaper at Hazelwood High School. The newspaper was published using school funds and was part of a journalism class. The principal ordered the deletion of stories dealing with student pregnan-

cies and the impact of parental divorce on students. The student editors sued, claiming their First Amendment rights had been violated. The Court agreed that students do not "shed their constitutional rights to freedom of speech or expression at the schoolhouse gate" and that they cannot be punished for expressing on campus their personal views. But students do not have exactly the same rights as adults if the exercise of those rights impedes the educational mission of the school. Students may lawfully say things on campus, as individuals, that they cannot say if they are part of school-sponsored activities, such as plays or school-run newspapers, that are part of the curriculum. School-sponsored activities can be controlled so long as the controls are "reasonably related to legitimate pedagogical concerns."[33]

Church and State

Everybody knows, correctly, the language of the First Amendment that protects freedom of speech and the press, though most people are not aware of how complex the legal interpretations of these provisions have become. But many people also believe, wrongly, that the language of the First Amendment clearly requires the "separation of church and state." It does not.

What that amendment actually says is quite different and maddeningly unclear. It has two parts. The first, often referred to as the **free-exercise clause,** states that Congress shall make no law prohibiting the "free exercise" of religion. The second, which is called the **establishment clause,** states that Congress shall make no law "respecting an establishment of religion."

The Free-Exercise Clause

The free-exercise clause is the clearer of the two, though by no means is it lacking in ambiguity. It obviously means that Congress cannot pass a law prohibiting Catholics from celebrating Mass, requiring Baptists to become Episcopalians, or preventing Jews from holding a *bar mitzvah*. Since the First Amendment has been applied to the states via the due-process clause of the Fourteenth Amendment, it means that state governments cannot pass such laws

Religious Issues on Which the Supreme Court Is Silent

Often the cases that the Supreme Court doesn't decide are just as important as the ones it does decide. Here are some cases involving claims of religious freedom that were decided by lower courts. Since the Supreme Court refused to hear an appeal of these decisions, the lower court decisions, at least for now, are the law.

Reading the Bible In a Colorado public school, classrooms occasionally have a silent reading period during which the students and teachers can read various books. One teacher silently read his Bible during this period. There is no evidence his students knew what he was reading; however, the principal of the school told the teacher he could not read the Bible because *if* the students found out it might influence them to read the Bible also. A federal court upheld the principal.

Mentioning God A professor of physiology at the University of Alabama occasionally mentioned in class the importance to him of his Christian faith. He also gave an after-class lecture on "Evidences of God in Human Physiology." Attendance was optional. The university ordered him not to present any comments from a Christian perspective in class. A federal court upheld the university.

Spouse abuse and religion The New Orleans Baptist Theological seminary expelled a student when it learned from the police that he had abused his wife. The state courts ordered him reinstated because spouse abuse did not bear on his academic qualifications for a degree. The seminary argued that giving him a degree would entitle him to be a Baptist minister, and that spouse abuse was incompatible with a religious vocation. The seminary lost.

Americans, even a few bikers such as this one in Iowa, are more religious than the people of other industrialized nations, with the result that the Supreme Court must confront endless church-state issues.

SOURCE: Adapted from Michael McConnell, "Freedom From Religion?" *The American Enterprise* (January/February 1993): 32–43.

either. In general the courts have treated religion like speech: you can pretty much do or say what you want so long as it does not cause some serious harm to others.

Even some laws that do not appear on their face to apply to churches may be unconstitutional if their enforcement imposes particular burdens on churches or greater burdens on some churches than others. For example, a state cannot apply a license fee on door-to-door solicitors when the solicitor is a Jehovah's Witness selling religious tracts.[34] By the same token, the courts ruled that the city of Hialeah, Florida, cannot ban animal sacrifices by members of an Afro-Caribbean religion called Santeria. Since killing animals is generally not illegal (if it were, there could be no hamburgers or chicken sandwiches served in Hialeah's restaurants, and rat traps would be unlawful), the ban in this case was clearly directed against a specific religion and hence was unconstitutional.[35]

Having the right to exercise your religion freely does not mean, however, that you are exempt from laws binding other citizens, even when the law goes against your religious beliefs. A man cannot have more than one wife, even if (as once was the case with Mormons) polygamy is thought desirable on religious grounds.[36] For religious reasons you may oppose being vaccinated or having blood transfusions, but if the state passes a compulsory vaccination law or orders that a blood transfusion be given to a sick child, the courts will not block them on grounds of religious liberty.[37] Similarly, if you belong to an Indian tribe that uses a drug, peyote, in religious ceremonies, you cannot claim that your freedom was abridged if the state decides to ban the use of peyote, provided the law applies equally to all.[38] Since airports have a legitimate need for tight security measures, begging can be outlawed in them even if some of the people doing the begging are part of a religious group (in this case, the Hare Krishnas).[39]

Unfortunately some conflicts between religious belief and public policy are even more difficult to settle. What if you believe on religious grounds that war is immoral? The draft laws have always exempted a conscientious objector from military duty, and the Court has upheld such exemptions. But the Court has gone further: it has said that people cannot be drafted even if they do not believe in a Supreme Being or belong to any religious tradition, so long as their "consciences, spurred by deeply held moral, ethical, or religious beliefs, would give them no rest or peace if they allowed themselves to become part of an instrument of war."[40] Do exemptions on such grounds create an opportunity for some people to evade the draft because of their political preferences? In trying to answer such questions, the courts often have had to try to define a religion—no easy task.

And even when there is no question about your membership in a bona fide religion, the circumstances under which you may claim exemption from laws that apply to everybody else are not really clear. What if you, a member of the Seventh-Day Adventists, are fired by your employer for refusing

When a Hare Krishna hands out flowers, is he exercising his First Amendment rights?

on religious grounds to work on Saturday, and then it turns out that you cannot collect unemployment insurance because you refuse to take an available job—one that also requires you to work on Saturday? Or what if you are a member of the Amish sect, which refuses, contrary to state law, to send its children to public schools past the eighth grade? The Court has ruled that the state must pay you unemployment compensation and cannot require you to send your children to public schools beyond the eighth grade.[41]

These last two decisions, and others like them, show that even the "simple" principle of freedom of religion gets complicated in practice and can lead to the courts' giving, in effect, preference to members of one church over members of another.

The Establishment Clause

What in the world did the members of the First Congress mean when they wrote into the First Amendment language prohibiting Congress from

Religious Groups on Campus

What rights do religious groups have in schools and colleges? For publicly supported schools, the Supreme Court has held that

- It does not violate the establishment clause of the First Amendment for a public university to grant equal access to its facilities to religious as well as nonreligious groups.

- If a school allows its property to be used to present all views on an issue except a religious one, then it has violated the Constitution.

- If a school or university subsidizes student publications or organizations, then it cannot deny that subsidy to a religious newspaper or organization.

In short, the state must be neutral toward religion, and it cannot evade that obligation to be neutral by claiming that *any* involvement with religion violates the establisment clause of the First Amendment.

---

making a law "respecting" an "establishment" of religion? The Supreme Court has more or less consistently interpreted this vague phrase to mean that the Constitution erects a "wall of separation" between church and state.

That phrase, so often quoted, is not in the Bill of Rights nor in the debates in the First Congress that drafted the Bill of Rights; it comes from the pen of Thomas Jefferson, who was opposed to having the Church of England as the established church of his native Virginia. (At the time of the Revolutionary War there were established churches—that is, official, state-supported churches—in at least eight of the thirteen former colonies.) But it is not clear that Jefferson's view was the majority view.

During much of the debate in Congress the wording of this part of the First Amendment was quite different and much plainer than what finally emerged. Up to the last minute the clause was intended to read "no religion shall be established by law" or "no national religion shall be established." The meaning of those words seems quite clear: whatever the states may do, the federal government cannot create an official, national religion or give support to one religion in preference to another.[42]

But Congress instead adopted an ambiguous phrase, and so the Supreme Court had to decide

what it meant. It has declared that these words do not simply mean "no national religion" but mean as well no government involvement with religion at all, even on a nonpreferential basis. They mean, in short, erecting a "wall of separation" between church and state.[43] Though the interpretation of the establishment clause remains a topic of great controversy among judges and scholars, the Supreme Court has more or less consistently adopted this **wall-of-separation principle.**

Its first statement of this interpretation was in 1947. The case involved a New Jersey town that reimbursed parents for the costs of transporting their children to school, including parochial (in this case Catholic) schools. The Court decided that this reimbursement was constitutional, but it made it clear that the establishment clause of the First Amendment applied (via the Fourteenth Amendment) to the states and that it meant, among other things, that the government cannot require a person to profess a belief or disbelief in any religion; it cannot aid one religion, some religions, or all religions; and it cannot spend any tax money, however small the amount might be, in support of any religious activities or institutions.[44] The reader may wonder, in view of the Court's reasoning, why it allowed the town to pay for busing children to Catholic schools. The answer that it gave is that busing is a religiously neutral activity, akin to providing fire and police protection to Catholic schools. Busing, available to public- and private-school children alike, does not breach the wall of separation.

Since 1947 the Court has applied the wall-of-separation theory to strike down as unconstitutional every effort to have any form of prayer in public schools, even if it is nonsectarian,[45] voluntary,[46] or limited to reading a passage of the Bible.[47] Since 1992 it has even been unconstitutional for a public school to ask a rabbi or minister to offer a prayer—an invocation or a benediction—at the school's graduation ceremony.[48] Moreover, the Court has held that laws prohibiting teaching the theory of evolution or requiring giving equal time to "creationism" are religiously inspired and thus unconstitutional.[49] A public school may not allow its pupils to take time out from their regular classes for religious instruction if this occurs within the schools, though "released-time" instruction is all right if it is done outside the public school building.[50] The school prayer decisions in particular have provoked a storm of controversy, but efforts to get Congress to propose to the states a constitutional amendment authorizing such prayers have failed.

Almost as controversial have been Court-imposed restrictions on public aid to parochial schools, though here the wall-of-separation principle has not been used to forbid any and all forms of aid. For example, it is permissible for the federal government to provide aid for constructing buildings on denominational (as well as nondenominational) college campuses[51] and for state governments to loan free textbooks to parochial-school pupils,[52] grant tax-exempt status to parochial schools,[53] allow parents of parochial-school children to deduct their tuition payments on a state's income tax returns,[54] and pay for a deaf child's sign language interpreter at a Catholic school.[55] But the government cannot pay a salary supplement to teachers who teach secular subjects in parochial schools,[56] reimburse parents for the cost of parochial-school tuition,[57] supply parochial schools with services such as counseling,[58] give money with which to purchase instructional materials, require that "creationism" (the Biblical doctrine that God created mankind) be taught in public schools, or create a special school district for Hasidic Jews.[59]

If you find it confusing to follow the twists and turns of Court policy in this area, you are not alone. The wall-of-separation principle has not been easy to apply, and with its membership undergoing change, the Court has begun to alter its position on church-state matters. (O'Connor, Rehnquist, Scalia, Kennedy, and Thomas have generally supported lowering—or perhaps perforating—the wall a bit.) The Court has tried to sort out the confusion by developing a three-part test to decide under what circumstances government involvement in religious activities is improper.[60] That involvement is constitutional if it meets these tests:

1. It has a secular purpose.

2. Its primary effect neither advances nor inhibits religion.

3. It does not foster an excessive government entanglement with religion.

No sooner had the test been developed than the Court decided that it was all right for the government

A major free speech issue arises when parents object to the books their children are required to read in school, as here in Greenville, Tennessee.

of Pawtucket, Rhode Island, to erect a nativity scene as part of a Christmas display in a local park. But five years later it said that Pittsburgh could not put a nativity scene in front of the courthouse but could display a menorah (a Jewish symbol of Chanukah) next to a Christmas tree and a sign extolling liberty.[61]

Confused? It gets worse. Though the Court has struck down prayer in public schools, it has upheld prayers in Congress (since 1789, the House and Senate open each session with a prayer).[62] A public school cannot have a chaplain, but the armed services can. The Court has said that the government cannot "advance" religion, but it has not objected to the printing of the phrase "In God We Trust" on the back of every dollar bill.

It is obvious that despite its efforts to set forth clear rules governing church-state relations, the Court's actual decisions are hard to summarize. It is

CRITICAL Thinking

How Would You Decide?

Suppose that you are on the Supreme Court. In each of the actual cases summarized below, you are asked to decide whether the First Amendment to the Constitution permits or prohibits a particular action. What would be your decision? (How the Supreme Court actually decided is given on page 564.)

CASE 1: Jacksonville, Florida, passed a city ordinance prohibiting drive-in movies from showing films containing nudity if the screen was visible to passersby on the street. A movie theater manager protested, claiming that he had a First Amendment right to show such films, even if they could be seen from the street. Who is correct?

CASE 2: Dr. Benjamin Spock wanted to enter Fort Dix Military Reservation in New Jersey to pass out campaign literature and discuss issues with service personnel. The military denied him access on grounds that regulations prohibit partisan campaigning on military bases. Who is correct?

CASE 3: A town passed an ordinance forbidding the placing of "For Sale" or "Sold" signs in front of homes in racially changing neighborhoods. The purpose was to reduce "white flight" and panic selling. A realty firm protested, claiming that its freedom of speech was being abridged. Who is correct?

CASE 4: A girl in Georgia was raped and died. A local television station broadcast the name of the girl, having obtained it from court records. Her father sued, claiming that his family's right to privacy had been violated, and pointed to a Georgia law that made it a crime to broadcast the name of a rape victim. The television station claimed that it had a right under the First Amendment to broadcast the name. Who is correct?

CASE 5: Florida passed a law giving a political candidate the right to equal space in a newspaper that had published attacks on him. A newspaper claimed that this violated the freedom of the press to publish what it wants. Who is correct?

CASE 6: Zacchini is a "human cannonball" whose entire fifteen-second act was filmed and broadcast by an Ohio television station. Zacchini sued the station, claiming that his earning power had been reduced by the film because the station showed for free what he charges people to see at county fairs. The station replied that it had a First Amendment right to broadcast such events. Who is correct?

---

deeply divided—some would say deeply confused—on these matters, and so the efforts to define the "wall of separation" will continue to prove to be as difficult as the Court's earlier efforts to decide what is interstate and what is local commerce (see Chapter 3).

Crime and Due Process

Whereas the central problem in interpreting the religion clauses of the First Amendment has been to decide what they mean, the central problems in interpreting those parts of the Bill of Rights that affect people accused of a crime have been to decide not only what they mean but also how to put them into effect. It is not obvious what constitutes an "unreasonable search," but even if we settle that question, we still must decide how best to protect people against such searches in ways that do not unduly hinder criminal investigations.

There are at least two ways to provide that protection. One is to let the police introduce in court evidence relevant to the guilt or innocence of a person, no matter how it was obtained, and then, after the case is settled, punish the police officer (or his or her superiors) if the evidence was gathered improperly (for example, by an unreasonable search). The other way is to exclude improperly gathered evidence from the trial in the first place, even if it is relevant to determining the guilt or innocence of the accused.

Most democratic nations, including England, use the first method; the United States uses the second. Because of this, many of the landmark cases decided by the Supreme Court have been bitterly controversial. Opponents of these decisions have argued that a guilty person should not go free just because the police officer blundered, especially if the mistake was minor.[63] Supporters rejoin that there is no way to punish errant police officers effectively other than by excluding tainted evidence; moreover, nobody should be convicted of a crime except by evidence that is above reproach.[64]

The Exclusionary Rule

The American method relies on what is called the **exclusionary rule**. That rule holds that evidence gathered in violation of the Constitution cannot be used in a trial. The rule has been used to implement two provisions of the Bill of Rights—the right to be free from unreasonable searches and seizures (Fourth Amendment) and the right not to be compelled to give evidence against oneself (Fifth Amendment).*

Not until 1949 did the Supreme Court consider whether to apply the exclusionary rule to the states. In a case decided that year the Court made it clear that the Fourth Amendment prohibited the police from carrying out unreasonable searches and obtaining improper confessions but held that it was not necessary to use the exclusionary rule to enforce those prohibitions. It noted that other nations did not require that evidence improperly gathered had to be excluded from a criminal trial. The Court said that the local police should not improperly gather and use evidence, but if they did, the remedy was to sue the police department or punish the officer.[65]

But in 1961 the Supreme Court changed its mind about the use of the exclusionary rule. It all began when the Cleveland police broke into the home of Dollree Mapp in search of drugs and, finding none, arrested her for possessing some obscene pictures that they found there. The Court held that this was an unreasonable search and seizure because the police had not obtained a search warrant, though they had ample time to do so. Furthermore,

such illegally gathered evidence could not be used in the trial of Mapp.[66] Beginning with this case—*Mapp v. Ohio*—the Supreme Court required the use of the exclusionary rule as a way of enforcing a variety of constitutional guarantees.

Search and Seizure

After the Court decided to exclude improperly gathered evidence, the next problem was to decide what evidence was improper. What happened to Dollree Mapp was an easy case: hardly anybody argued that it was reasonable for the police to break into someone's home without a warrant, ransack their belongings, and take whatever they could find that might be incriminating. But that left a lot of hard choices still to be made.

When can the police search you without its being unreasonable? Under two circumstances—when they have a search warrant and when they have lawfully arrested you. A **search warrant** is an order from a judge authorizing the search of a place; the order must describe what is to be searched and seized, and the judge can issue it only if he or she is persuaded by the police that good reason (**probable cause**) exists to believe that a crime has been committed and that the evidence bearing on that crime will be found at a certain location. (The police can also search a building if the occupant gives them permission.)

In addition, you can be searched if the search occurs when you are being lawfully arrested. When can you be arrested? You can be arrested if a judge has issued an arrest warrant for you, if you commit a crime in the presence of a police officer, or if the officer has probable cause to believe that you have committed a serious crime (usually a felony). If you are arrested and no search warrant has been issued, the police, and not a judge, decide what they can search. What rules should they follow?

In trying to answer that question, the courts have elaborated a set of rules that are complex, subject to frequent change, and quite controversial. In general, the police, after arresting you, can search

• You

• Things in plain view

• Things or places under your immediate control

---

* We shall consider here only two constitutional limits—those bearing on searches and confessions. Thus we will omit many other important constitutional provisions affecting criminal cases, such as rules governing wiretapping, prisoner rights, the right to bail and to a jury trial, the bar on ex post facto laws, the right to be represented by a lawyer in court, the ban on "cruel and unusual" punishment, and the rule against double jeopardy.

How the Court Decided

The United States Supreme Court answered the questions on page 562 in the following way:

CASE 1: The drive-in movie won. The Supreme Court, 6–3, decided that the First Amendment protects the right to show nudity; it is up to the unwilling viewer on the public streets to avert his or her eyes.

Erznoznik v. Jacksonville,
422 U.S. 205 (1975)

CASE 2: The military won. The Supreme Court, 6–2, decided that military reservations are not like public streets or parks, and thus civilians can be excluded from them, especially if such exclusion prevents the military from appearing to be the handmaiden of various political causes.

Greer v. Spock, 424 U.S. 828 (1976)

CASE 3: The realtor won. The Supreme Court, 8–0, decided that the First Amendment prohibits the banning of signs, even of a commercial nature, without a strong, legitimate state interest. Banning the signs would not obviously reduce "white flight," and the government has no right to withhold information from citizens for fear that they will act unwisely.

Linmark Associates, Inc. v. Willingboro,
431 U.S. 85 (1977)

CASE 4: The television station won. The Court, 8–1, decided that the First Amendment protects the right to broadcast the names of rape victims obtained from public (that is, court) records.

Cox Broadcasting Corp. v. Cohn,
420 U.S. 469 (1975)

CASE 5: The newspaper won. The Supreme Court decided unanimously that the First Amendment prohibits the state from intruding into the function of editors.

Miami Herald Publishing Co. v. Tornillo,
418 U.S. 241 (1974)

CASE 6: Zacchini, the human cannonball won. The Supreme Court, 5–4, decided that broadcasting the entire act without the performer's consent jeopardized his means of livelihood, even though the First Amendment would guarantee the right of the station to broadcast newsworthy facts about the act.

Zacchini v. Scripps-Howard Broadcasting Co.,
433 U.S. 562 (1977)

As a practical matter, things "in plain view" or "under your immediate control" mean the room in which you are arrested but not other rooms of the house.[67] If the police want to search the rest of your house or a car parked in your driveway, they will first have to go to a judge to obtain a search warrant. But if the police arrest a college student on campus for drinking under age and then accompany that student back to his or her dormitory room so that the student can get proof that he or she was old enough to drink, the police can seize drugs that are in plain view in that room.[68] And if marijuana is growing in plain view in an open field, the police can enter and search that field even though it is fenced off with a locked gate and a "No Trespassing" sign.[69]

But what if you are arrested while driving your car—how much of it can the police search? The answer to that question has changed almost yearly. In 1979 the Court ruled that the police could not search a suitcase taken from a car of an arrested person, and in 1981 it extended this protection to any "closed, opaque container" found in the car.[70] But the following year the Court decided that all parts of a car, closed or open, could be searched if the officers had probable cause to believe that the car contained contraband (that is, goods illegally possessed).[71]

In this confusing area of the law the Court is attempting to protect those places in which a person has a "reasonable expectation of privacy." Your body is one such place, and so the Court has held that the police cannot compel you to undergo surgery to remove a bullet that might be evidence of your guilt or innocence in a crime.[72] But the police can require you to take a Breathalyzer test to see whether you have been drinking while driving.[73] Your home is another place where you have an expectation of privacy, but a barn next to your home is not, nor is your backyard viewed from an airplane, nor is your home if it is a motor home that can be driven away, and so the police need not have a warrant to look into these places.[74]

If you work for the government, you have an expectation that your desk and files will be private; nonetheless, your supervisor may search the desk and files without a warrant, provided that he or she is looking for something related to your work.[75] But bear in mind that the Constitution only protects you against *the government;* a private employer has a great deal of freedom to search your desk and files.

Some people had hoped that the Court would develop a general right of privacy so that nothing done in your home among consenting adults would be subject to government regulation. Support for this hope was given by the Court's decisions forbidding states from prohibiting the sale of contraceptives. But when the Court was asked to pass on the constitutionality of a Georgia statute that made it illegal to engage in homosexual activities, it held, by a narrow five-to-four vote, that the right to privacy does not extend to such activities, and so the Georgia statute may stand.[76]

Testing for Drugs and AIDS If the government can under some circumstances search your desk and files without a warrant, can it require you to undergo a test for AIDS or for drug use?

In the mid-1980s the deadly AIDS virus became a major public health issue. Because it disproportionately affected homosexuals, testing people to see whether they had the disease raised fears among some that the tests would be used to discriminate against homosexuals in employment and the issuance of life insurance. But others worried that failing to test for the virus would cause people to be needlessly exposed to the risk of death. In 1987 President Reagan called for AIDS tests for new immigrants, federal prisoners, and certain other categories of people.

Drug testing has begun to work its way through the courts. In the wake of growing public concern about the spread of drug abuse, President Reagan in 1986 signed an executive order requiring many federal-government employees to be tested. Numerous

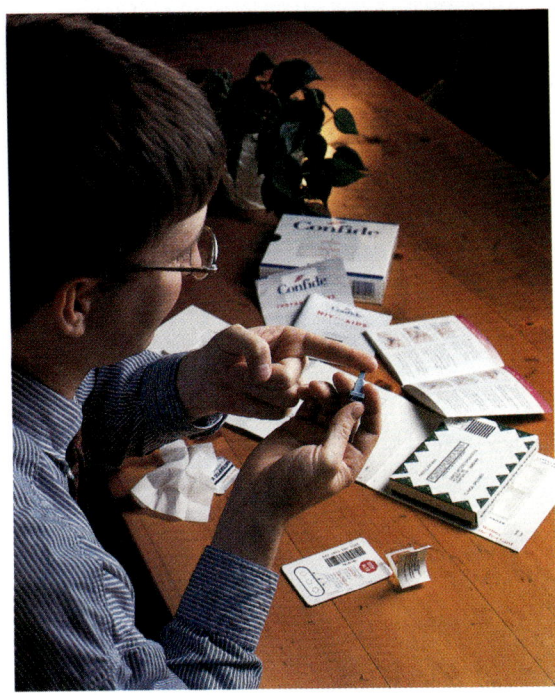

There are now home tests that can be used to detect the AIDS virus.

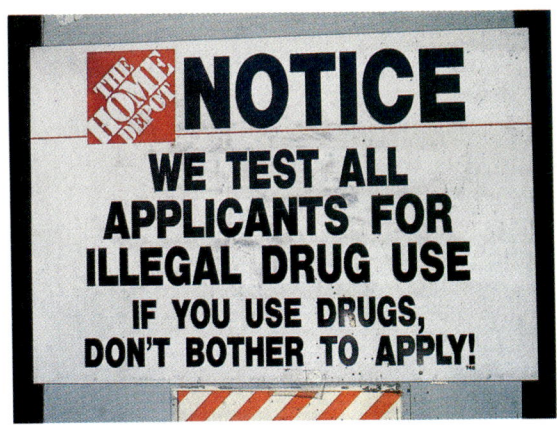

Since the U.S. Constitution only controls government actions, it does not affect drug testing by private businesses.

private firms and major league sports organizations had already required such testing of job applicants and athletes. There is no obvious constitutional reason why a *private* organization should not be able to

The Miranda Rule

*T*he Supreme Court has interpreted the due-process clause to require that local police departments issue warnings of the sort shown below to people whom they are arresting.

PHILADELPHIA POLICE DEPARTMENT
STANDARD POLICE INTERROGATION CARD

WARNINGS TO BE GIVEN ACCUSED

We are questioning you concerning the crime of (state specific crime).

We have a duty to explain to you and to warn you that you have the following legal rights:

A.   You have a right to remain silent and do not have to say anything at all.

B.   Anything you say can and will be used against you in Court.

C.   You have a right to talk to a lawyer of your own choice before we ask you any questions, and also to have a lawyer here with you while we ask questions.

D.   If you cannot afford to hire a lawyer, and you want one, we will see that you have one provided to you free of charge before we ask you any questions.

E.   If you are willing to give us a statement, you have a right to stop any time you wish.

75-Misc.-3   (Over)
(6-24-70)

Ernesto A. Miranda was convicted in Arizona of rape and kidnapping. When the Supreme Court overturned the conviction, it issued a set of rules—the "Miranda rules"—governing how police must conduct an arrest and interrogation.

test its members. But the Constitution restricts what the *government* may do; so is drug testing by a government agency a proper or an improper "search" of a person?

At first some federal district courts took the view that the mandatory drug testing of, say, fire fighters was an unreasonable search unless the fire fighter who was tested had been suspected of some wrongdoing. But in 1989 the Supreme Court held that certain kinds of employees could be subjected to drug tests without a search warrant or even any individualized suspicion. These were employees involved in law enforcement (in particular, Customs Service agents) and railroad employees involved in accidents. In short, a concern for public safety or national security can justify government-ordered drug tests. Using the same reasoning, the Court has upheld state laws that authorize the police to set up roadblocks and randomly check drivers to see if they are sober.[77] The Court has also upheld the random drug testing of high school athletes.[78]

Confessions and Self-Incrimination

The constitutional ban on being forced to give evidence against oneself was originally intended to prevent the use of torture or "third-degree" police tactics to extract confessions. But it has since been extended to cover many kinds of statements uttered not out of fear of torture but from lack of awareness of one's rights, especially the right to remain silent, whether in the courtroom or in the police station.

For many decades the Supreme Court had held that involuntary confessions could not be used in federal criminal trials but had not ruled that they were barred from state trials. But in the early 1960s it changed its mind in two landmark cases—*Escobedo* and *Miranda.*[79] The story of the latter and of the controversy that it provoked is worth telling.

Ernesto A. Miranda was convicted in Arizona of the rape and kidnapping of a young woman. The conviction was based on a written confession that Miranda signed after two hours of police questioning. (The victim also identified him.) Two years earlier the Court had decided that the rule against self-incrimination applied to state courts.[80] Now the question arose of what constitutes an "involuntary" confession. The Court decided that a confession should be presumed involuntary unless the person in custody had been fully and clearly informed of his or her right to be silent, to have an attorney present during any questioning, and to have an attorney provided free of charge if he or she could not afford one. The accused may waive these rights and offer to talk, but the waiver must be truly voluntary. Since Miranda did not have a lawyer present when he was questioned and had not knowingly waived his right to a lawyer, the confession was excluded from evidence in the trial and his conviction was overturned.[81]

Miranda was tried and convicted again, this time on the basis of evidence supplied by his girlfriend, who testified that he had admitted to her that he was guilty. Nine years later he was released from prison; four years after that he was killed in a barroom fight. When the Phoenix police arrested the prime suspect in Ernesto Miranda's murder, they read him his rights from a "Miranda card."

Everyone who watches cops-and-robbers shows on television probably knows the "Miranda warning" by heart (see the box on page 566). The police now read it routinely to people whom they arrest, both on and off television. It is not clear whether it has much impact on who does or does not confess or what effect, if any, it may have on the crime rate.

In time the Miranda rule was extended to mean that you have a right to a lawyer when you appear in a police lineup[82] and when you are questioned by a psychiatrist to determine whether you are competent to stand trial.[83] The Court threw out the conviction of a man who had killed a child, because the accused, without being given the right to have a lawyer present, had led the police to the victim's body.[84] You do not have a right to a Miranda warning, however, if while in jail you confess a crime to another inmate who turns out to be an undercover police officer.[85]

Relaxing the Exclusionary Rule

Cases such as *Miranda* were highly controversial and led to efforts in Congress to modify or overrule the decisions by statute—without much coming of the attempts. But as the rules governing police conduct became increasingly more complex, pressure mounted to find an alternative. Some thought that any evidence should be admissible, with the question of police conduct left to lawsuits or other ways of punishing official misbehavior. Others felt that the exclusionary rule served a useful purpose but had simply become too technical to be an effective deterrent to police misconduct (the police cannot

obey rules that they cannot understand). And still others felt that the exclusionary rule was a vital safeguard to essential liberties and should be kept intact.

The courts themselves began to adopt the second position, deciding a number of cases in ways that retained the exclusionary rule but modified it by limiting its coverage (police were given greater freedom to question juveniles)[86] and by incorporating what was called a **good-faith exception.** For example, if the police obtain a search warrant that they believe is valid, the evidence that they gather will not be excluded if it later turns out that the warrant was defective for some reason (such as the judge's having used the wrong form).[87] And the Court decided that "overriding considerations of public safety" may justify questioning a person without first reading the person his or her rights.[88] Moreover, the Court changed its mind about the killer who led the police to the place where he had disposed of his victim's body. After the man was convicted a second time and again appealed, the Court in 1984 held that the body would have been discovered anyway; thus evidence will not be excluded if it can be shown that it would "inevitably" have been found.[89]

SUMMARY

Civil liberties questions are in some ways like and in some ways unlike ordinary policy debates. Like most issues, civil liberties problems often involve competing interests—in this case conflicting rights or conflicting rights and duties—and so we have groups mobilized on each side of issues involving free speech and crime control. Like some other issues, civil liberties problems can also arise from the successful appeals of a policy entrepreneur, and so we have periodic reductions in liberty resulting from popular fears, usually aroused during or just after a war.

But civil liberties are unlike many other issues in at least one regard: more than struggles over welfare spending or defense or economic policy, debates about civil liberties reach down into our fundamental political beliefs and political culture, challenging us to define what we mean by religion, Americanism, and decency.

The most important of these challenges focuses on the meaning of the First Amendment: What is "speech"? How much of it should be free? How far can the state go in aiding religion? How do we strike a balance between national security and personal expression? The zigzag course followed by the courts in judging these matters has, on balance, tended to enlarge freedom of expression.

Almost as important has been the struggle to strike a balance between the right of society to protect itself from criminals and the right of people (including criminals) to be free from unreasonable searches and coerced confessions. As with free speech cases, the courts have generally broadened the rights at some expense to the power of the police. But in recent years the Supreme Court has pulled back from some of its more sweeping applications of the exclusionary rule.

The resolution of these issues by the courts is political in the sense that differing opinions about what is right or desirable compete, with one side or another prevailing (often by a small majority). In this competition of ideas federal judges, though not elected, are often sensitive to strong currents of popular opinion. When entrepreneurial politics has produced new action against apparently threatening minorities, judges are inclined, at least for a while, to give serious consideration to popular fears and legislative majorities. And when no strong national mood is discernible, the opinions of elites influence judicial thinking (as described in Chapter 14).

At the same time, courts resolve political conflicts in a manner that differs in important respects from the resolution of conflicts by legislatures or executives. First, the very existence of the courts, and the relative ease with which one may enter them to advance a claim, facilitates challenges to accepted values. An unpopular political or religious group may have little or no access to a legislature, but it will have substantial access to the courts. Second, judges often settle controversies about rights not simply by deciding the case at hand but by formulating a general rule to cover like cases elsewhere. This has an advantage (the law tends to become more consistent and better known) but a disadvantage as well: a rule suitable for one case may be unworkable in another. Judges reason by analogy and sometimes assume that two cases are similar when in fact there are important differences. A definition of "obscenity" or of "fighting words" may suit one situation but be inadequate in another. Third, judges interpret

the Constitution, whereas legislatures often consult popular preferences or personal convictions. However much their own beliefs influence what judges read into the Constitution, almost all of them are constrained by its language.

Taken together, the desire to find and announce rules, the language of the Constitution, and the personal beliefs of judges have led to a general expansion of civil liberties. As a result, even allowing for temporary reversals and frequent redefinitions, any value that is thought to hinder freedom of expression and the rights of the accused has generally lost ground to the claims of the First, Fourth, Fifth, and Sixth Amendments.

KEY TERMS

McCarthyism   *p. 548*

freedom of expression   *p. 550*

freedom of religion   *p. 550*

prior restraint   *p. 551*

clear-and-present danger test   *p. 551*

due-process clause   *p. 552*

libel   *p. 553*

symbolic speech   *p. 556*

free-exercise clause   *p. 557*

establishment clause   *p. 557*

wall-of-separation principle   *p. 560*

exclusionary rule   *p. 563*

search warrant   *p. 563*

probable cause   *p. 563*

good-faith exception   *p. 567*

SUGGESTED READINGS

Abraham, Henry J. *Freedom and the Court.* 6th ed. New York: Oxford University Press, 1994. Analysis of leading Supreme Court cases on civil liberties and civil rights.

Amar, Akhil Reed. *The Constitution and Criminal Procedure: First Principles*. New Haven, Conn.: Yale University Press, 1997. A brilliant critique of how the Supreme Court has interpreted those parts of the Constitution bearing on search warrants, the exclusionary rule, and self-incrimination.

Berns, Walter. *The First Amendment and the Future of American Democracy*. New York: Basic Books, 1976. A look at what the Founders intended by the First Amendment that takes issue with contemporary Supreme Court interpretations of it.

Clor, Harry M. *Obscenity and Public Morality*. Chicago: University of Chicago Press, 1969. Argues for the legitimacy of legal restrictions on obscenity.

Levy, Leonard W. *Legacy of Suppression: Freedom of Speech and Press in Early American History*. Rev. ed. New York: Oxford University Press, 1985. Careful study of what the Founders and the early leaders meant by freedom of speech and press.

Pritchett, C. Herman. *Constitutional Civil Liberties*. Englewood Cliffs, N.J.: Prentice-Hall, 1984. An excellent summary and analysis of the constitutional law governing civil liberties.

19

Civil Rights

★ Blacks and the political system

★ Role of the NAACP

★ Role of the courts

★ Testing of "separate-but-equal" education

★ Getting civil rights on the national political agenda

★ Civil disobedience and violence

★ How civil rights legislation was passed

★ The resurgence of the feminist movement

★ The Supreme Court's "reasonableness" test

★ What happened to the ERA

★ The struggle over abortion

★ Women and the economy

★ Affirmative action

In 1830 Congress passed a law requiring all Indians east of the Mississippi River to move to the Indian Territory west of the river, and the army set about implementing it. In the 1850s a major political fight broke out in Boston over whether the police department should be obliged to hire an Irish officer. Until 1920 women could not vote in most elections. In the 1930s the Cornell University Medical School had a strict quota limiting the number of Jewish students who could enroll. In the 1940s the army, with the approval of President Franklin D. Roosevelt, removed all Japanese-Americans from their homes in California and placed them in relocation centers far from the coast.

In all such cases some group, usually defined along racial or ethnic lines, was denied access to facilities, opportunities, or services that were available to other groups. Such cases raise the issue of **civil rights.** The pertinent question regarding civil rights is not whether the government has the authority to treat different people differently; it is whether such differences in treatment are reasonable. All laws and policies make distinctions among people—for example, the tax laws require higher-income people to pay taxes at a higher rate than lower-income ones—but not all such distinctions are defensible. The courts have long held that classifying people on the basis of their income and taxing them at different rates is quite permissible because such classifications are not arbitrary or unreasonable and are related to a legitimate public need (that is, raising revenue). Increasingly, however, the courts have said that classifying people on the basis of their race, or ethnicity, is unreasonable. These are **suspect classifications,** and while not every law making such classifications has been ruled unconstitutional, they have all become subject to especially strict scrutiny.[1]

Given the theory of policy-making described so far in this book, it may seem surprising that specific groups, particularly those that constitute only a small minority of the population, should require any special protection at all. We have seen how easy it is for many small groups—businesses, occupations, unions—to practice client politics. They can obtain some special advantage (a grant, a license, a subsidy) or avoid some threatened regulation because, being small, they find it easy to organize and to escape general public notice. Yet Native Americans, blacks, Japanese-Americans, and Mexican-Americans are also relatively small groups whose demands seemingly place little burden on the majority population. Despite this, they have been more often the victims than the clients of the policy-making process.

To explain the victimization of certain groups and the methods by which they have begun to overcome it, we shall consider chiefly the case of black Americans. Black-white relations have in large measure defined the problem of civil rights in this country; most of the landmark laws and court decisions have involved black claims. The strategies employed by or on behalf of blacks have typically set the pattern for the strategies employed by other groups. At the end of this chapter we shall look at the related but somewhat different issues of women's rights and gays' rights.

A segregated bus station in Durham, North Carolina, in 1940.

The Black Predicament

Though constituting more than 12 percent of the population, blacks until fairly recently could not in many parts of the country vote, attend integrated schools, ride in the front seats of buses, or buy homes in white neighborhoods.

One reason is that the perceived costs of granting these demands to blacks were not widely distributed among the public at large but instead were concentrated on some relatively small and readily organized group. Although today white citizens generally do not feel threatened when a black family moves into Cicero, Illinois, a black child goes to school at Little Rock Central High School, or a black organization organizes voters in Neshoba County, Mississippi, at one time most whites in Cicero, Little Rock, and Neshoba County felt deeply threatened by these things (and even now some whites still do). In the language of this book, civil rights in these places was not a matter of client politics but of competitive or interest group politics. This was especially the case in those parts of the country, notably the Deep South, where blacks were often in the majority. There the politically dominant white minority felt keenly the potential competition for jobs, land, public services, and living space posed by large numbers of people of another race. But even in the North, black gains often appeared to be at the expense of lower-income whites who lived or worked near them, not at the expense of upper-status whites who lived in suburbs.

The interest group component of racial politics put blacks at a decided disadvantage: they were not allowed to vote at all in many areas; they could vote only with great difficulty in others; and even in those places where voting was easy, they often lacked the material and institutional support for effective political organization. If your opponent feels deeply threatened by your demands and in addition can deny you access to the political system that will decide the fate of those demands, you are, to put it mildly, at a disadvantage. Yet from the end of Reconstruction down to the 1960s—for nearly a century—many blacks in the South found themselves in just such a position.

A second reason why the restrictions on black Americans continued for so long is that majoritarian politics worked to the disadvantage of blacks. Because of white attitudes, this was the case even when white and black interests were not directly in competition. To the dismay of those who prefer to explain political action in terms of economic motives, people often attach greater importance to the intangible costs and benefits of policies than to the tangible ones. Thus, even though the average black represented no threat to the average white, antiblack attitudes—racism—produced some appalling actions. Between 1882 and 1946, 4,715 people, about three-fourths of them blacks, were lynched in the United States.[2] Some lynchings were carried out by small groups of vigilantes acting with much ceremony, but others were the actions of frenzied mobs. In the summer of 1911 a black charged with murdering a white man in Livermore, Kentucky, was dragged by a mob to the local theater, where he was hanged. The audience, which had been charged admission, was invited to shoot the swaying body (those in the orchestra seats could empty their revolvers, those in the balcony were limited to a single shot).[3]

Though the public in other parts of the country was shocked by such events, little was done: lynching was a local, not a federal, crime. It obviously would not require many lynchings to convince blacks in these localities that it would be foolhardy to try to vote or enroll in a white school. And even in those states where blacks did vote, popular attitudes were not conducive to blacks' buying homes or taking jobs on an equal basis with whites. Even among those professing to support equal rights, a substantial portion opposed black efforts to obtain them and federal action to secure them. In 1942 a national poll showed that only 30 percent of whites thought that black and white children should attend the same schools; in 1956 the proportion had risen, but only to 49 percent, still less than a majority. (In the South white support for school integration was even lower—14 percent favored it in 1956, about 31 percent in 1963.) As late as 1956 a majority of southern whites were opposed to integrated public transportation facilities. Even among whites who generally favored integration, there was in 1963 (*before* the ghetto riots) considerable opposition to the black civil rights movement: nearly half of the

Jim Crow

Thomas D. ("Daddy") Rice, a white entertainer, began around 1828 to stage a vaudeville sketch in which he blacked his face with burned cork and sang a ditty that acquired the title "Wheel About and Turn About and Jump, Jim Crow." Thus was born what later became the immensely popular minstrel shows, a burlesque by whites of black songs and speech mannerisms. The term **Jim Crow,** from Rice's song, soon came to be a slang expression for blacks and was later applied to laws and practices that segregated blacks from whites.

whites who were classified in a survey as moderate integrationists thought that demonstrations hurt the black cause; nearly two-thirds disapproved of actions taken by the civil rights movement; and over a third felt that civil rights should be left to the states.[4]

In short, the political position in which blacks found themselves until the 1960s made it difficult for them to advance their interests through a feasible legislative strategy: their opponents were aroused, organized, and powerful. Thus if black interests were to be championed in Congress or state legislatures, blacks would have to have white allies. Though some such allies could be found, they were too few to make a difference in a political system that gives a substantial advantage to strongly motivated opponents of any new policy. For that to change, one or both of two things would have to happen: additional allies would have to be recruited (a delicate problem, given that many white integrationists disapproved of aspects of the civil rights movement), or the struggle would have to be shifted to a policy-making arena in which the opposition enjoyed less of an advantage.

Partly by plan, partly by accident, black leaders followed both of these strategies simultaneously. By publicizing their grievances and organizing a civil rights movement that (at least in its early stages) concentrated on dramatizing the denial to blacks of essential and widely accepted liberties, blacks were able to broaden their base of support both among political elites and among the general public and thereby to raise civil rights matters from a low to a high position on the political agenda. By waging a patient, prolonged, but carefully planned legal struggle, black leaders shifted decision-making power on key civil rights issues from Congress, where they had been stymied for generations, to the federal courts.

After this strategy had achieved some substantial successes—after blacks had become enfranchised and legal barriers to equal participation in political and economic affairs had been lowered—the politics of civil rights became more conventional. Blacks were able to assert their demands directly in the legislative and executive branches of government with reasonable (though scarcely certain) prospects of success. Civil rights became less a matter of gaining entry into the political system and more one of waging interest group politics within that system. At the same time, the goals of civil rights politics were broadened. The struggle to gain entry into the system had focused on the denial of fundamental rights (to vote, to organize, to obtain equal access to schools and public facilities); later the dominant issues were manpower development, economic progress, and the improvement of housing and neighborhoods.

The Campaign in the Courts

The Fourteenth Amendment was both an opportunity and a problem for black activists. Adopted in 1868, it seemed to guarantee equal rights for all: "No state shall make or enforce any law which shall abridge the privileges or immunities of citizens of the United States; nor shall any state deprive any person of life, liberty, or property, without due process of law; nor deny to any person within its jurisdiction the equal protection of the laws."

The key phrase was "equal protection of the laws." Read broadly, it might mean that the Constitution should be regarded as color-blind: no state law could have the effect of treating whites and blacks differently. Thus a law segregating blacks and whites into separate schools or neighborhoods would be unconstitutional. Read narrowly, "equal protection" might mean only that blacks and whites had certain fundamental legal rights in common, among them the right to sign contracts, to serve on juries, or to buy and sell property, but otherwise they could be treated differently.

Historians have long debated which view Congress held when it proposed the Fourteenth Amendment. What forms of racial segregation, if any, were still permissible? Segregated trains? Hotels? Schools? Neighborhoods?

The Supreme Court took the narrow view. Though in 1880 it declared unconstitutional a West Virginia law requiring juries to be composed only of white males,[5] it decided in 1883 that it was unconstitutional for Congress to prohibit racial discrimination in public accommodations such as hotels.[6] The difference between the two cases seemed, in the eyes of the Court, to be this: serving on a jury was an essential right of citizenship that the state could not deny to any person on racial grounds without violating the Fourteenth Amendment, but registering at a hotel was a convenience controlled by a private person (the hotel owner), who could treat blacks and whites differently if he or she wished.

The major decision that was to determine the legal status of the Fourteenth Amendment for over half a century was *Plessy* v. *Ferguson*. Louisiana had passed a law requiring blacks and whites to occupy separate cars on railroad trains operating in that state. When Adolph Plessy, who was seven-eighths white and one-eighth black, refused to obey the law, he was arrested. He appealed his conviction to the Supreme Court, claiming that the law violated the Fourteenth Amendment. In 1896 the Court rejected his claim, holding that the law treated both races equally even though it required them to be separate. The equal-protection clause guaranteed political and legal but not social equality. "Separate-but-equal" facilities were constitutional because if "one race be inferior to the other socially, the Constitution of the United States cannot put them on the same plane."[7]

"Separate but Equal"

Thus began the **separate-but-equal doctrine**. Three years later the Court applied it to schools as well, declaring in *Cumming* v. *Richmond County Board of Education* that a decision in a Georgia community to close the black high school while keeping open the white high school was not a violation of the Fourteenth Amendment because blacks could always go to private schools. Here the Court seemed to be saying that not only could schools be separate, they could even be unequal.[8]

What the Court has made, the Court can unmake. But to get it to change its mind requires a long, costly, and uncertain legal battle. The National Association for the Advancement of Colored People (NAACP) was the main organization that waged that battle. Formed in 1909 by a group of whites and blacks in the aftermath of a race riot, the NAACP did many things—lobbying in Washington and publicizing black grievances, especially in the pages of *The Crisis,* a magazine edited by W. E. B. Du Bois—but its most influential role was played in the courtroom.

It was a rational strategy. Fighting legal battles does not require forming broad political alliances or changing public opinion, tasks that would have been very difficult for a small and unpopular organization. A court-based approach also enabled the organization to remain nonpartisan.

But it was a slow and difficult strategy. The Court had adopted a narrow interpretation of the Fourteenth Amendment. To get the Court to change its mind would require the NAACP to bring before it cases involving the strongest possible claims that a black had been unfairly treated—and under circumstances sufficiently different from those of earlier cases that the Court could find some grounds for changing its mind.

The steps in that strategy were these: First, persuade the Court to declare unconstitutional laws creating schools that were separate but obviously unequal. Second, persuade it to declare unconstitutional laws supporting schools that were separate

Shown above is the cover of the first issue of *The Crisis,* the magazine started by the NAACP in 1910 to raise black consciousness and publicize racist acts.

but unequal in not-so-obvious ways. Third, persuade it to rule that racially separate schools were inherently unequal and hence unconstitutional.

Can Separate Schools Be Equal?

The first step was accomplished in a series of court cases stretching from 1938 to 1948. In 1938 the Court held that Lloyd Gaines had to be admitted to an all-white law school in Missouri because no black law school of equal quality existed in that state.[9] In 1948 the Court ordered the all-white University of Oklahoma Law School to admit Ada Lois Sipuel, a black, even though the state planned to build a black law school later. For education to be equal, it had to be equally available.[10] It still could be separate,

Critical Thinking

The Black College Predicament

Howard University in Washington, D.C., a traditionally black college.

Until the Supreme Court desegregation rulings, blacks in most parts of the South could attend only segregated, all-black colleges. After a long struggle, blacks won admission to previously all-white colleges and universities.

This left an unanswered question: what should happen to the previously all-black schools, some of which had a long and illustrious history? Theoretically, whites would be free to enroll in traditionally black schools just as blacks were free to enter all-white ones, but in fact very few whites applied to the all-black schools. Moreover, some black educators believe that attending a predo-

minately black school is helpful to many black students, just as some female educators believe that going to an all-women college makes sense for many female students. The United Negro College Fund raises money for predominately black colleges.

But the Supreme Court, having ruled that separate schools are inherently unequal, opposed segregation. In 1992 it decided that the state-funded maintenance in Mississippi of eight universities, some of which were predominately black, was unconstitutional.* This ruling challenges public funding for all colleges and universities that have a predominately minority or female enrollment.

Should black colleges be abolished? Should colleges serving specific groups be banned even when no one is excluded from attending any school on the basis of race? Should blacks or women who prefer a more segregated environment be forced to attend mostly white and coeducational schools?

* United States v. Fordice, 112 S.Ct. 2727 (1992).

---

however: the university admitted Ms. Sipuel but required her to attend classes in a section of the state capitol, roped off from other students, where she could meet with her law professors.

The second step was taken in two cases decided in 1950. Heman Sweatt, a black, was treated by the University of Texas Law School much as Ada Sipuel had been treated in Oklahoma: "admitted" to the all-white school but relegated to a separate building. Another black, George McLaurin, was allowed to study for his Ph.D. in a "colored section" of the all-white University of Oklahoma. The Supreme Court unanimously decided that these arrangements were

unconstitutional because, by imposing racially based barriers on the black students' access to professors, libraries, and other students, they created unequal educational opportunities.[11]

The third step, the climax of the entire drama, began in Topeka, Kansas, where Linda Brown wanted to enroll in her neighborhood school but could not because she was black and the school was by law reserved exclusively for whites. When the NAACP took her case to the federal district court in Kansas, the judge decided that the black school that Linda could attend was substantially equal in quality to the white school that she could not attend. Thus, denying her access to the white school was constitutional. To change that, the lawyers would have to persuade the Supreme Court to overrule the district judge on the grounds that racially separate schools were unconstitutional even if they were equal. In other words, the separate-but-equal doctrine would have to be overturned by the Court.

It was a risky and controversial step to take. Many states, Kansas among them, were trying to make their all-black schools equal to those of whites by launching expensive building programs. If the NAACP succeeded in getting separate schools declared unconstitutional, the Court might well put a stop to the building of these new schools. Blacks could win a moral and legal victory but suffer a practical defeat—the loss of these new facilities. Despite these risks, the NAACP decided to go ahead with the appeal.

Brown v. Board of Education

On May 17, 1954, a unanimous Supreme Court, speaking through an opinion written and delivered by Chief Justice Earl Warren, found that "in the field of public education the doctrine of 'separate but equal' has no place" because "separate educational facilities are inherently unequal."[12] *Plessy* v. *Ferguson* was overruled, and "separate but equal" was dead.

The ruling was a landmark decision, but the reasons for it and the means chosen to implement it were as important and as controversial as the decision itself. There were at least three issues. First, how would the decision be implemented? Second, on what grounds were racially separate schools unconstitutional? Third, what test would a school system have to meet in order to be in conformity with the Constitution?

Implementation The *Brown* case involved a class-action suit; that is, it applied not only to Linda Brown but to all others similarly situated. This meant that black children everywhere now had the right to attend formerly all-white schools. This change would be one of the most far-reaching and conflict-provoking events in modern American history. It could not be effected overnight or by the stroke of a pen. In 1955 the Supreme Court decided that it would let local federal district courts oversee

the end of segregation by giving them the power to approve or disapprove local desegregation plans. This was to be done "with all deliberate speed."[13]

In the South "all deliberate speed" turned out to be a snail's pace. Massive resistance to desegregation broke out in many states. Some communities simply defied the Court; some sought to evade its edict by closing their public schools. In 1956 over one hundred southern members of Congress signed a "Southern Manifesto" that condemned the *Brown* decision as an "abuse of judicial power" and pledged to "use all lawful means to bring about a reversal of the decision."

In the late 1950s and early 1960s the National Guard and regular army paratroopers were used to escort black students into formerly all-white schools and universities. It was not until the 1970s that resistance collapsed and most southern schools were integrated. The use of armed force convinced people that resistance was futile; the disruption of the politics and economy of the South convinced leaders that it was imprudent; and the voting power of blacks convinced politicians that it was suicidal. In addition, federal laws began providing financial aid to integrated schools and withholding it from segregated ones. By 1970 only 14 percent of southern black schoolchildren still attended all-black schools.[14]

The Rationale As the struggle to implement the *Brown* decision continued, the importance of the rationale for that decision became apparent. The case was decided in a way that surprised many legal scholars. The Court could have said that the equal-protection clause of the Fourteenth Amendment makes the Constitution, and thus state laws, color-blind. Or it could have said that the authors of the Fourteenth Amendment meant to ban segregated schools. It did neither. Instead it said that segregated education is bad because it "has a detrimental effect upon the colored children" by generating "a feeling of inferiority as to their status in the community" that may "affect their hearts and minds in a way unlikely ever to be undone."[15] This conclusion was supported by a footnote reference to social science studies of the apparent impact of segregation on black children.

Why did the Court rely on social science as much as or more than the Constitution in support-

On September 25, 1957, troops of the 101st Airborne Division escorted nine black children into Little Rock (Arkansas) Central High School to begin its integration.

ing its decision? Apparently for two reasons. One was the justices' realization that the authors of the Fourteenth Amendment may *not* have intended to outlaw segregated schools. The schools in Washington, D.C., were segregated when the amendment was proposed, and when this fact was mentioned during the debate, it seems to have been made clear that the amendment was not designed to abolish this segregation. When Congress debated a civil rights act a few years later, it voted down provisions that would have ended segregation in schools.[16] The Court could not easily base its decision on a constitutional provision that had, at best, an uncertain application to schools. The other reason grew out of the first. On so important a matter the chief justice wanted to speak for a unanimous court. Some justices did not agree that the Fourteenth Amendment made the Constitution color-blind. In the interests of harmony the Court found an ambiguous rationale for its decision.

Desegregation versus Integration   That ambiguity led to the third issue. If separate schools were inherently unequal, what would "unseparate" schools

look like? Since the Court had not said that race was irrelevant, an "unseparate" school could be either one that blacks and whites were free to attend if they chose or one that blacks and whites in fact attended whether they wanted to or not. The first might be called a desegregated school, the latter an integrated school. Think of the Topeka case. Was it enough that there was now no barrier to Linda Brown's attending the white school in her neighborhood? Or was it necessary that there be black children (if not Linda, then some others) actually going to that school together with white children?

As long as the main impact of the *Brown* decision lay in the South, where laws had prevented blacks from attending white schools, this question did not seem important. Segregation by law (**de jure segregation**) was now clearly unconstitutional. But in the North, laws had not kept blacks and whites apart; instead all-black and all-white schools were the result of residential segregation, preferred living patterns, informal social forces, and administrative practices (such as drawing school district lines so as to produce single-race schools). This was often called segregation in fact (**de facto segregation**).

In 1968 the Supreme Court settled the matter. In New Kent County, Virginia, the school board had created a "freedom-of-choice" plan under which every pupil would be allowed without legal restriction to attend the school of his or her choice. As it turned out, all the white children chose to remain in the all-white school, and 85 percent of the black children remained in the all-black school. The Court rejected this plan as unconstitutional because it did not produce the "ultimate end," which was a "unitary, nonracial system of education."[17] In the opinion written by Justice William Brennan, the Court seemed to be saying that the Constitution required actual racial mixing in the schools, not just the repeal of laws requiring racial separation.

This impression was confirmed three years later when the Court considered a plan in North Carolina under which pupils in Mecklenburg County (which includes Charlotte) were assigned to the nearest neighborhood school without regard to race. As a result, about half the black children now attended formerly all-white schools, with the other half attending all-black schools. The federal district court held that this was inadequate and ordered some children to be bused into more distant schools in order to achieve a greater degree of integration. The Supreme Court, now led by Chief Justice Warren Burger, upheld the district judge on the grounds that the court plan was necessary to achieve a "unitary school system."[18]

This case—*Swann v. Charlotte-Mecklenburg Board of Education*—pretty much set the guidelines for all subsequent cases involving school segregation. The essential features of those guidelines are as follows:

- To violate the Constitution, a school system, by law, practice, or regulation, must have engaged in discrimination. Put another way, a plaintiff must show an intent to discriminate on the part of the public schools.

- The existence of all-white or all-black schools in a district with a history of segregation creates a presumption of intent to discriminate.

- The remedy for past discrimination will not be limited to freedom of choice, or what the Court called "the walk-in school." Remedies may include racial quotas in the assignment of teachers and

In 1963 Governor George Wallace of Alabama stood in the doorway of the University of Alabama to block the entry of black students. Facing him is United States Deputy Attorney General Nicholas Katzenbach.

pupils, redrawn district lines, and court-ordered busing.

- Not every school must reflect the social composition of the school system as a whole.

Relying on *Swann*, district courts have supervised redistricting and busing plans in localities all over the nation, often in the face of bitter opposition from the community. In Boston the control of the city schools by a federal judge, W. Arthur Garrity, lasted for more than a decade and involved him in every aspect of school administration.

One major issue not settled by *Swann* was whether busing and other remedies should cut across city and county lines. In some places the central-city schools had become virtually all black. Racial integration could be achieved only by bringing black pupils to white suburban schools or moving white pupils into central-city schools. In a series of split-vote decisions the Court ruled that court-ordered intercity busing could be authorized only if it could be demonstrated that the suburban areas as

Antibusing protesters buried a school bus (unoccupied) to dramatize their cause.

well as the central city had in fact practiced school segregation. Where that could not be shown, such intercity busing would not be required. The Court was not persuaded that intent had been proved in Atlanta, Detroit, Denver, Indianapolis, and Richmond, but it was persuaded it had been in Louisville and Wilmington.[19]

The importance that the Court attaches to intent means that if a school system that was once integrated becomes all black as a result of whites' moving to the suburbs, the Court will not require that district lines constantly be redrawn or new busing plans adopted to adjust to the changing distribution of the population.[20] This in turn means that as long as blacks and whites live in different neighborhoods

for whatever reason, there is a good chance that some schools in both areas will be heavily of one race. If mandatory busing or other integration measures cause whites to move out of a city at a faster rate than they otherwise would (a process often called "white flight"), then efforts to integrate the schools may in time create more single-race schools. Ultimately integrated schools will exist only in integrated neighborhoods or where the quality of education is so high that both blacks and whites want to enroll in the school even at some cost in terms of travel and inconvenience.

Mandatory busing to achieve racial integration has been a deeply controversial program and has generated considerable public opposition. Surveys show that a majority of people oppose it.[21] As recently as 1992, a poll showed that 48 percent of whites in the Northeast and 53 percent of southern whites felt that it was "not the business" of the federal government to ensure "that black and white children go to the same schools."[22] Presidents Nixon, Ford, and Reagan opposed busing; all three supported legislation to prevent or reduce it, and Reagan petitioned the courts to reconsider busing plans. The courts refused to reconsider, and Congress has passed only minor restrictions on busing.

The reason why Congress has not followed public opinion on this matter is complex. It has been torn between the desire to support civil rights and uphold the courts and the desire to represent the views of its constituents. Because it faces a dilemma, Congress has taken both sides of the issue simultaneously.

During the 1970s the House of Representatives passed bills restricting busing, but the Senate amended them to allow busing ordered by a court. The result was no policy at all. In 1981 the Senate approved a bill forbidding federal judges from ordering busing except in very narrow circumstances, but it never became law. Although a House version of these bills was adopted in 1982, it too never became law. Throughout the 1980s Congress did enact laws forbidding the use of federal funds to bus schoolchildren for purposes of racial integration; these laws had little effect, however, since a judge could still order states and cities to pay the costs. By the late 1980s busing was a dying issue in Congress, in part because no meaningful legislation seemed

Chronology of Major Events in the Civil Rights Movement, 1955–1968

Dec. 5, 1955	Blacks in Montgomery, Alabama, begin yearlong boycott of bus company; the Reverend Martin Luther King, Jr., emerges as leader.
Feb. 1, 1960	First sit-in demonstration. Black students at North Carolina Agricultural and Technical College sit in at a dime-store lunch counter in Greensboro.
May 4, 1961	Freedom rides begin as blacks attempt to ride in white sections of interstate buses. Violence erupts, a bus is burned, U.S. marshals are dispatched to restore order.
Sept. 30, 1962	Violence greets effort of James Meredith, a black, to enroll in University of Mississippi.
Apr. 3, 1963	Demonstrations by blacks begin in Birmingham, Alabama; police retaliate.
June 12, 1963	Medgar Evers, Mississippi state chairman of NAACP, murdered in Jackson.
Aug. 28, 1963	March on Washington by 250,000 whites and blacks.
Fall 1963	Blacks boycott schools in several northern cities to protest *de facto* segregation.
June 1964	Three civil rights workers killed in Neshoba County, Mississippi.
Summer 1964	First ghetto riots by blacks in northern cities, beginning in Harlem on July 18.
Jan. 2, 1965	King begins protest marches in Selma, Alabama; police attack marchers in February and March.
Aug. 11, 1965	Black riots in Watts section of Los Angeles and on West Side of Chicago.
June 6, 1966	James Meredith shot (but not killed) while on protest march in Mississippi.
Summer 1966	Black ghetto riots in Chicago, Cleveland, New York, and other cities; King leads protest marches in Chicago.
Summer 1967	Riots or violent demonstrations in 67 cities.
Apr. 4, 1968	Martin Luther King, Jr., murdered in Memphis, Tennessee.

possible and in part because popular passion over busing had somewhat abated.

Then, in 1992, the Supreme Court made it easier for local school systems to reclaim control over their schools from the courts. In DeKalb County (a suburb of Atlanta), the schools had been operating under court-ordered desegregation plans for many years. Despite this effort full integration had not been achieved, largely because the county's neighborhoods had increasingly become either all black or all white. The Court held that the local schools could not be held responsible for segregation caused solely by segregated living patterns and so the courts would have to relinquish their control over the schools.[23]

The Campaign in Congress

The campaign in the courts for desegregated schools, though slow and costly, was a carefully managed effort to alter the interpretation of a constitutional provision. But to get new civil rights laws out of Congress required a far more difficult and de-

In 1960 black students from North Carolina Agricultural and Technical College staged the first "sit-in" when they were refused service at a lunch counter in Greensboro (left). Twenty years later, graduates of the college returned to the same lunch counter (right). Though prices had risen, the service had improved.

Rosa Parks was arrested for refusing to move to the segregated section at the back of a bus in Montgomery, Alabama.

centralized strategy, one that was aimed at mobilizing public opinion and overcoming the many congressional barriers to action.

The first problem was to get civil rights on the political agenda by convincing people that something had to be done. This could be achieved by dramatizing the problem in ways that tugged at the conscience of whites who were not racist but were ordinarily indifferent to black problems. Brutal lynchings of blacks had shocked these whites, but lynchings were becoming less frequent in the 1950s, and obviously black leaders had no desire to provoke more lynchings just to get sympathy for their cause.

Those leaders could, however, arrange for dramatic confrontations between blacks claiming some obvious right and the whites who denied it to them. Beginning in the late 1950s these confrontations began to occur in the form of sit-ins at segregated lunch counters and "freedom rides" on segregated bus lines. At about the same time, efforts were made to get blacks registered to vote in counties where whites had used intimidation and harassment to prevent it.

The best-known campaign occurred in 1955–1956 in Montgomery, Alabama, where blacks, led by a young minister named Martin Luther King, Jr., boycotted the local bus system after it had a black woman, Rosa Parks, arrested because she refused to surrender her seat on a bus to a white man.

These early demonstrations were based on the philosophy of **nonviolent civil disobedience**—that is, peacefully violating a law, such as one requiring blacks to ride in a segregated section of a bus, and allowing oneself to be arrested as a result.

But the momentum of protest, once unleashed, could not be centrally directed or confined to nonviolent action. A rising tide of anger, especially among younger blacks, resulted in the formation of more militant organizations and the spontaneous eruption of violent demonstrations and riots in dozens of cities across the country. From 1964 to 1968 there were in the North as well as the South four "long, hot summers" of racial violence.

The demonstrations and rioting succeeded in getting civil rights on the national political agenda, but at a cost: many whites, opposed to the demonstrations or appalled by the riots, dug in their heels and fought against making any concessions to "lawbreakers," "troublemakers," and "rioters." In 1964 and again in 1968 over two-thirds of the whites interviewed in opinion polls said that the civil rights movement was pushing too fast, had hurt the black cause, and was too violent.[24]

In short there was a conflict between the agenda-setting and coalition-building aspects of the civil rights movement. This was especially a problem since conservative southern legislators still controlled many key congressional committees that had for years been the graveyard of civil rights legislation. The Senate Judiciary Committee was dominated by a coalition of southern Democrats and conservative Republicans, and the House Rules Committee was under the control of a chairman hostile to civil rights bills, Howard Smith of Virginia. Any bill that passed the House faced an almost certain filibuster in the Senate. Finally, President John F. Kennedy was reluctant to submit strong civil rights bills to Congress.

Four developments made it possible to break the deadlock. First, public opinion was changing. As Figure 19.1 shows, between 1959 and 1965 the proportion of southern whites who said that they were willing to have their children attend a school that was half black more than doubled (though it was

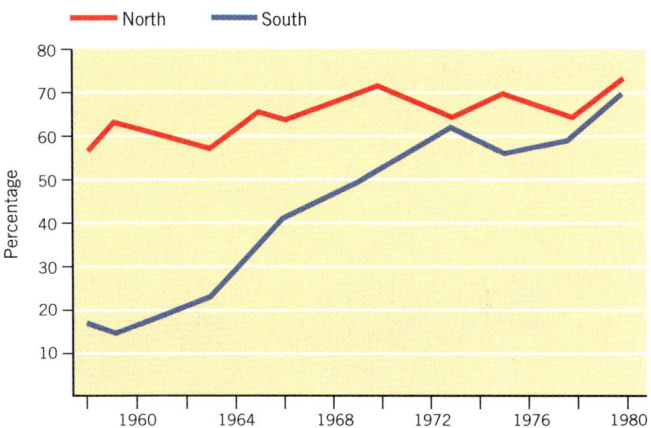

FIGURE 19.1 Changing White Attitudes Toward School Integration

Percentage of whites saying that they did not object to their children's attending a school with a half-black, half-white enrollment.

SOURCE: Reprinted by permission of the publisher from *Racial Attitudes in America: Trends and Interpretations* by Howard Schuman, Charlotte Steeh, and Lawrence Bobo, Cambridge, Mass.: Harvard University Press, Copyright © 1985 by the Presidents and Fellows of Harvard College.

still less than a majority), while the proportion of northern whites giving the same answer was high (over 60 percent) throughout that period. About the same change could be found in attitudes toward allowing blacks equal access to hotels and buses.[25] Of course support in principle for these civil rights measures was not necessarily the same as support in practice; nonetheless there clearly was occurring a major shift in popular approval of at least the principles of civil rights. At the leading edge of this change were young, college-educated people.[26]

Second, certain violent reactions by white segregationists to black demonstrators were vividly portrayed by the media, especially television, in ways that gave to the civil rights cause a powerful moral force. In May 1963 the head of the Birmingham police, Eugene "Bull" Connor, ordered his men to use attack dogs and high-pressure fire hoses to repulse a peaceful march by blacks demanding desegregated public facilities and increased job opportunities. The pictures of that confrontation (such as the one on page 584) created a national sensation and contributed greatly to the massive participation, by whites and blacks alike, in the "March on Washington" that summer. About a quarter of a million people gathered in front of the Lincoln Memorial to

This picture of a police dog lunging at a black during a racial demonstration in Birmingham, Alabama, in May 1963 was one of the most influential news photographs ever published. It was widely reprinted throughout the world and was frequently referred to in congressional debates on the civil rights bill of 1964.

hear the Reverend Dr. King deliver a stirring and widely hailed address, often called the "I Have a Dream" speech. The following summer in Neshoba County, Mississippi, three young civil rights workers (two white and one black) were brutally murdered by Klansmen aided by the local sheriff. When the FBI identified the murderers, the effect on national opinion was galvanic: no white southern leader could any longer offer persuasive opposition to federal laws protecting voting rights when white law enforcement officers had killed students working to protect those rights. And the next year a white woman, Viola Liuzzo, was shot and killed while driving a car used to transport civil rights workers. Her death was the subject of a presidential address.

Third, President John F. Kennedy was assassinated in Dallas, Texas, in November 1963. Many people originally (and wrongly) thought that he had

been killed by a right-wing conspiracy. Even after the assassin had been caught and revealed to have left-wing associations, the shock of the president's murder—in a southern city—helped build support for efforts by the new president, Lyndon B. Johnson (himself a Texan), to obtain passage of a strong civil rights bill as a memorial to the slain president.

Fourth, the 1964 elections not only returned Johnson to office with a landslide victory but also sent a huge Democratic majority to the House and retained the large Democratic margin in the Senate. This made it possible for northern Democrats to outvote or outmaneuver southerners in the House.

The cumulative effect of these forces led to the enactment of five civil rights laws between 1957 and 1968. Three (1957, 1960, and 1965) were chiefly directed at protecting the right to vote; one (1968) was aimed at preventing discrimination in housing; and one (1964), the most far-reaching of all, dealt with voting, employment, schooling, and public accommodations.

The passage of the 1964 act was the high point of the legislative struggle. Liberals in the House had drafted a bipartisan bill, but it was now in the House Rules Committee, where such matters had often disappeared without a trace. In the wake of Kennedy's murder a discharge petition was filed, with President Johnson's support, to take the bill out of committee and bring it to the floor of the House. But the Rules Committee, without waiting for a vote on the petition (which it probably realized it would lose), sent the bill to the floor, where it passed overwhelmingly. In the Senate an agreement between Republican Minority Leader Everett Dirksen and President Johnson smoothed the way for passage in several important respects. The House bill was sent directly to the Senate floor, thereby bypassing the southern-dominated Judiciary Committee. Nineteen southern senators began an eight-week filibuster against the bill. On June 10, 1964, by a vote of seventy-one to twenty-nine, cloture was invoked and the filibuster ended—the first time in history that a filibuster aimed at blocking civil rights legislation had been broken.

Since the 1960s, congressional support for civil rights legislation has grown—so much so, indeed, that labeling a bill a civil rights measure, once the

President Lyndon Johnson signs the Civil Rights Act of 1965 in the company of the Reverend Martin Luther King, Jr., and the Reverend Ralph Abernathy.

kiss of death, now almost guarantees its passage. For example, in 1984 the Supreme Court decided that the federal ban on discrimination in education applied only to the "program or activity" receiving federal aid and not to the entire school or university.[27] In 1988 Congress passed a bill to overturn this decision by making it clear that antidiscrimination rules applied to the entire educational institution and not just to that part (say, the physics lab) receiving federal money. When President Reagan vetoed the bill (because, in his view, it would diminish the freedom of church-affiliated schools), Congress overrode the veto. In the override vote every southern Democrat in the Senate and almost 90 percent of those in the House voted for the bill. This was a dramatic change from 1964, when over 80 percent of the southern Democrats in Congress voted against the Civil Rights Act (see Figure 19.2).

This change partly reflected the growing political strength of southern blacks. In 1960 less than one-

FIGURE 19.2 Growing Support among Southern Democrats in Congress for Civil Rights Bills

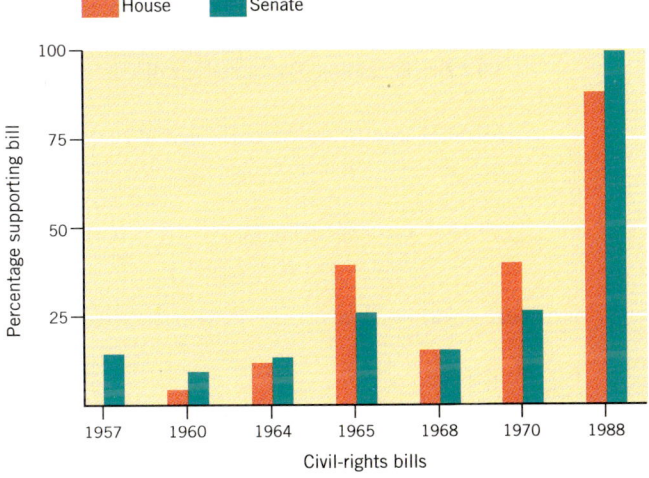

SOURCES: Congressional Quarterly, *Congress and the Nation*, vols. I, II, III, VII.

Key Provisions of Major Civil Rights Laws

1957   **Voting** Made it a federal crime to try to prevent a person from voting in a federal election. Created the Civil Rights Commission.

1960   **Voting** Authorized the attorney general to appoint federal referees to gather evidence and make findings about allegations that blacks were being deprived of their right to vote. Made it a federal crime to use interstate commerce to threaten or carry out a bombing.

1964   **Voting** Made it more difficult to use devices such as literacy tests to bar blacks from voting.
Public accommodations Barred discrimination on grounds of race, color, religion, or national origin in restaurants, hotels, lunch counters, gasoline stations, movie theaters, stadiums, arenas, and lodging houses with more than five rooms.
Schools Authorized the attorney general to bring suit to force the desegregation of public schools on behalf of citizens.
Employment Outlawed discrimination in hiring, firing, or paying employees on grounds of race, color, religion, national origin, or sex.
Federal funds Barred discrimination in any activity receiving federal assistance.

1965   **Voter registration** Authorized appointment by the Civil Service Commission of voting examiners who would require registration of all eligible voters in federal, state, and local elections, general or primary, in areas where discrimination was found to be practiced or where less than 50 percent of voting-age residents were registered to vote in 1964 election. The law was to have expired in 1970, but Congress has since extended it; it will expire in 2007.
Literacy tests Suspended use of literacy tests or other devices to prevent blacks from voting.

1968   **Housing** Banned, by stages, discrimination in sale or rental of most housing (excluding private owners who sell or rent their homes without the services of a real estate broker).
Riots Made it a federal crime to use interstate commerce to organize or incite a riot.

1972   **Education** Prohibited sex discrimination in education programs receiving federal aid.

1988   **Discrimination** If any part of an organization receives federal aid, no part of that organization may discriminate on the basis of race, sex, age, or physical handicap.

1991   **Discrimination** Made it easier to sue over job discrimination and collect damages; overturned certain Supreme Court decisions.

third of voting-age blacks in the South were registered to vote; by 1971 more than half were, and by 1984 two-thirds were. In 1991 over seven thousand blacks held elective office in the South (see Table 19.1). But this was only half of the story. Attitudes among white political elites and members of Congress had also changed. This was evident as early as 1968, when Congress passed a law barring discrimination in housing even though polls showed that only 35 percent of the public supported the measure.

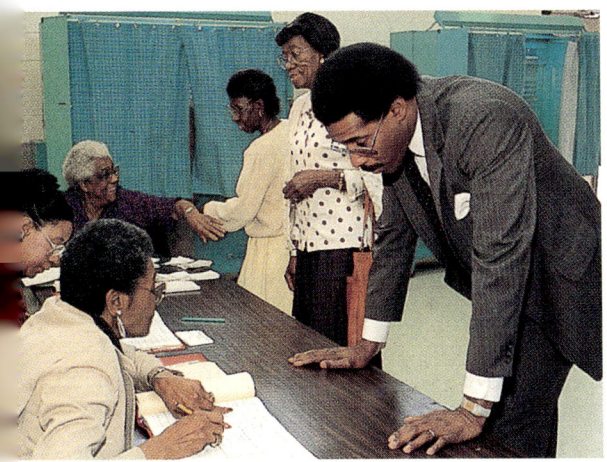

Nearly six million blacks are registered to vote in the eleven southern states.

TABLE 19.1   Increase in Number of Black Elected Officials

Office	1970	1991	1993
Congress and state legislatures	182	476	561
City and county offices	715	4,493	4,819
Judges and sheriffs	213	847	922
Boards of education	362	1,629	1,682
Total	1,472	7,445	7,984

SOURCES: *Statistical Abstract of the United States, 1990,* 260; *Statistical Abstract of the United States, 1992,* 267; *Statistical Abstract of the United States, 1995,* 287.

Civil rights is not an issue easily confined to schools, housing, and jobs. Sometimes it is extended to crime. When crack cocaine became a popular drug, it was cheap and easily sold on street corners.

When the public demanded that the police get tough on crack dealers, arrests followed. Since the great majority of arrested dealers were black, there was a sharp increase in black drug dealers going to prison. Some blacks claimed that they were being singled out by the police because of their race. The Supreme Court disagreed, holding that no evidence had been presented to show that drug dealers of other races had not been prosecuted.[28]

In 1971 Jesse Jackson was arrested at a sit-in held to demand that a grocery chain hire more blacks. In 1984 he was a candidate for the Democratic nomination for president and addressed the Democratic National Convention in San Francisco.

Women and Equal Rights

The political and legal efforts to secure civil rights for blacks were accompanied by efforts to expand the rights of women. There was an important difference between the two movements, however: whereas blacks were arguing against a legal tradition that explicitly aimed to keep them in a subservient status, women had to argue against a tradition that claimed to be protecting them. For example, in 1908 the Supreme Court upheld an Oregon law that limited female laundry workers to a ten-hour workday against the claim that it violated the Fourteenth Amendment. The Court justified its decision with this language:

> The two sexes differ in structure of body, in the functions to be performed by each, in the amount of physical strength, in the capacity for long-continued labor, particularly when done standing, . . . the self-reliance which enables one to assert full rights, and in the capacity to maintain the struggle for subsistence. This difference justifies a difference in legislation and upholds that which is designed to compensate for some of the burdens which rest upon her.[29]

The feminist movement that resurfaced not long after the civil rights movement questioned the claim that women differed from men in ways that justified differences in legal status. Congress responded by passing laws that required equal pay for equal work, prohibited discrimination on the basis of sex in employment and among students in any school or university receiving federal funds, and banned discrimination against pregnant women on the job.[30]

At the same time, the Supreme Court was altering the way it interpreted the Constitution. The key passage was the Fourteenth Amendment, which prohibits any state from denying to "any person" the "equal protection of the laws." For a long time the traditional standard, as we saw in the 1908 case, was a kind of protective paternalism. By the early 1970s, however, the Court had changed its mind. In deciding whether the Constitution bars all, or some, or no sexual discrimination, the Court had a choice between two standards. The first is the *reasonableness* standard. This says that when the government treats some classes of people differently from others—for example, applying statutory rape laws to men but not to women—the different treatment must be reasonable and not arbitrary. The second is the **strict scrutiny** standard. This says that some instances of drawing distinctions between different groups of people—for example, by treating whites and blacks differently—are inherently suspect; thus the Court will subject them to strict scrutiny to ensure that they are clearly necessary to attain a legitimate state goal.

When women complained that some laws treated them unfairly, the Court adopted a standard somewhere between the reasonableness and strict scrutiny tests. Thus a law that treats men and women differently must be more than merely reasonable, but the allowable differences need not meet the strict scrutiny test.

And so in 1971 the Court held that an Idaho statute was unconstitutional because it required that males be preferred over females when choosing people to administer the estates of deceased children. To satisfy the Constitution, a law treating men and women differently "must be reasonable, not arbitrary, and must rest on some ground of difference having a fair and substantial relation to the object of legislation so that all persons similarly circumstanced shall be treated alike."[31] In later decisions some members of the Court wanted to make classifications based on sex inherently suspect and subject to the strict scrutiny test, but no majority has yet embraced this position.[32]

But sexual classifications can also be judged by a different standard. The Civil Rights Act of 1964 prohibits sex discrimination in the hiring, firing, and compensation of employees. The 1972 Civil Rights Act bans sex discrimination in local education programs receiving federal aid. These laws apply to *private* and not just government action.

Over the years the Court has decided many cases involving sexual classification. The following lists provide several examples of illegal sexual discrimination (violating either the Constitution or a civil rights act) and legal sexual distinctions (violating neither).

Illegal discrimination

- A state cannot set different ages at which men and women legally become adults.[33]

- A state cannot set different ages at which men and women are allowed to buy beer.[34]

- Women cannot be barred from jobs by arbitrary height and weight requirements.[35]

- Employers cannot require women to take mandatory pregnancy leaves.[36]

- Girls cannot be barred from Little League baseball teams.[37]

- Business and service clubs, such as the Junior Chamber of Commerce and Rotary Club, cannot exclude women from membership.[38]

- Though women as a group live longer than men, an employer must pay them monthly retirement benefits equal to those received by men.[39]

- High schools must pay the coaches of girls' sports the same as they pay coaches of boys' sports.[40]

Decisions allowing differences based on sex

- A law that punishes males but not females for statutory rape is permissible; men and women are not "similarly situated" with respect to sexual relations.[41]

- All-boy and all-girl public schools are permitted if enrollment is voluntary and quality is equal.[42]

- States can give widows a property-tax exemption not given to widowers.[43]

- The navy may allow women to remain officers longer than men without being promoted.[44]

The lower federal courts have been especially busy in the area of sexual distinctions. They have said that public taverns may not cater to men only and that girls may not be prevented from competing against boys in noncontact high school sports; on the other hand, hospitals may bar fathers from the delivery room. Women may continue to use their maiden names after marriage.[45]

In 1996 the Supreme Court ruled that women must be admitted to the Virginia Military Institute, until then an all-male state-supported college that

Though many women have enlisted in the armed forces, the Supreme Court in 1981 held that Congress could exclude women from the draft.

had for many decades supplied what it called an "adversative method" of training to instill physical and mental discipline in cadets. In practical terms this meant being very tough on students. The Court said that for a state to justify spending tax money on a single-sex school, it must supply an "exceedingly persuasive justification" for excluding the other gender. Virginia countered by offering to support an all-female training course at another college, but this was not enough.[46] This decision came close to imposing the strict scrutiny test, and so it has raised important questions about what could happen to all-female or traditionally black colleges that accept state money.

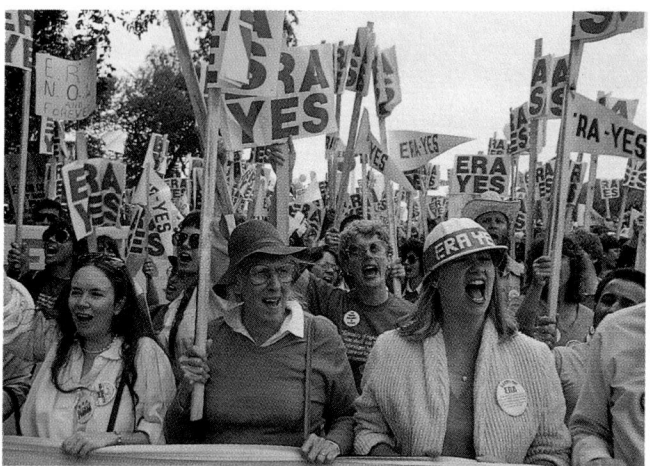

Despite a long campaign, women could not get the Equal Rights Amendment ratified by enough states.

Perhaps the most far-reaching cases defining the rights of women have involved the draft and abortion. In 1981 the Court held in *Rostker* v. *Goldberg* that Congress may require men but not women to register for the draft without violating the due-process clause of the Fifth Amendment.[47] In the area of national defense the Court will give great deference to congressional policy (Congress had already decided to bar women from combat roles). For many years women could be pilots and sailors but not on combat aircraft or combat ships. In 1993 the secretary of defense opened air and sea combat positions to all persons regardless of gender; only ground-troop combat positions are still reserved for men. The issue, as we shall see, played a role in preventing the ratification of the Equal Rights Amendment to the Constitution, because of fears that it would reverse *Rostker* v. *Goldberg,* and remains controversial.

The ERA

The extension to women, by law and court order, of a wide range of rights was sufficiently steady to make it seem for a while that the passage of an Equal Rights Amendment (ERA) to the Constitution was a foregone conclusion. That amendment, which had been before Congress since 1923, read in its operative clause as follows: "Equality of rights under the law shall not be denied or abridged by the United States or any State on account of sex."

When Congress in 1972 passed this amendment and sent it to the states for consideration, the prospects for its prompt ratification seemed excellent. It had sailed through Congress by votes of 84–8 in the Senate and 354–24 in the House; it had been endorsed by every president from Harry Truman to Jimmy Carter and by both political parties; opinion polls showed the public to be in favor of it; and women—the group to be benefited—accounted for half the voting population.

The optimism of its backers appeared for the moment to be justified. Within the first year the legislatures of twenty-two states ratified the ERA, most by overwhelming votes. By 1974–1975, however, it was clearly in trouble: it barely squeaked through the Montana senate and the North Dakota house, and two states (Nebraska and Tennessee) voted to rescind their earlier ratifications. By 1978 the ratification effort was stalled. Thirty-five states had ratified, three short of the necessary three-fourths; three states had rescinded their earlier ratifications; and repeated efforts to get the ERA ratified in such key states as Illinois and Florida had come to naught. Moreover, the time originally allowed for the ratification process—until March 22, 1979—was about to expire.

Congress was persuaded to extend the period allowed for ratification to June 30, 1982, but to little avail—none of the fifteen states refusing to ratify changed its position. Thus the ERA is no longer before the states. How can this dramatic reversal in the fortunes of this measure be explained?

What began as an apparently noncontroversial matter ended up being deeply controversial. That fact alone worked against it: since three-fourths of the states must ratify an amendment to the Constitution, the ERA's opponents needed to get only thirteen of the country's ninety-nine* state legislative houses to vote no. Legislators do not like to take positions on controversial matters, so they were espe-

---

* Forty-nine states have two house (bicameral) legislatures; one state, Nebraska, has a one-house (unicameral) legislature.

cially reluctant to support the ERA, since many of the supposed beneficiaries—in this case women—were themselves opposed to the amendment. One issue that was particularly important was the draft: many legislators and voters otherwise favoring the ERA worried that its passage would require that women be drafted for combat duty. Proponents of the ERA, such as the National Organization for Women (NOW), had difficulty countering that argument. Another issue that was highly controversial was whether the ERA would eliminate laws that protected women in the workplace (such as maximum-hour or minimum-wage laws). This was a concern of the Mormon Church and the National Council of Catholic Women.

In the end the ERA came to symbolize conflict over a broad range of cultural values in the United States. Then a series of political events sealed the fate of the bill. In 1980 the Republican party withdrew its endorsement of the ERA, and the people elected as president a man known to oppose it. In 1982 a federal judge in Idaho held that Congress had acted unconstitutionally when it extended the deadline for ratification and refused to allow states to rescind their earlier ratifications. Congress had not produced the two-thirds majority necessary to resubmit the ERA to the states.

Abortion

As the struggle over the ERA faded, the struggle over abortion intensified. Until 1973 it was up to the states to decide whether and under what circumstances women could obtain an abortion. For example, New York allowed abortion on demand during the first twenty-four weeks of pregnancy, but Texas banned abortion except when the mother's life was threatened.

By a seven-to-two vote in the 1973 case *Roe* v. *Wade,* the Supreme Court struck down the Texas law (and all similar state laws).[48] The majority argued that the due-process clause of the Fourteenth Amendment implies a "right to privacy" that protects a woman's freedom to choose, during the first three months of pregnancy, whether to have an abortion. (During the second three months, or trimester, the states were allowed to regulate abor-

The Constitutional Position of Abortion Laws as of 1994

This is what the majority of the Court held in the 1992 *Casey* decision:

1. "It is a constitutional liberty of the woman to have some freedom to terminate her pregnancy. . . . No state may prohibit a woman from terminating her pregnancy" before the fetus becomes "viable."

2. After the fetus has become viable, a state may "regulate, and even proscribe, abortion except where it is necessary . . . for the preservation of the life and the health of the mother."

3. States may put restrictions on the right to an abortion, but these restrictions must not place an "undue burden" on the exercise of a woman's rights.

Planned Parenthood v. Casey, 112 S.Ct. 291 (1992).

tion procedures to protect the mother's health; during the final trimester, states might ban abortions.)

In reaching this decision, the Court denied that it was trying to decide when human life began—at the moment of conception, at the moment of birth, or somewhere in between. But that is not how critics of the decision saw things. To them life begins at conception, and so the human fetus is a "person" entitled to the equal protection of the laws guaranteed by the Fourteenth Amendment. People feeling this way began to use the slogans "right to life" and "pro-life." Supporters of the Court's action saw matters differently. In their view, no one can say for certain when human life begins; what one *can* say, however, is that a woman is entitled to choose whether or not to have a baby. These people took the slogans "right to choose" and "pro-choice."

Almost immediately the congressional allies of pro-life groups introduced constitutional amendments to overturn *Roe* v. *Wade,* but none passed Congress. Nevertheless, abortion foes did persuade Congress, beginning in 1976, to bar the use of federal funds to pay for abortions except when the life of the mother is at stake. This provision was known as the

Hyde Amendment, after its sponsor, Representative Henry Hyde. The chief effect of the amendment has been to deny the use of Medicaid funds to pay for abortions for low-income women. (In 1980 the Supreme Court upheld the constitutionality of the Hyde amendment.)[49] During the Bush administration the government carried the spirit of this amendment one step further by barring the use of federal funds for family planning clinics that provided abortion counseling. Called a "gag rule" by some, this policy was repealed by the Clinton administration.

Despite pro-life opposition, the Supreme Court for sixteen years steadfastly reaffirmed and even broadened its decision in *Roe* v. *Wade.* It struck down laws requiring, before an abortion could be performed, a woman to have the consent of her husband, an "emancipated" but underage girl to have the consent of her parents, or a woman to be advised by her doctor as to the facts about abortion.[50]

But in 1989, under the influence of justices appointed by President Reagan, it began in the *Webster* case to uphold some state restrictions on abortions.

When that happened, many people predicted that in time *Roe* v. *Wade* would be overturned, especially if President Bush was able to appoint more justices. He appointed two (Souter and Thomas), but *Roe* survived. The key votes were cast by Justices O'Connor, Souter, and Kennedy. In 1992, in its *Casey* decision, the Court by a vote of 5–4 explicitly refused to overturn *Roe,* declaring that there was a right to abortion. At the same time, however, it upheld a variety of restrictions imposed by the state of Pennsylvania on women seeking abortion. These included a mandatory twenty-four-hour waiting period between the request for an abortion and the performance of it, the requirement that teenagers obtain the consent of one parent (or, in special circumstances, of a judge), and a requirement that women contemplating an abortion be given pamphlets about alternatives to it. Similar restrictions had been enacted in many other states, all of which looked to the Pennsylvania case for guidance as to whether they could be enforced. In allowing these restrictions, the Court overruled some of its own earlier decisions.[51] On the other hand, the Court did strike down a state law that would have required married women to obtain the consent of their husbands before having an abortion. The key provisions of the *Casey* decision are summarized in the box on page 591.

Women and the Economy

With the defeat of the ERA, women's organizations increasingly turned their attention to economic issues. Some women had begun to think of these matters as more important than the ERA, because economic issues addressed the actual benefits women might obtain from society rather than simply the legal claims they could make on it.

A split had long existed among feminists on this score. One group, traditional liberals, wanted to press for equal rights; for them the ERA was the ultimate goal. If all legal barriers to female participation were struck down, then women would take advantage of their opportunities and advance themselves as far as their interests led them, they argued. But another group saw the economic status of women as perhaps more important than their legal one.

It has been illegal since 1964 to discriminate on the basis of sex in employment. Despite this fact, the earnings of women are lower than those of men. Moreover, one group of women—those with children sired by men who have deserted or divorced them—are especially vulnerable to economic hardship.

Female-headed households are much more likely to be living in poverty than households headed by an intact couple. Finally, pregnant women have often found it necessary to give up their jobs if there is no provision for pregnancy leave.

These concerns reflect changes not only in women's political beliefs but also in their economic circumstances. In 1960 only about one-sixth of all married women with children under the age of six were in the labor force. By 1980 that proportion had risen to nearly half, and by 1991 it was nearly 60 percent. (Being "in the labor force" means that a person is either working at a job or looking for one.) In 1988 more than 60 percent of all working mothers made use of some form of day care for their children, either in the home of another person or in a

A law passed in 1993 guarantees that employees of large firms can take unpaid pregnancy and child-care leave.

group day care center.[52] Mothers who had been deserted by or divorced from the fathers of their children were, in a significant fraction of cases, not receiving the child support payments due them.

Women's organizations began pressing Congress and the courts for laws and rulings that would address these new interests, often referred to as women's-economic-equity issues. Their lobbying included demands for

- **Government-funded day care.** In general liberals have favored generous programs of this sort (in order to help working mothers), while many conservatives have opposed them (in order to keep responsibility for raising children fixed on the family). In 1984 Congress passed and the president signed a compromise plan that authorized several million dollars in federal aid to states to support or provide information about local day care services.

- **Child support enforcement.** In 1984 Congress passed and the president signed a bill that requires the states to set up procedures for withholding from the paychecks of men and women (in those few cases where it is applicable to

women) overdue court-ordered child support payments to the spouses who have custody of their children. In 1988 this provision became part of a much larger welfare reform plan.

- **Pregnancy leave.** In 1978 Congress passed a law amending the 1964 Civil Rights Act to prohibit employers from discriminating against pregnant women in the hiring, firing, or promoting of workers. It also required health and disability plans to cover pregnant workers. In 1987 the Supreme Court upheld state laws that required employers to provide parental leave to women and to guarantee that they could resume their jobs when their leave ended.[53] For several years efforts to enact a federal parental leave law either failed in Congress or were blocked by presidential vetoes. In 1993, however, a law providing up to twelve weeks of unpaid leave to workers to deal with births, adoptions, or serious illnesses within their families was passed and signed by President Clinton.

- **Comparable worth.** The most controversial of the "economic equity" proposals has involved the doctrine of "comparable worth." Since 1963 federal law has required that people receive "equal pay for substantially equal work." But this has left many women's groups dissatisfied on the grounds that women are concentrated in certain kinds of jobs that traditionally pay lower wages than the jobs men usually hold. For example, women tend to be nurses, secretaries, and sales clerks, whereas men tend to be plumbers, truck drivers, and bricklayers. Even if all nurses are paid equally and all plumbers are paid equally, plumbers may wind up earning more than nurses.

The doctrine of **comparable worth** requires that a worker's compensation be determined by the "worth" of his or her work, not by what it commands in the market. To measure "worth," each job must be ranked by an expert in terms of its intrinsic difficulty. Points are assigned based on the skill, training, and responsibility inherent in each job. For example, when the city of San Jose, California, adopted a comparable-worth plan, it decided that its painters (most of whom were men) were worth 173 points and its secretaries (most of whom were women) were worth 177 points. Since the city's secretaries on average were earning much less than its painters, the city agreed to raise the pay of the secretaries.[54]

Several other governments (including those of the states of Minnesota and Washington) have adopted comparable-worth plans for government employees, and many other states are studying the idea. The 1984 Democratic presidential platform endorsed the comparable-worth concept. But many critics argue that there is no objective way of comparing the worth of different jobs other than seeing what wages they can command in a free market. Moreover, wage differences may have nothing to do with the sex or race of the job holder. For example, professors of law, medicine, and computer sciences earn more at most universities than do professors of history, Spanish, or fine arts. This would probably be true no matter what the race or sex of those holding these professorships, because lawyers, doctors, and computer scientists have job opportunities open to them outside the university that historians and Spanish instructors do not. Neither the Supreme Court nor Congress has yet spoken definitively on this question.

Affirmative Action

A common thread running through the politics of civil rights is the argument between equality of results and equality of opportunity.

Equality of Results   One view, expressed by most civil rights and feminist organizations, is that the burdens of racism and sexism can be overcome only by taking race or sex into account in designing remedies. It is not enough to give rights to people; they must be given benefits. If life is a race, everybody must be brought up to the same starting line (or possibly even to the same finish line). This means that the Constitution is not and should not be color-blind or sex-blind. In education this implies that the races must actually be mixed in the schools, by busing if necessary. In hiring it means that **affirmative action**—preferential hiring practices—must be used to find and hire women, blacks, and other minorities. Women should not simply be free to enter the labor force; they should be given the material necessities (for example, free day care) that will help them enter it. On payday workers' checks should reflect not just the results of people's competing in the marketplace but the results of plans designed to ensure that people earn comparable amounts for comparable jobs. Of late, affirmative action has been defended in the name of diversity or multiculturalism—the view that every institution (firm, school, or agency) and every college curriculum should reflect the cultural (that is, ethnic) diversity of the nation.

Equality of Opportunity   The second view holds that if it is wrong to discriminate *against* blacks and women, it is equally wrong to give them preferential treatment over other groups. To do so constitutes **reverse discrimination**. The Constitution and laws should be color-blind and sex-neutral. In this view, allowing children to attend the school of their choice is sufficient; busing them to attain a certain racial mixture is wrong. Eliminating barriers to job opportunities is right; using numerical "targets" and "goals" to place minorities and women in specific jobs is wrong. If people wish to compete in the market, they should be satisfied with the market verdict concerning the worth of their work.

A Nation of Immigrants

As we approach the twenty-first century, immigration is bound to alter the American political, cultural, and legal landscapes in ways that can be only dimly perceived at present. In the first decade of the twentieth century, immigration was virtually unrestricted and nearly 8.8 million persons, most of them from Europe, came to the United States. In the 1980s some 5.8 million people were admitted to the United States, and about 2.7 million who had resided here illegally were legalized under new federal immigration laws.

From 1911 to 1920 the average annual rate of immigration was 5.7 per 1,000 U.S. residential population. Between 1921 and 1930 the immigration rate dipped to 3.5. The adoption of restrictive immigration laws and uncompromising enforcement procedures kept the rate below 1.0 from 1931 to 1950. Despite a sharp increase in the number of people all around the world seeking to come to America because of famine, political persecution, civil war, and other reasons, the rate remained between 1.0 and 2.1 during the period 1951 to 1980. In the 1980s, however, changes both in immigration laws and in the enforcement of existing laws contributed to a steady increase in the immigration rate. As the table below shows, the immigration rate climbed between 1984 and 1990, catapulting from 2.6 in 1988 to 6.1 in 1990. Most of today's immigrants come from Asia, Mexico, Central America, and Africa, not Europe.

These immigration trends presage a historic demographic shift and pose profound legal questions related to civil rights laws and the meaning of citizenship. In the early 1990s the many aspects of immigration law, policy, and practice remained largely unsettled. For example, state and federal courts were still undecided on the question of what obligations employers have in hiring aliens, legal and illegal. Even so, some things about the civil rights of aliens and the concomitant responsibilities of naturalized citizens were largely settled (see box on page 596).

Immigrants do not take only entry-level jobs; many bring important skills, such as these Vietnamese working in a dentist's office.

Year	Number	Rate[a]
1984	544,000	2.3
1985	570,000	2.4
1986	602,000	2.5
1987	602,000	2.5
1988	643,000	2.6
1989	1,091,000	4.4
1990	1,536,000	6.1

[a]Number of immigrants per 1,000 U.S. residential population.
SOURCE: Adapted from *Statistical Abstract of the United States, 1992*, 10.

These two views are intertwined with other deep philosophical differences. Supporters of equality of opportunity tend to have orthodox beliefs; they favor letting private groups behave the way that they want (and so may defend the right of a men's club to exclude women). Supporters of the opposite view are likely to be progressive in their beliefs and insist that private clubs meet the same standards as schools or business firms. Adherents to the equality-of-opportunity view often attach great importance to traditional models of the family and so are skeptical of day care and federally funded abortions. Adherents to the equality-of-results view prefer greater freedom of choice in lifestyle questions and

Becoming a Citizen

For persons born in the United States, the rights of U.S. citizenship have been ensured, in constitutional theory if not in everyday practice, since the passage of the Fourteenth Amendment in 1868 and the civil rights laws of the 1960s. The Fourteenth Amendment conferred citizenship upon "all persons born in the United States . . . and subject to the jurisdiction thereof." Subsequent laws also give citizenship to children born outside the United States to parents who are American citizens.

But immigrants, by definition, are not born with the rights of U.S. citizenship. Instead, those seeking to become U.S. citizens must, in effect, assume certain responsibilities in order to become citizens. The statutory requirements for naturalization, as they have been broadly construed by the courts, are as follows:

- Five years' residency, or three years if married to a citizen.

- Continuous residency since filing of the naturalization petition.

- Good moral character, which is loosely interpreted to mean no evidence of criminal activity.

- Attachment to constitutional principles. This means that potential citizens had to answer basic factual questions about American government (e.g., "Who was the first president of the United States?") and publicly denounce any and all allegiance to their native country and its leaders (e.g., Italy and the king of Italy), but devotion to constitutional principles is now regarded as being implicit in the act of applying for naturalization itself.

- Being favorably disposed to "the good order and happiness of the United States."*

Today about 97 percent of aliens who seek citizenship are successful in meeting these requirements and becoming naturalized citizens of the United States.

* 8 U.S.C. 1423, 1427 (1970); Girouard v. United States, 328 U.S. 61 (1946).
SOURCE: *The New York Times* (July 25, 1993): 33. Copyright © 1993 by the *New York Times*. Reprinted by permission.

---

so take the opposite position on day care and abortion.

Of course the debate is more complex than this simple contrast suggests. Take, for example, the question of affirmative action. Both the advocates of equality of opportunity and those of equality of results might agree that there is something odd about a factory or university that hires no blacks or women, and both might press it to prove that its hiring policy is fair. Affirmative action in this case can mean *either* looking hard for qualified women and minorities and giving them a fair shot at jobs *or* setting a numerical goal for the number of women and minorities that should be hired and insisting that that goal be met. Persons who defend the second course of action call these goals "targets"; persons who criticize that course call them "quotas."

The issue has largely been fought out in the courts. Between 1978 and 1990 about a dozen major cases involving affirmative action were decided by the Supreme Court; in about half it was upheld, and in the other it was overturned. The different outcomes reflect two things—the differences in the facts of each case and the arrival onto the Court of three justices (Kennedy, O'Connor, and Scalia) appointed by a president, Ronald Reagan, who was opposed to at least the broader interpretation of affirmative action. As a result of these decisions, the law governing affirmative action is now complex and confusing.

Consider one issue: should the government be allowed to use a quota system to select workers, enroll students, award contracts, or grant licenses? In the *Bakke* decision in 1978, the Court said that the medical school of the University of California at Davis could not use an explicit numerical quota in admitting minority students but could "take race into account."[55] So no numerical quotas, right? Wrong. Two years later the Court upheld a federal rule that set aside 10 percent of all federal construction contracts for minority-owned firms.[56] All right, maybe quotas can't be used in medical schools, but they can be used in the construction industry. Not exactly. In 1989 the Court overturned a Richmond, Virginia, law that set aside 30 percent of its construction contracts for minority-owned firms.[57] Well, maybe the Court just changed its mind between 1980 and 1989. No. One year later it upheld a federal rule that gave preference to minority-owned firms in the awarding of broadcast licenses.[58] Then in 1993 it upheld the right of white contractors to challenge minority set-aside laws in Jacksonville, Florida.[59]

It is too early to try to make sense of these twists and turns, especially since a deeply divided Court is still wrestling with these issues and Congress (as

The Rights of Aliens

*A*merica is a nation of immigrants. Some have arrived legally, others illegally. An illegal, or undocumented, alien is subject to being deported. With the passage in 1986 of the Immigration Reform and Control Act, illegal aliens who have resided in this country continuously since before January 1, 1982, are entitled to amnesty—that is, they can become legal residents. However, the same legislation stipulated that employers (who once could hire undocumented aliens without fear of penalty) must now verify the legal status of all newly hired employees; if they knowingly hire an illegal alien, they face civil and criminal penalties.

Aliens—people residing in this country who are not citizens—cannot vote or run for office. Nevertheless, they must pay taxes just as if they were citizens. And they are entitled to many constitutional rights, even if they are in this country illegally. This is because most of the rights mentioned in the Constitution refer to "people" or "persons," not to "citizens." For example, the Fourteenth Amendment bars a state from depriving "*any person* of life, liberty, or property, without due process of law" or from denying "to *any person* within its jurisdiction the equal protection of the laws" [italics added]. As a result, the courts have held that

- The children of illegal aliens cannot be excluded from the public school system.[1]

- Legally admitted aliens are entitled to welfare benefits.[2]

- Illegal aliens cannot be the object of reprisals if they attempt to form a labor union where they work.[3]

- The First Amendment rights of free speech, religion, press, and assembly and the Fourth Amendment protections against arbitrary arrest and prosecution extend to aliens as well as to citizens.[4]

- Aliens are entitled to own property.

The government can make rules that apply to aliens only, but they must justify the reasonableness of the rules. For example:

- The Immigration and Naturalization Service has broader powers to arrest and search illegal aliens than police departments have to arrest and search citizens.[5]

- States can limit certain jobs, such as police officer and school teacher, to citizens.[6]

- The president or Congress can bar the employment of aliens by the federal government.[7]

- States can bar aliens from serving on a jury.[8]

- Illegal aliens are not entitled to obtain a Social Security card.

---

[1] Plyler v. Doe, 457 U.S. 202 (1982).

[2] Graham v. Richardson, 403 U.S. 365 (1971).

[3] Sure-Tan v. National Labor Relations Board, 467 U.S. 883 (1984).

[4] Chew v. Colding, 344 U.S. 590 (1953).

[5] U.S. v. Brignoni-Ponce, 422 U.S. 873 (1975); INS v. Delgado, 466 U.S. 210 (1984); INS v. Lopez-Mendoza, 486 U.S. 1032 (1984).

[6] Cabell v. Chavez-Salido, 454 U.S. 432 (1982); Foley v. Connelie, 435 U.S. 291 (1978); Amblach v. Norwick, 441 U.S. 68 (1979).

[7] Hampton v. Mow Sun Wong, 436 U.S. 67 (1976).

[8] Schneider v. New Jersey, 308 U.S. 147 (1939).

---

with the Civil Rights Act of 1991) is modifying or superseding some earlier Court decisions. But a few general standards seem to be emerging. In simplified form, they are as follows:

- The courts will subject any quota system created by state or local governments to "strict scrutiny" and will look for a "compelling" justification for it.

- Quotas or preference systems cannot be used by state or local governments without first showing that such rules are needed to correct an actual past or present pattern of discrimination.[60]

- In proving that there has been discrimination, it is not enough to show that blacks (or other minorities) are statistically underrepresented among employees, contractors, or union members; you must

The Rights of the Disabled

*I*n 1990 the federal government passed the Americans with Disabilities Act (ADA), a sweeping law that extended many of the protections enjoyed by women and racial minorities to disabled persons.

WHO IS A DISABLED PERSON?

Anyone who *has* a physical or mental impairment that substantially limits one or more major life activities (for example, holding a job), anyone who has a *record* of such impairment, or anyone who is *regarded* as having such an impairment is considered disabled.

WHAT RIGHTS DO THE DISABLED HAVE?

Employment The disabled may not be denied employment or promotion if, with "reasonable accommodation," they can perform the duties of that job. (Excluded from this protection are people who currently use illegal drugs, gamble compulsively, or are homosexual or bisexual.) Reasonable accommodation need not be made if this would cause "undue hardship" on the employer.

Government Programs and Transportation Disabled persons may not be denied access to government programs or benefits. New buses, taxis, and trains must be accessible to disabled persons, including those in wheelchairs.

Public Accommodations The disabled must enjoy "full and equal" access to hotels, restaurants, stores, schools, parks, museums, auditoriums, and the like. To achieve equal access, owners of existing facilities must alter them "to the maximum extent feasible"; builders of new facilities must ensure that they are readily accessible to disabled persons, unless this is structurally impossible.

Telephones The ADA directs the Federal Communications Commission to issue regulations to ensure that telecommunications devices for hearing- and speech-impaired people are available "to the extent possible and in the most efficient manner."

Congress The rights under this law apply to employees of Congress.

Rights Compared The ADA does not enforce the rights of the disabled in the same way as the Civil Rights Act enforces the rights of blacks and women. Racial or gender discrimination must end *regardless of cost;* denial of access to the disabled must end unless "undue hardship" or excessive costs would result.

identify the actual practices that have had this discriminatory impact.[61]

- Quotas or preference systems that are created by *federal* law will be given greater deference, in part because Section 5 of the Fourteenth Amendment gives to Congress powers not given to the states to correct the effects of racial discrimination.[62]

- It may be easier to justify in court a voluntary preference system (for example, one agreed to in a labor-management contract) than one that is required by law.[63]

- Even when you can justify special preferences in *hiring* workers, the Court is not likely to allow racial preferences to govern who gets *laid off.* A worker laid off to make room for a minority worker loses more than does a worker not hired in preference to a minority applicant.[64]

Complex as they are, these rulings still generate a great deal of passion. Supporters of the decisions barring certain affirmative action plans hail these decisions as steps back from an emerging pattern of reverse discrimination. In contrast, civil rights organizations have denounced those decisions that have overturned affirmative action programs. In 1990 their congressional allies introduced legislation that would reverse several decisions. In particular this legislation would put the burden of proof on the employer, not the employee, to show that the underrepresentation of minorities in the firm's work force was the result of legitimate and necessary business decisions and not the result of discrimination. If the employer could not prove this, the aggrieved employee would be able to collect large damage awards. (In the past, he or she could only collect back pay.) In 1991 the bill was passed and was signed by President Bush.

In thinking about these matters, most Americans distinguish between compensatory action and preferential treatment. They define **compensatory action** as "helping disadvantaged people catch up, usually by giving them extra education, training, or services." A majority of the public supports this. They define preferential treatment as "giving minorities preference in hiring, promotions, college admissions, and contracts." Large majorities oppose this.[65] These views reflect an enduring element in American political culture—a strong commitment to individualism ("nobody should get something without deserving it") coupled with support for help for the disadvantaged ("somebody who is suffering through no fault of his or her own deserves a helping hand").

Where does affirmative action fit into this culture? Polls suggest that if affirmative action is defined as "helping," people will support it, but if it is defined as "using quotas," they will oppose it.[66] The conflict in the courts over affirmative action—and the conflicting rulings the courts have issued—reflect this deeper conflict in American opinion.

The courts are likewise divided on this matter. In 1996 the federal appeals court for the fifth circuit (covering Louisiana, Mississippi, and Texas) decided that the University of Texas Law School's refusal to admit a white woman, Cheryl Hopwood, even though her academic record was much better than that of many black and Hispanic students who had been admitted, was unconstitutional. The school said it gave preference to racial minorities to achieve diversity among its students, but the appeals court held that diversity was not a sufficiently compelling state interest to justify racial preferences. When the school appealed the decision to the Supreme Court, it refused to hear the matter because, by then, the school had stopped using racial admissions criteria.[67] This means that no law school in Louisiana, Mississippi, and Texas can use race at all in making admissions decisions, but those in the other states still can.

What may be the most important recent Supreme Court decision on affirmative action was made in 1995. A small construction company named Adarand tried to get a contract to build guard rails along a highway in Colorado. Though it was the low bidder, it lost the contract because of a government policy that favors small businesses owned by "socially and economically disadvantaged individuals"—that is, by racial and ethnic minorities. In a 5-4 decision the Court agreed with Adarand and sent the case back to Colorado for a new trial.

The essence of its decision was that *any* discrimination based on race must be subject to strict scrutiny, even if its purpose is to help, not hurt, a racial minority. Strict scrutiny means two things:

• Any racial preference must serve a "compelling government interest."

Government-subsidized job training programs are examples of compensatory action.

• The preference must be "narrowly tailored" to serve that interest.[68]

To serve a compelling governmental interest, it is likely that any racial preference will have to remedy a clear pattern of past discrimination. No such pattern had been shown in Colorado.

This decision prompted a good deal of political debate about affirmative action. The Republicans introduced a bill in Congress to ban it, but they later withdrew the bill. In California, however, an initiative was put on the 1996 ballot to prevent state authorities from using "race, sex, color, ethnicity, or national origin as a criterion for either discriminating against, or granting preferential treatment to, any individual or group" in public employment, public education, or public contracting. When the votes were counted, it passed. Other states are now discussing similar measures.

Gays and the Supreme Court

As conflicts over homosexuality have risen in political importance, the Supreme Court has had to confront the issue of gay rights more frequently. Because the nation is divided about it, one shouldn't be surprised to learn that the Court is also.

When some Georgians protested that a state law barring homosexual actions between two consenting adults was unconstitutional, the Court by a 5-4 vote decided that there was no constitutional reason to prevent a state from passing such a law.[69] Homosexuality in that state remained illegal.

In many cities in Colorado, ordinances were passed to ban discrimination against people because of their sexual orientation. Most voters did not approve of this, and so in response they adopted a state constitutional amendment that made it illegal to pass any law to protect persons based on their "homosexual, lesbian, or bisexual orientation." The amendment did not penalize gays and lesbians; instead, it said that they could not become the object of specific legal protection of the sort that has traditionally been given to racial or ethnic minorities. The Court struck down this amendment on the grounds that it violated the equal protection clause of the Constitution by singling out as unworthy of protection one specific group of citizens.[70]

So now we have an odd condition: a state can pass a law banning homosexual activities, but it cannot pass a law preventing the cities within that state from reversing that ban. (The decision that overturned the Colorado amendment did not mention the decision sustaining the Georgia law.)

Presently the status of civil rights for homosexuals remains unclear. Complicating matters is the role of gays in the military. In 1993 the Clinton administration instituted the policy of "don't ask, don't tell" in the military, but the Court has yet to speak authoritatively about what this means in practice.

SUMMARY

The civil rights movement in the courts and in Congress profoundly changed the nature of black participation in politics by bringing southern blacks into the political system so that they could become an effective interest group. The decisive move was to enlist northern opinion in this cause, a job made easier by the northern perception that civil rights involved simply an unfair contest between two minorities—southern whites and southern blacks. That perception changed when it became evident that the court rulings and legislative decisions would apply to the North as well as to the South, leading to the emergence of northern opposition to court-ordered busing and affirmative action programs.

By the time this reaction developed, the legal and political system had been changed sufficiently to make it difficult if not impossible to limit the application of civil rights laws to the special circumstances of the South or to alter by legislative means the decisions of federal courts. Though the courts can accomplish little when they have no political allies (as revealed by the massive resistance to early school desegregation decisions), they can accomplish a great deal, even in the face of adverse public opinion, when they have some organized allies (as revealed by their ability to withstand antibusing moves).

The feminist movement has paralleled in organization and tactics many aspects of the black civil rights movement, but with important differences. Women sought to repeal or reverse laws and court rulings that in many cases were ostensibly designed to protect rather than subjugate them. The conflict between protection and liberation was sufficiently intense to defeat the effort to ratify the Equal Rights Amendment.

The most divisive civil rights issues in American politics are abortion and affirmative action. From 1973 to 1989 the Supreme Court seemed committed to giving constitutional protection to all abortions within the first trimester; since 1989 it has approved various state restrictions on the circumstances under which such abortions can be obtained.

There has been a similar shift in the Court's view of affirmative action. Though it will still approve some quota plans, it now insists that they pass strict scrutiny to ensure that they are used only to correct a proven history of discrimination, that they place the burden of proof on the party alleging discrimination, and that they be limited to hirings and not extended to layoffs. Congress has modified some of these rulings with new civil rights legislation.

KEY TERMS

civil rights   *p. 571*

suspect classifications   *p. 571*

Jim Crow   *p. 573*

separate-but-equal doctrine   *p. 575*

de jure segregation   *p. 578*

de facto segregation   *p. 578*

nonviolent civil disobedience   *p. 583*

strict scrutiny   *p. 588*

comparable worth   *p. 594*

affirmative action   *p. 594*

equality of opportunities   *p. 594*

reverse discrimination   *p. 594*

compensatory action   *p. 598*

SUGGESTED READINGS

Flexner, Eleanor. *Century of Struggle: The Women's Rights Movement in the United States.* Rev. ed. Cambridge, Mass.: Harvard University Press, 1975. A historical account of the feminist movement and its political strategies.

Franklin, John Hope. *From Slavery to Freedom.* 5th ed. New York: Knopf, 1980. A survey of black history in the United States.

Kluger, Richard. *Simple Justice.* New York: Random House/Vintage, 1977. Detailed and absorbing account of the school-desegregation issue, from the Fourteenth Amendment to the *Brown* case.

Kull, Andrew. *The Color-Blind Constitution.* Cambridge, Mass.: Harvard University Press, 1993. A history of efforts, none yet successful, to make the Constitution color-blind.

Mansbridge, Jane J. *Why We Lost the ERA.* Chicago: University of Chicago Press, 1986. Explains why the Equal Rights Amendment did not become part of the Constitution.

Orfield, Gary. *Congressional Power: Congress and Social Change.* New York: Harcourt Brace Jovanovich, 1975. Analysis of the legislative politics of the major civil-rights laws.

Pritchett, C. Herman. *Constitutional Civil Liberties.* Englewood Cliffs, N.J.: Prentice-Hall, 1984. Chapters 10 and 12 provide an excellent summary of the constitutional basis of civil rights.

Wilhoit, Francis M. *The Politics of Massive Resistance.* New York: George Braziller, 1973. The methods—and ultimate collapse—of all-out southern resistance to school desegregation.

Woodward, C. Vann. *The Strange Career of Jim Crow.* New York: Oxford University Press, 1957. Brief, lucid account of the evolution of Jim Crow practices in the South.

Foreign Policy

★ War, peace, and global diplomacy—
majoritarian issues

★ Preeminence of the president

★ Relationship of president and Senate

★ Checks on presidential power

★ Foreign policy machinery

★ The White House, the State Department,
and the NSC

★ Impact of public opinion

★ Origins of elite opinion

★ Isolationism, antiappeasement, and
disengagement

★ Post–cold war policy

W hen Iraq invaded Kuwait in August 1990, President Bush sent U.S. troops to the Persian Gulf, initially in small numbers to defend neighboring Saudi Arabia but later in large numbers to force Iraq out of Kuwait. He obtained the backing of the United Nations Security Council and the military support of many other nations.

This forced Americans once again to face a key foreign policy issue: can the president send troops into combat on his own authority, or does he need a congressional declaration of war? President Bush said he did not need such a declaration, citing the action of previous presidents who had made war without it. Congress responded by quoting the Constitution, which gives to Congress the power to declare war. On January 13, 1991, the immediate issue was settled when Congress passed (though by a narrow margin in the Senate) a resolution authorizing the president to use force in the Gulf. On January 16 we attacked. On March 3 Iraq gave up.

But the largest issue remains unsettled. Is our Constitution, or democratic politics generally, well suited to the needs of diplomacy in the modern age? Tocqueville said that the conduct of foreign affairs requires precisely those qualities most lacking in a democratic nation: "A democracy can only with great difficulty regulate the details of an important undertaking, persevere in a fixed design, and work out its execution in spite of serious obstacles. It cannot combine its measures with secrecy or await their consequences with patience."[1] In plain language, a democracy is forced to play foreign policy poker with its cards turned up. As a result, aggressors, from Hitler to Saddam Hussein, will bluff us or misjudge us.

Others, however, find fault not with the system but with what they view as the reckless policies of American presidents. If Congress had been more involved, they say, we would not have gotten bogged down in Vietnam, tried to trade arms for hostages in Iran, or supported the rebels in Nicaragua.

Happily, most foreign policy issues are not matters of war or peace. But the same issues can be found in them all: How great are the powers of the

603

president? What role should Congress play? How important is public opinion? When do interest groups make a difference? To answer those questions we must first distinguish among foreign policy issues that involve majoritarian, interest group, and clientele politics.

Kinds of Foreign Policy

The majoritarian component of foreign policy includes those decisions (and nondecisions) that are perceived to confer widely distributed benefits and impose widely distributed costs. The decision to go to war is an obvious example of this. So, too, are the establishment of military alliances with Western Europe, the negotiation of a nuclear test ban treaty or a strategic arms limitation agreement, the response to the crisis posed by the Soviet blockade of West Berlin or the placement of Soviet offensive missiles in Cuba, the decision to aid the contras in Nicaragua, and the opening up of diplomatic relations with the People's Republic of China. These may be good or bad policies, but such benefits and such costs as they have accrue to the nation generally. Some argue that the costs of many of these policies are in fact highly concentrated—for example, soldiers bear the burden of a military operation—but that turns out, on closer inspection, not to shape the positions that people take on issues of war and peace. Though soldiers and their immediate families may feel the costs of a war to an especially high degree, public opinion surveys taken during the Vietnam War showed that having a family member in the armed forces did not significantly affect how people evaluated the war.[2] There is a sense that, during wartime, we are all in this together.

Foreign policy decisions may also reflect interest group politics. Tariff decisions confer benefits on certain business firms and labor unions and impose costs on other firms and unions. If the price of Japanese steel imported into this country is increased by tariffs, quotas, or other devices, this helps the American steel industry and the United Steelworkers of America. On the other hand, it hurts those firms (and associated unions) that had been purchasing the once-cheap Japanese steel.

Examples of client politics also occur in foreign affairs. Washington often provides aid to American corporations doing business abroad because the aid helps those firms directly without imposing any apparent costs on an equally distinct group in society. Our policy toward Israel has in part reflected the fact that Jews in this country feel strongly about the need to support a Jewish state abroad and are well organized to make those concerns felt. (Other factors also help explain our support of Israel; it is by no means a pure case of client politics.) Arab-Americans have begun to organize and to press on the government concerns very different from the pro-Israel arguments. We may in fact be witnessing a change of our policy toward Israel from one chiefly influenced by client politics to one more subject to interest group politics.

Who has power in foreign policy depends very much on what kind of foreign policy we have in mind. Where it is of a majoritarian nature, the president is clearly the dominant figure, and much, if not everything, depends on his beliefs and skills and on those of his chief advisers. Public opinion will ordinarily support this presidential leadership, but it will not guide it. As we shall see, public opinion on majoritarian foreign policy issues usually reflects a disposition to trust the president. But woe to the president who by his actions forfeits that trust.

When interest group or client politics are involved, Congress plays a much larger role. Although Congress plays a subsidiary role in the conduct of foreign diplomacy, the decision to send troops overseas, or the direction of intelligence operations, it plays quite a large role in decisions involving foreign economic aid, the structure of the tariff system, the shipment of weapons to foreign allies, the creation of new weapons systems, and the support of Israel.

And Congress is the central political arena on those occasions when entrepreneurial politics shapes foreign policy. If a multinational corporation is caught in a scandal, congressional investigations shake the usual indifference of politicians to the foreign conduct of such corporations. If presidential policies abroad lead to reversals, as when in 1986 presidential aides sought to trade arms for U.S. hostages in Iran and then use some profits from the arms sales to support the anti-Marxist contras fighting in Nicaragua, Congress becomes the forum for investigations and criticism. At such moments Congress often seeks to expand its power over foreign affairs.

North American Free Trade Agreement

Snatching a Foreign Policy Victory from the Jaws of a Domestic Policy Defeat

*T*he passage of the North American Free Trade Agreement (NAFTA) in November 1993 was a stunning victory for President Clinton and a vivid illustration of how presidents tend to get their way with Congress more often in foreign policy matters than in matters of domestic policy. More precisely, it illustrates how a president can sometimes get his way with Congress by emphasizing the foreign policy benefits of a proposal when the domestic policy benefits of that same proposal are in doubt.

Essentially, NAFTA eliminates most tariff and other trade barriers among the United States, Mexico, and Canada within fifteen years. In the long run American consumers and workers are virtually certain to benefit from NAFTA, but in the short term a number of jobs will probably be lost in sectors where Mexico or Canada (or both) have an economic advantage and can produce and sell goods more cheaply than can U.S. firms.

During the 1992 presidential campaign President Bush supported NAFTA, but it wasn't until he succeeded Bush that President Clinton really got behind the plan. Clinton's initial reluctance to support NAFTA was understandable. Although Republicans in Congress had gone on record in support of NAFTA, many of the Democratic leaders in Congress were strongly opposed to the policy, and the anti-NAFTA coalition was broad and powerful. It included traditional Democratic constituencies such as organized labor, influential blocs on Capitol Hill such as the Congressional Black Caucus, key Democratic House members such as Majority Leader Richard A. Gephardt of Missouri and Majority Whip David E. Bonior of Michigan, and influential American po-

For many years before the passage of the North American Free Trade Agreement (NAFTA), "maquiladora" factories in Mexico made things for export to the United States duty free.

litical personalities such as conservative columnist Pat Buchanan, consumer advocate Ralph Nader, the Reverend Jesse Jackson, and Ross Perot.

Early in the NAFTA debate, Clinton argued that NAFTA was crucial to his economic program and a boon to the creation of high-skill, high-wage jobs. He also used a divide-and-conquer strategy, making deals to protect certain industries (for example, citrus, sugar, and vegetable growers) from any adverse effects but denying others (for example, glasswear manufacturers) similar concessions. Still, as late as September, just two months before the final vote, most observers gave NAFTA almost no chance of passage.

As the debate wore on, however, Clinton began to pitch NAFTA in foreign policy terms. The White House arranged for a highly publicized pro-NAFTA gathering featuring several ex-presidents and former secretaries of state. President Clinton stressed that failure to ratify NAFTA would not only invite Germany and Japan to capture the increasingly lucrative Mexican market but would also damage the country's international prestige and the president's standing as a world leader. Indeed, President Clinton was scheduled to attend an international economic summit only days after the NAFTA vote: was he to represent the country as a free-trading giant or a protectionist mouse?

In the end, NAFTA passed in the House by a vote of 234–200 and in the Senate by a vote of 61–38. Although a majority of House Democrats voted against NAFTA, many of those who were initially leaning against the agreement, in Washington and in the country at large, were undoubtedly moved to support it (or at least relax their opposition to it) by the president's successful effort to play up the foreign policy aspects of the issue.

Domestic interest groups powerfully affect the making of foreign policy, such as when Jewish-Americans denounce Palestinian terrorists and Arab-Americans support self-government for Palestinians.

In this chapter we will be chiefly concerned with foreign policy insofar as it displays the characteristics of majoritarian politics. Limiting the discussion in this way permits us to focus on the grand issues of foreign affairs—war, peace, and global diplomacy. It allows us to see how choices are made in a situation in which public majorities support but do not direct policy, in which opinion tends to react to events, and in which interest groups are relatively unimportant.

The Constitutional and Legal Context

The Constitution defines the authority of the president and of Congress in foreign affairs in a way that, as Edward Corwin put it, is an "invitation to struggle."[3] The president is commander in chief of the armed forces, but Congress must authorize and appropriate money for those forces. The president ap-points ambassadors, but they must be confirmed by the Senate. The president may negotiate treaties, but the Senate must ratify these by a two-thirds vote. Only Congress may regulate commerce with other nations and "declare" war. (In an early draft of the Constitution the Framers gave Congress the power to "make" war but changed this to "declare" so that the president, acting without Congress, could take military measures to repel a sudden attack.) Because power over foreign affairs is shared by the president and Congress, conflict between them is to be expected in this area.

Yet almost every American thinks instinctively that the president is in charge of foreign affairs, and what popular opinion supposes, the historical record confirms. Presidents have asserted the right to send troops abroad on their own authority in more than 125 instances.[4] Only five of the twelve major wars that this country has fought have followed a formal declaration of war by Congress.[5] The

The president dominates the politics of grand diplomacy, as did President Clinton when he met with Palestinian President Yasser Arafat, Israeli Prime Minister Benjamin Netanyahu, and King Hussein of Jordan.

State Department, the Central Intelligence Agency, and the National Security Agency are almost entirely "presidential" agencies, with only modest congressional control. The Defense Department, though keenly sensitive to congressional views on weapons procurement and the location of military bases, is very much under the control of the president on matters of military strategy. While the Senate has since 1789 ratified well over a thousand treaties signed by the president, the president during this period has also signed around seven thousand executive agreements with other countries that did not require Senate ratification and yet have the force of law.[6]

Presidential Box Score

When the president seeks congressional approval for foreign policy matters, he tends to win more often than when he asks for support on domestic matters. Between 1948 and 1964 Congress approved 73 percent of the president's defense measures, 71 percent of his treaty and foreign aid proposals, 59 percent of his other foreign policy measures—but only 40 percent of his domestic programs. One student of the

presidency, Aaron Wildavsky, concluded that the American political system has "two presidencies"— one in domestic affairs that is relatively weak and closely checked, and another in foreign affairs that is quite powerful.[7] As we shall see, this view considerably overstates presidential power in certain areas.

By the standards of American government (limiting our attention to majoritarian issues of diplomacy and military deployment), the president is indeed strong, much stronger than the Framers in 1789 may have intended and certainly stronger than many members of Congress would prefer. Examples abound:

- 1801: Thomas Jefferson sent the navy to deal with the Barbary pirates.

- 1845: James K. Polk sent troops into Mexico to defend newly acquired Texas.

- 1861: Abraham Lincoln blockaded southern ports and declared martial law.

- 1940: Franklin D. Roosevelt sent fifty destroyers to England to be used against Germany, with which we were then technically at peace.

Shifting Patterns of Leadership in Foreign Policy

*D*epending on the personalities, skills, and interest of those involved, leadership in making American foreign policy may be found centered in the White House (the president and his national security adviser) or in the State Department (the secretary of state).

Periods of White House dominance

President	Secretary of State
Franklin D. Roosevelt	Cordell Hull (1933–1944)
John F. Kennedy (and National Security Adviser McGeorge Bundy)	Dean Rusk (1961–1969)
Richard M. Nixon (and National Security Adviser Henry A. Kissinger)	William P. Rogers (1969–1973)

Periods of leadership by the secretary of state

Secretary of State	President
George O. Marshall (1947–1949) and Dean Acheson (1949–1953)	Harry S Truman
John Foster Dulles (1953–1959)	Dwight D. Eisenhower
Henry A. Kissinger (1973–1977)	Gerald R. Ford
Warren Christopher (1993–1996)	Bill Clinton

Periods of tension between the White House and secretary of state

President	Secretary of State
Jimmy Carter	Cyrus Vance (1977–1980)
Ronald Reagan	George Shultz (1982–1989)

John F. Kennedy with Dean Rusk

- 1950: Harry Truman sent American troops into South Korea to help repulse a North Korean attack on that country.

- 1960s: John F. Kennedy and Lyndon Johnson sent American forces into South Vietnam without a declaration of war.

- 1983: President Reagan sent troops to overthrow a pro-Castro regime in Grenada.

- 1987: President Reagan sent the navy to protect oil tankers in the Persian Gulf.

- 1989: President Bush ordered the U.S. invasion of Panama to depose dictator Manuel Noriega.

- 1990: President Bush ordered troops to Saudi Arabia in response to Iraq's invasion of Kuwait.

However, by the standards of other nations, even other democratic ones, the ability of an American president to act decisively often appears rather modest. England was dismayed at the inability of Woodrow Wilson in 1914–1915 and Franklin Roosevelt in 1939–1940 to enter into an alliance when England was engaged in a major war with Germany. Wilson was unable to bring this country into the League of Nations. Gerald Ford could not intervene covertly in Angola in support of an anti-Marxist faction. President Reagan was heavily criticized in Congress for sending fifty-five military advisers to El Salvador and a few hundred Marines to Lebanon.

After President Bush sent U.S. troops to the Persian Gulf in 1990, he began a long debate with Congress over whether he would need a formal declaration of war before the troops were sent into combat. And a treaty signed by the president is little more than his promise to try to get the Senate to go along. (He can sign executive agreements without Senate consent, but most of these are authorized in advance by Congress.)[8]

By contrast, the leaders of other democratic nations (to say nothing of totalitarian ones) are often able to act with much greater freedom. While Reagan was arguing with Congress over whether we should assign any military advisers to El Salvador, the president of France, François Mitterrand, ordered twenty-five hundred combat troops to Chad with scarcely a ripple of opposition. A predecessor of Mitterrand, Charles de Gaulle, brought France into the Common Market over the explicit opposition of the French Assembly and granted independence to Algeria, then a French colony, without seriously consulting the Assembly.[9] The British prime minister brought his country into the European Common Market despite popular opposition and can declare war without the consent of Parliament.[10]

Evaluating the Power of the President

Whether one thinks the president too strong or too weak in foreign affairs depends not only on whether one holds a domestic or international point of view but also on whether one agrees or disagrees with his policies. Historian Arthur M. Schlesinger, Jr., thought that President Kennedy exercised commendable presidential vigor when he made a unilateral decision to impose a naval blockade on Cuba to induce the Soviets to remove missiles installed there. However, he viewed President Nixon's decision to extend United States military action in Vietnam into neighboring Cambodia as a deplorable example of the "imperial presidency."[11] To be sure, there were important differences between these two actions, but that is precisely the point: a president strong enough to do something that one thinks proper is also strong enough to do something that one finds wrong.

The Supreme Court has fairly consistently supported the view that the federal government has powers in the conduct of foreign and military policy beyond those specifically mentioned in the Constitution. The leading decision, rendered in 1936, holds that the right to carry out a foreign policy is an inherent attribute of any sovereign nation:

The power to declare and wage war, to conclude peace, to make treaties, to maintain diplomatic relations with other sovereignties, if they had never been mentioned in the Constitution, would have vested in the Federal Government as necessary concomitants of nationality.[12]

The individual states have few rights in foreign affairs.

Moreover, the Supreme Court has been most reluctant to intervene in disputes over the conduct of foreign affairs. When various members of Congress brought suit challenging the right of President

Nixon to enlarge the war in Vietnam without congressional approval, the court of appeals handled the issue, as one scholar was later to describe it, with all the care of porcupines making love. The court said that it was a matter for the president and Congress to decide and that if Congress was unwilling to cut off the money to pay for the war, it should not expect the courts to do the job for it.[13]

The Supreme Court upheld the extraordinary measures taken by President Lincoln during the Civil War and refused to interfere with the conduct of the Vietnam War by Presidents Johnson and Nixon.[14] After Iran seized American hostages in 1979, President Carter froze Iranian assets in this country. To win the hostages' freedom, the president later agreed to return some of these assets and to nullify claims on them by American companies. The Court upheld the nullification because it was necessary for the resolution of a foreign policy dispute.[15]

How great the deference to presidential power may be is vividly illustrated by the actions of President Franklin Roosevelt in ordering the army to move over one hundred thousand Japanese—the great majority of them born in this country and citizens of the United States—from their homes on the

In 1962 President Kennedy forced the Soviet Union to withdraw the missiles it had placed in Cuba after their presence was revealed by aerial photography.

Japanese-Americans awaiting transportation under military guard from their homes on the West Coast to relocation camps in the interior, where they remained for the duration of World War II.

Checks on Presidential Power

If there is a check on the powers of the federal government or the president in foreign affairs, it is chiefly political rather than constitutional. The most important check is Congress's control of the purse strings. In addition, Congress has imposed three important kinds of restrictions on the president's freedom of action, all since Vietnam:

1. Limitations on the president's ability to give military or economic aid to other countries   For example, between 1974 and 1978 the president could not sell arms to Turkey because of a dispute between Turkey and Greece over control of the island of Cyprus. The pressure on Congress from groups supporting Greece was much stronger than that from groups supporting Turkey. In 1976 Congress prevented President Ford from giving aid to the pro-Western faction in the Angolan civil war. Until the method was declared unconstitutional, Congress for many years could use a legislative veto, a resolution disapproving of an executive decision (see Chapter 13), to block the sale by the president of arms worth more than $25 million to another country.

2. The War Powers Act   Passed in 1973 over a presidential veto, this law placed the following restrictions on the president's ability to use military force:

- He must report in writing to Congress within forty-eight hours after he introduces U.S. troops into areas where hostilities have occurred or are imminent.

- Within sixty days after troops are sent into hostile situations, Congress must, by declaration of war or other specific statutory authorization, provide for the continuation of hostile action by U.S. troops.

- If Congress fails to provide such authorization, the president must withdraw the troops (unless Congress has been prevented from meeting as a result of an armed attack).

- If Congress passes a concurrent resolution (which the president may not veto) directing the removal of U.S. troops, the president must comply.

West Coast to inland "relocation centers" for the duration of World War II. Though this action was a wholesale violation of the constitutional rights of U.S. citizens and was unprecedented in American history, the Supreme Court decided that with the West Coast vulnerable to attack by Japan, the president was within his rights to declare that people of Japanese ancestry might pose a threat to internal security; thus the relocation order was upheld.[16] (No Japanese-American was ever found guilty of espionage or sabotage.) One of the few cases in which the Court denied the president broad wartime powers occurred in 1952, when by a 5-4 vote it reversed President Truman's seizure of the steel mills—a move that he had made in order to avert a strike that, in his view, would have imperiled the war effort in Korea.[17]

Under the War Powers Act the president has reported the use of troops to Congress on several occasions:

- President Ford three times sent armed forces to evacuate people from Communist-controlled areas in Cambodia and Vietnam.

- President Ford ordered the military to free the crew of the merchant ship *Mayaguez,* captured by Cambodia.

- President Carter sent troops (unsuccessfully) to rescue the Americans held hostage in Iran.

- President Reagan sent troops to try to restore order in Lebanon and to expel a pro-Cuban regime from the island of Grenada.

- President Bush invaded Panama.

No president has acknowledged the constitutionality of the War Powers Act. In its 1983 decision in the *Chadha* case the Supreme Court in effect struck down the part of the War Powers Act that authorizes the use of a legislative veto as well as all statutes authorizing legislative vetoes to control arms sales abroad.[18] The other parts of the War Powers Act—the notification provisions and the requirement that troops be withdrawn in sixty days unless war is formally declared—have not yet been tested in court.

Even if the law should be sustained by the courts, its practical political significance is unclear. Few members of Congress would challenge a military operation that was successful, as were the Panama and Grenada invasions. Some would rebuke the president for engaging in one that was swift and unsuccessful—but only after the fact. No one knows what effect the law would have if a president committed American forces to a protracted engagement of the sort that we had in Vietnam. Even after that war had become unpopular, Congress continued to appropriate money for its conduct. Not once from 1966 to 1973 did Congress cut off funds for the war or require the withdrawal of American troops by some specific date. When in 1982 President Reagan sent the Marines ashore in Beirut, Lebanon, as a peacekeeping force, Congress after much discussion passed a joint resolution authorizing them to remain there for up to eighteen months. The president

Rivalry Versus Cooperation: The President and the Senate

Because the Senate must ratify treaties and consent to the appointment of ambassadors and other high foreign policy officials, it has the opportunity to play a large role in the conduct of foreign affairs. The key figure in the Senate is usually the chairman of the Senate Foreign Relations Committee.

Depending on personalities and circumstances, the president and the chairman have sometimes been able to work together closely but at other times have been bitter, outspoken rivals. In general, cooperation occurs when there is a widely shared foreign policy worldview; rivalry erupts when worldviews diverge.

Periods of shared worldviews and political cooperation

President	Chairman of Foreign Relations Committee
Franklin D. Roosevelt	Tom Connally (1941–1947, 1949–1953)
Harry S Truman	Arthur H. Vandenberg (1947–1949)

Periods of competing worldviews and political rivalry

President	Chairman of Foreign Relations Committee
Woodrow Wilson	Henry Cabot Lodge (1919–1924)
Lyndon B. Johnson	J. William Fulbright (1959–1975)
Richard M. Nixon	J. William Fulbright (1959–1975)
Bill Clinton	Jesse Helms (1995–)

Harry S Truman with Senator Arthur Vandenberg

Despite predictions by critics that the United States would become bogged down in a long, costly ground war, the U.S. offensive against Iraq lasted only four days and took very few U.S. lives.

did not request this resolution, and it is not clear what would have happened had Congress not acted as it did. In time President Reagan withdrew the Marines, not because of congressional demands but because the situation in Lebanon had deteriorated to the point where our military presence had little peacekeeping value.

3. Intelligence oversight   Owing to the low political stock of President Nixon during the Watergate scandal and the revelations of illegal operations by the Central Intelligence Agency (CIA) within the United States, Congress required that the CIA notify appropriate congressional committees about any proposed covert action (between 1974 and 1980 it had to notify *eight* different committees). Today it must keep two groups, the House and the Senate Intelligence Committees, "fully and currently informed" of all intelligence activities, including covert actions. The committees do not have the authority to disapprove such actions.

However, from time to time Congress will pass a bill blocking particular covert actions. This happened when the Boland Amendment (named after its sponsor, Representative Edward Boland) was passed on several occasions between 1982 and 1985. Each version of the amendment prevented, for specifically stated periods, intelligence agencies from supplying military aid to the Nicaraguan contras. One of the issues raised during the Iran-contra investigation was whether the aid supplied by the staff of the National Security Council was illegal because it was provided by an "intelligence agency" within the meaning of the law.

The Machinery of Foreign Policy

From the time that Thomas Jefferson took the job in Washington's first administration until well into this century, foreign policy was often made and almost always carried out by the secretary of state. No more. When America became a major world power during and after World War II, our commitments overseas expanded dramatically. With that expansion two things happened. First, the president began to put foreign policy at the top of his agenda and to play a larger role in directing it. Second, that policy was shaped by the scores of agencies (some brand new) that had acquired overseas activities.

Today Washington, D.C., has not one State Department but many. The Defense Department has military bases and military advisers abroad. The Central Intelligence Agency has intelligence officers abroad, most of them assigned to "stations" that are part of the American embassy but not under the full control of the American ambassador there. The Departments of Agriculture, Commerce, and Labor have missions abroad. The Federal Bureau of Investigation and the Drug Enforcement Administration have agents abroad. The Agency for International Development has offices to dispense foreign aid in host countries. The United States Information Agency runs libraries, radio stations, and educational programs abroad.

Every new secretary of state bravely announces that he is going to "coordinate" and "direct" this enormous foreign policy establishment. He never does. The reason is partly that the job is too big for any one person and partly that most of these agencies owe no political or bureaucratic loyalty to the secretary of state. If anyone is to coordinate them, it will have to be the president. But the president cannot keep track of what all these organizations are doing in the more than 140 nations and fifty international organizations where we have representatives, nor in the more than eight hundred international conferences that we attend each year.

So he has hired a staff to do the coordinating for him. That staff is part of the National Security Council (NSC), a committee created by statute and chaired by the president, whose members include by law the vice president and the secretaries of state and defense, by custom the director of the CIA and the chairman of the Joint Chiefs of Staff, and often the attorney general. Depending on the president, the NSC can be an important body in which to hammer out foreign policy. Attached to it is a staff headed by the national security adviser. That staff, which usually numbers a few dozen men and women, can be (again, depending on the president) an enormously powerful instrument for formulating and directing foreign policy.

Nominally that staff exists only to bring before the president a balanced account of the views of the heads of the major government agencies with a stake

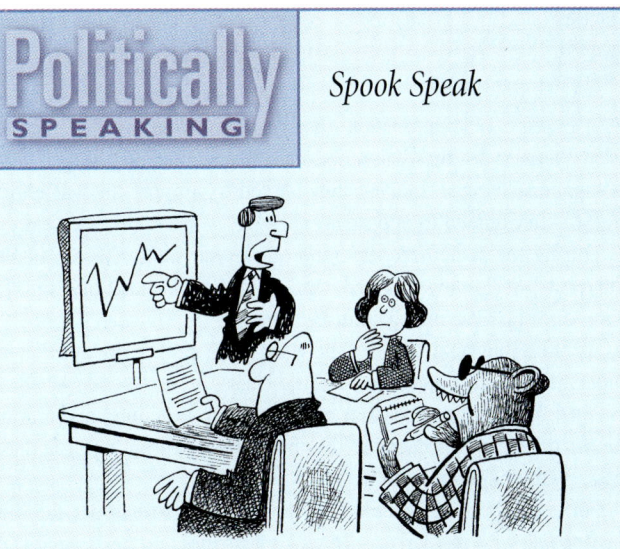

Politically SPEAKING

Spook Speak

Spook Speak is the jargon used by the Central Intelligence Agency and other intelligence organizations to refer to their activities and procedures. The terms include

- *Asset:* A foreign person who cooperates with the CIA, by furnishing information or assistance, but is not a CIA employee.

- *Black-bag job:* Secretly entering a home or office, without a warrant, to search it or plant a listening device.

- *Cover:* A false name and identity used to conceal the real identity of an intelligence officer or activity.

- *Covert action:* Secret or clandestine activity designed to influence events or governments abroad, including financial payments, propaganda, and military action.

- *Double agent:* An asset who is working both sides of the street, giving information or assistance to the intelligence service of one country while pretending to work for the service of another.

- *Family jewels:* The most important secrets (files or operations) of an intelligence agency.

- *Mole:* A person employed by one intelligence service who is actually spying on it for a hostile service.

- *Proprietary:* A private business firm that is actually owned and controlled by an intelligence agency: for example, an airline company that transports cargo for the CIA.

- *Safe house:* An innocent-appearing house or apartment used to hide intelligence officers or their assets.

SOURCE: Adapted from *Safire's Political Dictionary* by William Safire. Copyright © 1968, 1972, 1978 by William Safire. Reprinted by permission of Random House, Inc. and the author.

The Influence of the National Media

*B*etween 1964 and 1968 the position taken on the war in Vietnam by the major national magazines and the principal newspapers changed. In 1964 they tended to support the war effort; by 1968 they tended to oppose it.

During the same time the Survey Research Center (SRC) of the University of Michigan asked citizens for their positions on the war—once in 1964 and again in 1968.

As the table below shows, between 1964 and 1968 opinion of upper-middle-class and lower-middle-class people on the war effort changed much more than that of working-class people, *and* among the former, opinions changed the most among those who regularly read several magazines and newspapers.

For example: in 1964, a total of 78 percent of those upper-middle-class people who regularly read many magazines and newspapers felt that we should take a stronger stand in Vietnam, even if it meant invading North Vietnam. By 1968 only 40 percent of this group felt that way, a shift of 38 percent. By contrast, upper-middle-class people who did not regularly read several magazines and newspapers changed by only half as much—from 59 percent favoring a stronger stand in 1964 to 41 percent favoring it in 1968, an 18 percent shift. And among working-class people there was scarcely any media effect at all—a decline of 7 percent in the proportion favoring a stronger stand for both those who read a lot and those who did not.

Decline in Support for a Stronger Stand in Vietnam, by Social Class and Media Readership

	1964	1968	Change
Read several magazines and newspapers regularly			
Upper-middle class	78%	40%	−38
Lower-middle class	50	19	−31
Working class	55	48	−7
Do not read several magazines or newspapers			
Upper-middle class	59	41	−18
Lower-middle class	41	33	−8
Working class	45	38	−7

NOTE: Upper-middle class = white-collar workers earning over $10,000; Lower-middle-class = white-collar workers earning under $10,000; Working class = blue-collar workers. Omitted are non-whites, southerners, and persons with no opinion on the war.
SOURCE: James D. Wright, "Life, Time and the Fortunes of War." Published by permission of Transaction, Inc., from *Transaction,* vcol. 9, no. 3, copyright © January 1972 by Transaction, Inc.

in foreign policy decisions, to help the president choose among the options that these advisers identify, and to oversee the implementation of the presidential decision. These decisions are usually in the form of a National Security Decision Directive, or NSDD, signed by the president.

Presidents Truman and Eisenhower made only limited use of the NSC staff, but beginning with President Kennedy it has grown greatly in influence. Its head, the national security adviser, has come to rival the secretary of state for foreign policy leadership, especially when the adviser is a powerful personality such as Henry Kissinger. President Reagan attempted to downgrade the importance of the national security adviser, but ironically it was one of his relatively low-visibility appointees, Admiral John Poindexter, and his subordinate, Lieutenant Colonel Oliver North, who precipitated the worst crisis of the Reagan presidency when, allegedly without informing the president, they tried to use cash realized from the secret sale of arms to Iran to finance guerrillas fighting against the Marxist government of Nicaragua. The sale and the diversion became known, North was fired, a congressional investigation ensued, criminal charges were filed against Poindexter and North, and the president's political position was weakened.

But even in ordinary times the NSC staff is the rival of the secretary of state, except during that period in the Ford administration when Henry Kissinger held *both* jobs.

The way in which the machinery of foreign policy making operates has two major consequences for the substance of that policy. First, as former Secretary of State George Shultz asserted, "It's never over." Foreign policy issues are endlessly agitated, rarely settled. The reason is that the rivalries *within* the executive branch intensify the rivalries *between* that branch and Congress. In ways already described, Congress has steadily increased its influence over the conduct of foreign policy. Anybody in the executive branch who loses out in a struggle over foreign policy can take his or her case (usually by means of a well-timed leak) to a sympathetic member of Congress, who then can make a speech, hold a hearing, or introduce a bill.

The plan to have the NSC staff manage the Iran arms sale and the raising of private money for the contras may have been motivated by a desire to keep these controversial matters out of the leaky, conflict-ridden machinery by which foreign policy is normally made. If so, the effort was an exercise in futility; for no matter who carries out a policy, if it is controversial it will become public. Americans often worry that their government is keeping secrets from them. In fact there are no secrets in Washington—at least not for long.

The interests of the various organizations making up the foreign policy establishment profoundly affect the positions that they take. Because the State Department has a stake in diplomacy, it tends to resist bold or controversial new policies that might upset established relationships with other countries. Part of the CIA has a stake in gathering and analyzing information; that part tends to be skeptical of the claims of other agencies that their overseas operations are succeeding. Another part of the CIA conducts covert operations abroad; it tends to resent or ignore the skepticism of the intelligence analysts. The air force flies airplanes and so tends to be optimistic about what can be accomplished through the use of air power in particular and military power in general; the army, on the other hand, which must fight in the trenches, is often dubious about the prospects for military success.

Foreign Policy and Public Opinion

These organizational conflicts shape the details of foreign policy, but its broad outlines are shaped by public and elite opinion.

World War II was the great watershed event in American foreign policy. Before that time a clear majority of the American public opposed active involvement in world affairs. The public saw the costs of such involvement as being substantially in excess of the benefits, and only determined, skillful leaders were able, as was President Roosevelt during 1939–1940, to affect in even a limited fashion the diplomatic and military struggles then convulsing Europe and Asia.

Our participation in the war produced a dramatic shift in popular opinion that endured for three decades, supplying broad (though often ambiguous) public support for an internationalist for-

eign policy. World War II had this effect, alone among all wars that we have fought, for several reasons. First, it was almost the only universally popular war in which we have been engaged, one that produced few, if any, recriminations afterward. Second, the war seemed successful: an unmitigated evil (the Nazi regime) was utterly destroyed; an attack on our own land (by Japan at Pearl Harbor) was thoroughly avenged. Third, that war ended with the United States recognized as the dominant power on earth, owing to its sole possession of the atomic bomb and its enormous military and economic productivity.

In 1937, fully 94 percent of the American public preferred the policy of doing "everything possible to keep out of foreign wars" to the policy of doing "everything possible to prevent war, even if it means threatening to fight countries that fight wars." In 1939, after World War II had begun in Europe but before Pearl Harbor was attacked, only 13 percent of Americans polled thought that we should enter the war against Germany. Just a month before Pearl Harbor only 19 percent felt that the United States should take steps, at the risk of war, to prevent Japan from becoming too powerful.[19] Congress reflected the noninterventionist mood of the country: in the summer of 1941, with war breaking out almost everywhere, the proposal to continue the draft passed the House of Representatives by only one vote.

The Japanese attack on Pearl Harbor on December 7 changed all that. Not only was the American war effort supported almost unanimously, not only did Congress approve the declaration of war with only one dissenting vote, but World War II—unlike World War I—produced popular support for an active assumption of international responsibilities that continued after the war had ended.[20] Whereas after World War I a majority opposed U.S. entry into the League of Nations, after World War II a clear majority favored our entry into the United Nations.[21]

This willingness to see the United States remain a world force persisted until the 1960s, when the inconclusive war in Vietnam led an increasing proportion of citizens to return to isolationist sentiments. The number of people thinking that we should "keep independent" in world affairs as opposed to

The battleship *West Virginia* burning after being hit by Japanese warplanes at Pearl Harbor on December 7, 1941.

"working closely with other nations" rose from 10 percent in 1963 to 22 percent in 1969.[22] Even so, as late as 1967, after more than two years of war in Vietnam, 44 percent of Americans believed that this country had an obligation to "defend other Vietnams if they are threatened by communism."[23]

But the support for an internationalist American foreign policy was, and is, highly general and heavily dependent on the phrasing of poll questions, the opinions expressed by popular leaders, and the impact of world events. Public opinion, while more internationalist than once was the case, is both mushy and volatile. Just prior to President Nixon's decision to send troops into Cambodia, only 7 percent of the people said that they supported such a move. After the troops were sent and Nixon made a speech explaining his move, 50 percent of the public said that they supported it.[24] Similarly, only 49 percent of the people favored halting the American bombing of North Vietnam before President Johnson ordered such a halt in 1968; afterward 60 percent of the public said that it supported such a policy.[25]

Backing the President

Much of this volatility in specific opinions (as opposed to general mood) reflects the already-mentioned deference to the "commander in chief" and a desire to support the United States when it confronts other nations. Table 20.1 shows the proportion of people who said that they approved of the way the president was doing his job before and after various major foreign policy events. Each foreign crisis increased the level of public approval of the president, often dramatically. The most vivid illustration of this was the Bay of Pigs fiasco: an American-supported, American-directed invasion of Cuba by anti-Castro Cuban émigrés was driven back into the sea. President Kennedy accepted responsibility for the aborted project. His popularity *rose*. (Comparable data for domestic crises tend to show no similar effect.)

This tendency to "rally 'round the flag" has been carefully studied and seems to operate on behalf of any president engaged in any foreign policy initia-

TABLE 20.1 **Popular Reactions to Foreign Policy Crises**

Percentage of public saying that they approve of the way the president is handling his job

Foreign Policy Crisis		Before	After
1960	American U-2 spy plane shot down over Soviet Union	62%	68%
1961	Abortive landing at Bay of Pigs in Cuba	73	83
1962	Cuban missile crisis	61	74
1975	President Ford sends marine to rescue the *Mayaguez*	40	51
1979	American embassy in Teheran seized by Iranians	32	61
1980	Failure of military effort to rescue hostages in Iran	39	43
1983	U.S. invasion of Grenada	43	53
1989	U.S. invasion of Panama	71	80
1990	U.S. troops to Persian Gulf	60	75

SOURCE: Updated from Theodore J. Lowi, *The End of Liberalism* (New York: Norton, 1969), 184. Poll data are from Gallup poll. Time lapse between "before" and "after" samplings of opinion was in no case more than one month.

tive, whether force is used or not. One analysis of the standing of presidents in public opinion from Truman through Johnson (1945–1968) found that, even allowing for the effects of ups and downs in the economy and the decay in presidential popularity that almost always occurs during a presidential term of office, every president enjoys a boost in popularity immediately after an international crisis or major diplomatic event.[26] There is at least one exception to this tendency. The revelation that the Reagan administration was trying to swap arms for hostages in Iran led to a *drop* in the president's popularity—perhaps because the effort had been secret and was revealed by critics of it.

If presidents derive more political rewards from playing a foreign policy role rather than a domestic one, we would expect that most presidents would prefer the foreign policy role and that some presidents might even deliberately manufacture diplomatic "successes" to bolster their sagging popularity. Most presidents since 1941 have in fact felt that their most important tasks were in the field of foreign affairs, but the reality of global instability has probably had as much to do with that pattern as the political rewards of diplomacy. When presidents travel abroad, it is always as much for domestic political consumption as for any substantive effect. Since the rewards are so great, one wonders why any president would shun even risky international ventures.

One reason is that, though the president wins popular support during the early stages of an international crisis, that support tends to deteriorate if the crisis is not soon resolved or if a protracted and costly stalemate ensues. World War II is the only major war about which we have opinion data in which public support remained high throughout. World War I, though it commanded popular support at the time, led to bitter recriminations afterward; by 1937 nearly two-thirds of the American people thought that it was a mistake for the United States to have entered it.[27] Support for Truman's decision to send troops to Korea declined as the war went on: whereas initially about two-thirds of the people backed the decision, two years later only a bit more than a third thought that it had been a good idea.[28] Support for the decision of President Johnson to send troops to Vietnam followed almost exactly the same pattern: initial support gave way to mounting skepticism as the war dragged on inconclusively.[29] Though in retrospect we think of Vietnam as bitterly controversial and Korea as much less so, in fact *public* opinion was pretty much the same in both cases. What was different is that *elite* opinion protested our involvement in Vietnam, but not our participation in Korea.

The clearest lesson that history offers a president on the exercise of his war-making powers is this: either fight a popular crusade or fight only short wars that you can win quickly. Given the edge enjoyed by

FIGURE 20.1　Trends in Support for the Vietnam War, by Education

FIGURE 20.2　Trends in Support for the Vietnam War, by Age

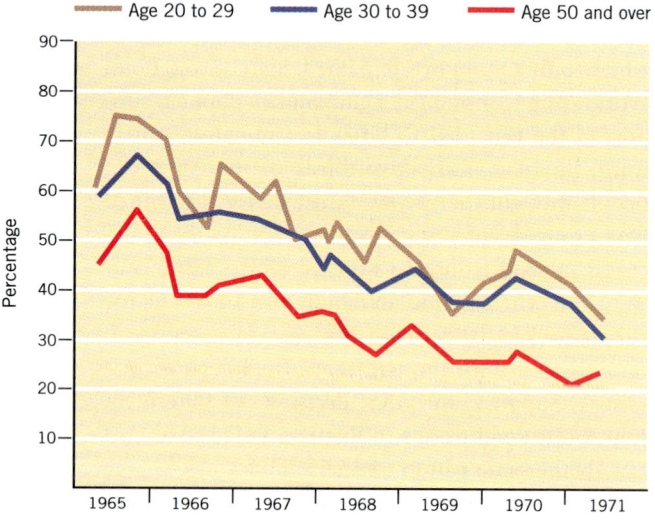

SOURCE: John E. Mueller, *War, Presidents, and Public Opinion* (New York: Wiley, 1973), 125, 139. Reprinted in 1985 by University Press of America, Lanham, Md., by permission of the author.

Democrats in party identification, it is noteworthy that two of the five times since 1945 that a Republican has won the presidency have been in the midst of an unpopular war—Eisenhower in 1952 and

Nixon in 1968. On a third occasion—Reagan in 1980—fifty-two Americans were being held hostage in Iran. It is not true that Democrats start wars and Republicans end them, but protracted military stalemates can help the party out of power get elected.

Mass versus Elite Opinion

The average citizen tends to be rather uninformed about world affairs (except when the United States is directly and dramatically involved), to support the president in most of his undertakings, and to judge the success of those undertakings largely on practical grounds. By contrast, members of the political elite tend to be well informed, to give much less support to the president, and to judge the success of his undertakings on philosophical rather than practical grounds.

In 1984, for example, fewer than half the voters knew that the United States was backing the government of El Salvador; a fifth thought, wrongly, that we were backing the rebels; and the rest did not know whom we were backing. In Nicaragua only a third thought, correctly, that we were supporting the rebels; a quarter thought that we were supporting the government.[30] Perhaps because of their lack of knowledge (but more likely because of their innate caution), the voters have repeatedly indicated that they oppose sending American troops to El Salvador or anywhere else in Central America. But if past experience (such as the Grenada invasion) is any guide, the public will give strong support to the president if he should decide to send in troops.

If troops are sent into the area, mass opinion will judge the success of the military action largely on pragmatic grounds. If we are successful, the people will approve. If we suffer important defeats or the war drags on, they will reduce their approval. During Vietnam, for example, the average citizen reacted adversely to the war when American troops suffered losses or seemed to be on the defensive.[31]

Elite opinion, on the other hand, is better informed but more volatile and moralistic. Initially, college-educated people gave *more* support to the war in Vietnam than those without college training; by the end of the war, however, college-educated support had decreased dramatically (see Figure

20.1). The reasons for that decline in support differed. Whereas the average citizen was upset when the United States seemed to be on the *defensive* in Vietnam, college-educated voters tended to be more upset when the United States was on the *offensive*.[32]

Though the average citizen did not want our military in Vietnam in the first place, he or she felt that we should support our troops once they were there. The average person also was deeply opposed to the antiwar protests taking place on college campuses. When the Chicago police roughed up antiwar demonstrators at the 1968 Democratic convention, public sentiment was overwhelmingly on the side of the police.[33] Contrary to myths much accepted at the time, younger people were *not* more opposed to the war than older ones (see Figure 20.2). There was no "generation gap."

By contrast, college-educated citizens, thinking at first that troops should be involved, soon changed their minds, decided that the war was wrong, and grew increasingly upset when the United States seemed to be enlarging the war (by invading Cambodia, for example). College students protested against the war largely on moral grounds, and their protests received more support from college-educated adults than from other citizens.

The cleavage between mass and elite opinion is even wider if you restrict the definition of *elite* to only those involved in making foreign policy rather than including all college-educated people. In Table 20.2 we see the differences in foreign policy views of a cross section of American citizens and a group of 341 leaders active in government, academia, the mass media, and various organizations concerned with foreign affairs.[34]

In general the leaders have a more liberal and internationalist outlook than the public: they are more likely to favor giving economic aid to other countries, defending our allies, reducing tariffs, and opposing oppressive regimes. The public, on the other hand, wants the United States to be less active overseas and worries about protecting the jobs of American workers. Accordingly, it wants the United States to keep tariffs high, protect American jobs from foreign competition, protect American businesses abroad from foreign threats, and give less economic aid to other nations.

TABLE 20.2 How the Public and the Elite See Foreign Policy, 1990

| | Percentage Agreeing | |
	Public	Leaders
It is very important to:		
Protect the jobs of American workers	65%	39%
Defend U.S. allies	61	56
Have worldwide arms control	53	80
Improve living standard in under-developed nations	41	42
Protect the interests of U.S. business abroad	63	27
Prevent the spread of nuclear weapons	59	94
Improve the global environment	58	72
Contain communism	56	10
U.S. should send troops if:		
Soviets invade Europe	58	87
Iraq invades Saudi Arabia[a]	52	89
Arabs invade Israel	43	70
U.S. should give economic aid to:		
Soviet Union	40	71

[a] Question asked after Iraq's invasion of Kuwait in August 1990.
SOURCE: *American Public Opinion and U.S. Foreign Policy, 1991* (Chicago: Chicago Council on Foreign Relations, 1991), 15, 34, 37.

Cleavages Among Foreign Policy Elites

As we have seen, public opinion on foreign policy is permissive and a bit mushy: it supports presidential action without giving it much direction. Elite opinion therefore acquires extraordinary importance. Of course events and world realities are also important, but since events have no meaning except as they are perceived and interpreted by people who must react to them, the attitudes and beliefs of those people in and out of government who are actively involved in shaping foreign policy often assume decisive importance. Contrary to the views of people who think that some shadowy, conspiratorial group of insiders runs our foreign policy, the foreign policy elite in this country is deeply divided.

Politically SPEAKING

Iron Curtain and Cold War

The **iron curtain** was neither iron nor a curtain; it was the political barrier, maintained by the Soviet Union, to free travel and communication between Eastern and Western Europe. In 1989 the iron curtain began to collapse. The phrase was given its present meaning by Winston Churchill in a speech that he delivered at Westminster College in Fulton, Missouri, on March 5, 1946: "From Stettin in the Baltic to Trieste in the Adriatic, an iron curtain has descended across the continent. Behind that line lie all the capitals of the ancient states of central and eastern Europe."

The **cold war** refers to the nonmilitary struggle between the United States (and its allies) and the former Soviet Union (and its allies). (A *cold war* is distinguished from a *hot*, or *shooting*, war.) The phrase was coined by journalist Herbert Bayard Swope in 1946 and popularized by columnist Walter Lippmann.

SOURCE: Adapted from *Safire's Political Dictionary* by William Safire. Copyright © 1968, 1972, 1978 by William Safire. Reprinted by permission of Random House, Inc. and the author.

That elite consists not only of those people with administrative positions in the foreign policy field—the senior officials of the State Department and the staff of the National Security Council—but also the members and staffs of the key congressional committees concerned with foreign affairs (chiefly the Senate Foreign Relations Committee and the House Foreign Affairs Committee) and various private organizations that help shape elite opinion, such as the members of the Council on Foreign Relations and the editors of two important publications, *Foreign Affairs* and *Foreign Policy.* To these must be added influential columnists and editorial writers whose work appears regularly in the national press. One could extend the list by adding ever-wider circles of people with some influence (lobbyists, professors, leaders of veterans' organizations); this would complicate without changing the central point: elite beliefs are probably more important in explaining foreign policy than in accounting for decisions in other policy areas.

How a Worldview Shapes Foreign Policy

These beliefs can be described in simplified terms as **worldviews** (or, as some social scientists put it, as paradigms)—more or less comprehensive mental pictures of the critical problems facing the United States in the world and of the appropriate and inappropriate ways of responding to these problems. The clearest, most concise, and perhaps most influential statement of one worldview that held sway for many years was in an article published in 1947 in *Foreign Affairs,* entitled "The Sources of Soviet Conduct."[35] Written by a "Mr. X" (later revealed to be George F. Kennan, director of the Policy Planning Staff of the State Department and thereafter ambassador to Moscow), the article argued that the Russians were pursuing a policy of expansion that could only be met by the United States' applying "unalterable counterforce at every point where they show signs of encroaching upon the interests of a peaceful and stable world." This he called the strategy of "containment," and it became the governing principle of American foreign policy for at least two decades.

There were critics of the containment policy at the time—Walter Lippmann, in his book *The Cold War,* argued against it in 1947[36]—but the criticisms were less influential than the doctrine. A dominant worldview is important precisely because it prevails over alternative views. One reason why it prevails is that it is broadly consistent with the public's mood. In 1947, when Kennan wrote, popular attitudes toward the Soviet Union, favorable during World War II when Russia and America were allies, had turned quite hostile. In 1946 less than one-fourth of the American people believed that Russia could be trusted to cooperate with this country,[37] and by 1948 over three-fourths were convinced that the

Alternative Worldviews of the United States: Relations During the Cold War

Containment View

Communism is a monolithic threat.

If we don't intervene overseas, we may get dragged into war.

We must nip aggression in the bud.

Only American military superiority will contain Soviet expansionism and preserve peace.

> *Let every nation know that we shall pay any price, bear any burden, meet any hardship, support any friend, oppose any foe to assure the survival and success of liberty.*

President John F. Kennedy,
inaugural address, 1960

Disengagement or Vietnam View

Communism is a divided movement.

If we do intervene overseas, we are sure to get into a war.

We are not the world's police force.

Only arms limitation treaties and reductions in military force will preserve peace.

> *[It means] an even more positive commitment to coexistence with the Communist countries. It means a much more determined effort to get military competition with the Soviets under control. . . . It means abandoning the Sub-Imperial ambitions in the Third World and recognizing instead that there is little we can do to influence political development in this part of the world and less that we need to do now.*

John Kenneth Galbraith,
writing in *Esquire*, March 1972

SOURCE: Adapted from Michael Roskin, "From Pearl Harbor to Vietnam: Shifting Generational Paradigms and Foreign Policy," *Political Science Quarterly* 89 (Fall 1974): 576.

Soviet Union was trying not simply to defend itself but to become the dominant world power.[38]

Such a worldview was also influential because it was consistent with events at the time: Russia had occupied most of the previously independent countries of Eastern Europe and was turning them into puppet regimes. When governments independent of both the United States and the Soviet Union attempted to rule in Hungary and Czechoslovakia, they were overthrown by Soviet-backed coups. A worldview also becomes dominant when it is consistent with the prior experiences of the people holding it.

Three Worldviews Every generation of political leaders comes to power with a foreign policy worldview shaped, in large measure, by the real or apparent mistakes of the previous generation.[39] This pattern can be traced back, some have argued, to the very beginnings of the nation. Frank L. Klingberg traces the alteration since 1776 of national "moods" (here called worldviews) that favored first "extroversion" (or an active, internationalist policy) and then "introversion" (a less-active, even isolationist posture).[40]

Since the 1920s American elite opinion has moved through three dominant worldviews:

Politically SPEAKING — *Domino Theory*

In 1954 President Eisenhower said that "you have a row of dominoes set up; you knock over the first one, and what will happen to the last one is that it will go over very quickly." He used this analogy to justify giving economic aid to South Vietnam to prevent it, and thus its Southeast Asian neighbors, from being taken over by communists.

Supporters of aid to South Vietnam accepted this **domino theory;** opponents of that aid denied the theory, arguing (as did novelist Norman Mailer) that these countries were not dominoes but "sand castles" that were being engulfed by a "tide of nationalism."

In the 1980s the domino theory was part of the argument about whether we should help El Salvador and support the contras in Nicaragua as a way of keeping Central America from being dominated by Marxist governments.

For the record: after South Vietnam fell to communist North Vietnam, two other nearby dominoes—Cambodia and Laos—also went communist, but Thailand did not.

SOURCE: Adapted from *Safire's Political Dictionary* by William Safire. Copyright © 1968, 1972, 1978 by William Safire. Reprinted by permission of Random House, Inc. and the author.

A meeting that named an era: In Munich, British Prime Minister Neville Chamberlain attempted to appease the territorial ambitions of Hitler. Chamberlain's failure brought World War II closer.

isolationism, antiappeasement (or the "Munich–Pearl Harbor" paradigm), and disengagement. **Isolationism** was the view adopted as a result of our unhappy experience in World War I. Our efforts to help European allies had turned sour: thousands of American troops had been killed in a war that had seemed to accomplish little and certainly had not made the world, in Woodrow Wilson's words, "safe for democracy." As a result, in the 1920s and 1930s elite opinion (and popular opinion) opposed getting involved in European wars.

The **containment** (or **antiappeasement**) paradigm was the result of World War II. At a conference in Munich, efforts of British and French leaders to satisfy Hitler's territorial demands in Europe had led not to "peace in our time," as Prime Minister Neville Chamberlain of Britain had claimed, but to ever-greater territorial demands and ultimately to world war. This crisis brought to power men determined not to repeat their predecessors' mistakes: "Munich" became a synonym for weakness, and leaders such as Winston Churchill made antiappeasement the basis of their postwar policy of resisting Soviet expansionism. Churchill summed up the worldview that he had acquired from the Munich era in a famous speech delivered in 1946 in Fulton, Missouri, in which he coined the term *Iron Curtain* to describe Soviet policy in Eastern Europe.

Pearl Harbor was the death knell for isolationism. Senator Arthur H. Vandenberg of Michigan, a staunch isolationist before the attack, became an ardent internationalist not only during but after the war. He later wrote of the Japanese attack on Pearl Harbor on December 7, 1941: "That day ended isolationism for any realist."[41]

The events leading up to World War II were the formative experiences of those leaders who came to power in the 1940s, 1950s, and 1960s. What they took to be the lessons of Munich and Pearl Harbor were applied repeatedly—in building a network of defensive alliances in Europe and Asia during the late 1940s and 1950s, in operating an airlift to aid West Berlin when road access to it was cut off by the Russians, in coming to the aid of South Korea, and finally in intervening in Vietnam. Most of these applications of the containment worldview were successful in the sense that they did not harm American interests, they proved welcome to allies, or they prevented a military conquest.

The **disengagement** (or "Vietnam") view resulted from the experience of the younger foreign policy elite that came to power in the 1970s. Unlike previous applications of the antiappeasement view, our entry into Vietnam had led to a military defeat and a domestic political disaster. There were three ways of interpreting that crisis: (1) we applied the correct worldview in the right place but did not try hard enough; (2) we had the correct worldview but tried to apply it in the wrong place under the wrong circumstances; (3) the worldview itself was wrong. By and large the critics of our Vietnam policy tended toward the third conclusion, and thus when they supplanted in office the architects of our Vietnam policy, they inclined toward a worldview based on the slogan "no more Vietnams." Critics of this view called it the "new isolationism," arguing that it would encourage Soviet expansion.

How elites think about Vietnam affects their foreign policy views right down to the present. The answers to poll questions differ sharply depending on the respondents' opinion of the war in Vietnam. The foreign policy leaders who thought that the war in Vietnam was "fundamentally wrong and immoral" were only half as likely as those who were not so critical of Vietnam to support the use of U.S. troops to protect South Korea from a North Korean invasion or to remove Soviet missiles from Nicaragua.[42]

To a great extent the foreign policy elite that held the disengagement view came to power during the

TABLE 20.3 Cleavages in the Elite: Reagan Administration Officials versus Other Foreign Policy Leaders

	Percentage Agreeing	
	Reagan Officials	Other Leaders
In foreign policy Congress is too strong	77%	28%
Favor a nuclear freeze	40	82
Goal of containing communism is very important	86	40
Vietnam war was immoral	5	45
Favor military aid to rebels fighting communist-supported governments	100	48
Favor negotiating with terrorists	0	23
In Middle East I sympathize more with Israel	32	63
U.S. efforts to overthrow leftist government of Nicaragua were "excellent" or "good"	70	15

SOURCE: *American Public Opinion and U.S. Foreign Policy, 1987* (Chicago: Chicago Council on Foreign Relations, 1987), 38.

administration of President Jimmy Carter. They were replaced during the administration of President Ronald Reagan by leaders who held a different view. The elite that is out of power stays active by participating in the work of think tanks, foundations, and universities—liberal ones when conservatives are in power, conservative ones when liberals are in power.

Just how deep the cleavages in elite opinion can be is shown in Table 20.3. On virtually every issue there were huge differences in opinion between Reagan administration officials and foreign policy leaders who were out of government. The Reagan officials worried about the power of Congress, thought that containing communism was very important, supported military aid to the contras in Nicaragua and to insurgents in other countries where they were opposing communist governments, and rejected the idea that the war in Vietnam had been immoral. The foreign policy elite not in office expressed very nearly the opposite of these views. When Bill Clinton became president, he brought to the White House attitudes shaped by his youthful opposition to American involvement in Vietnam.

U.S. Marines escorting emergency food supplies to rural villages in Somalia.

The language of Vietnam continues to color discussions of foreign policy. Almost every military initiative since then has been debated in terms of whether it would lead us into "another Vietnam": sending the Marines to Lebanon, invading Grenada, dispatching military advisers to El Salvador, supporting the contras in Nicaragua, helping South American countries fight drug producers, sending troops to the Persian Gulf to force Iraq to abandon its invasion of Kuwait, sending troops to Somalia, and using American air power in Bosnia.

The Beginning of a New Era

After more than forty years, the cold war ended. After nearly three-quarters of a century, the Soviet Union collapsed. A new era in American foreign policy began.

These dramatic changes started in 1985 when Mikhail Gorbachev became the Soviet leader. A dedicated communist, he discovered that communism was not working. The Soviet Union and its empire were on the brink of economic collapse. Neither the USSR nor its satellite governments in Eastern Europe could feed their people. In Poland a workers' movement, Solidarity, had challenged the government. Disparate ethnic groups inside the USSR were seething with discontent. Inefficiency and corruption were rampant.

Americans holding the antiappeasement view welcomed the fall of the iron curtain and the creation of freely elected governments in Czechoslovakia, East Germany, Hungary, and Poland, but they warned that the Soviet Union remained a powerful and dangerously unpredictable force in the world. Gorbachev, they said, may have let go of his empire, but it was only out of economic necessity, not due to any fundamental change in Soviet thinking. Given this view, these elites urged the United States not to dismantle its armed forces, not to give direct economic aid to the USSR until it had created more democratic political institutions and a freer economic system, and to be wary of signing any further arms-reduction treaties until it was clear that the USSR had actually abandoned its efforts to impose its will on other nations.

Foreign policy elites holding the disengagement outlook took a more optimistic view of the changes under way in Moscow. They argued that these changes fundamentally and irreversibly reduced the Soviet threat to the United States and that our policy should be based on that assessment. Since Europe was now safe from Soviet attack, our forces there could be dramatically reduced. Since the USSR no longer had the will to attack the United States, our ballistic missiles, designed to deter such an attack, could be cut back as well. Since the Soviet Union faced an economic crisis that, if not resolved, might lead to more dangerous leaders' coming to power,

U.S. MILITARY INTERVENTION IN THE MIDDLE EAST

the United States should give economic aid to Gorbachev.

These rival predictions were quickly put to the test in ways that surprised almost everybody. The strength of a worldview is that it draws lessons from history; the weakness of one is that it can be upset by an unexpected turn in history. This turn began on August 19, 1991, when certain top Soviet officials, including the head of the KGB (the Soviet secret police), launched a coup against Gorbachev. He was held captive in his summer home while KGB, military, and party leaders announced that they had assumed power. Boris Yeltsin, the president of Russia, denounced the coup and stated that he would not surrender certain Moscow government buildings to the forces controlled by the coup leaders. He called upon Western leaders not to recognize the new government being installed by the coup; they did not. He urged the people of Moscow to rally to his defense. And they did.

On August 21, two days after it began, the coup collapsed and Gorbachev was released. Soon thereafter the plotters were arrested. Yeltsin, whom many Western leaders had previously dismissed as a buffoon who drank too much, had become a hero. Yeltsin (who as president of Russia headed the largest single part of the USSR) forced Gorbachev to relinquish his powers and his office. But more than Gorbachev was overthrown; the Soviet Union itself was abolished.

Third World

Originally a French term (*triers monde*) referring to nations neutral in the cold war between the United Nations and the Soviet Union, the **Third World** now means almost any underdeveloped nation in Africa, Asia, Latin America, or the Middle East.

When the oil-producing nations, such as Saudi Arabia, became wealthy after having succeeded in raising oil prices in the early 1970s, some observers began to use a new phrase, the *Fourth World,* to refer to underdeveloped nations that had no oil reserves and thus had to pay heavily for imported oil.

And some nations, such as Taiwan and the Republic of Korea, once thought to be part of the Third World because they were underdeveloped have made such startling economic progress that they are now referred to as the "newly industrialized nations" (NINs).

SOURCE: Adapted from *Safire's Political Dictionary* by William Safire. Copyright © 1968, 1972, 1978 by William Safire. Reprinted by permission of Random House, Inc. and the author.

On December 8, the leaders of Russia, the Ukraine, and Byelorussia announced that the Soviet Union no longer existed and that each of them, along with several other regions of the former USSR, would become independent states with their own representation in foreign capitals. In order to provide some kind of union for the management of common problems, including what to do with the massive Soviet armed forces, the Commonwealth of Independent States was formed. It was governed by a loose confederation (not too different from the system set up by the Articles of Confederation, under which the United States governed itself after declaring its independence from England). The once formidable Soviet Union had fragmented, dramatically altering the landscape of world politics.

America's Role in the New Era

The end of the cold war did not mean the end of American foreign policy challenges. In some ways, the new challenges were more difficult to manage. Before, many people thought that it was only necessary to decide on the magnitude of the Soviet threat and prepare accordingly. With the collapse of the Soviet Union it became necessary to prepare for any number of hard-to-predict threats. These threats included the following:

- **More coups in Russia:** The coup that toppled Gorbachev may not be the last one. Yeltsin or one of his successors could be overthrown. Reactionary leaders desirous of ending Yeltsin's cooperation with the West could come to power, gaining control of the still formidable Russian armed forces and its arsenal of nuclear weapons.

- **Fighting within and among the remnants of the Soviet empire:** Ethnic warfare erupted in many regions within the former Soviet Union and between Serbs and Croatians within the former nation of Yugoslavia. These conflicts, especially in Yugoslavia, drew other nations in.

- **Ancient antagonisms in such explosive regions as the Middle East:** When there were two rival superpowers, there were limits to how far a Middle Eastern nation might go in challenging its neighbors, for fear of provoking a response from the United States or the USSR. But with only one superpower, the United States (which was cutting back on its military strength), left there were fewer checks on Middle Eastern military threats.

- **The spread of nuclear weapons:** Saddam Hussein tried to build his own nuclear bomb, and no doubt he and other nations will try again. Many people believe that such weapons exist in North Korea.

- **The rise of China:** The Chinese economy is growing rapidly but the country remains under communist control. Some day China may be a large military power in Asia.

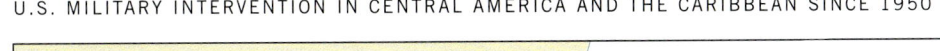

U.S. MILITARY INTERVENTION IN CENTRAL AMERICA AND THE CARIBBEAN SINCE 1950

UNITED STATES

ATLANTIC OCEAN

GULF OF MEXICO

BAHAMAS

1962: U.S. naval blockade of Cuba to prevent installation of Soviet missiles.

1965: U.S. troops occupy Dominican Republic to block takeover by Communist regime.

Havana

CUBA

VIRGIN ISLANDS (U.S.)

1961: U.S.– sponsored invasion of Cuba fails at Bay of Pigs.

MEXICO

JAMAICA

HAITI DOMINICAN REPUBLIC

PUERTO RICO (U.S.)

BELIZE

GUATEMALA

1980–?: U.S. conducts joint military operations with Honduras.

CARIBBEAN SEA

HONDURAS

1954: U.S. helps overthrow Marxist government in Guatemala.

1982–1989: CIA supports anti-government guerrillas in Nicaragua.

GRENADA

EL SALVADOR NICARAGUA

1981: U.S. military advisers sent to help government of El Salvador.

COSTA RICA Panama Canal Zone

1983: U.S. troops invade Grenada to oust pro-Cuba government.

PACIFIC OCEAN

PANAMA

1989: U.S. invades Panama, ousts dictator Manuel Noriega.

COLOMBIA

VENEZUELA

How the United States reacts to these possibilities will be heavily influenced by elite opinion. Some argue that the United States cannot be the "world's policeman" and so should cut back drastically on its armed forces. Others rejoin that while the United States should not intervene everywhere, it is the only power capable of preventing the rise of regional aggressors (such as Saddam Hussein in Iraq), and so it must remain strong, albeit with armed forces organized and equipped in ways different from what was necessary when the USSR posed the major threat.

This disagreement reflects a long-standing conflict between two worldviews. To some extent, the difference between the containment and the disengagement worldviews corresponds to the difference between conservatives and liberals. But not entirely: when Pat Buchanan, a conservative, challenged George Bush for the 1992 presidential nomination, he argued for the disengagement (or even the old isolationist) worldview. And when the army in Haiti overthrew its democratically elected president, some liberals, such as Senator John Kerry (D., Mass.), argued for a U.S. invasion to put the Haitian president back in power.

The Growing Role of the United Nations

The United Nations has had a long history of efforts to settle conflicts between member nations. Between 1948 and 1993 it sent more than thirty missions to monitor cease-fire agreements, observe national elections to make sure they were fair, or provide security for humanitarian operations. Most of these missions involved small numbers of troops contributed by United Nations members. Before 1991 it was rare for either the Soviet Union or the United States to provide any of these peacekeeping forces; the antagonism between the two great powers made such cooperation almost impossible, and the presence of either one alone in a UN force would have undercut the UN's appearance of neutrality.

UNITED NATIONS DEPLOYMENTS, 1993

With the collapse of the Soviet Union and the end of the cold war, the United Nations is no longer dominated by the conflict between the United States and the Soviet Union. The United Nations' military effort in Kuwait was organized and largely controlled by the United States and was not opposed by Russia. UN peacekeeping missions have also become more numerous. The UN played a role in sending troops that attempted to restore order in Somalia and that tried to protect humanitarian aid being shipped into what once was Yugoslavia. By 1993 U.S. troops were part of UN missions in seven different locations around the globe.

Some American leaders welcomed this development as the beginning of a new era in which the U.S. would use force in other parts of the world only, or chiefly, as part of a UN effort involving many nations. But other leaders worried that the U.S., as the sole remaining military superpower, ought not to let its forces be directed by an international organization in which the U.S. had but one vote.* The former leaders want the U.S. to work through the UN;

* In the UN General Assembly the U.S. has one vote out of 184 members; in the Security Council the U.S. has one vote out of fifteen, but that one Security Council vote entitles it to block any action of which it disapproves.

the latter ones do not want to see U.S. policy controlled by other nations (many of which have dictatorial or hostile governments). As political conflict erupts around the globe with seemingly increasing frequency and intensity, the United States' relationship to the United Nations is likely to continue to be an important foreign policy issue. Liberals, especially those with a disengagement worldview, often want the United States to use military force abroad only as part of a United Nations effort. Conservatives, especially those with an antiappeasement worldview, tend to favor acting without United Nations authority or controls.

SUMMARY

The great issues of national diplomacy are shaped by majoritarian politics. The president is the dominant figure, political ideology is important, and interest groups are only moderately important (unless the diplomatic issue involves differential costs and benefits, as it does when dealing with foreign trade).

But the majority opinion is weakly defined. It prefers that the United States mind its own business; when this country does become involved overseas, public opinion does not have strongly held views about most of our international activities, except to urge that we put American interests, especially economic ones, first. However, in a crisis or the aftermath of a bold presidential initiative, popular opinion tends to follow the presidential lead.

Given the loose and permissive quality of public opinion, elite opinion is usually very important. Foreign policy activists tend to hold to one or another rather well defined worldview, or paradigm (ideology, if you prefer). Before World War II the elite view was *isolationist;* after Pearl Harbor and lasting until Vietnam it displayed the *containment* or antiappeasement perspective; since Vietnam it has been deeply divided between those who still favor containment and those who favor *disengagement* from military commitments.

Elite views are also shaped by the organizational interests of the machinery by which foreign policy is made. That machinery is so large and complex as to be beyond the control of the secretary of state, who is often reduced to being one player among many. Through the National Security Council and the national security adviser, the president tries to coordinate that machinery, but sometimes he does so in ways that make the NSC staff independent players with their own agenda.

These executive branch divisions exacerbate the conflict between the president and Congress over the direction of foreign policy. Since the early 1970s Congress has become more assertive, passing laws (sometimes over presidential vetoes) that curb the president's ability to sell arms abroad or engage in covert operations (the Boland Amendments), that attempt to limit the president's ability to commit troops overseas (the War Powers Act), and that require the CIA to report to congressional committees.

KEY TERMS

worldviews   *p. 620*

isolationism   *p. 622*

containment (or antiappeasement)   *p. 622*

disengagement   *p. 623*

Spook Speak   *p. 613*

iron curtain   *p. 620*

cold war   *p. 620*

domino theory   *p. 622*

Third World   *p. 626*

SUGGESTED READINGS

Allison, Graham T. *Essence of Decision: Explaining the Cuban Missile Crisis.* Boston: Little, Brown, 1971. Shows how the decision made by a president during a major crisis was shaped by bureaucratic and organizational factors.

Blechman, Barry M., and Stephen S. Kaplan. *Force without War: U.S. Armed Forces as a Political Instrument.* Washington, D.C.: Brookings Institution, 1978. Describes how and with what effect American military power is used as an instrument of foreign policy.

Cohen, Benjamin J. *The Question of Imperialism.* New York: Basic Books, 1973. Careful analysis of theories claiming that economic motives control American foreign policy.

Destler, I. M. *Presidents, Bureaucrats, and Foreign Policy.* Princeton, N.J.: Princeton University Press, 1972. Analyzes the perennial struggle between the White House and the State Department.

Dougherty, James, and Robert Pfaltzgraff. *American Foreign Policy: FDR to Reagan.* New York: Harper & Row, 1986. Brief history of U.S. foreign policy since 1932.

Henkin, Louis. *Foreign Affairs and the Constitution.* New York: Norton, 1975. How the Supreme Court has interpreted the constitutional sources of the government's war and foreign policy powers.

Hilsman, Roger. *The Politics of Policymaking in Defense and Foreign Affairs.* Englewood Cliffs, N.J.: Prentice-Hall, 1987. Good review of the various theories of how foreign policy is made, by a scholar who was also a State Department official in the 1960s.

Kissinger, Henry. *White House Years.* Boston: Little, Brown, 1979. A brilliant insider's account of the politics and tactics of "high diplomacy" during the Nixon administration.

Mueller, John E. *War, Presidents, and Public Opinion.* New York: Wiley, 1973. Best summary of the relationship between presidential foreign policy decisions and public opinion.

Wittkopf, Eugene R. *Faces of Internationalism: Public Opinion and American Foreign Policy* (Durham, N.C.: Duke University Press, 1990). A useful review of public opinion toward America's international roles.

21

Military Policy

★ How the military is organized

★ Interservice rivalry

★ The defense budget

★ Defense spending

★ What we get for our money

★ The "$435 hammer"

★ Congress versus the president

The politics of the military are captured in movies about the military. In *Heartbreak Ridge* the American invasion of Grenada is a skillful maneuver by tough Marines led by sergeant-major Clint Eastwood. But in *Platoon* land warfare is a bloody, confused, brutal experience with angry men and incompetent leaders. In *Top Gun* Tom Cruise, a sassy but superb naval aviator, flies an F-14 jet fighter with extraordinary precision. But in *Dr. Strangelove* pilots are dolts led by mindless generals and mad scientists.

The inconsistent images are matched by apparently inconsistent facts: in 1985 most Americans applauded the beautifully coordinated maneuver in which navy fighters forced down an Egyptian airliner carrying the terrorists who had hijacked a cruise ship; two years earlier most Americans were enraged by stories that "idiots" in the navy had paid $435 for a common hammer.

One view of the military holds that national defense is a vital function of the federal government whose goals and means are determined by debates about the international balance of power. As in any large venture, there are honest mistakes, agonizing struggles, and bureaucratic stupidities. This view sees defense policy making as an example of majoritarian politics, often reinforced by deep feelings of patriotism but sometimes fouled up by inevitable human error.

Another view is that defense policy making is nothing but a gigantic boondoggle that exposes innocent men and women to unnecessary hazards to satisfy the demands of client groups and special interests or to advance dubious national objectives that sometimes are merely a cloak for the economic imperialism of multinational corporations.

In the first view, the benefits and costs of national defense are widely distributed: everybody is protected, every taxpayer foots the bill, and accordingly, the size and purpose of our military establishment broadly reflects the realities of our international situation and the shape of public opinion. Before World War II we had a small standing army because there were no obvious threats to our security and because

631

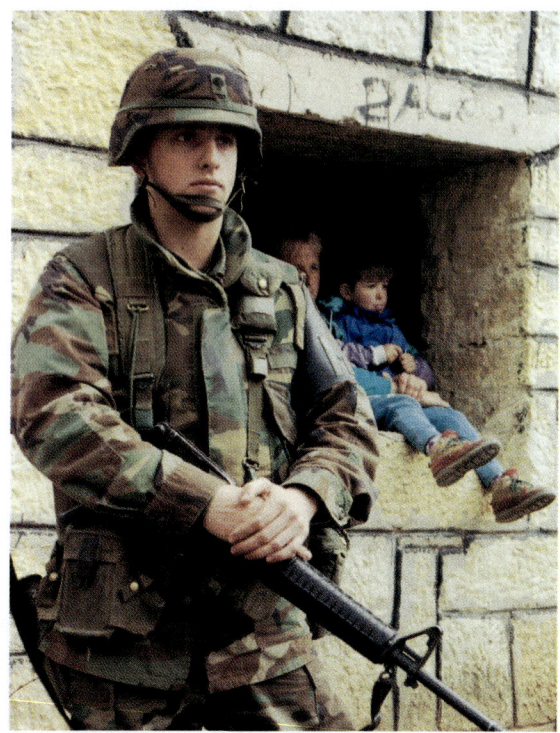

Increasingly, U.S. troops are used not to fight wars but to maintain peace, as here in Bosnia.

public opinion was isolationist. Since that time, according to this view, we have maintained a large military establishment because our role in the world has grown and public opinion has been concerned about the Soviet threat. We do not always agree about military matters—the debate over the wisdom of our intervention in Vietnam was bitter and lasting—but at least we are debating national purpose, not private advantage.

In the second view, the only real beneficiaries of military spending are generals, admirals, big corporations, and members of Congress whose districts get fat defense contracts. Everyone pays, but only some well-placed clients benefit. The size of the defense budget reflects the lobbying skills of Pentagon bureaucrats, not the realities of any threat to the United States. Reductions in international tensions and the U.S.–Soviet arms race were frustrated by the stake that the **military-industrial complex** (the sup-

posedly unified political bloc consisting of the Defense Department and industries that build military weapons) had in large defense budgets. Adherents to this view of the military argue that although we have seen cuts in defense spending since the end of the cold war, the defense budget would be even lower were it not for the continuing power of the military-industrial complex.

To understand what the people who hold these views are arguing about, we must first examine the structure of defense decision making and describe how the defense budget is determined. Then we'll turn to the politics of billion-dollar missiles and $435 hammers.

The Structure of Defense Decision Making

The formal structure within which decisions about national defense are made was in large part created after World War II, but it reflects concerns that go back at least to the time of the Founding. Chief among these is the persistent desire by citizens to ensure civilian control over the military.

The National Security Act of 1947 and its subsequent amendments created the Department of Defense (see Figure 21.1). It is headed by the secretary of defense, under whom serve the secretaries of the army, the air force, and the navy as well as the Joint Chiefs of Staff. The secretary of defense, who must be a civilian (though one former general, George C. Marshall, was allowed by Congress to be the secretary), exercises, on behalf of the president, command authority over the defense establishment. The secretary of the army, the secretary of the navy,* and the secretary of the air force also are civilians and are subordinate to the secretary of defense. Unlike him, they do not attend cabinet meetings or sit on the National Security Council. In essence, they manage the "housekeeping" functions of the various armed services, under the general direction of the secretary of defense and his deputy and assistant secretaries of defense.

* The secretary of the navy manages two services: the navy and the Marine Corps.

FIGURE 21.1 Department of Defense

DEPARTMENT OF DEFENSE

SOURCE: *The United States Government Manual, 1996–97.*

The four armed services are separate entities; by law they cannot be merged or commanded by a single military officer, and each has the right to communicate directly with Congress. There are two reasons for having separate uniformed services functioning within a single department: the fear of many citizens that a unified military force might become too powerful politically, and the desire of each service to preserve its traditional independence and autonomy. The result, of course, is a good deal of interservice rivalry and bickering, but this is precisely what Congress intended when it created the Department of Defense. Rivalry and bickering, it was felt, would ensure that Congress would receive the maximum amount of information about military affairs and would enjoy the largest opportunity to affect military decisions.

Interservice rivalry has provided just this kind of opportunity to Congress. In 1948 the air force wanted to take over naval aviation; the navy counterattacked by criticizing the effectiveness of air force bombers and argued instead for building large aircraft carriers. When the navy was refused permission to build the "supercarriers" that it had in mind, several admirals resigned in protest. In the 1960s the navy and air force argued again, this time over a new fighter aircraft (the TFX), only one type of which was to be built. The air force wanted a plane to fly over long distances and to carry nuclear weapons; the navy wanted one to take off and land from aircraft carriers and to fly at high speed for short distances. The air force was seeking to enlarge the role of manned aircraft as a major part of our deterrent forces; the navy wanted to preserve the role of the carrier as a strategic force.

Though disputes like these often employ the usual techniques of bureaucratic infighting—leaking information to the press, mobilizing sympathetic members of Congress, hiring rival civilian "experts"—they are not *merely* infighting, for they focus attention on major issues of defense policy.

Since the end of World War II Congress has aimed both to retain a significant measure of control over the military's decision making and to ensure the adequacy of the nation's defenses. Congress does not want a single military command headed by an all-powerful general or admiral, but neither does it want the services to be so autonomous or their heads so equal that coordination and efficiency suffer. In 1986 Congress passed and the president signed a defense reorganization plan known as the Goldwater-Nichols Act, which increased the power of the officers who coordinate the activities of the different services. The 1947 structure was left in place, but with revised procedures.

Joint Chiefs of Staff   The Joint Chiefs of Staff (JCS) is a committee consisting of the uniformed heads of each of the military services (the army, navy, air force, and Marine Corps), plus a chairman and a (nonvoting) vice chairman, also military officers, who are appointed by the president and confirmed by the Senate. The JCS does not have command authority over troops, but it plays a key role in national defense planning. Before 1986 the JCS was a committee of equals. Since each service had one vote, the JCS operated by consensus: it rarely, if ever, made a decision opposed by any single service (and thus it rarely made an important decision). Since 1986 the chairman of the Joint Chiefs has been designated the president's principal military adviser, in an effort to give him more influence over the JCS. It remains to be seen whether the JCS will be any better equipped to make tough decisions under the new law than it was under the old.

Joint Staff   Assisting the JCS is the Joint Staff, consisting of several hundred officers from each of the four services. The staff draws up plans for various military contingencies. Before 1986 each staff member was loyal to the service whose uniform he or she wore. As a result the staff was often "joint" in name only, since few members were willing to take a position opposed by their service for fear of being passed over for promotion. The 1986 law changed this in two ways: First, it gave the chairman of the JCS control over the Joint Staff; now it works for the chairman, not for the JCS as a group. Second, it required the secretary of defense to establish guidelines to ensure that officers assigned to the Joint Staff (or to other interservice bodies) were promoted at the same rate as officers whose careers were spent entirely with their own services.

Unified Commands   Most of the combat forces of the United States are assigned to one or another of

The Joint Chiefs of Staff as of October 1996, from left to right: Adm. Jay L. Johnson, U.S. Navy; Gen. Dennis J. Reimer, U.S. Army; Gen. Joseph W. Ralston, U.S. Air Force, Vice Chairman; Gen. John M. Shalikashvili, U.S. Army, Chairman; Gen. Ronald R. Fogleman, U.S. Air Force; Gen. Charles C. Krulak, U.S. Marine Corps.

eight "unified commands" or two "specified commands." Five of the unified commands control our forces assigned to geographic areas—Europe, the Pacific (including the Far East and Southeast Asia), the Atlantic, Central America (called the Southern Command), and the Middle East (called the Central Command). Three handle specialized forces—space and its defense, transportation, and special operations (such as the army Rangers and navy Seal Teams). The specified commands are responsible for strategic missiles and bombers and for defense forces in the United States. Before 1986 these commands were often unified in name only: each service component (for example, the navy) would tend to take orders from its own brass in Washington rather than from the commander in chief (CINC) of the unified command. The 1986 law gave more power to the CINCs. The Central Command in the Middle East ("CentCom") was in charge of our forces fighting against Iraq.

The Services   Each military service is headed by a civilian secretary—one for the army, the navy (including the Marine Corps), and the air force—plus a senior military officer: the chief of staff of the army, the chief of naval operations, the comman-

dant of the Marine Corps, and the chief of staff of the air force. The civilian secretaries are in charge of purchasing, auditing, congressional relations, and public affairs. The military chiefs oversee the discipline and training of their uniformed forces and in addition represent their services on the Joint Chiefs of Staff.

The Chain of Command   Under the Constitution the president is the commander in chief of the armed forces. The chain of command runs from him to the secretary of defense (also a civilian), and from him to the various unified and specified commands. These orders may be transmitted through the Joint Chiefs of Staff or its chairman, but by law the chairman of the JCS does not have command authority over the combat forces. Civilians are in charge at the top to protect against excessive concentration of power.

No one yet knows how well the 1986 changes will work, though many analysts viewed the quick victory in the 1991 Persian Gulf War as evidence of its success.[1] Critics of the Pentagon have been urging changes along these lines at least since 1947. But others say that unless the armed services are actually merged, interservice rivalry will continue. Still others argue that even the degree of coordination intended by the 1986 act is excessive; the country, in their view, is better served by having wholly autonomous services. What is striking is that many members of Congress who once would have insisted on the latter view voted for the 1986 law without question, thus indicating a greater willingness to permit some degree of concentration of power in the military.

The Defense Budget

There are two important things to know about the defense budget—how big it is and how it is divided up. The first reflects majoritarian politics, the second interest group bargaining, with the "interests" in this case being the military services and their allies in Congress.

Total Spending

Throughout most of our history, the United States has not maintained large military forces during peacetime. For instance, the percentage of the gross national product (GNP) spent on defense in 1935,

on the eve of World War II, was about the same as it was in 1870, when we were on the eve of nothing in particular.[2] We armed when a war broke out, then we disarmed when the war ended. But all of that changed after World War II, when defense spending declined sharply but did not return to its prewar levels. And in 1950 our defense expenditures soared again.

In that year we rearmed to fight a war in Korea, but when it was over we did not completely disarm. The reason was our containment policy toward the Soviet Union. For about forty years—from the outbreak of the Korean War in 1950 to the collapse of the Soviet Union in 1991—American military spending was driven by our desire to contain the Soviet Union and its allies. The Soviet Union had brought under its control most of Eastern Europe; would it also invade Western Europe? Russia had always wanted access to the oil and warm-water ports of the Middle East; would the Soviets someday invade or subvert Iran or Turkey? The Soviet Union was willing to help North Korea invade South Korea and North Vietnam to invade South Vietnam; would it next use an ally to threaten the United States? Soviet leaders supported "wars of national liberation" in Africa and Latin America; would they suc-

The Pentagon, headquarters of the United States armed forces.

FIGURE 21.2 Trends in Military Spending

NOTE: Budget authority figures for years before 1985 have been recalculated to disregard the effect of inflation and show costs in 1985 dollars.
SOURCE: Adapted and updated from *The New York Times* (May 14, 1985). Copyright © 1985 by The New York Times Company. Reprinted by permission. Updated by the author.

ceed in turning more and more nations against the United States?

To meet these threats the United States built up a military system that was designed to repel a Soviet invasion of Western Europe and at the same time help allies resist smaller-scale invasions or domestic uprisings. Figure 21.2 depicts the dramatic increase in military spending in 1950. It also shows that even after we decided to have a large military force, there were many ups and downs in the actual level of spending. After the Korean war was over we spent less; when we became involved in Vietnam we spent more; when the Soviet Union invaded Afghanistan we spent more again. These changes in spending tended to reflect changes in public opinion about the defense budget (see Figure 21.3, page 638).

As Figure 21.3 shows, for the past thirty years the American public generally has said that we spend too much on defense. With the exception of the period from the mid-1970s to the early 1980s, public opinion has favored downward pressure on defense spending. Typically that view shifts only

when a war or crisis occurs, such as Korea, Sputnik, Berlin, Vietnam, or Afghanistan. But until around 1991, any decreases in military spending were limited by the continuing fear of Soviet domination. For decades, America raised and lowered its defense spending, but always with an eye on the ever-increasing Soviet military budget.

Then, suddenly, the Soviet Union ceased to exist. The troops that once occupied Eastern Europe and Afghanistan withdrew to Russia; there were huge cuts in Russian military spending; and military and economic aid to its long-time ally, Cuba, was suspended. For the first time since 1950, American leaders were faced with defining the principles of our military policy (and thus the size of our defense budget) in the absence of a Soviet threat.

The debate that occurred, and is still continuing, largely reflected personal beliefs and political ideologies[3] (that is, *majoritarian* politics). Liberals demanded sharp cuts in defense spending, weapons procurement, and military personnel, arguing that with the Soviet threat ended it was time to collect

FIGURE 21.3   Public Sentiment on Defense Spending, 1960–1990

— Spending too much   — Spending too little

Percentage favoring position

SOURCE: Gallup Poll data, reported by Kim Neighbor.

our "peace dividend" and divert funds from the military to domestic social programs. Conservatives agreed that some military cuts were in order, but they argued that the world was still a dangerous place and therefore that a strong (and well-funded)

Saddam Hussein, ruler of Iraq.

military remained essential to the nation's defense. This disagreement reflected different predictions about what the future would be like. Many liberals (and some conservatives, such as Pat Buchanan, who believed that America should "stay at home") argued that we could not afford to be the "world's policeman." Many conservatives (and some liberals) responded by saying that Russia was still a military powerhouse that might once again fall under the control of ruthless leaders and that many other nations hostile to the United States (such as Libya, North Korea, Iran, and Iraq) were becoming potential adversaries as they tried to build or acquire nuclear weapons and missile systems.

Saddam Hussein soon provided evidence that international aggression had by no means ended with the demise of the Soviet Union. In 1990 Iraq invaded and conquered Kuwait, a small oil-producing country in the Persian Gulf. President Bush, moving to protect our allies in the Middle East (such as Saudi Arabia), sent U.S. forces to the region. This effort was joined by forces from several other nations and given the blessing of the United Nations. When the Iraqi forces refused to withdraw from Kuwait, the United States and its allies attacked, in January 1991. In short order Iraq's forces were driven out of Kuwait, with remarkably few allied casualties. Although Saddam Hussein managed to salvage enough of his military forces to remain in power in

Iraq, the short-lived war was viewed by most Americans as an astounding military success.

Operation Desert Storm (as it was called) postponed the debate over military spending but did not end it. The U.S. victory was so swift and stunning that it convinced many people that this country could not be challenged by anyone. Some held that we could afford to rely on "smart weapons" and other sophisticated military technology and did not need a lot of men and women under arms. Some believed we should not intervene in the affairs of other nations except, as in Desert Storm, as part of a United Nations effort that would provide us with the support of many allies. Others argued that high technology and smart weapons were desirable because they would make it easier for the United States to intervene effectively in future conflicts, with or without the UN. Critics declared that smart weapons might work brilliantly in fighting Iraq, but for other kinds of wars only ground troops could win. They also argued that the U.S. could not let its

military and foreign policy be controlled by the United Nations, a body of many diverse interests, in which the United States has only one vote.

Not long after Desert Storm we sent troops to aid a UN peacekeeping effort in Somalia, a country where millions of people were starving because a civil war had disrupted the economy and blocked the distribution of relief supplies sent from abroad. While this was going on, the former nation of Yugoslavia collapsed into a civil war marked by unspeakable atrocities perpetrated against innocent civilians. Initially the United States was reluctant to get involved, but it ultimately brokered a peace with the combatants in November 1995. As President Clinton entered his second term, U.S. troops continued to serve as part of a NATO peacekeeping force in Bosnia.

Just as important as the debate over U.S. involvement in these world events was the reality of how defense spending was allocated within the overall federal budget. Defense spending is almost the only

FIGURE 21.4 The Federal Government Dollar Fiscal Year 1997 Estimates

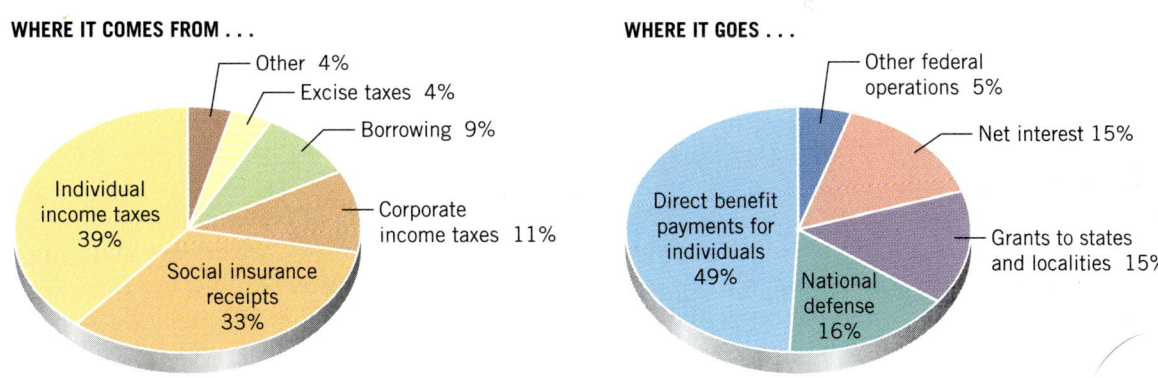

WHERE IT COMES FROM . . .

- Other 4%
- Excise taxes 4%
- Borrowing 9%
- Corporate income taxes 11%
- Individual income taxes 39%
- Social insurance receipts 33%

WHERE IT GOES . . .

- Other federal operations 5%
- Net interest 15%
- Grants to states and localities 15%
- Direct benefit payments for individuals 49%
- National defense 16%

RECEIPTS, OUTLAYS, AND SURPLUS OR DEFICIT
(In billions of dollars)

	1995 Actual	Estimate						
		1996	1997	1998	1999	2000	2001	2002
Receipts	1,355	1,427	1,495	1,578	1,653	1,734	1,820	1,912
Outlays	1,519	1,572	1,635	1,676	1,717	1,761	1,812	1,868
Surplus/deficit (−)	−164	−146	−140	−98	−64	−28	8	44

SOURCE: Budget Supplement—*Budget of the United States Government, Fiscal Year 1997.*

TABLE 21.1	U.S. Military Forces Before and After the Breakup of the Soviet Union	
Service	Before 1991	End FY 1996
Army		
Active divisions	18	10
National Guard divisions	10	8+
Navy		
Aircraft carriers	15	11/1
Training carriers	1	0
Ships	546	359
Air Force		
Active fighter wings	24	13
Reserve fighter wings	12	7
Marine Corps		
Active duty troops	197,000	174,000
Reserve troops	44,000	42,000
Strategic Nuclear Forces		
Ballistic missile submarines	34	17
Strategic bombers	301	173
ICBMs	1,000	580

SOURCE: *Congressional Quarterly Weekly Report* (September 4, 1993): 2350; 1996 Annual Defense Report.

part of the federal budget that can easily be cut by the president and Congress. Presidents looking for money to reduce the deficit or to finance new programs are irresistibly drawn to the defense budget. President Bush had begun to make cuts in military spending following the breakup of the Soviet Union. By 1993 the army had been reduced from eighteen divisions to fourteen, the navy from 546 ships to 443; the air force from 24 wings of fighter planes to 16. President Clinton sought to make even deeper cuts. To do so he instructed his secretary of defense to conduct a "bottom-up" review of our defense needs. This review concluded that the biggest threat now facing the United States arose from the possibility of smaller, "regional" wars breaking out in various parts of the world—wars like the Iraqi invasion of Kuwait. The secretary and the Joint Chiefs of Staff decided that the United States had to have a military force capable of fighting two regional wars at the same time. The forces they proposed would even further reduce the army (to 10 divisions), the navy (from 443 to 346 ships, including 12 aircraft carriers), and the air force (from 16 to 13 fighter wings). Only the Marine Corps was spared deep cuts, on the theory that the Marines are specially trained and equipped to intervene in remote parts of the world (see Table 21.1). There were also to be cuts in the number of new weapons purchased.

But making big cuts in new weapons carries a risk: if the cuts are too deep, the companies with the ability to make these weapons will go out of business. For example, there are only two American companies capable of building modern submarines and only a few that can build high-performance combat aircraft. The Pentagon plan, therefore, called for purchasing some submarines and aircraft that were not strictly necessary in order to keep these production lines, and the skilled workers employed by them, in existence. Furthermore, the military services have been cutting back on procurement of current weapons over the past few years so that they can save money for next-generation systems. The services are not buying as many "new" weapons, but they have not lost interest in developing the very "newest" ones. As we shall see, keeping a defense plant open is not simply a question of defense policy; it also is a matter of interest group and client politics.

By the beginning of President Clinton's second term, many members of Congress had shifted their attention to cutting domestic programs in an effort to balance the budget by 2002. Still, with many members concerned that our military forces have been cut either too fast or not fast enough, the debate about the level of military spending is likely to go on for many years.

Allocating Defense Dollars

Presidents may set total military spending, within limits, but they have a much harder time changing the allocation of funds among the various services. If majoritarian politics governs the first decision, interest group politics shapes the second.

In the United States—and probably in every nation—the army, the navy, the Marine Corps, and the air force can each mobilize important political allies if threatened with a loss of resources relative to the other services. It is thus much easier for a president or secretary of defense to require that all services accept an across-the-board budget cut, equally applicable to all, than to compel one service to accept a cut while another service enjoys an increase.

The Joint Chiefs of Staff, composed of representatives of each service, usually will unanimously recommend policies that benefit all services equally and reluctantly accept policies that penalize all equally. Members are obviously incapable of making choices that would favor one service over another. In any coordinating committee each member will tacitly agree to support the favored positions of every other member in exchange for support for his own favored position. Though there have been exceptions when the Joint Chiefs have split on major issues, in general they follow this pattern.

This pattern of equal support for each service is reinforced by the members of the congressional committees who handle military authorizations and appropriations. At one time each military service was overseen by separate committees in the House and Senate, but after World War II these committees were merged into the House Armed Services Committee and the Senate Armed Services Committee. There remain within these committees strong congressional advocates of one or the other service. For example, within the House Armed Services Committee there is the Subcommittee on Seapower, whose members regularly support larger budget authorizations for the navy than even the Pentagon requests. In 1978 the subcommittee proposed a 68 percent increase in the Carter administration's request for funds with which to build navy ships.

As a result of these constraints, the share of the total defense budget going to each service changes very slowly. Each major service usually receives roughly a third of the defense budget. In peacetime the army's share will be somewhat lower, since the number of soldiers tends to fluctuate between wartime and peacetime more than the number of sailors or air force personnel.

The key allocation decisions thus become incremental ones—decisions about what new things to add to a service's existing budget rather than decisions about transferring a function from one service to another. Usually these involve the purchase of major new weapons. Over one-third of the total defense budget is devoted to weapons research, development, and procurement. The more expensive of these weapons systems, such as the B-1 and B-2 bombers, the MX missile, the Trident nuclear submarine, and the M1 tank, become the subject of intense political debate involving the Pentagon, the White House, Congress, and various interest groups. Interest groups include not only weapons manufacturers but scientists and private defense budget analysts in such think tanks as RAND, the Brookings Institution, and the American Enterprise Institute.

In these debates many factors—strategic, economic, and political—come to the fore. The proposal to build the B-1 bomber, for example, involved arguments over whether we needed a supersonic intercontinental bomber; whether such a bomber, even if valuable, would cost too much; and whether making such an investment would have desirable effects on the economy of those states in which major components would be produced. Each year funds were requested for developing the B-1, a prolonged discussion occurred, frequently with close votes in Congress. President Carter terminated the program, but President Reagan revived it, and the bombers were built.

The congressional role in deciding on weapons systems has changed somewhat over the years. Before World War II Congress often made, based on military advice, the most detailed decisions concerning what equipment to buy, what bases to open, and where ships and army units were to be located. During the war it retreated from this activist stance in deference to military opinion; the all-out nature of the war effort and the popularity of the cause dissuaded members of Congress from acting in a way that might be interpreted as hindering the fighting forces.

After the war Congress again became assertive, but typically in favor of different or larger military programs than those proposed by the president. For example, Congress favored a larger Marine Corps and a larger air force than President Truman. When Congress appropriated more money for these purposes than Truman wanted, he refused to spend it.

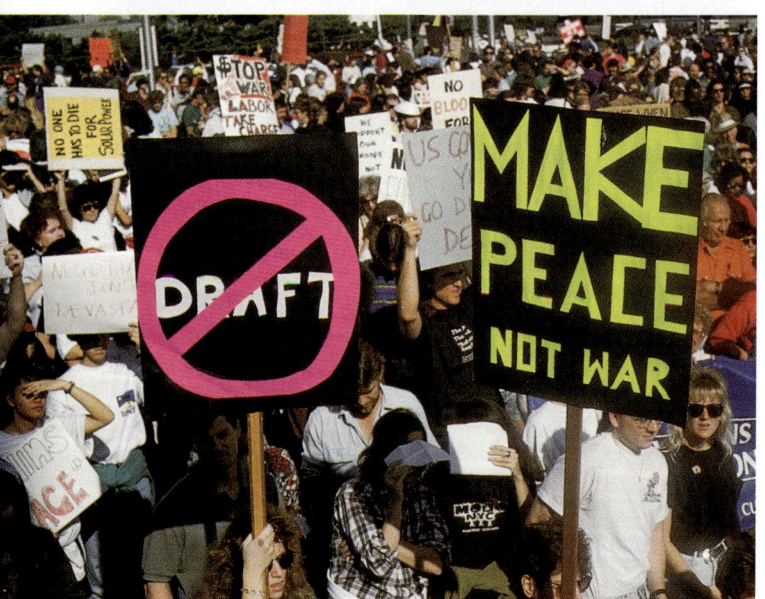

The national mood has changed with regard to military affairs. An enthusiastic parade celebrated the end of the war in Europe on May 7, 1945, and the role of the armed forces in that conflict. Forty years later, protesters objected vehemently to money spent on weapons.

Congress was also deeply involved in postwar decisions regarding the B-36 bomber, the navy's "supercarriers," the choice among competing missile systems, and the building of new fighter aircraft such as the TFX. While a senator, John F. Kennedy criticized President Eisenhower's emphasis on strategic weapons (bombers and missiles armed with nuclear bombs) at the expense of conventional ground forces. After he became president in 1961, Kennedy began to build up these ground forces and encouraged the creation of the "Green Beret" special forces units.

Throughout this period Congress was expanding its power to affect certain military decisions. In the 1950s it made military-construction appropriations subject to an annual authorization. In the 1960s it made the procurement of weapons systems subject to annual authorization.

During the latter part of the 1960s congressional interest in these matters sharpened and shifted its tone. Congress began to take a more critical stance toward the military. This reflected the growing unpopularity of the war in Vietnam, the increase in the influence of interest groups (such as liberal scientists with experience in weapons research) that opposed various new weapons systems, and a lessened popular confidence in military expertise. Unlike in the late 1940s and early 1950s, when the decision to go ahead with the development of the hydrogen bomb, for example, was made by the president acting alone, without extensive congressional debate, since the late 1960s almost every new weapons system has been subjected to intensive discussion.

For example, in 1969 the proposed antiballistic missile system barely survived congressional and interest group opposition (in the Senate a motion to defeat the plan lost in a tie vote, 50-50). Ultimately the president scaled down the plan to just one installation, and in 1975 Congress voted to close down even that facility.

In the 1980s the most controversial new weapons system was the strategic defense initiative (SDI), more popularly called "Star Wars." President Reagan proposed building a system that would intercept enemy missiles before they could reach this country. No one doubted that such a system would be complex and costly. The debate over it reflected both majoritarian politics, with heavy attention to philosophical and ideological issues, and interest group politics, with keen rivalries among the armed services and prospective contractors.

The philosophical issues included the system's cost and feasibility as well as its likely success at actually knocking down enemy missiles or deterring an enemy from launching missiles. Conservatives argued that, though costly, it was feasible and a better way of protecting the United States than relying on our ability to blow up Soviet cities after they had attempted to blow up ours. Liberals argued that it would undermine the system of "mutual assured destruction" (MAD)—whereby each of the superpowers deterred the other through the threat of massive retaliation—and thus increase the risk of war.

The interest group politics involved the armed services and the contractors. Many service leaders privately did not favor Star Wars because its enormous cost would divert resources from their traditional missions, whether it worked or not. The air force, for example, operated the land-based intercontinental ballistic missiles (ICBMs) on which "mutual assured destruction" depended. If Star Wars were effective, the need for these missiles might be greatly reduced. But many defense contractors and the states in which they were located favored SDI because it held out the promise of big contracts.

Like any major new defense measure, SDI had to go through a two-stage political process in Congress. In the first stage, members debate the merits of the proposal. Ideology plays a large role. If the proposal is adopted, then members maneuver to get contracts for their districts. Constituency interests play a large role. In the first stage strong conservatives will vote for increased military spending even though it may not benefit their district, and strong liberals will oppose it even if a bigger defense budget might be good for theirs. But in the second stage both wings of Congress work to get the benefits. For example, Edward Kennedy of Massachusetts is an outspoken critic of defense spending but extremely effective in getting jet engine contracts for the General Electric plant in Massachusetts.

What Do We Buy for Our Money?

We buy people, of course—soldiers, sailors, airmen, and airwomen (see Table 21.1). They are the most expensive part of the defense budget. Then we buy hardware, of roughly two kinds—big-ticket items, like aircraft carriers and bombers, and small-ticket items, like hammers and screwdrivers. Each of these kinds of hardware has its own politics. Finally, we buy "readiness"—training, supplies, munitions, fuel, and food.

Personnel

Efforts to develop our military forces before World War II reflected the considerable American discomfort with a strong central government. The U.S. did not institute a peacetime draft until 1940, when the rest of the world was already at war, and the draft was renewed the following year (only a few months before Pearl Harbor) by only a one-vote margin in the House. Until 1973 the United States relied on the draft to obtain military personnel. Then, at the end of the Vietnam War, it replaced the draft with the all-volunteer force (AVF). After getting off to a rocky start, the AVF began to improve thanks to increases in military pay and rising civilian unemployment. Abolishing the draft had been politically popular: nobody likes being drafted, and even in congressional districts that otherwise are staunch supporters of a strong defense, the voters tell their representatives that they do not want to return to the draft.

Of late the size of the armed forces has been shrinking; in 1994 there were 1.6 million men and women in uniform, down from 2.1 million just six years earlier. This decline may make finding recruits easier than it would have been had the armed forces remained at their cold war size.

The problem of finding recruits has been politically less important than the question of who shall be a recruit. There has been a steady increase in the percentage of women in the military (in 1990 they constituted 10 percent of the total). For a long time, however, they were barred by law from serving in combat roles. (What constitutes a "combat role" is a bit difficult to say, since even personnel far from the main fighting can be hit by an enemy bomb or artillery shell.) In 1993 Congress ended the legal ban on assigning women to navy combat ships and air force fighter jets, and by 1994 between four and five hundred women were serving on three aircraft carriers. Congress must still be consulted in advance if women are to serve in ground combat forces (such

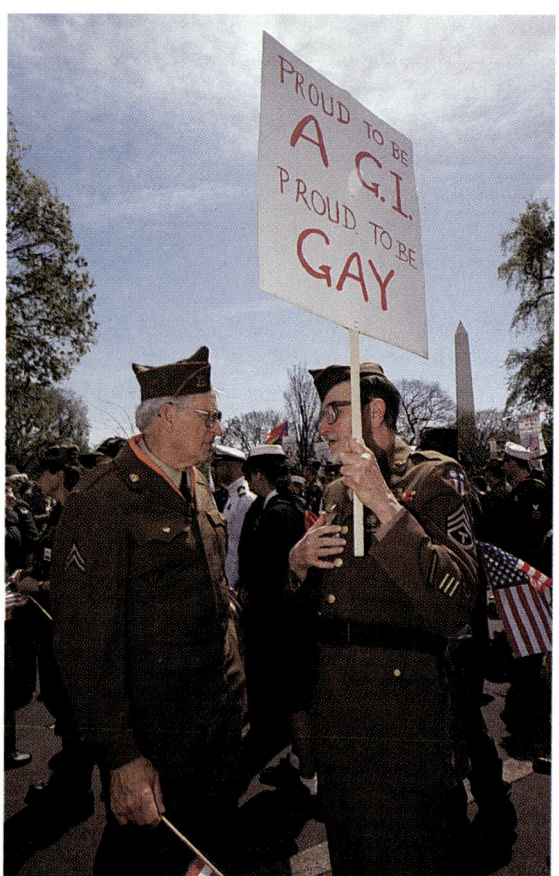

The military modified its ban on gays and lesbians serving in the armed forces: now the policy is "don't ask, don't tell."

as in front-line infantry or tank units), but soon they may be in those positions as well.

The presence of homosexuals in the military has proved much harder to resolve. Until 1993 it was the long-standing policy of the U.S. armed forces to bar homosexuals from entering the military and to discharge them if they were discovered serving. Gay and lesbian rights organizations had long protested this exclusion. In 1993 a gay soldier won a lawsuit against the army for having discharged him; he settled for back pay and retirement benefits in exchange for a promise not to reenlist. In 1993 another judge ordered the navy to reinstate a discharged sailor who had revealed on national television that he was a homosexual. In response to the growing controversy, presidential candidate Bill Clinton promised to lift the official ban on gays and lesbians serving in the military if he were elected to office.

Once in office he discovered that it was not that easy. Many members of the armed forces believed that knowingly serving alongside and living in close quarters with gays and lesbians would create unnecessary tension and harm military morale and troop solidarity. The Joint Chiefs of Staff opposed lifting the ban, and several key members of Congress said they would try to pass a law reaffirming it. President Clinton was forced to settle for a compromise: "don't ask, don't tell." Under this policy, persons entering or serving in the military will not be asked to reveal their sexual orientation and will be allowed to serve provided they do not engage in homosexual conduct. If a person says he or she is a homosexual it will not be automatic grounds for discharge, but it may be grounds for launching an investigation to see whether rules against homosexual conduct have been violated.

In 1994 the new Pentagon rules designed to implement this policy went into effect. They are sure to lead to new lawsuits. For example, what constitutes homosexual conduct? Going to a gay bar? Holding hands in public with a person of the same sex?

Big-Ticket Hardware

Whenever the Pentagon buys a new submarine, airplane, or missile, we hear about **cost overruns.** In the 1950s actual costs were three times greater than estimated costs; by the 1960s things were only slightly better—actual costs were twice estimated costs.[4]

There are five main reasons for these overruns. First, it is hard to know in advance what something that has never existed before will cost once you build it. People who have remodeled their homes know this all too well. So do government officials who build new subways or congressional office buildings. It is no different with a B-2 bomber or a Trident submarine.

Second, people who want to persuade Congress to appropriate money for a new airplane or submarine have an incentive to underestimate the cost. To get the weapon approved, its sponsors tell Congress how little it will cost; once the weapon is under construction, the sponsors go back to Congress for additional money to cover "unexpected" cost increases. Similarly, contractors who want the Pentagon to build their new device have an incentive to underestimate the costs and then increase them after the contract is granted.

Third, the Pentagon officials who decide what kind of new aircraft they want are drawn from the ranks of those who will fly it. These officers naturally want the best airplane (or ship or tank) that money can buy. As air force General Carl "Tooey" Spaatz once put it: "A second-best aircraft is like a second-best poker hand. No damn good."[5] But what exactly is the "best" airplane? Is it the fastest one? Or the most maneuverable one? Or the most reliable one? Or the one with the longest range? Pentagon officials have a tendency to answer: "All of the above." Of course, trying to produce all of the above is incredibly expensive (and sometimes impossible). But asking for the expensive (or the impossible) is understandable, given that the air force officers who buy it will also fly it. This tendency to ask for everything at once is called **gold plating.**

Fourth, many new weapons are purchased from a single contractor. This is called sole-sourcing. A contractor is hired to design, develop, and build an airplane. As a result there is no competition, and so the manufacturer has no strong incentive to control costs. And if the sole manufacturer gets into financial trouble, the government, seeking to avoid a shutdown of all production, has an incentive to bail the company out.

Fifth, when Congress wants to cut the military budget, it often does so not by canceling a new weapons system but by stretching out the number of years during which it is purchased. Say that Congress wants to buy one hundred F-14s, twenty-five a year for four years. To give the appearance of cutting the budget, it will decide to buy only fifteen the first year and take five years to buy the rest. Or it will authorize the construction of twenty now and then ask again next year for the authority to build more. But start-and-stop production decisions and stretching out production over more years drives up the cost of building each unit. If Ford built cars this way, it would go broke.

There are ways to cope with four of these five problems. You cannot do much about the first, ignorance, but you can do something about low estimates, gold plating, sole-sourcing, and stretch-outs. If the Pentagon would give realistic cost estimates initially (perhaps verified by another agency); if it would ask for weapons that meet a few critical performance requirements instead of every requirement that can be thought of; if two or more manufacturers were to compete in designing, developing, and manufacturing new weapons; and if Congress were to stop trying to "cut" the budget using the smoke-and-mirrors technique of stretch-outs, then we would hear a lot less about cost overruns.

Some of these things are being done. There is more competition and less sole-sourcing in weapons procurement today than once was the case.[6] But the political incentives to avoid other changes are very powerful. Pentagon officers will always want "the best." They will always have an incentive to understate costs. Congress will always be tempted to use stretch-outs as a way of avoiding hard budget choices.

Small-Ticket Items

It may be easy to understand why jet fighters cost so much, but what about $435 hammers?

In fact there never was a $435 hammer. It was a myth. The myth grew out of a complicated Pentagon accounting procedure that was exploited for publicity purposes by a member of Congress who thought he had found a hot issue. If you want to understand why somebody might think that the navy had paid $435 for a hammer, read the accompanying box on page 646.

The issue in buying small-ticket items is not the hammer problem, it is the coffee maker problem. Everybody knows what a hammer is and where to buy one—for about $20, tops. But a coffee maker, *if it is especially designed to function on a military plane,* is another matter. If the plane is going to lurch about in rough air, if the coffee maker has to fit into an odd place, it will occur to somebody in the Pentagon that what is needed is a specially designed coffee maker.

The $435 Hammer

For a long time the Pentagon paid its suppliers using an accounting method called the equal-allocation formula. Here is how it worked:

Suppose that you are selling the Pentagon equipment with which to fix a radar set. There are 250 of these parts, some extremely complex and costly (such as a piece of computer hardware) and others very simple and cheap (such as a hammer). Your total cost is the cost of manufacturing each item, plus your overhead costs. These overhead costs include the rent for your factory, the salary for your bookkeepers, and your taxes and insurance premiums. You want to charge the Pentagon an amount that will reimburse you for the cost of making these gadgets and for your overhead (plus a profit). How do you show overhead on the bill that you send to the government?

There are two ways. One is to figure out how much overhead was in fact needed to produce each of the 250 items. That is very complicated. The other way is simply to allocate your overhead equally to each item. If your total overhead is $100,000, under the "equal-allocation formula" you arbitrarily assign to each part an equal share of the overhead. That means that each part is billed to the government as if it were responsible for eating up $400 worth of overhead ($100,000 divided by 250 parts equals $400 per part). The government may be paying the right price for the whole package of parts, but theoretically it is paying too little for the computer hardware and too much for the hammer. On the invoice it looks as though the hammer costs $435 because $400 of overhead was arbitrarily assigned to it. (Of course, $35 may still be too much to pay for a hammer, but at least it is not totally outrageous.)

A sailor who gets the package of parts spots the $435 hammer price and wonders how anybody in his or her right mind could pay that much. He tells the press. A member of Congress picks up on the story. Nobody takes time to learn how the accounting rules work. And thus a myth is born.

The equal-allocation rule was eventually abolished. Now a different accounting system is in place. But whether there has been any real improvement in how the Pentagon buys hammers is unclear. The original hammer may have cost too much; no one knows. Future hammer purchases may cost too much; no one knows. The real problems in procurement—as described in the text—are left unattended.

SOURCE: Based on James Fairhall, "The Case for the $435 Hammer," *Washington Monthly* (January 1987): 47–52. See also Steven Kelman, "The Grace Commission: How Much Waste in Government?" *The Public Interest* (Winter 1985): 62–87.

Once somebody thinks like that, the coffee maker is purchased in the same way as a new jet fighter, and with results just as bad. The design is gold-plated (for example, "Let's have a coffee maker that can fly upside down"), the contract is let out to a sole source with no competition, the cost is underestimated, and the production run is limited to ten coffee makers. The result? A coffee maker that costs $7,600.[7]

Readiness

Presumably we have a peacetime military so that we will be ready for wartime. Presumably, therefore, the peacetime forces will devote a lot of their time and money to improving their readiness.

Not necessarily. The politics of defense spending are such that readiness often is given a very low priority. Here is why.

The Pentagon budget is very large. Frequently Congress will want to make cuts, especially during a period when the federal budget is running a big deficit and the former Soviet Union has collapsed. Where shall it make the cuts?

Client politics influences the decision. In 1990 Congress was willing to cut almost anything, provided it wasn't built or stationed in some member's district. That doesn't leave much. Plans to stop producing F-14 fighters for the navy were opposed by members from Long Island, where the Grumman manufacturing plant is located. Plans to kill the Osprey aircraft for the Marines were opposed by members from the places where it was to be built. Plans to close bases were opposed by every member with a base in his or her district.

That leaves training and readiness. These things, essential to military effectiveness, have no constituencies and hence few congressional defenders. When forced to choose, the services themselves often prefer to allocate scarce dollars to developing and buying new weapons than to spending for readiness. Moreover, the savings from buying less fuel or having fewer exercises shows up right away, while the savings from canceling an aircraft carrier may not show up for years. Not surprisingly, training and readiness are usually what get the ax.

In fiscal 1987 Congress cut heavily into readiness.[8] What is surprising is that some new weapons were canceled and some old bases closed. In January 1991 the secretary of defense startled everyone by terminating the contract to build an advanced tactical fighter (the A-12) for the navy on the grounds that the contractors (all well connected in Congress) had wasted too much money with too little to show for it.

Bases

At one time the opening and closing of military bases was pure client politics, which meant that a lot of bases were opened and hardly any were closed. Almost every member of Congress fought to get a base in his or her district, and *every* member fought to keep an existing base open. Even the biggest congressional critics of the U.S. military, people who would vote to take a gun out of a soldier's hand, would fight hard to keep a base in their district open and operating.

In 1988 Congress finally concluded that no base would ever be closed unless the system for making decisions was changed. It created a Commission on Base Realignment and Closure, consisting of private citizens (originally twelve, later eight) who would consider recommendations from the secretary of defense. By law, Congress would have to vote within forty-five days for or against the commission's list as a whole, without having a chance to amend it. In 1989 Congress considered the commission's first report, which called for closing eighty-six bases and slimming down five others. With no chance to pick the bases each member wanted to protect and knowing that the country had more bases than it needed, Congress let the report stand, and the closings began.

In 1991 it went through the same process again, finally voting to accept (technically, voting not to block) a commission report calling for closing thirty-four more bases and altering many others.

Congress, it appears, has finally figured out how to make some decisions that most members know are right but that each member individually finds it politically necessary to oppose.

Congress versus the Executive

Defense policy, like Edward S. Corwin said about foreign policy, is an "invitation to struggle." Until World War II, Congress made detailed decisions about what weapons to buy, what bases to build, and where troops should be sent. Even during the Civil War, Congress, restless with President Lincoln's conduct of that struggle, attempted to influence his selection of commanding generals.

During World War II and for some time thereafter, Congress played a more passive role, deferring to the president and the military chiefs. But since the war in Vietnam, and especially since the Carter-Reagan arms buildup began, Congress has reasserted its interest in detailed decisions, something now called, by its critics, **micromanaging.**

The change is easily measured. In 1962 the Senate and House Armed Services Committees held twenty-seven hearings and published 1,400 pages of testimony about the defense budget. In 1985 the two committees held eighty hearings and published 11,246 pages of testimony. The number of congressional subcommittees concerned with defense matters more than tripled from 1970 to 1985. The Military Reform Caucus has taken a keen interest in military policy, even though only a quarter of its 133 members sit on defense-oversight committees. Whereas in 1977 the defense budget was debated in the House for two days and no amendment was offered, in 1986 it was debated for nine days and 116 amendments were offered.[9]

Part of this increased congressional interest in defense policy reflects changes in the executive branch. A large peacetime military is bound to attract congressional attention. Part of the increased interest has little to do with defense and a lot to do with serving constituents in an era of budget deficits. During the Reagan presidency the military spending bill was one of the few veto-proof bills Congress could pass, and so members tried to attach to it a lot of pet projects. And part of the increased attention reflects the already-noted shifts in the ideology of members of Congress, as well as the more general resurgence of congressional assertiveness since the 1970s.

What Would You Do?

MEMORANDUM

TO: The president
FROM: National security advisor
SUBJECT: Hostages

The problem: The six Americans held hostage in the Middle East are beginning their second year of captivity. One, a CIA officer with extensive knowledge of our intelligence apparatus in the region, is undergoing torture at an unknown location. It has been the policy of this administration not to negotiate with terrorists. Criticism of this refusal is being heard more frequently from hostage families and their sympathizers in Congress and the press. The terrorist groups are demanding that we end our support of Israel. A government in the region has secretly indicated that, in exchange for military supplies, it may be able to help win the release of "some" hostages.

Your options:

1. Maintain the "no-negotiations" policy but use quiet diplomacy with friendly nations in the region to see whether they can intercede with the terrorist groups on behalf of the hostages.
Advantages: (a) Our "no-negotiations" policy remains credible, and this will deter other terrorist groups from thinking that they can win concessions by capturing Americans. (b) This policy is consistent with our insistence that U.S. allies not negotiate with terrorists. *Disadvantages:* (a) There is no evidence that our traditional policy will get the hostages released. (b) Public sympathy for the hostages may increase, and this will lead to more criticism of this administration for failing to free captive Americans.

2. Secretly exchange arms for the release of Americans.
Advantages: (a) Some or all hostages may be released. (b) We may earn the goodwill of more moderate elements in the area and thereby increase our influence there. *Disadvantages:* (a) We may deliver arms and no hostages will be released. (b) If secret arms deliveries become public, we will be heavily criticized for abandoning our "no-negotiations" policy.

3. Use military units to find and free the hostages.
Advantage: The hostages may be freed without our having to make any concessions. *Disadvantages:* (a) The military is not optimistic that it can find and free the hostages, who are being kept in hidden, scattered sites. (b) The hostages may be killed during the rescue effort.

Your decision: Option 1 _____   Option 2 _____   Option 3 _____

SUMMARY

The politics of defense, like that of everything else, is different in the United States. Congress plays a much larger role in the details of military policy than does the parliament of a European democracy. The separation of powers among the branches of the U.S. government is a doctrine that is also applied to the military services, under the theory that divided and rivalrous armed forces are a better way of protecting civilian control than would be a unified and coordinated military.

Civilian control is vested in the president, who is commander in chief; the chain of command runs from him to the secretary of defense, who sends orders to the various unified commands. The Joint Chiefs of Staff is a planning and advisory body, not a centralized command. The defense-reorganization act of 1986 increased somewhat the influence of the chairman of the Joint Chiefs and of the commanders of the unified commands.

Decisions regarding total military spending and the acquisition of new weapons systems are made via majoritarian politics, with a large role played by the ideology of the president and members of Congress, by international realities, and by public opinion. The allocation of contracts and (until the system was changed) the maintenance of military bases have traditionally reflected interest group politics.

The problems that we encounter in recruiting personnel, buying big-ticket and small-ticket items, and achieving readiness reveal the different kinds of defense politics at work. In general these decisions reflect a combination of ignorance (what will work?), organizational needs (the attractions of gold plating and the convenience of sole sourcing), and constituency pressures (avoid the draft, keep contractors happy, and cut the budget with stretch-outs and by underfunding readiness).

KEY TERMS

military-industrial complex   *p. 632*

cost overruns   *p. 644*

gold plating   *p. 645*

micromanaging   *p. 647*

SUGGESTED READINGS

Art, Robert J. *The TFX Decision: McNamara and the Military.* Boston: Little, Brown, 1968. An interesting case study of how the decision was made to acquire a controversial new fighter aircraft.

Blackwell, James A., Jr., and Barry M. Blechman, eds. *Making Defense Reform Work.* Washington: Brassey's, 1990. A series of reports based on the 1987 Project on Monitoring Defense Reorganization, sponsored by the Foreign Policy Institute at Johns Hopkins and the Center for Strategic and International Studies. The project examined the effects of the Goldwater-Nichols Act and the recommendations of the Packard Commission.

Cohen, Eliot. *Citizens and Soldiers.* Ithaca, N.Y.: Cornell University Press, 1985. An analysis of how the United States recruits soldiers, comparing the draft and the all-volunteer force.

Fox, J. Ronald. *The Defense Management Challenge: Weapons Acquisition.* Boston: Harvard Business School Press, 1988. A perceptive explanation of the problems in the way we acquire weapons systems, with suggestions for change.

Halperin, Morton H. *Bureaucratic Politics and Foreign Policy.* Washington, D.C.: Brookings Institution, 1974. Analysis of how the tasks and missions of military and intelligence agencies affect the kind of positions that they take and the political strategies that they employ.

Perry, Mark. *Four Stars: The Inside Story of the Forty-Year Battle Between the Joint Chiefs of Staff and America's Civilian Leaders.* Boston: Houghton Mifflin, 1989. An engaging account of the conflict surrounding the JCS from its creation in 1947 through passage of the Goldwater-Nichols Act in 1986.

22

Environmental Policy

- ★ Controversial nature of environmental policy

- ★ Role of the American political system

- ★ Entrepreneurial politics: factory pollution

- ★ The Clean Air Act

- ★ Majoritarian politics: automobile pollution

- ★ Extended deadlines

- ★ Interest group politics: acid rain

- ★ Congressional stalemate and compromise

- ★ Client politics: pesticides

- ★ Defining the problem

- ★ Rules versus incentives

- ★ Results

Everybody loves the environment. A large majority of the American public believes that the government should do more to protect it. Over 80 percent of college freshmen believe that the government is not doing enough to control pollution, far more than the number who think the government is doing too little about disarmament, protecting the consumer, or controlling handguns.[1] No one wants to be called a "polluter."

Why, then, is environmental policy so controversial? There are three reasons. First, every governmental policy, including one established to protect the environment, creates both winners and losers. The losers are the people who must pay the costs without getting enough of the benefits. Sometimes those losers are influential interest groups. But sometimes the losers are average citizens. They may love the environment, but not enough to change the way they live in order to enhance it. For example, automobile exhausts are a major cause of smog, but not many people like the idea of being told to leave their cars at home and take the bus to work.

Second, many environmental issues are enmeshed in scientific uncertainty: the experts either do not know or they disagree about what is happening and how to change it. For example, some people worry that society is burning so much fuel (thus producing a lot of carbon dioxide) and cutting down so many trees (thus reducing the plants available to convert carbon dioxide back into oxygen) that the earth will soon become a greenhouse: the excess carbon dioxide in the earth's atmosphere will prevent heat from escaping, and so the earth will get warmer, with disastrous effects for humanity. But scientists do not know how large the greenhouse effect is, whether it will lead to a harmful amount of global warming, or (if it will) what should be done about it.[2]

Third, much environmental policy takes the form of entrepreneurial politics—mobilizing decision makers with strong, often emotional appeals in order to overcome the political advantages of the client groups that oppose a change. To make these appeals, people who want change must stir up controversy and find villains. Many times this produces desirable changes. But it can also lead to distorted priorities. For example, it is much easier to make dramatic and politically powerful arguments about a pesticide that causes a minute increase in the risk of cancer than it is to dramatize the runoff into our rivers and oceans of polluted water from farms and city streets.

The American Context

Environmental policy, like welfare policy, is shaped by the unique features of American politics. Almost every industrialized nation has rules to protect the environment, but in this country those rules are designed and enforced in a way that would be baffling to someone in, say, Sweden or England.

First, environmental policy making here is much more adversarial than it is in most European nations. In this country there have been bitter and lasting conflicts over the contents of the Clean Air Act. Minimum auto emissions standards are uniform across the nation, regardless of local conditions (states can set higher standards if they wish). Many rules for improving air and water quality have strict deadlines and require expensive technology. Hundreds of inspectors enforce these rules, and hundreds of lawyers bring countless lawsuits to support or challenge this enforcement. Government and business leaders have frequently denounced each other for being unreasonable or insensitive. So antagonistic are the interests involved in environmental policy that it took thirteen years, from 1977 to 1990, to agree on a congressional revision of the Clean Air Act.

In England, by contrast, rules designed to reduce air pollution were written by government and business leaders acting cooperatively. The rules are neither rigid nor nationally uniform; they are flexible and allow plenty of exceptions to deal with local variations in business needs. Compliance with the rules depends mostly on voluntary action, not formal enforcement. Lawsuits are rare. Business and government officials do not routinely accuse each other of being unreasonable. You might think that all this sweetness and light was the result of having meaningless rules, but not so. As David Vogel has shown, the improvement in air and water quality in

Everyone wants clean air, but few people are willing to give up the personal freedom that their automobiles afford them.

England has been at least as great as, if not greater than, that in the United States.[3]

A second feature of environmental policy here is that, as in so many other policy areas, what is done depends heavily on the states. Though there are uniform national air quality standards, how those standards are achieved is left to the states (subject to certain federal controls). Though sewage treatment plants are in large measure paid for by Washington, they are designed, built, and operated by state and local governments. Though the federal government decrees that radioactive waste must be properly disposed of somewhere, the states have a big voice in where that is. When Congress decided in 1982 to select places in which to dispose of such waste, it announced that sites would be chosen on the basis of "science." But of course no state wanted to get such wastes, so all objected. In the congressional committee that made the final decision in 1988, Nevada had the least influence, and so Nevada got the waste. In a federal system of government, "science" rarely makes allocative decisions; local politics usually does.

Federalism reinforces adversarial politics: one of the reasons environmental issues are so contentious in this country is that cities and states fight over what standards should apply where. But federalism is not the whole story. The separation of powers guarantees that almost anybody who wants to wield influence over environmental policy will have an opportunity to do so. In England, and in most European nations, the centralized, parliamentary form of government means that the opponents of a policy have less leverage.*

It would take a book almost as long as this one to describe all the environmental laws and regulations now in effect in this country and to discuss the endless controversies over how those rules should be changed or expanded. In Table 22.1 you can find a summary of some of the more important federal laws governing air and water pollution, environmental impact statements, and open spaces.

In this chapter we want to explain how environmental policy is made. Controversies over controlling pollution from stationary sources, such as factories and power plants, take the form of *entrepreneurial politics*—many people hope to benefit from rules that impose costs on a few firms. Policies intended to reduce air pollution caused by automobiles involve *majoritarian politics*—many people hope to benefit, but many people (anyone who owns a car) will have to pay the cost. The fight over acid rain has largely been a case of *interest group politics*—regions hurt by acid rain (mainly in the Northeast) argue with regions that produce a lot of acid rain (mainly in the Midwest) about who should pay. Finally, there are examples of *client politics* at work—for example, when farmers manage to minimize federal controls over the use of pesticides. Most people are unaware of what food contains what pesticide or which, if any, are harmful; farmers are keenly aware of the economic benefits of pesticides and are well organized to defend them.

---

* Here, environmental pressures are brought by interest groups; in Europe, where such groups have less influence, environmentalists form or enter political parties so as to be represented in the legislature.

TABLE 22.1	Major Federal Environmental Laws
1963	Clean Air Act
1964	Wilderness Act
1965	Highway Beautification Act Water Quality Act
1967	Air Quality Act
1968	Wild and Scenic Rivers Act
1969	National Environmental Policy Act Endangered Species Conservation Act
1970	Clean Air Amendments Water Quality Improvement Act
1972	Federal Water Pollution Control Act Marine Mammal Protection Act Marine Protection, Research, and Sanctuaries Act Coastal Zone Management Act Federal Environmental Pesticide Control Act Noise Control Act
1973	Endangered Species Act
1974	Safe Drinking Water Act
1976	Federal Land Policy and Management Act National Forest Management Act Resource Conservation and Recovery Act Toxic Substances Control Act
1977	Clean Air Act Amendments Clean Water Act Surface Mining Control and Reclamation Act
1978	Outer Continental Shelf Lands Act Amendments
1980	Comprehensive Environmental Response, Compensation, and Liability Act ("Superfund") Alaska National Interest Lands Conservation Act
1984	Hazardous and Solid Waste Amendments
1986	Safe Drinking Water Amendments Superfund Amendments and Reauthorization Act
1987	Water Quality Act
1988	Endangered Species Act Reauthorization Federal Insecticide, Fungicide, and Rodenticide Act Amendments
1990	Clean Air Act Amendments Pollution Prevention Act

SOURCE: *Congressional Quarterly Weekly Report* (January 20, 1990): 154.

Entrepreneurial Politics: Pollution from Factories

The environmental movement was created by entrepreneurial politics. Throughout the 1960s, public awareness of the problem of pollution had been growing, but any effort to pass tough laws to reduce

Major Environmental Issues

Smog The Clean Air Act (passed in 1970; amended in 1977 and 1990)

- **Stationary sources:** EPA sets national air quality standards; states must develop plans to attain them. If state plan is inadequate, EPA sets a federal plan. Local sources that emit more than a certain amount of pollutants must install pollution control equipment.

- **Gasoline-powered vehicles:** Between 1970 and 1990, pollution from cars was cut by between 60 and 80 percent. Between 1991 and 1998 there must be another 30 percent reduction. All states must have an auto pollution inspection system.

- **Cities:** Classifies cities in terms of how severe their smog problem is and sets deadlines for meeting federal standards.

Water Clean Water Acts of various years state that there is to be no discharge of wastewater into lakes and streams without a federal permit; to get a permit, cities and factories must meet federal discharge standards.

Toxic Wastes EPA is to clean up abandoned dump sites with money raised by a tax on the chemical and petroleum industries and from general revenues. (Many thousands of such sites exist.)

Environmental Impact Statements Since 1969, any federal agency planning a project that would significantly affect the human environment must prepare in advance an environmental impact statement (EIS).

Acid Rain The Clean Air Act of 1990 requires a reduction of 10 million tons of sulfur dioxide (mostly from electric-generating plants that burn coal) by 1995. The biggest sources must acquire government allowances (which can be traded among firms) setting emission limits.

pollution coming from stationary sources—such as factories, power plants, or oil fields—had to overcome the strategic political advantage enjoyed by the sources of pollution. These sources were well organized to resist the costs of a cleanup, which might be high; the people who would benefit from the cleanup were numerous but unorganized.

On January 28, 1969, an oil well off the coast of California blew out, dumping thousands of gallons of oil on the beaches of Santa Barbara. Coming as it did at the end of the 1960s, when protest movements of every sort were commonplace, the event provided environmentalists with a horror story (the oil spill) and a demon (the oil companies) that could serve as rallying cries for a new environmental movement. On April 22, 1970, that movement came together around a national event—the first Earth Day celebration. By the end of the year, President Nixon had created, by executive order, the Environmental Protection Agency (EPA), and Congress had passed the new Clean Air Act setting national air quality standards that had to be met by certain deadlines.

Though the state governments were given the job of devising plans to achieve these standards (some states already had their own pollution control laws), it was clear that factories and power plants would have to install expensive new equipment to cut down on the amount of pollutants they produced. Especially hard hit were steel mills, smelters, and electric utilities (particularly those that burned coal). These firms and organized coal producers (the National Coal Association) had for years been able to keep the federal government from adopting tough standards, but in 1970 the protests of utilities, firms, and producers were pretty much ignored.

The oil spill and Earth Day had generated bad publicity for any source of pollution, but headlines alone don't produce new laws. Members of Congress must be induced to act. The key congressional actor was Senator Edmund Muskie (D., Maine). He chaired the subcommittee that wrote environmental laws; just as important, he wanted to run for president in 1972. As Muskie began drafting the 1970 law, consumer activist Ralph Nader attacked him for offering proposals that Nader claimed were too weak and for "selling out" to industry.[4] Muskie in fact wanted a tough bill, but in the face of Nader's accusations and the publicity they generated, he had no choice but to make it tougher still. The Clean Air Act was signed into law in December 1970.

There are many other examples of policy entrepreneurs taking advantage of an aroused public opinion to put in place new laws, either by collaborating with congressional leaders or, as in the case of the Clean Air Act, by embarrassing them. In direct response to the Santa Barbara oil spill, in 1970

Congress passed the Water Quality Improvement Act, which among other things made oil companies liable for up to $14 million in cleanup costs. Two years later it passed (over President Nixon's veto) a bill creating tough new standards and deadlines for reducing water pollution. Though strongly opposed by many industries, the bill required oil companies to install, by 1977, the "best practicable" technology for treating discharges into U.S. waterways and, by 1983, the "best available" technology. The goal was to eliminate *all* pollutant discharges into U.S. waters by 1985. The EPA was to implement the law; in addition, citizens were given the right to sue the EPA if they believed it insufficiently vigorous in carrying out its duties.

All of these bills reflected the widespread national concern with environmental issues in the early 1970s. That concern arose almost overnight and caught politicians and interest groups by surprise. In May 1969 only 1 percent of the American people told pollsters that they thought pollution was an important national problem; one year later about 25 percent thought so. An estimated 20 million people participated in Earth Day, the membership of existing environmental organizations such as the Sierra Club and the Audubon Society rose dramatically, and several new organizations—Friends of the Earth, the Environmental Defense Fund, and others—were formed.[5] In the face of this groundswell, the lobbying efforts of industry were mostly ineffective. As is often the case with entrepreneurial politics, leadership tended to come from Congress rather than from the president.

In the late 1980s and early 1990s the conditions existed for another wave of entrepreneurial politics aimed at environmental issues. The oil spill from the *Exxon Valdez* tanker off the Alaskan coast had much the same galvanizing effect as the Santa Barbara oil spill had had twenty years earlier. In April 1990 there was another Earth Day celebration, this one even larger than the first in 1970. Public opinion polls showed that a growing number of Americans believed that the quality of the environment was worse than it had been five years earlier and that "continuing environmental improvements must be made *regardless of cost*" (see Figure 22.1).

The difficulty with improving things "regardless of cost" is not only that the cost is likely to be very

In the wake of the *Exxon Valdez* oil spill, Americans began to express their concerns about the environment with renewed vigor.

FIGURE 22.1 Willing to Pay

QUESTION *Do you agree or disagree with the following statement? Protecting the environment is so important that requirements and standards cannot be too high, and continuing environmental improvements must be made regardless of cost.*

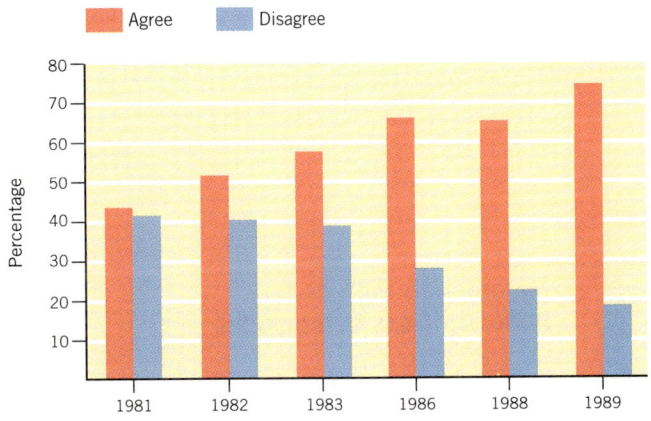

SOURCE: *Congressional Quarterly Weekly Report* (January 20, 1990): 142.

FIGURE 22.2   Sources of Toxins in the Air

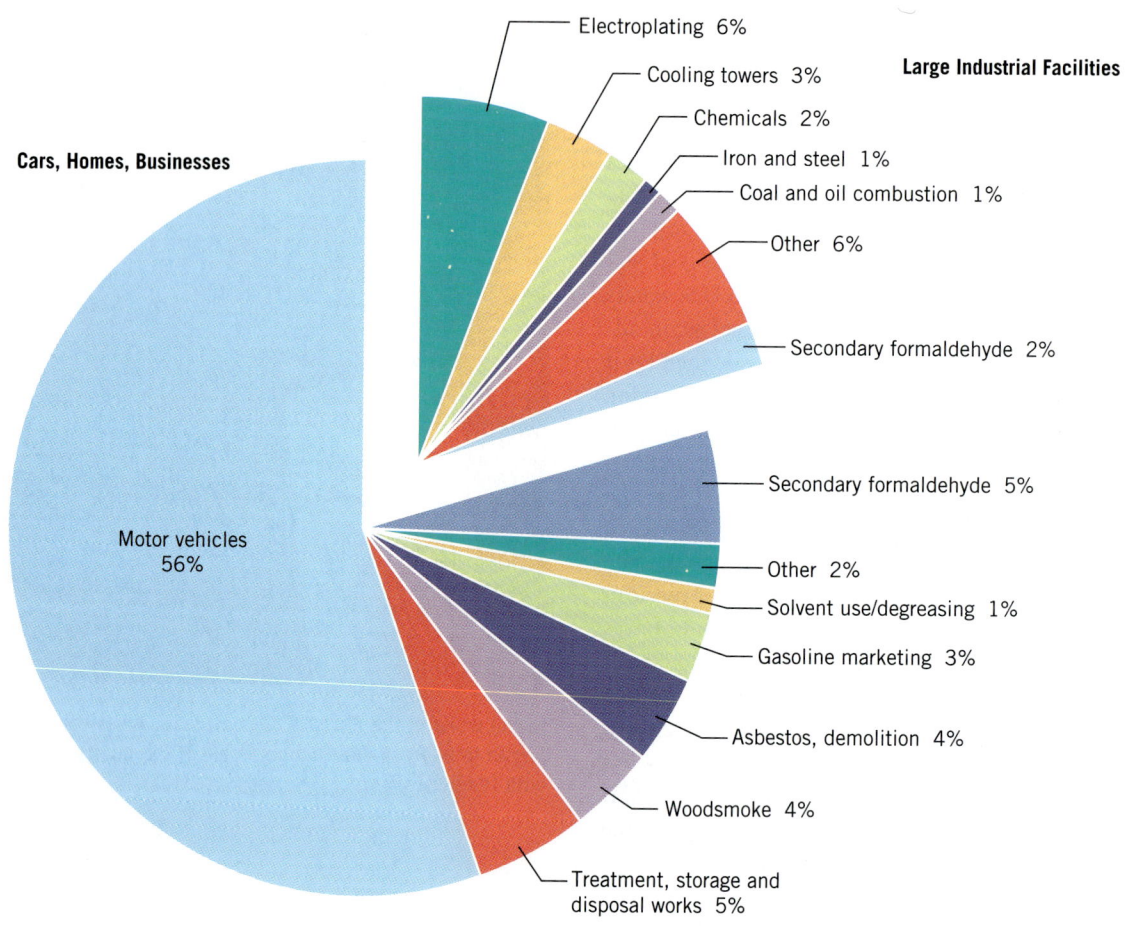

Electroplating 6%

Large Industrial Facilities

Cooling towers 3%

Chemicals 2%

Iron and steel 1%

Coal and oil combustion 1%

Other 6%

Secondary formaldehyde 2%

Cars, Homes, Businesses

Motor vehicles
56%

Secondary formaldehyde 5%

Other 2%

Solvent use/degreasing 1%

Gasoline marketing 3%

Asbestos, demolition 4%

Woodsmoke 4%

Treatment, storage and
disposal works 5%

(Does not add to 100% due to rounding)

SOURCE: *Congressional Quarterly Weekly Report* (January 20, 1990): 143.

high but also that it will fall mostly on the average citizen, not on some special interest group. The reason: the biggest single source of pollutants in the atmosphere is the automobile (see Figure 22.2). And that, as the next section shows, leads to a very different kind of politics.

Majoritarian Politics: Pollution from Automobiles

The Clean Air Act of 1970 also imposed tough restrictions on the amount of pollutants that could come out of automobile tail pipes. Indeed, most of the debate over that bill centered on this issue.

Initially the auto emissions control rules followed the pattern of entrepreneurial politics: an aroused public with media support demanded that automobile companies be required to make their cars less polluting. It seemed to be "the public" against "the interests," and the public won: by 1975 new cars would have to produce 90 percent less of two pollutants (hydrocarbons and carbon monoxide), and by 1976 achieve a 90 percent reduction in another (nitrous oxides). This was a tall order. There was no time to redesign automobile engines or to find an alternative to the internal combustion engine; it would be necessary to install devices (called catalytic converters) on exhaust pipes that would transform pollutants into harmless gases.

But a little-noticed provision in the 1970 law soon shoved the battle over automobile pollution into the arena of majoritarian politics. That provision required states to develop land-use and transportation rules to help attain air quality standards. What that meant in practice was that in any area where smog was still a problem, even after emission controls had been placed on new cars, there would have to be rules restricting the public's use of cars.

There was no way cities such as Denver, Los Angeles, and New York could get rid of smog just by requiring people to buy less-polluting cars—the increase in the number of cars or in the number of miles driven in those places outweighed the gain from making the average car less polluting. That meant that the government would have to impose such unpopular measures as bans on downtown parking, mandatory use of buses and carpools, and even gasoline rationing.

Efforts to do this failed. Popular opposition to such rules was too great, and the few such rules that were put into place didn't work. Congress reacted by postponing the deadlines by which air quality standards in cities would have to be met; the EPA reacted by abandoning any serious effort to tell people when and where they could drive.[6]

Even the effort to clean up the exhausts of new cars ran into opposition. Some people didn't like the higher cost of cars with catalytic converters; others didn't like the loss in horsepower that these converters caused (many people disconnected them). The United Auto Workers union began to worry that antismog rules would hurt the U.S. auto industry and cost them their jobs. Congress took note of these complaints and decided that despite a lot of effort, new cars could not meet the 90 percent emission reduction standard by 1975–1976, and so in 1977 it amended the Clean Air Act to extend these deadlines by up to six years.

The Clean Air Act, when revised again in 1990, set new, tougher auto emission control standards—but it pushed back the deadline for compliance with them, in stages, to 1995. It reiterated the need for getting rid of smog in the smoggiest cities and proposed a number of ways to do it—but it set the deadline for compliance in the worst area (Los Angeles) at twenty years in the future.

The public will support tough environmental laws when somebody else pays or when the costs are

Some states reserve a highway lane for people driving in carpools.

hidden (as in the price of a car); it will not give as much support when it believes that it is paying, especially when the payment takes the form of changing how and when it uses the family car. Here are more examples of each kind of majoritarian politics.

Majoritarian Politics When People Believe the Costs Are Low The National Environmental Policy Act (NEPA), passed in 1969, contained a provision requiring that an **environmental impact statement** (EIS) be written before any federal agency undertakes an activity that will "significantly" affect the quality of the human environment. (Similar laws have been passed in many states, affecting not only what government does but what private developers do.) Because it required only a "statement" rather than some specific action and because it was a pro-environment law, NEPA passed by overwhelming majorities.

As it turned out, the EIS provision was hardly innocuous. Opponents of virtually any government-sponsored project have used the EIS as a way of blocking, changing, or delaying the project. Hundreds of lawsuits have been filed to challenge this or that provision of an EIS or to claim that a project was not supported by a satisfactory EIS. In this way environmental activists have challenged the Alaska pipeline, a Florida canal, and several nuclear power plants, as well as countless dams, bridges, highways, and office buildings. Usually the agency's plan is upheld, but this does not mean that the EIS is unimportant: the EIS induces the agency to think through what it is doing, and it gives critics a chance to examine, and often to negotiate, the content of those plans.

Despite the grumbling of many people adversely affected by fights over an EIS (someone once complained that Moses would never have been able to part the Red Sea if he had had to file an EIS first), popular support for it remains strong because the public at large does not believe that it is paying a high price and does believe that it is gaining a significant benefit.

Majoritarian Politics When People Believe the Costs Are High From time to time someone proposes that gasoline taxes be raised sharply. Such taxes would discourage driving, and this not only would conserve fuel but also would reduce smog. Almost everyone would pay, but almost everyone would

benefit. However, it is only with great difficulty that the public can be persuaded to support such taxes. The reason is that the people pay the tax first, and the benefit, if any, comes later. Unlike Social Security, where the taxes we pay now support cash benefits we get later, gasoline taxes support noncash benefits (cleaner air, less congestion) that many people doubt will ever appear or, if they do, will not be meaningful to them.[7]

When gasoline taxes have been raised, it has usually been because the politicians did not push the tax hike as an environmental measure. Instead they promised that in return for paying higher taxes the public would receive some concrete benefits—more highways, more buses, or a reduction in the federal deficit (as happened with the gas tax hike of 1990 and again in 1993).

Interest Group Politics: Acid Rain

Sometimes the rain, snow, or dust particles that fall onto the land are acidic. This is called **acid rain**. One source of that acid precipitation is burning fuel, such as certain types of coal, that contains a lot of sulfur. Some of the sulfur (along with nitrogen) will turn into sulfuric (or nitric) acid as it comes to earth. Steel mills and electric power plants that burn high-sulfur coal are concentrated in the Midwest and Great Lakes regions of the United States. The prevailing winds tend to carry those sulfurous fumes eastward, where some fall to the ground.

That much seems certain. Everything else has been surrounded by controversy. Many lakes and rivers in the eastern United States and in Canada have become more acidic, and some forests in these areas have died back. Some part of this is the result of acid rain from industrial smokestacks, but some part of it is also the result of naturally occurring acids in the soils and rainfall. How much of the acidification is man-made and how much is a result of the actions of Mother Nature is unclear. Some lakes are not affected by acid rain; some are. Why some are affected more than others is unclear. The long-term effects of higher acid levels in lakes and forests are also unclear.

These scientific uncertainties were important because they provided some support for each side in

Acid rain may cause damage to forests.

a fierce interest group battle. Residents of Canada and New England complained bitterly of the loss of forests and the acidification of lakes, blaming it on midwestern smokestacks. Midwestern businesses, labor unions, and politicians denied that their smokestacks were the major cause of the problem (if, indeed, there was a problem) and argued that, even if they were the cause, they shouldn't have to pay the cost of cleaning up the problem.

Here was a classic case of two well-organized parties, one hoping to reap benefits and the other fearing to pay costs, locked in a struggle over a policy proposal. Even before people were aware that acid rain might be a problem, these two groups were fighting over how, if at all, sulfur emissions should be reduced. (In the early 1970s, sulfur coming out of smokestacks was believed to pose a health hazard.)

An attempt to deal with the issue in 1977 reflected the kind of bizarre compromises that some-times result when politically opposed forces have to be reconciled. There were essentially two alternatives. One was to require power plants to burn low-sulfur coal. This would undoubtedly cut back on sulfur emissions, but it would cost money, because, as can be seen in the map below, low-sulfur coal is mined mostly in the West, hundreds of miles away from the midwestern coal-burning industries. The other way would be to require power plants to install scrubbers—complicated and very expensive devices that would take sulfurous fumes out of the gas before it came out of the smokestack. In addition to their cost, the trouble with scrubbers was that they didn't always work and that they generated a lot of unpleasant sludge that would have to be hauled away and buried somewhere. Their great advantage, however, was that they would allow midwestern utilities to continue their practice of using cheap, high-sulfur coal.

THE POLITICS OF ENERGY: SOURCES OF FOSSIL FUELS IN THE UNITED STATES

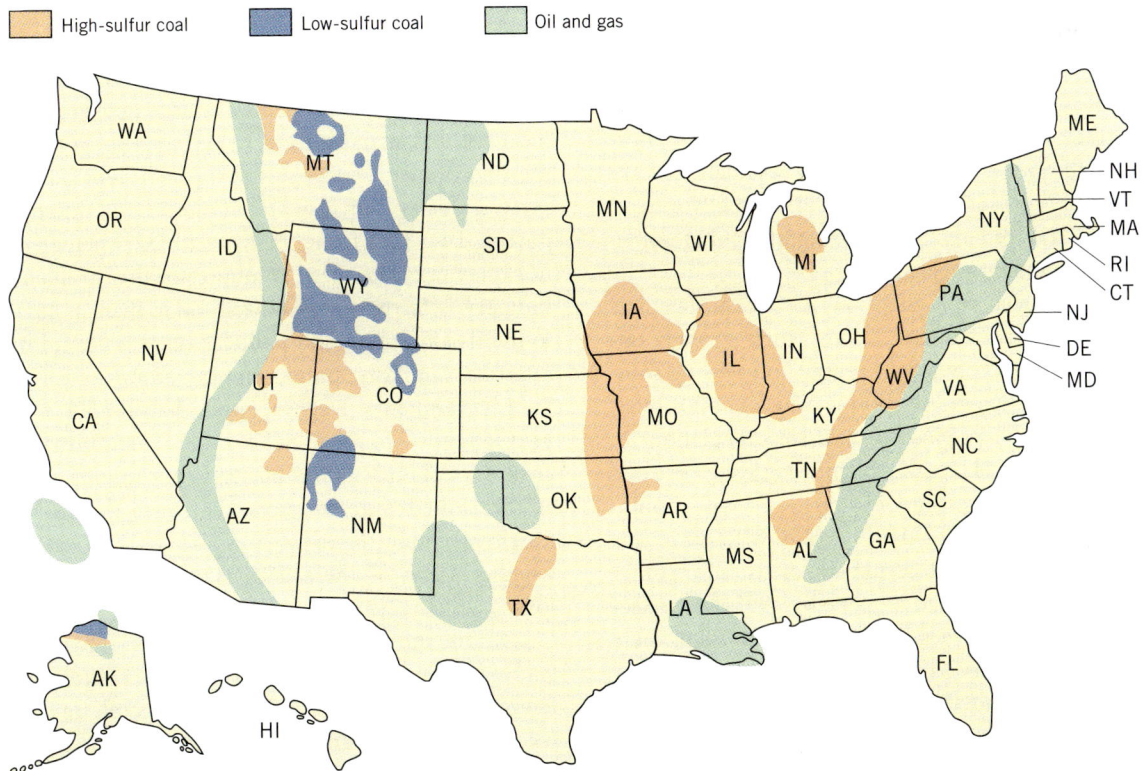

SOURCE: *Congressional Quarterly Weekly Report* (January 20, 1990): 160.

Congress voted for the scrubbers for all new coal-burning plants, even if they burned low-sulfur coal. In the opinion of most economists, this was the wrong decision,[8] but it had four great political advantages. First, the jobs of miners in high-sulfur coal mines would be protected. They had powerful allies in Congress. Second, environmentalists liked scrubbers, which they seemed to regard as a definitive, technological "solution" to the problem, an approach far preferable to relying on incentives to induce power plants to buy low-sulfur coal. Third, scrubber manufacturers liked the idea, for obvious reasons. Finally, some eastern governors liked scrubbers because if all new plants had to have them, it would be more costly, and thus less likely, for existing factories in their states to close down and move into the West.

The 1977 law in effect required scrubbers on all new coal-burning plants—even ones located right next to mines where they could get low-sulfur coal. As two scholars later described the law, it seemed to produce "clean coal and dirty air."[9]

The 1977 bill did not solve much. Many of the scrubbers, as predicted, didn't work very well. And there remained the question of what to do about existing power plants and factories. In the early 1980s the Reagan administration took the position that too little was known to warrant strong action; more research was needed first. The Canadian government and members of Congress from the Northeast took a very different view, demanding that something be done immediately.

For thirteen years there was a political stalemate in Congress, as is often the case when strongly opposed interest groups fight it out. And when a solution was finally agreed upon, it was a compromise. President Bush proposed a two-step regulation. In the first phase 111 power plants would be required to reduce their emission of sulfur by a fixed amount. They could decide for themselves how to do it: buy low-sulfur coal, install scrubbers, or use some other technology. This would be done by 1995. In the second phase, with a deadline in the year 2000, there would be sharper emission reductions for many more plants, and this would probably require the use of scrubbers. To create some flexibility in how much each utility must cut its emissions, there was created a system of sulfur dioxide allowances that

could be bought and sold. Coal miners complained that they would lose jobs during phase one, and so they were promised some financial compensation if they were laid off as a result of their employers' complying with the new limits. This compromise became part of the Clean Air Act of 1990.

Interest group politics permeates many aspects of environmental policy making. When cities or states consider land-use controls and zoning ordinances, they are weighing the competing demands of established residents (who often want as little new growth in their communities as possible) against demands of developers who want to build additional housing.

Interest group politics often lacks the moral fervor of entrepreneurial politics and rarely taps the deep streams of public opinion that are reflected in majoritarian politics. As environmental policy has become more complex and as people have adjusted to existing laws, however, new interest groups have been formed that have a stake in how things are done. As a result it becomes harder and harder to change existing policies. The heady victories of the early 1970s are hard to duplicate today because groups that were once unorganized are now well organized.

For example, there is now a large and growing industry that makes products designed to improve the environment. As we saw in the acid rain controversy, industry can play an important role in supporting laws that favor their machines, whether or not they are the best solution to the problem. Industry is far better organized today than in 1970 to use its employees and political allies to defend its interests. Similarly, public-interest groups, such as the Environmental Defense Fund, that did not exist in 1965 now compete with other environmental groups for money and publicity. Labor unions, such as the United Auto Workers, that once fought for tough air pollution laws now are worried about whether some of these laws may cost them their jobs.

Despite the rise of all of these interests, the political momentum remains with the policy entrepreneurs. Environmentalism is seen as good politics (see Figure 22.3), and few members of Congress want to be caught on the wrong side of the vote on an environmental bill.

Client Politics: Agricultural Pesticides

Some client groups have so far escaped this momentum. One such group is organized farmers, who have more or less successfully resisted efforts to restrict, sharply, the use of pesticides or to control the runoff of pesticides from farmlands.

For a while it seemed as though farmers would also fall before the assaults of policy entrepreneurs. When Rachel Carson published *Silent Spring* in 1962, she set off a public outcry about the harm to wildlife caused by the indiscriminate use of DDT, a common pesticide. In 1972 the EPA banned the use of DDT.

That same year Congress directed the EPA to evaluate the safety of all pesticides on the market; unsafe ones were to be removed. However, that is easier said than done. One reason is that there are over fifty thousand pesticides now in use, with five thousand new ones introduced every year.[10] Testing all of these chemicals is a huge, vastly expensive, and very time-consuming job, especially since any health effects on people may not be observed for several years.[11] Another reason is that pesticides have many beneficial uses; therefore someone has to balance the gains and the risks of using a given pesticide and compare the relative gains and risks of two similar pesticides.

But even if the science were easy, the politics would not be. American farmers are the most productive in the world, and most of them believe that they cannot achieve that output (and thus their present incomes) without using pesticides. These farmers are well organized to express their interests and well represented in Congress (especially on the House and Senate Agricultural Committees). Complicating matters is the fact that the subsidies the taxpayers give to farmers often encourage them to produce more food than they can sell and thus to use more pesticides than they really need. Though many of these chemicals do not remain in the crops that are harvested, large amounts sink into the soil, contaminating water supplies. But these problems are largely invisible to the public and are much harder to dramatize than, say, the discovery of a toxic waste dump like that at Love Canal, New York.

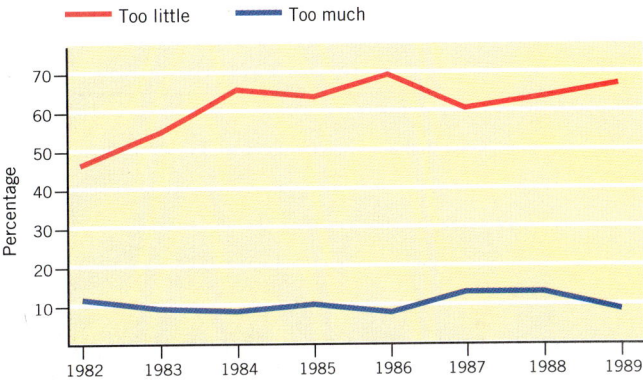

FIGURE 22.3 Government Regulation

QUESTION *In general do you think there is too much, too little . . . government regulation and involvement in the area of environmental protection?**

* Others responded "right amount" or "don't know."

SOURCE: *Congressional Quarterly Weekly Report* (January 20, 1990): 185.

Though attacked by environmental organizations, farm groups have been generally successful at practicing client politics. The EPA's budget for reviewing pesticides has been kept small (the longtime chairman of the House Appropriations Committee, Jamie Whitten, was a supporter of farmers and a critic of environmentalists).[12] Very few pesticides have been taken off the market, and those that have have tended to be ones that, because they were involved in some incident receiving heavy media coverage (such as the effect of DDT on birds), easily fell prey to entrepreneurial politics.

A similar kind of client politics exists in the timber industry. Wood product companies and loggers want access to forests under the control of the U.S. Forest Service. Though only 13 percent of all cut timber comes from these forests and two-thirds of the U.S. forest system is already off-limits to logging, environmentalists want further restrictions, especially to prevent clear-cutting (cutting down all the trees in a given area) and to prevent harvesting trees from the old-growth forests of Oregon and Washington. But Congress has generally supported the timber industry, ordering the Forest Service to sell harvesting rights at below-market prices, in effect subsidizing the industry. Some activists hope to

Environmentalists use the protection of an endangered species, such as the spotted owl, as a way of reducing timber harvests.

convert this client politics into entrepreneurial politics by demanding that clear-cutting in certain forests be stopped in order to protect endangered species, such as the spotted owl.

The Environmental Uncertainties

Making environmental policy strikes many people as easy—identify a problem, raise a fuss, defeat "the interests," and enjoy the benefits. In fact it is much harder than that to have a sane environmental policy.

First, what is the problem? Nobody likes smog, and human waste or oil slicks floating off our beaches are obviously bad. But many other problems are much less clear-cut. Science doesn't know whether we are experiencing a dangerous level of global warming or how bad the greenhouse effect is, if it exists at all. Pesticides that cause cancer in animals when given in megadoses may or may not cause cancer in people when absorbed in nominal amounts.

Second, if there is a problem, what goals do we want to achieve? We want reasonably clean air and water, of course, but how clean is reasonably clean? Since the cost of removing from the air the last 10 percent of some pollutants is often greater than the cost of removing the first 90 percent, how clean is clean enough? If making air and water cleaner is costly in terms of jobs, energy, and economic growth, how big a price are we willing to pay? When the cost of gasoline shot up in 1973–1974, many voters became much less interested in nonpolluting cars if the devices that reduced the pollution also reduced the cars' gas mileage.

Third, how do we want to achieve our goals? Issuing rules and enforcing them in court often seem the easiest things to do, but they are not always the wisest. That **command-and-control strategy** assumes that the rule makers and rule enforcers know how to achieve the greatest environmental gain at the least cost. In fact no one knows how to do that, because local circumstances, technological problems, and economic costs are so complex. Under what circumstances can we use incentives and market prices to get people voluntarily to clean up their act by using their own imagination?

All of these uncertainties have become part of the endless political controversies surrounding the administration of the Environmental Protection Agency. For example:

What Is the Problem?   The EPA was given responsibility to administer certain laws governing air, water, and pesticides (among others). But it is rarely left alone to define these problems; any new environmental scandal leads to popular and congressional demands that it drop everything and solve that crisis. When toxic chemicals were found at Love Canal and Virginia Beach, these dramatic discoveries put other, less dramatic, but often more important problems onto the back burner.

What Are the Costs and Benefits?   Everyone wants a healthy environment, but people do not distinguish accurately between realistic and unrealistic threats or between reasonable and unreasonable costs. The biggest scare is cancer, even though every form of cancer has been steadily declining for many years (except lung cancer, which is caused primarily by smoking, not environmental hazards). People fear the unknown—many are afraid of flying, for example, even though flying is vastly safer than driving. People fear strange threats, such as toxic chemicals, even though they may never hurt anyone. People applaud dramatic governmental steps without asking whether they actually help anyone. For example, the government has mandated that all asbestos must be removed from public school buildings. Though intense exposure to asbestos can cause health problems, removing all the asbestos from old school buildings helps almost no one and may hurt the asbestos removers. The problem for government officials is to keep policies aimed at real risks—they do exist—and to not be diverted by popular concerns over unreal ones. In a free society, that is not easy.

What Are Our Goals? When the EPA was told by Congress to eliminate *all* pollutants entering our waterways by 1985, to cut auto emissions by 90 percent within five years, and to eliminate smog in *all* cities, Congress should have known that these goals were utterly unrealistic. When the EPA realized that it could not achieve these goals, it was forced to ask for extensions in deadlines and for revisions in laws. This gave it the appearance of knuckling under to industry pressure.[13]

How Do We Achieve Our Goals? Initially the EPA was zealous about using a command-and-control strategy to improve air and water quality. For example, to reduce water pollution discharged from factories, the EPA issued rules broken down into 642 industry subcategories, and even then there was a lot of local variation that it could not take into account.[14] When the cost of doing this sort of thing got out of control, the EPA during the Carter administration began to devise incentives to replace some rules. These included offsets, bubbles, and banks:

- **Offsets.** If a company wants to open a new plant in an area with polluted air, it can do so if the pollution it generates is offset by a reduction in pollution from another source in that area. To

achieve that reduction, the new company may buy an existing company and close it down.

- **Bubble standard.** A bubble is the total amount of air pollution that can come from a given factory. A company is free to decide which specific sources within that factory must be reduced and how to meet the bubble standard.

- **Pollution allowances** (or **banks**). If a company reduces its polluting emissions by more than the law requires, it can either use this excess to cover a future plant expansion or sell it to another company as an offset.

Once, only affected businesses complained about the high cost, slow progress, and legal complexity of environmental regulations. Increasingly, however, pro-environment interest groups and the government itself have become aware of the difficulties that arise when the government relies on a command-and-control strategy that is indifferent to costs and excessively reliant on lawsuits.

When the Clinton administration took office in 1993, it had the strong support of environmental-

Cleaning up the more than 1,200 major toxic waste sites nationwide will take decades.

FIGURE 22.4   Quality of Life

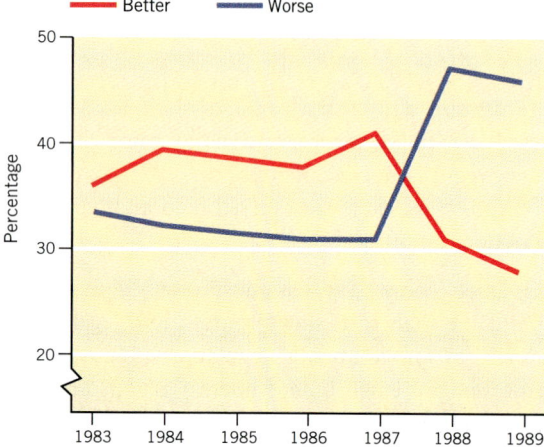

QUESTION

Overall quality of the environment around here: better or worse than it was five years ago?

■— Better   ■— Worse

SOURCE: *Congressional Quarterly Weekly Report* (January 20, 1990): 138.

ists. Vice President Gore was a visible and influential supporter of environmental protection; he had even written a book on the subject. Secretary of the Interior Bruce Babbitt was also a staunch environmentalist. But instead of just pushing ahead with more command-and-control policies, the new administration began to reexamine these approaches. It suggested, for example, that the Superfund law, intended to clean up toxic waste dumps, was in fact not cleaning up many sites; instead it was encouraging armies of lawyers to bring lengthy and costly lawsuits to determine who was responsible for the toxic waste.

American politics, though often messy, confusing, and conflict-ridden, sometimes changes as people learn from their experiences. Indeed, our political system causes learning (and undergoes change) precisely *because* it is messy, confusing, and conflict-ridden. Problems that once looked simple ("There is too much pollution") and policies that once sounded straightforward ("We'll tell people to stop polluting") must often be tempered and modified once they are tested by the complexities of reality.

The Results

Though Americans think that their environment has gotten worse, in fact many aspects of it have gotten better since 1970 (see Figure 22.4). There is now much less carbon monoxide, sulfur dioxide, and lead in the atmosphere than once was the case. It is less clear whether there have been equally noticeable improvements in water quality, in large part because much of the gunk that flows into our rivers, lakes, and oceans does not come from some fixed source (such as a sewer) that can be easily isolated; a lot comes from runoff from the ground as a result of rain washing pollutants off urban streets and farmlands and into the water.

Hazardous waste is found at thousands of known locations (and perhaps hundreds more unknown ones). The cleanup job is so great that it will be years before much progress can be shown. Getting big reductions in dangerous pesticides requires first reaching agreement on what is a dangerous pesticide and then finding a way of minimizing the harm to agriculture that would be caused by the reduction.

SUMMARY

Environmental issues illustrate all four styles of policy-making.

Entrepreneurial politics: an unorganized public is to benefit at the expense of a well-organized group. An example is the effort to reduce air and water pollution from stationary sources, such as factories. Such politics requires mobilizing the media, dramatizing the issue, and convincing members of Congress that their political reputations will suffer if they do not cast the right vote. To prevent client groups from taking over the implementation of these laws, the bills are written to make it easy to use the courts to force action.

Majoritarian politics: an unorganized public is to benefit at its own expense. Examples include reducing auto emissions by imposing transportation controls, raising gasoline taxes, and requiring environmental impact statements. Interest groups tend not to be the decisive players. Whether the proposal wins or loses depends on how the public generally evaluates the costs. They like environmental impact statements but oppose higher gasoline taxes and restrictions on private automobile use. Dramatizing a crisis tends to be less effective because the public at large, and not some small interest, must pay for any benefits.

Interest group politics: two organized groups with a material stake in the outcome fight over who will pay and who will benefit. An example is the controlling of acid rain. When faced with two or more powerful interests, Congress tends not to pass broad, sweeping bills but to find workable compromises.

Client politics: an organized group gets a benefit; an unorganized public must pay. Examples include the use of agricultural pesticides and timber cutting in U.S. forests. Client politics depends on the client group's having strategically placed allies in Congress and on its potential opponents' being unable to convert this policy system into a pattern of entrepreneurial politics (by dramatizing a crisis, for example).

In general, entrepreneurial politics has played the dominant role in most environmental issues. The prevalence of entrepreneurial politics in this arena is largely due to (1) the success of policy entrepreneurs in sensitizing public opinion to these matters and (2) the growth of a variety of public-interest lobbies with close ties to the media and with the ability to threaten recalcitrant legislators with attacks on their reputations.

Unlike economic or welfare issues, environmental issues lend themselves to entrepreneurial politics because the problems can be portrayed in life-threatening terms, the goals can be related to what most people believe is the good life, and the costs can be minimized, deferred, or (seemingly) placed on small groups.

KEY TERMS

environmental impact statement   *p. 657*

acid rain   *p. 658*

command-and-control strategy   *p. 662*

offsets   *p. 663*

bubble standard   *p. 663*

pollution allowances *or* banks   *p. 663*

SUGGESTED READINGS

Easterbrook, Gregg. *A Moment on Earth.* New York: Viking, 1995. A comprehensive account of what we have accomplished and what remains to be done regarding the environment, written by a hard-headed environmentalist.

Landy, Mark K., Marc J. Roberts, and Stephen R. Thomas. *The Environmental Protection Agency: Asking the Wrong Questions.* New York: Oxford University Press, 1990. Careful review of how the EPA tries to manage complex environmental problems under laws and policies that force it to focus on "what causes cancer."

Meier, Kenneth J. *Regulation: Politics, Bureaucracy, and Economics.* New York: St. Martin's Press, 1985, chap. 6. Good brief overview of the laws and agencies that define our environmental policy.

Melnick, R. Shep. *Regulation and the Courts: The Case of the Clean Air Act.* Washington, D.C.: Brookings Institution, 1983. Thoughtful analysis of the extraordinary role played by the courts in implementing the Clean Air Act.

Rosenbaum, Walter A. *Environmental Politics and Policy.* 2d ed. Washington, D.C.: Congressional Quarterly Press, 1991. Analysis of the politics of environmental issues, including air and water pollution, the use of chemicals, nuclear power, and preserving open space.

Vogel, David. *National Style of Regulation: Environmental Policy in Great Britain and the United States.* Ithaca, N.Y.: Cornell University Press, 1986. An explanation of why environmental politics in the United States is so adversarial.

PART FIVE

The Nature of American Democracy

"Justice is the end of government. It is the end of civil society. It ever has been and ever will be pursued until it be obtained, or until liberty be lost in the pursuit."

— Federalist no. 51

23

Who Governs?

★ What policies the government adopts

★ The politics of various policies

★ Evaluating the traditional theories of political power: Marxist, elitist, bureaucratic, pluralist

I t is time to try to answer the questions with which this book began. We want to know who governs and to what ends. In this chapter we shall try to answer the first question; in the next we shall say something about the second.

Describing, however precisely, government institutions and political organizations is a necessary but not sufficient condition for deciding who governs. Simply by choosing what to emphasize and what to leave out, one can write an account of the presidency that makes that institution seem "imperialistic" or a "pitiful, helpless giant" (to use the contrasting imagery of Arthur Schlesinger and Richard Nixon). And depending on what issues one picks, one can characterize Congress as a gathering of zealots that whoops new legislation through in record time (as it did when it passed the Social Security Act and the law outlawing mandatory retirement) or as an elephantine institution bogged down by its own convoluted procedures and internal quarrels (as it was when it labored for months over an energy bill and health care reform).

Since we want to know who governs largely because our lives are affected by the distribution of political power, it seems only reasonable to try to answer the question of governance by examining, as systematically as we can, what policies the government adopts (or fails to adopt). A scheme for classifying public policies was presented in Chapter 15. It does not deserve to be called a theory, for there are many policies that do not fit well into the classification, and the distinctions that it suggests are crude and oversimplified. It does have at least two advantages, though: it requires us to look at a comprehensive list of policies (or nonpolicies) rather than permitting us to generalize about politics on the basis of a few issues in which we happen to be interested at the moment, and it calls attention to important ways in which those policies are thought to affect people (the distribution of perceived costs and benefits). Let us begin by summarizing what we have learned about the politics of making four kinds of policies and then use that information as evidence to evaluate the competing theories of political power that were described in Chapter 1.

669

Four Kinds of Politics

Majoritarian Politics

The costs and benefits of a proposed course of action are sometimes seen by people as being widely distributed: everybody, or almost everybody, or very broad groups of people stand to gain or lose in roughly the same way. We have seen several examples: the old-age and survivors' insurance provided under the 1935 Social Security Act; the medical benefits offered under the 1965 Medicare Act; the fair-trade requirements of the Sherman Antitrust Act of 1890 and the Federal Trade Commission Act of 1914; the general foreign policy posture of the United States (internationalist or isolationist); the decisions to go to war in 1941, 1950, the 1960s, and 1991 (and to *not* go to war in 1914 and 1954); those features of macroeconomic policy that seem to contribute to price stability and reasonably full employment; and the failure of attempts to reduce automobile use. All these examples, though different in substance, have in common the fact that similar political institutions and actors tend to play the leading policy-making roles.

Public Opinion   Because matters like those listed above are highly visible and seem to affect the country as a whole, public opinion about them is usually discernible. Sometimes public opinion is quite specific, such as when polls showed that a majority of Americans wanted something very much like what the Social Security and Medicare Acts ultimately provided. Sometimes public opinion provides only a general direction but no particular details to policy makers, such as when it inclines toward internationalism or isolationism.

And sometimes the public wants things that turn out to be inconsistent, such as stable prices, full employment, and high levels of government spending, all at the same time. But policy makers are aware that public opinion does exist and that, even when it lacks detail or consistency, it is ignored only at a politician's peril. Citizens expect leadership and are willing to tolerate both delays and gambles in its exercise, but in the long run officials who ignore the thrust of public opinion or devise policies that supply more costs than benefits are likely to suffer at the

polls. The Republicans who opposed much of the New Deal misread public opinion or thought that they could defy it; they learned differently in the Democratic sweep of 1936. Democratic politicians were supported for a while in their military policy in Vietnam, but by 1968 a majority of people had decided that the policy was more of a burden than a benefit and wanted a change. In 1980 the public was upset by inflation and the hostage crisis in Iran; in 1992 they were concerned about the economy and crime.

The president and his principal advisers tend to play a leading, if not dominant, role in majoritarian politics. People hold the president responsible for the economy, for national defense, for social welfare, and for foreign policy. Sometimes, as with foreign policy and military spending, that accountability is well placed, for the president, constitutionally and institutionally, plays the dominant role in these decisions. Sometimes, as with the state of the economy, the president may be as much a victim as an architect of the current state of affairs, but no matter: he must act as if he could control things, because people believe that he should be able to control them.

Ideological Debate   A proposal to adopt a wholly new program that applies to many people often precipitates an intense, sometimes ideological debate. Social Security and Medicare were enacted after just such a debate; the Family Assistance Plan was *not* enacted as a consequence of such a debate. The struggles over whether to enter World War II (neutrality versus interventionism) in 1939–1941, over strategic military doctrine in the 1960s and again in the 1970s, over policy toward Central America in the 1980s, over whether the nation should continue to follow Keynesian fiscal policy or instead adopt the big tax cuts suggested by supply-side economists—all these were genuine debates in which ideas as much as interests played a decisive role.

Worldview   The outcome of such debates is often the institutionalization of a new worldview. In the 1950s the interventionists won out over the isolationists; the advocates of a federal social-welfare policy defeated the supporters of private charity and local relief programs; and the critics of big business won at least a rhetorical advantage over the defenders of large industrial trusts. In these struggles a crisis often provided the decisive leverage: what the Great Depression did for welfare policy, the attack on Pearl Harbor did for foreign policy and World War II did for fiscal policy. When the constraints of public opinion are loose, as they are in foreign policy, the worldview that is significant is that of policy elites who operate in or close to government. When the constraints are tighter, as they are in macroeconomic policy, elected officials discover that their freedom of action is narrowed. Incumbent politicians must balance national interests, as they define them, against their need to get reelected, which often leads them to fund certain programs—the "sacred cows"—more generously than others and to sweeten a general tax cut with specific benefits for particular groups.

But a crisis is not the only force that alters a popular or elite worldview. Higher education, the mass media, changing perceptions of the causes and consequences of various human problems—all have had an effect on people's ideas of what is desirable public policy. The history of welfare legislation provides a good example of how a worldview changes and evolves. It shows how a nation with a strong belief in self-reliance and the value of work has slowly modified (but not abandoned) those ideas, first accepting aid to the elderly and the infirm (on an insurance basis), then endorsing aid to the unemployed and the indigent, and then accepting some limited forms of direct income support for the poor (whatever their age or work experience) in the form of food stamps.

But thus far the changing popular definition of social justice has not included large-scale income redistribution. And one particularly visible form of welfare—Aid to Families with Dependent Children—because it was not seen as a majoritarian policy but one in which a client group ("them") benefited at the expense of society at large ("us"), has been discontinued.

Political Parties When Congress is adopting new majoritarian policies, political parties tend to be relatively important. Many of the key issues in social welfare, economic policy, and foreign affairs pit a substantial majority of Democrats against a substantial majority of Republicans. In policies of this sort Congress has acted more like a parliament than an assemblage of independent legislators, debating

The separation of powers can lead to stalemate, as when President Reagan repeatedly threatened to veto spending bills passed by a Democratic Congress.

broad issues in partisan and even ideological terms. Often no new policy can win if the parties are relatively evenly balanced in Congress, because though Congress may debate in a parliamentary style, it lacks the parliamentary discipline to prevent a few defectors from one party or the other from blocking change. As a result the victory of a new idea often requires an election that gives one party an extraordinary majority.

A majoritarian policy, once adopted *and* proved to be popular, tends to lose its ideological significance and to attract bipartisan support, especially when government can readily increase the level of benefits to the public (as with Social Security and Medicare). However, if costs become very high—as they may have for Medicare—the "easy politics" of continually increasing benefits may come under closer scrutiny.

Interest Group Politics

When the costs of a policy are perceived to be concentrated on one distinct, relatively small group and the benefits on a different, equally distinct and small group, interest group politics dominates the policy-making process. Interest groups are active to some degree in almost all policy-making, of course, but they are the *dominant* political forces when costs and benefits are distributed in this way. Labor legislation—the National Labor Relations Act, the Taft-Hartley Act, the Landrum-Griffin Act, and other bills—are obvious examples of this. So also are the struggles between cable and over-the-air television broadcasters, between domestic ethnic groups over certain foreign policy matters, and between importers and exporters over tariff laws and regulations. Similarly, interest group politics is evident in the tension between the Midwest and Northeast over acid rain, between opposed interests in cases involving rights in conflicts (such as the right to a fair trial versus the right to publish news), between parties competing before certain regulatory commissions (such as the Environmental Protection Agency or the Occupational Safety and Health Administration), and between blacks and whites in local communities with segregated schools.

Changing Cleavages in Society   The sources of interest group policy proposals are to be found in changing economic and social cleavages in society. The rise of new technologies, the altered shape of markets, the rise and decline of regions, and changes in the organizational skills and resources of previously unorganized (or weakly organized) groups provide opportunities for new interest group proposals. The debate over the Commerce Act of 1887 was set off by declining profits on the long-haul railroads, high monopolistic prices on many short-haul lines, rivalry among port cities for cheap access to the agricultural heartland of the country, and the rising importance of national and international markets for commercial farmers. Every interest had an incentive to organize for political action.

Though usually interest group policies by their very nature stimulate the organization of all relevant interests, sometimes one group is able to block the organizing efforts of its rival. Many industries were able to do this in the nineteenth and early twentieth centuries with respect to would-be labor unions; whites were able to do this in many communities with respect to blacks and other racial minorities. These restraints on equality of organizational opportunity were made possible by the privileged access that one group already had to the coercive powers of the government. Industries could for many years count on the police and the army as al-

lies in breaking strikes, just as southern whites could use laws and administrative regulations to keep large numbers of blacks from voting.

That privileged power position was sustained by widely shared attitudes. Many people disapproved of unions or objected to strikes that seemed intended to win exclusive control by a union over entry into a particular job market. Similarly, many citizens either were prejudiced against blacks or disapproved of blacks' efforts to alter the distribution of political power. When these restraints on equal organizational opportunity existed, the disadvantaged group has had to employ a variety of tactics to change popular attitudes, attract legislative allies, and enlist the sympathy of the courts.

Political Parties   When a policy is proposed by one interest group and opposed by another of comparable political power, the political parties will often be deeply divided and, as a consequence, play little or no role in the resolution of the matter. The issue cuts across partisan lines, and unlike parties in some European democracies, American parties are too weak to overcome deep internal divisions. The passage of the Commerce Act, for example, was not a partisan matter, and both Democrats and Republicans were split for decades over the question of civil rights. A few interest group conflicts follow party lines—for example, labor-management issues have tended to parallel Democratic-Republican differences. But these are the exceptions.

Continuing Struggle   Interest group politics does not end with the passage or defeat of the initial proposal. The struggle continues in other places—in the bureaucracy, before the courts, and in subsequent legislative sessions. The interest group struggle that resulted in the passage of the National Labor Relations Act and the Occupational Safety and Health Act was transferred from the lobbies of Congress to the offices and corridors of the National Labor Relations Board and the Occupational Safety and Health Administration. Such agencies are less likely to be "captured" by any single interest than are those created as a result of client politics. Nor will the affected interest groups accept gracefully the decisions of the bureaucracy: appeals will be taken to the federal courts, and efforts will be made to get the law amended.

Public opinion and presidential leadership have some effect on the outcome of these struggles, but except in the formative stages that effect will ordinarily be weak. The public at large cannot possibly become so well informed or so concerned as to shape in important ways the conflict between well-organized, vitally involved opponents. The president can tilt the balance of power one way or another by whom he chooses to appoint to key bureaucratic agencies, but rarely does a president try to shape directly, deeply, or in detail the outcome of these conflicts. The public and the president are usually content to hope that the "right persons" are put in charge of refereeing interest group conflicts. And except to report on the more important outcomes and occasional scandals associated with interest group politics, the mass media rarely play an important role.

Client Politics

Sometimes the benefits of a policy are concentrated on one relatively small, easily organized group, and the costs are widely distributed over the public at large. In these cases client politics arises. We find this happening when the merchant marine receives a government subsidy, when veterans obtain special benefits, when farmers defeat efforts to curtail sharply the use of pesticides, and when various occupations are allowed by state licensing laws to govern themselves. Client politics is also at work when a community wishes to obtain a flood-control project or retain a military base, or when an economic or other interest obtains a "loophole" in the tax laws. Client politics need not involve obvious economic groups. We see client politics in action when teachers, organized as the National Education Association, seek the creation of a cabinet-level Department of Education; when organized Native Americans work to make certain that the Bureau of Indian Affairs is sensitive to their demands; when professors insist that only other professors decide on what research projects the National Science Foundation will spend its money; and when civil rights groups dominate the work of the Office for Civil Rights.

Visibility Client politics is low-visibility politics: neither the public at large nor (usually) the mass media have much interest in or knowledge about

Some "Rules" of Politics

*H*ere are some generalizations about American politics, distilled from what has been said in this book, offered in nervous awareness that our political system has a way of proving everybody wrong. (Before the 1960s it was a "rule" of politics that no Catholic could be elected president. John F. Kennedy took care of that.)

- Policies, once adopted, tend to persist whatever their value. (It is easier to start new programs than to end old ones.)

- Almost all electoral politics is local politics. (Members of Congress who forget "home base" tend not to remain in Congress for long.)

- Whatever the size of their staff and budget, Congress and the White House will always be overworked. (More resources produce more work, which requires more resources.)

- Each branch of government tends to emulate the others. (Congress will become more bureaucratized to cope with an executive branch that is becoming more bureaucratized; judges will become more activist as Congress becomes more activist.)

- Proposals that seem to confer widespread and immediate benefits will be enacted whatever their long-term costs.

- Proposals that seem to confer delayed benefits will be enacted only if their costs are unknown, concealed, or deferred.*

- Nobody—businesspeople, bureaucrats, members of Congress, judges, professors—likes competition, and everybody will do whatever he or she can to reduce or eliminate it.

- "Planning" in government takes place after a crisis takes place.

- The mass media never cover a story about things that are going well. Thus the number of "problems" in society is a function of the number of reporters.

- If you want something, you are claiming a right; if your opponent wants something, he or she is protecting a vested interest.

* This rule appears in William C. Mitchell, "The Anatomy of Public Failure: A Public Choice Perspective," paper no. 13 (Los Angeles: International Institute for Economic Research, 1978).

the policies involved. That can change, however. The regulations restricting the importation of foreign oil so that some oil companies are benefited became controversial because of the steep rise in oil prices in the early 1970s. The costs that consumers had to bear suddenly became so visible and so high that no client group in the oil industry could any longer hope that its benefits would go unnoticed. Similarly, for decades technological advances steadily reduced the cost of electricity, so the public was indifferent to the fact that state utility commissions charged with regulating the price of electricity usually did so in a perfunctory manner. When electricity prices began rising steeply in the 1970s, however, consumers complained, and many state utility commissions began to take a tough line against utilities. Subsidies to tobacco farmers were largely ignored until many people became concerned about the harmful effects of cigarette smoking on health.

Noneconomic groups can also see their favored-client position deteriorate as a result of external forces. Extremist political groups may easily take advantage of the protection that they enjoy from the First Amendment during tranquil times; when a national crisis, such as a war, occurs, the public may suddenly decide that the costs of free speech have become too great and demand restrictions.

Political Parties Political parties ordinarily play only a small role in client politics, for an obvious reason: when a group makes an unopposed request, it would be foolhardy for most legislators to suppose that they had anything to gain by voting against it. Such measures typically pass with the support of lopsided majorities in both parties. Sometimes that outcome is facilitated by grouping a number of client proposals in one package (a "pork barrel") so that there is something for everybody.

The political problem of a client group is ordinarily not that of winning a majority on the final vote but of getting its proposal brought up for a vote at all. Thousands of groups want things from the government; the limits of time and of congressional-committee interest reduce the number that will succeed. Finding a strategically placed congressional sponsor is essential. Because of the importance of having a sponsor and the ease of avoiding publicity, many of the cases of political corruption occur in the arena of client politics. Some members of Congress think that they can charge for their services and get away with it. This is not to say that most or even many client-serving policies are the result of improper influence, but only that the condi-

tions here are more conducive to such influence than they are in majoritarian politics.

Identifying the Clients Occasionally a client-serving policy will be devised and proposed not by the client group itself but by a self-appointed (or "vicarious") representative. The Economic Opportunity Act of 1964 was intended to benefit the urban poor, especially in minority neighborhoods, but it was not carried through Congress by an organization representing the urban poor. This was done by professionals, bureaucrats, and political executives who thought that it was time to act on behalf of the poor. Because they framed their proposals in harmony with the existing consensus on how needy people should be helped (chiefly with services rather than money), and because their proposals seemed then to impose no costs on any other distinct segment of society, the easy passage of the Economic Opportunity Act revealed a kind of client politics. Conflict later erupted, however, when mayors discovered that the Community Action Programs were a challenge to the institutional authority of city hall. From then on the matter became one of interest group politics.

Serving the Clients Client-serving programs have led to the creation of client-serving government agencies. Some scholars speak of how agencies like the Civil Aeronautics Board and the Federal Communications Commission have been "captured" by groups they are supposed to regulate, but this is a misreading of history. These agencies and others like them were formed specifically to serve the interests of domestic aviation and radio broadcasting, just as the Veterans Administration (later renamed the Department of Veterans Affairs) was created to serve the interests of veterans. At the time that these laws were passed, and for many years thereafter, people saw nothing wrong with such promotional ventures.

Important political changes have substantially reduced the freedom of action of client-serving agencies. The greater ease with which one can form and sustain groups purporting to represent mass or diffuse interests and the larger range of questions in which federal courts now intervene have made low-visibility client politics less common than in the past. Even tobacco farmers have had to accept lesser subsidies because of popular concerns over smoking. Consumer advocate groups, environmental protection groups, and organizations representing liberal and conservative causes use sophisticated fund-raising methods and take advantage of the easier access that plaintiffs have to courts (owing to changed rules on standing and provisions for fee shifting). By these methods such groups have reduced the extent to which diffuse interests go unrepresented in the arena of client politics, but they have created new problems because that representation is often inaccurate.

Moreover, the proliferation of regulatory agencies in the government has resulted in the creation of offsetting pressure against some client interests. Client politics comes about because the majority of the people who must bear the costs (at a small per-person amount) of a client group's benefits have no incentive to organize to contest those benefits. The government, because it can sustain organizations through taxation rather than having to depend on voluntary contributions, can create agencies to contest client claims. Thus the Antitrust Division of the Justice Department has challenged some of the practices of client-serving regulatory agencies, as when it criticized airline regulations for failing to promote competition.

Entrepreneurial Politics

Though opposition to client politics may eventually be institutionalized in the form of a new government agency, initially such opposition requires some form of entrepreneurial politics. An indifferent public can only be mobilized through skilled leadership that attracts substantial media attention. If real or imaginary threats to public well-being are pointed out, a congressional majority can be led to favor policies that will impose substantial costs on even a well-organized minority. This happened when congressional—and ultimately popular—majorities were led to support policies that set tough standards on air and water pollution or tightened the regulations on patent medicines and prescription drugs. It also happened when the public was aroused against socialists, anarchists, communists, and other radical political groups, and against high taxes.

Entrepreneurs can be found in the federal government, such as Dr. Harvey Wiley, the government chemist who dramatized the need for regulation of patent medicines, and Senator Estes Kefauver, who won headlines with his investigations of, first, organized crime and, later, the pharmaceutical industry. There was also Attorney General A. Mitchell Palmer and Senator Joseph McCarthy, who in different eras stimulated national passions directed at supposed subversives. Senator Bill Bradley and Representative Jack Kemp aroused interest in tax reform. And entrepreneurs can be found outside the federal government: Ralph Nader criticized various business practices, Upton Sinclair wrote about the conditions in meat-packing plants, and Howard Jarvis led a grassroots attack on high property taxes in California.

Compelling Symbols Policy entrepreneurs must achieve by emotional pleas what appeals to narrow self-interest cannot. Thus the rationale for a new policy must be presented in dramatic terms and evoke powerful symbols in the public's mind—

Policy entrepreneurs can sometimes defeat client interests, as when cigarette companies were required to display health warnings on all packaging and advertisements.

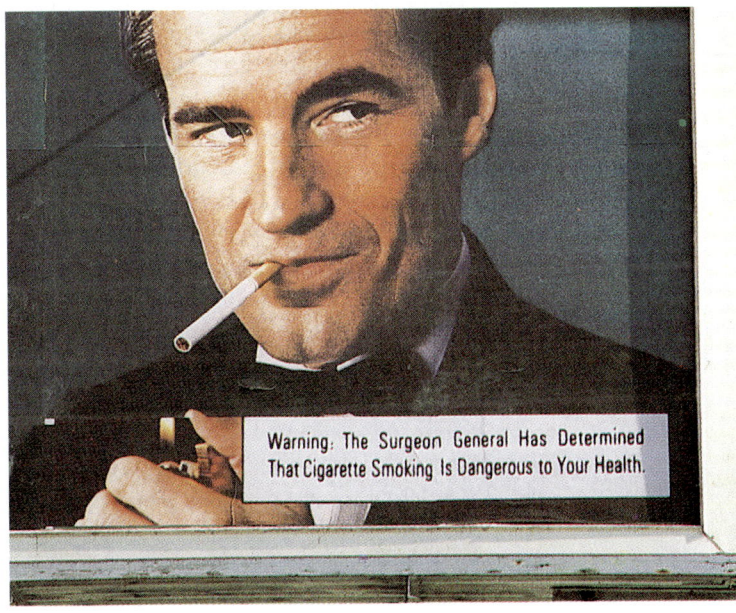

Warning: The Surgeon General Has Determined That Cigarette Smoking Is Dangerous to Your Health.

"clean air," "pure water," "Americanism," "sinister plots," "tax cheats," "confiscatory taxes," and so on. Legislative and administrative action based on such appeals is often cast in equally bold terms, with strict standards, stern penalties, and short deadlines. Since the success of such proposals depends on arousing or taking advantage of a popular mood, the kinds of policies that can be adopted depend on the kinds of symbols to which people will respond. These symbols change from one generation to the next.

At one time atheists and communists seemed especially threatening forces; at another time people were largely indifferent to such groups. In an earlier era citizens might have accepted high levels of atmospheric pollution; in the modern era even low levels are a cause for popular concern. Some people may be indifferent to the plight of coal miners, who suffer injury and death to satisfy our need for coal as an energy source, but be deeply upset by even the chance of an accident at a nuclear power plant.

Sometimes no compelling symbol can be found. Advocates of strict gun control, for example, have found it difficult to mobilize an intense popular majority. This fact is sometimes explained by the power of the National Rifle Association. No doubt that group is influential, but so also have been the automobile industry, local pharmacists, and the American Medical Association. Nevertheless, each of these other groups has lost decisively on important issues because each was unable to defeat powerful symbolic appeals.

Promotion by the Media   The mass media are of great importance in entrepreneurial politics, especially key reporters and editors who decide to give serious attention to the proponent of a policy. Often a tacit alliance exists between a policy entrepreneur, who supplies facts and arguments, and a reporter, who produces vivid feature stories. These stories often stimulate routine coverage of the issue by the press generally. Though political parties will play some role in this—one party is usually more sympathetic to the change than the other—that role is less significant than when majoritarian politics are involved. To the extent that the symbols are powerful, members of both parties feel compelled to pay them lip service.

Capture of the Agencies   The government agencies created as a result of entrepreneurial politics are often vulnerable to "capture" by the interest group adversely affected by the policy. Since the policy adopted imposes significant costs on an organized group, that group has a strong incentive to weaken the administration of that policy. The pharmaceutical industry, for example, was from time to time able to weaken the enforcement of the food and drug laws by the Food and Drug Administration. In recognition of this possibility advocates of such laws will sometimes create agencies that will encourage interest group competition (the regulations of the Environmental Protection Agency, for instance, impose costs on industries that must abide by them and create benefits for other industries that sell the equipment necessary to comply with the regulations).

The Courts   The courts play an important role in entrepreneurial politics. All affected parties, whether they be business firms or political movements, will seek court assistance in defending or resisting the new policy. Usually the courts have deferred to the popular mood, at least initially, and thus upheld new environmental regulations or new restrictions on free speech. In time, however, and especially as popular passions abate, the courts tend to evolve balancing tests to assess the fairness of the regulations following from the new policy.

Competing Theories of Political Power

In Chapter 1 we briefly sketched several competing theories of the distribution of political power in modern society. Each of these theories—the Marxist, the pluralist, the bureaucratic, the elitist—is an attempt to characterize the political system *as a whole*. From the evidence summarized earlier in this chapter, the reader may already have surmised what in fact is the case—that no single description of the entire political system seems adequate, as different policies tend to arise out of somewhat different political processes.

Of course, there is one description of the entire system that is roughly accurate: ours is a representative democracy with a high degree of personal freedom in the area of speech and opinion. But though that says a great deal, it does not say everything; in particular it does not say much about the very different forms that "representative democracy" may take in particular policy areas. This point will become clearer if we review the more familiar theories of politics in light of what we have learned about policy-making. We should bear in mind that even a fairly extensive review of policies will of necessity omit much that is important and that policies, perceptions of policies, and the political system itself are constantly changing.

Marxist Theory

Orthodox Marxist theory argues that the economic structure—and in particular the pattern of ownership of the means of production—shapes politics and determines political outcomes. The aspects of American policy-making most frequently cited in support of this view are foreign policy, defense policy, and economic regulation. With regard to foreign and defense policies we have seen that political con-

siderations—public opinion, perceptions of international military and diplomatic necessities, and the worldview of government elites—and not corporate ones are the decisive factors. Political considerations account for at least the major diplomatic and military initiatives of this country and explain the overall level of defense spending. Economic regulations can be of very different kinds depending on whether they are the product of interest group conflicts (the National Labor Relations Act), entrepreneurial skill (much environmental legislation), or client politics (an agency such as the Maritime Administration).

A Marxist—or more accurately, an economic-determinist—theory of politics may be applicable in cases where an economic client obtains a governmental advantage. An economic determinist can point to such client politics as maritime and dairy subsidies; price supports for large farmers; import quotas for sugar, beef, steel, and other products; and favorable tax treatment for various economic groups. But even with respect to client politics, economic determinism gives an incomplete explanation, because a large and growing number of instances of client politics reflects the demands of

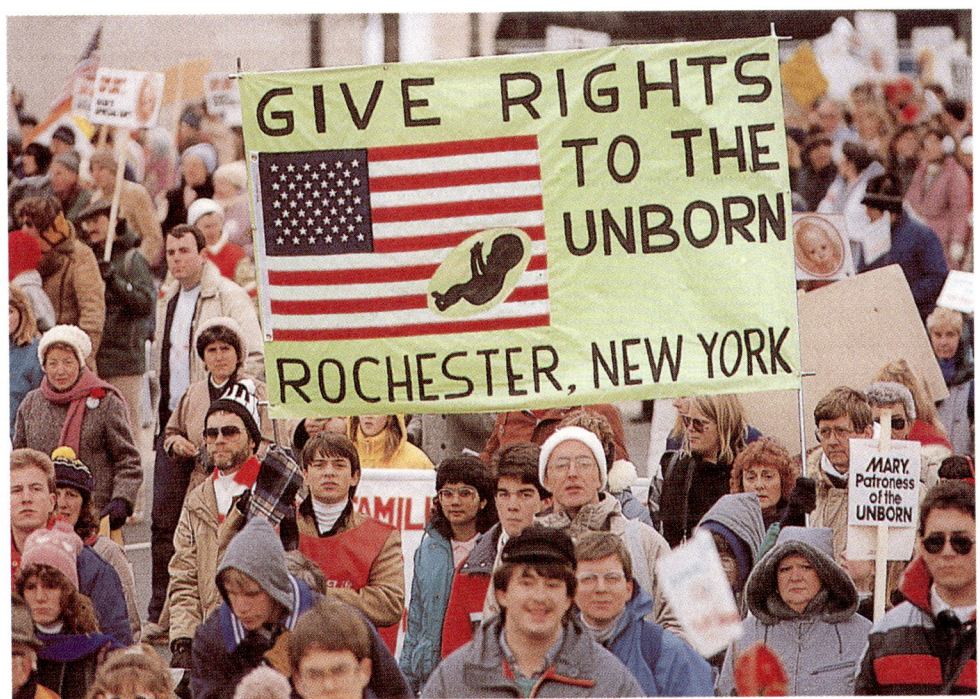

It is hard to explain the importance of such issues as abortion by Marxist theories of politics.

noneconomic organizations. The most notable instances are those of ethnic, racial, and women's groups. The special status that such groups enjoy with the Office for Civil Rights, the Equal Employment Opportunity Commission, the Civil Rights Commission, and the Civil Rights Division of the Justice Department is not the result of their economic power, nor are the benefits that they seek exclusively economic.

Moreover, even client politics takes place within the boundaries of public and elite opinion. One can easily explain in economic terms how the Civil Aeronautics Board (CAB) was created, since much of the work of that agency was directly beneficial to and protective of the major airline companies. It is harder to explain why the CAB was abolished and how the protected status of the airlines was removed over their intense opposition or how bills to increase competition among bankers, truckers, and securities brokers became law or why the auto industry was unable to prevent the passage of the Clean Air Act.

A Marxist might rejoin that the principal influence of economic, and especially corporate, power is not in the details of legislation but in the control of the agenda of politics, the shaping of the major thrust of policy (especially economic policy), and the distribution of political resources among potential participants in politics. There have been periods in American history where such influences have been important.

In an era of limited government, especially before the 1930s, many problems and practices never became political issues at all. Efforts to put them on the political agenda were met with the argument, often decisive, that it was wrong or illegitimate for the government to play any part in such matters as social welfare, income distribution, labor disputes, or the conditions of the workplace.

Since the 1930s, and in particular since the 1960s, it is hard to think of any problem, real or imagined, that has not found its way onto the political agenda. The "legitimacy barrier" has long since collapsed; politics today is not just about a few obviously public things but about nearly everything.

Similarly, at one time access to political resources—money and votes—was sharply limited. Political funds came predominantly from the wealthy, and voting was heavily influenced by party

bosses and machines. Newcomers to politics often experienced difficulty in obtaining either funding or votes. But in the modern era a remarkable transformation occurred. There was a wholesale redistribution of political resources, without a prior redistribution of income:

- Nominees for office were selected by primary elections rather than by party organizations.
- The partisan and elite media were in part replaced by the mass media.
- Racial and sexual barriers to voting were torn down.
- Issue organizations became easier to form and to maintain as a result of the role of private foundations, direct-mail fund-raising techniques, government grants and contracts, and fee shifting in court suits.

Moreover, the making of economic policy was profoundly altered when elite opinion accepted the propriety of budget deficits and of public responsibility for the maintenance of a high-employment economy. Once the earlier constraints had been removed—the belief that balanced budgets were essential and that economic growth should be maintained by governmental aids to investment but not to consumption—public officials were free to pursue economic policies with an eye chiefly to their impact on majority opinion.

In sum, though many examples of policymaking are dominated by economic advantage, no simple theory of economic determinism offers an accurate, comprehensive view of American politics.

Elitist Theory

In one sense almost all politics is elitist, in that almost all government decisions are made by the few rather than the many. But elitist theory says more than this: it asserts that it is always the same elite that makes policy, whatever the nature of the issue; that this elite acts in concert or at least has a common social, economic, or occupational background; and that the elite is only weakly influenced, if at all, by popular opinion.

One could describe client politics as a partial confirmation of elite theory. Obviously, when a few individuals—businesspeople, union leaders, professors, state welfare directors—acquire substantial influence over a broad policy area from which they benefit, they are an elite. But these examples illustrate the inherent ambiguity in elite theory. It makes all the difference whether a small group has power because it constitutes the direct *beneficiary* of some policy (as with dairy farmers, merchant seamen, or university research laboratories) or because it has certain general *characteristics* (wealth, prestige, social standing) that enable it to influence even policies that do not affect its interests. Elite theory subscribes to the latter view of elites—that they are powerful simply because of their personal attributes.

Client politics should not be regarded as a confirmation of elite theory but as an illustration of how the distribution of the costs and benefits of a proposed public policy differentially influences the abilities of the affected groups to shape that policy. The power of an activist federal judiciary is a better illustration of elite theory—not because judges are well paid or prestigious but because they are drawn from a profession (law) that provides them with cues and rewards that influence their decisions. Judges make decisions without being closely constrained by interest groups or voters but with considerable attention to the world of legal scholarship.

Foreign policy making is an especially interesting case of elite influence, because, unlike in client politics, the power of the elite does not depend on its ability to win votes, mobilize interest groups, raise campaign funds, or represent ethnic or racial blocs. The influence of this elite depends on its members' being part of a group that shares certain ideas and that has acquired experience in managing or writing about foreign affairs. At one time the foreign policy elite was also distinctive for its common social background—well-to-do, white, Anglo-Saxon Protestants who had attended Ivy League colleges. That is much less the case today. At present the members of the foreign policy elite are distinctive more for their ideas than for their origins. These ideas are formed by experience, academic training, and personal ideology and tend to change from one generation to the next.

The most popular version of elitist theory today holds that career politicians in Congress make decisions without any serious regard for social reality or public opinion. But if that is true, how did these people get so much power? The answer, of course, is that we elected them to Congress, usually by big margins. Once, when people complained of elites, they had in mind business or labor leaders whom no one had elected. Today we complain of elites that the people have chosen.

Bureaucratic Theory

The bureaucratization of almost all aspects of life, public and private, is one of the dominant facts of modern society. Some have argued that the number, size, and influence of government bureaucracies have become so great that elected officials and their key advisers are almost powerless to affect policy: whatever top officials propose, the bureaucracy can subvert. Criticisms of the bureaucratic state have evoked a rich verbal imagery: "leading the bureaucracy is like pushing a wet string" or "changing the bureaucracy is like moving a cemetery."

But it is as easy to overestimate as to underestimate bureaucratic power. Bureaucracy—that is, government by large organizations made up of appointed career officials—is most influential when the law confers on such officials wide discretion (or freedom to choose among alternative courses of action). Such broad discretion exists with respect to the procurement of weapons, the enforcement of civil rights laws, the making of foreign policy, and the regulation of business.

Some of this discretionary authority is inevitable. There is no way, for example, that Congress could write into law the precise specifications of the fighter planes that the air force should buy or set the exact rates that railroads should charge for various classes of freight. But some discretion is the result of Congress's being unwilling to make choices that could, in fact, be made. Congress could, for example, clarify the ambiguous laws now governing methods for allocating TV licenses. Indeed, it has tried to do this but found that congressional opinion is so divided that the choice must be left, willy-nilly, to judicial and administrative officials.

Bureaucrats have the least power when their task is specified by statute and in exact language. This is the case in the area of the Social Security laws that tell the administrator exactly how much money is to

Despite the growth of the federal government, state and local governments retain more power here than in almost any other nation. This is the Texas legislature.

be sent to what classes of people how often. Bureaucratic discretion is similarly narrow when it comes to providing benefits to veterans and farmers. This is not to say that agencies working in these areas do not have bureaucratic problems, such as red tape or delays. They do, as do all large organizations, private or public. But those are very different problems from the kinds that are created by the existence of bureaucratic discretion.

Congress has of late taken note of this and tried to reduce bureaucratic discretion in some areas. Clean air and clean water laws specify rather exact standards for pollution control; the Endangered Species Act gave nearly absolute protection to such endangered creatures as spotted owls (until it was revised in 1978); drug laws require the banning of certain foodstuffs and chemicals if they have *any* tendency to produce cancer. But if exact standards solve certain problems, they create others, such as the problem of keeping down the social cost of applying such strict standards.

There is at least one other way, besides being given discretionary authority, in which the bureaucracy has become more powerful. Increasingly the bureaucracy has become a source of the agenda of

politics. The Economic Opportunity Act of 1964, the Medicare Act of 1965, proposals for new weapons systems, and many other important measures came not from private demands made on government but from government's generating demands on itself. Any president who tries to formulate a legislative program quickly discovers that he is heavily dependent on the bureaucracy for most of his ideas, just as any president who tries to reorganize the executive branch soon learns that his chief opponents are his nominal subordinates, the bureau chiefs.

In short, the power of a bureaucracy may not depend so much on the kinds of politics (interest group, client, or whatever) that led to its creation as on the clarity and consistency of the congressional laws governing it and on the political constraints that make it more concerned with following rules than serving people.

Pluralist Theory

The view that policies are shaped by conflict and bargaining among organizations representing affected groups is obviously an accurate description of what we have called interest group politics. We have also seen the limits of the pluralist model: it overestimates the extent to which interest groups will form and be active. In client politics the large number of people who bear the widely distributed costs of a client-serving program have no incentive to organize and must rely instead on the vicarious (and perhaps inaccurate) representation supplied by "public-interest" lobbies. In majoritarian politics important decisions can be made as the result of direct presidential leadership of, and congressional response to, majority views, with interest groups playing only a marginal role.

With the rise of entrepreneurial politics and the collapse of some of the barriers to political participation, the pluralist theory has in a sense become more applicable to American government. Ironically, during the period (generally the 1950s) in which the theory was most influential, it was least accurate. Many interests (consumers, for example) were not represented in politics at all, and some groups in society (blacks, for example) were encountering barriers to political action. Today a greater variety of interests and of people are represented one way or another in Washington than ever before. Indeed, some see in this an "atomization" of politics that has sharply reduced the power of the government to do anything at all.[1]

But if the pluralist theory has become more descriptive of politics today, it still remains an incomplete one, not only because it does not take into account client or majoritarian politics but also because it offers no clear explanation of the special nature of entrepreneurial politics. The policy entrepreneur as folk hero is not a new phenomenon, but it has become a commonplace one. This could not have happened without the rise of a national mass media and a shift in beliefs among the upper middle class (or at least that part of it called the "new class" in Chapter 5) in a direction that is supportive of certain kinds of entrepreneurship. Nor does pluralism take fully into account the extraordinary role played by the judiciary, an institution that can only with difficulty be described as a "group" with "interests." Rather, the courts are a constitutionally based source of authority, the exercise of which depends crucially on the ideas and beliefs of its individual members.

SUMMARY

There is no single answer to the question "Who governs?" Everything depends on what policy is being proposed and on the opportunities that different proponents and opponents have to mobilize on their own behalf different parts of the fragmented institutions and processes of government. A crude classification can be made of some of the ways in which power is distributed by looking at the perceived costs and benefits of a policy. There are four types of policies: majoritarian, interest group, client, and entrepreneurial.

Using these four types, we can evaluate the claims made by advocates of the Marxist, elitist, bureaucratic, and pluralist theories of politics. No single theory is generally true, though some theories are correct in some cases. Any classification scheme and any evaluation of political theories must constantly be revised to account for changes in social reality, public perceptions of that reality, and ideas that people have about the proper purposes of government.

682

24

To What Ends?

★ Growth of government

★ Competing interests

★ Constraints on growth

★ Rise of an activist government

★ Disenchantment with government performance

★ The influence of structure

★ The influence of ideas

★ Government reform

The most striking change in American government has been the dramatic expansion in the scope of its activities. Until well into the twentieth century, who ruled in Washington, or to what ends, made little difference in the lives of most citizens except in wartime or when a dispute arose over the management of the nation's currency. National politics was not a career for many members of Congress; governors and mayors were more in the public eye than presidents; most citizens never came into contact with a federal official except when they received their mail.

When the federal establishment was relatively small, one could supply a fairly simple answer to the question of what ends the government served. If the Republicans were in power, the government sought high tariffs, tight money, and, for a while, the punishment of the southern states that had seceded from the Union. If the Democrats were in power, the government tended to lower tariffs, enlarge the money supply, and reach an accommodation with the South. From time to time circumstances altered this tidy pattern—a brief flirtation with "Manifest Destiny" and the acquisition of an overseas empire, the recurrence of various social issues such as temperance and the enfranchisement of women, the bitter struggle between labor and management over union organization, for example.

Today if one wants to know the objectives of government, the answer is "practically everything." The expansion of the scope of government has meant the proliferation of the goals of government. No single philosophy animates public policy, because public policy is not responsive to any single set of interests or influenced by any single set of political resources. Washington has policies (such as highway construction and mortgage insurance) that make it easier to move out of cities and policies (such as giving grants for neighborhood development) intended to encourage people to stay in cities. It has policies (such as pollution standards) designed to protect the environment, even at the cost of economic growth, and policies (such as tax deductions for investments) designed to stimulate economic growth. The government is formally committed to the goal of equal opportunity for all regardless of race and to programs that encourage employers to give special consideration to certain racial and ethnic groups in their hiring policies. In its foreign policy the government urges other nations to observe human rights and at the same time offers aid and alliances to nations that ignore fundamental rights.

Competing Interests

It is not perversity or stupidity that leads the federal government to pursue so many apparently inconsistent goals. Because the interests and opinions of people conflict, the policies of any government seeking to serve those interests and opinions will of necessity be inconsistent. People want different things. There is no "public opinion"; rather there are the differing opinions of many competing publics. As long as government is small, the competing desires of people are either reconciled by private arrangements (the market, voluntary agreements) or they are ignored. A large and active government might, of course, seek to be consistent, to follow a single philosophy, to serve some interests and not others. But if it is popularly elected, no such government will long survive.

A popular majority is a coalition of people who want different things from government; to win and hold that majority, the government must do many different things. But since it cannot do everything that a majority of the people want, it will lose the support of some, who will then join with others formerly in the minority to form a new majority coalition wanting a slightly different set of policies. A new government is elected, and the process starts over again. In the long run politicians win elections by promising to do things for people who either are not represented by or are disappointed by the party in power. Promises often become programs.

Politicians are not being venal when they try to win votes by making promises. They are being democratic. Politicians who fail to make promises (usually) fail to win elections; politicians who fail to deliver on their promises may not win reelection.

Restraints on the Growth of Government

For the better part of a century and a half, democratic politics in this country did not produce a rapid growth in the power and scope of the federal government. There were three reasons for this. First, the prevailing interpretation of the Constitution sharply limited what policies the federal government could adopt. The Supreme Court restricted the authority of the government to regulate business and prevented it from levying an income tax. Most important, the Supreme Court refused, with some exceptions, to allow the delegation of broad discretionary power to administrative agencies. This changed somewhat in the early decades of this century and changed fundamentally in the 1930s.

But the Supreme Court could not have maintained this position for as long as it did if it had acted in the teeth of popular opposition. The second restraint on the growth of government was popular opinion. It was not thought legitimate for the federal government to intervene deeply in the economy (even the American Federation of Labor, led by Samuel Gompers, resisted federal involvement in labor-management issues). It was certainly not thought proper for Washington to upset racial segregation as it was practiced in both the North and the South.

It took constitutional amendments to persuade Congress that it had the authority to levy an income tax or to prohibit the sale of alcoholic beverages. Even in the 1930s public opinion polls showed that as many as half the voters were skeptical of a federal unemployment compensation program. Public opinion, of course, changed as a result of crises (such as the Great Depression), the spread of higher education, and other factors difficult to assess. Today people will quarrel about the *wisdom* of some government policy, but few any longer argue that the government has no *right* to enact the policy. Almost any policy—except for those that might restrict First Amendment and other fundamental freedoms—that can attract majority support can be enacted into law without a serious challenge to its legitimacy or constitutionality.

Third, the political system designed by the Framers was based on the assumption that the key problem was to prevent the government from doing too much. The separation of powers and other constitutional checks and balances were intended to make it difficult to enact a new policy unless that policy had broad support. No single faction would be able to dominate the government. For a long period things worked pretty much as intended: it was difficult to introduce significant new programs except in emergency circumstances or when approval was both enduring and widespread. But the same arrangements that make adopting new programs difficult make eliminating or revising old programs equally difficult. The very separation of powers that ensured that any new proposal would confront entrenched critics also ensured that any existing programs would have entrenched defenders.

Ronald Reagan learned this when he took office in 1981 after promising to reduce the size of government. He did persuade Congress to cut taxes, but his plans to cut domestic spending resulted in only small declines in some programs and actual increases in many others. Though some programs, such as public housing, were hard hit, most were not, and agricultural subsidies increased dramatically. After Vice President Al Gore released his report on "reinventing government," not much happened. A large government has become a permanent fixture, mostly because that is what people want.

Consequences of Activist Government

It is tempting to make a sweeping judgment about a large and activist government, either praising it because it serves a variety of popular needs or condemning it because it is a bureaucratic affliction. Such generalizations are not entirely empty, but neither are they very helpful. The worth of any given program, or of any collection of programs, can be assessed only by a careful consideration of its costs and benefits, of its effects and side effects. But we may discover some general political consequences of the enlarged scope of government activity.

Politically SPEAKING — *Political Proverbs*

"If you can't stand the heat, get out of the kitchen."
—President Harry S Truman

"You scratch my back, I'll scratch yours."
—Attributed to Simon Cameron, secretary of war in the cabinet of Abraham Lincoln

"To the victor belong the spoils of the enemy."
—Senator William Marcy of New York, 1832

"How you stand depends on where you sit."
—Attributed to Rufus Miles, formerly of the U.S. Budget Bureau

"If it ain't broke, don't fix it."
—Bert Lance, director of the Office of Management and Budget under President Jimmy Carter

"Whenever you have to start explaining—you're in trouble."
—Representative Barber Conable of New York

SOURCE: From *Safire's Political Dictionary* by William Safire. Copyright © 1968, 1972, 1978 by William Safire. Reprinted by permission of Random House, Inc. and the author.

First, as the government gets bigger, its members must spend more time managing the consequences—intended and unintended—of existing programs and less time debating at length new ideas. As a result, all parts of the government, not just the executive agencies, become more bureaucratized. The White House Office and the Office of Management and Budget (OMB) grow in size and influence, as do the staffs of Congress. At the same time, private organizations (corporations, unions, universities) that deal with the government must also become more bureaucratic. The government hires more people when it is running eighty programs concerned with employment than when it is running two. By the same token, a private employer will hire (and give power to) more people when it is complying with eighty sets of regulations than when it is complying with two.

Second, the more government does, the more it will appear to be acting in inconsistent, uncoordinated, and cumbersome ways. When people complain of red tape, bureaucracy, stalemates, and confusion, they often assume that these irritants are caused by incompetent or self-seeking public officials. There is incompetence and self-interest in government just as in every other part of society, but these character traits are not the chief cause of the problem. As citizens, we want many different and often conflicting things. The result is the rise of competing policies, the division of labor among separate administrative agencies, the diffusion of accountability and control, and the multiplication of paperwork. And because Americans are especially energetic about asserting their rights, we must add to the above list of problems the regular use of the courts to challenge policies that we do not like.

Third, an activist government is less susceptible to control by electoral activity than a passive one. When the people in Washington did little, elections made a larger difference in policy than when they began to do a lot. We have pointed out in this book the extent to which both political parties and voter turnout have declined. There are many reasons for this, but an important one is often forgotten. If elections make less of a difference—because the few people for whom one votes can do little to alter the ongoing programs of government—then it may make sense for people to spend less time on party or electoral activities and more on interest group activities aimed at specific agencies and programs.

Citizens are more likely to be drawn into direct contact with politicians in America than they are in other countries. Here, people in Syracuse, New York, discuss with a city leader how the streets are fixed.

The rapid increase in the number and variety of interest groups and their enlarged role in government is not pathological. It is a rational response to the fact that elected officials can tend to only a few things, and therefore we must direct our energies at the appointed officials (and judges) who tend to all other government matters. Every president tries to accomplish more, usually by trying to reorganize the executive branch. But no president and no reorganization plan can affect more than a tiny fraction of the millions of federal employees and thousands of government programs. "Coordination" from the top can at best occur selectively, for a few issues of exceptional importance.

Finally, the more government tries to do, the more things it will be held responsible for and the greater the risk of failure. From time to time in the nineteenth century, the business cycle made many people unhappy with the federal government—recall the rise of various protest parties—though then the government did very little. If federal officials were lucky, popular support would rise as soon as economic conditions improved. If they were unlucky and a depression lasted into the election campaign, they would be thrown out of office. Today, however, the government—and the president in particular—is held responsible for crime, drug abuse, abortion, civil rights, the environment, the elderly, the status of women, the decay of central cities, the price of gasoline, and international tensions in half a dozen places on the globe.

No government and no president can do well on all or even most of these matters most of the time. Indeed, most of these problems, such as crime, may be totally beyond the reach of the federal government, no matter what its policy. It should not be surprising, therefore, that opinion surveys taken since the early 1960s have shown a steep decline in public confidence in government. There is no reason to believe that this represents a loss of faith in our form of government or even in the design of its institutions, but it clearly reflects a disappointment in, and even cynicism about, the performance of government.

Disenchantment with government performance is not unique to the United States; it appears to be a feature of almost every political system in which public opinion is accurately measured. The disen-

The Crime Bill

chantment is in fact probably greater elsewhere. Americans who complain of high taxes might feel somewhat differently if they lived in Sweden, where taxes are nearly twice as high as here. Those who grouse about bureaucrats in this country probably have never dealt with the massive, centralized bureaucracies of Italy or France. People who are annoyed by congestion, pollution, and inflation ought to arrange a trip to Rome, Mexico City, or Tokyo. However frustrating private life and public affairs may be in this country, every year thousands living in other nations become immigrants to this country. Few Americans choose to emigrate to other places.

The enormous expansion of the scope and goals of the federal government has not been random or unguided. The government has tended to enlarge its powers more in some directions than in others; certain kinds of goals have been served more frequently than others. Though many factors shape this process of selection, two are of special importance. One is our constitutional structure, the other our political culture.

The Influence of Structure

To see the influence of structure, it is necessary to perform a mental experiment. Suppose that the Founders had adopted a centralized, parliamentary regime instead of a decentralized, congressional one.

They had the British model right before their eyes. Every other European democracy adopted it. What difference would it have made had we followed the British example?

No one can be certain, of course, because the United States and Great Britain differ in many ways, and not just in their political forms. At best our mental experiment will be an educated guess. But the following possibilities seem plausible.

A parliamentary regime of the British sort centralizes power in the hands of an elected prime minister with a disciplined partisan majority in the legislature and frees him or her from most of the constraints created by independent congressional committees or independent, activist courts. Had the Framers adopted a parliamentary system, we might see these features in the political life of the United States today:

- *Quicker adoption of majoritarian policies, such as those in the area of social welfare.* Broad popular desires would be translated sooner into national policy when they are highly salient and conform to the views of party leaders.

- *More centralization of bureaucratic authority—more national planning, less local autonomy.* More decisions would be made bureaucratically, both because bureaucracies would be proportionately larger and because they would have wider discretionary authority delegated to them. (If the prime minister heads *both* the executive branch and the legislature, he or she sees no reason why decisions cannot be made as easily in one place as the other.) Local authorities would not have been able to prevent groups of citizens (such as blacks) from voting or otherwise participating in public life by maintaining segregated facilities at the local level.

- *Fewer opportunities for citizens to challenge or block government policies of which they disapprove.* Without independent and activist courts, without local centers (state and city) of autonomous power, U.S. citizens would have less of a chance to organize to stop a highway or an urban-renewal project, for example, and hence fewer citizen organizations with these and similar purposes would exist.

- *Greater executive control of government.* If a situation like Watergate occurred, we would never know about it. No legislative investigating committees would be sufficiently independent of executive control to be able to investigate claims of executive wrongdoing.

- *Similar foreign policy.* We probably would have fought in about the same number of wars and under pretty much the same circumstances.

- *Higher and more centralized taxation.* Taxes would be higher, and a larger share of our tax money would be collected at the national level. Thus we would find it harder to wage a "tax revolt" (since it is easier to block local spending decisions than national ones).

If this list of guesses is even approximately correct, it means that you would get more of some things that you want and less of others. In general it would have been easier for temporary majorities to govern and harder for individuals and groups to protect their interests.

The Founders would probably not be surprised at this list of differences. Though they could not have foreseen all the events and issues that would have led to these outcomes, they would have understood them, because they thought that they were creating a system designed to keep central power weak and to enhance local and citizen power. They would have been amazed, of course, at the extent to which central power has been enhanced and local power weakened in the United States, but if they visited Europe, they would learn that by comparison American politics remains far more sensitive to local concerns than does politics abroad.

The Influence of Ideas

The broadly shared political culture of Americans has also influenced the policies adopted by the U.S. government. Paramount among these attitudes is the preoccupation with rights. More than the citizens of perhaps any other nation, Americans define their relations with one another and with political authority in terms of rights. The civil liberties protected by the Bill of Rights have been assiduously defended and their interpretation significantly broadened even while the power of government has been growing.

For example, we expect that the groups affected by any government program will have a right to play a role in shaping and administering that program. In consequence, interest groups have proliferated. We think that citizens should have the right to select the nominees of political parties as well as to choose between the parties; hence primary elections have largely replaced party conventions in selecting candidates. Individual members of Congress assert their rights, and thus the power of congressional leaders and committee chairman has steadily diminished. We probably use the courts more frequently than the citizens of any other nation to make or change public policy; in doing so, we are asserting one set of rights against a competing set. The procedural rules that set forth how government is to act—the Freedom of Information Act, the Privacy Act, the Administrative Procedure Act—are more complex and demanding than the rules under which any other democratic government must operate. Each rule exists because it embodies what somebody has claimed to be a right: the right to know information, to maintain one's privacy, to participate in making decisions, and to bring suit against rival parties.

The more vigorously we assert our rights, the harder it is to make government decisions or to manage large institutions. We recognize this when we grumble about red tape and bureaucratic confusion, but we rarely give much support to proposals to centralize authority or simplify decision making. We seem to accept whatever it costs in efficiency or effectiveness in order to maintain the capacity for asserting our rights.

We do not always agree on which rights are most important, however. In addition to the influence of the widely shared commitment to rights generally, government is also shaped by the views that certain political elites have about which rights ought to be given the highest priority. Elite opinion tends to favor freedom of expression over freedom to manage or dispose of property. Mass opinion, though it has changed a good deal in the last few decades, is less committed to the preferred position of freedom of expression. Rank-and-file citizens often complain

A policy dilemma: nuclear power plants reduce our dependence on foreign and nonrenewable energy sources but sharpen our concerns over safety.

that what the elite calls essential liberty should instead be regarded as excessive permissiveness. People who own or manage property often lament the extent to which the rights governing its use have declined.

The changes in the relative security of personal and property freedom are linked to a fundamental and enduring tension in American thought.

Tocqueville said it best: Americans, he wrote, "are far more ardently and tenaciously attached to equality than to freedom." Though democratic communities have a "natural taste for freedom," that freedom is hard to preserve, because its excesses are immediate and obvious and its advantages are remote and uncertain. The advantages of equality, on

How American Politics and Government Have Changed

Old System	New System
Congress:	
Chairmen relatively strong	Chairmen relatively weak
Small staffs	Large staffs
Few subcommittees	Many subcommittees
Interest groups:	
A few large blocs (farmers, business, labor)	Many diverse interests that form ad hoc coalitions
Rely on "insider" lobbying	Mobilize grass roots
Presidency:	
Small staff	Large staff
Reaches public via press conferences	Reaches public via radio and television
Courts:	
Allow government to exercise few economic powers	Allow government to exercise broad economic power
Take narrow view of individual freedoms	Take broad view of individual freedoms
Political parties:	
Dominated by state and local party leaders meeting in conventions	Dominated by activists chosen in primaries and caucuses
Policy agenda:	
Brief agenda	Long agenda
Key questions:	
Should the federal government enter a new policy area?	How can we fix or pay for an existing policy?
Key issue:	
Would a new federal program abridge states' rights?	Would a new federal program prove popular?

resist, in the long run if not the short, the passions of temporary majorities seeking to curtail such liberties. But he did not underestimate the extent to which in the economic and social realms Americans would decide that improving the conditions of life would justify restrictions on the right to dispose of property and to manage private institutions. At first the conflict was between liberty and equality of opportunity; more recently it has become a conflict—among political elites if not within the citizenry itself—between equality of opportunity and equality of results.

The fact that decisions can be influenced by opinions about rights indicates that decisions can be influenced by opinions generally. As the political system has become more fragmented and more individualized as a result of our collective assertion of rights, it has come more under the sway of ideas. When political parties were strong and congressional leadership was centralized (as in the latter part of the nineteenth and the early part of the twentieth centuries), gaining access to the decision-making process in Washington was difficult, and the number of new ideas that stood a chance of adoption was small. However, those proposals that could command leadership support were more easily adopted: though there were powerful organizations that could say no, those same organizations could also say yes.

Today these and other institutions are fragmented and in disarray. Individual members of Congress are far more important than congressional leaders. Political parties no longer control nominations for office. The media have given candidates direct access to the voters; campaign finance laws have restricted, but not eliminated, the influence that interest groups can wield by spending money. Forming new, issue-oriented lobbying groups is much easier today than formerly, thanks to the capability of computers and direct-mail advertising.

These idea-based changes in institutions affect how policy is made. When there is widespread enthusiasm for an idea—especially among political elites but also in the public at large—new programs can be formulated and adopted with great speed. This happened when Lyndon Johnson's Great Society legislation was proposed, when the environmental and consumer protection laws first arrived

the other hand, are readily apparent, and its costs are obscure and deferred.[1]

Tocqueville may have underestimated the extent to which political liberties would endure, because he did not foresee the determination of the courts to

Four Simple Rules for Improving Government

1. **No law is valid unless the members of Congress voting for it have read it.** The Ninety-seventh Congress considered over ten thousand bills and enacted over five hundred. The tax bill alone ran to several hundred pages. What is your guess as to the number of these bills that the average member of Congress reads?

2. **No law or regulation is valid if it is incomprehensible to the average citizen.** Section 509(a) of the Internal Revenue Code reads as follows: "For purposes of paragraph (3), an organization described in paragraph (2) shall be deemed to include an organization described in section 501 (c) (4), (5), or (6) which would be an organization described in paragraph (2) if it were an organization described in section 501 (c) (3)." Any questions?

3. **No law is valid if it does not clearly state its goals and the means to attain them.** The law creating the Federal Communications Commission instructs it to award radio and television licenses on the following principle: to serve "the public interest, convenience, or necessity." Now you know.

4. **No law passed by Congress is valid if it does not apply to Congress itself.** For decades Congress exempted itself and its employees from many laws regulating the workplace, such as the minimum-wage and worker-safety laws. But in 1995 it voted to make itself subject to many of these. Will it continue to do this in the future?

SOURCE: Adapted from Irving Younger, "Socrates and Us," *Commentary* (December 1980): 46–49. Reprinted by permission. All rights reserved.

on the public agenda, and when campaign finance reform was proposed in the wake of Watergate. So long as such symbols have a powerful appeal, so long as a consensus persists, change is possible. But when these ideas lose their appeal—or are challenged by new ideas—the competing pressures make change extremely difficult. Environmentalism today is challenged by concerns about creating jobs and economic growth; social legislation is challenged by skepticism about its effectiveness and concern over its cost; campaign finance reforms are, to some critics, merely devices for protecting incumbents.

This may all seem obvious to a reader raised in the world of contemporary politics. But it is different in degree if not in kind from the way in which politics was once carried out. In the 1920s, the 1930s, the 1940s—even in the 1950s—people described politics as a process of bargaining among organized interests or "blocs," representing business, farming, labor, ethnic, and professional groups. With the expansion of the scope of government policy, there are no longer a few major blocs that sit astride the policy process. Instead, thousands of highly specialized interests and constituencies seek above all to protect whatever benefits, intangible as well as tangible, they get from government. This vast array of specialized interests can often be mobilized (or overcome) to produce broad changes. In the 1960s and early 1970s there was change aplenty. But when enthusiasm wanes, when symbols lose their appeal, when ideologies are in conflict, the political process becomes slow, cautious, and localistic. This, of course, was what the Founders intended, but they intended it for a government far smaller and less active than what we now have.

We have a large government—and large expectations about what it can achieve. But the government finds it increasingly difficult to satisfy those expectations. The public's acceptance of an activist role for government has been accompanied by a decline in public confidence in those who manage that government. We expect more and more from government but are less and less certain that we will get it, or get it in a form and at a cost that we find acceptable. This perhaps constitutes the greatest challenge to statesmanship in the years ahead: to find a way to serve the true interests of the people while restoring and retaining their confidence in the legitimacy of government itself.

PART SIX

State and Local Government

"The powers reserved to the several States will extend to all the objects which, in the ordinary course of affairs, concern the lives, liberties, and properties of the people, and the internal order, improvement, and prosperity of the State."

— FEDERALIST NO. 45

25

State and
Local
Government

- ★ Jacksonians versus Progressives

- ★ State constitutions

- ★ Governors

- ★ State legislatures

- ★ "Reformed" versus "unreformed" cities

- ★ Mayors and councils

- ★ Taxes and tax revolts

- ★ Federal versus local crime control

State governments are not miniature versions of the federal government, and municipal governments are not miniature versions of state ones. There is almost as much variation in the forms and operations of governments *within* the United States as there is between the United States and other democratic nations.

At all levels, government in the United States is in some sense democratic, but consider these variations on that theme:

- In the national government the president and vice president are the only elected executive officers; in most states the executive power is divided among several elected officials—a governor, attorney general, secretary of state, and treasurer. In some states the people even elect commissioners in charge of agriculture, insurance, education, and public utilities.

- In Congress party leaders have little influence over who becomes chairmen of the standing committees; in many state legislatures party leaders can select and dismiss committee chairmen almost at will.

- At the national level executive and legislative powers are divided between two separately elected branches of government; in many American cities the legislature (a city council) chooses the executive (a mayor or city manager).

- Federal judges are appointed by the president and confirmed by the Senate; many state judges are elected by the people.

- The people never vote directly on any matter decided by the national government; the people do vote directly on a host of matters decided by many state and local governments.

- The Constitution of the United States is brief, general, and rarely amended; the constitutions of many states are long, detailed, and frequently amended.

The constitution and politics of each state, like those of the United States, have been profoundly

Andrew Jackson appealed to the people's distrust of strong executive powers, a distrust that is reflected in many state constitutions.

shaped by important philosophical beliefs as to the nature and scope of government. These changing beliefs help explain the differences among state governments and between the state and national governments.

State Constitutions and Political Philosophy

The Antifederalists may have lost their struggle to prevent the ratification of the United States Constitution, but the principles that they espoused—numerous elected officials, short terms of office, weak executives—triumphed in many states and cities.

The original thirteen states had been British colonies, ruled in most cases by a royal governor selected by the king. The American Revolution put an end to that and ushered in a period in which executive power was held in deep suspicion. Accordingly, the new state constitutions vested most governmen-

tal authority in the legislatures and kept the newly elected governors relatively weak. In many states the legislature picked the governor and the judges. In only a few states could the governor veto legislative acts. Though the legislatures were dominant in these new state governments, they were not selected by a wholly popular electorate, for the right to vote was restricted to persons who owned a certain amount of property and (sometimes) to persons of particular religious beliefs.

The Jacksonian Era

In the early nineteenth century the right to vote was significantly extended, due in part to party competition and in part to rising land values that weakened the old property-based barriers to voting. Soon most white males were eligible to vote. The mood of these voters was distinctly antigovernment. Many state constitutions were revised in the two decades preceding 1840 in ways intended to make state governments both more democratic and weaker. The requirement that voters must be property owners was eliminated altogether, and restrictions on the power of state governments were devised. For example, many legislatures were forbidden from meeting more often than once every two years or for more than a few weeks at a time. The theory was that if the politicians could not meet, they could not do much harm. Moreover, specific restrictions were placed on what kinds of laws the legislatures could pass. These included limits on the amount of debt that states could incur and prohibitions on raising the salaries of state officials or chartering private banks.

In some ways the powers of the governors were increased by filling the office through direct popular election, lengthening the term of office, and allowing governors to veto legislative acts. But these changes were not really intended to make the governor powerful; they were designed only to make the governor a more effective check on the legislature. In short, the principle of separation of powers was being vigorously pursued.

To keep the governor weak, executive authority in state governments was divided among a host of elected officials—treasurers, auditors, secretaries of state, attorneys general, superintendents of education, even surveyors and state printers. In New York, for example, executive power was divided among a dozen or so elected officials. (It was ironic that this should be described as the era of "Jacksonian democracy," for the man in whose name the assault on executive authority was proceeding at the state level was himself substantially enlarging the power of the presidency at the national level.) Essentially the same changes were occurring at the local level. The power of mayors was reduced and that of city councils enlarged.

The result of all these changes was the radical decentralization of political authority at the state and local level. Whereas at the national level liberty was to be preserved by checks and balances among the three branches of government, at the local level it was to be maintained by multiplying the number of elected officials and keeping each as weak as possible. This decentralization meant that for anything to get done at all in state or local government, a large number of legally independent elected officials would have to agree.

But unlike the national government, state and local governments had a lot of work to do. They had to pave streets, build city halls, run schools and jails, and deal with the poor and helpless. Some way had to be found for all the independent elected officials to agree on a program. The way was provided by the political parties.

Political parties grew in power not only because they were needed to get voters out to the polls but also because they helped to make the decentralized state and local governments function. If a party in New York or New Jersey could elect a slate of candidates—say, for governor, lieutenant governor, treasurer, attorney general, state senator, and state representative—it could put into office people beholden to it. A party leader could make certain that a bill was enacted into law by inducing each party member holding office to support it. If somebody refused to go along, that official could be dropped from the party slate in the next election. Moreover, party leaders often controlled valuable **patronage**— jobs, contracts, and money that could be given to or withheld from officeholders to reward or punish their party loyalty. Thus the local political parties, especially those that were party machines, came to dominate many state and local governments.

The Progressive Response

The benefits of party government—in making certain that decentralized state and local governments could function—were purchased at a price: corruption and inefficiency. Tammany Hall dominated the politics of New York City; the political machine of the Southern Pacific Railroad dominated California. Many upper-middle-class citizens thought that the costs of party or machine rule were too high and began a variety of reform efforts. These efforts, called the **progressive movement,** began in earnest after the Civil War and reached a peak during the early years of the twentieth century. Though there were many differences among progressives, most shared a desire to purify politics and to make government more efficient by attacking the sources of partisan influence.

Among the changes that they proposed were these:

- Make elections nonpartisan so that political parties will not play a role in them.

- Reduce the number of state officials so that executive authority is concentrated in the hands of the governor.

- Put the management of city affairs into the hands of an appointed, professional city manager.

- Reduce the size of state legislatures and city councils so that the close ties between legislators and local interests are reduced.

- Check the power of legislatures and city councils by giving the people the right to vote directly on important measures (the *initiative, referendum,* and *recall,* to be described).

- Eliminate patronage; make all appointments to administrative positions on the basis of merit.

In the early 1900s the progressives won power in a number of states, including California, Minnesota, and Wisconsin, where they proceeded to put their proposals into effect. They failed to make much headway in other states, such as Illinois, Massachusetts, and New York. But the struggle continues. From the beginning of the twentieth century right down to the present, much of the conflict in state and local government is between those who prefer the **Jacksonian model** of government and those who prefer the **progressive model.** The modern-day Jacksonians are those who want to have a lot of elected officials closely accountable to the voters, who believe that the average citizen and not some appointed expert should have the most authority, who want specific neighborhoods and not the "city as a whole" represented on city councils, and who expect legislators to intervene in government decisions on behalf of the interests of individual citizens. The modern-day progressives are those who prefer few elected officials, power concentrated more in executive than in legislative hands, greater reliance on experts, and city-council members elected from the city at large rather than from small districts.

In the late 1960s and early 1970s progressive sentiment was once again on the rise. Between 1965 and 1976 nine states adopted new constitutions and many others amended theirs; the new provisions tended to increase the authority of the governor. But similar changes were less apparent in city government. It may be that progressives were more successful at the state level because voters saw state issues

(such as taxes and welfare programs) in terms of the need for greater efficiency and lower costs but saw city issues (such as school integration and neighborhood services) in terms of a need for greater citizen participation and closer checks on the power of experts. Moreover, Jacksonian systems are better adapted to giving representation to racial and ethnic groups (many of which tend, as we shall see, to be underrepresented in governments based on progressive principles), and it has been the cities, more than the states, that have been the arena of racial and ethnic politics.

The conflict between these two conceptions of politics, coupled with the normal struggles among competing interests, have given an amazing variety to state and local government in this country. Scarcely any other nation uses as many different political systems to manage local affairs. The continued existence of this variety is testimony to the special importance that Americans attach to local issues.

The Legal Basis of State and Local Government

That importance was evident in the debates over the initial ratification of the Constitution and the insistence of many that a Bill of Rights be added to it that would, in part, reaffirm the special place of the states. The Tenth Amendment specifies that "powers not delegated to the United States by the Constitution, nor prohibited by it to the States, are reserved to the States respectively, or to the people."

For decades, this amendment had little effect on what Washington could do. As late as 1985, the Supreme Court suggested that it was up to politicians, not judges, to decide what independence, if any, cities and states might enjoy from federal control. But of late the Court has begun to give new life to the Tenth Amendment. In 1992 it told the federal government that it could not force states to enact a certain reglatory program. In 1997 it said that the national government could not require local law enforcement officials to conduct background checks on people trying to buy guns, as had been required by the Brady Law. A five-to-four majority has begun

The Top Ten States in Spending

Educational Spending per Pupil (1995–1996)	Average AFDC Monthly Payment (1995–1996)
New Jersey	Alaska
New York	Hawaii
Alaska	Vermont
Connecticut	California
Rhode Island	Massachusetts
Delaware	New York
Massachusetts	Rhode Island
D.C.	New Hampshire
Pennsylvania	Washington
Michigan	Connecticut

SOURCE: Taken from *CQ Fact Finder 1996: Rankings Across America* by Harold A. Hovey, tables L-8, H-15. Copyright 1996, Congressional Quarterly Inc. Reprinted with permission.

to reassert the view that the Constitution creates a system of "dual sovereignty" under which states, or officials in states, retain certain powers free of federal authority.[1]

Though the states have many fewer *exclusive* powers than they once had, they still have many powers that are *shared* with the federal government. In general the states can do anything that is not prohibited by the Constitution or preempted by federal policy and that is consistent with their own constitution. One generally recognized state power is the police power.

The **police power** refers to those laws and regulations, not otherwise unconstitutional, that promote health, safety, and morals. Thus the states can enact and enforce criminal laws, require children to attend school and citizens to be vaccinated, and restrict (subject to many limitations) the availability of pornographic materials or the activities of prostitutes and drug dealers. As a practical matter the most important activities of state and local governments involve public education, law enforcement and criminal justice, health and hospitals, roads and highways, public welfare, and control over the use of land.

The Constitutional Framework of State Government

How the states manage these functions is determined by state constitutions. Though they are like the federal Constitution in their setting forth the offices that are to exist, the powers that they are to have, and the manner in which they are to be filled, these documents are unlike the federal Constitution in that they go well beyond these structural matters to include all sorts of specific arrangements that one might suppose could be left to ordinary legislation. For example, the California constitution sets forth rules governing the duration of wrestling matches, and the Georgia constitution provides a $250,000 reward to the first person who strikes oil in the state. One reason that state constitutions are so detailed is that they are often easy to amend; usually an amendment requires only a two-thirds vote of the legislature (in fourteen states it requires only a simple majority vote) followed by a majority vote of the citizens in the next election. And in many states, such as California, voters can amend the constitution without going through the legislature if they can get enough signatures to put a proposed amendment

Public education is one of the primary responsibilities of state and local government.

```
              SACRAMENTO COUNTY
              GENERAL ELECTION
               November 5, 1996
```

Vote YES or NO	MEASURE 209
210 YES	PROHIBITION AGAINST DISCRIMINATION OR PREFERENTIAL TREATMENT BY STATE AND OTHER PUBLIC ENTITIES. INITIATIVE CONSTITUTIONAL AMENDMENT. Generally prohibits discrimination or
211 NO	preferential treatment based on race, sex, color, ethnicity, or national origin
in public employment, education, and contracting. Fiscal Impact: Could affect state and local programs that currently cost well in excess of $125 million annually. Actual savings would depend on various factors (such as future court decisions and implementation actions by government entities).	

Vote YES or NO	MEASURE 210
215 YES	MINIMUM WAGE INCREASE. INITIATIVE STATUTE. Increases the state minimum wage for all industries to $5.00 per hour on March 1, 1997, and
216 NO	to $5.75 per hour on March 1, 1998. Fiscal Impact: Unknown impact on government revenues. Annual wage-related costs to state and local gov-
ernments of $120 million to $300 million (depending on federal action), partly offset by net savings, in the low tens of millions, in health and welfare programs.	

Vote YES or NO	MEASURE 211
219 YES	ATTORNEY-CLIENT FEE ARRANGEMENTS. SECURITIES FRAUD. LAWSUITS. INITIATIVE STATUTE. Prohibits restrictions on attorney-client
220 NO	fee arrangements, except as allowed by laws existing on January 1, 1995. Prohibits deceptive conduct by any person in securities transactions
resulting in loss to retirement funds, savings. Imposes civil liability, punitive damages. Fiscal Impact: Probably minor net fiscal impact on state and local governments.	

Vote YES or NO	MEASURE 212
223 YES	CAMPAIGN CONTRIBUTIONS AND SPENDING LIMITS. REPEALS GIFT AND HONORARIA LIMITS. RESTRICTS LOBBYISTS. INITIATIVE STAT-
224 NO	UTE. Repeals gift/honoraria limits. Limits contributions to $200 in state and $100 in other campaigns. Imposes spending limits. Prohibits lobbyist
contributions. Fiscal Impact: Costs of up to $4 million annually to state and local governments for implementation and enforcement; unknown, but probably not significant, state and local election costs. Increases state revenues about $6 million by eliminating tax deduction for lobbying.	

Vote YES or NO	MEASURE 213
228 YES	LIMITATION ON RECOVERY TO FELONS, UNINSURED MOTORISTS, DRUNK DRIVERS. INITIATIVE STATUTE. Denies recovery of all damages
229 NO	to convicted felons for crime-related injury. Denies recovery of noneco- nomic damages (e.g., pain, suffering) to drunk drivers, if convicted, and
most uninsured motorists. Fiscal Impact: Probably minor net fiscal impact on state and local government.	

Vote YES or NO	MEASURE 214
232 YES	HEALTH CARE. CONSUMER PROTECTION. INITIATIVE STATUTE. Regulates health care businesses. Prohibits discouraging health care pro-
233 NO	fessionals from informing patients or advocating treatment. Requires health care businesses to establish criteria for payment and facility staff-
ing. Fiscal Impact: Increased state and local government costs for existing health programs and benefits, probably in the tens to hundreds of millions of dollars annually.	

Continue Voting on Next Page ➡

SB-009.001   212-10

This page from the 1996 California ballot shows some of the measures voters had to decide as a result of the use of the initiative procedure.

banking. Exactly this was done, and so for many decades branch banking was unconstitutional in the state of Illinois.

States frequently write entirely new constitutions. Ten states have had five or more constitutions in their history. Louisiana has had eleven and Georgia ten. (The oldest state constitution still in effect, albeit much amended, is that of Massachusetts, adopted in 1780.)[2] But such changes are at times deeply controversial. In 1975 Texas tried unsuccessfully to adopt a new constitution. It was defeated by the voters in part because many people thought that the new constitution, by authorizing the legislature to meet annually, might lead to higher taxes—a worry that dates back at least to 1830.[3]

Eighteen state constitutions provide for legislation by **initiative.** This is a method that allows voters to place legislative measures (and sometimes constitutional amendments) directly on the ballot by getting enough signatures (usually between 5 percent and 15 percent of those who voted in the last election) on a petition. Forty-nine states also allow for the **referendum,** a procedure that enables voters to reject a measure adopted by the legislature. Often the legislature will handle controversial issues by means of a referendum: it will vote to enact the measure but require that, before it takes effect, it go before the voters at the next election. Sometimes the constitution specifies that certain kinds of legislation (for example, a tax increase) must be subject to a referendum whether the legislature wishes it or not. The **recall** is a procedure, in effect in fifteen states, whereby the voters can remove an elected official from office. If enough signatures are gathered on a petition, the official must go before the voters, who can vote to leave the person in office, remove the person from office, or remove the person and replace him or her with someone else.

The initiative, referendum, and recall show how far many state constitutions are from the federal one. The Founders would never have dreamed of giving voters these kinds of powers over federal lawmaking. As we saw in Chapter 2, the Constitution is based on a republican, not a democratic, principle: laws are to be made by the representatives of citizens, not by the citizens directly. The reason for this is to filter temporary popular passions through the medium of prolonged deliberation and discussion.

on the ballot (in California, 8 percent of the number that voted in the last gubernatorial election). As a result, the California constitution has been amended well over four hundred times.

Another reason for all this detail is that, since the early nineteenth century, citizens and interest groups have not trusted state governments to do the right thing and so have told them what to do or not do by writing it into the constitution. If you were a small-town banker living in Illinois, for example, you might worry that someday the legislature might allow big-city banks to open branches in your town to compete with you. One way to prevent that would be to amend the constitution to prohibit branch

TABLE 25.1   Winners and Losers Among the States

State with the highest birth rate:	Utah
State with the lowest birth rate:	Vermont
State with the highest percentage of female legislators:	Washington
State with the lowest percentage of female legislators:	Alabama
State whose soldiers scored highest on the Armed Forces Qualification Test:	Oregon
State with the highest percentage of students finishing high school:	Minnesota
State with the lowest percentage of students finishing high school:	Mississippi
State with the highest abortion rate:	California
State with the lowest abortion rate:	Wyoming
State with the highest divorce rate:	Alabama*
State with the lowest divorce rate:	Massachusetts
State with the fattest citizens:	Michigan
State with the thinnest citizens:	Colorado
State with the highest crime rate:	Florida
State with the lowest crime rate:	West Virginia
State with the highest voting turnout:	South Dakota
State with the lowest voting turnout:	West Virginia

*Not counting Nevada, where many go to get divorced.

SOURCE: Harold A. Hovey, *State Fact Finder: Rankings Across America, 1996* (Washington, D.C.: Congressional Quarterly Press, 1996), various pages.

Observers are divided over whether such filtering is also desirable at the state level.

The Constitutional Basis of Local Government

The existence of the states is guaranteed by the federal Constitution: no state can be divided without its consent, each state must have two representatives in the Senate, every state is assured of a republican form of government, and powers not granted to Congress are (theoretically) reserved for the states. But cities, towns, and counties enjoy no such protection. They exist at the pleasure of the states. Indeed, states have frequently abolished certain kinds of local governments, such as independent school districts.

Most Americans live in cities. Legally a city is a **municipal corporation** that has been chartered by the state to exercise certain defined powers and provide certain specific services. There are two kinds of such charters: special-act charters and general-act charters. A **special-act charter** applies to a certain

named city (for example, New York City) and lists what that city can and cannot do. A **general-act charter** applies to a number of cities that fall within a certain classification, usually based on city population. Thus in some states all cities over 100,000 population will be governed on the basis of one charter, while all cities between 50,000 and 99,999 population will be governed on the basis of a different one.

In accordance with the legal principle known as **Dillon's rule,** the terms of these charters are to be interpreted very narrowly. Under this rule (named after a lawyer who wrote a book on the subject in 1911), a municipal corporation can exercise only those powers expressly given it or those powers necessarily implied by, or essential to the accomplishment of, these stated powers.[4] Any doubts about what a city can do under its charter are to be resolved against the city. This means that a city cannot operate a peanut stand at the city zoo unless the state legislature has specifically given the city that power by law or charter.

City officials, needless to say, intensely dislike these restrictions and so argue in favor of a different kind of authorizing law, called a **home-rule charter.** Such a charter, now in effect in many cities, especially larger ones, reverses Dillon's rule and allows the city government to do anything that is not prohibited by the charter or by state law. In theory the charter creates a form of government (or allows the city to choose among several forms), states what the government can do in general terms, lists some restrictions and prohibitions, and then allows the city to exercise its powers broadly: "You're on your own, govern yourself." In practice many home-rule charters have not been as flexible as this, since city laws (that is, ordinances) cannot be in conflict with state laws, and the states often pass laws that interfere with what home-rule cities want to do.

You might think that everybody living in a city would like home rule, since that means that the people in the city can govern themselves. Not so. Many interest groups in a city—business, labor, civil rights groups, and the like—often welcome the chance to get the state to pass a law requiring the city to do something contrary to what the city's voters want. Whether these groups will favor home rule depends on whether they think that they will win or lose in city politics. In this sense city-state relations are just like state-federal relations: the increase in the power and intrusiveness of higher levels of government is often the result of the activities of groups that lost out in the struggle for power at the lower level.

Cities are not, of course, the only kind of local government. As can be seen in Table 25.2, there are in this country over eighty-six thousand local governments, of which municipalities make up less than one-fourth. The other governments are these:

Counties   These are the largest territorial units between a state and a city or town. Every state but two (Connecticut and Rhode Island) has a system of county government. (In Louisiana counties are called parishes; in Alaska they are called boroughs.) Numbering more than three thousand, county governments are especially important in rural areas where people do not live in incorporated cities or towns. Most are governed by an elected board of county supervisors or commissioners with a separately elected sheriff, county clerk, coroner, prosecutor (or district attorney), and various other officers. A few counties, especially those with a large, urbanized population (as in Nassau and Suffolk counties in New York), also elect a county executive who functions much like the mayor of a city, and some (as in Los Angeles County) appoint a professional county administrator who is in charge of the day-to-day running of county administrative affairs.

Towns and Townships   In some eastern and midwestern states counties are divided into townships. Most have no separate government, but there are exceptions. In New England and New York, town governments are important. A town was once a village (some are still called that) to which farmers from the surrounding area went to transact business. Such governmental business as they had was conducted by an annual gathering of all the citizens eligible to vote; these citizens would pass on proposals and choose officials to handle matters between town meetings. The New England **town meeting** continues that tradition in dozens of small towns across that region. As some of these towns grew in population, a meeting of all the adult citizens became impractical. A few of these towns became cities, but some preserved the town meeting system, modifying it only by reducing the number of persons who attended to one or two hundred by having voters elect town meeting representatives. This system is called the **representative town meeting.**

TABLE 25.2   **Number of Governments in the United States**

Type of Government	1992	1982	1972
Total	86,748	82,688	78,269
U.S. government	1	1	1
State governments	50	50	50
Local governments	86,697	82,637	78,218
County	3,043	3,041	3,044
Municipal	19,296	19,083	18,517
Township	16,666	16,748	16,991
School district	14,561	15,032	15,781
Special district	33,131	28,733	23,885

SOURCE: *Municipal Yearbook, 1986* (Washington, D.C.: International City Management Association) and *Governing* (April 1993): 15.

Special Districts There are more than thirty-three thousand special-district governments (sometimes called authorities) in the United States. They have specific responsibility for some single governmental function—handling sewage treatment and the supply of water, managing airports and bridges, or getting rid of mosquitoes. The biggest is the New York Port Authority, which operates airports, bridges, and bus terminals. Most are much smaller. The number of special-district governments has increased in recent years. Their proponents claim that they make possible more efficient management; their critics argue that they so diffuse responsibility for governmental functions as to make them hard to control.

School districts (there are more than fourteen thousand of them) are a familiar example of special-district governments. Though arrangements vary from state to state, often the voters elect school board members (the school board thus becomes a miniature legislature), who then choose a school superintendent (the executive). Where the progressive tradition is strong, the emphasis is on finding an "expert" school superintendent and giving him or her a great deal of power to run the schools on the basis of the best professional opinion. Where the Jacksonian tradition is strong, the emphasis is on finding a local person to be school superintendent and having the school board become deeply involved in the details of school management.

The Structure of State Government

Politically the essential difference among state governments is not whether they are big or small, urban or rural, but whether they embody the Jacksonian or the progressive philosophy of governance. Some states, such as California and Wisconsin, have governmental institutions that represent the high-water mark of progressive thinking—a strong governor, relatively few other elected executive officials, a more or less full-time, professional legislature, and a tradition of active (and expensive) governmental involvement in various policy areas such as welfare and education. Other states, such as Indiana, Louisiana, and Texas, were largely unaffected by the progressive movement and have institutions that reflect a desire

In mid-1997, two women served as state governors: Jeanne Shaheen (above) of New Hampshire and Christine Todd Whitman of New Jersey.

for limited government by part-time officeholders: a weak governor who cannot serve more than one or two consecutive terms, many elected executive officials, a legislature that meets infrequently or for only a brief period, and a tradition of relatively limited (and less well funded) state activity.

To speak of two styles of state politics is, of course, to oversimplify matters greatly. California has some features of the Jacksonian system, such as an elected superintendent of instruction, and Texas has some features of the progressive system, such as a governor who can serve an unlimited number of terms. And state politics is changing—more and more states have moved in the progressive direction. Moreover, the states differ in many ways in addition to their governmental systems—some have rural populations that want small government concerned about the needs of farmers; others have large urban populations that generate a wider variety of political demands. But the oversimplification is a useful one, for it reminds us that institutions make a difference in how politics works and that institutions arise out of competing philosophies as to what constitutes good government.

California

California's politics reflects two deep divisions in the state—between north and south and between liberals and conservatives. Its congressional delegation, the largest in the nation, is perhaps the most divided ideologically: California Democrats are more liberal than Democrats elsewhere, and California Republicans are more conservative than Republicans elsewhere. The state's governors have ranged from the conservative Ronald Reagan to the liberal Jerry Brown. Today California has two Democratic senators, both of them women (Barbara Boxer and Dianne Feinstein). But for many years the state sent one Democrat and one Republican to the Senate.

The governor serves a four-year term, to which he or she can be reelected once. The governor shares authority with six other elected executive officers, an elected Board of Equalization, and several quasi-independent commissions (such as the one that runs the universities). The number of appointments that the governor can make is limited by a strong civil service system, but the governor does have a line-item veto and substantial reorganization authority.

The legislature, which meets annually, is one of the most professionalized in the nation; its forty senators (who serve four-year terms) and eighty Assembly members (who serve two-year terms) are among the best paid and best staffed in the country. The speaker of the Assembly is very powerful, appointing all committee chairmen and most committee members.

California's political parties are organizationally quite weak, a legacy of the progressive reforms begun in 1911. The real influence in elections comes not from party leaders but from elected officials and interest groups, professional campaign management firms, newspaper endorsements, and television advertising.

The initiative, referendum, and recall are heavily used in California. Between 1981 and 1990, fifty-eight statewide initiative measures got on the ballot and twenty-seven were approved. The famous Proposition 13, which cut property taxes, was an initiative measure approved in 1978. So important are these petitions that firms have sprung up that are in the business of gathering signatures.

Governors

By considering various aspects of the formal (that is, legal) authority of governors—their tenure in office, their ability to appoint subordinates and reorganize the executive branch, and their budgetary and veto powers—it is possible to distinguish between those who are relatively strong and those who are relatively weak. Thad L. Beyle did this and came up with the following ranking:

- *Very strong governors:* New Jersey, Pennsylvania, Utah, Hawaii, Maryland, Massachusetts, Minnesota, New York

- *Weak governors:* Mississippi, Texas, South Carolina, New Hampshire, North Carolina, Nevada[5]

The other governors were in between, with those in California and Connecticut tending toward the "very strong" end of the scale and those in Missouri, Ohio, and Virginia tending toward the "weak" end. Note that states with strong governors tend to be populous, urban states and those with weak ones tend to be rural or southern states. It is important to bear in mind, however, that these rankings are based only on legal authority; personal skill, the strength of political parties and interest groups allied with the governor, and the governor's use of the media all affect how much actual power he or she will have.

The typical governor, if there is such a thing, is elected for a four-year term and (in thirty-eight states) can serve for only two terms. In the typical state the governor does *not* run as a team with the candidate for lieutenant governor, so that unlike the case of the U.S. president and vice president, it is possible for the governor to be from one party and the lieutenant governor to be from a different one (this has happened in California and some other states). There is a growing tendency, however, to change the rules to require that the two candidates run as a team; that rule is now in effect in twenty-seven states.

Most governors have the authority to prepare the state budget, veto legislation, take command of their state's National Guard, and grant pardons or clemency to persons convicted of a crime. In forty-three states the governor can use a *line-item veto:* that is, he or she can veto one provision of some or all bills without vetoing the entire bill. In some states the governor can go even further than this—he or she can reduce the amount appropriated for a specific purpose. The legislature can override the line-item veto or the appropriation reduction, usually by a two-thirds vote.

The power of the governor to appoint other executive officers varies greatly from place to place. The limitations on the appointive power are of two kinds—constitutional and legal. The constitutional limitation arises from the requirement that certain executive offices be filled by direct election. About thirty states elect six or more executive officials in addition to the governor and lieutenant governor; these tend to be southern and midwestern states with a strong Jacksonian tradition. About twenty elect five or fewer; these tend to be eastern or far western states. Just Maine, New Hampshire, New Jersey, and Tennessee follow the national practice of electing only the chief executive. Over the last quarter century there has been a trend toward reducing the number of elected executive officers.

The political limitation arises from civil service laws. In progressive states, such as California, these laws are very strong and restrict the governor from making more than a small number of appointments entirely at his or her discretion. In many Jacksonian states, such as Indiana, the civil service laws are weak and the governor can make thousands of patronage appointments. Once again, the link between constitutional philosophy and the appointive process is not perfect. Some states, such as Pennsylvania, that have powerful governors and only a few elected executives also have extensive opportunities for patronage appointments. And things are changing: whereas in 1958 only half of all state jobs were under the civil service, today the great majority are.

Just as the constitutional base and political powers of the governor's office have been changing, so also has the kind of person who becomes governor. In the past a few governors, such as Al Smith in New York and Earl Warren in California, were important figures, but many were unimpressive time-servers who did little more than cut ribbons to open new public buildings and pose for the cameras. The states were not so much "laboratories of democracy" as havens for second-rate politicians. That seems to have changed.

A new breed of governor has come to the fore, bringing energy and intelligence to an office that has grown in both importance and power. Many new national policies have been modeled on ones pioneered in the states. For example, the Family Support Act of 1988 and the Welfare Reform Act of 1996 designed to encourage welfare recipients to become self-supporting, were based in part on work-oriented welfare programs begun by governors in California, Massachusetts, Michigan, New Jersey, Wisconsin, and elsewhere. Federal efforts to improve education have grown out of meetings of the governors from states that have experimented with school reform plans. Three of the last four presidents—Jimmy Carter, Ronald Reagan, and Bill Clinton—came to the White House as former governors, as did thirteen presidents before them.

From 1970 until 1994, Democrats held a majority of the governorships, and they did this despite the increasing tendency of white southerners to vote for Republican candidates. In 1994 that changed. Republicans lost none of the statehouses they already controlled and won eleven more while four Democratic incumbents were defeated. For the first time in a quarter century, Republicans had more governorships (thirty-one) than did the Democrats (eighteen) (see map, page 706). The Republicans now controlled the statehouses in eight of the ten largest states and in half of the Southern ones.

Until the 1994 election, Democrats had been doing a better job of winning governorships than of winning the presidency. There were several reasons for this. Presidential elections are often influenced more by the economic condition of the nation and the character of the candidates than by party loyalty. State elections, by contrast, are more likely to reflect traditional party allegiances; for a long time more voters have been Democratic than Republican. Another reason is that in most states gubernatorial elections are no longer held on the same day as presidential ones. In the 1930s thirty-three states chose their governors in the same election as they chose the president. In 1992 only twelve states did this. As a result the popularity of a Republican presidential candidate cannot readily be transferred to a Republican gubernatorial candidate—having the two chosen in different years cuts the president's coattails. Moreover, the president's party often loses popularity during off-year elections, just at the time when most governors are being elected.

Like most recent presidents, most governors face legislatures in which one or both houses are con-

PARTY CONTROL OF STATE GOVERNORSHIPS, 1995

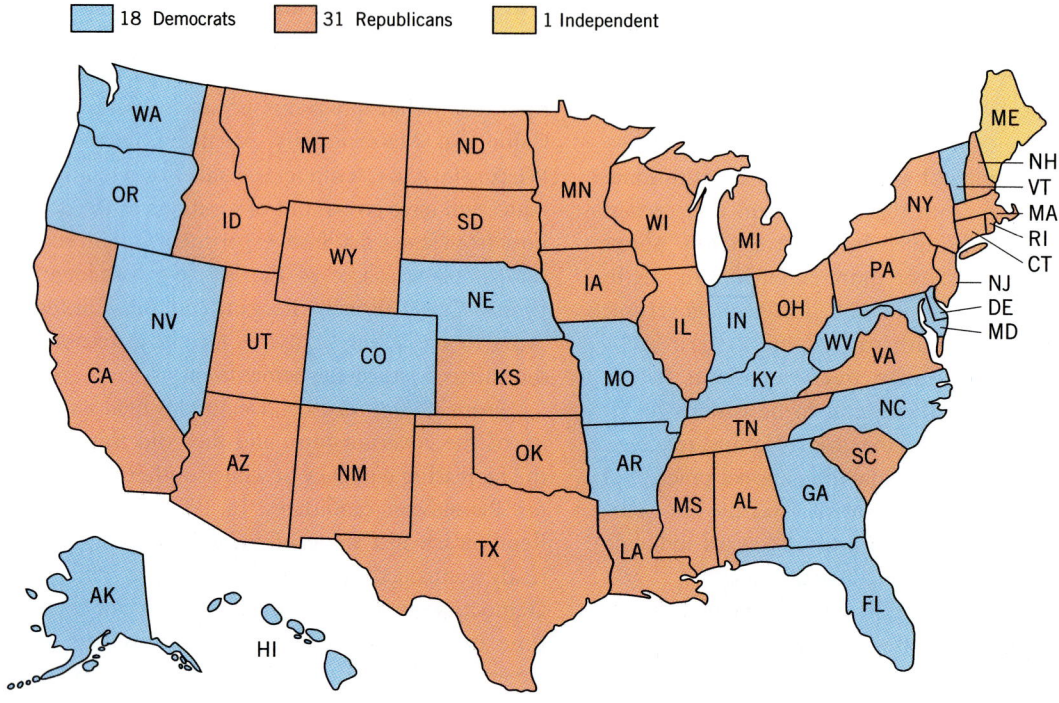

trolled by the opposition party. In 1952, about 80 percent of the states had a government in which the same party controlled the governor's office and both houses of the legislature; by 1986, only about 40 percent had unified governments (see Figure 25.1). The main reason for the decline in unified state governments has been the inability of Republicans to elect state legislators. Once, a Republican governor could count on having a Republican-controlled legislature; no more. In 1993 eighteen states had Republican

FIGURE 25.1 The Decline of Unified State Government

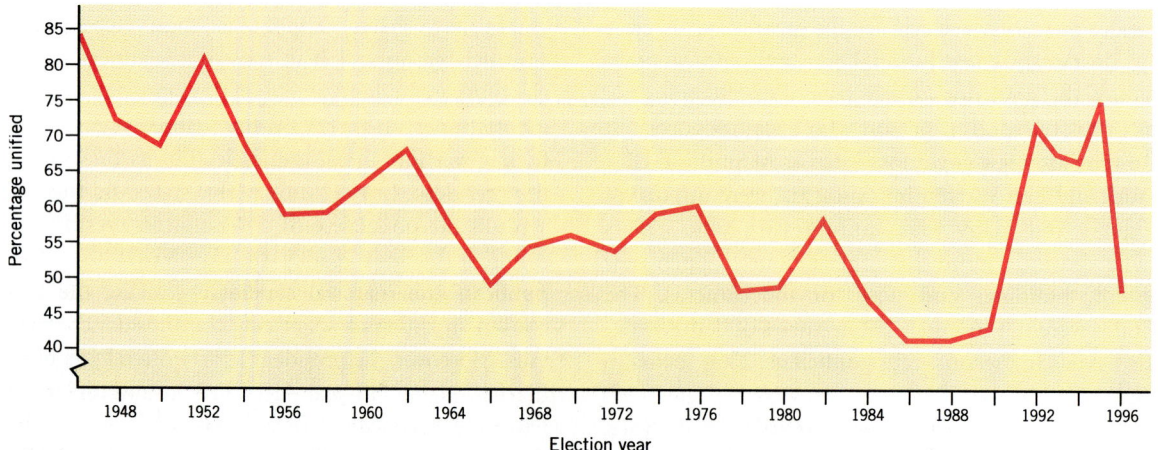

SOURCE: Morris Fiorina, *Divided Government* (New York: Macmillan, 1992), 25. Updated by the author.

governors; in only three (Arizona, New Hampshire, and Utah) did the Republicans also control the legislatures. After the 1996 election, divided control continued to be the rule rather than the exception. Before it, thirty-one states had divided rule; after it, twenty-eight did. Republican governors did make some progress; before the election, only three of them had legislatures of the same party, but after it fifteen did. Even so, Republican governors had to face legislatures with at least one house under Democratic control in such important states as California, New York, and Texas.

State Legislatures

State legislatures are not small-scale versions of Congress. Though all but Nebraska's have two houses, the way in which they are elected, organized, and led often differs greatly from what one finds in Washington. A member of Congress represents a large district (half a million people), is paid a good salary, has a large staff, and works at his or her job full-time; in many states exactly the opposite is true.

Elections and Electoral Districts Many state legislators are not even chosen from single-member districts but rather from multimember ones. About a third of all members of the lower houses of the state legislatures (and about one-eighth of all state senators) are elected from districts that choose more than one legislator.[6] Until 1980, for example, three members of the Illinois house were chosen from each electoral district. Each voter in those districts could cast three votes, giving one to each of three candidates, or three to one candidate and none to any other, or some other combination. This meant that a passionate Republican could give all three of his or her votes to a single Republican candidate, and if enough other passionate Republicans did the same thing, a Republican could be elected from a district where the vast majority of voters were Democrats.

In most states the effect of multimember districts (as well as other factors) is to give the dominant political party a big advantage—if it wins 55 to 60 percent of the popular vote in a state, it will win 65 to 70 percent of the legislative seats.[7]

Except in Nebraska, all state legislators run under a party label. Just as with members of Con-

The People's Representatives Speak

When you have over a half million elected officials at the state and local levels, you should not assume that they all will speak with the clarity and wisdom of Winston Churchill.

Take lawmakers in Michigan. Reporters covering that state's legislature have written down some of the flakier examples of official phrase making. Each exchange was heard by at least two reporters.

"There comes a time to put principle aside and do what's right."

"I don't see anything wrong with saving human life. That would be good politics, even for us."

"Some of our friends wanted it in the bill, some of our friends wanted it out. Jerry and I are going to stick with our friends."

"From now on, I'm watching everything you do with a fine-toothed comb."

"The chair would wish the members would refrain from talking about the intellectual levels of other members. That always leads to problems."

"Mr. Chairman, fellow members and guests. That's a god-damn lie."

"I don't think you appreciate how difficult it is to be a pawn of labor."

"Let's violate the law one more time."

"Now we've got them right where they want us."

"Mr. Speaker, what bill did we just pass?"

SOURCE: Adapted from Eugene Carlson, " 'Now,' the Senator Said, 'We've Got Them Right Where They Want Us,' " *Wall Street Journal* (March 19, 1982): 27. Reprinted by permission of the Wall Street Journal, © 1982 Dow Jones & Company, Inc. All rights reserved worldwide.

gress, they get on the ballot by winning a primary election. But in some states political parties play a much bigger role in deciding who gets the nomination than they do in others. In Connecticut and Pennsylvania, party leaders will often help recruit candidates and give to favored candidates a party endorsement. In other states, such as Minnesota and Washington, party organizations are much weaker, candidates are likely to be self-selected (rather than party-recruited), and only a minority of the primary candidates will be endorsed by party leaders.[8]

The Determinants of Legislative Elections Traditional party loyalties have kept southern state legislatures overwhelmingly Democratic even though these states have increasingly voted for the Republican candidate for president and, of late, have begun to elect Republican governors in large numbers (there were five Republican governors in the South in 1996).

Outside the South, state legislative elections tend to be influenced by some of the same forces that shape national elections. For example, since 1950 the president's political party has lost seats in the state legislatures (outside the South) in every election occurring between the regular presidential elections. This is strikingly similar to the losses that the president's party almost always suffers in congressional seats, and it suggests that voters approach state legislative elections in much the same way as they approach congressional ones.

Further evidence of this is a fact discovered by political scientist John Chubb: the condition of the *national* economy has a strong effect on *state* legislative elections, just as it does on national ones.[9]

Once elected, legislators tend to be about as safe in most states as they are in the U.S. House of Representatives. In most years, about 90 percent of all state legislators who stand for reelection are reelected, just as in the U.S. House.[10] (However, fewer state legislators stand for reelection, and so the turnover in membership is higher in state legislatures than in Congress.) But in 1992 public criticism of career politicians reduced the rate at which state legislators were reelected (down to "only" about 70 percent), just as it cut the reelection rate of members of Congress. Proposals to place term limits on state and national legislators passed in each of the fourteen states that had them on the ballot.

There are about 7,400 legislative seats in the American states; Democrats have won a majority of them in virtually every election for the last forty years, including 1994. The Republicans have closed the gap a bit, even in the South. In 1994 they took control of the lower houses in both North and South Carolina for the first time in this century. As of 1996, eighteen states were under Republican control, nineteen were under Democratic sway, and

PARTY CONTROL OF LEGISLATIVE CHAMBERS, 1995

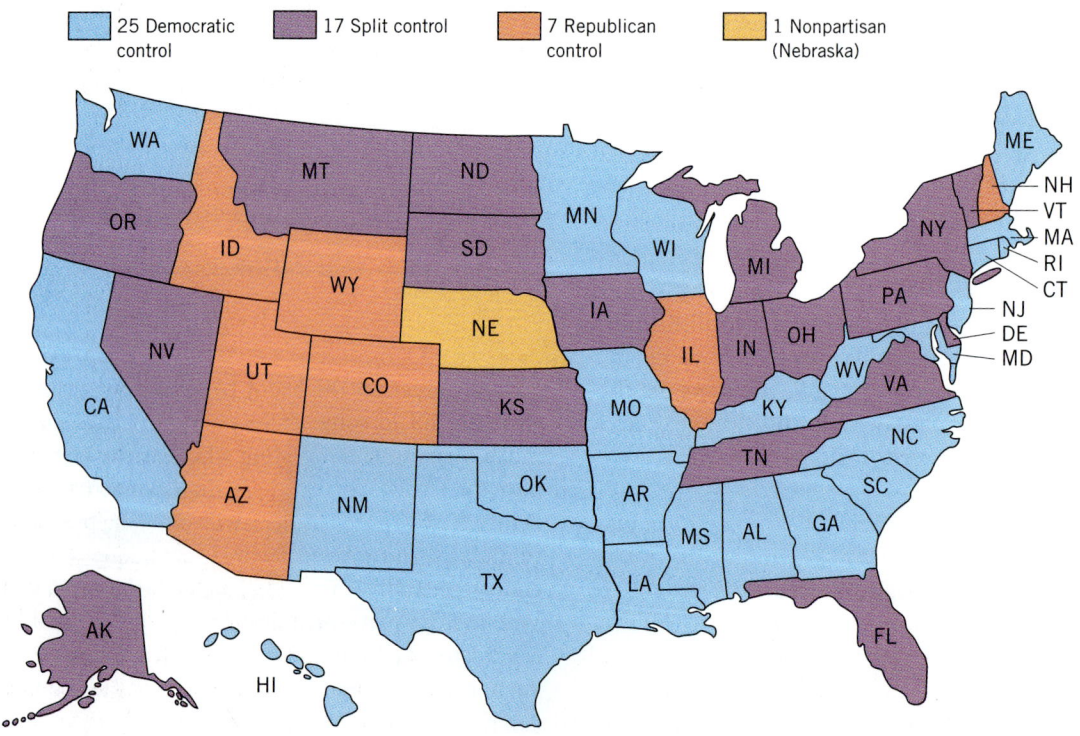

PERCENTAGE OF STATE LEGISLATORS WHO ARE WOMEN, 1993

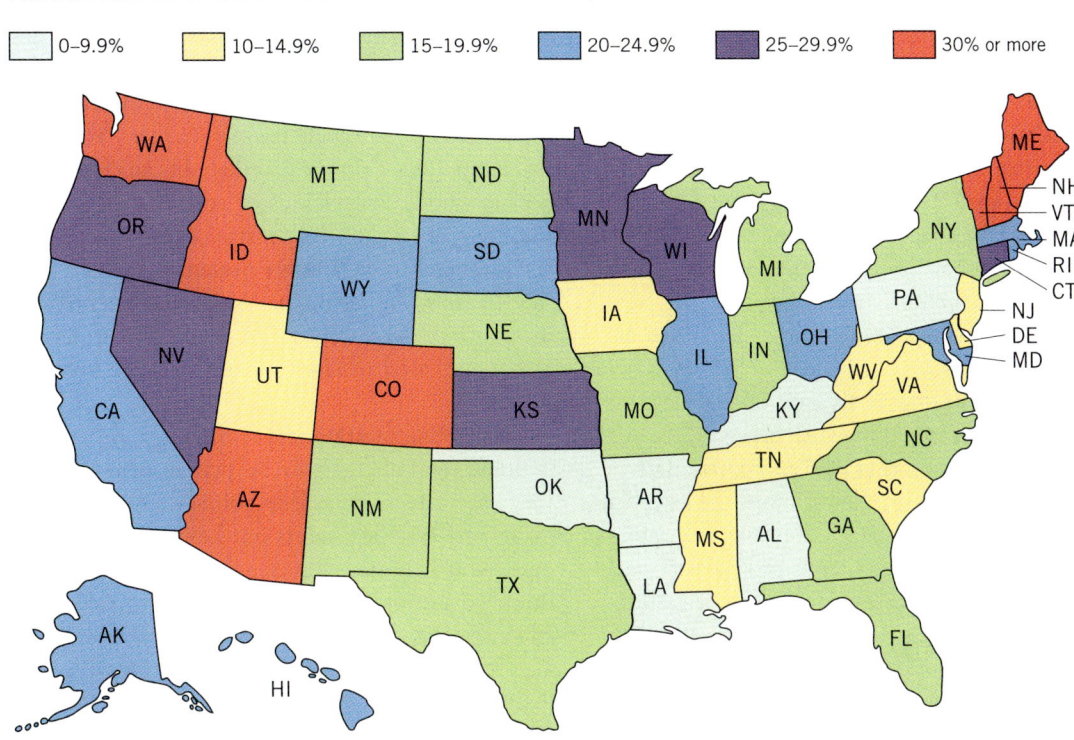

☐ 0–9.9%   ☐ 10–14.9%   ☐ 15–19.9%   ☐ 20–24.9%   ☐ 25–29.9%   ☐ 30% or more

SOURCE: Rob Gurwitt, "Legislatures: The Faces of Change," *Governing* (February 1993): 30.

fourteen had divided control. (One state, Nebraska, has a nonpartisan legislature. See map at left.) In 1992 women and minorities made big gains in state capitols when 125 more women, 65 more blacks, and 27 more Hispanics entered office (see map above). One-fifth of all legislators are female.

Apportionment   Once, many state legislatures were unrepresentative of the people of the state, as a result of malapportionment. District lines were drawn so as to give an enormous advantage to some parts of the state, usually rural ones, at the expense of other parts, usually urban and suburban ones. Before 1964, for example, a vote cast in a rural county would, on the average, be worth twice as much as one cast in a big city, because in the former there would be only half as many voters per elected representative as in the latter.[11] In certain states the underrepresentation was much greater than these national averages suggest. Los Angeles County, with almost 40 percent of California's population, had but one state senator (out of forty). In 1964 the

United States Supreme Court ruled, in the case of *Reynolds* v. *Sims*,[12] that the populations of each district in a given house of a state legislature had to be substantially equal. The rule to be followed was "one person, one vote."

As a result of this decision many state legislatures had to be redistricted. The consequences were often dramatic. In Georgia, for example, the number of representatives from urban areas increased by a factor of ten in the lower house of the legislature and by a factor of twenty in the upper house.[13] In other states the chief beneficiaries were suburban rather than urban voters. Moreover, the partisan and racial composition of state legislatures began to change. In the South Republicans (from suburban districts) and blacks (from urban districts) increased in number. Urban and suburban interests got more attention from state government, and rural interests got somewhat less. But some of these gains for big cities have proved to be short-lived. As people have moved out of large, older cities and into the suburbs, the continuing process of reapportionment means that many big cities have lost voting strength in their state capitols, and suburbs have gained strength.

Professional versus Amateur Legislators Though state legislative districts are about the same size within a given state, they of course differ greatly in size across states. A California legislative district may have 300,000 people in it while one in New Hampshire may have only 2,000.[14] Thus in California legislative politics is big business; in New Hampshire it is a folksy, friends-and-neighbors affair.

States differ not only in the size of their legislatures but also in the extent to which being a legislator is a full-time job. California paid its representatives (in 1995) $72,000 a year; New Hampshire pays its representatives $100 a year. California legislators work in an institution with a large, professional staff and many conveniences; New Hampshire legislators are pretty much on their own. Twenty-seven states pay their legislators $15,000 a year or more; thirteen pay them less (often much less) than $10,000 a year.

There has been a significant increase in the number of legislatures that have been professionalized. A **professional legislature** has some or all of the following characteristics:

- It meets during most of the year.

- Its members are relatively well paid.

- Its members regard being a legislator as their main job.

- Members and committees have sizable, year-round staffs.

California has a professional legislature, as do Illinois, Massachusetts, Michigan, Minnesota, New York, New Jersey, Ohio, Pennsylvania, and Wisconsin. By contrast, New Hampshire, Texas, Wyoming, and many other states have an **amateur,** or part-time, **legislature.** One of the striking features of professionalized legislatures is the low turnover among members. In eight of the ten professionalized legislatures listed above, turnover in the 1988 election was less than 10 percent.

The rise of the professional legislature means an increase in the number of legislators whose full-time occupation is politics. This fact may help explain why Democrats do better at winning elections to state legislatures than do Republicans. As Morris Fiorina and Alan Ehrenhalt have pointed out, the two parties differ in the kinds of people who are active in them.[15] Republican party activists are often older persons, especially lawyers, farmers, and business executives. Conservative Republicans tend to be people who are suspicious of government, wishing that it were smaller. By contrast, Democratic party activists tend to be younger persons for whom politics (or work for various social movements involved in politics) has been a full-time career. Liberal Democrats tend to like government and want it to do more.

If this line of argument is correct, it means that Republicans will tend to be people who, because they have careers outside of politics, will find it easy to be part-time legislators but hard to be full-time ones. And it means that Republicans, because they think government should do relatively little, may enjoy serving in a legislature that does little but dislike serving in one that does a lot. As a result, Republicans will be less likely than Democrats to be vigorous, persistent, and skillful candidates for elective office, and so Democrats will win a larger-than-expected share of seats in the legislatures. The result will be a tendency toward divided government—Republican governors who do not have a Republican legislature.

Party Organization Party leaders in Congress are important but have only a little power; they cannot choose committee chairmen or remove members from committees. But party leaders in many state legislatures often have a great deal of power.

A few states, mostly in the South (Alabama, Louisiana, Mississippi, New Hampshire, South Carolina, and Texas), have no distinct majority and minority leaders, in part because there are so few Republicans in these legislatures as to make party organization almost meaningless. Nebraska has no party leaders because its state legislators are all elected on a nonpartisan ballot.

In the rest of the states the influence of party leaders varies considerably. In Massachusetts and California, for example, the speaker of the lower house handpicks committee members and committee chairmen. Chairmen who act against the speaker's wishes risk losing their chairmanships and all the accompanying powers and privileges. Similarly, the speaker of the House in Michigan is a dominant figure; as one state legislator put it, "nothing happens without the speaker's approval."[16] In New York party discipline is quite strong; as one former speaker of the Assembly said, "never once in the fifteen years I've been here have we failed to get a Republican majority for a 'must' piece of legislation."[17] In a few states not only do party caucuses meet regularly to decide what positions their parties will take on pending legislation, those decisions are binding on party members. But in other states party leaders have relatively little influence.

Party leaders derive their power not only from their ability to pick committee chairmen (posts that often carry higher salaries and more fringe benefits than ordinary legislative seats) but also from the legislative patronage that they have to dispense (a lot in states such as New York, New Jersey, and Pennsylvania) and from the campaign funds that they frequently control. In California, for example, the last few speakers of the Assembly (Jesse Unruh, Leo McCarthy, and Willie Brown) have raised millions of dollars from interest groups. The speakers then passed out this money to support the reelection campaigns of loyal legislators.

One would like to know how effective all this leadership is in producing party-line voting in the state legislatures. But we don't know: the research on this subject is too fragmentary to permit one to say much. It appears that in the legislatures of states such as California, Colorado, Rhode Island, and Pennsylvania there has been a high level of party voting and in states such as Montana, Washington, and Wyoming there has not been much.[18]

No one is quite certain why some states are more partisan than others, though it appears that the urbanized, industrialized states tend to have more party-line votes than do more rural states. But there are at least two qualifications that have to be made to this—and any other—generalization about legislative voting. One is that the patterns change over time. A second is that the concept of party is relatively meaningless in one-party states. In Alabama, Georgia, Louisiana, or Mississippi almost everybody in the legislature is a Democrat. The real cleavages in these states tend to be between urban and rural or

Texas

*P*olitics in Texas has traditionally been a contest among Democrats whose campaigns focused on the state's small towns but were financed by big-city oil and banking money. But that is changing. Liberal Democrats, with support in the big cities and among ethnic minorities, have been growing in influence. In response, people who were once conservative Democrats increasingly have been campaigning and voting as Republicans, at least for statewide and national office. As a result, the old one-party politics of Texas has given way to two-party politics.

The emergence of a two-party Texas is especially important given the state's power in national affairs. It has the third-largest congressional delegation, two of its citizens have been president (Lyndon Johnson and George Bush), and in recent years it has produced two powerful speakers of the House (Sam Rayburn and Jim Wright), a Senate majority leader (Johnson), and two secretaries of the treasury (John Connally and Lloyd Bentsen).

Since 1978 both parties have had a good shot at winning the governorship; Republican William Clements won in that year, Democrat Mark White in 1982, Clements again in 1986, Democrat Ann Richards in 1990, and Republican George W. Bush in 1994. Currently both senators are Republican (Phil Gramm and Kay Bailey Hutchinson). In both houses of the state legislature, however, Democrats enjoy large majorities.

The governor serves a four-year term and can be reelected, but his or her executive authority must be shared with six other elected statewide officials and an elected Railroad Commission. The detailed, Jacksonian-style constitution places sharp limits on government power. The lieutenant governor is not elected on the same slate as the governor and enjoys considerable independent power as a result of his ability, as presiding officer of the Senate, to pick its committee members and chairmen. The speaker is equally influential in the House. The Texas legislature is a part-time venture, meeting only in odd-numbered years and paying its members $7,200 a year.

The state is fiscally conservative: it has no state income tax, and it spends less per capita than most other states. The recession in the oil industry hurt the state in the 1980s, but in the 1990s it was enjoying an economic revival and industrial diversification.

liberal and conservative legislators, not between Democrats and Republicans.

Committees   State legislatures, like Congress, have committees, in which much of the real lawmaking work is done. But state committees are often much less important than their congressional counterparts, and for good reason. Where the party leaders are powerful, committee chairmen will be less powerful. One indication of committee weakness is the turnover in their membership—it is often higher in the states than in Congress. Another is that seniority often counts for much less in picking a state committee chairman than it does in choosing a chairman in Congress.

In sum, the legislatures of many of the bigger, industrialized, northern states tend to be more partisan, more highly organized, and more tightly led than is Congress, whereas legislatures in small, rural, and southern states tend to be somewhat less structured than Congress. Committees tend to be somewhat less important in the states than in Congress.

State Courts

In general the structure of state courts looks much like the federal system. There are many trial courts in most states and usually a single supreme court. In most states there are also intermediate appeals courts. But when examined more closely, state courts turn out to be much more diverse and specialized than federal ones. Let us start at the bottom and work up.

Trial Courts   There are two kinds. First, there are minor courts (in cities they are usually called municipal courts; in rural areas they are sometimes called justices of the peace) that handle traffic tickets, small claims, and minor criminal offenses. Second, there are trial courts with broad jurisdiction over all criminal and civil matters. These are called, variously, superior courts, county courts, circuit courts, district courts, or courts of common pleas. (In New York they are called supreme courts, but they are not really supreme.) People charged with serious crimes are tried in these courts, and major lawsuits are settled there. At this level there may also be specialized courts to handle probate

(that is, the wills and estates of deceased persons) and juvenile or family matters. Most general jurisdiction trial courts are part of a county government, though the judges may be selected by the governor.

Appeals Courts   At the top of the system there are the state equivalents to the United States Supreme Court. In most states it is called the state supreme court, but in Maine and Massachusetts it is called the Supreme Judicial Court and in Maryland and New York the Court of Appeals. (Two states have separate supreme courts for civil and criminal matters.) State supreme courts, like their federal counterpart, have the power to declare acts of state government to be unconstitutional. They can also claim that federal laws are unconstitutional, but such decisions almost always get reviewed by the United States Supreme Court. Between the highest court and the trial courts there are, in most states, appeals courts on which several judges sit.

Choosing Judges   There is a bewildering variety of methods for choosing judges. In general, states that reflect the Jacksonian tradition elect their judges, and states that embody the progressive tradition appoint theirs. The Jacksonians believe that election guarantees that the judges will be close to the people; the progressives argue that appointment ensures that the judges will be competent. But within this framework are countless combinations and exceptions.

To simplify matters a bit, let us look at five methods for picking judges:

1. *Partisan elections.* In fifteen states judges run for office as Democrats or Republicans. Among the larger states that use this method are Illinois, New York, North Carolina, Pennsylvania, and Texas. In five of these states, including New York, partisan elections are used for some but not all courts.

2. *Nonpartisan elections.* In sixteen states judges run for office in nonpartisan elections. Among the larger states using this method are Michigan, Minnesota, Ohio, and Wisconsin. Five of these states combine this method with another for different courts.

3. *Appointment by governor.* In ten states the governor appoints the judges. These include Maryland, Massachusetts, and New Jersey. Three of these states combine this method with another for different courts.

4. *Appointment by legislature.* In four states the judges are appointed by the legislature. These are Connecticut, Rhode Island (appeals judges only), South Carolina, and Virginia.

5. *"Missouri Plan."* In this system, used in whole or in part by sixteen states, the judge is first appointed and then must face the electorate at the end of his or her first term. The governor makes the appointment from a list of candidates produced by a screening committee of citizens and lawyers. When the judge completes the first term of office, his or her name goes on the ballot with the question, "Shall Judge A be retained in office?" There is no opponent (except in California, where trial court judges, but not appellate judges, face an opponent). If more people vote "yes" than "no" on retaining the judge in office, the judge stays. Among the states using this plan are California, Colorado, Florida (appeals judges), Indiana (appeals judges), Iowa, Missouri, Nebraska, and Utah.[19]

Experts argue over what difference, if any, the selection method makes in the quality of judges. No one knows for certain, in part because people disagree as to what constitutes a good judge. We do know a few facts, however. First, not many people vote in those elections where judges are chosen. Second, most incumbent judges don't face an opponent when they stand for reelection. Third, the Missouri Plan results in the defeat of only a tiny proportion of all judges who run. Sometimes, though, that small fraction can include some celebrated cases. One such was Chief Justice Rose Bird of California, who in 1986 was defeated by a massive campaign to unseat her because of decisions that she had written preventing the carrying out of the death penalty in various criminal cases. Fourth, elected and appointed judges do not differ greatly in their decisions, though elected Democrats tend to be somewhat more liberal than elected Republicans.

Political Culture

These facts and figures, though important, do not capture the flavor of daily life in state government, because each state has a style, or political culture, that is often quite distinctive. Alan Rosenthal suggests some of this with these thumbnail sketches:

> *In New York professional politics, political wheeling and dealing, and frantic activity are characteristic. In Virginia, one gets a sense of tradition, conservatism, and gentility, and the General Assembly has been described by its admirers as the "first men's club" in the state. Louisiana's politics are wild and flamboyant. By contrast, moderation and caution are features of Iowa. A strong disposition of compromise pervades Oregon. . . . In Kansas hard work, respect for authority, fiscal prudence, and a general conservatism and resistance to rapid social change are pervasive features of the state environment. Indiana is intensely partisan, Wyoming is mainly individualistic and Ohio is fundamentally conservative. In Hawaii the relatively recent political dominance of Japanese, and the secondary status of Chinese, native Hawaiians, and Haoles (whites) makes for tough ethnic politics. Yankee Republicans used to run Massachusetts, but now the Irish dominate. . . . Mormonism, of course, dominates Utah.*[20]

The Structure of Local Government

Just as states tend to reflect either the Jacksonian or the progressive political culture, so also do cities, especially big cities, differ in this way. Many scholars distinguish between **unreformed cities** and **reformed cities.** They do not mean by this that unreformed cities are bad and reformed ones good, only that in the latter case the progressive impulse has made greater headway. These differences can be summarized, in oversimplified form, as follows:

Unreformed (Jacksonian) city	Reformed (progressive) city
Elections partisan	Elections nonpartisan
City council elected from districts	City council elected at large

Unreformed (Jacksonian) city	Reformed (progressive) city
Executive powers in hands of mayor	Executive powers in hands of appointed city manager
Weak civil service	Strong civil service

In general, unreformed large cities are found in the older states of the Northeast, while reformed cities are more characteristic of the younger states of the West and Southwest. Among cities that most nearly resemble the Jacksonian (or unreformed) model are Baltimore, Chicago, Cleveland, New York, Philadelphia, and St. Louis. Among those that most nearly approximate the progressive (or reformed) model are Cincinnati, Dallas, Kansas City, San Diego, and San Jose. Los Angeles and Detroit are interesting mixed cases. Los Angeles elects its council members by district and has no city manager, but it is nonpartisan and has a strong civil service tradition. Detroit elects its council members at large but has a strong mayor.

Today some observers believe that a mixture of the two traditions is best suited for big-city governance. A strong elected mayor gives the city a single, visible symbol of popular desires and community attachments, and district elections ensure that neighborhoods will have a say in how things are done, but it is also necessary to have a nonpartisan

civil service headed by a professional city administrator who serves under the mayor. In theory this would strike a balance between representation and efficiency. A few cities have experimented with such combinations, but opinions differ as to their success.

Complicating the distinction between "reformed" and "unreformed" has been the controversy over the racial consequences of at-large elections. Originally at-large elections were favored by progressives because they would allow the "best people" to run for the city council without regard to where they lived in the city and without having to represent on the council the interests of a particular neighborhood; such council members would presumably be free to do what was good for the city "as a whole." Jacksonians opposed at-large elections precisely because they tended to result in elections' being won by well-known people (most of whom all lived in one part of town) who would not tend to the interests of particular neighborhoods.

Recently, however, the choice between at-large and district representation has been made more difficult because of the effect of each system on the chances that black (and other minority-group) representatives will get elected. The federal courts have interpreted the voting rights laws to mean that it is not enough for blacks to have a chance to register, vote, and run for office; these laws also require that blacks (and other minorities) have a reasonable chance of *winning* the election. In a city where blacks are in the minority, few if any will be elected to the city council in an at-large election. In cities that use neighborhood districts, it is much easier for blacks to get elected. The federal courts have required many cities and counties (chiefly but not only in the South) to switch from at-large to district elections.

Mayor-Council Plan

The most common form of city government is one in which authority is vested in an elected mayor and council. It is typical of very small cities (those under 10,000 population) and very large cities (those over 250,000 population). (See Table 25.3.) A **mayor-council system** can be of two sorts. **Weak-mayor systems** have, as the name implies, a mayor who does not have much power over the administration

FIGURE 25.2   Weak-Mayor–Council Form of Government

TABLE 25.3 Forms of City and Town Government, 1992

Form of Government	All Cities
Mayor-council	15,125
Council-manager	3,131
Commission	351
Other	531
Total	19,138

SOURCE: U.S. Census Bureau, *1992 Census of Municipal Governments.*

of the system (he or she often must share executive authority with various boards and commissions) and does not have a lot of influence in the city council (see Figure 25.2). Often the mayor is chosen by the city council from among its members rather than being directly elected by the citizens. But even when directly elected, some mayors can be weak. The mayor of Los Angeles, for example, has relatively few appointive powers. The mayor can select the chief of police, but only from a short list produced by the civil service system, and once selected the chief serves for a fixed term and reports to a separate police commission.

Strong-mayor systems have a directly elected mayor with substantial authority over the administrative branch of government and important budgetary powers (see Figure 25.3). The mayors of Boston and New York City are strong mayors. In general the larger cities have moved to increase the authority of their mayors, but this process has not moved as rapidly or as far as it has for governors.

Council-Manager Plan

Under the **council-manager system** the people vote only for city council members, who then appoint a professional city manager to take charge of most or all of the city's administration (see Figure 25.4). Usually elections in council-manager cities are nonpartisan and at-large, and civil service is quite strong. The council-manager plan is the most common form in middle-sized cities, those with a population of between ten thousand and two hundred thousand. In some cities managers are in fact local politicians, but in most they have been specially trained for this career and often come to their job from another city.

FIGURE 25.3 Strong-Mayor–Council Form of Government

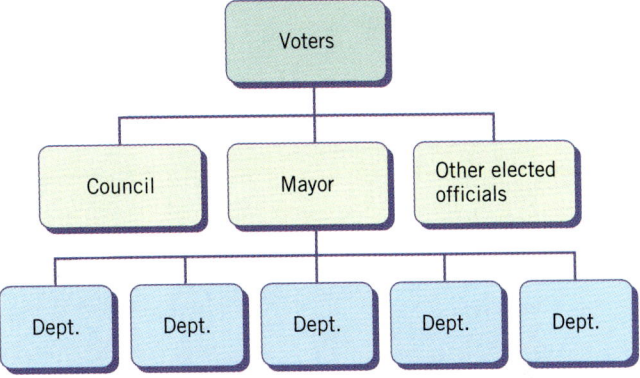

SOURCE: Adapted from Institute of Public Affairs. The University of Texas at Austin, *Forms of City Government*, 7th ed. (Austin: 1968), 4.

FIGURE 25.4 City-Manager Form of Government

Commission Plan

In a few cities government is in the hands of an elected commission that does not have a single head of the executive branch. Instead each commissioner takes responsibility for some part of city administration. One commissioner may oversee the fire and police departments; another may supervise roads and highways. The commission plan is not very popular, as it seems to make management more complex and leadership more divided, but a few big cities, including St. Paul, Tulsa, and Mobile, still have it.

Mayor Rudolph Giuliani of New York City (left), Mayor Richard Riordan of Los Angeles (right).

Metropolitan Government

Some people think that the structure of governance in our big cities is out of date. In places such as Boston, Chicago, and St. Louis, the central city is run by one government and the surrounding suburbs are run by others. But the problems of the metropolitan area do not respect city boundaries. Crime, traffic congestion, and air pollution move across these political boundaries as if they did not exist. Moreover, people in the suburbs often work and shop in the central cities but do not pay taxes there, and so the big cities must pay for programs aimed at slums, poverty, big welfare rolls, and run-down schools with money that is collected only from city residents.

People who worry about such matters advocate finding some way to govern the metropolitan area as a whole. One method is for the central city to annex the surrounding suburbs. Some cities have done just this. Houston has expanded its city limits so that it now encompasses a land area in excess of 565 square miles. (By contrast, Philadelphia, with about the same population as Houston, occupies a land area only one-fourth as large.) But **annexation** will be resisted by suburbs, especially in the older metropolitan areas. Boston, for example, has a land area of only forty-seven square miles and has no chance of persuading any of the surrounding towns to become

part of the city. Annexation may be possible when suburban and central-city residents are about the same in race, social class, and political interest, but as soon as the central city becomes known for having a lower-income, minority population with many problems, white suburbanites are not likely to favor annexation.

Another way to deal with metropolitan problems is to strengthen county government or even to consolidate city and county government into one. The governments of the city and county of San Francisco are one and the same, as are (with some exceptions) those of the city of Boston and Suffolk county in Massachusetts. New York City is the result of a merger, dating back to the turn of the century, of five counties (now called boroughs)—Brooklyn, the Bronx, Manhattan, Queens, and Staten Island. **City-county consolidation** today is unlikely for the same reason that annexation is unlikely.

County government can perform a major role even without consolidation by providing services on contract. In Los Angeles, for example, the county offers a variety of services that local communities can purchase by signing a contract. The Los Angeles Sheriff's Office provides, for a fee, police protection to cities in the county that do not want the expense or bother of running their own police departments. Similar services are provided to many communities on Long Island in New York by the Nassau County government. This system offers the advantages of professional management and broad coverage without the political problems of merger.

A third way of managing metropolitan problems is to create a **metropolitan government.** This is a system for governing the entire area while leaving some autonomy in the hands of local governments. It is a kind of federal system, with the metropolitan area government handling the areawide problems and city governments handling the local matters. Metropolitan governments have been created in Dade County (Miami), Florida, and Nashville, Tennessee, among other places. But most metropolitan areas have resisted this method, because local communities want to be independent. Many people believe that they have a right to choose their own kind of town, and town government, just as they choose their own home and car. Suburban cities develop a distinctive lifestyle and want to preserve it.

In view of the problems with annexation, consolidation, and metropolitan government, the most common method of dealing with metropolitan problems is to create special districts or authorities to manage specific services, such as water supply, sewage treatment, airports and highways, or bus and subway systems. These districts can tax the residents throughout the area and can borrow money to build transportation or water systems. They often are quite efficient, but some people worry that they quickly become remote from popular control.

In general, politics within most metropolitan areas is not under any kind of central leadership. Instead it is carried on by a process of bargaining among local governments. The arena in which the struggle proceeds is usually the state legislature, though an increasing number of metropolitan areas are creating councils of governments (sometimes known as COGs) in which mayors and city managers meet to see whether they can work out agreements on a voluntary basis.

Politics and Policies

Policy-making in the states differs from that in the federal government for at least two important reasons. First, most states have to work harder to live within their means than does Washington. In more than thirty states the constitution requires that the legislature pass a balanced budget. Congress, by contrast, can vote for an unbalanced budget—that is, one that calls for spending more money than is coming in—any time it wants. It is more difficult for many states to borrow money than it is for the national government. In eleven states it takes an extraordinary majority in the legislature to authorize borrowing; in other states the voters must approve borrowing in a referendum. Neither provision applies to Congress. Owing to these and other factors, the total debt owed by all state governments is only about one-tenth of that owed by Washington. As a result, state politics is fiscally more constrained than national politics. Many governors lose elections because they raised taxes;[21] only rarely is a president defeated because of taxes. The reason: it is easier for a president to avoid new taxes by tolerating deficits.

Second, states (and cities) compete with one another to attract businesses, residents, and tourists. To do this they struggle to provide a "good business climate," which means, among other things, keeping taxes down, regulations simple, and costs under control. Because of political pressures for more services and regulations, some states lose out in this competition for jobs. For example, the high cost of doing business in California has caused many firms to move to Arizona, Nevada, Utah, and other less costly states. By contrast, the federal government does not have to do as much to maintain a good business climate. Though it worries a bit about foreign competition, even if an American firm decides to build a factory abroad, Washington can still tax the profits when they are brought back into this country.

States with a Jacksonian style of government are, it seems, a bit more likely to maintain a political climate attractive to business. A weak or divided state government will find it hard to raise taxes or impose new regulations; a state that, because of the progressive tradition, has a strong governor and a professionalized legislature will find it easier to do these things. Moreover, states with a Jacksonian style are more common in those parts of the country, such as the South, where a tradition of limited government is strong and where economic elites have great power.

New York

Traditionally the big split in New York politics has been between New York City and upstate. Part of it has been ideological (the city is more liberal than upstate) and part of it monetary (the city and the state disagree over who should pay for what services). The key figures in this struggle are the governor and the mayor of New York City.

For many years New York has had a series of strong governors, several of whom became presidential candidates. Elected for a four-year term to which they can be reelected, New York's governors share their authority with only two other statewide officers (besides the lieutenant governor)—an attorney general and a controller. The governor can make many appointments, with a large supply of patronage at his disposal.

The legislature is among the best paid in the country. Its sixty-one senators and one hundred fifty Assembly members meet annually and are well organized along party lines. The Republicans control the Senate, the Democrats the Assembly. A great deal of power is wielded by the Senate president pro tem and the Assembly speaker, each of whom has considerable influence on committee assignments.

New York's Democratic and Republican parties have been neighborhood-based, patronage-fed organizations virtually since the founding of the Republic, though today the legendary Tammany Hall (the Democratic party of Manhattan) is but a pale shadow of its former self. In the city a reform movement that began in the late 1950s has gradually replaced the old-style bosses with younger, more issue-oriented activists and with black and Hispanic district leaders. Other parties—the Liberal, the Right-to-Life, and the Conservative—have also been influential in the state.

In New York City the Democratic party consists of an uneasy alliance among blacks, middle-income white ethnics, and liberal (often Jewish) activists. This alliance has become strained by issues such as crime, taxes, and racial integration. Responding to popular concerns about crime and city services, Democrat Edward Koch put together a right-of-center, personality-based political coalition that reelected him several times, but by 1989 he could no longer hold his following together in the face of scandals among some associates. He lost to David Dinkins, who became the first black mayor of New York City. But after only one term in office, Dinkins was defeated by Republican Rudolph Giuliani, a white, who revived the old Koch political coalition.

Jacksonian states, especially those without many big cities, have emphasized limited government, which business often finds attractive and labor finds unattractive. Progressive states, particularly those with a largely urbanized population, have tended to emphasize redistributing income and regulating business. For example, California and Wisconsin were among the first states to create, and have been among the most generous in financing, state universities, aid to families with dependent children (AFDC), and environmental protection laws.[22]

The same tendency can be found in city governments. Those with a "reformed" form of government (for example, council-manager) were among the first to fluoridate their water supplies[23] and have worked hardest to keep the police out of local politics and operating in accordance with whatever is thought to be "professional" police practice.[24]

There are many exceptions to this generalization, however. Illinois has many features of the Jacksonian tradition, such as elected judges and patronage-oriented political parties, but it has not been reluctant to develop and pay for new programs. New York City has hardly been an example of a reformed city government, but it has been a pioneer in producing expensive schools, hospitals, and public housing projects.

Politics and Representation

Progressive states and "reformed" cities differ not only in their taxing and spending policies but also in how they secure representation for their citizens. As we have already seen, cities with at-large, nonpartisan elections make it harder for blacks and other spatially concentrated minorities to win office. Cities with district, partisan elections make it easier for such groups to enter office.

But the very "unreformed" cities that ease the entry of minorities into politics are also the cities that make it hard to adopt the kinds of programs that minorities often want. As a result, a political system that facilitates representation is often one that impedes change.

For example: Blacks are politically very liberal—they want the government to do a lot about their concerns regarding integration, reducing poverty, and enhancing education. And like every racial or ethnic group, they want their share of elected and appointed offices. But the institutions most likely to adopt liberal policies are ones in which political authority is centralized, tax monies are ample, experts are influential, and local interests are kept in the background—precisely the kinds of institutions that will underrepresent racial or neighborhood interests. Cities with at-large, nonpartisan elections are likely to have fewer black elected officials (relative to the size of the black population) than cities with district-based, partisan elections. Blacks have most frequently come to power in unreformed cities with a weak tax base, a decaying array of municipal services, and a relatively small supply of trained experts.

Moreover, the old political machines that once made governing possible in the unreformed cities—the Daley machine in Chicago, Tammany Hall in New York—have been so weakened by a combination of political reforms and ethnic conflicts that, just as blacks begin to take control in the old cities, they discover that the traditional instrument of municipal power, the party, is no longer of much value. Harold Washington, a black, became mayor of Chicago and immediately became embroiled in a struggle with white aldermen and ward committeemen representing the remnants of the old Daley machine. Washington triumphed, leading to a period in which racial politics largely replaced machine politics. After Washington died in 1987, a new election in which voters cast their ballots along racial lines resulted in the election of a white mayor, Richard Daley, son of the old boss. Though the younger Daley had his father's name, he did not have his power. Eventually another black will probably become mayor of Chicago, but that person will not be able to run the city as it was once run.

Of course, blacks have also come to power in cities without a tradition of machine politics. Tom Bradley became mayor of Los Angeles, Coleman Young mayor of Detroit, and Marion Barry mayor of Washington, D.C. (By 1993 there were black mayors in 356 American cities and Hispanic mayors in 202.) They have had to negotiate alliances with other interests, such as downtown businesspeople and white liberals, in order to govern. It is difficult, however, for these mayors to increase their formal authority. The mayor of Los Angeles (until 1993 Tom Bradley, now Richard Riordan) would no

doubt like to get tighter control over many quasi-independent boards, commissions, and administrators, but this is not easily done, and so the pursuit of any political agenda will confront many roadblocks.

Taxes and Tax Revolts

Politics in states and cities is often dominated by the issues of taxing and spending, not only because government at these levels must try harder to live within their means but also for three other reasons:

First, states and cities provide services—schooling, law enforcement, fire protection, hospital care, road maintenance—directly to the citizen. Voters can see and even touch what state and local government does; they can only guess about much of what the federal government does. Because state and local services are so close to the daily lives of the people, the quality of these services is often a hot political issue.

Where Do You Pay the Most Taxes?

State and local tax payments in 1990 for a family of four earning $25,000 per year:

Portland, Oregon	$3,457
Milwaukee, Wisconsin	$3,436
Philadelphia, Pennsylvania	$3,192
Detroit, Michigan	$2,980
Baltimore, Maryland	$2,826
Newark, New Jersey	$2,800
New York, New York	$2,647
Providence, Rhode Island	$2,641
Cleveland, Ohio	$2,484
Washington, D.C.	$2,372
Honolulu, Hawaii	$2,112

SOURCE: *Statistical Abstract of the United States, 1992,* 303.

Second, state and local taxes are more visible than federal ones. The voters must write checks to pay the property taxes on which cities rely for about three-fourths of their revenue. Voters pay cash at the check-out counter for the sales taxes on which the states rely for about half their revenues (see Figure 25.5). The federal income tax, by contrast, is mostly collected by withholding it from our paychecks. It is money we never see, and often we can look forward to getting a refund after we file our tax return.

Third, many state and local taxes do not reflect how much money people earn. People must pay the same sales tax whether they are rich or poor. People must pay their property taxes whether they earned a lot of money that year or were laid off and earned next to nothing. By contrast, how much we pay in federal income taxes depends on how much we earn—in good years we pay more, in poor years we pay less.

These factors mean that city and state politicians are more likely than federal ones to be hit by demands for more services or lower taxes. People want more police on the streets but don't want to pay for them. Often some compromise can be worked out, but sometimes the voters' anger at their tax bills makes any compromise impossible. When that happens we have a **tax revolt**—a citizen-initiated demand for lower taxes.

This is especially likely to occur when property taxes rise faster than personal income. Suppose you buy a modest home at a time when you can afford the taxes. Then your neighborhood or city becomes very popular, with people moving in by the thousands. The value of your home suddenly skyrockets. The local tax assessor keeps raising the stated value of your home, and that means the property taxes you pay go up even if the tax *rate* does not change. But during all of this your income does not go up. As a result, you discover you can't afford to pay your property taxes. So you join a tax revolt.

Probably the first and certainly the best known of these revolts was Proposition 13, a measure adopted by the voters of California in 1978. Under it, the property taxes on a piece of land or a house had to be limited to 1 percent of the property's market value. Property assessments could not go up by more than 2 percent a year, and new state taxes would require a two-thirds vote of the legislature. Many city governments had to reduce taxes, and

some had to reduce services (some were able to maintain services by adopting other taxes, assessing fees for various services, or increasing their efficiency). The state government, which at the time had a budget surplus, also came to the aid of local governments by increasing its share of the costs of certain programs. As a result, more and more of California's public expenditures were being paid for out of state income and sales taxes.

In the wake of Proposition 13 several other states adopted tax-limitation or spending-limitation measures. Massachusetts voters enacted Proposition $2\frac{1}{2}$, and Missouri and Texas amended their constitutions to restrict the growth in revenues (Missouri) or expenditures (Texas) to the rate of growth in personal income. Other states adopted similar plans.

State and local governments tried to cope with tax revolts and declining federal aid in several ways. They began to tighten up the administration of their programs in hopes of saving money. In some places they reduced services (several cities laid off many police officers). They charged fees for various services, such as school band programs, that once were paid for out of taxes. They turned over some previously public services, such as trash collection, to private contractors who operated on a fee-for-service basis. And more than forty states created state-run lotteries, earmarking a portion of the profits for aid to education or for subsidies to city and town governments. In 1995 lottery sales were nearly $31.9 billion, with the states retaining about $11 billion in proceeds.

State Policies and Federal Politics: The Case of Crime Control

The importance of the decisions made by state and local governments and the diversity in the ways in which those decisions are made are two of the most distinctive features of the American political system. We often quote a maxim familiar to all elected officials: "all politics is local politics." This is not literally true—a lot of important decisions are made with an eye chiefly on their national or international implications. But it is true enough for many policies and especially true for electoral politics.

FIGURE 25.5 Where the Money Comes From and Where the Money Goes, 1990

STATE GOVERNMENT

Revenue Sources

Expenditures

LOCAL GOVERNMENT

Revenue Sources

Expenditures

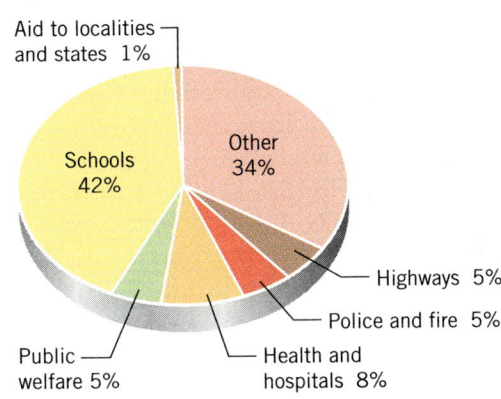

SOURCE: *Significant Features of Fiscal Federalism, 1992* (Washington, D.C.: Advisory Commission on Intergovernmental Relations, 1992), Tables 5, 9, 61, 77, 79.

State or local governments, after all, is where most members of Congress and many members of the national administration get their start. (For example, between 1950 and 1980 one-fourth of all ex-governors who stayed in politics wound up in Congress and 40 percent were appointed to federal administrative posts.) They learn politics by practicing local politics. In so doing, they learn that to get and keep national office, one must be seen as serving local interests.

As we have seen, the states and the federal government are locked in a continuing struggle over policy. The states want Washington to pay for new programs but to let the states decide what those programs should consist of and how they should be run. Washington wants the states to pay a larger share, but it hopes to decide what programs will be supported by this money. The balance of power has continually shifted back and forth between them, with different laws, numerous political personalities, and changes in public opinion influencing their repositioning. One of the most vivid examples of this ever-changing relationship is in the area of crime control.

You might think that crime control would always have been on the federal agenda. After all, America has always had crime, and crime is an ideal issue for majoritarian politics: if crime is reduced, all of us (except criminals) benefit and all of us (especially criminals) pay. Any president or member of Congress would be delighted to take credit for reducing crime.

But before the late 1960s, crime was rarely on the federal agenda. There were two reasons for this. First,

Major Federal Anti-Crime Laws, 1980–1994

Comprehensive Crime Control Act (1984) Established the Sentencing Commission to produce sentencing guidelines for federal judges that would provide greater "certainty and fairness" in punishing those who broke federal laws.

Anti-Drug Abuse Act (1986) Toughened penalties for drug dealers and other federal offenders, made it easier to seize the assets (money, homes, cars, etc.) of convicted drug dealers, and provided money for state and local governments to combat crime and drug abuse.

Anti-Drug Abuse Act (1988) Created the Office of National Drug Control Policy (commonly known as the "Drug Czar"), specified how money should be allocated between treatment and enforcement, authorized the death penalty for drug dealers who commit murders, required that contractors doing work for the federal government certify that they have a drug-free work place, and denied federal benefits (such as the right to live in public housing) to drug dealers.

Crime Control Act (1990) Addressed a wide range of criminal activities, including international money laundering, selling drugs in or near schools, and the sale of drug paraphernalia.

Anti-Car Theft Act (1992) Made car-jacking (stealing a car from its driver at gunpoint) a federal crime.

Brady Bill (1993) Required that anyone purchasing a hand gun wait five days before taking delivery so that a mandatory records check can be made to see if the purchaser has a criminal record.

Crime Act (1994) Expanded federal death penalty; mandated life imprisonment for federal criminals convicted of three violent or drug offenses; banned certain assault weapons; and authorized $8 billion to hire 100,000 more police officers, $8 billion to build prisons for state offenders, and $7 billion for various crime prevention programs.

many people thought the national government had no constitutional right to play a role in crime control. Criminal laws were passed by state legislatures and enforced by city police chiefs and county prosecutors. Nowhere did the Constitution give to Washington the power to have a police force or to pass laws making personal behavior—stealing, killing, raping—federal crimes. We are so used to having a Federal Bureau of Investigation (FBI) that we forget that it did not exist until the 1920s and that then it was controversial because people worried about a "national police force." When Congress passed a law against prostitution in 1910 it had to justify its enactment by relying on the commerce clause of the Constitution. Since Congress could regulate interstate commerce, it could regulate prostitutes who moved across state lines. It used a similar justification for a law banning the interstate transportation of stolen vehicles. When the infant son of the heroic aviator Charles Lindbergh was kidnapped in 1932, there was a demand that Congress do something. It responded by making it a federal offense to transport a kidnapped person across state lines.

The second limitation on the federal role came from the widespread assumption that local matters ought to be handled by local authorities. Local politicians reinforced this view by defending "states' rights." One reason for this position was the fear in many southern states that if the federal government started passing criminal laws it might make civil rights violations (which were a routine part of southern political life at that time) a federal crime. But there was another reason: Americans had not yet come to expect that Washington would, should, or could do much about local matters.

The role of the federal government in crime slowly grew as the power to regulate interstate commerce was more broadly interpreted by the Supreme Court (see Chapter 3), making it possible to apply federal criminal statutes to more and more local activities. For example, the Consumer Credit Protection Act of 1968 made loan sharking* a federal crime. When this law was challenged, the Supreme Court

---

* A loan shark is a person who loans money to people at illegally high interest rates and enforces repayment of the loan by the threat of force.

said that even if loan sharking was a purely local activity, it might "affect" interstate commerce and so Congress was entitled to regulate it.[25]

The growing crime rate and political opportunism also drove this growth of federal power. In the early 1960s the number of reported crimes began to rise dramatically, an increase that within ten years would double the rate of violent crime. America had become a nation of city dwellers, and this increase hit the big cities especially hard. In 1964 Republican Barry Goldwater ran against President Lyndon Johnson on a platform that, among other things, accused the Democrats of tolerating "crime in the streets." Goldwater lost, but Johnson responded to the Goldwater attack by appointing a national commission to make recommendations on how to improve law enforcement. Four years later Richard Nixon defeated Hubert Humphrey after a campaign that made "law and order" a key issue. Nixon carried out his campaign pledge to get tough on crime by appointing "law and order" attorneys to the Justice Department and by strengthening the federal drug enforcement agency.

Crime has been on the national agenda ever since. During the 1980s, Congress passed at least one new crime or drug control bill every two years (see box on page 722). In the 1960s and early 1970s, crime was an issue pressed by Republicans, but of late it has become a bipartisan issue with many of the toughest proposals coming from some Democrats in Congress. In 1993 President Clinton signed the Brady bill, which required a five-day waiting period for the purchase of a handgun.

The Distributive Politics of "100,000 Cops"

During his 1994 State of the Union address, President Clinton pledged to put 100,000 additional police officers on the streets of America's neighborhoods. On September 13, 1994, with strong bipartisan support, the President signed into law the Violent Crime Control and Law Enforcement Act of 1994. One major provision of the Act created a federal office of Community Oriented Policing (COPS) and authorized $8.8 billion over six years for grants to local policing agencies to add 100,000 officers and teach officers to "enhance their conflict resolution, mediation, problem solving, service, and other skills." The "100,000 cops" plan was quite popular with voters and with many mayors. President Clinton used the plan effectively in his 1996 reelection bid. But how did the COPS program actually work, and what, if any, impact on crime did it have?

By mid-1996, only about 17,000 local police officers were funded via the COPS program, roughly 14,000 of them existing officers redeployed from other assignments to patrol the streets.

The COPS money was spread across literally hundreds of cities and small towns. A single-spaced printout of the jurisdictions granted COPS funds in May 1996 ran to thirty-seven pages. Sunnyvale, California, officials calculated that hiring six new police officers would cost $6.3 million, to which the COPS program would contribute only $450,000. They turned down the COPS money.

Crime in many cities dropped between 1990 and 1996, but not for reasons that are clearly related to the COPS program, which did not take effect in many places until 1995. For example, crime in Boston had been dropping for five years when, at the end of 1995, the city added its first 61 COPS-funded officers to its force of over 2,100 officers.

Whatever its impact on crime, or lack thereof, the COPS program illustrates the distributive politics of federal social policy. While some crime experts argued in 1994 and thereafter that targeting the federal funds (and the local police) towards high-crime big-city neighborhoods would be best, there was no chance that Congress would approve any plan that failed to spread the money around.

Crime: Rhetoric Versus Reality

There are two main problems with the enlarged federal role in crime control. First, the vast majority of the people and money involved in fighting crime are still to be found at the local level. Second, nobody—not the president, not any police chief, not any judge, not any professor—really knows how to cut the crime rate dramatically, or at least cut it dramatically while still preserving our essential freedoms.

In 1990, state and local governments spent nearly nine dollars on crime control for every one dollar spent by the federal government. There are thirteen times as many inmates in state prisons as there are in federal ones. The vast majority of law enforcement officers are local police officers. Even the Washington, D.C., police force is under the control of a mayor, not Congress or the president. The president cannot appoint a single police chief. Washington has become a partner of the states in the war on crime, but it is still very much a junior partner, and that is not likely to change.

Washington has spent billions of dollars and passed many get-tough crime bills, but crime rates have been largely unaffected by any of this. There are many reasons for our inability to design an effective crime control strategy for a free society. It is rather easy to steal something, hit someone, or sell drugs when no police officer is looking. Even doubling or tripling the number of officers on the street will not make it much more likely that a criminal will be caught in the act. Most of us don't steal, hit, or deal in drugs; the reasons some people do are varied and complex.

Many criminals come from homes that are broken, unhappy, or abusive, but the government doesn't know how to create intact, happy, and caring families. Many criminals have parents who are criminals or who abuse alcohol and drugs, yet it is very hard for the government to prevent the problems of parents from becoming the problems of their children. The moral values that keep some individuals from engaging in criminal acts are not shared by all members of our society, and morality is not something that can be easily created by plan.

In some communities the lack of jobs and the evident success of drug dealers have reduced the incentive to find legitimate work and increased the rewards and glamour of crime and drug dealing. It is not easy to create jobs in such neighborhoods; businesses don't want to locate there because the crime rate is high. In many crime-ridden neighborhoods, gangs often rule the streets, shooting their rivals and sometimes killing innocent bystanders. It is not easy to break up these gangs, however, because they provide safety and income for their members—safety that the police can't provide and income that local businesses can't supply.

All this makes for a difficult kind of majoritarian politics. When you create a Social Security program and pay benefits to retired people, the rate of poverty among the elderly goes down. When you

pass an environmental law requiring that less polluting engines be installed in new automobiles, the amount of pollution in the air goes down. But when you pass an anti-crime bill, the crime rate does not necessarily go down.

This means that the options Washington has are rather few: make speeches denouncing crime (but criminals don't listen), spend more money on crime control (but federal money is only a drop in the national crime-control bucket), or make penalties for breaking federal laws more severe (but most criminals are prosecuted under state laws). Because a president can do so little about crime, he is always vulnerable to political attacks in an election if he has the bad luck to be in office when crime rates are high or rising. And since the early 1960s, every president until Bill Clinton's second term has been in that unenviable position.

The Changing Face of Crime-Control Policy

Given the fact that the states and localities will always play the lead role in crime control, Washington has been limited to trying various combinations of three different strategies:

1. *It has supplied help—money, technical assistance, computerized information, fingerprint records, and statistics—to local law enforcement agencies.* The federal government has funded research on new crime-control techniques, coordinated some local investigations that cut across state lines, and investigated criminal organizations that were too big to be investigated by local authorities.

2. *It has made some things that were once just state crimes into federal crimes.* For example, Washington has made bank robbery, car-jacking, and drug dealing federal crimes. This means that the FBI and the Drug Enforcement Administration (DEA) can get involved in investigating these matters; with respect to drug trafficking, even the military has been involved. And it means that federal prosecutors can try some cases and, on occasion, get tougher penalties imposed than can state prosecutors. The federal government has also passed laws especially aimed at organized

crime so that federal investigators can bring charges against gangsters who may have corrupted or overpowered local authorities.

3. *It has brought under some degree of federal regulation activities that may contribute to crime.* For example, Washington controls who and what kinds of products (such as drugs) can enter the country, it has rules for buying handguns and certain other weapons, and it inspects the flow of money through banks to see if any of it is the result of fraud, organized crime, or drug trafficking.

During the late 1960s and most of the 1970s, Washington emphasized the first of these strategies. This was done through the Law Enforcement Assistance Administration (LEAA), created in 1968, and its successor agencies, such as the National Institute of Justice (NIJ), the Bureau of Justice Statistics (BJS), and the Bureau of Justice Assistance (BJA), all located in the U.S. Department of Justice. The LEAA, NIJ, and BJA were essentially funding agencies that shipped federal money to states, counties, and cities to help them fight crime. They were specifically prohibited from getting involved in the direction or operation of local law enforcement. The law creating LEAA, for example, barred any federal official from directing, supervising, or controlling any local police force or state law enforcement agency.

As a check-writing machine, LEAA was a great success. Between 1969 and 1977, it sent about $8 billion to the states and localities. But crime continued to go up, and so it came as no surprise when, in the 1976 election campaign, Democratic candidate Jimmy Carter attacked Republican presidents Richard Nixon and Gerald Ford for having presided over a crime wave and for LEAA's failure to do anything about it. LEAA was in particular criticized for letting local authorities buy almost anything they wanted with federal dollars. After Carter was elected, LEAA was reorganized and its budget sharply cut; most of its functions were transferred to NIJ and later BJA, but with nowhere near as much money as LEAA once had. But crime rates continued to rise.

President Carter was then vulnerable to attack on the crime issue, and in the 1980 campaign Republican candidate Ronald Reagan was quick to go on the offensive. Reagan and his successor, George Bush, began to shift federal crime-control policies toward the second and third strategies listed above. With bipartisan support in Congress, Washington began to emphasize direct federal involvement in law enforcement. It did this by expanding the number of local crimes that were now also federal crimes, toughening the sentences violating federal criminal statutes, and (especially) getting federal agencies more deeply involved in combatting drug trafficking.

Since the 1960s, governors and mayors had wanted Washington to send them money to combat crime. They got money from LEAA until it was abolished by Ronald Reagan; then, between 1989 and 1992, Washington nearly quadrupled (from $118 million to $423 million) the amount of drug-fighting money it was sending to the states and cities each year. Traditionally the states had not wanted direct federal involvement in enforcing the laws, except for the cooperation of the FBI, but increasingly they began asking for more direct federal involvement. If they thought that the state penalty for, say, car-jacking or drug dealing was too lenient, they would urge the federal government either to make this a federal crime or, if it was already a federal offense, increase the penalties. That way, a person arrested for such a crime could be subjected to federal prosecution. The states also pressed Washington to get the military involved in stopping international drug trafficking.

For all of the changes that have occurred since the 1960s, law enforcement remains a local matter. Of the three areas of possible involvement in law enforcement—making policy, administering justice, and supplying funds—the federal government has sometimes emphasized one, sometimes another, but never has it taken the lead in all three. The localism of American politics—a localism supported by constitutional tradition and (more importantly) public sentiment—is clearly evident in the independence state and local governments continue to exercise in fighting crime. Though the federal government has expanded its supportive role in recent decades, crime control remains the province of local police officers and state troopers, who have very little connection to the policies of Washington.

SUMMARY

State and local governments tend to reflect variations on two different views of the public interest: a Jacksonian tradition that seeks to keep government close to the people (leading to many elected offices, weak governors and mayors, small electoral districts, a suspicion of experts, detailed state constitutions, and patronage politics) and a progressive, or "reformed" tradition that seeks to make government stronger and more efficient (leading to strong governors, appointed city managers, large electoral districts, professionalized legislatures, nonpartisan elections, brief state constitutions, and a comprehensive civil service in which expertise is rewarded).

State government is by no means a small version of national government, as can be seen by the many executive and judicial posts that are filled, at the state level, by popular election and by the much greater strength of party leaders in many state legislatures. Local government shows an even greater variety, with large and small cities governed under the mayor-council system, middle-sized cities governed by the council-manager form, and some places governed by town meetings, representative town meetings, or commissions.

Within these institutions there is a struggle among rival interests and preferences shaped, in great part, by a concern over taxes and the competitive economic position of states and localities. They also continually negotiate with the federal government over crime control and many other matters, looking to increase federal funding without giving up their autonomy.

KEY TERMS

patronage   *p. 697*
progressive movement   *p. 697*
Jacksonian model   *p. 698*
progressive model   *p. 698*
police power   *p. 699*
initiative   *p. 700*
referendum   *p. 700*
recall   *p. 700*
municipal corporation   *p. 701*
special-act charter   *p. 701*

general-act charter   *p. 701*
Dillon's rule   *p. 701*
home-rule charter   *p. 702*
town meeting   *p. 702*
representative town meeting   *p. 702*
professional legislature   *p. 710*
amateur legislature   *p. 710*
unreformed cities   *p. 713*
reformed cities   *p. 713*
mayor-council system   *p. 714*
weak-mayor system   *p. 714*
strong-mayor systems   *p. 715*
council-manager system   *p. 715*
annexation   *p. 716*
city-county consolidation   *p. 716*
metropolitan government   *p. 717*
tax revolt   *p. 720*

SUGGESTED READINGS

Banfield, Edward C., and James Q. Wilson. *City Politics.* Cambridge, Mass.: Harvard University Press, 1963. An argument about how political culture or ethos shapes the politics of American cities.

Council of State Governments. *Book of the States.* Lexington, Ky.: Council of State Governments, annual. Yearly publication of facts and figures on state government.

Elazar, Daniel J. *American Federalism: A View from the States.* 3d ed. New York: Harper & Row, 1984. Insightful discussion of state political cultures.

Fesler, James W., ed. *The Fifty States and Their Local Governments.* New York: Knopf, 1967. Though dated, it remains a good source on the constitutional background of state and local government.

Gray, Virginia, and Herbert Jacob, eds. *Politics in the American States.* 6th ed. Washington, D.C.: CQ Press, 1996. An excellent collection of articles on state governmental institutions, processes, and policies.

International City Managers Association. *Municipal Yearbook.* Washington, D.C.: ICMA, annual. A yearly publication with facts and figures about American local government.

Pierce, Neal R., and Jerry Hagstrom. *The Book of America: Inside 50 States Today.* New York: Norton, 1983. A lively and informative account by two first-class journalists of how each of the fifty states is governed.

Rosenthal, Alan. *The Third House.* Washington, D.C.: CQ Books, 1993. Examines lobbying in state governments; many vivid examples.

The Declaration of Independence

In Congress, July 4, 1776

The Unanimous Declaration of the Thirteen United States of America

When, in the course of human events, it becomes necessary for one people to dissolve the political bands which have connected them with another, and to assume, among the powers of the earth, the separate and equal station to which the laws of nature and of nature's God entitle them, a decent respect to the opinions of mankind requires that they should declare the causes which impel them to the separation.

We hold these truths to be self-evident: That all men are created equal; that they are endowed by their Creator with certain unalienable rights; that among these are life, liberty, and the pursuit of happiness; that, to secure these rights, governments are instituted among men, deriving their just powers from the consent of the governed; that whenever any form of government becomes destructive of these ends, it is the right of the people to alter or to abolish it, and to institute new government, laying its foundation on such principles, and organizing its power in such form, as to them shall seem most likely to effect their safety and happiness. Prudence, indeed, will dictate that governments long established should not be changed for light and transient causes; and accordingly all experience hath shown that mankind are more disposed to suffer, while evils are sufferable, than to right themselves by abolishing the forms to which they are accustomed. But when a long train of abuses and usurpations, pursuing invariably the same object, evinces a design to reduce them under absolute despotism, it is their right, it is their duty, to throw off such government, and to provide new guards for their future security. Such has been the patient sufferance of these colonies; and such is now the necessity which constrains them to alter their former systems of government. The history of the present King of Great Britain is a history of repeated injuries and usurpations, all having in direct object the establishment of an absolute tyranny over these states. To prove this, let facts be submitted to a candid world.

He has refused to assent to laws, the most wholesome and necessary for the public good.

He has forbidden his governors to pass laws of immediate and pressing importance, unless suspended in their operation till his assent should be obtained; and, when so suspended, he has utterly neglected to attend to them.

He has refused to pass other laws for the accommodation of large districts of people, unless those people would relinquish the right of representation in the legislature, a right inestimable to them, and formidable to tyrants only.

He has called together legislative bodies at places unusual, uncomfortable, and distant from the depository of their public records, for the sole purpose of fatiguing them into compliance with his measures.

He has dissolved representative houses repeatedly, for opposing, with manly firmness, his invasions on the rights of the people.

He has refused for a long time, after such dissolutions, to cause others to be elected; whereby the legislative powers, incapable of annihilation, have returned to the people at large for their exercise; the state remaining, in the mean time, exposed to all dangers of invasions from without and convulsions within.

He has endeavored to prevent the population of these states; for that purpose obstructing the laws for naturalization of foreigners; refusing to pass others to encourage their migration hither, and raising the conditions of new appropriations of lands.

He has obstructed the administration of justice, by refusing his assent to laws for establishing judiciary powers.

He has made judges dependent on his will alone, for the tenure of their offices, and the amount and payment of their salaries.

He has erected a multitude of new offices, and sent hither swarms of officers to harass our people, and eat out their substance.

He has kept among us, in times of peace, standing armies, without the consent of our legislatures.

He has affected to render the military independent of, and superior to, the civil power.

He has combined with others to subject us to a jurisdiction foreign to our constitution, and unacknowledged by our laws, giving his assent to their acts of pretended legislation:

For quartering large bodies of armed troops among us:

For protecting them, by a mock trial, from punishment for any murders which they should commit on the inhabitants of these states;

For cutting off our trade with all parts of the world;

For imposing taxes on us without our consent;

For depriving us, in many cases, of the benefits of trial by jury;

For transporting us beyond seas, to be tried for pretended offenses;

For abolishing the free system of English laws in a neighboring province, establishing therein an arbitrary government, and enlarging its boundaries, so as to render it at once an example and fit instrument for introducing the same absolute rule into these colonies;

For taking away our charters, abolishing our most valuable laws, and altering fundamentally the forms of our governments;

For suspending our own legislatures, and declaring themselves invested with power to legislate for us in all cases whatsoever.

He has abdicated government here, by declaring us out of his protection and waging war against us.

He has plundered our seas, ravaged our coasts, burned our towns, and destroyed the lives of our people.

He is at this time transporting large armies of foreign mercenaries to complete the works of death, desolation, and tyranny already begun with circumstances of cruelty and perfidy scarcely paralleled in the most barbarous ages, and totally unworthy the head of a civilized nation.

He has constrained our fellow-citizens, taken captive on the high seas, to bear arms against their country, to become the executioners of their friends and brethren, or to fall themselves by their hands.

He has excited domestic insurrection among us, and has endeavored to bring on the inhabitants of our frontiers the merciless Indian savages, whose known rule of warfare is an undistinguished destruction of all ages, sexes, and conditions.

In every stage of these oppressions we have petitioned for redress in the most humble terms; our repeated petitions have been answered only by repeated injury. A prince, whose character is thus marked by every act which may define a tyrant, is unfit to be the ruler of a free people.

Nor have we been wanting in our attentions to our British brethren. We have warned them, from time to time, of attempts by their Legislature to extend an unwarrantable jurisdiction over us. We have reminded them of the circumstances of our emigration and settlement here. We have appealed to their native justice and magnanimity; and we have conjured them, by the ties of our common kindred, to disavow these usurpations, which would inevitably interrupt our connections and correspondence. They, too, have been deaf to the voice of justice and of consanguinity. We must, therefore, acquiesce in the necessity which denounces our separation, and hold them, as we hold the rest of mankind, enemies in war, in peace friends.

We, therefore, the representatives of the United States of America, in General Congress assembled, appealing to the Supreme Judge of the world for the rectitude of our intentions, do, in the name and by the authority of the good people of these colonies, solemnly publish and declare, that these United Colonies are, and of right ought to be, FREE AND INDEPENDENT STATES; that they are absolved from all allegiance to the British crown, and that all political connection between them and the state of Great Britain is, and ought to be, totally dissolved; and that, as free and independent states, they have full power to levy war, conclude peace, contract alliances, establish commerce, and do all other acts and things which independent states may of right do. And for the support of this declaration, with a firm reliance on the protection of Divine Providence, we mutually pledge to each other our lives, our fortunes, and our sacred honor.

JOHN HANCOCK [*President*]
[*and fifty-five others*]

The Constitution of the United States

Preamble

We the People of the United States, in Order to form a more perfect Union, establish Justice, insure domestic Tranquility, provide for the common defence, promote the general Welfare, and secure the Blessings of Liberty to ourselves and our Posterity, do ordain and establish this Constitution for the United States of America.

ARTICLE I.

Bicameral Congress

Section 1. All legislative Powers herein granted shall be vested in a Congress of the United States, which shall consist of a Senate and House of Representatives.

Membership of the House

Section 2. The House of Representatives shall be composed of Members chosen every second Year by the People of the several States, and the Electors in each State shall have the Qualifications requisite for Electors of the most numerous Branch of the State Legislature.

No person shall be a Representative who shall not have attained to the age of twenty five Years, and been seven Years a Citizen of the United States, and who shall not, when elected, be an Inhabitant of that State in which he shall be chosen.

Representatives and direct Taxes shall be apportioned among the several States which may be included within this Union, according to their respective Numbers, which shall be determined by adding to the whole Number of free Persons, including those bound to Service for a Term of Years, and excluding Indians not taxed, three fifths of all other Persons.[1] The actual Enumeration shall be made within three Years after the first Meeting of the Congress of the United States, and within every subsequent Term of ten Years, in such Manner as they shall by Law direct. The Number of Representatives shall not exceed one for every thirty Thousand, but each State shall have at Least one Representative; and until such enumeration shall be made, the State of New Hampshire shall be entitled to chuse three, Massachusetts eight, Rhode-Island and Providence Plantations one, Connecticut five, New-York six, New Jersey four, Pennsylvania eight, Delaware one, Maryland six, Virginia ten, North Carolina five, South Carolina five, and Georgia three.

When vacancies happen in the Representation from any State, the Executive Authority thereof shall issue Writs of Election to fill such Vacancies.

Power to impeach

The House of Representatives shall chuse their Speaker and other Officers; and shall have the sole Power of Impeachment.

Membership of the Senate

Section 3. The Senate of the United States shall be composed of two Senators from each State, *chosen by the Legislature thereof,*[2] for six Years; and each Senator shall have one Vote.

NOTE: The topical headings are not part of the original Constitution. Excluding the Preamble and Closing, those portions set in italic type have been superseded or changed by later amendments.
1. Changed by the Fourteenth Amendment, section 2.
2. Changed by the Seventeenth Amendment.

Immediately after they shall be assembled in Consequence of the first Election, they shall be divided as equally as may be into three Classes. The Seats of the Senators of the first class shall be vacated at the Expiration of the second Year, of the second Class at the Expiration of the fourth Year, and of the third Class at the Expiration of the sixth Year, so that one third may be chosen every second Year; *and if Vacancies happen by Resignation, or otherwise, during the Recess of the Legislature of any State, the Executive thereof may make temporary Appointments until the next Meeting of the Legislature, which shall then fill such Vacancies.*[3]

No Person shall be a Senator who shall not have attained to the Age of thirty Years, and been nine Years a Citizen of the United States, and who shall not, when elected, be an Inhabitant of that State for which he shall be chosen.

The Vice President of the United States shall be President of the Senate, but shall have no Vote, unless they be equally divided.

The Senate shall chuse their other Officers, and also a President pro tempore, in the Absence of the Vice President, or when he shall exercise the Office of President of the United States.

Power to try impeachments

The Senate shall have the sole Power to try all Impeachments. When sitting for that Purpose, they shall be on Oath or Affirmation. When the President of the United States is tried the Chief Justice shall preside: And no Person shall be convicted without the Concurrence of two thirds of the Members present.

Judgment in Cases of Impeachment shall not extend further than to removal from Office, and disqualification to hold and enjoy any Office of honor, Trust or Profit under the United States: but the Party convicted shall nevertheless be liable and subject to Indictment, Trial, Judgment and Punishment, according to Law.

Laws governing elections

Section 4. The Times, Places and Manner of holding Elections for Senators and Representatives, shall be prescribed in each State by the Legislature thereof; but the Congress may at any time by Law make or alter such Regulations, except as to the Places of chusing Senators.

The Congress shall assemble at least once in every Year, and such Meeting shall be on the *first Monday in December, unless they shall by Law appoint a different Day.*[4]

Rules of Congress

Section 5. Each House shall be the Judge of the Elections, Returns and Qualifications of its own Members, and a Majority of each shall constitute a Quorum to do Business; but a smaller number may adjourn from day to day, and may be authorized to compel the Attendance of absent Members, in such Manner, and under such Penalties as each House may provide.

Each House may determine the Rules of its Proceedings, punish its Members for disorderly Behaviour, and, with the Concurrence of two thirds, expel a Member.

Each House shall keep a Journal of its Proceedings, and from time to time publish the same, excepting such Parts as may in their Judgment require Secrecy; and the Yeas and Nays of the Members of either House on any question shall, at the Desire of one fifth of those Present, be entered on the Journal.

---

3. Changed by the Seventeenth Amendment.
4. Changed by the Twentieth Amendment, section 2.

Neither House, during the Session of Congress, shall, without the Consent of the other, adjourn for more than three days, nor to any other Place than that in which the two Houses shall be sitting.

Salaries and immunities of members

Section 6.   The Senators and Representatives shall receive a Compensation for their Services, to be ascertained by Law, and paid out of the Treasury of the United States. They shall in all Cases, except Treason, Felony and Breach of the Peace, be privileged from Arrest during their Attendance at the Session of their respective Houses, and in going to and returning from the same; and for any Speech or Debate in either House, they shall not be questioned in any other Place.

Bar on members of Congress holding federal appointive office

No Senator or Representative shall, during the Time for which he was elected, be appointed to any civil Office under the Authority of the United States, which shall have been created, or the Emoluments whereof shall have been encreased during such time; and no Person holding any Office under the United States, shall be a Member of either House during his Continuance in Office.

Money bills originate in House

Section 7.   All Bills for raising Revenue shall originate in the House of Representatives; but the Senate may propose or concur with Amendments as on other Bills.

Procedure for enacting laws; veto power

Every Bill which shall have passed the House of Representatives and the Senate, shall, before it become a Law, be presented to the President of the United States; If he approve he shall sign it, but if not he shall return it, with Objections to that House in which it shall have originated, who shall enter the Objections at large on their Journal, and proceed to reconsider it. If after such Reconsideration two thirds of that House shall agree to pass the Bill, it shall be sent, together with the Objections, to the other House, by which it shall likewise be reconsidered, and if approved by two thirds of that House, it shall become a Law. But in all such Cases the Votes of both Houses shall be determined by yeas and Nays, and the Names of the Persons voting for and against the Bill shall be entered on the Journal of each House respectively. If any Bill shall not be returned by the President within ten Days (Sundays excepted) after it shall have been presented to him, the Same shall be a Law, in like Manner, as if he had signed it, unless the Congress by their Adjournment prevent its Return, in which Case it shall not be a Law.

Every Order, Resolution, or Vote to which the Concurrence of the Senate and House of Representatives may be necessary (except on a question of Adjournment) shall be presented to the President of the United States; and before the Same shall take Effect, shall be approved by him, or being disapproved by him, shall be repassed by two thirds of the Senate and House of Representatives, according to the Rules and Limitations prescribed in the Case of a Bill.

Powers of Congress
—*taxes*

Section 8.   The Congress shall have Power To lay and Collect Taxes, Duties, Imposts and Excises, to pay the Debts and provide for the common Defence and general Welfare of the United States; but all Duties, Imposts and Excises shall be uniform throughout the United States.

—*borrowing*

To borrow Money on the credit of the United States;

—*regulation of commerce*

To regulate Commerce with foreign Nations, and among the several States, and with the Indian Tribes;

—*naturalization and bankruptcy*

To establish an uniform Rule of Naturalization, and uniform Laws on the subject of Bankruptcies throughout the United States;

—money

To coin Money, regulate the Value thereof, and of foreign Coin, and fix the Standard of Weights and Measures;

—counterfeiting

To provide for the Punishment of counterfeiting the Securities and current Coin of the United States;

—post office

To establish Post Offices and post Roads;

—patents and copyrights

To promote the Progress of Science and useful Arts, by securing for limited Times to Authors and Inventors the exclusive Right to their respective Writings and Discoveries;

—create courts

To constitute Tribunals inferior to the Supreme Court;

—punish piracies

To define and punish Piracies and Felonies committed on the high Seas, and Offences against the Law of Nations;

—declare war

To declare War, grant Letters of Marque and Reprisal, and make Rules concerning Captures on Land and Water;

—create army and navy

To raise and support Armies, but no Appropriation of Money to that Use shall be for a longer Term than two Years;

To provide and maintain a Navy;

To make Rules for the Government and Regulation of the land and naval Forces;

—call the militia

To provide for calling forth the Militia to execute the Laws of the Union, suppress Insurrections and repel Invasions;

To provide for organizing, arming, and disciplining, the Militia, and for governing such Part of them as may be employed in the Service of the United States, reserving to the States respectively, the Appointment of the Officers, and the Authority of training the Militia according to the discipline prescribed by Congress;

—govern District of Columbia

To exercise exclusive Legislation in all Cases whatsoever, over such District (not exceeding ten Miles square) as may, by Cession of Particular States, and the Acceptance of Congress, become the Seat of the Government of the United States, and to exercise like Authority over all Places purchased by the Consent of the Legislature of the State in which the Same shall be, for the Erection of Forts, Magazines, Arsenals, dock-Yards and other needful Buildings;—And

—"necessary-and-proper" clause

To make all Laws which shall be necessary and proper for carrying into Execution the foregoing Powers, and all other Powers vested by this Constitution in the Government of the United States, or in any Department or Officer thereof.

Restrictions on powers of Congress

—slave trade

Section 9. The Migration or Importation of such Persons as any of the States now existing shall think proper to admit, shall not be prohibited by the Congress prior to the Year one thousand eight hundred and eight, but a Tax or duty may be imposed on such Importation, not exceeding ten dollars for each Person.

—habeas corpus

The Privilege of the Writ of Habeas Corpus shall not be suspended, unless when in Cases of Rebellion or Invasion the public Safety may require it.

—no bill of attainder or ex post facto law

No bill of Attainder or ex post facto Law shall be passed.

No Capitation, or other direct, Tax shall be laid, *unless in Proportion to the Census or Enumeration herein before directed to be taken.*[5]

—no interstate tariffs

No Tax or Duty shall be laid on Articles exported from any State.

—no preferential treatment for some states

No Preference shall be given by any Regulation of Commerce or Revenue to the Ports of one State over those of another; nor shall Vessels bound to, or from, one State, be obliged to enter, clear or pay Duties in another.

---

5. Changed by the Sixteenth Amendment.

—*appropriations*

No Money shall be drawn from the Treasury, but in Consequence of Appropriations made by Law; and a regular Statement and Account of the Receipts and Expenditures of all public Money shall be published from time to time.

—*no titles of nobility*

No Title of Nobility shall be granted by the United States: And no Person holding any Office of Profit or Trust under them, shall, without the Consent of the Congress, accept of any present, Emolument, Office, or Title, of any kind whatever, from any King, Prince, or foreign State.

Restrictions on powers of states

Section 10. No State shall enter into any Treaty, Alliance, or Confederation; grant Letters of Marque and Reprisal; coin Money; emit Bills of Credit; make any Thing but gold and silver Coin a Tender in Payment of Debts; pass any Bill of Attainder, ex post facto Law, or Law impairing the Obligation of Contracts, or grant any Title of Nobility.

No State shall, without the Consent of Congress, lay any Imposts or Duties on Imports or Exports, except what may be absolutely necessary for executing its inspection Laws; and the net Produce of all Duties and Imposts, laid by any State on Imports or Exports, shall be for the Use of the Treasury of the United States; and all such Laws shall be subject to the Revision and Controul of the Congress.

No State shall, without the Consent of Congress, lay any Duty of Tonnage, keep Troops, or Ships of War in time of Peace, enter into any Agreement or Compact with another State, or with a foreign Power, or engage in War, unless actually invaded, or in such imminent Danger as will not admit of delay.

ARTICLE II.

Office of president

Section 1. The executive Power shall be vested in a President of the United States of America. He shall hold his Office during the Term of four Years, and, together with the Vice President, chosen for the same Term, be elected, as follows

Election of president

Each State shall appoint, in such Manner as the Legislature thereof may direct, a Number of Electors, equal to the whole Number of Senators and Representatives to which the State may be entitled in the Congress: but no Senator or Representative, or Person holding an Office of Trust or Profit under the United States, shall be appointed an Elector.

The Electors shall meet in their respective States, and vote by Ballot for two Persons, of whom one at least shall not be an Inhabitant of the same State with themselves. And they shall make a List of all the Persons voted for, and of the Number of Votes for each; which List they shall sign and certify, and transmit sealed to the Seat of the Government of the United States, directed to the President of the Senate. The President of the Senate shall, in the Presence of the Senate and House of Representatives, open all the Certificates, and the Votes shall then be counted. The Person having the greatest Number of Votes shall be the President, if such Number be a Majority of the whole Number of Electors appointed; and if there be more than one who have such Majority, and have an equal Number of Votes, then the House of Representatives shall immediately chuse by Ballot one of them for President; and if no Person have a Majority, then from the five highest on the List said House shall in like Manner chuse the President. But in chusing the President, the Votes shall be taken by States, the Representation from each State having one Vote; a quorum for this Purpose shall consist of a Member or Members from two thirds of the States, and a Majority of all the States shall be necessary to a Choice. In every Case, after the Choice of the President, the Person having the greatest Number of Votes of the Electors shall be the Vice President.

But if there should remain two or more who have equal Votes, the Senate shall chuse from them by Ballot the Vice President.[6]

The Congress may determine the Time of chusing the Electors, and the Day on which they shall give their Votes, which Day shall be the same throughout the United States.

Requirements to be president

No Person except a natural born Citizen, or a Citizen of the United States, at the time of the Adoption of this Constitution, shall be eligible to the Office of President; neither shall any person be eligible to that Office who shall not have attained to the Age of thirty five Years, and been fourteen Years a Resident within the United States.

In Case of the Removal of the President from Office, or of his Death, Resignation, or Inability to discharge the Powers and Duties of the said Office, the Same shall devolve on the Vice President, and the Congress may by Law provide for the Case of Removal, Death, Resignation or Inability, both of the President and Vice President, declaring what Officer shall then act as President, and such Officer shall act accordingly, until the Disability be removed, or a President shall be elected.[7]

Pay of president

The President shall, at stated Times, receive for his Services, a Compensation, which shall neither be increased nor diminished during the Period for which he shall have been elected, and he shall not receive within that Period any other Emolument from the United States, or any of them.

Before he enter on the Execution of his Office, he shall take the following Oath or Affirmation:—"I do solemnly swear (or affirm) that I will faithfully execute the Office of President of the United States, and will to the best of my Ability preserve, protect and defend the Constitution of the United States."

Powers of president —*commander in chief*

Section 2. The President shall be Commander in Chief of the Army and Navy of the United States, and of the Militia of the several States, when called into the actual Service of the United States; he may require the Opinion, in writing, of the principal Officer in each of the executive Departments, upon any Subject relating to the Duties of their respective Offices, and he shall have Power to grant Reprieves and Pardons for Offences against the United States, except in Cases of Impeachment.

—*pardons*

—*treaties and appointments*

He shall have Power, by and with the Advice and Consent of the Senate, to make Treaties, provided two thirds of the Senators present concur; and he shall nominate, and by and with the Advice and Consent of the Senate, shall appoint Ambassadors, other public Ministers and Consuls, Judges of the supreme Court, and all other Officers of the United States, whose Appointments are not herein otherwise provided for, and which shall be established by Law: but the Congress may by Law vest the Appointment of such inferior Officers, as they think proper, in the President alone, in the Courts of Law, or in the Heads of Departments.

The President shall have Power to fill up all Vacancies that may happen during the Recess of the Senate, by granting Commissions which shall expire at the End of their next Session.

Relations of president with Congress

Section 3. He shall from time to time give to the Congress Information of the State of the Union, and recommend to their Consideration such Measures as he shall judge

---

6. Superseded by the Twelfth Amendment.
7. Modified by the Twenty-fifth Amendment.

necessary and expedient; he may, on extraordinary Occasions, convene both Houses, or either of them, and in Case of Disagreement between them, with Respect to the Time of Adjournment, he may adjourn them to such Time as he shall think proper; he shall receive Ambassadors and other public Ministers; he shall take Care that the Laws be faithfully executed, and shall Commission all the Officers of the United States.

Impeachment

Section 4. The President, Vice President and all civil Officers of the United States, shall be removed from Office on Impeachment for, and Conviction of, Treason, Bribery, or other high Crimes and Misdemeanors.

ARTICLE III.

Federal courts

Section 1. The judicial Power of the United States, shall be vested in one supreme Court, and in such inferior Courts as the Congress may from time to time ordain and establish. The Judges, both of the supreme and inferior Courts, shall hold their Offices during good Behaviour, and shall, at stated Times, receive for their Services, a Compensation, which shall not be diminished during their Continuance in Office.

Jurisdiction of courts

Section 2. The judicial Power shall extend to all Cases, in Law and Equity, arising under this Constitution, the Laws of the United States, and Treaties made, or which shall be made, under their Authority;—to all Cases affecting Ambassadors, other public Ministers and Consuls;—to all Cases of admiralty and maritime Jurisdiction;—to Controversies to which the United States shall be a Party;—to Controversies between two or more States;—*between a State and Citizens of another State;*[8]—between Citizens of different States;—between Citizens of the same State claiming Lands under Grants of different States, and between a State, or the Citizens thereof, and foreign States, Citizens or Subjects.

—*original*

—*appellate*

In all Cases affecting Ambassadors, other public Ministers and Consuls, and those in which a State shall be Party, the supreme Court shall have original Jurisdiction. In all the other Cases before mentioned, the supreme Court shall have appellate Jurisdiction, both as to Law and Fact, with such Exceptions, and under such Regulations as the Congress shall make.

The Trial of all Crimes, except in Cases of Impeachment, shall be by Jury; and such Trial shall be held in the State where the said Crimes shall have been committed; but when not committed within any State, the Trial shall be at such Place or Places as the Congress may by Law have directed.

Treason

Section 3. Treason against the United States, shall consist only in levying War against them, or in adhering to their Enemies, giving them Aid and Comfort. No Person shall be convicted of Treason unless on the Testimony of two Witnesses to the same overt Act, or on Confession in open Court.

The Congress shall have Power to declare the Punishment of Treason, but no Attainder of Treason shall work Corruption of Blood, or Forfeiture except during the Life of the Person attainted.

---

8. Modified by the Eleventh Amendment.

ARTICLE IV.

Full faith and credit

Section 1. Full Faith and Credit shall be given in each State to the public Acts, Records, and judicial Proceedings of every other State. And the Congress may by general Laws prescribe the Manner in which such Acts, Records and Proceedings shall be proved, and the Effect thereof.

Privileges and immunities

Section 2. The Citizens of each State shall be entitled to all Privileges and Immunities of Citizens in the several States.

Extradition

A person charged in any State with Treason, Felony, or other Crime, who shall flee from Justice, and be found in another State, shall on Demand of the executive Authority of the State from which he fled, be delivered up, to be removed to the State having Jurisdiction of the Crime.

No Person held to Service or Labour in one State, under the Laws thereof, escaping into another, shall, in Consequence of any Law or Regulation therein, be discharged from such Service or Labour, but shall be delivered up on Claim of the Party to whom such Service or Labour may be due.[9]

Creation of new states

Section 3. New States may be admitted by the Congress into this Union; but no new State shall be formed or erected within the Jurisdiction of any other State; nor any State be formed by the Junction of two or more States, or Parts of States, without the Consent of the Legislatures of the States concerned as well as of the Congress.

Governing territories

The Congress shall have Power to dispose of and make all needful Rules and Regulations respecting the Territory or other Property belonging to the United States; and nothing in this Constitution shall be so construed as to Prejudice any Claims of the United States, or of any particular State.

Protection of states

Section 4. The United States shall guarantee to every State in this Union a Republican Form of Government, and shall protect each of them against Invasion; and on Application of the Legislature, or of the Executive (when the Legislature cannot be convened) against domestic Violence.

ARTICLE V.

Amending the Constitution

The Congress, whenever two thirds of both Houses shall deem it necessary, shall propose Amendments to this Constitution, or, on the Application of the Legislatures of two thirds of the several States, shall call a Convention for proposing Amendments, which, in either Case, shall be valid to all Intents and Purposes, as Part of this Constitution, when ratified by the Legislatures of three fourths of the several States, or by Conventions in three fourths thereof, as the one or the other Mode of Ratification may be proposed by the Congress; Provided that no Amendment which may be made prior to the Year One thousand eight hundred and eight shall in any Manner after the first and fourth Clauses in the Ninth Section of the first Article; and that no State, without its Consent, shall be deprived of its equal Suffrage in the Senate.

---

9. Changed by the Thirteenth Amendment.

ARTICLE VI.

Assumption of debts of Confederation

All Debts contracted and Engagements entered into, before the Adoption of this Constitution, shall be as valid against the United States under this Constitution, as under the Confederation.

Supremacy of federal laws and treaties

This Constitution, and the Laws of the United States which shall be made in Pursuance thereof; and all Treaties made, or which shall be made, under the Authority of the United States, shall be the Supreme Law of the Land; and the Judges in every State shall be bound thereby, any Thing in the Constitution or Laws of any State to the Contrary notwithstanding.

No religious test

The Senators and Representatives before mentioned, and the Members of the several State Legislatures, and all executive and judicial Officers, both of the United States and of the several States, shall be bound by Oath or Affirmation, to support this Constitution; but no religious Test shall ever be required as a Qualification to any Office or public Trust under the United States.

ARTICLE VII.

Ratification procedure

The Ratification of the Conventions of nine States, shall be sufficient for the Establishment of this Constitution between the States so ratifying the Same.

Done in Convention by the Unanimous Consent of the States present the Seventeenth Day of September in the Year of our Lord one thousand seven hundred and Eighty seven and of the Independence of the United States of America the Twelfth In witness whereof We have hereunto subscribed our Names,

G̿ºWASHINGTON—*Presid*ᵗ.
and deputy from Virginia

New Hampshire	{ JOHN LANGDON NICHOLAS GILMAN	*Connecticut*	{ Wᴹ. SAMᴸ. JOHNSON ROGER SHERMAN	
Massachusetts	{ NATHANIEL GORHAM RUFUS KING	*New York*	ALEXANDER HAMILTON	
New Jersey	{ WIL: LIVINGSTON DAVID BREARLEY Wᴹ. PATERSON JONA: DAYTON	*Maryland*	{ JAMES MᶜHENRY DAN OF Sᵀ THOˢ. JENIFER DANᴸ CARROLL	
		Virginia	{ JOHN BLAIR— JAMES MADISON JR.	
Pennsylvania	{ B FRANKLIN THOMAS MIFFLIN ROBᵀ MORRIS GEO. CLYMER THOˢ FITZSIMONS JARED INGERSOLL JAMES WILSON GOUV MORRIS	*North Carolina*	{ Wᴹ. BLOUNT RICHᴰ DOBBS SPAIGHT HU WILLIAMSON	
		South Carolina	{ J. RUTLEDGE CHARLES COTESWORTH PINCKNEY CHARLES PINCKNEY PIERCE BUTLER	

Delaware	{ Geo: Read Gunning Bedford jun John Dickinson Richard Bassett Jaco: Broom	*Georgia*	{ William Few Abr Baldwin

[The first ten amendments, known as the "Bill of Rights," were ratified in 1791.]

AMENDMENT I.

Freedom of religion, speech, press, assembly

Congress shall make no law respecting an establishment of religion, or prohibiting the free exercise thereof, or abridging the freedom of speech, or of the press; or the right of the people peaceably to assemble, and to petition the Government for a redress of grievances.

AMENDMENT II.

Right to bear arms

A well regulated Militia, being necessary to the security of a free State, the right of the people to keep and bear Arms, shall not be infringed.

AMENDMENT III.

Quartering troops in private homes

No Soldier shall, in time of peace be quartered in any house without the consent of the Owner, nor in time of war, but in a manner to be prescribed by law.

AMENDMENT IV.

Prohibition against unreasonable searches and seizures

The right of the people to be secure in their persons, houses, papers, and effects, against unreasonable searches and seizures, shall not be violated, and no Warrants shall issue, but upon probable cause, supported by Oath or affirmation, and particularly describing the place to be searched, and the persons or things to be seized.

AMENDMENT V.

Right when accused; "due-process" clause

No person shall be held to answer for a capital, or otherwise infamous crime, unless on a presentment or indictment of a Grand Jury, except in cases arising in the land or naval forces, or in the Militia, when in actual service in time of War or public danger; nor shall any person be subject for the same offence to be twice put in jeopardy of life or limb; nor shall be compelled in any criminal case to be a witness against himself, nor be deprived of life, liberty, or property, without due process of law, nor shall private property be taken for public use, without just compensation.

AMENDMENT VI.

Rights when on trial

In all criminal prosecutions, the accused shall enjoy the right to a speedy and public trial, by an impartial jury of the State and district wherein the crime shall have been committed, which district shall have been previously ascertained by law, and to be informed of the nature and cause of the accusation; to be confronted with the witnesses against him; to have compulsory process for obtaining witnesses in his favor, and to have the Assistance of Counsel for his defence.

AMENDMENT VII.

Common-law suits

In Suits at common law, where the value in controversy shall exceed twenty dollars, the right of trial by jury shall be preserved, and no fact tried by a jury, shall be otherwise reexamined in any Court of the United States, than according to the rules of the common law.

AMENDMENT VIII.

Bail; no "cruel and unusual" punishments

Excessive bail shall not be required, nor excessive fines imposed, nor cruel and unusual punishments inflicted.

AMENDMENT IX.

Unenumerated rights protected

The enumeration in the Constitution, of certain rights, shall not be construed to deny or disparage others retained by the people.

AMENDMENT X.

Powers reserved for states

The powers not delegated to the United States by the Constitution, nor prohibited by it to the States, are reserved to the States respectively, or to the people.

AMENDMENT XI.
[*Ratified in 1795.*]

Limits on suits against states

The Judicial power of the United States shall not be construed to extend to any suit in law or equity, commenced or prosecuted against one of the United States by Citizens of another state, or by Citizens or Subjects of any Foreign State.

AMENDMENT XII.
[*Ratified in 1804.*]

Revision of electoral-college procedure

The Electors shall meet in their respective states and vote by ballot for President and Vice President, one of whom, at least, shall not be an inhabitant of the same state with themselves; they shall name in their ballots the person voted for as President, and in distinct ballots the person voted for as Vice President, and they shall make distinct lists of all persons voted for as President, and of all persons voted for as Vice President, and of the number of votes for each, which lists they shall sign and certify, and transmit sealed to the seat of government of the United States, directed to the President of the Senate;—The President of the Senate shall, in the presence of the Senate and House of Representatives, open all the certificates and the votes shall then be counted;—The person having the greatest number of votes for President, shall be the President, if such number be a majority of the whole number of Electors appointed; and if no person have such majority, then from the persons having the highest numbers not exceeding three on the list of those voted for as President, the House of Representatives shall choose immediately, by ballot, the President. But in choosing the President, the votes shall be taken by states, the representation from each state having one vote; a quorum for this purpose shall consist of a member or members from two-thirds of the states, and a majority of all the states shall be necessary to a choice. *And if the House of Representatives shall not choose a President whenever the right of choice shall devolve upon them, before the fourth day of March next following, then the Vice President shall act as President, as in the case of the death or other constitutional disability of the President.*—[10] The person having the greatest number of votes as Vice President, shall be the Vice President, if such number be a majority of the whole number of Electors appointed, and if no person have a majority, then from the two highest numbers on the list, the Senate shall choose the Vice President; a quorum for the purpose shall consist of two-thirds of the whole number of Senators, and a majority of the whole number shall be necessary to a choice. But no person constitutionally ineligible to the office of President shall be eligible to that of Vice President of the United States.

AMENDMENT XIII.
[*Ratified in 1865.*]

Slavery prohibited

Section 1.   Neither slavery nor involuntary servitude, except as a punishment for crime whereof the party shall have been duly convicted, shall exist within the United States, or any place subject to their jurisdiction.

Section 2.   Congress shall have power to enforce this article by appropriate legislation.

AMENDMENT XIV.
[*Ratified in 1868.*]

Ex-slaves made citizens

Section 1.   All persons born or naturalized in the United States and subject to the jurisdiction thereof, are citizens of the United States and of the State wherein they reside. No State shall make or enforce any law which shall abridge the privileges or immunities of citizens of the United States; nor shall any State deprive any person of life, liberty, or property, without due process of law; nor deny to any person within its jurisdiction the equal protection of the laws.

"Due-process" clause applied to states
"Equal-protection" clause

Reduction in congressional representation for states denying adult males the right to vote

Section 2.   Representatives shall be apportioned among the several States according to their respective numbers, counting the whole number of persons in each State, excluding Indians not taxed. But when the right to vote at any election for the choice of electors for President and Vice President of the United States, Representatives in Congress, the Executive and Judicial officers of a State, or the members of the Legislature thereof, is denied to any of the male inhabitants of such State, being *twenty-one*[11] years of age and citizens of the United States, or in any way abridged, except for participation in rebellion, or other crime, the basis of representation therein shall be reduced in the proportion which the number of such male citizens shall bear to the whole number of male citizens twenty-one years of age in such State.

Southern rebels denied federal office

Section 3.   No person shall be a Senator or Representative in Congress, or elector of President and Vice President, or hold any office, civil or military, under the United

---

10. Changed by the Twentieth Amendment, section 3.
11. Changed by the Twenty-sixth Amendment.

States, or under any State, who, having previously taken an oath, as a member of Congress, or as an officer of the United States, or as a member of any State legislature, or as an executive or judicial officer of any State, to support the Constitution of the United States, shall have engaged in insurrection or rebellion against the same, or given aid or comfort to the enemies thereof. But Congress may by a vote of two-thirds of each House, remove such disability.

Rebel debts repudiated

Section 4.   The validity of the public debt of the United States, authorized by law, including debts incurred for payment of pensions and bounties for services in suppressing insurrection or rebellion, shall not be questioned. But neither the United States nor any State shall assume or pay any debt or obligation incurred in aid of insurrection or rebellion against the United States, or any claim for the loss or emancipation of any slave; but all such debts, obligations and claims shall be held illegal and void.

Section 5.   The Congress shall have power to enforce, by appropriate legislation, the provisions of this article.

AMENDMENT XV.
[*Ratified in 1870.*]

Blacks given right to vote

Section 1.   The right of citizens of the United States to vote shall not be denied or abridged by the United States or by any State on account of race, color, or previous condition of servitude.

Section 2.   The Congress shall have power to enforce this article by appropriate legislation.

AMENDMENT XVI.
[*Ratified in 1913.*]

Authorizes federal income tax

The Congress shall have power to lay and collect taxes on incomes, from whatever source derived, without apportionment among the several States, and without regard to any census or enumeration.

AMENDMENT XVII.
[*Ratified in 1913.*]

Requires popular election of senators

The Senate of the United States shall be composed of two Senators from each State, elected by the people thereof, for six years; and each Senator shall have one vote. The electors in each State shall have the qualifications requisite for electors of the most numerous branch of the State legislatures.

When vacancies happen in the representation of any State in the Senate, the executive authority of such State shall issue writs of election to fill such vacancies: Provided, That the legislature of any State may empower the executive thereof to make temporary appointments until the people fill the vacancies by election as the legislature may direct.

This amendment shall not be so construed as to affect the election or term of any Senator chosen before it becomes valid as part of the Constitution.

AMENDMENT XVIII.
[*Ratified in 1919.*]

Prohibits manufacture and
sale of liquor

Section 1. *After one year from the ratification of this article the manufacture, sale, or transportation of intoxicating liquors within, the importation thereof into, or the exportation thereof from the United States and all territory subject to the jurisdiction thereof for beverage purposes is hereby prohibited.*

Section 2. *The Congress and the several States shall have concurrent power to enforce this article by appropriate legislation.*

Section 3. *This article shall be inoperative unless it shall have been ratified as an amendment to the Constitution by the legislatures of the several States, as provided in the Constitution, within seven years from the date of the submission hereof to the States by the Congress.*[12]

AMENDMENT XIX.
[*Ratified in 1920.*]

Right to vote for women

The right of citizens of the United States to vote shall not be denied or abridged by the United States or by any State on account of sex.

Congress shall have power to enforce this article by appropriate legislation.

AMENDMENT XX.
[*Ratified in 1933.*]

Federal terms of office to
begin in January

Section 1. The terms of the President and Vice President shall end at noon on the 20th day of January, and the terms of Senators and Representatives at noon on the 3d day of January, of the years in which such terms would have ended if this article had not been ratified; and the terms of their successors shall then begin.

Section 2. The Congress shall assemble at least once in every year, and such meeting shall begin at noon on the 3d day of January, unless they shall by law appoint a different day.

Emergency presidential
succession

Section 3. If, at the time fixed for the beginning of the term of the President, the President elect shall have died, the Vice President elect shall become President. If a President shall not have been chosen before the time fixed for the beginning of his term, or if the President elect shall have failed to qualify, then the Vice President elect shall act as President until a President shall have qualified; and the Congress may by law provide for the case wherein neither a President elect nor a Vice President elect shall have qualified, declaring who shall then act as President, or the manner in which one who is to act shall be selected, and such person shall act accordingly until a President or Vice President shall have qualified.

---

12. Repealed by the Twenty-first Amendment.

Section 4.   The Congress may by law provide for the case of the death of any of the persons from whom the House of Representatives may choose a President whenever the right of choice shall have devolved upon them, and for the case of the death of any of the persons from whom the Senate may choose a Vice President whenever the right of choice shall have devolved upon them.

Section 5.   Sections 1 and 2 shall take effect on the 15th day of October following the ratification of this article.

Section 6.   This article shall be inoperative unless it shall have been ratified as an amendment to the Constitution by the legislatures of three-fourths of the several States within seven years from the date of its submission.

AMENDMENT XXI.
[*Ratified in 1933.*]

Repeals Prohibition

Section 1.   The eighteenth article of amendment to the Constitution of the United States is hereby repealed.

Section 2.   The transportation or importation into any State, Territory, or possession of the United States for delivery or use therein of intoxicating liquors, in violation of the laws thereof, is hereby prohibited.

Section 3.   This article shall be inoperative unless it shall have been ratified as an amendment to the Constitution by conventions in the several States, as provided in the Constitution, within seven years from the date of submission hereof to the States by the Congress.

AMENDMENT XXII.
[*Ratified in 1951.*]

Two-term limit for president

Section 1.   No person shall be elected to the office of the President more than twice, and no person who has held the office of President, or acted as President, for more than two years of a term to which some other person was elected President shall be elected to the office of President more than once. But this Article shall not apply to any person holding the office of President when this Article was proposed by the Congress, and shall not prevent any person who may be holding the office of President, or acting as President, during the term within which this Article becomes operative from holding the office of President or acting as President during the remainder of such term.

Section 2.   This Article shall be inoperative unless it shall have been ratified as an amendment to the Constitution by the legislatures of three-fourths of the several States within seven years from the date of its submission to the States by the Congress.

AMENDMENT XXIII.
[*Ratified in 1961.*]

Right to vote for president in District of Columbia

Section 1.   The District constituting the seat of Government of the United States shall appoint in such manner as the Congress may direct:

A number of electors of President and Vice President equal to the whole number of Senators and Representatives in Congress to which the District would be entitled if it were a State, but in no event more than the least populous State; they shall be in addition to those appointed by the States, but they shall be considered, for the purposes of the election of President and Vice President, to be electors appointed by a State; and they shall meet in the District and perform such duties as provided by the twelfth article of amendment.

Section 2. The Congress shall have power to enforce this article by appropriate legislation.

AMENDMENT XXIV.
[*Ratified in 1964.*]

Prohibits poll taxes in federal elections

Section 1. The right of citizens of the United States to vote in any primary or other election for President or Vice President, for electors for President or Vice President, or for Senator or Representative in Congress, shall not be denied or abridged by the United States or any State by reason of failure to pay any poll tax or other tax.

Section 2. The Congress shall have the power to enforce this article by appropriate legislation.

AMENDMENT XXV.
[*Ratified in 1967.*]

Presidential disability and succession

Section 1. In case of the removal of the President from office or of his death or resignation, the Vice President shall become President.

Section 2. Whenever there is a vacancy in the office of the Vice President, the President shall nominate a Vice President who shall take office upon confirmation by a majority vote of both Houses of Congress.

Section 3. Whenever the President transmits to the President pro tempore of the Senate and the Speaker of the House of Representatives his written declaration that he is unable to discharge the powers and duties of his office, and until he transmits to them a written declaration to the contrary, such powers and duties shall be discharged by the Vice President as Acting President.

Section 4. Whenever the Vice President and a majority of either the principal officers of the executive departments or of such other body as Congress may by law provide, transmit to the President pro tempore of the Senate and the Speaker of the House of Representatives their written declaration that the President is unable to discharge the powers and duties of his office, the Vice President shall immediately assume the powers and duties of the office as Acting President.

Thereafter, when the President transmits to the President pro tempore of the Senate and the Speaker of the House of Representatives his written declaration that no inability exists, he shall resume the powers and duties of his office unless the Vice President and a majority of either the principal officers of the executive department[s] or of such other body as Congress may by law provide, transmit within four days to the President pro tempore of the Senate and the Speaker of the House of Representatives their written declaration that the President is unable to discharge the powers and duties of his office. Thereupon Congress shall decide the issue, assembling within forty-eight hours for that purpose if not in session. If the Congress, within twenty-one days after receipt of the latter written declaration, or, if Congress is not in session, within twenty-one days after Congress is required to assemble, determines by two-thirds vote of both Houses that the President is unable to discharge the powers and duties of his office, the Vice President shall continue to discharge the same as Acting President; otherwise, the President shall resume the powers and duties of his office.

AMENDMENT XXVI.
[*Ratified in 1971.*]

Voting age lowered to eighteen

Section 1.   The right of citizens of the United States, who are eighteen years of age or older, to vote shall not be denied or abridged by the United States or by any State on account of age.

Section 2.   The Congress shall have power to enforce this article by appropriate legislation.

AMENDMENT XXVII.
[*Ratified in 1992.*]

Congressional pay raises

No law varying the compensation for the services of the Senators and Representatives shall take effect, until an election of Representatives shall have intervened.

The Federalist No. 10

———

November 22, 1787

James Madison

TO THE PEOPLE OF THE STATE OF NEW YORK.

Among the numerous advantages promised by a well constructed Union, none deserves to be more accurately developed than its tendency to break and control the violence of faction. The friend of popular governments, never finds himself so much alarmed for their character and fate, as when he contemplates their propensity to this dangerous vice. He will not fail therefore to set a due value on any plan which, without violating the principles to which he is attached, provides a proper cure for it. The instability, injustice and confusion introduced into the public councils, have in truth been the mortal diseases under which popular governments have every where perished; as they continue to be the favorite and fruitful topics from which the adversaries to liberty derive their most specious declamations. The valuable improvements made by the American Constitutions on the popular models, both ancient and modern, cannot certainly be too much admired; but it would be an unwarrantable partiality, to contend that they have as effectually obviated the danger on this side as was wished and expected. Complaints are every where heard from our most considerate and virtuous citizens, equally the friends of public and private faith, and of public and personal liberty; that our governments are too unstable; that the public good is disregarded in the conflicts of rival parties; and that measures are too often decided, not according to the rules of justice, and the rights of the minor party; but by the superior force of an interested and over-bearing majority. However anxiously we may wish that these complaints had no foundation, the evidence of known facts will not permit us to deny that they are in some degree true. It will be found indeed, on a candid review of our situation, that some of the distresses under which we labor, have been erroneously charged on the operation of our governments; but it will be found, at the same time, that other causes will not alone account for many of our heaviest misfortunes; and particularly, for that prevailing and increasing distrust of public engagements, and alarm for private rights, which are echoed from one end of the continent to the other. These must be chiefly, if not wholly, effects of the unsteadiness and injustice, with which a factious spirit has tainted our public administrations.

By a faction I understand a number of citizens, whether amounting to a majority or minority of the whole, who are united and actuated by some common impulse of passion, or of interest, adverse to the rights of other citizens, or to the permanent and aggregate interests of the community.

There are two methods of curing the mischiefs of faction: the one, by removing its causes; the other, by controlling its effects.

There are again two methods of removing the causes of faction: the one by destroying the liberty which is essential to its existence; the other, by giving to every citizen the same opinions, the same passions, and the same interests.

It could never be more truly said than of the first remedy, that it is worse than the disease. Liberty is to faction, what air is to fire, an aliment without which it instantly expires. But it could not be a less folly to abolish liberty, which is essential to political life, because it nourishes faction, than it would be to wish the annihilation of air, which is essential to animal life, because it imparts to fire its destructive agency.

The second expedient is as impracticable, as the first would be unwise. As long as the reason of man continues fallible, and he is at liberty to exercise it, different opinions will be formed. As long as the connection subsists between his reason and his self-love, his opinions and his passions will have a reciprocal influence on each other; and the former will be objects to which the latter will attach themselves. The diversity in the faculties of men from which the rights of property originate, is not less an insuperable obstacle to a uniformity of interests. The protection of these faculties is the first object of Government. From the protection of different and unequal faculties of acquiring property, the possession of different degrees and kinds of property immediately results: and from the influence of these on the sentiments and views of the respective proprietors, ensues a division of the society into different interests and parties.

The latent causes of faction are thus sown in the nature of man; and we see them every where brought into different degrees of activity, according to the different circumstances of civil society. A zeal for different opinions concerning religion, concerning Government and many other points, as well of speculation as of practice; an attachment to different leaders ambitiously contending for pre-eminence and power; or to persons of other descriptions whose fortunes have been interesting to the human passions, have in turn divided mankind into parties, inflamed them with mutual animosity, and rendered them much more disposed to vex and oppress each other, than to cooperate for their common good. So strong is this propensity of mankind to fall into mutual animosities, that where no substantial occasion presents itself, the most frivolous and fanciful distinctions have been sufficient to kindle their unfriendly passions, and excite their most violent conflicts. But the most common and durable source of factions, has been the various and unequal distribution of property. Those who hold, and those who are without property, have ever formed distinct interests in society. Those who are creditors, and those who are debtors, fall under a like discrimination. A landed interest, a manufacturing interest, a mercantile interest, a monied interest, with many lesser interests, grow up of necessity in civilized nations, and divide them into different classes, actuated by different sentiments and views. The regulation of these various and interfering interests forms the principal task of modern Legislation, and involves the spirit of party and faction in the necessary and ordinary operations of Government.

No man is allowed to be judge in his own cause; because his interest would certainly bias his judgment, and, not improbably, corrupt his integrity. With equal, nay with greater reason, a body of men, are unfit to be judges and parties, at the same time; yet, what are many of the most important acts of legislation, but so many judicial determinations, not indeed concerning the rights of single persons, but concerning the rights of large bodies of citizens, and what are the different classes of legislators, but advocates and parties to the causes which they determine? Is a law proposed concerning private debts? It is a question to which the creditors are parties on one side, and the debtors on the other. Justice ought to hold the balance between them. Yet the parties are and must be themselves the judges; and the most numerous party, or, in other words, the most powerful faction must be expected to prevail. Shall domestic manufactures be encouraged, and in what degree, by restrictions on foreign manufactures? are questions which would be differently decided by the landed and the manufacturing classes; and probably by neither, with a sole regard to justice and the public good. The apportionment of taxes on the various descriptions of property, is an act which seems to require the most exact impartiality; yet, there is perhaps no legislative act in which greater opportunity and temptation are given to a predominant party, to trample on the rules of justice. Every shilling with which they over-burden the inferior number, is a shilling saved to their own pockets.

It is in vain to say, that enlightened statesmen will be able to adjust these clashing interests, and render them all subservient to the public good. Enlightened statesmen will not always be at the helm: Nor, in many cases, can such an adjustment be made at all, without taking into view indirect and remote considerations, which will rarely prevail over the immediate interest which one party may find in disregarding the rights of another, or the good of the whole.

The inference to which we are brought, is, that the *causes* of faction cannot be removed; and that relief is only to be sought in the means of controlling its *effects.*

If a faction consists of less than a majority, relief is supplied by the republican principle, which enables the majority to defeat its sinister views by regular vote: It may clog the administration, it may convulse the society; but it will be unable to execute and mask its violence under the forms of the Constitution. When a majority is included in a faction, the form of popular government on the other hand enables it to sacrifice to its ruling passion or interest, both the public good and the rights of other citizens. To secure the public good, and private rights, against the danger of such a faction, and at the same time to preserve the spirit and the form of popular government, is then the great object to which our inquiries are directed: Let me add that it is the great desideratum, by which alone this form of government can be rescued from the opprobrium under which it has so long labored, and be recommended to the esteem and adoption of mankind.

By what means is this object attainable? Evidently by one of two only. Either the existence of the same passion or interest in a majority at the same time, must be prevented; or the majority, having such co-existent passion or interest, must be rendered, by their number and local situation, unable to concert and carry into effect schemes of oppression. If the impulse and the opportunity be suffered to coincide, we well know that neither moral nor religious motives can be relied on as an adequate control. They are not found to be such on the injustice and violence of individuals, and lose their efficacy in proportion to the number combined together; that is, in proportion as their efficacy becomes needful.

From this view of the subject, it may be concluded, that a pure Democracy, by which I mean, a Society, consisting of a small number of citizens, who assemble and administer the Government in person, can admit of no cure for the mischiefs of faction. A common passion or interest will, in almost every case, be felt by a majority of the whole; a communication and concert results from the form of Government itself; and there is nothing to check the inducements to sacrifice the weaker party, or an obnoxious individual. Hence it is, that such Democracies have ever been spectacles of turbulence and contention; have ever been found incompatible with personal security, or the rights of property; and have in general been as short in their lives, as they have been violent in their deaths. Theoretic politicians, who have patronized this species of Government, have erroneously supposed, that by reducing mankind to a perfect equality in their political rights, they would, at the same time, be perfectly equalized and assimilated in their possessions, their opinions, and their passions.

A republic, by which I mean a government in which the scheme of representation takes place, opens a different prospect, and promises the cure for which we are seeking. Let us examine the points in which it varies from pure democracy, and we shall comprehend both the nature of the cure and the efficacy which it must derive from the union.

The two great points of difference, between a democracy and a republic, are, first, the delegation of the government, in the latter, to a small number of citizens, elected by the rest; secondly, the greater number of citizens, and greater sphere of country, over which the latter may be extended.

The effect of the first difference is, on the one hand, to refine and enlarge the public views, by passing them through the medium of a chosen body of citizens, whose wisdom may best discern the true interest of their country, and whose patriotism and love of justice, will be least likely to sacrifice it to temporary or partial considerations. Under such a regulation, it may well happen, that the public voice, pronounced by the representatives of the people, will be more consonant to the public good, than if pronounced by the people themselves, convened for the purpose. On the other hand the effect may be inverted. Men of factious tempers, of local prejudices, or of sinister designs, may by intrigue, by corruption, or by other means, first obtain the suffrages, and then betray the interest of the people. The question resulting is, whether small or extensive republics are most favorable to the election of proper guardians of the public weal, and it is clearly decided in favor of the latter by two obvious considerations.

In the first place, it is to be remarked that, however small the republic may be, the representatives must be raised to a certain number, in order to guard against the cabals of a few; and that however large it may be, they must be limited to a certain number, in order to guard against the confusion of a multitude. Hence, the number of representatives in the two cases not being in proportion to that of the constituents, and being proportionally greatest in the small republic, it follows, that if the proportion of fit characters be not less in the large than in the small republic, the former will present a greater option, and consequently a greater probability of a fit choice.

In the next place, as each Representative will be chosen by a greater number of citizens in the large than in the small Republic, it will be more difficult for unworthy candidates to practise with success the vicious arts, by which elections are too often carried; and the suffrages of the people being more free, will be more likely to center on men who possess the most attractive merit, and the most diffusive and established characters.

It must be confessed, that in this, as in most other cases, there is a mean, on both sides of which inconveniences will be found to lie. By enlarging too much the number of electors, you render the representatives too little acquainted with all their local circumstances and lesser interests; as by reducing it too much, you render him unduly attached to these, and too little fit to comprehend and pursue great and national objects. The Federal Constitution forms a happy combination in this respect; the great and aggregate interests being referred to the national, the local and particular, to the state legislatures.

The other point of difference is, the greater number of citizens and extent of territory which may be brought within the compass of Republican, than of Democratic Government; and it is this circumstance principally which renders factious combinations less to be dreaded in the former, than in the latter. The smaller the society, the fewer probably will be the distinct parties and interests composing it; the fewer the distinct parties and interests, the more frequently will a majority be found of the same party; and the smaller the number of individuals composing a majority, and the smaller the compass within which they are placed, the more easily they will concert and execute their plans of oppression. Extend the sphere, and you take in a greater variety of parties and interests; you make it less probable that a majority of the whole will have a common motive to invade the rights of other citizens; or if such a common motive exists, it will be more difficult for all who feel it to discover their own strength, and to act in unison with each other. Besides other impediments, it may be remarked, that where there is a consciousness of unjust or dishonorable purposes, communication is always checked by distrust, in proportion to the number whose concurrence is necessary.

Hence it clearly appears, that the same advantage, which a Republic has over a Democracy, in controlling the effects of factions, is enjoyed by a large over a small Republic—is enjoyed by the Union over the States composing it. Does this advantage consist in the substitution of Representatives, whose enlightened views and virtuous sentiments render them superior to local prejudices, and to schemes of injustice? It will not be denied, that the Representation of the Union will be most likely to possess these requisite endowments. Does it consist in the greater security afforded by a greater variety of parties, against the event of any one party being able to outnumber and oppress the rest? In an equal degree does the increase variety of parties, comprised within the Union, increase this security? Does it, in fine, consist in the greater obstacles opposed to the concert and accomplishment of the secret wishes of an unjust and interested majority? Here, again, the extent of the Union gives it the most palpable advantage.

The influence of factious leaders may kindle a flame within their particular States, but will be unable to spread a general conflagration through the other States: a religious sect, may degenerate into a political faction in a part of the Confederacy but the variety of sects dispersed over the entire face of it, must secure the national Councils against any danger from that source: a rage for paper money, for an abolition of debts, for an equal division of property, or for any other improper or wicked project, will be less apt to pervade the whole body of the Union, than a particular member of it; in the same proportion as such a malady is more likely to taint a particular county or district, than an entire State.

In the extent and proper structure of the Union, therefore, we behold a Republican remedy for the diseases most incident to Republican Government. And according to the degree of pleasure and pride, we feel in being Republicans, ought to be our zeal in cherishing the spirit, and supporting the character of Federalists.

PUBLIUS

The Federalist No. 51

———

February 6, 1788

James Madison

TO THE PEOPLE OF THE STATE OF NEW YORK.

To what expedient then shall we finally resort for maintaining in practice the necessary partition of power among the several departments, as laid down in the constitution? The only answer that can be given is, that as all these exterior provisions are found to be inadequate, the defect must be supplied, by so contriving the interior structure of the government, as that its several constituent parts may, by their mutual relations, be the means of keeping each other in their proper places. Without presuming to undertake a full development of this important idea, I will hazard a few general observations, which may perhaps place it in a clearer light, and enable us to form a more correct judgment of the principles and structure of the government planned by the convention.

In order to lay a due foundation for that separate and distinct exercise of the different powers of government, which to a certain extent, is admitted on all hands to be essential to the preservation of liberty, it is evident that each department should have a will of its own; and consequently should be so constituted, that the members of each should have as little agency as possible in the appointment of the members of the others. Were this principle rigorously adhered to, it would require that all the appointments for the supreme executive, legislative, and judiciary magistracies, should be drawn from the same fountain of authority, the people, through channels, having no communication whatever with one another. Perhaps such a plan of constructing the several departments would be less difficult in practice than in it may in contemplation appear. Some difficulties however, and some additional expense, would attend the execution of it. Some deviations therefore from the principle must be admitted. In the constitution of the judiciary department in particular, it might be inexpedient to insist rigorously on the principle; first, because peculiar qualifications being essential in the members, the primary consideration ought to be to select that mode of choice, which best secures these qualifications; secondly, because the permanent tenure by which the appointments are held in that department, must soon destroy all sense of dependence on the authority conferring them.

It is equally evident that the members of each department should be as little dependent as possible on those of the others, for the emoluments annexed to their offices. Were the executive magistrate, or the judges, not independent of the legislature in this particular, their independence in every other would be merely nominal.

But the great security against a gradual concentration of the several powers in the same department, consists in giving to those who administer each department, the necessary constitutional means, and personal motives, to resist encroachments of the others. The provision for defense must in this, as in all other cases, be made commensurate to the danger of attack. Ambition must be made to counteract ambition. The interest of the man must be connected with the constitutional right of the place. It may be a reflection on human nature, that such devices should be necessary to control the abuses of government. But what is government itself but the greatest of all reflections on human nature? If men were angels, no government would be necessary. If angels were to govern men, neither external nor internal controls on government would be necessary. In framing a government which is to be administered by men over men, the great difficulty lies in this: You must first enable the government to control the governed; and in the next place, oblige it to control itself. A dependence on the people is no doubt the primary control on the government; but experience has taught mankind the necessity of auxiliary precautions.

This policy of supplying by opposite and rival interests, the defect of better motives, might be traced through the whole system of human affairs, private as well as public. We see it particularly displayed in all the subordinate distributions of power; where the constant aim is to divide and arrange the several offices in such a manner as that each may be a check on the other; that the private interest of every individual, may be a sentinel over the public rights. These inventions of prudence cannot be less requisite in the distribution of the supreme powers of the state.

But it is not possible to give each department an equal power of self defense. In republican government the legislative authority, necessarily, predominates. The remedy for this inconvenience is, to divide the legislative into different branches; and to render them by different modes of election, and different principles of action, as little connected with each other, as the nature of their common functions, and their common dependence on the society, will admit. It may even be necessary to guard against dangerous encroachments by still further precautions. As the weight of the legislative authority requires that it should be thus divided, the weakness of the executive may require, on the other hand, that it should be fortified. An absolute negative, on the legislature, appears at first view to be the natural defense with which the executive magistrate should be armed. But perhaps it would be neither altogether safe, nor alone sufficient. On ordinary occasions, it might not be exerted with the requisite firmness, and on extraordinary occasions, it might be prefidiously abused. May not this defect of an absolute negative be supplied, by some qualified connection between this weaker department, and the weaker branch of the stronger department, by which the latter may be led to support the constitutional rights of the former, without being too much detached from the rights of its own department?

If the principles on which these observations are founded be just, as I persuade myself they are, and they be applied as a criterion, to the several state constitutions, and to the federal constitution, it will be found, that if the latter does not perfectly correspond with them, the former are infinitely less able to bear such a test.

There are moreover two considerations particularly applicable to the federal system of America, which place the system in a very interesting point of view.

First. In a single republic, all the power surrendered by the people, is submitted to the administration of a single government; and usurpations are guarded against by a division of the government into district and separate departments. In the compound republic of America, the power surrendered by the people, is first divided between two distinct governments, and then the portion allotted to each, subdivided among distinct and separate departments. Hence a double security arises to the rights of the people. The different governments will control each other; at the same time that each will be controlled by itself.

Second. It is of great importance in a republic, not only to guard the society against the oppression of its rulers; but to guard one part of the society against the injustice of the other part. Different interests necessarily exist in different classes of citizens. If a majority be united by a common interest, the rights of the minority will be insecure. There are but two methods of providing against this evil: The one by creating a will in the community independent of the majority, that is, of the society itself, the other by comprehending in the society so many separate descriptions of citizens, as will render an unjust combination of a majority of the whole, very improbable, if not impracticable. The first method prevails in all governments possessing an hereditary or self appointed authority. This at best is but a precarious security; because a power independent of the society may as well espouse the unjust views of the major, as the rightful interests, of the minor party, and may possibly be turned against both parties. The second method will be exemplified in the federal republic of the United States. While all authority in it will be derived from and dependent on the society, the society itself will be broken into so many parts, interests and classes of citizens, that the rights of individuals or of the minority, will be in little danger from interested combinations of the majority. In a free government, the security for civil rights must be the same as for religious rights. It consists in the one case in the multiplicity of interests, and in the other, in the multiplicity of sects. The degree of security in both cases will depend on the number of interests and sects; and this may be presumed to depend on the extent of country and number of people comprehended under the same government. This view of the subject must particularly recommend a proper federal system to all the sincere and considerate friends of republican government: Since it shows that in exact proportion as the territory of the union may be formed into more circumscribed confederacies or states, oppressive combinations of a majority will be facilitated, the best security under the republican form, for the rights of every class of citizens, will be diminished; and consequently, the stability and independence of some member of the government, the only other security, must be proportionally increased. Justice is the end of government. It is the end of civil society. It ever has been, and ever will be pursued, until it be obtained, or until liberty be lost in the pursuit. In a society under the forms of which the stronger faction can readily unite and oppress the weaker, anarchy may as truly be said to reign, as in a state of nature where the weaker individual is not secured against the violence of the stronger: And as in the latter state even the stronger individuals are prompted by the uncertainty of their condition, to submit to a government which may protect the weak as well as themselves: So in the former state, will the more powerful factions or parties be gradually induced by a like motive, to wish for a government which will protect all parties, the weaker as well as the more powerful. It can be little doubted, that if the state of Rhode Island was separated from the confederacy, and left to itself, the insecurity of rights under the popular form of government within such narrow limits, would be displayed by such reiterated oppressions of factious majorities, that some power altogether independent of the people would soon be called for by the voice of the very factions whose misrule had proved the necessity of it. In the extended republic of the United States, and among the great variety of interests, parties and sects which it embraces, a coalition of a majority of the whole society could seldom take place on any other principles than those of justice and the general good; and there being thus less danger to a minor from the will of the major party, there must be less pretext also, to provide for the security of the former, by introducing into the government a will not dependent on the latter; or in other words, a will independent of the society itself. It is no less certain than it is important, notwithstanding the contrary opinions which have been entertained, that the larger the society, provided it lie within a practicable sphere, the more duly capable it will be of self government. And happily for the *republican cause,* the practicable sphere may be carried to a very great extent, by a judicious modification and mixture of the *federal principle.*

PUBLIUS

Presidents and Congresses, 1789–1997

Year	President and vice president	Party of president	Congress	House Majority party	House Minority party	Senate Majority party	Senate Minority party
1789–1797	**George Washington** John Adams	None	1st 2d 3d 4th	38 Admin 37 Fed 57 Dem-Rep 54 Fed	26 Opp 33 Dem-Rep 48 Fed 52 Dem-Rep	17 Admin 16 Fed 17 Fed 19 Fed	9 Opp 13 Dem-Rep 13 Dem-Rep 13 Dem-Rep
1797–1801	**John Adams** Thomas Jefferson	Federalist	5th 6th	58 Fed 64 Fed	48 Dem-Rep 42 Dem-Rep	20 Fed 19 Fed	12 Dem-Rep 13 Dem-Rep
1801–1809	**Thomas Jefferson** Aaron Burr (to 1805) George Clinton (to 1809)	Dem-Rep	7th 8th 9th 10th	69 Dem-Rep 102 Dem-Rep 116 Dem-Rep 118 Dem-Rep	36 Fed 39 Fed 25 Fed 24 Fed	18 Dem-Rep 25 Dem-Rep 27 Dem-Rep 28 Dem-Rep	13 Fed 9 Fed 7 Fed 6 Fed
1809–1817	**James Madison** George Clinton (to 1813) Elbridge Gerry (to 1817)	Dem-Rep	11th 12th 13th 14th	94 Dem-Rep 108 Dem-Rep 112 Dem-Rep 117 Dem-Rep	48 Fed 36 Fed 68 Fed 65 Fed	28 Dem-Rep 30 Dem-Rep 27 Dem-Rep 25 Dem-Rep	6 Fed 6 Fed 9 Fed 11 Fed
1817–1825	**James Monroe** Daniel D. Tompkins	Dem-Rep	15th 16th 17th 18th	141 Dem-Rep 156 Dem-Rep 158 Dem-Rep 187 Dem-Rep	42 Fed 27 Fed 25 Fed 26 Fed	34 Dem-Rep 35 Dem-Rep 44 Dem-Rep 44 Dem-Rep	10 Fed 7 Fed 4 Fed 4 Fed
1825–1829	**John Quincy Adams** John C. Calhoun	Nat-Rep	19th 20th	105 Admin 119 Jack	97 Jack 94 Admin	26 Admin 28 Jack	20 Jack 20 Admin
1829–1837	**Andrew Jackson** John C. Calhoun (to 1833) Martin Van Buren (to 1837)	Democrat	21st 22d 23d 24th	139 Dem 141 Dem 147 Dem 145 Dem	74 Nat Rep 58 Nat Rep 53 AntiMas 98 Whig	26 Dem 25 Dem 20 Dem 27 Dem	22 Nat Rep 21 Nat Rep 20 Nat Rep 25 Whig
1837–1841	**Martin Van Buren** Richard M. Johnson	Democrat	25th 26th	108 Dem 124 Dem	107 Whig 118 Whig	30 Dem 28 Dem	18 Whig 22 Whig
1841	**William H. Harrison*** John Tyler	Whig					
1841–1845	**John Tyler** (VP vacant)	Whig	27th 28th	133 Whig 142 Dem	102 Dem 79 Whig	28 Whig 28 Whig	22 Dem 25 Dem
1845–1849	**James K. Polk** George M. Dallas	Democrat	29th 30th	143 Dem 115 Whig	77 Whig 108 Dem	31 Dem 36 Dem	25 Whig 21 Whig
1849–1850	**Zachary Taylor*** Millard Fillmore	Whig	31st	112 Dem	109 Whig	35 Dem	25 Whig
1850–1853	**Millard Fillmore** (VP vacant)	Whig	32d	140 Dem	88 Whig	35 Dem	24 Whig
1853–1857	**Franklin Pierce** William R. King	Democrat	33d 34th	159 Dem 108 Rep	71 Whig 83 Dem	38 Dem 40 Dem	22 Whig 15 Rep

NOTES: Only members of two major parties in Congress are shown; omitted are independents, members of minor parties, and vacancies.

Party balance as of beginning of Congress.

Congresses in which one or both houses are controlled by party other than that of the president are shown in color.

During administration of George Washington and (in part) John Quincy Adams, Congress was not organized by formal parties; the split shown is between supporters and opponents of the administration.

ABBREVIATIONS: **Admin** = Administration supporters; **AntiMas** = Anti-Masonic; **Dem** = Democratic; **Dem-Rep** = Democratic-Republican; **Fed** = Federalist; **Jack** = Jacksonian Democrats; **Nat Rep** = National Republican; **Opp** = Opponents of administration; **Rep** = Republican; **Union** = Unionist; **Whig** = Whig.

* Died in office.

				House		Senate	
Year	President and vice president	Party of president	Congress	Majority party	Minority party	Majority party	Minority party
1857–1861	**James Buchanan**	Democrat	35th	118 Dem	92 Rep	36 Dem	20 Rep
	John C. Breckinridge		36th	114 Rep	92 Dem	36 Dem	26 Rep
1861–1865	**Abraham Lincoln***	Republican	37th	105 Rep	43 Dem	31 Rep	10 Dem
	Hannibal Hamlin (to 1865)		38th	102 Rep	75 Dem	36 Rep	9 Dem
	Andrew Johnson (1865)						
1865–1869	**Andrew Johnson**	Republican	39th	149 Union	42 Dem	42 Union	10 Dem
	(VP vacant)		40th	143 Rep	49 Dem	42 Rep	11 Dem
1869–1877	**Ulysses S. Grant**	Republican	41st	149 Rep	63 Dem	56 Rep	11 Dem
	Schuyler Colfax (to 1873)		42d	134 Rep	104 Dem	52 Rep	17 Dem
	Henry Wilson (to 1877)		43d	194 Rep	92 Dem	49 Rep	19 Dem
			44th	169 Dem	109 Rep	45 Rep	29 Dem
1877–1881	**Rutherford B. Hayes**	Republican	45th	153 Dem	140 Rep	39 Rep	36 Dem
	William A. Wheeler		46th	149 Dem	130 Rep	42 Dem	33 Rep
1881	**James A. Garfield***	Republican	47th	147 Rep	135 Dem	37 Rep	37 Dem
	Chester A. Arthur						
1881–1885	**Chester A. Arthur**	Republican	48th	197 Dem	118 Rep	38 Rep	36 Dem
	(VP vacant)						
1885–1889	**Grover Cleveland**	Democrat	49th	183 Dem	140 Rep	43 Rep	34 Dem
	Thomas A. Hendricks		50th	169 Dem	152 Rep	39 Rep	37 Dem
1889–1893	**Benjamin Harrison**	Republican	51st	166 Rep	159 Dem	39 Rep	37 Dem
	Levi P. Morton		52d	235 Dem	88 Rep	47 Rep	39 Dem
1893–1897	**Grover Cleveland**	Democrat	53d	218 Dem	127 Rep	44 Dem	38 Rep
	Adlai E. Stevenson		54th	244 Rep	105 Dem	43 Rep	39 Dem
1897–1901	**William McKinley***	Republican	55th	204 Rep	113 Dem	47 Rep	34 Dem
	Garret A. Hobart (to 1901)		56th	185 Rep	163 Dem	53 Rep	26 Dem
	Theodore Roosevelt (1901)						
1901–1909	**Theodore Roosevelt**	Republican	57th	197 Rep	151 Dem	55 Rep	31 Dem
	(VP vacant, 1901–1905)		58th	208 Rep	178 Dem	57 Rep	33 Dem
	Charles W. Fairbanks		59th	250 Rep	136 Dem	57 Rep	33 Dem
	(1905–1909)		60th	222 Rep	164 Dem	61 Rep	31 Dem
1909–1913	**William Howard Taft**	Republican	61st	219 Rep	172 Dem	61 Rep	32 Dem
	James S. Sherman		62d	228 Dem	161 Rep	51 Rep	41 Dem
1913–1921	**Woodrow Wilson**	Democrat	63d	291 Dem	127 Rep	51 Dem	44 Rep
	Thomas R. Marshall		64th	230 Dem	196 Rep	56 Dem	40 Rep
			65th	216 Dem	210 Rep	53 Dem	42 Rep
			66th	240 Rep	190 Dem	49 Rep	47 Dem
1921–1923	**Warren G. Harding***	Republican	67th	301 Rep	131 Dem	59 Rep	37 Dem
	Calvin Coolidge						
1923–1929	**Calvin Coolidge**	Republican	68th	225 Rep	205 Dem	51 Rep	43 Dem
	(VP vacant, 1923–1925)		69th	247 Rep	183 Dem	56 Rep	39 Dem
	Charles G. Dawes		70th	237 Rep	195 Dem	49 Rep	46 Dem
	(1925–1929)						
1929–1933	**Herbert Hoover**	Republican	71st	267 Rep	167 Dem	56 Rep	39 Dem
	Charles Curtis		72d	220 Dem	214 Rep	48 Rep	47 Dem
1933–1945	**Franklin D. Roosevelt***	Democrat	73d	310 Dem	117 Rep	60 Dem	35 Rep
	John N. Garner		74th	319 Dem	103 Rep	69 Dem	25 Rep
	(1933–1941)		75th	331 Dem	89 Rep	76 Dem	16 Rep
	Henry A. Wallace		76th	261 Dem	164 Rep	69 Dem	23 Rep
	(1941–1945)		77th	268 Dem	162 Rep	66 Dem	28 Rep
	Harry S Truman (1945)		78th	218 Dem	208 Rep	58 Dem	37 Rep
1945–1953	**Harry S Truman**	Democrat	79th	242 Dem	190 Rep	56 Dem	38 Rep
	(VP vacant, 1945–1949)		80th	245 Rep	188 Dem	51 Rep	45 Dem
	Alben W. Barkley		81st	263 Dem	171 Rep	54 Dem	42 Rep
	(1949–1953)		82d	234 Dem	199 Rep	49 Dem	47 Rep

* Died in office.

Year	President and vice president	Party of president	Congress	House Majority party	House Minority party	Senate Majority party	Senate Minority party
1953–1961	**Dwight D. Eisenhower**	Republican	83d	221 Rep	211 Dem	48 Rep	47 Dem
	Richard M. Nixon		84th	232 Dem	203 Rep	48 Dem	47 Rep
			85th	233 Dem	200 Rep	49 Dem	47 Rep
			86th	283 Dem	153 Rep	64 Dem	34 Rep
1961–1963	**John F. Kennedy***	Democrat	87th	263 Dem	174 Rep	65 Dem	35 Rep
	Lyndon B. Johnson						
1963–1969	**Lyndon B. Johnson**	Democrat	88th	258 Dem	177 Rep	67 Dem	33 Rep
	(VP vacant, 1963–1965)		89th	295 Dem	140 Rep	68 Dem	32 Rep
	Hubert H. Humphrey (1965–1969)		90th	247 Dem	187 Rep	64 Dem	36 Rep
1969–1974	**Richard M. Nixon†**	Republican	91st	243 Dem	192 Rep	57 Dem	43 Rep
	Spiro T. Agnew††		92d	254 Dem	180 Rep	54 Dem	44 Rep
	Gerald R. Ford§						
1974–1977	**Gerald R. Ford**	Republican	93d	239 Dem	192 Rep	56 Dem	42 Rep
	Nelson A. Rockefeller§		94th	291 Dem	144 Rep	60 Dem	37 Rep
1977–1981	**Jimmy Carter**	Democrat	95th	292 Dem	143 Rep	61 Dem	38 Rep
	Walter Mondale		96th	276 Dem	157 Rep	58 Dem	41 Rep
1981–1989	**Ronald Reagan**	Republican	97th	243 Dem	192 Rep	53 Rep	46 Dem
	George Bush		98th	269 Dem	165 Rep	54 Rep	46 Dem
			99th	253 Dem	182 Rep	53 Rep	47 Dem
			100th	257 Dem	178 Rep	54 Dem	46 Rep
1989–1993	**George Bush**	Republican	101st	262 Dem	173 Rep	55 Dem	45 Rep
	Dan Quayle		102d	267 Dem	167 Rep	56 Dem	44 Rep
1993–	**Bill Clinton**	Democrat	103d	258 Dem	176 Rep	57 Dem	43 Rep
	Albert Gore, Jr.		104th	230 Rep	204 Dem	53 Rep	47 Dem
			105th	228 Rep	206 Dem	55 Rep	45 Dem

* Died in office.   † Resigned from the presidency.   †† Resigned from the vice presidency.   § Appointed vice president.

Glossary

Acid rain Precipitation in the form of rain, snow, or dust particles, the increased acidity of which is caused by environmental factors such as pollutants released into the atmosphere. (22)

Activist An individual, usually outside of government, who actively promotes a political party, philosophy, or issue he or she cares about. (6)

Activist approach (judicial) The view that judges should discern the general principles underlying the Constitution and its often vague language and assess how best to apply them in contemporary circumstances, in some cases with the guidance of moral or economic philosophy. (14)

Ad hoc structure A method of organizing a president's staff in which several task forces, committees, and informal groups of friends and advisers deal directly with the president. (12)

Adversarial press A national press that is suspicious of officialdom and eager to break an embarrassing story about a public official. (10)

Affirmative action The requirement, imposed by law or administrative regulation, that an organization (business firm, government agency, labor union, school, or college) take positive steps to increase the number or proportion of women, blacks, or other minorities in its membership. (19)

Amateur legislature A state legislature consisting of part-time representatives whose primary job is outside of government. *See also* Professional legislature (25)

Amendment (constitutional) Change in, or addition to, a constitution. Amendments are proposed by a two-thirds vote of both houses of Congress or by a convention called by Congress at the request of two-thirds of the state legislatures and ratified by approval of three-fourths of the states. (2)

Amicus curiae A Latin term meaning "a friend of the court." Refers to interested groups or individuals, not directly involved in a suit, who may file legal briefs or make oral arguments in support of one side. (14)

Annexation (city) A policy of incorporating an area into an adjoining city. (25)

Annual authorizations *See* Authorization legislation (13)

Antifederalists Opponents of a strong central government who campaigned against ratification of the Constitution in favor of a confederation of largely independent states. Antifederalists successfully marshaled public support for a federal bill of rights. After ratification, they formed a political party to support states' rights. *See also* Federalists (2)

Appropriation A legislative grant of money to finance a government program. *See also* Authorization (13)

Articles of Confederation A constitution drafted by the newly independent states in 1777 and ratified in 1781. It created a weak national government that could not levy taxes or regulate commerce. In 1789 it was replaced by our current constitution in order to create a stronger national government. (2)

Assistance program A government program financed by general income taxes that provides benefits to poor citizens without requiring contributions from them. (17)

Australian ballot A government-printed ballot of uniform size and shape to be cast in secret that was adopted by many states around 1890 in order to reduce the voting fraud associated with party-printed ballots cast in public. (6)

Authority The right to use power. (1)

Authorization legislation Legislative permission to begin or continue a government program or agency. An authorization bill may grant permission to spend a certain sum of money, but that money does not ordinarily become available unless it is also appropriated. Authorizations may be annual, multiyear, or permanent. *See also* Appropriation (13)

Background story (news) A public official's explanation of current policy provided to the press on the condition that the source remain anonymous. (10)

Benefit Any satisfaction, monetary or nonmonetary, that people believe they will enjoy if a policy is adopted. *See also* Cost (15)

Bicameral legislature A lawmaking body made up of two chambers or parts. The U.S. Congress is a bicameral legislature composed of a Senate and a House of Representatives. (11)

Bill of attainder A law that declares a person, without a trial, to be guilty of a crime. The state legislatures and Congress are forbidden to pass such acts by Article I of the Constitution. (2)

Bill of rights The first ten amendments to the U.S. Constitution, containing a list of individual rights and liberties, such as freedom of speech, religion, and the press. (2)

Blanket primary A primary election that permits all voters, regardless of party, to choose candidates. A Democratic voter, for example, can vote in a blanket pri-

Blanket primary (continued)
mary for both Democratic and Republican candidates for nomination. (8)

Block grants Grants of money from the federal government to states for programs in certain general areas rather than for specific kinds of programs. *See also* Grants-in-aid; Categorical grants (3)

Boycott A concerted effort to get people to stop buying goods and services from a company or person in order to punish that company or to coerce its owner into changing policies. (15)

Brief A legal document prepared by an attorney representing a party before a court. The document sets forth the facts of the case, summarizes the law, gives the arguments for its side, and discusses other relevant cases. (14)

Bubble standard The total amount of air pollution that can come from a given factory. A company is free to decide which specific sources within that factory must be reduced and how to meet the bubble standard. (22)

Budget A document that announces how much the government will collect in taxes and spend in revenues and how those expenditures will be allocated among various programs. (16)

Budget deficit A situation in which the government spends more money than it takes in from taxes and fees. (16)

Budget resolution A proposal submitted by the House and Senate budget committees to their respective chambers recommending a total budget ceiling and a ceiling for each of several spending areas (such as health or defense) for the current fiscal year. These budget resolutions are intended to guide the work of each legislative committee as it decides what to spend in its area. (16)

Budget surplus A situation in which the government takes in more money than it spends. (16)

Bureaucracy A large, complex organization composed of appointed officials. The department and agencies of the U.S. government make up the federal bureaucracy. (13)

Bureaucratic theory (politics) A theory that appointed civil servants make the key governing decisions. (1)

Bureaucrats (government) The appointed officials who operate government agencies from day to day. (1)

Cabinet By custom, the cabinet includes the heads of the fourteen major executive departments. (12)

Categorical grants A federal grant for a specific purpose defined by federal law: to build an airport, for example, or to make welfare payments to low-income mothers. Such grants usually require that the state or locality put up money to "match" some part of the federal grant, though the amount of matching funds can be quite small. *See also* Grants-in-aid; Block grant (3)

Caucus (congressional) An association of members of Congress created to advocate a political ideology or a regional, ethnic, or economic interest. (7, 11)

Caucus (nominating) An alternative to a state primary in which party followers meet, often for many hours, to select party candidates. (7)

Checks and balances The power of the legislature, executive, and judicial branches of government to block some acts by the other two branches. *See also* Separation of powers (2)

Christmas-tree bill *See* Riders (11)

Circular structure A method of organizing a president's staff in which several presidential assistants report directly to the president. (12)

City-county consolidation A policy of merging city and county governments into one. For example, the city and county of San Francisco are the same. (25)

Civic competence A belief that one can affect government policies. (4)

Civic duty A belief that one has an obligation to participate in civic and political affairs. (4)

Civil law The body of rules defining relationships among private citizens. It consists of both statutes and the accumulated customary law embodied in judicial decisions (the "common law"). *See also* Criminal law (14)

Civil rights The rights of citizens to vote, to receive equal treatment before the law, and to share equally with other citizens the benefits of public facilities (such as schools). (19)

Class-action suit A case brought into court by a person on behalf of not only himself or herself but all other persons in the country under similar circumstances. For example, in *Brown* v. *Board of Education of Topeka, Kansas,* the Court decided that not only Linda Brown but all others similarly situated had the right to attend a local public school of their choice without regard to race. (14)

Class consciousness An awareness of belonging to a particular socioeconomic class whose interests are different from those of others. Usually used in reference to workers who view their interests as opposite to those of managers and business owners. (4)

Clear-and-present danger test A legal interpretation that reconciled two views of the First Amendment right of free speech, the first that Congress could not pass any law to restrict speech and the second that it could punish harms caused by speech. Proposed by Supreme Court Justice Oliver Wendell Holmes in 1919, it held that Congress could only punish speech that created a "clear and present danger" of bringing about the actions that Congress is authorized to prevent. (18)

Client politics The politics of policy making in which some small group receives the benefits of the policy and the public at large bears the costs. Only those who benefit have an incentive to organize and press their case. (15, 17)

Closed primary A primary election limited to registered party members. Prevents members of other parties from crossing over to influence the nomination of an opposing party's candidate. *See also* Open primary; Primary election (8)

Closed rule An order from the House Rules Committee in the House of Representatives that sets a time limit on debate and forbids a particular bill from being amended on the legislative floor. *See also* Open rule; Restrictive rule (11)

Cloture rule A rule used by the Senate to end or limit debate. Designed to prevent "talking a bill to death" by filibuster. To pass in the Senate, three-fifths of the entire Senate membership (or sixty senators) must vote for it. *See also* Filibuster (11)

Coalition An alliance among different interest groups (factions) or parties to achieve some political goal. An example is the coalition sometimes formed between Republicans and conservative Democrats. (2)

Coattails The tendency of lesser-known or weaker candidates to profit in an election by the presence on the ticket of a more popular candidate. (8)

Cold War Refers to the nonmilitary struggle between the United States (and its allies) and the former Soviet Union (and its allies) following World War II. (A cold war is distinguished from a *hot* or *shooting war*.) (20)

Command-and-control strategy A strategy to improve air and water quality, involving the setting of detailed pollution standards and rules. (22)

Committee clearance The ability of a Congressional committee to review and approve certain agency decisions in advance and without passing a law. Such approval is not legally binding on the agency, but few agency heads will ignore the expressed wishes of committees. (13)

Comparable worth A doctrine that would require salaries to be determined by the "worth" of the job, not by what it commands in the market. (19)

Compensatory action An action designed to help members of disadvantaged groups, especially minorities and women, catch up, usually by giving them extra education, training, or services. (19)

Competitive service The government offices to which people are appointed on grounds of merit as ascertained by a written examination or by having met certain selection criteria (such as training, educational attainments, or prior experience). *See also* Excepted service (13)

Concurrent resolution An expression of congressional opinion without the force of law that requires the approval of both the House and Senate but not of the president. Used to settle housekeeping and procedural matters that affect both houses. *See also* Simple resolution; Joint resolution (11)

Concurring opinion A Supreme Court opinion by one or more justices who agree with the majority's conclusion but for different reasons. *See also* Opinion of the Court; Dissenting opinion (14)

Conditions of aid Federal rules attached to the grants that states receive. States must agree to abide by these rules in order to receive the grant. (3)

Confederation or **confederal system** A political system in which states or regional governments retain ultimate authority except for those powers that they expressly delegate to a central government. The United States was a confederation from 1776 to 1787 under the Articles of Confederation. *See also* Federalism; Unitary system (2)

Conference committees *See* Joint committees (11)

Congressional campaign committee A party committee in Congress that provides funds to members who are running for re-election or to would-be members running for an open seat or challenging a candidate from the opposition party. (7)

Conservative In general, a person who favors more limited and local government, less government regulation of markets, more social conformity to traditional norms and values, and tougher policies toward criminals. *See also* Liberal (5)

Conservative coalition An alliance between Republicans and conservative Democrats. (11)

Constitutional Convention A meeting of delegates in 1787 to revise the Articles of Confederation, which produced a totally new constitution still in use today. (2)

Constitutional court A federal court exercising the judicial powers found in Article III of the Constitution and whose judges are given constitutional protection: they may not be fired (they serve during "good behavior") nor may their salaries be reduced while they are in office. The most important constitutional courts are the Supreme Court, the ninety-four district courts, and the courts of appeals (one in each of eleven regions plus one in the District of Columbia). *See also* District courts; Courts of appeals; Federal-question cases (14)

Containment or **Antiappeasment** The view that the United States should contain aggressive nations (such as the former Soviet Union). *See also* Isolationism (20)

Cost Any burden, monetary or nonmonetary, that some people must bear, or think that they must bear, if a policy is adopted. *See also* Benefit (15)

Cost overruns Actual costs that are several times greater than estimated costs. These occur frequently among private contractors producing new weapons for the Pentagon. (21)

Council-manager system A system in which people vote only for city-council members, who then appoint a professional city manager to take charge of most or all of the city's administration. Elections in council-manager cities are usually nonpartisan. This plan is most common in cities with a population between 10,000 and 200,000. (25)

Courts of appeals The federal courts with authority to review decisions by federal district courts, regulatory commissions, and certain other federal courts. Such courts have no original jurisdiction; they can hear only appeals. There are a total of twelve courts of appeals in the United states and its territories. *See also* Constitutional courts; District courts. (14)

Criminal law The body of rules defining offenses that, though they harm an individual (such as murder, rape, and robbery), are considered to be offenses against society as a whole and as a consequence warrant punishment by and in the name of society. *See also* Civil law (14)

Critical or **Realigning periods** Periods during which a sharp, lasting shift occurs in the popular coalition supporting one or both parties. The issues that separate the two parties change, and so the kinds of voters supporting each party change. (8)

Cue (political) A signal telling a congressional representative what values (e.g., liberal or conservative) are at stake in a vote—who is for, who against a proposal—and how that issue fits into his or her own set of political beliefs or party agenda. (9)

De facto segregation Racial segregation in schools that occurs, not because of laws or administrative decisions, but as a result of patterns of residential settlement. To the extent that blacks and whites live in separate neighborhoods, neighborhood schools will often be segregated "de facto." *See also* De jure segregation (19)

De jure segregation Racial segregation that occurs because of laws or administrative decisions by public agencies. When state laws, for example, required blacks and whites to attend separate schools or sit in separate sections of a bus, "de jure" segregation resulted. *See also* De facto segregation (19)

Delegated powers Powers expressly granted to the national government by the Constitution. These powers, found in Article I, section 8, include the authority to provide for the common defense, to coin money, and to regulate commerce. *See also* Concurrent powers; Implied powers (2)

Democracy A term used to describe a political system in which the people are said to rule, directly or indirectly. *See also* Democratic centralism; Participatory democracy; Representative democracy (1)

Democratic centralism A government said to be democratic if its decisions will serve the "true interests" of the people whether or not the people affect the decision making or select the decision makers. Using this definition, various authoritarian regimes have claimed to be "democratic." *See also* Direct or participatory democracy; Representative democracy (1)

Descriptive representation A correspondence between the demographic characteristics of representatives and those of their constituents. (11)

Devolution The current effort to scale back the size and activities of the national government and to shift responsibility for a wide range of domestic programs from Washington to the states. In recent years these areas have included welfare, health care, and job training. (2)

Dillon's rule A legal principle that holds that the terms of city charters are to be interpreted narrowly. Under this rule (named after a lawyer who wrote a book on the subject in 1911), a municipal corporation can exercise only those powers expressly given it or those powers necessarily implied by, or essential to the accomplishment of, these stated powers. (25)

Direct or **Participatory democracy** A political system in which all or most citizens participate directly by either holding office or making policy. The town meeting, in which citizens vote on major issues, is an example of participatory democracy. (1, 12)

Discharge petition A device by which any member of the House, after a committee has had a bill for thirty days, may petition to have it brought to the floor. If a majority of the members agree, the bill is discharged from the committee. The discharge petition was designed to prevent a committee from killing a bill by holding it for too long. (11)

Discretionary authority The extent to which appointed bureaucrats can choose courses of action and make policies that are not spelled out in advance by laws. (13)

Disengagement A view that U.S. involvement in Vietnam had led to a military defeat and political disaster and that further similar involvements should be avoided. Also known as "new isolationism." *See also* Isolationism; Containment (20)

Dissenting opinion A Supreme Court opinion by one or more justices in the minority to explain the minority's disagreement with the Court's ruling. *See also* Opinion of the Court; Concurring opinion (14)

District courts The lowest federal courts where federal cases begin. They are the only federal courts where trials are held. There are a total of ninety-four district courts in the United States and its territories. *See also* Courts of appeals; Constitutional courts; Federal-question cases (14)

Diversity cases Cases involving citizens of different states over which the federal courts have jurisdiction as described in the Constitution. *See also* Federal-question cases (14)

Divided government A government in which one party controls the White House and another party controls one or both houses of Congress. *See also* Unified government (12)

Division vote A congressional voting procedure in which members stand and are counted. *See also* Voice vote; Teller vote; Roll call (11)

Domino theory An influential theory first articulated by President Eisenhower holding that if an important nation were to fall into communist hands, other neighboring countries would follow suit. Eisenhower used the metaphor of a row of dominoes falling in sequence to illustrate his point. (20)

Double-tracking A procedure to keep the Senate going during a filibuster in which the disputed bill is shelved temporarily so that the Senate can get on with other business. *See also* Filibuster; Cloture rule (11)

Dual federalism A constitutional theory that the national government and the state governments each have defined areas of authority, especially over commerce. (3)

Due-process clause Protection against arbitrary deprivation of life, liberty, or property as guaranteed in the Fifth and Fourteenth Amendments. (18)

Earned Income Credit A provision of a 1975 tax law that entitles working families with children to receive money from the government if their total income falls below a certain level. (17)

Economic planning An economic philosophy that assumes that the government should plan, in varying ways, some part of the country's economic activity. For instance, in times of high inflation, it suggests that the government regulate the maximum prices that can be charged and wages that can be paid, at least in the larger industries. Another form of planning, called *industrial policy,* would have the government planning or subsidizing investments in industries that need to recover or in new industries that could replace them. (16)

Elite An identifiable group of persons who possess a disproportionate share of some valued resource—such as money or political power. (1)

Elitist theory A theory that a few top leaders make the key decisions without reference to popular desires. (1)

Entrepreneurial politics Policies benefiting society as a whole or some large part that impose a substantial cost on some small identifiable segment of society. *See also* Policy entrepreneurs (15)

Environmental impact statement A report required by federal law that assesses the possible effect of a project on the environment if the project is subsidized in whole or part by federal funds. (22)

Equal-time rule A rule of the Federal Communications Commission (FCC) stating that if a broadcaster sells time to one candidate for office, he or she must be willing to sell equal time to opposing candidates. (10)

Equality of opportunities A view that it is wrong to use race or sex either to discriminate against or give preferential treatment to blacks or women. *See also* Reverse discrimination (19)

Establishment clause A clause in the First Amendment to the Constitution stating that Congress shall make no law "respecting an establishment of religion." (18)

Exclusionary rule A rule that holds that evidence gathered in violation of the Constitution cannot be used in a trial. The rule has been used to implement two provisions of the Bill of Rights—the right to be free from unreasonable searches or seizures (Fourth Amendment) and the right not to be compelled to give evidence against oneself (Fifth Amendment). *See also* Good-faith exception (18)

Ex post facto law A Latin term meaning "after the fact." A law that makes criminal an act that was legal when it was committed, or that increases the penalty for a crime after it has been committed, or that changes the rules of evidence to make conviction easier; a retroactive criminal law. The state legislatures and Congress are forbidden to pass such laws by Article I of the Constitution. (2)

External efficacy *See* Political efficacy. (4)

Faction According to James Madison, a group of people who seek to influence public policy in ways contrary to the public good. (2)

Fairness doctrine A former rule of the Federal Communications Commission (FCC) that required broadcasters to give time to opposing views if they broadcast a program giving one side of a controversial issue. (10)

Feature stories Media reports about public events knowable to any reporter who cares to inquire, but involving acts and statements not routinely covered by a group of reporters. Thus a reporter must take the initiative and select a particular event as newsworthy, decide to write about it, and persuade an editor to run it. (10)

Federalism A political system in which ultimate authority is shared between a central government and state or regional governments. *See also* Confederation; Unitary state (2, 3)

Federalist Papers A series of eight-five essays written by Alexander Hamilton, James Madison, and John Jay (all using the name "Publius") that were published in New York newspapers in 1787–1788 to convince New Yorkers to adopt the newly proposed Constitution. They are classics of American constitutional and political thought. (2)

Federalists Supporters of a stronger central government who advocated ratification of the Constitution. After ratification they founded a political party supporting a strong executive and Alexander Hamilton's economic policies. *See also* Antifederalists (2)

Federal-question cases Cases concerning the Constitution, federal law, or treaties over which the federal courts have jurisdiction as described in the Constitution. *See also* Diversity cases (14)

Federal system A system in which sovereignty is shared so that on some matters the national government is supreme

Federal system (continued)
and on others the state, regional, or provincial governments are supreme. (3)

Fee shifting A law or rule that allows the plaintiff (the party that initiates the lawsuit) to collect its legal costs from the defendant if the defendant loses. *See also* Plaintiff (14)

Filibuster An attempt to defeat a bill in the Senate by talking indefinitely, thus preventing the Senate from taking action on it. From the Spanish *filibustero* which means a "freebooter," a military adventurer. (11)

Fiscal policy An attempt to use taxes and expenditures to affect the economy. (16)

Fiscal year The period from October 1 to September 30 for which government appropriations are made and federal books are kept. A fiscal year is named after the year in which it ends—thus "fiscal 1995" (or "FY 95") refers to the twelve-month period ending September 30, 1995. (16)

Franking privilege The ability of members of Congress to mail letters to their constituents free of charge by substituting their facsimile signature (frank) for postage. (11)

Freedom of expression The constitutional rights of Americans to "freedom of speech, or of the press, or the right of people peaceably to assemble, and to petition the government for a redress of grievances" as outlined in the First Amendment to the Constitution. (18)

Freedom of religion The religious rights of Americans outlined in the First Amendment to the Constitution. The amendment states that "Congress shall make no law respecting an establishment of religion; or abridging the free exercise thereof." (18)

Free-exercise clause A clause in the First Amendment to the Constitution stating that Congress shall make no law prohibiting the "free exercise" of religion. (18)

Gender gap Differences in the political views and voting behavior of men and women. (5)

General-act charter A charter that applies to a number of cities that fall within a certain classification, usually based on city population. Thus in some states, all cities with populations over 100,000 will be governed on the basis of one charter, while all cities with populations between 50,000 and 99,999 will be governed by a different one. *See also* Special-act charter (25)

General election An election used to fill an elective office. *See also* Primary election (8)

Gerrymandering Drawing the boundaries of political districts in bizarre or unusual shapes to make it easy for candidates of the party in power to win elections in those districts. (11)

Gold plating The tendency of Pentagon officials to ask weapons contractors to meet excessively high requirements. (21)

Good-faith exception Admission at a trial of evidence that is gathered in violation of the Constitution if the violation results from a technical or minor error. *See also* Exclusionary rule (18)

Grandfather clause A clause added to registration laws allowing people who did not meet registration requirements to vote if they or their ancestors had voted before 1867 (before blacks were legally allowed to vote). This was to exempt poor and illiterate whites from registration requirements established to keep former slaves from voting. The Supreme Court declared the practice unconstitutional in 1915. (6)

Grants-in-aid Federal funds provided to states and localities. Grants-in-aid are typically provided for airports, highways, education, and major welfare services. *See also* Categorical grants; Block grants (3)

Great Compromise or **Connecticut Compromise** A compromise at the Constitutional Convention in 1787 that reconciled the interests of small and large states by allowing the former to predominate in the Senate and the latter in the House. Under the agreement, each state received two representatives in the Senate, regardless of size, but was allotted representatives on the basis of population in the House. (2)

Home-rule charter A charter that allows the city government to do anything that is not prohibited by the charter or by state law. (25)

Ideological-interest group A political organization that attracts members by appealing to their political convictions with a coherent set of (usually) controversial principles. (9)

Ideological party A party that values principled stands on issues above all else, including winning. It claims to have a comprehensive view of American society and government radically different from that of the established parties. (7)

Impeachment A formal accusation against a public official by the lower house of a legislative body. Impeachment is merely an accusation and not a conviction. Only one president, Andrew Johnson in 1868 was ever impeached. He was not, however, convicted, for the Senate failed by one vote to obtain the necessary two-thirds vote required for conviction. (12)

Incentive (political) A valued benefit obtained by joining a political organization. (9)

Income strategy A policy of giving poor people money to help lift them out of poverty. (17)

Incumbent The person currently in office. (8)

Industrial policy *See* Economic planning (16)

In forma pauperis A procedure whereby a poor person can file and be heard in court as a pauper, free of charge. (14)

Initiative A procedure allowing voters to submit a proposed law to a popular vote by obtaining a required number of signatures. *See also* Referendum (25)

Insider stories Information not usually made public that becomes public because someone with inside knowledge tells a reporter. The reporter may have worked hard to learn these facts, in which case it is called "investigative reporting," or some official may have wanted a story to get out, in which case it is called a "leak." (10)

Insurance program A self-financing government program based on contributions that provide benefits to unemployed or retired persons. (17)

Interest group An organization of people sharing a common interest or goal that seeks to influence the making of public policy. (9)

Interest-group politics The politics of policy making in which one small groups bears the costs of the policy and another small group receives the benefits. Each group has an incentive to organize and to press its interest. *See also* Majoritarian politics; Client politics (15)

Internal efficacy *See* Political efficacy (4)

Iron Curtain A metaphor first used by Winston Churchill to describe a military and political barrier maintained by the former Soviet Union to prevent free travel and communication between Eastern and Western Europe. (20)

Iron triangle A close relationship between an agency, a congressional committee, and an interest group that often becomes a mutually advantageous alliance. *See also* Issue network; Client politics (13)

Isolationism The view that the United States should withdraw from world affairs, limit foreign aid, and avoid involvement in foreign wars. *See also* Containment (20)

Issue network A network of people in Washington-based interest groups, on congressional staffs, in universities and think tanks, and in the mass media who regularly discuss and advocate public policies—say, health care or auto safety. Such networks are split along political, ideological, and economic lines. (13)

Jacksonian model (government) A model of government favored by those who want many elected officials closely accountable to the voters, who believe that average citizens rather than appointed experts should have the most authority, who want specific neighborhoods and not the "city as a whole" represented on city councils, and who expect legislators to intervene on behalf of individual citizen interests. *See also* Progressive model (25)

Jim Crow A slang expression for African Americans that emerged in the 1820s and came to signify the laws and governmental practices designed to segregate blacks from whites, especially in the American South. (19)

Joint committees Committees on which both representatives and senators serve. An especially important kind of joint committee is the *conference committee* made up of representatives and senators appointed to resolve differences in the Senate and House versions of the same piece of legislation before final passage. *See also* Standing committees (11)

Joint resolution A formal expression of congressional opinion that must be approved by both houses of Congress and by the president. Joint resolutions proposing a constitutional amendment need not be signed by the president. *See also* Concurrent resolution; Simple resolution (11)

Judicial review The power of the courts to declare acts of the legislature and of the executive to be unconstitutional and hence null and void. (2, 14)

Keynesianism An economic philosophy that assumes that the market will not automatically operate at a full-employment, low-inflation level. It suggests that the government should intervene to create the right level of demand by pumping more money into the economy (when demand is low) and taking it out (when demand is too great). (16)

Laissez-faire An economic theory that government should not regulate or interfere with commerce. (13)

Lame duck A politician who is still in office after having lost a re-election bid. (12)

Legislative court A court that is created by Congress for some specialized purpose and staffed with judges who do not enjoy the protection of Article III of the Constitution. Legislative courts include the Court of Military Appeals and the territorial courts. (14)

Legislative veto The rejection of a presidential or administrative-agency action by a vote of one or both houses of Congress without the consent of the president. In 1983 the Supreme Court declared the legislative veto to be unconstitutional. (12, 13)

Legitimacy Political authority conferred by law, public opinion, or constitution. (1)

Liberal In general, a person who favors a more active federal government for regulating business, supporting social welfare, and protecting minority rights, but who prefers less regulation of private social conduct. *See also* Conservative (5)

Libertarians People who wish to maximize personal liberty on both economic and social issues. They prefer a small, weak government that has little control over either the economy or the personal lives of citizens. (5)

Line-item veto The power of an executive to veto some provisions in an appropriations bill while approving others. The president does not have the right to

Line-item veto *(continued)*
exercise a line-item veto and must approve or reject an entire appropriations bill. *See also* Pocket veto; Veto message (2, 12)

Literacy test A requirement that citizens pass a literacy test in order to register to vote. It was established by many states to prevent former slaves (most of whom were illiterate) from voting. Illiterate whites were allowed to vote by a "grandfather clause" added to the law saying that you could vote, even though you did not meet the legal requirements, if you or your ancestors voted before 1867. (6)

Litmus test In chemistry, a way of finding out whether a liquid is acid or alkaline. The term is used in politics to mean a test of ideological purity, a way of finding out whether a person is a dyed-in-the-wool liberal or conservative or what his or her views are on a controversial question. (14)

Loaded language Words that reflect a value judgment, used to persuade the listener without making an argument. For example, if someone likes a politician, he might call him "the esteemed Senator Smith"; if he doesn't like him, he might refer to him as "right-wing or radical senators such as Smith." (10)

Lobby An interest group organized to influence governmental decisions, especially legislation. To *lobby* is to attempt to influence such decisions. A *lobbyist* is a person attempting to influence government decisions on behalf of the group. (9)

Lobbyist *See* Lobby (9)

Logrolling Mutual aid among politicians, whereby one legislator supports another's pet project in return for the latter's support of his. The expression dates from the days when American pioneers needed help from neighbors in moving logs off of land to be farmed. (15)

Majoritarian politics The politics of policy making in which almost everybody benefits from a policy and almost everybody pays for it. *See also* Interest-group politics; Client politics (15, 17)

Majority leader The legislative leader elected by party members holding the majority of seats in the House of Representatives or the Senate. *See also* Minority leader (11)

Majority-minority districts Congressional districts designed to make it easier for citizens of a racial or ethnic minority to elect representatives. (11)

Malapportionment Drawing the boundaries of political districts so that districts are very unequal in population. (11)

Mandates Rules imposed by the federal government on the states as conditions for obtaining federal grants or requirements that the states pay the costs of certain nationally defined programs. (3)

Marginal district Political districts in which the candidate elected to the House of Representatives wins in a close election, typically with less than 55% of the vote. (11)

Market (television) An area easily reached by a television signal. There are about two hundred such markets in the country. (10)

Marxist theory (politics) A theory that those who control the economic system also control the political one. (1)

Material incentives Benefits that have monetary value; including money, gifts, services, or discounts received as a result of one's membership in an organization. (9)

Mayor-council system The most common form of city government in which authority is vested in an elected mayor and council. It is typical of very small cities (those under 10,000 population) and very large cities (those over 250,000 population). (25)

McCarthyism Making a charge that unfairly or dishonestly tarnishes the motives, attacks the patriotism, or violates the rights of individuals, especially of political opponents. Refers to the numerous unsubstantiated accusations of communism made against public and private individuals by Senator Joseph McCarthy in the 1950s. (18)

Means test An income qualification that determines whether one is eligible for benefits under government programs reserved for lower-income groups. (17)

Metropolitan government A government for a metropolitan area that includes county, city, and suburban governments. (25)

Micromanaging A term used to criticize congressional involvement in reviewing the detailed decisions of the executive branch. (21)

Middle America A phrase coined by the late Joseph Kraft in a 1968 newspaper column to refer to Americans who have moved out of poverty but are not yet affluent and who cherish traditional middle-class values. (5)

Military-industrial complex An alleged alliance among key military, governmental, and corporate decision makers involved in weapons procurement and military support systems. The phrase was coined by Dwight D. Eisenhower who warned Americans about its dangers. (21)

Minority leader (floor leader) The legislative leader elected by party members holding a minority of seats in the House of Representatives or the Senate. *See also* Majority leader (11)

Monetarism An economic philosophy that assumes inflation occurs when there is too much money chasing too few goods. Monetarism suggests that the proper thing for government to do is to have a steady, predictable increase in the money supply at a rate about equal to the growth in the economy's productivity. (16)

Monetary policy An attempt to alter the amount of money in circulation and the price of money (the interest rate) to affect the economy. (16)

Motor-voter bill A bill passed by Congress in 1993 to make it easier for Americans to register to vote. The law, which went into effect in 1995, requires states to allow voter registration by mail, when one applies for a driver's license, and at state offices that serve the disabled or poor. (6)

Muckraker A journalist who searches through the activities of public officials and organizations seeking to expose conduct contrary to the public interest. The term was first used by President Theodore Roosevelt in 1906 to warn that antibusiness journalism, while valuable, could be excessively negative. (10)

Mugwumps or Progressives The faction in the Republican party of the 1890s to the 1910s composed of reformers who opposed the use of patronage and party bosses and favored the leadership of experts. After 1910, they evolved into a nonpartisan "good government" movement that sought to open up the political system and curb the abuses of parties. *See also* Political machine (7)

Multiple referral A congressional process whereby a bill may be referred to several committees that consider it simultaneously in whole or in part. For instance, the 1988 trade bill was considered by fourteen committees in the House and nine in the Senate simultaneously. (11)

Municipal corporation A legal term for a city. It is chartered by the state to exercise certain powers and provide certain services. *See also* Special-act charter; General-act charter (25)

Name-request job A job to be filled by a person whom a government agency has identified by name. (13)

National chairman (party) A paid, full-time manager of a party's day-to-day work who is elected by the national committee. (7)

National committee A committee of delegates from each state and territory that runs party affairs between national conventions. (7)

National convention A meeting of party delegates elected in state primaries, caucuses, or conventions that is held every four years. Its primary purpose is to nominate presidential and vice-presidential candidates and to ratify a campaign platform. (7)

Necessary-and-proper clause or Elastic clause The final paragraph of Article I, section 8, of the Constitution, which authorizes Congress to pass all laws "necessary and proper" to carry out the enumerated powers. Sometimes called the "elastic clause" because of the flexibility that it provides to Congress. (3)

Nonviolent civil disobedience A philosophy of opposing a law one considers unjust by peacefully violating it and allowing oneself to be punished as a result. (19)

Norm A standard of right or proper conduct that helps determine the range of acceptable social behavior and policy options. (5)

Nullification A theory first advanced by James Madison and Thomas Jefferson that the states had the right to "nullify" (that is, declare null and void) a federal law that, in the states' opinion, violated the Constitution. The theory was revived by John C. Calhoun of South Carolina in opposition to federal efforts to restrict slavery. The North's victory in the Civil War determined once and for all that the federal union is indissoluble and that states cannot declare acts of Congress unconstitutional, a view later confirmed by the Supreme Court. (3)

Office-bloc ballot A ballot listing all candidates for a given office under the name of that office; also called a "Massachusetts" ballot. *See also* Party-column ballot (8)

Offsets An environmental rule that a company in an area with polluted air can offset its own pollution by reducing pollution from another source in the area. For instance, an older company that can't afford to pay for new anti-pollution technologies may buy pollution credits from a newer company that has reduced its source of pollution below the levels required by law. (22)

Open primary A primary election that permits voters to choose on election day the primary in which they wish to vote. They may vote for candidates of only one party. *See also* Blanket primary; Closed primary; Primary election; Presidential primary (8)

Open rule An order from the House Rules Committee in the House of Representatives, that permits a bill to be amended on the legislative floor. *See also* Closed rule; Restrictive rule (11)

Opinion of the Court A Supreme Court opinion written by one or more justices in the majority to explain the decision in a case. *See also* Concurring opinion; Dissenting opinion (14)

Orthodox (social) People who believe that moral rules are derived from the commands of God or the laws of nature, commands and laws that are relatively clear, unchanging, and independent of individual moral preferences. They are likely to believe that traditional morality is more important than individual liberty and should be enforced by government and communal norms. *See also* Progressive (social) (4)

Party-column ballot A ballot listing all candidates of a given party together under the name of that party; also called an "Indiana" ballot. *See also* Office-bloc ballot (8)

Party unity vote A vote in which a majority of voting Democrats oppose a majority of voting Republicans.

Party vote There are two measures of such voting. By the strictest measure, a party vote occurs when 90 percent or more of the Democrats in either house of Congress vote together against 90 percent or more of the Republicans. A looser measure counts as a party vote in any case where at least 50 percent of the Democrats vote together against at least 50 percent of the Republicans. (11)

Patronage *See* Political machine (25)

Peace dividend Vast sums of money that some assumed would be freed up for domestic spending by cuts in post–Cold War defense spending. (16)

Per curiam opinion A brief, unsigned opinion issued by the Supreme Court to explain its ruling. *See also* Opinion of the Court (14)

Perks A short form of perquisites meaning the "fringe benefits of office." Among the perks of political office for high-ranking officials are limousines, expense accounts, free air travel, fancy offices, and staff assistants. (12)

Personal following The political support provided to a candidate on the basis of personal popularity and networks. (7)

Plaintiff The party that initiates a lawsuit to obtain a remedy for an injury to his or her rights. (14)

Pluralist theory (politics) A theory that competition among all affected interests shapes public policy. (1)

Plurality system An electoral system, used in almost all American elections, in which the winner is the person who gets the most votes, even if he or she does not receive a majority of the votes. (7)

Pocket veto One of two ways for a president to disapprove a bill sent to him by Congress. If the president does not sign the bill within ten days of his receiving it and Congress has adjourned within that time, the bill does not become a law. *See also* Veto message; Line-item veto (12)

Police power The power of a state to promote health, safety, and morals. (25)

Policy entrepreneurs Those in and out of government who find ways of pulling together a legislative majority on behalf of unorganized interests. *See also* Entrepreneurial politics (15)

Political action committee (PAC) A committee set up by and representing a corporation, labor union, or special-interest group that raises and spends campaign contributions on behalf of one or more candidates or causes. (8)

Political agenda A set of issues thought by the public or those in power to merit action by government. (15)

Political culture A broadly shared way of thinking about political and economic life that reflects fundamental assumptions about how government should operate. It is distinct from *political ideology* which refers to a more or less consistent set of views about the policies government ought to follow. Up to a point, people sharing a common political culture can disagree about ideology. *See also* Political ideology (4)

Political-editorializing rule A rule of the Federal Communications Commission that if a broadcaster endorses a candidate, the opposing candidate has a right to reply. (10)

Political efficacy, sense of A citizen's belief that he or she can understand and influence political affairs. This sense is divided into two parts—internal efficacy (confidence in a citizen's own abilities to understand and take part in political affairs) and external efficacy (a belief that the system will respond to a citizen's demands). (4)

Political elite *See* Elite (political) (5)

Political ideology A more or less consistent set of views as to the policies government ought to pursue. *See also* Political culture (4, 5)

Political machine A party organization that recruits its members by dispensing *patronage*—tangible incentives such as money, political jobs, an opportunity to get favors from government—and that is characterized by a high degree of leadership control over member activity. (7)

Political party A group that seeks to elect candidates to public office by supplying them with a label—a "party identification"—by which they are known to the electorate. (7)

Political question An issue that the Court refuses to consider because it believes the Constitution has left it entirely to another branch to decide. Its view of such issues may change over time, however. For example, until the 1960s, the Court refused to hear cases about the size of congressional districts, no matter how unequal their populations. In 1962, however, it decided that it was authorized to review the constitutional implications of this issue. (14)

Poll A survey of public opinion. *See also* Random sample (5)

Poll tax A requirement that citizens pay a tax in order to register to vote. It was adopted by many states in order to prevent former slaves (most of whom were poor) from voting. It is now unconstitutional. *See also* Grandfather clause; Literacy test (6)

Pollution allowances or **Banks** A reduction in pollution below that required by law that can be used to cover a future plant expansion or sold to another company whose pollution emissions are above the legal requirements. (22)

Populists People who hold liberal views on economic matters and conservative ones on social matters. They prefer a strong government that will reduce economic inequality, regulate businesses, and impose stricter social and criminal sanctions. The name and views have their origins in an agriculturally-based social movement and party of the 1880s and 1890s that sought to curb the power of influential economic interests. (5)

Pork-barrel legislation Legislation that gives tangible benefits (highways, dams, post offices) to constituents in several districts or states in the hope of winning their votes in return. (11)

Pork-barrel projects *See* Pork-barrel legislation (15)

Position issue An issue dividing the electorate on which rival parties adopt different policy positions to attract voters. *See also* Valence issue (8)

Power The ability of one person to get another person to act in accordance with the first person's intentions. (1)

Presidential primary *See* Primary election (8)

Price-and-wage controls *See* Economic planning (16)

Primary election (direct primary) An election prior to the general election in which voters select the candidates who will run on each party's ticket. Before presidential elections, a *presidential primary* is held to select delegates to the presidential nominating conventions of the major parties. *See also* Closed primary; Open primary (8)

Prior restraint The traditional view of the press's free speech rights as expressed by William Blackstone, the great English jurist. According to this view, the press is guaranteed freedom from censorship—that is, rules telling it in advance what it can publish. After publication, however, the government can punish the press for material that is judged libelous or obscene. (18)

Private bill A legislative bill that deals only with specific, private, personal, or local matters rather than with general legislative affairs. The main kinds include immigration and naturalization bills (referring to particular individuals) and personal-claim bills. *See also* Public bill (11)

Probable cause *See* Search warrant (18)

Process regulation Rules regulating manufacturing or industrial processes, usually aimed at improving consumer or worker safety and reducing environmental damage. (15)

Professional legislature A state legislature that meets during most of the year, consists of legislators who are well paid and regard their position as their main job, and that provides legislators and legislative committees with sizable, year-round staffs. *See also* Amateur legislature (25)

Progressive model A model of government favored by those who prefer to have few elected officials, power concentrated more in executive than in legislative hands, greater reliance on experts, and city-council members elected from the city at large rather than from small districts. (25)

Progressive movement A movement that began in earnest after the Civil War and reached a peak during the early years of the twentieth century. Its principal aims were to purify politics and make government more efficient by attacking the sources of partisan influence. *See also* Mugwumps or Progressives (25)

Progressives (social) People who believe that moral rules are derived in part from an individual's beliefs and the circumstances of modern life. They are likely to favor government tolerance and protection of individual choice. (4)

Prospective voting Voting for a candidate because one favors his or her ideas for addressing issues after the election. (Prospective means "forward-looking.") *See also* Retrospective voting (8)

Public bill A legislative bill that deals with matters of general concern. A bill involving defense expenditures is a public bill; a bill pertaining to an individual's becoming a naturalized citizen is not. *See also* Private bill (11)

Public-interest lobby A political organization the stated goals of which will principally benefit nonmembers. (9)

Purposive incentive The benefit that comes from serving a cause or principle from which one does not personally benefit. (9)

Pyramid structure A method of organizing a president's staff in which most presidential assistants report through a hierarchy to the president's chief of staff. (12)

Quorum call A calling of the roll in either house of Congress to see whether the number of representatives in attendance meets the minimum number required to conduct official business. (11)

Random sample A sample selected in such a way that any member of the population being surveyed (e.g., all adults or voters) has an equal chance of being interviewed. (5)

Ratings An assessment of a representative's voting record on issues important to an interest group. Such ratings are designed to generate public support for or opposition to a legislator. (9)

Reaganomics The federal economic policies of the Reagan Administration elected in 1981. These policies combined a monetarist fiscal policy, supply-side tax cuts, and domestic budget-cutting. Their goal was to reduce the size of the federal government and stimulate economic growth. *See also* Supply-side theory; Monetarism (16)

Recall A procedure, in effect in fifteen states, whereby the voters can vote to remove an elected official from office. (25)

Red tape Complex bureaucratic rules and procedures that must be followed to get something done. (13)

Referendum The practice of submitting a law to a popular vote at election time. The law may be proposed by a voter's initiative or by the legislature. *See also* Initiative (25)

Reformed cities Cities based on the progressive model of government. They have nonpartisan elections, a city council elected at large, a strong civil service, and their executive powers in the hands of an appointed city manager. *See also* Unreformed cities (25)

Registered voters People who are registered to vote. While almost all adult American citizens are theoretically eligible to vote, only those who have completed a registration form by the required date may do so. (6)

Religious tradition The moral teachings of religious institutions on religious, social and economic issues. (5)

Remedy A judicial order preventing or redressing a wrong or enforcing a right. (14)

Representative democracy A political system in which leaders and representatives acquire political power by means of a competitive struggle for the people's vote. This is the form of government used by nations that are called democratic. (1, 12)

Representative town meeting A town meeting that consists of one- to two-hundred town meeting representatives elected by all voters eligible to vote in the town. *See also* Town meeting (25)

Republic A form of democracy in which power is vested in representatives selected by means of popular competitive elections. *See also* Representative democracy (2)

Restrictive rule An order from the House Rules Committee in the House of Representatives that permits certain kinds of amendments but not others to be made to a bill on the legislative floor. *See also* Closed rule; Restrictive rule (11)

Retrospective voting Voting for or against the candidate or party in office because one likes or dislikes how things have gone in the recent past. (Retrospective means "backward-looking.") *See also* Prospective voting (8)

Revenue sharing A law providing for the distribution of a fixed amount or share of federal tax revenues to the states for spending on almost any government purpose. Distribution was intended to send more money to poorer, heavily taxed states and less to richer, lightly taxed ones. The program was ended in 1986. (3)

Reverse discrimination Using race or sex to give preferential treatment to some people. (19)

Riders Amendments on matters unrelated to a bill that are added to an important bill so that they will "ride" to passage through the Congress. When a bill has lots of riders, it is called a Christmas-tree bill. (11)

Right-of-reply rule A rule of the Federal Communications Commission that if a person is attacked on a broadcast (other than in a regular news program), that person has the right to reply over that same station. (10)

Roll call or **Record vote** A congressional voting procedure that consists of members answering "yea" or "nay" to their names. When roll calls were handled orally, it was a time-consuming process in the House. Since 1973 an electronic voting system permits each House member to record his or her vote and learn the total automatically. *See also* Voice vote; Division vote; Teller vote (11)

Routine stories Media reports about public events that are regularly covered by reporters and that involve simple, easily described acts or statements. For example, the president takes a trip or Congress passes a bill. (10)

Runoff primary A second primary election held in some states when no candidate receives a majority of the votes in the first primary; the runoff is between the two candidates with the most votes. Runoff primaries are common in the South. (8)

Safe district A district in which incumbents win by margins of 55 percent or more. (11)

Sampling error The difference between the results of two surveys or samples. For example, if one random sample shows that 60 percent of all Americans like cats and another random sample taken at the same time shows that 65 percent do, the sampling error is 5 percent. (5)

Search warrant An order from a judge authorizing the search of a place; the order must describe what is to be searched and seized, and the judge can only issue it if he or she is persuaded by the police that good reason (probable cause) exists that a crime has been committed and that the evidence bearing on the crime will be found at a certain location. (18)

Select committees Congressional committees appointed for a limited time and purpose. *See also* Standing committees; Joint committees (11)

Selective attention Paying attention only to those parts of a newspaper or broadcast story with which one agrees. Studies suggest that this is how people view political ads on television. (10)

Separate-but-equal doctrine The doctrine, established in *Plessy* v. *Fergusson* (1896), in which the Supreme Court ruled that a state could provide "separate but equal" facilities for blacks. (19)

Separation of powers A principle of American government whereby constitutional authority is shared by three separate branches of government—the legislative, the executive, and the judicial. *See also* Checks and balances (2)

Sequential referral A congressional process by which a Speaker may send a bill to a second committee after the first is finished acting, or may refer parts of a bill to separate committees. (11)

Sequester Automatic, across-the-board cuts in certain federal programs that are triggered by law when Congress and the president cannot agree on a spending plan. (16)

Service strategy A policy of providing poor people with education and job training to help lift them out of poverty. (17)

Shays's Rebellion A rebellion in 1787 led by Daniel Shays and other ex-Revolutionary War soldiers and officers to prevent foreclosures of farms as a result of high interest rates and taxes. The revolt highlighted the weaknesses of the Confederation and bolstered support for a stronger national government. (2)

Silent majority A phrase used to describe people, whatever their economic status, who uphold traditional values, especially against the counterculture of the 1960s. (5)

Simple resolution An expression of opinion either in the House of Representatives or the Senate to settle housekeeping or procedural matters in either body. Such expressions are not signed by the president and do not have the force of law. *See also* Concurrent resolution; Joint resolution (11)

Social movement A widely shared demand for change in some aspect of the social or political order. The civil-rights movement of the 1960s was such an event as are broadly based religious revivals. A social movement may have liberal or conservative goals. (9)

Social status or **Socio-economic status** A measure of one's social standing obtained by combining factors such as education, income, and occupation. (5)

Soft money Funds solicited from individuals, corporations, and unions that are spent on party activities, such as voter-registration campaigns and voting drives, rather than on behalf of a specific candidate. These funds need not be reported to the Federal Election Commission. (8)

Solidary incentives The social rewards that lead people to join local or state political organizations. People who find politics fun and want to meet others who share their interests are said to respond to solidary incentives. (7, 9)

Sophomore surge An increase in the votes that congressional candidates usually get when they first run for re-election. (11)

Sound bite A brief statement no longer than a few seconds used on a radio or television news broadcast. (10)

Sovereign immunity A doctrine that a citizen cannot sue the government without its consent. By statute, Congress has given its consent for the government to be sued in many cases involving a dispute over a contract or damage done as a result of negligence. (14)

Sovereignty Supreme or ultimate political authority; a sovereign government is one that is legally and politically independent of any other government. (3)

Special-act charter A charter that denies the powers of a certain named city and lists what the city can and cannot do. *See also* General-act charter (25)

Split-ticket (voting) Voting for candidates of different parties for various offices in the same election. For example, voting for a Republican for senator and a Democrat for president. *See also* Straight-ticket voting (8)

Spoils system Another phrase for political patronage—that is, the practice of giving the fruits of a party's victory, such as jobs and contracts, to the loyal members of that party. (13)

Sponsored party A local or state political party that is largely staffed and funded by another organization with established networks in the community. One example is the Democratic party in and around Detroit which has been developed, led, and to a degree financed by the political-action arm of the United Auto Workers union. (7)

Spots (campaign) Short television advertisements used to promote a candidate for government office. *See also* Visual (8)

Standing A legal concept establishing who is entitled to bring a lawsuit to court. For example, an individual must ordinarily show personal harm in order to acquire standing and be heard in court. (14)

Standing committee A permanently established legislative committee that considers and is responsible for legislation within a certain subject area. Examples are the House Ways and Means Committee and the Senate Judiciary Committee. *See also* Select committees; Joint committees (11)

Stare decisis A Latin term meaning "Let the decision stand." The practice of basing judicial decisions on precedents established in similar cases decided in the past. (14)

Straight-ticket voting Voting for candidates who are all of the same party. For example, voting for Republican candidates for senator, representative, and president. *See also* Split-ticket voting (8)

Strict-constructionist approach (judicial) The view that judges should decide cases on the basis of the language of the Constitution. (14)

Strict scrutiny The standard by which the Supreme Court judges classifications based on race. To be accepted, such a classification must be closely related to a "compelling" public purpose. (19)

Strong-mayor system A system with a directly elected mayor who has substantial authority over the administrative branch of government and important budgetary powers. *See* Weak-mayor system (25)

Substantive representation The correspondence between representatives' opinions and those of their constituents. *See also* Descriptive representation (11)

Superdelegates Party leaders and elected officials who become delegates to the national convention without having to run in primaries or caucuses. Party rules determine the percentage of delegate seats reserved for party officials. (7)

Supply-side theory An economic philosophy that holds that sharply cutting taxes would increase the incentive that people have to work, save, and invest. Greater investments would lead to more jobs, a more productive economy, and more tax revenues for the government. (16)

Suspect classifications Classifications of people on the basis of their race and ethnicity. The courts have ruled that laws classifying people on these grounds will be subject to "strict scrutiny." (19)

Symbolic speech An act that conveys a political message, such as burning a draft card to protest the draft. (18)

Tax revolt A citizen-initiated movement to limit or reduce taxes. (25)

Teller vote A congressional voting procedure in which members pass between two tellers, the "yeas" first and

Teller vote *(continued)*
then the "nays." Since 1971 the identities of members in a teller vote can be "recorded." *See also* Voice vote; Division vote; Roll call (11)

Third World Originally a French term (*tiers monde*) referring to nations neutral in the cold war between the United States and the former Soviet Union. The term now refers to the group of developing nations in Africa, Asia, Latin America, and the Middle East. *See also* Cold War (20)

Town meeting A meeting of all town citizens to vote on budgets and proposals. *See also* Representative town meeting (25)

Trial balloon (political) Information provided to the media by an anonymous public official as a way of testing the public reaction to a possible policy or appointment. (10)

Trust funds Funds for government programs that are collected and spent outside the regular government budget; the amounts are determined by preexisting law rather than by annual appropriations. The Social Security trust fund is the largest of these. *See also* Appropriations (13)

Two-party system An electoral system with two dominant parties that compete in state or national elections. Third parties have little chance of winning. (7)

Unalienable rights Rights thought to be based on nature and Providence rather than on the preferences of people. (2)

Unified government A government in which the same party controls both the White House and both houses of Congress. When Bill Clinton became president in 1993, it was the first time since 1981 (and only the second time since 1969) that the same party was in charge of the presidency and Congress. *See also* Divided government (12)

Unitary systems Systems in which sovereignty is wholly in the hands of the national government so that subnational political units are dependent on its will. *See also* Federalism; Federal system (3)

Unreformed cities Cities based on the Jacksonian model of government. They have partisan elections, a city council elected from districts, and their executive powers are in the hands of the mayor. *See also* Reformed cities (25)

Valence issue An issue on which voters distinguish rival parties by the degree to which they associate each party or candidate with conditions, goals, or symbols the electorate universally approves or disapproves of. Examples of such issues are economic prosperity and political corruption. *See also* Position issue (8)

Veto message One of two ways for a president to disapprove a bill sent to him by Congress. The veto message must be sent to Congress within ten days after the president receives it. *See also* Pocket veto; Line-item veto (12)

Visual (campaign) A campaign activity that appears on a television news broadcast. *See also* Spots (8)

Voice vote A congressional voting procedure in which members shout "yea" in approval or "nay" in disapproval; allows members to vote quickly or anonymously on bills. *See also* Division vote; Teller vote; Roll call (11)

Voting-age population The citizens who are eligible to vote after reaching a minimum age requirement. In the United States, a citizen must be at least eighteen years old in order to vote. (6)

Wall-of-separation principle A Supreme Court interpretation of the Establishment clause in the First Amendment that prevents government involvement with religion, even on a nonpreferential basis. (18)

Weak-mayor system A mayor-council system in which the mayor does not have much power over the administration of the system (he or she often must share executive authority with various boards and commissions) and does not have a lot of influence in the city council. *See also* Strong-mayor system (25)

Whip A senator or representative who helps the party leader stay informed about what party members are thinking, rounds up members when important votes are to be taken, and attempts to keep a nose count on how the voting on controversial issues is likely to go. (11)

White primary The practice of keeping blacks from voting in primary elections (at the time, the only meaningful election in the one-party South was the Democratic primary) through arbitrary implementation of registration requirements and intimidation. Such practices were declared unconstitutional in 1944. (6)

Work ethic A belief in the importance of hard work and personal achievement. (4)

Worldviews (foreign policy) More or less comprehensive mental pictures of the critical problems facing the United States in the world and of the appropriate and inappropriate ways of responding to these problems. (20)

Writ of certiorari A Latin term meaning "made more certain." An order issued by a higher court to a lower court to send up the record of a case for review. Most cases reach the Supreme Court through the writ of certiorari, issued when at least four of the nine justices feel that the case should be reviewed. (14)

Writ of habeas corpus A Latin term meaning "you shall have the body." A court order directing a police officer, sheriff, or warden who has a person in custody to bring the prisoner before a judge and show sufficient cause for his or her detention. The writ of habeas corpus was designed to prevent illegal arrests and imprisonment. (2)

References

Chapter 1 *The Study of American Government*

1. Aristotle, *Politics*, iv, 4, 1290[b]. More precisely Aristotle's definition was this: democracy is a "constitution in which the free-born and poor control the government—being at the same time a majority." He distinguished this from an oligarchy, "in which the rich and well-born control the government—being at the same time a minority." Aristotle listed several varieties of democracy, depending on whether, for example, there was a property qualification for citizenship.
2. Joseph A. Schumpeter, *Capitalism, Socialism, and Democracy,* 3d ed. (New York: Harper Torchbooks, 1950), 269. (This book was first published in 1942.)
3. Karl Marx and Friedrich Engels, "The Manifesto of the Communist Party," in *The Marx-Engels Reader,* 2d ed., ed. Robert C. Tucker (New York: Norton, 1978), 469–500.
4. C. Wright Mills, *The Power Elite* (New York: Oxford University Press, 1956).
5. Richard Rovere, *The American Establishment* (New York: Harcourt Brace, 1962).
6. H. H. Gerth and C. Wright Mills, eds., *From Max Weber: Essays in Sociology* (London: Routledge & Kegan Paul, 1948), 232–235.
7. Among the authors whose interpretations of American politics are essentially pluralist is David B. Truman, *The Governmental Process,* 2d ed. (New York: Knopf, 1971).
8. Alexis de Tocqueville, *Democracy in America,* ed. Phillips Bradley (New York: Knopf, 1951), vol. 2, book 2, ch. 8, 122.
9. Derek C. Bok and John T. Dunlop, *Labor and the American Community* (New York: Simon & Schuster, 1970), 134.

Chapter 2 *The Constitution*

1. Quoted in Bernard Bailyn, *The Ideological Origins of the American Revolution* (Cambridge, Mass.: Harvard University Press, 1967), 61, n. 6.
2. Quoted in Bailyn, *op. cit.,* 135–137.
3. Quoted in Bailyn, *op. cit.,* 77.
4. Quoted in Bailyn, *op. cit.,* 160. Italics in the original.
5. *Federalist* No. 37.
6. Gordon S. Wood, *The Creation of the American Republic* (Chapel Hill: University of North Carolina Press, 1969). See also *Federalist* No. 49.
7. Letter of George Washington to Henry Lee (October 31, 1787). In John C. Fitzpatrick, ed., *Writings of George Washington* (Washington, D.C.: Government Printing Office, 1939), vol. 29, 34.
8. Letters of Thomas Jefferson to James Madison (January 30, 1787) and to Colonel William S. Smith (November 13, 1787), in Bernard Mayo,

ed., *Jefferson Himself* (Boston: Houghton Mifflin, 1942), 145.
9. *Federalist* No. 51.
10. *Federalist* No. 48.
11. *Federalist* No. 51.
12. *Ibid.*
13. *Ibid.*
14. "The Address and Reasons of Dissent of the Minority of the State of Pennsylvania to Their Constituents," in *The Anti-Federalist,* ed. Cecelia Kenyon (Indianapolis, Ind.: Bobbs-Merrill, 1966), 39.
15. Max Farrand, *The Framing of the Constitution of the United States* (New Haven, Conn.: Yale University Press, 1913), 185.
16. See, for example, John Hope Franklin, *Racial Equality in America* (Chicago: University of Chicago Press, 1976), ch. 1, esp. 12–20.
17. Max Farrand, *The Records of the Federal Convention of 1787,* 4 vols. (New Haven, Conn.: Yale University Press, 1911–1937).
18. Theodore J. Lowi, *American Government: Incomplete Conquest* (Hinsdale, Ill.: Dryden Press, 1976), 97.
19. Article I, section 2, para. 3.
20. Article I, section 9, para. 1.
21. Article IV, section 2, para. 3.
22. Charles A. Beard, *An Economic Interpretation of the Constitution* (New York: Macmillan, 1913), esp. 26–51, 149–151, 324–325.
23. Forrest McDonald, *We the People* (Chicago: University of Chicago Press, 1958); Robert E. Brown, *Charles Beard and the Constitution* (Princeton: Princeton University Press, 1956).
24. Robert A. McGuire, "Constitution Making: A Rational Choice Model of the Federal Convention of 1787," *American Journal of Political Science* 32 (May 1988): 483–522. See also Forrest McDonald, *Novus Ordo Seclorum* (Lawrence, Kan.: University of Kansas Press, 1985), 221.
25. McDonald, *Novus Ordo Seclorum,* 202–221.
26. Robert A. McGuire and Robert L. Ohsfeldt, "Economic Interests and the American Constitution: A Quantitative Rehabilitation of Charles A. Beard," *Journal of Economic History* 44 (June 1984): 509–519.
27. Lloyd N. Cutler, "To Form a Government," *Foreign Affairs* (Fall 1980), 126–143.

Chapter 3 *Federalism*

1. Woodrow Wilson, *Constitutional Government in the United States* (New York: Columbia University Press, 1908; reprinted 1961), p. 173.
2. David B. Truman, "Federalism and the Party System," in *Federalism: Mature and Emergent,* ed. Arthur MacMahon (Garden City, N.Y.: Doubleday, 1955), 123.

3. Harold J. Laski, "The Obsolescence of Federalism," *New Republic* (May 3, 1939), 367–369.
4. Riker, *op. cit.,* 154.
5. Daniel J. Elazar, *American Federalism: A View from the States* (New York: Crowell, 1966), 216.
6. Martin Diamond, "The Federalists' View of Federalism," in *Essays in Federalism,* ed. George C. S. Benson (Claremont, Calif.: Institute for Studies in Federalism, 1961), 21–64; and Samuel H. Beer, "Federalism, Nationalism, and Democracy in America," *American Political Science Review* 72 (March 1978): 9–21.
7. United States v. Sprague, 282 U.S. 716 (1931).
8. Garcia v. San Antonio Metropolitan Transit Authority, 105 S. Ct. 1005 (1985), overruling National League of Cities v. Usery, 426 U.S. 833 (1976).
9. McCulloch v. Maryland, 4 Wheat, 316 (1819).
10. This was in part overruled in Pollock v. Farmers' Loan & Trust Co., 157 U.S. 429 (1895); overruled in South Carolina v. Baker, No. 94 (1988).
11. Texas v. White, 7 Wall. 700 (1869).
12. Champion v. Ames, 188 U.S. 321 (1903).
13. Hoke v. United States, 227 U.S. 308 (1913).
14. Clark Distilling Co. v. W. Md. Ry., 242 U.S. 311 (1917).
15. Hipolite Egg Co. v. United States, 220 U.S. 45 (1911).
16. United States v. E. C. Knight Co., 156 U.S. 1 (1895).
17. Paul v. Virginia, 8 Wall. 168 (1869).
18. Veazie Bank v. Fenno, 8 Wall. 533 (1869).
19. Brown v. Maryland, 12 Wheat. 419 (1827).
20. Wickard v. Filburn, 317 U.S. 111 (1942); NLRB v. Jones & Laughlin Steel Corp., 301 U.S. 58 (1937).
21. Kirschbaum Co. v. Walling, 316 U.S. 517 (1942).
22. Goldfarb v. Virginia State Bar, 421 U.S. 773 (1975); Flood v. Kuhn, 407 U.S. 258 (1972).
23. United States v. California, 332 U.S. 19 (1947).
24. Morton Grodzins, *The American System* (Chicago: Rand McNally, 1966), 49–50.
25. Morton Keller, *Affairs of State* (Cambridge, Mass.: Harvard University Press, 1977), 310, 381–382.
26. Edward C. Banfield, "Making a New Federal Program: Model Cities, 1964–1968," in *Policy and Politics in America,* ed. Allan P. Sindler (Boston: Little, Brown, 1973), 124–158.
27. Neal R. Pierce, "Partnership for City Aid," *Boston Globe* (March 30, 1978).
28. Samuel H. Beer, "The Modernization of American Federalism," *Publius* 3 (Fall 1973), esp. 74–79; and Beer, "Federalism . . . ," *op. cit.,* 18–19.
29. Calculated from *Special Analyses: Budget of the*

U.S. Government, Fiscal Year 1979 (Washington, D.C.: Government Printing Office, 1978), 187.

30. Quoted in *National Journal* (September 18, 1976), 1321.

31. R. Douglas Arnold, "The Local Roots of Domestic Policy," in *The New Congress,* ed. Thomas E. Mann and Norman J. Ornstein (Washington, D.C.: American Enterprise Institute, 1981), 268.

32. Congressional Budget Office, *Federal Constraints on State and Local Government Actions* (Washington, D.C.: Government Printing Office, 1979).

33. Civil Rights Act of 1871, as amended in 1875: *United States Code,* Title 42, section 1983.

34. *Nation's Business,* December 1993, p. 12.

35. *Federally Induced Costs Affecting State and Local Governments* (U.S. Advisory Commission on Intergovernmental Relations, September 1994), p. v.

36. *United States Code,* Title 23, section 131 (1976).

37. *Congressional Record* 126 (February 5, 1980), S1009–S1013.

38. *Ibid.,* S1010.

39. *Statistical Abstract of the United States, 1990,* 371.

40. Charles Murray, "Does Welfare Bring More Babies?" *The American Enterprise* (Jan./Feb. 1994): 55.

41. Richard P. Nathan and Fred Doolittle, *Reagan and the States* (Princeton, N.J.: Princeton University Press, 1987), p. 7.

42. George Peterson et al., *The Reagan Block Grants: What Have We Learned?* (Washington, D.C.: The Urban Institute Press, 1986), pp. 21–27.

43. R. Kent Weaver, "Deficits and Devolution in the 104th Congress," unpublished draft paper, Washington, D.C., Brookings Institution, April 1996.

44. Richard P. Nathan, "Hard Road Ahead: Block Grants and 'The Devolution Revolution,'" Discussion Paper, Washington, D.C., Center for Public Management, Brookings Institution, October 27, 1995.

45. *The Public Perspective,* April/May 1995, p. 5.

Chapter 4   *American Political Culture*

1. Alexis de Tocqueville, *Democracy in America,* ed. Phillips Bradley (New York: Knopf, 1951), vol. 1, 288. (First published in 1835.)

2. *Ibid.,* vol. 1, pp. 319–320.

3. Ibid., vol. 1, p. 319.

4. Donald J. Devine, *The Political Culture of the United States* (Boston: Little, Brown, 1972), 185; Herbert McClosky and John Zaller, *The American Ethos: Public Attitudes toward Capitalism and Democracy* (Cambridge, Mass.: Harvard University Press, 1984), ch. 3, esp. 74–75.

5. McClosky and Zaller, *op. cit.,* 74–77.

6. *Ibid.,* 66.

7. Gunnar Myrdal, *An American Dilemma: The Negro Problem in Modern Democracy* (New York: Harper, 1944), intro. and ch. 1.

8. Frank R. Westie, "The American Dilemma: An Empirical Test," *American Sociological Review* 30 (August 1965): 536–537.

9. Eric L. McKitrick, "Party Politics and the Union and Confederate War Efforts," in *The American Party Systems,* 2d ed., ed. William Nisbet Chambers and Walter Dean Burnham (New York: Oxford University Press, 1975), 117–121.

10. McClosky and Zaller, *op. cit.,* 174.

11. Sidney Verba and Gary R. Orren, *Equality in America: The View from the Top* (Cambridge, Mass.: Harvard University Press, 1985), 146–147.

12. McClosky and Zaller, *op. cit.,* 82–84.

13. *Ibid.,* 93, 95.

14. Verba and Orren, *op. cit.,* 74; McClosky and Zaller, *op. cit.,* 126.

15. Verba and Orren, *op. cit.,* 72, 254.

16. Donald Kinder and David Sears, "Symbolic Racism versus Racial Threats to the Good Life," *Journal of Personality and Social Psychology* 40 (1981): 414–431.

17. Paul M. Sniderman and Michael Gray Hagen, *Race and Inequality: A Study in American Values* (Chatham, N.J.: Chatham House, 1985), 111.

18. *Ibid.,* 37–38.

19. Theodore Caplow and Howard M. Bahr, "Half a Century of Change in Adolescent Attitudes: A Replication of a Middletown Survey by the Lynds," *Public Opinion Quarterly* 43 (1979): 1–17, table 1.

20. Thomas J. Anton, "Policy-Making and Political Culture in Sweden," *Scandinavian Political Studies* 4 (1969): 88–100; M. Donald Hancock, *Sweden: The Politics of Post-Industrial Change* (Hinsdale, Ill.: Dryden Press, 1972); Sten Johansson, "Liberal-Democratic Theory and Political Processes," in *Readings in the Swedish Class Structure,* ed. Richard Scarse (New York: Pergamon Press, 1976); Steven J. Kelman, *Regulating America, Regulating Sweden: A Comparative Study of Occupational Safety and Health Policy* (Cambridge, Mass.: MIT Press, 1981), 118–123.

21. Lewis Austin, *Saints and Samurai: The Political Culture of American and Japanese Elites* (New Haven, Conn.: Yale University Press, 1975).

22. Gabriel Almond and Sidney Verba, *The Civic Culture* (Princeton, N.J.: Princeton University Press, 1963), 169, 185. See also Gabriel Almond and Sidney Verba, eds., *The Civic Culture Revisited* (Boston: Little, Brown, 1980).

23. Sidney Verba et al., *Voice and Equality: Civic Voluntarism in American Politics* (Cambridge, Mass.: Harvard University Press, 1995), pp. 69, 70.

24. Gordon Heald, "A Comparison between American, European, and Japanese Values," as quoted in Richard Rose, "Public Confidence, Popular Consent: A Comparison of Britain and the United States," *Public Opinion* (February–March 1984), 11.

25. Gallup International Poll for the European Value System Study, 1982.

26. Paul M. Sniderman, *A Question of Loyalty* (Berkeley: University of California Press, 1981).

27. Seymour Martin Lipset, *The First New Nation* (New York: Doubleday Anchor Books, 1967), 170–171.

28. Verba and Orren, *op. cit.,* 255.

29. Max Weber, *The Protestant Ethic and the Spirit of Capitalism,* trans. Talcott Parsons (New York: Scribner's, 1930). (First published in 1904.)

30. Erik H. Erickson, *Childhood and Society* (New York: Norton, 1950), ch. 8.

31. The phrase "culture war" is from James Davison Hunter, *Culture Wars: The Struggle to Define America* (New York: Basic Books, 1991). This discussion draws heavily on Professor Hunter's analysis.

32. *Ibid.,* 96–97, 116–117. See also Robert Lerner, Stanley Rotham, and S. Robert Lichter, "Christian Religious Elites," *Public Opinion* 11 (March/April 1989): 54–58.

33. Schlozman and Verba, *op. cit.,* 218–224, 237.

34. Arthur H. Miller, "Political Issues and Trust in Government: 1964–1970," *American Political Science Review* 68 (September 1974): 95–272. These data were updated from figures supplied by the Survey Research Center, University of Michigan.

35. Jack Citrin, "Comment: The Political Relevance of Trust in Government," *American Political Science Review* 68 (September 1974): 973–988; James S. House and William M. Mason, "Political Alienation in America, 1958–1968," *American Sociological Review* 40 (April 1975): 123–147; Seymour Martin Lipset and William Schneider, *The Confidence Gap: Business, Labor, and Government in the Public Mind* (New York: Free Press, 1983), ch. 12.

36. Citrin, *op. cit.,* 975.

37. Robert E. Lane, "The Politics of Consensus in the Age of Affluence," *American Political Science Review* 59 (December 1965): 874–875; Lane, "The Decline of Politics and Ideology in a Knowledgeable Society," *American Sociological Review* 31 (October 1966): 649–662; Lipset and Schneider, *op. cit.,* 14–15.

38. Arthur Miller, "Is Confidence Rebounding?" *Public Opinion* (June–July 1983), 16–20.

39. Lipset and Schneider, *op. cit.,* 21–22; Warren E. Miller, "Crisis in Confidence II—Misreading the Public Pulse," *Public Opinion* (October–November 1979), 12–13.

40. Data from the Survey Research Center, University of Michigan. See also Norman H. Nie, Sidney Verba, and John R. Petrocik, *The Changing American Voter* (Cambridge, Mass.: Harvard University Press, 1976), 125–128.

41. Samuel H. Barnes and Max Kaase, eds., *Political Action: Mass Participation in Five Democracies* (Beverly Hills, Calif.: Sage, 1979), 541–542, 574.

42. James W. Prothro and Charles M. Grigg, "Fundamental Principles of Democracy: Bases of Agreement and Disagreement," *Journal of Politics* 22 (Spring 1960); 275–294.

43. Herbert McClosky and Alida Brill, *Dimensions of Tolerance: What Americans Believe about Civil Liberties* (New York: Russell Sage Foundation, 1983), 124.

44. *Ibid.,* 62, 66, 70, 118, 131.

45. *Ibid.,* 435; James A. Davis, "Communism, Cohorts, and Categories: American Tolerance in 1954 and 1972–1973," *American Journal of Sociology* 81 (1975): 491–513; and Clyde A. Nunn, Harry J. Crockett, Jr., and J. Allen Williams, Jr., *Tolerance for Nonconformity: A National Survey of Changing Commitment to Civil Liberties* (San Francisco, Calif.: Jossey-Bass, 1978). But compare the different conclusion in John L. Sullivan, James Pierson, and George E. Marcus, *Political Tolerance and American Democracy* (Chicago: University of Chicago Press, 1982).

Chapter 5 *Public Opinion*

1. George W. Bishop, Alfred J. Tuchfarber, and Robert W. Oldendick, "1984: How Much Can We Manipulate and Control People's Answers to Public Opinion Surveys?" paper delivered at the 1984 annual meeting of the American Political Science Association; Howard Schuman and S. Presser, *Questions and Answers in Attitude Surveys* (New York: Academic Press, 1981), ch. 5.

2. Data from the National Election Survey, 1986, as tabulated by Professor John Zaller, University of California at Los Angeles.

3. M. Kent Jennings and Richard G. Niemi, "The Transmission of Political Values from Parent to Child," *American Political Science Review* 62 (March 1968): 173.

4. Robert D. Hess and Judith V. Tomey, *The Development of Political Attitudes in Children* (Chicago: Aldine, 1967), 90.

5. Several studies of child-parent agreement on party preference are summarized in David O. Sears, "Political Behavior," in *The Handbook of Social Psychology,* 2d ed., ed. Gardner Lindzey and Elliot Aronson (Reading, Mass.: Addison-Wesley, 1969), vol. 5, 376.

6. Norman H. Nie, Sidney Verba, and John R. Petrocik, *The Changing American Voter* (Cambridge, Mass.: Harvard University Press, 1976), ch. 4.

7. Robert S. Erickson and Norman R. Luttbeg, *American Public Opinion: Its Origins, Content, and Impact* (New York: Wiley, 1973), 197; and Seymour Martin Lipset, *Revolution and Counterrevolution,* rev. ed. (Garden City, N.Y.: Doubleday Anchor Books, 1970), 338–342.

8. *The Baron Report* (June 18, 1984).

9. ICPSR American National Election Study, 1992: Pre- and Post-Election Surveys.

10. Alexander M. Astin, *Four Critical Years: Effects of College on Beliefs, Attitudes, and Knowledge* (San Francisco: Jossey-Bass, 1978), 36–38.

11. Institute of Politics, Harvard University, *Campaign '84 and Beyond* (1986), 12.

12. Erikson and Luttbeg, *op. cit.,* 138; Terry S. Weiner and Bruce K. Eckland, "Education and Political Party: The Effects of College or Social Class?" *American Journal of Sociology* 84 (1979): 911–928.

13. Astin, *op. cit.,* 38.

14. John Zaller, "The Effects of Political Awareness on Public Opinion and Voting Behavior," *American Political Science Review,* forthcoming.

15. Everett Carl Ladd, Jr., and Seymour Martin Lipset, *The Divided Academy: Professors and Politics* (New York: McGraw-Hill, 1975), 26–27, 55–67, 184–190.

16. *Statistical Abstract of the United States, 1984,* 144.

17. J. L. Spaeth and Andrew M. Greeley, *Recent Alumni and Higher Education* (New York: McGraw-Hill, 1970), 100-110; and Erland Nelson, "Persistence of Attitudes of College Students Fourteen Years Later," *Psychological Monographs* 68 (1954): 1–13.

18. Kenneth A. Feldman and Theodore M. Newcomb, *The Impact of College on Students* (San Francisco: Jossey-Bass, 1969), vol. 1, 99–100, 312–320.

19. John McAdams, "Testing the Theory of the New Class," *Sociological Quarterly* 28 (1987): 23–49.

20. M. Kent Jennings, "Residues of a Movement: The Aging of the American Protest Generation," *American Political Science Review* 81 (1987): 367–382.

21. Kay Lehman Schlozman and Sidney Verba, *Insult to Injury: Unemployment, Class, and Political Response* (Cambridge, Mass.: Harvard University Press, 1979), 115–118; David Butler and Donald Stokes, *Political Change in Great Britain* (New York: St. Martin's Press, 1969), 70, 77; Erikson and Luttbeg, *op. cit.,* 184; *National Journal* (November 8, 1980), 1878.

22. V. O. Key, Jr., *Public Opinion and American Democracy* (New York: Knopf, 1961), 122–138.

23. Richard E. Dawson, *Public Opinion and Contemporary Disarray* (New York: Harper & Row, 1973), ch. 4.

24. Seymour Martin Lipset, "Two Americas, Two Value Systems: Blacks and Whites," *Working Papers in Political Science* P–91–1, Hoover Institution, Stanford University (November 1991): 18.

25. *Ibid.,* 15.

26. *Differences in Black and White Opinion on Important Issues of Public Policy* (Washington, D.C.: The Center for New Black Leadership, February 1996).

27. Nie, Verba, and Petrocik, *op. cit.,* 253–256.

28. Schlozman and Verba, *op. cit.,* 172.

29. Susan Welch and Lorn Foster, "Class and Conservatism in the Black Community," paper delivered at the 1986 annual meeting of the American Political Science Association. See also Franklin D. Gilliam, Jr., "Black America: Divided by Class?" *Public Opinion* (February–March 1986): 53–57.

30. Linda S. Lichter, "Who Speaks for Black America?" *Public Opinion* (August–September 1985): 41ff.

31. Bruce Cain and Roderick Kiewiet, "California's Coming Minority Majority," *Public Opinion* (February–March 1986): 50–52.

32. F. Chris Garcia et al., "The Effects of Ethnic Partisanship on Electoral Behavior: An Analysis and Comparison of Latino and Anglo Voting in the 1988 United States Presidential Election," paper delivered at the Annual Meeting of the American Political Science Association, September 3–6, 1992.

33. Robert Suro, "Poll Finds Hispanic Desire to Assimilate," *The New York Times* (December 15, 1992), A18, citing the findings of the National Latino Survey led by Rodolfo O. de la Garza.

34. Nie, Verba, and Petrocik, *op. cit.,* 247–250.

35. Philip E. Converse, "The Nature of Belief Systems in Mass Publics," in *Ideology and Discontent,* ed. David Apter (New York: The Free Press of Glencoe, 1964), 206–261.

36. Christopher H. Achen, "Mass Political Attitudes and the Survey Response," *American Political Science Review* 69 (December 1975): 1218–1231.

37. Seymour Martin Lipset and Earl Raab, *The Politics of Unreason* (New York: Harper & Row, 1970), ch. 11; James A. Stimson, "Belief Systems: Constraint, Complexity, and the 1972 Election," *American Journal of Political Science* 19 (1975): 393–417; and Herbert McClosky and John Zaller, *The American Ethos* (Cambridge, Mass.: Harvard University Press, 1984), ch. 8.

38. Estimates of size of four groups averaged from 1993–1994 data presented by Everett Carll Ladd, "A New View of the Electorate," *The American Enterprise,* May/June 1994, p. 91.

39. Zaller, *op. cit.;* and Stimson, *op. cit.* See also Allen H. Barton and R. Wayne Parsons, "Measuring Belief System Structures," *Public Opinion Quarterly* 41 (1977): 159–180.

40. McAdams, *op. cit.*

41. Seymour Martin Lipset and David Riesman, *Education and Politics at Harvard* (New York: McGraw-Hill, 1975), ch. 8.

42. McAdams, *op. cit.*

43. *Ibid.*

44. John Zaller, *The Nature of Mass Opinion* (Cambridge: Cambridge University Press, 1992).

45. *Ibid.*

Chapter 6 *Political Participation*

1. David Glass, Peverill Squire, and Raymond Wolfinger, "Voter Turnout: An International Comparison," *Public Opinion* (December–January 1984): 49–55. See also G. Bingham Powell, Jr., "Voting Turnout in Thirty Democracies: Partisan, Legal, and Socio-Economic Influences," in *Electoral Participation: A Comparative Analysis,* ed. Richard Rose (Beverly Hills, Calif.: Sage Publications, 1980).

2. Morton Keller, *Affairs of State* (Cambridge, Mass.: Harvard University Press, 1977), 523.

3. United States v. Reese, 92 U.S. 214 (1876); United States v. Cruikshank, 92 U.S. 556 (1876); and Ex parte Yarbrough, 110 U.S. 651 (1884).

4. Guinn and Beall v. United States, 238 U.S. 347 (1915).

5. Smith v. Allwright, 321 U.S. 649 (1944).

6. Schnell v. Davis, 336 U.S. 933 (1949).

7. Congressional Quarterly, *Congress and the Nation,* vol. 3: 1969–1972 (Washington, D.C.: Congressional Quarterly, 1973), 1006; and *Statistical Abstract of the United States, 1975,* 450.

8. *Historical Statistics of the United States: Colonial Times to 1970*, part 2, 1071–1072.

9. Walter Dean Burnham, "The Changing Shape of the American Political Universe," *American Political Science Review* 59 (March 1965): 11; and William H. Flanigan and Nancy H. Zingale, *Political Behavior of the American Electorate*, 3d ed. (Boston: Allyn & Bacon, 1975), 15.

10. Burnham, *op. cit.*; E. E. Schattschneider, *The Semisovereign People* (New York: Holt, Rinehart and Winston, 1960), chs. 5, 6.

11. Keller, *op. cit.*, 523.

12. *Ibid.*, 524.

13. Philip E. Converse, "Change in the American Electorate," in *The Human Meaning of Social Change*, ed. Angus Campbell and Philip E. Converse (New York: Russell Sage Foundation, 1972), 263–338.

14. Michael W. Traugott and John P. Katosh, "Response Validity in Surveys of Voting Behavior," *Public Opinion Quarterly* 43 (1979): 359–377; Aage R. Clausen, "Response Validity: Vote Report," *Public Opinion Quarterly* 32 (1969): 588–606.

15. Sidney Verba et al., *Voice and Equality: Civic Voluntarism in American Politics* (Cambridge, Mass.: Harvard University Press, 1995), p. 79.

16. *Ibid.*, p. 77.

17. Wolfinger and Rosenstone, *op. cit.*, esp. 102; and John P. Katosh and Michael W. Traugott, "Costs and Values in the Calculus of Voting," *American Journal of Political Science* 26 (1982): 361–376.

18. David C. Leege and Lyman A. Kellstedt, *Rediscovering the Religious Factor in American Politics* (Armonk, N.Y.: M. E. Sharpe, 1993), 129–131.

19. Verba and Nie, *op. cit.*, 151–157; and Milbrath and Goel, *op. cit.*, 120.

20. Jack Citrin, "The Alienated Voter," *Taxing and Spending* (October 1978), 1–7; Austin Ranney, "Nonvoting is Not a Social Disease," *Public Opinion* (October–November 1983): 16–19; Glass, Squire, and Wolfinger, *op. cit.*

21. Dunn v. Blumstein, 405 U.S. 330 (1972).

22. Wolfinger and Rosenstone, *op. cit.*

23. Richard G. Smolka, *Election Day Registration: The Minnesota and Wisconsin Experience* (Washington, D.C.: American Enterprise Institute, 1977), 5.

24. Gary R. Orren, "The Linkage of Policy to Participation," in *Presidential Selection*, ed. Alexander Heard and Michael Nelson (Durham, N.C.: Duke University Press, 1987).

25. Glass, Squire, and Wolfinger, *op. cit.*, 52.

26. Powell, *op. cit.*; Robert W. Jackman, "Political Institutions and Voter Turnout in Industrial Democracies," *American Political Science Review* 81 (1987): 405–423.

27. Roy Texeira, "Will the Real Nonvoter Please Stand Up?" *Public Opinion* (July/August 1988): 43; Texeira, "Registration and Turnout," *Public Opinion* (January/February 1989): 12.

28. Richard A. Brody, "The Puzzle of Political Participation in America," in *The New American Political System*, ed. Anthony King (Washington, D.C.: American Enterprise Institute, 1978),

315–323; and Charles Lewis Taylor and Michael C. Hudson, *World Handbook of Political and Social Indicators*, 2d ed. (New Haven, Conn.: Yale University Press, 1972), table 3.1.

29. Richard Smolka, quoted in William J. Crotty, *Political Reform and the American Experiment* (New York: Crowell, 1977), 86–87.

30. Sidney Verba et al., "Race, Ethnicity, and the Resources for Participation: the Role of Religion," paper delivered at the 1992 Annual Meeting of the American Political Science Association, September 3–6, 1992.

Chapter 7 *Political Parties*

1. Leon D. Epstein, "Political Parties," in *Handbook of Political Science*, ed. Fred I. Greenstein and Nelson W. Polsby (Reading, Mass.: Addison-Wesley, 1975), vol. 4, 230.

2. Quoted in Henry Adams, *History of the United States of America during the Administrations of Jefferson and Madison*, abridged edition, ed. Ernest Samuels (Chicago: University of Chicago Press, 1967), 147.

3. Robert Kuttner, "Fat and Sassy," *The New Republic* (February 23, 1987), 21–23.

4. Morton Keller, *Affairs of State* (Cambridge, Mass.: Harvard University Press, 1977), 239.

5. Quoted in Keller, *op. cit.*, 256.

6. Martin Shefter, "Parties, Bureaucracy, and Political Change in the United States," in *The Development of Political Parties*, Sage Electoral Studies Yearbook, vol. 4, ed. Louis Maisel and Joseph Cooper (Beverly Hills, Calif.: Sage Publications, 1978).

7. James Q. Wilson, *The Amateur Democrat: Club Politics in Three Cities* (Chicago: University of Chicago Press, 1962).

8. Samuel J. Eldersveld, *Political Parties: A Behavioral Analysis* (Chicago: Rand McNally, 1964), 278, 287.

9. Robert H. Salisbury, "The Urban Party Organization Member," *Public Opinion Quarterly* 29 (Winter 1965–1966): 550–564.

10. *Ibid.*, 557, 559.

11. Eldersveld, *op. cit.*; and J. David Greenstone, *Labor in American Politics* (New York: Knopf, 1969), 187.

12. David R. Mayhew, *Placing Parties in American Politics* (Princeton, N.J.: Princeton University Press, 1986), chs. 2, 3.

13. *Boston Globe* (July 9, 1984), 1.

14. William Nisbet Chambers and Walter Dean Burnham, eds., *The American Party Systems: Stages of Political Development*, 2d ed. (New York: Oxford University Press, 1975), 6.

15. Williams v. Rhodes, 393 U.S. 23 (1968).

16. James Q. Wilson, *Political Organizations* (New York: Basic Books, 1973), ch. 12; and Samuel Stouffer, *Communism, Conformity, and Civil Liberties* (Garden City, N.Y.: Doubleday, 1955).

17. On 1972 and 1976 see Jeane Kirkpatrick, *The New Presidential Elite* (New York: Russell Sage Foundation and Twentieth Century Fund, 1976), 297–315; on 1980 see *New York Times* (August 13, 1980).

18. Nelson W. Polsby, *Consequences of Party Reform* (New York: Oxford University Press, 1983), 9–11, 64.

19. *Ibid.*, 158. But compare John G. Geer, "Voting in Presidential Primaries," paper delivered to the 1984 annual meeting of the American Political Science Association.

20. Michael J. Malbin, "Democratic Party Rules Are Made to be Broken," *National Journal* (August 23, 1980), 1388.

21. Kirkpatrick, *op. cit.*, ch. 4.

Chapter 8 *Elections and Campaigns*

1. Fred Barnes, "Charade on Main Street," *The New Republic* (June 15, 1987), 15–17. See also Hugh Winebrenner, *The Iowa Precinct Caucuses: The Making of a Media Event* (Ames, Iowa: Iowa State University Press, 1987).

2. Arthur H. Miller et al., "A Majority Party in Disarray: Policy Polarization in the 1972 Election," *American Political Science Review* 70 (1976): 757.

3. Thomas E. Patterson and Robert D. McClure, *The Unseeing Eye: The Myth of Television Power in National Politics* (New York: Putnam, 1976); and Xandra Kayden, *Campaign Organization* (Lexington, Mass.: D. C. Heath, 1978), ch. 6.

4. Gerald M. Pomper et al., *The Election of 1980* (Chatham, N.J.: Chatham House, 1981), 75, 105–107.

5. Buckley v. Valeo, 424 U.S. 1 (1976).

6. Gary C. Jacobson, *The Politics of Congressional Elections*, 2d ed. (Boston, Mass.: Little, Brown, 1987), 49.

7. Donald Philip Green and Jonathan S. Krasno, "Salvation for the Spendthrift Incumbent: Reestimating the Effects of Campaign Spending in House Elections," *American Journal of Political Science* 32 (1988): 884–960; Stephen Ansolabehere, "Winning is Easy But It Sure Ain't Cheap," Working Paper 90-1, Center for American Politics and Public Policy, UCLA (1990); Robert S. Erickson and Thomas R. Palfrey, "The Puzzle of Incumbent Spending in Congressional Elections," *Social Science Working Paper* 806 (California Institute of Technology, August 1992).

8. Angus Campbell, Philip E. Converse, Warren E. Miller, and Donald E. Stokes, *The American Voter* (New York: Wiley, 1960), ch. 8.

9. V. O. Key, Jr., *The Responsible Electorate* (Cambridge, Mass.: Harvard University Press, 1966).

10. Morris P. Fiorina, *Retrospective Voting in American National Elections* (New Haven, Conn.: Yale University Press, 1981).

11. Jay P. Greene, "Forewarned Before Forecast: Presidential Election Forecasting Models and the 1992 Election," *P.S.: Political Science and Politics* (March 1993): 20.

12. In 1988, Dukakis led Bush by 17 percent in polls taken shortly after Dukakis was nominated, only to see Bush win handily. In 1980 Carter led Reagan in the early polls.

13. Robert Axelrod, "Where the Votes Come From:

An Analysis of Electoral Coalitions, 1952–1968," *American Political Science Review* 66 (1972): 11–20; and Axelrod, "Communication," *American Political Science Review* 68 (1974): 718–719.

14. Walter Dean Burnham, *Critical Elections and the Mainsprings of American Politics* (New York: Norton, 1970), 10.

15. James L. Sundquist, *Dynamics of the Party System* (Washington, D.C.: Brookings Institution, 1973), ch. 7.

16. Edward G. Carmines and James A. Stimson, "Issue Evolution, Population Replacement, and Normal Partisan Change," *American Political Science Review* 75 (March 1981): 107–118; and Gregory Markus, "Political Attitudes in an Election Year," *American Political Science Review* 76 (September 1982): 538–560.

17. Ray Wolfinger and Michael G. Hagen, "Republican Prospects: Southern Comfort," *Public Opinion* (October–November 1985), 8–13. But compare Richard Scammon and James A. Barnes, "Republican Prospects: Southern Discomfort," *Public Opinion* (October–November 1985), 14–17.

18. Jerrold G. Rusk, "The Effect of the Australian Ballot Reform on Split-Ticket Voting: 1876–1908," *American Political Science Review* 64 (December 1970): 1220–1238.

19. Gerald M. Pomper, *Elections in America* (New York: Dodd, Mead, 1971), 178.

20. Benjamin Ginsberg, "Elections and Public Policy," *American Political Science Review* 70 (March 1976): 41–49.

Chapter 9 *Interest Groups*

1. L. Harmon Zeigler and Hendrik van Dalen, "Interest Groups in the States," in *Politics in the American States*, 2d ed., ed. Herbert Jacob and Kenneth N. Vines (Boston: Little, Brown, 1974), 122–160; and Edward C. Banfield and James Q. Wilson, *City Politics* (Cambridge, Mass.: Harvard University Press, 1963), chs. 18, 19.

2. Joseph LaPalombara, *Interest Groups in Italian Politics* (Princeton, N.J.: Princeton University Press, 1964).

3. Kay Lehman Schlozman and John T. Tierney, "More of the Same: Washington Pressure Group Activity in a Decade of Change," *Journal of Politics* 45 (1983): 356.

4. The use of injunctions in labor disputes was restricted by the Norris–LaGuardia Act of 1932; the rights to collective bargaining and to the union shop were guaranteed by the Wagner Act of 1935.

5. *Historical Statistics of the United States, Colonial Times to 1970*, vol. 1, 386.

6. The distinction is drawn from Kay Lehman Schlozman and John T. Tierney, *Organized Interests and American Democracy* (New York: Harper & Row, 1985).

7. Jeffrey M. Berry, *The Interest Group Society* (Boston: Little, Brown, 1984), 20–21.

8. *Ibid.*, 24, 130.

9. Gabriel A. Almond and Sidney Verba, *The Civic Culture* (Princeton, N.J.: Princeton University Press, 1963), 302; Derek C. Bok and John T. Dunlop, *Labor and the American Community* (New York: Simon & Schuster, 1970), 49; *Statistical Abstract of the United States, 1975*, 373.

10. Almond and Verba, *op. cit.*, 194.

11. *Ibid.*, 207.

12. Mancur Olson, Jr., *The Logic of Collective Action* (Cambridge, Mass.: Harvard University Press, 1965), 153–157.

13. Bok and Dunlop, *op. cit.*, 134.

14. Henry J. Pratt, *The Liberalization of American Protestantism* (Detroit: Wayne State University Press, 1972), ch. 12; Gerhard Lenski, *The Religious Factor* (Garden City, N.Y.: Doubleday, 1961), ch. 4.

15. Jane J. Mansbridge, *Why We Lost the ERA* (Chicago: University of Chicago Press, 1986), ch. 10. See also Joyce Gelb and Marian Lief Palley, *Women and Public Choices* (Princeton, N.J.: Princeton University Press, 1982), ch. 3; Jo Freeman, *The Politics of Women's Liberation* (New York: McKay, 1975), ch. 3; Maren Lockwood Carden, "The Proliferation of a Social Movement: Ideology and Individual Incentives in the Contemporary Feminist Movement," *Research in Social Movements*, vol. 1 (1978), 179–196; and Dom Bonafede, "Still a Long Way to Go," *National Journal* (September 13, 1986), 2175–2179.

16. Mansbridge, *op. cit.*, 130–131.

17. Jeffrey M. Berry, *Lobbying for the People* (Princeton, N.J.: Princeton University Press, 1977), 71–76.

18. Berry, *Interest Group Society, op. cit.*, 88.

19. Schlozman and Tierney, *Organized Interests and American Democracy, op. cit.*, table 5–4.

20. *New York Times* (December 8, 1983), 1.

21. Raymond A. Bauer, Ithiel de Sola Pool, and Lewis Anthony Dexter, *American Business and Public Policy* (New York: Atherton, 1963), ch. 30.

22. Berry, *Lobbying for the People, op. cit.*, 136–140.

23. Margaret Ann Latus, "Assessing Ideological PACs: From Outrage to Understanding," in *Money and Politics in the United States*, ed. Michael Malbin (Chatham, N.J.: Chatham House, 1984), 143; and data supplied by the Federal Election Commission, March 1992.

24. *Ibid.*, 144.

25. Malbin, *op. cit.*, table A.8, 290–291.

26. Michael J. Malbin, "Looking Back at the Future of Campaign Finance Reform: Interest Groups and American Elections," in Malbin, *Money and Politics, op. cit.*, 248; James B. Kau and Paul H. Rubin, *Congressmen, Constituents and Contributors* (Boston: Martinus Nijhoff, 1982); Henry W. Chappell, Jr., "Campaign Contributions and Voting on the Cargo Preference Bill: A Comparison of Simultaneous Models," *Public Choice* 36 (1981): 301–312; W. P. Welch, "Campaign Contributions and Voting: Milk Money and Dairy Price Supports," *Western Political Quarterly* 35 (1982): 478–495; John R. Wright, "PACs, Contributions, and Roll Calls: An Or-

ganizational Perspective," *American Political Science Review* 79 (1985): 400–414. But compare Benjamin Ginsberg and John C. Green, "The Best Congress Money Can Buy," in Ginsberg and Alan Stone, eds., *Do Elections Matter?* (Armonk, N.Y.: M. E. Sharpe, 1986), 75–89.

27. William T. Gormley, "A Test of the Revolving Door Hypothesis at the FCC," *American Journal of Political Science* 23 (1979): 665–683; Paul J. Quirk, *Industry Influence in Federal Regulatory Agencies* (Princeton, N.J.: Princeton University Press, 1981); and Jeffrey E. Cohen, "The Dynamics of the 'Revolving Door' on the FCC," *American Journal of Political Science* 30 (1986): 689–708.

28. Suzanne Weaver, *Decision to Prosecute* (Cambridge, Mass.: MIT Press, 1977), 154–163.

29. United States v. Harriss, 347 U.S. 612 (1954).

30. *United States Code,* Title 26, section 501(c)(3).

31. James Q. Wilson, *Political Organizations* (New York: Basic Books, 1973), 321.

Chapter 10 *The Media*

1. R. L. Lowenstein, *World Press Freedom, 1966* (Columbia, Mo.: Freedom of Information Center, 1967), publication No. 11.

2. D. E. Butler, "Why American Political Reporting Is Better than England's," *Harper's* (May 1963), 15–25.

3. *New York Times* (March 15, 1975).

4. *New York Times* (January 28, 1974).

5. Douglass Cater, *The Fourth Branch of Government* (Boston: Houghton Mifflin, 1959), 76; and William L. Rivers, "The Press as a Communication System," in *Handbook of Communication*, ed. Ithiel de Sola Pool *et al.* (Chicago: Rand McNally, 1973), 522–526.

6. Quoted in F. L. Mort, *American Journalism, 1690–1960,* 3d ed. (New York: Macmillan, 1962), 529, as cited in Rivers, *op. cit.*, 526.

7. Kiko Adatto, *Picture Perfect: The Art and Artifice of Public Image Making* (New York: Basic Books, 1993).

8. Edward Jay Epstein, *News from Nowhere: Television and the News* (New York: Random House, 1973), 37.

9. Allen H. Barton, "Consensus and Conflict among American Leaders," *Public Opinion Quarterly* 38 (Winter 1974–1975): 507–530.

10. Paul H. Weaver, "The New Journalism and the Old—Thoughts after Watergate," *The Public Interest* (Spring 1974), 67–88.

11. William C. Adams, "Media Coverage of Campaign '84: A Preliminary Report," *Public Opinion* (April–May 1984), 9–13.

12. Near v. Minnesota, 283 U.S. 697 (1931).

13. *New York Times* v. United States, 403 U.S. 713 (1971).

14. *New York Times* v. Sullivan, 376 U.S. 254 (1964).

15. Miami Herald Publishing Co. v. Tornillo, 418 U.S. 241 (1974).

16. Yates v. United States, 354 U.S. 298 (1957).

17. Branzburg v. Hayes, 408 U.S. 665 (1972).

18. Zurcher v. *Stanford Daily,* 436 U.S. 547 (1978),

overturned by the Privacy Protection Act of 1980 (P.L. 96–440).

19. *National Journal* (April 16, 1983), 787.

20. Benjamin I. Page, "The Media As Political Actors," *PS: Political Science & Politics,* March 1996, p. 21.

21. Thomas E. Patterson and Robert D. McClure, *The Unseeing Eye: The Myth of Television Power in National Elections* (New York: Putnam, 1976); and Herbert Asher, *Presidential Elections and American Politics* (Homewood, Ill.: Dorsey Press, 1976), 239–240 (and studies cited therein).

22. David O. Sears and Richard E. Whitney, "Political Persuasion," in Pool, *op. cit.,* 253–289.

23. Robert S. Erickson, "The Influence of Newspaper Endorsements in Presidential Elections: The Case of 1964," *American Journal of Political Science* 20 (May 1976): 207–233.

24. Maxwell E. McCombs and Donald R. Shaw, "The Agenda Setting Function of the Mass Media," *Public Opinion Quarterly* 36 (Summer 1972): 176–187; Shanto Iyengar and Donald R. Kinder, *News That Matters* (Chicago: University of Chicago Press, 1987).

25. G. Ray Funkhouser, "The Issues of the Sixties," *Public Opinion Quarterly* 37 (Spring 1973): 62–75.

26. Joseph Wagner, "Media Do Make a Difference: The Differential Impact of Mass Media in the 1976 Presidential Race," *American Journal of Political Science* 27 (August 1983): 407–430.

27. Benjamin I. Page, Robert Y. Shapiro, and Glenn R. Dempsey, "What Moves Public Opinion?" *American Political Science Review* 81 (March 1987): 23–43.

28. George Jergens, "Theodore Roosevelt and the Press," *Daedalus* (Fall 1982), 113–133; and Henry Fairlie, "The Rise of the Press Secretary," *New Republic* (March 18, 1978), 20–23.

29. Michael J. Robinson, "A Twentieth Century Medium in a Nineteenth Century Legislature: The Effects of Television on the American Congress," in *Congress in Change,* ed. Norman J. Ornstein (New York: Praeger, 1975), 240–261.

30. S. Robert Lichter and Stanley Rothman, "Media and Business Elites," *Public Opinion* (October–November 1981), 42–46.

31. Robert Lichter, "Consistently Liberal: But Does It Matter?," unpublished draft paper, forthcoming in *Media Critic,* p. 26.

32. Michael J. Robinson, "Just How Liberal Is the News? 1980 Revisited," *Public Opinion* (February–March 1983), 55–60; Maura Clancey and Michael J. Robinson, "The Media in Campaign '84: General Election Coverage," *Public Opinion* (December–January 1985); Elizabeth Kolbet, "Maybe the Media Did Treat Bush Harshly," *The New York Times* (November 22, 1992), E2.

33. Peter Braestrup, *Big Story* (Boulder, Col.: Westview Press, 1977), 2 vols.

Chapter 11 *Congress*

1. *Congressional Quarterly Weekly,* January 7, 1995, p. 18.

2. H. Douglas Price, "Careers and Committees in the American Congress," in *The History of Parliamentary Behavior,* ed. William O. Aydelotte (Princeton, N.J.: Princeton University Press, 1977), 28–62; John F. Bibby, Thomas E. Mann, and Norman J. Ornstein, *Vital Statistics on Congress, 1980* (Washington, D.C.: American Enterprise Institute, 1980), 53–54; Thomas E. Cavanaugh, "The Dispersion of Authority in the House of Representatives," *Political Science Quarterly* 97 (1982–1983): 625–626; *Congressional Quarterly Weekly Reports.*

3. David R. Mayhew, *Congress: The Electoral Connection* (New Haven, Conn.: Yale University Press, 1974); Bibby, Mann, and Ornstein, *op. cit.,* 14–15.

4. Mayhew, *op. cit.;* Morris P. Fiorina, *Congress: Keystone of the Washington Establishment* (New Haven, Conn.: Yale University Press, 1977).

5. Rhodes Cook, "House Republicans Scored a Quiet Victory in '92," *Congressional Quarterly* (April 17, 1993), 966.

6. Bruce E. Cain and David Butler, "Redrawing District Lines: What's Going On and What's At Stake," *The American Enterprise* (July/August 1991), 37.

7. Gary C. Jacobson, "The Persistence of Democratic House Majorities: Structure or Politics," paper delivered at the 1990 Annual Meeting of the American Political Science Association (San Francisco, California, August 30–September 2, 1990): 2.

8. Wesberry v. Sanders, 376 U.S. 1 (1964).

9. Linda Greenhouse, "Court Questions Districts Drawn To Aid Minorities," *New York Times* (June 29, 1993), A1, A12.

10. Dave Kaplan, "Constitutional Doubt is Thrown on Bizarre-Shaped Districts," *Congressional Quarterly* (July 3, 1993), 1761–1763.

11. John Leo, "Electioneering By Race" *U.S. News and World Report* (September 28, 1992), 33.

12. Kaplan, *op. cit.;* Greenhouse, *op. cit.*

13. Holly Idelson, "Supreme Court Considers Racially Conscious Map," *Congressional Quarterly* (April 24, 1993), 1034; Kaplan, *op. cit.;* Greenhouse, *op. cit.*

14. Hannah F. Pitkin, *The Concept of Representation* (Berkeley: University of California Press, 1967).

15. Carol M. Swain, *Black Faces, Black Interests: The Representation of African-Americans in Congress* (Cambridge, Mass.: Harvard University Press, 1993), 207.

16. Richard F. Fenno, Jr., "U.S. House Members and Their Constituencies: An Exploration," *American Political Science Review* 71 (September 1977), 883–917, esp. 914.

17. John A. Ferejohn, *Pork Barrel Politics* (Stanford, Calif.: Stanford University Press, 1974).

18. Douglas Arnold, *Congress and the Bureaucracy* (New Haven, Conn.: Yale University Press, 1979).

19. *Congressional Quarterly Weekly Report,* December 3, 1994, pp. 3430–3435.

20. In 1993, the 103rd Congress also contained a lot of newly elected Democratic members eager to change House rules. But they voted for the old rules and procedures because that is what their party leaders wanted.

21. Barbara Sinclair, *The Transformation of the United States Senate* (Baltimore, Md.: Johns Hopkins University Press, 1989).

22. Norman J. Ornstein, Thomas E. Mann, and Michael J. Malbin, *Vital Statistics on Congress, 1995–1996* (Washington, D.C.: Congressional Quarterly Press, 1996), pp. 199–200.

23. Gary C. Cox and Matthew D. McCubbins, *Legislative Leviathan* (Berkeley: University of California Press, 1993); David W. Rhode, *Parties and Leaders in the Postreform House* (Chicago: University of Chicago Press, 1991).

24. Susan Webb Hammond, "Congressional Caucuses in the 104th Congress," draft chapter for Lawrence Dodd and Bruce Oppenheimer, eds., *Congress Reconsidered* (Washington, D.C.: Congressional Quarterly Press, 1997), p. 6. We are most grateful to her for permitting us to draw on this chapter prior to its publication. The remainder of this section on caucuses is drawn directly from her work.

25. *Ibid.,* p. 34.

26. Steven S. Smith, "Revolution in the House: Why Don't We Do It on the Floor?" discussion paper No. 5 (Washington, D.C.: Brookings Institution, September 1986).

27. Richard F. Fenno, Jr., *Congressmen in Committees* (Boston: Little, Brown, 1973).

28. Bibby, Mann, and Ornstein, *op cit.,* 65–74.

29. Fiorina, *op cit.*

30. Bibby, Mann, and Ornstein, *op. cit.* 60.

31. Michael J. Malbin, "Delegation, Deliberation, and the New Role of Congressional Staff," in *The New Congress,* ed. Thomas E. Mann and Norman J. Ornstein (Washington, D.C.: American Enterprise Institute, 1981), 134–177, esp. 170–171.

32. Lawrence H. Chamberlain, "The President, Congress, and Legislation," in *The Presidency,* ed. Aaron Wildavsky (Boston: Little, Brown, 1969), 444–445; Ronald C. Moe and Steven C. Teel, "Congress as a Policy-Maker: A Necessary Reappraisal," *Political Science Quarterly* 85 (September 1970), 443–470.

33. Richard E. Cohen, "Challenging the House's Traffic Cop," *The National Journal* (April 4, 1993), 1002.

34. Thomas E. Mann and Norman J. Ornstein, *Renewing Congress: A Second Report* (Washington, D.C.: American Enterprise Institute, 1993), p. 49.

35. Malcolm E. Jewell and Samuel C. Patterson, *The Legislative Process in the United States,* 3d ed. (New York: Random House, 1977), 439.

36. Warren E. Miller and Donald E. Stokes, "Constituency Influence in Congress," in *Elections and the Political Order,* ed. Angus Campbell *et al.* (New York: Wiley, 1966), 359.

37. John E. Jackson, *Constituencies and Leaders in Congress* (Cambridge, Mass.: Harvard University Press, 1974).

38. Jerrold E. Schneider, *Ideological Coalitions in Congress* (Westport, Conn.: Greenwood Press, 1979), 134, 195.

39. Michael Foley, *The New Senate: Liberal Influence on a Conservative Institution, 1959–1972*

(New Haven, Conn.: Yale University Press, 1980), 242.

40. Based on results of interviews with one thousand randomly selected Americans conducted by the American Talk Issues Foundation, March 10–15, 1993.

41. As quoted in Edward L. Lascher *et al.,* "Policy Views, Constituency Pressure, and Congressional Action on Flag Burning," *Public Choice* 6 (1993), 90.

42. *Ibid.,* 98.

43. Survey by NBC News/*Wall Street Journal,* April 11–14, 1992, as reported in *The American Enterprise* (January/February 1993), 97.

44. Michael J. Malbin and Gerald Benjamin, eds., *Limiting Legislative Terms* (Washington, D.C.: Congressional Quarterly Press, 1992).

45. *Decisionmaking in the Federal Government: The Wallace S. Sayre Model,* 20–21.

46. Steve Goldstein, "All-Star Tickets Find Their Way to Congress," *The Philadelphia Inquirer* (July 14, 1993), A1, A8.

47. Thomas E. Mann and Norman J. Ornstein, *Renewing Congress: A Second Report* (Washington, D.C.: Brookings Institution and American Enterprise Institute, 1993), 71–72.

48. As reported in *New York Times* editorial, "Postmark Politics," July 13, 1993, p. A18.

49. Mann and Ornstein, *op. cit.,* 72.

50. *Ibid.,* 18.

51. *Ibid.,* 15–17.

52. *Ibid.,* 15–31.

53. *Ibid.,* 68–69.

54. *Ibid.,* 69.

55. Dennis F. Thompson, *Ethics in Congress: From Individual to Institutional Corruption* (Washington, D.C.: Brookings Institution, 1995), p. 191.

56. *Ibid.,* p. 3.

Chapter 12 *The Presidency*

1. Jean Blondel, *An Introduction to Comparative Government* (New York: Praeger, 1969), as cited in Nelson W. Polsby, "Legislatures," in *Handbook of Political Science,* ed. Fred I. Greenstein and Nelson W. Polsby (Reading, Mass.: Addison-Wesley, 1975), vol. 5, 275.

2. Donald F. Kettl, *Deficit Politics: Public Budgeting in Its Institutional and Historical Context* (New York: Macmillan, 1992), 13.

3. Morris P. Fiorina, *Divided Government* (New York: Macmillan, 1992), 86–111.

4. David Mayhew, *Divided We Govern: Party Control, Lawmaking, and Investigations, 1946–1990* (New Haven, CT: Yale University Press, 1991), 76.

5. Mark A. Peterson, *Legislating Together: The White House and Congress from Eisenhower to Reagan* (Cambridge: Harvard University Press, 1990).

6. Richard E. Cohen, *Washington At Work: Back Rooms and Clean Air* (New York: Macmillan, 1992), 154–155.

7. *Ibid.,* 169.

8. Kettl, *op. cit.,* 138.

9. Woodrow Wilson, *Congressional Government*

(New York: Meridian Books, 1956), 167–168, 170. (First published in 1885.)

10. Stephen Hess, *Organizing the Presidency* (Washington, D.C.: Brookings Institution, 1976), 3; R. W. Apple, "Clinton's Refocusing," *The New York Times* (May 6, 1993), A22; Michael K. Frisby, "Power Switch," *The Wall Street Journal* (March 26, 1993), A1, A7.

11. David T. Stanley *et al., Men Who Govern* (Washington, D.C.: Brookings Institution, 1967), 41–42, 50.

12. Daniel J. Elazar, "Which Road to the Presidency?" in *The Presidency,* ed. Aaron Wildavsky (Boston: Little, Brown, 1969), 340.

13. James David Barber, *The Presidential Character: Predicting Performance in the White House,* 3d ed. (Englewood Cliffs, N.J.: Prentice-Hall, 1985).

14. Richard E. Neustadt, *Presidential Power,* rev. ed. (New York: Wiley, 1976), ch. 4.

15. Walter D. Burnham, "Insulation and Responsiveness in Congressional Elections," *Political Science Quarterly* 90 (Fall 1975): 412–413; George C. Edwards III, *Presidential Influence in Congress* (San Francisco: Freeman, 1980), 70–78; Warren E. Miller, "Presidential Coattails: A Study in Political Myth and Methodology," *Public Opinion Quarterly* 19 (Winter 1955–1956): 368; and Miller, "The Motivational Basis for Straight and Split Ticket Voting," *American Political Science Review* 51 (June 1957): 293–312.

16. Edwards, *op. cit.,* 86–100; Douglas Rivers and Nancy L. Rose, "Passing the President's Program: Public Opinion and Presidential Influence in Congress," paper delivered at the 1981 annual meeting of the Midwestern Political Science Association.

17. Marbury v. Madison, 1 Cranch 137 (1803).

18. United States v. Nixon, 418 U.S. 683 (1974).

19. Joseph A. Califano, Jr., *A Presidential Nation* (New York: Norton, 1975), 51.

20. Marcus Cunliffe, *American Presidents and the Presidency* (New York: American Heritage Press/McGraw-Hill, 1972), 63, 65.

21. *Ibid.,* 214.

22. Adapted from Paul C. Light, *The President's Agenda* (Baltimore, Md.: Johns Hopkins University Press, 1982), 217–225.

Chapter 13 *The Bureaucracy*

1. Charles E. Lindblom, *Politics and Markets* (New York: Basic Books, 1977), 114.

2. Article II, section 2, para. 2.

3. Article II, section 3.

4. Calculated from data in *Historical Statistics of the United States: Colonial Times to 1970* (Washington, D.C.: Government Printing Office, 1975), vol. 2, 1102–1103.

5. Panama Refining Co. v. Ryan, 293 U.S. 388 (1935).

6. Hampton Jr. & Co. v. United States, 276 U.S. 394 (1928).

7. Edward S. Corwin, *The Constitution and What It Means Today,* 13th ed. (Princeton, N.J.: Princeton University Press, 1973), 151.

8. Bruce D. Porter, "Parkinson's Law Revisited: War and the Growth of American Government," *Public Interest* (Summer 1980), 50–68.

9. See the cases cited in Corwin, *op. cit.,* 8.

10. *U.S. Statutes,* vol. 84, sec. 799 (1970).

11. *Historical Statistics of the United States,* vol. 2, 1107.

12. *Statistical Abstract of the United States, 1975* (Washington, D.C.: Government Printing Office, 1975), 242.

13. Donald F. Kettl *et al., Civil Service Reform: Building a Government That Works* (Washington, D.C.: Brookings Institution, 1996), p. 18.

14. *Ibid.,* p. 15.

15. Hugh Heclo, "Issue Networks and the Executive Establishment," in *The New American Political System,* ed. Anthony King (Washington, D.C.: American Enterprise Institute, 1978), 87–124.

16. *National Journal* (July 18, 1981), 1296–1299.

17. Quoted in Hugh Heclo, *A Government of Strangers* (Washington, D.C.: Brookings Institute, 1977), 225.

18. J. Donald Kingsley, *Representative Bureaucracy* (Yellow Springs, Ohio: Antioch Press, 1944).

19. See Richard P. Nathan, *The Plot That Failed: Nixon and the Administrative Presidency* (New York: Wiley, 1975).

20. Stanley Rothman and S. Robert Lichter, "How Liberal Are Bureaucrats?" *Regulation* (November–December, 1983), 17–18.

21. Kenneth Meier and Lloyd Nigro, "Representative Bureaucracy and Policy References: A Study of the Attitudes of Federal Executives," *Public Administration Review* 36 (July–August 1976): 458–467; Bernard Mennis, *American Foreign Policy Officials* (Columbus, Ohio: Ohio State University Press, 1971).

22. Joel D. Aberbach and Bert A. Rockman, "Clashing Beliefs within the Executive Branch: The Nixon Administration Bureaucracy," *American Political Science Review* 70 (June 1976): 456–468.

23. David Stockman, *The Triumph of Politics* (New York: Harper and Row, 1986).

24. James Q. Wilson, *Bureaucracy* (New York: Basic Books, 1989), ch. 6.

25. Heclo, "Issue Networks and the Executive Establishment," *op. cit.,* 87–124.

26. Richard F. Fenno, Jr., *The Power of the Purse* (Boston: Little, Brown, 1966), 450, 597.

27. John E. Schwartz and L. Earl Shaw, *The United States Congress in Comparative Perspective* (Hinsdale, Ill.: Dryden Press, 1976), 262–263; *National Journal* (July 4, 1981), 1211–1214.

28. Immigration and Naturalization Service v. Chadha, 103 S. Ct. 2764 (1983); Maine v. Thiboutot, 100 S. Ct. 2502 (1980).

29. See cases cited in Corwin, *op. cit.,* 22.

30. Steven Kelman, "The Grace Commission: How Much Waste in Government?" *Public Interest* (Winter 1985), 62–87.

31. Daniel Katz *et al., Bureaucratic Encounters* (Ann Arbor: Survey Research Center, University of Michigan, 1975), 63–69, 118–120, 184–188.

32. *From Red Tape to Results: Creating a Government That Works Better and Costs Less,* report

of the National Performance Review, Vice President Al Gore, September 7, 1993.

Chapter 14   *The Judiciary*

1. Henry J. Abraham, *The Judicial Process,* 3d ed. (New York: Oxford University Press, 1975), 279–280.
2. Robert G. McCloskey, *The American Supreme Court* (Chicago: University of Chicago Press, 1960), 27.
3. Marbury v. Madison, 5 U.S. 137 (1803); and McCulloch v. Maryland, 17 U.S. 316 (1819).
4. Martin v. Hunter's Lessee, 14 U.S. 304 (1816); and Cohens v. Virginia, 19 U.S. (1821).
5. Gibbons v. Ogden, 22 U.S. (1824).
6. Quoted in Albert J. Beveridge, *The Life of John Marshall* (Boston: Houghton Mifflin, 1919), vol. 4, 551.
7. Dred Scott v. Sandford, 60 U.S. 393 (1857).
8. Abraham, *op. cit.,* 286.
9. *In re* Debs, 158 U.S. 564 (1895).
10. Pollock v. Farmers' Loan & Trust Co., 157 U.S. 429 (1895).
11. United States v. Knight, 156 U.S. 1 (1895).
12. Cincinnati, N.O. & T.P. Railway Co. v. Interstate Commerce Commission, 162 U.S. 184 (1896).
13. Hammer v. Dagenhart, 247 U.S. 251 (1918).
14. Lochner v. New York, 198 U.S. 45 (1905).
15. McCloskey, *op. cit.,* 151.
16. Munn v. Illinois, 94 U.S. 113 (1877).
17. Dayton-Goose Creek Railway Co. v. United States, 263 U.S. 456 (1924).
18. Atchison, Topeka, and Santa Fe Railroad Co. v. Matthews, 174 U.S. 96 (1899).
19. Mugler v. Kansas, 123 U.S. 623 (1887).
20. St. Louis Consolidated Coal Co. v. Illinois, 185 U.S. 203 (1902).
21. New York Central Railroad Co. v. White, 243 U.S. 188 (1917).
22. German Alliance Insurance Co. v. Lewis, 233 U.S. 389 (1914).
23. Morton Keller, *Affairs of State* (Cambridge, Mass.: Harvard University Press, 1977), 369. See also Mary Cornelia Porter, "That Commerce Shall Be Free: A New Look at the Old Laissez-Faire Court," in *The Supreme Court Review,* ed. Philip B. Kurland (Chicago: University of Chicago Press, 1976), 135–159.
24. Chief of Capitol Police v. Jeannette Rankin Brigade, 409 U.S. 972 (1972).
25. Aptheker v. Secretary of State, 378 U.S. 500 (1964).
26. Trop v. Dulles, 356 U.S. 86 (1958); Afroyim v. Rusk, 387 U.S. 253 (1967); and Schneider v. Rusk, 377 U.S. 163 (1964).
27. Lamont v. Postmaster General, 381 U.S. 301 (1965); and Blount v. Rizzi, 400 U.S. 410 (1971).
28. Richardson v. Davis, 409 U.S. 1069 (1972); U.S. Department of Agriculture v. Murry, 413 U.S. 508 (1973); Jimenez v. Weinberger, 417 U.S. 628 (1974); and Washington v. Legrant, 394 U.S. 618 (1969).
29. U.S. v. Lopez, 115 S. Ct. 1624 (1995).
30. Seminole Tribe v. Florida, 116 S. Ct. 1114 (1996).

31. Robert A. Carp and C. I. Rowland, *Policymaking and Politics in the Federal District Courts* (Knoxville, Tenn.: University of Tennessee Press, 1983), 38; Sheldon Goldman, "Voting Behavior on the United States Courts of Appeals, Revisited," *American Political Science Review* 69 (1975): 491–506; C. Heal Tate, "Personal Attribute Models of the Voting Behavior of U.S. Supreme Court Justices," *American Political Science Review* 75 (1981): 355–367.
32. Henry J. Abraham, *Justices and Presidents* (New York: Oxford University Press, 1974), 75.
33. United States v. Lanza, 260 U.S. 377 (1922). Cf. Abbate v. United States, 359 U.S. 187 (1959) and Bartkus v. Illinois, 359 U.S. 121 (1989).
34. Gideon v. Wainwright, 372 U.S. 335 (1963). The story is told in Anthony Lewis, *Gideon's Trumpet* (New York: Random House, 1964).
35. Erwin Griswold, "Rationing Justice: The Supreme Court's Case Load and What the Court Does Not Do," *Cornell Law Review* 60 (1975): 335–354.
36. Paul A. Freund, *Report of the Study Group on the Caseload of the Supreme Court* (Washington, D.C.: Federal Judicial Center, 1972).
37. Alyeska Pipeline Service Co. v. Wilderness Society, 421 U.S. 240 (1975).
38. Flast v. Cohen, 392 U.S. 83 (1968), which modified the earlier Frothingham v. Mellon, 262 U.S. 447 (1923); United States v. Richardson, 418 U.S. 166 (1974).
39. Brown v. Board of Education of Topeka, 347 U.S. 483 (1954).
40. Baker v. Carr, 369 U.S. 186 (1962).
41. See Louise Weinberg, "A New Judicial Federalism?" *Daedalus* (Winter 1978), 129–141.
42. "The Supreme Court, 1989 Term" *Harvard Law Review* 104 (1990): 360. See also Lawrence Baum, *The Supreme Court,* 2d ed. (Washington, D.C.: Congressional Quarterly Press, 1985), 138–139.
43. "The Supreme Court, 1989 Term," *op. cit.,* 360.
44. Quoted in Abraham, *The Judicial Process, op. cit.,* 330.
45. A. P. Blaustein and A. H. Field, "Overruling Opinions in the Supreme Court," *Michigan Law Review* 47 (1958): 151; Henry J. Abraham, *The Judicial Process,* 4th ed. (New York: Oxford University Press, 1980), 349.
46. Colegrove v. Green, 328 U.S. 549 (1946).
47. The Court abandoned the "political question" doctrine in Baker v. Carr, 369 U.S. 186 (1962), and began to change congressional-district apportionment in Wesberry v. Sanders, 376 U.S. 1 (1964).
48. Donald L. Horowitz, *The Courts and Social Policy* (Washington, D.C.: Brookings Institution, 1977), 6.
49. Gates v. Collier, 349 F. Supp. 881 (1972).
50. Lau v. Nichols, 414 U.S. 563 (1974).
51. *International Directory of Bar Associations,* 4th ed. (Chicago: American Bar Foundation, 1983).
52. Joel B. Grossman and Austin Sarat, "Litigation in the Federal Courts: A Comparative Perspective," *Law and Society Review* 9 (Winter 1975): 321–346.

53. Administrative Office of the U.S. Courts, *Annual Report, 1988,* 109.
54. Jack W. Peltason, *Fifty-Eight Lonely Men: Southern Federal Judges and School Desegregation* (New York: Harcourt Brace, 1961).
55. Anthony Patridge and William B. Eldridge, *The Second Circuit Sentencing Study* (Washington, D.C.: Federal Judicial Center, 1974).
56. Abington School District v. Schempp, 374 U.S. 203 (1963).
57. Robert H. Birkby, "The Supreme Court and the Bible Belt," *Midwest Journal of Political Science* 10 (1966): 3.
58. *Ibid.,* 41–42.
59. *Ibid.,* 332
60. *Ex parte* McCardle, 74 U.S. 506 (1869).
61. Walter F. Murphy, *Congress and the Court* (Chicago: University of Chicago Press, 1962); and C. Herman Pritchett, *Congress versus the Supreme Court* (Minneapolis: University of Minnesota Press, 1961).
62. Gregory A. Caldeira, "Neither the Purse Nor the Sword: Dynamics of Public Confidence in the U.S. Supreme Court," *American Political Science Review* 80 (1986): 1209–1226. See also Joseph T. Tannenhaus and Walter F. Murphy, "Patterns of Public Support for the Supreme Court: A Panel Study," *Journal of Politics* 43 (1981): 24–39.

Chapter 15   *The Policy-Making Process*

1. E. E. Schattschneider, *The Semisovereign People* (New York: Holt, Rinehart and Winston, 1960), 68.
2. Jack L. Walker, "Setting the Agenda in the U.S. Senate: A Theory of Problem Selection," *British Journal of Political Science* 7 (1977): 343, 441.
3. *Statistical Abstract of the United States, 1975* (Washington, D.C.: Government Printing Office, 1975), 342–343, 349.
4. Alexis de Tocqueville, *The Old Regime and the French Revolution,* trans. Gilbert Stuart (Garden City, N.Y.: Doubleday Anchor Books, 1955), 176–177. (First published in 1856.)
5. David O. Sears and J. B. McConahay, *The Politics of Violence* (Boston: Houghton Mifflin, 1973). Compare Abraham H. Miller *et al.,* "The New Urban Blacks," *Ethnicity* 3 (1976): 338–367.
6. Daniel Patrick Moynihan, *Maximum Feasible Misunderstanding* (New York: Free Press, 1969), ch. 2.
7. Nelson W. Polsby, "Goodbye to the Senate's Inner Club," in *Congress in Change: Evolution and Reform,* ed. Norman J. Ornstein (New York: Praeger, 1975), 208–215.
8. *Federalist* No. 62.
9. Walker, *op. cit.,* 434, 439, 441.
10. This is a revised version of a theory originally presented in James Q. Wilson, *Political Organizations* (New York: Basic Books, 1973), ch. 16. There are other ways of classifying public policies, notably that of Theodore J. Lowi, "American Business, Public Policy, Case Studies, and Political Theory," *World Politics* 16 (July 1964).

11. Donald F. Kettl, *Sharing Power: Public Governance and Private Markets* (Washington, D.C.: Brookings Institution, 1993). Lawrence J. Hajna, "Superfund: Costly Program Under Fire," *Courier-Post* (February 13, 1994), 6A.

12. Edward S. Greenberg, *Serving the Few: Corporate Capitalism and the Bias of Government Policy* (New York: Wiley, 1974).

13. Charles E. Lindblom, *Politics and Markets* (New York: Basic Books, 1977).

14. Joseph Schumpeter, *Capitalism, Socialism, and Democracy* (New York: Harper & Row, 1950).

15. Louis Galambos, *The Public Image of Big Business in America, 1880–1940* (Baltimore, Md.: Johns Hopkins University Press, 1975).

16. Suzanne Weaver, *Decision to Prosecute: Organization and Public Policy in the Antitrust Division* (Cambridge, Mass.: MIT Press, 1977); Robert H. Bork, *The Antitrust Paradox* (New York: Basic Books, 1978).

17. Richard A. Posner, *Antitrust Law: An Economic Perspective* (Chicago: University of Chicago Press, 1976), 25.

18. Alan J. Seltzer, "Woodrow Wilson as 'Corporate-Liberal': Toward a Reconsideration of Left Revisionist Historiography," *Western Political Quarterly* 30 (June 1977): 183–212.

19. Weaver, *op. cit.*, and Robert A. Katzmann, *Regulatory Bureaucracy: The Federal Trade Commission and Antitrust Policy* (Cambridge, Mass.: MIT Press, 1980).

20. Charles R. Plott, "Occupational Self-Regulation: A Case Study of the Oklahoma Dry Cleaners," *Journal of Law and Economics* 8 (October 1965): 195–222.

21. Paul H. MacAvoy, ed., *Federal Milk Marketing Orders and Price Supports* (Washington, D.C.: American Enterprise Institute, 1977).

22. *Ibid.*, 111.

23. *Congressional Quarterly Weekly Report* (April 21, 1990), 1184–1188.

24. Paul J. Halpern, "Consumer Politics and Corporate Behavior: The Case of Automobile Safety" (unpublished Ph.D. dissertation, Harvard University, 1972).

25. Upton Sinclair, *The Jungle* (New York: Doubleday, Page and Co., 1906).

26. Mark V. Nadel, *The Politics of Consumer Protection* (Indianapolis, Ind.: Bobbs-Merrill, 1971), 143–144.

27. Alfred A. Marcus, *Promise and Performance: Choosing and Implementing an Environmental Policy* (Westport, Conn.: Greenwood Press, 1980).

28. Nadel, *op. cit.*, 66–80.

29. Martha Derthick and Paul J. Quirk, *The Politics of Deregulation* (Washington, D.C.: Brookings Institution, 1985).

30. Executive Orders 11821 (1974), 12044 (1978), and 12291 (1981).

Chapter 16 Economic Policy

1. Edward R. Tufte, *Political Control of the Economy* (Princeton, N.J.: Princeton University Press, 1978), 84; Douglas A. Hibbs, Jr., "The Mass Public and Macroeconomic Performance: The Dynamics of Public Opinion toward Unemployment and Inflation," *American Journal of Political Science* 23 (1979): 705–731.

2. D. Roderick Kiewiet, *Macroeconomics and Micropolitics: The Electoral Effect of Economic Issues* (Chicago: University of Chicago Press, 1983); Morris P. Fiorina, "Economic Retrospective Voting in American National Elections: A Micro-Analysis," *American Journal of Political Science* 22 (1978): 426–443; Donald R. Kinder and D. Roderick Kiewiet, "Sociotropic Politics: The American Case," *British Journal of Political Science* 11 (1981): 129–161.

3. *New York Times–*CBS News poll cited in Douglas A. Hibbs, Jr., "President Reagan's Mandate from the 1980 Elections: A Shift to the Right?" *American Politics Quarterly* 10 (1982): 387–420.

4. Hibbs, "The Mass Public . . . ," *op. cit.*

5. *Ibid.*

6. Kiewiet, *op. cit.*

7. Michael S. Lewis-Beck, "Comparative Economic Voting: Britain, France, Germany, Italy," *American Journal of Political Science* 30 (1986): 315–346.

8. Douglas A. Hibbs, Jr., "Political Parties and Macroeconomic Policy," *American Political Science Review* 71 (1977): 1467–1487.

9. Kiewiet, *op. cit.*, 69.

10. *Congressional Quarterly Weekly Report* (November 3, 1990), 3710–3717; *National Journal* (November 3, 1990), 2674.

11. Pollock v. Farmers' Loan & Trust Co., 157 U.S. 429, 158 U.S. 601 (1895).

12. NBC News/*Wall Street Journal* poll, as reported in *National Journal* (July 12, 1986), 1741.

Chapter 17 Social Welfare

1. For a general discussion see Charles E. Gilbert, "Welfare Policy," in *Handbook of Political Science*, ed. Fred I. Greenstein and Nelson W. Polsby (Reading, Mass.: Addison-Wesley, 1975), vol. 6, ch. 4.

2. Congressional Quarterly, *Congress and the Nation, 1945–1964* (Washington, D.C.: Congressional Quarterly Service, 1965), 1225.

3. Harold E. Raynes, *Social Security in Britain: A History* (London: Pitman, 1960), ch. 18. See also Hugh Heclo, *Modern Social Politics in Britain and Sweden* (New Haven: Yale University Press, 1974).

4. Histories of the 1935 act include Edwin E. Witte, *The Development of the Social Security Act* (Madison: University of Wisconsin Press, 1962). A different view, offering a neo-Marxist interpretation of the act, can be found in Frances Fox Piven and Richard A. Cloward, *Regulating the Poor* (New York: Pantheon, 1971).

5. The development of Medicare is described in Sundquist, *op. cit.*, and Theodore Marmor, "Doctors, Politics, and Health Insurance for the Aged: The Enactment of Medicare," in *Cases in Contemporary American Government*, ed. Allan Sindler (Boston: Little, Brown, 1969).

6. Michael Harrington, *The Other America* (Baltimore, Md.: Penguin Books, 1962).

7. Michael E. Schiltz, *Public Attitudes toward Social Security, 1935–1965*, Research Report No. 3, Social Security Administration, U.S. Department of Health, Education, and Welfare (Washington, D.C.: Government Printing Office, 1970), 36, 98, 128, 140.

8. Alicia H. Munnell, *The Future of Social Security* (Washington, D.C.: Brookings Institution, 1977), appendix.

9. Martha Derthick, "How Easy Votes on Social Security Came to an End," *Public Interest* (Winter 1979), 96.

10. Schiltz, *Public Attitudes Toward Social Security, op. cit.*, ch. 4, pp. 154–165.

11. Charles Murray, *Losing Ground: American Social Policy, 1950–1980* (New York: Basic Books, 1984). A critique of Murray is William J. Wilson, *The Truly Disadvantaged* (Chicago: University of Chicago Press, 1987), esp. chs. 3 and 4.

12. *Congressional Quarterly Weekly Report* (March 26, 1983), 596–600.

13. Congressional Quarterly, *Congress and the Nation*, Vol. VII, 1985–1988 (Washington, D.C.: Congressional Quarterly, 1990), 551.

14. G. J. Borjas, R. B. Freeman, and L. F. Katz, "Labor Market Effects of Immigration and Trade," in George J. Borjas and Richard B. Freeman, *Immigration and the Work Force* (Chicago: University of Chicago Press, 1992), 242–243.

Chapter 18 Civil Liberties

1. Zamora v. Pomeroy, 639 F. 2d 662 (1981); Goss v. Lopez, 419 U.S. 565 (1975); Tinker v. Des Moines Community School District, 393 U.S. 503 (1969); Smith v. Goguen, 415 U.S. 566 (1974); New Jersey v. T.L.O. 469 U.S. 325 (1985).

2. Sheppard v. Maxwell, 384 U.S. 333 (1966); New York Times Co. v. United States, 403 U.S. 713 (1971); and Kunz v. New York, 340 U.S. 290 (1951).

3. William Blackstone, *Commentaries*, vol. IV (1765), 151–152.

4. Jefferson's remarks are from a letter to Abigail Adams (quoted in Walter Berns, *The First Amendment and the Future of American Democracy* [New York: Basic Books, 1976], 82) and from a letter to Thomas McKean, governor of Pennsylvania, February 19, 1803 (Paul L. Ford, ed., *The Writings of Thomas Jefferson: 1801–1806*, vol. 8 [New York: Putnam, 1897], 218).

5. Schenck v. United States, 249 U.S. 47 (1919), 52.

6. Gitlow v. New York, 268 U.S. 652 (1925), 666.

7. Fiske v. Kansas, 274 U.S. 380 (1927); Stromberg v. California, 283 U.S. 359 (1931); Near v. Minnesota, 283 U.S. 697 (1931); De Jonge v. Oregon, 299 U.S. 353 (1937).

8. Dennis v. United States, 341 U.S. 494 (1951), 510ff. The test was first formulated by Judge Learned Hand of the Court of Appeals: see Dennis v. United States, 183 F.2d 201 (1950), 212.

9. Yates v. United States, 354 U.S. 298 (1957).

10. Brandenburg v. Ohio, 395 U.S. 444 (1969).

11. Village of Skokie v. National Socialist Party, 432 U.S. 43 (1977); 366 N.E.2d 349 (1977); and 373 N.E.2d 21 (1978).
12. R.A.V. v. City of St. Paul, 112 S. Ct. 2538 (1992).
13. Wisconsin v. Mitchell, No. 92–515 (1993).
14. C. Herman Pritchett, *Constitutional Civil Liberties* (Englewood Cliffs, N.J.: Prentice-Hall, 1984), 100.
15. *New York Times* v. Sullivan, 376 U.S. 254 (1964); but compare Time, Inc. v. Firestone, 424 U.S. 448 (1976).
16. Henry J. Abraham, *Freedom and the Court,* 4th ed. (New York: Oxford University Press, 1982), p. 193, fn 189.
17. Justice Stewart's famous remark was made in his concurring opinion in Jacobellis v. Ohio, 378 U.S. 184 (1964), 197.
18. Miller v. California, 413 U.S. 15 (1973).
19. Jenkins v. Georgia, 418 U.S. 153 (1974).
20. Schad v. Borough of Mt. Ephraim, 452 U.S. 61 (1981).
21. Barnes v. Glen Theatre, 111 S. Ct. 2456 (1991).
22. American Booksellers Association v. Hudnut, 771 F.2d 323 (1985), affirmed at 475 U.S. 1001 (1986).
23. Renton v. Playtime Theatres, 475 U.S. 41 (1986). See also Young v. American Mini-Theatres, Inc., 427 U.S. 50 (1976).
24. Revo v. American Civil Liberties Union, 95–511.
25. United States v. O'Brien, 391 U.S. 367 (1968).
26. Texas v. Johnson, 109 S. Ct. 2533 (1989).
27. The Court had earlier held unconstitutional statutes that made it illegal to mutilate the flag [Street v. New York, 394 U.S. 576 (1967)], deface the flag [Spence v. Washington, 418 U.S. 405 (1974)], or treat the flag contemptuously by, for example, sewing it to the seat of your pants [Smith v. Goguen, 415 U.S. 566 (1974)]. U.S. v. Eichman, 496 U.S. 310 (1990).
28. First National Bank of Boston v. Bellotti, 435 U.S. 765 (1978). 44 Liquormart v. Rhode Island, 116 S. Ct. 1495 (1996).
29. Federal Election Commission v. Massachusetts Citizens for Life, Inc., 479 U.S. 238 (1986).
30. Pacific Gas and Electric Co. v. Public Utilities Commission, 475 U.S. 1 (1986). Some limitations on corporate speech have been upheld, including a state law prohibiting a firm from spending money on candidates for elective office. Austin v. Michigan Chamber of Commerce, 100 S. Ct. 1391 (1990).
31. Board of Trustees of the State University of New York v. Fox, 492 U.S. 469 (1989).
32. Bates v. State Bar of Arizona, 433 U.S. 350 (1977); Edenfield v. Bane, 113 S. Ct. 1792 (1993).
33. Hazelwood School District v. Kuhlmeier, et al. 484 U.S. 260 (1988).
34. Murdock v. Pennsylvania, 319 U.S. 105 (1943).
35. Church of the Lukumi Babalu Aye v. City of Hialeah, No. 91–948 (1993).
36. Reynolds v. United States, 98 U.S. 145 (1878).
37. Jacobson v. Massachusetts, 197 U.S. 11 (1905).
38. Employment Division, Department of Human Resources of Oregon v. Smith, 110 S. Ct. 1595 (1990).
39. Society for Krishna Consciousness v. Lee, 112 S. Ct. 2701 (1992).
40. Welsh v. United States, 398 U.S. 333 (1970); Pritchett, *op. cit.,* 140–141.
41. Sherbert v. Verner, 374 U.S. 398 (1963); Wisconsin v. Yoder, 406 U.S. 205 (1972); Hobbie v. Unemployment Appeals Commission of Florida, 480 U.S. 136 (1987); Estate of Thornton v. Caldor, Inc., 472 U.S. 703 (1985).
42. Berns, *op. cit.*
43. Pritchett, *op.cit.,* 145–147
44. Everson v. Board of Education, 330 U.S. 1 (1947).
45. Engel v. Vitale, 370 U.S. 421 (1962).
46. Lubbock Independent School District v. Lubbock Civil Liberties Union, 669 F.2d 1038.
47. School District of Abington Township v. Schempp, 374 U.S. 203 (1963).
48. Lee v. Weisman, 112 S. Ct. 2649 (1992).
49. Epperson v. Arkansas, 393 U.S. 97 (1968); McLean v. Arkansas Board of Education, 529 F. Supp. 1255 (1982).
50. McCollum v. Board of Education, 333 U.S. 203 (1948); Zorach v. Clauson, 343 U.S. 306 (1952).
51. Tilton v. Richardson, 403 U.S. 672 (1971).
52. Board of Education v. Allen, 392 U.S. 236 (1968).
53. Walz v. Tax Commission, 397 U.S. 664 (1970).
54. Mueller v. Allen, 463 U.S. 388 (1983).
55. Zobrest v. Catalina Foothills School District, No. 92–94 (1993).
56. Lemon v. Kurtzman, 403 U.S. 602 (1971).
57. Committee for Public Education v. Nyquist, 413 U.S. 756 (1973).
58. Meek v. Pittenger, 421 U.S. 349 (1975) and Wolman v. Walter, 433 U.S. 229 (1977).
59. Edwards v. Aguillard, 482 U.S. 578 (1987); Board of Education of Kiryas Joel Village School v. Louis Grumet, 114 S. Ct. 2481 (1994).
60. Lemon v. Kurtzman, 403 U.S. 602 (1971).
61. Lynch v. Donnelly, 465 U.S. 668 (1984); Allegheny v. ACLU, 109 S. Ct. 3086 (1989).
62. Marsh v. Chambers, 492 U.S. 573 (1983).
63. Stephen R. Schlesinger, *Exclusionary Injustice: The Problem of Illegally Obtained Evidence* (New York: Dekker, 1975).
64. Yale Kamisar, "Does (Did) (Should) the Exclusionary Rule Rest on a 'Principled Basis' Rather Than an 'Empirical Proposition'?" *Creighton Law Review* 16 (1982–1983): 565–667.
65. Wolf v. Colorado, 338 U.S. 25 (1949).
66. Mapp v. Ohio, 367 U.S. 643 (1961).
67. Chimel v. California, 395 U.S. 752 (1969).
68. Washington v. Chrisman, 455 U.S. 1 (1982).
69. Oliver v. United States, 466 U.S. 170 (1984).
70. Arkansas v. Sanders, 442 U.S. 753 (1979); Robbins v. California, 453 U.S. 420 (1981).
71. United States v. Ross, 456 U.S. 798 (1982).
72. Winston v. Lee, 470 U.S. 753 (1985).
73. South Dakota v. Neville, 459 U.S. 553 (1983); Schmerber v. California, 384 U.S. 757 (1966).
74. United States v. Dunn, 480 U.S. 294 (1987); California v. Ciraolo, 476 U.S. 207 (1986); California v. Carney, 471 U.S. 386 (1985).
75. O'Connor v. Ortega, 480 U.S. 709 (1987).
76. Bowers v. Hardwick, 478 U.S. 186 (1986).
77. National Treasury Employees Union v. von Rabb, 489 U.S. 656 (1989); Skinner v. Railway Labor Executives' Association, 489 U.S. 602 (1989); Michigan v. Sitz, 496 U.S. 444 (1990).
78. Vernonia School District v. Acton, 115 S. Ct. 2386 (1995).
79. Escobedo v. Illinois, 378 U.S. 478 (1964); Miranda v. Arizona, 384 U.S. 436 (1966).
80. Malloy v. Hogan, 378 U.S. 1 (1964).
81. Miranda v. Arizona, 384 U.S. 436 (1966).
82. Gilbert v. California, 388 U.S. 263 (1967); Kirby v. Illinois, 406 U.S. 682 (1972).
83. Estelle v. Smith, 451 U.S. 454 (1981).
84. Brewer v. Williams, 430 U.S. 387 (1977).
85. Illinois v. Perkins, 496 U.S. 292 (1990).
86. Fare v. Michael C., 442 U.S. 707 (1979).
87. United States v. Leon, 468 U.S. 897 (1984); Massachusetts v. Sheppard, 468 U.S. 981 (1984).
88. New York v. Quarles, 467 U.S. 649 (1984); See also Arizona v. Fulminante, 111 S. Ct. 1246 (1991).
89. Nix v. Williams, 467 U.S. 431 (1984).

Chapter 19   *Civil Rights*

1. United States v. Carolene Products Co., 304 U.S. 144 (1938); San Antonio Independent School District v. Rodriguez, 411 U.S. 1 (1973).
2. Gunnar Myrdal, *An American Dilemma* (New York: Harper, 1944), ch. 27.
3. Richard Kluger, *Simple Justice* (New York: Random House/ Vintage Books, 1977), 89–90.
4. Paul B. Sheatsley, "White Attitudes toward the Negro," in *The Negro American,* ed. Talcott Parsons and Kenneth B. Clark (Boston: Houghton Mifflin, 1966), 305, 308, 317.
5. Strauder v. West Virginia, 100 U.S. 303 (1880).
6. Civil Rights Cases, 109 U.S. 3 (1883).
7. Plessy v. Ferguson, 163 U.S. 537 (1896).
8. Cumming v. Richmond County Board of Education, 175 U.S. 528 (1899).
9. Missouri *ex rel.* Gaines v. Canada, 305 U.S. 337 (1938).
10. Sipuel v. Board of Regents of the University of Oklahoma, 332 U.S. 631 (1948).
11. Sweatt v. Painter, 339 U.S. 629 (1950); McLaurin v. Oklahoma State Regents for Higher Education, 339 U.S. 637 (1950).
12. Brown v. Board of Education of Topeka, 347 U.S. 483 (1954).
13. Brown v. Board of Education of Topeka, 349 U.S. 294 (1955). This case is often referred to as "Brown II."
14. Frederick S. Mosteller and Daniel P. Moynihan, eds., *On Equality of Educational Opportunity* (New York: Random House, 1972), 60–62.
15. Brown v. Board of Education of Topeka, 347 U.S. 483 (1954).
16. C. Herman Pritchett, *Constitutional Civil Liberties* (Englewood Cliffs, N.J.: Prentice-Hall, 1984), 250–251, 261.
17. Green *et al.* v. County School Board of New Kent County, 391 U.S. 430 (1968).

18. Swann v. Charlotte-Mecklenburg Board of Education, 402 U.S. 1 (1971).
19. Busing *within* the central city was upheld in Armour v. Nix, 446 U.S. 930 (1980); Keyes v. School District No. 1, Denver, 413 U.S. 189 (1973); Milliken v. Bradley, 418 U.S. 717 (1974); Board of School Commissioners of Indianapolis v. Buckley, 429 U.S. 1068 (1977); and School Board of Richmond v. State Board of Education, 412 U.S. 92 (1972). Busing *across* city lines was upheld in Evans v. Buchanan, 423 U.S. 963 (1975), and Board of Education v. Newburg Area Council, 421 U.S. 931 (1975).
20. Pasadena City Board of Education v. Spangler, 427 U.S. 424 (1976).
21. See, for example, Herbert McClosky and John Zaller, *The American Ethos* (Cambridge, Mass.: Harvard University Press, 1984), 92, 100; and data reported in Chapter 5 of this text.
22. NES, *1952–1990 Cumulative Data File, 1992 NES Pre/Post Election Study* (1992).
23. Freeman v. Pitts, 112 S. Ct. 1430 (1992).
24. Robert S. Erikson and Norman R. Luttbeg, *American Public Opinion* (New York: Wiley, 1973), 49; and Hazel Erskine, "The Polls: Demonstrations and Race Riots," *Public Opinion Quarterly* 31 (Winter 1967–1968): 654–677.
25. Howard Schuman, Charlotte Steeh, and Lawrence Bobo, *Racial Attitudes in America* (Cambridge, Mass.: Harvard University Press, 1985), 69, 78–79.
26. *Ibid.*, 102, 110, 127–135.
27. Grove City College v. Bell, 465 U.S. 555 (1984).
28. U.S. v. Armstrong, 116 S. Ct. 1480 (1996).
29. Mueller v. Oregon, 208 U.S. 412 (1908).
30. Equal Pay Act of 1963; Civil Rights Act of 1964, Title VII, and 1978 amendments thereto; Education Amendments of 1972, Title IX.
31. Reed v. Reed, 404 U.S. 71 (1971).
32. Frontiero v. Richardson, 411 U.S. 677 (1973).
33. Stanton v. Stanton, 421 U.S. 7 (1975).
34. Craig v. Boren, 429 U.S. 190 (1976).
35. Dothard v. Rawlinson, 433 U.S. 321 (1977).
36. Cleveland Board of Education v. LaFleur, 414 U.S. 632 (1974).
37. Fortin v. Darlington Little League, 514 F.2d 344 (1975).
38. Roberts v. United States Jaycees, 468 U.S. 609 (1984); and Board of Directors Rotary International v. Rotary Club of Duarte, 481 U.S. 537 (1987).
39. Arizona Governing Committee for Tax Deferred Annuity and Deferred Compensation Plans v. Norris, 463 U.S. 1073 (1983).
40. E.E.O.C. v. Madison Community Unit School District No. 12, 818 F.2d 577 (1987).
41. Michael M. v. Superior Court, 450 U.S. 464 (1981).
42. Vorchheimer v. School District of Philadelphia, 430 U.S. 703 (1977).
43. Kahn v. Shevin, 416 U.S. 351 (1974).
44. Schlesinger v. Ballard, 419 U.S. 498 (1975).
45. Bennett v. Dyer's Chop House, 350 F. Supp. 153 (1972); Morris v. Michigan State Board of Education, 472 F.2d 1207 (1973); Fitzgerald v. Porter Memorial Hospital, 523 F.2d 716

(1975); Kruzel v. Podell, 226 N.W.2d 458 (1975).
46. U.S. v. Virginia, 116 S. Ct. 2264 (1996).
47. Rostker v. Goldberg, 453 U.S. 57 (1981).
48. Roe v. Wade, 410 U.S. 113 (1973).
49. Harris v. McRae, 448 U.S. 297 (1980); Beal v. Doe, 432 U.S. 438 (1977); Maher v. Roe, 432 U.S. 464 (1977).
50. Planned Parenthood Federation of Central Missouri v. Danforth, 428 U.S. 52 (1976); Bellotti v. Baird, 443 U.S. 622 (1979); Akron v. Akron Center for Reproductive Health, 462 U.S. 416 (1983); Thornburgh v. American College of Obstetricians and Gynecologists, 476 U.S. 747 (1986). But compare with Planned Parenthood Association of Kansas City v. Ashcroft, 462 U.S. 476 (1983).
51. Planned Parenthood v. Casey, 112 S. Ct. 2791 (1992).
52. *Statistical Abstract of the United States, 1992* (Washington, D.C.: Government Printing Office, 1987), 374, 388.
53. California Federal Savings and Loan Association v. Guerra, 479 U.S. 272 (1987).
54. John R. Bunzel, "To Each According to Her Worth?" *Public Interest,* no. 67 (Spring 1982): 77–93.
55. Regents of the University of California v. Bakke, 438 U.S. 265 (1978).
56. Fullilove v. Klutznick, 448 U.S. 448 (1980).
57. City of Richmond v. J.A. Croson Co., 488 U.S. 469 (1989).
58. Metro Broadcasting v. FCC, 497 U.S. 547 (1990).
59. Northeastern Florida Contractors v. Jacksonville, 91–1721 (1993).
60. Firefighters Local Union No. 1784 v. Stotts, 467 U.S. 561 (1984); Wygant v. Jackson Board of Education, 476 U.S. 267 (1986); City of Richmond v. J.A. Croson Co., 488 U.S. 469 (1989).
61. Local No. 28 of the Sheet Metal Workers' International Association v. Equal Employment Opportunity Commission, 478 U.S. 421 (1986); Wards Cove Packing Co. v. Atonio, 490 U.S. 642 (1989); Price Waterhouse v. Hopkins, 490 U.S. 228 (1989). (Note: Wards Cove and Price were both superseded in part by the Civil Rights Act of 1991, as discussed in the text of memo above.)
62. Fullilove v. Klutznick, 448 U.S. 448 (1980); Metro Broadcasting v. FCC, 497 U.S. 547 (1990).
63. United Steelworkers of America v. Weber, 443 U.S. 193 (1979); Johnson v. Santa Clara County Transportation Agency, 480 U.S. 616 (1987).
64. Wygant v. Jackson Board of Education, 476 U.S. 267 (1986); U.S. v. Paradise, 480 U.S. 149 (1987).
65. Seymour Martin Lipset and William Schneider, "An Emerging National Consensus," *The New Republic* (October 15, 1977), 8–9.
66. Poll data cited in John R. Bunzel. "Affirmative Re-Actions," *Public Opinion* (February–March 1986), 45–49.
67. Hopwood v. State of Texas, 78 F.3rd 932 (1996); Texas v. Hopwood, 135 L. Ed.2d 1095 (1996).

68. Adarand Constructors v. Pena, 115 S. Ct. 2097 (1995).
69. Bowers v. Hardwick, 478 U.S. 186 (1986).
70. Romer v. Evans, 116 S. Ct. 1620 (1996).

Chapter 20 *Foreign Policy*

1. Alexis de Tocqueville, *Democracy in America,* vol. 1, ed. Phillips Bradley (New York: Knopf, 1951), 235.
2. Richard Lau, Thad A. Brown, and David O. Sears, "Self-Interest and Civilians' Attitudes toward the Vietnam War," *Public Opinion Quarterly* 42 (1978): 464–481.
3. Edward S. Corwin, *The President: Office and Powers* (New York: New York University Press, 1940), 200.
4. Louis Henkin, *Foreign Affairs and the Constitution* (New York: Norton, 1972), 53, 306 n 43.
5. Louis W. Koenig, *The Chief Executive,* 3d ed. (New York: Harcourt Brace Jovanovich, 1975), 217.
6. Louis Fisher, *President and Congress* (New York: Free Press, 1972), 45; United States v. Belmont, 301 U.S. 324 (1937).
7. Aaron Wildavsky, "The Two Presidencies," in *The Presidency,* ed. Wildavsky (Boston: Little, Brown, 1969), 231.
8. Loch Johnson and James M. McCormick, "The Making of International Agreements: A Reappraisal of Congressional Involvement," *Journal of Politics,* 40 (1978), 468–478.
9. Bernard E. Brown, "The Decision to End the Algerian War," in *Cases in Comparative Politics,* ed. James B. Christoph (Boston: Little, Brown, 1965), 154–180; Roy C. Macridis, "De Gaulle and NATO," in *Modern European Governments,* ed. Macridis (Englewood Cliffs, N.J.: Prentice-Hall, 1968), 92–115; and Schwartz and Shaw, *op. cit.,* 235–236.
10. Peter G. Richards, *Parliament and Foreign Affairs* (London: George Allen & Unwin, 1967), 37–38; and John E. Schwartz and L. Earl Shaw, *The United States Congress in Comparative Perspective* (Hinsdale, Ill.: Dryden Press, 1976), 235.
11. Arthur M. Schlesinger, Jr., *A Thousand Days: John F. Kennedy in the White House* (Boston: Houghton Mifflin, 1965), chs. 30, 31. Schlesinger, at p. 841, described Kennedy's actions as a "brilliantly controlled," "matchlessly calibrated" combination of "nerve and wisdom." His view of Nixon's actions was a good deal less charitable in *The Imperial Presidency* (Boston: Houghton Mifflin, 1974), ch. 7.
12. United States v. Curtiss-Wright Export Co., 299 U.S. 304 (1936).
13. Mitchell v. Laird, 488 F. 2d 611 (1973).
14. Prize Cases, 67 U.S. 635 (1863); Mora v. McNamara, 389 U.S. 934 (1964); Massachusetts v. Laird, 400 U.S. 886 (1970).
15. Dames and Moore v. Regan, 435 U.S. 654 (1981).
16. Korematsu v. United States, 323 U.S. 214 (1944).
17. Youngstown Sheet & Tube Co. v. Sawyer, 343 U.S. 579 (1952).

18. Immigration and Naturalization Service v. Chadha, 103 S. Ct. 2764 (1983).
19. Robert S. Erikson and Norman R. Luttbeg, *American Public Opinion* (New York: Wiley, 1973), 50–51.
20. William R. Caspary, "The 'Mood Theory': A Study of Public Opinion and Foreign Policy," *American Political Science Review* 64 (June 1970): 536–547.
21. Erikson and Luttbeg, *op. cit.*, 52.
22. John E. Mueller, *War, Presidents, and Public Opinion* (New York: Wiley, 1973), 110.
23. *Ibid.*, 112.
24. Milton J. Rosenberg, Sidney Verba, and Philip E. Converse, *Vietnam and the Silent Majority* (New York: Harper & Row, 1970), 26–27.
25. Erikson and Luttbeg, *op. cit.*, 155.
26. Mueller, *op. cit.*, ch. 9.
27. *Ibid.*, 169.
28. *Ibid.*, 45–47.
29. *Ibid.*, 54–56.
30. ABC–*Washington Post* poll as cited in *National Journal* (July 28, 1984), 1450.
31. Howard Schuman, "Two Sources of Antiwar Sentiment in America," *American Journal of Sociology* 78 (1973): 513–536.
32. *Ibid.*
33. Philip E. Converse, Warren E. Miller, Jerrold G. Rusk, and Arthur C. Wolfe, "Continuity and Change in American Politics: Parties and Issues in the 1968 Election," *American Political Science Review* 63 (December 1969): 1083–1105; and John P. Robinson, "Public Reaction to Political Protest: Chicago, 1968," *Public Opinion Quarterly* 34 (Spring 1970): 1–9.
34. Chicago Council on Foreign Relations, *American Public Opinion and U.S. Foreign Policy, 1983* (Chicago: Council on Foreign Relations, 1983), 13, 25, 37.
35. X, "The Sources of Soviet Conduct," *Foreign Affairs* 25 (July 1947): 566.
36. Walter Lippmann, *The Cold War* (New York: Harper Brothers, 1947).
37. Erikson and Luttbeg, *op. cit.*, 52.
38. Mueller, *op. cit.*, 40.
39. Michael Roskin, "From Pearl Harbor to Vietnam: Shifting Generational Paradigms and Foreign Policy," *Political Science Quarterly* 89 (Fall 1974): 567.
40. Frank L. Klingberg, "The Historical Alternation of Moods in American Foreign Policy," *World Politics* 4 (1952): 239–273.
41. Roskin, *op. cit.*, 567.
42. *American Public Opinions and U.S. Foreign Policy, 1987* (Chicago: Chicago Council on Foreign Relations, 1987), 33.

Chapter 21 *Military Policy*

1. Katherine Boo, "How Congress Won the War in the Gulf," *Washington Monthly* (October 1991), pp. 31–37.
2. Stanley Lieberson, "An Empirical Study of Military-Industrial Linkages," in *Testing the Theory of the Military Industrial Complex*, ed. Steven Rosen (Lexington, Mass.: D.C. Health/Lexington Books, 1973), 74.
3. Arnold Kanter, "Congress and the Defense Budget: 1960–1970," *American Political Science Review* 66 (1972): 129–143.
4. Robert J. Art, "Why We Overspend and Underaccomplish: Weapons Procurement and the Military-Industrial Complex," in Rosen, *op. cit.*, 249.
5. Quoted in Robert J. Art, *The TFX Decision: McNamara and the Military* (Boston: Little, Brown, 1968), 126.
6. Bill Keller, "Compctition: A Pentagon Battlefield," *New York Times* (May 12, 1985), section 3, p. 1.
7. James Fairhall, "The Case for the $435 Hammer," *Washington Monthly* (January 1987), 50.
8. Harry Summers, "Nuts, Bolts, & Death," *Washington Monthly* (January 1987), 51–52.
9. David C. Morrison, "Chaos on Capitol Hill," *National Journal* (September 27, 1986), 2302–2307.

Chapter 22 *Environmental Policy*

1. Alexander W. Astin, et al., *The American Freshman: National Norms for 1989* (Los Angeles: UCLA Graduate School of Education, 1989), 89.
2. On the greenhouse effect, see Philip D. Jones and Tom L. Wigley, "Global Warming Trends," *Scientific American* (August 1990), 84–91; Gordon J. MacDonald, "Scientific Basis for the Greenhouse Effect," *Journal of Policy Analysis and Management* 7 (1988): 425–444; S. Fred Singer, *Global Warming: Do We Know Enough to Act?* Paper 104, Center for the Study of American Business, Washington University (March 1991).
3. David Vogel, *National Styles of Regulation* (Ithaca, N.Y.: Cornell University Press, 1986), 19–30.
4. Alfred Marcus, *Promise and Performance: Choosing and Implementing an Environmental Policy* (Westport, Conn.: Greenwood Press, 1980), ch. 2; Charles O. Jones, *Clean Air* (Pittsburgh, Penn.: University of Pittsburgh Press, 1975).
5. David Vogel, *Fluctuating Fortunes: The Political Power of American Business* (New York: Basic Books, 1989), 65.
6. R. Shep Melnick, *Regulation and the Courts: The Case of the Clean Air Act* (Washington, D.C.: Brookings Institution, 1983), ch. 9.
7. Pietro S. Nivola, *The Politics of Energy Conservation* (Washington, D.C.: Brookings Institution, 1986), 11–12, 244–247.
8. Robert W. Crandall, "Pollution, Environmentalists, and the Coal Lobby," in Roger G. Noll and Bruce M. Own, eds., *The Political Economy of Deregulation* (Washington, D.C.: American Enterprise Institute, 1983), 84–96; and Crandall, *Controlling Industrial Pollution* (Washington, D.C.: Brookings Institution, 1983).
9. Bruce A. Ackerman and William T. Hassler, *Clear Coal/Dirty Air* (New Haven, Conn.: Yale University Press, 1981).
10. Meier, *op. cit.*, 159.
11. Robert Dorfman, "Lessons of Pesticide Regulation," in Wesley A. Magat, ed., *Reform of Environmental Regulation* (Cambridge, Mass.: Ballinger, 1982), 13–30.
12. *Congressional Quarterly Weekly Report* (January 12, 1990), 166–170.
13. R. Shep Melnick, "Deadlines, Cynicism, and Common Sense," *The Brookings Review* (Fall 1983), 21–24.
14. Meier, *op. cit.*, 156–157.

Chapter 23 *Who Governs?*

1. Anthony King, "The American Polity in the Late 1970s: Building Coalitions in the Sand," in *The New American Political System,* ed. King (Washington, D.C.: American Enterprise Institute, 1978), 391; and James Q. Wilson, "American Politics, Then and Now," *Commentary* (February 1979), 39–46.

Chapter 24 *To What Ends?*

1. Alexis de Tocqueville, *Democracy in America,* ed. Phillips Bradley (New York: Knopf, 1951), vol. 2, book 2, ch. 1.

Chapter 25 *State and Local Government*

1. The 1985 case was Garcia v. San Antonio Metropolitan Transit Authority, 105 S. Ct. 1005. The newer cases are New York v. United States, 504 U.S. 144 (1992) and Printz v. United States, 95–1478 (1997).
2. *Book of the States, 1984–1985* (Lexington, Ky.: Council of State Governments, 1985), 221.
3. Beryl E. Pettus and Randall W. Bland, *Texas Government Today* (Homewood, Ill.: Dorsey Press, 1979).
4. John F. Dillon, *Commentaries on the Law of Municipal Corporation,* 5th ed. (Boston: Little, Brown, 1911), vol. 1, sec. 237.
5. Thad L. Beyle, "Governors," in *Politics in the American States,* 4th ed., ed. Virginia Gray, Herbert Jacob, and Kenneth N. Vines (Boston: Little, Brown, 1983), 202.
6. Samuel C. Patterson, "Legislators and Legislatures in the American States," in Gray, Jacob, and Vines, *op. cit.*, 141.
7. Patterson, *op. cit.*, 142.
8. Richard J. Tobin and Edward Keynes, "Institutional Differences in the Recruitment Process: A Four-State Study," *American Journal of Political Science* 19 (1975): 671–676, quoted in Patterson, *op. cit.*, 144.
9. John E. Chubb, "Institutions, the Economy, and the Dynamics of State Elections," Brookings Discussion Paper no. 7 (Washington, D.C.: Brookings Institution, 1986).
10. Patterson, *op. cit.*, 148–149, 153.
11. Paul T. David and Ralph Eisenbergh, *Devaluation of the Urban and Suburban Vote* (Charlottesville, Va.: University of Virginia Bureau of Public Administration, 1961), 8, cited in Thomas R. Dye, *Politics in States and Communities* (Englewood Cliffs, N.J.: Prentice-Hall, 1969), 122.
12. 377 U.S. 533 (1964).

13. Timothy G. O'Rourke, *The Impact of Reapportionment* (New Brunswick, N.J.: Transaction Books, 1980), ch. 7.
14. Patterson, *op. cit.*, 145.
15. Morris Fiorina, *Divided Government* (New York: Macmillan, 1992); Fiorina, "Divided Government in the American States," paper presented to the Midwestern Political Science Association (March 1993); Alan Ehrenhalt, *The United States of Ambition: Politicians, Power, and the Pursuit of Office* (New York: Random House/Times Books, 1991).
16. Quoted in Patterson, *op. cit.*, 161.

17. Quoted in Alan Rosenthal, *Legislative Life: People, Process, and Performance in the States* (New York: Harper & Row, 1981), 168.
18. Sarah McCally Morehouse, *State Politics, Parties and Policy* (New York: Holt, Rinehart and Winston, 1981), 295.
19. Adapted from Herbert Jacob, "Courts," in Gray, Jacob, and Vines, *op. cit.*, 238.
20. Rosenthal, *op. cit.*, 112–113.
21. Larry Sabato, *Goodbye to Good-Time Charlie: The American Governorship Transformed,* 2d ed. (Washington, D.C.: Congressional Quarterly Press, 1983), 108–109; Beyle, *op. cit.*, 215.

22. Virginia Gray, "Politics and Policy in the American States," in Gray, Jacob, and Vines, *op. cit.*, ch. 1.
23. Donald B. Rosenthal and Robert L. Crain, "City Government and Fluoridation," in *City Politics and Public Policy,* ed. James Q. Wilson (New York: Wiley, 1968).
24. James Q. Wilson, *Varieties of Police Behavior* (Cambridge, Mass.: Harvard University Press, 1968), 257–277.
25. Perez v. United States, 404 U.S. 146 (1971).

Index

Note: Page numbers followed by (fig.) indicate
figures and tables referred to in text.

AARP, *see* American Association of Retired Persons
Abernathy, Ralph, 585
Abortion, 45, 98, 591–592
    anti-abortion groups, 247, 476, 556, 592
    as campaign issue, 220
    public opinion on, 125, 136
    state court rulings, 465
    Supreme Court on, 448, 469, 476, 591–592
Acheson, Dean, 608
Acheson's rule, 428
Acid rain, 653, 654, 658–660, 661(fig.)
ACLU (American Civil Liberties Union), 454, 458
Acquired immunodeficiency syndrome (AIDS), 139,
    565
Activism, 112, 138, 152
    activist approach to judicial review, 440
    gay-rights activists, 262
    influence on nominating conventions, 191, 200
    judicial, *see* Judicial activism
    prospective voting by, 218
    right-to-life activists, 247, 476, 556, 592
    role in nominations, 191, 201, 203
    see also Political participation; Political elites
Activist government, 685–687
ADA (Americans with Disabilities Act) [1990], 70,
    73, 598
Adams, John, 5, 26, 168, 303, 384, 412
    on appointments, 411
    conflict with Democratic-Republicans, 95
    election of 1800, 442
    on English politics, 20
    Marbury v. *Madison,* 442
    presidency of, 371, 372, 374, 380
    on revolution, 21
    as vice president, 401, 411
Adams, John Quincy, 201, 370, 384
Adams, Samuel, 26, 34
Ad hoc structure of White House office, 377, 378
Administrative Procedure Act (1946), 426, 689
Adversarial politics, federalism and, 653
Adversarial press, 291–293
Advertising, 204, 219
    effects on political attitudes, 115, 284
    freedom of expression in, 557
    negative, 210, 219, 293
    see also Direct-mail solicitations
AFBF (American Farm Bureau Federation), 236, 237,
    238, 252
AFDC, *see* Aid to Families with Dependent Children
    (AFDC)
Affirmative action, 133
    equality of opportunity and, 594–599
    equality of results and, 594, 595–596
Afghanistan, Soviet invasion of, 637
AFL-CIO, 12, 183, 458
    as interest group, 236, 248–249
    ratings of legislators by, 254, 325
Age Discrimination Act, 351

Agencies
    congressional staff agencies, 334
    consumer-protection agencies, 418
    culture of, 424–425
    "executive" agencies, 381–382
    federal, 382
    independent and quasi-independent, 381–382
    regulatory, *see* Regulatory agencies
    view of recruitment and retention, 419–420
    see also Bureaucracy; *specific agencies*
Agency "capture," 487, 490, 672, 676
Agency for International Development, 425, 613
Agency-specific recruitment, 416
Agnew, Spiro, resignation of, 404
Agricultural Adjustment Act, 487
Agricultural Marketing Service, 487
Agricultural Research Service, 432
Agricultural Stabilization and Conservation Service,
    432
Agricultural subsidies, 415, 661
    milk subsidies, 487–488, 546
    tobacco subsidies, 493–495, 524, 674, 675
Agriculture
    pesticides, 653, 661–662
    price supports, 481, 487–488
Agriculture Department, 413, 421, 428, 487, 488, 613
AIDS (acquired immunodeficiency syndrome), 139,
    565
Aid to Families with Dependent Children (AFDC),
    524, 530, 539, 671, 718
    compared to Medicaid, 78–79
    conversion to block grant program, 75–77, 537,
    538
    role of policy intellectuals, 540
Air Force, 634, 640, 640(fig.)
Airline Deregulation Act (1978), 494
Airline regulation, 481, 488, 493, 494
Alabama, 460, 461, 579, 582–583
Alexander, Lamar, 212
Alger, Horatio, 98
Allen, George, 62
All-volunteer force (AVF), 643
Almond, Gabriel, 91, 240
Amateur legislature, 710, 711
Amendments to Constitution, 44, 45. *See also specific*
    amendments
American Association of Retired Persons (AARP), 78,
    241–242, 263, 264
American Civil Liberties Union (ACLU), 454, 458,
    547
American Cotton Manufacturers Institute, 239–240
American Council on Education, 240
American Enterprise Institute, 640
American Farm Bureau Federation (AFBF), 236, 237,
    238, 252
American Federation of Labor, 684
American Independent party, 186, 187
Americanism, 89, 131
American Jewish Committee, 237
American ("Know-Nothing") party, 187
American Legion, 241

American Medical Association, 237, 529, 530, 536,
    676
American Nazi party, 552–553
American Public Transit Association, 240
American Revolution, 18, 23
Americans for Constitutional Action, 254, 325
Americans for Democratic Action, 254, 325
Americans with Disabilities Act (ADA) [1990], 70,
    73, 598
American Telephone and Telegraph (AT&T), 485, 493
American way of life, 89
Amicus curiae brief, 457–458
Anderson, John, 137, 185, 186, 205, 221
Andrus, Cecil D., 243
"Angry white males," 221
Annexation, 716
Annual authorizations, 430, 642
Anti-abortion organizations, 247, 476, 556, 592
Antiappeasement, 620, 621, 622, 623, 624, 627
Antiballistic missile system, 642
Anti-Car Theft Act (1992), 722
Anti-Defamation League, 237
Anti-Drug Abuse Act (1986), 722
Anti-Drug Abuse Act (1988), 722
Antifederalists, 33, 35, 167, 696
    Congress and, 348, 349
    views of governmental strength, 42
Antifeminist movement, 247
Anti-gun-control lobby, 256
Anti-Jackson Republicans (1831), 169
Anti-Masonic party (1831), 169
Anti-Saloon League, 188
Antitrust Division of Justice Department, 484, 675
Antitrust legislation, 61, 444, 484–487
Antiwar movement, 187, 262, 289, 619
Apathy, of voters, 143, 144
Appointments, presidential, 354, 382–384, 415
    agencies, commissions and judgeships, 381–382
    bureaucratic appointments, 411–412, 416
    cabinet appointments, 364, 380–381, 381(fig.)
    judicial appointments, 447–450, 713
    state and local, 695, 705, 713
Appropriations, 429
Appropriations Committee (House), 353, 429–430,
    509, 661
Aquino, Corazon, 369
Aristotle, 6, 33–34
Arizona, 220, 245
Arkansas, 578
Armed Services Committees, congressional, 345, 641,
    647
Army, 640, 640(fig.)
Arnold, Thurman, 484
Arthur, Chester A., 374
Articles of Confederation (1781), 23–24, 26–27,
    56–57, 626
    New Jersey Plan and, 31, 33
    Virginia Plan, 29–30
Ash Council, 434, 435
Asian-Americans, 126, 126(fig.), 609–610
Assassination attempts, 256, 401

Assassinations, 369, 401, 403, 417, 584
Asset, CIA definition of, 613
Assistance programs, 527, 528
Associated Press, 270, 276, 289
At-large elections, 714
AT&T (American Telephone and Telegraph), 485, 493
Attitudinal voting, in Congress, 344
Attorney general, 613
Audubon Society, 655
Australian ballot, 151, 164
Austria, 236
Authority, 5–6
    centralization of, 688
    decentralization of, 165, 697
    discretionary, 415, 679, 680
    under Federalism, 165–166
    of president, 44, 46
    see also Power; *specific kinds of power*
Authorization legislation, 429
Automobile emissions, 653, 654, 656–658
Auto-safety law (1966), 489, 490
AVF (all-volunteer force), 643

Babbitt, Bruce, 664
Background briefings, 291
Background stories, 295
Baker, Howard, 197
Bakke, Allan, 458
Bakke case, 458, 597
Balanced budget, 717
Balanced budget amendment (proposed), 45, 47, 48, 513
Bane, Mary Jo, 540
Banfield, Edward C., 540
Banking, 59–60
Bank of the United States, 59–60
Barber, James David, 386
Barry, Marion, 719
Barton, Clara, 423
Bayh, Birch, 183
Bay of Pigs, 616
Beard, Charles, 41
Bell, Alexander Graham, 423
Beneficiaries of programs, 525(fig.), 531–532
    groups as, 478, 482
    legitimacy of, 524, 525, 527, 533–534, 535(fig.)
Benefit (of proposed policy), *see* Costs and benefits
Bentsen, Lloyd, 320, 351, 370, 711
Berman, Howard L., 180
Bernstein, Carl, 279
Beyle, Thad L., 704
Bias
    of electronic media, 283, 287–288, 288(fig.)
    of interest groups, 250–252
    upper-class bias, 250–251
Bicameral legislature, 302, 590
Big-ticket hardware, 644–645
Bill of attainder, 37
Bill of Rights, 38–39, 545–546
    Antifederalist proposal for, 36
    gender not mentioned, 43
    intentions of, 552
    state bills of rights, 22, 38, 39, 698
    see also specific amendments
Bills
    anti-busing bills, 580
    marking up, 338
    pollution-control bills, 489
    private and public, 336
    riders and Christmas-trees, 340, 341

study by committees, 337–340, 339(fig.)
    see also Legislation; Legislative process
Bingham, George Caleb, 36
Bipartisan relations with Congress, 399
Bird, Rose, 713
BJA (Bureau of Justice Assistance), 725
BJS (Bureau of Justice Statistics), 725
Black, Hugo, 440, 554
Black-bag job, 613
Black colleges, 576
Blackmun, Harry, 448, 458
Blacks
    in AFDC program, 524
    in bureaucracy, 420, 421(fig.)
    city and state representation, 718–719
    civil rights and, 572–574
    in Congress, 307–308, 309(fig.)
    majority-minority districts and, 316–317
    in major political parties, 187
    political disadvantages of, 573–574
    political opinions of, 125(fig.), 125–126, 126(fig.)
    political strength of, 585–586
    riots of mid–1960s, 476, 583
    voter participation, 148, 148(fig.), 158–159, 159(fig.), 221, 222
    voting restrictions, 144, 148
    voting rights, 147–148
Blackstone, William, 550–551
Blair, Tony, 365
Blanket primary, 202
Block grants, 51, 67, 68, 69, 74, 75–77
Blount, William, 42
"Blue Dog Democrats," 329
Boland, Edward, 612
Boland Amendment (1982–1985), 612
Boll Weevils, 359
Bolton, Frances, 317
Bolton, Oliver, 317
B–1 bomber, 640
Bonior, David E., 321, 605
Boone, Daniel, 36
Border Patrol, 426
Boren's laws, 428
Bork, Robert, 440, 449, 450
Bosnia, 639
Boston, 236
"Bowling alone," 160–161
Boxer, Barbara, 704
Boycotts, 486, 582–583
Bradley, Bill, 197, 675
Bradley, Tom, 719
Brady, Jim, 256
Brady, Sarah, 256
Brady Bill (1993), 256, 698, 722, 723
Braestrup, Peter, 289
Brandeis, Louis, 464
Brandenburg, Clarence, 552
Braun, Carol Moseley, 308, 327
Breckinridge, John C., 225
Brennan, William J., Jr., 458, 462, 579
Breyer, Stephen, 458
Bribery, 350–351
Brief, 457
Brill, Alida, 104
Broder, David, 197
Brookings Institution, 538, 640
Brown, Jerry, 704
Brown, Linda, 455, 456, 576–577, 578
Brown, Pat, 183
Brown, Ronald H., 178

Brown, Willie, 711
Brownlow, Louis, 434
Brownlow Commission, 434, 435
Brown v. Board of Education (1954), 455, 577–581
    desegregation *versus* integration and, 578–581
    implementation of ruling, 577
    rationale behind, 577–578
Bryan, William Jennings, 170–171, 225, 226, 227
Bubble standard, 663
Buchanan, James, 384
Buchanan, Pat, 212, 605, 627
Buckley v. *Valeo* (1976), 264
Budget and Accounting Act (1921), 376
Budgetary constraints in policy making, 397
Budget Committees (House and Senate), 509
Budget deficit, 325, 352, 512–513
Budget Reconciliation Act (1993), 514
Budget Reform Act (1974), 395
Budget reforms, 513
Budget resolution, 511
Budgets, 511–516, 512(fig.), 515(fig.)
    budget agreement of 1990, 513–514
    collapse of Soviet Union and, 514, 640, 640(fig.)
    defense spending, *see* Defense budget
Buffalo, New York, 483
Bull Moose (Progressive) party, 185, 187, 188
Bundling, 264
Bundy, McGeorge, 608
Bunning, Jim, 350
Bunyan, John, 271
Bureaucracy, 128, 173, 409–437, 688
    agency abbreviations, 431
    allied agencies, 428–429
    appointments, 411–412
    attempts at reform, 434, 435–436
    bureaucratic pathologies, 432–435
    bureaucratic power, 414–415, 415(fig.), 688
    compared with other countries, 409–411
    congressional oversight of, 429–432
    congressional staffs as, 332–334, 333(fig.)
    constraints on, 425–428
    culture of, 424–425
    growth of, 411–414
    hostility toward, 434–435
    House Appropriations Committee and, 429–430
    investigations of, 431–432
    language of, 425
    "laws" of procedure, 427
    layers of, 410
    legislative committees and, 429–430
    legislative veto and, 430
    realities of, 426
    recruitment and retention in, 415–420
    right of removal in, 411
    role in policy-making, 476
    service role of, 412–414
    spoils system in, 411–412, 417
    White House as, 376, 377(fig.)
Bureaucratic theory, 679–680
Bureaucrats, 10
    appointments of, 411–412, 416
    getting rid of, 418–419, 424
    personal attitudes of, 422–424
    personal attributes of, 420–422, 420–422(figs.)
    political sabotage by, 422–424
    typical daily schedule, 417
Bureau of Competition (FTC), 423–424
Bureau of Economics (FTC), 423–424
Bureau of Indian Affairs, 673

Bureau of Justice Assistance (BJA), 725
Bureau of Justice Statistics (BJS), 725
Bureau of the Budget, *see* Office of Management and Budget
Burger, Warren, 448, 458, 469, 579
Burnett, Carol, 553
Burns, Arthur F., 509
Burr, Aaron, 370
Bus Deregulatory Reform Act (1982), 494
Bush, George, 9, 197, 228, 364, 369, 711, 725
　campaign of 1988, 199, 200, 218, 219, 230, 403, 513
　campaign of 1992, 206, 231, 288, 365, 627
　decline in popularity, 390, 391(fig.)
　deregulation and, 495
　on downsizing congressional staff, 353
　election of 1992, 123, 185, 212, 218, 500
　mandates signed into law, 70
　PAC contributions to, 264
　Persian Gulf War, 603
　personality and character, 385, 386
　policies, 397, 499, 608, 611, 640, 660
　presidency of, 374, 400, 429, 598
　support of NAFTA, 605
　Supreme Court nominations, 439, 458
　as vice president, 401
Bush, George W., 711
Bush administration, 70, 592
Business, 130, 222, 717
　business-oriented interest groups, 246, 250, 251, 252
　civil liberties for corporations, 444, 556–557
　PACs sponsored by, 259
　political influence of, 473
　tax reform and, 514, 518
Business regulation, 483–491
　client politics and, 487–488
　entrepreneurial politics and, 488–491
　interest group politics and, 485–487
　majoritarian politics and, 484–485
　Supreme Court views of regulation, 444
　telecommunications deregulation and, 277
　of tobacco industry, 493–495
Busing
　to achieve desegregation, 71, 448, 469, 579–581
　media coverage of, 290
　proposed amendment prohibiting, 45
Butler, B. F., 481

CAB, *see* Civil Aeronautics Board (CAB)
Cabinet
　appointments to, 364, 380–381, 381(fig.)
　rivalry with White House staff, 384
Cable News Network (CNN), 272, 274, 276, 287
Cable television networks, 272, 274, 276, 277, 287
Calhoun, John C., 60–61, 373
California, 243, 315, 451, 541, 654, 697
　anti-affirmative-action bill, 599
　constitution of, 699–700
　government of, 704, 710
　Hispanic vote in, 220
　malapportionment in, 709
　Proposition 13 (1978), 483, 704, 720
　public opinion of immigration, 126, 126(fig.), 128
　term limit initiative, 348
California Public Utility Commission, 556
Calorie Control Council, 257
Cambodia, 616
Cameron, Simon, 383, 685
Campaigners, 152–153

Campaign finance laws, 258, 263
Campaign fund raising, 198, 199, 207(fig.), 207–214
　compared with other countries, 211, 214
　effects of reform, 209, 210(fig.), 211–212
　ethics and, 355–356
　federal matching funds, 198, 199, 208
　finance rules, 209–211
　sources of money, 208(fig.), 208–209
　winning and, 212–214
Campaign oratory, 205–206
Campaigns, 219–220
　elections and, 195–233
　rules for radio and television, 282–283
　see also Congressional campaigns; Presidential campaigns
Campbell, Ben Nighthorse, 308
Canada, 91, 605
Candidates, evaluation by voters, 219
Cannon, Howard, 493
Cannon, Joseph G., 304, 305, 321, 330
Capital grants, 75
Carlyle, Thomas, 432
Carnal Knowledge, 555
Carp, Robert A., 448
Carson, Rachel, 661
Carter, Jimmy, 118, 212, 243, 274, 285, 685, 705
　on "American malaise," 99
　appointments, 464, 509
　campaigns, 199, 203, 205, 230, 725
　Congress and, 365, 398
　decline in popularity, 390, 391(fig.)
　deregulation and, 493, 495
　elections, 130, 137, 216, 218, 221, 227, 500
　legislation, 338, 342
　media and, 278, 295
　personality and character, 385
　policy-making, 396, 397, 608, 609, 611, 623, 640
　presidency of, 364, 366, 377–378, 384, 387, 392, 429, 449, 479
　reorganization efforts, 400, 434
Carter administration, 487, 663
Carver, George Washington, 228
Categorical grants, 66–68, 69, 74
Catholics, as voting bloc, 222, 223(fig.)
Caucuses, 190–191, 195–196, 199, 247, 331
　Iowa caucuses, 200–201, 279
　party caucuses, 303–305
　policy leadership and, 326–327, 328(fig.), 329
Caucus system, 169
CBC (Congressional Black Caucus), 327, 329, 605
CBO (Congressional Budget Office), 334, 511
CEA (Council of Economic Advisers), 379, 519
Center for Participation in Democracy, 359
Central Intelligence Agency (CIA), 379, 607, 612, 613, 615
CETA (Comprehensive Employment and Training Act), 67
Chadha case (1983), 430, 611
Chain of command in military, 635–636
Chamberlain, Neville, 622
Chamber of Commerce, 237, 238, 240, 325, 536
Chapman's rules of committees, 428
Chase, Salmon P., 383
Chase, Samuel, 464
Checks and balances, 34–35, 302
　judicial review, 439–440
　on power of judiciary, 463–469
　as restraint on government, 685
Chicago, 236
Chief Justices, 440(fig.)

Children's Protection and Toy Safety Act (1969), 488
Child support enforcement, 593
China, 541, 626
Chinese-Americans, 144
Chinese Revolution, 18
Christian Coalition, 94, 117–118, 180, 181
Christmas-tree bill, 340
Christopher, Warren, 608
Chubb, John, 708
Churchill, Winston, 364, 620, 622, 707
CIA (Central Intelligence Agency), 379, 607, 612, 613, 615
CINCs (commanders in chief) of unified command, 635
Circular structure, of White House office, 377, 378
Cities, 72–73, 719, 720
　chartered by states, 701
　commission plan, 715
　council-manager plan, 715, 715(fig.)
　home-rule charters, 701–702
　mayor-council plan, 714(fig.), 714–715, 715(fig.)
　metropolitan government and, 716–717
　reformed and unreformed, 713–714, 718
　see also Local governments; *specific cities*
Citizens, 37, 38, 71, 138, 283–284, 688
Citizenship, 595, 596
Citrin, Jack, 221
City-county consolidation, 716
Civic competence, 91
Civic duty, 86, 91
Civil Aeronautics Board (CAB), 253, 674, 678
　abolition of, 12, 494
　airline regulation by, 488, 493, 494, 495
Civil disobedience, 583
Civilian Conservation Corps, 528
Civilian secretaries of armed forces, 635
Civil law, 452
Civil liberties, 545–568
　American preoccupation with, 688–691
　for corporations and groups, 556–557
　crime and due process, 562–567
　cultural conflicts and, 549(fig.), 549–550, 550(fig.)
　establishment clause and, 557, 559–562
　First Amendment and, *see* First Amendment
　free-exercise clause, 557–559
　obscenity and, 554–556
　policy entrepreneurs and, 547–549
　politics, culture and, 546–550
　religious issues and, 558, 560
　rights in conflict and, 546–547
　separation of church and state, 557–562
　symbolic speech and, 555, 556
Civil rights, 12, 70, 135, 230, 571–600
　affirmative action and, 594–599
　black predicament and, 572–574
　Congress and, 305–306, 581–587, 583(fig.), 585(fig.), 587(fig.)
　courts and, 445, 461, 574–581
　immigration and, 595, 597
　schools and, 575–577
　separate-but-equal doctrine and, 574–577
　for women, 588–592
Civil Rights Act, 351
Civil Rights Act (1957), 584, 586
Civil Rights Act (1960), 584, 586
Civil Rights Act (1964), 460–461, 584, 586, 588
Civil Rights Act (1965), 584, 585, 586
Civil Rights Act (1968), 584, 586
Civil Rights Act (1972), 584, 586, 588
Civil Rights Act (1988), 584, 586

Civil Rights Act (1991), 584, 586, 597
Civil Rights Commission, 678
Civil Rights Division of Justice Department, 678
Civil rights legislation, 337, 344, 584, 585
    media and, 583–584
    public opinion and, 583, 583(fig.)
    see also specific laws
Civil-rights movement, 187, 244
    disruptive tactics of, 262
    major events in, 581
    preferential treatment and, 90
    role of religion, 93–94
Civil service, 179–180, 412, 435–436
Civil Service Commission, 586
Civil Service Reform Act (1978), 419
Civil War, 5, 59, 89, 464–465
    effects of, 169–170, 412, 413
    Lincoln's foreign policy, 607, 609
    presidential powers during, 373
    slavery issue and, 41, 61
Clarity, free speech and, 554
Clarke, Gary, 78
Class-action suits, 455–456, 462, 577–581
Class consciousness, 96
Classes, *see* Social class
Clay, Henry, 169, 303, 321, 373
Claybrook, Joan, 490
Clayton, Eva, 316
Clayton Act (1914), 484, 485
Clean Air Act (1970), 257, 374, 488, 672, 678
    1977 amendment, 655
    1990 amendment, 374, 654, 655, 660
    automobile emissions, 656
    smog issue and, 654
"Clean election" initiative, 264
Clean water acts, 654
Clear-and-present-danger test, 551–552
Clements, William, 711
Cleveland, Grover, 171, 201
    presidency of, 373, 374, 375, 376, 417
    use of vetoes, 374, 393(fig.), 393–394
Client-based welfare programs, 524, 530(fig.), 530–532
Client politics, 253, 260, 428, 523, 673–675
    business regulation and, 487–488
    deregulation and, 493, 495
    environmental policy and, 661–662
    in foreign policy, 604
    military and, 631, 632, 646–647
    policy-making process and, 481–482, 487–488
    political power and, 673–675
    political theories and, 677–678, 679, 681
    practiced by groups, 571–572
    social welfare and, 533–534, 534(fig.), 535(fig.)
    tax loopholes and, 519
Clinton, Bill, 9, 160, 178, 197, 243, 301, 705
    campaign of 1992, 199, 205, 206, 213, 231, 353, 365
    campaign of 1996, 205, 221, 231
    civil litigation and, 395
    congressional election of 1994 and, 216, 217
    economic policy, 499, 514–515
    election of 1992, 123, 130, 185, 212, 218, 292, 365, 500
    election of 1996, 130, 212–213, 221, 536
    electronic town meetings, 12
    foreign policy, 608, 611, 623
    health care plan, 254, 536
    line-item veto and, 47–48
    media and, 286, 288

military policy, 134, 600, 640, 644
    NAFTA and, 605
    PAC contributions to, 264
    party fund-raising, 174
    personality and character, 385, 386
    pledge to end welfare, 78
    policy-making constraints, 397
    presidency of, 325, 364, 366, 369, 377, 378, 400, 429, 639, 723
    success rate with Congress, 398–399
    Supreme Court appointees, 458
    Telecommunications Act (1996), 277
    welfare cuts, 76–77
Clinton, Chelsea, 231
Clinton, George, 26
Clinton, Hillary Rodham, 231, 292, 377, 536
Clinton administration
    budget bill of 1993, 514–515
    environmental policy of, 663–664
    makeup of cabinet, 364
    on school prayer, 468
Closed primary, 202
Closed rules, 339, 339(fig.)
Clothespin vote, 200
Cloture, 307, 340, 341, 584
CNN (Cable News Network), 272, 274, 276, 287
Coal, environment and, 654, 659–660
Coalition, 37
Coalition, the, 329
Coal-mine-safety law (1969), 490
Coattails, 196, 197, 389(fig.), 389–390
Coca-Cola Company, 257
COGs (councils of governments), 717
Cohen, Wilbur, 529
Cold War, 620
Cold War, The (Lippmann), 620
Colonial America, opinions on liberty, 20–21
Colorado, 62, 348, 599, 600
Command-and-control strategy, 662
Commanders in chief (CINCs) of unified command, 635
Commentaries (Blackstone), 550–551
Commerce, regulation of, 61, 443
Commerce Act (1887), 672
Commerce Department, 613
Commercial advertising, 204
Commission on Base Realignment and Closure (1988), 647
Commission plan, 715
Committee chairmen, 330–331
Committee Clearance, 430
Committee of Detail, 32
Committee of the Whole, 340, 342
Committee on Committees, congressional, 320, 322
Committee on Economic Security, 528
Committee on Standards of Official Conduct (House), 351
Committees, 329–332
    conference committees, 330, 342–343
    joint committees, 330, 353
    PACs, *see* Political action committees (PACs)
    reducing number of, 352–353, 353(fig.)
    select committees, 330, 353
    standing committees, 305, 329, 330
    of state legislatures, 712
    study of bills by, 337–340, 339(fig.)
    see also specific committees
Commodity Credit Corporation (Department of Agriculture), 487
Common Cause, 250, 251, 264

Common Market, 608–609
Commonwealth of Independent States (Soviet), 626
Communalists, 153
Communist Control Act (1954), 548
Communist party, 187, 548, 552
Community Action Programs, 674
Community Development Block Grants, 67
Community Oriented Policing (COPS) program, 723
Comparable worth doctrine, 593–594
Compensatory action, 598–599
Competing interests, 58, 684, 686
Competitive service, 415
Comprehensive Crime Control Act (1984), 722
Comprehensive Employment and Training Act (CETA), 67
Compulsory voting, 155
Computers, 206, 413. *See also* Internet
Conable, Barber, 685
Concurrent resolution, 336
Conditions of aid, 69
Confederal system, 53, 56(fig.)
Confederation, 53, 58, 626
Conference committees, 330, 342–343
Confessions, due process and, 566–567
Confidentiality, 280–282, 394–395
Conflict, 89, 491
    in bureaucracy, 432, 433, 434
    cultural conflicts, 549(fig.), 549–550, 550(fig.)
    rights in conflict and, 546–547
Conflict of interest, 261
Congress, 34, 147, 299–360, 318
    bureaucracy and, 411–412, 429–432, 435, 679
    calendars of, 338
    caucuses, 326–327, 328(fig.), 329
    changes in, 690
    civil rights and, 581–587, 583(fig.), 585(fig.), 587(fig.)
    committees, 329–332
    compared with parliamentary system, 299–302, 363–365, 366
    conflict over distribution of power, 303
    control of, 166, 170–171, 191
    devolution and, 51
    economic policy and, 509–510
    effect of procedures on policy, 512
    elections, *see* Congressional elections
    ethics and, 354–357
    federalism and, 80–82
    House-Senate differences, 343
    ideological consistency of, 138
    immigration law and policy, 128
    judiciary and, 464–467
    legislative process in, *see* Legislative process
    media coverage of, 286–287
    methods of raising pay, 356
    move for direct democracy in, 346–347
    movement to reform, 346, 350–353
    PAC influence on, 260
    pay increase amendment, 45
    political parties and, 319–329, 324(fig.), 324–326, 325(fig.)
    powers of, 300, 302, 373–374, 393
    president and, 375–376, 387, 389, 389(fig.), 390, 391(fig.), 398–399
    public pressure on, 257
    regulation of lobbying, 262–263
    rights of disabled persons, 598
    right to charter national bank, 59–60
    role in foreign policy, 604, 606
    role in military policy, 634, 641–642, 647

staffs and specialized offices, *see* Congressional staffs
strength of party structures, 323–324
subjecting to law, 351–352
term limits for, 348–350
voting in, 341–353, 532–533, 533(fig.)
see also House of Representatives; Legislation; Senate; *specific laws*
Congressional Accountability Act (1995), 351
Congressional Black Caucus (CBC), 327, 329, 605
Congressional Budget Act (1974), 511, 512
Congressional Budget and Impoundment Control Act (1974), 360
Congressional Budget Office (CBO), 334, 511
Congressional campaigns, 173, 208(fig.), 208–209
Congressional elections, 196, 314–319
of 1938, 387
of 1980, 346
of 1982, 173, 232
of 1986, 173, 214, 450
of 1988, 196, 214, 228
of 1992, 118–119, 119(fig.), 207, 308, 316, 327
of 1994, 118, 216–217, 221, 309, 312–313, 327
of 1996, 213
at-large *vs.* district elections, 147
compared to presidential elections, 196
districts and, 312, 314–315, 315(fig.), 316–317
female candidates, 118–119, 119(fig.)
midterm elections, 218
primary elections, 317–319
social welfare votes and, 533
Congressional Government (Wilson), 375
Congressional Record, 318
Congressional Research Service (CRS), 334
Congressional staffs, 332–334, 333(fig.), 353
Connally, John, 711
Connally, Tom, 611
Connecticut, 40, 256
Connecticut (Great) Compromise, 31–32
Connor, Eugene "Bull," 583
Conscientious objectors, 559
Consent of governed, 21–22, 29
Conservatism, 130, 132–133, 133(fig.)
of college students, 120, 121(fig.)
in public-interest organizations, 243
on SDI ("Star Wars"), 643
in Senate, 345, 346
on Supreme Court, 440
think tanks, 244
view of social welfare, 532, 534, 541
views of military spending, 638
Conservative coalition, 313–314
Conservative/strict constructionist bloc, in Supreme Court, 458
Considine, Bob, 546
Consistency of attitude, 131–132, 135, 137, 138
Constituency caucuses, 327, 328(fig.)
Constituents, 80–81, 333, 344, 358–359
Constitutional Convention (1787), 16, 24–29
delegates to, 24, 26–27, 29, 31, 32
economic interests, 41–42
effects of Shays's Rebellion, 25–26
Great (Connecticut) Compromise, 31–32
models of confederacies, 24–26
motives of delegates, 41–44
New Jersey Plan, 31, 33
resolution of political issues in, 29–32
Virginia Plan, 29–30
Constitutional courts, 447
Constitutional reform, 44, 46–48, 513

Constitutional system, interest groups and, 235
Constitution of the United States, 5, 32–35, 373, 442, 450
Antifederalist view of, 35–38
application to women, 43
as basis for sweeping court orders, 460–461
Bill of Rights, *see* Bill of Rights; *individual amendments*
bureaucracy and, 413
on cabinet office, 364
cases affecting interpretation, 452
checks and balances in, 34
commerce clause, 61
criticisms of, 47–48
economic interests as factor, 41–42
Eighth Amendment to, 460
Eleventh Amendment to, 446–447, 450, 465
equality issue and, 42–44
Fifteenth Amendment to, 147–148, 445, 465
Fifth Amendment to, 563, 590
First Amendment to, 210, 262, 264, 280, 455, 462, 549–562, 564, 670
Fourteenth Amendment to, 39, 186, 316, 440, 444, 445, 455, 465, 552, 574
Fourth Amendment to, 562–567
human nature as factor, 33–35
interpretation by judiciary, 462
on jurisdiction of Supreme Court, 442
key principles of, 33
methods of amending, 44
as model for Confederate constitution, 89
Nineteenth Amendment to, 43, 149
personal liberty and, 19–24, 35–41, 94
presidential powers and, 375
ratification of, 42
Second Amendment to, 256
separation of church and state, 455
Seventeenth Amendment to, 307
Sixteenth Amendment to, 14, 414, 465, 517, 519
slavery issue and, 21, 39–41, 42
state-federal relations and, 57, 58
Tenth Amendment to, 58, 62, 69, 71, 698
Thirteenth Amendment to, 465
Twelfth Amendment to, 370
Twenty-fifth Amendment to, 380, 403, 404
Twenty-second Amendment to, 369, 400
Twenty-seventh Amendment to, 45
Twenty-sixth Amendment to, 45, 149, 465
Twenty-third Amendment to, 149
ways of amending, 44
see also Constitutional Convention (1787)
Constitutions, 52–53
federal, *see* Constitution of the United States
state, *see* State constitutions
Consumer advocates, 482
Consumer Credit Protection Act (1968), 722–723
Consumer Federation of America, 254
Consumer-protection agencies, 418
Containment
policy toward Soviet Union, 636–637
as worldview, 620, 621, 622, 623, 624, 627
Continental Congress, 24, 40, 42
Contractual obligations, 37
"Contract with America," 78, 79, 217, 306
Convention system, 169
Coolidge, Calvin, 374, 401
Copartisan relations with Congress, 399
COPS program (Community Oriented Policing), 723
Corporations, *see* Business
Corruption, 172, 179–180, 230, 674

"constituent service" and, 358–359
Ethics in Government Act (1978), 261
Corwin, Edward S., 606, 647
Cost argument, 491
Cost of Living Council, 414
Cost (of proposed policy), *see* Costs and benefits
Cost overruns, 644–646
Costs and benefits, 477
benefits of proposed policy, 478, 662–663
of environmental quality, 655(fig.), 655–656, 656(fig.), 662–663
narrowly concentrated, 479, 479(fig.)
in policy-making process, 477–479
of social welfare, 534–535, 537
widely distributed, 479, 479(fig.), 491
Council-manager system, 715, 715(fig.)
Council of Economic Advisers (CEA), 379, 519
Council on Foreign Relations, 620
Councils of governments (COGs), 717
Counties, 702, 716–717
Coups, Soviet, 625, 626
Court costs, 453–456
Court of Military Appeals, 447
Courts, 38, 105, 128, 454, 690
checks and balances of, 34
civil rights and, 574–581
class-action suits, 455–456, 462, 577–581
court costs and, 453–456
district courts, 447
entrepreneurial politics and, 676
failure to comply with, 463, 464
federal, *see* Federal courts
jurisdiction of, 442, 450–453, 466–467
legal standing and, 454–455, 456, 462
municipal courts, 712
political liberties and, 445–447, 690
role in policy-making, 476
territorial courts, 447
see also Judiciary; Supreme Court
Courts of appeals, 419, 447, 712
Cover, 613
Covert action, 613
Cox Broadcasting Corp. v. *Cohn* (1975), 562, 564
Cranston, Alan, 358–359
Crawford, William H., 370
Crime Act (1994), 722
Crime control, 721–725
Crime Control Act (1990), 722
Criminal justice, 721–725
civil rights and, 586
compared with other countries, 562–563
crime rates, 216, 278
due process and, 562–567
effects of federalism on, 55
major federal anti-crime laws, 722
police, *see* Police
Criminal law, 452, 463, 465
Criminals, motivations of, 724
Crisis, The, 575
Critical periods, 224–228
Cronkite, Walter, 285
Cross-partisan relations with Congress, 399
CRS (Congressional Research Service), 334
C-SPAN, 287
Cuba, 270–271, 616, 637
Cuban-Americans, 220, 222
Cuban immigration (1980), 541
Cultural conflict, 98–99, 549(fig.), 549–550, 550(fig.)
Cultural differences, effects on political system, 91, 93, 94(fig.)

Cultural elite, liberalism of, 120
Culture, civil liberties and, 546–550
Cumming v. *Richmond County Board of Education* (1899), 575
Cuomo, Mario, 197
Currency, right to issue, 60, 64
Customs Service, 426, 432

Dairy industry, 487–488, 546
Daley, Richard, 719
Davis, John W., 176
Day care, 592–593
DEA (Drug Enforcement Administration), 426, 432, 613, 724
Death penalty, 465, 722
Deaver, Michael K., 261
Debates, 287, 637–638, 670
   floor debates, 340–341
   on meaning of federalism, 59–68
   televised, 204–205, 207
Debs, Eugene, 186
Declaration of Independence, 18, 93
DeConcini, Dennis, 358–359
De facto segregation, 578
Defense budget, 636–643
   big-ticket hardware, 644–645
   components of, 640(fig.), 643–647
   effect of Soviet collapse on, 514, 640, 640(fig.)
   equal-allocation formula, 645, 646
   federal budget and, 639(fig.), 639–640
   military base closings, 647
   personnel, 643–644
   small-ticket items, 645–646
   total spending, 636–640, 637–640(figs.)
   training and readiness, 646–647
Defense decision-making, 632, 633(fig.)
   chain of command in, 635–636
   Joint Chiefs of Staff, 634, 635
   Joint Staff, 634
   military services, 635
   Unified Commands, 634–635
Defense Department, 421, 607, 613, 632
   annual authorizations, 430
   bureaucratic constraints on, 425–426
de Gaulle, Charles, 608–609
De jure segregation, 578
Delaware, 40
Delegates to nominating conventions
   apportioning, 175–178, 177(fig.)
   influence of "new" delegates, 191
   selection of, 202
   voter attitudes and, 189(fig.), 189–190
Dellums, Ron, 345
Democracy
   under Constitution, 33
   definitions of, 5–7
   direct, *see* Direct democracy
   distribution of power in, 7–12
   as element of political system, 86
   representative, *see* Representative democracy
Democracy in America (de Tocqueville), 86, 160
Democratic centralism, 6
Democratic National Committee (DNC), 172–173
Democratic National Convention, 183, 191, 586, 619
Democratic party, 171, 173, 177, 177(fig.), 711
   antiwar movement and, 187, 619
   control of state legislatures, 708–709, 710
   divisions in, 313–314, 346
   dominance of, 224, 224(fig.), 312, 312(fig.)
   effect of social movements on, 181

effects of strain within middle class, 139
governorships, 705
national conventions, *see* National nominating conventions
participation in caucuses, 200–201
party identification, 115(fig.), 115–116, 215(fig.), 215–216
role of blacks in, 187
rules changes in, 176–177
in South, 127, 127(fig.), 130, 130(fig.), 183, 184(fig.), 216–217
Tammany Hall, 171, 179, 181, 697, 718, 719
see also Political parties
Democratic Party v. *La Follette* (1981), 202
Democratic-Republican caucus, 304
Democratic Study Group, 327, 345
Denmark, 214
Department of Commerce, 413, 421
Department of Defense, 632, 633(fig.)
Department of Education, 381, 381(fig.), 410, 673
Department of Health, Education and Welfare, 400
Department of Health and Human Services, 410
Department of Housing and Urban Development (HUD), 232, 381, 410, 428
Department of Labor, 410, 413
Department of State, 411
Department of the Interior, 428
Department of the Treasury, 421
Department of Transportation, 400, 433
Department of Veterans Affairs, 428
Depository Institution Deregulation and Monetary Control Act (1980), 494
Deregulation, 277, 282, 493, 494, 495
Derthick, Martha, 493
Descriptive representation, 316
Desegregation
   distinguished from integration, 578–581
   federal oversight of, 577
   mandates, 71
   social science as support for, 577–578
Devolution, 51, 75–80, 81(fig.)
Dickinson, John, 20
Dillon's rule, 701, 702
Dinkins, David, 718
Direct democracy, 6, 8, 180–181
   arguments for, 7
   representative democracy compared, 7, 9, 11, 346–347
Direct election, 32
Direct-mail solicitations
   as campaign tool, 206, 219
   by interest groups, 250, 257–258
   money raised by, 249, 251
   see also Advertising
Direct political action, 13
Dirksen, Everett, 584
Disabled persons
   Americans with Disabilities Act (ADA), 70, 73, 598
   Rehabilitation Act (1973), 72–73
   rights of, 598
Discharge petition, 338–339
Discretionary authority, 415, 679, 680
Discrimination
   Age Discrimination Act, 351
   intent to discriminate, 579, 580
   quotas and, 597, 598
   reverse discrimination, 458, 594
   sex discrimination, 586, 592
Disengagement worldview, 621, 623, 624–625, 627

Disruptive tactics, of interest groups, 261–262
Dissenting opinion, 458
Distribution of power, 15–16, 178
   congressional conflict over, 303
   in democracy, 7–12
   effects of issues on, 477–479
Distributive politics, 723
District courts, 447
District elections, 714
District of Columbia, 45, 149, 370
Diversity cases, 450
Divided government, 365–367, 435. *See also* Policy gridlock
Division vote, 342
Dixiecrats, 186, 187, 188
DNC (Democratic National Committee), 172–173
Doctrine of nullification, 60–61, 62
Dole, Elizabeth, 275
Dole, Robert, 112–113, 197, 275
   campaign of 1988, 200
   elections, 212–213, 217, 221, 231, 536
Domino theory, 622
Donnelly, Ignatius, 169
Dornan, Robert, 212
Double agent, 613
Double-tracking, 341
Douglas, Stephen A., 225
Douglas, William O., 464
Douglass, Frederick, 176
Draft
   draft resistance, 551, 556
   peacetime draft, 643
   women and, 589, 590
Dred Scott (1857), 443–444, 465, 467
Drug abuse, public opinion on, 125, 133
"Drug Czar," 722
Drug Enforcement Administration (DEA), 426, 432, 613, 724
Drug testing, due process and, 565–566
Dual federalism, 61, 62
Dual sovereignty doctrine, 451–452, 699
Du Bois, W. E. B., 240, 575
Due process, 562–567
   confessions and self-incrimination, 566–567
   drug and AIDS testing, 565–566
   exclusionary rule, 563, 567
   Miranda rule, 566–567
   search and seizure, 563–566
Due-process clause, 552, 557–558, 590, 591
Dukakis, Michael, 197, 292
   campaign of 1988, 199, 218, 219, 230
   caucuses and, 191
   "faithless electors," 370
Dulles, John Foster, 608
Dunlop, John, 383
Duplication, in bureaucracy, 432, 433, 434

Earned Income Credit, 531, 537
Earned Income Tax Credit (EITC), 527, 538–539
Earth Day, 654, 655
Economic-determinist theory, 677–678
Economic individualism, 90, 90(fig.)
Economic inequality, tolerance for, 90
Economic interests, party affiliations and, 168
Economic issues, 186, 187, 230
   elections and, 216, 225–226, 226
   immigration and, 541–542
   influence of political elites, 139–140
   interest group formation and, 237–238

ratings of legislators on, 325–326
religion and, 117
retrospective voting and, 218, 219(fig.)
women and, 592–594
Economic Opportunity Act (1964), 674, 680
Economic planning, 505–506
Economic policy, 135, 137, 499–521, 500(fig.), 670
budgetary process and, 511–516, 512(fig.), 515(fig.)
Congress and, 509–510
economic-determinist theory and, 678
economic health and, 500–504
economic realities and, 499–500
economic theories and political needs, 504–507
Federal Reserve Board and, 508, 509
policy-making machinery, 507–510
spending and, 510–511, 511(fig.)
taxation and, 516(fig.), 516–520
terminology, 507
Economics
Constitutional Convention and, 41–42
government as reflection of economic forces, 8–9
property rights, 20, 597, 689
ratification of Constitution and, 42
Economic system
comparison with other countries, 92–93, 93(fig.), 94(fig.)
political system and, 89–90, 90(fig.)
Economic theories, 504–507
economic planning, 505–506
errors in, 505
ideology and, 506
Keynesianism, 504–505
monetarism, 504
Reaganomics, 506–507
supply-side theory, 506, 519
Economists, 423, 424, 519
Economy
effect on state elections, 708
regulation by Supreme Court, 444–445
women and, 592–594
Education
effect on opinions, 134, 138, 139, 619
interest group membership and, 238, 251, 252(fig.)
political attitudes and, 119–121, 120(fig.), 121(fig.)
political participation and, 153, 153(fig.), 154
qualifications for voting, 148, 151
sex discrimination prohibited, 586
social class and, 124
state court rulings, 465
voting record and, 223(fig.)
see also Schools
Ehrenhalt, Alan, 710
Ehrlichman, John, 394
Eighth Amendment, 460
Eisenhower, Dwight D., 100, 222, 224, 364, 401
attempts at reorganization, 399, 400
domino theory, 622
elections, 389, 389(fig.), 618
personality and character, 384–385
policy-making, 397, 608, 614, 642
presidency of, 375, 377, 380, 392, 400, 401, 403, 474, 476
social welfare and, 528
success rate with Congress, 398
use of vetoes, 393(fig.), 393–394
EIS (environmental impact statement), 654, 655–656
EITC (Earned Income Tax Credit), 527, 538–539

Elazar, Daniel J., 54, 55
Elections, 195–233
campaigns, see Campaigns; Congressional campaigns; Presidential campaigns
compared with other countries, 195
decline of parties and, 224(fig.), 228–229
early variations in, 147
effects on policy, 229, 232
outcomes of, 224(fig.), 224–229
party realignments and, 224–228
predicting outcome of, 218–219
state legislatures, 707
winner-take-all feature, 185, 186, 370
see also Congressional elections; Presidential elections; Voting
Electoral coalitions, 220–222, 223(fig.)
Electoral college, 32, 185, 368, 370–371
Electorate, 144–152
realignments of, 224–228
state and federal control of, 147–149, 148(fig.)
voter turnout, 144–145, 145(fig.), 149–152, 150(fig.), 196
Electronic media, 272–275, 274(fig.)
bias in, 283, 287–288, 288(fig.)
competition in, 276, 277
deregulation movement, 282
Internet, 12, 272, 273, 556
private ownership of, 268
regulation of, 276, 277, 282
see also Radio; Television
Electronic town meetings, 12, 273
Eleventh Amendment, 446–447, 450, 465
Elites
characteristics of, 679
cultural elite, 120
pluralist view of, 10, 12
power elites, 9–10
see also Political elites
Elitist theory, 678–679
Ellwood, David, 540
El Salvador, 618, 622
Employer mandates, 536
Employment
civil rights acts and, 584, 586
preference systems in, 598
rights of disabled persons, 598
sex discrimination in, 592
temporary and white-collar, 416
see also Unemployment
Employment and Training Administration, 410
Endangered Species Act, 680
"End Poverty in California" program, 528
Energy Department, 430
England, see Great Britain
Enhanced rescission authority, see Line-item veto
Entitlement grants, 75, 352
Entrepreneurial politics, 675–676
agency "capture" and, 676
business regulation and, 488–491
of congressional staffs, 333
environmental policy and, 483, 651–652, 653–656, 655(fig.), 656(fig.)
in foreign policy, 604
importance of media in, 676, 681
pluralist theory and, 681
policy-making process and, 482–483
tax reform and, 519
Environmental Action, 245, 246, 258
Environmental Defense Fund, 245, 246, 250, 655, 660
Environmental impact statement (EIS), 654, 655–656

Environmental movement, 243, 245, 246
Environmental policy, 70, 489, 651–665
acid rain, 653, 654, 658–660, 661(fig.)
agricultural pesticides, 653, 661–662
automobile emissions, 653, 654, 656–658
client politics and, 661–662
compared with other countries, 652–653
entrepreneurial politics and, 483, 651–652, 653–656, 655(fig.), 656(fig.)
federal laws, 653(fig.)
industrial pollution, 653–656, 655(fig.), 656(fig.)
interest group politics and, 658–660, 661(fig.)
majoritarian politics and, 653, 656–658
results of, 664, 664(fig.)
uncertainties in, 651, 658–659, 662–664
Environmental Protection Agency (EPA), 410, 421, 428, 654
agency capture and, 490, 676
federal courts and, 490–491
hazardous waste and, 654, 664
pesticide ban, 661
Superfund program and, 483, 664
EPA, see Environmental Protection Agency (EPA)
Equal-allocation formula, in defense budget, 645, 646
Equal Employment Opportunity Commission, 678
Equality
Constitution and, 42–44
de Tocqueville on, 689–690
political vs. economic equality, 86
Equality of opportunity, 594–599
Equality of results, 594, 595–596
Equal justice principle, 460
Equal Pay Act, 351
Equal Rights Amendment (ERA), 45, 246–247, 590–591
Equal time rule, 282
ERA, see Equal Rights Amendment (ERA)
Erikson, Erik, 96
Ernoznik v. Jacksonville (1975), 562, 564
Escobedo case, 566
Espionage Act (1917), 547–548, 551
"Establishment, the," 10
Establishment clause, 557, 559–562
Ethics
Congress and, 354–357, 492
Ethics in Government Act (1978), 261
ethics violations, 355
"Keating Five," 368–359
media and, 294
Ethics Committees, congressional, 353, 355, 492
Ethics in Government Act (1978), 261
Ethnic minorities
bureaucracy and, 420, 421(fig.)
city and state representation, 718–719
civil liberties of, 546
cleavages in public opinion and, 126, 126(fig.)
immigration law and policy and, 128–129
Jacksonian model of government and, 698
voter participation and, 158–159, 159(fig.)
Ethnic warfare, 626, 628
Europe
bureaucracy in, 410–411
elections in, 195
political parties in, 165, 166
see also specific countries
Evers, Medgar, 581
Exclusionary rule, 563, 567
"Executive" agencies, 381–382
Executive branch, see Cabinet; Presidency; President; Presidential power

Executive departments, 380–381, 381(fig.). *See also* Cabinet; *specific departments*
Executive Office of the President, 379–380, 400, 434
Executive privilege, 34, 394–395
Ex post facto law, 37
External efficacy, 102

Factional parties, 188, 189
Factions, 30, 34–35, 37
    ideological, 180–181
    interest groups and, 235
    in political parties, 167, 171, 173, 180–181, 371
    political power of, 54–55
    public opinion and, 112
    see also Special interests
Fairness doctrine, 282
"Fair share" of national income, 525
Family, 96, 97, 115(fig.), 115–117
Family and Medical Care Leave Act, 351
Family Assistance Plan (1969), 130, 670
Family jewels, CIA definition of, 613
Family Support Act (1988), 705
Farber, Myron, 280–282
Farmers
    foreign competition and, 510
    interest groups of, 236, 237, 238, 251–252
    milk subsidies, 487–488, 546
    organizations of, 236, 237
    price supports and, 481, 487–488
    tobacco subsidies, 493–495, 524, 674, 675
    voting records of, 222
FBI (Federal Bureau of Investigation), 410, 426, 429, 613, 722, 724
FCC, *see* Federal Communications Commission (FCC)
FDA, *see* Food and Drug Administration (FDA)
FEA (Federal Energy Administration), 254
Feature stories, 288–290
FEC (Federal Election Commission), 209–210, 264
Federal Acquisition Streamlining Act (1994), 436
Federal Bureau of Investigation (FBI), 410, 426, 429, 613, 722, 724
Federal Communications Commission (FCC), 253–254, 428, 674, 691
    appeals of rulings, 452
    regulation of media, 206, 276, 277, 282, 493
    rights of disabled persons and, 598
Federal courts
    on affirmative action, 599
    appointments to, 447–450
    black civil rights movement and, 574
    development of, 441–447
    growth of mandates and, 71
    increase in cases, 462, 463(fig.)
    judicial activism in, 461–462, 463(fig.)
    jurisdiction of, 450–453, 466
    legislation and, 462–463
    litmus test for, 448(fig.), 449–450, 450(fig.)
    nation-state relationship and, 441, 443
    oversight of desegregation, 577
    partisanship and, 447
    policy-making by, 459–461
    political liberties and, 445–447
    powers of, 459–463
    pressure on regulatory agencies by, 490–491
    scope of governmental powers and, 444–445
    senatorial courtesy and, 448–449
    on sexual distinctions, 589
    slavery issue and, 443–444
    structure of, 447–450
    see also Courts; State courts; Supreme Court

Federal crimes, 722, 724–725
Federal Deposit Insurance Corporation, 426–427
Federal Election Commission (FEC), 209–210, 264
Federal Energy Administration (FEA), 254
Federal government
    conflict with states, 721
    control of electorate, 147–149, 148(fig.)
    policy entrepreneurs in, 675
    right to issue currency, 60, 64
    role in crime control, 722–725
    supremacy of, 441, 443
    Supreme Court cases and, 458
    see also Congress; House of Representatives; Judiciary; Presidency; President; Senate; Supreme Court
Federal Home Loan Bank Board, 358
Federal Housing Finance Board, 426–427
Federal income tax, 3, 14, 516–519, 517(fig.)
    Budget Reconciliation Act (1993) and, 514
    cuts in 1981, 512
    declared illegal (1895), 444, 465, 516–517
    grants-in-aid and, 63–64
    loopholes in, 516, 517–519
    tax rates, 517, 517(fig.)
    World War II use of, 414
    see also Taxation
Federalism, 33, 51–82
    adversarial politics and, 653
    checks and balances of, 34–35
    Congress and, 80–82
    debate on meaning of, 59–68
    decentralized political authority and, 165
    devolution in, 51, 75–80
    doctrine of nullification and, 60–61
    dual federalism, 61, 62
    grants-in-aid and, *see* Grants-in-aid
    lines of power in, 56(fig.)
    national welfare policy and, 526–527
    as protector of personal liberty, 56(fig.), 56–59
    Supreme Court interpretations, 59–60
Federalist Papers, 28, 30, 53, 57–58
    answers to Antifederalists, 36–37
    No. 10, 28, 30, 54–55, 235, 347
    No. 51, 28, 30, 37
    No. 78, 441
    on power of federal government, 58–59
Federalists, 35, 225
    conflict with Democratic-Republicans, 95
    founding of party, 167
    views of governmental strength, 42
    see also Jeffersonian Republicans
Federal judges, 382, 405, 464
Federal Maritime Commission, 488
Federal power, 57–59
    efforts to cut, 13, 74, 75, 76, 232
    powers of courts, 459–463
    scope of, 444–445
    see also Federalism; *specific branches, offices, and agencies*
Federal-question cases, 450
Federal Regulation of Lobbying Act (1946), 262–263
Federal Reserve Board, 426–427, 509
Federal Reserve System, 509
Federal spending
    defense budget, *see* Defense budget
    economic policy and, 510–511, 511(fig.)
    grants-in-aid, *see* Grants-in-aid
    Reagan's attempts to cut, 512
Federal system, *see* Federalism
Federal Trade Commission Act (1914), 484, 485, 670
Federal Trade Commission (FTC), 261, 421, 423–424

Federation of Business and Professional Women, 246
Fee shifting, 454
Feinstein, Dianne, 704
Feminist movement, 90, 245–247, 262, 555
Fenno, John, 269
Fernandez, Joseph, 98
Ferraro, Geraldine, 201
Fifteenth Amendment, 147–148, 445, 465
Fifth Amendment, 563, 590
Filibuster, 305, 307, 308, 341, 584
Finance Committee (Senate), 320, 332, 509, 519, 536
Fiorina, Morris, 710
Firearm Owners Protection Act (1986), 256
First Amendment, 210, 262, 264, 280, 455, 462, 670
    definition of person, 556–557
    definition of speech, 553–556
    establishment clause, 559–562
    Fourteenth Amendment and, 557–558, 560
    free-exercise clause, 557–559
    public religious displays and, 549–550
    religion and, 557–562
    restrictions on speech, 554
    rights of immigrants under, 597
    speech and national security, 550–553
    Supreme Court rulings, 562, 564
First Great Awakening, 93
First Hoover Commission, 434, 435
Flag burning, 347, 556
Flat tax, 14
Florida, 220, 541
Foley, Thomas, 322, 348, 360
Food and Drug Administration (FDA), 257, 261, 421, 490, 676
Food Stamps, 523, 524, 527, 531, 537
Forbes, Steve, 212
Ford, Gerald, 201, 285, 580
    assassination attempt, 401
    campaign of 1976, 190, 205, 474, 725
    deregulation and, 493, 495
    foreign policy, 608, 610, 611
    personality and character, 385
    presidency of, 383, 387, 392, 404, 405, 458, 479
Foreign affairs, 13, 15, 133, 325–326, 332
Foreign Affairs, 620
Foreign Affairs Committee (House), 620
Foreign aid, 399
Foreign Investors Act (1966), 340
Foreign policy, 603–629
    cleavages among elites, 619–624
    congressional approval of, 344, 607–609
    constitutional and legal context of, 606–612
    elitist theory and, 679
    majoritarian politics in, 604, 670
    media influence on, 614
    under parliamentary system, 688
    political cooperation on, 611
    post-cold-war era, 624–628
    public opinion and, 615–619
    role of United Nations, 627–628
Foreign Policy, 620
Foreign Relations Committee (Senate), 320, 332, 611, 620
Foundations, grants made by, 249–250
Fourteenth Amendment, 39, 186, 316, 440, 444, 445, 455, 465, 552
    abortion and, 591–592
    black civil rights movement and, 574
    citizenship and, 596
    due-process clause, 557–558, 591
    equal rights for women and, 588
    First Amendment and, 557–558, 560

quotas and preference systems, 598
reasonableness standard, 588, 597
rights of immigrants under, 597
strict scrutiny standard, 588, 597
Fourth Amendment, 562–567, 597
Fourth World, 626
France, 608–609
bureaucracy in, 410, 686
campaign fund raising compared, 214
interest groups in, 236
media in, 267, 268
systems of government, 53, 54, 185
Frankfurter, Felix, 460
Franking privilege, 214, 310, 351
Franklin, Benjamin, 26, 31
Franks, Gary, 327
Fraternal Order of Police, 256, 547
Frazer, Victor, 327
"Freedom-of-choice" desegregation plan, 579
Freedom of expression, 550
commercial and noncommercial speech, 557
national security and, 550–553
nature of speech and, 553–556
restrictions on, 554
Freedom of Information Act (1966), 268, 426, 689
Freedom of religion, 550, 559
Freedom of the press, 465
Freedom rides, 581, 582
Free-enterprise economic system, 89–90
Free-exercise clause, 557–559
"Free rider" problem, 480
Free Soil party, 187
French Revolution, 18, 475–476
Freneau, Philip, 269
Friedman, Milton, 540
Friends of the Earth, 655
FTC (Federal Trade Commission), 261, 421, 423–424
Fulbright, J. William, 611
Fulton, Robert, 443
Fundamentalism, 116(fig.), 117–118
Fund raising
for campaigns, *see* Campaign fund raising
interest groups and, 249–250, 258–260, 259(fig.),
260(fig.)

Gaines, Lloyd, 575
Galbraith, John Kenneth, 621
Gallatin, Albert, 303
Gallup, George, 122, 123, 347
GAO (General Accounting Office), 334
Gardner, John, 250
Garfield, James A., 401, 403, 417
Garner, John Nance, 403
Garrity, W. Arthur, 579
Gasoline taxes, 658
Gatekeeper role, of media, 278
Gay rights, 465, 599–600. *See also* Homosexuality
Gay-rights activists, 262
Gazette of the United States, 269
Gender
omitted from Constitution, 43
political attitudes and, 118(fig.), 118–119,
119(fig.)
of senators and representatives, 307–308, 309(fig.)
views on abortion and, 134
voting record and, 223(fig.)
see also Women
Gender gap, 118, 118(fig.)
Gender-sensitive policies, 118, 118(fig.)
General Accounting Office (GAO), 334
General-act charter, 701

General election, 202
General Election Project (1992), 231
General Motors, 242–243
General revenue sharing (GRS), 66–68
General Services Administration, 435
Geographic region, public opinion and, 126–127,
127(fig.), 130, 130(fig.)
George III, King of England, 21
Georgia, 555, 599–600, 699, 700, 709
Gephardt, Richard A., 197, 264, 519, 605
Germany, 91, 214, 240, 526, 615
Gerry, Elbridge, 32, 38, 41, 314
Gerrymandering, 314–315, 316
Gideon, Clarence Earl, 452, 453, 454
Gilder, George, 540
Gingrich, Newt, 217, 264, 360
ethics violations, 355
as Speaker of the House, 305, 321, 322, 323, 330
Ginsburg, Ruth Bader, 458, 459
Gitlow, Benjamin, 552
Giuliani, Rudolph W., 73, 716, 718
Glazer, Nathan, 540
Glenn, John, 197, 358–359
GNP (gross national product), 636
Gold plating, 645, 646
Goldwater, Barry
campaign of 1964, 189, 190, 191, 205, 216, 230,
284, 723
conservatism of, 132–133
election of 1964, 532
Goldwater-Nichols Act (1986), 634
Gompers, Samuel, 684
Good-faith exception, 567
GOPAC, 264
Gorbachev, Mikhail, 624, 625, 626
Gore, Al, 174, 197, 205, 515, 685
environmental policy and, 664
National Performance Review, 435
as vice president, 403
Gorton, Slade, 450
Gover, Al, 377
Government, 687–688, 695–696
activist government, 685–687
changes in system, 690
competing interests and, 684
competition between branches, 291–292
expansion of scope of, 683–684
ideas and, 688–692
policies of, 238
powers of, 444–445
restraints on growth of, 684–685
rights of disabled persons and, 598
rules for improving, 691
strength of, 24, 29, 31, 35, 36–37
see also Federal government; Local governments;
State governments
Governmental associations, 239
Government employee unions, 248–249, 249(fig.)
Government-funded day care, 593
Government Printing Office, 270
Governors, 698, 704–707, 706(fig.), 711
appointments of judiciary, 713
direct popular election of, 696
in intergovernmental lobbying, 66, 66(fig.)
line-item veto power, 704–705
Grace, J. Peter, 433
Grace Commission, 433, 434
Gramm, Phil, 212, 513, 711
Gramm-Rudman Balanced Budget Act (1985), 513
Grand Army of the Republic, 238
Grandfather clause, 148

Grange, The, 236, 237, 484, 485
Grant, Ulysses S., 373
Grants-in-aid, 63–64, 69–75, 415
block grants, 51, 75–77
categorical grants and revenue sharing, 66–68
for interest groups, 250
intergovernmental lobbies for, 66, 66(fig.)
mandates and, 70(fig.), 70–71, 73
Medicaid *versus* AFDC, 78–79
national needs and, 64(fig.), 65(fig.), 65–66
restrictions attached to, 71–75
slowdown in, 68–69
Grass-roots lobbying, 255
Grassroots organizations, 178, 263
Gravel, Mike, 203, 318
Gravel v. United States (1972), 318
Gray, Edwin, 358
Great Britain, 20, 164, 240, 381, 526
colonial opinions of, 20
compared with United States, 91, 214, 410, 411
criminal justice in, 562–563
effect of elections on policy, 229, 232
environmental policy in, 652
interest groups in, 235–236
media in, 267
as model of government structure, 687–688
parliamentary system, 33, 299–302, 363–365, 366,
653
role of judiciary, 439–440
see also Parliamentary systems
Great (Connecticut) Compromise, 31–32
Great Depression, 226, 247, 414
impact on policy, 474–475, 671
welfare programs and, 527, 528
Great Society programs, 476, 690–691
Greenback party, 187, 226
Greer v. Spock (1976), 562, 564
Gridlock, *see* Policy gridlock
Gross national product (GNP), 636
Groups
as beneficiaries of programs, 478, 482
client politics practiced by, 571–572
legitimacy of, 478, 482
role in policy-making process, 475–476
see also Interest groups
GRS (general revenue sharing), 66–68
Gubernatorial campaigns, 203, 213
Gulf War, procurement for, 436
Gun control, 62, 256, 344
Brady Bill (1993), 256, 698, 722, 723
entrepreneurial politics and, 676
NRA and, 256, 676
state court rulings, 465
Gun-Free School Zones Act (1990), 62, 446

Haddon, William, Jr., 257, 490
Hagen, Michael Gray, 90
Haig, Alexander, 382
Haiti, 541
Haldeman, H. R., 394
Hamilton, Alexander, 5, 38, 269, 303, 380, 383
conflict with Democratic-Republicans, 95
on English politics, 20
executive monarchy proposal, 367
on federalism, 58, 59
on judiciary, 441
presidency of, 371, 372
quarrel with Jefferson, 167
role at Constitutional Convention, 26, 31
on strong national government, 24
see also Federalist Papers

Hammond, Susan Webb, 327, 329
Hancock, John, 23, 24
Handgun Control, Inc., 256
Handicapped Children's Protection Act (1986), 70
Harding, Warren G., 180, 204, 551
Harkin, Tom, 197
Harlan, John, 464
Harmelin, Ronald A., 55
Harris, Louis, 122, 123
Harrison, Benjamin, 201, 203
Harrison, William Henry, 373, 384, 401
Hart, Gary, 279
Harvard Law Review, 458
Hastings, Alcee, 464
Hatch Act (1939), 179
Hawaii, 243, 245
Hawthorne, Nathaniel, 423
Hayden, Carl, 317
Hayes, Rutherford B., 176, 374
Hazardous waste, 654, 664
Health Care Financing Administration (HCFA), 78, 410
Health care reform, 254, 348
Hearst, William Randolph, 270–271
Heclo, Hugh, 428
Heinz, John III, 274
Helms, Jesse, 611
Henry, Patrick, 20, 26, 27, 38
Henry Wallace Progressive party, 187
Here-and-now argument, 491
Highway funding, conditions for, 72
Hill, Anita F., 439, 449
Hispanics
  bilingual education and, 550
  influence in House, 308
  majority-minority districts and, 316
  mayors, 719
  political opinions of, 126, 126(fig.)
  as voting bloc, 220, 221–222
Hitler, Adolf, 622
Hollerith, Herman, 413
Hollerith machine, 413
Holmes, Oliver Wendell, 448, 551, 552
Homeless, aid to, 537, 541
Homosexuality
  AIDS and, 139, 565
  conflict over, 98, 599–600
  military and, 134, 600, 644
  public opinion on, 134
  see also Gay rights
"Honeymoon" (presidential popularity), 390, 392
Hoover, Herbert, 285, 399
Hoover Commissions, 434, 435
Hopwood, Cheryl, 599
Horse-race reporting, 283
Hostage crisis, 390, 609, 648
House Judiciary Committee, 287
House of Representatives, 31, 32, 36, 196, 315, 318, 322, 340, 353, 368
  Appropriations Committee, 353, 429–430, 509, 661
  blacks and women in, 307–308, 309(fig.)
  civil rights and, 305–306, 580
  committees, 89, 305, 329, 330, 331, 509
  early powers of, 303–304
  ethics rules, 355, 356
  evolution of, 303–306, 357–360
  issues in common with voters, 345, 346(fig.)
  political parties and, 305, 320–322
  procedural changes made, 300–301, 303, 332

Rules Committee, 305, 306, 321, 339–340, 358, 360, 584
  rules on gifts, 350–351
  salaries and allowances, 301–302
  voting methods, 341–342
  Ways and Means Committee, 332, 358, 509, 519, 529, 536
  see also Congress; Senate
Housing, civil rights acts and, 586
HUD (Department of Housing and Urban Development), 232, 381, 410, 428
Hughes, Charles Evans, 464
Hull, Cordell, 608
Humphrey, Hubert, 183, 191, 278, 403, 530
  campaign of 1968, 190, 205, 723
  presidential elections of 1968, 186–187
Hunt, James B., 176
Hunt Commission, 176, 177
Hussein, Saddam, 626, 627, 638–639
Hutchinson, Kay Bailey, 711
Hutchinson v. *Proxmire* (1979), 318
Hyde, Henry, 591–592
Hyde Amendment, 591–592

ICBMs (intercontinental ballistic missiles), 643
ICC (Interstate Commerce Commission), 413, 444
Ideological parties, 180–181, 186, 187
Ideology, *see* Political ideology
Ignorance, public opinion and, 112–113
"I Have a Dream" speech, 583–584
Illegal search and seizure, 563–566
Illegal (undocumented) aliens, 541
Illinois, 220, 541
Illinois Farm Bureau, 241
Immigration
  cultural conflicts and, 549, 549(fig.)
  demographics, 129, 549, 550(fig.), 595
  economic effects of, 541–542
  immigrants' civil rights, 597
  political machine and, 179
  public opinion on, 126, 126(fig.), 128–129
  undocumented aliens, 541
  voting restrictions on aliens, 144, 151
Immigration and Naturalization Service (INS), 128, 597
Immigration Reform and Control Act (1986), 597
Imminent danger, free speech and, 554
Impeachment
  of Andrew Johnson, 304
  of presidents, 404–405
  of Richard Nixon, 287
Imperialism, in bureaucracy, 432–433, 434
"In-and-outers," 382–383
Incentives to join organizations, 241–243
Incitement, 280
Income inequality, 502–503, 502–503(figs.)
Income strategy, in social welfare, 534
Incumbency, 196, 197, 212, 218, 317–318
  advantages of, 309–310, 313
  campaign strategy and, 198–199
  composition of Congress and, 308–310, 310(fig.), 311(fig.), 312
  franking privilege and, 214, 310, 351
  pocketbook issues and, 500
Independent agencies and commissions, 381–382
"Independent" voters, 215(fig.), 216
Indiana, 245, 283, 555
Indiana (party-bloc) ballot, 229
Individual responsibility, 86, 598–599
Industrial pollution, 653–656, 655(fig.), 656(fig.)

Inflation, 500
In forma pauperis, 454
Information, 138, 253–254
Initiative, 172, 700, 704
Insider stories, 289, 291
Insider strategy, 254–255
INS (Immigration and Naturalization Service), 128, 597
Institute for Legislative Action, 256
Institutional interest groups, 239–240, 249
Institutions, 476–477, 690–691
Insurance (contributory) welfare programs, 527, 528
Integration, desegregation and, 578–581
Intellectuals, 120, 540
Intelligence Committees (House and Senate), 612
Intent to discriminate, 579, 580
Interagency cooperation, 75
Intercontinental ballistic missiles (ICBMs), 643
Interest group politics, 671–673
  allocating military spending and, 640–643
  environmental policy and, 658–660, 661(fig.)
  in foreign policy, 604
  pluralist theory and, 680–681
  policy-making process and, 480–481, 485–487
  racial politics, 571, 572, 574
Interest groups, 218, 235–265, 454, 494, 687, 690, 702
  civil liberties and, 546, 556–557, 689
  disruptive tactics of, 261–262
  effect on economic policy, 510
  environmental movement and, 245, 246
  feminist movement and, 245–247
  fund raising efforts, 249–250, 258–260, 259(fig.), 260(fig.)
  identifying, 220–221
  immigration law and policy, 128–129
  influence on antitrust legislation, 486–487
  information-gathering by, 253–254
  mass media, *see* Media
  membership groups, 240–241
  opinions on federal spending, 510–511, 511(fig.)
  PACs and, 258–260, 259(fig.), 260(fig.), 264
  in policy-making, 395
  public support of, 254–255, 257–258
  ratings of legislators by, 254, 325–326
  regulation of, 262–263, 265
  "revolving door" and, 260–261
  social movements and, 239, 244–249
  telecommunications deregulation and, 277
  unions as, 247–249, 248(fig.), 249(fig.)
  upper-class bias of, 250–251
  see also Lobbies
Intergovernmental lobbies, 66, 66(fig.)
Interior secretary, 384
Internal efficacy, 102
Internal Revenue Service, 263
Internal Security Act (1950), 548
International Relations Committee (House), 332
Internet, 12, 272, 273, 556
Interstate commerce, 61, 446–447
Interstate Commerce Commission (ICC), 413, 444, 493, 494
Interstate Commerce Commission Termination Act (1995), 494
Intraparty caucuses, 327, 328(fig.)
Iowa caucuses, 200–201, 279
Iran, 390, 609, 648
Iran-contra affair, 290, 612, 614, 617
Iraq, 612, 638–639
Iron curtain, 620, 622
Iron triangle, 428, 493

Irving, Washington, 423, 432
Isolationism worldview, 622–623
Israel, 164, 195, 214, 363–364
Issue networks, 428–429
Issue public, 255
Issues, 216–219
    economic, *see* Economic issues
    "hot button" issues, 212
    pocketbook issue, 500
    position and valence issues, 230–231
    prospective and retrospective voting, 218–219,
      219(fig.)
    see also specific issues
Italy, 91, 155, 165, 214, 236, 410–411, 686

Jackson, Andrew, 146, 269, 304, 401, 412
    assassination attempt, 401
    attack on Supreme Court, 443
    coattails, 197
    conflict with Congress, 373
    elections, 168, 225, 370
    presidency of, 372–373, 374
Jackson, Henry, 278
Jackson, Jesse, 156, 586, 605
    candidacies of, 187
    caucuses and, 191
    convention delegates and, 178
    promotion of boycotts, 486
    PUSH, 250
Jacksonian Democrats, 168–169, 225, 372–373
Jacksonian model of government, 697–698, 703, 705
    business development and, 717
    election of judges, 712
    state constitutions, 696–697, 711
    state governments, 718
    unreformed cities, 713–714
Jacobson, Gary C., 213–214, 313
Japan, 91, 214, 363–364, 615
Japanese-Americans, 126, 609–610
Jarvis, Howard, 483, 675
Jay, John, 28
JCS, *see* Joint Chiefs of Staff (JCS)
Jefferson, Thomas, 5, 269, 303, 304, 380, 383, 384,
    411, 412
    conflict with Federalists, 95
    Constitutional Convention and, 24, 26, 27
    election of 1800, 201, 370, 442
    on equality, 42
    on essential rights, 20
    on federalism, 58
    founding of party, 168
    on freedom of religion, 560
    on independence, 21
    Marbury v. *Madison,* 442
    on nullification, 60
    opposition to slave trade, 40
    presidency of, 367, 370, 371, 372, 373, 401, 551,
      607
    quarrel with Hamilton, 167
    Sedition Act (1798) and, 547, 551
    on Shays's Rebellion, 26
    support of states' rights, 58
    as vice president, 401, 403
Jeffersonian Republicans, 225
    founding of party, 167
    Marbury v. *Madison* and, 442, 443
Jehovah's Witnesses, 558
Jewish voters, 221
Jim Crow, 573
John Q. Public, 113

Johnson, Andrew, 201, 304, 384, 405
Johnson, Hiram, 172
Johnson, Lyndon B., 187, 278, 285, 364, 369, 401, 711
    campaigns, 205, 230, 279, 284, 723
    civil rights legislation and, 584, 585
    decline in popularity, 390, 390(fig.)
    election of 1964, 130, 201, 222, 358, 529, 532
    foreign policy, 608, 609, 611, 616, 617
    Great Society programs, 476, 690–691
    Medicare Act (1965), 530
    Model Cities plan, 64
    personality and character, 385, 386
    presidency of, 295, 365, 366, 383, 387, 392, 395,
      397, 400, 509
    as Senate majority leader, 319–320
    social welfare and, 528
    as vice president, 403
    Vietnam War and, 616, 617
Joint Chiefs of Staff (JCS)
    budget cuts and, 641
    Defense Department and, 632, 633(fig.)
    foreign policy and, 613
    homosexuals in military and, 644
    role in military policy, 634, 635, 640
Joint Committee on Reorganization, 434
Joint committees, 330, 353
Joint resolution, 337
Joint Staff, 634
Jones, Charles O., 399
Jones, Paula, 395
Jordan, Hamilton, 378
Journalism, 271, 278. *See also specific media*
Judges
    federal, 382, 405, 464
    impeachment of, 405, 464
    placing of mandates by, 71
    state judges, 712–713
    see also Courts; Judiciary; Supreme Court; *specific*
      courts
Judicial activism, 444, 446–447, 461–462, 463(fig.),
    467
Judicial power
    federal courts, 459–463
    lawyers and, 461–462
    policy-making process, 459–461
    proposals to curtail, 48
    of Supreme Court, 441, 443–444
Judicial review, 33, 439–440
Judiciary, 439–469, 440(fig.)
    checks on power of, 463–469
    congress and, 464–467
    constitutional interpretation by, 462
    federal, *see* Federal courts; Federal judges
    pluralist theory and, 681
    public opinion and, 467(fig.), 467–469
    school prayer issue, 465–466, 468
    state, 695
    Supreme Court, *see* Supreme Court
    see also Courts; Judges; *specific courts*
Judiciary Act (1789), 442
Jungle, The (Sinclair), 489
Justice Department, 277, 426–427, 457, 725
    annual authorizations, 430
    Antitrust Division, 484, 675
    Civil Rights Division, 678
Justices of Supreme Court, 456(fig.)
Justices of the peace, 712

Kamarck, Elaine, 377
Kansas-Nebraska Act (1854), 308

Kassebaum, Nancy Landon, 317
Katzenbach, Nicholas, 579
Keating, Charles Jr., 358–359, 492
"Keating Five," 358–359
Keep Commission, 434
Kefauver, Estes, 284, 285, 488, 489, 675
Keller, Morton, 198
Kelman, Steven, 436
Kelso, Frank B., II, 635
Kemp, Jack, 197, 212, 213, 519, 675
Kennan, George F., 620
Kennedy, Anthony, 450, 458, 459, 468, 562, 592, 596
Kennedy, Edward M., 258, 493, 643
    challenge of pocket veto, 392–393
    personal following of, 182, 183
Kennedy, John F., 230, 364, 673
    assassination of, 369, 401, 584
    Bay of Pigs fiasco, 616
    campaign of 1960, 205, 206
    election of 1960, 130, 222, 389, 389(fig.)
    foreign policy, 608, 609, 614, 616, 621
    party machine and, 180
    personal following of, 182, 183
    personality and character, 385
    presidency of, 295, 365, 380, 392, 394, 395, 397,
      400, 583
    social welfare and, 528
    on strategic weapons, 642
Kennedy, Joseph III, 182
Kennedy, Robert F., 182, 183, 187, 204
Kentucky Resolution, 60
Kerrey, Bob, 197
Kerry, John, 627
Key, V. O., Jr., 124, 216–217
Keyes, Alan, 212
Keynesianism, 504–505
KGB coup, 625
Kidnapping, 722
Kinder, Donald, 90
King, Martin Luther, Jr., 94, 581, 583, 585
King, Rodney, 451
Kinsley, Michael, 272
Kirk, Paul, 177
Kissinger, Henry A., 378, 383, 394, 608, 614
Klingberg, Frank L., 621
"Know-Nothing" (American) party, 187
Knox, Henry, 367
Koch, Edward, 72, 73, 718
Koppel, Ted, 287
Korean-Americans, 126
Korean War, 548, 552, 617, 636, 637, 637(fig.)
Kraft, Joseph, 113
Kristol, William, 254
Ku Klux Klan, 262, 552
Kunz, Carl Jacob, 547
Kuwait
    Iraqi invasion of, 638–639
    United Nations effort in, 628

Labor Department, 613
Labor movement, 187
Labor unions, 236, 237–238, 247, 248(fig.)
    demand for government protection, 485–486
    demand for safety law, 475
    environmental policy and, 657, 660
    interest group policies and, 672
    as interest groups, 244, 247–249, 248(fig.),
      249(fig.)
    members as voting bloc, 222, 223(fig.)
    PACs sponsored by, 259

Labor unions (*cont.*)
  parties sponsored by, 182
  Supreme Court and, 444
  see also AFL-CIO; *specific unions*
La Follette, Robert, 172, 183
La Follette Progressive party, 187, 188
Laissez-faire, 413
Lame duck, 404
Lamm, Richard, 185, 213
Lance, Bert, 685
Land-grant colleges, 63
Landrum-Griffin Act (1959), 486, 672
Laski, Harold, 53
Lasswell, Harold, 55
Latinos, 158–159, 159(fig.). *See also* Hispanics
Law
  civil and criminal, 452, 463, 465
  differential application of, 55, 691
  see also Legislation; Legislative process; *specific laws*
Law Enforcement Assistance Act, 67
Law Enforcement Assistance Administration (LEAA), 725
Lawsuits, 71, 243, 463
  class-action suits, 455–456, 462, 577–581
  libel suits, 553
  against president, 395
Lawyers, 239
  class-action suits and, 456
  in FTC, 423, 424
  power of courts and, 461–462
  before Supreme Court, 457
LEAA (Law Enforcement Assistance Administration), 725
Leadership PACs, 264
League of Conservation voters, 254
League of Nations, 608, 615
League of Women Voters, 241, 245, 246, 264
Least-restrictive means, 554
Lebanon, 611–612
Legal standing, in court, 454–455, 456, 462
Legislation
  antitrust, 61, 444, 484–485
  authorization legislation, 429
  civil rights, 337, 344, 583–584, 585
  federal courts and, 462–463
  pork-barrel, 350, 352
  tax legislation, 332
  vague language in, 463
Legislative courts, 447
Legislative process, 334–343
  factors in voting, 343–353
  floor debates, 340–341
  introducing bills, 336–337
  relative speed of, 334–335, 347–348
  role of congressional staffs, 333
  study by committees, 337–340, 339(fig.)
  voting methods, 341–343
Legislative Reorganization Act (1946), 330
Legislative veto, 400, 430, 610, 611
Legislators, 254, 319, 330–331
Legislatures
  amateur, 710, 711
  bicameral, 302, 590
  under Great Compromise, 31
  presidency and, 364–365
  professional, 710
  state legislatures, *see* State legislatures
  unicameral, 590
  in Virginia Plan, 30

see also Congress; House of Representatives;
  Parliamentary systems; Senate
Legitimacy
  of beneficiaries, 524, 525, 527, 533–534, 535(fig.)
  of government, 5, 21–22, 369, 372, 474–477, 678
  of groups, 478, 482
Levin, Adam K., 283
Libel, civil liberties and, 553
Libel law, 267
Libelous material, 280
Liberal/activist bloc, 458
Liberalism, 130, 132–133, 133(fig.), 244, 440
  of blacks, 125
  in civil service, 421, 422(fig.)
  college education and, 119–121, 120(fig.), 121(fig.), 138
  in environmental interest groups, 245, 246
  of journalists, 287–288, 288(fig.)
  on SDI ("Star Wars"), 643
  in Senate, 245, 246
  view of social welfare, 532, 534, 541
  views of military spending, 637–638
Libertarian party, 135, 137, 187
Liberty, 18, 19–24, 37, 86
  Antifederalist view of, 35–38
  bureaucracy as protection for, 435–436
  Constitution and, 19–24, 35–41, 94
  federal courts and, 445–447
  federalism as protector of, 56(fig.), 56–59
  as natural right, 27, 29
  protection of personal liberties, 35–41
  strength of government and, 35–37
  see also Civil liberties; First Amendment
Library of Congress, 334
Lieb, Martin, 436
Lieutenant governor, 704
Lilie, Stuart A., 135
Lincoln, Abraham, 180, 197, 370, 423, 685
  assassination of, 401
  elections, 225, 373
  Gettysburg Address, 111
  presidency of, 373, 376, 380, 383, 401, 607, 609, 647
Lincoln Savings and Loan, 358–359, 492
Lindbergh, Charles, 722
Line-item veto
  by governors, 704–705
  by president, 47–48, 393, 513
Line Item Veto Act (1996), 47–48
Linmark Associates, Inc. v. *Willingboro* (1977), 562, 564
Lippmann, Walter, 620
Lipset, Seymour Martin, 93, 125, 135
Literacy tests, 148, 586
Litmus test, 448(fig.), 449–450, 450(fig.)
Little Rock, 578
Liuzzo, Viola, 584
Loaded language, 122, 281
Loan sharking, 722–723
Lobbies, 12, 236, 255, 263, 494
  anti-gun-control lobby, 256
  congressional regulation of, 262–263
  intergovernmental, 66, 66(fig.)
  public-interest lobbies, 239, 242–243, 249, 251, 660
  see also Interest groups
Lobbyist, 236
Local governments, 410, 487, 555, 695, 697, 713–717
  cities, *see* Cities
  client politics and, 481–482
  commission plan, 715

constitutional basis of, 701–703, 702(fig.)
  council-manager plan, 715, 715(fig.)
  counties, 702, 716–717
  crime control and, 720–725
  federal law enforcement assistance, 724
  grants-in-aid to, 64(fig.), 65(fig.), 65–66
  in intergovernmental lobbying, 66, 66(fig.)
  mayor-council plan, 714(fig.), 714–715, 715(fig.)
  metropolitan government, 716–717
  special districts, 703, 717
  towns and townships, 702
Locke, John, 27, 29
Lodge, Henry Cabot, 611
Logrolling, 481, 482
Long, Huey, 188, 528, 529
Los Angeles, 236
Losing Ground (Murray), 540
Lott, Trent, 212
Louisiana, 700
Love Canal dump site, 483, 661, 662
Lowi, Theodore, 40
Low-income families
  aid to poor, 537
  effects of welfare reform on, 538–539
  voting record and, 222, 223(fig.)
Lugar, Dick, 212
Lynchings, 573

McAdams, John, 139
McCain, John, 358–359
McCarthy, Eugene, 187, 279
McCarthy, Joseph R., 292, 548, 675
McCarthy, Leo, 711
McCarthyism, 548
McClosky, Herbert, 104, 135
McCulloch, James, 59, 60
McCulloch v. *Maryland* (1819), 59–60, 441
McGovern, George, 74, 149, 176, 187, 191, 201, 203, 205, 279
McKinley, William, 226, 227, 271, 376, 401
McLaurin, George, 576
McNabb, Eula, 249
McNamara, Robert S., 394
McPeak, Merrill A., 635
Maddox, William S., 135
Madison, James, 38, 168, 304, 317, 401
  conflict with Federalists, 95
  creation of Department of State, 411
  economic interests, 41
  on equality, 42
  on factions, 34–35, 37, 54–55, 235
  on federalism, 57–58
  Federalist Papers, 28, 29, 30, 347
  Marbury v. *Madison*, 442
  on nullification, 60
  opinions of Pennsylvania constitution, 25
  opposition to equal representation of states, 31–32
  role at Constitutional Convention, 24, 26, 27, 29, 32
  on self-interest, 34
  on strength of government, 36–37
MAD (mutual assured destruction), 643
Magaziner, Ira, 377
Magazines
  influence on foreign policy, 614
  opinion magazines, 271–272, 272(fig.)
  see also Newspapers
Magnet, Myron, 540
Magnuson, Warren, 489

Mailer, Norman, 622
Majoritarian politics, 8, 479(fig.), 479–480, 523, 688
 blacks at disadvantage, 573
 business regulation and, 484–485
 cost of, 657–658
 crime control and, 724
 economic policy and, 500
 environmental policy and, 653, 656–658
 in foreign policy, 604, 670
 ideological debate and, 670
 income tax and, 517, 519
 military and, 631–632, 637–638
 political parties and, 671
 political power and, 670–671
 public opinion and, 670
 social welfare and, 532–533, 533(fig.)
 worldview and, 670–671
Majoritarian programs, 527–530
Majority leaders, congressional, 319–320, 322
Majority-minority districts, 316–317
Majority rule, 32–33
Malapportionment, 314–315, 456
Mandates
 defined, 69–70
 grants-in-aid and, 70(fig.), 70–71, 73
Mann, Thomas E., 352–353
Mansbridge, Jane, 246
Mansfield, Mike, 320
Mapp, Dollree, 563
Mapp v. *Ohio* (1961), 563
Marbury, William, 442
Marbury v. *Madison* (1803), 441, 442
March on Washington (1963), 583–584
Marcos, Ferdinand, 369
Marcy, William, 412, 685
Marginal districts, 309
Marine Corps, 640, 640(fig.)
Markets (television), 282–283
Markey, Edward, 249
Marshall, George C., 632
Marshall, George O., 608
Marshall, John, 59–60, 62
 Marbury v. *Madison,* 442
 on national supremacy, 441, 444, 467
Marshall, Thurgood, 458, 464, 468
Marshall Plan (1946), 365
Marx, Karl, 8, 10, 483–484
Marxists, 8–9, 473
Marxist theory, 677–678
Mason, George, 5, 32, 40, 41, 42
Massachusetts, 38, 40, 156, 185, 556
 constitution of, 25, 700
 Proposition 2½, 720
Massachusetts Citizens for Life, 556
Massachusetts (office-bloc) ballot, 229
Massachusetts Spy, 19
Mass transit, 69, 72–73
Matching funds, 66–67
Material incentives, 241–242
Mayhew, David, 183, 365
Mayor-council system, 714(fig.), 714–715, 715(fig.)
Mayors
 intergovernmental lobbying, 66, 66(fig.)
 mayor-council system, 714(fig.), 714–715, 715(fig.)
 strong elected mayors, 714
 strong-mayor systems, 715, 715(fig.)
 weak-mayor systems, 714–715, 715(fig.)
Mead, Lawrence, 540
Means test, 523, 524, 527, 528

Meat Inspection Act (1906), 489
Media, 267–295
 campaigning and, 282–283
 civil rights legislation and, 583–584
 compared with other countries, 267–268, 276
 competition in, 275–276, 277
 confidentiality of sources and, 280–282
 Congress and, 286–287, 309
 effects on politics, 283–285
 government and, 267–268, 285–287, 295
 importance in entrepreneurial politics, 676, 681
 interpreting news stories, 287(fig.), 287–295, 288(fig.), 289(fig.)
 journalism, *see* Newspapers
 presidency and, 285–286
 regulation of, 276, 279–283, 295
 roles of, 278–279, 477
 see also Electronic media; *specific media*
Medicaid program, 75–77, 232, 523, 527, 531
 abortion and, 592
 compared to AFDC, 78–79
 costs of, 539
Medicare Act (1965), 530, 532, 670, 680
Medicare Catastrophic Coverage Act (1988), 535, 537
Medicare program, 232, 523, 527, 670
 costs of, 535, 537
 as uncontrollable expenditures, 515, 515(fig.)
Meese, Edwin III, 462
Membership groups, 240–241
Mencken, H. L., 279
Menino, Thomas, 716
Meredith, James, 581
Merit system of recruitment, 417, 433
Merit Systems Protection Board (MSPB), 419
Merrill, Michael, 349
Meskimen's law, 428
Metropolitan government, 716–717
Mexican-Americans, 220, 222
Mexico, 91, 541, 605
Mfume, Kwiese, 329
Miami Herald Publishing Co. v. *Tornillo* (1974), 562, 564
Michigan, 707
Micromanaging, 647
Middle America, 113
Middle class, 139, 177, 177(fig.)
Middle East, 626
Mideast oil crisis, 479
Mikulski, Barbara, 176, 181
Miles, Rufus, 685
Military, 634, 635, 641, 643–644
 civilian control of, 632
 homosexuals in, 134, 600, 644
 role in crime control, 724, 725
 views of, 631–632
 women in, 589, 590, 643–644
Military-industrial complex, 632, 640
Military policy, 631–649
 base closings, 647
 decision-making structure, 632, 633(fig.), 634–636
 defense budget and, *see* Defense budget
 on homosexuality, 134, 600, 644
 military preparedness and, 405–406
 role of Congress in, 634, 641–642, 647
 trends in spending, 637, 637(fig.)
 War Powers Act, 610–612
Military Reform Caucus, 647
Milk subsidies, 487–488, 546
Miller, G. William, 509
Mills, C. Wright, 9–10

Mills, Wilbur, 529
Minnesota, 553, 593
Minority leader (House), 322
Minority leader (Senate), 319
Miranda, Ernesto A., 566–567
Miranda rule, 566–567
Mississippi, 148, 148(fig.)
Missouri, 483
Missouri Compromise, 443–444
"Missouri plan" judicial appointments, 713
Mistrust of government, 91, 94–95, 318, 686
 government responsiveness and, 102–103, 103(fig.)
 political culture and, 99–102, 100(fig.), 101(fig.)
 political participation and, 154
 scandals and, 102, 309, 313
 state governments, 700
Mitterand, François, 608–609
Mobilization politics, 198
Model Cities plan, 64
Mole, 613
Mondale, Walter, 119, 177, 197, 205, 279, 403, 479, 519
Monday Morning, 264
Monetarism, 504
Monroe, James, 168, 304, 317, 371, 384, 401
Morality, conflict over, 98–99
Moral Majority, 94, 118
Mormon Church, 591
Morris, Gouverneur, 32, 368
Morris, Robert, 42
Motor Carrier Act (1980), 494
Motor Vehicle Air Pollution Control Act (1965), 488
Motor-voter bill (1993), 144–145, 145(fig.)
Moynihan, Daniel Patrick, 299, 320, 356, 383, 476, 536
MSPB (Merit Systems Protection Board), 419
Muckraker, 271
Mugwumps, 171, 188
Multiculturalism, 593
Multiple referral, 338
Mundy, Carl E., 635
Munich-Pearl Harbor paradigm, 622–623
Municipal bonds, 60
Municipal corporations, 701
Municipal courts, 712
Murdoch, Rupert, 276
Murphy's law, 428
Murray, Charles, 534, 540
Muskie, Edmund, 64, 191, 257, 279, 488, 489, 490, 654
Mutual assured destruction (MAD), 643
Myrdal, Gunnar, 88–89

NAACP, *see* National Association for the Advancement of Colored People (NAACP)
Nader, Ralph, 242–243, 257, 418, 429, 605, 675
 auto safety issue and, 489, 490
 interest group formation, 237
 as policy entrepreneur, 482, 488
 pollution-control issue and, 488, 654
NAFTA (North American Free Trade Agreement), 605
Name-request jobs, 417–418
NARAL (National Abortion Rights Action League), 247
Narrowly concentrated costs and benefits, 479, 479(fig.)
NASA (National Aeronautics and Space Administration), 430

Nast, Thomas, 169
Nathan, Richard P., 74, 78–79
National Abortion Rights Action League (NARAL), 247
National Aeronautics and Space Administration (NASA), 430
National Alliance of Business, 250
National Association for the Advancement of Colored People (NAACP), 237, 240–241, 329
  formation of, 575
  organization of civil rights cases, 454, 455, 456, 458, 576
  tax status of, 263
National Association of Counties, 240
National Association of Manufacturers, 237
National Bureau of Standards, 413
National Catholic Welfare Conference, 237
National chairman, 173
National Coal Association, 654
National committee, 173
National Conservative Caucus, 251
National Council of Catholic Women, 591
National Council of the Churches of Christ (NCC), 244
National Daylight Saving Coalition, 244, 245
National Education Association, 183, 258, 673
National Endowment for the Arts, 98
National Environmental Policy Act (NEPA) [1969], 426, 655
National Farmers' Union, 236, 237
National Federation of Republican Women, 247
National Gazette, 269
National Guard, 577
National Highway Traffic Safety Administration, 257, 490
National Institute of Justice (NIJ), 725
National Intelligencer, 269
National Labor Relations Act, 672
National Labor Relations Board (NLRB), 485–486, 672
National Legal Center for the Public Interest, 250
National nominating conventions, 173, 174–178, 177(fig.)
  beginning of, 304
  controlling, 199
  delegates to, *see* Delegates to nominating conventions
  effects of media on, 284
  organizations represented, 183
National Organization for Women (NOW), 183, 247, 591
National Performance Review (NPR), 377, 434, 435
National Rifle Association (NRA), 256, 676
National Science Foundation, 673
National security, 550–553, 566
National Security Act (1947), 632, 633(fig.)
National Security Agency, 607
National Security Council (NSC), 612, 613–614, 620, 632
National Security Decision Directive (NSDD), 614
National Traffic and Motor Vehicle Safety Act (1966), 488
National Wildlife Federation, 245, 246
National Women's Political Caucus, 247
Nation-state relationship, *see* State-federal relationship
Naturalization requirements, 596
Navy, 634, 640, 640(fig.)
NCC (National Council of the Churches of Christ), 244

Nebraska, 707, 710
"Necessary and proper" clause, 59–60, 302
Negative advertising, 210, 219, 293
NEPA (National Environmental Policy Act), 426, 655
Netherlands, 195
Neustadt, Richard, 382, 387
Neutrality, 554
Nevada, 653
"New class," 138–139
New Deal, 62, 132, 232, 476
  bureaucracy and, 414
  origins of, 188
New Deal coalition, 139, 224
New England, 167
New England town meeting, 6, 8, 702
New Hampshire, 710
New Jersey, 256, 443, 541
New Jersey Plan, 31, 33
Newly industrialized nations (NINs), 626
News, 287–289(figs.), 287–295
  ethical considerations, 294
  leaks, 291–293, 293(fig.)
  slanted stories, 288–291, 289(fig.)
  see also Media; *specific media*
Newspapers, 269–275, 276, 278, 281, 284
  competition between, 275–276
  controlled by political parties, 269
  electronic media compared, 272, 279
  influence on foreign policy, 614
  party-controlled press, 269
  popular press, 270–271
  role in policy-making, 477
  see also Magazines
New York City, 283
  proportional representation in, 185
  structure of government, 718
  Tammany Hall, 171, 179, 181, 697, 718, 719
New York Custom House, 179
New York Daily News, 270
New York Port Authority, 703
New York State, 443, 541, 552, 697, 718
  governors, 718
  Hispanic vote in, 220
  ratification of Constitution, 38
New York Times, 270, 278, 477, 547
New York v. United States (1992), 62
Nicaragua, 618, 622
Nie, Norman, 152
NIJ (National Institute of Justice), 725
Nineteenth Amendment, 43, 149
NINs (newly industrialized nations), 626
Nixon, Richard M., 187, 222, 288, 364, 580
  appointments, 448, 460, 468
  Budget Reform Act (1974) and, 395
  campaigns, 205, 206, 208, 216, 230, 723, 725
  criticism of civil service, 420
  decline in popularity, 390, 391(fig.)
  elections, 149, 201, 203, 389, 389(fig.), 618
  impeachment of, 287
  "new federalism" of, 74
  personality and character, 385
  policies, 397, 509, 608, 609, 611, 616, 654, 655
  presidency of, 377, 378, 383, 392, 394, 399–400, 404, 414, 474, 479, 509
  resignation of, 405
  treatment of media, 295
  as vice president, 401, 403
  Vietnam War and, 616
  Watergate burglary, 100, 405, 612
Nixon, Walter, 464

NLRB (National Labor Relations Board), 485–486, 672
Nofziger, Lyn, 261
Nomenklatura, 138
Nominations, *see* Presidential nominations
Noncareer executive assignments (NEA jobs), 417
Nonpartisan ballot, 707, 710
Nonpartisan election of judges, 712
Nonviolent civil disobedience, 583
Nonvoting, 143–146, 144(fig.), 145(fig.)
North, Oliver, 290, 614
North American Free Trade Agreement (NAFTA), 605
North Carolina, 316, 579, 582
NOW (National Organization for Women), 183, 247, 591
NPR (National Performance Review), 377, 434, 435
NRA (National Rifle Association), 256
NSC (National Security Council), 612, 613–614, 620, 632
Nuclear power plants, 290
Nullification, 60–61, 62

OASDI (Old Age, Survivors, and Disability Insurance), 527
Obscenity, 280, 554–556
Occupation, voting record and, 223(fig.)
Occupational Safety and Health Act (1970), 475, 486, 490, 672
Occupational Safety and Health Administration (OSHA), 351, 410, 428, 486–487, 490, 672
Ocean Dumping Ban Act (1988), 70
O'Connor, Sandra Day, 458, 459, 464, 468, 469, 562, 592, 597
Office-bloc (Massachusetts) ballot, 229
Office for Civil Rights, 673, 678
Office of Compliance, 351
Office of Management and Budget (OMB), 376, 377, 379–380, 422, 686
Office of National Drug Control Policy ("Drug Czar"), 722
Office of Personnel Management (OPM), 379, 415–416
Office of Special Counsel, 422
Office of Technology Assessment (OTA), 334
Office of the President, 376–382, 377(fig.)
  agencies and commissions, 381–382
  cabinet, 380–381, 381(fig.)
  Executive Office, 379–380, 400, 434
  organization of, 377–379, 379(fig.)
Office of Thrift Supervision, 426–427
Office of U.S. Trade Representative, 379
Offsets, 663
Ohio, 552
Oil spills, 654, 655
Oklahoma, 348
Old Age, Survivors, and Disability Insurance (OASDI), 527
"Old boys' network," 418
OMB (Office of Management and Budget), 376, 377, 379–380, 422, 686
O'Neill, Thomas P. "Tip," 319, 322, 360
One-issue parties, 187
Open Meeting Law (1976), 426
Open primary, 202
Open rules, 339, 339(fig.)
Operational grants, 75
Operation Desert Storm, 638–639
Opinion magazines, 271–272, 272(fig.)

Opinion of the Court, 458
Opinion polls, 88, 113(fig.), 113–114, 114(fig.), 122–123
OPM (Office of Personnel Management), 379, 415–416
Organizational voting, 344
Organizations, 164–165, 198, 199
Original intent, 462
Ornstein, Norman J., 352–353
Orren, Gary, 92
Orthodoxy, political, 98–99, 595
OSHA, *see* Occupational Safety and Health Administration (OSHA)
OTA (Office of Technology Assessment), 334
Otis, James, 40
O'Toole's corollary to Murphy's law, 428
Outsider strategy, 255
Oversight Committee (House), 351
Owens, William A., 635

PAC, *see* Political action committees (PACs)
Pacific Gas and Electric Company, 556
Packwood, Robert, 355, 519
Paine, Thomas, 25
Palmer, A. Mitchell, 548, 675
Panama Canal treaties (1978), 257, 287, 344
Panetta, Leon E., 377
Parental leave law, 593
Parent-Teacher Association (PTA), 161
Parent-Teachers Association (PTA), 241
Parkinson's laws, 428
Parks, Rosa, 582–583
Parliamentary systems, 33, 46, 653, 688
    bureaucracy compared, 410, 411
    cabinet officers in, 383
    compared with Congress, 299–302, 363–365, 366
    effect of elections on policy, 229
    role of judiciary, 439–440
    social welfare and, 688
    see also Great Britain
Parochial participants, 153
Participatory democracy, *see* Direct democracy
Partisan election of judges, 712
Partisan relations with Congress, 399
Partisanship, in federal courts, 447
Part-time legislature, 710, 711
Party affiliations, 168, 170–171, 373
Party-bloc (Indiana) ballot, 229
Party caucuses, *see* Caucuses
Party identification, 163, 164, 164(fig.), 165
    formation of, 115(fig.), 115–116
    presidential elections and, 215(fig.), 215–216
Party symbols, 169
Party unity vote, 324
Paterson, William, 27, 31
Patriotism, 92, 93(fig.)
Patronage, 411–412, 417, 697, 705, 711
Peace dividend, 514
Pearl Harbor, 615, 616, 622–623, 670
Peckham, Rufus, 440
Pendleton Act (1883), 417
Penniman, Howard, 211
Pennsylvania, 25, 38, 40, 592
Pension Office, 413
Pentagon, 636
Pentagon Papers, 318, 547
Penthouse magazine, 553
Per curiam opinion, 458
Perkins, Frances, 383

Perks, 380
Perot, Ross, 9, 187, 274, 605
    campaigns, 123, 173, 185, 186, 188–189, 206, 213, 218, 231, 365
    decline of, 213
    infomercials, 206
    mistrust of government and, 102
Persian Gulf War, 608, 635, 638–639
Personal conduct, 135, 137
Personal followings, 182–183
Personal-interest caucuses, 327, 328(fig.)
Personal Responsibility and Work Opportunity Reconciliation Act (1996), 76–77, 537, 538–539, 540
Pesticides, 661–662
Peter principle, 428
Peterson, Mark A., 374
Pharmaceutical industry, 490, 676
Pharmaceutical Manufacturers' Association, 490
Pickett, Owen, 345
PIRGs (Public Interest Research Groups), 243
Pitkin, Hannah F., 316
Plaintiff, 454
Planned Parenthood v. *Casey* (1992), 591, 592
Plessy, Adolph, 574–575
Plessy v. *Ferguson* (1896), 574–575, 577
Plunkitt, George Washington, 179
Pluralism, 10, 12, 473
Pluralist theory, 680–681
Plurality system, 184–185, 186
Pocketbook issue, 500
Pocket veto, 392–393
Poindexter, John, 614
Poland, 624
Police, 38, 723
    Fraternal Order of Police, 256, 547
    rules for conduct of, 563–566, 567
Police power, 699
Policy Committees, congressional, 320, 322
Policy development, 395–398
Policy entrepreneurs, 482, 478–481, 519, 675, 681
    civil liberties and, 546, 547–549
    Medicare plan and, 529–530
    symbols used by, 675–676
Policy gridlock, 348, 365–367
Policy intellectuals, 540
Policy-making process, 396–397, 473–495, 506, 677
    agenda for, 474–477
    in business regulation, 483–491
    client politics and, 481–482, 487–488
    costs and benefits in, 477–479, 491, 662–663
    deregulation and, 493, 494
    entrepreneurial politics and, 482–483, 488–491
    groups, role of, 475–476
    institutions, role of, 476–477
    interest group politics and, 480–481, 485–487
    legitimate scope of action, 474–477
    majoritarian politics and, 479(fig.), 479–480, 484–485
    media, role of, 477
    power of federal courts and, 459–461
    presidential programs, 395–400
    reducing subsidies, 493–495, 524
    savings and loan crisis, 492
    sources for, 395–398
    in states, 717–719
Political action, 13, 240
Political action committees (PACs)
    interest groups and, 258–260, 259(fig.), 260(fig.), 264

    as source of campaign funds, 198, 208(fig.), 209–211, 210(fig.), 214
    spending by, 259(fig.), 259–260
Political agenda, 474–477
Political attitudes, 114–121
    education and, 119–121, 120(fig.), 121(fig.)
    family and, 115(fig.), 115–117
    gender and, 118(fig.), 118–119, 119(fig.)
    religion and, 116(fig.), 117–118
Political change, 12–13, 15
Political cues, 254
Political culture, 85–106, 166, 546, 713
    adversarial spirit of, 94–95, 410, 461
    compared with other nations, 90–94
    cultural conflict and, 98–99
    economic system and, 89–90, 90(fig.), 92–93, 93(fig.), 94(fig.)
    mistrust of government, 99–102, 100(fig.), 101(fig.)
    political efficacy and, 102–103, 103(fig.)
    political systems, 86, 88–89, 91–92, 92(fig.), 93(fig.)
    political tolerance in, 102–106, 105(fig.), 106(fig.)
    religion and, 93–94, 94(fig.), 95(fig.)
    sources of, 94–99
Political editorializing rule, 282
Political efficacy, 102–103, 103(fig.)
Political elites, 8
    explanatory theories, 8–10, 12
    foreign policy elites, 619–624, 671
    ideology of, 137–138
    mass views shaped by, 139–140, 617
    nature of opinions, 618(fig.), 618–619, 619(fig.)
    as "new class," 138–139
    sensitivity of judiciary to, 467
    views of civil liberties, 689
    see also Activism
Political ideology, 87, 130–139, 131(fig.)
    attitudinal voting in Congress, 345–346, 346(fig.)
    bureaucracy and, 421–422
    debate on military spending and, 637–638
    economic theories and, 506
    effects of family on, 116–117
    influence on nominating conventions, 191
    of journalists, 289–290
    majoritarian politics and, 670
    of political elites, 137–138
    terminology of, 132–133, 133(fig.)
Political institutions, 91–92, 92(fig.)
Political liberties, 445–447
Political machines, 178–180, 182, 697
Political participation
    activities, 145–146
    causes of, 153(fig.), 153–156
    forms of, 152(fig.), 152–153
    meaning of participation rates, 156, 157–159(figs.)
    see also Activism; Voting
Political parties, 133, 134, 163–193, 690
    client politics and, 674
    comparison with other countries, 163–166, 164(fig.)
    in Congress, 322, 323–326, 324(fig.), 325(fig.), 345
    convention delegates and, *see* Delegates to nominating conventions
    effects of campaign financing reform on, 211
    effects of Civil War, 169–171
    formation of party identification, 115(fig.), 115–116
    fund raising activities, 210–211

Political parties (*cont.*)
    ideological factions in, 180–181, 366
    interest group politics and, 672
    Jacksonian Democrats, 168–169, 225, 372–373
    judicial behavior and, 448
    majoritarian politics and, 671
    modern party structure, 172–178
    national conventions, *see* National nominating
        conventions
    newspapers controlled by, 269
    organization of Senate and, 319–320
    in parliamentary system, 300
    partisan loyalties, 219
    personal followings and, 182–183
    platforms, 232
    political machines, 178–180
    as presidential audience, 138
    presidential nominations, 189–191
    primaries, *see* Primary elections
    ratios on committees, 330
    realignments, 224–228
    reform era, 171–172
    rise and decline of, 80, 166–172, 224(fig.),
        228–229
    role in elections, 195–196
    role in political culture, 166
    selection of committee chairmen, 331
    social class and, 124
    solidary groups, 182
    state and local, *see* State and local political parties
    symbols, 169
    two-party system, 183–186, 184(fig.)
    voting and, 145, 150, 154, 155, 191–192, 192(fig.)
    see also specific parties
Political power, 4–5, 54
    bureaucratic theory of, 679–680
    client politics and, 673–675
    distribution of, *see* Distribution of power
    elitist theory of, 678–679
    entrepreneurial politics and, 675–676
    of federal courts, 459–463
    interest group politics and, 671–673
    majoritarian politics and, 670–671
    Marxist theory of, 677–678
    pluralist theory of, 680–681
    see also Presidential power; *specific powers and
        kinds of power*
Political proverbs, 685
Political questions, 460
Political subculture, 87
Political systems, 82(fig.), 91–92, 93(fig.)
Political tolerance, 102–106, 105(fig.), 106(fig.), 134
Political values, 89, 473, 491–493
Politicians, 387, 501, 504
Politics, 12, 198, 546–550, 653, 723
    client, *see* Client politics
    effects of media on, 283–285
    entrepreneurial, *see* Entrepreneurial politics
    federal grants-in-aid and, 64
    interest group, *see* Interest group politics
    majoritarian politics, *see* Majoritarian politics
    racial, 571, 572, 574
    "rules" of, 673
    of Social Security, 533
Politics of Deregulation, The (Derthick & Quirk), 493
Polk, James K., 373, 607
Poll tax, 148
Pollution allowances (banks), 663
Pollution-control laws, 70
Popular majority, 684

Populist party, 186, 187, 226
Populists, 137
Pork-barrel legislation, 350, 352
Pork-barrel projects, 481–482, 674
Position issues, 230
Postal Service, 410, 412
Post Office Department, 411
Poverty, *see* Low-income families
Powell, Lewis, 458
Power
    bureaucratic power, 414–415, 415(fig.), 688
    of Congress, 373–374
    distribution of, *see* Distribution of power
    federal, *see* Federal power
    of federal courts, 459–463
    under Federalism, 56(fig.), 57–58
    of government, 444–445
    judicial, *see* Judicial power
    of regulatory agencies, 413
    in unitary systems, 54, 56(fig.)
    veto power, *see* Veto power
    see also Political power; Presidential power
Power elites, 9–10
Preferences, 15, 190
Preferential treatment, 90, 597–599
Preferred position, free speech and, 554
Presidency, 363–406, 367, 690
    appointive powers of, *see* Appointments,
        presidential
    concerns of Founders, 367–368
    congressional power and, 373–374
    divided government and, 365–367
    early presidents, 371–372
    electoral college and, 368, 370–371
    evolution of, 367–374
    executive privilege, 392–395
    impeachment, 404–405
    Jacksonian Democrats and, 372–373
    media and, 285–286
    other countries compared, 363–365
    peaceful transitions, 369–370, 400–405
    problems of succession to, 403–404
    reliance on persuasion, 386–392
    term of office issue, 368–370
    two-party system and, 185–186
    veto, *see* Veto power
    vice-presidential succession to, 401, 403
    see also Office of the President; President; *specific .
        presidents*
President, 34, 364, 371–372, 376, 406
    access to, 378–379
    appointments by, *see* Appointments, presidential
    attempts to reorganize, 398–400
    audiences, 386–387, 388(fig.)
    bills introduced by, 336
    bureaucracy and, 435
    character of, 384–386
    as commander in chief, 375, 635
    Congress and, 398–399, 611
    decline in popularity, 390–392(figs.), 392
    defense budget cuts and, 647
    executive privilege, 394–395
    foreign policy, *see* Foreign policy
    impoundment of funds by, 395
    increase in authority of, 44, 46
    legislature and, 364–365
    media and, 285–286
    military preparedness and, 405–406
    popularity and influence, 285–286, 387, 389–390,
        389–391(figs.)

    programs of, 395–400
    public appearances, 387, 388(fig.)
    role in majoritarian politics, 670
    role in military policy, 647
    signature or veto of bills, *see* Veto power
    treatment of media, 295
    see also Office of the President; Presidency; *specific
        presidents*
Presidential campaigns, 197–199, 219–220
    of 1840, 154, 230
    of 1888, 198, 203
    of 1920, 204
    of 1960, 205, 206
    of 1962, 488
    of 1964, 205, 216, 230, 284, 723
    of 1968, 204, 205, 230, 279, 723
    of 1972, 205, 208, 216, 279, 488
    of 1976, 199, 203, 205, 230, 474, 725
    of 1980, 199, 205, 282, 288, 725
    of 1984, 199, 205, 216, 230, 279, 288, 479
    of 1988, 197, 199, 200, 218, 219, 230, 513
    of 1992, 78, 197, 199, 205, 206, 213, 231, 288,
        289(fig.), 605, 627
    of 1996, 174, 199, 205, 208, 211, 221, 231
    fund raising for, *see* Campaign fund raising
    mobilization politics and, 198
    nominations, 199
    organizations for, 198, 199
    primary *versus* general, 199–207
    role of media in, 203–207, 219
    sources of funds, 208
    strategy and themes, 198–199
    tone, timing, and targets of, 199
Presidential elections, 166
    of 1796, 168
    of 1800, 201, 225, 368, 370
    of 1804, 168, 304
    of 1808, 304
    of 1812, 304
    of 1816, 168, 169, 304
    of 1820, 168
    of 1824, 168, 169, 201, 368, 370
    of 1828, 168, 225
    of 1832, 168–169
    of 1836, 169
    of 1840, 168
    of 1860, 185–186, 225, 232
    of 1864, 201
    of 1888, 201
    of 1892, 186
    of 1896, 170, 225, 226, 227, 231
    of 1912, 185, 186, 187, 188
    of 1932, 225, 226, 228, 232, 527
    of 1936, 228, 445, 529, 670
    of 1944, 130
    of 1948, 130, 186, 189
    of 1952, 618
    of 1956, 389, 389(fig.)
    of 1960, 123, 130, 389, 389(fig.)
    of 1964, 130, 189, 201, 232, 358, 529, 532, 584
    of 1968, 186–187, 189, 618, 670
    of 1972, 149, 191, 201, 203, 389, 389(fig.)
    of 1976, 118, 123, 130
    of 1980, 118, 123, 186, 189, 227, 232, 389(fig.),
        389–390, 500, 509, 618, 670
    of 1984, 118, 156, 201, 232
    of 1988, 207, 370
    of 1992, 123, 130, 185, 186, 207, 292, 365, 500, 670
    of 1996, 130, 185, 192, 192(fig.), 206, 212–213,
        221, 232, 536

critical elections, 216–217
decided by House, 368, 370
deciding factors in, 215–222
electoral coalitions, 220–222, 223(fig.)
"faithless electors," 370
fund raising for, 209
issues and, 216–219
party identification and, 215(fig.), 215–216
role of voting blocs, 220, 221
variations in early elections, 147
Presidential nominations, 189–191. *See also* Delegates
  to nominating conventions; National
  nominating conventions
Presidential power, 373, 374–376, 405–406
  appointive powers, *see* Appointments, presidential
  Congress and, 373–374, 375–376
  under Constitution, 375
  evaluating, 609–610
  in foreign policy, 604, 606–612
  intelligence oversight and, 612
  military or economic aid, 610
  under parliamentary system, 688
  persuasion and, 386–392
  restrictions on, 610–612
  veto power, *see* Veto power
  War Powers Act and, 610–612
Presidential Power (Neustadt), 387
Presidential primary, *see* Primary elections
President pro tempore (Senate), 319
President's Commission on Administrative
  Management, 378
President's Commission on Economy and Efficiency,
  434
President's Committee on Administrative
  Management, 434, 435
Press conferences, 273, 387, 388(fig.)
Press secretary, 285–286
Primary elections, 166, 190–191, 199, 202
  of 1968, 187
  of 1984, 177, 178
  of 1992, 178, 190, 316
  congressional, 317–319
  fund raising for, 209
  media coverage of, 279
  white primary, 148
Print media, 614. *See also* Magazines; Newspapers
Prior restraint, 551, 554
Privacy, 280, 564–565, 591
Privacy Act (1974), 426, 689
Private bill, 336
Private property, 444
Privileged speech doctrine, 318
Probable cause, 563
Process regulation, 495
Professional legislature, 710
Professional societies, 238, 251
Progressive income tax system, 14
Progressive model of government, 697–698
  election of judges, 712
  governmental structure, 703
  reformed cities, 713–714
  schools and, 703
  state governments, 718
Progressive movement, 697–698
Progressive party, *see* Bull Moose (Progressive) party
Progressives, 98–99, 171
  equality of opportunity and, 595
  social welfare and, 526
Prohibition, 188, 219–220
Prohibition party, 187

Pro-life organizations, 247, 476, 556, 592
Property rights, 20, 597, 689
Proportional representation, 178, 185
Proposition 2½, 720
Proposition 13 (1978), 7, 483, 704, 720
Proprietary, CIA definition of, 613
Prospective voting, 218
Prostitution, 722
Protestantism, 96
Protest marches, 581
Proxmire, William, 318
PTA (Parent-Teacher Association), 161
Public accommodations, civil rights and, 584, 586,
  598
Public appearances by president, 387, 388(fig.)
Public bill, 336
Public Citizen, 243, 264
Public demonstrations, 156
Public interest, 15, 347
Public-interest law firms, 243
Public-interest lobbies, 239, 242–243, 249, 251, 660
Public Interest Research Groups (PIRGs), 243
Public opinion, 111–140
  on abortion, 136
  approval of president, 616–618, 617(fig.)
  civil rights legislation and, 583, 583(fig.)
  cleavages in society and, 672
  of client-based welfare programs, 531
  competing interests and, 684
  of defense spending, 637, 638(fig.)
  elite opinion contrasted, 618(fig.), 618–619,
    619(fig.)
  of environment, 664, 664(fig.)
  on foreign policy, 615–619
  on homosexuality, 134
  on immigration, 128–129
  interest group politics and, 672, 673
  judiciary and, 467(fig.), 467–469
  majoritarian politics and, 670
  media and, 284–285, 292
  political ideology and, 130–139, 131(fig.)
  as restraint on government, 684
  social welfare and, 540
  of Soviet Union, 620–621
  on telecommunications deregulation, 277
Public policy, *see* Policy; Policy-making process;
  specific policies and kinds of policy
Public pressure, by interest groups, 257
Public safety, Fourth Amendment rights and, 566,
  567
Public schools, *see* Schools
Public support for social welfare, 537, 541–542
Puerto Ricans, 222
Pulitzer, Joseph, 270
Pure conservatives, 135
Pure Food and Drug Act (1906), 488
Pure liberals, 135
Puritanism, 96
Purposive incentives, 242, 247
PUSH, 250
Putnam, Robert D., 160–161
Pyramid structure, of White House office, 377,
  378

Quasi-independent agencies, 381–382
Quirk, Paul, 493
Quorum, 340
Quorum call, 340
Quotas, discrimination and, 597, 598

Raab, Earl, 135
Race
  adequate representation and, 317
  at-large elections and, 714
  cleavages in public opinion and, 125(fig.),
    125–126, 126(fig.)
  political participation and, 153–154
  of senators and representatives, 307–308, 309(fig.)
  voting record and, 223(fig.)
Race relations, 88–89
Racial discrimination, 582–583
  black colleges and, 576
  intent to discriminate, 579, 580
  majority-minority districts and, 316–317
  reverse discrimination and, 458, 594
  separate-but-equal doctrine, 574–577
  voting restrictions, 144, 148
  see also Brown v. *Board of Education;*
    Desegregation; Segregation
Racial politics, 571, 572, 574
Racism, 573
"Radical Republicans," 304
Radio
  advertising, 219
  rules for campaigns, 282–283
  see also Electronic media; Television
Radioactive waste disposal, 652–653
Railroad Revitalization and Regulatory Reform Act
  (1976), 494
Rainey, Joseph H., 317
Randolph, Edmund, 27, 29, 32, 367
Random sample, 122
RAND (think tank), 640
Rangel, Charles, 259
Rankin, Jeannette, 317
Rather, Dan, 287
Ratification of amendments, 45
Ratification of Constitution, 35, 38–39, 42
Ratings of legislators, 254, 325–326
Rayburn, Sam, 305, 321–322, 326, 711
Reagan, Ronald, 99, 111, 119, 135, 137, 164, 190, 197,
    222, 243, 364, 384, 401, 580, 704, 705
  appointments, 382, 458, 464, 468, 490, 596
  assassination attempt, 256, 401, 403
  block grants, 74
  campaigns, 199, 205, 216, 230, 288, 725
  civil rights legislation and, 585
  congressional election of 1982 and, 216
  deregulation and, 493, 495
  economic policy and, 499, 512, 513, 515
  election of 1980, 123, 124, 218, 221, 227, 346,
    389(fig.), 389–390, 500, 618
  election of 1984, 124, 137, 201
  foreign policy, 608, 611–612, 614, 623
  military policy, 640
  opinions of women on, 118
  personality and character, 385–386
  policy-making, 396, 397
  presidency of, 377, 378, 382, 389, 400, 422, 428,
    429, 449, 450, 474, 565, 725
  "Star Wars" (SDI), 642–643
Reagan administration
  antitrust activities, 485
  efforts to cut federal power, 13, 74, 75, 76, 232,
    685
  environmental and, 490, 660
  Iran-contra affair, 290, 612, 614, 617
  mistrust of government and, 99, 102
  opposition to mandates, 70
  reduced grants to interest groups, 250

Reaganomics, 506–507
Realigning periods, 224–228
Reasonable expectation of privacy, 564–565
Reasonableness standard, 588, 597
Recall, 700, 704
Recession, 390
Reconstruction, 373
Red Scare, 548
Red tape, 427–428, 432, 433, 434
Reed, Ralph, 118
Reed, Thomas B., 304, 305, 321, 330
Reelection, 368, 708
Referendum, 172, 346, 700, 704
Reformed cities, 713–714, 718
Reform movements
    civil service reform, 412, 435–436
    congressional reform, 346, 350–353
    as ideological parties, 181
    political parties and, 171–172
Reform party, 185, 187, 188–189
Regulatory agencies, 413, 415, 490–491, 675
Rehabilitation Act (1973), 72–73, 433
Rehnquist, William H., 112, 439, 440, 449, 458, 459,
    468, 562
Relative deprivation, 475–476
Religion, 37, 95, 96, 99, 153
    as campaign issue, 220
    civil liberties and, 550, 558, 559, 560
    decline in church attendance, 160–161
    First Amendment and, 557–562
    First Great Awakening, 93
    free-exercise clause, 557–559
    interest group formation and, 238–239
    political attitudes and, 116(fig.), 117–118
    religious display on public property, 549–550
    role in political culture, 93–94, 94(fig.), 95(fig.),
        96
    schools and, 558, 560
    views on abortion and, 134
    voting and, 222, 223(fig.)
Religious tradition, 117
Remedies (judicial), 460
Remington, Frederic, 271
Reorganization Act (1939), 400
Representational voting, 343–345
Representative democracy, 6, 7, 33, 34, 676–677
    direct democracy compared, 7, 9, 11, 346–347
    distribution of power in, 7–12
    gridlock as consequence of, 180–181
Representative town meeting, 702
Republic, 32
Republican Congressional Committee, 173
Republican National Committee (RNC), 173, 174
Republican party, 170, 171, 173, 177, 177(fig.),
    225
    attempt to abolish caucuses, 32
    Christian Coalition and, 118
    "Contract with America," 78, 79
    control of Congress, 300–301, 345–346
    control of state legislatures, 708–709, 710
    defection of Southern Democrats to, 216–217
    dominance of, 224, 224(fig.)
    effect of social movements on, 181
    governorships, 705
    national conventions, *see* National nominating
        conventions
    party identification, 115(fig.), 115–116, 215(fig.),
        215–216
    at state and local levels, 183–184, 184(fig.)
    see also Jeffersonian Republicans

Republican Senatorial Committee, 173
Republican Study Committee (House), 345
Residential segregation, 578
Resolution Funding Corporation, 426–427
Resolution Trust Corporation, 426–427
Restrictive rules, 339, 339(fig.)
Retinitis Pigmentosa Foundation, 244, 245
Retrospective voting, 218–219, 219(fig.)
Revenue sharing, 66–68
Reverse discrimination, 458, 594
"Revolving door," 260–261
Reynolds v. Sims (1964), 709
Rhode Island, 26, 40
Ribicoff, Abraham, 489
Rice, Donna, 279
Rice, Thomas D. ("Daddy"), 573
Richards, Ann, 711
Riders, 340, 341
Riegle, Donald, 358–359
Right-of-reply rule, 282
Right-to-life activists, 247, 476, 556, 592
Riker, William H., 53, 55
Riordan, Richard, 719
Rioting, 476, 548, 581, 583
RNC (Republican National Committee), 173,
    174
Roberts, Owen J., 445, 446
Robertson, Pat, 118, 180, 191, 200
Robertson's rule, 428
Rockefeller, Nelson, 205, 404
Rockefeller Family Fund, 250
Rockne, Knute, 423
Roemer, Tim, 283
Roe v. Wade (1973), 591, 592
Rogers, William P., 608
Roll-call vote, 342, 344, 345
Roosevelt, Franklin D., 176, 224, 285, 364
    assassination attempt, 401
    attempts at reorganization, 399, 400
    attempt to "pack" Supreme Court, 445–446, 464,
        466
    elections, 130, 225, 226, 228, 445, 527, 529
    foreign policy, 607, 611, 615
    internment of Japanese-Americans, 609–610
    liberalism of, 132
    New Deal, 5, 62, 414
    party machine and, 180
    presidency of, 365, 366, 374, 377, 380, 383, 387,
        392, 396, 400, 401, 403, 484, 571
    social welfare and, 527, 528, 529
    terms of office, 368–369, 384, 400
    use of vetoes, 393(fig.), 393–394
Roosevelt, Theodore, 188, 273, 285, 286, 384, 401
    assassination attempt, 401
    elections, 185, 187, 373
    libel suit, 553
    on muckraking, 271
    presidency of, 374, 448, 484
    social welfare and, 526
Rosenthal, Alan, 713
Rosker v. Goldberg, (1981), 590
Rostenkowski, Dan, 519
Rotary Club, 241
Routine stories, 288, 289
Rowland, C. K., 448
Rudman, Warren, 513
Rule of propinquity, 376–377
Rules Committee (House), 305, 306, 321, 339–340,
    358, 360, 584
Runoff primary, 202

Rural areas, 702, 703
Rusk, Dean, 608
Russian Revolution, 18

Safe districts, 309
Safe house, 613
Sampling error, 123
Santeria religion, 558–559
Savings and loan crisis, 358–359, 492
SBA (Small Business Administration), 428
Scaife foundations, 250
Scalia, Antonin, 458, 459, 468, 562, 596
Scandals, 230, 355, 449
    Lincoln Savings and Loan case, 358–359, 492
    mistrust of government and, 102, 309, 313
    Watergate, 100, 290, 390, 394, 405, 612
Schattschneider, E. E., 167
"Schedule C" jobs, 416–417
Schenck, Charles T., 551
Schick, Allen, 536
Schlesinger, Arthur M., Jr., 609, 669
Schlozman, Daniel Aaron, 251
Schlozman, Kay, 251
Schmidt, Helmut, 292
School-desegregation plans, as mandates, 71
School districts, 703
School prayer, 560–561
School prayer issue, 465–466, 468
Schools
    civil rights and, 575–577, 584, 586
    public aid to parochial schools, 561
    public school expenditures, 55
    religion and, 558, 560
    school districts, 703
    single-sex schools, 589
    see also Busing; Desegregation; Education;
        Segregation
Schumpeter, Joseph, 6, 7
Scorekeeper role, of media, 278–279
Scott, Dred, 443–444
Searches, law regarding, 281–282
Search warrant, 563
Sears, David, 90
Second Amendment, 256
Second Hoover Commission, 434
Secretary of state, 383
Secret Service, 376
Sectionalism, 170–171, 373
Securities and Exchange Act (1929), 489
Sedition, 547–548
Sedition Act (1798), 547, 551
Sedition Act (1918), 547–548, 551, 552
Segregation, 3–4
    colleges and universities, 575–576, 599
    de facto and de jure, 578
    of public transportation, 582–583
    residential, 578
    see also Brown v. Board of Education; Civil rights;
        Civil rights movement; Desegregation
Select committees, 330, 353
Selected stories, 290
Selective attention, 283
Self-incrimination, due process and, 566–567
Self-interest, 12, 34
Senate, 31, 287, 306–307, 318, 342, 403
    attitudinal voting in, 345–346
    blacks and women in, 308, 309(fig.)
    committees, 284, 320, 331, 332, 509, 519
    ethics rules, 355, 356
    floor debates, 340–341

political parties and, 319–320, 322
powers shared with president, 374
procedural changes, 332
role in policy-making, 476–477
Rule 22, 307, 308
selection of senators, 306–307
Senate Judiciary Committee, 583
Senatorial courtesy, 448–449
Senior Executive Service (SES), 419
Seniority, in Congress, 331
Sentencing Commission, 722
Separate-but-equal doctrine, 574–577
Separation of church and state, 557–562
Separation of powers, 33, 34
   constitutional reform of, 44, 46–47
   ethics and, 354
   executive privilege and, 394
   as restraint on government, 685
Sequential referral, 338
Sequester, 513
Service agencies, 412–414
Services, provided by government, 526, 719, 720
Service strategy, in social welfare, 534
SES (Senior Executive Service), 419
Seventeenth Amendment, 307
Sex discrimination, 586, 592
Shalala, Donna E., 377
Shalikashvili, John M., 635
Shapp, Milton, 203
"Share Our Wealth" program, 528, 529
Sharon, Ariel, 280, 553
Shaw v. *Reno* (1993), 316
Shays, Daniel, 25
Shays's Rebellion, 25–26, 29
Shelby, Richard, 216
Sheppard, Samuel H., 546
Sherman, John, 484
Sherman, Roger, 32, 38
Sherman Antitrust Act (1890), 484–485, 670
Shultz, George, 608, 614
Sierra Club, 240, 241, 245, 246, 263, 655
Silent majority, 113
Silent Spring (Carson), 661
Simon, Paul, 197
Simple resolution, 336
Sinclair, Barbara, 323–324
Sinclair, Upton, 489, 528, 675
Single-issue groups, 219–220, 318–319
Single-sex schools, 589
Sipuel, Ada Lois, 575–576
Sit-ins, 581, 582, 587
Sixteenth Amendment, 14, 414, 465, 517, 519
Skokie, Illinois, 552–553
Slavery
   agitation over, 169–170
   antislavery organizations, 238
   attempts to ban, 61
   as campaign issue, 219, 225, 230
   conflict in House of Representatives, 304
   Constitution and, 21, 39–41, 42
   federal courts and, 443–444
Small Business Administration (SBA), 428
Small-ticket items, 645–646
"Smart weapons," 639
Smith, Al, 176, 705
Smith, Howard, 583
Smith, Samuel Harrison, 269
Smith Act (1940), 548, 552
Smith's principle, 428
Smog, 654

Sniderman, Paul M., 90
"Soccer moms," 221
Social class, 8, 96, 98
   interest-group bias and, 250–251
   organizational membership and, 252(fig.)
   political elites as "new class," 138–139
   political participation and, 153–154, 158
   public opinion and, 121, 124–125
Socialist Labor party, 187
Socialist party, 186, 187, 188
Socialist Workers party, 187
Social movements
   for civil rights, *see* Civil rights movement
   environmental movement, 245, 246
   feminist movement, 90, 245–247, 262, 555
   as ideological parties, 181
   interest groups and, 238, 244–249
   for reform, *see* Reform movements
Social regulation, 495
Social science, desegregation and, 577–578
Social Security Act (1935), 405, 526, 528, 532, 670
Social Security program, 523, 533, 534, 670
   distributed benefits of, 479, 479(fig.), 491
   funding for, 405, 429–430
   as uncontrollable expenditure, 515, 515(fig.)
Social status of religious groups, 117
Social welfare, 523–543
   assistance programs, 527, 537, 541–542
   client-based welfare programs, 530(fig.), 530–532
   client politics and, 533–534, 534(fig.), 535(fig.)
   costs of, 534–535, 537
   factors affecting, 524–532, 525(fig.)
   health care plan, 254, 536
   insurance programs, 527
   majoritarian politics and, 527–530, 532–533, 533(fig.)
   parliamentary system and, 688
   public opinion and, 537, 540
   ratings of legislators on issues, 325–326
   representational voting on, 344
   role of federalism in, 526–527
   state responsibility for, 538–539
   see also Welfare; *specific welfare programs*
Soft money, 174, 211, 264
Soil Conservation Service, 425, 429
Solarz, Stephen, 316
Sole-sourcing, 645
Solicitor general, 457
Solidarity movement (Poland), 624
Solidary groups, 182
Solidary incentives, 182, 241, 246–247
Somalia, 639
Sophomore surge, 318
Sound bite, 274
Sources of news, 280–282, 281
Souter, David, 449, 458, 592
South, 130, 182–183
   conversion to Republican party, 216–217
   Democratic Party and, 127, 127(fig.), 130, 130(fig.), 183, 184(fig.)
   Jeffersonian Republicans in, 167–168
   political attitudes of, 126–127, 127(fig.), 130, 130(fig.)
   voting patterns of, 223(fig.), 227–228
"Southern Manifesto" (1956), 577
Southern Pacific Railroad, 697
Sovereign immunity, 455
Sovereignty, 53
Soviet Union, 6, 52–53
   collapse of, 514, 624–628, 637, 640, 640(fig.)

containment policy toward, 636–637
   invasion of Afghanistan, 637
   iron curtain and, 620, 622
   public opinion of, 620–621
   U.S. budget and, 514, 640, 640(fig.)
Spaatz, Carl "Tooey," 645
Spain, 270–271
Speaker of the House, 305
   control of Rules Committee, 339, 360
   Newt Gingrich, 305, 321, 322, 323
   powers of, 300–301, 303–304, 306, 321–322, 360
   revolt against, 304–305
Special-act charter, 701
Special-district governments, 703, 717
Special interests, 9, 347, 491, 692. *See also* Interest group politics; Interest groups
Specified commands, 635
Speech, nature of, 553–556
Spending
   on defense, *see* Defense budget
   federal, *see* Federal spending
   military spending, 636–638, 637(fig.), 640–643
   by political action committees, 259(fig.), 259–260
   by states, 698
Split ticket, 228(fig.), 228–229, 366
Spock, Benjamin, 562, 564
Spoils system, 411–412, 417
Sponsored parties, 182
Spook Speak, 613
Spots, 203
SSI (Supplemental Security Income), 527, 537, 538
Staggers Rail Act (1980), 494
Standard Oil Company, 484
Standing, 454–455, 456, 462
Standing committees, 305, 329, 330
Standing votes, 345
Starck, Pete, 536
Stare decisis, 460
Starr, Kenneth, 101
"Star Wars" (SDI), 642–643
State and Local Fiscal Assistance Act (1972), 67
State and local political parties, 178–183
   ideological parties, 180–181
   personal followings, 182–183
   political machine and, 178–180, 182
   two-party system and, 183–184, 184(fig.)
State constitutions, 25, 695, 699–701
   bills of rights in, 22, 38, 39, 698
   political philosophy and, 696–698
State courts, 465, 712–713
State Department, 421, 425, 430, 607, 615, 620
State-federal relationship
   Constitution and, 57, 58
   federal courts and, 441, 443
   under federalism, 57, 61, 63
   as source of political conflict, 51
State governments, 487, 695, 696, 697, 705, 713
   constitutional framework of, *see* State constitutions
   courts, 712–713
   crime control and, 720–725
   decline in unified governments, 705–707, 706(fig.)
   federal bureaucracy and, 410
   federal controls on, 69–70
   governors, *see* Governors
   grants-in-aid to, 64(fig.), 65(fig.), 65–66
   in intergovernmental lobbying, 66, 66(fig.)
   legal basis of, 698–699
   legislatures, 707–712
   policy-making in, 717–719

State governments (*cont.*)
  representation in, 718–719
  structure of, 703–713
  taxation, 719–720, 721(fig.)
State legislatures, 704, 707–712, 718
  appointments of judiciary, 713
  apportionment, 709–710
  elections, 707, 708–709
  governors and, 705–707, 706(fig.)
  legislative phrase-making, 707
  party organization, 710–712
  professional *versus* amateur, 710
State militias, 63
States, 58, 178, 576, 698, 701, 701(fig.)
  control of electorate, 147–149, 148(fig.)
  deregulation of telecommunications, 277
  federal government and, *see* State-federal relationship
  implementation of Clean Air Act, 654
  responsibility for social welfare, 538–539
  rivalry for grants-in-aid, 68–69
  role in environmental policy, 652
  voting restrictions, 144, 148, 696
  welfare programs, 526–527
States' bills of rights, 22, 38, 39, 698
States' rights, 38, 58–59, 722
States' Rights Democrats, 186, 187
Steel industry, 464, 510, 610
Steering and Policy Committee, congressional, 322, 360
Steering Committee (Senate), 320
Steffens, Lincoln, 271
Stevens, John Paul, 458
Stevens, Thaddeus, 304
Stevenson, Adlai, 169, 190, 284
Stewart, Potter, 554
Stockman, David, 380, 422
STOP ERA, 247
Straight ticket, 228
Strategic defense initiative (SDI), 642–643
Strategic weapons, 642
Stretch-outs, 645
Strict-constructionism, 440
Strict scrutiny standard, 588, 597
Study commission on executive reorganization, 434
Subcabinet, 382
Subcommittee on Seapower, 640
Subcommittees, 331, 352, 428
Subsidies, *see* Agricultural subsidies
Substantive representation, 316–317
Succession Act (1886), 403–404
Succession to presidency, 401, 403–404
Suffrage, 147–148, 220
Sugar quotas, 488
Sullivan, "Big Tim," 150
Sullivan, Gordon R., 635
Supercarriers, 634
Superdelegates, 177
Superfund program (1980), 483, 664
Supplemental Security Income (SSI), 527, 537, 538
Supply-side economic theory, 506, 519
Supreme Court, 36, 452
  on abortion, 448, 469, 476, 591–592
  on affirmative action, 596–597, 599
  attempt of FDR to "pack," 445–446, 464, 466
  attempts to define obscenity, 554–555
  on campaign financing, 210
  on civil rights, 445
  on confidentiality of sources, 280–282
  on congressional investigative power, 431

on convention delegate selection, 202
on discretionary power of bureaucracy, 415
on federalism, 59–60
on First Amendment rights, 562, 564
on foreign and military policy, 609
on freedom of religion, 558
growth of mandates and, 71
immigration law and policy, 128
income tax declared illegal, 444, 465, 516–517
increase in workload of, 453
influences on, 457–458
on Internet pornography, 556
interpretation amendments, 62, 71, 575
interpretations of federalism, 59–60
judicial activism of, 446–447
judicial review power, 33
justices of, 456(fig.)
on lawsuits against president, 395
on legislative veto, 430
litmus test issue and, 449
on malapportionment, 315, 456, 709
on male/female differences, 588
on mandatory busing, 579, 581
powers of, 441, 443–444
proposals to curtail, 48
on regulation of commerce, 61, 443
regulation of economy, 444–445
on regulatory agencies, 413
rejection of nominees, 448(fig.), 449–450, 450(fig.)
as restraint on government, 684
on restriction of third parties, 186
reversal of decisions, 460
reviews of state court decisions, 712
school desegregation ruling (1954), 476
school prayer issue, 465–466, 468, 560–561
standards for civil rights cases, 596–598
state court rulings and, 465
on state-federal relations, 61, 63
term limit ruling, 349–350
voting patterns in, 458–459
on voting rights, 149
on Watergate tapes, 394
see also Courts; Federal courts; *specific cases*
Survey Research Center (University of Michigan), 614
Suspect classifications, 571
Swain, Carol M., 317
Swann v. *Charlotte-Mecklenburg Board of Education* (1971), 579
Sweatt, Heman, 576
Sweatt, Robert W., 73
Sweden, 91, 92–93, 93(fig.), 410, 526, 686
Sweet, Robert W., 73
Swing bloc, in Supreme Court, 458
Swing voters, 220
Swope, Herbert Bayard, 620
"Symbolic racism," 90
Symbolic speech, 555, 556
Symbols, 169, 675–676

Taft, William Howard, 187, 238, 369, 384, 464
Taft-Hartley Act (1947), 486, 671
Tammany Hall, 171, 179, 181, 697, 718, 719
Taney, Roger B., 443, 445, 464, 467
TANF (Temporary Assistance for Needy Families), 527, 537
Tariffs, 516
Task Force on Regulatory Relief (1981), 495
Taxation, 14, 47, 516(fig.), 516–520, 719
  Antifederalist proposal for, 36
  gasoline taxes, 658

history of, 516–519, 517(fig.)
under parliamentary system, 688
property taxes, 720
state and local, 719–720, 721(fig.)
by states, 60
see also Federal income tax
Tax codes, 263
Tax legislation, 332
Tax loopholes, 516, 517–519
Tax reform, 519–520
Tax Reform Act (1986), 197, 365, 516, 518, 519
Tax revolt, 720
Taylor, Zachary, 197, 373, 403
Teamsters Union, 493, 494
Telecommunications Act (1996), 277
Telephones, rights of disabled persons, 598
Teles, Steven, 540
Television
  cable television, 272, 274, 276, 277, 287
  compared to newspapers, 279
  major networks, 273–274, 274(fig.), 276
  role in presidential campaigns, 203–207, 219
  see also Electronic media; Radio
Teller vote, 342
Temporary Assistance for Needy Families (TANF), 527, 537
Temporary employees, 416
Tenth Amendment, 58, 62, 69, 71, 698
Term limits, 348–350, 402
  alternatives to, 349
  as early issue, 368–370
  movement for, 308–309
  at state level, 348, 708
  see also Incumbency
Territorial courts, 447
Tet Offensive, 289
Texas, 220, 314, 541, 711
TFX fighter aircraft, 634, 642
Thatcher, Margaret, 364
Think tanks, 244
Third parties, 170, 180–181, 185–186, 225
Third World, 626
Thirteenth Amendment, 465
Thomas, Clarence, 350, 439, 440, 449, 458, 562, 592
Thompson, Dennis F., 358–359
Thrift Institutions Restructuring Act (1982), 494
Thurber, James, 423
Thurmond, J. Strom, 186, 317
Tilden, Samuel J., 176
Timber industry, 661–662
Time magazine, 553
Times Beach, Missouri, 483
Tinsdale, Elkanah, 314
Tocqueville, Alexis de, 160, 161
  Democracy in America, 86, 160
  on democratic government, 85–86
  on equality, 689–690
  on French Revolution, 475–476
  on religion, 93
  on self-interest, 12
Town meetings
  electronic, 12, 273
  New England, 6, 8, 702
Townsend, Francis E., 528
Toxic Substances Control Act (1976), 488
Trade associations, 239
Trade bill (1988), 510
Trade restrictions, 510
Transportation, rights of disabled persons, 72–73, 598
Treasury Department, 411, 426–427, 519

Treaty of Versailles, 307
Trial balloon, 281
Trial by jury, 37
Trial courts, state, 712
Truman, David B., 53
Truman, Harry S, 130, 186, 401, 530, 685
    assassination attempt, 401
    attempts at reorganization, 399, 400
    decline in popularity, 390, 390(fig.)
    foreign policy, 608, 611, 614, 617
    impoundment of funds, 395
    policies, 397, 509, 640–641
    presidency of, 383, 387, 392, 400
    on primaries, 190
    seizure of steel mills, 464, 610
    social welfare and, 528
    use of vetoes, 393(fig.), 393–394
    as vice president, 403
Trust funds, 429–430
Twelfth Amendment, 370
Twenty-fifth Amendment, 380, 403, 404
Twenty-second Amendment, 369, 400
Twenty-seventh Amendment, 45
Twenty-sixth Amendment, 45, 149, 465
Twenty-third Amendment, 149
Two-party system, 172(fig.), 183–186, 184(fig.)
Tyler, John, 401
Tyner, James N., 179

UI (Unemployment Insurance), 527
Uncontrollable expenditures, 515, 515(fig.)
Unemployment
    economic class and, 96, 98
    effect on federal spending, 515–516
    as pocketbook issue, 500
    see also Employment
Unemployment Insurance (UI), 527
Unheavenly City, The (Banfield), 540
Unicameral legislature, 590
Unified commands, 634–635
Unified government, 365
Unions, *see* Labor unions
Unitary systems, 52, 53, 54, 56, 56(fig.)
United Auto Workers (UAW), 182, 657, 660
United Nations, 615
    peacekeeping missions, 626, 639
    role in foreign policy, 627–628
United Press International, 276, 289
United States Chamber of Commerce, 237, 238, 240, 325, 536
United States Code, 454
United States Court of Appeals, 419
United States Information Agency, 613
United States v. *Fordice* (1992), 576
United States v. *Lopez,* 62
United States v. *Nixon* (1973), 394
United We Stand America, 264. *See also* Reform party
Universal enrollment (voting registration), 155
University of California, 458, 597
University of Michigan, 614
University of Oklahoma, 576
University of Oklahoma Law School, 575–576
University of Texas Law School, 576, 599
Unreformed cities, 713–714
Unruh, Jesse, 711
Unsafe at Any Speed (Nader), 489
Urban and suburban populations
    metropolitan government and, 716–717
    reapportionment and, 709–710
    structure of state government and, 703

Urban League, 237
U.S. Census, 69
U.S. census, 413
U.S. Committee Against Nuclear War, 249
U.S. Conference of Mayors, 71
U.S. Forest Service, 429, 661
USS Maine, 271

Valence issues, 230–231
Van Buren, Martin, 169, 230, 401, 412
Vance, Cyrus, 382–383, 608
Vandenberg, Arthur H., 611, 622–623
Velasquez, Nydia M., 316
Verba, Sidney, 91, 92, 152, 240
Veto message, 392
Veto power, 343, 392–394, 393(fig.)
    legislative veto, 400, 430, 610, 611
    line-item veto, 47–48, 393, 513
    pocket veto, 392–393
    presidential use of, 343, 372, 373, 374, 392–394, 393(fig.)
Vice presidency, 401, 403, 411
Vietnam War, 318, 390, 392, 624
    elite views of, 623
    foreign policy, 609
    media coverage of, 278, 289
    military spending and, 637, 637(fig.)
    political conflict over, 101
    public opinion on, 615–616, 617, 618(fig.), 618–619
Vietnam worldview, 621, 623, 624–625, 627
Violent Crime Control and Law Enforcement Act (1994), 723
Virginia, 38, 39, 256, 579, 596
Virginia Military Institute, 589
Virginia Plan, 29–30
Virginia Resolution, 60
Visuals, 203–204, 274
Vogel, David, 652
Voice vote, 342, 345
Voter backlash, 217
Voter registration, 143, 144(fig.), 145
    black civil rights and, 582–583
    civil rights acts and, 584, 586, 587
    impediments to, 154–155
    registration regulations, 151
    voter turnout and, 144–145, 145(fig.)
Voters, 143, 144, 217, 499
    ethnicity of, 158–159, 159(fig.)
    opinions on federal spending and, 510–511, 511(fig.)
    political parties and, 177, 177(fig.), 191–192, 192(fig.)
    two-party system and, 186
    see also Voting
Voter turnout, 144–145, 145(fig.), 149–152, 150(fig.), 196
Voting, 144–152, 155–156, 158
    age and voting record, 223(fig.)
    bloc voting, 220, 221
    civil rights acts and, 584, 586
    comparison with other countries, 143, 144(fig.), 156, 158, 158(fig.)
    media patterns of, 288, 289(fig.)
    nonvoting, 143–146, 144(fig.), 145(fig.)
    partisan divisions in, 224, 224(fig.)
    pocketbook issues and, 500–501
    political machine and, 179–180
    social class and, 124
    Southern patterns of, 223(fig.), 227–228

    at state and local levels, 695
    Twenty-sixth Amendment, 45, 149, 465
    women and, 43, 54, 144, 148–149, 220
    see also Nineteenth Amendment
Voting-age population, 143, 144(fig.)
Voting fraud, 150
Voting restrictions, 144, 148–149, 151, 220, 696
Voting Rights Act (1965), 148, 232
Voting Rights Act (1970), 149
Voting Rights Act Amendment (1982), 70
Voting specialists, 152

Wagner Act (1935), 485–486
Wallace, George, 130, 148, 183, 278, 579
    election of 1968, 186, 187
    election of 1972, 191
Wallace, Henry, 186, 187
Wall-of-separation principle, 560
War
    defense spending and, 636
    freedom of speech and, 551–552
    government bureaucracy and, 413–414
    impact on policy, 474
    see also specific wars
War Department, 411
War Powers Act (1973), 360, 610–612
Warren, Earl, 446, 577, 705
Washington, George, 5, 303
    American Revolution and, 23
    economic interests of, 42
    on political parties, 167
    presidency of, 367, 368, 371, 372, 380, 383, 401, 405
    role at Constitutional Convention, 26, 29
    on Shays's Rebellion, 25–26
    on strong national government, 24
    term of office self-limited, 368
Washington, Harold, 719
Washington Globe, 269
Waste, in bureaucracy, 433–434
Watchdog role of media, 279
Watergate, 100, 290, 390, 394, 405, 612
Water pollution, 663
Water Quality Improvement Act (1970), 488, 489, 654–655
Watt, James, 243, 490
Watt, Melvin, 316
Watts, J. C., 327
Waxman, Henry A., 180
"Waxman-Berman organization," 180
Ways and Means Committee (House), 332, 358, 509, 519, 529, 536
Weak-mayor systems, 714–715, 715(fig.)
Wealth, liberalism and, 138
WEAL (Women's Equity Action League), 247
Weaver, R. Kent, 77, 79
Weaver, Robert, 383
Weber, Max, 10, 96
Webster, Daniel, 373, 403
Wednesday Club, 345
Weinberger, Caspar, 112
Welfare
    devolution of, 76–77
    political machine as informal system, 179, 180
    public perceptions of, 78, 79
Welfare Reform Act (1996), 542, 705
Westmoreland, William, 454
West Virginia, 150–151
Whig party, 169, 225, 373
Whip, 319, 320, 321

Whistle Blower Protection Act (1989), 422
Whistler, James, 423
"Whistle-stop" tours, 205
White, Byron, 458
White, Mark, 711
White-collar government employees, 416
White flight, 580–581
White House office, *see* Office of the President
White House press corps, 286, 295
White House staff, 12, 400
    as bureaucracy, 376, 377(fig.), 686
    cabinet-staff rivalry, 384
    NSC foreign policy staff, 613–614
White primary, 148
Whitewater, 292
Whitlock, Brand, 170
Whitman, Christine Todd, 47
Whitman, Walt, 423
Whitten, Jamie, 661
Wholesome Poultry Act (1968), 488
Widely distributed costs and benefits, 479, 479(fig.)
Wildavsky, Aaron, 607
Wilderness Society, 245, 246
Wilentz, Sean, 349
Wiley, Harvey, 488, 675
"Williamsburg Resolve, The," 62
Wilson, Edith Galt, 403
Wilson, James, 32, 41, 367
Wilson, William Julius, 540
Wilson, Woodrow, 187, 224, 369, 375, 403
    on filibusters, 307

    foreign policy, 608, 611, 622
    presidency of, 374, 401, 485, 622
    on state-federal relations, 51–52
    wartime powers of, 413–414
Winchell, Walter, 546
Winner-reward system of delegate distribution, 178
Winograd, Morley, 176
Wire services, role of, 270, 276
Wirthlin, Richard, 174
Woman's party, 187
Women
    in bureaucracy, 420, 421(fig.)
    cabinet appointments of, 383–384
    as candidates for Congress, 118–119, 119(fig.)
    child support enforcement and, 593
    civil rights and, 588–592
    comparable worth doctrine and, 593–594
    day care and, 592, 593
    economy and, 592–594
    in House of Representatives, 307–308, 309(fig.)
    in military, 589, 590, 643–644
    omitted from Constitution, 43
    parental leave law, 593
    in Senate, 308, 309(fig.)
    sexual classification and, 588–589
    as state legislators, 709
    valence issues and, 231
    voting, 43, 54, 147–148
    voting restrictions, 144, 148–149, 220
Women's Equity Action League (WEAL), 247
Woodward, Bob, 279

Work ethic, 96
Work requirements, 537
Worldviews
    containment (antiappeasement) view, 620, 621, 622, 623, 624, 627
    disengagement (Vietnam) view, 621, 623, 624–625, 627
    foreign policy elites and, 619–620, 671
    isolationism, 622–623
    in majoritarian politics, 670–671
World War I, 186, 548, 617
World War II, 414, 548, 552, 647, 670
    expansion of foreign policy and, 612–613, 615
    public opinion and, 615, 617, 642
World Wide Web, *see* Internet
Wornick, Susan, 280
Wright, Jim, 292, 322, 355, 360, 519, 711
Writ of certiorari, 452–453, 457
Writ of habeas corpus, 37
Writ of mandamus, 442

Yale Law Journal, 458
Yellow journalism, 271
Yeltsin, Boris, 6, 625, 626
Young, Coleman, 719
Yugoslavia (former), 626, 628

Zacchini v. *Scripps-Howard Broadcasting Co.* (1977), 562, 564
Zaller, John, 120, 135, 139
Zoning ordinances, pornography and, 556

Photograph Credits

Illustrations other than political cartoons by Patrice Rossi, Rossi & Associates. Maps by Maryland Carto-Graphics, Inc. Politically Speaking cartoons by Peter Wallace. Background photograph on all part and chapter pages by Robert Llewellyn.

Chapter 1

p. 2, D. W. Hamilton/The Image Bank; p. 5, David R. Frazier/Folio; p. 6, David Burnett/Contact Press Images; p. 7, Randy Taylor/Sygma; p. 8, George A. Robinson,/fStop Pictures; p. 9, David Young-Wolff/PhotoEdit; p. 10, *left*, The Granger Collection, New York; p. 10, *right*, German Information Center; p. 11, Focus on Sports; p. 13, *top*, Andrew Holbrooke; p. 13, *bottom*, D. Tulis/Atlanta Journal Constitution/Sygma.

Chapter 2

p. 18, Pete Souza/Folio; p. 20, Library of Congress; p. 21, William Walcutt, *Pulling Down the Statue of George III at Bowling Green,* 1857, oil on canvas, $51^5/_8 \times 77^5/_8''$. Lafayette College Art Collection, Easton, Pennsylvania; p. 23, Rare Books Division, The New York Public Library, Astor, Lenox, and Tilden Foundations; p. 24, Dennis Degnan/Uniphoto; p. 25, The Print and Picture Collection, The Free Library of Philadelphia; p. 26, *left*, Corbis-Bettmann; p. 26, *right*, Courtesy, American Antiquarian Society; p. 27, *first*, Library of Congress; p. 27, *second*, U. S. Government Printing Office; p. 27, *third*, Bowdoin College Museum of Art, Brunswick, Maine. Bequest of the Honorable James Bowdoin III; p. 27, *fourth*, Library of Congress; p. 27, *fifth*, By permission of the Houghton Library, Harvard University; p. 27, *sixth*, The New Jersey Bank; p. 28, *upper left*, Library of Congress; p. 28, *lower left*, Collection of The New-York Historical Society; p. 28, *center*, Courtesy, American Antiquarian Society; p. 28, *right*, Library of Congress; p. 36, George Caleb Bingham, *Daniel Boone Escorting Settlers through the Cumberland Gap,* 1851–52. Oil on canvas, $36^1/_2 \times 50^1/_4''$. Washington University Gallery of Art, St. Louis. Gift of Nathaniel Phillips, 1890; p. 39, Chicago Historical Society; p. 40, Doonesbury, © 1987 G. B. Trudeau. Reprinted with permission of Universal Press Syndicate. All rights reserved; p. 41, *left*, Courtesy of The Bostonian Society/Old State House; p. 41, *right*, National Collection of Fine Arts, Smithsonian Institution/Art Resource; p. 45, Gary Brookins, Richmond Times-Dispatch; p. 47, Allan Tannenbaum/Sygma.

Chapter 3

p. 50, Bob Daemmrich; p. 52, Reuters/Corbis-Bettmann; p. 54, The Granger Collection, New York; p. 59, Bowdoin College Museum of Art, Brunswick, Maine. Bequest of the Honorable James Bowdoin III;

p. 60, The Granger Collection, New York; p. 63, Courtesy of The Regents of the University of California, Berkeley Campus; p. 67, Rick Friedman/The Picture Cube; p. 72, Marion Bernstein; p. 74, *left*, J. P. Laffont/Sygma; p. 74, *right*, Christopher Little/Outline; p. 80, Paul S. Conklin.

Chapter 4

p. 84, Clint Clemens/Gamma Liaison; p. 86, The Granger Collection, New York; p. 87, *left*, Charles Harbutt/Magnum; p. 87, *center*, Jim McHugh/Sygma; p. 87, *right*, Sylvia Johnson/Woodfin Camp & Associates; p. 88, Corbis-Bettmann; p. 89, UPI/Corbis-Bettmann; p. 92, Les Stone/Sygma; p. 95, Alan Oddie/PhotoEdit; p. 97, *top*, State Historical Society of Wisconsin–WHi(V24)2013; p. 97, *left*, Alan Carey/Image Works; p. 97, *right*, M. Hayman/Photo Researchers; p. 98, Claudio Edinger/Gamma-Liaison; p. 100, UPI/Corbis-Bettmann; p. 101, *left*, Jean-Claude Lejeune; p. 101, *right*, Charles Gatewood/Magnum; p. 102, Reuters/Jeff Mitchell/Archive Photos; p. 104, © Richard B. Levine.

Chapter 5

p. 110, Bob Daemmrich; p. 112, Drew Harmon/Folio; p. 115, Drawing by Richter; © 1991 The New Yorker Magazine, Inc.; p. 117, Robert Burroughs/Gamma Liaison; p. 123, Doonesbury, © G. B. Trudeau 1980. Reprinted with permission of Universal ıress Syndicate. All rights reserved; p. 127, Shelly Katz/Gamma Liaison; p. 134, Judy G. Rolfe/Uniphoto; p. 136, Tony Savino/Sygma; p. 137, *left*, Misha Erwitt/Magnum; p. 137, *right*, Brooks Draft/Sygma.

Chapter 6

p. 142, Bob Daemmrich; p. 145, Washington Secretary of State; p. 146, Abby Aldrich Rockefeller Folk Art Center, Williamsburg, VA; p. 147, *top*, The Granger Collection, New York; p. 147, *bottom*, Smithsonian Institution, Department of Social History; p. 149, Library of Congress; p. 154, The Granger Collection, New York; p. 155, The League of Women Voters; p. 156, Bob Daemmrich/Stock Boston; p. 162, Corbis/Bettmann.

Chapter 7

p. 165, Peter Menzel/Stock Boston; p. 167, Paul S. Conklin; p. 168, Tennessee Historical Society, p. 170, Burt Glinn/Magnum; p. 171, UPI/Corbis-Bettmann; p. 173, Reuters/Peter Morgan/Archive Photos; p. 174, AP/Wide World Photos; p. 175, *bottom*, L. Stone/Sygma; p. 175, *top*, Library of Congress; p. 176, AP/Wide World Photos; p. 177, Corbis-Bettmann; p. 179,

By permission of the Houghton Library, Harvard University; p. 180, Reuters/Robert Giroux/Archive Photos; p. 181, Mike Greenlar/The Image Works; p. 181, James Colburn/IPOL; p. 183, Henri Dauman/Magnum; p. 188, *top*, Library of Congress; p. 188, *bottom*, Corbis-Bettmann.

Chapter 8

p. 194, M. Granitsas/The Image Works; p. 198, *left*, Smithsonian Institution, Department of Social History; p. 198, *right*, Smithsonian Institution, Department of Social History; p. 200, Steve Liss/Gamma Liaison; p. 201, Diego Goldberg/Sygma; p. 202, *both*, State of Wisconsin Elections Board; p. 203, Library of Congress; p. 204, *top*, Corbis-Bettmann; p. 204, *bottom*, UPI/Corbis-Bettmann; p. 205, Reuters/Win McNamee/Archive Photos; p. 206, *top*, National Broadcasting Company; p. 206, *bottom*, Steve Lehman/Saba Press; p. 207, AP/Wide World Photos; p. 220, Bob Daemmrich/The Image Works; p. 222, Michael Evans/Sygma; p. 227, *left*, The Granger Collection, New York; p. 227, *right*, Historical Pictures Service/Stock Montage; p. 228, UPI/Corbis-Bettmann; p. 229, *top*, Indiana State Elections Board; p. 229, *bottom*, Commonwealth of Massachusetts Secretary of State.

Chapter 9

p. 234, Bob Daemmrich; p. 237, *left*, Michael Schumann/Saba Press; p. 237, *right*, Michael Schumann/Saba Press; p. 239, Terry Ashe/Uniphoto; p. 240, Historical Pictures Service/Stock Montage; p. 241, *top*, Michael Newman/PhotoEdit; p. 241, *bottom*, Barry Staver; p. 242, Copyright © 1978 The New York Times Co. Reprinted by Permission; p. 248, Bob Daemmrich/The Image Works; p. 253, J. P. Laffont/Sygma; p. 254, David Young-Wolff/PhotoEdit; p. 255, Paul S. Conklin; p. 256, John Ficara/Sygma; p. 257, Matt Freedman; p. 258, Courtesy National Education Association; p. 262, Bruce Allen/IPOL.

Chapter 10

p. 266, Dennis Brack/Black Star; p. 269, By permission of the Houghton Library, Harvard University; p. 270, *top*, Copyright © 1987 by The New York Times Co. Reprinted by Permission; p. 270, *bottom*, N.Y. Daily News, L.P. reprinted with permission; p. 273, *top*, David Young-Wolff/PhotoEdit; p. 273, *bottom left*, UPI/Corbis-Bettmann; p. 273, *bottom right*, Paul S. Conklin/Uniphoto; p. 275, AP/Wide World Photos; p. 278, Lyndon Baines Johnson Library; p. 280, Molly Lynch/WCVB TV; p. 285, UPI/Corbis-Bettmann; p. 286, *top*, Brown Brothers; p. 286, *bottom*, Les Stone/Sygma; p. 290, Terry Ashe/Uniphoto.

Chapter 11

p. 298, Dennis Brack/Black Star; p. 300, AP/Wide World Photos; p. 301, Paul S. Conklin; p. 303, Library of Congress; p. 305, *left*, Library of Congress; p. 305, *center*, Library of Congress; p. 305, *right*, AP/Wide World Photos; p. 307, General Research Division, The New York Public Library, Astor, Lenox, and Tilden Foundations; p. 314, Corbis-Bettmann; p. 317, UPI/Corbis-Bettmann; p. 321, *left*, Erik Lesser/ Gamma Liaison; p. 321, *right*, House of Representatives Majority Whip's Office; p. 327, AP/Wide World Photos; p. 336, Office of the Clerk, Legislative Resource Center, U.S. House of Representatives; p. 337, AP/Wide World Photos; p. 338, Office of the Clerk, Legislative Resource Center, U.S. House of Representatives; p. 342, *left*, Keith Jewell/U.S. House of Representatives; p. 342, *right*, Keith Jewell/ U.S. House of Representatives; p. 354, Cartoon by NEWSTAFF/Cullum. Copyright The Birmingham News. Reprinted with permission; p. 355, AP/Wide World Photos.

Chapter 12

p. 362, Mark E. Gibson/Folio; p. 365, Corbis-Bettmann; p. 367, Corbis-Bettmann; p. 369, *top*, Noel-Figaro/Gamma Liaison; p. 369, *bottom left*, Library of Congress; p. 369, *bottom right*, AP/Wide World Photos; p. 372, The Granger Collection, New York; p. 375, Wally McNamee/Woodfin Camp & Associates; p. 376, White House Photo Office; p. 383, *left*, Franklin D. Roosevelt Library; p. 383, *right*, Lyndon Baines Johnson Library; p. 384, *left*, The Granger Collection, New York; p. 385, Reuters/Luc Novovitch/Archive Photos; p. 386, *left*, UPI/Corbis-Bettmann; p. 386, *right*, © 1997, The Washington Post. Reprinted with permission; p. 394, Fred J. Maroon; p. 396, AP/Wide World Photos; p. 401, Michael Evans/The White House; p. 403, Historical Pictures Service/Stock Montage.

Chapter 13

p. 408, Peter Menzel/Stock Boston; p. 413, *left*, Smithsonian Institution Photo No. 79-10952; p. 413, *right*, Mark Mangold, Bureau of the Census; p. 416, AP/Wide World Photos; p. 418, Jeff MacNelly. Reprinted by permission, Tribune Media Services; p. 425, With permission of Bob Thaves; p. 423, *left*, National Archives; p. 423, *right*, National Portrait Gallery, Smithsonian Institution; p. 433, Stephen Ferry/Gamma Liaison.

Chapter 14

p. 438, Spencer Grant/Gamma Liaison; p. 440, Wally McNamee/Woodfin Camp & Associates; p. 442, *left*, National Portrait Gallery, Smithsonian Institution; p. 442, *right*, Library of Congress; p. 443, *left*, Library of Congress; p. 443, *center*, The Granger Collection, New York; p. 443, *right*, Collection of the New-York Historical Society; p. 445, Corbis-Bettmann; p. 450, *left*, Wally McNamee/Woodfin Camp & Associates; p. 450, *right*, Terry Ashe/Gamma Liaison; p. 453, *bottom*, National Archives; p. 453, *top*, Flip Schulke; p. 455,

Carl Iwasaki/Life Magazine © 1954 Time, Inc.; p. 457, Erich Solomon/Magnum; p. 459, Collection, The Supreme Court of the United States, courtesy The Supreme Court Historical Society. Photographed by Richard Strauss, Smithsonian Institution; p. 461, Alex Webb/Magnum; p. 464, *left*, Brown Brothers; p. 464, *right*, UPI/Corbis-Bettmann; p. 466, Ellis Herwig/ Stock Boston.

Chapter 15

p 472, David Graham; p. 477, AP/Wide World Photos; p. 478, T. Michaels/The Image Works; p. 482, Peter Menzel/Stock Boston; p. 484, Brown Brothers; p. 485, Ken Rogers/Black Star; p. 487, Susan McCartney/ Photo Researchers; p. 488, Corbis-Bettmann; p. 489, Brown Brothers; p. 490, Jeffrey D. Smith/Woodfin Camp & Associates.

Chapter 16

p. 498, Dennis Brack/Black Star; p. 501, Rod Rolle/Gamma Liaison; p. 504, Ed Kashi/Gamma Liaison; p. 506, UPI/Corbis-Bettmann; p. 506, Karen Vismara/Black Star; p. 506, UPI/Corbis-Bettmann; p. 506, Tony Korody/Sygma; p. 507, Tom McHugh/Photoresearchers; p. 509, Brad Markel/ Gamma Liaison; p. 520, Jeff MacNelly. Reprinted by permission, Tribune Media Services.

Chapter 17

p. 522, Tony Freeman/PhotoEdit; p. 528, UPI/Corbis-Bettmann; p. 529, *left*, UPI/Corbis-Bettmann; p. 529, *right*, AP/Wide World Photos; p. 530, Yoichi Okamoto/Lyndon Baines Johnson Memorial Library; p. 531, *top*, Steven Rubin/The Image Works; p. 531, *bottom*, © 1997 Kevin Horan/Chicago; p. 538, Corbis-Bettmann; p. 541, Reuters/John Gibbons/ Archive Photos.

Chapter 18

p. 544, William Bradstreet/Folio; p. 547, The Granger Collection, New York; p. 551, Corbis-Bettmann; p. 553, William Campbell/Sygma; p. 554, M. Douglas/ The Image Works; p. 555, From *In Opposition*, ©1968, Benedict Fernandez; p. 556, Les Stone/Sygma; p. 558, Max Winter/Stock Boston; p. 559, Owen Franken/ Stock Boston; p. 561, Rob Nelson/Stock Boston; p. 565, *top*, Ed Lallo/Gamma Liaison; p. 565, *bottom*, Tony Freeman/PhotoEdit; p. 566, *bottom*, ©The Arizona Republic 1997. Photo by Ludd Keaton. Used with permission. Permission does not imply endorsement.

Chapter 19

p. 570, Photo by Jim Prigoff. Mural by Culture on the Corner, Mel Simmons, Director, 1996; p. 572, Library of Congress; p. 573, By permission of the Houghton Library, Harvard University; p. 575, By permission of the Houghton Library, Harvard University; p. 576, Dennis Brack/Black Star; p. 578, UPI/Corbis-Bettmann; p. 579, Steve Shapiro/Black Star; p. 580,

Ted Crowell/Black Star; p. 582, *bottom*, AP/Wide World Photos; p. 582, *top left*, UPI/Corbis-Bettmann; p. 582, *top right*, AP/Wide World Photos; p. 584, AP/Wide World Photos; p. 585, Yoichi Okamoto/ Lyndon Baines Johnson Library; p. 587, *bottom left*, AP/Wide World Photos; p. 587, *bottom right*, AP/Wide World Photos; p. 587, *top*, Peter Blakeley/ Saba Press; p. 589, Topham/The Image Works; p. 590, Paul S. Conklin; p. 593, David J. Sams/Stock Boston; p. 595, J. P. Laffont/Sygma; p. 599, Rhoda Sidney/The Image Works.

Chapter 20

p. 602, AP/Wide World Photos; p. 605, Bob Daemmrich/Image Works; p. 606, *left*, P. Gifford/ Gamma Liaison; p. 606, *right*, Penny Prince/Gamma Liaison; p. 607, Brad Markel/Gamma Liaison; p. 608, UPI/Corbis-Bettmann; p. 609, UPI/Corbis-Bettmann; p. 610, National Archives; p. 611, AP/Wide World Photos; p. 612, Bill Gentile/SIPA; p. 616, U.S. Navy; p. 621, *left*, Henri Dauman/Magnum; p. 621, *right*, Michael D. Sullivan/Black Star; p. 622, Corbis-Bettmann; p. 624, Alexandra Avakian/Contact Press.

Chapter 21

p. 630, C. Johnson/Gamma Liaison; p. 632, AP/Wide World Photos; p. 635, Helene C. Stikkel/Department of Defense; p. 638, Pierre Perrin/Gamma Liaison; p. 636, Robert Llewellyn; p. 642, *top*, UPI/Corbis-Bettmann; p. 642, *bottom*, Joseph Sohm/Photo Researchers; p. 644, Lisa Quinones/Black Star.

Chapter 22

p. 650, Jeff Lepore/Photo Researchers; p. 652, John Lawlor/Tony Stone Images; p. 655, David Young-Wolff/PhotoEdit; p. 657, Stephen Frisch/Stock Boston; p. 658, John Elk III/Stock Boston; p. 662, William Campbell/Sygma; p. 663, Bill Horsman/Stock Boston.

Chapter 23

p. 668, Al Messerschmidt/Folio; p. 671, AP/Wide World Photos; p. 675, ©1997 Kevin Horan/Chicago; p. 677, Susan Steinkamp/Saba Press; p. 680, Bob Daemmrich/The Image Works.

Chapter 24

p. 682, Drew Harmon/Folio; p. 686, Kevin Jacobus/The Syracuse Newspapers/The Image Works; p. 687, Mike Ramirez/Copley News Service; p. 689, Tony O'Brien/Stock Boston; p. 691, Bob Daemmrich/ Stock Boston.

Chapter 25

p. 694, Paul S. Conklin; p. 696, National Archives; p. 699, Kolvoord/The Image Works; p. 700, County of Sacramento Voter Registration and Elections; p. 703, Barry Carr/Fosters Daily Democrat; p. 716, *right*, Bart Bartholomew/Black Star; p. 716, *left*, Victor Malafrone/Archive Photos.